TOWARD A PRACTICE OF AUTONOMOUS SYSTEMS

Complex Adaptive Systems

John H. Holland, Christopher Langton, and Stewart W. Wilson, advisors

Adaptation in Natural and Artificial Systems: An Introductory Analysis with Applications to Biology, Control, and Artificial Intelligence, MIT Press/Bradford Books edition, John H. Holland

Toward a Practice of Autonomous Systems: Proceedings of the First European Conference on Artificial Life, edited by Francisco J. Varela and Paul Bourgine

TOWARD A PRACTICE OF AUTONOMOUS SYSTEMS

Proceedings of the First European Conference on Artificial Life

edited by Francisco J. Varela and Paul Bourgine

A Bradford Book

The MIT Press
Cambridge, Massachusetts
London, England

Second printing, 1994

This book was printed and bound in the United States of America.

Library of Congress Cataloging-in-Publication Data

European Conference on Artificial Life (1st : 1991 : Paris, France)
Toward a practice of autonomous systems : proceedings of the first European Conference on Artificial Life / edited by Francisco J. Varela and Paul Bourgine.
p. cm. — (Complex adaptive systems)
Selected papers from the first European Conference on Artificial Life, held in Paris, France in December 1991.
Includes bibliographical references and index.
ISBN 0-262-72019-1
1. Robotics—Congresses. 2. Artificial intelligence—Congresses. I. Varela, Francisco J., 1945– II. Bourgine, Paul. III. Title. IV. Series.
TJ210.3.E87 1991
629.8'92—dc20 92-1350
CIP

CONTENTS

SWARM INTELLIGENCE

LEARNING AND EVOLUTION

PREFACE

Artificial Life is a recent conceptual step in modern science concerting a number of apparently disparate research efforts on a common ground. After the pioneering efforts at the Santa Fe Institute, USA where the first two gatherings on artificial life marked the birth of the discipline, it seemed to us that it was the right time to host the first european meeting on artificial life. It became known as ECAL 91, and it took place in Paris on December 11-13,1991 most appropriately at the cité des Sciences et de l'Industrie, France's ultramodern science museum.

Our main guiding thought was to put the accent on all aspects of research concerned with autonomous systems . Besides examining research results, another major objective was to engage both practicing scientists and philosophers to examine the epistemological basis of this new field. Only through sustained analysis of the main concepts and ideas can we prepare a fertile terrain for important advances of this new research trend. These proceedings follow the sequence of presentations during the Conference itself, with the exception of the posters which have been incorporated into the Section that seemed most appropriate.

ECAL 91 could not have taken place without the invaluable help of a number of people and organizations. First of all we are especially grateful to members of the program committee:

Hugues Bersini	(Belgium)
Rodney Brooks	(USA)
Jacques Demongeot	(France)
Brian Goodwin	(UK)
Stuart Kauffman	(USA)
Chris G. Langton	(USA)
Jean-Arcady Meyer	(France)
Domenico Parisi	(Italie)
Hans-Paul Schwefel	(Germany)

They provided us with continued assistance throughout the whole organization process, from the elaboration of the scope, from the selection of paper to the final preparation of the meeting.

The members of the Artificial Intelligence Laboratory of the CEMAGREF have assured every effort to make this conference a success. We thank in particular Isabelle Alvarez, Laurent Bochereau, Guillaume Deffuant, Vincent Douzal and Thierry Fuhs.

We also wish to thank the following sponsors for the great confidence they have shown in this project. They together provided all the actual means vital to the realization of the conference; without them this conference would not have been possible:

- cité des Sciences et de l'Industrie
- Banque de France
- Fondation de France
- Electricité de France
- CEMAGREF
- CNR, Roma
- AFCET
- CREA, Ecole Polytechnique
- OFFILIB
- Sun Microsystems France

We especially wish to express our gratitude to la cité des Sciences et de l'Industrie for having generously placed at our disposal the Salle Laser, in which the conference was held, and to Joël de Rosnay and Marie-Christine Hergault for their constant help in organizing the conference and communicating with the media.

Thanks also to Louis Bec, responsible for the artistic conception of the ECAL 91 Poster and the Proceedings cover.

Last but not least, our heartfelt thanks to all the participants in this volume. Without their enthusiasm and creative work there would have been nothing to present at all.

Paul Bourgine and Francisco J. Varela
Conference Co-Chairs

Towards a Practice of Autonomous Systems

Paul Bourgine
Laboratoire d'Intelligence Artificielle
CEMAGREF,
BP 121
92185 Antony Cedex

Francisco J. Varela
CREA,
Ecole Polytechnique,
1 rue Descartes
75005 Paris

1 NEW TRENDS

Artificial Life is the most recent expression of a relatively long tradition of thought which searches the core of basic cognitive and intelligent abilities in the very capacity for being alive. Metaphorically, this current of thought would see in a modest insect, rather than in the symbolic abilities of an expert, the best prototype for intelligence.

This recent surge of interest in 'artificial' life has to be understood in the background of the tradition inaugurated in earnest with cybernetics, seeking explicitly common grounds for the living and the artificial. In the early 50's, pioneering work of people such as Grey Walter and his turtles and W.Ross Ashby and his ultra-stable machine, were not given all the attention they deserved, as research efforts swung towards symbolic computation as the prime mover for research leading to what is still today the dominant form of artificial intelligence and cognitive science. After 30 years of a research program emphasizing symbolic computations and abstract representations, we can now benefit from this accumulated experience and the more recent re-discovery of connectionist models and neural networks which have come to pose important challenges to the dominant computationalist tradition (Meyer and Wilson, 1991).

The guiding intuition to both cybernetic forerunners and current proponents of artificial life is quite similar: the need to understand the class of processes that endow living creatures with their characteristic autonomy Autonomy in this context refers to their basic and fundamental capacity to be, to assert their existence and to bring forth a world that is significant and pertinent without be pre-digested in advance. Thus the autonomy of the living is understood here both in regards to its actions and to the way it shapes a world into significance. This conceptual exploration goes hand in hand with the design and construction of autonomous agents and suggest an enormous range of applications at all scales, from cells to societies.

From what we have said already, it is clear that in our view, AL has to go further in its self-definition. According to a recent formulation: "Artificial Life is a field of study devoted to understanding life by attempting to abstract the fundamental dynamical principles underlying biological phenomena, and recreating these dynamics in other physical media - such as computers - making them accessible to new kinds of experimental manipulation and testing" (Langton et al. 1991:xiv). Rather we think artificial life can be better defined as a research program concerned with autonomous systems, their characterization and specific modes of viability. This view is not in contradiction with the previously quoted one; rather, we claim that the foregoing definition needs to be made more precise, by focusing on those dynamical processes that assure the key features of autonomy more than any other dynamical principles present in living systems. Furthermore, it is by focusing on living autonomy that one can naturally go beyond the tempting route of characterizing living phenomena entirely by disembodied abstractions, since the autonomy of the living naturally brings with it the situated nature of its cognitive performances.

As white light seen through a prism, the autonomy of the living is articulated by a number of constitutive capacities such as viability, abduction and adaptability concepts on which research can actually advance. This first European Meeting on Artificial Life was intentionally focused on such key points of research, in an attempt to reveal common trends and to examine conceptual foundations. Whence the title: towards a practice of autonomous systems. Needless to say, not every contributor shares our viewpoint on the matter, but they share it to a sufficient extent to respond enthusiastically to our call for papers under this description.

This is the view that animates this book. The rest of this Introduction is our attempt to clarify further the cluster of key notions: autonomy, viability, abduction and adaptation. These notions form the conceptual scaffolding within which the individual contribution contained in this volume can be placed. Hopefully, these global concepts represent fundamental signposts for future research that can spare us a mere flurry of modelling and simulations into which this new field could fall.

2 AUTONOMY AND OPERATIONAL CLOSURE

At first glance, when studying a (natural or artificial) behaving system, one has two alternative ways of addressing it. If the system is considered as an heteronomous device, it is addressed as an input/output device, essentially defined by a set of instructions and the related control that will act upon it. In contradistinction, if a system is considered as an autonomous device, the center of attention is placed on emergent behaviors and internal self-organizing processes which define what counts as relevant interactions.

Obviously, living systems are the prime example of autonomous devices, and the most important source of examples of generalizable insights. It is on this basis that Varela (1979) proposed the following:

Hypothesis 1 (Closure Thesis): *Every autonomous system is operationally closed .*

The notion of closure here is intended in its algebraic sense : a domain K has closure if all operations defined in it remain within the same domain. The operation of a system has therefore closure, if the results of its action remain within the system itself. This notion of closure has nothing in common with the idea of a closed system or closedness, which means an incapacity to interact. Obviously we are interested in interacting systems ; the main point is the nature of internal dynamics of the systems which determine how the arriving interactions are interpreted, rather than being pre-given as information-rich inputs. One of the most paradigmatic cases of operational closure is the very origin of life as the emergent unit of minimal cellular organization, where the biochemical closure of membrane constitution and metabolic repair make the cell a viable self-distinguishing autopoietic unit (as discussed more extensively elsewhere in Varela *et al* .1974; Varela, 1991).

For our purposes here, we wish to focus on the operational closure of sensory-motor action. We claim that contemporary neurosciences - like cell biology for the case of the cellular organization - gives enough elements to conceive the basic organization of a cognitive self in terms of the operational closure of the nervous system (Maturana and Varela, 1980; Varela, 1979, 1991). Again this is not interactional closedness; we speak of closure to highlight the self-referential quality of the interneuron network and the perceptuo-motor surfaces whose correlations it subserves. More specifically, the nervous system is the operational closure of reciprocally related modular sub-networks giving rise to ensembles of coherent activity in such a way that :

(i) they continuously mediate invariant patterns of sensory-motor correlation of the sensory and effector surfaces;

(ii) they give rise to a behavior for the total organism as a mobile unit in space.

The operational closure of the nervous system thus brings forth a specific mode of coherence, which is embedded in the organism. This coherence is a cognitive self: a unit of perception/motion in space, sensory-motor invariances mediated through the interneuron network. The passage to cognition occurs at the level of a behavioral entity, and not, as in the basic cellular self, as a spatially bounded entity. The key to this cognitive process is the nervous system through its distinctive operational closure. In other words, the cognitive self is the manner in which the organism, through its own self-produced activity, becomes a distinct entity in space, though always coupled to its corresponding environment from which it remains nevertheless distinct. A distinct coherent self which, by the very same process of constituting itself, configures an external world of perception and action.

These two cases, the cellular unit constituted via the metabolic network and the constitution of a cognitive agent via the nervous system, are two prime example of the way in which the Closure Thesis is validated. Its intent is to make the admittedly intuitive notion of autonomy into a more pragmatic one, in the same spirit of, say, how Church's Thesis works by identifying calculability with recursivity on the basis of accumulated experience. Similarly, our experience of autonomy as manifested in living systems makes it plausible that we can generalize : autonomy is always obtained when we endow the system with a rich enough closure of its constitutive process.

3 ABDUCTION AND VIABILITY

Autonomous systems must be, in harmony with Hypothesis 1, endowed with the capacity to be viable in the face of an unpredictable or unspecified environment. The concept of viability can be made quite precise, as discussed by J.P.Aubin (1991). The key idea is that one considers the dynamical description *f* of a system's closure as giving rise, not to an unique solution, but to an ensemble of possible solutions. One works with differential inclusions (Aubin and Celina, 1989) rather than with the more familiar differential equations. From amongst the ensemble of possible trajectories, the system must "choose" one so as not to depart from a domain of constraints which guarantee its continuity, the viability subspace *K*.

Aubin has developed these ideas mostly in reference on how an heteronomous system is kept viable by an observer introducing the appropriate control parameters, which are different from the state parameters. This is clearly inadequate for autonomous systems since they are not endowed with an external controller giving well defined inputs. The system is defined by its closure, the embodiment of sensori-motor cycles configuring what counts as perception and action. Every state change $s(t)$ is the basis for the new state given by the closure dynamics $f(s(t))$ eventually modulated by the coupling with independent and unspecified perturbations. If we consider for clarity the discrete case, this can be written as:

$$s(t+1) \in f(s(t)))$$

The system will cease to operate when there are no more accessible states : its domain of dis-organization is thus defined. The viability domain can only be defined relative to *f*. In the classical theory of viability and control, one assumes *K* known and the observer or the system chooses the next state if one exists within *K*:

$$\forall s \in \mathrm{K} \quad \mathrm{f(s)} \cap \mathrm{K} \neq \emptyset$$

This point of view is too demanding for an appropriate theory of autonomous systems, since is supposes an omniscient control from outside, even if the controlling agent is supposed to be not human but environmental optimizing parameters. For an autonomous unit we must modify the definition as follows :

$$\forall s \in K \quad f(s) \subset K$$

This says that the function f for an autonomous system must guess, at any moment, a set of solutions that are all viable by eliminating all others. This capacity is best expressed in the notion of abduction. C.S. Peirce states abduction as "the mind's capacity to guess the hypothesis with which experience must be confronted, leaving aside the vast majority of possible hypothesis without examination" (Peirce, 6.530). This is the reverse of the usual logical implication arrow, which is close to what we need for an autonomous behavior. To fix ideas let us give a logical characterization of abduction as follows:

Definition: An abductive machine is a function $f{:}A \rightarrow 2^B$ which interprets the indices in a space A to produce a restricted domain of hypothesis in a space B.

This abductive capacity is both an eliminating capacity and a hermeneutic (i.e interpretive) capacity. We can evaluate these capacities in probabilistic terms by assuming a uniform measure μ on B, so that

- the eliminating abductive capacity is $1-\dfrac{\mu(f(s))}{\mu(B)}$
- the hermeneutic abductive capacity is $\dfrac{\mu(f(s)\cap K)}{\mu(f(s))}$

We are less interested here in the eliminating capacity than in the hermeneutic capacity. Let us remark that the hermeneutic capacity of all states of K is one, but, clearly, the above definition of a viability domain does not give the system a finite horizon of life. Once the system steps into its viability domain, it will remain for ever within it. For a more realistic description, we consider domains where the hermeneutic capacity is only close to one.

We will now utilize the hermeneutic abductive capacity as a key notion for the understanding of autonomous devices with a large adaptability, since they do not know *a priori* their viability domain (Bourgine, 91):

Hypothesis 2:
Every autonomous system behaves as an abductive machine with a hermeneutic acquired capacity close to unity along its trajectory of states.

It is clear that in living systems the hermeneutic capacity is almost always close to unity, since they realize an enormous numbers of sensori-motor cycles and yet remain viable. Everything happens as if the living system had the capacity to find viable behavior within a given life horizon, and thus as if both Hypothesis 1 and 2 were valid. Notice how operational closure and viability domain are closely linked although not equivalent. The first refers to the algebraic closure of the system on the basis of its previous state and its coupling; the second to the fact that it remains within bounds so that its operation may continue and hence within the viability domain. Hypothesis 1 and 2 represent, so to speak, the two complementary sides of the same process.

This situation has been the result of millions of years of natural evolution, and it thus differs strongly from the case of artificial devices. But it makes it clear that one central topic in artificial life is how to define and implement, as part of the systems closure, effective abduction processes. This demands a further clarification of what such abduction capacities might be, which is the theme of the next section.

4 VIABILITY AND METADYNAMICS

One important key to abduction capacities, proper to living systems endowed with a nervous system, has been widely explored recently in the form of distributed processes within a very well connected network. To the extent that such studies are based on network architectures such as those found in all unsupervised learning schemes, their operational closure is guaranteed.

In general we wish to characterize an adapting process as a metadynamical procedure, that is, a procedure g which changes the dynamics f of the system after each time step. Thus the unit is expressed by the triplet:

$$Unit(g,f,s)(t) \rightarrow Unit(g,f+\delta f,s)(t+1)$$

There are at least three important manners in which such metadynamics have been conceived so far, and it useful to see them as variants of the same research as just described:

1. Neuronal strategies: the nodes of the networks are fixed (and considered as some form of idealized neurons), but their connections are allowed to vary according to various algorithms, such as Hebb's rule or its variants (see e.g. Amit, (1989) for review of this large literature). The constraints for an autonomous system is that learning should be either by reinforcement (various models) or by unsupervised learning (again various models available) (Kohonen, 1984). Metadynamics which assume a direct supervised learning such as back-propagation, are less directly applicable for implementation of autonomous devices for obvious reasons.

2. Genetic strategies: here the emphasis of the metadynamics is not so much on a fixed set of nodes in a network (neuronal or not), but on the way in which one can apply rules for the replacement and updating of the participating nodes. A classical approach is via recombination of the previously existing nodes, much like in genetic recombination of chromosomal DNA. This approach was originally developed by Holland (1975, 1987) and is in full expansion (Grefenstette and Goldberg, 1991).

3. Immunitary strategies: like the previous case, connections between cells are not modified *per se*, but the list of active or participating agents changes continuously. The difference with genetic algorithms is that the new participating nodes are not recombinations of previously existing ones, but newly recruited nodes from a large potential pool. The core of this most recent of metadynamical processes is inspired by the amazing adaptability of the immune system (Bersini and Varela, 1991).

In all these cases, the operational closure of the system is respected by a trajectory, not only in state space but in continual change in the defining dynamics, which maximizes the chances that the choice of the next state will remain in the viability domain. Thus the observation of natural systems teaches us yet another lesson: metadynamical capacities are essential for their capacity for viability, and, by the same token, for their adaptability in vastly different and unpredictable environments .

5 ARTIFICIAL LIFE: PERSPECTIVES

In this introductory essay we have tried to be explicit about some key notions which are shared by various researchers in artificial life. We reiterate that in order to avoid falling into the trap of a mere fashionable buzz word, or a fascination with technological wizardry without direction, it is important not to lose sight of the deep issues that animate this re-surgence of research. Our view, as we stated at the outset, is that AL finds its *elan* because it (re-) discovers the central role of the basic abilities of living system as the key to any form of knowledge from simple sensori-motor capacities all the way to symbolic interaction. Therefore, the key is the identification of such basic living properties and our stance here is that autonomy is the emblematic quality which needs to be unfolded into clear and practical concepts as expressed in our two Hypotheses.

In contrast with classical models in AI and cognitive science, AL if understood as we have presented it here, leaves behind the notion of knowledge as being a form of problem-solving of problems already posed; knowledge becomes instead the capacity to pose the relevant problems which are solved in order to preserve viability (Bourgine & Le Moigne, 87). These two positions are sufficiently different to become a "nouvelle AI" in the words R.Brooks (Steels, 1992). Inside cognitive science there has also an historical progression, which began with classical cognitivism (or computationalism), continued with connectionism which opened the way to a full appreciation of issues dear to AL. The last step in this progression has been characterized by one of us as an enactive view of cognitive processes , which also places the autonomy of the system as its center and is thus naturally close to AL (Varela, 1989; 1991).

The comparative table below is an attempt to evoke a progressive shift of research trends and their corresponding emphasis in some dimensions of analysis (Varela, 1989; Bourgine, 1991).

To conclude, this first ECAL is a living proof that the issues just discussed are being addressed by a growing community of researchers from all disciplinary fields, and that theoretical, conceptual and engineering progress is quite possible in notions that until recently were dismissed as merely metaphorical. The practice of autonomous systems is not any longer a matter of mere vague speculation in contrast to a well developed theory of control systems. It is the necessary enlargement of the field of science to encompass what is most interesting in life and knowledge.

	Cognitivism --> Connectionism --> Enaction	
problems:	well defined	not representable
resolution:	heuristic methods	adaptive methods
reasoning:	deduction	abduction
behavior:	given	emergent
knowledge:	symbolic	know-how
characterization	controlled	autonomous
success criteria:	validity	viability

6 REFERENCES

Amit,D. (1989), Neural Networks, Cambridge U.Press,1989.

Aubin, J.P.(1991) Viability Theory, Birhäuser, Berlin

Aubin,J.P. and C.Celina, (1989) Differential Inclusions, Springer-Verlag, Berlin.

Bersini,H. and F.Varela, (1991), Hints for adaptive problem solving gleaned from immune networks, in: H.-P.Schwefel and R.Männer (Eds.), Parallel Problem Solving from Nature, Lecture Notes in Computer Science N°496, Springer Verlag, Berlin, pp.343-354.

Bourgine P., Le Moigne J.L. (1987), The intelligence of economics and the economics of intelligence,in: Economics and Artificial Intelligence, Ed. J.L. Roos, Pergamon Press, 1987.

Bourgine P. (1991) , Heuristic and Abduction, Report n° 65, Dept. of Computer Science, University of Caen .

Grefenstette, J .J. and D .E. Goldberg (1991) (Eds.) Genetic Algorithms, Morgan Kauffman, 1991

Holland, J.H.(1975), Adaptation in natural and artificial systems. Ann Arbor : the university of Michigan Press.

Holland, J.H., (1980), Adaptive algorithms for discovering and using general patterns in growing knowledge-bases, Int.J.Policy Analysis Inform. Syst. 4 : 245-268.

Holland J.H. (1987), Genetic algorithms and classifier systems : foundations and future directions, Proc. Second ICGA .

Kohonen T.(1984) Self-Organization and Associative Memory. Springer Verlag, Berlin.

Langton, C., Taylor,C, J.D.Farmer, S.Rasmunssen, (1991) Artificial Life II, Addisson- Wesley, New Jersey.

Meyer J.A., Wilson S.W. (1991), From animals to animats, M.I.T./Bradford Books, Cambridge,MA.

Maturana,H. and F.Varela,(1980) Autopoeisis and Cognition: The realization of the Living, D.Reidel, Boston.

Steels, L. (1992) (Ed.), Situated Cognition, Emergent Functionality and Symbol Grounding, Artificial Intelligence Journal, (in press)

Varela, F., Maturana,H. and R.Uribe, (1974) Autopoeisis: the organization of the living, its characterization and a model, BioSystems 5:187-195.

Varela, F., (1979) Principles of Biological Autonomy, Elsevier/North-Holland, New York.

Varela, F. (1989) Connaître: Les sciences congnitives, Eds. du Seuil. Paris.

Varela, F., (1991) Organism: A meshwork of selfless selves, in: A.Tauber (Ed.) Organism and the Origin of Self, Kluwer Associates, Dordrecht, pp.79-107.

AUTONOMOUS ROBOTS

Artifical Life and Real Robots

Rodney A. Brooks
MIT Artificial Intelligence Laboratory
545 Technology Square
Cambridge, MA 02139, USA
brooks@ai.mit.edu

Abstract

The first part of this paper explores the general issues in using Artifical Life techniques to program actual mobile robots. In particular it explores the difficulties inherent in transferring programs evolved in a simulated environment to run on an actual robot. It examines the dual evolution of organism morphology and nervous systems in biology. It proposes techniques to capture some of the search space pruning that dual evolution offers in the domain of robot programming. It explores the relationship between robot morphology and program structure, and techniques for capturing regularities across this mapping.

The second part of the paper is much more specific. It proposes techniques which could allow realistic explorations concerning the evolution of programs to control physically embodied mobile robots. In particular we introduce a new abstraction for behavior-based robot programming which is specially tailored to be used with genetic programming techniques. To compete with hand coding techniques it will be necessary to automatically evolve programs that are one to two orders of magnitude more complex than those previously reported in any domain. Considerable extensions to previously reported approaches to genetic programming are necessary in order to achieve this goal.

1 Introduction

In recent years a new approach to Artificial Intelligence has developed which is based on building behavior-based programs to control situated and embodied robots in unstructured dynamically changing environments [**Brooks 91c**]. Rather than modularize perception, world modeling, planning, and execution, the new approach builds intelligent control systems where many individual modules directly generate some part of the behavior of the robot. In the purest form of this model each module incorporates its own perceptual, modeling, and planning requirements. An arbitration or mediation scheme, built within the framework of the modules, controls which behavior-producing module has control of which part of the robot at any given time. The programs are layered in their construction, but are non-hierarchical in their control flow, with lower levels taking care of more primitive activities and higher levels taking care of more sophisticated ones (see [**Brooks 86**] and [**Brooks 90b**] for an introduction and review, and [**Brooks 91c**] for a survey of the field).

This work draws its inspirations from neurobiology, ethology, psychophysics, and sociology. The approach grew out of dissatisfactions with traditional robotics and Artificial Intelligence, which seemed unable to deliver real-time performance in a dynamic world. The key idea of the new approach is to advance both robotics and AI by considering the problems of building an autonomous agent that physically is an autonomous mobile robot, and that carries out some useful tasks in an environment which has not been specially structured or engineered for it.

While robots built on these principles have been demonstrated learning calibration information [**Viola 90**], behavior coordination [**Maes and Brooks 90**], and representations of the world [**Mataric 90**], progress in learning new behaviors has proven more difficult. Today, we are constrained to programming each new behavior by hand.

Work in Artificial Life has developed techniques for evolving programs for controlling situated, but unembodied (i.e., simulated), robots (e.g., [**Langton 87**], [**Langton et al 90**]). At some level one of the goals of Artificial Life is to move out of the digital medium into that of embodied systems. Is there a match between AL and AI? This paper explores the prospects for using Artificial Life techniques to evolve programs to control physically embodied mobile robots, so that we no longer have to do it all by hand.

There have been no reports to date of programs evolved for embodied robots. There has been work on learning new behaviors using reinforcement learning, e.g., [**Kaelbling 90**] and [**Mahadevan and Connell 90**] used Q-learning ([**Watkins 89**]). The major drawback is the large number of runtime trials, many more than needed by real animals, and the need for carefully "shaping" the learning by splitting up the taks into little pieces that the robot learns sequentially. It seems that real animals have innate built-in structures that facilitate learning particular constrained classes of behaviors. The vast numbers of trials necessary are spread over the generations, and runtime learning has a more constrained space in which it must search.

Recently **[Langton 91]** suggested using genetic programming for behavior-based embodied robots to overcome these limitations.

2 Genetic Programming

One way to solve the programming problem might be to use Artificial Life techniques to evolve behavior-based programs.

Previously many workers have used genetic algorithms to program software agents, typically running in cellular worlds. [**Collins and Jefferson 90**] is a good example. It demonstrates the evolution of both neural networks and finite state machines through a genetic algorithm running on a bit string representation.

More conventional computer programs have also been processed with genetic algorithms, such as the pioneering work of [**Friedberg 58**], [**Friedberg et al 59**], and more recently that of [**Ray 90**]. Robot programs, and in particular behavior-based robot programs, are much more complex than any programs that have been reported in the literature to have been so evolved. A reasonable comparison might be in terms of the memory taken to represent the programs. By this measure behavior-based robot programs are three orders of magnitude larger than those mutated competitively by genetic techniques.

Recently, however, [**Koza 90**] has shown a number of stimulating results by applying genetic algorithms directly to lisp-like programs rather than to more traditional bit strings [**Holland 75**]. He has been very successful in a number of domains with this technique, rekindling earlier interest in the idea of mutating lisp program structures directly [**Lenat 77**]. [**Koza 91**] shows an example of synthesizing the base behaviors of [**Mataric 90**]'s behavior-based robot programs. He makes a number of simplifying assumptions, and reduces the search space significantly by carefully selecting the primitives by hand after examining Mataric's source code. His programs only run in simulation rather than on a physically embodied robot, but the results are nevertheless significant enough to warrant further exploration of this technique.

Before these techniques can be adopted and modified for programming physically embodied mobile robots there are a number of problems which must be addressed:

- Most likely the evolution of robot programs must be carried out on simulated robots—unfortunately there is a vast difference (which is not appreciated by people who have not used real robots) between simulated robots and physical robots and their dynamics of interaction with the environment.
- The structure of the search space of possible programs is very dependent on the representation used for programs and the primitives available to be incorporated. Careful design is necessary.
- Natural evolution co-evolved the structure of the physical entities and their neural controllers in a way which arguably cut down the size of its search space. Can some equivalent tricks be played when evolving programs for robots?

3 Simulations of Physical Robots

The number of trials needed to test individuals precludes using physical robots for testing the bulk of the control programs produced for them by genetic means. The obvious choice is to use simulated robots and then run the successful programs on the physical robots.

Previously we have been very careful to avoid using simulations ([**Brooks 90b, 91b, 91c**]) for two fundamental reasons.

- Without regular validation on real robots there is a great danger that much effort will go into solving problems that simply do not come up in the real world with a physical robot (or robots).
- There is a real danger (in fact, a near certainty) that programs which work well on simulated robots will completely fail on real robots because of the differences in real world sensing and actuation—it is very hard to simulate the actual dynamics of the real world.

3.1 Artifactual Problems

There has been a tendency to use cellular representations of space for simulating robots in Artificial Life (e.g., [**Langton et al 90**]) and Artificial Intelligence (e.g., [**Pollack and Ringuette 90**] and [**Wang and Beni 90**]).

These representations are good for conducting computational experiments, and help uncover many fundamental issues. Unfortunately they do not shed light on all the problems which will be encountered when using physically embodied robots. For the physical robot perspective, cellular worlds have three problems. First, there is no notion of the uncertainty that the real world presents—see the subsection below for more discussion of this point. Second, there is a tendency to not only postulate sensors which return perfect information (e.g., the cell ahead *contains food*—no real perception system can do such a thing), but there is a real danger of confusing the global world view and the robot's view of the world. Third, the dynamics actually tend to be more brittle than in the real world where noise and stochastic processes smooth things out quite a bit.

The dynamics mentioned in the last point often leads to problems which do not occur in the real world. A good example is being concerned with how two robots resolve a conflict when their paths must cross a single cell simultaneously. This and other equally artifactual problems are the main concern of a number of papers in this area.

But the same intellectual problem of worrying about simulated problems which do not actually appear in the real world is more general than just for cellular simulations. A number of papers have appeared that are concerned with path planning for mobile robots in non-grid worlds, i.e., in two dimensional Euclidean space. Some of these papers expend much effort on solving the problem of the paths of two robots crossing each other and introduce elaborate protocols to avoid deadlock. But real robots would never reach the state of perfect deadlock which are postulated in these papers. They would never run down their respective corridors perfectly and arrive at identical times. Simple reactive strategies would suffice to break any possible deadlock, just as random variations in ethernet controllers break deadlocks on rebroadcast.

Thus, while simulated worlds are in many ways simpler than the real world, they are paradoxically sometimes harder to operate within.

3.2 Real Worlds

For a physically embodied robot in the real world there are a number of key points to understand.

- Sensors deliver very uncertain values even in a stable world.
- The data delivered by sensors are not direct descriptions of the world as objects and their relationships.
- Commands to actuators have very uncertain effects.

A particular sensor, under ideal experimental conditions, may have a particular resolution. Suppose the sensor is a sonar. Then to measure its resolution an experiment will be set up where a return signal from the test article is sensed, and the resolution will be compared against measurements of actual distance. The experiment might be done for a number of different surface types. But when that sensor is installed on a mobile robot, situated in a cluttered, dynamically changing world, the return signals that reach the sensor may come from many possible sources. The object nearest the sensor may not be made of one of the tested materials. It may be at such an angle that the sonar pulse acts as though it were a mirror, and so the sonar sees a secondary reflection. The secondary lobes of the sonar might detect something in a cluttered situation where there was no such interference in the clean experimental situation. All sensors have comparable sets of problems associated with them. They simply do not return clean accurate readings. At best they deliver a fuzzy approximation to what they are apparently measuring, and often they return something completely different.

Even given these difficulties, sensor readings are not the same as a description of the world. Sensors measure certain quantities or indirect aspects of the world. They do separate objects from the background. They do not identify objects. They do not give pose information about objects. They do not separate out static objects, moving objects, and effects due to self motion. They do not operate in a stable coordinate system independent of the uncertain motion of the robot. They do not integrate other sensory modalities into a single consistent picture of the world. A robot operating in the real world needs a complex perceptual system. As much as 50% of the human brain seems to be devoted to perception. Off the shelf perceptual systems are not available, however. All of the problems listed above are active areas of research by perception researchers. And, as argued elsewhere [**Brooks 91a, 91b**], it may be impossible to treat perception as a black box with a clean interface to the rest of intelligence.

Just as sensors do not deliver simple descriptions of the world, high level action commands need many layers of refinement before they become appropriately orchestrated motor currents. In any case, the desired action and the achieved action may differ widely depending on the intricate details of the situation at hand. On flat smooth floors, odometry errors soon accumulate to the point that a a robot needs to recalibrate its position to some external reference. Besides a large unsystematic component, odometry may also have systematic aspects, e.g., depending on the relative nap of the carpet on which the robot is operating—this has lead some researchers to try to sense the nap! The situation is much more difficult to model, of course, when the robot is in contact with an obstacle.

Sensing, and action are intimately tied together in a physical robot. They both rely on, and at the same time generate, the dynamics of the interaction of the robot with the world. Simple state space models of the world do not suffice in the internal control program of a physically embodied mobile robot.

4 Morphological Development

We now turn to the nature of the search space in which the genetic programming techniques must work.

In nature, evolution experiments with both the morphology of the individual and its neural circuitry cotemporaneously, and through the same genetic mechanism. There are two important consequences of this, both of which reduce the space which evolution must search.

- The control program is evolved incrementally. Evolution is restricted initially to a small search space. The size of the space grows over many generations, but by then there is a good partial solution already found which forms the basis for searching the newer parts of the space.
- Symmetric or repeated structures naturally have symmetric or repeated neural circuits installed—they do not need to be individually evolved (e.g., a single encoding specifies the wiring of both a right and a left leg, and likewise each added segment containing a leg pair in a mutant *Drosophila* comes with neural circuitry).

Our approach to behavior-based programming of robots has always been to build layers incrementally [**Brooks 86**]. For genetic programming we suggest that the robot (both simulated and physical) should initially be operated with only some of its sensors, and perhaps only some of its actuators. Programs can be evolved for this simplified robot, much as our hand written programs ([**Brooks 90b**]) start out with layers which only use some of the capabilities of the robot. Once fundamental behaviors are present, additional sensors and actuators can be made available so that higher level behaviors can be evolved. The particular fitness function used to control the evolutionary search can be varied over time to emphasize the use of new capabilities and the need to develop higher level behaviors. There might also be some advantage to biasing the genetic operators towards operating more on the newer behaviors than on the early. (Although it certainly makes sense for the crossover operator to take pieces of old behavior—e.g., an orienting behavior-based on a sensor activated early in the evolutionary search would be a good prototype for an orienting behavior using a new sensor.)

In our hand written programs we capture symmetry and repeated structure by the use of macros. For example, on the six-legged robot Genghis ([**Brooks 89**]) there is a macro version of the leg control behaviors which gets instantiated six times, once for each leg. This suggests two ideas to again reduce the genetic search space.

- The language that is subject to genetic programming should include a macro capability. As the search learns how to use these effectively it will greatly accelerate the production of good programs.
- There must be some way to reference the symmetries and regularities of the morphological structure of the robot, in order to invoke the macros correctly. This morphological descriptor will be a constant for each particular class of robot. The constant could be evolved, but it would be much quicker to have that as an available constant somewhere in the original pool of ancestral programs.

5 Evolving Behavior-Based Programs

[**Koza 91**] reports on a genetic programming implementation in simulation of the navigation behaviors of [**Mataric 90**]'s robot Toto. The programming language he uses is a carefully chosen subset of Lisp. While adequate for the task Koza reports, based on our experience with physical robots, it is perhaps not sufficient for the more general case.

[**Langton 91**] has suggested the idea of genetically programming a physical robot using the Behavior Language (BL) defined in [**Brooks 90a**]. Unfortunately, there are many drawbacks to using BL directly.

[**Lenat and Brown 84**] analyze the the apparent success of the discovery system AM [**Lenat 77**]. They point out the crucial way in which the syntax of the Lisp programs being mutated mirrored the semantics of the world of simple mathematics concepts being explored. We can likewise expect performance of a crossover based genetic programming system to critically depend on the syntax of the language used and the way in which crossover mutates a program's semantics.

In this section we try to identify the choices made by Koza which led to his success, and compare them to what is available in BL. We propose a higher level language, called GEN, which can be compiled into BL as the target language for genetically programming physical robots.

5.1 Primitives for Genetic Programming of Robots

[**Koza 90**] uses a representation for Lisp programs which is crucial to the easy application of crossover. He treats an S-expression as a tree rooted with the first elements, and with one branch for each of the subsequent elements. E.g., the expression `(* 1 2 3)` is thought of as a tree with four nodes, a depth of two and a branching factor of three at the root node. Koza calls each thing which can occur at a non-terminal node a function, but that terminology differs from modern Lisp terminology. In fact his operators are often special forms or macros.

For instance, he might use `IF-SENSOR` as an operator which accesses some hidden state (or perceptual information) and depending on its value either evaluate the first argument or the second argument—thus it is not a function in the usual sense of being applied to all its evaluated arguments. Such embedded conditionals seem to be the only conditional forms used by Koza. This is for a very good reason. Pure Lisp can be thought of as a type-free language. But, in fact some values, such as the test argument to a conditional, are treated as booleans. Although everything is trivially coercible to a boolean, including a conditional requiring a boolean test would greatly increase the search space and drastically lower the density of semantically useful program trees.

In **[Koza 91]** careful analysis of **[Mataric 90]**'s original code was done in order to pick just the right set of conditionals with access to hidden state which is to be tested.

Without the hindsight from a successful implementation GEN must allow more general testing than Koza allows. But the heuristic of embedding predicates in conditional special forms (implemented as macros) is a good one.

Koza hides critical constants in these special forms also. **[Ray 90]** points out the difficulty in having too many constants around in the genetic pool, and instead evolves simple constructive program segments to build them. Primitives to make this easy would be a good idea in GEN also.

5.2 Variables and Lexicality

Real BL programs use many named state variables. Sometimes these are simply used as semaphores, sometimes they are used as counters, sometimes they are used for calibration offsets, and sometimes they are used to store sensor readings, or processed sensor readings, for later comparison.

As with Lisp and BL, lexical contours should be able to be introduced at any point in a program (both languages use `LET` to do this). Variable names as such can not be used conveniently if crossover is to occur, as the produced programs will not be lexically meaningful very often. Instead some sort of indexing scheme is needed. A global index for a behavior is not a good idea, because then it will be hard to use crossover to duplicate little pieces of code with local variables. Instead we propose using a single form `(variable-ref)`, and specific operators to move up and down the lexical contour tree, and to rotate around the set of variables introduced at a particular contour (often there will be just a single variable).

P	N	T	D	B	AD	AB	behavior name
3	61	25	4	4	4.8	1.6	CORRECT
3	79	35	4	6	4.5	1.7	ALIGN
2	97	41	3	5	4.9	1.7	STROLL
3	64	29	4	6	4.0	1.7	SIDES
3	96	41	4	6	5.0	1.7	VALLUMFILIA
3	24	21	2	7	1.9	7.0	PRINT-PPORT
1	10	3	4	3	2.5	1.3	GET-PPORT-DATA
1	3	1	3	2	1.7	1.0	GET-SONAR-DATA
8	230	147	5	7	3.1	2.7	BASEMON
12	229	129	6	12	3.0	2.2	BASE
1	49	28	5	9	4.2	2.3	DEBUG
40	942	500	6	12	3.8	2.0	total

Figure 1: A statistical summary of a BL program to drive the robot TOTO in its wall following. It includes various debugging behaviors and display code. The columns are P, number of processes, N, total number of nodes, T, total number of terminals, D, maximum depth, B, maximum branching factor, AD, average depth of all nodes, AB, average breadth at non-terminal nodes, and the name chosen by the programmer as the behavior name.

5.3 Depth and Breadth

In Koza's re-implementation of Toto's navigation behaviors the best solution found has 157 nodes of which 65 are terminals, and the tree has depth 12. Figure 1 shows the statistics for Mataric's original BL program for the same task. Overall it has 942 nodes, and 500 terminals, and coincidentally a maximum depth of 12.

The difference can be accounted for by three components:

1. There are a number of housekeeping operations, reporting, and debugging features included in the original BL program. These can be left out of GEN programs also.

2. The techniques used by Koza to compress the trees are not present in the BL programs. GEN will be able to get some of this benefit, but not all, as it needs to be more general than the minimal set of primitives used by Koza.

3. The code produced by Koza has only been tested in simulation, and relies a little on the simplicty of the the simulated emvironment. GEN programs for embodied robots may need to be slightly more complex than this.

It seems reasonable to assume that a general purpose GEN language program for this task might come out a factor of two to three bigger than Koza's program.

Evolving a program of that size certainly seems within reach—it is not a drastic step up from Koza's results.

For comparison, figure 2 shows the statistics for a walking program for the six-legged robot Attila. Again there are a number of debugging aids and tools included in this program, along with some low level substrate processes (which need not be evolved).

5.4 Mappings

Earlier it was pointed out that there needs to be some way to relate the evolved program to the morphological regularities in the structure of the robot. There is an additional related problem which if not handled well will generate a search space with only a low density of useful program fragments.

Typically on real robots a ring of 8, say, bump sensors, or infrared proximity sensors, will be accessible as a single byte of 8 one bit values. The mapping between arrangment of those bits and the morphology of the sensors is usually quite arbitrary, and indeed there may be no natural semantically valid arrangement of the bits.

Careful attention must be paid to this issue to provide appropriate mapping primitives so that the evolvoing programs can pull out the right boolean bits. One simple heuristic for the robot designer is to make all such mappings consistent where possible on a particular robot design, thus maximizing the benefits for crossover of program fragments in adopting new sensors.

6 Reconnecting to Reality

Eventually the programs developed by genetic programming are to be run on physically embodied robots. There are a number of concerns in connecting the programs back to this reality.

6.1 Calibration

It is our experience that supposedly identical physical robot components are not identical. We have experienced this with very different sensing and actuator responses from supposedly identical legs on a six legged robot. We have also experienced this with 20 small wheeled robots (R-1's).

On reflecting on our past practices, we realized that when programming just a single robot system we had experimented by hand and built appropriate constants into our programs to handle the responses of our sensors and actuators. When we had the same code running on multiple copies of a robot, or robot component, we found this approach inadequate. We have found it necessary therefore to build in adpative elements into the run-time structures of our programs which change thresholds and timeout intervals. This is not yet a formalized process, but we need to find a set of primitives that allow such adpative elements to be constructed easily.

The implication of this for genetic programming of physical robots is clear. There must be a set of primitives available to the system so that adaptive elements can be constructed. Further, the simulation must have enough variance in it that these adaptive elements are essential to successfully run the programs on the simulated robots, so that the adaptive elements will be there when it comes time to validate on physical robots.

6.2 Adapting the Simulation

When the programs which have been evolved on the simulated robots are tried on embodied robots there will be two types of information available.

1. How well the programs work on embodied robots.
2. How different the performance of the programs is on the simulated robots and the embodied robots.

The first type of information can be used to inform the genetic programming system, as would any simulated test of the generated programs.

The second type of information should be used to tune up the simulation to better match reality. One would expect that this would be done by hand. However there is a more tantalizing possibility. Perhaps this information could be used to co-evolve the simulator using genetic programming techniques—especially if the simulator were written in the same sort of BL as the robots were programmed (our current simulator is partially written in BL). The idea would be to run the evolved robot programs on the embodied robots, then with those programs fixed, evolve the simulator until it better matched what happened in reality. There are deep issues in finding measures to compare the performance of the simulator to reality, since the robots won't be going through exactly the same sequence of operations. Eventually, perhaps, this may be a viable approach.

7 Progress

At the time of writing no complete experiments have been carried out using the ideas in this paper.

We have built a simulator for multiple R-2 robots[1]. It is not grid-based, but instead the coordinates of a robot can be arbitrary floating point numbers within the workspace. R-2 robots have a two wheeled differential drive with passive castors for stability. The simulator handles arbitrary independent velocities on the two wheels. There is a simple physics associated with

[1] Manufactured by IS Robotics.

motion of a robot when it has collided with an obstacle (which are all modeled as immovable cylinders). The sensors currently modeled are a ring of eight bump sensors, a ring of eight infrared proximity sensors, and three forward looking beacon sensors. We expect to add more sensor models. No explicit uncertainty is built into the sensor or actuator models. However, the BL program which runs the robots refers to the real time clock of the computer on which the simulation is run. Noise is therefore introduced into the system by the load on the computer, and by the interjection of the Lisp garbage collector.

The complete simulation is about 500 lines of combined Common Lisp and BL code. We have no hypothesis at this point about how well programs developed on the simulator will transfer to the real robot. This will be a critical data point in evaluating the utility of the approach.

The Behavior Language compiler has been modified so that other programs can call it, rather than having to go through the previous interface optimized for people using it to program physical robots. It already had a backend which produced a byte-code program for which a Common Lisp program provides an interpreter. Thus, BL programs can be automatically compiled and run on a simulation machine. In addition, a higher level language known as GEN has been partially built which compiles into BL programs. GEN is based on the ideas explored in the previous sections.

8 Conclusion

The key ideas presented in this paper are:

- Use genetic programming techniques to build behavior-based programs which can run real robots (this idea is due to **[Langton 91]**).
- Evolution and runtime adaptation are two separate issues.
- All robots will need runtime adaptation elements.
- Evolution of control structure needs to run in parallel with evolution of morphology—in robots this can be simulated by progressively enabling more sensors and actuators as layers of behaviors evolve for those already operational.
- Regularity (e.g., symmetry or repeated structures) in morphological structure should be mirrored in regularity in the control structure, and thus needs to be representable in the control language.
- Special care must be taken in design of the control language to minimize the depth and breadth of useful program trees.
- To make crossover useful in a control language with variables, a new method for representing variable references was introduced.
- There are real methodological dangers in using simulations as a testing medium in which to evolve programs which are intended eventually to run on physical robots—great care must be taken to develop a sufficient validation regime.

There are many possible approaches to using Artificial Life techniques for programming physical robots. We have chosen one particular approach here, but many of the points of concern will be common with other approaches.

Acknowledgements

Maja Mataric, Ian Horswill and Anita Flynn provided helpful comments on drafts of this paper.

Support for this research was provided in part by the University Research Initiative under Office of Naval Research contract N00014-86-K-0685, in part by the Advanced Research Projects Agency under Office of Naval Research contract N00014-85-K-0124, in part by the Hughes Artificial Intelligence Center, and in part by Mazda Corporation.

References

[Brooks 86] "A Robust Layered Control System for a Mobile Robot", Rodney A. Brooks, *IEEE Journal of Robotics and Automation*, RA-2, April, 14–23.

[Brooks 89] "A Robot that Walks: Emergent Behavior from a Carefully Evolved Network", Rodney A. Brooks, *Neural Computation*, 1:2, Summer, 253–262.

[Brooks 90a] "The Behavior Language; User's Guide", Rodney A. Brooks, *MIT A.I. Lab Memo* 1227, April.

[Brooks 90b] "Elephants Don't Play Chess", Rodney A. Brooks, *in* **[Maes 90]**, 1990, 3–15.

[Brooks 91a] "Intelligence without Representation", Rodney A. Brooks, *Artificial Intelligence 47*, Jan., 139–159.

[Brooks 91b] "Intelligence without Reason", Rodney A. Brooks, *IJCAI-91*, Sydney, Australia, Aug., 569–595.

[Brooks 91c] "New Approaches to Robotics", Rodney A. Brooks, *Science 253*, Sep., 1227–1232.

[Collins and Jefferson 90] "AntFarm: Towards Simulated Evolution", Robert J. Collins and David R. Jefferson, *in* **[Langton et al 90]**, 579–601.

[Friedberg 58] "A Learning Machine, Part I", R. M. Friedberg, *IBM Journal of Research and Development 2*, 2–13.

[Friedberg et al 59] "A Learning Machine, Part II", R. M. Friedberg, B. Dunham, and J. H. North, *IBM Journal of Research and Development 3*, 282–287.

[Holland 75] "Adaptation in Natural and Artificial Systems", John H. Holland, *University of Michigan Press*, Ann Arbor, MI.

[Kaelbling 90] "Learning in Embedded Systems", Leslie Pack Kaelbling, *Ph.D. Thesis*, Stanford.

[Koza 90] "Evolution and Co-Evolution of Computer Programs to Control Independently-Acting Agents", John R. Koza, *Proc. First Int. Conf. on Simulation of Adaptive Behavior, Paris, MIT Press*, Cambridge, MA, 1990, 366–375.

[Koza 91] "Evolving Emergent Wall Following Robotic Behavior Using the Genetic Programming Paradigm", John R. Koza, *ECAL, Paris*, Dec.

[Langton 87] "Proceedings of Artificial Life", Christopher G. Langton *(ed), Addison-Wesley*, appeared 1989.

[Langton 91] *Personal communication*, Christopher G. Langton, September.

[Langton et al 90] "Proceedings of Artificial Life, II", Christopher G. Langton, Charles Taylor, J. Doyne Farmer, and Steen Rasmussen *(eds), Addison-Wesley*, appeared 1991.

[Lenat 77] "The Ubiquity of Discovery", Douglas B. Lenat, *IJCAI-77*, Cambridge, MA, Aug., 1093–1105.

[Lenat and Brown 84] "Why AM and EURISKO Appear to Work", Douglas B. Lenat and John Seely Brown, *Artificial Intelligence 23*, 269–294.

[Maes 90] "Designing Autonomous Agents: Theory and Practice from Biology to Engineering and Back", Pattie Maes *(ed), MIT Press*, Cambridge, MA, 1990.

[Maes and Brooks 90] "Learning to Coordinate Behaviors", Pattie Maes and Rodney A. Brooks, *AAAI-90*, Boston, MA, 1990, 796–802.

[Mahadevan and Connell 90] "Automatic Programming of Behavior-based Robots using Reinforcement Learning", Sridhar Mahadevan and Jonathan Connell, *IBM T.J. Watson Research Report*, Dec.

[Mataric 90] "A Distributed Model for Mobile Robot Environment–Learning and Navigation", Maja J Mataric, *MIT A.I. Lab Technical Report* 1228, May.

[Pollack and Ringuette 90] "Introducing the Tileworld: Experimentally Evaluating Agent Architectures", Martha E. Pollack and Marc Ringuette, *AAAI-90*, Boston, MA, August, 183–189.

[Ray 90] "An Approach to the Synthesis of Life", Thomas S. Ray, *in* **[Langton et al 90]**, 371–408.

[Viola 90] "Adaptive Gaze Control", Paul A. Viola, *MIT SM Thesis*, 1990.

[Wang and Beni 90] "Distributed Computing Problems in Cellular Robotic Systems", Jing Wang and Gerardo Beni, *IEEE/RSJ International Workshop on Intelligent Robots and Systems*, Ikabara, Japan, 819–826.

[Watkins 89] "Learning from Delayed Rewards", Christopher Watkins, *Ph.D. Thesis*, King's College, Cambridge.

P	N	T	D	B	AD	AB	behavior name
6	470	258	6	21	4.1	2.2	MONITOR
2	39	25	5	4	3.2	2.6	PARAMS
2	55	28	4	5	5.5	2.0	R3-FIND
2	55	28	4	5	5.5	2.0	R2-FIND
2	55	28	4	5	5.5	2.0	R1-FIND
2	55	28	4	5	5.5	2.0	L3-FIND
2	55	28	4	5	5.5	2.0	L2-FIND
2	55	28	4	5	5.5	2.0	L1-FIND
3	61	34	5	9	3.8	2.1	STANDUP
1	3	2	2	2	1.7	2.0	ROLLER
2	8	4	3	2	2.0	1.5	R3-SLEG
2	8	4	3	2	2.0	1.5	R2-SLEG
2	8	4	3	2	2.0	1.5	R1-SLEG
2	8	4	3	2	2.0	1.5	L3-SLEG
2	8	4	3	2	2.0	1.5	L2-SLEG
2	8	4	3	2	2.0	1.5	L1-SLEG
6	101	51	9	9	5.1	1.9	FLIPPER
2	34	13	5	3	3.9	1.5	FLIPPED?
1	23	13	3	8	2.6	2.2	CALIBRATE
17	485	224	5	10	3.8	1.8	R3-ALEG
17	485	224	5	10	3.8	1.8	R2-ALEG
17	485	224	5	10	3.8	1.8	R1-ALEG
17	485	224	5	10	3.8	1.8	L3-ALEG
17	485	224	5	10	3.8	1.8	L2-ALEG
17	485	224	5	10	3.8	1.8	L1-ALEG
2	20	9	5	2	3.2	1.6	TILTER
2	11	6	3	2	2.4	1.8	TILTINTERFACE
2	123	53	3	17	6.2	1.7	STATIC-CALIBRATE
3	21	12	4	2	2.8	2.0	PANIC-MAINTAIN
9	151	78	5	17	3.0	1.9	HEADER
2	65	26	5	8	3.8	1.6	SLEEP
4	24	14	4	2	2.7	2.0	DROWSINESS-MAINTAIN
3	61	33	6	10	3.3	2.1	I2CBUS
2	31	13	8	2	5.5	1.6	LISTEN-HOST
176	4526	2176	9	21	4.0	1.9	total

Figure 2: A statistical summary of a walking program for the robot Attila. The columns have the same labels as those in figure 1. Notice that some behaviors are duplicated six times—once for each leg of the robot.

Concept Formation as Emergent Phenomena

Mukesh J Patel
School of Cognitive and Computer Sciences
The University of Sussex
Brighton, UK
mukesh@cogs.susx.ac.uk

Uwe Schnepf
AI Research Division
GMD
Sankt Augustin
Germany
usc@gmdzi.gmd.de

Abstract

Concept formation is a complex learning phenomenon which has yet to be given an adequate account. Following a discussion of some of the shortcomings of recent models of concept formation, our novel approach, focussing on the agent-environment interaction as the key to concept formation, is described. The methodological tools relevant to our ecological approach are explained. An outline of an adaptive complex autonomous system with appropriate computational features (such as classifier systems) to enable us to investigate the nature of concept formation as an emergent phenomenon is presented. Finally, a prototype implementation (robot) designed to enable us to investigate the dynamic nature of concept formation is described.

1 Introduction

A novel approach to the study of concept formation will be described here. It is aimed at overcoming limitations of one sort of models of concept formation in Psychology and Artificial Intelligence (AI) that do not give an adequate account of the process of learning and assimilating new concepts. Recent developments in the field of Complex Adaptive Systems in general and Artificial Life in particular provides a better methodology for investigating the process of simple concept formation. More specifically, the aim is to exploit powerful learning (search) techniques such as genetic algorithms (GA) and parallel distributed processing (PDP) in order to investigate concept formation in an artificial organism[1]. This is essentially a bottom-up approach, free of any preconceptions about the nature and structure of concepts. Learning about the world is not determined by preconceived conceptualisation, as is often the case in knowledge representation in AI. Instead, we assume that an agent (or artificial organism) learns and forms concepts about its environment by performing goal directed behaviour, such as survival and improved fitness. These aspects have an important affect on how concepts are formed and what they represent. In other words, the approach enables the investigation of concept formation as emergent properties of the dynamic process of interaction between an organism and its environment motivated by a set of goals that typically ensure an organism's continued survival.

[1]An *artificial organism* refers to a computational structure which reflects to some extent the characteristics of real organisms in terms of autonomy, desires, goals, needs etc., and which has the ability to sense and act in its (eventually computational) environment according to these characteristics.

2 Evaluation of Models of Concepts

In this section, after a brief description of a widely accepted notion of a concept, we will evaluate some AI and Cognitive Psychology accounts (or models) of concepts. Concepts are the representational equivalent of words or phrases referring to objects or events in the world. Each concept is normally assumed to be defined by a set of features. These features correspond to various properties of objects and events (in the world). For example, the concept of table would have a feature to denote presence of legs which would be assigned the value, "legs present". How "legs" are defined or came to mean what they do for this concept is rarely addressed. Instead, most accounts concentrate on the role of features (as symbolic representations) in concept formation and the relationship between concepts (Keil 1989). Since features represent invariant properties across objects and events, their semantic value is assumed to be determined by this correlation. In order to be formally sound the number and semantic value of basic features remains fixed, ensuring compositional semantics. This assumption has an important implication for modelling emergent phenomenon.

The classical model is one of the earliest and the most basic, rigid and limited in scope. It assumes clear boundaries between concepts and a hierarchical structure to represent relationships between concepts. The nature and function of features determine the clarity of boundaries between concepts. This formal account of concepts fails to predict a large portion of psychological data (Wrobel 1991). For example, there is evidence to suggests that concepts are not very clearly defined in practise (Smith and Medin 1981) and that some concepts seem to have a more central (or basic) role than others (Rosch et al. 1976) thus upsetting the notion of a hierarchical representational structure. This class of concepts is regarded as equivalent of "natural" categories though that has not proved particularly insightful as far as our understanding of the nature and role of concepts in cognition is concerned. Further, instantiated members of a concept are not considered to be equal; some members are regarded as more typical than others (Rosch and Mervis 1975).

Alternative models to account for psychological data incompatible with the predictions of the classical model have been proposed. Some psychological models account for a large portion of empirical data (see for example, Keil 1989), and that certain AI implementations perform specific task with a fair degree of success (Feldman 1986 and Hinton 1986). A probabilistic based model assigns different saliency (or weight) to features between and within sets defining concepts. This, coupled with a threshold based decision procedure, gives a more realistic account of the role of concept in cognitive processes and (human) behaviour. Exemplar based models are an alternative attempt at overcoming the limitations of the basic classical model (Rosch 1978). These models predict that concepts are defined by exemplars which if properly defined can determine gradations in, and typicality of, membership.

While these psychological models seem to provide better accounts of empirical evidence, they are difficult to implement, and so a majority of AI or Machine Learning implementations are based on the classical model. These implementation are largely designed to exploit the formal syntactic properties of the classical model, and are not concerned with semantic representation issues (for examples of implementations see Shavlik and Diettrich 1990). They assume a top down decomposition of concepts and are confined to issues related to symbolic level encodings with fixed semantics. This paradigm pervades research work in AI and has shortcomings similar to those encountered in other fields such as planning and knowledge representation where cognitive processes are modelled as purely syntactic phenomena. The semantic values are fixed beforehand and really function as little more than labels to be interpreted by the user. Though perfectly adequate as logically constructed inference engines operating over well-formed syntactic structures, such models generally ignore the role of semantics and *context* in influencing, altering and constraining concept formation and use.

Our approach is aimed at breaking this chain of recursive syntactic definitions, and to do away with the homunculus metaphor which dominates current AI. None of the models outlined above provide adequate accounts of *concept formation*, which we will suggest partly explains their overall shortcomings. The assumption that concepts are defined by sets of features overlooks other factors which determine their formation and subsequent use. The role of contextual factors may alter the relative saliency of features, which could explain how meaning (intension) of concepts can vary across situations (Barsalou 1982) or how relationship between concepts can be sensitive to context (Tversky 1977). Finally, these models of concept are based on the information processing approach which suffers from a number of shortcomings.

3 Information Processing and Concept Formation

Why is it useful for an agent or organisms to form concepts? Concepts are derived from individual instances but are not confined in their application to just those individuals; they can be applied to classify novel objects and events. The process of concept formation is the process of learning about and encoding invariant properties shared by a set of objects or events in the world. Any agent with an ability to form concepts would therefore gain in efficiency in interacting with its environment. Without concepts an agent's repertoire of sophisticated sensory-motor and cognitive behaviour would be limited to simple reflexive actions in response to a finite set of stimuli. Hence, concept formation and use is part of an agents enhanced survival strategy: A proposition that has very important consequences on how meaning is assigned to concepts.

How are concepts formed? The information processing approach attempts to answer only part of the question: How are similarities and differences between objects and events in the world identified, abstracted and encoded for classification of subsequent instances of similar objects and events? This question is based on the assumption that information is a property of the world which via transducers determine the formal structure and semantics of an organism's concepts. Below we show that accounts of concept formation based on this assumption are necessarily inadequate. And that the shortcomings can be overcome when emphasis is shifted to a more ecological approach focusing on the determinants of rendering continuous, dynamic and random data into discrete, static and deterministic encodings with the appropriate semantics as emergent properties of the agent-environment interaction.

If it is a matter of gathering information from the world then it will not be easy to motivate the formation of an initial, basic set of features, for the following reasons. Assume that an agent encodes some invariant property in the world. By what process does the agent assign meaning to that encoding? Innate meaning for such primitive feature would be one way of doing so but that is not particularly insightful, and identifying these innate representations is fraught with problems. The feature can be assigned an arbitrary (but consistent) semantic value, but this renders the idea of information as a property of the world superfluous. Information is supposed to satisfy the requirements of correspondence between the world and internal representations which arbitrary assignments cannot guarantee. This problem is confounded by the fact that there is no independent way of verifying the assumed correspondence between internal representation and the object and events in the world. So encoding may have (internally) consistent semantics but there is no way of checking their validity (something similar was pointed out by Wittgenstein 1922).

This problem resolves itself if the correspondence assumption is abandoned, which then allows for arbitrary but consistent assignment of semantic values. However, even this weaker position assumes that the world is already divided up into discrete objects and events and the task of the agent is to engage in seeking out pattern of regularities. This seems like a reasonable assumption but the perceived regularities could equally be a consequence of perceptual and cognitive processes designed to search for maximal difference between perceived boundaries and minimal difference within them. If so, the assumed correspondence is suspect; if the agent can determine how the world is perceived then its representation may bear little resemblance to how the world actually is. The point is that any account that assumes that the world is something distinct from the agent lays itself open to the charge of being unable to motivate its semantics. One solution would be to treat the interaction between an agent and its environment as a "complete reality" (Maturana 1981).

There is a further problem that the information processing view cannot resolve without severely limiting the explanatory power of computational models based on it. In order to construct concepts to represent invariant properties shared by similar objects in the world one needs to know about the correspondence between concepts and the properties they are to represent. But that knowledge of correspondence is only available *after* the relevant concept have been formed. In other words, a concept cannot be formed unless it already exists. Without motivating its semantics independent of the encodings of invariant properties it would be difficult to have concepts corresponding to objects and events in the world. Typically, computational models *avoid* this problem by fixing the number and possible semantics values of features, and putting constraints on their role in concept formation. But in so doing they fail to give an account for the occurrence of totally novel features (or concepts) – otherwise known as the New Term Problem.

It is worth repeating that the issue it not that there exists a correspondence between objects in the world and an internal *encoding* of it. That has to be logically necessary in any model of cognition which admits the possibility of internal representations. However, in the information processing approach it is unclear how the internal encoding is assigned meaning such that it can be said to *represent* some property of the world. The correspondence between objects and encodings though necessary, is not sufficient to explain this process by which encodings are rendered into representations. Other factors such as context make this correspondence very complicated. Our approach is designed to take account of this complexity but, unlike other alternatives, it does not appeal either to an anti-representational position (e.g., Brooks 1987), or to truth-conditional semantics (e.g., Dowty, Wall and Peters 1981). It incorporates the notion of grounding semantics (Harnad 1990) which attempts to resolve the New Term Problem by grounding the semantics of symbols (or features) — that is, the semantic value of concepts is determined during the learning stage of the agent. By avoiding *post hoc* assignment of meaning to symbols or concepts, it would be possible to give more realistic accounts of complex cognitive processes. However, this approach to concept formation still assumes that symbols end up with more or less fixed semantics after the learning phase is over. From the complex adaptive systems' approach this is neither feasible nor desirable. Instead we propose a radical shift in focus; abandon the information processing paradigm, and concentrate on investigating cognitive processes as part of the complete interaction between an agent and its environment.

4 Ecological Approach and Emergent Phenomena

Our novel approach to concept formation is based on four basic assumptions:

1. Abandon the notion that the world contains information (logical or necessary truths) which agents strive to learn and encode as internal representations.

2. Dynamic cognitive processes such as concept formation are modelled as part of complete reality and not regarded as formal syntactic phenomena confined to an abstract symbolic level detached from the rest of an agent's sensory and affective systems.
3. Assume a correlation between invariant properties in the world and internal encodings but do not motivate semantics on this basis.
4. Motivate the representational content of encodings on goal-related task or strategy — encodings have meaning because their correspondence to certain actions and its outcomes has some *purpose* for the organism.

A study motivated by these four requirements is analogous to observational studies typically used in ethology and certain branches of developmental psychology, except that computer based implementations provide more control over variables that influence learning. A more detailed description and justification of this approach can be found in Sejnowski, Koch and Churchland (1988). Here we elaborate on some of the consequences of the above assumptions. First, the world contains no *a priori* information: Instead it contains *data* which the agent renders into *information*. So information is a synthesis of agent-environment interaction and therefore, relative and subjective. This perspective enables us to address the more realistic issue of why agents need to gather information. They need to do so because it enables the agent to carry out goal oriented tasks more efficiently. The information content of the data from the world is determined by the agent according to its past relevant experiences, present perception of its environment, and future goals. The agent is not regarded as perceiving or acting in the *world* but interacting within an *environmental niche*.

The second assumption follows from the first. If information is actively (and subjectively) constructed from data from the world then even the most abstract or symbolic cognitive process is determined by such subjective interpretation. Thus, this approach is not concerned about *a priori* absolute truths or similar certainties in assigning semantics. So highly formal and abstract (syntactic) accounts of cognitive processes are considered inadequate from the ecological perspective which assumes that semantics are not fixed though they may be stable over a long period of time. An agent in constant interaction with its environment is actively engaged in constructing discrete internal representations appropriate in a particular context or for a specific task *within that environment*. And this activity affects not only meaning, or representational contents of encodings (by being updated, modified, or even discarded for better conceptualisations) but also processes which function over encodings. In an implementation of an artificial organism, it is possible to analyse in details such changes in patterns of internal encoding to determine the influence of specific factors on concept formation.

The agent-environment interaction results in the transformation from a continuous, fluid world into reasonably stable representations. In seeking this transformation the agent is in constant search for invariant patterns or properties in the world. Hence, the reason for the third assumption, that there is a correspondence between invariant properties in the world and internal encodings of them. The agent's goal would determine which invariant properties are encoded. However, correspondence in itself is not sufficient to assign semantic values to encodings of invariance. That is determined by the fourth assumption. The assignment of semantics which has an element of intensionality is best described with an example. Assume a very simple organism whose survival depends on being able to distinguishing between food and non-food in the world, and that it learns to distinguish between the two by trial and error. On finding some food, it can assign the accompanying internal encodings the (semantic) content "food". The internal pattern can also have semantic values associated with corresponding sensory-motor activity related to that particular act of locating food. Thus encodings have semantic values determined by some goal oriented behaviour of the organisms. This process need not be very complicated but must include a facility to compare patterns of invariance across different events of locating food. This process of comparision and association between internal encodings of invariance patterns is expected to manifest new or novel (emergent) patterns which can be interpreted as analogous to concept formation.

Overall, the emphasis is on modelling cognition as biological function (Varela 1986): Concept formation is not regarded as an abstract, formal cognitive process detached from the rest of the organism or its environment. Our research objective is to explain the nature of simple concept formation as mediated by interaction between an agent and its environment. To do so adequately it is necessary to explain the process of transition from continuous (noisy), dynamic, variable data to static, discrete, internal states — representations of invariant features. An ecological, bottom-up approach coupled with powerful search and learning algorithms such as Classifier Systems provides the opportunity to explore this transition process as analogous to assigning semantics during concept formation. The focus is on processes which account for successful searches for invariance in the data from the environment. More generally, it is not in the nature of this methodological approach to assume that learning comes to an end at a particular stage, though the incremental learning may diminish to a vanishingly small point.

As concepts play an important role in the functioning of an agent, any account of them must also give an account of the relationship between concepts and sensory-motor behaviour. Meaning of representations is not independent of its effect and affect on behaviour. Further, the relationship between sensory-motor data from the environment and internal representations of concepts needs to be taken into account because it serves to determine (or "ground") their semantic values and helps define their role in cognition in terms of other concepts[2]. A good grasp of processes involved in the transition from continuous data to discrete internal encoding, and, the assignment of semantic value (partly determined by sensory-motor behaviour) would help develop a model of concept formation as emergent properties of interaction between an agent and its environment. The emergent properties of internal encodings of invariance can be reliably correlated with interpretable sensory-motor behaviour. This allows us to observe learning and behaviour as emergent properties of dynamic and adaptive processes of agent-environment interaction.

The ecological approach increases the level of complexity of concept formation phenomena, but it also overcomes the limitations of models based on more simplistic approaches, such as the ones described in the previous section. However, even very simple models based on simulations or artificial organisms (robots) based on a bottom-up adaptive approach have proved to be extremely insightful as recent work has shown (see review by Meyer and Guillot 1990).

5 Methodology: Motivation and Description

The overall object of the exercise is to study the behaviour of an autonomous system or agent in its (unstructured) environment. The agent-environment interaction can either be simulated on a computer or implemented in an autonomous system such as a robot. It has been argued by Harnad (1990) that there are non-trivial differences between these two approaches. In a simulated environment, no matter how realistic, the data input or its *perception* by the agent is not direct, that is, it is as continuous or variable as it might be perceived by transducers directly from the environment. However, simulations are not a complete waste of time. They represent a very efficient tool to study the emergence of activity of autonomous system in a more realistic time scale. As will be seen both approaches have a role to play in this study.

[2]Thus individual concepts are not construed as independent of each other; the meaning of a concept is necessarily dependent on the meaning of other concepts.

The important issue here is the notion of autonomy. In our case the term does not imply that the autonomous system has self-contained on-board computing facilities and power supply, but that the system is self-determinant. Its activities are determined by an internal reference scheme and needs. Of course, initially these referential structures have to be programmed in, or incorporated in the design of the system. So they provide a framework for future interaction with the environment — learning about it and adapting to it - but do not predetermine the nature, process or content of any such interactions.

One suitable method to incorporate basic needs and demands into the system is to use reinforcement learning procedures. Reinforcement learning takes place as a result of agent-environment interaction (see Fig. 1). The autonomous system has no knowledge about its environment, or about objects, properties of objects, rules or plans. The learning system interacts with its environment via detectors and effectors. The detectors gather data from the environment, and the effectors facilitate action within the environment (often determined by data gathered by the detectors). This distinction is for a practical purpose; in reality the agent is not regarded as distinct from the environment, as its activity can lead to simultaneous changes in both, the environment and the agent which in turn can alter the relation between the two.

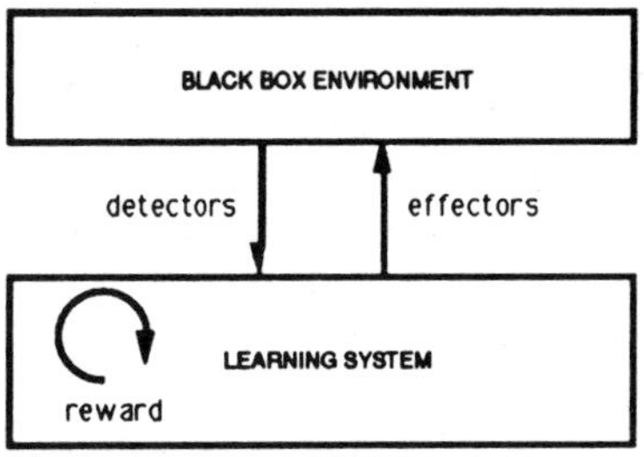

Figure 1: Reinforcement learning

In this approach action and therefore learning is determined solely by the agent's goal of maximising a reward (which is one of initial parameters incorporated to ensure autonomy as described above). But this aim does not render specific behaviour predictable. The learning procedures enable the autonomous system to build up internal representations of objects, events, etc. The structuring of the data (that is, its transition into information as defined above) on the basis of internal feedback will contribute to a dynamic construction process necessary for basic cognitive processes of pattern recognition, generalisation, abstraction and concept formation. During this process, objects and features in the real world are correlated with useful behaviour of the robot. The more complex the structures developed, the more complex the robot's evolving behaviour will be. An important point here is the basic mechanism which constructs this correlation and which will outlined in the following section.

5.1 Behavioural Organisation as Inductive Process

Induction is an inferential process that *expands knowledge in the face of uncertainty*. In this process, probabilistic and statistical inferences are highly relevant. Traditionally, inferential processes are characterised as a process of search through a state space that has an initial state, one or more goals, and a set of operators that can transform one state into another. These techniques apply operators to fixed problem representations mainly in the symbolic domain yielding syntactic structures. Learning is not usually involved and the system needs predetermined knowledge to solve a problem, where the problem must be well-defined (in terms of initial state, goal-state, and operators). But there are only a few classes of problems sufficiently well-defined. Usually problems are ill-defined, and even worse, arbitrarily ill-defined.

We intend to utilise induction as a more dynamic inferential process motivated by problem solving behaviour, which is partly based on Holland et al.ś (1986) emphasis on the relation between goal-directed problem solving behaviour and induction of new rules. They suggest that induction is directed by problem solving activity, and, that it proceeds on the bases of feedback from success or failure of predictions. However, this problem solving behaviour is still confined to a fairly abstract symbolic, syntactic domain very much within the mainstream information processing paradigm evaluated above.

Alternatively, we wish to apply inductive processes to behavioural organisation and non-symbolic internal encoding (representations). In order to do so, it assumed that an organism, even at a fairly basic level of behavioural organisation, has the ability to apply inferential rules to events which can generate hypotheses applicable to subsequent events. Induction supports this process of hypotheses generation and testing, and learning which will allow us to address general issues such as, how can a cognitive system process data (from the world) and store knowledge so as to benefit from experience? And, how can a system organise its experience so as to provide some basis for behaviour in novel situations? As well as helping us to explore these questions, induction processes need to be suitably constrained to limit unchecked generation of fruitless or trivial hypotheses derived from otherwise useful generalisations. Hence, the study of induction is the study of how knowledge is modified through use.

Our robot will incorporate the ability to adapt to experiences mainly on the basis of an internal semantic rather than syntactic structures or pragmatic aspects. So novel (or emergent) behaviour is expected to accompany novel internal encodings with semantics that match the behaviour. Encodings will capture regularities which will determine their relative stability of semantic values. Further, such (initially simple) internal encodings (of general properties of environmental stimuli) would be expected to enhance future construction of information from data.

5.2 The System Constraints

A computational structure which is expected to bring about the emergence of cognitive capabilities has to feature three important aspects:

1. It has to be modular and parallel in order to represent many concurrent processes activated by signals from a number of sensory-motor inputs.
2. The individual modules need to be able to learn from experience.
3. The interaction between the various modules has to be dynamic in order to guarantee flexibility and plasticity.

This cognitive architecture serves one main purpose, namely to control the activity of our autonomous system (robot). Two basic features facilitate this. First, it is pre-disposed to elicit some sorts of behaviour and avoid others; this is incorporated by introducing a set of desirable goals that can be achieved by appropriate behaviour. However, these goals are not explicit but expressed as reward and punishment functions which serve to distinguish between useful and useless behaviour.

The second basic feature of the system is that it can learn simple behaviour in response to stimuli in its an environment. In order to do so it needs to be able to learn about and encode internal representations of salient features in the environment. This learning will be embedded in the robot's knowledge about its spatial position in the environment and the relative positions of its sensory organs and motor controls. The system is provided feedback by an evaluation mechanism based on beneficial goals which the organism is expected to achieve. Achieving such goals will only be possible when the agent forms the necessary concepts — that is, having the correct internal states which enable the organism to perform appropriate behaviour. (We will return to the issue of distinguishing concepts as internal encoding in a later section). The evaluation mechanism is expected to incorporate thresholds which determine when a particular behaviour is elicited. The complete control architecture for behavioural organisation is shown in Fig. 2.

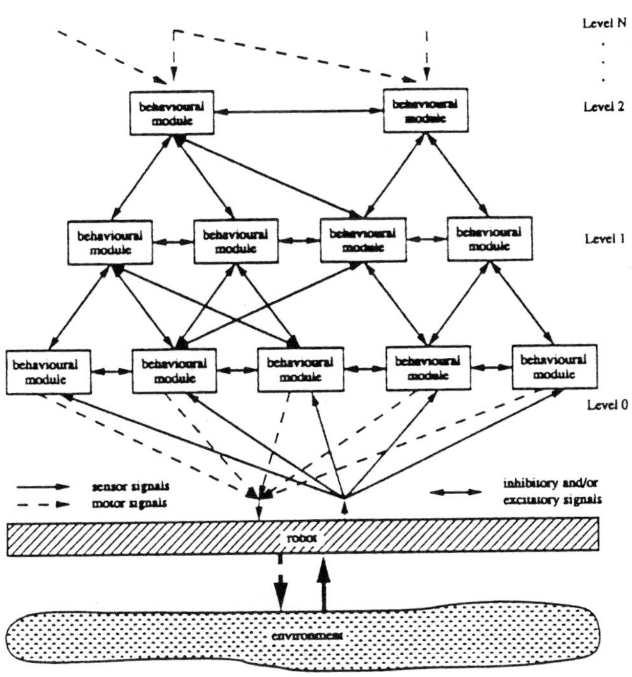

Figure 2: Behavioural organisation in an artificial organism

This behavioural organisation is derived from ethological models based on animal studies (see Schnepf 1990 for more details).

We selected learning classifier systems as the most appropriate computation device to implement this model which could support inferential based inductive learning as will be briefly explained in the next section.

5.3 Learning Classifier Systems

A classifier system is a kind of rule-based or production system. Learning classifier systems provide the adaptivity necessary for reinforcement learning and inductive processes (see Holland et al. 1986) and support learning which has the flexibility and the power necessary for inductive search for appropriate patterns corresponding to appropriate behaviour (in a given situation).

The rules, or *classifiers*, consist of a condition and action part which are formed by a very low level syntax usually consisting of a three letter alphabet containing the letters *0, 1,* and *# (don't care)*. A message list is used to provide environmental messages which are matched against the condition parts of existing classifiers of the rule base. If more than one classifier matches the environmental message, an additional parameter, each matching classifier's *strength*, is used to determine which classifier is chosen to perform its action (see Fig. 3). In accordance with its action's effectiveness measured by an internal feedback scheme which compares the environmental and the agent's internal state before

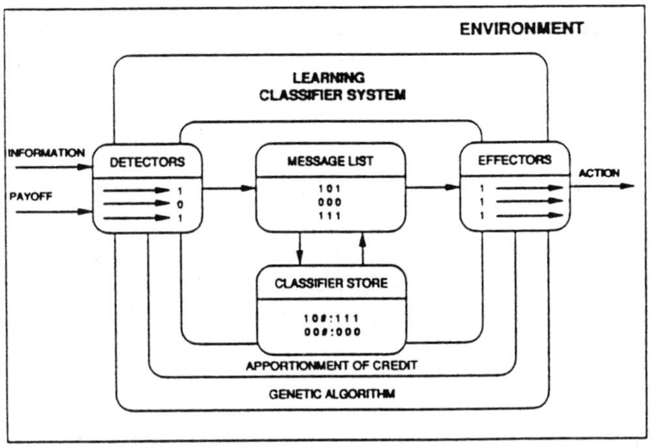

Figure 3: A learning classifier system and its environment

and after the action taken, the robot receives positive or negative feedback. Additionally, adaptive generation of new rules is based on the effectiveness of existing rules. This step is performed by a genetic algorithm, or a more general evolutionary algorithm.

To summarise, the three main components of a learning classifier system are: First, a rule and message system which resembles a production rule system in structure and performance. Second, an apportionment of credit system which handles feedback of success or failure of rule execution. Third, a genetic algorithm which generates new rules on the basis of effective existing ones. Together, these components form an adaptive mechanism capable of modelling non-trivial learning about appropriate environmental features by an agent.

In standard classifier systems, adaptive rule learning is performed by one processing unit, that is, a classifier system has a cluster of rules as the largest group of situation-action pairs related to each other[3]. Consequently, the complexity of action sequences (referred to as behavioural sequences) to be learnt and performed is not very high. Additional disadvantages of such systems arise from the apportionment of credit problem over long sequences of chained rules (see Wilson and Goldberg 1989). In order to achieve more complex behavioural sequences reflecting the process of concept formation, we designed a system with many classifier systems operating in parallel. The task of each classifier system is to learn short rule sequences (which at first sight looks like limiting the capabilities of each classifier system unnecessarily). This has the advantage that short rule sequences are reinforced more easily, and so

[3]This is independent of whether the chosen approach is Michigan or Pittsburgh. In the former, one classifier system consists of a collection of condition-action rules, whereas in the Pittsburgh approach, a classifier system consists of strings which represent complete rule sets themselves.

are learnt more quickly. The system is also expected to learn to organise individual classifier systems with enough flexibility to achieve more complex behaviours. This allows the addition of an extra dimension for the organisation of rules and rule clusters as stated above. Future work is expected to clarify, how the technique chosen to mediate between the different classifier systems (spreading of excitation and inhibition) influences the coordination of these rule clusters, and how this activity can be described in the context of induction.

6 Computational Model and Implementation

As shown in Fig. 2 behavioural modules are the basic components of our cognitive architecture. These modules are linked up to communicate either excitatory or inhibitory signals to each other, and collectively satisfy the constraints described above. A behavioural module (see Fig. 4) reflects the structure and functionality of a learning classifier system. It operates in the same way as a classifier system; environmental stimuli are accessed by each behavioural module where classifiers compete to achieve the best match, thus determining the selection of the rule that eventually fires resulting eventually in the accompanying sensory-motor behaviour. In addition to the three main components already mentioned, each classifier system has an important feature to support self-organising computational structures so necessary for inferential processes (as explained above). This is called the ***activation filter*** which serves two main purposes. First, it realises the activation and inhibition spreading between the different behavioural modules. Second, it determines the weight of the emitted motor or excitatory/inhibitory signals. Each will be described in more detail.

Excitation and Inhibition Each behavioural module has a record of the behavioural modules located at the same or subordinate levels of the behavioural hierarchy. Modules at the same level communicate mutual inhibition. Each module sends out inhibitory signals corresponding to its own excitatory status which helps to inhibit the control from passing on to one of the neighbouring modules. On the other hand, modules in different levels communicate both, excitatory and inhibitory signals. The "flow" of communication is directed towards the lower levels in the behavioural hierarchy, except at *Level 0* where modules send out motor signals. Why particular modules receive excitatory and others inhibitory signals from superordinate levels will be explained below.

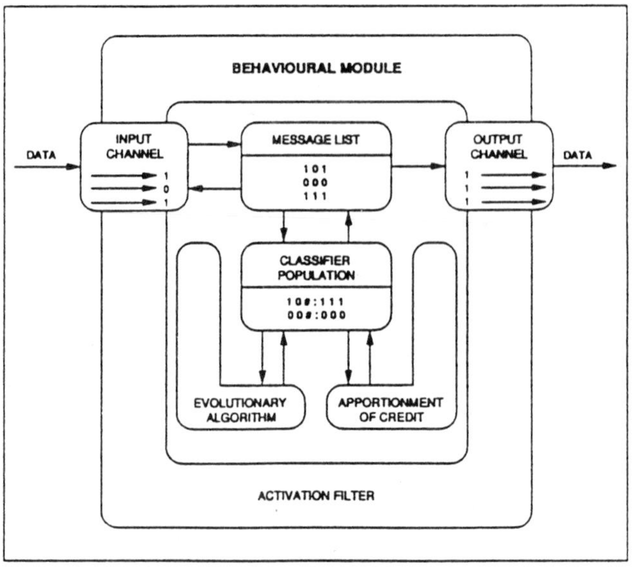

Figure 4: Behavioural module

Weighting Each behavioural module receives environmental stimuli data which are matched against existing rules of the classifier population inside a module. The activation filter keeps a record of the match between the selected classifier and the stimuli. The degree of this match determines the weight (or strength) of the emitted signal from the relevant module. Apart from determining the weight of the emitted signal, a module also assigns its input inhibitory and excitatory signals to the emitted signal (that is, as motor signals or excitatory/inhibitory signals). Thus, the emitted signals are weighted according to the inhibitory and excitatory signal received by the module. At the bottom of the hierarchy, weighted motor signals determine the motor behaviour of the artificial organism.

6.1 Concepts in Classifier Systems

Having defined the computational backbone of our model, we will outline the definition of *concept* in terms of distributed learning classifier systems. Since, in our design, one classifier system consists of a collection of condition-action rules (Michigan approach), the basic syntactic structures of each classifier system are rules with pairs of condition-action parts. Information learnt via interacting with the environment is stored in the classifier system's rule set. The dynamic interaction and internal organisation of these rules will determine concept formation activities identifiable in the rule set.

First, individual rules representing stimuli-response pairs are learnt as a result of agent-environment interaction. Although the formation of appropriate feature detectors (internal and external stimuli) and motor signals by means of rule generation is trigggered by objects and events of the real world, we do not conbsider these rules as concepts, since their formation is directed towards stimuli-response-pairs without using internal models. The second stage would be a cluster of rules which act independently of each other but which are linked as a result of agent-environment interaction — that is, applying one rule results in the application of another rule more appropriate in this new context. Also here, no internal representations can be identified in the formation of these rule clusters. Next, a cluster of rule which act in unison by posting internal messages — that is, the action part of a classifier is not directed to effectors, but to the message list where the action part is used as a new message which is matched against the condition part of other existing classifiers in the rule set. This stage would be the first instantiation of an internal encoding of a specific aspect of the environment, since the rules acting as internal message generators can be regarded as models of aspects of the environment. These models might be able to represent abstract properties of the environment since more general rules (with many "don't cares" in the condition part) can trigger evaluation of other rules which finally end up producing a particular output. Such rule clusters could further form groups to support more complex concepts. This grouping is performed by the coordination of classifier system activities through superordinate classifier systems by means of lateral excitation and inhibition. The usage, the persistence, and the dynamic properties of these concept clusters remains highly speculative at this stage of the research and is subject to a reformulation as a result of further research.

6.2 Implementation as a Robot

Given our emphasis on autonomy as a non-trivial requirement for study of complex cognitive processes such as concept formation, the use of a real robot, no matter how basic, is necessary. Autonomy affords viability which enables an autonomous learning system to deal with and learn from an unstuctured environment. Simulation, though useful as will see, alone cannot provide for this as only direct access to the world can provide a truely unstructured environment, which a system internally structures as a result of perceiving and interacting with it. An autonomous agent with a set of basic demands and skills, in direct interaction with the environment is far more likely to develop novel complex cognitive processes and encodings.

Here we will describe the implementation of our autonomous system in a robot. The mobile robot is equipped with sensors such as encoders, ultrasonic and touch sensors. It has onboard computing facilities consisting of a parallel computing environment which is a transputer based MIMD architecture capable of supporting complex and asynchronous parallel programming tasks. The simple effectors consist of two powered wheels to control forward and reverse movements, and turning. The power source is an onboard battery unit. The robot has the following two main components:

- An onboard computing unit consisting of several cards such as a transputer mother board card, a transputer card which controls the robot's sensors and effectors, or several cards for TTL and analogue I/O.
- The robot is built on a simple moving platform with six wheels and various sensors such as eight ultrasonic sensors (forming a so-called ring of confidence), sixteen touch sensors (so-called whiskers), two simple visual sensors (photo resistors), and two encoders for recording performed motor sequences.

6.3 Simulated Training and Learning Scenario

Simulations play an important role in the development and training phase of the control algorithm. There are two reasons for this. First, simulations are helpful in the training of adaptive and learning control algorithms which require a large numbers of act-sense cycles with feedback assignment. Reinforcement learning in a robot interacting with a real environment would take far too long. A powerful workstation running a complex simulation of the learning scenario would be faster. Second, simulation would avoid damaging the robot. During the early stage of learning the robot is bound to perform futile or senseless actions which are better confined to a simulation. Thus, a well-defined, fairly complex but suitabley constrained simulated environment is useful during the early stages of training an adaptive autonous system.

Following the simulation stage, the robots initial learning task will be to guide itself through a maze which requires fairly complex learning abilities and behaviour. The motivation to learn about the maze will be provided by rewards of "food", that is, a metaphorical term for something desirable to the robot. While learning about the maze and seeking out "food" sources the robot will be expected to build maps of its behavioural organisation based on its activity patterns. Such maps would represent information about paths to "food" sources. All activity will be determined by the internal measuring scale of the robot provided by the feedback model. Once a useful path has been learnt, the robot should be able to follow it in subsequent trials. Such internal encoding of certain properties of environment, such as a path through a maze, is expected to provide insights into how abstractions and generalisation are constructed while learning to perform such complex activities.

7 Conclusion

The set of tools and our methodological approach will enable us to observe the relationship between sensory-motor perception and action within a specific environment. The relationship between sensors and effectors, as mediated by internally represented concepts will be explored. We hope to describe the nature of properties and processes involved in invariant features extraction from raw continuous data, and how this information affects sensory-motor behaviour in increasingly complex scenarios. Our novel but simple approach is not expected to give an account of the effect of memory or past experience on behaviour in a particular context. Apart from making the issue too complicated we feel that the primary goal of understanding the nature of concept formation needs to be well accounted for before attempting to explain a more complicated system.

Acknowledgements

We would like to thank Ulrich Licht and Jörg Prust from the Artificial Intelligence Research Division of GMD who were strongly involved in designing and building the robot and developing the basic robot control algorithms.

References

Barsolou, L. W. 1982. Context-independent and context-dependent information in concepts. *Memory and Cognition*, 10:82-93.

Brooks, R. A. 1987. Intelligence without Representation. In *Proceedings of the Workshop on Foundations of Intelligence.* MIT:Endicott House.

Dowty, D. R., R. E. Wall, and S. Peters. 1981. *Introduction to Montague Semantics.* London:Reidel.

Feldman, J. A. 1986. *Neural Representation of Conceptual Knowledge.* University of Rochester, Dept. of Computer Science, TR 189.

Harnad, S. 1990. The Symbol Grounding Problem. *Physica D*, 42:335-346.

Hinton, G. E. 1986. Learning distributed representations of concepts. In *Proceedings of the Eighth Annual Conference of the Cognitive Science Society*, Amherst, MA.

Holland, J. H, J. H. Keith, E. N. Richard, and R. T. Paul. 1986. *Induction.* Cambridge: MIT Press.

Keil, F. 1989. *Concepts, Kinds and Cognitive Development.* Cambridge: MIT Press.

Maturana, H. 1981. Autopoiesis. In *Autopoiesis: A Theory of Living Organization*, edited by M. Zeleny. New York: North-Holland.

Meyer, J.-A., and A. Guillot. 1990. *From animals to animats: Everything you wanted to know about the simulation of adaptive behavior.* Ecole Normale Superieure, Paris, Technical Report BioInfo-90-1.

Rosch, E., and C. B. Mervis. 1975. Family resemblances: Studies in the internal structure of categories. *Cognitive Psychology*, 7:573-605.

Rosch, E., C. B. Mervis, W. D. Gray, D. M. Johnson, and P. Boyes-Braem. 1976. Basic Objects in Natural Categories. *Cognitive Psychology*, 8:382-439.

Rosch, E. 1978. *Principles of Categorization.* In *Cognition and Categorization*, edited by E. Rosch and B. B. Lloyd. Hillsdale: Erlbaum.

Schnepf, U. 1991. Robot Ethology: a Proposal for the Research in Intelligent Autonomous Systems. In *From animals to animats: proceedings of the First International Conference on Simulation of Adaptive Behavior.* Cambridge: MIT Press/Bradford Books.

Sejnowski, T. J., C. Koch, and P. S. Churchland. 1988. Computational Neuroscience. *Science*, 241:1299-1306.

Shavlik, J. W., and T. G. Dietterich, eds. 1990. *Readings in Machine Learning.* San Mateo: Morgan Kaufman.

Smith, E. E., and D. L. Medin. 1981. *Categories and Concepts.* London: Harvard University Press.

Tversky, A. 1977. Features of similarity. *Psychological Review*, 84:327-352.

Varela, F. J. 1986. *The Science and Technology of Cognition: Emerging Trends.* unpublished mss.

Wilson, St. W., and D. E. Goldberg. 1989. A Critical Review of Classifier Systems, in *Proceedings of the Third International Conference on Genetic Algorithms*, Fairfax.

Wittgenstein, L. 1922. *Tractatus Logico-philosophicus.* Translated by D. F .Pears and B. F. McGuinness, London:RKP (1961 edition).

Wrobel, S. 1991. *Concept Formation in Man and Machines: Fundamental Issues.* GMD Working Paper no. 560. Sankt Augustin, Germany.

Distributed Adaptive Control: A Paradigm for Designing Autonomous Agents

Rolf Pfeifer* and Paul Verschure
AI Lab, Institute for Informatics
University of Zurich-Irchel
Winterthurerstrasse 190, CH-8057 Zurich
Switzerland
e-mail: pfeifer@ifi.unizh.ch, verschur@ifi.unizh.ch

Abstract

Over the last decade AI has been criticized on many grounds. Parallel models of computation, e.g. neural networks, have been proposed as an alternative. Indeed, these models do solve a number of problems of AI in interesting ways, e.g. learning, generalization, and fault and noise tolerance. However, it can be shown that they do not solve some of the fundamental conceptual problems of traditional AI such as grounding or situatedness. In order to approach these problems a biologically inspired paradigm for designing autonomous agents is proposed. In contrast to other approaches to autonomous agents, our own focuses on adaptation, i.e. the dynamics of the acquisition of "knowledge" in the interaction with the environment. It is shown that this way a number of the fundamental problems of AI can be solved in natural ways, others "disappear" since they are artifacts of the traditional approach. Moreover, we conjecture that with this approach more robustness can be achieved.
Keywords: autonomous agents, distributed adaptive control, situatedness, grounding

1 Introduction

Over the last decade AI has been criticized on many grounds. Typical criticisms are that AI models are brittle, that learning is mostly ad hoc and not principled, that they cannot generalize and that they are too much like digital computers. Neural networks have been advocated as the solution to the problems of AI. Indeed, neural network models do solve a number of them in interesting ways, e.g. learning, generalization, and fault and noise tolerance. However, they do not automatically solve some of the fundamental conceptual problems of traditional AI such as grounding and situatedness. Symbol grounding refers to the difficulty of relating symbols to the real world (e.g. Harnad, 1990). Normally such a mapping is only present in the mind of the observer, but does not exist from the point of view of a system that has to intereact with the real world (Clancey, 1989). Situatedness roughly means the following (e.g. Winograd & Flores, 1986, Suchman, 1987, Agre & Chapman, 1988): if a system has to act in a particular situation in the real world, there will always be relevant factors which could not have been forseen by the designer because the real world is constantly changing, only partially knowable, and intrinsically unpredictable. In other words, however detailed the models may be, and however large the library of models, there will always be situations which have not been covered. If a system is "situated" it can get the information it needs to act directly from the particular situation it is in.

Now, most neural network models, in particular the large class of backpropagation models, start with a designer-defined domain ontology. This is the reason why, for the better part, neural network models — though they do acquire their knowledge through learning — are neither grounded nor situated. It has been argued — and it is argued in

*This research was partly supported by the Swift AI Chair, Free University of Brussels

this paper — that new approaches to the study of intelligence are needed which differ radically from those of traditional AI. Our results indicate that these fundamental problems of AI can be addressed by building autonomous agents, a suggestion which has also been made by others (e.g. Malcolm, Smithers, & Hallam, 1989, Brooks, 1991).

Now, robotics has always been an important discipline in AI since its beginning but it has received renewed attention in recent years. The history of robotics has taught us, however, that merely building robots will not provide the solutions. Classical robots are typically based on a functional decomposition, leading to a so-called "sense-think-act" cycle: they map sensory input onto internal models before deciding on a particular action (Malcom, Smithers, & Hallam, 1989) which leads — among other things — to enormous requirements for computing power. This can be seen as a symptom of more fundamental problems which are entailed by the idea of mapping inputs onto internal designer defined models. The resulting systems will be neither situated nor will their knowledge be grounded (e.g. Clancey, 1989). Most traditional AI programs are one way or another model based in this sense. Thus, building robots alone is not sufficient as long as traditional techniques are used — something is needed in addition.

Brooks (1986, 1991) argues that robots, in order to be situated, should have an architecture based on a behavioral decomposition, rather than on a functional one. Indeed, the subsumption architecture represents a significant departure from traditional approaches: subsumption-based robots can pursue several behaviors in parallel without the need to map complex sensory inputs onto complex internal models before acting. While Brooks' line of work has proved very successful (see Brooks, 1991 for a review), it is lacking adaptivity and flexibility. Since the behaviors are implemented by augmented finite state machines (in which all input-output relations and interconnections have to be prespecified), great efforts may be required by the designer for a very particular solution (as argued by Maes, 1990). Therefore, the resulting robot still only embodies designer knowledge as in the traditional AI case.

Therefore, what is needed are mechanisms by which the robot can acquire its own" knowledge". Nature has endowed most creatures with flexibile mechanisms which enable them to more optimally adapt to their environments (e.g. habituation, sensitisation, associative learning). In fact, it has been shown that even a creature as small as *C. elegans* with only 302 neurons is capable of associative learning (Kumar et al., 1989). In other words, we can safely assume that such mechanisms will be present in most, even the simplest, animals. It seems natural to include them in our endeavors to understand and build intelligent systems. Obvious candidates for the implementation of adaptive mechanisms are neural networks. There is a lot of neural network based work in robotics and computer vision. But, as mentioned above, employing neural network technology as such will not suffice.

As an alternative we propose the paradigm of "Distributed Adaptive Control" which combines physical embodiment and behavior-based design with the flexibility of neural networks (or, more generally, dynamical systems). It will be shown that this approach leads to situated adaptive systems.

2 Outline of "Distributed Adaptive Control"

The paradigm of "Distributed Adaptive Control (DAC)" can be translated into a number of steps for building autonomous agents:

1. Define the physical setup of the robot with its sensors and effectors and specify the types of environments in which the robot is to function. This is the framework determining the interaction potential of the robot.

2. Define the "value scheme". The value scheme comprises a set of basic sense-act reflexes (direct connections of sensory patterns to motor actions), a set of elementary drives, as well as the specific properties of the sensors and effectors. The value scheme is predefined. It provides the constraints on the self-organization.

3. Define the network architecture and the learning mechanisms. The assumptions about the value scheme are translated into a network architecture. Sensory input is projected into a

set of corresponding network layers. A minimal set of assumptions to achieve adaptive behavior is (a) that the sense-act reflexes be implemented by linking the respective sensory layers to the motor system, and (b) that there be an associative mechanism to enable the transfer of these reflexes to more sophisticated sensors[1].

4. Let the robot interact with its environment. Analyze the robot's behavior by informal and systematic observation, and by formal analyses. Relate its behavior to the dynamics of the network.

A central aspect of this approach is that the design should be entirely robot-centered, i.e. in the design process, everything has to be seen from the robot's point of view. The impact of this "rule" will be demonstrated. The approach is now illustrated with a simulation example.

3 A simulation example

Only a short description is given here. For more detail the reader is referred to Verschure, Kröse, & Pfeifer (submitted).

1. Defining the robot and the environment: First, the robot consists of three types of sensors, a collision detector, a target detector and a range finder, as well as a means of locomotion. The environment, shown in Figure 1[2] consists of an enclosure with walls and a number of obstacles (the trajectory will be explained later). The size, shape, and number of obstacles can vary.

2. Defining the value scheme: Second, the value scheme needs to be specified. It is predefined by the designer and is considered fixed for the period of the simulations. It contains the following elements. There are a number of "sense-act-reflexes", e.g. "whenever a collision occurs, retract and turn in the other direction", or "whenever a target is detected turn towards the target". There is also a basic drive which is simply to move straight ahead. In the current simulation no other drives have been implemented. When the robot touches an object on the left part of the front, the left collision detector lights up and analogously for the right side. The range finder has a focus of attention around 0 degrees, i.e. the center of the front (39 to -39 degrees), giving a distance profile with a resolution of 3 degrees.

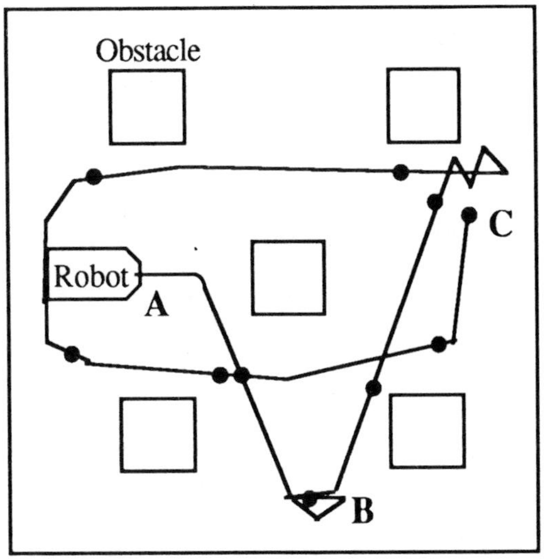

Figure 1: Robot setup including the first thousand simulation steps. The black dots mark 100 steps. (a) is the starting point, (b) shows a region where it is touching and wondering around, and (c) shows the robot's position after 1000 steps.

An example of a range finder profile is shown in Figure 2 The signals from the sensors have to be translated into inputs for the neural architecture. This is achieved by transducer functions. In the case of the collision detector, the input to the neural structures is 1 if it is on, otherwise 0. Similarly for the target detector, whenever a target is detected within a certain angular segment from the front, there is an input of 1 into that part of the neural structure, otherwise the input is 0. There are two segments in the front of the the robot (0 to 5 degrees, 0 to -5 degrees — the *inner* region) and two on each side (5 to 180 degrees, -5 to -180 degrees — the *outer region*). The reason for having two regions is that the robot should turn faster if the target is detected in the outer region.

[1]This minimal set of assumptions was implemented in our example and will be illustrated in Section 3. But more complex architectures are possible and need to be explored.

[2]The figures have been manually redrawn for purposes of presentation.

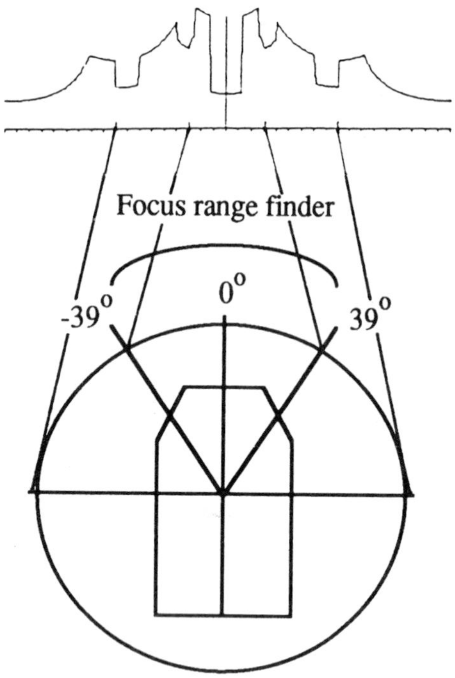

Figure 2: Robot with range finder profile

To get the input from the range finder, distance is transformed in the following way. If d is the distance, the input to the neural structure is 1/exp(d). The main reason for this particular choice is that nearby objects are more important than distant ones. These assumptions are treated in more detail in the discussion section.

3. Defining the architecture and the learning mechanisms: As a third step these assumptions have to be translated into mechanisms. Since the space of possible architectures is indefinitely large it is important to find appropriate constraints. Neurobiology or animal biology can provide valuable intuitions (e.g. Anderson & Donath, 1990, Verschure & Coolen, 1991). Our approach is based on a model of classical conditioning proposed by Verschure & Coolen (1991) which incorporates constraints from the field of animal learning (e.g. the Rescorla Wagner law) and neurobiology (e.g. the use of Hebbian learning).

Figure 3 shows the network architecture. There is an approach and an avoidance layer. Whenever a node in one of these layers is turned on, i.e. its activation set to 1, it will automatically trigger a motor response via a so-called command layer. In the present implementation the approach and avoidance layers have hardwired connections to the command layer and cannot be changed. The command layer consists of so-called command-neurons (Kupfermann & Weiss, 1978) which automatically trigger certain motor responses whenever they are activated. For the avoidance behavior there are two nodes, one which triggers "retract and turn left" and one for "retract and turn right". For target detection, there are four nodes capable of triggering the following responses: "turn 1 degree to left", "turn 1 degree to right", "turn 9 degrees to left", and "turn 9 degrees to right", each corresponding to a different angular range.

It is clear now, that with these characteristics of the network architecture and the sensors, the reflexes defined in the value scheme are implemented.

The activation of the neurons in the approach and avoidance layers is as follows:

$$s_i^\lambda = f[c_i^\lambda + \sum_{j=1}^{N} s_j K_{ij}^\lambda] \tag{1}$$

s_i^λ is the activation of node i in layer λ (the approach or the avoidance layer), c_i^λ the input from the respective sensors (the collision or the target detector), s_j the activation of the range finder layer, K_{ij}^λ the connection strengths between range finder and approach or avoidance layer, and f a threshold function.

The approach and avoidance layer are connected via an inhibitory element which gives the avoidance reflex preference over the approach one. The activation of the inhibitory element, a, is given by:

$$a(t+1) = \zeta a(t) + \frac{1}{M}\sum_{i=1}^{M} s_i \tag{2}$$

ζ denotes the decay rate, M the number of units in the avoidance layer, and s_i the activation of element i of the avoidance layer. There is a threshold for the output function, i.e. inhibition only takes place if the activation value of the inhibitory unit exceeds a threshold. This unit will inhibit the response triggered by the approach layer, rather than inhibit activity in this field. In this way, the "intertia" of the positive response remains in place.

The avoidance and the approach layers are fully interconnected with other sensory input, in our case, the range finder. The weights are updated following a Hebbian learning mechanism with active decay:

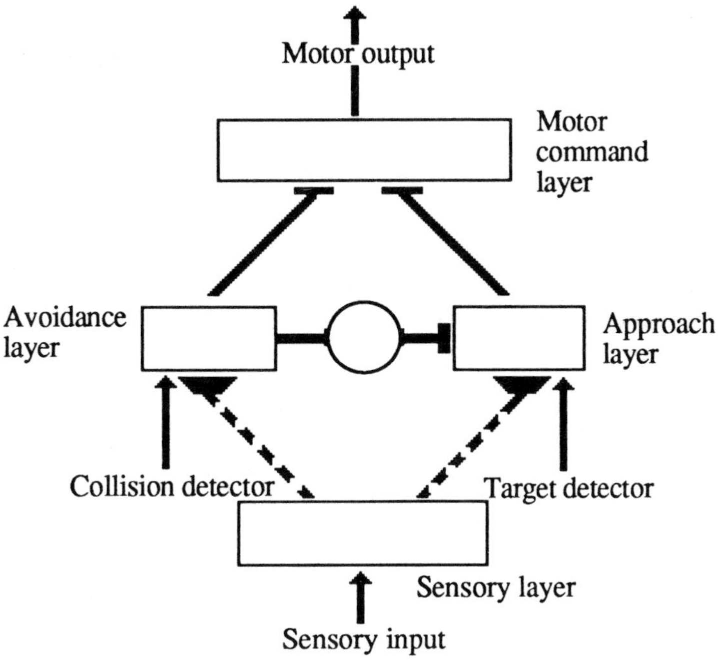

Figure 3: Network architecture

$$\Delta K_{ij}^{\lambda} = \frac{1}{N}[\eta^{\lambda} s_i^{\lambda} s_j - \epsilon \bar{s}^{\lambda} K_{ij}^{\lambda}] \quad (3)$$

In equation 3 η^{λ} denotes the learning rate for the connections between the range finder layer and layer λ, N the number of units in the range finder layer, ϵ the decay rate, $\bar{s}^{\lambda}$ the average activity of layer λ. The term $\bar{s}^{\lambda}$ makes the decay dependent on activation in layer λ which is the reason for calling it *active* decay. In most systems, decay is occurring continuously which implies that the system eventually looses all its memory traces, whereas in ours decay only occurs during learning.

An important assumption in this approach is that there is no distinction between a learning and a performance phase[3]. If there were, the robot itself would have to decide when it is a good time to stop learning. Since the world is continuously changing and unpredictable this would be hard to do. The better solution is to look for mechanisms which lead to equilibrium behavior if the environment is stable. Although in this situation the system will not learn anything new the learning mechanism is still active and need not be artificially turned off. However, if the environment changes, learning will immediately start having an effect again. This is achieved by the weight change mechanisms described by equation 3.

4. Letting the robot interact and analyzing its behavior: For the purposes of the current discussion only the main results are outlined. The values of the individual parameters have been described elsewhere (Verschure, Kröse, & Pfeifer, submitted). We first describe the simulation experiments. The results will be discussed in Section 4.

Avoidance behavior: First we start with an environment in which there is no target. The environment and the first one thousand steps are shown in Figure 1.

Initially the robot collides with the wall and with objects, i.e. its avoidance behavior is controlled by the collision detector. Gradually control shifts to the range finder through an associative mechanism. In other words, the range finder input has become *conditioned* on the avoidance response. In numbers: during the first 100 steps 29 avoidance movements are triggered by physical collisions. After 600 steps this number has dropped to 0.

Another experiment conducted with this setup was to put the robot into a corner near one of the obstacles after it had learned to avoid obstacles. The only way for it to keep moving is to back out

[3]Such a distinction is present in most neural network models, in particular in the backpropagation paradigm.

of the impasse and turn away, which is precisely what it does — without collision!

Approach and avoidance behavior: Figure 4 shows an environment with an attractive force. The target will only affect the robot when it is whithin the range of the outer circle. It will stop moving around if it is sufficiently close to the target, i.e. within the inner circle (c). The simulation consisted of 20 trials, each starting with the robot in position (a). The initial trajectories are not shown in the figure. During the first trial the robot collided 23 times before it stopped (i.e. before it reached the target). The number of collisions are successively reduced until they disappear. Figure 4 shows the trajectory after 20 trials. In this trial the attractive force was removed from the environment.

4 Discussion

Let us now look at the simulation results and discuss a number of fundamental issues. We will take the frame-of-reference problem into account (Clancey, 1989) and carefully specify who's perspective we are assuming: the designer's, the observer's or the robot's.

4.1 The emergence of structured behavior

Let us consider avoidance-learning for a moment. Every collision establishes a sense-act-reflex which is the basis for the associative mechanism to become effective. As the robot accumulates experience over time, control slowly shifts from the collision-driven type (which is predefined) to the more sophisticated range finder-driven one (which is learned). It can be seen that the trajectory in Figure 1 smoothes out over time. Since it starts turning before it actually collides with the obstacle, it looks as if the robots starts *anticipating* obstacles. But there is no component for anticipation in the system, rather the anticipatory behavior *emerges* out of the interaction of a number of processes[4]. The reason for this is as follows. If the robot approaches an object from a certain direction and collides with it the particular pattern in the range finder will be learned via weight-modification (equation 3). If at a later occasion the robot approaches an object from the same direction, a similar pattern will start to develop in the range finder. Because of the similarity, at a certain point, this pattern will lead to sufficient activation in the avoidance layer to trigger the response: the robot has learned to anticipate obstacles. But the anticipation will not extend its scope indefinitely. It is limited by the particular transducer function (the inverse exponential — if the objects are too far away, the activation they provide will be zero) and by the decay term in equation 3. The important point is that an *equilibrium* develops, which is different from static stability. This is the very reason why there is no need for a distinction into a learning and a performance phase, as mentioned above.

Let us now turn to the experiment in which the robot was put into the corner near one of the obstacles. Although this situation has not been forseen by the designer, and thus there is no rule for backing out of an impasse, this is what the robot does. Again, this behavior is emergent.

One way of analyzing the network is by propagating activity back from, say the avoidance layer to the range finder layer. This will lead to prototypical patterns which can help us to develop an intuitive understanding. They can in some sense be said to reflect a "representation" of the system-environment interaction which is encoded in the weights. In the example, one of the prototypical patterns can be interpreted as meaning something like "a situation in which it is a good idea to retract and turn left". The "backing out" can be understood as a succession of "retract and turn" behaviors each of which is triggered by patterns similar to the prototypical ones.

A more complicated form of emergence is seen in Figure 4. Initially the behavior of the robot is the same as in the avoidance experiment (not shown in the figure). Only as it gets into the range of the target it turns towards its center and stops if it reaches the inner circle. In these simulation runs the target was always put behind a hole in the wall. Thus it was possible for the robot to associate range finder patterns corresponding to "near

[4] Originally we had planned to get anticipatory behavior by introducing several network layers to keep some information about the recent past. This turned out not to be necessary.

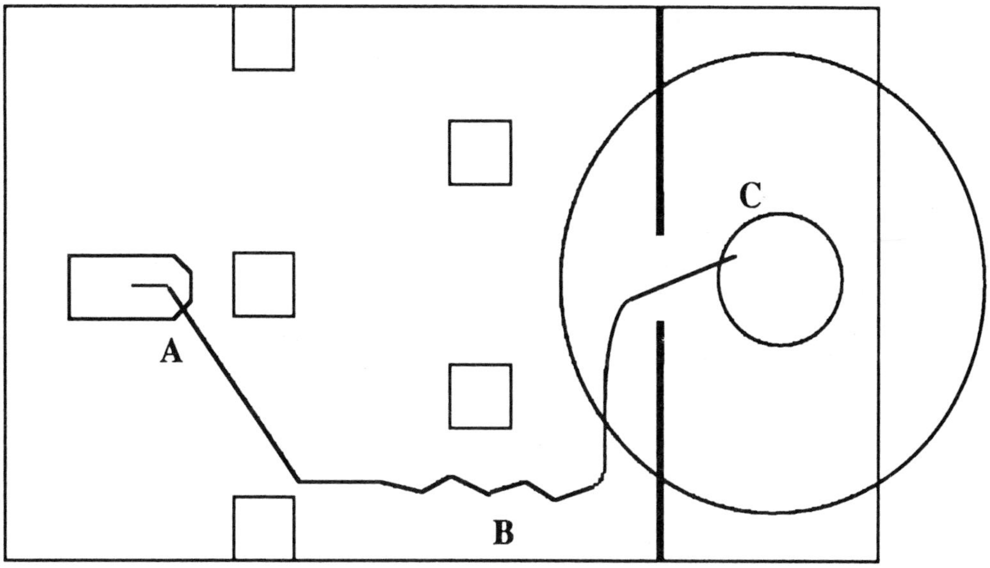

Figure 4: Simulation including an attractive force.

the wall" with "near target". Assuming that the robot is near the wall and near the target, there is an attractive "force" pulling the robot towards the target, but there is also a repulsive one from the wall pushing the robot in the other direction. And it is encoded in the architecture that the repulsive one has priority. This way the wiggly trail of Figure 4 comes about: a succession of attraction and repulsion (b). Whether a range finder pattern acts as an attractive or repellant force is not a function of the environment but of the system's "interpretation" of this pattern due to its learning history. In an environment in which targets are always behind holes in walls the robot will develop wall-following behavior due to this regularity. Again, wall-following is emergent[5]: the behavior of the robot looks very goal-directed — it seems to search for a target — although neither goals nor plans are part of the robot's design.

From these remarks it can be seen that even in this extremely simple case, it is a difficult task to predict the robot's behavior, given its design and a particular environment. This is especially true whenever learning and interaction with an environment are involved. Before we can design complicated robots we first need to develop a sound understanding of the relation between architecture (value scheme, morphology, and system dynamics), environment, and the resultant behaviors. A precondition for understanding this relationship is to view the world through the robot's "eyes", a perspective people seem to have a hard time to adopt. This leads us to our next point.

4.2 Designer- vs. robot-centered design: grounding and situatedness

In our "rules" we mentioned that everything must be seen from the robot's point of view. This is a crucial point. For example, it has been mentioned that the symbol grounding problem is essentially an artifact of the introduction of a designer or an observer who tries to describe the behavior of a system by means of symbols. But autonomous systems, by definition, must learn from their own experience. Only then can we expect them to develop "genuine intelligence".

(1) The value scheme: For the robot the value scheme is the teacher: it enables learning (through the activation of basic behaviors) and constrains the self-organization. Thus, in a sense, supervised learning does take place, but the supervision is not done by some outside observer or designer, but by the way in which the value system is activated by the environment. In other words, the robot, through the value scheme, provides its own rein-

[5] For a an approach to a theory of emergent functionality, see Steels, 1990.

forcement. This way it can learn from its very own perspective.

(2) Transducer functions: In section 3 we mentioned that by using 1/exp(d) as the input to the range finder layer we (the designers) are deciding that nearby objects are more important for the robot than distant ones. This way the robot does not get any information about distance (it does not "see" distance), but rather, in a sense, risk of hitting. In our view, it would be a mistake to feed distance into the robot. What the robot needs to know to *act* is risk, not distance[6]. We are stressing this point since, as human observers, it is hard *not* to think of distance as the most natural thing.

(3) Neural structures: The neural structures for associating sensory information with action, provide the means by which the system can acquire its own "knowledge" of its interaction with the world over time. This enables the system to adapt to a larger variety of different environmental conditions than systems lacking a general learning component as, for example, Brooks' subsumption architecture (Brooks, 1986). In addition, *any* "knowledge" acquired by the robot will automatically be *grounded* in its experience. For example, the knowledge about "situations — defined in terms of prototypical range finder patterns — in which it is a good idea to retract and turn left" would be fully grounded in the agent's experience which is, in the end, determined by the interaction between architecture and environment. Thus, our approach is also a step towards solving the *grounding* problem. We deliberately omit the word "symbol": there is no need to solve the *symbol* grounding problem since there are no designer defined symbols in the system that have to be grounded. The designer defined basic reflexes are part of the initial set up and are by definition grounded. If they are inappropriate the robot will be maladapted and may not survive.

If a strict robot-centered design point of view is adopted, as suggested, the resulting agent will be a situated one. Since it acquires its own knowledge as it interacts with its environment through learning mechanisms, there is no need for a designer to predefine all potentially relevant situations the agent might encounter. Given the indefinitely large number of possible range finder patterns, the latter would be very difficult if not impossible to do. And the more complex the sensors get, the more difficult it will be. For example, in traditional design, the situation of an impasse would have to be predefined along with the actions to take. For a situated system this is not necessary since it can act appropriately (i.e. showing coherent behavior without colliding) by taking advantage of its current physical environment, i.e. of the sensory inputs which are mediated by the traces of its past experiences to indicate the appropriate action. This leads, as we have seen, for example, to this behavior of "backing out". This direct interaction minimizes computation so that the robot can act in real time. It should be mentioned that there is a true real-time constraint for the robot: since it keeps moving, which is its basic motivation, it *must* act quickly if it is to avoid collisions. In this sense, the agent's behavior is reactive. However, it also learns to anticipate obstacles which makes it less reactive, but also dependent on its "knowledge" about the environment. Only when an unexpected (novel) situation appears (e.g. smaller obstacles) the purely reactive component comes in again. From this discussion it is obvious that situated agents capable of incorporating experience will be robust: they will show appropriate behavior in situations which have not been predefined by the designer. Moreover, we believe that robust systems can never be constructed on top of designer defined knowledge structures.

4.3 Limitations and further work:

The model presented is limited in several ways. Currently all layers in the system are directly linked to sensors and/or motor actions. In a next step we will try to integrate this information in a higher-order layer. Since this higher-order layer will no longer be coupled directly to sensors or motor actions, this will enable the robot to take its experience more strongly into account. For example, the construction of navigation related maps can be addressed in this way. In other words, it will be able to act more "intelligently". Another step will be to extend the value scheme to include the notion of internal needs. Moreover, the informal discus-

[6] Similar observations have been made in the area of computer vision, where time-to-contact rather than distance is the important variable (e.g. Lee, 1976).

sions reported here must sprebe augmented by systematic investigation and formal analyses. It can be expected that additional insight will be gained by implementing the model on real robots. This work is currently in progress[7].

5 Conclusions

We have discussed a paradigm for designing autonomous systems. It promises to resolve a number of fundamental problems of AI in natural ways (such as situatedness and robustness), others will not need to be solved since they are artifacts of the traditional approach (e.g. symbol grounding). We have also shown that our approach is superior to others in certain ways since through its embeddedness in a learning system it is capable of adapting to an environment in a robust way. The DAC paradigm promises to be a valuable conceptual tool which will help us design better autonomous agents. This will in turn enable us to more effectively explore the foundations of intelligent systems — which has always been the goal of the scientific branch of AI. It can be seen, in a sense, as a "step toward the counter-representationalist position" (Bersini, 1990). Although we believe that the approach will scale up to more complex behaviors, this is essentially an empirical question.

References

[1] Agre, P.E., & Chapman, D. (1987). Pengi: An implementation of a theory of activity. *AAAI-87*, Seattle, WA, 268-272.

[2] Anderson, T.L. & Donath, M. (1990). Animal behavior as a paradigm for develop robot autonomy. *Robotics and Autonomous Systems, 6,* 145-168.

[7]We might mention that we have just tried the approach in a real robot, Lola, which has been developed at the AI Lab of the Free University of Brussels. Although it was done with very different types of sensors (unreliable infrared) it worked fine. And here is one detail: if the robot works without the learning, it can easily get stuck in corners, if the learning as added, it has so far not been getting trapped at all (in the regular hallways of the university). We are currently systematically analyzing these results.

[3] Bersini, H. (1990). A step toward the counter-representationalist position. *Proceedings ECAI-90,* 107-114.

[4] Brooks, R.A. (1991). Intelligence without reason.*Proceedings IJCAI-91, 569-595.*

[5] Brooks, R.A. (1986). A robust layered control system for a mobile robot. *IEEE Journal of Robotics and Automation, RA-2,* 14-23.

[6] Clancey, W.J. (1989). The frame-of-reference problem in cognitive modeling. *Annual conference of the cognitive science society,* 107-114.

[7] Harnad, S. (1990). The symbol grounding problem. *Physica D, 42(1-3),* 335-346.

[8] Kupferman, I., & Weiss, K.R. (1978). The command neuron concept. *Behavioral and Brain Sciences, 1,* 3-39.

[9] Kumar, N., Williams, M., Bulotti, & van der Kooy, D. (1989). Evidence for associative learning in the nematode *C. elegans. Society for Neuroscience Abstracts, 15,* 1141.

[10] Lee, D.N. (1976). A theory of visual control of braking based on information about time to collision. *Perception, 5,* 437-459.

[11] Maes, P. (1990). Situated agents can have goals. *Robotics and Autonomous Systems, 6,* 49-70.

[12] Malcolm, C.A., Smithers, T., & Hallam, J. (1989). An emerging paradigm in robot architecture. In: T. Kanade, F.C.A. Groen, & L.O. Herzberger (eds.). *Intelligent Autonomous Systems, 2,* 546-564.

[13] Steels, L., (1990). Towards a theory of emergent functionality. In: J.-A. Meyer, & S. W. Wilson (eds.). *From animals to animats.* Cambridge, Mass.: MIT Press, 451-461.

[14] Suchman, L.A. (1987). *Plans and situated actions. The problem of human machine interaction.* Cambridge University Press.

[15] Verschure, P.F.M.J. & Coolen, A.C.C, (1991). Adaptive fields: distributed representations of classically conditioned associations. *Network, 2.*

[16] Verschure, P.F.M.J, Kröse, B.J.A., & Pfeifer, R. (submitted). Distributed adaptive control: the self-organization of structured behavior. Techreport Nr. 91.15, Institute for Informatics, University of Zurich.

[17] Winograd, T., & Flores, F. (1986). *Understanding computers and cognition.* Reading, Mass.: Addison-Wesley.

Taking Eliminative Materialism Seriously: A Methodology for Autonomous Systems Research

Tim Smithers[†]

Artificial Intelligence Laboratory
Vrije Universiteit Brussel
Pleinlaan 2
1050 Brussels
Belgium

Telephone: + 32 2 641 29 65
Fax: + 32 2 641 28 70
E-mail: tim@arti.vub.ac.be

Abstract

Traditionally autonomous systems research has been a domain of Artificial Intelligence. We argue that, as a consequence, it has been heavily influenced, often tacitly, by folk psychological notions. We believe that much of the widely acknowledged failure of this research to produce reliable and robust artificial autonomous systems can be apportioned to its use and dependence upon folk psychological constructs. As an alternative we propose taking seriously the Eliminative Materialism of Paul Churchland. In this paper we present my reasons for adopting this radical alternative approach and briefly describe the bottom-up methodology that goes with it. We illustrate the discussion with examples from our work on autonomous systems.

1 Introduction

Any theory of intelligent behaviour must serve to explain how and why biological systems, whose behaviour we describe as intelligent, perform the way they do. It should also support the effective design and construction of artificial systems whose behaviour is similarly task achieving and adaptable. What follows from this is that our attempts to develop such a theory can be pursued in two different ways. One way is to study the biological systems whose behaviour we wish to understand and explain. This is the aim of the biological sciences, in particular psychology, neuroscience, and ethology. The second approach involves building and experimenting with artificial systems, in other words, building robots, or autonomous systems, as we will call them here. It is in this second approach that we are primarily engaged, but not in isolation from the closely related work in the biological sciences.

Autonomous systems research is about designing, constructing, and experimenting with artificial systems that engage in specific kinds of task achieving behaviour in particular real environments, and which do so reliably and robustly with respect to the normal variations and events in these environments. To be effective this research, just like any other, needs a sound methodology, one that sets up a framework upon which to hang theoretical developments and one which supports effective experimental procedures. It should also be as free as possible from inappropriate pre- or folk-theoretic prejudices and presumptions.

Traditionally autonomous systems research has been a domain of Artificial Intelligence (AI). As a result it has been strongly influenced by the metaphors and folk-theories that have dominated AI since its earliest days. In particular, the intentional terms and propositional attitudes of folk psychology have been used, almost exclusively, to describe the behaviour of autonomous

[†] The author currently holds the SWIFT AI chair at the VUB AI Lab and is on leave from Department of Artificial Intelligence, University of Edinburgh.

systems.[1] These folk theoretic descriptions have in turn been used to inform and specify the design of artificial systems. For example, we will typically say that some robot needs to *know* K so that it can *believe* B which, given its *desire* D, will lead it to adopt *goal* G to achieve task T. This *Knowledge Level* description ([Newell, 1982]) of behaviour is then used as a specification for a *Symbol Level* design that identifies what symbolic representation structures, and computational operations and processes are required to engender such Knowledge Level behaviour. When this symbol system is implemented in a robot what we typically see is some set of 'perception' subsystems that feed a symbolic 'world model' which in turn supports symbolic 'reasoning processes' used to construct the plans of actions the robot must execute in order to achieve its goals. We call this the *sense-think-act* cycle and it is to be found in some form or other in the vast majority of artificial autonomous systems—see [Malcolm, et al, 1989] for a fuller exposition of this classical approach to autonomous systems research.

Three striking observations can be made of most past and present autonomous systems research in AI: first, the heavy influence and use of folk psychological notions is often only implicit; second, many of the practitioners are apparently unaware of or unconcerned by this implicit use and dependence upon a folk theory; and third, despite considerable effort, this research has very little to show in the way of successful autonomous systems—as opposed to the numerous successful knowledge-base systems designed to help or support human users. We still have no robots whose performance comes anywhere near that of even simple behaving biological systems. We believe that this tacit dependence upon folk psychology and apparent lack of success are not unconnected, and that the blame for much of this lack of success can be attached to the tacit (and often unappreciated) use of folk psychology to provide the methodological framework.[2] In an attempt to correct this situation we have become attracted to a radically different stance championed by Paul Churchland, that of *Eliminative Materialism*.[3]

In this paper we briefly set out what eliminative materialism is. We then explain what it means to take eliminative materialism seriously and why doing so offers a suitable methodology for autonomous systems research. We will conclude by illustrating how this methodology is being used to direct our research into autonomous systems and to shape the technology we are developing to support it.

2 Eliminative Materialsim

Eliminative materialism presents the thesis that folk psychology—our every day conception of such psychological phenomena as 'thinking', 'believing', 'desiring', 'feeling', 'remembering', fearing', etc.—is a radically false theory of intelligent behaviour; "... a theory so fundamentally defective that both the principles and the ontology of that theory will eventually be displaced, rather than smoothly reduced, by completed neuroscience", [P.M. Churchland, 1989a, page 1]. In place of folk psychology it proposes that research into the structure, activity, and mechanisms of the brain, from its micro-structure to its macro-structure, will lead us to a new kinematic and dynamical theory of what are currently referred to as the cognitive activities underlying intelligent behaviour in autonomous biological systems. It further proposes that such a theory will be uniform across the brains (nervous systems) of all (terrestrial) biological systems (not just human brains) and that it will properly connect with theories in evolutionary biology and nonequilibrium thermodynamics, [P.M. Churchland, 1989a, page 17]. According to eliminative materialism, then, a detailed neurophysiological-based understanding of ourselves (a materialistic understanding) will eventually displace (eliminate) our current mentalistic self-conception in the way oxidation theory (and modern chemistry in general) simply displaced the phlogiston theory of matter transformation, [P.M. Churchland, 1979, chapter 1].[4]

Though radical, what we find refreshing in this proposal is that it places what we believe to be an appropriate emphasis on the fundamentally material nature of any proper theory of intelligent behaviour, as opposed to the traditional emphasis on the 'mental' and the 'mind'. In referring specifically to an understanding of brain processes and mechanisms and the overall

[1] The term *folk psychology* is used to refer to the commonsense psychological terms such as 'believe', 'desire', 'fear', 'feel', 'imagine', 'prefer', 'think', etc. whose every day use is governed by a loose knit network of largely tacit principles, platitudes, and paradigms, and *not* by some system of well founded, coherent, and consistent natural laws, as is required of any scientific theory. See [Stich, 1986, chapter 1] for a good introduction to the concept of folk psychology and some historical context.

[2] For a different, but not unrelated, analysis of the reasons for the failure of classical robotics research and symbolic AI in general, see [Brooks, 1986a] and [Brooks, 1991]. See also [Moravec, 1988] for an analysis which presents a very different outlook on the future of man and robots.

[3] Here we use the term 'stance' in the same way Dennett does in his *intentional stance*, [Dennett, 1987]. Dennett's intentional stance is, by the way, an earlier attraction of ours which we have subsequently abandoned due to its failure to offer non-arbitrary accounts of how so called mental states relate to brain states. See [P.M. Churchland, 1988] for a concise but persuasive statement of this criticism.

[4] For a different view on the likely role of folk psychology in a science of cognition, but not one simply dismissive of Eliminative Materialism, see [Stich, 1986, chapter 10].

architecture together with the relationship any such understanding must have with evolutionary biology and nonequilibrium thermodynamics, it points the way to what we believe is likely to be a more fruitful and successful theory of intelligent behaviour, one unencumbered by historically rooted and inappropriate philosophies of mind.

To date, advocates of this alternative approach to a science of cognition have pointed to work in the biological sciences, and to neuroscience and computational neuroscience in particular, as the basis for its development, see [P.S. Churchland, 1986], for example. We believe that research into artificial autonomous systems can also contribute to this programme. We also believe that to take eliminative materialism seriously in autonomous systems research is likely to lead to much greater success in understanding how to design and build such systems: an understanding of the mechanisms, processes and architectures, competence theories, and associated task-environment decriptions of artificial autonomous systems.

3 On Agents, Environments, and Behaviour

Before setting out in more detail what taking Eliminative Materialism seriously means for us, we first need to establish some *working characterisations* of what it is to be an agent, an environment, and thus what behaviour is. But first a word about working characterisations.

Working characterisations are those essential yet hazardous devices of research which enable us to initially and temporarily set up some structure over what we are interested in studying and eventually understanding. To serve us well, to do useful work for us, we must guard against such characterisations becoming dogmatised, defended for their familiarity, or taken as well established definitions. As working characterisations they must be modified (modernised) or even abandoned as our investigations and discoveries proceed. Eventually some of them may take their rightful places in well formed theories, but this is not necessarily the case. Their best work may be done as stepping stones on the way to better characterisations and theoretical constructs. With these thoughts in mind here is how we are currently seeking to characterise what an agent is, what an environment is, and thus what behaviour is.

We characterise an agent as a coherent system of processes (typically organised in a function differentiating architecture) that reliably and robustly affects specific changes on its environment while receiving any affects from its environment which may be (direct or indirect) consequences of its actions or may simply be the affects of unrelated events occurring in the environment impinging upon it. In other words, an agent is a system which affects and which is affected by the environment it acts on. We call this being embedded in an environment. In this way agents are to be properly seen as components of their environment, not as something separate (or separable) from it.

We characterise an environment as a system of processes (not necessarily coherent, and so not organised in an architecture) which are affected by and/or affect an agent. Such a set of processes is typically a subset of the processes that constitute what we call the real world. In this sense the environment of one agent may not intersect the environment of another agent; each agent has its own reality. We call this *robot reality* to distinguish it from our own (human) reality—the two, as it turns out, are often quite different, which is one of the reasons for the frequent failure of our intuitions (particularly folk psychological ones) in coming to understand the mechanisms and processes that underlie intelligent behaviour.

Given these characterisations of an agent and an environment we can characterise behaviour as the dynamics of the interaction space between agent processes and environment processes. An autonomous agent is thus a system which is responsible for (primarily causal in) the establishment and maintenance of some particular kind of dynamic form in the interaction space between it and its environment. The behaviour we are interested in is thus properly seen as a dynamic property of this interaction space. It is *not* a property of our agent and so it cannot properly be studied by observing and analysing just the agent processes. From this characterisation of behaviour we can see that it is necessarily an *emergent* phenomenon. It cannot be said to arise simply from the internal processes (workings) of the agent. The modern emphasis on 'emergent' behaviour to distinguish it from 'determined' behaviour shows the effects of the folk psychological notions traditionally employed to characterise behaviour. Behaviour has never been a phenomenon determined and generated by an agent alone. Characterising and thus investigating behaviour as something generated by an agent is one of the more serious flaws seen in most contemporary autonomous systems research.

The term 'agent' is, of course, a favourite of the folk psychological ontology. It consequently carries with it notions of intentionality and purposefulness that we wish to avoid. Here we use the term divested of such associated baggage. We simply appeal to the observational fact that there is a class of systems which can be picked out of the general observable goings on which engage their surrounding processes in a coherent and effective way. These systems, which we want to call agents, consist of not just a collection of arbitrary processes, but are formed from particular sets of processes whose dynamic combination leads them to interact with all the other processes that constitute their environment in ways that result in reproducible, reliable, and robust task achieving behaviour. For us the possibility of agenthood is not so much a folk psychological attribute as a biological fact. We leave the explanation of how such systems came about and how they are possible to the evolution biologists, the biochemists, and those investigating the far from equilibrium dynamic processes which seem to play a key role in their evolution in biology. Our aim is to build upon, in a continuous way, the understanding and theories we see developing in these other sciences.

Our working characterisations of agents, environments, and behaviour may seem strange when compared to the more usual notions used or implied by classical autonomous systems research. Their construction is heavily influenced by our desire to develop a theoretical account of intelligent behaviour which will take us smoothly from the very simplest of agent-environment systems to the more complex forms. In adopting this eliminative materialsim stance we are necessarily limited by our current understanding and we are thus constrained to start by investigating relatively simple systems. This is, as we say, for pragmatic reasons, not because we believe that more complex systems are just bigger versions of simpler ones: they almost certainly are not. However, if our approach is to be of any value, the theoretical notions we develop and test out on simple systems must support us when we come to investigate more complex examples.

4 The Problem of Autonomous Systems

Having set out our working characterisations of the three essential components of intelligent behaviour we can now attempt a statement of what the problem of autonomous systems is, from an eliminative materialism stance.

> The problem is, given the requirement for some kind of reliable and robust task achieving behaviour in some given environment, what is the necessary and sufficient set of competences that an auronomous systems must have to be able to achieve the specified task in the given environment, what set of processes can or must be used to engender these competences and how are they organised in an architecture, and what mechanisms and structural properties can or must be used to realise such a set of processes, and hence such an agent?

From this statement of the problem we can identify a set of four different kinds of, or levels of (as we will call them her) understanding that we must develop in order to fully understand an autonomous system. They are:

- *Task and Environment:* This level defines that overall task, or tasks, of the agent and the environment in which it must successfully and reliably achieve its task—its niche, in ethological terms. A simple example might be, move around my office without getting trapped by any of the furniture and people in it.
- *Competence Theory:* This level defines the necessary and sufficient competence required by an agent to reliably achieve the specified task in the given environment. Here a competence means a particular ability or skill, such as move around the environment without getting stuck. For our simple example we would need competences like move (forward, backwards, left and right turn) and avoid obstacles.
- *Processes and Architecture:* This level identifies the set of processes that when organised in a particular architecture (so that they interact in the appropriate way) engender the required competences when they interact with environment processes. Again, for our simple example, the set of processes would include motor-sensory processes connecting motor actions to sensor systems, and probably some kind of process to modify and adjust the motor-sensory relationships embodied in the former processes.
- *Mechanisms and Strucural Components:* This level identifies the mechanisms and structural components used to implement the specified processes and architecture. Example mechanisms would typically involve electric motors, sensor devices such as Infra-red emitter-detector pairs, electronic amplification, and computations.

In the next section we introduce a way of talking about behaviour which is both free of folk psychological notions and which we believe will be easier to relate to a specification of the necessary and sufficient set of competences, the processes and their organisation required to engender these competences, and the mechanisms and strurctural components that can be used to implement the processes. In other words, the basis for a materialistic theory of intelligent behaviour which eliminates folk psychological notions.

5 Dynamical Systems

The interaction space between an agent and its environment forms the phase space of a dynamical system; a dynamical system produced by the interaction of agent processes and those environment processes that constitute the agent's reality. We can therefore describe behaviour in terms of properties of this dynamical system. This is both convenient and attractive. It is convenient because the mathematical modelling and analysis of dynamical systems and complex dynamical systems can be drawn upon to develop formal descriptions and specifications of behaviour.[5] It is attractive because the science of dynamical and complex dynamical systems, and the far from equilibrium phenomena that are an important property of such systems, seems to us to offer a path to the uniform theory of intelligent behaviour that Eliminative Materialism attempts to promote. It also offers a basis for relating a theory of intelligent behaviour to the closely related theories of evolutionary biology and nonequilibrium thermodynamics—which is again one of the stated aims of Eliminative Materialism.

5.1 Some Illustrative Examples

To illustrate the use of dynamical systems to describe and analyse the behaviour of artificial autonomous systems we will discuss some experiments in our mobile robotics research—see [Donnett & Smithers, 1991], [Nehmzow, et al, 1989], [Nehmzow & Smithers, 1991a], and [Nehmzow, et al, 1991], for further details of this work. We have concentrated on building and using small rather simple mobile robots. They typically have a small number of binary sensors built using microswitches, infra-red (IR) emitters and IR-sensitive diodes, and light dependent resistors (LDRs), and simple motor control giving forward and reverse at two speeds for two motors.

5.1.1 Obstacle Avoidance and Point Attractors

If an agent is to move about its environment, a basic competence it must have is to avoid obstacles. In other words, it must not get stuck. It doesn't matter how easy or difficult engineering this competence is in a mobile robot, it has to have it, else it won't be a mobile robot for long. Obstacle avoidance and don't get stuck are rather 'loaded' ways of talking about what is a very basic kind of behaviour. That is, such folk psychological descriptions tend to be taken as indicating the need for such systems to be able to identify obstacles so that they may be avoided and to have explicit strategies for getting out of trouble. If these indications are taken too seriously then we might be tempted (as indeed many mobile robot builders are) to design and construct obstacle recognition and explicit strategy planning subsystems for our mobile robots. Neither are necessary for this kind of competence.

A better description of this basic behaviour is that there must be no point attractors in the interaction space of the agent-environment system, at least not under normal conditions,[6] only point repellors that coresspond to the so called obstacles. Taking this 'no point attractors only point repellors in the interaction space' description we can use it more effectively as a specification for the kind of processes that we must build into our mobile robot, at least to engender this particular competence. Thus, the dynamics of the agent processes when interacting with the dynamics of its environment must not induce point attractors but must produce point repellors. The agent processes that we are specifying here are the motor-sensory processes that it must be equipped with to interact with its environment. The question is therefore, what are the necessary dynamics of the motor-sensory processes that will, when they interact with the environment dynamics, produce a dynamical system (an interaction space) which has only point repellors in and no point attractors?

We have been investigating two different kinds of mechanisms which can be used to implement such processes in our simple mobile robots. In the first case, see [Nehmzow, et al, 1989], we investigated the use of a self modifying mechanism based upon a simple pattern associator and a condition monitor. Essentially this is a mechanism which initially learns and then adaptively changes the mapping from sensory signals to motor control signals so as to establish and maintain obstacle avoidance behaviour in a particular environment. By monitoring certain internally measurable conditions of the robot the function used to map sensor space into motor space (implemented using the pattern associator) is constantly adjusted so that the dynamics of the motor-sensory control process, when interacting with the environment, results in a dynamical system which

[5]There are now many texts on dynamical systems, but two that we have found to be good introductions to the subject are [Arrowsmith & Place, 1990] and [Sandefur, 1990]. The former is a good formal treatment, the latter a more informal and applications oriented treatment. Another relevant text here, by someone whose writings we also find inspiring and influential, is [Rosen, 1970].

[6]Except, perhaps, for those required as part of some other task achieving behaviour, locating and docking with a recharging station, for example.

has no point actractors.[7] What this work shows, for a very simple robot in a very simple environment—for a simple interaction space—is that no one function (fixed) transformation will do for all situations. In other words, even for simple interaction spaces, preventing point attractors occuring requires an agent with motor-sensory processes which are not of the fixed reactive type frequently employed in mobile robot simulations, and frequently presumed to be adequate for competent autonomous behaviour.

In the second investigation we are using a Lego vehicle, see [Donnett & Smithers, 1991], to implement mechanisms that preserve the qualitative properties of the sensor-to-motor mapping function but which adjust it quantitatively in order to adapt the dynamics of the sensor-motor process to the particular environmental conditions the vehicle is in. In this experiment we are using a robot which has three different types of sensor systems, one with two binary bump sensors, one with two three-state whisker sensors ('not bent', 'bent left', and 'bent right'), and one with three binary infra-red sensors. These three sensor systems are arranged in a layered fashion (not unlike Brooks' Subsumption Architecture, [Brooks, 1986b]). Each layer implements a mapping of sensor space onto motor space. Additional mechanisms are implemented to monitor sensor signals from each type of system and to adjust the parameters of the relevant transformation function to adapt the dynamics of the respective sensor-motor system to the current environment dynamics, and hence to prevent point attractors occurring in the interaction space. In these experiments we are using a rather more complex environment than in the previous case, my office. This contains instances of all the usual office furniture—desks, tables, filing cabinets, chairs (four-legged and typists' swivel chairs)—together with a varying number of people and constitutes a difficult environment for our Lego vehicle, and thus a more complex interaction space. This work is still ongoing, but one of the most striking results so far is the realisation that getting the dynamics of the vehicle's motor-sensory processes right frequently requires implementing some subtle and neat tricks in the mechanisms that implement and adjust the mapping functions. For example, treating the infra-red sensors as simple binary (on/off) sensors hardly ever works, better schemes involve sampling their output signals over time and using information about the history of motor commands to continuously adjust the sampling size to maintain a constant proportion of 'on' signals to 'off' signals in each sample. The current sample size can then be used to categorise different situations and so be used to adjust the sensor-to-motor transformation to suit.[8] Similar experiences were observed in work done in four MSc student projects which used Lego vehicles, see [Ardin, 1990], [Dallas, 1990], [Mein, 1991], and [Pebody, 1991], the second and fourth projects involved groups of four and three vehicles respectively to investigate mechanism for co-operative and co-ordintated behaviour.

What we conclude from these experiences is that getting the dynamics right involves constantly adjusted mechanisms (nothing new to the control engineer) and, more importantly, it involves getting some very low level details of the mechanisms right. Preventing point attractors in the interaction space of an agent-environment system requires a careful study of the details of the dynamics of the particular interaction space. This we believe can only successfully be done (at least given our present understanding of all that is involved) by building real complete systems and testing them in their real environments.[9]

5.1.2 Exploration and Limit Cycles

Building mobile robots which prevent point attractors in their interaction spaces typically results in systems which move about in a chaotic manner. It is only for very simple robots in very simple environments that the dynamics of the interaction space is such that the behaviour is predictable. More usually the inevitable contingencies and tiny variations in the details of the interactions between agent and environment are such that the resulting behaviour, though deterministic, is unpredictable in form, not just in detail. This is the case for our Lego vehicle as it moves about in my office, for example.

Chaotic movement about an environment is not good for effective exploration and mapping behaviour. In a different series of experiments, see [Nehmzow & Smithers, 1991a], [Nehmzow, et al, 1991], and [Nehmzow & Smithers, 1991b], we have been investigating the use of self-organising networks as the basis for a location recognition competence in a mobile robot—as part of a more powerful navigation

[7] This type of control system is related to, and was inspired by, the Tensor Network Theory (TNT) of sensory-motor coordination developed by Pellionisz and Llinás, see [Pellionisz & Llinás, 1980], and [Pellionisz, 1985], for example. For a simple but effective explanation of the essential ideas of TNT see Churchland's Crab [P.M. Churchland, 1989a, page 82] or [P.S. Churchland, 1986, page 420].

[8] Another interesting aspect of this scheme is that it illustrates the tight coupling between sensor and motor processes. Indeed they are not well characterised as separate kinds of processes. In biological systems too, it is often the case that early processing of sensor signals is significantly influenced by signals from other (functionally different) parts of the nervous system.

[9] In saying this we do not mean to rule out the use of simulations, but we do mean to rule out only using simulations. A careful and disciplined use of both real experimental systems and faithful and validated simulations of aspects of them is typically required for this kind of work.

competence we are still working on. One important result from this work is that random motion in an environment to be mapped is not a good idea. What works rather better is some kind of structured motion. For our simple mobile robot this kind of motion is most easily achieved by having it follow the walls of its enclosure. A similar technique of wall following has been successfully used by students required to build Lego vehicles that visit all four corners of the Laboratory without making use of any internal map-like representations of the environment.

In terms of the dynamics of the interaction space we can see that such structured motions are examples of limit cycles in the interaction space. The wall following competences used by our robots can thus be understood as employing mechanisms which establish and maintain the desired limit cycles in their interaction spaces. The reliability and robustness of such exploration and location recognition competences is therefore a matter of the stability of the limit cycles. If the dynamics of the interaction space of a particular agent operating in a particular environment contains only weakly stable limit cycles then our agent will be easily disturbed (and possibly prevented) from effectively exploring and mapping its environment. Investigating mobile robot control schemes that are able to establish and maintain sufficiently stable limit cycles to support exploration and mapping competences in dynamic environments is one of the subjects of our current work.

5.2 More Complex Behaviour

Preventing point attractors (not getting stuck) and establishing and maintaining limit cycles (structured motion) in agent-environment interaction spaces are relatively simple problems compared to the more complex kinds of behaviour we would like to have autonomous systems produce. But, point attractors and limit cycles are relatively simple aspects of dynamical systems. We are sufficiently encouraged by our use of these ideas so far to believe that they will continue to be useful in trying to understand, investigate, and characterise more complex kinds of processes that can be used to realise more complex competences—which result in interaction spaces having numbers of attractors of different types in them, which may themsleves behave dynamically with respect to the others, for example. We see these dynamical system constructs as being a new way to both describe observed behaviour and to understand and specify the complex processes (cognitive processes) that underly intelligent behaviour.

One aspect of such behaviour that has already been worked on is action selection in situations where more than one action is valid or in situations in which a sequence of actions must be performed. Of particular interest here is a technique developed by Maes, see [Maes, 1989a], [Maes, 1989b], and [Maes & Brooks, 1990], which uses a dynamical system to select and coordinate actions in an autonomous system. See also [Pebody, 1991]. We are currently attempting to implement such a scheme in another MSc project using a Lego vehicle. Another area of related work is on emergent functionality, [Steels, 1991], and the use of analogical representations, [Steels, 1990], both of which depend in essential ways on the dynamics of the processes involved and on the details of the mechanisms used to implememt them. Understanding how such processes and mechanisms are to be effectively combined with the processes and mechanisms described above for preventing point attractors s and establishing limit cycles is something we are looking forward to and working towards.

A different set of ideas that we also see as closely related to our dynamical systems approach is due to Maturana and Varela, [Maturana & Varela, 1987]. In their theory of *autopoetic* systems they present what we believe to be the important concept of structural coupling between the dynamics of the agent processes and those processes that make up its environment. According to this idea, once established, autopoetic systems are subject to ongoing interactions with their environment, which may result in internal structural changes: during continuous interaction between agent and environment the agent both continuously classifies its situation in the environment in terms of its internal structure and continuously modifies its internal structure according to the dynamics of the processes that consititute it.

6 A Methodology

We started this paper with the assertion that by taking Eliminative Materialism seriously we could develop a more effective methodology for autonomous systems research. We will finish by setting out what we think this methodology entails. These points draw on our experiences so far in trying to reject folk psychological notions while investigating the mechanisms and structural components, processes and architectures, competence theories, and task-environment specifications that are needed to fully explain and thus understand autonomous intelligent behaviour. Taking Eliminative Materialism seriously in our autonomous system research means for us:

- Treating intelligent behaviour as particular properties of the dynamical system that results from the interaction between an agent and its environment. In this way we can form a language for talking about and describing behaviour which is both free of (eliminates) folk psychological notions and easier to relate to the competence, processes and architecture, and mechanisms and structural components (material) that might be used to realise the required agent dynamics.

- Building complete real artificial autonomous systems in order to effectively study the details of interaction spaces. Or, to borrow from Clarke, [Clarke, 1987][10], finding out what 'being there' really means, and not investigating what we suppose it means using simulations.

- Starting with the logically prior competences, such as preventing point attractors and establishing and maintaining point repellors and limit cycles in interaction spaces, and only moving to investigate more complex competences when we are secure in our understanding of these basic ones. This is not as simple as it might seem since it is not at all clear what is more complex or what is basic—see [McGonigle, 1991] for some good advice on this aspect.

- Designing and producing a technology suitable for building and effectively experimenting with artificial autonomous systems. This is what Lego vehicles were, and continue to be, developed for and have proved very effective at. One crucial ability that Lego vehicle technology allows us, an that most other robot building technologies do not, is to easily and significantly vary the robot morphology and sensor-motor configuration.[11]

We believe that by adopting these tenets we will be adopting a more effective and more successful methodology in our autonomous system research. We further believe that carrying out the 'artificial neurophysiological' investigations of real robots in the terms we suggest here is not only to take Eliminative Materialism seriously in our methodology, but that it is also a way to make an effective contribution to the programme of Eliminative Materialism as a whole. We believe it will lead us to develop new non-folk psychological concepts for talking about the complex cognitive processes that underly the competences that an autonomous agent must have in order to behave intelligently in its environments.

[10] Who, in this paper, advocates the building of robots (real ones) as a necessary part of Cognitive Science.

[11] It is sometimes far easier to change a vehicle's dynamics by changing its physical shape and/or structure than it is by trying to program it. Sometimes it is the only way.

Acknowledgements

The work of the 'Really Useful Robots' project is supported by a grant from the UK Science and Engineering Research Council (GR/F/5852.3) and the development of the Lego vehicles technology and support for the associated Intelligent Sensing and Control Laboratory is provided by the Department. The participation of Paul Ardin, Jim Dallas, John Hallam, Brendan McGonigle, Richard Mein, Ulrich Nehmzow, and Miles Pebody in some of the work reported here is acknowledged and much appreciated. Amaia Bernaras, David Connah (and other members of the Artificial Intelligence Group at Phillips Research Laboratories, Redhill), Dave Corne, John Hallam, Mitch Harris, Leslie Kaelbling, Chris Malcolm, Ulrich Nehmzow, Rolf Pfeifer, and Barbara Webb, read and usefully commented on earlier versions of this paper.

References

[Ardin, 1990] Paul Ardin, 1990, *The Development of Tactile and Opptokinetic Competences in a Mobile Robot*, MSc. Thesis, Department of Artificial Intelligence, University of Edinburgh.

[Arrowsmith & Place, 1990] D.K. Arrowsmith and C.M. Place, 1990, *An Introduction to Dynamical Systems*, Cambridge University Press.

[Brooks, 1986a] Rodney A. Brooks, 1986, *Achieving Artificial Intelligence Through Building Robots*, AI Memo 899, MIT AI Laboratory, May 1986.

[Brooks, 1986b] Rodney A. Brooks, 1986, *A Robust Layered Control System for a Mobile Robot*, IEEE Journal of Robotics and Automation, RA-2, April, 1986, pp 14–23.

[Brooks, 1991] Rodney A. Brooks, 1991, *Intelligence Without Reason*, to appear in the proceedings of the International Joint Conference on Artificial Intelligence, Sydney, Australia, 24–30 August, 1991.

[P.M. Churchland, 1979] Paul M. Churchland, 1979, *Scientific realism and the Plasticity of Mind*, Cambridge University Press.

[P.M. Churchland, 1989a] Paul M. Churchland, 1989, *A Neurocomputational Perspective: The Nature of Mind and the Structure of Science*, A Bradford Book, the MIT Press.

[P.M. Churchland, 1988] Paul M. Churchland, 1988, *On the Ontological Status of Intentional States: Nailing Folk Psychology to Its Perch*, in Behavioural and Brain Sciences, vol 11, no 3, pp 507–508.

[P.S. Churchland, 1986] Patricia Smith Churchland, 1986, *Neurophilosophy: Towards a Unified Science of the Mind/Brain*, A Bradford Book, the MIT Press.

[Clarke, 1987] Andy Clarke, 1987, *Being there: Why Implementation Matters to Cognitive Science*, Artificial Intelligence Review, vol 1, pp 231–244.

[Dallas, 1990] Jim Dallas, 1990, *Co-operative Search Behaviour in a Group of Lego Robots*, MSc. Thesis, Department of Artificial Intelligence, University of Edinburgh.

[Dennett, 1987] Daniel C. Dennett, 1987, *The Intentional Stance*, A Bradford Book, the MIT Press.

[Donnett & Smithers, 1991] Jim G. Donnett and Tim Smithers, 1991, *Lego Vehicles: A Technology for Studying Intelligent Systems*, in Jean-Arcady Meyer and Stewart W. Wilson (Eds.), *From Animals to Animats*, A Bradford Book, the MIT Press, pp 540–549; proceedings of the International Conference on the Simulation of Adaptive Behaviour: From Animals to Animats, held in Paris, 24–28 September, 1990.

[Gould, 1989] Stephen Jay Gould, 1989, *Wonderful Life, The Burgess Shale and the Nature of History*, Hutchison Radius.

[Hansell, 1984] Michael H. Hansell, 1984, *Animal Architecture and Building Behaviour*, Longman.

[Malcolm, et al, 1989] Chris M. Malcolm, Tim Smithers, and John Hallam, 1989, *An Emerging Paradigm in Robot Architecture*, an invited paper in Proceedings of the Second Intelligent Autonomous Systems Conference, Amsterdam, 11–14 December 1989, pp 284–293, edited by T Kanade, F.C.A. Groen, and L.O. Hertzberger, and published by Stichting International Congress of Intelligent Autonomous Systems.

[Maes, 1989a] Pattie Maes, 1989, *How to do the Right Thing*, Connection Science, vol 1, no 3, pp 291–323.

[Maes, 1989b] Pattie Maes, 1989, *The Dynamics of Action Selection*, Procedings of the International Joint Conference on Artificial Intelligence (IJCAI-89), Detroit, pp 991–997.

[Maes & Brooks, 1990] Pattie Maes and Rodney A. Brooks, 1990, *Learning to Co-ordinate Behaviours*, in Proceddings of the AAAI-90 conference, pp 796–802.

[Maturana & Varela, 1987] Humberto R. Maturana and Francisco J. Varela, 1987, *The Tree of Knowledge: The Biological Roots of Human Understanding*, New Science Library.

[McGonigle, 1991] Brendan McGonigle, 1991, *Incrementing Intelligent Systems by Design*, in Jean-Arcady Meyer and Stewart W. Wilson (Eds.), *From Animals to Animats*, A Bradford Book, the MIT Press, pp 525–531; proceedings of the International Conference on the Simulation of Adaptive Behaviour: From Animals to Animats, held in Paris, 24–28 September, 1990.

[Mein, 1991] Richard Mein, 1991, *Co-operative Behaviour in Uniformly and Differentially Programmed Lego Vehicles*, MSc. Thesis, Department of Artificial Intelligence, University of Edinburgh.

[Moravec, 1988] Hans Moravec, 1988, *Mind Children, The Future of Robot and Human Intelligence*, Harvard University Press.

[Nehmzow, et al, 1989] Ulrich Nehmzow, John Hallam, and Tim Smithers, 1989, *Really Useful Robots*, Proceedings of the Second Intelligent Autonomous Systems Conference, Amsterdam, 11–14 December 1989, pp 284–293, edited by T Kanade, F.C.A. Groen, and L.O. Hertzberger, and published by Stichting International Congress of Intelligent Autonomous Systems.

[Nehmzow & Smithers, 1991a] Ulrich Nehmzow and Tim Smithers, 1991, *Mapbuilding Using Self-Organising Networks in "Really Useful Robots"*, in Jean-Acardy Meyer and Stewart W. Wilson (Eds.), *From Animals to Animats*, A Bradford Book, MIT Press, 1991, pp 152–159; proceedings of the International Conference on the Simulation of Adaptive Behaviour: From Animals to Animats, held in Paris, 24–28 September, 1990.

[Nehmzow & Smithers, 1991b] Ulrich Nehmzow and Tim Smithers, 1991, *Using Motor Actions for Location recognition*, this volume.

[Nehmzow, et al, 1991] Ulrich Nehmzow, Tim Smithers, and John Hallam, 1991, *Location Recognition in a Mobile Robot Using Self-Organising Feature Maps*, to appear in the Proceedings of the International Workshop on Information Processing in Autonomous Mobile Robots, held in Munich, March 1991, and published by Springer-Verlag. Also available as DAI Research Paper No 520, Department of Artificial Intelligence, University of Edinburgh.

[Newell, 1982] Allan Newell, 1982, *The Knowledge Level*, Artificial Intelligence Journal, vol 18, pp 87–127.

[Pebody, 1991] Miles Pebody, 1991, *How to Make a Lego Vehicle do the Right Thing*, MSc. Thesis, Department of Artificial Intelligence, University of Edinburgh.

[Pellionisz & Llinás, 1980] A. Pellionisz and R. Llinás, 1980, *Tensorial Approach to the geometry of Brain Function: Cerebellar Coordination via a Metric Tensor*, Neuroscience, vol 5. pp 1125–1136.

[Pellionisz, 1985] A. Pellionisz, 1985, *Tensorial Aspects of the Multidimensional Approach to the vestibulo-Oculomotor Reflex and Gaze*, chapter 19 in A. Berthoz and G. Melvill Jones (Eds.), *Adaptive Mechanisms in Gaze Control*, Elsevier, 1985, pp 281–296.

[Rosen, 1970] Robert Rosen, 1970, *Dynamical System Theory in Biology*, Wiley-Interscience, a division of John Wiley and Sons, Inc.

[Sandefur, 1990] James T. Sandefur, 1990, *Discrete Dynamical Systems, Theory and Applications*, Clarendon Press, Oxford.

[Steels, 1990] Luc Steels, 1990, *Exploiting Analogical Representations*, in Pattie Maes (Ed.), *Designing Autonomous Agents, Theory and Practice from Biology to Engineering and Back*, A Bradford Book, the MIT Press, pp 71–88. Also in Robotics and Autonomous Systems Journal, vol 6.

[Steels, 1991] Luc Steels, 1991, *Towards a Theory of Emergent Functionality*, in Jean-Acardy Meyer and Stewart W. Wilson (Eds.), *From Animals to Animats*, A Bradford Book, MIT Press, 1991, pp 451–461; proceedings of the International Conference on the Simulation of Adaptive Behaviour: From Animals to Animats, held in Paris, 24–28 September, 1990.

[Stich, 1986] Stephen Stich, 1986, *From Folk Psychology to Cognitive Science, The Case Against Belief*, A Bradford Book, the MIT Press.

An Adaptable Mobile Robot

Leslie Pack Kaelbling*
lpk@cs.Brown.edu
Computer Science Department
Box 1910
Brown University
Providence, RI 02912 USA

Abstract

This paper reports on the design and construction of a mobile robot that adapts to its environment. We start by considering the necessity for adaptability in artificial agents and proposing a reinforcement learning framework for describing the processes of adaptation. We then go on to present a simple algorithm for reinforcement learning and conclude by describing its application to a physical mobile robot. The overall goal of this work is to understand the utility of adaptability in engineered artificial agents, rather than to model natural adaptability.

The Necessity of Adaptability

One motive for making artificial agents adaptable is that many natural agents are adaptable and that there is a strong analogical similarity between natural and artificial agents. For engineering purposes, however, we must only adopt techniques of agent design that either simplify the design and construction of artificial agents or cause the agents ultimately to perform better. We argue that it is crucial for artificial agents to be capable of adapting their behavior to their environments.

The designer of an agent is given a specification of an environment or a class of environments in which the agent must work and a specification of the task the agent is to perform. The environment description may include the physical morphology and primitive sensorimotor capabilities of the agent, or those may be left to vary as part of the design. The word "task" is used very broadly here: a task could be as simple as to keep moving without bumping into things or as complex as to research the geological make-up of an unexplored planet. Because we are interested in agents that have a long-term interaction with an environment, tasks will not be specifications of short-term achievement goals that terminate before the end of the agent's "life."

*This work was carried out at Teleos Research and was supported in part by the Air Force Office of Scientific Research under contract F49620-89-C-0055, in part by the System Development Foundation, and in part by Teleos Research IR&D.

It is theoretically possible, given complete specifications of the task and the environment, to design an agent that optimally carries out the task in the environment. However, this strict prerequisite is rarely, if ever, satisfied. When the environment is not completely known to the designer ahead of time, the agent must itself be designed to adapt to its environment.

The dictionary [Morris, 1969] defines "adapt" as: "to adjust to a specified use or situation." We use the term "adaptation" rather than "learning" in order to focus attention on the improvement of behavior by making it more appropriate for the environment in which the agent is situated. The term "learning" has been used for a much wider variety of processes, including so-called "symbol-level learning" [Dietterich, 1986] in which no information is gained, but the internal processes of the agent are made more efficient.

We must make our agents adaptable when the specification of the environment and the agent's sensorimotor capabilities is incomplete, incorrect, or simply at an inappropriate level of abstraction. Here is a motivational story:

> I once spent a long time trying to program a mobile robot to use ultrasonic sensors to navigate down a hallway. I had a physical specification of the environment (it was the hallway I was sitting in) and fairly accurate manufacturers' specifications for the sensors and motors of the robot. Theoretically, I had enough knowledge to write the correct program and be done with it. However, the specifications of the abilities of the robot and of the properties of the environment were impossible for me to translate directly into the correct program. So, I worked in a debugging cycle that went like this:
>
> - Write a program for the robot;
> - Run the program on the robot watch it drive into a wall;
> - Analyze the behavior of the robot and see where the program was mistaken;
> - Fix the problem in the program;

- Run the program on the robot and watch it drive into a wall (this time for a different reason!);

and so on. The result of this cycle was that I learned a good deal about the nature of the interaction between the robot's sensors and the physical environment. Using this information, I *adapted* the robot's behavior so that it would perform its task correctly. A much more efficient strategy would have been for me to design a behavior for the robot that would, *itself*, adapt to the environment it was in.

The need for adaptability is even more pronounced when the specification of the environment is quite weak, allowing for a variety of different types of environments or even environments whose characteristics change over time. In that case, no amount of off-line learning on the part of the designer will allow a correct fixed strategy to be obtained, because the correct behavior will vary from run to run and even from time to time during the course of a single run.

Reinforcement Learning

One way to view the problem of constructing adaptable behaviors for agents is as a *reinforcement learning* problem. In reinforcement learning, the goal of the agent's designer is for the agent to learn what actions it should perform in which situations in order to maximize an external measure of success. All of the information the agent has about the external world is contained in a series of inputs that it receives from the environment. These inputs may encode information ranging from the output of a vision system to a robot's current battery voltage. The agent can be in many different states of information about the environment, and it must map each of these information states, or situations, to a particular action that it can perform in the world. The agent's mapping from situations to actions is referred to as an *action map*. Part of the agent's input from the world encodes the agent's *reinforcement*, which is a scalar measure of how well the agent is performing in the world. The agent should learn to act in such a way as to maximize the total reinforcement it gains over its lifetime.

As a concrete example, consider a simple robot with two wheels and two photo-sensors. It can execute five different actions: stop, go forward, go backward, turn left, and turn right. It can sense three different states of the world: the light in the left eye is brighter than that in the right eye, the light in the right eye is brighter than that in the left eye, and the light in both eyes is roughly equally bright. Additionally, the robot is given high values of reinforcement when the average value of light in the two eyes is increased from the previous instant. In order to maximize its reinforcement, this robot should turn left when the light in its left eye is brighter, turn right when the light in its right eye is brighter, and move forward when the light in both eyes is equal. The problem of learning to act is to discover such a mapping from information states to actions.

Thus, the problem of learning to act can be cast as a function-learning problem: the agent must learn a mapping from the situations in which it finds itself, represented by streams of input values, to the actions it can perform. In the simplest case, the mapping will be a pure function of the current input value, but in general it can have state, allowing the action taken at a particular time to depend on the entire stream of previous input values.

In the past few years there has been a great deal of work in the artificial intelligence (AI) and theoretical computer science communities on the problem of learning pure Boolean-valued functions [Haussler, 1988, Michalski, 1983, Mitchell, 1982, Quinlan, 1983, Valiant, 1984]. Unfortunately, this work is not directly relevant to the problem of reinforcement learning because of the different settings of the problem. In the traditional function-learning work, often referred to in the AI community as "concept learning," a learning algorithm is presented with a set or series of input-output pairs that specify the correct output to be generated for that particular input. This setting allows for effective function learning, but differs from the situation of an agent trying to learn an action map. The agent, finding itself in a particular input situation, must generate an action. It then receives a reinforcement value from the environment, indicating how valuable the current world state is for the agent. The agent cannot, however, deduce the reinforcement value that would have resulted from executing any of its other actions. Also, if the environment is noisy, as it will be in general, just one instance of performing an action in a situation may not give an accurate picture of the reinforcement value of that action.

Reinforcement learning reduces to concept learning when the agent has only two possible actions, the world generates Boolean reinforcement that depends only on the most recently taken action, there is exactly one action that generates the high reinforcement value in each situation, and there is no noise. In this case, from performing a particular action in a situation, the agent can deduce that it was the correct action if it was positively reinforced; otherwise it can infer that the other action would have been correct.

Reinforcement learning has its name because of its similarity to models used in psychological studies of behavior-learning in humans and animals [Estes, 1950]. It is also referred to as "learning with a critic," in contrast with the "learning with a teacher" of traditional supervised concept learning [Widrow *et al.*, 1973].

A Simple Reinforcement-Learning Algorithm

The *interval estimation* algorithm is a simple but effective method for learning from reinforcement. It is based on the idea of storing an estimate of the expected reinforcement for each action in each input situation *and* some information about how good that estimate is. The standard statistical technique of constructing confidence-interval estimates of quantities provides us with a method for doing this. The size of the confidence interval is a measure of the lack of information about the quantity being estimated. The interval estimation method can be applied in a wide variety of environments. The simplest form, in which reinforcement is Boolean, is presented here; extensions to the basic algorithm and an analysis of its performance can be found elsewhere [Kaelbling, 1990, Kaelbling, 1991].

The initial state of the algorithm consists of two two-dimensional arrays, both indexed by the set of possible inputs and the set of possible actions. Elements of the array n are integers encoding the number of times that the action has been executed in the input situation; elements of the array x are integers encoding the number of times it has succeeded (resulted in reinforcement value 1). To update the state of the algorithm in response to an interaction with the world, we must know i, the input that the agent received, a, the action it took, and r, the resulting reinforcement value. The update phase increments $n[i,a]$ by 1 and increments $x[i,a]$ by r. To generate a new action in response to an input i, the algorithm chooses the action a that maximizes

$$ub(x[i,a], n[i,a]) \ ,$$

where

$$ub(x,n) = \frac{\frac{x}{n} + \frac{z^2_{\alpha/2}}{2n} + \frac{z_{\alpha/2}}{\sqrt{n}}\sqrt{\left(\frac{x}{n}\right)\left(1-\frac{x}{n}\right) + \frac{z^2_{\alpha/2}}{4n}}}{1 + \frac{z^2_{\alpha/2}}{n}}$$

and $z_{\alpha/2} > 0$.

The value of $ub(x[i,a], n[i,a])$ is the upper bound of a confidence interval estimate of the underlying probability of receiving reinforcement value 1 given that action a is executed in input situation i. If n is the number of trials and x the number of successes arising from a series of Bernoulli trials with probability p, the upper bound of a $100(1-\alpha)\%$ confidence interval for p can be approximated by $ub(x,n)$. [1] Given an input situation, the action with the highest upper bound on expected reinforcement in that situation is taken.

[1]This is a somewhat more complex form than usual, designed to give good results for small values of n [Larsen and Marx, 1986]. The more standard form is

$$\frac{x}{n} + \frac{z_{\alpha/2}}{\sqrt{n}}\sqrt{\left(\frac{x}{n}\right)\left(1-\frac{x}{n}\right)} \ ,$$

which is the sample mean plus the product of interval size parameter, z, and the sample standard deviation.

a0s	a0t	a0b	a1s	a1t	a1b
(14 /	19)	.88194	(0 /	1)	.79346
(81 /	138)	.66567	(0 /	2)	.65763
(85 /	147)	.65507	(0 /	3)	.56151

Figure 1: A sample run with $p_0 = .55$, $p_1 = .45$, and $z_{\alpha/2} = 1.96$. In this case, it converges very quickly.

Initially, each of the actions will have an upper bound of 1, and action 0 will be chosen arbitrarily. As more trials take place, the bounds will tighten. The interval estimation method balances acting to gain information with acting to gain reinforcement by taking advantage of the fact that there are two reasons that the upper bound for an action might be high: because there is little information about that action, causing the confidence interval to be large, or because there is information that the action is good, causing the whole confidence interval to be high. The parameter $z_{\alpha/2}$ is the value that will be exceeded by the value of a standard normal variable with probability $\alpha/2$. It controls the size of the confidence intervals and, thus, the relative weights given to acting to gain information and acting to gain reinforcement. As α increases, more instances of reinforcement value 0 are required to drive down the upper bound of the confidence intervals, causing more weight to be placed on acting to gain information. By the DeMoivre-Laplace theorem [Larsen and Marx, 1986], these bounds will converge, in the limit, to the true underlying probability values, and, hence, if each action is continually attempted, this algorithm will converge to the optimal strategy.

In order to provide intuition about the workings of the interval-estimation algorithm, Figures 1 and 2 show output from two sample runs in a simulated environment in which there is only one input situation and the actions a_0 and a_1 succeed with probabilities p_0 and p_1. The listings show the number of success and trials of a_0 (the columns headed a0s and a0t), the upper bound on the confidence interval of p_0 (the column headed a0b) and the same for a_1 and p_1 (columns headed a1s, a1t, and a1b). These statistics are just shown at interesting points during the run of the algorithm. In Figure 1, the first few trials of a_1 fail, causing the estimate of p_1 to be quite low; it will be executed a few more times, once the upper bound for p_0 is driven near .56. The run shown in Figure 2 is somewhat more characteristic. The two actions have similar probabilities of success, so it takes a long time for one to establish dominance.

Experiments with a Mobile Robot

This section describes the application of the interval estimation algorithm to a mobile-robot learning sce-

a0s	a0t	a0b	a1s	a1t	a1b
(4 /	7)	.84178	(1 /	3)	.79235
(39 /	75)	.62931	(22 /	45)	.62996
(226 /	394)	.62150	(22 /	46)	.61863
(358 /	631)	.60549	(31 /	59)	.64734
(963 /	1789)	.56128	(52 /	111)	.56080
(5548 /	9888)	.57084	(52 /	112)	.55630

Figure 2: Another sample run with $p_0 = .55$, $p_1 = .45$, and $z_{\alpha/2} = 1.96$. This time, the two actions battle for a long time, but a_0 is clearly winning after 10,000 trials.

Figure 3: Spanky, a mobile robot.

nario. There have been very few implementations of reinforcement-learning algorithms on real robotic hardware. Three notable examples are: Nehmzow, Smithers, and Hallam's [Nehmzow *et al.*, 1990] work on a reinforcement-like robot-learning problem; Maes and Brooks' [Maes and Brooks, 1990] use of a simple algorithm to learn to coordinate predefined behaviors on a walking robot; and Mahadevan and Connell's [Mahadevan and Connell, 1991] work on learning individual behaviors given a subsumption structure for them.

The robot pictured in Figure 3 was used to experiment with reinforcement-learning algorithms. It has two drive wheels, one on each side, which allow it to move forward and backward along circular arcs. A set of five "feelers" allow it to detect obstacles to its front and sides, the round bumper detects contact anywhere on its perimeter, and four photosensors, facing forward, backward, left, and right, measure the light levels in each direction.

Task

In this task, the robot is given negative reinforcement, normally distributed with mean -2 and standard deviation 0.5 whenever the round bumper makes contact with any physical object. If the bumper is not engaged, the robot is given positive reinforcement, normally distributed with mean 1 and standard deviation 0.2, whenever the light in its front sensor gets brighter. If the bumper has not engaged and the brightness has not increased, it is given "zero" reinforcement, normally distributed with mean 0 and standard deviation 0.2.

The robot interacts with the world by making fixed-length motions, either forward or rotating in place to the left or right. The agent gets the following five bits of input:

Bits 0 and 1: Which direction is currently the brightest? 0 = front, 1 = left, 2 = right, 3 = back.

Bit 2: Is the rightmost feeler engaged?

Bit 3: Is the leftmost feeler engaged?

Bit 4: Is (at least) one of the middle three feelers engaged?

The robot was constructed with fairly inexpensive and highly inaccurate sensors and effectors. The description above gives a rough interpretation of the inputs and actions, but during the course of execution that interpretation is very frequently violated. A nominally optimal behavior that was hand-programmed was only able to get positive reinforcement about 40 percent of the time.

The agent must learn a mapping from this input space to its three actions that maximizes its local reinforcement. It develops a behavior that avoids bumping into obstacles and tends to move toward the light.

Results

The robot was run, using the interval-estimation algorithm, in this domain for more than 20 trials. It always learned a good local strategy for the domain with the length of time to learn the strategy varying from 2 to 10 minutes depending on how favorable its initial interactions with the world were. These experiments allow us to say, qualitatively, that the learning algorithm worked successfully. As we construct more learning methods, though, it would be useful to have a quantitative evaluation of the learning method, as well.

Ideally, this section would describe a long series of trials of the algorithm on the real mobile robot. Unfortunately, it is difficult to conduct such trials fairly in the physical system. The first problem is that a human must intervene whenever the robot approaches the light source and move the robot to a new location. The second problem is that it takes a long time to conduct the experiments. The time that it takes the robot to move greatly dominates the computation time of the learning algorithms, and this particular

ALG	*er*
IE	.6439
random	.3074
optimal	.6695

Table 1: Average reinforcement in artificial mobile robot environment over 100 runs of length 2000.

robot must have human supervision. So, for quantitative experiments with multiple trials, we will make use of an artificial domain. The domain is, superficially, a simulation of the robot domain described above. However, it is not of high fidelity, which causes this to be a substantially different problem than that of running on the actual robot. Still, it serves as an interesting and slightly complex domain for testing reinforcement-learning algorithms.

In the artifical robot domain, noise is added to the action and perception of the robot. Each action of the artificial robot is, with probability .1, changed to a randomly chosen action; each perception of the state of the world is, with probability .1, changed to a randomly chosen world state. This noise is in no way intended to model the noise occurring in the physical robot domain. Whenever the robot reaches the light source in the artificial world, the light is "teleported" to a new randomly-chosen location.

The results of the interval estimation algorithm for 100 runs of length 2000 are shown in Table 1. The optimal expected reinforcement value was estimated by running a hand-crafted non-learning behavior in the environment under the same conditions as the experimental algorithms. Similarly, the expected reinforcement of a random strategy was estimated by running a random strategy in the world. The learning curves of the interval estimation, optimal, and random algorithms are shown in Figure 4. Each point on the curve shows the average reinforcement (over the 100 runs) at each point in time during the run. To simplify the graph, buckets of 100 time steps are averaged together. As we can see, the interval estimation algorithm rapidly converges to optimal performance.

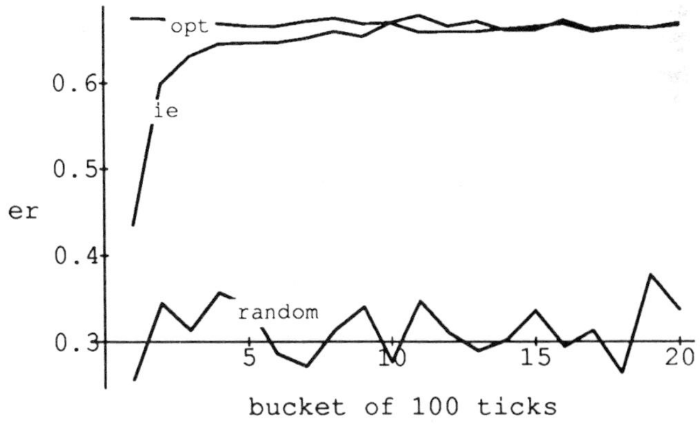

Figure 4: Learning curves for the artificial mobile robot task.

New Directions

This paper illustrates the application of a very simple reinforcement-learning algorithm to the mobile robot domain. The result is a robust artificial agent that can adjust to different environments and wirings of its sensors. There is a whole range of possible extensions to this work, some of which are being successfully tackled and others of which are still very open problems.

Delayed Reinforcement

The previous mobile robot domain can be complicated by giving the robot a large reinforcement value only when it reaches the light source. In order to tackle such problems, the learning algorithm must be modified to take actions that optimize some measure of future reinforcement rather than just the next step. Watkins' *Q-learning* algorithm [Barto *et al.*, 1989, Watkins, 1989] and its modification to use the interval estimation method [Kaelbling, 1990] can be used effectively on delayed-reinforcement problems.

The Q-learning algorithm estimates the value of taking action a in state s by $Q(a, s)$, which is the expected sum of discounted future reward given that action a is taken in state s and that the agent continues with the optimal strategy. The Q values can be estimated by

$$r + \gamma \max_{a'} Q(a', s') \ ,$$

where r is the instantaneous reward received for executing a in s; s' is the next state of the world; and γ is a discounting factor, which governs how important reward in the distance future is to the current choice of action. Watkins showed that, with a simple moving average, the estimated Q values will converge to the true values. This proof hinged on the requirement that every state be visited infinitely often. Of course, this requirement will never be satisfied in a practical setting, but it again highlights the need for a principled exploration method. One way to control exploration is to apply the interval estimation technique to the estimation of Q values: use standard statistical methods to construct confidence interval estimates on Q values and take the action with the highest upper bound. The details of the statistics are different than described above because the Q values are not Boolean. Confidence intervals for the normal distribution or non-parametric methods can be used to compute the upper bounds.

This particular robotic problem is considerably more difficult than other domains used for delayed reinforcement, such as the cart-pole domain [Anderson, 1987, Connell and Utgoff, 1987, Michie and Chambers, 1968, Selfridge and Sutton, 1985]. In the cart-pole domain, the robot receives a large negative reinforcement value whenever the pole falls over. In the absence of a good control strategy, the pole will fall over quite readily, giving the learner a lot of good data early on. In the more difficult robot domain, the robot may execute its initial random strategy for a very long time before it accidentally encounters the light source. Informal experiments with the real mobile robot were only successful if a human took an active role near the beginning of the run, putting the robot in situations from which it was relatively easy to reach the light and, therefore, get useful reinforcement data.[2] A set of formal experiments with the artificial analogue of the delayed-reinforcement robot domain, without shaping, were carried out [Kaelbling, 1990], but required on the order of 10,000 learning instances to converge to an appropriate strategy. The majority of that time was spent acting randomly before stumbling upon the goal state.

Generalization

Another major concern in developing reinforcement-learning algorithms that will work in more complex environments is the problem of generalization. Many of the early algorithms for reinforcement learning, including the interval estimation algorithm, require an enumeration of all possible inputs to the agent. For interesting real-world agents, the number of inputs can become enormous, causing a combinatorial explosion in the run-time and space requirements for the algorithms. In addition, such algorithms completely compartmentalize the information they have about individual input situations. If they learn to perform a particular action in a particular input situation, that has no influence on what they will do in similar input situations. In realistic environments, an agent cannot expect ever to encounter all of the input situations, let alone have enough experience with each one to learn the appropriate response. Thus, it is important to develop algorithms that will generalize across input situations.

It is important to note, however, that in order to find algorithms that are time and space efficient and that have the ability to generalize over input situations, we must give up something. What we will be giving up is the possibility of learning any arbitrary action mapping. In the worst case, the only way to represent a mapping is as a complete look-up table, which is what the enumerative algorithms do. There are many useful and interesting functions that can be represented much more efficiently, and the continuing research in this area must rest on the hope and expectation that an agent can learn to act effectively in interesting environments without needing action maps of pathological complexity.

Input generalization can be added to reinforcement-learning algorithms by adopting methods for function approximation, such as radial-basis functions [Poggio and Girosi, 1989], CMAC [Albus, 1981], or backpropagation [Rumelhart *et al.*, 1986]. A more directly statistical approach, which creates a decision tree by finding the most "relevant" input bits, is used in the G algorithm [Chapman and Kaelbling, 1991]. The G algorithm is based on Q-learning, but only partitions the world states according to those bits have a statistically significant impact on the Q values. This allows the algorithm to learn effectively in domains with many irrelevant bits, with many orders of magnitude improvement in running time of the algorithm and in the number of interactions with the world before convergence to a correct strategy. Strategies for which individual input bits are relevant but not statistically correlated with results (such as parity functions) cannot be learned by this algorithm, however.

[2] This process is an instance of a class of methods for expediting learning that are referred to by psychologists [Hilgard and Bower, 1975] as "shaping."

Conclusion

It is crucial for artificial agents to be able to adapt to their environments. Reinforcement learning provides a useful framework for expressing the process of adaptability and comparing the performance of candidate algorithms. Current reinforcement-learning algorithms can be made to work robustly on simple problems, but there are a variety of dimensions in which they must be improved before it will be possible to construct artificial agents that adapt to complex domains.

References

Albus, James S. 1981. *Brains, Behavior, and Robotics*. BYTE Books, Subsidiary of McGraw-Hill, Peterborough, New Hampshire.

Anderson, Charles W. 1987. Strategy learning with multilayer connectionist representations. In *Proceedings of the Fourth International Workshop on Machine Learning*, Ann Arbor, Michigan. 103–114.

Barto, A. G.; Sutton, R. S.; and Watkins, C. J. C. H. 1989. Learning and sequential decision making. Technical Report 89-95, Department of Computer and Information Science, University of Massachusetts, Amherst, Massachusetts. Also published in *Learning and Computational Neuroscience: Foundations of Adaptive Networks*, Michael Gabriel and John Moore, eds. The MIT Press, Cambridge, Massachusetts, 1991.

Chapman, David and Kaelbling, Leslie Pack 1991. Input generalization in delayed reinforcement learning: An algorithm and performance comparisons. In *Proceedings of the International Joint Conference on Artificial Intelligence*, Sydney, Australia.

Connell, Margaret E. and Utgoff, Paul E. 1987. Learning to control a dynamic physical system. In *Proceedings of the Sixth National Conference on Artificial Intelligence*, volume 2, Seattle, Washington. Morgan Kaufmann. 456–460.

Dietterich, Thomas G. 1986. Learning at the knowledge level. *Machine Learning* 1(3):287–315.

Estes, William K. 1950. Toward a statistical theory of learning. *Psychological Review* 57:94–107.

Haussler, David 1988. Quantifying inductive bias: AI learning algorithms and Valiant's learning framework. *Artificial Intelligence* 36(2):177–222.

Hilgard, Ernest R. and Bower, Gordon H. 1975. *Theories of Learning.* Prentice Hall, Englewood Cliffs, New Jersey, fourth edition.

Kaelbling, Leslie Pack 1990. *Learning in Embedded Systems.* Ph.D. Dissertation, Stanford University, Stanford, California.

Kaelbling, Leslie Pack 1991. An interval estimation algorithm for reinforcement learning. Forthcoming.

Larsen, Richard J. and Marx, Morris L. 1986. *An Introduction to Mathematical Statistics and its Applications.* Prentice-Hall, Englewood Cliffs, New Jersey.

Maes, Pattie and Brooks, Rodney A. 1990. Learning to coordinate behaviors. In *Proceedings of the Eighth National Conference on Artificial Intelligence*, Boston, Massachusetts. Morgan Kaufmann.

Mahadevan, Sridhar and Connell, Jonathan 1991. Automatic programming of behavior-based robots using reinforcement learning. In *Proceedings of the Ninth National Conference on Artificial Intelligence*, Anaheim, California.

Michalski, Ryszard S. 1983. A theory and methodology of inductive learning. In Michalski, Ryszard S.; Carbonell, Jaime G.; and Mitchell, Tom M., editors 1983, *Machine Learning: An Artificial Intelligence Approach.* Tioga. chapter 4.

Michie, D. and Chambers, R. A. 1968. BOXES: An experiment in adaptive control. In Dale, E. and Michie, D., editors 1968, *Machine Intelligence 2.* Oliver and Boyd, Edinburgh.

Mitchell, Tom M. 1982. Generalization as search. *Artificial Intelligence* 18(2):203–226.

Morris, William, editor 1969. *The American Heritage Dictionary of the English Language.* American Heritage Publishing and Houghton Mifflin, Boston.

Nehmzow, Ulrich; Smithers, Tim; and Hallam, John 1990. Steps towards intelligent robots. Technical Report 502, Department of Artificial Intelligence, University of Edinburgh, Edinburgh, Scotland.

Poggio, Tomaso and Girosi, Federico 1989. A theory of networks for approximation and learning. Technical Report AIM-1140, MIT Artificial Intelligence Laboratory, Cambridge, Massachusetts.

Quinlan, J. Ross 1983. Learning efficient classification procedures and their application to chess end games. In Michalski, Ryszard S.; Carbonell, Jaime G.; and Mitchell, Tom M., editors 1983, *Machine Learning: An Artificial Intelligence Approach.* Tioga. chapter 15.

Rumelhart, D. E.; Hinton, G. E.; and Williams, R. J. 1986. Learning internal representations by error propagation. In Rumelhart, David E. and McClelland, James L., editors 1986, *Parallel Distributed Processing*, volume 1. MIT Press. chapter 8.

Selfridge, Oliver G. and Sutton, Richard S. 1985. Training and tracking in robotics. In *Proceedings of the Ninth International Joint Conference on Artificial Intelligence*, Los Angeles, California. Morgan Kaufmann. 670–672.

Valiant, L. G. 1984. A theory of the learnable. *Communications of the ACM* 27(11):1134–1142.

Watkins, Christopher John Cornish Hellaby 1989. *Learning from Delayed Rewards.* Ph.D. Dissertation, King's College, Cambridge.

Widrow, Bernard; Gupta, Narendra K.; and Maitra, Sidhartha 1973. Punish/reward: Learning with a critic in adaptive threshold systems. *IEEE Transactions on Systems, Man, and Cybernetics* SMC-3(5):455–465.

Learning Behavior Networks from Experience

Pattie Maes
MIT Media-Lab Rm. 489
20 Ames Street
Cambridge, MA 02139
pattie@media.mit.edu

Abstract

In earlier work we presented a model for motivational competition and selection of behaviors in an artificial creature. The model makes usage of a *behavior network*, which encodes information about predecessor, successor and conflictor links among behaviors. This paper describes an algorithm for learning the links among behaviors from experience. The learning algorithm is completely integrated in the behavior selection model: as the creature accumulates more experience about the actual effects of behaviors, its behavior selection gradually becomes more optimal. In the tradition of behavior-based systems, the learning capability is implemented in a completely distributed, decentralized way. The model allows to control the degree to which knowledge is innate (versus learned), as well as the degree to which the learning is biased (or innate). Some similarities between this learning model and animal learning, in particular *operant conditioning*, are discussed.

1 Introduction

One of the goals of Artificial Life is to model and build artificial creatures: computer-based systems that operate completely autonomously and exhibit life-like behavior. The particular problem that I concentrate on is how such creatures can select the behavior to perform next (given that they have many competing motivations and many sensor data), and how they can improve their behavior selection policy on the basis of experience. The latter problem is the specific focus of this paper. Adaptability is a crucial characteristic of living systems. To a large degree adaptability can be obtained by the evolution of the species. However, psychologists also recognize the utility of learning by individual organisms (Walker 1987). Not only humans, but also lower level animals, change their behavior over time, thereby improving their efficiency at achieving particular desired states. In particular, learning by the individual is necessary for living systems to adapt to those aspects of the environment that are not stable over long periods of time.

In (Maes 1989) (Maes 1991b) I proposed a mechanism for motivational competition and selection of behavior. One important characteristic of this mechanism is that the selection of behavior is modeled as an emergent property of a parallel process. This is in contrast with mechanisms for behavior selection and motivational competition proposed earlier, which are based on a hierarchical, preprogrammed control structure (see Coderre 1989, for an Artificial Life reference, and the classical planning literature from Artificial Intelligence). In this earlier work I showed that selection of behavior can be modeled in a bottom-up way using an activation/inhibition dynamics among the different behaviors that can be selected. There is no weighing up of behaviors in a cognitive manner and neither are hierarchical or bureaucratic structures imposed.

The central structure used by the algorithm is called the *behavior network*. The nodes of this network represent the different behaviors (or activities) in which the creature can engage. The links are of three different types and represent causal relations among the behaviors (predecessor, successor, conflictor relations). These links are used in specific ways in a spreading activation process which causes activation energy to accumulate in the most "relevant" behaviors. One of limitations of the model was that the feedback from the environment was never used to improve the behavior network, so as to better represent the actual causal relations among behaviors. For example, if the network encoded the knowledge that "scratching" leads to the condition "food available", and this effect never actually occurs in a particular environment (e.g. an environment that is paved), then the creature would not learn to adapt its network. Similarly, if certain causal links were missing in the network, the creature would never learn these associations.

In this paper, we present a major extension to this model which allows the creature to build and improve the behavior network on the basis of experience. The algorithm is completely distributed and decentralized: each of the behaviors in the network adapts the weights of its links to other behaviors so as to better reflect the actual probabilities of causal relations with specific other behaviors. It does so by monitoring certain expectations or noticing new correlations. The behavior selection model and learning algorithm are completely integrated. An interesting property of the algorithm is that an elegant balance between exploration (trying something new) and exploitation (doing what you know works) is obtained as an emergent property of the spreading activation dynamics coupled to the idea of probabilistic selection of behaviors.

Another interesting property of the algorithm is that it allows for *partial learning* to take place: one can choose how much is innate (built in) in the creature's behavior versus how much is actually learned (in contrast with Neural Networks, which put the whole burden on learning or Symbolic AI Systems which put the whole burden on programming). Even more, the algorithm allows to model a form of *instinctive learning* in which a specific learning bias is innate (the creature applies heuristics for deciding which correlations to evaluate first or only considers particular correlations for learning). The learning algorithm models a lot of what has been called *instrumental conditioning* (or operant conditioning) in the Animal Behavior literature (Walker 1987). It requires the repertoire of behaviors that the creature can engage in to be built in (no new activities can be learned) and focuses on learning their effects (and thereby indirectly also when they are relevant and should be applied).

The paper is structured as follows. Section 2 presents a brief overview of the behavior network formalism and behavior selection algorithm. Section 3 presents the learning algorithm. This algorithm could possibly be used in coexistence with any other behavior selection algorithm that uses a representation of behaviors in terms of conditions and (probabilistic) expected effects. Section 4 illustrates the results obtained on the basis of an example of a "simulated robot pet". Experiments are under way to implement the same network on a real robot. Section 5 discusses the assumptions and limitations of the algorithm and sketches future extensions. The relation of this work to Artificial Life and theories of Animal Behavior is described in Section 6. Finally section 7 discusses related work.

2 Behavior Networks

In the style of Behavior-Based Artificial Intelligence (Brooks 1991) (Maes 1991a), we view a creature as consisting of a distributed, decentralized set of *competence modules*, also called *behaviors*[1], that it can engage in. A competence module is a black box that realizes a specific competence. For example, a robot "pet" would have competence modules for "going towards a human", "wandering around", "seeking recharging station", "recharging", etc. A competence module is *executable* if all of its *conditions* are fulfilled (these are like "stimuli" that have to be observed for the competence module to be able to run). E.g. the condition for "going towards a person", might be that the robot observes a person in its neighborhood. An executable module can be *activated*, which means that some processes are executed that implement the competence (i.e. the creature takes some real actions as dictated by that module).

A creature also has a set of *goals* (or *motivations*) which each have a particular strength. The robot pet, for example, is motivated to "receive attention from people", "avoid pain (bumping into things)", "keep its battery charged", "explore its environment", and so on. The strengths of the goals vary over time. The strength at time t is determined by a user-defined function (this is a function of the strength of the goal at the previous timestep, the module that was last activated and the current time). Every goal (motivation) is associated with one or more behaviors, which (partially) fulfill the motivation when activated. Following the literature on Ethology, we call these *consummatory behaviors*, and the remaining behaviors *apetitive behaviors*. For example, the motivation "keep battery charged" is associated with the consummatory behavior "recharging". Finally a creature has sensor inputs, which again vary over time. In both our simulated and robotic creatures, we abstract the sensor data into a finite set of binary *perceptual conditions*, such as "obstacle within 1-foot range of creature", "person on the left", "person on the right", "wall on the left", and so on.

In earlier work (Maes 1991b), I presented a bottom-up mechanism for behavior selection in such a creature. The mechanism determines which behavior is the most "relevant" for the creature to be engaged in at a particular moment. The different behaviors (or competence modules) of the creature are linked in a network representing the causal links between the behaviors[2]:

- There is a *predecessor link* from behavior A to behavior B for condition C if B (through its actions) causes condition C of A to become true
- There is a *conflictor link* from behavior A to behavior B for condition C if B (through its actions) causes condition C of A to become false
- There is a *successor link* from behavior A to behavior B if there are one or more predecessor links from B to A

This network is used for a specific spreading activation process which causes activation energy to accumulate in the most relevant behaviors. It implements behavior selection in a completely distributed way through a competition among behaviors for activation energy. The method solves the problem of behavior selection in a satisfiable way, and has the advantages over traditional AI methods that it is completely distributed and decentralized, and therefore more flexible, faster and fault-tolerant (Maes 1989).

[1]Notice that in the Ethology literature, the word "behavior" is rather used to denote externally observable activity, rather than an identifyable structure or process within an animal.

[2]Notice that there can be more than one predecessor link or more than one conflictor link between two modules A and B. There can even be a conflictor link as well as a predecessor link between two modules for the same condition.

The spreading activation process has two components, an *external* one and an *internal* one. The external spreading activation is defined as follows: every motivation (goal) increases the activation level of those behaviors that are associated with that motivation (consummatory behaviors) with an amount proportional to the motivation's strength[3]. Further, every one of the currently observed sensor data increases the activation level of the behaviors that have that sensor datum in their condition-list.

The internal spreading activation is defined as follows: every executable behavior spreads activation energy to its successors (this implements "habits" or routine behavior), every non-executable module spreads activation energy to its predecessors for those conditions that are not true (so that the predecessors become active and cause the conditions to become true), and finally every behavior decreases the activation level of its conflictors for those conditions that are true (to decrease the chance that the conflictors become active and undo the conditions of the behavior)[4]. The amount of activation energy spread (or taken away) is always proportional to the activation level of the module that is the source of the spreading.

This spreading activation process goes on continuously. The activation level of a behavior represents the "relevance" of that particular behavior at that moment in time. As soon as one of the executable modules reaches a global threshold, it is *selected* and executed (its processes run and make the creature perform physical actions). After the module has been executed, its activation level is reset to 0. We wait till the module has finished taking actions, before selecting the next module to activate.

When these networks are run, paths of highly activated nodes emerge, linking the sensor data to the motivations (goals). The resulting behavior selection has been shown to be data-driven (opportunistic), goal-driven (the more a behavior contributes to goals, the higher its activation level), sensitive to goal conflicts and it has a certain inertia or bias (towards previous behavior sequences). In previous papers I have argued that this behavior selection mechanism has advantages over other mechanism presented, in particular, explicit deliberation (or traditional AI planning models) and hardwired schemes (or so-called reactive systems) (Maes 1989) (Maes 1991d). I also argued in (Maes 1991b) that this scheme produces resulting behavior that is very "animal-like". Nevertheless, the learning algorithm discussed in the next section could be decoupled from this particular method of behavior selection. The only assumption made is that the learning goal is to build up a network of causal relations among active modules.

[3] There can be negative goals, or goals with a negative strength, that take away activation energy.

[4] Notice that a module might be a conflictor as well as a predecessor for a particular condition. For example, the module "following walls" can cause the condition "at recharging station" to become true as well as false. Only one of these links is used in spreading activation at any particular time, though, because conflictor links are only used when the condition is observed to be true, while predecessor links are used when the condition is false. So if a (sub)goal is to be at the recharging station, then "following walls" would be encouraged to become active when that goal is not fulfilled and would be discouraged from becoming active when that goal is fulfilled.

3 Learning Causal Links among Behaviors

3.1 The Need for Learning

The behavior selection model presented above assumes the existence of a behavior network that correctly models all the successor, predecessor and conflictor relations among behaviors. It is useful for a creature to be able to learn these links from experience because often the *programmed* or "innate" network is incomplete (missing links) and incorrect (wrong links). Furthermore, it is necessary for a creature to have this ability in order to adapt to the non-static aspects of the environment: components may break down (we would like a graceful degradation), the environment may change over time, and so on. Finally, most environments are of a probabilistic nature, which means that it is also useful for the creature to learn about the *reliability* of links, or the probability that a link is actually manifested. For example, it is useful for our robot pet to know in how many cases the module "find recharging station using IR (infra-red sensors)" resulted in the desired effect of being at the recharging station versus the number of cases the module "following walls" produced that same effect.

The goal of the learning algorithm is to improve the links of the behavior networks so as to better reflect the real causal relations (and their reliability) among behaviors. The better the links of the network reflect reality, the better the behavior selection will be. If a creature has a complete and correct model of the effects of behaviors, then the spreading activation process computes what we have shown is a good measure for the "relevance" of a behavior in a particular context (Maes 1989). The learning task can be defined as follows. Given a set of competence modules with an initial condition list, a set of initial links (with their reliability estimate) and a set of motivations (positive and negative ones), and given a noisy, dynamic, non-deterministic environment, the task is to have every module learn its conflictor links, successor links and predecessor links with their respective reliability.

3.2 Changes to the Behavior Selection Model

In order to accommodate learning two changes had to be made to the behavior selection model described in section 2. First of all, links are given *weights*. The weight for some link from module A to module B is represented as a fraction $\frac{S}{T}$, where S represents the number of successes, and T represents the number of trials or experiments with that link. E.g. if there is a predecessor link for the condition "at recharging station" from module "recharging" to module "find recharging station using IR" with weight $\frac{7}{11}$, then in 7 out of 11 cases, activating "find recharging station using IR" resulted in the observation "at recharging station". The weights of links represent the *reliability* of a particular causal relation between modules.

The weights of links are used in the spreading activation process: when one module spreads activation energy to another one, it not only spreads an amount proportional to its own activation level, but also multiplies this amount by the weight of the link[5]. For example, suppose the module "recharging" spreads activation energy towards its predecessors for the condition "at recharging station", and the predecessor link to "find recharging station using IR" has a weight of $\frac{4}{6}$, while the predecessor link to "following walls" has a weight of $\frac{1}{6}$, then the former module will receive four times more activation energy from "recharging" than the latter one (and thus have a higher chance of being selected).

A second change that was made to the behavior selection model is that instead of selecting the most active module whose activation level surpasses the threshold, we now wait till the network comes to an equilibrium, and then select one of the executable modules randomly with a probability proportional to their activation levels. As a consequence the creature does not always select the module that is the most relevant at a particular moment. Instead less-activated modules are occasionally selected. This results in an elegant tradeoff between exploitation and exploration during learning. Eventually the system reduces the amount of experimentation: when the learning has been going on for a while, the weights of links have values close to either 0 or 1, which means that a module either receives almost no activation energy through its links or a lot of activation energy[6], consequently, the chances that a module that has not proven to be useful becomes selected are very small.

3.3 The Learning Algorithm

Initialization of the Links.
The designer of a creature can choose to initialize some of the links of the network. All other links will be nonexistent (or have an initial weight = 0). The weight $\frac{S_0^i}{T_0^i}$ chosen for a link reflects the designer's estimate of the *reliability* of that link. The denominator T_0^i reflects the "rigidity" of the weight, or how difficult it will be to change the weight through real world feedback. For example, if we want the creature to have a bias towards believing that module A might make condition C of module B come true, we could choose the initial weight for this predecessor link to be $\frac{1}{2}$. Or if we want the creature to "stubbornly" believe that this is true, even after accumulating a lot of evidence for the link not being there, we could set the initial weight to $\frac{5{,}000}{10{,}000}$. Section 4.5 below discusses the selection of the initial weights in more detail.

Creating a Predecessor or Conflictor Link.
Learning happens as follows. Every competence module (or behavior) of the artificial creature continuously monitors its conditions[7]. Whenever one of its conditions changes state (from being observed, or "true", to no longer being observed, or vice versa), the module holds the module that was active most recently responsible for this change of state[8]. If there was no link yet from the module to the last module for the condition that changed value, then a new link is created with initial weight $\frac{S_0}{T_0}$. For example, if we chose S_0 and T_0 to be 1, then a new link is created with weight $\frac{1}{1}$. If the change of state was such that the condition changed from being observable (true) to being unobservable, then the link created is a *conflictor* link. In the case that the condition became observable, the link created is a *predecessor* link. For example, if the creature was executing "following walls" and suddenly it finds itself at the recharging station, all those modules that have "at recharging station" as one of their conditions, will create a predecessor link to "following walls". Or also, if "at recharging station" suddenly becomes false, and the most recently active module is "wandering around", then the same modules will create a conflictor link to "wandering around" for the condition "at recharging station".

Reinforcing a Predecessor or Conflictor Link.
If there already exists a predecessor (respectively conflictor) link from the monitoring module to the most recently active module, then the weight of that link is increased. Specifically, if there was already a link with weight $\frac{S}{T}$, then the new weight for that link becomes $\frac{S+1}{T+1}$ (one more trial and one more success). For example, if there is a predecessor link from "recharging" to "find recharging station using IR" for condition "at

[5] In the original behavior network model described above, links can be viewed as having a weight = 1.

[6] In section 6 we discuss the cases in which the weight of a link does not converge to 0 or 1.

[7] The creature is not able to sense the entire environment at all times. It senses its local environment and "represents" it in "deictic representations" (Agre 1988), such as "at recharging station", "obstacle in front of me", etc. "False" is equated with "no longer observed". For example, if the creature sees a door in front of it, and decides to move to the left, then afterwards "door in front" will no longer be observed and thus no longer true. "Move to left" will be held responsible for this change.

[8] In dynamic environments, some of the changes in the environment are not caused by the creature itself (but for example by other creatures). We assume that (i) a majority of the changes happening in the local neighborhood of the creature are caused by the creature, and (ii) that other changes happen in randomly distributed ways (so that they do not bring the weights of links out of balance but can instead be treated as noise).

recharging station" with a weight $\frac{3}{4}$, then if once more the recharging station was found by using the IR's, this weight will be increased to $\frac{4}{5}$. Notice that in the limit, for $n \rightarrow \infty$, $\frac{S_0+n}{T_0+n} \rightarrow 1$. So, no matter which initial weight we adopt, if there is a strong correlation, the weight of the link will converge to 1.

Weakening a Predecessor or Conflictor Link.
Every module monitors its existing predecessor and conflictor links. Whenever it notices a counter example for a link, i.e. the condition did not change state as the predecessor or conflictor module became active[9], the monitoring module weakens the predecessor (resp. conflictor) link from $\frac{S}{T}$ to $\frac{S}{T+1}$. The number of trials T is incremented while the number of successes S is not. For example, if the weight of the predecessor link from "recharging" to "following walls" is $\frac{1}{6}$ and "following walls" is activated and does not result in the recharging station to be observed, then the weight of the link is decremented to $\frac{1}{7}$. Notice again that in the limit, for $n \rightarrow \infty$, $\frac{S_0}{T_0+n} \rightarrow 0$. So, no matter which initial weight we adopt, if there is a not a strong correlation, the weight of the link will converge to 0.

Creating, Reinforcing and Weakening a Successor Link.
Every module also monitors which module is active right after the monitoring module has been active itself. If it did not yet have a successor link to that module, it creates one with initial weight $\frac{S_0}{T_0}$. If there was already a link with weight $\frac{S}{T}$, the weight is increased to $\frac{S+1}{T+1}$. The weights of all the other successor links are decreased from $\frac{S}{T}$ to $\frac{S}{T+1}$ (because this constitutes a negative example for these successor links)[10].

3.4 Complexity of the Algorithm

If there are m modules, and n is the mean number of conditions of a module, then the maximum number of links that has to be learned about is: $(2n+1)m^2$. This number is the result of summing (i) m^2 successor links (a module can have any other module as successor), (ii) nm^2 predecessor links (for each of its conditions, a module can have any other module as predecessor), and (iii) nm^2 conflictor links (for each of its conditions, a module can have any other module as conflictor). For example, in the case of the simulated robot pet, m is about 10 and n is 2, which means that the maximum number of links to be learned about is 500.

If we want to keep the number of links linear with respect to the number of modules, we could limit the number of links maintained per module and per condition to K, which means that the complexity or number of links to be learned about is reduced to $K(2n+1)m$. Practically this could be implemented by discarding the least good link (i.e. the one with the smallest weight $\frac{S}{T}$) when the limit of K links has been achieved. Another way in which the complexity can be reduced is by limiting the set of modules that one module can learn about to a particular fixed selection. We could for example subdivide the behaviors or modules of the creature into groups that possibly might have causal relations and only learn links among members of the same group.

4 Results: A Learning Creature

The above described learning algorithm has been implemented and runs on a Symbolics 3600 LISP machine. We tested the algorithm on several examples including a simulated "robot pet". Figure 1, 2 and 3 illustrate some of the results of the simulator experiments. We are currently working on a physical version of the robot pet and a graphical interface for the simulated version. The robot pet has several motivations among which are to receive attention from people, to keep its battery charged, to explore its neighborhood and to avoid bumping into things. Its repertoire of behaviors includes modules such as "wandering around", "following walls", "find recharging station using IR", "recharging", "ask human to bring me to recharging station", "go towards human", and so on. Its perceptual conditions include "at recharging station", "battery low", "next to human", etc. The environment and the effects of actions are being simulated by a non-deterministic, probabilistic simulator. For example, the creature has a chance of 30 percent to detect a human in its neighborhood, activating "find recharging station using IR" has a 75 percent chance of resulting in the creature finding the recharging station, etc. Below we describe some of the results obtained in the experiments. Section 5 describes some of the limitations discovered.

4.1 Learning a network from Scratch

The first experiment consisted of learning the network from scratch. The algorithm was successful, in that the longer we ran it, the more the weights of the links got closer to the actual reliabilities of relations between modules. Initially, the module selection is completely random, because there are no links yet, and so only the external spreading activation plays a role. This means that all executable modules accumulate the same amount of activation energy (from the currently observed sensor data) and thus have equal chances of being activated. If one of the executable modules also receives activation energy from the goals, it will have a greater chance of being selected. Since a module's

[9] More specifically, in the case of a predecessor link, the condition was false and after the predecessor module became active, the condition was still false. Or for a conflictor link, the condition was observed (true) and after the conflictor module has been active, it is still true.

[10] The role of successor links are to speed up the selection of familiar behavior sequences (sequences of behaviors that usually follow one another). As a result the creature demonstrates typical "habits", or "routines" (as in Agre 1988). Once it activates a module that is part of a strong successor chain, it is very likely to continue activating modules along that chain.

```
-------------------------------
TIME: 11
state of the environment:
  (BATTERY-HIGH RECHARGING
   NEXT-TO-HUMAN IR-LIGHT-RECEIVED
   AT-RECHARGING-STATION
   RADIO-SIGNAL-RECEIVED)
goals of the environment:
  (AVOID-OBSTACLES BATTERY-HIGH)
modules selectable:
  ((RANDOM-WALK 11.458042696445729)
   (RECHARGE 11.080059690149668)
   (GO-TO-RECHARGING-STATION-IR-ROUTINE
    11.458042696445729)
   (GO-TO-RECHARGING-STATION-RADIO-ROUTINE
    11.458042696445729)
   (GO-TO-RECHARGING-STATION-ASK-HUMAN
    11.440735324473643)
   (GO-TO-RECHARGING-STATION-MAP-BASED
    11.440735324473643))
module becoming active:
  GO-TO-RECHARGING-STATION-MAP-BASED
learning:
  conflictor link reinforced from RECHARGE to
      GO-TO-RECHARGING-STATION-MAP-BASED
      for AT-RECHARGING-STATION, weight 1
  successor link reinforced from RECHARGE to
      GO-TO-RECHARGING-STATION-MAP-BASED,
      weight 1
  conflictor link reinforced from
      GO-TO-RECHARGING-STATION-ASK-HUMAN to
      GO-TO-RECHARGING-STATION-MAP-BASED
      for NEXT-TO-HUMAN, weight 1
-------------------------------
TIME: 12
state of the environment:
  (IR-LIGHT-RECEIVED
   BATTERY-HIGH
   RADIO-SIGNAL-RECEIVED)
goals of the environment:
  (AVOID-OBSTACLES BATTERY-HIGH)
no module becoming active
-------------------------------
```

Figure 1: Excerpt from a trace of the system. At timestep 11 module go-to-recharging-station-map-based is selected. This module takes the robot away from the recharging station (were it just recharged before).

```
GO-TO-RECHARGING-STATION-IR-ROUTINE * * * * * * *
RECHARGE * * * * * RANDOM-WALK * * * * *
GO-TO-RECHARGING-STATION-IR-ROUTINE * * * *
RECHARGE * * RANDOM-WALK * * * * * * RANDOM-WALK *
* RANDOM-WALK * * * RANDOM-WALK * * * *
GO-TO-HUMAN * * RANDOM-WALK * * AVOID-OBSTACLE * *
RANDOM-WALK * GO-TO-RECHARGING-STATION-MAP-BASED
* GO-TO-HUMAN * *
GO-TO-RECHARGING-STATION-RADIO-ROUTINE * * * * * *
* * * * * RECHARGE * * * * * AVOID-OBSTACLE * * *
* * RANDOM-WALK * * * * * AVOID-OBSTACLE * * * *
RANDOM-WALK * * * * RANDOM-WALK * AVOID-OBSTACLE *
* GO-TO-RECHARGING-STATION-IR-ROUTINE * * * * * *
RECHARGE * * * * RANDOM-WALK * * * * *
AVOID-OBSTACLE * * * * * RANDOM-WALK * * * *
RANDOM-WALK * * * *
GO-TO-RECHARGING-STATION-RADIO-ROUTINE * * * * * *
RECHARGE * * * * * RECHARGE * * * *
GO-TO-RECHARGING-STATION-RADIO-ROUTINE * * * * *
RANDOM-WALK * * *
GO-TO-RECHARGING-STATION-MAP-BASED
* RANDOM-WALK * * * * RANDOM-WALK *
GO-TO-RECHARGING-STATION-RADIO-ROUTINE * *
GO-TO-RECHARGING-STATION-RADIO-ROUTINE * *
GO-TO-RECHARGING-STATION-MAP-BASED * * * * * * *
RECHARGE * * * * * RANDOM-WALK * * *
AVOID-OBSTACLE
* * * * GO-TO-HUMAN * * * * *
GO-TO-RECHARGING-STATION-MAP-BASED * * * * * * * *
RECHARGE * * * * *
GO-TO-RECHARGING-STATION-MAP-BASED * RANDOM-WALK *
* GO-TO-RECHARGING-STATION-RADIO-ROUTINE * *
GO-TO-RECHARGING-STATION-MAP-BASED * * * *
GO-TO-RECHARGING-STATION-IR-ROUTINE * * * * * * *
RECHARGE * * * * RANDOM-WALK * * *
GO-TO-RECHARGING-STATION-IR-ROUTINE * * * *
RANDOM-WALK * * * * * * RANDOM-WALK * * * *
GO-TO-HUMAN * * *
GO-TO-RECHARGING-STATION-IR-ROUTINE * *
GO-TO-RECHARGING-STATION-IR-ROUTINE * * * * * * *
* * * * RECHARGE * * AVOID-OBSTACLE * * * * * *
RANDOM-WALK * * AVOID-OBSTACLE * * * * *
GO-TO-RECHARGING-STATION-MAP-BASED * * * *
GO-TO-RECHARGING-STATION-RADIO-ROUTINE *
GO-TO-HUMAN * * *
GO-TO-RECHARGING-STATION-ASK-HUMAN * * * * * *
RECHARGE * * * *
GO-TO-RECHARGING-STATION-IR-ROUTINE
```

Figure 2: Trace of the simulated robot's behavior selection. After 800 cycles the robot prefers to search for the recharging station by asking a human (if one is around), followed by using its infra-red sensors, then by using its map, and finally by using the radio sensor.

```
LINKS LEARNED BY AVOID-OBSTACLE:
predecessors for OBSTACLE:
  <RANDOM-WALK 23/66>
conflictors for OBSTACLE:
successors:
  <GO-TO-RECHARGING-STATION-MAP-BASED 1/1>

LINKS LEARNED BY RECHARGE:
predecessors for AT-RECHARGING-STATION:
  <RANDOM-WALK 1/20>
  <GO-TO-RECHARGING-STATION-MAP-BASED 8/14>
  <GO-TO-RECHARGING-STATION-IR-ROUTINE 18/19>
  <GO-TO-RECHARGING-STATION-ASK-HUMAN 5/5>
  <GO-TO-RECHARGING-STATION-RADIO-ROUTINE 6/15>
conflictors for AT-RECHARGING-STATION:
  <GO-TO-RECHARGING-STATION-RADIO-ROUTINE 4/5>
  <RANDOM-WALK 24/27>
  <AVOID-OBSTACLE 5/5>
  <GO-TO-HUMAN 2/2>
  <GO-TO-RECHARGING-STATION-MAP-BASED 1/2>
  <GO-TO-RECHARGING-STATION-IR-ROUTINE 2/6>
successors:
  <GO-TO-RECHARGING-STATION-IR-ROUTINE 1/2>
  <AVOID-OBSTACLE 1/2>

LINKS LEARNED BY
GO-TO-RECHARGING-STATION-ASK-HUMAN:
predecessors for NEXT-TO-HUMAN:
  <GO-TO-HUMAN 12/12>
conflictors for NEXT-TO-HUMAN:
  <RANDOM-WALK 2/2>
  <GO-TO-RECHARGING-STATION-IR-ROUTINE 2/2>
  <GO-TO-RECHARGING-STATION-RADIO-ROUTINE 2/3>
  <GO-TO-RECHARGING-STATION-MAP-BASED 1/1>
successors:
  <RECHARGE 1/1>

...
```

Figure 3: Some of the links learned by the simulated robot after 900 timesteps, starting from an empty network. Notice how the weights on the predecessor links for module "recharge" start to approach the probability that the different modules produce the result "at recharging station". The probabilities built into the simulator were: asking a human (100% reliable), using the infra-red sensors (75% reliable), using the map (50% reliable), and using the radio (25% reliable).

activation level is reset to 0 after it has been selected and activated, the chances that each of the executable modules are tried are even better.

Very quickly, the behavior selection becomes more meaningful and more goal-oriented. For example, if a chain of predecessor related modules A B C leads to the fulfilment of a motivation M (C is a consummatory behavior for motivation M), then if C has had an opportunity to observe that B is its predecessor and B has had an opportunity to learn that A is its predecessor, then activation energy will spread from C to B to A according to how strong M is and how strong the learned links are. Notice that if the sequence A B D E leads to another motivation M' being fulfilled, then the same "knowledge" that A can make B executable, is also applicable in this new context. The solution is a *compositional* one, because knowledge learned in the context of one motivation (or goal) can be applied in the context of another one.

Notice that the tradeoff between exploration (trying something new) and exploitation (doing what you know works) is an emergent property of the spreading activation dynamics and behavior selection model. Even more, there is an emergent notion of "temperature" or degree of randomness: the more the weights on links converge to either 0 or 1 (the more has been learned), the less likely it is that a module is selected because of experimentation purposes. This is the case because the modules that have proven successful will have activation levels that are much higher than average.

4.2 Partial Programming

In other experiments we gave the network some initial knowledge, varying from a light bias, a strong bias, to almost fixed (unchangeable) knowledge. We also experimented with giving the network wrong knowledge (links that should not be there). Section 6 discusses how these partial programming techniques can be used to implement "instinctive knowledge" as well as "instinctive learning". A light bias can be implemented by initializing some of the weights of the links to $\frac{S_0^i}{T_0^i}$, where T_0^i is small.

E.g. if the programmer believes the creature should prefer using the module "find recharging station using IR" to search for the recharging station, we can create an initial link from "recharging" to this module with weight $\frac{1}{2}$. Since T is small in this case, the creature will be able to adapt quickly if this knowledge would be wrong. E.g. after 2 counter examples (it did not find the recharging station using this module), the weight of the link is already reduced to $\frac{1}{4}$, which means that it is already much less likely that this module will be selected whenever the creature wants to find the recharging station.

4.3 Learning Reliabilities of Behaviors

The algorithm makes it possible for the creature to learn how reliably certain modules produce certain effects.

The reliability of module M producing effect C is reflected in the predecessor (or conflictor) links from other modules to M for condition C. These measures of reliability are automatically taken into account by the behavior selection process. If module M has a reliability (weight) of $\frac{3}{10}$ and module M' has a reliability of $\frac{6}{10}$ for changing the state of condition C, then M' will get double as much activation energy from those modules that want C to change state, and therefore will have double as much chances of being selected. So the chances of being selected are proportional to the reliability of modules. Sometimes this results in the creature preferring one sequence of behaviors to the goal (or motivation) over a shorter sequence that is less reliable. E.g., if a human will bring the robot to the recharging station with 100 percent reliability when asked to do so, and "seek human" has a 60 percent chance of succeeding, then the robot might prefer this solution for finding the recharging station over "find recharging station using IR", if the latter has a reliability of less than 60 percent.

4.4 Adapting to an Altered Situation

The learning algorithm not only allows a creature to learn causal relations among behaviors in a noisy, nondeterministic environment, but it also allows the creature to adapt to a new environment (or to behaviors having effects that change over time). For example, if suddenly people in the robot's neighborhood are not cooperative any more, the robot will learn to adapt the reliability of modules such as "ask human to bring me to the recharging station". These modified reliabilities will also be reflected in the creature's behavior selection. How long it takes for the network to adapt depends on the size of the denominator T of the links involved. The creature is also able to adapt when components break down. For example, if the infra-red sensors break down or become unreliable, modules using these sensors will become less reliable and therefore less likely to be selected.

4.5 Selecting the Parameters

The algorithm provides a set of parameters that can be used to implement a range of different learning styles. For example, the initial values S_0 and T_0 can be used to implement *one shot learning* ($S_0 = 1$ and $T_0 = 1$), or cautious learning ($S_0 << T_0$ and T_0 big), and so on. Depending on the environment and the task at hand, one might prefer one over the other. E.g. in a very deterministic environment one might want to make usage of one shot learning. In future work we want to experiment with having a *meta-network* select and tune these parameters automatically (cfr. Maes 1991c for a similar idea).

5 Limitations and Future Extensions

The learning algorithm described above has several limitations. Some of these limitations were known to us beforehand (simplifying assumptions), while others were discovered as we were running experiments. In future research we hope to deal with most of these limitations.

5.1 Immediate feedback

One of the simplifying assumptions made by the algorithm is that the effects of modules are "fairly" immediate (before the next module is activated). This is not always the case in real applications (in particular when the real robot is involved). For example, it takes a while for a human to carry the robot to the recharging station. The robot might select a next competence module before the carrying job has ended. One solution to this problem would be to create (or reinforce) a link not only to the previously active module but also the one active before that, and so on, with the weight (or weight increase) inversely proportional to the time past since the modules were active. In the example, if the robot decided to activate another module and then ends up at the recharging station (because a person put it there), then the link to both of these modules would be reinforced.

A related problem is that some modules have to be activated several times before the results are observable. For example, "follow walls" has to be activated several times before a door will be perceived. Another solution to this and the above problem could be to introduce the concept of *average time until consummation*. Once selected a module would be active for this duration unless the conditions become false (e.g suddenly there is no wall to follow any more). The average time until consummation for a module could also be learned from experience.

5.2 Hidden Conditions

Another major simplifying assumption is that the effect of a behavior does not depend on implicit conditions. An effect E of module M should be learnable, independent of what happened before M (whether M' or M" was active before M). This implies that if an ordered behavior sequence has to be learned, the behaviors have to be linked by predecessor links. Non-ordered behavior sequences can also be learned if one subsequence deals with one subgoal and another subsequence deals with another subgoal of a more general goal. An example of something that cannot be learned would be that going backwards from the recharging station, followed by going forwards results in the robot being back at the recharging station (because going forwards does not generally result in being at the recharging station). A solution to this problem would be to hypothesize that the effects of a module depend on a hidden condition whenever the weights do not converge (i.e. the weights do not get within a small distance of either 0 or 1).

If a result of a module is not reliable one could keep track of whether the result is produced more reliably when an extra condition is observed to be true or false. This solution was adopted in some of my earlier work on learning to coordinate behaviors (Maes and Brooks 1990).

5.3 Learning about Goals

The algorithm assumes that the creature knows which modules achieve the global goals (motivations). One way in which the system can be made to learn about goals is by including a dummy module in the network which has as conditions, those perceptual conditions that describe the goal. For example, if we want a legged robot to learn to walk, then this goal can be described as a conjunction of the condition "avoid bottom touching the ground" and "make forward movement". If we include a dummy module in the network that has these conditions and is associated with the goal (motivation) "walk", then the creature is able to learn which modules achieve this goal. This way we can deal with conjunctive goals and negative goals. Disjunctive goals (the goal is true if A or B is observed) can be dealt with by having two or more such dummy modules. The type of goals that cannot be dealt with are goals that cannot be specified as a conjunction, disjunction or negation of perceptual conditions. Further, the algorithm cannot yet deal with parallel behaviors. It only allows one module to be active at a time, which again limits the types of goals that can be learned about. Some goals might involve multiple behaviors being active at the same time (cfr. Maes and Brooks 1990).

5.4 Learning new Behaviors

The algorithm does not support the learning of new behaviors. The assumption that is made is that the repertoire of innate behaviors is sufficient and granular enough to learn how to achieve the goals (motivations). Techniques such as those used by Drescher (1991) could be employed to extend an initial repertoire of modules with more specialized modules and composed modules.

Another assumption that is made is that the relevant perceptual conditions are already extracted from the raw sensor data and are represented in the form of binary variables.

6 Relevance to Artificial Life

The behavior selection and learning architecture described above fits completely within the spirit of Artificial Life. It emphasizes issues such as distributedness, parallelism, emergence and adaptivity which have been recognized to be key characteristics of living systems (Langton 1989). There are no central components: the global behavior is an emergent property of the local activity (spreading activation and creating and modifying links) of behaviors. The result is a very adaptive, flexible and robust system.

It is certain that animals adapt not only through natural selection but also through individual learning. An advantage of the algorithm described above is that one can decide how much "knowledge" is innate versus learned. The initial links (and their weights) represent the innate knowledge of an artificial creature. An initial link with a very high denominator T can be used to implement innate reflexes and habits. By initializing all of the links and choosing big denominators T, one can implement a hard-wired, non adaptive creature. On the other extreme, one can model a creature that has to learn everything from scratch, by starting with a network with no links. One can also implement a form of "instinctive learning"[11] by building in some experimentation bias through the initial weights and links.

The architecture was not developed with the intention of maximizing biological validity. As it turns out, however, there are many interesting parallels between animal learning and the learning method described in this paper. Different types of learning have been observed in animals (Walker 1987) (McFarland 1987). Our learning algorithm is closest to what has been termed *operant conditioning* or also *instrumental conditioning* in the Animal Behavior literature: an animal can learn that it has to perform (a sequence of) behaviors for some motivationally significant event to happen (e.g. to obtain food). It learns to perform a particular behavior because it has particular consequences.

Furthermore, as in our model, it is the case that an animal can learn that different behaviors lead to different results: an animal can learn to do X when it wants to obtain water and Y when it wants to obtain food. Also, as in our model, it is the case that an animal cannot learn completely new behaviors, but rather it learns which of the behaviors in its innate repertoire are instrumental in achieving a particular result. One cannot teach an animal to do just anything in order to get food: the behaviors we want it to perform have to be in its behavioral repertoire. Another similarity is that the strength of the motivation (e.g. how hungry or thirsty the animal is) modulates the degree to which external cues arouse ideas of the reward (food, water) and the intensity with which any such ideas are followed by instrumental behaviors (Walker 1987). Finally another similarity is the development of habits (behavior sequences which sometimes lose their usefulness, but are still performed anyway)(Walker 1987). When certain successor links in a creature have very high weights, the creature might activate a sequence of behaviors only because it has activated this sequence many times before (without it being related to one of the goals or motivations).

[11]It turns out that a lot of learning is preprogrammed in animals, e.g. a bee learns which features of a flower are most indicative of the richness of the food source. It tests a particular set of features in a particular preprogrammed order. E.g. first smell, then shape, etc.

7 Related Work

Reinforcement learning (RL) algorithms (Sutton 1991) deal with the problem of learning an action (behavior) selection policy so that a scalar, externally received reinforcement signal is maximized over time. They learn a table of Q-values Q(s,a) which represent the value of selecting action a in state s. The complexity of RL algorithms is higher than that of the algorithm discussed in this paper. The main problem of RL is generalizing over states. This problem is solved in our algorithm by only maintaining data about those classes of states that are preconditions of a competence module (i.e. those bits are important, the other ones are not taken into account or are "generalized"). The second main difference is that the goals (and also subgoals) an RL system learns about are implicit. As a consequence, what is learned in the context of one goal, cannot be applied in the context of another goal (all of the Q-values are goal-dependent). Finally it is more difficult to include domain knowledge in RL systems (because all they maintain are values, there is no structure or model of the environment). Some of the advantages of RL systems over the algorithm presented here are their method of temporal credit assignment (which is more general) and the fact that a goal can be specified through reinforcement.

Classifier systems have been suggested as a model for animal behavior and learning (Wilson 1987)(Holland et. al. 1986). The same remark about the implicitness of goals holds here.

Finally the *schema mechanism* (Drescher 1991) also learns about effects of actions, but is not coupled to a performance system. The learning is not goal-driven enough and as a result the learning is slow (there is too much that can be learned). Advantages of Drescher's work are its way of composing schemata and extending the vocabulary (or set of perceptual conditions).

Acknowledgements

I would like to thank John Bresina, Chris Langton, Stewart Wilson and Jonathan Connell for their helpful comments on a previous version of this paper.

References

Agre, P.E. 1988. *The Dynamic Structure of Everyday Life.* PhD thesis. MIT Artificial Intelligence Laboratory. TR 1085.

Brooks, R.A. 1991. Elephants Don't Play Chess. In *Designing Autonomous Agents*, edited by P. Maes. Bradford-MIT Press. Also in *Special Issue on Autonomous Agents*, Journal of Robotics and Autonomous Systems, Vol. 6(1&2), North-Holland.

Coderre, B. 1989. Modeling Behavior in Pet World. In *Artificial Life*,. edited by C. Langton. Addison Wesley.

Drescher, G.L. 1991. *Made-Up Minds: A Constructivist Approach to Artificial Intelligence.* MIT Press.

Holland, J., 1986. Escaping Brittleness: the Possibilities of General Purpose Machine Learning Algorithms applied to Parallel Rule based Systems. In *Machine Learning, an Artificial Intelligence Approach*, edited by R. Michalski, J. Carbonell and T. Mitchell, Vol. 2, Morgan Kaufmann.

Langton, C. 1989. Artificial Life. In *Artificial Life*, edited by C. Langton. Addison Wesley.

Maes, P. 1989. How To Do the Right Thing. *Connection Science Journal* 1(3).

Maes, P. and Brooks, R.A. 1990. Learning to Coordinate Behaviors. *Proceedings of AAAI-90*, 1990.

Maes, P. (editor) 1991a. *Designing Autonomous Agents.* Bradford-MIT Press, 1991. Also: *Special Issue on Autonomous Agents*, Journal of Robotics and Autonomous Systems, 6(1&2).

Maes, P. 1991b. A Bottom-up mechanism for Behavior Selection in an Artificial Creature. In *Proceedings of the first International Conference on Simulation of Adaptive Behavior*, edited by J.A. Meyer and S. Wilson, MIT Press.

Maes, P. 1991c. Adaptive Action Selection. *Proceedings of the Cognitive Science Conference 1991.*

Maes, P. 1991d. Situated Agents can Have Goals. In *Designing Autonomous Agents*, edited by P. Maes. Bradford-MIT Press. Also in *Special Issue on Autonomous Agents*, Journal of Robotics and Autonomous Systems, Vol. 6(1&2), North-Holland.

McFarland, D. (editor) 1987. *The Oxford Companion to Animal Behavior.* Oxford University Press.

Sutton, R. 1991. Reinforcement Learning Architectures for Animats. In *Proceedings of the first International Conference on Simulation of Adaptive Behavior*, edited by J.A. Meyer and S. Wilson, MIT Press.

Walker, S. 1987. *Animal Learning, an Introduction.* Routledge and Kegan Paul, series on introductions to Modern Psychology.

Wilson, S. 1987. Classifier systems and the Animat Problem. In *Machine Learning Journal*, Vol. 2.

Characterizing Adaptation by Constraint

Ian Horswill
MIT Artificial Intelligence Lab
545 Technology Square
Cambridge, MA 02139
ian@ai.mit.edu

October 11, 1991

Abstract

A key problem in the study of both biological and artificial creatures is the description of the relationship between a creature and its habitat. This paper discusses the use of formal constraints as a theoretical tool for describing a creature's adaptation to its environment. Such constraints (1) define a set of environments in which the creature can operate successfully, (2) play a direct explanatory role in a theory of the creature's interaction with its environment, and (3) form a unit of theory independent of the particular creature or information processing system which can be applied to the design or analysis of other systems.[1]

1 Adapted systems

What is the nature of the world that we may live in it? Creatures, be they biological or artificial, are not general purpose systems which perform arbitrary tasks in arbitrary domains. I cannot for example perform very well under water or in hard vacuum without augmenting myself with very special equipment. Similarly, my visual system is hard-wired to believe that the sun is above my head rather than below my feet. We generally think of creatures as being adapted to performing specific sorts of tasks or activities within specific habitats. This specialization is embodied, among other places, in the perceptual and control systems of the creature.

Specialized processing is important for a number of reasons. Research on general systems has proven difficult, and while this does not mean that general systems are impossible, it does suggest that research on specialized processing might not only be easier but might also lead to insights about more general types of processing. From an engineering standpoint, we know that generality tends to be expensive and so we expect computational systems for performing specific tasks in specific environments to be easier to build and less costly on average than systems which perform a superset of the tasks or which operate within a superset of domains. In general we expect to find trade-offs between the complexities of domains, tasks, and machinery. Finally, specialized processing is interesting from a scientific standpoint specifically because it is used so much in nature. To understand an animal, we want not only to understand what computations it performs, but also what trade-offs have been made by nature. We want to understand what computations it *doesn't* do and why it doesn't do them.

This raises the question of what a theory of specialized processing would look like. We can imagine a three-place relation, the "implements" relation, which would hold between a machine, an activity, and a habitat when the machine could implement the activity in the habitat. Ideally, one might want to characterize the implements relation well enough that given specifications of an activity and a habitat, we could determine what the simplest class of machinery was which could implement it. Given a class of machinery and a habitat, we could also solve for the class of tasks (possibly null) which the machinery could implement in the environment. Of course this isn't realistic. It seems difficult enough to completely understand individual systems, tasks and environments, much less to completely characterize the structure of the spaces of possible machines, tasks and environments. Moreover, notions such as "activity" and "habitat" are fuzzy at best. The notion of "machinery" is somewhat better understood, but we still have nothing like an exhaustive taxonomy of it[2].

Nevertheless, the question of how to characterize the

[1] Support for this research was provided in part by the University Research Initiative under Office of Naval Research contract N00014-86-K-0685, and in part by the Advanced Research Projects Agency under Office of Naval Research contract N00014-85-K-0124.

[2] Note however that Rosenschein and Kaelbling have made considerable progress on the problem of deriving machinery from formal descriptions of activities and habitats, for certain classes of machinery, activities and habitats [7].

relationship between a system, its habitat, and its activity is crucial. Frequently artificial creatures are described only at the level of their mechanism, without analyzing why they work, what the limits of their operation are, or what we can learn for them to design other systems. We need ways of making clear the role of specialization in simplifying their construction. Furthermore, we need to do so in a manner which not only illuminates the system in question, but which also makes clear more general lessons which can be applied to other systems.

2 Constraints

In this paper I propose the use of *habitat constraints* as one way of analyzing a creature's adaptation to its environment. Habitat constraints describe conditions on the structures and processes of a creature's environment which allow the creature to function.

Habitat constraints are useful in three ways. First, they form a useful descriptive language for habitats. As with the extension of a predicate in formal logic, a constraint implicitly defines a set of habitats. Conversely, we can partially characterize a particular habitat in terms of a set of constraints which it satisfies.

Second, constraints are useful in characterizing computational problems because their form can directly illuminate the relationship between a creature's habitat and the computations involved in guiding its activity. Constraints play an *explanatory role* in a description of the creature's activity, the constraints roughly playing the role of premises in a formal correctness proof[3]. Conversely, an existing explanation of the creature's activity can be used to derive a set of constraints which collectively define the space of habitats in which the creature can operate.

Most importantly, these constraints can be abstracted from an explanation of one creature and then compared to other creatures or used in the design of new creatures. Thus *a constraint forms an independent unit of theory with value of its own.*

To illustrate the use of such constraints, I'll present a simple visual proximity detector which is in day-to-day use in piloting a robot. I will then discuss the detector in terms of a pair of habitat constraints, the background texture constraint and the ground plane constraint, which help to explain the functioning of the detector and which can also be abstracted from the detector for designing and explaining other systems.

[3] I say "roughly" here because nothing as satisfying as a true correctness proof is generally possible since most domains are not completely, or at least not practically, formalizable.

3 A simple visual proximity detector

Proximity detection is the problem of determining whether there is an object within a given range of the creature. What makes proximity detection relatively simple is what it does not involve: it does not require reporting how many objects are in the scene, their exact distances or shapes, or what their boundaries are. It requires only a one-bit answer. This reduced information requirement allows the use of simple machinery.

Formally, proximity detection is the problem of determining whether there is an object within some region of 3-space, R, defined relative to the creature's body. For the system described here, R is a wedge-shaped region (see figure 1).

The detector is presently used to prevent the robot from colliding with obstacles as it drives through an office environment. The detector uses a combination of texture and motion as a cue to the presence of an object in a region of the image. The environment has relatively little texture so the presence of texture, particularly moving texture, is a cue to the presence of an obstacle.

The detector was initially developed as an experiment in normal flow field estimation[4]. It was not actually a very good flow field estimator however it proved, more or less by accident, to be a very effective object detector in our environment. In fact, the analysis provided below suggests that texture information should be sufficient (see sections 3.2 and 4). This is not good top-down design in the style of the Marr paradigm [6] or an introductory computer science class but it is the way the system was actually developed. A great deal of research, particularly research which involves making real robots work in real environments, seems to involve a large amount of experimentation. Unfortunately, a common practice is to simply report the success without attempting to explain why it worked or why the previous attempts failed.

3.1 Algorithm

The system first digitizes the image at low resolution[5]. This resolution is well below the projected frequency of the texture of the carpet so the carpet should appear to have roughly constant intensity.

Next the system finds pixels with significant intensity gradients. To do this it first smoothes the image[6].

[4] The optic flow field is the field of apparent 2D motions of points in the image. The normal flow at a point is the component of optic flow in the direction of the spatial gradient of intensity at that point. In the case of an edge, the gradient (and therefore the normal flow) is normal to the edge itself, hence the name.

[5] 64×48 pixels in the current implementation

[6] Smoothing is a process of averaging pixels with their neighbors to reduce noise. Since image noise is generally of very high

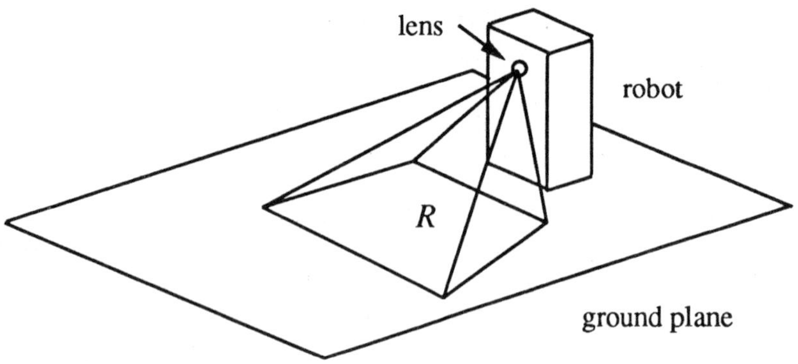

Figure 1: The sensitive region R.

Since the carpet has roughly constant intensity, it should never respond to the carpet, only to objects lying on the carpet. For each pixel with a significant gradient, it computes the normal component of the optic flow field[7] using the optic flow constraint equation [3, p. 283]:

$$\vec{I}_{xy} \cdot \vec{f} = -I_t$$

where $\vec{I}_{xy}$ is the spatial gradient of image intensity at some point, $\vec{f}$ is the image flow, and I_t is the temporal gradient of intensity. The equation is equivalent to stating that the component of flow in the direction of the gradient, called the normal flow, is the quotient of the temporal and spatial gradients:

$$f_{\perp} = -\frac{I_t}{||\vec{I}_{xy}||}$$

The magnitude of $f_{\perp}$ is a lower bound on the magnitude of the actual flow of the patch in the image. The total normal flow integrated over an image patch will be linear in total true flow integrated over the patch. If the orientations of the edge segments in the patch are uniformly distributed, then it will be proportional to the true flow.

The system then integrates the normal flow over the lower region of the image, which corresponds to points in the world close to the robot, to form a measure of the likelihood of the presence of an object. If the flow exceeds a threshold, the detector signals the presence of an object.

3.2 Problems and misfeatures

There are a number of known failure modes of the detector. They can be divided into false positives (stopping when there is no obstacle) and false negatives (crashing). The false negatives are caused by thin objects such as chair legs, which have relatively little texture and generate very little visual motion when the robot moves toward them, and dark areas or blank surfaces, where the robot simply cannot see any texture. False positives are caused by strong shadows or boundaries between differently colored carpets which trigger the detector. Incorrectly set apertures can also cause crashes by making all pixels appear black or white, thus making gradient estimation impossible.

Another issue is that it is not clear how the use of motion information contributes to detecting objects. The analysis of section 4 predicts that a texture detector should be sufficient, and in fact the detector does work well if the motion computation is replaced by one which simply marks each pixel with a one if it has a significant gradient and a zero otherwise. However the resulting detector seems to be somewhat less sensitive and so I have continued to use the motion-based system in my day-to-day work.

Finally, the filter used for smoothing, a simple 2x2 kernel, would normally be considered a bad filter in computer vision. The filter was chosen for implementation reasons. However, the analysis below suggests that *any* low-pass filter would produce acceptable results (see section 4.1).

3.3 Performance

The detector is intended for use in an autonomous navigation system currently under development. It is presently in day-to-day use as an autopilot. It allows users to drive the robot in a specified direction without having to worry about collisions. The detector stops forward motion of the robot whenever a nearby object is detected. With the exception of the failure modes noted above, the system works very well.

The detector is used in live demonstrations in which visitors are encouraged to try to crash the robot. Out

frequency and the averaging process is essentially one of low-pass filtering, the smoothing has the effect of reducing noise while preserving much of the original signal.

[7]The optic flow field is the field of apparent 2D motions of points in the image.

of roughly a dozen such demonstrations there has been only one crash. It was apparently due to the camera's aperture being incorrectly set. The system performed well when the aperture was widened.

4 Analysis

The purpose of this paper is not to argue that this is the perfect proximity detector. Even in the domain in which it operates successfully there are numerous obvious modifications which could be made to it, some of which might increase performance while others might hurt performance. For example, the resolution or the smoothing algorithm might be changed, the use of motion might be abandoned for the simple use of texture, it could be used in conjunction with other cues, and so on. I have experimented with some of these, and have reported on the one which I use in my daily research work.

The point I wish to make is that all of these systems share properties which are more important than the specifics of the algorithm. Proximity detection can be divided into two subproblems: separating objects from the background and sorting them by distance from the robot. This detector and its progeny all rely on special properties of the environment to simplify each of these computational tasks. These properties can be abstracted from the detectors and phrased as habitat constraints which directly illuminate the way in which they simplify their respective computational problems.

4.1 Background texture constraint

Separating objects from the background is a common problem in visual processing. It can be an arbitrarily difficult task if we consider pathological backgrounds such as a house of mirrors or pathological objects such as chameleons. On the other hand, it can be very easy if there is some property of objects which is not shared by the background. One such salience property is texture. A particularly simple case is when the background has no texture at all, in which case the presence of texture is a cue to the presence of an object. We can formalize a version of this as the background texture constraint.

Definition 1 *An environment satisfies the background texture constraint if there is a large band of spatial frequencies* $\Omega = (\omega_0, \omega_1)$*, called the* zero band*, which have no energy in the markings of surfaces forming the background (floors, walls, etc.).*

Many surfaces such as carpets, painted walls, stucco, wood paneling, and wall-papered surfaces with fine patterns have such zero bands. Other surfaces such as checkerboard floors do not. The backgrounds of many office environments are comprised of large surfaces whose textures share common zero bands. These environments satisfy the constraint.

To make precise the computational value of this constraint, consider a local, linear filter directed at some surface patch of the world[8]. The simplest case is when the surface patch is a plane whose surface reflectance is a sine wave grating with orientation defined by the vector $\vec{\omega}$:

$$R(x, y) = \frac{1}{2}(\sin\frac{x}{\omega_x} + \sin\frac{y}{\omega_y}) + \frac{1}{2}$$

If this patch is viewed in the fronto-parallel plane at unit distance through a lens of unit focal length, with even illumination of unit intensity, then the image intensity $I(x, y)$ at a point (x, y) in the image will simply be $R(x, y)$. If however we increase the distance or decrease the focal length by a factor c, then we will have that

$$I(x, y) = R(\frac{x}{c}, \frac{y}{c}) = \frac{1}{2}(\sin\frac{cx}{\omega_x} + \sin\frac{cy}{\omega_y}) + \frac{1}{2}$$

Thus the projected image will still be a sine-wave grating but of frequency $c\vec{\omega}$. If we instead rotate the patch around the x axis by an angle θ and ignore perspective effects, then the effect is simply to shrink the image along the y axis:

$$I(x, y) = R(x, y\cos\theta) = \frac{1}{2}(\sin\frac{x}{\omega_x} + \sin\frac{y\cos\theta}{\omega_y}) + \frac{1}{2}$$

resulting in the appearance of yet another grating, this time of frequency $(\omega_x, \frac{\omega_y}{\cos\theta})$. Similarly, a rotation about the y axis will result in multiplying the apparent x component of $\vec{\omega}$. Finally, a rotation about an axis perpendicular to the image plane will simply rotate the frequency vector by the same amount.

Thus any simple grating viewed from any position will appear as a grating with identical amplitude but with a frequency vector modified by a scaling of its two components and possibly a rotation. Since the projection process is linear in that the projection of the superposition of two signals is the superposition of their projections, this rule will carry over to the surface patch's Fourier transform: the transform of the patch's projection will be the transform of the patch, rotated and then stretched or contracted along each axis (see figure 2).

The result of the foregoing analysis is that frequency bands of the surface patch are transformed into elliptical regions of the frequency domain of its projection. Thus if the background has a zero band, its projection should have a zero-ellipse. In general, the distance, focal length

[8] Such a filter computes at every point in the image a weighted average of the intensities of the point and its neighbors. This can be viewed as amplifying certain frequencies in the image while attenuating others.

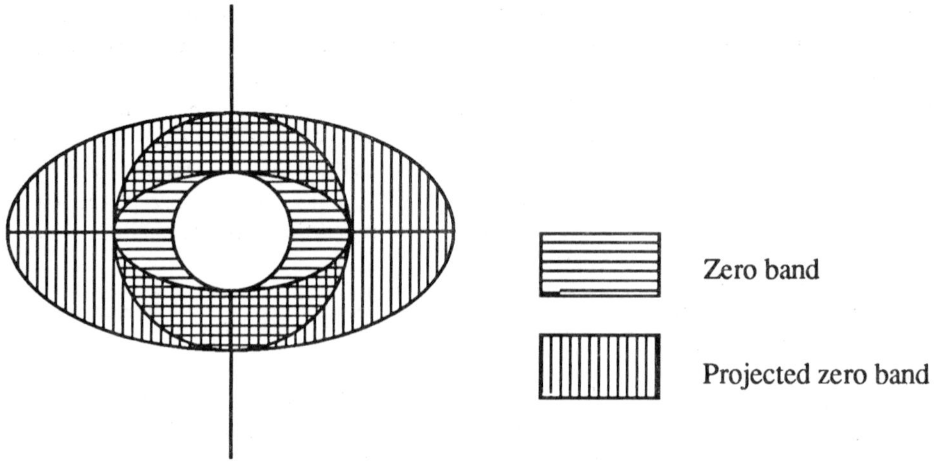

Figure 2: The effect of perspective projection on local frequency distributions.

and angles of the camera must be known to predict the ellipse.

An important special case where these parameters need not be known is when the texture of the background has no low frequency component other than dc[9]. This is the case used by the proximity detector. Here the zero band is simply the open interval $\Omega = (0, \omega_1)$. Suppose we view the texture from a distance greater than some d_{min} and bandpass filter the image. Since viewing the texture from an angle can only increase the apparent frequency of texture in the image, our bandpass filter should give zero energy whenever its cutoff frequency is below

$$\frac{d_{min}}{f}\omega_1$$

where f is the focal length of the camera.

The sampling and smoothing process of the detector described above form a low pass filter. The differentiation involved in computing the magnitude of the gradient on the other hand is a form of high pass filter. Thus the resulting transfer function has a bandpass shape, limited to the zero band. Any pixel which passes the gradient test of the algorithm must violate the background texture constraint and so is a candidate obstacle. Interestingly, this means that running the detector at higher resolution could actually cause it to fail.

4.2 Ground plane constraint

Another common problem is to separate nearby objects from ones which are more distant. This could be done by computing a depth map which would give the distance from the camera for each pixel. Such computations are expensive and unreliable however, at least at present. In land environments the creature rests on, and travels about, some sort of ground. Often the ground is a plane perpendicular to the force of gravity. If the camera is pointed forward and somewhat downward, then distant ground points will project to points "higher up" in the image than nearer ground points. The y (vertical) component of a point's projection in the image will be a monotonically increasing function[10] of the point's distance from the robot. If objects can be counted on to rest upon the ground plane, then their y coordinates[11] can be used as a sieve to separate distant objects from nearer objects. We can formalize this as the ground plane constraint.

Definition 2 *An environment satisfies the ground plane constraint if all objects, including the creature, rest upon a planar surface.*

Built environments such as houses and office buildings generally satisfy the ground plane constraint. The ground plane constraint allows us to focus processing on nearby objects by focusing it on a predefined region of the image.

4.3 Application to other systems and creatures

These constraints are not new. For example, the corridor- and object-following systems of Horswill and Brooks used both [4]. This work grew out of an desire to better understand their operation. The obstacle detector of Storjohann, et al. [8], uses a much stronger version of the ground plane constraint to simplify the stereo matching problem. The relationship between height in

[9] By "dc", I mean a constant term.

[10] It's precise form is a quotient of linear functions in the distance from the creature along the ground plane. The coefficients of the linear functions are determined by the parameters of projection.

[11] Technically, the smallest y coordinate of any point in the object's projection.

the image and depth has been known at least since Euclid [1, p. 41] and there is psychophysical evidence to suggest that people also use it [2].

The value of identifying these constraints is that they can be used in any environment which satisfies them. So the background texture constraint can always be used to segment objects from the background when the environment satisfies it. Similarly, the ground plane constraint can be used to focus attention on nearby objects or to compare distances.

5 Discussion

David Marr has extensively discussed the use of constraints to describe computational problems [6]. However, Marr was less interested in systems which operated in limited domains and so used constraints to characterize the world as a whole, rather than particular habitats. For Marr, a constraint was a constraint on *interpretation* which resolved ambiguities and allowed the formulation of an information-processing task as a well-defined problem.

Marr argued for the use of computational theories of information-processing problems as useful units of theory which are independent of the details of the specific algorithms which implement them [5]. He argued that one should progress from a computational theory (which included in it a set of contraints) to an algorithmic description independent of a particular implementation, and finally to an implementation of the algorithm.

This methodology is difficult to use for studying specialized processing because it seems to require a computational theory for every possible task-habitat pair. A coarser unit of theory is needed in addition, one which can make explicit the commonalities of related problems. Habitat constraints are a useful tool for this purpose. By making explicit individual properties of environments and the ways in which they facilitate different types of computational problems, habitats and computational tasks can be classified and their relationships drawn out.

An argument could be made that some sort of computational theory is implicit in any discussion of how a habitat constraint simplifies a computational problem, in effect that there are computational theories hidden in the descriptions of the constraints above. However, these computational theories would be of a very different sort than Marr proposed. Constraint descriptions do not formally define computational problems and so are incomplete as computational theories in Marr's sense. Another, perhaps more important, difference is that describing how constraints simplify a computation violates at least the letter of Marr's program of examining algorithmic issues only after having fixed a computational theory.

The important point is this. We need ways of describing and understanding those features of a habitat which allow its inhabitants to function. We need them both for the scientific problem of understanding natural creatures and for the engineering problem of building machines which can operate in environments of our choosing. Whatever their form, they must allow us to abstract away from the particulars of creature and environment and draw lessons of more general import.

In this paper I have sketched how we might do this by describing the relationship between a creature and its habitat in terms of constraints and their relationships to computational problems. It is too early to tell how far one can go with this method. Other tools will likely be needed. I hope this will encourage others to consider the problem.

Acknowledgments

Rod Brooks, Maja Mataric, David Michael, Lynn Stein, and Eric Grimson provided much needed feedback during the development of these ideas, and provided comments on drafts.

References

[1] James E. Cutting. *Perception with and Eye for Motion.* MIT Press, 1986.

[2] B. E. Dunn, G. C. Gray, and D. Thompson. Relative height on the picture-plane and depth perception. *Perceptual and Motor Skills*, 21:227–236, 1965.

[3] B. K. P. Horn. *Robot Vision.* MIT Press, 1986.

[4] Ian Horswill and Rod Brooks. Situated vision in a dynamic environment: Chasing objects. In *Proceedings of the Seventh National Conference on Artificial Intelligence*, August 1988.

[5] David Marr. Artificial intelligence—a personal view. *Artificial Intelligence*, 9:37–48, 1977.

[6] David Marr. *Vision.* W. H. Freeman and Co., 1982.

[7] Stanley J. Rosenschein and Leslie Pack Kaelbling. The synthesis of machines with provable epistemic properties. In Joseph Halpern, editor, *Proc. Conf. on Theoretical Aspects of Reasoning about Knowledge*, pages 83–98. Morgan Kaufmann, 1986.

[8] K. Storjohann, T. Zeilke, H. A. Mallot, and W. von Seelen. Visual obstacle detection for automatically guided vehicles. In *Proceedings of the IEEE International Conference on Robotics and Automation*, pages 761–766, May 1990.

On the Self-organizing Properties of Topological Maps

Didier Keymeulen Jo Decuyper *
didier@arti.vub.ac.be jo@arti.vub.ac.be
Artificial Intelligence Laboratory
Vrije Universiteit Brussel
Pleinlaan 2, B-1050 Brussels
Belgium

Abstract

Kohonen has proposed a way to implement self-organizing two-dimensional topological maps that can be used to map sensory inputs onto motor action in an artificial creature. He has shown that under certain conditions, such topological maps develop into automatic feature detectors without the need for an external teacher nor for a priori knowledge about the input space. In this paper we analyze these conditions and show that, under certain simplifying assumptions, they can be related to properties of the solutions of the field equations of electromagnetism. Our approach is based on the neural field theory introduced by Amari which contains as a special case the topological maps of Kohonen. We also discuss another example of a topological neural network which has been proposed to solve the path-finding problem in a maze. We show that in this case, the performance can be much improved by exploiting the relations between neural fields and the field theory of electromagnetism that we have pointed out.

1 Introduction.

Cognitive mapping is the complex process which computes a representation of the environment of an agent based on how this agent perceives his environment with his sensors (Yeap and Handley 1991). It is a general consensus in the field of artificial life that computing a cognitive map is fundamental to any living creature, be it a rat, a human or a robot. Building such a map forms a necessary step for example in the development of a navigational competence. The map-space in this case can be a two-dimensional grid of cells, a visibility graph or a self-organizing topological neural network such as proposed by Kohonen (1984).

There are essentially two different possiblities to construct cognitive maps. First, the structure of the map may be specified a priori by the designer. An example of this approach is the visibility graph (Lozano-Perez 1982). A second approach consists in using a self-organizing network that builds the map gradually as the result of the exploration of the environment by the creature (Nehmzow and Smithers 1991). The main advantages of this last approach are that the self-organizing capabilities of the network avoid the need for an external teacher and that no a priori knowledge about the domain must be available. On the other hand, a firm grip on the parameters of the system is needed in order to ensure the desired self-organizing properties.

Kohonen considers a two-dimensional layer of densily interconnected neurons and proposes necessary conditions for his topological map to converge. One of these conditions specifies that the lateral feedback between neurons must have the form of a *mexican hat*: i.e. local activation and global inhibition. He then derives the existence of a topology preserving map between the input space and the topological neural network.

The topological maps of Kohonen are in fact special cases of neural fields studied by Amari (1983). Neural fields are a continuum approximation to a certain type of recurrent neural networks. In this approximation it is assumed that neurons are uniformly distributed over a region of space. In the neural field theory it is shown that the equilibrium activation of a neural field must obey a non-linear integral equation. Because of its complexity, this equation cannot be solved in general. We study a special case of a neural field for which it is possible to solve explicitly the corresponding field equation. For this special case, we can show that if the connectivity between neural regions is similar to the *mexican hat*, then the equilibrium response of the neural field to a given input pattern will be localized. The radius of a responsive region depends inversely on the frequency of presenting the corresponding pattern during the learning phase. Our approach relies on mathematical tech-

*This research has been sponsored by the Belgian Government with the contract "Incentive Program For Fundamental Research In Artificial Intelligence ; Project : Self-organization in subsymbolic computation" and "Geconcerteerde Actie" ; Project : "Artificiële intelligentie, Parallelle Architecturen en Interfaces". Part of this research has also been funded by the Esprit Program with the contract P440: "Message Passing" niques borrowed from the theory of electrodynamics.

The paper is organized as follows. First we briefly review the field theory proposed by Amari and in particular the integral equation for the equilibrium activation of a neural field. Next we introduce the necessary material from the field theory of electrodynamics to enable us to solve the field equation for the simplified neural field. Following we derive the properties of the connectivity function and the existence of the topology preserving mapping between the input space and the neural field. In the last section we discuss one application namely the recent work by Lei, who uses a special type of Hopfield net for the solution of the path-finding problem in a maze (Lei 1990). We show that Lei's system is in fact an instance of a neural field such as described by Amari. The correspondence we have pointed out between the theory of electrodynamics and the neural field theory enables us to improve the convergence and performance of the Lei system.

2 Field theory for neural nets.

Some ten years ago Amari (1983) proposed a theory for neural nets which is based on the idea of the continuum limit of a dense distribution of neurons. In this model it is assumed that the individual neurons are no longer distinguishable. Instead they form a neural field which can be described in terms of field variables. The time evolution of these variables is governed by field equations which are the continuum analog of the dynamical equations for single neurons in neural networks.

To be more specific, consider a two-dimensional distribution of neurons described by a position vector $\vec{\xi}$. The equilibrium activation of the neural field after the learning phase is described by $\overline{U}(\vec{\xi},\tau)$. This activation corresponds to the response of the neural field at position $\vec{\xi}$ when the input pattern $\vec{x}(\tau)$ is presented. Following Amari we assume that the input space I can be completely characterized by a one-dimensional distribution of input vectors $\vec{x}(\tau)$ with a distribution denoted by $p(\tau)$.

The central issue in the neural field theory is the integral equation which has to be satisfied by $\overline{U}(\vec{\xi},\tau)$:

$$\overline{U}(\vec{\xi},\tau) = \int_{\Xi} w(\vec{\xi},\vec{\xi}')\, f[\overline{U}(\vec{\xi}',\tau)]\, d\vec{\xi}' + \int_{I} \lambda(\tau,\tau')\, p(\tau')\, f[\overline{U}(\vec{\xi},\tau')]\, d\tau' \quad (1)$$

where Ξ denotes the two-dimensional neural field and $w(\vec{\xi},\vec{\xi}')$ denotes the coupling function between neural regions $\vec{\xi}$ and $\vec{\xi}'$. The function f expresses the input-output relation of neurons and is usually taken to be a sigmoid. Finally, $\lambda(\tau,\tau')$ stands for the "overlap" between the input vectors $\vec{x}(\tau)$ and $\vec{x}(\tau')$ which in Amari's theory is given by the expression:

$$\lambda(\tau,\tau') = c\, \vec{x}(\tau)\cdot\vec{x}(\tau') - c'\, {x_0}^2 \quad (2)$$

Amari suggested to study the general field equation (1) in order to gain insight in the self-organizing properties of neural fields. In particular, the formation of topology preserving maps between the input space I and the neural field Ξ should be deducible from the properties of the solutions of this field equation. Unfortunately, (1) is far too difficult to be solved in general. Nevertheless, the work by Kohonen (1984) on topographic maps seems to support the thesis that such maps can be formed by a self-organizing process on a two-dimensional neural field. Also, Amari (1980) has shown that such self-organizing processes can occur in a simple one-dimensional neural field and for a simple input space.

Our goal in this paper is to establish a link between the field equation (1) and the theory of electromagnetic potentials in empty space. The link is the following: After the learning phase, a neural field will only admit those patterns of activation $(\overline{U}(\vec{\xi},\tau))$ for a given input $\vec{x}(\tau)$ which solve the field equation (1). On the other hand, the electromagnetic potential in empty space satisfies the wave equation:

$$\Delta\phi(\vec{x},t) - \frac{1}{c^2}\frac{\partial^2\phi(\vec{x},t)}{\partial t^2} = 0 \quad (3)$$

If we suppose that the solution has a sinusoidal dependence on time with a single frequency, it is possible to separate off the time term as a factor such that the potential has the form

$$\phi(\vec{x},t) = e^{-i\omega t}\psi(\vec{x}) \quad (4)$$

Then it follows that the spatial dependence satisfies the equation of Helmholtz:

$$\Delta\psi(\vec{x}) + k^2\psi(\vec{x}) = 0 \;\text{ where } k = \tfrac{w}{c} \quad (5)$$

This homogeneous, second-order, linear equation for the scalar field $\psi(\vec{x})$ is a typical form of general interest in Physics and Biology. We will show that the solution of the integral equation (1) corresponds to the solution of the Helmholtz equation (5) under certain simplifying assumptions. First we have to introduce the fundamental concept of a Green's function (Garabedian 1964). It will enable us to reformulate the Helmholtz equation as an integral equation.

2.1 Green's function and integral equations.

The general idea of electrostatics consists in considering a spatial distribution of charges and computing the corresponding potential. This potential in turn allows one to infer how a small test charge placed at a given location will be influenced by the charge distribution and therefore how it is going to move (Feynman, Leighton and Sands 1965) (Jackson 1975).

Mathematically speaking this problem corresponds to the solution of the Poisson equation subject to suitable boundary conditions:

$$\Delta\phi(\vec{x}) = -4\pi\rho(\vec{x}) \quad (6)$$

$$B_i\phi(\vec{x}) = 0 \quad (7)$$

Note that (5) can be considered as a special case of (6) if the charge distribution $\rho(\vec{x})$ depends itself on the potential $\phi(\vec{x})$ in a linear way. It should come as no surprise that the solutions of both problems are also related to each other.

Consider the Green's function $G(\vec{r}, \vec{r_0})$ of the Laplace operator Δ. It satisfies the equation [1] :

$$\Delta_{\vec{r}} G(\vec{r}, \vec{r_0}) = 4\pi\delta(\vec{r} - \vec{r_0}) \tag{8}$$

If we multiply (5) with $G(\vec{r}, \vec{r_0})$ and subtract from it (8) multiplied by $\psi(\vec{r})$ we obtain:

$$\begin{aligned} G(\vec{r}, \vec{r_0})\, \Delta_{\vec{r}}\psi(\vec{r}) - \psi(\vec{r})\, \Delta_{\vec{r}} G(\vec{r}, \vec{r_0}) \\ + k^2\, G(\vec{r}, \vec{r_0})\, \psi(\vec{r}) = \\ -4\pi\delta(\vec{r} - \vec{r_0})\, \psi(\vec{r}) \text{ for all } \vec{r}, \vec{r_0} \end{aligned} \tag{9}$$

Integrating this expression over a portion of space V_0 bounded by a closed surface S_0 we obtain:

$$\begin{aligned} &\int_{V_0} dv_0\, [G(\vec{r}, \vec{r_0})\, \Delta_{\vec{r_0}}\psi(\vec{r_0}) - \psi(\vec{r_0})\, \Delta_{\vec{r_0}} G(\vec{r}, \vec{r_0})] \\ &+ \int_{V_0} dv_0\, k^2\, G(\vec{r}, \vec{r_0})\, \psi(\vec{r_0}) = \begin{cases} -\psi(\vec{r}) & \text{if } \vec{r_0} \in V_0 \\ 0 & \text{otherwise} \end{cases} \end{aligned} \tag{10}$$

In deriving the previous equation we have used the symmetry of the Green's function and the δ-function for the permutation $\vec{r} \rightleftharpoons \vec{r_0}$. By Green's theorem (10) can be simplified into:

$$\begin{aligned} &\oint_{S_0} ds_0\, [G(\vec{r}, \vec{r_0})\nabla_{\vec{r_0}}\psi(\vec{r_0}) - \psi(\vec{r_0})\nabla_{\vec{r_0}} G(\vec{r}, \vec{r_0})] \\ &+ \int_{V_0} dv_0\, k^2\, G(\vec{r}, \vec{r_0})\, \psi(\vec{r_0}) = \begin{cases} -\psi(\vec{r}) & \text{if } \vec{r_0} \in V_0 \\ 0 & \text{else} \end{cases} \end{aligned} \tag{11}$$

If we assume that $\psi(\vec{r}) \sim \vartheta(\frac{1}{|\vec{r}|})$ when $|\, \vec{r}\, | \rightarrow \infty$ then the surface integral in (11) can be neglected in the limit $V_0 \rightarrow \infty$. It follows that the solutions of the Helmholtz equation (5) which satisfy the boundary conditions at ∞ must also satisfy the integral equation:

$$-\int_{V_0} dv_0\, k^2\, G(\vec{r}, \vec{r_0})\, \psi(\vec{r_0}) = \psi(\vec{r}) \tag{12}$$

where $G(\vec{r}, \vec{r_0})$ is the Green's function of the Laplace operator. This integral equation provides the link with the theory of neural fields.

2.2 Neural field theory and electromagnetism.

In order to relate the equilibrium potential of a neural field to the electromagnetic potential solving (12) we need to introduce some simplifying assumptions. Strictly speaking (1) is not an integral equation in the usual sense because of the double integral over the two different spaces Ξ and I. In principle this could be remedied by extending both integrations over the product space $\Xi \times I$ but this would not simplify the problem of getting the solution. Instead we assume that the input space has a particular structure: all input vectors have the same norm and the same mutual overlap with each other. Formally:

$$c\, \vec{x}(\tau) \cdot \vec{x}(\tau') - c' {x_0}^2 = \delta(\tau - \tau') \tag{13}$$

Under this assumption, the integral over the input space I is reduced to the single term:

$$p(\tau) f[\overline{U}(\vec{\xi}, \tau)] \tag{14}$$

and that the $\overline{U}$ has to satisfy the equation:

$$\begin{aligned} \overline{U}(\vec{\xi}, \tau) - p(\tau)\, f[\overline{U}(\vec{\xi}, \tau)] = \\ \int_{\Xi} d\vec{\xi'}\, w(\vec{\xi}, \vec{\xi'})\, f[\overline{U}(\vec{\xi'}, \tau)] \text{ for all} \tau \end{aligned} \tag{15}$$

This equation is still very difficult to solve in general due to the presence of the non-linear function f which is typically a sigmoid of the type $f[\overline{U}] = \frac{1}{1+e^{-\overline{U}}}$[2]. Therefore we consider as a first approach the linear approximation under the assumption that $|\, \overline{U}\, | \ll 1$. In that case we obtain the following integral equation for $\overline{U}$:

$$\begin{aligned} \overline{U}(\vec{\xi}, \tau)\, (1 - p(\tau)) = \\ \int_{\Xi} d\vec{\xi'}\, w(\vec{\xi}, \vec{\xi'})\, \overline{U}(\vec{\xi'}, \tau) \quad \text{for all} \tau \end{aligned} \tag{16}$$

Comparing (16) with (12) it follows that a possible equilibrium activation of a neural field when a pattern $\vec{x}(\tau)$ is presented, corresponds to the solution of the integral equation associated with the Helmholtz equation under the two conditions:

$$k^2 = \frac{1}{p(\tau) - 1} \tag{17}$$

$$w(\vec{\xi}, \vec{\xi'}) = G(\vec{\xi}, \vec{\xi'}) \tag{18}$$

where G is the Green's function for Δ.

2.3 Properties of the solution of the field equation.

For a *two-dimensional* neural field Ξ the corresponding Green's function is:

$$w(\vec{\xi}, \vec{\xi'}) \equiv G(\vec{\xi}, \vec{\xi'}) = log_e \frac{1}{|\, \vec{\xi} - \vec{\xi'}\, |} \tag{19}$$

The graph of this function is shown in figure 1. The interesting property is that it has essentially the same characteristic as the so-called 'mexican hat', i.e. positive near the origin and negative beyond a certain point. For neural field this implies that neuronal regions should be coupled in such a way that nearby regions activate each other while distant regions inhibit each other. In the Kohonen approach for example, such a coupling between regions is introduced in an ad hoc way (Kohonen 1984). The connection with the field

[1]The subscript $\vec{r}$ in $\Delta_{\vec{r}}$ indicates that the derivatives are to be taken with respect to the $\vec{r}$ variables.

[2]Schauder's fixed point theorem can be used to determine the existence of solutions of non-linear integral equations of the Fredholm type. However, we are interested in the properties of solutions and not in their mere existence (Hochstadt 1973).

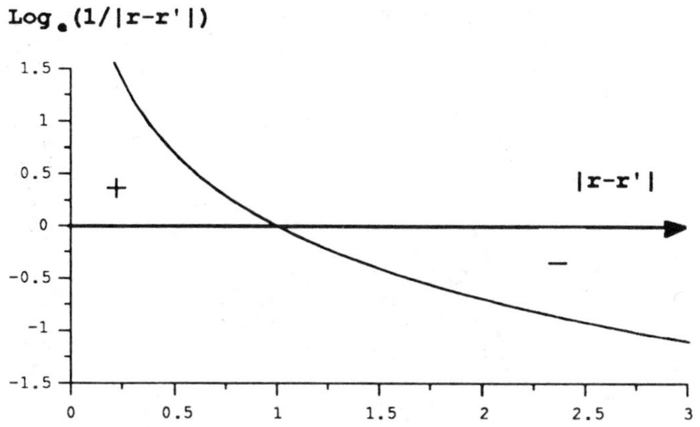

Figure 1: Connection function for the linear field approximation.

theory of electrostatics provides a way to understand the need for such a coupling in order to solve the field equations.

Under the assumptions we have introduced we can obtain explicit expressions for the solutions of the field equations. These correspond to the solutions of the Helmholtz equation (5) under the conditions (17)(18). We recall that $p(\tau)$ is a probability distribution and thus $0 \leq p(\tau) \leq 1$. It follows that the spatial dependence[3] is given by:

$$\psi(\vec{r}) \sim e^{-\kappa|\vec{r}|} \text{ with } \kappa^2 = -k^2 \tag{20}$$

Such a spatial dependence is of course exactly what one needs in order to get a localized response to a given input pattern. Note that the width of the responding region decreases with increasing frequency of presenting a pattern because of the relation

$$\kappa = \sqrt{\frac{1}{1-p(\tau)}} \tag{21}$$

This result seems to contradict the findings of Amari that the size of the neuronal region that responds to a given input pattern increases with the frequency of presenting this pattern during the learning phase. However, in his derivation Amari has assumed that the coupling between neurons is a constant (Amari 1980). It can be argued whether this is a plausible assumption given the fact that in the Kohonen type networks explicit use is made of a coupling in the form of a *mexican hat* in order to arrive at the self-organizing topological maps. Under the assumptions we have made, a more frequent presentation of an input pattern results in a more specific respons of the neural field in the sense of a smaller responsive region.

Given a neural field Ξ that has been trained with patterns from a given input space I, one can define a responsive region by the condition:

$$E(\tau) = \{\vec{\xi} \mid \overline{U}(\vec{\xi},\tau) \geq \theta\} \tag{22}$$

where θ is a given threshold. From (20) we infer that

$$E(\tau) = \{\vec{\xi} \mid |\vec{\xi}| \leq -\log_e \theta\sqrt{1-p(\tau)}\} \tag{23}$$

Because of our assumption that $|\overline{U}| \ll 1$ we may choose $\theta < 1$ such that (23) represents a non-empty set. It is clear that the radius of the responsive region is a continuous function of the distribution $p(\tau)$ and so is its inverse. This indicates that the topology of the input space, induced by the distribution $p(\tau)$ is mapped onto the topology in the Ξ space induced by the radius of the responsive regions, in a way which preserves the topology. However, our equations do not allow the deduction that nearby input patterns, measured by the overlap of input vectors, will get mapped onto nearby responsive regions.

3 Application of the neural field theory.

In the Hopfield's continuous state neuron model, the action potential u_i of a neuron satisfies the equations:

$$C_i\frac{du_i}{dt} = \sum_{j=1}^{N} T_{ij}U_j - \frac{u_i}{R_i} + I_i \tag{24}$$

$$U_i = g(u_i) \tag{25}$$

where T_{ij} are the weights of the connections between neurons, U_j is the output of neuron j, the term $\frac{u_i}{R_i}$ corresponds to a leakage and I_i represents an external stimulus. The weights can be chosen, subject to the condition $T_{i,j} = T_{j,i} \geq 0$, such that the dynamics of the neural network is governed by an ensemble of point attractors.

Lei (1990) studies an instance of this continuous neuron model for solving the path finding problem in maze . He introduces two extra conditions on the connection weights T_{ij}:

$$T_{ii} = -\sum_{j=1, j\neq i}^{N} T_{ij} \tag{26}$$

$$\frac{u_i}{R_i} \simeq 0 \tag{27}$$

Under these assumptions (24) reduces to:

$$C_i\frac{du_i}{dt} = \sum_{j=1, j\neq i}^{N} T_{ij}(U_j - U_i) + I_i \tag{28}$$

$$U_i = g(u_i) \tag{29}$$

Lei has shown that this neuronal model coincides with a fluid model where a fluid is allowed to flow over a 2-dimensional space under the action of gravity. He proposes to use this model for solving the path finding problem in a maze. In order to do this, the topology of

[3] We consider only spherically symmetrical solutions

the maze has to be encoded in the connection weights T_{ij}. Assume a 2-dimensional space with obstacles. This can be approximated by a lattice of cells which are either free or obstacle. With each cell corresponds a neuron and assume that the connections between neurons are limited to adjacent neurons. They are choosen such that if both neurons represent free space, the connection weight is 1 else it is 0. In order to find a path in the maze, a positive external input I is presented to the neuron corresponding to the start location and an equally large negative external input to the goal location. Lei has proven that this system always converges to a unique stable state regardless of the initial values of the activation of the neurons. In terms of the fluid model this state corresponds to a stationary flow between start and goal in a maze with reflective boundaries.

The correspondence between Lei's work and our approach to the field theory of neural nets by Amari can be seen as follows. By introducing the assumptions (26) on the connections and assuming that they are restricted to adjacent neurons on a 2-dimensional lattice, the neural network is effectively turned into a neural field similar to the Kohonen's topological maps. In the linear approximation $U_i \propto u_i$ and in a region of free space (28) corresponds to the diffusion equation for the activation field $U(\vec{x},t)$ with totally reflective boundaries:

$$\frac{\partial U(\vec{x},t)}{\partial t} = \Delta U(\vec{x},t) + I(\vec{x}) \tag{30}$$

where $I(\vec{x})$ stands for a source term. The stationary solution $\overline{U}(\vec{x})$, which is used by Lei for solving the path finding problem, satisfies the Poisson equation with Neuman boundary conditions:

$$\Delta\overline{U}(\vec{x}) = -I(\vec{x}) \tag{31}$$

$$\frac{\partial \overline{U}}{\partial n}\Big|_{boundary} = 0$$

This is the same equation as (6) where $4\pi\rho(\vec{x}) = I(\vec{x})$. The property of the solution of Lei's system, that it has no extrema except on the boundaries, follows directly from the properties of the solution of the Poisson equation. This is the reason why the system can be used to find the path in a maze. Indeed, Poisson's equation also describes the flow of an incompressible fluid in the presence of sources and sinks. Given this correspondance, several simplifications of Lei's system become possible. First, there is no need to consider non-linear neurons because the equilibrium potentials $\overline{U}$ may depend in any way on $\overline{u}$. However, the convergence of the system is drastically improved by considering a linear dependence: $U \propto u$. Second, some implicit limitations of the Lei system can be discarded. Lei assumes that there is only one possible way from the start to the goal and that this path is everywhere exactly one neuron wide, in order to assure that the gradient along the flow line is constant. Both these assumptions can be dropped in the linearized field approach. It suffices to look for a path corresponding to the steepest descent of the pressure field in a fluid system.

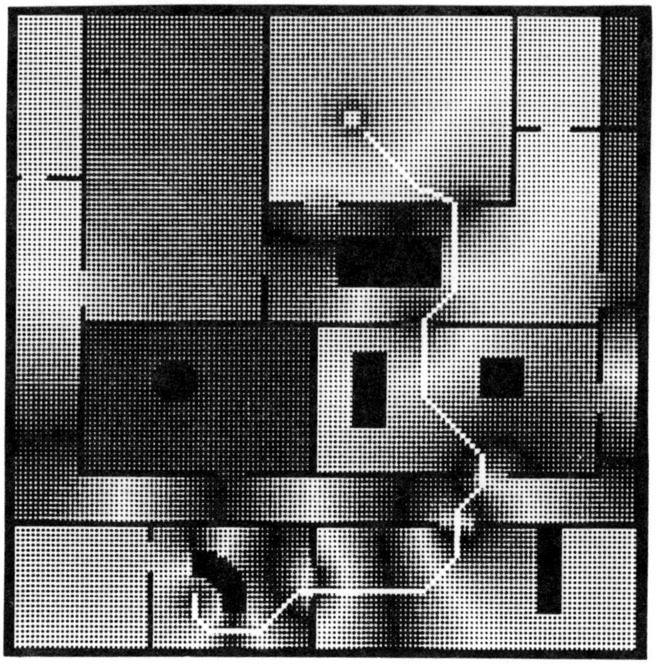

Figure 2: Path generated by the linear field approach.

We have implemented the linear field approach on a massively parallel machine of the type DAP[4] (Decuyper and Keymeulen 1991). It generates the shortest path between any start and goal position for an arbitrary topology. Furthermore if the topology is changed, for example by introducing a new obstacle, our system is capable of modifying the path by finding a new and optimal subpath around the obstacle. Figure (2) shows a path generated with our system. Further extensions to path planning are discussed in Keymeulen and Decuyper 1990.

4 Conclusion.

In this paper we have studied the conditions for self-organization in Kohonen's topological map. We exploit the fact that this map is a particular case of the general neural field theory proposed by Amari. Our approach is based on the analogy between a linear approximation of the field equation and the theory of electrodynamics. We have shown that well know features of neural fields, such as the interconnection between neuronal regions in the form of a 'mexican hat' and the localized respons to a input pattern, can be understood in this framework. More specifically, we have shown that the

[4]DAP is a trademark of Active Memory Technology

connectivity function is related to the Green's function of the Laplace operator and that the spatial properties of the activation potential of a neural field at equilibrium can be obtained from the corresponding solutions of the Helmholtz equation. We have also shown that this framework can be used to analyze a topological variant of a Hopfield net which has been proposed to solve the path finding problem in a maze. Through this analysis we were able to show that convergence can be improved and that some of the more cumbersome assumptions are not necessary in our linear field approach. We present an example of path finding using our implementation on a massively parallel DAP machine.

Acknowledgements.

It is a pleasure to thank Professor L. Steels for giving us the opportunity of doing this research in his lab. Thanks also to the other members of the complex dynamics group at the V.U.B. and especially to B. Manderick for his useful comments on this paper.

References

Amari, S. "Topographic organization of nerve fields". *Bull. Math. Biology* 42:339–364, September 1980.

Amari, S. "Field Theory of Self-Organising Neural Nets". *IEEE Transac. on Systems Man and Cybernetics* 13(5):741–748, September 1983.

Decuyper, J. and D. Keymeulen. 1991. "A Reactive Robot Navigation System Based on a Fluid Dynamics Metaphor". In Hans-Paul Schwefel and Reinhard Maenner, editors, *Parallel Problem Solving from Nature*, 348–355. Springer (Verlag), Berlin. Lecture Notes in Computer Science.

Feynman, R., R.B. Leighton and M. Sands. 1965. *Lectures on Physics.* Addison-Wesley.

Garabedian, P.R. 1964. *Partial Differential Equations.* John Wiley and Sons, New York-London-Sydney.

Hochstadt, H. 1973. *Integral Equations.* John Wiley and Sons, Inc., New York. Pure and Applied Mathematics, a Wiley-Interscience Series.

Jackson, I.D. 1975. *Classical electrodynamics.* Wiley, London.

Keymeulen, D. and J. Decuyper. 1990. "A Flexible Path Generator for a Mobile Robot: a Mathematical Approach". AI-memo 90-5, VUB AI-Lab.

Kohonen, T. 1984. *Self-Organisation and Associative Memory.* Springer-Verlag, Berlin-Heidelberg-New York-Tokyo. 2nd ed. 1988.

Lei, G. "A neuron model with fluid properties for solving labyrinthian puzzle". *Biological Cybernetics* 64(1): 61–67, November 1990.

Lozano-Perez. 1982. "Automatic Planning Manipulator Transfer Movements". In Brady and Al., editors, *Robot Motion: Planning and Control*, 499–535. MIT Press, Cambridge, Mass.

Nehmzow, U. and T. Smithers. 1991. "Mapbuilding using Self-Organising Networks in "Really Useful Robots". In J.A. Meyer and S.W. Wilson, editors, *Proceedings of the First International Conference on Simulation of Adaptive Behavior*, 152–158, Cambridge, Mass. MIT Press.

Yeap, W.K. and C.C. Handley. 1991. "Four Important Issues in Cognitive Mapping". In J.A. Meyer and S.W. Wilson, editors, *Proceedings of the First International Conference on Simulation of Adaptive Behavior*, 176–183, Cambridge, Mass. MIT Press.

Massively Parallel Evolution of Recurrent Networks: An Approach to Temporal Processing

Piet Spiessens and **Jan Torreele** *
AI Laboratory
Free University of Brussels
Belgium
e-mail: piet@arti.vub.ac.be
jant@arti.vub.ac.be

Abstract

In this paper we investigate an evolutionary approach to the problem of time-dependent processing with recurrent networks. Both structure and weights of these networks are evolved by a fine-grained parallel genetic algorithm. The parallel nature of this algorithm, which enables the co-evolution of clusters of networks, made it possible to successfully solve three non-trivial temporal processing problems. One of these problems consists of evolving a trail-following behaviour for an artificial ant.

1 Introduction

Many problems that an artificial animal (animat) has to face when it tries to survive in its environment have a temporal extent. Examples include the processing of sensory information, adaptive control and planning. These problems often require learning about temporal sequences with a priori unknown temporal properties.

The use of recurrent neural networks has proven to be a promising approach to the problem of time-dependent processing (Jordan, 1986; Pearlmutter, 1988; Pineda, 1989; Williams & Zipser, 1989). The recurrent connections in such networks allow the (intermediate) results of processing at time $t - \Delta t$ to influence the (intermediate) results of processing at time t, thereby shaping the network's subsequent behaviour by previous responses. Recurrent neural networks seem therefore suited to act as a computational substrate for time-dependent processing in an artificial animal.

1.1 The Problem of Recurrent Learning

Despite the fact that elegant and powerful algorithms—such as the Backpropagation Algorithm (Rumelhart et al., 1986)—have been developed for feedforward networks, no such algorithms are known today for their recurrent counterparts. Indeed, many of the learning algorithms devised for recurrent networks possess undesirable features such as the inability to perform on-line learning, growing memory or computational requirements, or the need for global information. See (Pineda, 1989) for an overview.

One of the main reasons for this is that in contrast with feedforward networks, recurrent networks have a complex dynamics. Even the smallest recurrent networks can engage in very complex and unanticipated behaviours. Although this is exactly what makes recurrent networks interesting from a computational point of view, it also makes them very hard to characterize and analyze. As a consequence, devising appropriate recurrent learning algorithms has proven to be extremely difficult. Due to this lack of insight into the networks' dynamics it is also virtually impossible for the designer to handcraft good initial network architectures.

1.2 An Evolutionary Approach

In this paper, we have studied an alternative approach to the problem of time-dependent processing with recurrent networks. We have used an evolutionary algorithm to simulate the dynamics of a population of recurrent networks which, under the influence of selective pressure, converges to a set of networks that successfully solve the task at hand. This evolutionary approach to the problem of time-dependent processing is appealing for several reasons. It tackles:

1. The *learning problem* for recurrent networks: It is well known that the error surface over the weight space of a neural network, given a non-trivial problem to be trained on, is typically highly rugged. This property is probably even more pronounced for recurrent networks and poses serious challenges to any gradient-based technique for finding optimal weights.
2. The *design problem* for recurrent networks: The use of an evolutionary algorithm also frees us from the need to design good initial architectures for the networks. By allowing the networks to modify their structure, network architectures appropriate for solving the problem under consideration can emerge as the evolution proceeds.

*This work is sponsored by IMPULS contract RF/AI/10: "A Cognitive Architecture for an Autonomous Agent based on Self-Organization"

Genetic Algorithms (GA's) are the most developed and most powerful class of evolutionary algorithms (see (Goldberg, 1989a) for an extensive overview). Nevertheless, the standard GA's do not seem to be ideal for evolving neural networks. Many researchers have found variants of the basic algorithm to be more appropriate (Whitley & Hanson, 1989; Torreele, 1991). In this paper we advocate the use of a fine-grained parallel genetic algorithm.

1.3 A Fine-Grained Parallel Genetic Algorithm

Although GA's are inspired by the Neo-Darwinian Evolution Theory, there are a number of important differences. A first difference is the global selection of genotypes. The selection step in a classical GA requires global information of the population because the average fitness of the genotypes is needed. In nature there is no global selection. Instead, natural selection is a local phenomenon, acting in an individual's local environment. A second difference is the random mating (recombination) of genotypes. In nature there is no random mating: each individual is restricted to the potential mates in its local environment.

The fine-grained parallel GA first introduced in (Manderick & Spiessens, 1989) fully eliminates the global character of GA's. In this algorithm, called FPGA, individuals of the population are placed on a toroidal grid and selection and crossover are restricted to small neighbourhoods on that grid. For the next generation, an individual on a particular location is selected from the individuals in the immediate neighbourhood of that location, and during crossover the mate is also selected from that neighbourhood.

The behaviour of a population under a fine-grained parallel GA is very different from the behaviour under a classical GA. Instead of a straightforward "survival of the fittest" behaviour, one observes a *co-evolution* of clusters of genotypes. This behaviour, which a.o. preserves the diversity in the population, has been shown to be very effective on hard optimization problems (Spiessens & Manderick, 1991; Mühlenbein, 1989). Another important feature of FPGA is that it is possible to implement it on a massively parallel machine. Such an implementation makes it feasible to work with very large populations in a reasonable amount of time. It is well known that the use of large populations dramatically improves the performance of GA's (Goldberg, 1989b).

In the remainder of this paper we will demonstrate how a fine-grained parallel genetic algorithm can be employed to evolve recurrent networks that perform time-dependent processing. The structure of the paper is as follows: first we outline the architecture and the dynamics of the recurrent networks. Then we describe the parallel genetic algorithm and the bitstring representation of the networks. In the next section we present results of our approach using three examples: The problem of generating a non-trivial temporal pattern, the problem of processing a sequence of inputs with a temporal information content, and finally, the problem of evolving purposeful behaviour for an artificial animal.

2 The Recurrent Neural Network Model

The recurrent networks investigated in this paper are composed out of Linear Threshold Elements (LTE's) operating in a discrete-time synchronous manner (figure 1a). LTE's are simple processing elements that linearly sum up their inputs, and compute their output by thresholding this sum:

$$x_k(t) = \sum_j w_{kj} y_j(t-1) \qquad (1)$$

$$y_k(t) = \begin{cases} 1 & \text{if } x_k(t) \geq \theta_k \\ 0 & \text{otherwise} \end{cases} \qquad (2)$$

where $x_k(t)$ is the total input of unit k at time t, $y_k(t)$ is the state of unit k at time t, w_{kj} is the weight of the connection from unit j to unit k and θ_k is the threshold of unit k. In our model, we have constrained the weights to be either $+1$ or -1. That is, the weights can be excitatory or inhibitory, but with the same amount. As a consequence, the threshold values of the units can be thought of as integers.

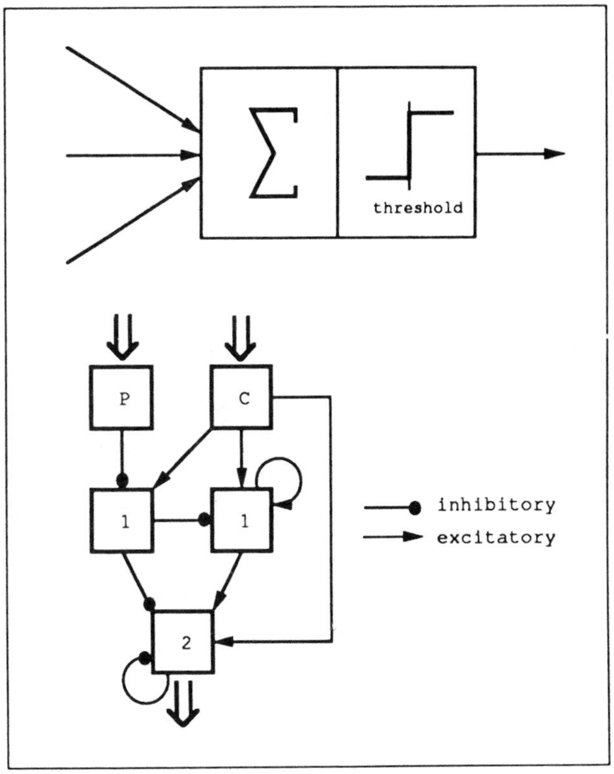

Figure 1: (a) A linear threshold element (LTE). (b) A recurrent network with linear threshold elements. The threshold values are displayed inside the units.

The units that receive external input are referred to as input units, and those that are observed from outside the network are output units. The remaining units are referred to as hidden, since they can only exchange signals with other parts of the network. External input is supplied by clamping the input units' state to zero or one. Notice that the set of input units can be empty. Even in the absence of external input, the networks can show a variety of complex behaviours.

One of the distinguishing properties of recurrent neural networks is that they have state. It is thus conceivable to configure them as simple memory elements. Figure 1b shows such a network. It has two input units: the unit marked with a "P" receives an arbitrary binary pattern, while the unit marked with a "C" is a cue. When the cue is being set to 1 the network remembers the corresponding bit on the pattern input, and sets it on the output neuron on the next occurrence of the cue. Since the delay between two occurrences of the cue can be arbitrarily long, this example clearly illustrates a type of task for which a simple recurrent network is well suited and which cannot be performed by feedforward networks or time-delay neural networks.

3 Co-evolution of Recurrent Networks

3.1 The Fine-Grained Parallel Genetic Algorithm

The fine-grained parallel genetic algorithm FPGA is described in figure 2. All the results in this paper are obtained with this algorithm running on a DAP 510, a massively parallel mesh-connected SIMD computer. Since there is no global control and only local communication in FPGA, the implementation on the DAP is straightforward. Each genotype is placed on a different processor, and it is therefore no problem to parallelize the evaluation and the mutation steps of the algorithm, since they require no interprocess communication. For the selection and the crossover steps it is necessary to get the individuals of the neighbouring processors to the processor itself. This can be done with very efficient machine-level shift operations.

The DAP implementation of FPGA is task-independent, i.e., the user must provide only an evaluation function which computes the fitness of a particular point in the search space. It is also possible to select various crossover operators (one-point, two-point, uniform) and various local selection strategies.

The local selection strategy used in all experiments in this paper is tournament selection. This strategy was chosen because previous experiments have shown it to be very effective (Spiessens & Manderick, 1991). Tournament selection in a particular neighbourhood simply operates by deterministically selecting the genotype with the highest fitness in that neighbourhood. We further used the 2-point crossover, and the parameters were set to: neighbourhood size = 4, crossover rate = 1.0, mutation rate = 0.01.

```
PARFOR each grid element el in the grid DO
  Initialization: Randomly generate an individual
    to occupy el
  Evaluation: Compute the fitness of individual(el)
  REPEAT
    Selection: Calculate the fitness-distribution of
      neighbourhood size individuals in the
      neighbourhood of el. Select according to
      this distribution an individual from the
      neighbourhood to become the new
      individual(el).
    Crossover: Randomly select an individual from
      the neighbourhood. Crossover this individual
      and individual(el) with probability
      crossover rate. Choose an individual from
      the offspring as the new individual(el).
    Mutation: Mutate individual(el) with
      probability mutation rate.
    Evaluation
  UNTIL some end-criterion
```

Figure 2: Outline of FPGA

3.2 A Genotype Representation for Recurrent Networks

Different strategies for representing neural networks exist, with varying degree of developmental specification. Weak specification schemes use loose descriptions of the networks as genotypes (Harp et al., 1989; Bergman, 1989). Strong representation schemes on the other hand, describe network architectures as well as other relevant parameters with a significant degree of detail (Miller et al., 1989).

As the networks investigated in this paper are very sensitive to only minor changes in their parameters or architecture, it is clear that weak specification schemes—such as the stochastic specification scheme used by (Bergman, 1989)—are not appropriate. We have chosen instead for a very strong specification scheme, in which networks are described in all their detail.

To accomplish this, the units of a network are arranged in a rectangular lattice. A neighbourhood structure is then defined over the lattice. This neighbourhood structure can be viewed as a repertoire of connections, that is, as a collection of other units from which a particular unit can eventually receive input. The neighbourhood structure can be problem-dependent, but is the same for all units in the network and once chosen, remains fixed during the course of evolution.

The networks are converted to bit string genotypes by concatenating the encodings of the network units on the lattice in a row-major order. Each individual unit has a binary code of M bits:

$$M = 2N + \lceil \log_2(2N) \rceil$$

where N is the number of neighbours in the neighbourhood structure. Of those M bits, $2N$ bits are used to encode the connectivity of the unit: for each of the N possible incoming connections, one bit is used to indicate the presence of that connection, and a second bit is used to encode the weight of the connection (+1 or −1). The remaining $\lceil \log_2(2N) \rceil$ bits represent the local threshold of the unit, encoded as an integer in the range $-N, \ldots, N-1$. This representation of the networks is closed: any bit string of length $K \times L \times M$ is a valid description of a $K \times L$-unit network on a $K \times L$ lattice.

4 Experiments and Results

We have successfully tested our approach on a number of small though interesting problems. In all of these experiments the networks had to learn to represent useful information about the temporal properties of the problem at hand. We report the results of the approach on three different temporal problems. The first problem demonstrates how the networks can be taught to generate a particular temporal pattern in the absence of any inputs. The second problem involves the extraction of time-dependent information from an input stream in order to categorize it. In the third problem a population of recurrent networks is evolved to allow an "artificial ant" to follow an irregular, broken trail.

4.1 The N-Blinker Problem

Even in the absence of any external inputs, recurrent networks are able to engage into particular temporal behaviours. Training a network to do so is difficult, because no external cues (i.e. inputs) are available to guide its internal dynamics.

Consider the problem of an output unit of a network required to stay active (state 1) for n time steps and then to become inactive (state 0) for another n time steps, repeating this cycle forever. We have named this problem the n-blinker. The problem is clearly of a nontrivial temporal nature. A possible solution would be for a network to develop a counter from 1 to n in its hidden units, together with a flip-flop-like element in its output unit.

We have performed a number of experiments to observe the algorithm's performance on the 4-blinker problem and on the 6-blinker problem, using a population of 2×2 networks with fully connected neighbourhood structure. A standard error measure was used to evaluate the networks' behaviour: they were run for a number of time steps (16 for the 4-blinker, 24 for the 6-blinker) and their fitness was computed by counting the number of correct outputs.

Figures 3 and 4 show the performance of the algorithm for the blinker problems, averaged over 20 runs. Different population sizes were used to demonstrate the importance of working with large populations on hard problems. It is clear that increasing the population size dramatically improves performance. For the 6-blinker problem, for instance, a solution was never found with a population size of 1,024. Note that the design of a network with only 4 units that solves the 6-blinker problem is challenging, because such a network has to autonomously generate a temporal sequence of length 12. Only very large populations provide enough clusters of partial solutions that co-evolve towards optimal networks.

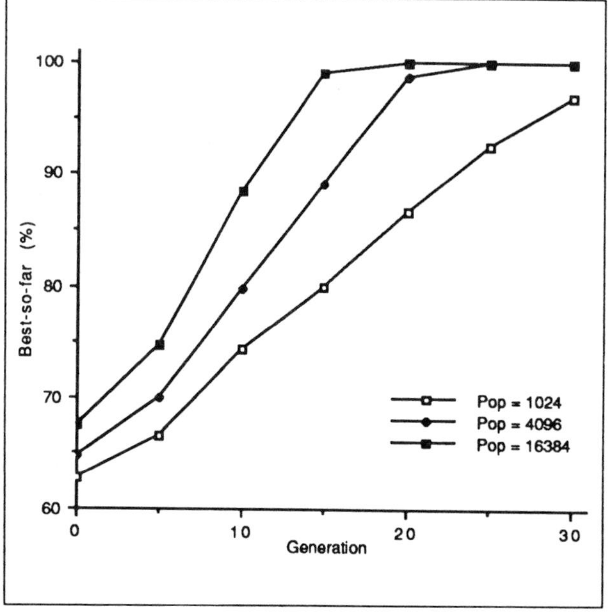

Figure 3: The performance of the algorithm on the 4-blinker problem, averaged over 20 runs.

A typical solution found for the 6-blinker problem is shown in figure 5. Figure 5a shows the architecture and the weights of the network. Figure 5b displays a trace of the activations of the network units during 12 successive time steps. One can clearly see that the network has developed a counter in its hidden units.

4.2 The Temporal 6-Multiplexer

The multiplexer problem is a categorization task for binary strings of length l. Each string belongs either to category "0" or to category "1". The category a string belongs to can be computed by using the first n bits of the string as an unsigned address that points to one of the remaining 2^n bits as the category (where $l = n + 2^n$). The multiplexer is a difficult problem that has been widely used as a testbed for neural network algorithms (e.g. (Barto, 1985)).

The multiplexer problem is typically not of a temporal nature. It can be transformed though into a nontrivial temporal problem for a recurrent network in the following way. An instance of the multiplexer is given as input to the network one bit at a time, i.e., the l bits of the binary string are sequentially clamped onto the input unit, from time t up to time $t+l-1$. The network is then expected to output the correct categorization of the string. This temporal version of the multiplexer incorporates several difficulties. In order to solve it, a network first has to decode the address bits. Next it has to figure out how many time steps it should wait

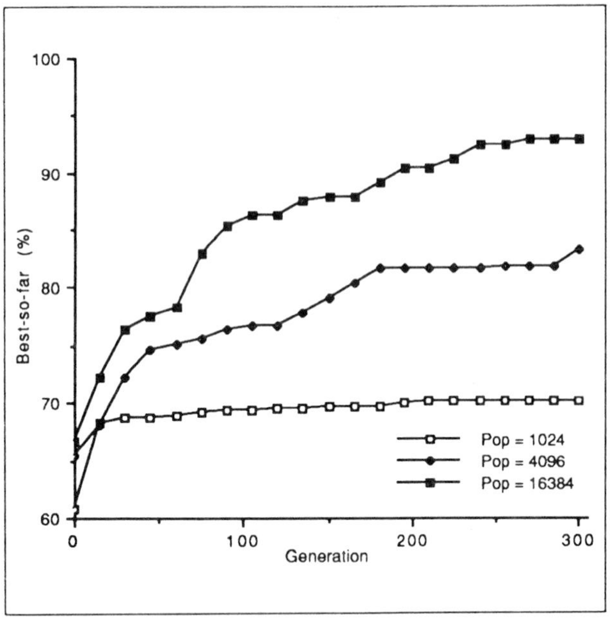

Figure 4: The performance of the algorithm on the 6-blinker problem, averaged over 20 runs.

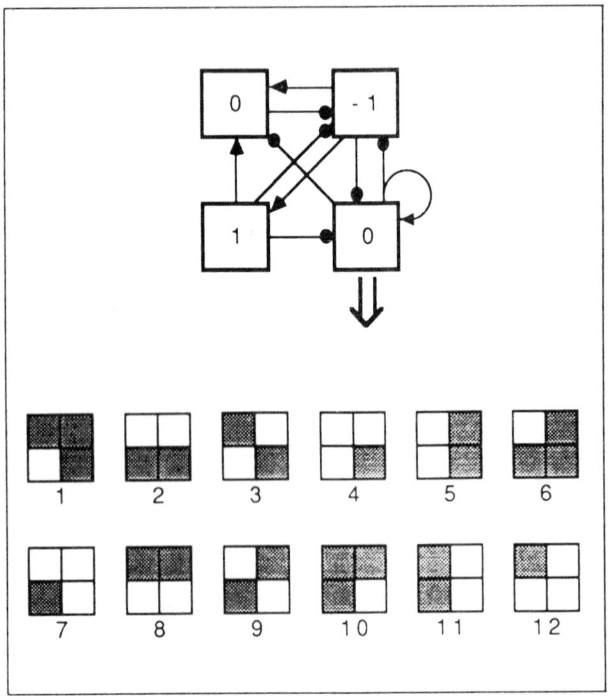

Figure 5: (a) A typical solution found for the 6-blinker problem. Threshold values are displayed inside the units. (b) The activations of the network during 12 successive time steps. The unit on the bottom right is the output unit.

before the appropriate data bit appears on the input unit, and finally it has to transmit this data bit to its output unit.

We have tested the algorithm on an instance of this problem, the temporal 6-multiplexer. Networks with 9 units arranged on a 3×3 lattice are used. The neighbourhood structure imposed on the networks is one with full connectivity. Two different units are chosen to be the input and the output unit of the networks respectively. An evaluation of a network consists of running it on the 64 different binary strings that have to be categorized. The fitness of a network is simply the number of bit strings for which it produces the correct classification on its output unit. In between the evaluations of each of the binary strings, the networks are re-initialized by setting the state of all its units to zero.

Figure 6 shows the performance of the algorithm on the 6-multiplexer, and figure 7 shows a typical solution found. In this experiment we have used a population size of 4,096 and the networks were coded by bit-strings of length 198 (4 threshold bits plus 18 connectivity bits per unit).

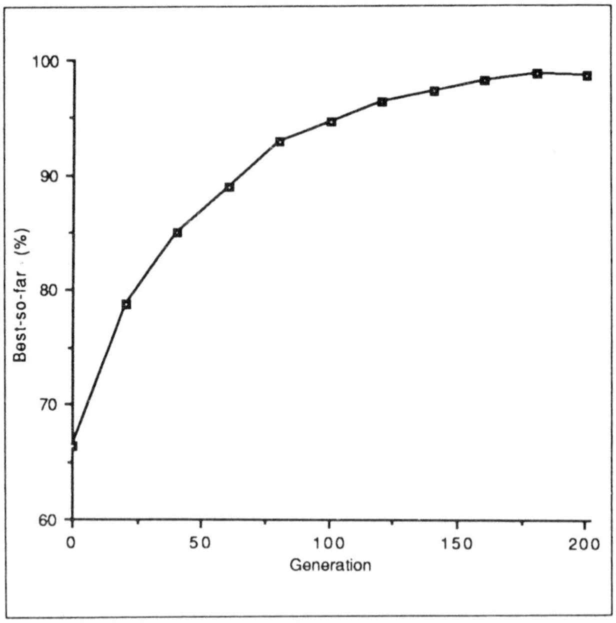

Figure 6: The performance of the algorithm on the 6-multiplexer problem, averaged over 10 runs.

As can be seen from figure 7, the algorithm has used its ability to evolve the structure of the networks in a purposeful way. From the 3×3 possible units, only 7 are effectively used, and from the 89 possible connections only 23 are used. Note that an a priori design of the network structure would not have been trivial.

4.3 The Artificial Ant Problem

The artificial ant problem is a planning problem in which a simple artificial organism (the "ant") has to

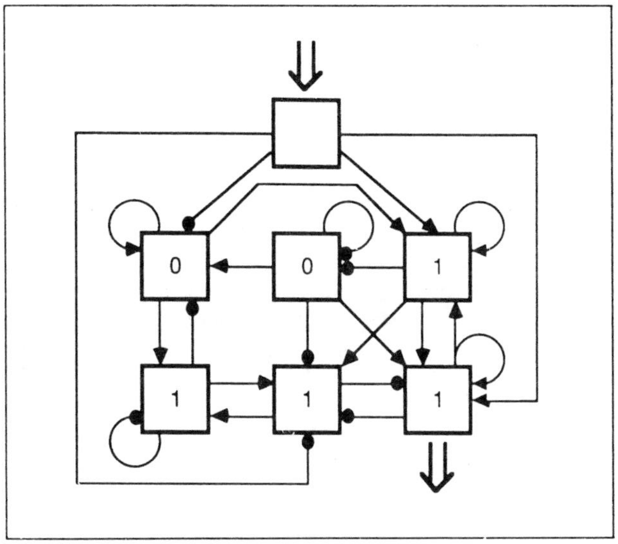

Figure 7: A typical solution for the 6-multiplexer problem. The threshold values are displayed inside the units.

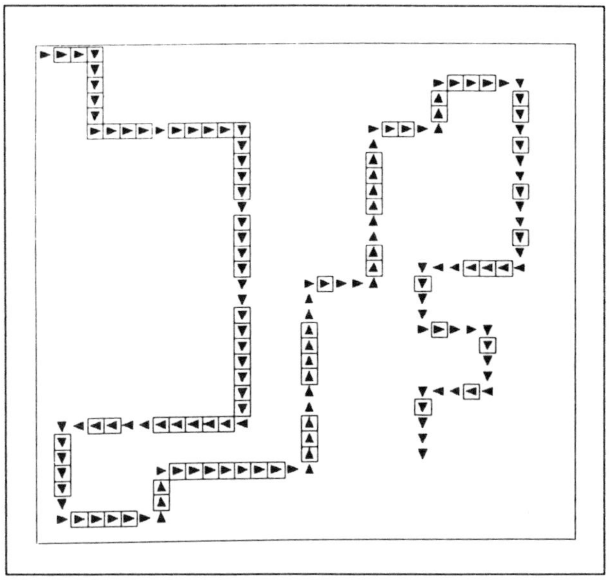

Figure 8: The Artificial Ant environment. The ant has learned the optimal path.

traverse an irregular, broken trail (Jefferson & Collins, 1990). This problem can be viewed as a synthesis of the two previous applications: the sequential processing of sensory data and the autonomous generation of sequences of actions with a temporal information content.

The ant's environment is a 32×32 toroidal grid, containing a noisy trail that consists of 89 stones (figure 8). The ant is initially located at the beginning of the trail. It has one simple sensor indicating the presence or absence of a stone in the location directly ahead. At each time step the ant can choose to move forward, to turn left, to turn right, or to do nothing. The objective of the ant is to traverse the entire trail within a limited number of time steps.

If we consider the fitness of an ant to be the amount of trail that it can follow during its lifetime, then a trail-following behaviour could be evolved by a GA. The fact that the fitness function only conveys information about the number of stones encountered makes this a hard problem. Firstly, this measure does not contain any feedback at all about the actual strategy the ant is following. A second difficulty is caused by the nature of the trail itself. The trail is quite simple in the beginning but gets increasingly more complex towards the end. Simple trail-following strategies will therefore acquire relatively high fitness values in the early stages of the search, taking over large parts of the population. In the later stages of the search these strategies will have to be transformed into more complex ones, while the necessary genetic material might not be present anymore. A last difficulty is caused by the fact that there are only 1024 distinct locations in the environment. Analysis shows that a robust strategy — i.e., a strategy that enables the ant to follow arbitrary paths with the same degree of difficulty — needs about 400 steps to traverse the entire trail (see also (Koza, 1990)). It is clear that a strategy that merely performs a random walk of length 400 will do reasonably well. The successfulness of these random strategies weakens the drive to evolve more intelligent alternatives.

Jefferson et al. (1990) have successfully solved the artificial ant problem problem using a conventional genetic algorithm which evolved a population of finite state automata. The problem was also tackled by Koza (1990). Using his genetic programming approach he discovered LISP S-expressions which enable the ant to traverse the entire trail.

In our approach to this problem we have used the fine-grained parallel genetic algorithm to evolve a population of recurrent networks with 3×3 units. The networks are encoded by bit-strings of length 198. One of the units is assigned to be the input of the network, implementing the ant's simple sensor. Two other units constitute the output of the network, coding for the ant's four possible actions. The neighbourhood structure is full connectivity.

Figure 9 shows the performance of the algorithm on the artificial ant problem, averaged over 10 runs. In 8 of the runs the optimal strategy was found well within 100 generations. It is instructive to also analyze the sometimes intricate strategies of non-optimal genotypes. Figure 10 shows such a strategy. In this example the network has learned to exploit statistical features of the environment. The fact that the gaps in the trail are on average 2 steps long is fruitfully exploited. Although this strategy is obviously far from optimal, the ant is able to traverse a considerable amount of trail.

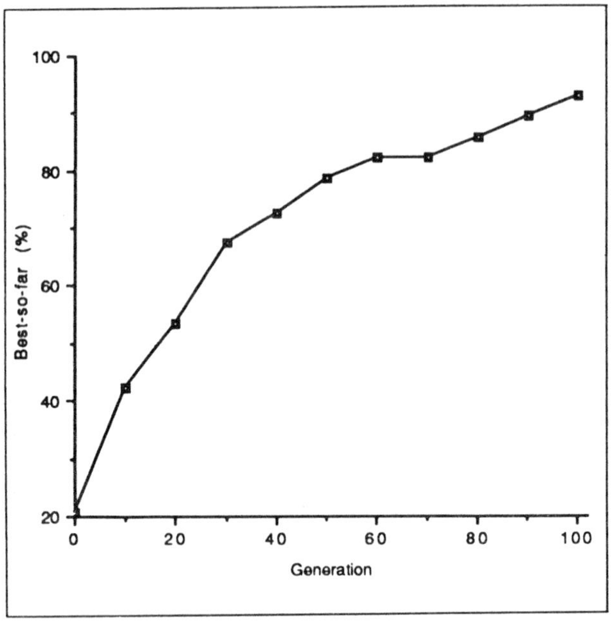

Figure 9: The performance of the algorithm on the Artificial Ant problem, averaged over 10 runs. The population size is 1024, the genotype length is 198.

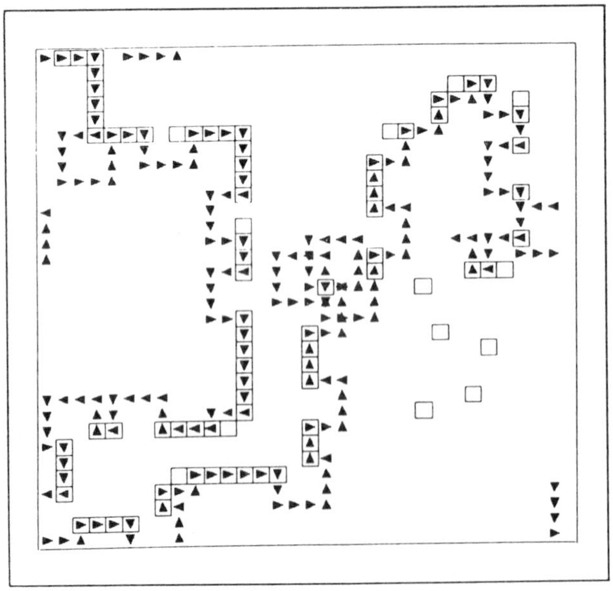

Figure 10: An ant that has learned to exploit statistical features of its environment.

5 Conclusion

One of the ingredients of intelligent behaviour is the ability to deal with problems that have a temporal extent. This often requires learning about temporal sequences with a priori unknown temporal properties. Recurrent networks have proven to be a promising approach to the problem of time-dependent processing. Unfortunately, these networks suffer from severe design and training problems. Motivated by this observation, we used a fine-grained parallel genetic algorithm to simulate the co-evolution of recurrent networks (both their structure and weights) without using any prior information about the temporal nature of the problem to be solved. We demonstrated the viability of our approach by tackling three non-trivial temporal problems. The first problem, called the n-blinker, involved the autonomous generation of a particular temporal pattern. The second problem, a temporal version of the 6-multiplexer, demonstrated how the networks can be taught to process a sequence of inputs with a temporal information content. The final problem consisted of evolving a trail-following behaviour for an artificial ant.

References

Barto, A. (1985). *Learning by Statistical Cooperation of Self-Interested Neuron-like Computing Elements.* COIN Technical Report 85-11, University of Massachusetts.

Belew, R. K. & Booker, L. B. (Eds.) (1991). *Proceedings of the Fourth International Conference on Genetic Algorithms.* Morgan Kaufmann, San Mateo, CA.

Bergman, A. (1989). Self-organization by simulated evolution. In E. Jen (Ed.), *Proceedings of the 1989 Complex Systems Summerschool* Santa Fe.

Goldberg, D. E. (1989a). *Genetic Algorithms in Search, Optimization, and Machine Learning.* Addison Wesley, Reading, MA.

Goldberg, D. E. (1989b). Sizing populations for serial and parallel genetic algorithms. In (Schaffer, 1989).

Harp, S. A., Samad, T., & Guha, A. (1989). Towards the genetic synthesis of neural networks. In (Schaffer, 1989).

Jefferson, D. & Collins, R. (1990). The genesys system: Evolution as a theme in artificial life. In *Proceedings of the Second Conference on Artificial Life*: Addison-Wesley, Redwood City, CA.

Jordan, M. I. (1986). Attractor dynamics and parallellism in a connectionist sequential machine. In *Proceedings of the Eighth Annual Conference of the Cognitive Science Society.*

Koza, J. R. (1990). Evolution and co-evolution of computer programs to control independently-acting agents. In *Proceedings of the First International Conference on Simulation of Adaptive Behaviour*: MIT Press, Cambridge, MA.

Manderick, B. & Spiessens, P. (1989). Fine-grained parallel genetic algorithms. In (Schaffer, 1989).

Miller, G. F., Todd, P. M., & Hegde, S. (1989). Designing neural networks using genetic algorithms. In (Schaffer, 1989).

Mühlenbein, H. (1989). Parallel genetic algorithms, population genetics and combinatorial optimization. In (Schaffer, 1989).

Pearlmutter, B. A. (1988). *Learning State Space Trajectories in Recurrent Neural Networks.* Technical Report Tech. Rep. CMU-CS-88-191, Carnegie Mellon University, Department of Computer Science.

Pineda, F. J. (1989). Recurrent backpropagation and the dynamical approach to adaptive computation. *Neural Computation*, 1(2).

Rumelhart, D. E., Hinton, G. E., & Williams, R. J. (1986). Learning internal representations by error propagation. In *Parallel Distributed Processing: Explorations in the Microstructure of Cognition.* Bradford Books, Cambridge, MA.

Schaffer, J. D. (Ed.) (1989). *Proceedings of the Third International Conference on Genetic Algorithms.* Morgan Kaufmann, San Mateo, CA.

Spiessens, P. & Manderick, B. (1991). A massively parallel genetic algorithm: Implementation and first analysis. In (Belew & Booker, 1991).

Torreele, J. (1991). Temporal processing with recurrent networks: An evolutionary approach. In (Belew & Booker, 1991).

Whitley, D. & Hanson, T. (1989). Optimizing neural networks using faster, more accurate genetic search. In (Schaffer, 1989).

Williams, R. J. & Zipser, D. (1989). Experimental analysis of the real-time recurrent learning algorithm. *Connection Science*, 1(1).

Neural Networks for Visual Tracking in an Artificial Fly

Dave Cliff
School of Cognitive and Computing Sciences, University of Sussex
Brighton BN1 9QH, England, U.K.
E-mail: davec@cogs.susx.ac.uk

Abstract

This paper reports on work using artificial life techniques to study issues in low-level animate vision. Animate vision is visual processing performed with dynamic control of the position/orientation of the image-acquisition device (eye/camera). Male *Syritta pipiens* hoverflies perform animate vision that is closely analogous to some aspects of human animate vision. This paper describes experiments with an artificial animal (i.e. an *animat*) called SyCo. SyCo has been constructed to explore possible processing strategies that reproduce, at the behavioural level, *Syritta*'s animate vision capabilities. The processing strategies are embodied within artificial neural networks which effect local, rather than centralized, control of flight behaviour. Each network is responsible for the generation of one particular visually-mediated behaviour. The design principles for SyCo have been influenced by Braitenberg's *Vehicles* and by Wilson's *Animats*: the emphasis is on minimalism so that specifications are simple rather than complex.

SyCo exists within a dynamic simulated environment that includes other flies. Typically SyCo will select another fly as a visual target, and then dynamically orient itself to keep the target in the centre of the field of view. Simultaneously, SyCo regulates a constant distance to the target. Distance regulation is achieved without explicit internal representation of distance. Seemingly complex behaviours arise from the interaction of a simple agent with its dynamic environment.

Keywords: Artificial Animals; Neural Networks; Animate Vision; Computational Neuroethology.

1 Introduction

Animate vision is the situation where a visual processing system has dynamic control over its image-acquisition system, e.g. we humans are capable of altering the orientation, focus, and convergence of our eyes.

Although animate vision is the *de facto* standard in the natural world (most sighted animals are capable of looking around), the computer vision community has, until recently, been prevented by technological limitations from studying *artificial* animate vision. The last few years have witnessed increasing interest in artificial animate vision (AAV), the motivation coming not only from the manifest need for AAV on autonomous robots but also from the realisation (e.g. Ballard 1987; D. S. Young 1989) that animate vision systems offer significant computational advantages for certain tasks in comparison to the conventional static approach.

Much work in AAV has been influenced by studies of primate animate vision. However, male *Syritta pipiens* hoverflies perform visually-guided behaviour which is functionally analogous to certain aspects of animate vision in primates (Land 1975). The work reported here uses Artificial Life techniques to study animate vision in *Syritta*.

An artificial animal, called SyCo,[1] is being developed with the ultimate intention of qualitatively replicating, at the behavioural level, *Syritta*'s animate vision capabilities. SyCo exists within a dynamic simulated environment that contains other flies with which SyCo interacts, thereby producing animate vision behaviour. SyCo could be classed as an *animat* (Wilson 1990), so a subtitle for this paper could be *animat animate vision*.

SyCo's internal processing is performed by artificial ("connectionist") neural nets. Inspired by Brooks's (1985) *subsumption architecture*, SyCo's networks are each autonomously responsible for generating one particular behaviour in its repertoire: the combined effect of these networks produces an overall competence.

A notable influence on the SyCo project is Braitenberg's (1984) book *Vehicles*, in particular his law of *uphill analysis and downhill design*, which states that it is much harder to analyse a pre-existing entity that exhibits a behaviour of interest than it is to design an artefact which reproduces the same behaviour.

To this end, the connectionist networks in SyCo have been created by design (i.e. "hardwired") rather than via a connectionist learning technique. The rationale for this approach is that using a learning algorithm, e.g. back-propagation (Rumelhart, Hinton, and

[1]From *Syritta computatrix*, the computational hoverfly. A name inspired by Arbib's computational frog *Rana Computatrix* (e.g. Arbib 1987).

Williams 1986), is not necessarily the most informative path to follow. If the network succeeds in generalising, then further investigation is required before the experimenter can state anything of interest; and if it fails, nothing has been gained. Given that some theoretical work is required in either eventuality, I feel that trying to design networks for SyCo from scratch forces the interesting work to be done sooner rather than later. Because most supervised connectionist learning techniques are defined in terms of a set of input data and a corresponding set of (desired) output data, there is a methodological danger in that they enable theory-free models to be constructed: the resulting trained network is essentially a black box. Designing a network to perform the same task *requires* some theory of how the network should operate.

This is not dismissing the use of learning in SyCo, just deferring it. Beer puts the case eloquently:

> "Our focus ...is ...not on the training of homogeneous neural networks, but on the design of heterogeneous ones. Only once the proper neural architectures for controlling the behavior of autonomous agents have been uncovered can we begin to examine ways in which the selective introduction of plasticity [i.e. learning] will increase the flexibility of the resulting controllers" (Beer 1990, p.62).

The networks used in SyCo consist of heterogeneous, richly interconnected, simple processing units. The networks are *minimal models*, i.e. the intention is to account for the given behaviours using as simple specifications as possible. This is in the spirit of the minimalism of Braitenberg's (1984) vehicles and Wilson's (1990) animats. It is also, to an extent, a consideration of biological feasibility: *Syritta*'s reaction times are sufficiently fast to indicate that there are no more than three or four interneurons in the pathway from sensory input to motor output.

This paper describes only two of the many networks that will be required in the ultimate SyCo. The two networks described here allow SyCo to follow a moving visual target. One network is responsible for orienting SyCo so it points at its selected target, and the other ensures that it keeps a roughly constant distance from the target. A significant result of this paper is that it is formally demonstrated that distance regulation is achievable *without explicit internal representation of distance*. Both the networks are based on speculative proposals by Collett and Land (1975). And can, to an extent, be viewed as a verification of their ideas.

For a full description of the current state of the SyCo project (and more details of the contents of this paper) see (Cliff 1991). This work is an instance of *computational neuroethology* (Cliff 1990b; Beer 1990).

The remainder of this paper is as follows. First, the relevant behaviours of *Syritta* are described. Then the two networks are discussed. The discussion focuses on theoretical issues: distance estimation is analysed in some detail. Results are then presented from a SyCo simulation session.

2 Visual Tracking Behaviour

The visually-guided flight-behaviour of *Syritta pipiens* has been documented in detail by Collett and Land (1975). Although the ultimate aim of the SyCo project is to study all of *Syritta*'s behaviours described by Collett and Land (C&L hereafter), this paper focuses only on a subset of behaviours concerned with tracking other flies.

Only Male *Syritta* perform visual tracking. Male *Syritta* have non-uniform, "foveal" vision, where the centre of the field of view is sampled at higher resolution than at the periphery. *Syritta* cannot move its eyes or head independently of its body, so changes in body orientation are the only way of changing the direction of view. Unlike most other flying insects, *Syritta* are capable of flying in directions different to the direction they are pointing in: they can move sideways or backwards relative to their longitudinal axis; and can hover, stationary, in the air for extended periods of time. Groups of *Syritta* tend to congregate in a horizontal plane level with the flowers that provide food. For this reason, C&L recorded only three degrees of freedom of flight: the forwards and sideways components of motion in the horizontal ($x-y$) plane and the angle of orientation relative to an arbitrary fixed world coordinate frame. These three parameters are referred to as $\dot{F}$, $\dot{S}$, and Φ_p respectively: see Figure 1. The velocity (temporal derivative) of orientation also enters the discussion: this is denoted by $\dot{\Phi}_p$.

The orientation of the target fly, Φ_t, is relevant because it affects the so-called "aspect angle" ξ, which is the angle made by the target's longitudinal axis and the line joining the target to the centre of the pursuing fly's head. Finally, the distance from the pursuing fly to the target is denoted by d. Figure 1 also shows the variables measured in tracking situations.

Syritta's tracking behaviour is more complex than simple pursuit. During tracking, the pursuing male fly points accurately towards the target fly, thereby fixating the image of the target in the fovea. C&L state that such foveal fixation is "...maintained by 'continuous' tracking in which the angular position of the target on the retina (θ_e) is continuously translated into the angular velocity of the tracking fly ($\dot{\Phi}_p$) with a latency of roughly 20ms." (Collett and Land 1975, p.1). If the target is outside the fovea, then it is fixated by means of a fast accurate turn of the body, referred to as a

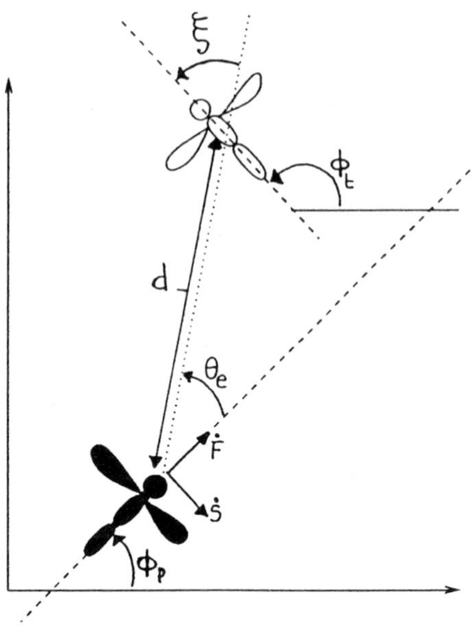

Figure 1: Variables measured in tracking situations. The tracking fly is shown shaded, a target fly is in outline. The orientations of the tracking fly (Φ_p) and of the target fly (Φ_t) are measured relative to a fixed arbitrary world coordinate frame. Components of motion are measured in the direction of ($\dot{F}$) and normal to ($\dot{S}$) the tracking fly's long axis. The angular eccentricity of the target fly (θ_e) is measured relative to tracking fly's long axis. Distance to the target (d) is measured from the tracking fly's head to the centre of the target's body. The "aspect angle" ξ is zero when the target's long axis is radial to the pursuing fly's head.

"saccade", which are performed intermittently. During saccades, $\dot{\Phi}_p$ can rise to values as high as $3000°\text{s}^{-1}$.

The distance to the target is regulated by the pursuing fly, which attempts to maintain an approximately constant distance in the range 5–15cm. The pursuing fly will move forwards or backwards depending on the difference between the actual and desired distances. While tracking a target, the pursuing fly will "retreat" from any other flies which appear too close (typically less than 3cm) in the peripheral visual field.

Mechanisms by which *Syritta* selects one fly as a target when there are several potential flies to choose from are not discussed by C&L.

3 Network Models

3.1 Overview

The aims of the work described here are to create artificial neural networks which can generate behaviour analogous to the foveal fixation and distance regulation discussed above.

Drawing inspiration from Brooks's *subsumption architecture* (Brooks 1985), the internal architecture of the fly is organised according to *behavioural* decomposition rather than *functional* decomposition. Each behaviour is generated by a neural network: one network performs foveal fixation, and another performs distance regulation. Both of these networks acts as a small autonomous agent, oblivious of the activities of any other networks.

Although only two behaviour-generating networks are discussed in this paper, other such networks are posited to exist within some form of subsumption architecture. These other networks would be responsible for behaviours like altitude regulation (as discussed in Section 3.4.1), retreating from non-target flies that come too close, and the optomotor response which helps maintain flight stability in turbulent air. If such networks generate conflicting control signals then competitive inhibition should resolve the conflict close to the point of motor actuation. (see (Cliff 1991) for further details).

As was discussed above, the networks in this model are created by "hardwiring" rather than using a network learning technique. The starting point for these two networks were speculative proposals by C&L (1975, pp.61–64) for possible neural architectures underlying the relevant behaviours. The networks described here constitute an extension of their work insofar as their proposals are not sufficiently detailed to be implemented directly, and indeed won't function without the addition of certain extra features (see Section 3.3). However, this work can be viewed as confirmation of their ideas. As far as I know, (T.S. Collett, Personal Communication 1991), C&Ls' proposals have not been simulated or verified by anyone else.

The similarities between the C&L network architecture and Brook's subsumption architecture (i.e. behavioural rather than functional decomposition; autonomously produced component behaviours combining to form an overall competence) are intriguing. Similarities between the organisational principles of insect sensorimotor control and the subsumption architecture have been noted by other authors (e.g. Altman and Kien 1989).

The units in the "neural" networks are simple processors. Each processing unit u_k takes on a positive activation value $a_k \in [0.0, 1.0]$. The resting a_k of most units is zero, although some units are spontaneously active, with unity activation in the absence of input. The activation a_k is a thresholded sum of the inputs impinging on the unit. The input i_{jk} from unit u_j to unit u_k is, in the simplest case, $a_j w_{jk}$ where w_{jk} is the connection strength: $w_{jk} \in [-1.0, 1.0]$. Connections from one unit to another can be *gated* by other units: in this case $i_{jk} = [0, (a_j w_{jk}) + \sum_{\forall l} a_l w_{ljk}]^+$ where w_{lji} is the (negative) weight of the gating connection from u_l on the connection between u_j and u_k, and $[x, y]^+$ denotes $\max(x, y)$. The output value o_k of u_k is a threshold function of its net input: either $o_k = [0, \sum_{\forall j} i_{jk}]^+$; or a unit step (Heaviside) function such that $o_k \in \{0, 1\}$. Each unit is either excitatory or inhibitory, but not both. That is, for unit k, $\exists c_k \in \{-1, 1\} : \forall j : w_{kj} \neq 0.0 \Rightarrow |w_{kj}|/w_{kj} = c_k$.

Although these units are similar in nature to the units employed in most other "neural network" models, it is important to note that no claims to neural reality are being made here. These units are minimal models of neurons, and nothing more than metaphorical allusion can be claimed of their relationship to biological reality. For example: neurological studies (e.g. D. Young 1989, pp.76–77) indicate that insect giant motion detector neurons are capable of localised habituation to image movement at individual synapses on their dendritic tree: it would require many SyCo units to replicate one such real neuron.

The remainder of this section discusses: the eye-model, which simulates *Syritta*'s foveal sampling of the optic array; then the networks that perform orientation for foveal fixation, and distance regulation.

The output of the networks are flight variables (θ_e and $\dot{F}$) which are assumed to be the inputs to flight-motor slave systems. For the orientation network, flight-motor actuation is simulated by applying the appropriate function (e.g. Equation 2) to the control input.

3.2 The Eye Model

C&L (1975, pp.3–9) provide details of the anatomy and optics of *Syritta*. *Syritta*'s head is approximately hemispherical (radius = 1mm), with the pole of the hemisphere being roughly on the long axis. The surface of the compound eyes occupies much of the surface of the head. The eye-surface is referred to here as the fly's retina. A significant fact is that the angle of view of a photoreceptor unit at a given point on the retina generally makes a non-zero angle with the normal to the retinal surface at that point. This allows the hemispherical retina to sample a total solid angle of around 300°. The area of the retina within about 13° of the long axis samples the area of the optic array 0–5° off the long axis: this roughly defines the foveal region.

C&L (1975, p.6, Fig.3) provide data for how the direction of view varies around the horizontal midline of male *Syritta*'s eye. They note that the angle of view varies approximately linearly in the foveal region, with the linearity reducing towards the periphery. The SyCo eye-model reflects this. Full details of the eye model are given in (Cliff 1991).[2] Here it suffices to note that the eye-model relates the off-axis eccentricity[3] (θ_r) of a point on the retina to the off-axis view-direction (θ_e) at that point:

[2] *Syritta*'s left and right eyes have a small region of frontally-directed binocular overlap, this is reflected in the full SyCo eye-model but is not yet incorporated in the work described here.

[3] The off-axis eccentricity of a point P is the angle $\angle POF$ where: O is the centre of the eye-sphere; and F is the point where the long axis intersects the frontal surface of the eye-sphere.

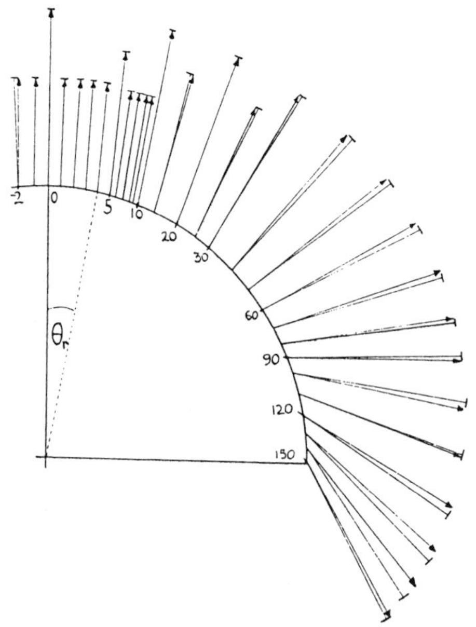

Figure 2: Comparison of $\theta_e = \mathcal{V}(\theta_r)$ and the original data. Vectors with arrowed heads are original data; vectors with tee-shaped heads are generated by $\mathcal{V}$. The eye surface is represented as a section of a circle. The tail of each vector is labelled with the view direction (in degrees) of the photoreceptor at that point on the eye surface.

$$\theta_e = \mathcal{V}(\theta_r) \quad (1)$$

In accordance with the biological data, $\mathcal{V}$ is linear in θ_r in the foveal region and quadratic in the periphery. Figure 2 shows a comparison between the original data and the view-directions generated by $\mathcal{V}$.

3.3 Orientation: Target fixation

C&L state that, when performing smooth tracking of a foveated target, the angular velocity $\dot{\Phi}_p$ of the pursuing fly is related to the angular position (off-axis eccentricity) of the image of the target θ_e by the relation:

$$\dot{\Phi}_p = k\theta_e \quad (2)$$

where $k \approx 30\text{s}^{-1}$. A similarly linear relation (with some saturation at the upper end of the range) is proposed by C&L to account for saccadic turns. The simple nature of this equation is interesting. It states that image *position* is sufficient to perform tracking: image *velocity* is not measured. C&L provide (1975 p.27) results from simulation studies using Equation 2 which are in good agreement with the observed data.

They also provide a speculative neural architecture for performing this calculation. Figure 3 shows a version of their network. The network is intended to serve for both smooth and saccadic tracking movements.

In its original formulation, the network has a number of problems: some form of competitive inhibition needs

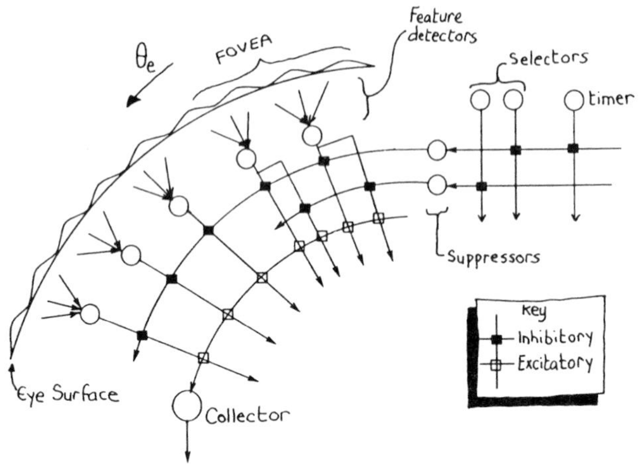

Figure 3: Orientation network for one eye (after (Collett and Land 1975, p.62, fig. 43a)). The retinal image is sampled by a number of *detector* units with distinct receptive fields. Each detector signals when small dark objects (i.e. flies) are present. The detectors feed onto a *collector* unit whose output determines the rate of turn. The connections from the detectors to the collector are gated by *suppressor* units which are spontaneously active. The smooth suppressor only gates connections to the collector in the foveal region. The suppressors are inhibited by *selector* units which determine whether smooth or saccadic tracking is performed. If neither selector is active, then the fly is not tracking other flies. A timer unit, active only intermittently, enables full inhibition of the saccadic suppressor, while the smooth selector is independently capable of complete disinhibition.

to be applied to the detectors before they feed on to the collector in order to prevent superposition effects; the smooth and saccadic selectors should be in competition to enforce mutual exclusion, and interocular effects have to be accounted for. Interocular effects are situations where conflicting signals from the left and right eyes have to be resolved. For example, if the left eye gives a response indicating a saccadic turn to the left, while the right eye is indicating that a very weak turn to the right should be made for smooth tracking, then the left eye should be ignored because the right eye is in the process of foveating a target. These problems have been remedied in the current SyCo model, leading to a situation where SyCo 'selects' one target-fly for tracking from a number of potential targets: see (Cliff 1991) for further details.

One detail omitted by C&L is how the fly might extract θ_e from its visual input: recall that θ_e is the off-axis eccentricity of the image of the target fly in the *optic array* of the pursuing fly. However, the fly's optic array is not uniformly represented on its *retina*: it is warped by nonlinearities in the view-direction function $\mathcal{V}$ (Equation 1). Thus, to effect the linear transformation between θ_e and $\dot{\Phi}_p$ in Equation 2, nonlinearities in $\mathcal{V}$ must be accounted for.

This is achieved in SyCo by setting the weights on the connections between the detectors and the collector to be proportional to $\mathcal{V}$. Specifically, if w_i denotes the weight from detector i to the collector, and the off-axis eccentricity of detector i on the retina (i.e. *not* the detectors view-direction, but its position on the eye) is θ_{ri}, then $w_i = \mathcal{V}(\theta_{ri})$. This results in the output of the collector being linearly proportional to the view-direction of the target (θ_e), rather than the retinal position of the active detector.

3.4 Distance Regulation from Image Height

As noted above, when male *Syritta* track other flies, they attempt to maintain a constant distance (within 5–15cm) between themselves and their targets.

C&L (1975, p.30) formulated an expression that relates the forwards velocity of the pursuing fly ($\dot{F}$: see Figure 1) to the difference between the current distance to the target (d) and the desired distance (d_0). Their formula is:

$$\dot{F} = k'(d - d_0) \tag{3}$$

where k' is a conversion constant of dimension s^{-1} in the range 10–20.

C&L (1975, pp.10–11) discuss a number of possible mechanisms by which the pursuing fly might measure the distance d, concluding that measuring the vertical height of the retinal image of the target was the most likely mechanism. Their reasoning was that the (horizontal) width of the target's image has a fourfold variance dependent on the target fly's aspect angle ξ, whereas the vertical height of the target's image is unaffected by these factors yet varies with the distance d.

As Bruce and Green (1985, p.264) point out, this argument is valid only so long as the two flies are at the same altitude. If the target fly and the pursuing fly are not at the same altitude, then the vertical height of the target's image is affected by the magnitude of the altitude difference. Bruce and Green go no further than making this qualitative observation, and I have been unable to locate any other discussion of this topic in the literature.

In order to design SyCo, a more rigorous theoretical analysis is required. The two key questions are:

- Can the effect of altitude be detected and compensated for when judging distance?
- What is the relationship between the vertical height of the retinal image of the target and the distance

to the target, given the non-uniform resolution of SyCo's eyes?

Mathematical analysis of these issues is presented below, followed by a brief description of the model network responsible for distance regulation. The distance-regulation mechanism is only operative for foveated targets, so the discussion that follows applies only to the fovea.

3.4.1 Altitude Effects

If the target fly's altitude is not very close to that of the pursuing fly, then the altitude difference affects the vertical height of the target's image of the pursuing fly. The effect of the altitude difference on vertical image height is greatest when the target fly is oriented radially with respect to the pursuing fly, so that $\xi = 0$.

Studying this worst case, let Δa denote the difference in altitude and d denote the horizontal distance (i.e. in the $x - y$ plane) between the two flies. We can take advantage of the inherent symmetry of the problem and restrict the study to cases where $\Delta a \geq 0$. The values Δa and d are measured between the centre of the target's body and the centre of the tracking fly's head. Furthermore we assume that the target is a cylinder of length l and diameter (width) w. This cylinder can be considered as the bounding volume for the target fly. If α_v denotes the vertical angular extent of the target's image in the pursuer's optic array, then it can be shown that:

$$\tan \alpha_v = \begin{cases} \frac{\Delta a l + dw}{\Delta a^2 + d^2 - \frac{1}{4}(l^2+w^2)} & : \Delta a > (w/2) \\ \frac{w(d-\frac{l}{2})}{(d-\frac{l}{2})^2 + \Delta a^2 - (\frac{w}{2})^2} & : \Delta a \in [0, w/2] \end{cases} \tag{4}$$

The expression for α_v when $\Delta a > (w/2)$ covers the case where the difference in altitude is such that the underside of the cylinder is visible. In order to answer the question posed above, *Can the effect of altitude be detected and compensated for when judging distance?*, it is sufficient to notice that α_v is symmetric in Δa and d, so w and l are the factors of interest. Because (for *Syritta*) $w = 2\ mm$ and $l =$ 8mm, α_v is more sensitive to changes in altitude than to changes in distance:

$$\frac{\partial \alpha_v}{\partial \Delta a} > \frac{\partial \alpha_v}{\partial d}$$

From this it can be inferred (and demonstrated: see (Cliff 1991)) that minor changes in altitude are detectable before comparatively large changes in distance. Once $\Delta a/d >\sim 0.01$, the lowest point of the target's image will be noticeably above the midline of the eye and correcting movements can be made to reduce Δa to zero. Therefore we assume the existence of mechanisms which regulate altitude, keeping Δa as close to zero as possible.

3.4.2 Distance from Image Height

When $a \approx 0$, approximations can be made (Cliff 1991) on Equation 4 which produce an estimate $\widehat{d}$ of the distance to the target, based on the vertical angular extent of the target in the pursuing fly's optic array:

$$\widehat{d} = \frac{w}{\alpha_v} \tag{5}$$

But equation 5 uses the vertical angular extent (α_v) of the target in the *optic array* of the pursuing fly. If the fly's eyes were uniform resolution then the relationship between α_v and the vertical angular height *on the fly's retina* would be simple. However, foveal vision implies that the optic array is not represented uniformly on the retina, so further analysis is required: the vertical angular height of the target's image on the retina (β_v) depends not only on the distance to the target, but also on the target's off-axis eccentricity θ_e. That is, $\beta_v = \mathcal{W}(d, \theta_e)$.

Now the view-direction function $\mathcal{V}$ is linear in the foveal region, i.e. $\mathcal{V} = c_1 + c_2\theta_r$, (n.b. c_1 is close to zero) so (cf. Equation 1):

$$\frac{d\theta_e}{d\theta_r} = c_2$$

and c_2 is small, hence $\frac{\partial \beta_v}{\partial \theta_e}$ is sufficiently small in the foveal area that we can safely ignore θ_e (see (Cliff 1991) for further details).

Further approximations can be made by assuming that the target is at the same altitude ($a \approx 0$) and that $d >\approx$ 1cm, and incorporating knowledge of the typical height of conspecifics (other *Syritta*), i.e. w. A good approximation $\widehat{d}$ to the true distance d is then given by:

$$\widehat{d} = \frac{1}{c_2\beta_v} \tag{6}$$

So the estimated distance-to-target $\widehat{d}$ is proportional to the reciprocal of the vertical angular extent of the image of the target, and this is true whether the height of the image is measured in the optic array *or* the retinal image. This theoretical result is supported in part by the available hoverfly neurological data: neurological studies of hoverfly visual interneurons (Collett and King 1975) revealed "feature detector" units that were sensitive to the angular height of small dark "blobs" moving through their receptive fields. The responses of these blob detectors scales roughly as the reciprocal of image height. This suggests that the detector units may give a response indicative of the distance to a target of known height. See (Cliff 1991) for further details.

Thus the term $d - d_0$ in Equation 3 can be replaced by $\widehat{d} - \widehat{d_0}$ where $\widehat{d_0}$ is calculated using Equation 5 with the value α_0 being the α_v corresponding to d_0. Substituting $\widehat{d} - \widehat{d_0}$ into Equation 3 and simplifying gives an approximation to $\dot{F}$:

$$\widehat{F} = k'w\left(\frac{1}{\alpha_v} - \frac{1}{\alpha_0}\right) \qquad (7)$$

This form of the equation is more appealing than Equation 3 for two reasons. First, it makes the role of w explicit; i.e. knowledge of the height of conspecifics is required in order to judge their distance. Second, it expresses forward velocity in terms of image height rather than in terms of distance: *distance regulation is achievable without any explicit internal representation of distance.* This point will be returned to in the conclusions.

3.4.3 Distance Regulation Network

The network that performs distance-regulation behaviour is inspired by C&Ls' proposal, but somewhat more complex because the C&L version allows the distance-measuring unit to take on both positive and negative activations and to both inhibit and excite other units simultaneously.

The network produces a signal proportional to the image height of a dark blob in its receptive field. The network operates on simulated 2D images which represent a visual signal after centre-surround (lateral inhibition) processing, so that the image-height measurements are derived from image *contrast* rather than image *intensity*.

The network is illustrated in schematic form in Figure 4. Assemblies of the processing units described above are configured to give a local estimate of image height at each column of the image. The input from each photoreceptor is weighted by a factor proportional to the angle of acceptance of that receptor, which helps to compensate for the non-uniform sampling of the optic array. The outputs from these height-sensitive subnetworks feed into two subnetworks: one comprises an array of veto units which operate to ensure that only blobs with approximately the correct aspect (height:length) ratio act as trigger features; the other network effects inhibition which limits excitation in the output stage of the network to the unit that is sampling the centre of the blob. Full details of this network are given in (Cliff 1991).

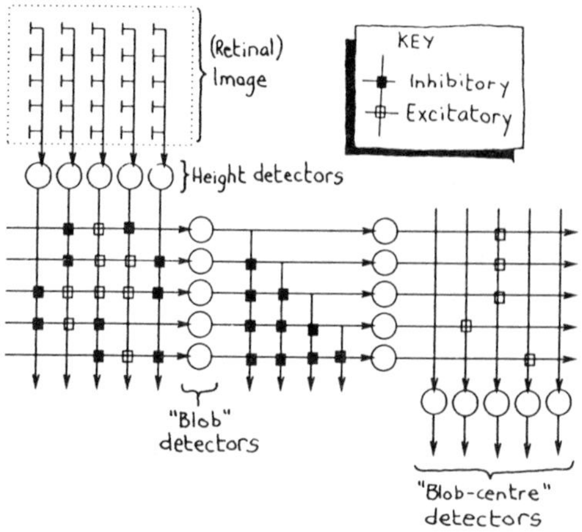

Figure 4: Distance regulation network (Schematic)

4 Results

The figures shown below illustrate SyCo operating in a dynamic simulated environment. To simplify the results, the environment contains only two other (target) flies. Simulations have been performed with more target flies: increasing the population does not degrade SyCo's performance, and the results are essentially the same as those shown here. The target flies move around the environment in a predetermined fashion. They are 'dumb', in that they don't perceive or react to changes around them.

The simulations shown here were performed by solving the projection equations for the eye (rather than using ray-tracing) to determine which detectors should be active. Noise is introduced by the quantisation inherent in using a finite number of non-overlapping receptive fields, and a small amount of simulated crosswinds/turbulence in the environment. Work is underway on a new SyCo that is tolerant to sensor noise and internal noise, and on embedding the networks described above in the ray-tracing system discussed in (Cliff 1990a).

Figure 5 shows an $x - y$ plot of the positions of the three flies every 0.04s, which demonstrates that, when the targets are stationary, SyCo will orient itself towards one of the targets and then move towards that target until the preferred distance d_0 is maintained.

Figures 6 and 7 shows the results from a simulation session in which the two target flies are moving on circular paths at constant angular velocities, opposite in sign but of the same order of magnitude.

Finally, Figure 8 shows $x - y$ plots for two further simulation sessions. The parameter settings and initial values for these sessions are the same as those for Figure 6: the only difference is in the random number seed which generates the (zero mean) noise in the simulation. Although the three sessions are all similar for roughly the first second (SyCo retreats from the targets), the minor changes in relative positions of the two targets that result from the different seed lead to observably different flight-paths for SyCo.

The results shown here are for orientation networks with 98 receptive fields in each eye. This requires a total of about 400 units with around 20000 connections. The constants k in Equation 2 and k' in Equation 7 are 30s^{-1} and 20s^{-1} respectively. The value of α_0 in Equation 7 corresponds to $d_0 = 10\text{cm}$. Data is generated at 50 frames per simulated second.

The graphs illustrate that SyCo manages to maintain the desired distance to the target, and furthermore fixates a selected target in the fovea when the magnitude of the target's image velocity $|\dot{\theta}_e| <\sim 30°s^{-1}$. Foveal fixation in real *Syritta* also breaks down when $|\dot{\theta}_e| >\sim 30°s^{-1}$ (Collett and Land 1975, p.20).

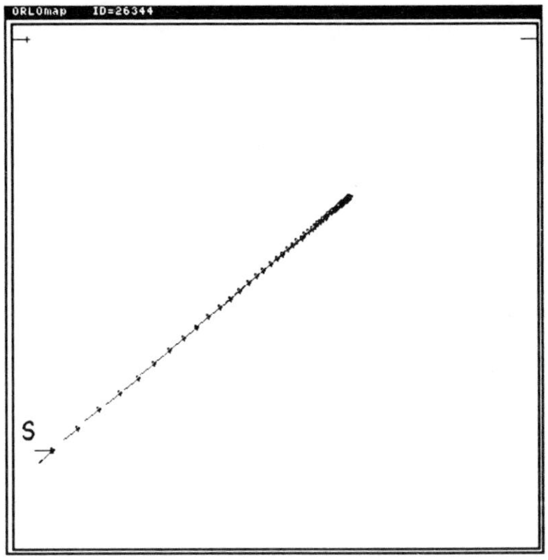

Figure 5: Positions of the three flies every 0.04s. The two targets are stationary (they are at the top left and right corners of the plot). SyCo starts at the point marked **S**, orients itself towards one of the targets, then reduces the distance to the preferred value d_0.

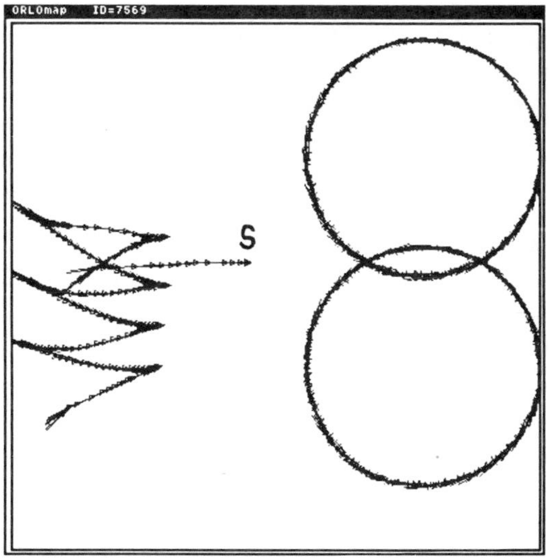

Figure 6: Two targets moving on circular paths (target 1 traces the upper circle). SyCo dynamically alters its position and orientation in order to foveate a target: same simulation session as shown in Figure 7.

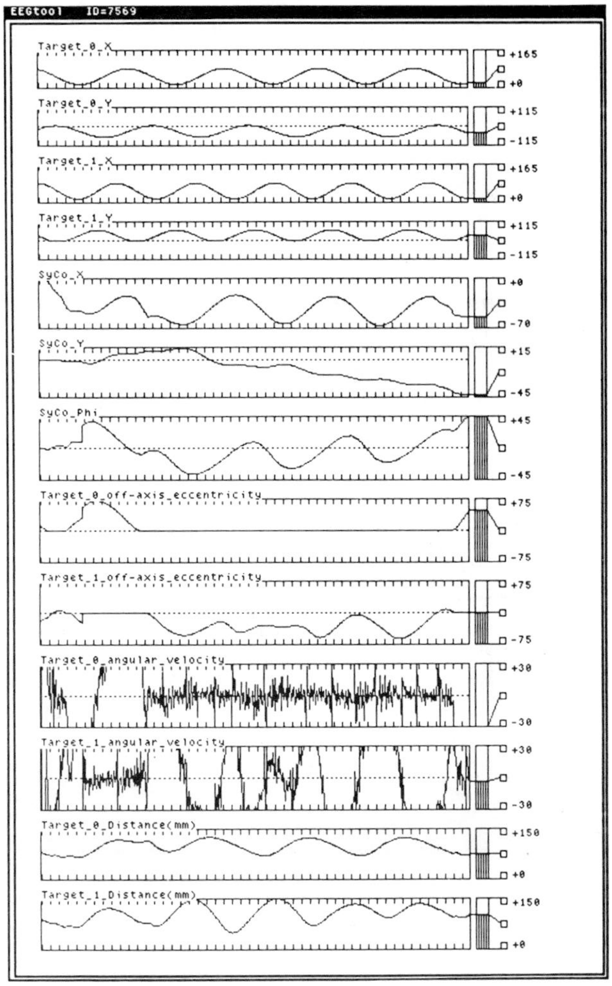

Figure 7: Results for experiment with two targets moving on circular paths (plotted in Figure 6). The abscissa is time (10.0s in total): tick-marks are every 0.2s. Angular measures are in degrees, distances in mm. From the top, the first four graphs give the $x - y$ positions of the two targets in space. The next two graphs show SyCo's $x - y$ position, followed by Φ_p. The graphs labelled `_off-axis_eccentricity` show θ_e for the two targets; those labelled `_angular_velocity` show $\dot{\theta}_e$ for the two targets. The final two graphs show the distances to the targets. A target is being tracked when both θ_e and $\dot{\theta}_e$ are close to zero: target 0 is tracked from $t = 0.1$ to $t = 0.6$ and $t = 2.2$ to $t = 9.6$; target 1 is tracked from $t = 1.0$ to $t = 2.5$ and from $t = 9.6$ to $t = 10.0$. The step change in Φ_p at $t = 1.0$ is a saccade, made to foveate target 1. Distance regulation is attempted, but because the targets are constantly moving, the required distance is only approximately maintained.

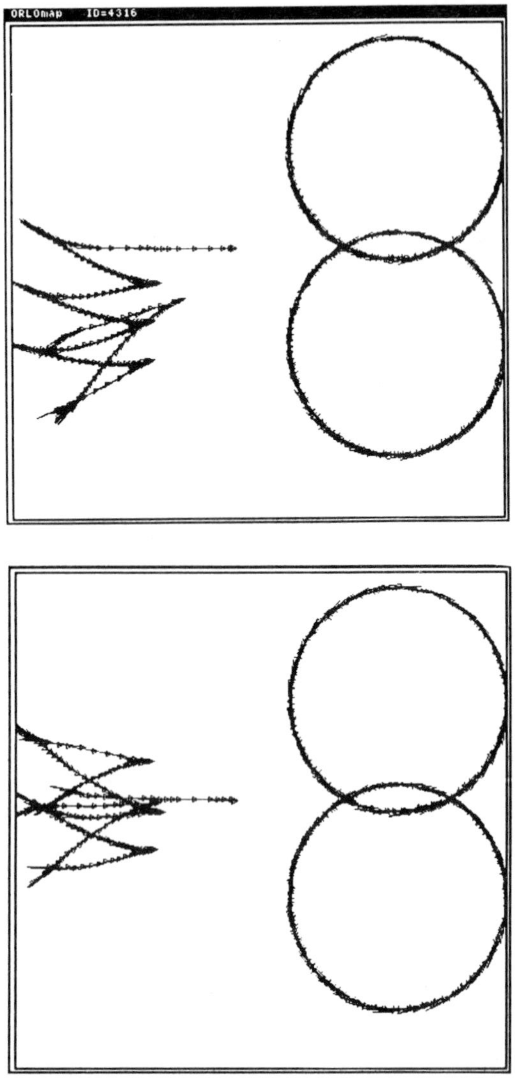

Figure 8: Positions of the three flies every 0.04s. Same initial conditions as the trace in Figure 6; minor variations in the positions of the two targets resulting from noise lead to observably different patterns of behaviour in SyCo.

5 Conclusions

The results illustrate that, qualitatively at least, SyCo performs visual tracking like *Syritta*. In accordance with C&Ls' proposals, the simple networks autonomously generate visual behaviours: orientation is maintained by measuring the target's image *position* rather than image *velocity*; and distance regulation is performed without SyCo having any internal representation of distance. C&L proposed that *Syritta* measure vertical image height, but did not perform the analysis leading to Equation 7. Nevertheless, it is interesting to note that their proposals predate the current vogue for behavioural decomposition and "Intelligence without Representation" (Brooks 1991) by over a decade.

The graphs of the previous section don't show the apparent complexity of SyCo's interaction with its environment. Viewing animation sequences of tracking in multi-fly environments, it is difficult not to ascribe *goals* or *intentions* to the SyCo-vehicle (an issue repeatedly emphasized in (Braitenberg 1984)). Yet the perceived complexity of SyCo's actions is not easily explained by examination of its internal architecture: SyCo comes close to Gibson's (e.g. 1979) notion of *direct perception*.

Rather, the complexity is an emergent phenomena or *gestalt* effect of the interaction of a simple agent with a (relatively) complex environment. This may have philosophical implications. SyCo is sufficiently simple that there seems to be no place for the ghost in the machine. If we ask (*pace* Nagel (1974)) *What is it like to be a hoverfly?*, a reasonable answer seems to be *Not much*!

Acknowledgements

Thanks to Inman Harvey, Hilary Tunley, David Young, and the (anonymous) reviewers for their comments.

References

Altman, J. S. and J. Kien. 1989. New models for motor control. *Neural Computation*, 1:173–183.

Arbib, M. A. 1987. Levels of modelling of mechanisms of visually guided behaviour. *The Behavioral and Brain Sciences*, 10:407–465.

Ballard, D. H. 1987. Eye movements and spatial cognition. TR 218, University of Rochester Computer Science Department, November 1987.

Beer, R. D. 1990. *Intelligence as Adaptive Behaviour: An Experiment in Computational Neuroethology*. Academic Press.

Braitenberg, V. 1984. *Vehicles: Experiments in Synthetic Psychology*. Cambridge MA: M.I.T. Press Bradford Books.

Brooks, R. A. 1985. A robust layered control system for a mobile robot. A.I. Memo 864, M.I.T. A.I. Lab, September 1985.

Brooks, R. A. 1991. Intelligence without representation. *Artificial Intelligence*, 47:139–159.

Bruce, V. and P. R. Green. 1985. *Visual Perception: physiology, psychology and ecology*. London: Lawrence

Erlbaum Associates.

Cliff, D. T. 1990a. The computational hoverfly; a study in computational neuroethology. In J.-A. Meyer and S. W. Wilson, editors, *From Animals to Animats: Proceedings of the First International Conference on Simulation of Adaptive Behavior (SAB90)*, pages 87–96, Cambridge MA: M.I.T. Press Bradford Books.

Cliff, D. T. 1990b. Computational neuroethology: A provisional manifesto. In J.-A. Meyer and S. W. Wilson, editors, *From Animals to Animats: Proceedings of the First International Conference on Simulation of Adaptive Behavior (SAB90)*, pages 29–39, Cambridge MA: M.I.T. Press — Bradford Books.

Cliff, D. T. 1991. *Animate Vision in an Artificial Fly: A Study in Computational Neuroethology.* DPhil thesis, University of Sussex School of Cognitive and Computing Sciences.

Collett, T. S. and A. J. King. 1975. Vision During Flight. In G. A. Horridge, editor, *The compound eye and vision of insects*, pages 437–466, Oxford: Clarendon Press.

Collett, T. S. and M. F. Land. 1975. Visual control of flight behaviour in the hoverfly, *Syritta pipiens* L. *Journal of Comparative Physiology*, 99:1–66.

Gibson, J. J. 1979. *The Ecological Approach to Visual Perception.* Boston: Houghton Mifflin.

Land, M. F. 1975. Similarities in the visual behaviour of arthropods and men. In M. S. Gazzaniga and C. Blakemore, editors, *Handbook of Psychobiology*, pages 49–72. Academic Press, New York, 1975.

Nagel, T. 1974. What is it like to be a bat? *Philosophical Review*, LXXXIII.

Rumelhart, D. E., G. E. Hinton, and R. J. Williams. 1986. Learning internal representations by error propagation. In D. E. Rumelhart and J. L. McClelland, editors, *Parallel Distributed Processing, Volume 1: Foundations*, pages 318–362. Cambridge MA: M.I.T. Press Bradford Books.

Wilson, S. W. 1990. The animat path to AI. In J.-A.-Meyer and S. W. Wilson, editors, *From Animals to Animats: Proceedings of the First International Conference on Simulation of Adaptive Behavior (SAB90)*, pages 15–21. Cambridge MA: M.I.T. Press Bradford Books,

Young, D. 1989. *Nerve Cells and Animal Behaviour.* Cambridge: Cambridge University Press:

Young, D. S. 1989. Logarithmic sampling of images for computer vision. In A. G. Cohn, editor, *Proceedings of the Seventh conference of the Society for the Study of Artificial Intelligence and Simulation of Behaviour*, pages 145–150. London: Pitman/Morgan Kaufmann.

An approach to sensorimotor relevance

Eric Dedieu & Emmanuel Mazer
LIFIA
46 av. Felix Viallet, 38031 Grenoble cedex — France
e-mail: manu@lifia.imag.fr

I— INTRODUCTION

During the last 20 years a great deal of work has been done to develop robot programming techniques. However, the current systems are limited when dealing with the variability of their environment even if it has been carrefully modelized.

The way robots are currently programmed lacks a proper interface between the physical world and their representation of it. The goal topic of this paper is "sensorimotor processing" as the search for such an interface. This problem addresses in fact the very conception of what a model is in robotics. Several researchers have already started to believe that the basic concepts used in robot programming were not suitable to develop advanced robot applications, as Varela (1988), Edelman (1987) or Brooks (1986).

Which conditions could be required for sensorimotor processing to yield a relevant environmental interface for a robot ? What methods could be used to develop such processing ? The present paper is a tentative proposition to answer these subjects.

Note: the term "sensorimotor" is used to stress that one cannot speak of sensory-flavored concepts, such as models or perception, without taking into account the action or the robot.

II— AN OVERVIEW OF SENSORIMOTOR PROCESSING IN ROBOTICS

Sensorimotor processing is a widely studied topic, from ethology and psychology to robotics, information sciences or artificial intelligence. Here we chose to tackle problems that appear mostly in robot programming, but we take a point of view that has a strong A.I. flavor.

Two main classes of robot programming systems exist today: model-based systems & reactive systems.

The model-based systems

These systems use a model of the environment which is given explicitely. A model is a collection of data structures that have a well defined function. For example the environment is modeled with predicates on symbols (STRIPS (Fikes & Nilson 1971)), with cartesian frames (LM (Mazer & Miribel 1984)) or with polyhedra (HANDEY (Lozano-Pérez *et al.* 1989)). A given environment is described to the system by instanciating the corresponding data structures, possibly from sensory values.

Classically, a problem is decomposed into levels which manipulate models of different natures, thus needing specific tools for each — often programming languages (e.g. in manipulation robotics it could be from top to bottom a predicate-based model, a grasp planner, a path planner, and a servo control level). In practice, this kind of hierarchical system is not reliable, because it does not take into account the complex interactions between the different levels.

Reactive programming

Considering the poor performances of model-based robots in non ad-hoc environments, a recent trend has been to program robots without any explicit model of the world. The most famous instance of this view is Brook's (1986, 1988) pioneer work on mobile robots. These are controlled using the «subsumption architecture», which implements parallel reactive loops between actual sensors and actuators. The collaboration of several "reflexes" then yields interesting globally "emerging" behaviors.

Most reactive architectures actually amount to rule-based systems where the left conditions of the rules are required to come from physical sensors. It was their key methodological contribution, but it is now their limit, too. Behaviors to be implemented must be designed according to the existence of specific sensors that permit to do it. In other words, behaviors are chosen because the programmer already had a good idea of *how* he could implement them from existing sensors. An a-priori arbitrary model of the environment still exists in this implicit sense.

A strong motivation for the subsumption architecture was to build robots incrementally, and make them evolve to become more and more complex. Yet the actual incrementability is very limited, because (i) one needs to construct a new specific sensor for each behavior, (ii) when adding a new behavior, one should take into account the *details* of implementation of already existing ones. After the original three-layer architecture described by Brooks (1986), other "incremental" constructions amounted to sequencing quite independent processes (Brooks 1988; Connell 1988). This is a very restricted kind of incrementality.

A basic issue for modeling

These two approaches, however different, have a common characteristic: the use of a modeling primitive (symbol, sensor,...) is specific to the function it was designed for. A model of the environment is something the programmer imposes to the robot according to his own conception.

III— THE PROBLEM OF RELEVANCE

We wish to substitute to the programmer's model a model that is grounded into the physical capabilities of the robot. We think any modeling primitive should be a generic available tool, i.e. its first interest is to be related to a property of the physical world, and only after that comes the issue of determining how to interpret and use it.

1) The inadequacy of "artificially implemented" modeling primitives

Physical and simulated robots

The use of a physical robot for experiments is a key point that has often been forgotten. There is a tremendous gap between robotic results in simulations and effective physical applications (further discussion in e.g. Smithers & Malcolm 1988; Aloimonos 1990; Brooks 1986). We think this gap comes from a bad approach to sensory processing.

Simulations often make very strong assumptions about the interface between a robot and its environment. It is often too obvious which sensory data are relevant to use (all!), in which way (often just take the direct value), and how to interpret them (as strongly related to explicit objects of the world...). Typical examples are Findler & Allan 1974, or Sutton 1990. Less trivial are the systems of Booker (1982) or Tyrrell and Mayhew (1990), however interesting they may be when not thinking of applying them to any physical situation related to what they aim to simulate. More convincing simulations are for example those of Beer (1989) or Cliff (1990).

An anecdote that occured to a physical robot

The following anecdote occured during the test of a small robot, the KitBorg (see section V.3). For observers, it was obviously just moving and avoiding obstacles, and did it pretty well. Actually, it was programmed by a light-seeking reactive behavior. Since "obstacles" were high enough to project a shadow, the robot was naturally avoiding them in the course of going towards the light source. It surprised both programmers and observers. Is that to say it was after all *not* avoiding obstacles ? Of course it was, we saw it !

The lessons we took from this story will appear in the course of the paper, because we'll use the same situation to illustrate the different topics we will discuss: all our examples will concern a robot equipped with a ring of sonars and a ring of photocells, which can be programmed to move towards light in a reactive way from the values of the photocells.

2) The "point of view of the robot": basic notions

A philosophical approach to representation

Focusing on the problem of representation as anything making the behaviour of a robot be "in touch" with environmental properties, we first wondered what kind of approach could account for Brooks' work. Our answer was that any action was potentially representing the environmental properties that made it "work". A robot program that lets the robot take an environmental property into account by its behaviour is as good a representation as a mathematical description of that property.

For example, an "obstacle" may be defined as anything raising above an horizontal plane (Mallot & al. 1989), or as a slow moving or stationary object (Lawton & al. 1990). By contrast, we claim that in themselves, Brooks robots (1986, 1988) or some robots described by Braitenberg (1983) are valid representations of obtacles, too.

We call this kind of representation "indirect", because the way the robot is programmed doesn't matter. An obstacle-avoiding robot may in fact be programmed to seek light; only the observed result is important. We'll call a representation "direct" when embodied in a data-structure that is present in the robot's hard- or software architecture (as would be e.g. a dedicated "obstacle detector").

Perception and action should not be independant

The first consequence of the notion of indirect representation is that what should be modeled is not the environment alone. The ongoing action is necessary, too, to determine what can and should be characterized by sensory processing. It is now commonly admitted in A.I. that the way a robot perceives its environment is biased by what it is doing. However, «what it is doing» almost always means «its goal», (Marr 1982; Aloimonos 1990). Here it merely means «how it is actually, physically, behaving».

Definition: a "context" is defined as an environment and an ongoing action the robot is having in this environment.

Sensorimotor channels

The goal of sensory processing can be seen as making a direct representation out of an indirect one. A sensorimotor channel is the data-structure that is to implement the former.

Definition: a "[sensorimotor] channel" is either (i) a physical sensor, or (ii) a device that delivers a numerical or vectorial value, which characterizes some property of the context, and which depends only on the values of other sensorimotor channels.

Definition: a sensorimotor channel is relevant if one can discover a relation between the values it delivers and one or several contextes. The most primitive relation would be the association of a boolean value and the presence/absence of some contextual event; but a relation may be more complex.

Intuitively, relevance should reflect the *potential* usefulness of a channel. This is to oppose to considering a channel having a functional design that tells how to use it.

Since channels have no a-priori design, they should be evolved empirically. The ideal robot we are imagining at this state would be a small electronique creture that moves around in its environment, gathers information, and tells the programmer: "Look Boss, I discovered lots of channels that are relevant. Please take them and program me back, so that I am useful; and while being useful I'll keep discovering more channels, the more as my behaviour is richer. How to use them for programming ? I don't know, that's your problem, you're a programmer after all, and I'm but a programming-tools generator...".

Note well that the programmer is free to use his knowledge or any available theory to direct the robot to evolve such or such channel. The programmer may (hopefully!) have a-prioris that influence the robot's evolution; the important issue is that the robot should not also "have" them explicit in a model, but genuinely discover some of their sensorimotor consequences.

Now the topic is set for the rest of the paper. Technical conditions for relevance will be proposed, together with a method for creating new sensorimotor channels.

IV— A TENTATIVE APPROACH TO SENSORIMOTOR RELEVANCE

1) A sensorimotor channel emerges by capturing sensorimotor dependances

The very fact of moving may constrain the sensorimotor situation of the robot so that it gets structured, i.e. has some properties that are caused by the context. For example, if a robot *is* avoiding obstacles, the turn angle and the sonar pattern are related, whether the robot was programmed for it on purpose, or for seeking light.

A channel is proposed to show up as the expression of a sensorimotor dependance that is likely to be due to a particular contextual event. We will say that a channel "tracks" a contextual event through a sensorimotor dependance this event induces. To develop this notion into an algorithmic method, we must make some hypothesis about the nature of the environment. We hope these hypothesis are reasonable; at least they are much weaker as those commonly take in model-based A.I.

2) Three fundamental hypothesis

Contextual stability of sensorimotor events

Many sensorimotor dependances that are to be captured are not context-specific: if they are related to contextual properties in a given context, they are likely to keep a similar relation in a large set of other contexts. However, they have to be first "grasped" in specific contexts before becoming useful in a larger extent (this extension stands for me as the very process one generally calls "abstraction").

For example, a relation between sonar patterns and motor values might be found during the light-seeking behaviour of a robot. This could be interpreted as a direct characterization of an obstacle, and used in other contexts (e.g. one in which the robot doesn't mind collisions because it is strong enough to push obstacles; yet it has to know in advance some characteristics of the obstacle it is going to push). Similarly, a relation found between photocell- and motor- values might be considered an obstacle detector in scarce contexts. However, as a shadow characterizer it might be more widely used.

Note well that generally, the interpretation given to a given channel may change depending of the context.

A dependance between normally independant sensorimotor data is due to the context

A dependance that concerns several channels that are normally independant will be regarded as related to properties of the context (Marr 1982; Lloyd 1988). For example, in our familiar example, a relation discovered between sonar patterns and photocell patterns tracks a contextual event, and a relation between sonars and motors as well (or photocells and motors). At a more primitive level, a correlation between two different photocell sensors tracks an event, too.

Interesting channels show a topological organization

Even between independant channels, not every type of relation is to be sought. We think that interesting ones that are likely to be found[1] are those which show a topological organization between the channel values on which they are built (discussion of this idea in Tattershall 1989). A typical kind of topological organization is dimensionality reduction: in a configuration space of dimension n, a sensory situation is represented by a point. Dimensionality reduction occurs if the set of points observed in a given context is restrained to some area of dimension $p<n$ (i.e., which could theoretically be described by only p parameters).

An appreciable effect of this organization is to allow channels to do classification by giving a name to a set of values that are topologically similar. Still more interesting is the possibility to give a value to characterize the tracked event: the interest of numerical values is in metric properties, and a topological organization is likely to define a natural notion of metric. (We allow a value to be integer, real, or vectorial. Note that the most primitive channels, physical sensors, are integer-valued when numeric and real-valued when analogic).

3) Method of sensorimotor channel creation

In an environment that fulfills the three above conditions, the programmer has four steps to follow. For each one, he may use his personal knowledge. The described method should be sufficient to guarantee the created channel is not an artificial modeling primitive.

- Choose an environment and design a robot program (whose implementation doesn't matter).
- Let the robot run the program in the environment. This determines a context, which in turn determines a sensorimotor history, which is either processed on line, or recorded to be analyzed later.
- Analyze the sensorimotor history to search topological dependances between independant existing channels. For this, he likely has to design a proper preprocessing of existing channel values to let dependances appear in the form he requires.
- Express the discovered dependance as a new channel that transforms other channels' values into a new value. The first possible way is to use a vector in the space in

[1] Other criterions of interest may be found for example in the behaviour of channel values with regard to time, or in their classification ability by mere clustering.

which the topological organization was found (see V.2). Another possibility is to map this space into another set (doing classification); if the latter set has metric properties (as the map has), it would be good that the two metrics be kept compatible.

4) Using a newly created sensory channel

The interpretation and use of the created channel is still to do. The "meaning" of the information it gives can only be found by indirect ways, for it is only defined by the history that explains the appearance of the new channel. It is highly context-dependant and subject to change. It is quite different from classical symbols which ideally should have an invariant "meaning" that guarantees its relevance without the robot having anything to add. So, this addresses directly the symbol-grounding problem.

Note that since channel deliver values, they can be seen, from a user's point of view, as kinds of "virtual" sensors implemented by software.

V— EXPERIMENTS & RESULTS

1) Influencial works

Pierce (1991) describes how a simulated robot may learn to characterize its motion by reference to the sensory outputs of a ring of sonars. Pierce & Kuipers (1990) show a similar robot characterizing a goal by finding a function of its sensory values which could be applied an optimization process that accounts for the goal.

Nehmzow & Smithers (1990) shows a physical robot using a self-organizing map to recognize its location in a maze. The recognition ability is specific to a wall-following behavior.

The Darwin II system (Edelman 1987) describes how the search for correlations between two maps greatly helps the categorization ability of both maps alone.

The ART system of Carpenter & Grossberg (1987) provides an interesting way of building models by discovering invariants. But its purposes are very different from ours: it is designed to process boolean patterns instead of numerical values, it has no concern about topology, and more critically it tries to classify *every* pattern it can get.

2) Implementation choices

Up to here, our approach was widely independant from existing computer tools.

The search for dependances that are mostly correlations has lead us to use neuronal networks. Because of our topological concerns, we finally focused on topologic maps (always bidimensional, for visualization necessities). A 2D topologic map permits to approximate a 2D surface S in a larger space, by implementing as a network proximity links between sample points of S (called prototypes). The self-organizing algorithm of Kohonen (1988) allows such maps to be developed by learning. Kohonen's algorithm has also statistical properties, and is often used to approximate statistical distributions without topologic concerns (e.g. Ans 1989).

If a set of samples cannot be approximated by a 2D surface, no topologic map will succeed to be built from them. So, topologic maps are linked to the problem of dimensionality reduction presented in IV.2 (on this read Tattershall (1989)).

The values on which the map will organize are existing channel values that have undergone some preprocessing, up to the programmer. We call these preprocessed values the channel's "primitive vector". The proposed method is actually a test for relevance: the programmer proposes a sensorimotor processing, and if it succeeds to create a channel in a "real" situation we call it relevant.

3) The static-world experiment

Experimental setup

We are using a small two-wheeled robot, the KitBorg (figure 1). It has an onboard NEC 78312 processor with an available RAM of 32 Kb. The onboard sensors are 4 photocells, 3 sonars, 2 infrared sensors, 1 microphone, and 2 wheel speed encoders. Sensor values are coded on one byte. Thanks to the open architecture of this robot, sensory hardware modifications are possible.

The KitBorg can be connected to a PC-compatible through a serial line. It is used to download programs, and reversely to transfer data from the robot to the PC. These data must then be transferred through the local net to a Sun4 workstation, where the analysis system lies.

Experimental goal

The situation we took as an example up to here is too complex for yielding an actual experiment. Rather, the first experiment will be to make the robot move in a contrasted static environment. In this context, the dynamic flow of cell data is widely dependant on the motion of the robot. There is a relation between cell data and motor data that is characteristic of the situation «moving in a static environment», and that's what we'd like the robot to capture. Note that such a relation might appear however complicated the motion is. Since this general relation is unlikely to be discovered at once, we won't start with a complex motion, and our first experiment will be to make the robot rotate with slowly varying speed.

Precisely, we'll try to find an association between the photocell values (properly preprocessed) and the motor values (which are restrained to a single commandable parameter: the rotation speed). Once we succeed to get a sensorimotor channel out of this experiment, we're going to use it to make the robot follow a now wholly-rotating world. This would be achieved by taking the value associated to the sensory situation, and taking its opposite as the direct acceleration to modify the motor command.

Note that while during learning the associated values were indeed motor speed-values, they are to be considered but pure sensory values once expressed as delivered by a channel. They are a resource for the programmer; only the simplicity of the experiment makes it possible to use them in an almost straightforward reactive loop by regarding them as opposites of accelerations.

An experimental session

We let the KitBorg move in a well-contrasted environment (in DC light). Rotation speed is an integer between -5 and +5. The resulting sensorimotor data is recorded up to the robot's memory limit: this gives ca. 2000 cells and motor values, sampled every 65ms. The recorded data are then transferred into the Sun workstation, where they are analyzed.

A 15x15 Kohonen map, called "sensory map", is built on a set of primitive vectors, to approximate this set with a fixed number of units. An associative network is then sought between this map and another map which accounts for the motor values. Note that the generalization ability of the associative network already depends on the topological properties of the sensory map: so in this experiment no explicit test for dimensionality reduction is necessary.

We developed a complete environment that permits to interactively produce maps (from a filtered and preprocessed set of channel values), activate them (from input patterns extracted from those same values or from the results of other similar recordings), and visualize the results in numerous useful ways. It is programmed on a SunSparc using Lucid Common Lisp 3.0.

Results

Currently, only analysis results have been obtained. They have still to be used to program the robot back, because we have difficulties to command the KitBorg directly from the Sun.

Many preprocessings have been tried, mostly disappointing. Currently, the best results are obtained when taking as channel primitives the shifts between pieces of signals read from two adjacent photocells. This unfortunately is very sensitive to the maximal rate we allow to change speed.

From a vector made of the three available such shifts out of our four photocells, the rotation speed can be estimated exactly for 35% of the samples, and with an error of 1 or less for 75% of them. 1% of the answers show an error of 5 or more. If we restrain to positive rotation speed, correct answers (error 0 or 1) raise to 80%, because more samples were available in the data that built the sensory map.

These weak results are partly due (we hope) to hardware problems. We didn't succed to calibrate our poor-quality photocells to make their values comparable. Maybe we're going to replace them by a camera on which we would only consider a row. Samely, motor control is unreliable; for example commanding a constant speed of 2 makes the actual speed (as read from sensors) vary quite randomly from 1 to 3.

Figure 2 is made the following way: a square zone is dedicated to a unit of the sensory map. For each sample, the best responding unit and the effective speed are recorded. The numbers in the square are the speed-codes which were current in at least 80% of the cases showing the unit as the best-responding one. If three values aren't enough to account for 80% of the responses, "???" is printed instead. The three values are ordered by decreasing occurences. Empty squares show units that responded less than 6 times (for 2000 samples).

Ideal properties for such a figure[1] should be (and they globally appear in the figure):
a • The units should be specific to a narrow range of contiguous speed-codes (required for classification abilities);
b • Close units should be specific to close ranges (required for generalization abilities).

Figure 3 shows the spatial representation of the same Kohonen sensory map that was used for obtention of figure 2. The 2D (surface) structure is very winding but is conspicuous in many areas. In fact, figure 2 is not so illustrative of our topological concern: the three axis are redundant ones, and so the resulting 2D structure is somewhat mysterious and empirically found (in the fact that maps organize always similarly in the same clearly 2D areas). The effective results derive from property 1 ("classification") of the map, that permits the associative network to focus on closer responses.

V — CONTRIBUTION & CONCLUSION

1) Fundamental critics

Some basic problems appeared that limited our ambition for this method as an effective modeling tool.
• Finding proper preprocessings appears as difficult a task as, say, finding sensory processings accounting for classical symbols (e.g. "chair-", "coffee-", or "predator-" sensors).
• Concrete convicing examples are hard to find: this is perhaps a sign that we skipped steps too ambitiously.
• The method lacks adaptativeness: in every experiment we devised, the procedure actually got a strong "supervised" flavor that we don't like. In the same spirit, we'd like the learning process to go on instead of stopping at the creation of the channel.
• Whereas sensory competence evolves, it seems hard to have motor competence follow, e.g. by developing "motor programs". It wasn't the purpose of our system to do it, yet the lack of it is to consider when pondering over the future of such a system.
• Formalization (looking towards probabilistic inference, Bessiere 1990) and "rethinking" of some choices (e.g. topologic maps) seem necessary.

Our current implementation could be ultimately regarded as the "test" part of a "generate and test" modeling procedure. However, the corresponding "generate" part is very difficult and is perhaps the key part.

The most appealing starting point for new investigations may be Varela's (1989) work on autonomous systems as defined from the inside: for the sake of formalization, it seems safer to describe the internal working of a system instead of the working of its environment, as would require e.g. the search for preprocessing. That way, "generate" might become a more tractable problem. Currently we have only very generic ideas on how this thread could be tackled.

---

[1] In fact, the original visualization tool is not like fig.2, it extensively uses colors. Fig. 2 was designed for the present (black & white) article.

2) Summary & conclusion

The subject of this paper was: which properties could have a satisfying interface between a physical robot's world model and its effective environment ?

After justifying the interest of such a question, we proposed a tentative answer in four parts:

- Environmental events that can be relevantly modelled are those which are expressable by a sensorimotor dependance in some particular situation. Such a situation is determined by the physical action of the robot as well as by its environment.
- Modeling primitives are "sensorimotor channels", data-structures that implement a sensorimotor dependance. They should have some given properties that define their "relevance".
- A method for ensuring such properties could be to develop a channel as an a-posteriori sensorimotor characterization of an encoutered situation. It is up to the user to put at first the robot in a situation fit for developing a useful channel.
- The numeric information the channels deliver must be interpreted by the user in order to use it. Channels should only be seen as available sensory resources.

We developed a simple system to study this approach. A physical robot was used in the experiments. Results are rather weak ; their main interest is to illustrate an original kind of concerns in robotics. Actually, this experimentation raised some very basic problems that will guide our future research.

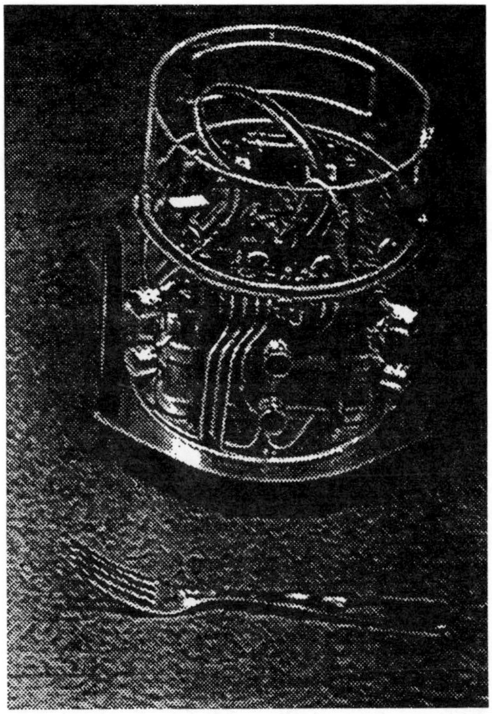

Figure 1: The KitBorg

Figure 2: The speed-codes associated to units of a 15x15 Kohonen map. The diplayed codes account for 80% of the responses of a given unit. If three codes aren't enough, "???" is written instead. White units are those which respond too seldom to be studied. Desired properties for this map are (1) units should be specific to narrow ranges (few contiguous values), and (2) near units should span near ranges. Note that code 5, parasitic in many places, appears when the robot doesn't move. It is a badly-handled situation.

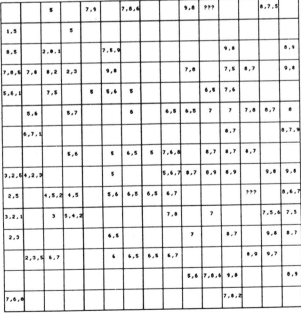

		5		7,9		7,8,6			9,8	???			8,7,5	
1,5			5											
8,5		2,8,1			7,5,9						9,8			8,9
7,8,5	7,8	8,2	2,3		9,8				7,8		7,5	8,7		9,8
5,6,1		7,5		5	5,6	5				6,5	7,6			
	5,6		5,7			6		6,5	6,5	7	7	7,8	8,7	8
	6,7,1										8,7			8,7,9
			5,6		5	6,5	5	7,6,8		8,7	8,7	8,7		
3,2,5	4,2,3				5			5,6,7	8,7	8,9	8,9		9,8	9,8
2,5		4,5,2	4,5		5,6	6,5	6,5	6,7				???		8,6,7
3,2,1		3	5,4,2					7,8		7			7,5,6	7,5
2,3					6,5				7		8,7		9,8	8,7
	2,3,5	6,7			6	6,5	6,5	6,7				8,9	9,7	
									5,6	7,8,6	9,8			8,9
7,6,8											7,8,2			

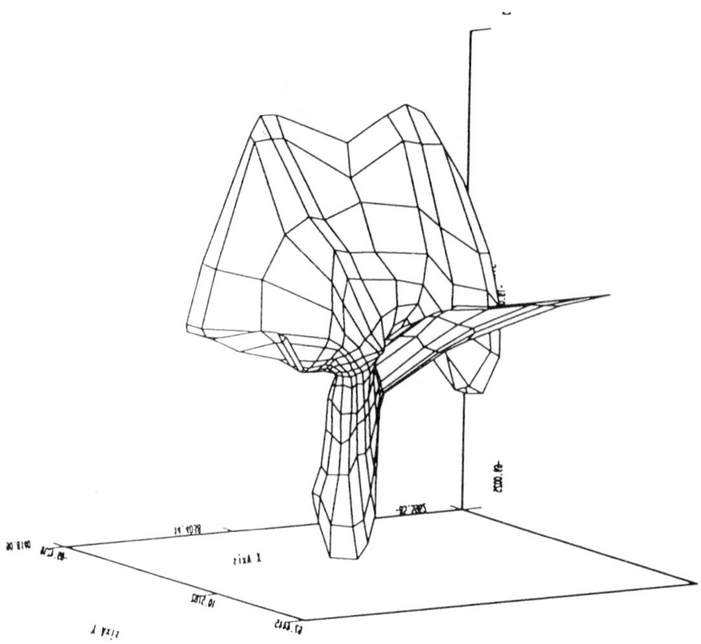

Figure 3: A spatial representation of the same map that was used to get fig. 2, and another map that was organized on the same data (in another order).

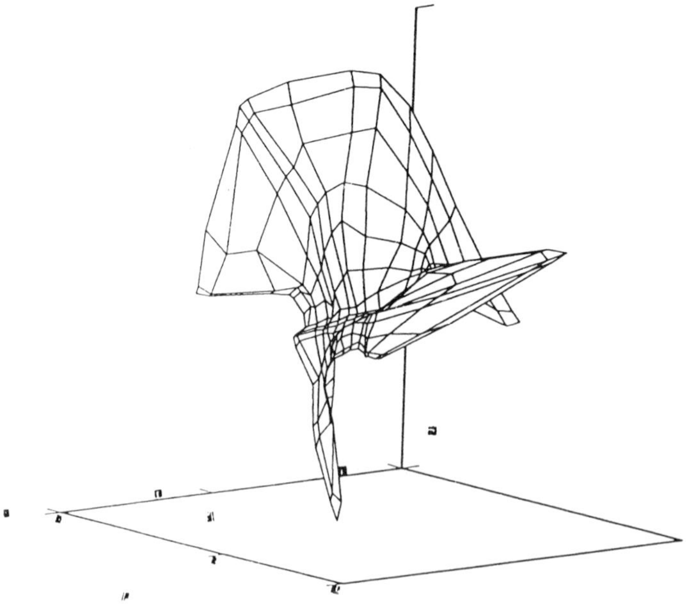

ACKNOWLEDGEMENTS: This work has been made possible by the Centre National de la Recherche Scientifique. Thanks to Pierre Bessière for his crucial influence on the current form of this paper.

REFERENCES:

Aloimonos 1990 — J. Aloimonos. *Purposive and qualitative active vision.* Computer vision lab., University of Maryland, 1990.

Ans 1989 — B. Ans. Learning arbitrary associations: a neuromimetic model. In G. Tiberghien, ed., *New theoretical issues in cognitive sciences,* E. Horwood, 1989.

Beer 1989 — R.D. Beer. *Intelligence as adaptive behavior: an experiment in computational neuroethology.* TR 89-167, Case Western Reserve University, Cleveland, 1989.

Bessière 1990 — P. Bessière. Toward a synthetic cognitive paradigm: Probabilistic inference. COGNITIVA 90, Madrid, 1990.

Booker 1982 — L.B. Booker. *Intelligent behavior as an adaptation to the task environment.* PhD Thesis, University of Michigan, 1982.

Braitenberg 1983 — V. Braitenberg. *Vehicles.* MIT Press/Bradford Books, 1983.

Brooks 1986 — R.A. Brooks. *Achieving artificial intelligence through building robots.* AI Memo 899, MIT, 1986.

Brooks 1988 — R.A. Brooks. *A robot that walks; emergent behaviors from a carefully evolved network.* AI Memo, MIT, september 1988.

Carpenter & Grossberg 1987 — G.A. Carpenter & S. Grossberg. A massively parallel architecture for a self-organizing neural pattern recognition machine. *Comp. vision, graphics and image processing* (37), 1987.

Cliff 1990 — D.T. Cliff. The computational hoverfly: a study in computational neuroethology. In Meyer & Wilson eds., *From animals to animats, proc. of SAB 90,* Paris, MIT Press, 1990.

Connell 1988 — J.H. Connell. *A behavior-based arm controller.* AI Memo 1025, MIT, 1988.

Edelman 1987 — G.M. Edelman. *Neural Darwinism.* Basic Books, New York, 1987.

Fikes & Nilson 1971 — R.E. Fikes & N.J. Nilson. Strips: a new approach of the application of theorem proving to problem solving. *Artificial intelligence journal.* 3,4 (2), 1971.

Findler & Allan 1974 — N. V. Findler & A. E. C. Allan. Studies on the behavior of an organism in a hostile environment. *Journal of the institution of computer science,* 4(3,4), 1974.

Kohonen 1988 — T. Kohonen. *Self-organization and associative memory.* Springer-Verlag, 2nd ed., 1988.

Lloyd 1989 — D. Lloyd. *Simple minds.* MIT Press/Bradford Books, 1989.

Lozano-Pérez *et al.* 1989 — T. Lozano-Pérez, J.L. Jones, E. Mazer & P.A. O'Donnel. Task-level planning of pick-and-place robot motions. *IEEE computer,* March 1989.

Marr 1982 — D. Marr. *Vision.* W.H. Freeman, 1982.

Mazer & Miribel 1984 — E. Mazer & J-F. Miribel. *Le langage LM: manuel de référence.* CEPADUES, 1984.

Pierce 1990 — D. Pierce. Learning turn-and-travel actions with an uninterpreted sensorimotor apparatus. In Meyer & Wilson eds., *From animals to animats, proc. of SAB 90,* Paris, MIT Press, 1990.

Smithers & Malcolm 1988 — T. Smithers & C. Malcolm. *Programming robotic assembly in terms of task-achieving behavioural modules.* DAI RP 417, University of Edinburgh, 1988.

Sutton 1990 — R. S. Sutton. Reinforcement learning architectures for animats. In Meyer & Wilson eds., *From animals to animats, proc. of SAB 90,* Paris, MIT Press, 1990.

Tattershall 1989 — G. Tattershall. Neural map applications. In I. Aleksander, ed., *Neural computing architectures,* MIT Press, 1989.

Tyrrell & Mayhew 1990 — T. Tyrrell & J.E.W. Mayhew. Computer simulation of an animal environment. In Meyer & Wilson eds., *From animals to animats, proc. of SAB 90,* Paris, MIT Press, 1990.

Varela 1988 — F.Varela. *Connaître les sciences cognitives: tendances et perspectives.* Seuil, Paris, 1988.

Varela 1989 — F. Varela. *Autonomie et connaissance: essai sur le vivant.* Seuil, Paris, 1989.

Using Motor Actions for Location Recognition*

Ulrich Nehmzow
Department of Artificial Intelligence
University of Edinburgh
ulrich@uk.ac.ed.aifh

Tim Smithers
Artificial Intelligence Laboratory
Vrije Universiteit Brussel
tim@be.ac.vub.artil

Abstract

We present a Behaviour-based mobile robot that is able to autonomously build internal representations of its environment and use these for location recognition. This is done by a process of self-organisation, no explicit world-model is given. The robot uses an artificial neural network for mapbuilding and additional adaptive processes to achieve successful location recognition. The robot reliably recognises locations in the world and can cope with the noise inherent to the real world.

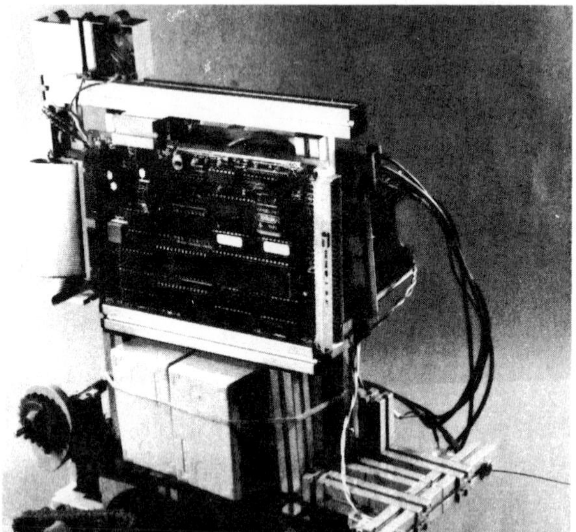

Figure 1: Alder, the first of the "Really Useful Robots".

1 Introduction

In an ongoing series of experiments we are using simple mobile robots to investigate mechanisms to support the autonomous acquisition of specified competences. These experiments form a part of our "Really Useful Robots" (RUR) project, the aim of which is to develop adaptive control schemes for autonomous mobile robots which are both flexible and robust with respect to variable and unforeseen situations. So far we have investigated schemes for learning obstacle avoidance, dead-end escape, wall-following and corridor-following competences, [Nehmzow, Hallam & Smithers '89], learning location recognition using sensor-based feature detectors, [Nehmzow & Smithers '91], and learning location recognition using motor command sequences, see [Nehmzow, Smithers & Hallam '91]. In this paper we present a new location recognition scheme which is not only more robust and reliable, but also simpler than our previous schemes. It again uses information derived from motor commands, rather than directly from sensors, which we believe to be novel in autonomous systems research.

Our previous experiments were done using "Alder", the first of our Really Useful Robots (see figure 1). Alder consists of a chassis built from Fischertechnik, an ARC52 controller which uses an INTEL 8052 eight-bit microprocessor and has an on-board BASIC interpreter, an interface card giving independent control for two motors (forward, reverse, and stop for each motor, but with no feedback of distance travelled or angle turned), and up to eight binary sensor inputs. For most of our experiments we have used two whisker sensors which act as omnidirectional tactile sensors. For the obstacle avoidance, dead-end escape, and wall following we used a behaviour-based controller together with a perceptron-like network to provide the necessary plastic element in the learning mechanism (see [Nehmzow, Hallam & Smithers '89] for more details).

For the location recognition experiments we have been using self-organising networks (see section 2.1). In our first experiment the self-organising process was fed with input vectors derived from a sensor-based feature detector programmed into the robot, [Nehmzow & Smithers '91]. The features that were detected and identified were the convex and concave corners of its enclosure (see figure 4), which it came across as it followed the wall around the internal perimeter. Although this scheme proved to be successful, we were dissatisfied with having to base it upon a hard-wired feature detector—we would prefer not to have to 'tell' the robot so much about its environment. In an attempt to do away with the feature detector we devised a location recognition scheme which uses vectors based upon motor commands. In this scheme an input vector to the self-organising network was constructed each time the motor states changed as a result of a new command. This meant that the number of input vectors produced was significantly larger than in the previous scheme. It also meant that it was harder to derive the information necessary to demonstrate location recognition. In the final scheme we used seven two-dimensional self-organising networks all working in parallel. Essentially this scheme performed a kind of frequency component analysis on the pseudo-periodic sequence of input vectors generated as the robot completed circuits of its enclosure. Although this scheme was successful, and it did remove the need for the explicitly programmed feature detector, we were again dissatisfied with it because of its high complexity and computational cost relative to the previous feature detector-based scheme. We also disliked the fact that the seven thresholds for the seven networks for location recognition had to be set by hand, thus making it dependent on 'magic numbers' which have to be set by the programmer.

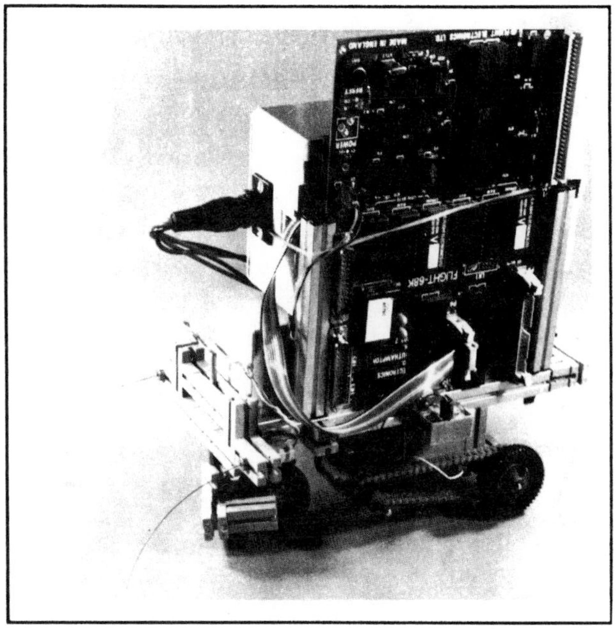

Figure 2: Cairngorm, the third of the "Really Useful Robots".

This led us to devise a new location recognition scheme which is the subject of the experiments presented here. For this scheme we have used a new robot, 'Cairngorm', the third of the Really Useful Robots[1], shown in figure 2.

Cairngorm also uses a chassis built from Fischertechnik, but has a more powerful controller based on a Motorola 68000 CPU and having 128 Kbytes of memory. Its motor control and sensor inputs are similar to that of Alder, but it is programmed in C, rather than BASIC. Otherwise it is essentially the same as Alder.

In the next section we describe the Behaviour-based controller and self-organising scheme used to support the new location recognition scheme. We then describe the experimental setup and procedure adopted; following that, we present our experimental results. We finish with a brief discussion and conclusions.

[1] A much larger mobile robot called 'Ben Hope' is the second in the series and is still under construction.

2 Behaviour-based Control and Mapbuilding Process

Cairngorm's control structure consists of three independent behaviours. They are responsible for obstacle avoidance, wall seeking, and mapbuilding, respectively. There is no direct communication between these behaviours except through the world. In combination they lead to successful location recognition behaviour. The mechanisms used in each of these behaviours will now be described in a little more detail.

The *obstacle avoidance* behaviour is a preprogrammed and fixed behaviour that makes the robot turn left for as long as either or both of the two whisker sensors (one on the left and one on the right) are on, i.e., are in contact with an obstacle (the robot is designed to follow a wall on its right hand side). As soon as there are no signals from the whisker sensors the robot resumes moving forwards.

The *wall seeking* behaviour is also a preprogrammed and fixed behaviour. If the robot has not experienced a whisker contact for some preset period of time (about three seconds in our experiments) it makes a right turn (towards the wall). It continues to turn until a signal from the right whisker, or both the right and left whiskers, is received (typically it is just the right-hand-side one), upon which the obstacle avoidance behaviour introduces a left turn away from the wall. The robot then continues to move forward until either the set period of time has elapsed again or it makes contact with an obstacle. In this way, the robot is able to both avoid obstacles, follow walls, and negotiate the corners of its enclosure without these being explicitly specified tasks achieved using explicitly programmed strategies. In this sense they are examples of emergent functionality as defined by [Steels '91].

In the experiment presented here both the obstacle avoidance and wall following behaviours were preprogrammed. However, we have previously shown that our robots can acquire this kind of obstacle avoidance and wall following competences through learning from interaction with their environments (see [Nehmzow, Hallam & Smithers '89] for details).

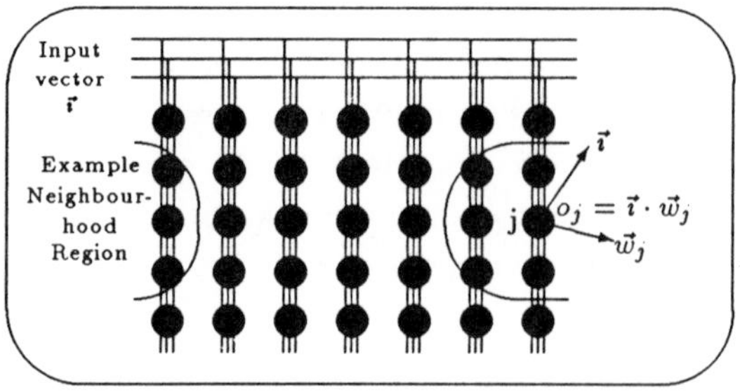

Figure 3: A two-dimensional self-organising network.

The third behaviour is *mapbuilding*. By 'mapbuilding' we mean something more like *taking notes* of particular experiences, rather than constructing a geographical map or floor-plan. For this a self-organising network (see [Kohonen '88]) is used. It is constructed ('trained') using input vectors derived from the motor action commands produced by the obstacle avoidance and wall-seeking behaviours. We next briefly review the details of this kind of network before describing in more detail the location recognition behaviour.

2.1 Self-Organising Networks

Consider the two-dimensional self-organising network (SON) given in figure 3.

Each cell j of the SON has an individual weight vector $\vec{w}_j$ of unit length. Each normalised input vector, $\vec{\imath}$, is fed to all cells[2]. The output o_j of cell j is determined by the dot product of input vector $\vec{\imath}$ and the weight vector $\vec{w}_j$ of cell j:

$$o_j = \vec{w}_j \cdot \vec{\imath} \tag{1}$$

The cell with the strongest response, the largest output value, is selected. This cell as well as all neighbouring cells within a defined neighbourhood region are then modified according to the following equation:

[2]For self-organisation, normalising the input vector is not strictly necessary. However, for numerical comparison of two responses of the network, which we do, it is.

$$\vec{w}_j(t+1) = \vec{w}_j(t) + \eta(\vec{\imath} - \vec{w}_j(t)) \tag{2}$$

where η is the so-called 'gain'—a value that determines the amount of change (it is typically set at 0.2). Weight vectors outside the specified neighbourhood[3] remain unchanged. After several 'epochs', i.e. presentations of input vectors to the network, the net develops regions which respond most strongly to particular types of input vectors. In this way a mapping is developed whereby different input vectors are mapped onto different regions of the network (always an injection, often a bijection).

2.2 Location Recognition Behaviour

On Cairngorm we have used a one-dimensional, ring-shaped SON of 50 cells, as in earlier experiments with Alder, with a neighbourhood region of one node either side. As the robot makes its way around its enclosure, wall-following and avoiding obstacles, a moving average of durations of turn actions is computed. If a turn action occurs which takes longer than the current average (a 'significant turn action') an input vector is constructed and fed into the self-organising network and the modification to the weight vectors of the net as defined above is performed. After about two to three times round the enclosure the one-dimensional ring develops a stable enough structure to be used to recognise particular locations. This is demonstrated by instructing the robot (by pressing a microswitch mounted on it) to store the excitation pattern of the self-organising ring when the robot is at the location that is to be recognised ('home' location). This stored pattern is then compared with all subsequent excitation patterns. If the pattern at the current location of the robot is found to be sufficiently similar to the stored one, the robot indicates that it has arrived back at the home location. The comparison is computed using the 'city-block' distance ϵ between two excitation patterns, and is given by:

[3] The neighbourhood size is often chosen to be decreasing over time, so that self-organisation occurs over larger areas of the network early on and then becomes more local, but in our case we keep the neighbourhood region fixed.

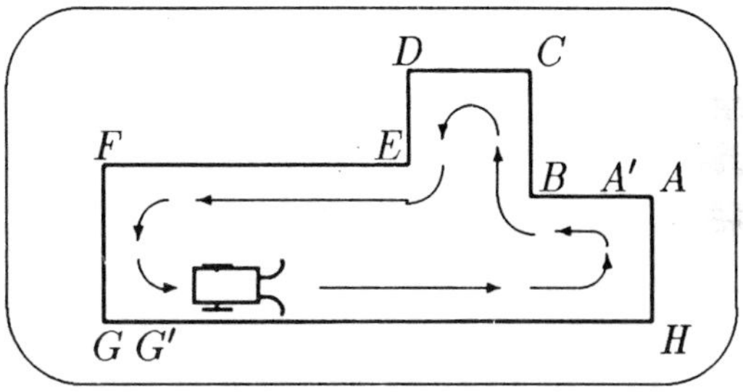

Figure 4: The experimental enclosure for location recognition.

$$\epsilon = \sum_{k=1}^{50} |o_{s_k} - o_{c_k}|, \tag{3}$$

where $\vec{o}_s$ is the stored excitation pattern, and $\vec{o}_c$ is the current excitation pattern. By using the city-block distance measure (or Euclidean distance measure, for that matter) we are effectively performing a vector quantisation, so the property of topology-preserving mapping of SON is not exploited. The advantage of this is that the network can be used for location recognition even in the early learning stages. However, once the net is well settled the index information of the most excited cell alone should suffice to recognize locations.

3 The Experimental Results

In this section we present our experimental results. We begin by describing the experimental setup.

3.1 Experimental Setup

The robot is placed in a simple enclosure, containing rightangled convex and concave corners as well as straight walls. Figure 4 shows the layout of the enclosure. The letters indicate locations where a turn action usually exceeds the average duration and therefore where an input vector to the SON is usually generated.

Once started, the robot follows the wall on its right hand side round the enclosure. This is

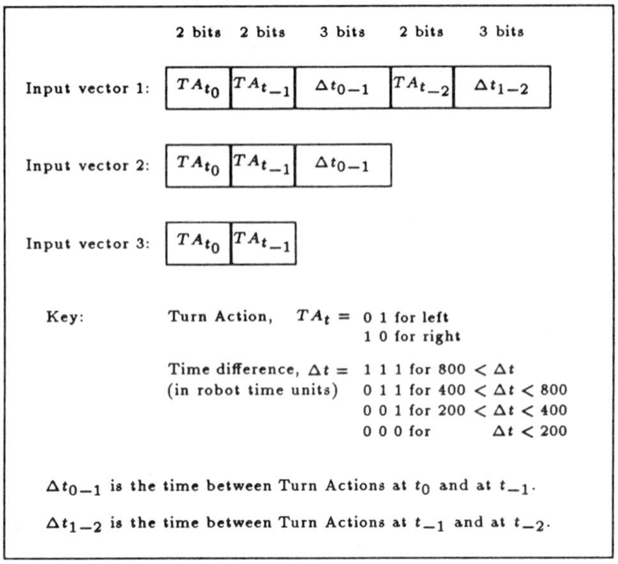

Figure 5: Input vector definition for the Self-Organising Controller.

achieved, as we mentioned before, by a combination of the obstacle avoidance and wall seeking behaviours. The mapbuilding behaviour monitors the turn actions commanded by the other two behaviours. Whenever a turn action takes longer than the current average turn action time, an input vector (see input vector 1, in figure 5), is generated and presented to the SON. The response of each cell in the ring is then determined and the relevant weight vectors are updated, as described in section 2.1. The robot is left to wall follow its way around the enclosure for typically two to three rounds, then a "home" corner is selected by pressing the microswitch mounted on the robot. This results in the current excitation pattern being stored in memory. From this point on all subsequent excitation patterns of the SON are compared to the stored pattern. If the city block distance between the goal-pattern and the current excitation patterns is less than $\frac{1}{3}$ of the average city-block distance, the robot assumes it is back at the goal location and a red light (mounted on the interface board) lights up.

As can be seen from input vector 1 in figure 5, the information used as input to the self-organising network consists of the type of the current turn action (right or left), and the types of the previous two turn actions, together with the elapsed time between each pair.

In order to investigate the performance of this location recognition scheme we used two other input vectors, see input vector 2 and 3 in figure 5, each one containing less information than the previous one. Input vector 2 consists of the types of the current and previous turn actions and the elapsed time between them, and input vector 3 consists of just the types of the current and previous turn actions. The experimental setup when using each of these three kinds of input vector was in all other respects the same.

The results obtained for all three input vectors are presented in the next section.

3.2 Experimental Results

Table 1 shows the location recognition results obtained using input vector 1 (see figure 5).

Location	Recognitions	Total no. of Visits
H	3	4
B	3	3
C	3	3
D	3	3
E	3	3
F	3	3
G	3	3
G'	2	4
A	3	3
A'	3	3

Table 1: Location recognition using input vector 1.

The letters refer to the locations shown in figure 4. Except for A' and G', they correspond to the corners of the enclosure. This is because turn actions that take longer than average are produced at these places. The locations A' and G' are produced because the robot typically takes two long turn actions to negotiate these particular corners.

The one 'missed' recognition at corner H occurred early on in the run and was due to the network not having settled down enough for a successful recognition to be registered. The two 'misses' at G' occurred because on these occasions the robot got round corner G with one turn action, and so the region of the SON corresponding to an input vector having G', G, and F was not excited by any input vector.

Table 2 indicates the pairs of locations which were confused during the run.

	A	A'	B	C	D	E	F	G	G'	H
A										
A'									X	
B										
C										
D										
E										
F										
G										
G'		X								
H										

Table 2: Confused locations when using input vector 1.

In this case it was only locations A' and G' which were confused. This occurs because the input vectors at these locations (built from H, A, A' and F, G, G' respectively) are similar, and thus excite the self-organising network in the same way.

Table 3 presents the location recognition results when using input vector 2. As can be seen, there is a degradation in performance with 'missed' locations occurring at D, F, and G. The failure to recognise location F here was due to an input vector not being generated at location E, thus leading to an 'odd' vector at F. This occurred only once and was the result of the inevitable variation in actual behaviour experienced when using real robots (even simple ones) in a real environment. This was, however, a one-off event and never observed to occur again.

Location	Recognitions	Total no. of Visits
H	3	3
B	3	3
C	3	3
D	3	4
E	3	3
F	3	4
G	4	5
G'	3	3
A	3	3
A'	3	3

Table 3: Location recognition using input vector 2.

	A	A'	B	C	D	E	F	G	G'	H
A		X			(X)			X	X	
A'	X							X	X	
B										
C										
D										
E										
F										
G	X	X			(X)				X	
G'	X	X						X		
H										

Table 4: Confused locations when using input vector 2.

The degradation in performance can be seen more clearly in table 4, which presents the pairs of confused locations. The bracketed pairs denote occasional confusions.

When we reduce the amount of information in the input vector still further, and use input vector 3, we obtain the results presented in tables 5 and 6. Here we can see that the robot is still able to recognise locations, but its ability to distinguish certain pairs of them is significantly diminished.

Location	Recognitions	Total no. of Visits
B	3	3
C	3	3
D	2	2
E	2	2
F	2	2
G	2	2

Table 5: Location recognition using input vector 3.

	A	A'	B	C	D	E	F	G	G'	H
A		X			X			X	X	X
A'	X				X			X	X	X
B						X				
C							X			
D	X	X						X	X	X
E			X							
F				X						
G	X	X							X	X
G'	X	X						X		X
H	X	X						X	X	

Table 6: Confused locations when using input vector 3.

As we would expect, the performance of the whole system depends on the information put into the self-orgainsing network. If the input vector contains insufficient information, then reliable location recognition is impossible. From the results presented above we can see that reducing the information content of the input vector does not affect the robot's ability to recognise a non-wall type environmental feature (corners in this case), but it does affect its ability to differentiate some pairs of such locations. The less informative the input vector, the more locations "look the same" to the robot.

4 Discussion

4.1 Discovering Significant Environment Structure

In our previous location recognition scheme based upon motor actions we required a set of seven self-organising two-dimensional networks to get the robot to reliably recognise (and distinguish between) locations. Yet in the scheme we presented above we only need one one-dimensional network (ring) to achieve similar performance results. We can explain this effect by observing that our new scheme works by filtering the sequence of motor commands so that only those *not* generated by following a straight wall are used to build input vectors to the self-organising structure, whereas in the previous scheme the set of seven networks had to do this filtering work implicitly.

Another way of viewing this is to say that the sequence of motor commands produced as the robot wall follows its way around the enclosure contains two kinds of structure. One kind occurs at a high frequency and is produced by the wall-following actions. The other kind has a lower frequency and is produced by the corners, or non-straight-wall features of the enclosure. It is this second type of structure in the motor action commands that contains information about significant structure in the robot's environment (corners in this case); the first type merely reflects the fact that the robot's environment has straight walls in it—a rather less useful piece of information for location recognition.

4.2 Setting Thresholds

When we first started to experiment with the scheme presented above, the turn action time threshold, used to distinguish wall-following actions from other actions, was set by hand. We arrived at the particular threshold value by carefully observing the robot's behaviour and choosing it such that it would differentiate between motor actions performed at a 'significant' location (usually a corner) and those performed elsewhere (while wall following). Later we implemented the moving average calculation, thus removing the need for this 'magic number' to be set by hand (by doing this we have effectively introduced two other values to be set: the time window over which the average duration of motor actions is computed and the proportion by which the duration of a motor action has to exceed this average to become a "significant action". However, both these values are not very critical and far easier to set than the previously needed thresholds). Similar mechanisms are found in biology. Pigeons, for example, extract the changes in air pressure generated by changes in altitude of a few feet by ignoring the total strength and only measuring differences around some mean, [Gould '82]. Using this simple device in our robot means that it does not need any predefined knowledge about thresholds and significant motor actions, it finds this out for itself. This approach has further advantages: The robot is able to adjust its assessment if the world or the robot change. Cairngorm's moves, for example, become slower with decreasing battery charge. If a fixed threshold for determining significant moves was used, the performance of the robot would change, simply because motor actions take longer. However, because the average turn action will also take longer, Cairngorm is able to adjust for this and so maintain its performance.

A similar threshold value is used in the comparison between the stored ('home') excitation pattern and all subsequent patterns. Once again, we started by determining the required value for this empirically and setting the value in the program by hand. But having devised the successful averaging mechanisms to set the turn action time threshold we decided to try a similar device for the comparison threshold. The robot thus computes a moving average of all the city-block distances between the stored and current excitation patterns. Once a distance is smaller than $\frac{1}{3}$ of this average distance, the robot indicates that it recognises the current pattern as being the same as the stored pattern, and thus that it recognises its current location as the 'home' location.

4.3 Why 'Motor Actions' and not 'Sensor Signals'?

Sensing and acting are so tightly coupled that it seems fair to say that they are two sides of the same coin. In earlier experiments we have used schemes based on sensory information to recognise locations (see section 1). In the experiments reported here we have obtained the same results as in the earlier work, using motor information rather than sensor information. This was done to prove exactly this point: that sensing and acting are tightly coupled.

There can be practical advantages in using motor action information: the amount of information to be processed is often smaller because the robot is effectively acting as an analog computing device. Also (and perhaps more importantly for practical applications), the controller becomes independent of the actual sensors used. If necessary, sensors can be replaced without affecting the actual controller.

4.4 Comparison with Animal Navigation

There are numbers of well studied examples of navigation by learned location recognition in the biological literature. In an exploratory phase bees store *visual images*, which are then associated with a motion vector that gives the direction towards the hive, see ([Waterman '89], [Gould & Gould '88] and [Cartwright & Collett '83]). When released some distance away from the hive, bees can find their way back using these acquired visual images by comparing them with the current images and calculating the appropriate flight direction to take them to their hive, [Collett '87]. In a similar way our robot stores "motor action images" and later compares stored images with current ones in order to recognise locations it has been at before. However, no vectors pointing homewards are associated with these images.

Other kinds of sensor-based navigation behaviour schemes have also been documented. For example, pigeons and salmon navigate using *olfactory information* ([Gould '82], [Hasler, Scholz & Horral '78]), and it seems possible that pigeons also use *acoustic (infrasound) and magnetic sensors* to find their way home [Gould '82]. Bees and ants also use the *polarisation of the light* of the sky to navigate [Wehner '76].

All these biological examples appear to just use sensor information and they are clearly reliable and robust. However, our experiments with simple robots have shown that motor-action based schemes can be used as well in order to achieve high degrees of reliability and robustness. The reasons for this apparent difference are not clear to us.

5 Summary and Future Work

In earlier work we demonstrated location recognition schemes using sensor-based feature detectors and using motor action changes. In this paper we present a new location recognition scheme, which again uses information about motor actions, but which is simpler and yet equally reliable and robust. As a part of this new scheme we have also incorporated automatic adaptive threshold setting mechanisms to reduce the number of parameters ('magic numbers') which have to be set by hand.

In our ongoing series of experiments to investigate the autonomous acquisition of specified competences we have demonstrated in separate schemes the acquisition of obstacle avoidance, wall-following, corridor following and location recognition competence by the robot. Our plan for the future is to put all these schemes together in one robot to demonstrate the staged learning of all the competences required for simple navigation in an autonomous robot.

Acknowledgements

The work reported here is supported by a grant from the UK Science and Engineering Research Council (grant number GR/F/5852.3). Other facilities were provided by the Department of Artificial Intelligence at Edinburgh University. We would like to thank John Hallam for the stimulating discussion about this work. We thank Claudia Alsdorf, Peter Forster and Barbara Webb for reading earlier versions of this paper and their helpful comments. Thanks also to the staff of the mechanical, electronic, and photographic workshops of the Department of Artificial Intelligence for their help and support.

References

[Cartwright & Collett '83] B.A. Cartwright and T.S.Collett, *Landmark Learning in Bees*, Journal of Comparative Physiology (1983) 151:521-543.

[Collett '87] T.S.Collett, *Insect Maps*, TINS, Vol. 10 No. 4, 1987.

[Gould '82] James L. Gould, *Ethology: The Mechanisms and Evolution of Behavior*, W.W. Norton and Co., New York 1982.

[Gould & Gould '88] James L. Gould and Carol Grant Gould, *The Honey Bee*, Scientific American Library 1988, p. 106.

[Hasler, Scholz & Horral '78] Arthur D. Hasler, A.T. Scholz and R.M. Horrall, *Olfactory Imprinting and Homing in Salmon*, American Scientist 66 (1978) pp. 347 - 55; quoted in [Gould '82].

[Kohonen '88]
Teuvo Kohonen, *Self-Organization and Associative Memory*, Springer Verlag, Berlin, Heidelberg, New York, 1988.

[Nehmzow, Hallam & Smithers '89]
Ulrich Nehmzow, John Hallam and Tim Smithers, *Really Useful Robots*, in: T. Kanade, F.C.A. Groen and L.O. Hertzberger (eds.), *Intelligent Autonomous Systems 2*, pp. 284–293, ISBN 90-800410-1-7, Amsterdam 1989.

[Nehmzow & Smithers '91]
Ulrich Nehmzow and Tim Smithers, *Mapbuilding using Self-Organising Networks*, in: Jean Arcady Meyer and Stewart Wilson (eds.), *From Animals to Animats*, pp. 152–159, MIT Press Cambridge Mass. and London, England, 1991.

[Nehmzow, Smithers & Hallam '91]
Ulrich Nehmzow, Tim Smithers and John Hallam, *Location recognition in a mobile robot using self-organising feature maps*, in: Günther Schmidt (ed.), *Information Processing in Autonomous Mobile Robots*, Springer Verlag, Berlin, Heidelberg, New York, 1991.

[Steels '91] Luc Steels, *Towards a theory of emergent functionality*, in Jean Arcady Meyer and Stewart Wilson (eds.), *From Animals to Animats*, pp. 451–461, MIT Press Cambridge Mass. and London, England, 1991.

[Waterman '89] Talbot H. Waterman, *Animal Navigation*, Scientific American Library 1989, p. 183.

[Wehner '76] Rüdiger Wehner, *Polarized-Light Navigation by Insects*, Scientific American 235 No. 1 (1976), pp.106-15.

[Willshaw & v.d.Malsburg '76] David J. Willshaw and Christoph von der Malsburg, *How patterned neural connections can be set up by self-organization*, Proc. R.Soc. London B. 194, pp.431-445 (1976).

The application of Temporal Difference Learning to the neural control of quadruped locomotion

Martin Snaith
Research Director
Technology Applications Group
5 Bolam's Mill
Alnwick. U.K.
+ 44 (0)665 604895
martin@tag.co.uk

Owen Holland
Research Director
Artificial Life Technologies
Clinton House, Church Place
Rodborough, Stroud. U.K.
+ 44 (0)453 752265
owen@tag.co.uk

Abstract

In order to investigate some aspects of the neural control of symmetrical jointed structures, a minimal four-legged walking platform was constructed. Each leg was equipped with a joint angle potentiometer and a foot pressure sensor, and was connected to the other legs through hard-wired reflexes modelled on those of a stick-insect and mediated by hardware analogue neurons. An off-board computer equipped with D-A and A-D facilities received the joint-angle information and sent an analogue control output to the hardware analogue control neurons; this control signal was derived from the joint-angle information and a number of externally supplied performance measures by a variety of methods, including nearest neighbor techniques and temporal differences. Although crude, the system proved capable of learning to produce gaits of the required character in spite of the complex interactions of the reflex system; in particular, some gaits outperformed the supposedly optimal 'engineered' gait used as a baseline index of preformance.

1. Introduction

Evidence from common observation shows the ability of natural systems both to learn and improve their ability to walk. What are the underlying mechanisms of this ability? Researchers have proposed various schemes to impart these abilities to a natural system or to a simple model of an animal. (Wilson's term animat [1] is gaining acceptance for this type of model.) But few trials on real animats have been attempted. We are undertaking a series of trials of various implementations of learning systems to promote a greater understanding of their characteristics. In order to keep the problem relatively tractable a simple quadrupedal robot with analogue foot and hip sensors has been constructed for this study. Simplicity of construction and movement have been uppermost in our minds to concentrate the study on the control paradigms rather than the constructional details.

2.1 The neural models used

In common with our work in the areas of navigation and mediation on wheeled and tracked robots [3,4,5] we use the simple SNF neural model [6]. The neurons used in this work are of the non-spiking type and are built out of convetional analogue hardware. The mathematical expression

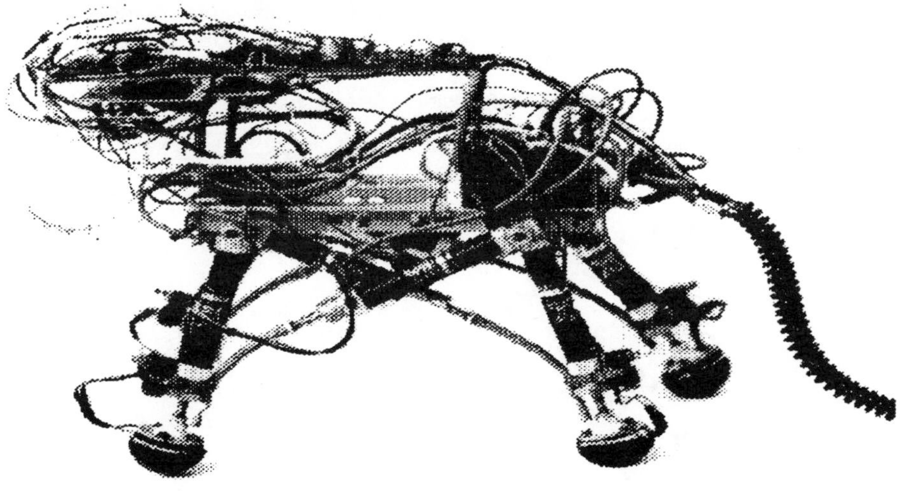

Figure 1 The small quadruped robot chassis used in this study.

of the transfer function is given by the equation :

$o(v,t) = \text{ceiling}\ [\text{floor}\ [g(m,t) * (\Sigma e_i(v,t) + \Sigma i_i(v,t))]]$

where: **g(m,t)** is a function of time and the modulation input. **e_i(v,t)** is the **I**th component of the excitation vector to the neuron (a function of the environment and time), **i_i(v,t)** if the **i**th component of the inhibition Input vector to the neuron. **ceiling** is a function which limits the output's positive excursion to 100% activity. **floor** is function which in this case limits the output's negitive excursion to 0% i.e. allows no negative excursion.

2.1.1 Comparison with the Koch neural model

At a recent workshop in Germany, Uwe Koch gave details of a hardware neuron model, constructed to be a close representation of a biologically plausible neuron [7]. In order to gain some appreciation of the relevance of studies using the simple SNF neuron, Koch and Snaith constructed a model of the Ludlow N-flop mediator [8] The transfer and hysteretic properties of the two models and their decay with parametric modulation was closely related. The reader is referred to [5] for a wider discussion of neural mediation studies.

2.2 The reflexoidal model chosen

After bench trials of more complex networks, including a twelve neuron, three reflex system which used both hip position and foot pressure sensors, an eight neuron network connected in a four pair configuration was used to model three simple leg reflexes: a power stroke, in which the leg is driven in the direction opposite to that of the required motion, provided that there is sufficient activity from the foot pressure sensor; a recovery stroke, in which the leg is retracted back to its rest position, provided there is little activity from the foot pressure sensor; and a step in which the leg is extended or retracted, although this reflex is generally triggered by the power stroke in the current study. The various conflicting reflexes are connected by mutual inhibition and the cooperative reflexes are connected by mutual excitation.

2.2.1 Stick insect walking study by Holk Cruse et al

The reflexes we use in this study are based, in a somewhat simplified form on studies of the walking mechanisms of the stick insect by Cruse et al [17]. These studies reveal a set of local interlinked mechanisms which are connected to leg position and force sensors on the leg of the insect. The legs are thought to be connected in local groups of four with inhibition and excitation paths both across the body and along the body. The simple mechanisms (reflexes) are thought to be self contained and not reliant upon central sequencing.

2.3 The choice of search paradigm

It was decided to give the learning system no direct access to the atate of the reflex neurons and their inputs. The state of the robot was therefore derived from four joint-angle potentiometers (one per leg). These signals underwent A-D conversion before being presented to an off-board computer as the state vector. The learning system produced a training vector with four elements; this underwent D-A conversion and each element was presented to the appropriate recovery neuron as a voltage. The robot would move in response to the input of a training vector; during training, the progress made was assessed when the movement had ceased or become oscillatory, and was then input as 'reward'.

3. The hybrid search / learning system

The state vector defined a point in the input space. Memory corresponding to a parametrically variable volume centred on that point was searched for the record of the training vector which had previously resulted in the highest return. (Return is defined as the cumulative total of individual rewards from the series formed by that vector and a parametrically variable number of vectors following it.) If the reward from the selected vector was above a threshold (calculated as below) the vector was output; otherwise the com-

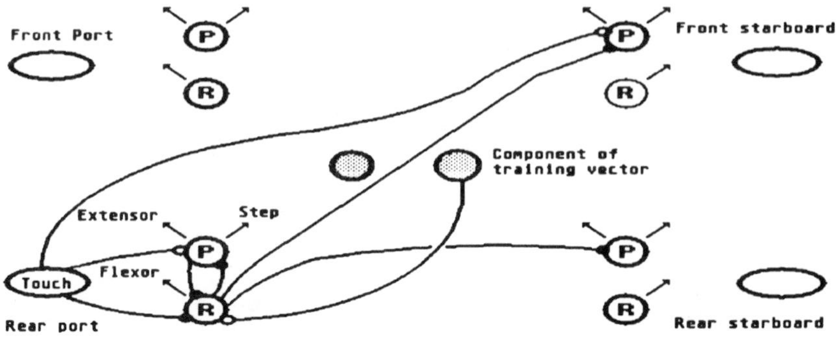

Figure 2.1 One leg of the reflexive network. The black circles are inhibitory inputs, the white excitatory. The sensors are shown as ellipses. Two training inputs are shown as in the oscillator experiments.

ponents of the vector were stochastically mutated by parametrically variable amounts before being output.

The threshold was determined by applying a temporal diference method (of the type TD[0]) to the successive rewards, producing a time-weighted estimate of forthcoming reward based on a linear combination of the elements of the state vector.

4.1 The sequenced state generator in action

As a baseline for walking, a pre-programmed gait was imposed on the robot by generating an appropriately structured sequence of strong excitations. A seven state gait proved to be easy to model and robust in use. Two diagonal pairs of legs, (front left paired with rear right and vice versa) provide the power stroke onto the extended front leg of the other power stroke pair, with the final member of this pair being recovered next in the gait cycle. This sequence is repeated for the other power stroke; seven states are required to produce a complete cycle. The small robot, with a step length of approximately 10cm, is able to move in a straight line across a reasonably level surface at a speed of 0.25m/sec. At speeds higher than this, mechanical instabilities produce a strongly curved trajectory which the system, lacking feedback, cannot correct.

4.1.1 The limitations of this approach

Because there is no modulation of the walking pattern by a 'perceptive' system, the sequenced state generator relies upon a stable environment. Should the robot be picked off the floor, the walking sequence continues. Similarly, if any major change occurs in the robot's internal state, such as a limb failing, the walking pattern can be disrupted. It is worth noting that there is some ability to cope with losing one reflex on a leg; for example, if the return stroke of a leg is disabled, the machine is still able to walk in a reasonably straight line. Though this may seem a trivial solution to the walking problem, it has been included both for completeness, and in order to act as a base level measure of performance against which the other approaches may be compared.

4.1.2 A possible extension

The addition to an established gait generator of a suitable 'perceptive' system, to provide correction for directional or other errors may yet prove to be the most effective approach to walking that is available at present. Despite the greater sophistication of our other trial systems, the sequencer still consistently produces the fastest regular walking pattern. We also note that the mechanically based, non-optimising walking machines of Todd [18] perform very well despite their apparant lack of sophistication. This may well be an example of good mechanical design (or morphological evolution) being at least as important in some cases as the optimisation of control algorithms.

4.2 The reflexoidal system in action

Using the network shown in figure 2.1 walking at a speed of 0.1m/sec was possible when external excitation was applied to the excitation inputs controlling the recovery stroke once the network has been set up. In this phase of the study the network is trained by a manual method using symmetrical constraints to reduce the phase space. [3,13]. The initially juddering walk is considerably smoothed by reducing the output bandwidth of the power stroke neurons. When picked up, the robot ceases walking in a stereotyped stance which has all four limbs ready for the power stroke. Stimulating the foot sensors produces an interestingly natural kick reaction - it is rather like picking up a pet rabbit.

4.2.1 Locking up into a semi-stable state

When the source of external stimulation is removed from the reflex network the robot comes to rest within four steps, in a stance in which a front leg is extended for a power stroke. If a force is applied to the rear of the chassis, walking resumes, ceasing when the force is removed. This semi-stable state is a characteristic of the avoidance and goal seeking navigation systems used on TAG's neuro-behavioural mobile robots; and if handled correctly can form the basis of a world mapping system [3,4,14].

4.2.2 Loosely coupled oscillator as excitation for the network

The eight neuron reflex model is able to walk unaided only when a cyclically varying external excitation source, such as an oscillator, is connected in anti-phase to the recovery neuron excitation inputs. The frequency of the gait produced by the reflex network is not the same as that applied by the oscillator. The oscillator can be run at a lower frequency than that of the gait without affecting the speed of motion. The role of the oscillator is apparently to prevent the network from locking into a particular state.

This particular solution is used as a control experiment to show that the reflexes of the platform are correctly configured, and that the learning sytem has a chance of producing a working solution.

4.3 The first search/learning system

Using a combination of a simple mutation operator to suggest future actions when no history is available to the system, and a minimum threshold of acceptance for any action based upon a learned prediction of return, it is possible to construct a first attempt at unsupervised training for a walking machine. The quality factors for training may be derived from the stereophonic images of a point noise source in the environment; at present these are usually substituted by the keyboard or a file.

4.3.1 Seeding the search

While the TD learning is used to increase the performance of the system, it needs some initial search strategy to generate the observation-outcome pairs; this mutates the current training vector within the limit of two system parameters: the maximum allowed single vector element mutation in one generation, and the maximum number of vector elements which can be mutated in one generation. Both seeding from supervised training and a correlation operator between state vector differential and training vector differential have been applied in successive experiments to promote convergence.

4.3.2 How to relate training sensors to the training vector

While there may be a correlation between the sensor position of the legs and the appropriateness of the current movement in some cases, this cannot be generally relied upon by a walking machine in the real world. The measurement of walking quality will generally be available from sensors other than leg position - sound or vision for example. To add to our difficulty, not only is there no guarantee of a simple correlation between quality measures and the training vector used to modulate the reflexes, but the dimensionality of the two vectors is different. This makes the production of a gradient operator for the correlation of the two surfaces (quality and training vector) a non-trivial task. Current paradigms seem to involve the reduction of vectorial quality measure to a scalar quantity (reward) with its associated loss of information, although we see in this particular study that the scalar quantity derived from the initial reward vectors does contain enough information to allow a gait to be found with no a priori knowledge.

4.3.3 Determination of previous state equivalence

A prerequisite to determining the best action to adopt in a particular state is the identification of that state. In a simulator this is trivial; real platforms must be able to cope with uncertainty in a similar way to other empirical studies. A guiding principle adopted in many experiments is to reject any reading of greater than three standard deviations from the mean of a population under study. A similar rule is used here to determine the acceptance of a particular stored previous state as being representative of the current state. The width of the acceptance window is parameterised and hence can manipulated by the experimentor or be subjected to the mutation operator.

5 Preliminary results

In order to satisfactorily compete against its less sophisticated forerunners, our current unsupervised learning arrangement needs time to search its memory, but it can come up with interesting gaits of its own within a few tens of trials on many occasions and within the first hundred on almost all of the trials so far. In the first successful trial with no a priori knowledge, i.e. no supervised training session or initialisation knowledge, the system learned to produce a gallop - it resolutely preferred 25cm inch lunges, followed by a period of inactivity, to a simple alternating gait or slight regular shuffle. A disadvantage of the present system is that an action with a large reward associated with it at one point of the input space tends to dominate the responses around the point in input space in which it occured, producing the phenominon known as 'stuck state' in which learning the rewards from other actions is prevented. Possible solutions involve the use of stochastic selection, or allowing learning to 'spread' to adjacent input states as in CMAC learning [23].

5.1 Extension of the trials

Other systems of self optimisation are candidates for trial on this platform to promote some understanding of their relative strengths when compared to the more design intensive, less self-optimising approaches. Implementations of CMAC and of recent work at MIT [15] are the most likely extensions. We are also looking at implementing a back-propagation of utility system [19], to search the same phase space. This interesting approach has been used successfully in the past on a number of working sytems [20,21]. The back-propogation of utility 'allows you to derive a schedule of actions, or adapt an optimal Action network, so as to maximise any performance index or utility function which you choose to specify, over multiple time periods' [22]. But the problem of how to relate multiple measures of quality to the modulation of the reflexes in a more direct way than that chosen so far remains for us to solve.

The use of learning may well prove to be no more than a sophisticated way of coding the designer's knowledge into an animat, more akin, albeit on a meta-level, to the encoding of heuristics in an expert system or behaviourally based architecture, than an algorithmic means of extending the knowledge horizon [16] of an animat. But the trials undertaken to date of this hybrid TD and mutation operator system do seem to allow some cause for optimism especially if we overcome the tendrency towards conservatism once a successful series of actions has been discovered.

References

[1] Wilson S, Conf. Proc. 'Simulation of Adaptive Behaviour in Animals and Animats' Paris September 1990.

[3] Snaith M. A. 'Neuro-Behavioural Control of Autonomous Mobile Robots.' Proc. IARP 2nd Workshop on Medical and Healthcare Robots. Newcastle UK Sept. 1989.

[4] Snaith M. A. 'A Virtual Field Uncertainty Recovery Strategy for Mobile Robot Navigation.' Workshop on Biology, Cognition and Robotics. GMD Sankt Augustin RG June 1990.

[5] Snaith M. A. & Holland O. 'An Investigation of two Mediation Strategies Suitable for Behavioural Control in Animals and Animats.' Proc. Conf. 'Simulation of Adaptive Behaviour.' Paris Sept 1990.

[6] Snaith M. A. 'SNFs and their Application to Autonomous Mobile Robots.' TAG internal paper Oct. 1989.

[7] Koch U. 'Simulation of Biological Neural Networks Using "Biological" Neurons.' Workshop on Biology, Cognition and Robotics. GMD Sankt Augustin RG June 1990.

[8] Ludlow A.R. 'The Behaviour of a Model Animal.' Behaviour vol 58, pp 131-172.

[9] Ashby W. Ross 'Design For a Brain' Chapman and Hall 1952.

[10] Sutton R. 'Reinforcement Learning Architectures for Animats.' Proc. Conf. 'Simulation of Adaptive Behaviour.' Paris Sept 1990.

[11] Sutton R. S.'Time-Derivative Models of Pavlovian Reinforcement' in Learning and Computational Science, J. W. Moore and M. Gabrial Eds. MIT Press 1989.

[13] Holland O. & Snaith M.A. 'The Blind Neural Network Maker: Can we use constrained embryologies to design animat nervous systems?' Proc. ICANN Helsinki 1991.

[14] Snaith M.A. & Holland O. 'A Feature Based Navigator for Mobile Robots.' presented at ICAR Pisa 1991.

[15] Maes P. & Brooks R.A. 'Learning to Co-ordinate Behaviours' AAAI Boston 1990.

[16] Popper K. 'The Open Society and Its Enemies.' Objective Knowledge: an evolutionary Approach, Oxford Clarendon Press.

[17] Todd J. Dept Mechanical Engineering Edinburgh University. 1990. (personal communication & video)

[18] Cruse H. 'What Mechanisms Co-ordinate Leg Movements in Walking Arthropods.' 'Workshop on Biology, Cognition and Robots.' Sankt Augustin GMD, RG 1990.

[19] Werbos P. 'Back propagation through time: what it does and how to do it.' Proc. IEEE August 1990.

[20] Jordan M. 'Generic constraints on underspecified target trajectories.' Proc. IJCNN 1989.

[21] Kawato M.'Computational schames and neural network models for formation and control of multi-joint arm trajectory.' Miller, Sutton and Wurbos 1990.

[22]Werbos P. 'Neurocontrol and related techniques.' p.348 para.3 in Maren, Harston and Pap 'Handbook of neural computing applications.' Academic Press 1990.

[23] Albus J. S. 'A new approach to manipulator control; the cerebellar model articulation controller (CMAC)' ASME Journal of Dynamic Systems, Measurement, and Control vol 97, pp 220-227

Evolution of Subsumption Using Genetic Programming

John R. Koza
Computer Science Department
Stanford University
Stanford, CA 94305 USA
E-MAIL: Koza@Sunburn.Stanford.Edu
PHONE: 415-941-0336 FAX: 415-941-9430

The recently developed genetic programming paradigm is used to evolve emergent wall following behavior for an autonomous mobile robot using the subsumption architecture.

1. INTRODUCTION AND OVERVIEW

The repetitive application of seemingly simple rules can lead to complex overall emergent behavior. Emergent functionality means that overall functionality is not achieved in the conventional tightly coupled, centrally controlled way, but, instead, indirectly by the interaction of relatively primitive components with the world and among themselves [Steels 1991]. Emergent functionality is one of the main themes of research in artificial life [Langton 1989].

In this paper, we use the genetic programming paradigm to evolve a computer program that exhibits emergent behavior and enables an autonomous mobile robot to follow the walls of an irregularly shaped room. The evolutionary process is driven only by the fitness of the programs in solving the problem.

2. BACKGROUND ON GENETIC ALGORITHMS

John Holland's pioneering 1975 *Adaptation in Natural and Artificial Systems* described how the evolutionary process in nature can be applied to artificial systems using the genetic algorithm operating on fixed length character strings [Holland 1975].

Holland demonstrated that a population of fixed length character strings (each representing a proposed solution to a problem) can be genetically bred using the Darwinian operation of fitness proportionate reproduction and the genetic operation of recombination. The recombination operation combines parts of two chromosome-like fixed length character strings, each selected on the basis of their fitness, to produce new offspring strings.

Current work in the field of genetic algorithms is reviewed in Goldberg [1989], Belew and Booker [1991], Davis [1987, 1991], Rawlins [1991] and Meyer and Wilson [1991].

3. BACKGROUND ON GENETIC PROGRAMMING

For many problems, the most natural representation for solutions are computer programs whose size, shape, and content have not been determined in advance. It is unnatural and difficult to represent computer programs of dynamically varying size and shape with fixed length character strings.

Although one might think that computer programs are so epistatic that they could only be genetically bred in a few especially congenial problem domains, we have shown that computer programs can be genetically bred to solve a surprising variety of problems in many different areas [Koza 1992], including

- emergent behavior (e.g. discovering a computer program which, when executed by all the ants in an ant colony, enables the ants to locate food, pick it up, carry it to the nest, and drop pheromones along the way so as to produce cooperative emergent behavior) [Koza 1991a],
- planning (e.g. navigating an artificial ant along an irregular trail) [Koza 1990b],
- finding minimax strategies for games (e.g. differential pursuer-evader games; discrete games in extensive form) by both evolution and co-evolution [Koza 1991b],
- optimal control (e.g. centering a cart and balancing a broom in minimal time by applying a bang-bang force to the cart) (Koza and Keane 1990a, 1990b],
- machine learning of functions (e.g. learning the Boolean 11-multiplexer function) [Koza 1991d],
- generation of random numbers (using entropy as fitness) [Koza 1991c],

- symbolic regression, integration, differentiation, and symbolic solution to general functional equations for a solution in the form of a function (including differential equations with initial conditions, and integral equations) [Koza 1990], and
- simultaneous architectural design and training of neural nets [Koza and Rice 1991a].

A videotape visualization of the application of genetic programming to planning, emergent behavior, empirical discovery, inverse kinematics, and game playing can be found in the *Artificial Life II Video Proceedings* [Koza and Rice 1991b].

3.1. OBJECTS IN GENETIC PROGRAMMING

In genetic programming, the individuals in the population are compositions of functions and terminals appropriate to the particular problem domain. The set of functions used typically includes arithmetic operations, mathematical functions, conditional logical operations, and domain-specific functions. The set of terminals used typically includes inputs (sensors) appropriate to the problem domain and possibly various constants. Each function in the function set should be well defined for any combination of elements from the range of every function that it may encounter and every terminal that it may encounter.

One can now view the search for a solution to the problem as a search in the hyperspace of all possible compositions of functions and terminals (i.e. computer programs) that can be recursively composed of the available functions and terminals.

The symbolic expressions (S-expressions) of the LISP programming language are an especially convenient way to create and manipulate the compositions of functions and terminals described above. These S-expressions in LISP correspond directly to the parse tree that is internally created by most compilers.

3.2. OPERATIONS IN GENETIC PROGRAMMING

The basic genetic operations for the genetic programming paradigm are reproduction (e.g. fitness proportionate reproduction) and crossover (recombination).

The reproduction operation copies an individual in the population into the new population for the next generation.

The crossover (recombination) operation is a sexual operation that operates on two parental LISP S-expressions and produces two offspring S-expressions using parts of each parent. The crossover operation creates new offspring S-expressions by exchanging sub-trees (i.e. sub-lists) between the two parents. Because entire sub-trees are swapped, this crossover operation always produces syntactically and semantically valid LISP S-expressions as offspring regardless of the crossover points.

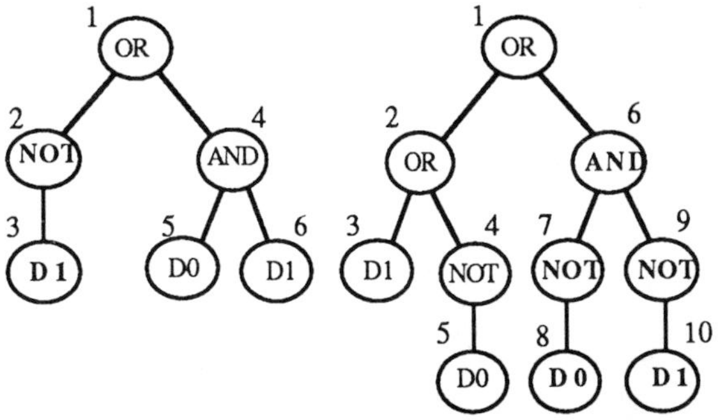

Figure 1: Two parental computer programs shown as trees with ordered branches. Internal points of the tree correspond to functions (i.e. operations) and external points correspond to terminals (i.e. input data).

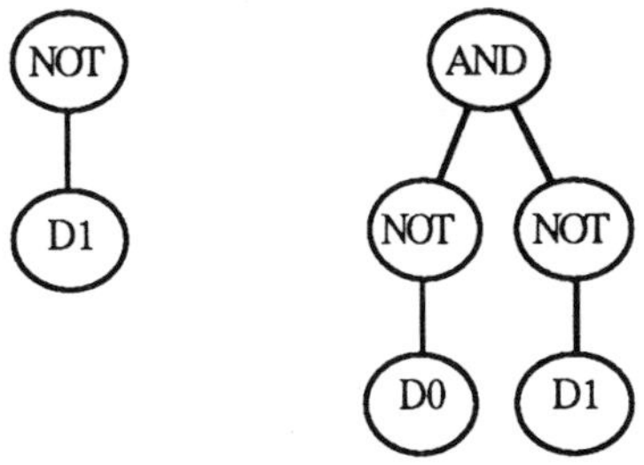

Figure 2: The two crossover fragments

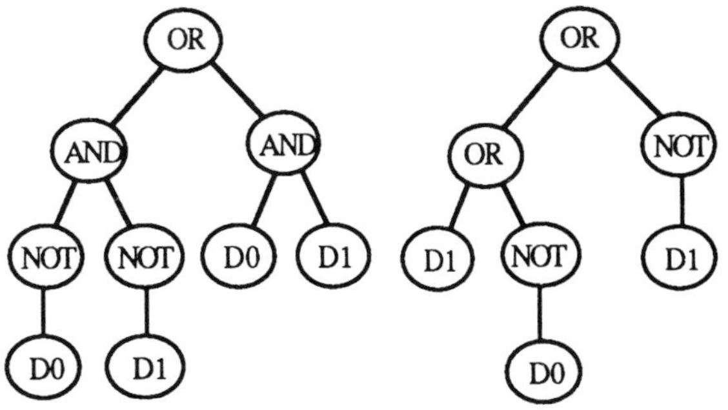

Figure 3: Offspring resulting from crossover

For example, consider the two parental S-expressions:

```
(OR (NOT D1) (AND D0 D1))

(OR (OR D1 (NOT D0))
    (AND (NOT D0) (NOT D1))
```

Figure 1 graphically depicts these two S-expressions as rooted, point-labeled trees with ordered branches. The numbers on the points of the tree are for reference only.

Assume that the points of both trees are numbered in a depth-first way starting at the left. Suppose that point no. 2 (out of 6 points of the first parent) is randomly selected as the crossover point for the first parent and that point no. 6 (out of 10 points of the second parent) is randomly selected as the crossover point of the second parent. The crossover points in the trees above are therefore the NOT in the first parent and the AND in the second parent.

Figure 2 shows the two crossover fragments are two sub-trees. These two crossover fragments correspond to the bold sub-expressions (sub-lists) in the two parental LISP S-expressions shown above.

Figure 3 shows the two offspring resulting from the crossover.

Note that the first offspring in Figure 3 is an S-expression for the Boolean even-parity (i.e. equal) function, namely

```
(OR (AND (NOT D0) (NOT D1)) (AND D0 D1)).
```

3.3. EXECUTION OF GENETIC PROGRAMMING

The genetic programming paradigm, like the conventional genetic algorithm, is a domain independent method. It proceeds by genetically breeding populations of computer programs to solve problems by executing the following three steps:

(1) Generate an initial population of random compositions of the functions and terminals of the problem (computer programs).

(2) Iteratively perform the following sub-steps until the termination criterion has been satisfied:

   (a) Execute each program in the population and assign it a fitness value according to how well it solves the problem.

   (b) Create a new population of computer programs by applying the following two primary operations. The operations are applied to computer program(s) in the population chosen with a probability based on fitness.

      (i) *Reproduction*: Copy existing computer programs to the new population.

      (ii) *Crossover*: Create two new computer programs by genetically recombining randomly chosen parts of two existing programs.

(3) The single best computer program in the population at the time of termination is designated as the result of the genetic programming paradigm. This result may be a solution (or approximate solution) to the problem.

4. THE WALL FOLLOWING PROBLEM

Mataric [1990] described the problem of controlling an autonomous mobile robot to perform the task of following the walls of an irregular room.

The robot is capable of executing the following five primitive motor functions: moving forward by a constant distance, moving backward by a constant distance, turning right by 30 degrees, turning left by 30 degrees, and stopping.

The robot has 12 sonar sensors which report the distance to the nearest wall. Each sonar sensor covers a 30 degree sector around the robot. In addition, there was a sensor for the STOPPED condition of the robot.

Figure 4 shows an irregularly shaped room and the distances reported by the 12 sonar sensors. The robot is shown at point (12, 16) near the center of the room. The north (top) wall and west (left) wall are each 27.6 feet long.

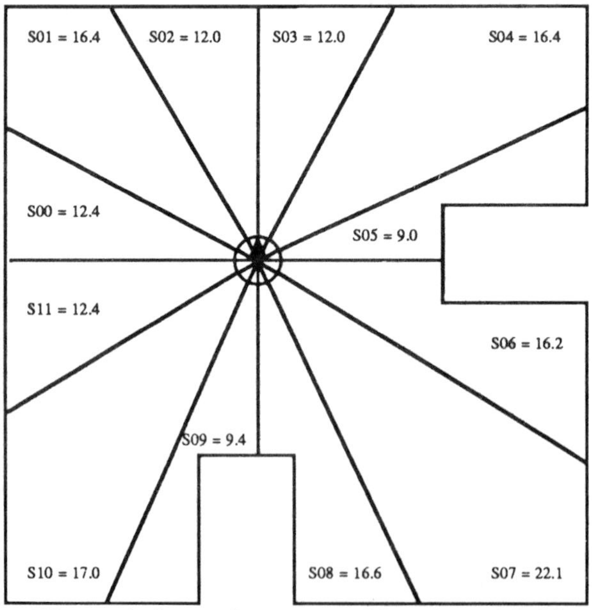

Figure 4: Irregular room with robot with 12 sonar sensors located near middle of the room

One can envision solving the wall following problem in one of three approaches, namely

(1) the conventional approach to building control systems for for autonomous mobile robots,

(2) the subsumption architecture, and

(3) genetic programming.

Regardless of which of these three approaches is used to solve the wall following problem, the 13 sensors can be viewed as the input to an as-yet unwritten computer program in a style appropriate to the three approaches. This as-yet unwritten program will process these inputs and will cause the activation, in some order, of the various primitive motor functions. This as-yet-unwritten program will be a composition of the five available primitive motor functions and the 13 available sensors.

Note that the 13 sensors and five primitive motor functions are the starting point of all three approaches. They are given as part of the statement of the problem.

5. THE CONVENTIONAL ROBOTIC APPROACH

The conventional approach to building control systems for autonomous mobile robots is to decompose the overall problem into a series of functional units that perform functions such as perception, modeling, planning, task execution, and motor control. A central control system then executes each functional unit in this decomposition and then passes the results on to the next functional unit in an orderly, closely coupled, and synchronized manner. For example, the perception unit senses the world and the results of this sensing are then passed to a modeling module which attempts to build an internal model of the perceived world. The internal model resulting from this modeling is then passed on to a planning unit which computes a plan. The plan might be devised by a consistent and logically sound technique (e.g. resolution and unification) or it might be devised by one of the many heuristic techniques of symbolic artificial intelligence. In any event, the resulting plan is passed on to the task execution unit which then executes the plan by calling on the motor control unit. The motor control unit then acts directly on the external world.

In this conventional approach, only a few of the functional units (e.g. the perception unit and motor control unit) typically are in direct communication with the world. All functional units must typically be executed in their intended orderly, closely coupled, and synchronized manner in order to make the robot do anything.

6. THE SUBSUMPTION ARCHITECTURE

The subsumption architecture decomposes the problem into a set of asynchronous task achieving behaviors [Brooks 1986, 1989]. The task achieving behaviors for an autonomous mobile robot might include behaviors such as avoiding objects, wandering, exploring, identifying objects, building maps, planning changes to the world, monitoring changes, and reasoning about behavior of the objects. The task achieving behaviors operate locally and asychronously and are only loosely coupled to one another. In contrast to the conventional approach, each of the task achieving behaviors is typically in direct communication with the world (and each other). The task achieving behaviors in the subsumption architecture are typically much more primitive than the functional units of the conventional approach.

In the subsumption architecture, various subsets of the task achieving behaviors typically exhibit some partial competence in solving a simpler version of the overall problem. Thus, the solution to a more complex version of a problem can potentially be built up by incrementally adding new independent acting parts to existing parts. In addition, the system may be fault tolerant in the sense that the failure of one part does not cause complete failure, but, instead, causes a gracefully degradation of performance to some lower level. In contrast, in the conventional approach, the various functional units have no functionality when operating separately and there is a complete suspension of all performance when one functional unit fails.

In the subsumption architecture, the task achieving behaviors each consist of an applicability predicate, a gate, and a behavioral action. If the current environment satisfies the applicability predicate of a particular behavior, the gate allows the output of the behavioral action to feed out onto the output line of that behavior. Potential conflicts among behavioral actions are resolved by a hierarchical arrangement of suppressor nodes. As a simple example, suppose that there are three task achieving behaviors with strictly decreasing priority. The applicability predicates and the suppressor nodes of these three behaviors are equivalent to the following composition of ordinary IF conditional functions:

```
(IF A-P-1 BEHAVIOR-1
          (IF A-P-2 BEHAVIOR-2
                    (IF A-P-3 BEHAVIOR-3)
```

In particular, if the first applicability predicate (A-P-1) is satisfied, then BEHAVIOR-1 is executed. Otherwise, if A-P-2 is satisfied, BEHAVIOR-2 is executed. Otherwise, the lowest priority behavior (i.e. BEHAVIOR-3) is executed.

Mataric (1990) has implemented the subsumption architecture for controlling an autonomous mobile robot by conceiving and writing a set of four programs for performing four task achieving behaviors. The four behaviors together enable a mobile robot called TOTO to follow the walls in an irregular room.

Starting with the five primitive motor functions and the 13 sensors that are part of the definition of the problem, Mataric applied her intelligence and ingenuity and conceived of a set of four task achieving behaviors which together enable a mobile robot to follow the walls in an irregular room. As a matter of preference, Mataric specifically selected her four task achieving behaviors so that their applicability predicates were mutually exclusive (thus eliminating the need for a conflict resolution architecture allowing one task achieving behavior to suppress the behavior of another).

Mataric then wrote a set of four LISP programs for performing the four task achieving behaviors. Mataric's four LISP programs corresponded to the four task achieving behaviors and were called STROLL, AVOID, ALIGN, and CORRECT. Each of these four task achieving behaviors interacted directly with the world and each other.

Various subsets of Mataric's four behaviors exhibited some partial competence in solving part of the overall problem. For example, the robot became capable of collission free wandering with only the STROLL and AVOID behaviors. The robot became capable of tracing convex boundaries with only the addition of only the ALIGN behavior to these first two behaviors. Finally, the robot became capable of general boundary tracing with the further addition of the CORRECT behavioral unit.

Mataric's four LISP programs included nine LISP functions (namely, COND, AND, NOT, IF, >, >=, =, <=, and >). In addition, her four programs internally made use of three constant parameters (defining an edging distance EDG, minimum safe distance MSD, and danger zone DZ), the minimum of all 12 sonar distances (called "Shortest Sonar" or SS), and eight other internally defined variables representing the minimum of various thoughtfully chosen subsets of the 12 sonar distances (e.g. the dynamically computed minimum of a particular three forward facing sensors).

In total, Mataric's four LISP programs consisted a composition of 151 functions and terminals.

The fact that Mataric was able to write four programs enabling an autonomous robot to perform the task of following the wall of an irregular room is evidence (based on this particular problem) for one of the claims of the subsumption architecture, namely, that it is possible to build a control system for an autonomous mobile robot using loosely coupled, asynchronous task achieving behaviors.

Note that if Mataric had wanted to write a computer program for wall following using conventional coupled synchronous robotic techniques, her program would have taken in the same 13 sensors as inputs and caused the activation, in some order, of the same five primitive motor functions as the output of the program.

The conception and design of suitable task achieving behaviors for the subsumption architecture requires considerable ingenuity and skill on the part of the human programmer.

7. APPLICATION OF GENETIC PROGRAMMING TO THE WALL FOLLOWING PROBLEM

The question arises as to whether an autonomous mobile robot can learn to perform wall following in an evolutionary way, and, in particular, by using genetic programming. This learning would include learning both the necessary task achieving behaviors (including the applicability predicates and behavioral actions) and the conflict resolution hierarchy.

There are five major steps in preparing to use the genetic programming paradigm, namely, determining:

(1) the set of terminals,
(2) the set of functions,
(3) the fitness function,
(4) the parameters and variables for controlling the run, and
(5) the criterion for designating a result and terminating a run.

The first major step in preparing to use genetic programming is to identify the set of terminals. The genetic programming paradigm genetically creates a computer program that takes certain inputs and produces outputs in order to successfully perform a specified task. The inputs to this program usually come from the statement of the problem. For the wall following problem, the potential inputs to the computer program consist of the 13 available sensors. These are the same 13 sensors which one would use if one were attempting to perform wall following with the conventional robotic approach or the subsumption architecture.

In reviewing the 13 sensors, we concluded that we had no use for the STOPPED sensor since our simulated robot could not be damaged by running into a wall in the course of a computer simulation. Moreover, we did not want our simulated robot to ever stop. Thus, we deleted the STOPPED sensor, the STOP primitive function, and the constant parameter for the danger zone DZ.

We retained Mataric's other two constant numerical parameters (i.e. the edging distance EDG and the minimum safe distance MSD). We retained Mataric's overall minimum sensor SS. However, we did not use any of her eight derived values representing specific subsets of sonar sensors. Human programmers find it convenient to create and refer to such intermediate variables in their programs.

Thus, our terminal set consisted of 15 items, namely,

```
T = {S00, S01, S02, S03, ...,
     S11, SS, MSD, EDG}
```

In other words, at each time step of the simulation, our simulated robot will have access to these 15 floating point values.

The second major step in preparing to use genetic programming is to identify a set of functions for the problem.

We start with the five given primitive motor functions that are part of the statement of this problem. As previously mentioned, we had no use for the STOP function. Since we want to evolve a subsumption architecture and we observed above that the subsumption architecture can be viewed as a composition of ordinary IF conditional functions, we included a single simple decision making function (IFLTE) in the function set. The function IFLTE (If-Less-Than-Or-Equal) takes four arguments. If the value of the first argument is less than or equal the value of the second argument, the third argument is evaluated and returned. Otherwise, the fourth argument is evaluated and returned.

We also included a connective function (PROGN2) in our function set. The connective function PROGN2 taking two arguments evaluates both of its arguments, in order, and returns the result of evaluating its second argument.

Thus, the function set F for this problem consists of four of the five given primitive motor functions (i.e. TR, TL, MF, and MB as described below), the decision function IFLTE, and the connective PROGN2. That is, the function set F is

```
F = {TR, TL, MF, MB, IFLTE,
     PROGN2}
```

The function TR (Turn Right) turns the robot 30 degrees to the right (i.e. clockwise).

The function TL (Turn Left) turns the robot 30 degrees to the left (i.e. counter-clockwise).

We achieved the same effect as the STOP function by letting our robot push up against the wall, and, if no change of state occurs after one time step, the robot is viewed as having stopped. Because we were not concerned with physically damaging our simulated robot, we did not include Mataric's primitive motor function STOP for stopping the robot (e.g. when it is about to invade the danger zone DZ and possibly damage itself).

The function MF (Move Forward) causes the robot to move 1.0 feet forward in the direction it is currently facing. If any of the six forward looking sonar sensors (i.e. S00 through S05) report a distance to any wall of less than 110% of the distance to be moved, no movement occurs.

The function MB (Move Backward) causes the robot to move 1.3 feet backwards. If any of the six backward looking sonar sensors (i.e. S06 though S11) report a distance to any wall of less than 110% of the distance to be moved, no movement occurs.

All sonar distances are dynamically recomputed after each execution of a move or turn. Each of the moving and turning functions returns the minimum of the two distances reported by the two sensors (i.e. S02 and S03) that look in the direction of forward movement (i.e. S02 representing the 11:30 o'clock direction and S03 representing the 12:30 o'clock direction).

The functions MF, MB, TR, and TL each take one time step (i.e. 1.0 seconds) to execute.

The third major step in preparing to use genetic programming is identification of the fitness function for evaluating how good a given computer program is at solving the problem at hand.

A wall following robot may be viewed as a robot that travels along the entire perimeter of the irregularly shaped room. Noting that the edging distance is 2.3 feet, we proceed to define the fitness measure for this problem by placing 2.3 foot square tiles along the perimeter of the room. Twelve such tiles fit along the 27.6 foot north wall and 12 such tiles fit along the 27.6 foot west wall. A total of 56 tiles are required to cover the entire periphery of the room.

Figure 5 shows the room with the 56 tiles (each with a filled circle at its center). The robot is shown in the middle of the room at its starting position (12, 16) facing in its starting direction (i.e. south).

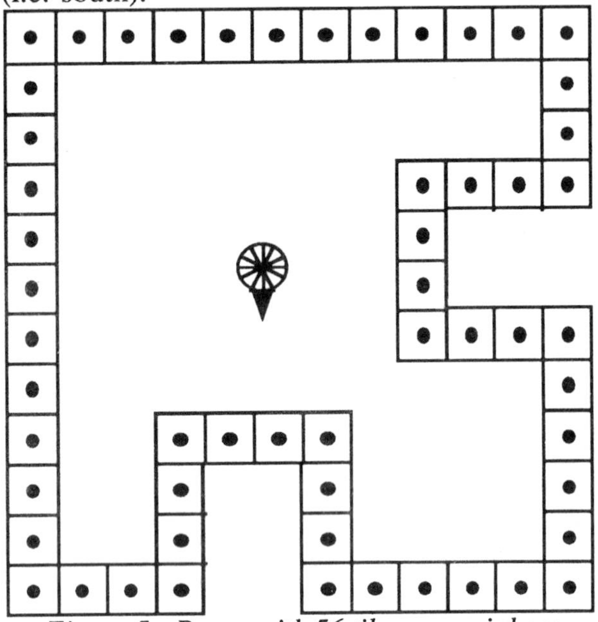

Figure 5: Room with 56 tiles on periphery showing robot at its starting position (12,16) facing south.

We defined the fitness of an individual S-expression in the population to be the number of tiles (from 0 to 56) that are touched by the robot within the allotted period of time (i.e. 400 time steps).

The fourth major step in preparing to use genetic programming is selecting the values of certain parameters. The population size is 1000 here. Each new generation is created from the preceding generation by applying the fitness proportionate reproduction operation to 10% of the population and by applying the crossover operation to 90% of the population (with both parents selected with a probability proportionate to fitness). In selecting crossover points, 90% were internal (function) points of the tree and 10% were external (terminal) points of the tree. For the practical reason of conserving computer time, the depth of initial random S-expressions was limited to 4 and the depth of S-expressions created by crossover was limited to 15.

Finally, the fifth major step in preparing to use genetic programming is the selection of the criterion for terminating a run and accepting a result. We will terminate a given run when either (i) genetic programming produces a computer program which achieves the maximal value for fitness (i.e. 56 out of 56), or (ii) 101 generations have been run.

Note that in performing these five preparatory steps, we made use only of the information provided in the basic statement of the problem (with the modifications needed because we did not intend to allow our simulated robot ever to stop during the course of our computer simulations). We *did not* use any of Mataric's thoughtfully chosen subsets of sensors nor did we use any knowledge about the four task achieving behaviors which Mataric conceived and defined. We *did*, however, define a way to measure fitness in performing wall following. We *did* use the 12 sonar sensors, two of the three constant numerical parameters, and four of the five primitive motor functions that were part of the statement of the problem.

8. RESULTS

In one run of the genetic programming paradigm on this problem, 57% of the individuals in the population in the initial random generation (i.e. generation 0) scored a fitness of zero (out of a possible 56). Many of these zero-scoring S-expressions merely caused the robot to turn without ever moving while others caused the robot to wander aimlessly in circles in the middle of the room. About 20% of the individuals from generation 0 were wall-bangers which scored precisely one because they headed for a wall and continued to push up against it.

The best single individual from generation 0 scored 17 (out of 56). This S-expression consists of 17 points (i.e. functions and terminals) and is shown below:

```
(IFLTE (PROGN2 MSD (TL))
       (IFLTE S06 S03 EDG (MF))
       (IFLTE MSD EDG S05 S06)
       (PROGN2 MSD (MF)))
```

Figure 6 shows the looping trajectory of the robot while executing this best-of-generation program for generation 0. The 39 filled circles along the periphery of the room represent the 39 of the 56 tiles that were not touched by the robot before it timed out. As can be seen, this individual starts in the middle of the room and circles on itself three times. It then begins a series of 11 loops which cause the robot to repeatedly hit the wall at irregular intervals. This looping leaves many intervening points along the wall untouched. This individual time outs on the west wall after 400 time steps. By generation 2, the best-of-generation individual scored 27. This S-expression consisted of 57 points.

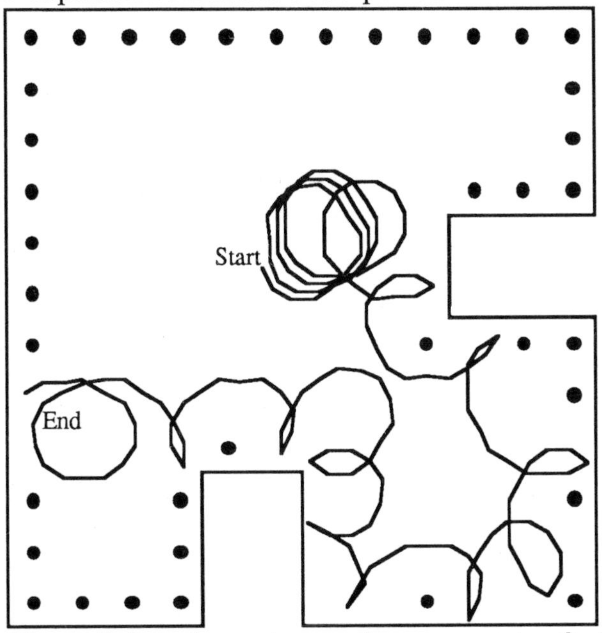

Figure 6: Looping trajectory from generation 0 of the best-of-generation individual (scoring 17).

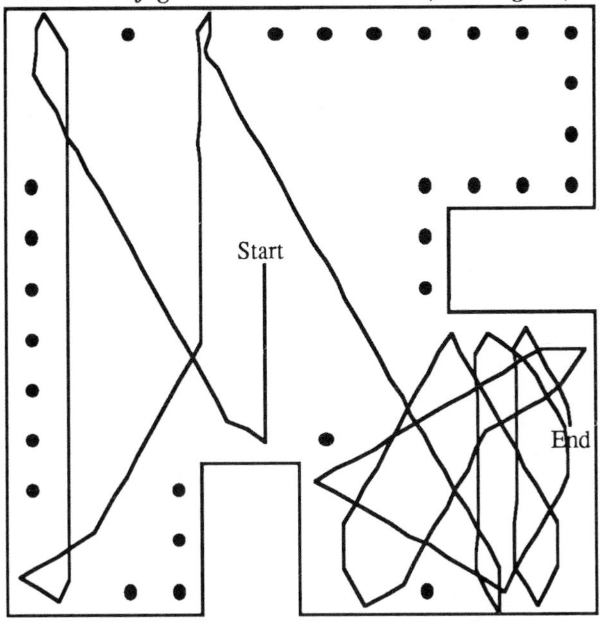

Figure 7: Ricocheting trajectory from generation 2 of the best-of-generation individual (scoring 27).

Figure 7 shows the ricocheting trajectory of the robot while executing this best-of-generation program for generation 2. As can be seen, this individual causes the robot to touch occasional points on the periphery of the room as the robot ricochets around the room 16 times.

Although this ricocheting individual from generation 2 is far from perfect, it is considerably better than the static and aimless wandering individuals (both scoring zero) from generation 0, the wall-banging individuals (scoring one) from generation 0, and the best-of-generation looping individual from generation 0 (scoring 17).

By generation 14, the best-of-generation S-expression scored 49 and consisted of 45 points. Figure 8 shows the trajectory of the robot while executing this best-of-generation program for generation 14. After once reaching a wall, this individual slithers in broad snake like motions along the walls and never returns to the middle of the room. In scoring 49 out of 56, it misses five corners and two points in the middle of walls.

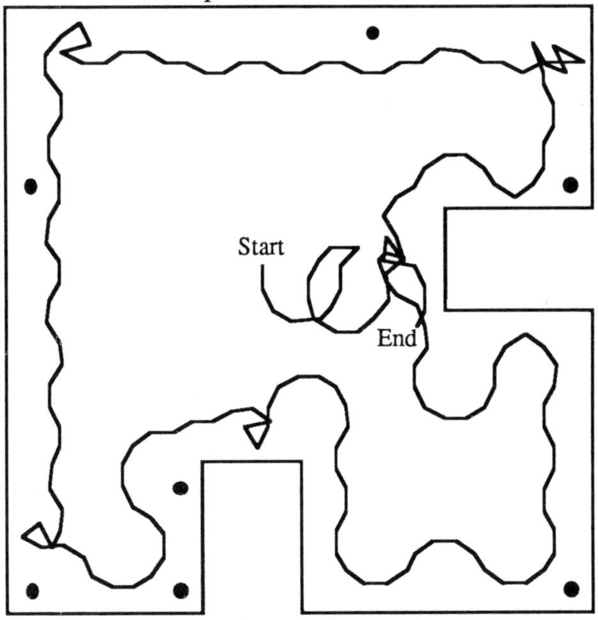

Figure 8: Broad snake like trajectory from generation 14 of best-of-generation individual (scoring 49 out of 56).

Finally, in generation 57, the best-of-generation S-expression scored a perfect 56 out of 56 This S-expression consisted of 145 points and is shown below:

```
(IFLTE (IFLTE S10 S05 S02 S05) (IFLTE (PROGN2
S11 S07) (PROGN2 (PROGN2 (PROGN2 S11 S05)
(PROGN2 (PROGN2 S11 S05) (PROGN2 (MF) EDG)))
SS) (PROGN2 (PROGN2 (IFLTE S02 (PROGN2 S11
S07) S04 (PROGN2 S11 S05)) (TL)) (MB)) (IFLTE
S01 EDG (TR) (TL))) (PROGN2 SS S08) (IFLTE
(IFLTE (PROGN2 S11 S07) (PROGN2 (PROGN2
(PROGN2 S10 S05) (PROGN2 (PROGN2 S11 S05)
(PROGN2 (MF) EDG))) SS) (PROGN2 (PROGN2 S01
(PROGN2 (IFLTE S07 (IFLTE S02 (PROGN2 (IFLTE
SS EDG (TR) (TL)) (MB)) S04 S10) S04 S10)
(TL))) (MB)) (IFLTE S01 EDG (TR) (TL)))
(PROGN2 S05 SS) (PROGN2 (PROGN2 MSD (PROGN2
S11 S05)) (PROGN2 (IFLTE (PROGN2 (TR) (TR))
(PROGN2 S01 (PROGN2 (IFLTE S02 (TL) S04 (MB))
```

```
(TL))) (PROGN2 S07 (PROGN2 (PROGN2 (MF) EDG)
EDG)) (IFLTE SS EDG (PROGN2 (PROGN2 (PROGN2
S02 S05) (PROGN2 (PROGN2 S11 S05) (PROGN2
(IFLTE S02 (TL) S04 S10) EDG))) SS) (TL)))
S08)) (IFLTE SS EDG (TR) (TL))))
```

This program consists of a composition of conditional statements which test various sensors from the environment and invoke various given primitive motor functions of the robot in order to perform wall following. In other words, this program is a program in the subsumption architecture.

We can simplify this S-expression to the following S-expression containing 59 points:

```
(IFLTE (IFLTE S10 S05 S02 S05)
       (IFLTE S07 (PROGN2 (MF) SS)
          (PROGN2 (TL) (MB))
          (IFLTE S01 EDG (TR) (TL)))
   *
   (IFLTE (IFLTE S07 (PROGN2 (MF) SS)
             (PROGN (IFLTE SS EDG (TR) (TL))
                    (MB) (TL) (MB))
             (IFLTE S01 EDG (TR) (TL)))
          SS
      (IFLTE (PROGN2 (TR) (TR))
             (PROGN2 (IFLTE S02 (TL) * (MB))
                     (TL))
         (MF)
         (TL))
      (IFLTE SS EDG (TR) (TL))))
```

In this S-expression, the asterisks indicate subexpressions that are free of side-effects and which are just returned as the value of the expression (i.e. are executed, but are inconsequential).

Figure 9 shows the trajectory of the robot while executing this best-of-generation program for generation 57. This individual starts by briefly moving at random in the middle of the room. However, as soon as it reaches the wall, it moves along the wall and stays close to the wall. It touches 100% of the 56 tiles along the periphery of the room.

Note that the progressive change in size and shape of the individuals in the population is a characteristic of genetic programming. The size (i.e. 145 points) and particular hierarchical structure of the best-of-generation individual from generation 57 was not specified in advance. Instead, the entire structure evolved as a result of reproduction, crossover, and the relentless pressure of fitness. That is, fitness caused the development of the structure.

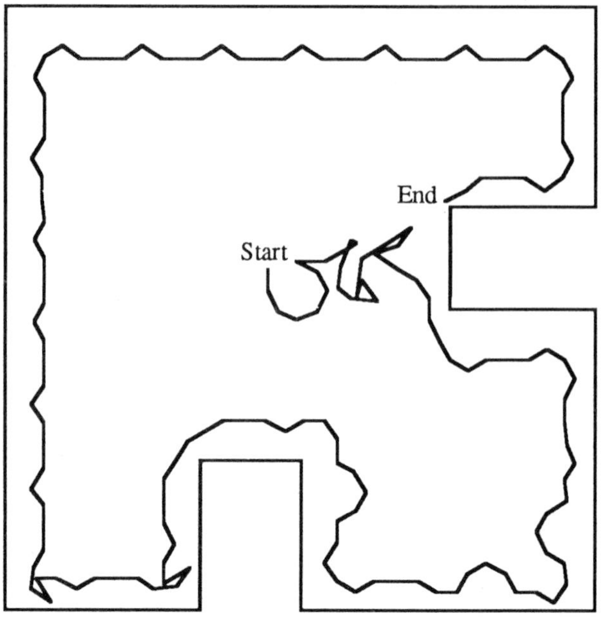

Figure 9: Wall following trajectory of the best-of-generation individual (scoring 56 out of 56) from generation 57.

Although a program written by a human programmer cannot be directly compared to the program generated using genetic programming, it is, nonetheless, interesting to note that the 145 points of this S-expression is similar to the 151 points in Mataric's four LISP programs.

We have obtained similar results on other runs of this problem.

9. CONCLUSIONS

We demonstrated that it is possible to use the genetic programming paradigm to breed a computer program to enable a robot to follow the wall of an irregular room.

The program we discovered consisted of a composition of conditional statements which tested various sensors from the environment and invoked various given primitive motor functions of the robot in order to perform wall following. In other words, this program is a program in the subsumption architecture. Thus, we have demonstrated the evolution of a program in the subsumption architecture using an evolutionary process that evolves structures guided only by a fitness measure.

The fact that it is possible to evolve a subsumption architecture to solve a particular problem suggests that this approach to decomposing problems may be useful in building up solutions to difficult problems by aggregating task achieving behaviors until the problem is solved.

10. ACKNOWLEDGMENTS

James P. Rice of the Knowledge Systems Laboratory at Stanford University made numerous contributions in connection with the computer programming of the above.

11. REFERENCES

Belew, Richard and Booker, Lashon (editors) *Proceedings of the Fourth International Conference on Genetic Algorithms*. San Mateo, Ca: Morgan Kaufmann Publishers Inc. 1991.

Brooks, Rodney. A robust layered control system for a mobile robot. *IEEE Journal of Robotics and Automation*. 2(1) March 1986.

Brooks, Rodney. A robot that walks: emergent behaviors from a carefully evolved network. *Neural Computation* 1(2), 253-262. 1989.

Davis, Lawrence (editor) *Genetic Algorithms and Simulated Annealing* London: Pittman 1987.

Davis, Lawrence. *Handbook of Genetic Algorithms*. New York: Van Nostrand Reinhold.1991.

Goldberg, David E. *Genetic Algorithms in Search, Optimization, and Machine Learning*. Reading, MA: Addison-Wesley 1989.

Holland, John H. *Adaptation in Natural and Artificial Systems*. Ann Arbor, MI: University of Michigan Press 1975.

Koza, John R. Hierarchical genetic algorithms operating on populations of computer programs. In *Proceedings of the 11th International Joint Conference on Artificial Intelligence*. San Mateo, CA: Morgan Kaufmann 1989.

Koza, John R. *Genetic Programming: A Paradigm for Genetically Breeding Populations of Computer Programs to Solve Problems*. Stanford University Computer Science Dept. Technical Report STAN-CS-90-1314. June 1990.

Koza, John R. Genetic evolution and co-evolution of computer programs. In Langton, Christopher, Taylor, Charles, Farmer, J. Doyne, and Rasmussen, Steen (editors). *Artificial Life II, SFI Studies in the Sciences of Complexity*. Volume X. Redwood City, CA: Addison-Wesley 1991. 603-629. 1991a.

Koza, John R. Evolution and co-evolution of computer programs to control independent-acting agents. In Meyer and Wilson below. 1991b.

Koza, John R. Evolving a computer program to generate random numbers using the genetic programming paradigm. In Belew and Booker above. 1991c.

Koza, John R. A hierarchical approach to learning the Boolean multiplexer function. In Rawlins below. 1991d.

Koza, John R. *Genetic Programming*. Cambridge, MA: MIT Press, 1992 (forthcoming).

Koza, John R. and Keane, Martin A. Genetic breeding of non-linear optimal control strategies for broom balancing. In *Proceedings of the Ninth International Conference on Analysis and Optimization of Systems*. Berlin: Springer-Verlag, 1990a.

Koza, John R. and Keane, Martin. Cart centering and broom balancing by genetically breeding populations of control strategy programs. In *Proceedings of International Joint Conference on Neural Networks, Washington, January, 1990*. Volume I. Hillsdale, NJ: Lawrence Erlbaum 1990b.

Koza, John R. and Rice, James P. Genetic generation of both the weights and architecture for a neural network. In *Proceedings of International Joint Conference on Neural Networks, Seattle, July 1991*. 1991a

Koza, John R. and Rice, James P. A genetic approach to artificial intelligence. In C. G. Langton (editor) *Artificial Life II Video Proceedings*. Addison-Wesley 1991. 1991b.

Meyer, Jean-Arcady and Wilson, Stewart W. *From Animals to Animats: Proceedings of the First International Conference on Simulation of Adaptive Behavior*. Paris. September 24-28, 1990. MIT Press, Cambridge, MA, 1991.

Mataric, Maja J. *A Distributed Model for Mobile Robot Environment-Learning and Navigation*. MIT Artificial Intelligence Laboratory technical report AI-TR-1228. May 1990.

Langton, Christopher G. *Artificial Life, Santa Fe Institute Studies in the Sciences of Complexity*. Volume VI. Redwood City, CA: Addison-Wesley. 1989.

Rawlins, Gregory (editor). *Proceedings of Workshop on the Foundations of Genetic Algorithms and Classifier Systems. Bloomington, Indiana. July 15-18, 1990*. San Mateo, CA: Morgan Kaufmann 1991.

Steels, Luc. Towards a theory of emergent functionality. In Meyer, Jean-Arcady and Wilson, Stewart W. *From Animals to Animats: Proceedings of the First International Conference on Simulation of Adaptive Behavior*. Paris. September 24-28, 1990. Cambridge, MA: MIT Press 1991.

SWARM INTELLIGENCE

Swarm-Made Architectures

Jean-Louis DENEUBOURG[1], Guy THERAULAZ[1, 2] and Ralph BECKERS[1]

[1] Unit of Theoretical Behavioural Ecology, Service de Chimie-Physique
CP 231, Université Libre de Bruxelles, 1050 Bruxelles, Belgium

[2] CNRS – UPR 38, 31 Chemin Joseph Aiguier, 13402 Marseille Cédex 09 France

Abstract

This paper deals with distributed problem solving in social insect colonies. We shows that different processes used by social insects could be used to solve different building problems or artefacts production. After defining some basic concepts of Swarm Intelligence we examine through the exemples of building behaviour in termite and wasp colonies how different types of constraints operates both on individual behaviour and on swarm dynamics.

1. Introduction

Are termites able to build Notre-Dame de Paris, could ants build the Golden Gate? Clearly, they don't build such structures. However, independently of this first observation, is there any reason why such "simple creatures" are unable to build at their scale corresponding structures ? At first sight, no reasons appear and any doubts are swept away when we observe the complexity of the artefacts produced by animals.

So the questions that appear, and around which this paper is centered, are "What are the rules governing the insects' behaviour to produce a nest" or "What rules should govern artificial creatures which must build Notre-Dame".

Building behaviour is widespread in the animal kingdom, the structures produced by animals having different purpose : reproduction, prey-capture, protection,... The first observation is that the structures'complexity is not related to what common sense calls cerebral capacity : Primates (except humans...) or dolphins are poor builders, whereas much simpler organisms such as arthropods are good builders. So we must not confuse the fact of building and the potential abilities of the organisms related to its brain.

Box 1
Swarm intelligence : basic concepts and fundamental properties

Swarm.

A swarm is defined as a set of (mobile) agents which are liable to communicate directly or indirectly (by acting on their local environment) with each other, and which collectively carry out a distributed problem solving (THERAULAZ *et al.*, 1990, THERAULAZ & GERVET, 1991). In this sense we refer to functional self-organisation (ARON *et al.*, 1990), since this emerges from the swarm's internal dynamics and its interaction with the environment (see also BENI, 1990 for special references with cellular robotics). The swarm functioning induces both the genesis of functional collective patterns which caracterize the differentiation and spatio-temporal organisation of the agents of the swarm and also the parallel organisation of the material elements in the environment upon which each agent acts.

It is clear that different factors, whether ecological or physiological, play a key role in the development of building behaviour, and these factors are not correlated to individual capacities (See HANSELL, 1984).

Box 2
Problem and collective problem solving

In the framework of swarm functioning the concept of a problem can be defined as a kind of description of the position of a biological or artificial agent, where a functional outcome is described as a goal even though some parameters having the possibity to evolve with time are described as constraints. One can consider the problem to be set when the goal, the constraints and the lawful procedure to move from an initial state S_0 to a final state S_f taking into account the swarm and the environment in which the swarm is scattered. It is worth noting that this definition not only applies to a swarm but also to a single agent. The swarm is characterized by the collective resolution of the problem (see THERAULAZ & GERVET, 1991 for a complete analysis). Depending on whether an artificial or biological system is considered, the description of the problem to be solved will take a different look:

• when we consider an artificial system the problem can be conceived before the design of the swarm whose local elementary behavioural rules will bring the system to solve this problem in a given environment ;
• but when we consider a biological system, the specification of the problem is equivalent to identifying a specific biological function (*e.g.* : the building behaviour, the task assignment).

The solution of the problem can be considered in both cases as a particular state of the swarm environment system through which the functional outcome looked for is reached. As a general rule, a number of solutions exist for a given problem, meaning that a given goal is compatible with several states of the system constituted by the swarm and its environment. Thus the "collective resolution of the problem" lies in the structural coevolutionary process between the swarm and its environment in which the functional outcome described as a goal is reached.

The diversity of the phylogenetic origins of the builders, the diversity of the materials used,... in other words, the diversity of living experience, makes that building behaviour is certainly a good subject matter for theoretical reflexion on behaviour and on swarm intelligence (see box 1).

Morevover building activity and the production of artefacts is a "Human Economical Activity", so building certainly will be one of the first tasks asked of "artificial creatures", tasks which are already assumed by our actual robots.

2. The right questions ?

The establishment of a link between the rules governing the units' behaviour (including interactions between these units) and the system's behaviour is common to numerous scientific activies. In behavioural science, computer science and all the sciences related to the problem of organization, traditionnaly the hierarchical blueprint was priviligied. Recently, an alternative was offered by the self-organization concept (which is far from new in physics and chemistry, see NICOLIS & PRIGOGINE, 1977). We see to-day the development and the analysis of multi-agent systems such as eco-problem-solving (FERBER, 1989), emergent functionality (STEELS, 1990, 1991), computational ecology (HUBERMAN, 1988) or cellular robotics (BENI, 1989, WANG & BENI, 1989). The self-organization blueprint shows that rather simple and decentralized units with strong interactions (*e.g.* with positive feed-back) are able to produce complex patterns and solve problems (see box 2).

But after an initial fascination, we quickly became unsatisfied and some questions appear:

• What are the links between the behavioural program and the structure produced ?

• How complex should the individual (behavioural) program be to produce global patterns ? By complexity, we refer here essentially to the number of factors (and their interplay) which influence the insect's behaviour.

• The animal evolves in an environment What are the components which must be

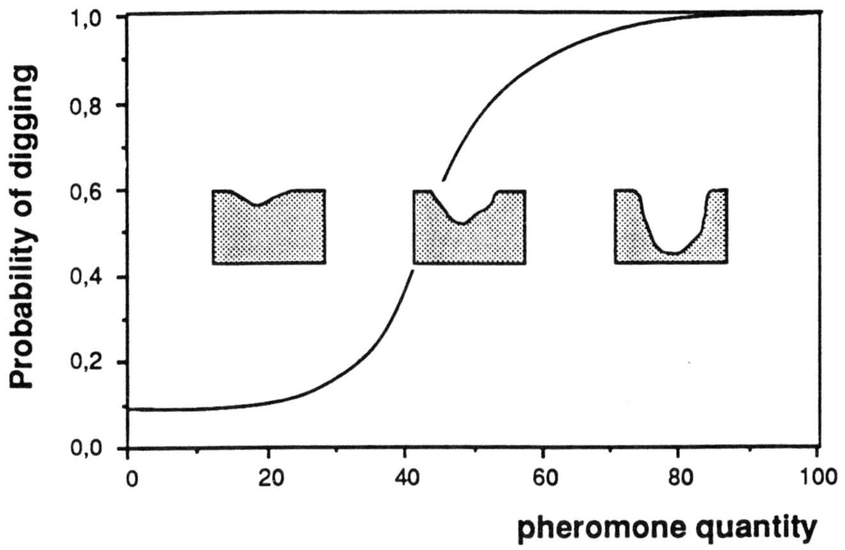

Fig. 1. Probability of digging as a function of chemical marking.

behaviourally coded and what can be obtained as a by-product of the physical constraints exploited by the program ?

• What are the constraints introduced on the program by the type of environnement, the material manipulated (silk, mud,...) or the tasks done (digging, weaving,...).

These questions are not specific to swarms or colonies, they are shared with all builders. However we shall see that the behavioural program for the same problem (*e.g.* digging) will depend on whether the builder is solitary or social and how the size of the society interacts with the program. Comparisons between solitary and social workers building similar structures in similar environments can provide information on the number of bluperints actually at work. The difference can appear for example at the level of the complexity needed to produce the right structure. However complexity is not the only characteristic of the behavioural program. Indeed these programs can be classified in different famillies such as stigmergy or the sequential (see the definitions below). So, for the same tasks, are some families of rules more adapted to solitary or to social agents ?

This is the link between the number of agents and the type of behavicural programs which shall be discusssed here, from a theoretical point of view, with the help of mathematical models.

3. Must a solitary worker's rules be different from a social worker's, with diggins as first exemple

3.1. A stigmergic script

This script is inspired by different biological observations and our first goal with such a model is to examine the power and the limit of given rules, rather than to fit theoretical and experimental results (a detailed presentation is in preparation, DENEUBOURG and BECKERS).

GRASSE introduced the concept of stigmergy (1959). The basic idea is that no direct interactions are necessary to coordinate the work of a group, but that the interactions between the nest and the workers is enough. The working termites modify their environment, providing new stimuli. These new stimuli induce new behavioural responses which in their turn modify the environment. With this succession of stimulus-reaction, the society is able to produce a structure. It is the work itself which assumes the coordination of the workers'activities.

The termites in the present script "use" a particular stigmergic mechanism which is an amplification. The termites move randomly in their nest and at each time-step, each termite is characterized by a probability P of digging and of extracting a soil particle. The model

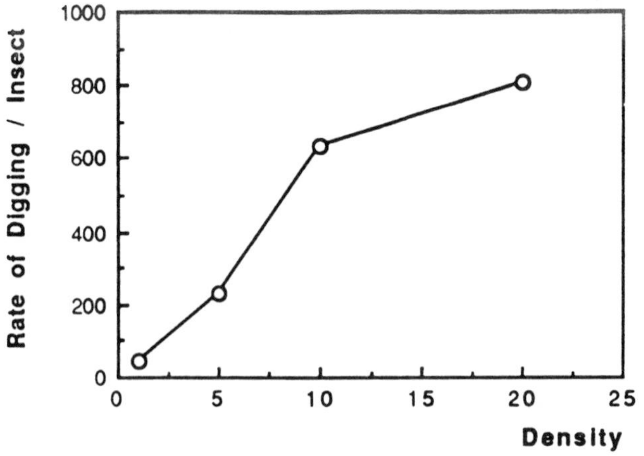

Fig.2.

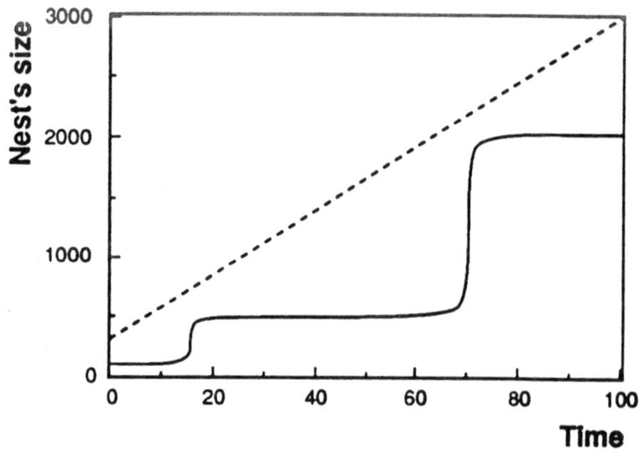

Fig. 3. Time evolution of the nest size. The dotted curve corresponds to the population growth

assumes that when a termite extracts a soil particule, it marks the neighbouring ground with a pheromone, or with a trail, and the probability of digging increases. This chemical marking stimulates the nestmates to dig (the probability of digging increases) at the same place or just in its neighbourhood (see fig.1). So the probability of digging is only determined by the local conditions.

The figure 2 shows that the digging rate per termite grows as the group's size (density) increases. In other words, the individual level of activity increases as the group increases.

3.2. Regulation of the nest volume

In a natural system, as the nest population grows, the digging activity increases to adapt the nest size to the total population. The algorithm described earlier doesn't contain any explicit instructions to "switch" the insects to digging (or non-digging) when the density reaches a certain threshold. However the algorithm does provide such regulation. Indeed, coupling the model with a slow population increase, the group is able to modulate the digging activities and to adapt the nest size to the population.

Different dynamics can be produced. We describe here only two extremes. The first and most intuitive is a continuous digging activity, producing a continuous increase in nest size. The second corresponds to a pulsatile growth of the nest size : brief periods of a high rate of digging, with long periods of negligeable digging between (*c.f.* fig. 3).

This behaviour is finally rather simple to understand. At low density, the digging activity is weak (see fig. 3). As the population increases, the density increases and a high level of activity is produced. This digging activity abruptly increases the nest size, but during this period the population doesn't really change. The consequence is that the termites' density falls and the rate of digging became negligeable until the density reaches again a high density. So without any explicit coding between nest size and colony population, a regulation is produced simply as a by-product of the rules used and the physical characteristics of the environment.

3.3. Selection of one site

The nest can be surrounded by heterogeneous material : for example one soft part easy to dig and one hard, more difficult to dig. The model simply assumes that when a termite tries to extract a soil particle in the soft part the probability of success is higher, and it is only when the extraction is successfull that pheromone is laid down. The environment's hardness-softness don't appear explicitly. Examining the decision as a function of the

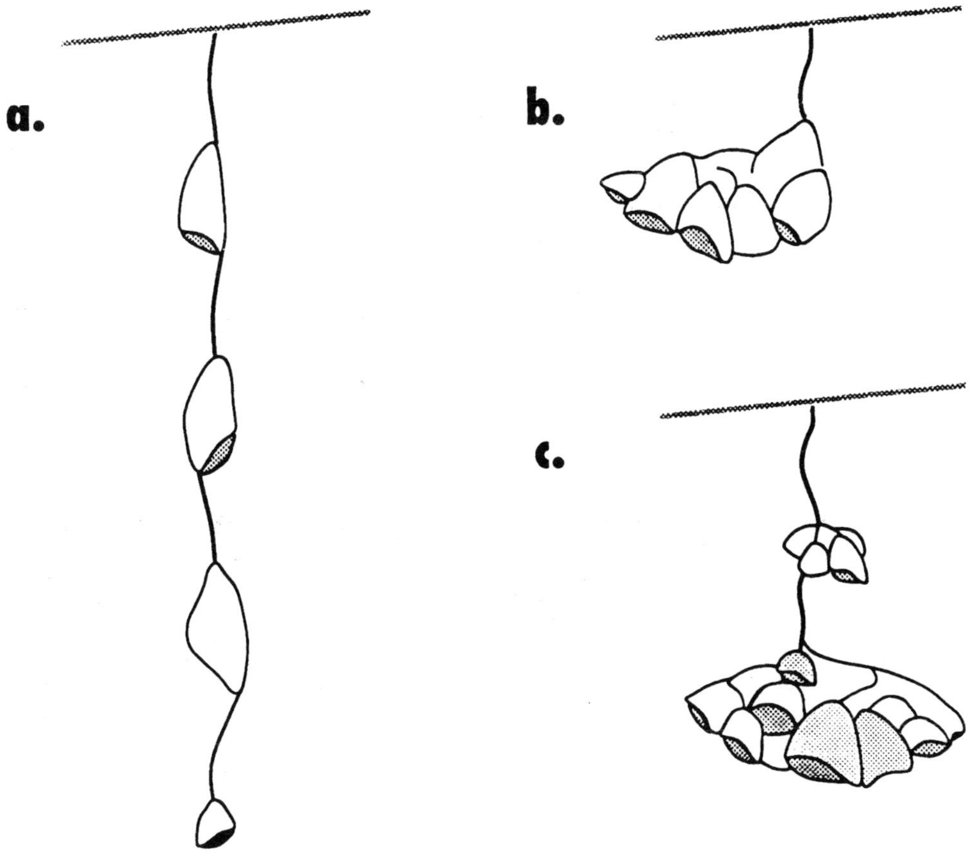

Fig. 4. Some aspects of the diversity of wasp nest architecture. The following genera and species are representative of the nest types shown : a. *Mischocyttarus punctatus* b. *Polistes* c. stenogastrinae, *Parischnogaster mellyi* . Redrawn from HANSELL 1984 and JEANNE 1975.

colony size (*e.g.* a group compared to a solitary individual), it appears that group is able to concentrate its activity on the soft part, neglecting the hard part, while the solitary cannot. Decreasing the strength of the positive feed-back, the group remains selective and the solitary individual increases its selectivity, but in this case its level of activity remains very low.

These examples show the power of such simple rules : regulation, selection of favorable sites, and roughly works for a solitary or social animal. However this example stresses the limit of a rule as a function of the number of agents : this rule appears much more powerful for a group than for a solitary worker, and so suggests the search of complexification or modification to produce a more efficient program for solitary builders.

The second case, discussed now, explores the limit of a stigmergic and of a sequential program as a function of the colony size.

4. Wasp builders

Figure 4 shows some aspects of the great diversity of nest architectures we observe in wasps. The variation of nest design extends from one cell per comb with an elongate form (a) to larger single combs (b) and multiple stacked combs with a varying number of cells per comb (c). Combs are suspended either to the substrate or from the rim of the cells of the upper comb.

One question we approach in this paper is why do these structures have the form they have ?

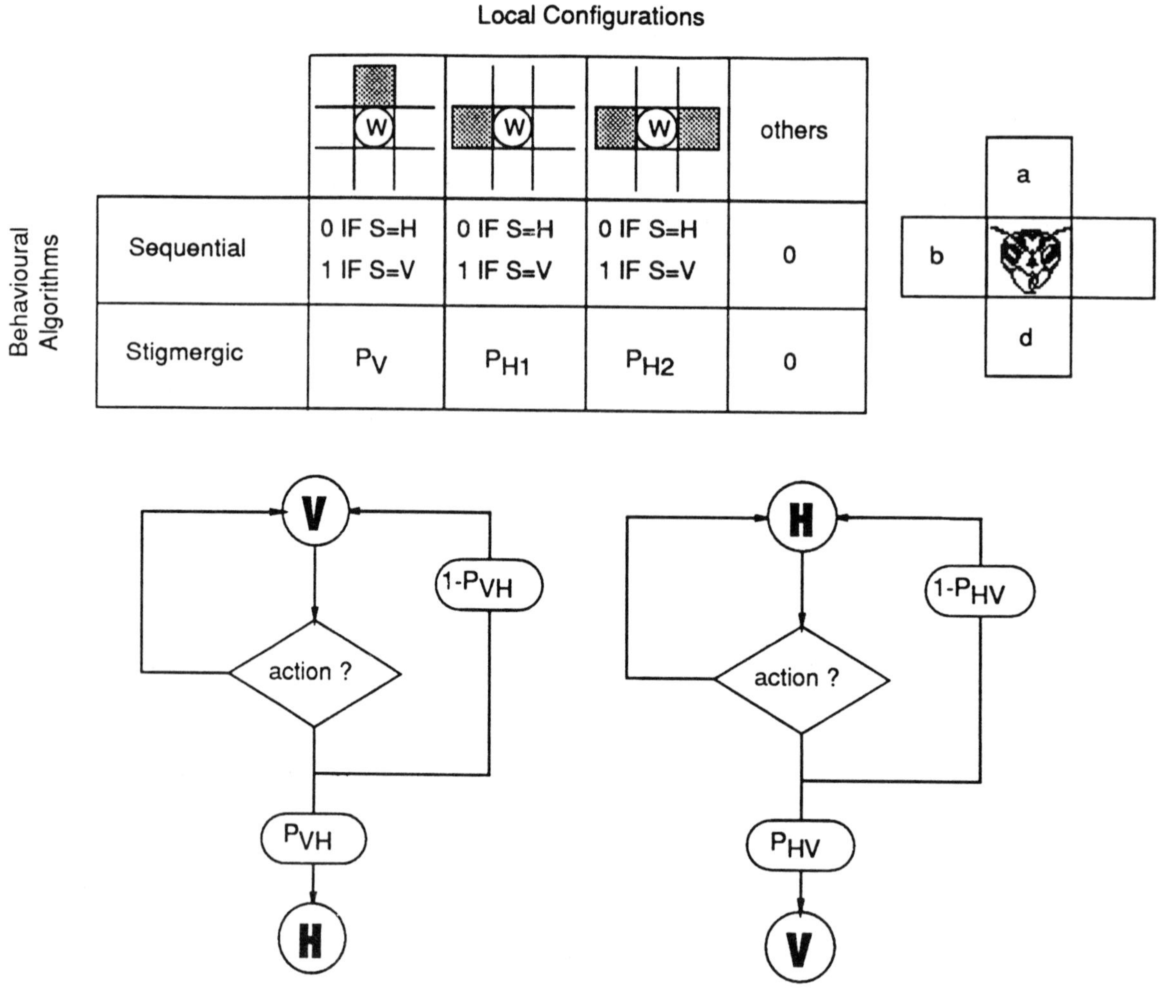

Fig. 5. Definition of the behavioural algorithms used by artificial wasps

4.1. The scripts

The environment is a lattice divided in n x m cells which can be empty (0) or full (1). The wasps move randomly on the nest and in its neighbourhood.

The stigmergic algorithm

In the case of the stigmergic script, as in the precedent case, only the local configuration met by the wasp determines its behaviour, which is here reduced to fill or not the corresponding cells.

From the 16 possible configurations, only three configurations stimulate the filling of the cell (see fig. 5). Two correspond to the horizontal mode and one to a vertical mode. Each mode is characterized by a probability P_{H1}, P_{H2} and P_V of filling the corresponding cell met by the wasp.

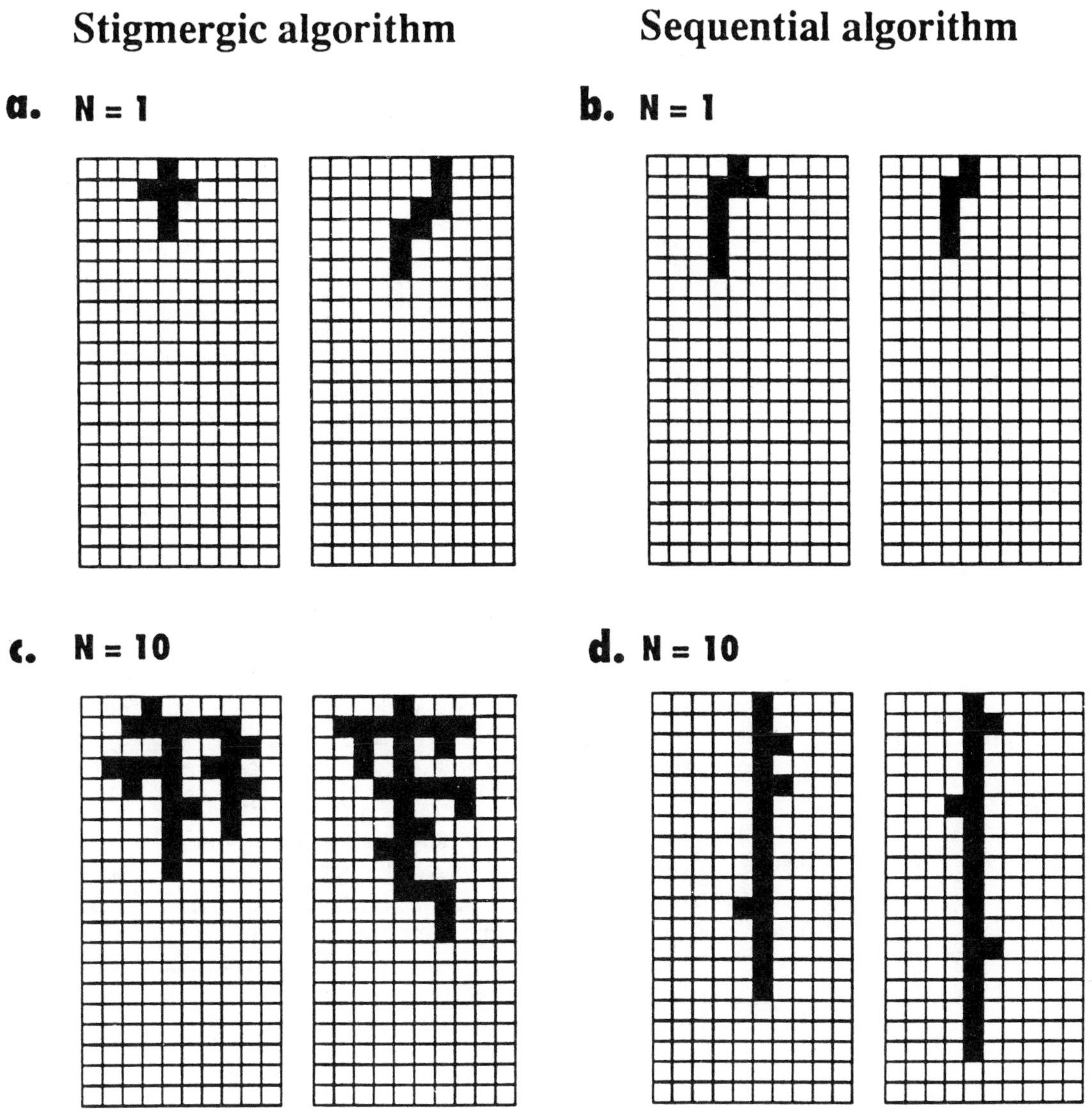

Fig. 6. Different patterns obtained with the sequential and stigmergic algorithms.
a. Solitary insect (N=1), sequential algorithm, $P_{VH} = 0.2$; $P_{HV} = 0.8$.
b. Solitary insect (N=1), stigmergic algorithm, $P_V = 0.8$; $P_{H1} = 0.2$; $P_{H2} = 0.4$.
c. Idem as a), but the structure is obtained with N=10 individuals.
c. Idem as b), but the structure is obtained with N=10 individuals.

The sequential algorithm.

In this case, the past activities of a wasp affect its building activity. The local configuration does not play a stimulating role, but only authorizes the wasp to fill, or not, the cell. It is the state of the wasp which controls its activity. At time t the wasps can be in the state "horizontal" or "vertical filling". The wasp in the state horizontal (vertical) can only fill a cell in the configuration "horizontal filling" ("vertical filling"). Having exhibited a vertical (horizontal) filling, the animal has a probability P_{VH} (P_{HV}) of becoming an horizontal (vertical) builder.

Comparing the rate of building per insect for different colony sizes, the sequential algorithm shows a decrease of efficiency. The stigmergic mechanism generally shows an increase as in the digging model.

Distributed Optimization by Ant Colonies

Alberto Colorni
Dipartimento di Elettronica
Politecnico di Milano
20133 Milano, Italy

Marco Dorigo
PM-AI&R Project
Dipartimento di Elettronica
Politecnico di Milano
20133 Milano, Italy
dorigo@ipmel2.elet.polimi.it

Vittorio Maniezzo
PM-AI&R Project
Dipartimento di Elettronica
Politecnico di Milano
20133 Milano, Italy
maniezzo@ipmel2.elet.polimi.it

Abstract

Ants colonies exhibit very interesting behaviours: even if a single ant only has simple capabilities, the behaviour of a whole ant colony is highly structured. This is the result of coordinated interactions. But, as communication possibilities among ants are very limited, interactions must be based on very simple flows of information. In this paper we explore the implications that the study of ants behaviour can have on problem solving and optimization. We introduce a distributed problem solving environment and propose its use to search for a solution to the travelling salesman problem.

1. Introduction

In this paper we propose a novel approach to distributed problem solving and optimization based on the result of low-level interactions among many cooperating simple agents that are not aware of their cooperative behaviour. Our work has been inspired by the study of ant colonies: in these systems each ant performs very simple actions and does not explicitly know what other ants are doing. Nevertheless everybody can observe the resulting highly structured behaviour.

In section 2 we explain the background on which our speculations have been built. We decided to develop a software environment to test our ideas on a very difficult and well known problem: the travelling salesman problem - TSP. We call our system, described in section 3, the ***ant system*** and we propose in this paper three possible instantiations to the TSP problem: the **ANT-quantity** and the **ANT-density** systems, described in section 4, and the **ANT-cycle** system, introduced in section 5. Section 6 presents some experiments, together with simulation results and discussion. In section 7 we sketch some conclusions and prefigure the directions along which our research work will proceed in the near future.

2. Motivations

The animal realm exhibits several cases of social systems having poor individual capabilities when compared to their complex collective behaviours. This is observed at different evolutionary stages, from bacteria (Shapiro 1988), to ants (Goss et al. 1990), caterpillars (Fitzgerald, Peterson 1988) molluscs and larvae. Moreover, the same causal processes that originate these behaviours are largely conserved in higher level species, like fishes, birds and mammals. These species make use of different communication media, adopted in less ubiquitous situation but essentially leading to the same patterns of behaviours (see for example the circular mills (Denebourg, Goss 1989)).

This suggests that the underlying mechanisms have proven evolutionarely extremely effective and are therefore worth of being analyzed when trying to achieve the similar goal of performing complex tasks by distributing activities over massively parallel systems composed of computationally simple elements.

One of the better studied natural cases of distributed activities regards ant colonies (Denebourg, Pasteels, Verhaeghe 1983): we outline here the main features of the models so far proposed to explain ant colonies behaviour. These features have been the basis for the definition of a distributed algorithm, that we have applied to the solution of "difficult" (NP-hard) computational problems.

The problem of interest is how almost blind animals manage to establish shortest route paths from their colony to feeding sources and back.

In the case of ants, the media used to communicate among individuals information regarding paths and used to decide where to go consists of *pheromone trails*. A moving ant lays some pheromone (in varying quantities) on the ground, thus marking the path it followed by a trail of this substance. While an isolated ant moves essentially at random, an ant encountering a previously laid trail can detect it and decide with high probability to follow it, thus reinforcing the

1990), collective choice (PASTEELS *et al.* 1987 ; BECKERS *et al.*, 1990 ; SEELEY *et al.*, 1991 ; CAMAZINE & SNEYD, 1991), the formation of trail networks (ARON *et al.* 1990), sorting (CAMAZINE, 1991 ; CAMAZINE *et al.*, 1990 ; DENEUBOURG *et al.* 1991), collective exploration (DENEUBOURG *et al.*, 1989 ; FRANKS 1989 ; FRANKS *et al.* 1991) and dynamical division of labour (DENEUBOURG *et al.* 1987 ; CORBARA *et al.* 1991 ; THERAULAZ *et al.*, 1991) synchronisation and the generation of oscillations (FRANKS *et al.* 1990 ; GOSS & DENEUBOURG, 1988 ; KRAFFT & PASQUET 1991). Such reflexions clearly lead us to imagine the development of new engeneering systems such as new transportations systems, new building monitoring,...

It is moving, from the point of view of nature lovers and admirers of technology, to imagine that the next robots could be the nephews of modest animals that have been on the earth for millions of years.

Acknowledgements

We thanks J. GERVET, S. GOSS and G. NICOLIS for their help and constant interest and stimulating discussions. This work was supported by the C.N.R.S. (Programme Cognisciences) and by the Belgium program on interuniversity attraction poles. Jean-Louis DENEUBOURG is a fellow of the Belgium F.N.R.S.

References

ARON S., DENEUBOURG J.L., GOSS S. & PASTEELS J.M. 1990. Functional self-organisation illustrated by inter-nest traffic in ants : the case of the Argentine ant, pp. 533-547. In: ALT W. & HOFFMANN G., Eds. Biological Motion, Lecture Notes in Biomathematics 89. *Springer-Verlag*.

BELIC M.R., SKARKA V., DENEUBOURG J.L. & LAX M. 1986. Mathematical model of a honeycomb construction. *Journal of Mathematical Biology*, 24: 437-449.

BENI G. 1989. The Concept of Cellular Robotic System, pp. 57-62. In: STEPHANOU H.E., MEYSTEL A., HERATH J. & LUH J.Y.S., Eds. *Proceedings of the 1988 IEEE International Symposium on Intelligent Control*, Arlington, VA.

BENI G. 1990. Key Issues of the Theory of Cellular Automata as Applied to Swarm Intelligence. In: MEYSTEL A., HERATH J. & GRAY S., Eds. *Proceedings of the 1990 IEEE International Symposium on Intelligent Control*, Philadelphia, PA. (in press).

BECKERS R., DENEUBOURG J.L., GOSS S. & PASTEELS J.M. 1990. Collective decision making through food recruitment. *Insectes Sociaux,* 37: 258-267.

BROOKS R.A. 1991. Intelligence Without Representation. *AI Journal*, 47: 139-160.

CAMAZINE S. 1991. Self-organizing pattern formation on the combs of honey bee colonies. *Behavioral Ecology and Sociobiology*, 28: 61-76.

CAMAZINE S. & SNEYD J. 1991. A mathematical model of colony-level nectar source selection by honey bees : self-organization through simple individual rules. *Journal of Theoretical Biology*, 149: 547-551.

CAMAZINE S, SNEYD J, JENKINS M.J. & MURRAY, J.D. 1990. A mathematical model of self-organized pattern formation on the combs of honey bee colonies. *Journal of Theoretical Biology*, 147: 553-571.

CORBARA B., DENEUBOURG J.L., FRESNEAU D., GOSS S., LACHAUD J.P. & PHAM-NGOC A. 1991. Simulation de la genèse d'une division du travail au sein d'une société de fourmis Ponerines : un modèle d'auto-organisation. *Actes Colloques Insectes Sociaux*, 7: 205-206.

DENEUBOURG, J.L. 1977. Application de l'ordre par fluctuations à la description de certaines étapes de la construction du nid chez les termites. *Insectes Sociaux*, 24 : 117-130.

DENEUBOURG J.L., PASTEELS J.M. & VERHAEGHE J.C. 1983. Probabilistic behaviour in ants : a strategy of errors. *Journal of Theoretical Biology*, 105: 259-271.

DENEUBOURG J.L., GOSS S., FRANKS & PASTEELS J.M. 1989. The blind leading the blind : modeling chemically mediated army ant raid patterns. *Journal of Insect Behavior,* 2: 719-725.

DENEUBOURG J.L., ARON S., GOSS S. & PASTEELS J.M. 1990. The self-organizing exploratory pattern of the argentine ant *Iridomyrmex humilis. Journal of Insect Behavior*, 3: 159-168.

DENEUBOURG J.L., GOSS S., PASTEELS J.M., FRESNEAU D. & LACHAUD J. P. 1987. Self-organization mechanisms in ant societies (II) : learning in foraging and division of labour, pp. 177-196. In: PASTEELS J.M. & DENEUBOURG J.L., Eds. From individual to collective behaviour in social insects. (*Experientia Supplementum* 54). *Basel: Birkhäuser Verlag.*

DENEUBOURG J.L., GOSS S., FRANKS N., SENDOVA-FRANKS A., DETRAIN C. & CHRETIEN L. 1991. The Dynamics of Collective Sorting : Robot-Like Ant and Ant-Like Robot, pp. 356-365. In: MEYER J.A. & WILSON S.W., Eds. Simulation of Adaptive Behavior : From Animals to Animats. *MIT Press/Bradford Books.*

FERBER J. 1989. Objets et agents : une étude des structures de représentation de communication en intelligence artificielle. Thèse de Doctorat d'état, Université Pierre et Marie Curie.

FRANKS N.R. 1989. Army ants: a collective intelligence. *American Scientist*, March-April: 139-145.

FRANKS N.R., BRYANT S., GRIFFITHS R. & HEMERIK L. 1990. Synchronization of the behaviour within nests of the ant *Letptothorax acervorum* (Fabricius) — I. Discovering the phenomenon and its relation to the level of starvation. *Bulletin of Mathematical Biology*, 52: 597-612.

FRANKS N.R., GOMEZ N., GOSS S. & DENEUBOURG J.L. 1991. The blind leading the blind : Testing a model of self-organization (Hymenoptera : Formicidae). *Journal of Insect Behavior,* 4: 583-607.

GOSS S. & J.L. DENEUBOURG J.L. 1988. Autocatalysis as a source of synchronised rhythmical activity. *Insectes Sociaux.*, 35: 310-315.

GRASSE, P.-P. 1959. La reconstruction du nid et les coordinations interindividuelles. La théorie de le stigmergie. *Insectes Sociaux*, 6: 41-84.

HANSELL M.H. 1984. Animal architecture and building behaviour. *Longman, London.*

HUBERMANN B.A. 1988. The Ecology of Computation. *North-Holland, Amsterdam.*

JEANNE R.L. 1975. The adaptiveness of social wasp nest architecture. *Quaterly Review of Biology*, 50: 267-287.

KRAFFT B. & PASQUET 1991. Synchronized and rhythmical activity during the prey capture in the social spider *Anelosimus eximius* (Arameae, Theridiidae). *Insectes Sociaux*, 38: 83-90.

NICOLIS G. & PRIGOGINE I. 1977. Self-organization in non-equilibrium systems. *Wiley, New-York.*

PASTEELS J.M., DENEUBOURG J.L. & GOSS S. 1987. Self-organization in ant societies (I): Trail recruitment to newly discovered food sources, pp. 155-175. In: PASTEELS J.M. & DENEUBOURG J.L., Eds. From individual to collective behaviour in social insects. (*Experientia Supplementum* 54). *Basel: Birkhäuser Verlag.*

SEELEY T.D., CAMAZINE S. & SNEYD, J. 1991. Collective decision-making in honey bees : how colonies choose among nectar sources. *Behavioural Ecology and Sociobiology*, 28: 277-290.

SKARKA V., DENEUBOURG J.L. & BELIC M.R. 1990. Mathematical model of building behavior of *Apis mellifera. Journal of Theoretical Biology* , 147: 1-16.

STEELS L. 1990. Cooperation between distributed agents through self-organisation, pp. 175-196. In: DEMAZEAU Y. & MULLER J.-P. Eds. Decentralized AI. *Elsevier Science Publishers B.V. (North-Holland).*

STEELS L. 1991. Toward a theory of emergent functionnality, pp. 451-461. In: MEYER J.A. & WILSON S.W., Eds. Simulation of Adaptive Behavior : From Animals to Animats. *MIT Press/Bradford Books.*

THERAULAZ G. & GERVET J. 1991. L'intelligence en essaim dans les sociétés d'insectes et les systèmes d'agents artificiels. *Psychologie Française*, n° Spécial Intelligence Animale (in press)

THERAULAZ G., GOSS S., GERVET J. & DENEUBOURG J.L. 1990. Swarm Intelligence in Wasps Colonies : a case for tasks assignment in multi-agents systems. In: MEYSTEL A., HERATH J. & GRAY S., Eds. *Proceedings of the 1990 IEEE International Symposium on Intelligent Control*, Philadelphia, PA. (in press).

THERAULAZ G., GOSS S., GERVET J. & DENEUBOURG J.L. 1991. Task differentiation in Polistes wasp colonies : a model for self-organizing groups of robots, pp. 346-355. In: MEYER J.A. & WILSON S.W., Eds. Simulation of Adaptive Behavior : From Animals to Animats. *MIT Press/Bradford Books* .

WANG J. & BENI G. 1989. Pattern Generation in Cellular Robotic Systems, pp. 63-69. In: STEPHANOU H.E., MEYSTEL A., HERATH J. & LUH J.Y.S., Eds. *Proceedings of the 1988 IEEE International Symposium on Intelligent Control*, Arlington, VA.

Distributed Optimization by Ant Colonies

Alberto Colorni
Dipartimento di Elettronica
Politecnico di Milano
20133 Milano, Italy

Marco Dorigo
PM-AI&R Project
Dipartimento di Elettronica
Politecnico di Milano
20133 Milano, Italy
dorigo@ipmel2.elet.polimi.it

Vittorio Maniezzo
PM-AI&R Project
Dipartimento di Elettronica
Politecnico di Milano
20133 Milano, Italy
maniezzo@ipmel2.elet.polimi.it

Abstract

Ants colonies exhibit very interesting behaviours: even if a single ant only has simple capabilities, the behaviour of a whole ant colony is highly structured. This is the result of coordinated interactions. But, as communication possibilities among ants are very limited, interactions must be based on very simple flows of information. In this paper we explore the implications that the study of ants behaviour can have on problem solving and optimization. We introduce a distributed problem solving environment and propose its use to search for a solution to the travelling salesman problem.

1. Introduction

In this paper we propose a novel approach to distributed problem solving and optimization based on the result of low-level interactions among many cooperating simple agents that are not aware of their cooperative behaviour. Our work has been inspired by the study of ant colonies: in these systems each ant performs very simple actions and does not explicitly know what other ants are doing. Nevertheless everybody can observe the resulting highly structured behaviour.

In section 2 we explain the background on which our speculations have been built. We decided to develop a software environment to test our ideas on a very difficult and well known problem: the travelling salesman problem - TSP. We call our system, described in section 3, the ***ant system*** and we propose in this paper three possible instantiations to the TSP problem: the **ANT-quantity** and the **ANT-density** systems, described in section 4, and the **ANT-cycle** system, introduced in section 5. Section 6 presents some experiments, together with simulation results and discussion. In section 7 we sketch some conclusions and prefigure the directions along which our research work will proceed in the near future.

2. Motivations

The animal realm exhibits several cases of social systems having poor individual capabilities when compared to their complex collective behaviours. This is observed at different evolutionary stages, from bacteria (Shapiro 1988), to ants (Goss et al. 1990), caterpillars (Fitzgerald, Peterson 1988) molluscs and larvae. Moreover, the same causal processes that originate these behaviours are largely conserved in higher level species, like fishes, birds and mammals. These species make use of different communication media, adopted in less ubiquitous situation but essentially leading to the same patterns of behaviours (see for example the circular mills (Denebourg, Goss 1989)).

This suggests that the underlying mechanisms have proven evolutionarely extremely effective and are therefore worth of being analyzed when trying to achieve the similar goal of performing complex tasks by distributing activities over massively parallel systems composed of computationally simple elements.

One of the better studied natural cases of distributed activities regards ant colonies (Denebourg, Pasteels, Verhaeghe 1983): we outline here the main features of the models so far proposed to explain ant colonies behaviour. These features have been the basis for the definition of a distributed algorithm, that we have applied to the solution of "difficult" (NP-hard) computational problems.

The problem of interest is how almost blind animals manage to establish shortest route paths from their colony to feeding sources and back.

In the case of ants, the media used to communicate among individuals information regarding paths and used to decide where to go consists of *pheromone trails*. A moving ant lays some pheromone (in varying quantities) on the ground, thus marking the path it followed by a trail of this substance. While an isolated ant moves essentially at random, an ant encountering a previously laid trail can detect it and decide with high probability to follow it, thus reinforcing the trail with its own pheromone. The collective behaviour that emerges is a form of *autocatalytic* behaviour — or *allelomimesis* — where the more are the ants following a trail, the more that trail becomes attractive for being followed. The process is thus characterized by a positive feedback loop, where the probability with which an ant chooses a path increases with the number of ants that chose the same path in the preceding steps.

In Fig.1 we present an example of how allelomimesis can lead to the identification of the shortest path around an obstacle (see also Goss et al. 1989). The experimental setting is the following: there is a path along which ants are walking (for example it could be a path from a food source A to the nest E - Fig.1a). Suddenly an obstacle appears and the previous path is cut off. So at position B the ants walking from E to A (or at position D those walking in the opposite direction) have to decide whether to turn right or left (Fig.1b). The choice is influenced by the intensity of the pheromone trails left by preceding ants. A higher level of pheromone on the right path gives an ant a stronger stimulus and thus a higher probability to turn right. The first ant reaching point B (or D) has the same probability to turn right or left (as there was no previous pheromone on the two alternative paths). Being path BCD shorter than BHD, the first ant following it will reach D before the first ant following path BHD. The result is that new ants coming from ED will find a stronger trail on path DCB, caused by the half of all the ants that by chance decided to approach the obstacle via ABCD and by the already arrived ones coming via BCD: they will therefore prefer (in probability) path DCB to path DHB. As a consequence, the number of ants following path BCD will be higher, in the unit of time, than the number of ants following BHD. This causes the quantity of pheromone on the shorter path to grow faster than on the longer one, and therefore the probability with which any single ant chooses the path to follow is quickly biased towards the shorter one. The final result is that very quickly all ants will choose the shorter path (Fig.1c). However, the decision of whether to follow a path or not is never deterministic, thus allowing a continuos exploration of alternative routes.

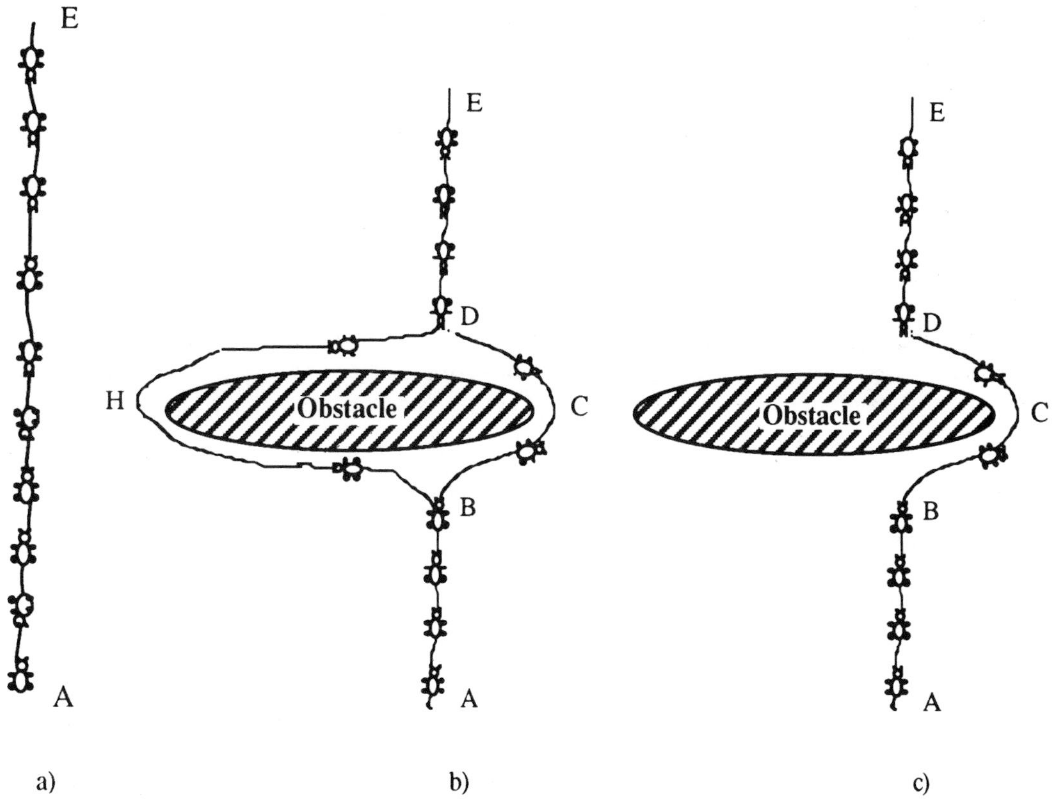

Fig.1 - a) Some ants are walking on a path between points A and E
b) An obstacle suddenly appears and the ants must get around it
c) At steady-state the ants choose the shorter path

Computational models have been developed, to simulate the food-searching process (Denebourg, Goss 1989), (Goss et al. 1990). The results are satisfactory, showing that a simple probabilistic model is enough to justify complex and differentiated collective patterns. This is an important result, where a minimal level of individual complexity can explain a complex collective behaviour.

An increase in the computational complexity of each individual, once established the lowest limit needed to account for the desired behaviours, can help in escaping from local optima and to face environmental changes. Trail laying regulated by feedback loop just eases ants to pursue the path followed by the first ant which reached its objective, but that path could easily be suboptimal. If we move from the goal of modeling natural reality to that of designing agents that perform food-seeking in the most efficient possible way, an increase in the individual agent's complexity could direct the search in front of an increment of computational cost. In this case we face the trade-off between individual performance and computational load caused by increasing population size: we are interested in the simplest models that take into account efficient shortest route identification and optimization.

3. The *Ant* system

We introduce in this section our approach to the distributed solution of a difficult problem by many locally interacting simple agents. As we are not interested in simulation of ant colonies, but in the use of artificial ant colonies as an optimization tool, our system will have some major differences with a real (natural) one: artificial ants will have some memory, they will not be completely blind and will live in a environment where time is discrete.

We call *ants* the simple interacting agents and *ant-algorithms* the class of algorithms we have defined. We first describe the general characteristics of the ant-algorithms and then introduce three of them, called **ANT-density**, **ANT-quantity** and **ANT-cycle**.

As a first test of the ant-algorithms, we decided to apply them to the well-known travelling salesman problem (TSP), to have a comparison with results obtained by other heuristic approaches: the model definition is influenced by the problem structure, however we refer the reader to (Colorni, Dorigo, Maniezzo 1991) to see how the same approach can be used to solve related optimization problems.

Given a set of n towns, the TSP problem can be stated as the problem of finding a minimal length closed tour that visit each town once. Let $b_i(t)$ (i=1, ..., n) be the number of ants in town i at time t and let

$$m = \sum_{i=1}^{n} b_i(t)$$

be the total number of ants.

Call $path_{ij}$ the shortest path between towns i and j; in the case of euclidean TSP (the one considered in this paper) the length of $path_{ij}$ is the Euclidean distance d_{ij} between i and j (i.e. $d_{ij}=[(x_1^i-x_1^j)^2 + (x_2^i-x_2^j)^2]^{1/2}$).

Let $\tau_{ij}(t+1)$ be the *intensity of trail* on $path_{ij}$ at time t+1, given by the formula

$$\tau_{ij}(t+1)=\rho\cdot\tau_{ij}(t)+\Delta\tau_{ij}(t,t+1) \qquad (1)$$

where

ρ is a coefficient such that $(1-\rho)$ represents *evaporation* ;

$$\Delta\tau_{ij}(t,t+1) = \sum_{k=1}^{m} \Delta\tau_{ij}^k(t,t+1)$$

$\Delta\tau_{ij}^k(t,t+1)$ is the quantity per unit of length of trail substance (pheromone in real ants) laid on $path_{ij}$ by the k-th ant between time t and t+1.

The intensity of trail at time 0, $\tau_{ij}(0)$, can be set to arbitrarily chosen values (in our experiments a very low value on every $path_{ij}$).

We call *visibility* the quantity $\eta_{ij} = 1/d_{ij}$, and define the transition probability from town i to town j as

$$p_{ij}(t) = \frac{[\tau_{ij}(t)]^\alpha\cdot[\eta_{ij}]^\beta}{\sum_{j=1}^{n} [\tau_{ij}(t)]^\alpha\cdot[\eta_{ij}]^\beta} \qquad (2)$$

where α and β are parameters that allow a user control on the relative importance of trail versus visibility. Therefore the transition probability is a trade-off between visibility, which says that close towns should be chosen with high probability, and trail intensity, that says that if on $path_{ij}$ there is a lot of traffic then it is highly desirable.

In order to satisfy the constraint that an ant visits n different towns, we associate to each ant a data structure (not biologically grounded), called *tabu list*[1], that memorizes the towns already visited up to time t and forbids the ant to visit them again before a cycle has been completed. When a cycle is completed the tabu list is emptied and the ant is free again to choose its way.

Different choices about how to compute $\Delta\tau_{ij}^{k}(t,t+1)$ and when to update the $\tau_{ij}(t)$ cause different instantiations of the ant-algorithm. In the next section we present three algorithms we used as experimental test-bed for our ideas. Their names are **ANT-density**, **ANT-quantity** and **ANT-cycle**.

4. The ANT-quantity and ANT-density algorithms

In the ANT-quantity model a constant quantity Q_1 of pheromone is left on $path_{ij}$ every time an ant goes from i to j; in the ANT-density model an ant going from i to j leaves Q_2 units of pheromone for every unit of length.

Therefore, in the ANT-quantity model

$$\Delta\tau_{ij}^{k}(t,t+1)=\begin{cases}\dfrac{Q_1}{d_{ij}} & \text{if k-th ant goes from i to j between t and t+1}\\ 0 & \text{otherwise}\end{cases} \tag{3}$$

and in the ANT-density model we have

$$\Delta\tau_{ij}^{k}(t,t+1)=\begin{cases}Q_2 & \text{if k-th ant goes from i to j between t and t+1}\\ 0 & \text{otherwise}\end{cases} \tag{4}$$

From these definitions it is clear that the increase in pheromone intensity on $path_{ij}$ when an ant goes from i to j is independent of d_{ij} in the ANT-density model, while it is inversely proportional to d_{ij} in the ANT-quantity model (i.e. shorter paths are made more desirable by ants in the ANT-quantity model, thus further reinforcing the visibility factor in equation (2)).

The **ANT-density** and **ANT-quantity** algorithms are then

1 Initialize:
  Set t:=0
  Set an initial value $\tau_{ij}(t)$ for trail intensity on every $path_{ij}$
  Place $b_i(t)$ ants on every node i
  Set $\Delta\tau_{ij}(t,t+1)$:= 0 for every i and j

2 Repeat until *tabu list* is full
  {this step will be repeated n times}

2.1 For i:=1 to n do {for every town}
  For k:=1 to $b_i(t)$ do
  {for every ant on town i at time t}
  Choose the town to move to, with probability p_{ij} given by equation (2), and move the k-th ant to the chosen location
  Insert the chosen town in the *tabu list* of ant k
  Set $\Delta\tau_{ij}(t,t+1) := \Delta\tau_{ij}(t,t+1) + \Delta\tau_{ij}^{k}(t,t+1)$
  computing $\Delta\tau_{ij}^{k}(t,t+1)$ as defined in (3) or in (4)

2.2 Compute $\tau_{ij}(t+1)$ and $p_{ij}(t+1)$ according to equations (1) and (2)

3 Memorize the shortest path found up to now and empty all tabu lists

4 If not(End_Test)
  {End_test is currently defined just as a test on the number of cycles}
  then
  set t:=t+1
  set $\Delta\tau_{ij}(t,t+1)$:=0 for every i and j
  goto step 2
  else
  print shortest path and Stop

In words the algorithms work as follows.

At time zero an initialization phase takes place during which ants are positioned on different towns and initial values for trail intensity are set on paths. Then every ant moves from town i to town j choosing the town to move to with a probability that is given as a function (with pa-

[1] Even though the name chosen recalls tabu search, proposed in (Glover 1989) and (Glover 1990), there are substantial differences between our approach and tabu search algorithms. We mention here (1) the absence of any aspiration function and (2) the difference of the elements recorded in the tabu list: permutations in the case of tabu search, cities in our case.

rameters α and β) of two desirability measures: the first (called trail - τ_{ij}) gives information about how many ants in the past have chosen that same $path_{ij}$, the second (called visibility - η_{ij}) says that the closer a town the more desirable it is (setting $\alpha = 0$ we obtain a stochastic greedy algorithm with multiple starting points, with $\alpha = 0$ and $\beta \rightarrow \infty$ we obtain the standard one): this implements a greedy constructive heuristic, in the following called *greedy force.*

Each time an ant makes a move, the trail it leaves on $path_{ij}$ is collected and used to compute the new values for path trails. When every ant has moved, trails are used to compute transition probabilities according to formulae (1) and (2).

After n moves the tabu list of each ant will be full: they will be emptied after having assessed the corresponding tours lengths and memorized the shortest tour for user convenience (its identification therefore is not an emergent property of the system). This process is iterated for an user-defined number of cycles.

5. The ANT-cycle algorithm

In the ANT-cycle system we introduced a major difference with respect to the two previous systems. Here $\Delta\tau^k_{ij}$ is not computed at every step, but after a complete tour (n steps). The value of $\Delta\tau^k_{ij}(t,t+n)$ is given by

$$\Delta\tau^k_{ij}(t,t+n)=\begin{cases}\frac{Q_3}{L^k} & \text{if k-th ant uses } path_{ij}\\ 0 & \text{otherwise}\end{cases}\qquad (5)$$

where Q_3 is a constant and L^k is the tour length of the k-th ant. This corresponds to an adaptation of the ANT-quantity approach, where trails are updated at the end of a whole cycle instead than after each single move.

The value of the trail is also updated every n steps according to a formula very similar to (1)

$$\tau_{ij}(t+n) = \rho\cdot\tau_{ij}(t)+\Delta\tau_{ij}(t,t+n) \qquad (1')$$

where $\Delta\tau_{ij}(t,t+n) = \sum_{k=1}^{m} \Delta\tau^k_{ij}(t,t+n)$

The **ANT-cycle** algorithm is then

1 Initialize:
    Set t:=0
    Set an initial value $\tau_{ij}(t)$ for trail intensity on every $path_{ij}$
    Place $b_i(t)$ ants on every node i
    Set $\Delta\tau_{ij}(t,t+n)$:= 0 for every i and j
2 Repeat until *tabu list* is full
    {this step will be repeated n times}
2.1 For i:=1 to n do {for every town}
    For k:=1 to $b_i(t)$ do
        {for every ant on town i at time t}
    Choose the town to move to, with probability p_{ij} given by equation (2), and move the k-th ant to the chosen location
    Insert the chosen town in the *tabu list* of ant k
2.2 Compute $\Delta\tau^k_{ij}(t,t+n)$ as defined in (5)
2.3 Compute $\Delta\tau_{ij}(t,t+n) = \sum_{k=1}^{m} \Delta\tau^k_{ij}(t,t+n)$
2.4 Compute the new values for $\tau_{ij}(t+n)$ and $p_{ij}(t+n)$ according to equations (1') and (2)
3 Memorize the shortest path found up to now and empty all tabu lists
4 If not(End_Test)
    {End_test is currently defined just as a test on the number of cycles}.
  then
    set t:=t+n
    set $\Delta\tau_{ij}(t,t+n)$:=0 for every i and j
    goto step 2
  else
    print shortest path and Stop

6. Computational results

The three reported algorithms have a performance which strongly depends on the parameter setting under which they are run. The parameters are: α (sensibility to trails), β (sensibility to distance), ρ (evaporation rate of pheromone trails) and Q_h (algorithm-specific, related to how much pheromone is laid down to form trails). Moreover, we are interested in studying how our algorithms scale up with the increase of the number of the towns in the tour and how the number of ants affects the overall performance.

Since we have not yet developed a mathematical analysis of the models, which would yield the optimal parameter setting in each situation, we ran several simulations, to collect statistical data for this purpose. The results are sketched in the following, for each algorithm.

ANT-quantity and ANT-density

The outcomes of these two models are very similar, except that the ANT-quantity has shown to be slightly more prone to get stuck in local minima (see (Colorni, Dorigo, Maniezzo 1991) for a more detailed analysis of their differences).

Simulations run on small-sized problems (10 cities, CCAO problem from (Golden, Stewart 1985), see Fig.2) and with initially an ant per city have shown that these two models are very sensitive to β, while their behaviour is almost unaffected by trails.

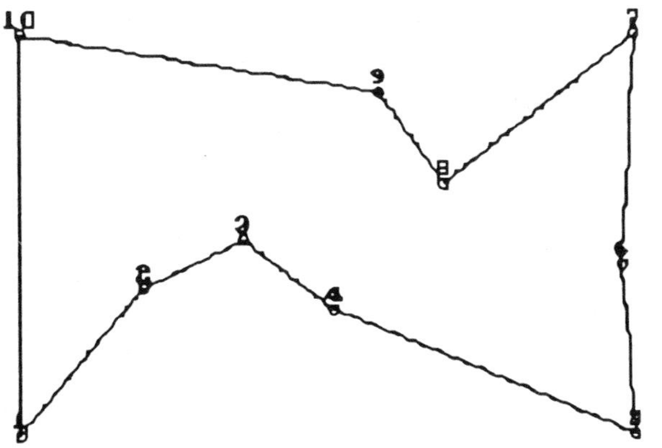

Fig.2 - CCA0 problem and relative optimal tour

We tested several values for each parameter, all the other being constant, over ten simulations for each setting in order to achieve some statistical information about the average evolution. The values tested were: $\alpha \in \{0, 0.5, 1, 2, 5, 10\}$, $\beta \in \{0, 0.5, 1, 2, 5, 10\}$, $\rho \in \{0.5, 0.7, 0.9\}$ and $Q_h \in \{10, 100, 10000\}$. The results show that for β=0 the algorithms were consistently incapable of finding the optimum, for β=0.5 it took them an average of 12.4 cycles to find it, for every $\beta \geq 1$ the optimum was found in about 3 or 4 cycles. These results hold for each combination of values of α, ρ and Q_h. With β=5 or β=10 we noticed an increase in the number of times in which the algorithms found the optimum at the first iteration, but it was not statistically significative (at a level of confidence of 0.05).

Parameters α, ρ and Q_h affected the time required to have a uniform behaviour in the ant population (i.e. the same tour followed by every ant). An increase of Q_h proved equivalent to an increase of α. Even though in no case we had a complete convergence after having found an optimum, in almost all the cases when the simulation was allowed to go on for some thousands of iterations, the average population tour converged to the best tour and the trail pattern converged to the single tour commonly followed.

More demanding tests were run on problems with 30, 50 and 75 cities, taken from (Lin, Kernigan 1973) and (Eilon, Watson-Gandy, Christofides 1969) (the data we used in our experiments can be found also in (Whitley, Starkweather, Fuquay 1989)). The results were consistent with those of the ten cities case: the most important parameter is β. Increasing sensibility to trail (or relative trail intensity) results in easing convergence, according to the inspiring autocatalytic paradigm. With problems of increasing size, the individuation of the best known solution becomes increasingly more rare; however in all cases the algorithms early individuated good solutions, exploring tours composed primarily of the contextually better edges so far individuated (see Fig.3).

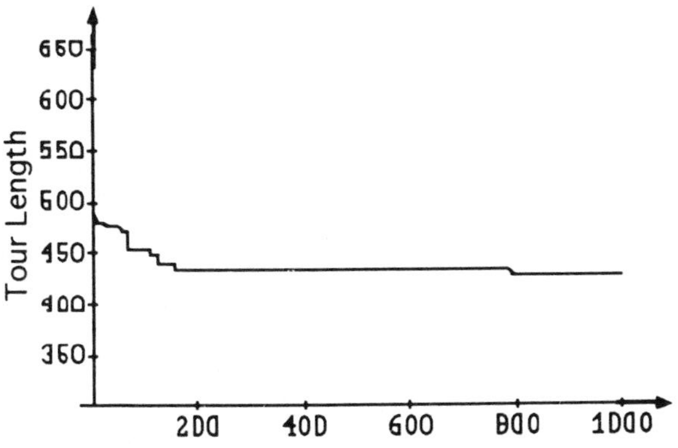

Fig.3 - A 1000 cycles run for the ANT-quantity on the 30 cities problem (α=2, β=5, ρ=0.7, Q_1=100)

In Fig.4 we present a typical run of the ANT-density algorithm for the 30 cities problem (Lin, Kernigan 1973) (parameters: 1 ant per city, $\alpha=1$, $\beta=5$, $\rho=0.7$, $Q_2=100$).

A second set of experiments was run, in order to assess the impact of the number of ants on the efficiency of the solving process. In this case, the test problem involved finding a tour in a 4 by 4 grid of evenly spaced points: this is a problem with a priori known optimal solution (16 if we put to 1 the edge distance of any four evenly neighbouring cities that form a square). In this case we determined the average number of cycles needed in each configuration to reach the optimum, if the optimum could be reached within 200 cycles. In Fig. 5 we present the results obtained for the ANT-density algorithm: on the abscissa there are the total number of ants used in each set of runs, on the ordinate there is the average number of cycles required to reach the optimum, multiplied by the number of ants used (in order to evaluate the efficiency per ant). When the majority of tests with a given configuration could not reach the optimum, we gave an high default value to the corresponding variable.

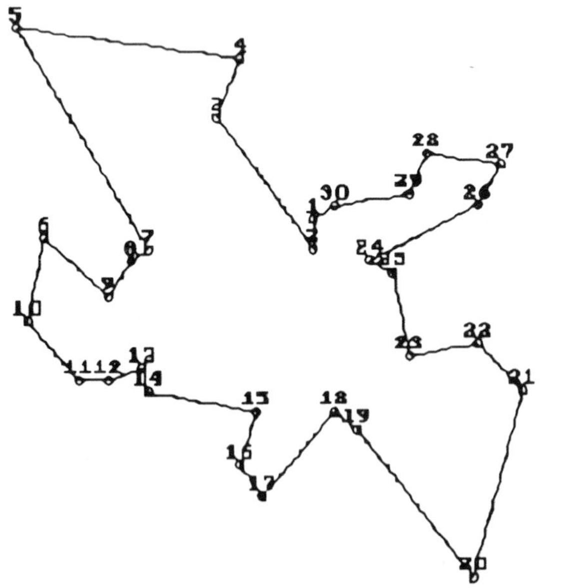

Fig.4 - A typical evolution of ANT-density (real length = 424.635; integer length = 421) on the 30 cities problem

It can be seen that only configurations with more than one ant per city were able to reach the optimum in less than 200 cycles, and an increase in the number of ants resulted in an increased efficiency of the overall system.

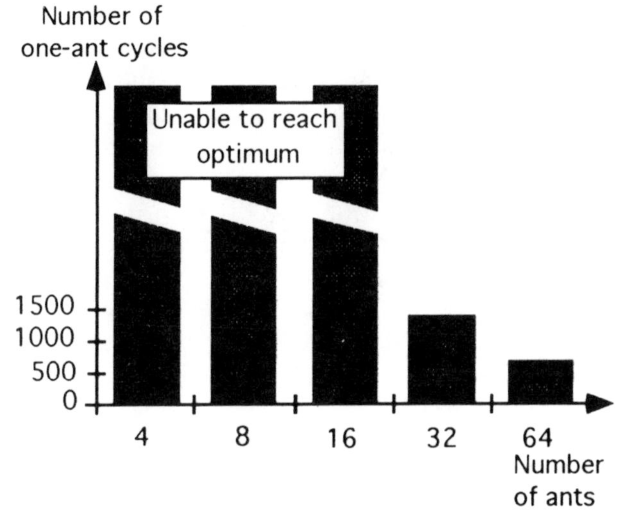

Fig.5 - Number of cycles required to reach optimum rated to the total number of ants for the 4x4 grid problem

ANT-cycle

This algorithm performs significantly better than the other two, especially on the harder problems, and is more sensible to variations of parameter values. Problem CCAO, used to roughly determine the sensitivity to each parameter, suggested the following results, changing parameters one at a time with respect to the default configuration $\alpha=1$, $\beta=1$, $\rho=0.7$, $Q_3=100$:

- α: small values of α (<1) lead to slow convergence, the slower the smaller. Moreover for low values of α most of the times only bad solutions can be found. For $\alpha\geq2$ we observed an early convergence to suboptimal solutions. The optimal range seems to be $1\leq\alpha\leq1.5$.
- β: for $\beta=0$ there is no convergence at all, progressively higher values lead to progressively quicker convergence. The behaviour is similar to that observed in the two other models, except that for $\beta>5$ the system quickly gets stuck in suboptimal tours.
- ρ: values below 0.5 slow down convergence, such as values above 0.8. There seems to be an optimum around 0.7.
- Q_3: we tested three values, $Q_3=1$, $Q_3=100$ and $Q_3=10000$ but the differences were not significant. Further experimentation is going on.

Experiments run on the 30 cities problem gave results in accordance to those of CCAO: slow or no convergence for $\beta \leq 1$, progressively quicker convergence for increasing betas, too quick for $\beta > 5$. Values of α in the range [1, 1.5] yield better results than higher or lower values, $\rho \approx 0.7$ is a good value for the coefficient related to evaporation, and $Q_3=100$ for the quantity of trail dropped. On this problem ANT-cycle reached the best-known result with a frequency over the number of test runs statistically higher than that of the other two algorithms and, on the whole, identification of good tours seems to be much quicker, even though we devised no index to quantify this. We also found a new optimal tour (see Fig.6) of length 423.741 (420 with distances rounded to integers; the previous best known tour on the same problem, published in (Whitley, Starkweather, Fuquay 1989) was of integer length 421); see (Colorni, Dorigo, Maniezzo 1991) or (Dorigo, 1991) for details.

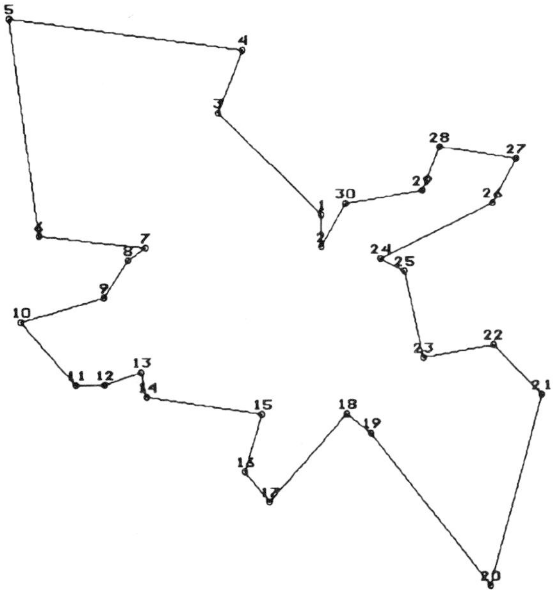

Fig. 6 - The new optimal tour obtained with 4200 iterations of ANT-cycle for the 30 cities problem ($\alpha=1$, $\beta=5$, $\rho=0.7$, $Q_3=100$). Real length = 423.741. Integer length = 420.

We tested the algorithm over the Eilon50 and Eilon75 problems (Eilon, Watson-Gandy, Christofides 1969) on a limited number of runs and with the number of cycles constrained to 3000. Under these restrictions we never got the optimum, but the quick convergence to satisfying solutions was maintained for both the problems (Fig. 7).

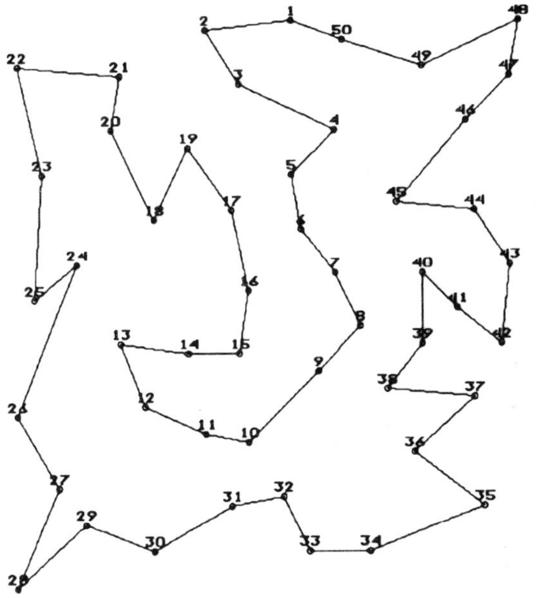

Fig.7 - A typical evolution of ANT-cycle on the Eilon50 problem ($\alpha=1$, $\beta=2$, $\rho=0.7$, $Q_3=100$). Real length = 441.572. Integer length = 438. Best known solution: integer length = 428.

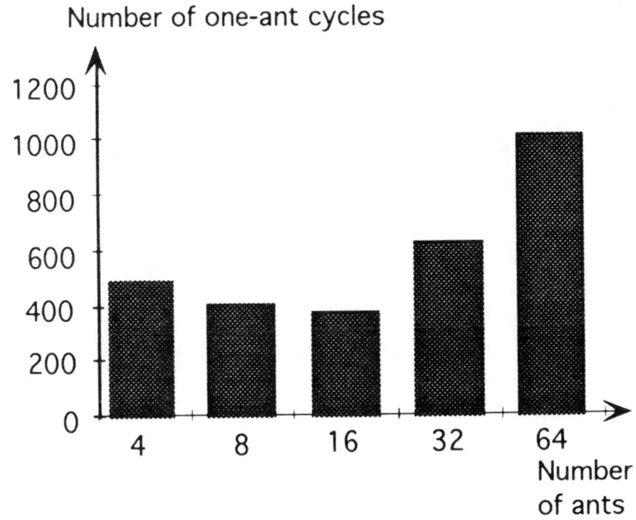

Fig.8 - Number of cycles required to reach optimum rated to the total number of ants for the 4x4 grid problem

The tests on the performance with increasing number of ants were conducted with the same modality described for the ANT-density and ANT-quantity systems. The results are shown in Fig.8: it is interesting to note that:

- the algorithm has been consistently able to identify the optimum with any number of ants;

- the computational overhead caused by the management of progressively more ants causes the overall efficiency to decrease with a high number of ants.

7. Conclusions and further work

In this paper we presented a new methodology based on an *autocatalytic* process and its application to the solution of a classical optimization problem. Simulation results are very encouraging and we believe the approach can be extended to a broader class of problems: we compared the results of our algorithm and those offered by other heuristic designed for the TSP over some well-known small-scale TSP instances (size 30, 50 and 75), always obtaining very good results, often better than those given by the other heuristics, although our algorithm requires a longer computational time. Still a basic questions remains largely with no answer: Why does the ant-algorithm work?

The general idea underlying this model is that of an autocatalytic process pressed by a greedy constructive heuristic (resulting in our so-called"*greedy force*"). The autocatalytic process alone tends to converge to a suboptimal path with exponential speed, while the greedy force alone is incapable to find anything but a suboptimal tour. When they work together it looks like the greedy force can give the right suggestions to the autocatalytic process and let it converge on very good, often optimal, solutions very quickly.

We believe that further work can be done along four main research directions:

- the formulation of a mathematical theory of the proposed model and of autocatalytic processes in general;
- the evaluation of the generality of the approach, through an investigation on which classes of problems can be well solved by this algorithm;
- the study of the implications that our model can have on artificial intelligence, particularly in the pattern recognition and machine learning fields;
- the possibility to exploit the inherent parallelism of the proposed model mapping it on parallel architectures.

References

Colorni A., Dorigo M., Maniezzo V. 1991. An Autocatalytic Optimizing Process. *Technical Report n. 91-016* Politecnico di Milano.

Denebourg J.L., Pasteels J.M., Verhaeghe J.C. 1983. Probabilistic Behaviour in Ants: a Strategy of Errors?. *J. theor. Biol.* 105:259-271.

Denebourg J.L., Goss S. 1989. Collective patterns and decision-making. *Ethology, Ecology & Evolution* 1:295-311.

Dorigo M. 1991. *Optimization, Learning and Natural Algorithms*. Ph.D. Thesis. Politecnico di Milano, in press.

Eilon S., Watson-Gandy T.H.., Christofides N. 1969. Distribution management: mathematical modeling and prcatical analysis. *Operational Research Quarterly*, 20.

Fitzgerald T.D., Peterson S.C. 1988. Cooperative foraging and communication in caterpillars. *Bioscience* 38:20-25.

Glover F. 1989. Tabu Search — Part I. *ORSA Jou. on Computing* 1:190-206.

Glover F. 1990. Tabu Search — Part II. *ORSA Jou. on Computing* 2:4-32.

Golden B., Stewart W.1985. Empiric analysis of heuristics. In *The Travelling Salesman Problem* edited by Lawler E.L., Lenstra J.K., Rinnooy-Kan A.H.G., Shmoys D.B. New York:Wiley.

Goss S., Aron S., Denebourg L., Pasteels J.M. 1989. Self-organized Shortcuts in the Argentine Ant. *Naturwissenschaften* 76.

Goss S., Beckers R., Deneubourg J.L., Aron S., Pasteels J.M. 1990. How Trail Laying and Trail Following Can Solve Foraging Problems for Ant Colonies. In *Behavioural Mechanisms of Food Selection* edited by R.N.Hughes. NATO ASI Series, Vol. G 20, Berlin:Springer-Verlag.

Lin S., Kernighan B.W. 1973. An effective Heuristic Algorithm for the TSP. *Operations research* 21.

Shapiro J.A. 1988. Bacteria as multicellular organisms. Scientific American, 82-89.

Whitley D., Starkweather T., Fuquay D. 1989. Scheduling Problems and Travelling Salesmen: the Genetic Edge Recombination Operator. *Proc. of the Third Int. Conf. on Genetic Algorithms*, Morgan Kaufmann.

Emergent Colonization in an Artificial Ecology

Andrew M. Assad
Department of Computer Science
University of Illinois, 1304 West Springfield Avenue, Urbana, IL 61801, USA
and
Norman H. Packard
Beckman Institute – Center for Complex Systems Research and the Physics Department
University of Illinois, 405 North Mathews Avenue, Urbana, IL 61801, USA.

Abstract.

This paper describes a computational model of organisms in an artificial ecology where colonization emerges through a process of resource gathering and exchange amongst an evolving population. Organismic fitness is defined implicitly as a result of local interactions of the artificial organsims with each other and their environment, with no explicit, global directive. The organisms move in the world, seeking different types of resources, and they have the capacity to trade with each other, according to a genetically encoded strategy. If the organisms can survive to the age of sexual maturity, they can reproduce, and their offspring's strategy is changed using crossover and mutation of the parents' strategies. The population is found to evolve a collection of strategies that tend to produce a spatial clustering behavior which is observable at the population level, but is not explicitly specified anywhere in the model. These clusters can be viewed as colonies since the organisms within them have actually evolved to rely to a large extent on the coherence of the cluster as an efficient resource distribution mechanism for their survival.

1. Introduction

Colonization is an important and widespread phenomenon found at almost every level of living biological systems. It is one of the clearest forms of emergence of a hierarchy in biological systems, and is one of the essential aspects of the evolution of higher organisms from lower ones. It is clear that many simple multicellular organisms are colonies of unicellular organisms, as occurs, for example, in the marine organism *man-of-war*.

Organisms of every kind, ranging from microscopic bacteria to humans and larger animals, form colonies around shared resources. Colonization appears to be a "natural" property that arises in any ecology where individual organisms must compete for spatially distributed resources, when the competition can be sufficiently complex.

Very simple forms of competition for a single resource are found to yield some macroscopic patterns in the population, but no colonization [1, 2]. The reason is simple: if all organisms are seeking the same resource in the world, it is advantageous to stay away from other organisms that have consumed resources in their own neighborhood. Thus, to make colonial aggregation even possible, it is necessary to have more than one resource. We have constructed a world with four resources, and four types of organism that can metabolize each type of resource. When a resource is not metabolized, it may be carried by an organism, and traded later, according to a genetically encoded strategy. The evolution of colonization takes place through the gradual changes in the organismic strategies.

Section 2 provides a brief survey of some recent discourse on *emergence* in the Artificial Life (ALife) literature as well as a definition of the term as it is employed in the title and throughout this paper. Section 3 is devoted to an examination of *colonization*, including a biological perspective as well as a definition of this behavior as it applies to this study. Section 4 describes the actual implementation of the artificial ecology. This description entails not only an examination of the basic "physics" of the artificial world, but also a detailed discussion of the world's artificial inhabitants and their characteristics and behavior. Section 5 presents results of the simulation. Finally, in section 6, the results are discussed and conclusions are drawn as to whether or not the simulation achieved the aforementioned objective of producing a truly *emergent* (as defined in Section 2) colonization behavior amongst the artificial inhabitants.

2. Emergence

Since its inception, the field of Artificial Life has consistently referred to the property of "emergent" phenomena as one of its primary distinguishing features. However, despite its frequent use in the literature, a clear, concise, and widely accepted definition of the term "emergent" has not yet been realized. Rather than attempting to propose such a standard, this section offers a definition that is relevant to the study at hand, and perhaps, will contribute to what may ultimately be an accepted definition.

In his opening essay to the Proceedings of the First Workshop on Artificial Life, Langton [3] includes *emergent behavior* as one of the fundamental characteristics of an ALife system. At first glance, his contrasting of emergent behavior with the *prespecified behavior* characteristic of AI systems seems to provide a sharp, intuitive distinction between the fields. However, upon further inspection this distinction may not be so clear.

We will be studying emergence in the realm of an ALife model, but it is worth noting that the concept has a rich history, which the ALife approach exemplified by this work will hopefully expand. The idea of emergence could perhaps be traced to Heraclitus and his theory of flux, and Anaxagoras, with his theory of *perichoresis*, which held that all discernable structure in the world is a result of a dynamical unmixing process (his version of emergence) that began with a homogeneous chaos.

In modern thought, the scientific paradigm beginning with Newton has been somewhat antithetical to the idea of emergence, as the power of the paradigm has often come from the exact derivability of phenomena (which, as we argue below, make a phenomena non-emergent). The first ideas of emergence in biological evolution were implicit in Darwin [4], though he was perhaps too conservative to voice the concept very loudly. Subsequently, Bergson, a rather nonconservative philosopher, voiced the concept rather more loudly [5].

Since these beginnings, discussion of emergence may have developed in two broad overlapping areas, theoretical biology and cybernetics [6, 7, 8, 9, 10, 11], and more recently and more or less independently in the area of computational models, starting with the work of McCullouch and Pitts [12], Kauffman [13], and Holland [14], though this early work on computational models does not always explicitly emphasize emergence. Computational emergence has only recently been named and studied in its own right [15], and is now the basis of most ALife studies [3]. Extended discussions of emergence in the context of ALife have been taking place on the network [16], and an extended bibliography may be found also be found there [17].

There is some controversy about whether true, life-like emergence can occur within a purely computational domain [6, 9, 18, 19]; we take the view here that some sort of nontrivial emergence can indeed occur in a purely computational domain, and we aim to demonstrate its occurrence by example.

Quite generally, emergence usually refers to two or more levels of description. In the simplest case of two levels (which is all we consider in this paper), we will call the level on which the model is defined in terms of interactions between components the *microscopic level*. The level on which phenomena emerge, as a global property of the collection of components, is the *macroscopic level*.

Typically, Alife models which produce unexpected macroscopic behavior that is not immediately predictable upon inspection of the specification of the system are said to exhibit some form of emergent behavior. Although certainly not a rigorous definition, this notion of emergence seems to be fairly pervasive in the literature. Thus, in many respects, "emergence" seems to be in the eye of the beholder. What is a wholly unexpected behavior from one perspective may be immediately obvious from another, though it is clear that some types of emergence (any emergence resulting in universal computation) must be able to produce truly unexpected behavior.

It is in this spirit of relativity that we propose a *scale* in which to measure emergence rather than a singular definition. While this scale does not circumvent the problem of lack of precision, it hopefully provides a common yardstick from which the level of emergence of a behavior can be estimated. The scale ranges from a "weak" or non-emergent level at the top to a "strong" or maximally emergent level at the bottom:

- *Non-emergent*: Behavior is immediately deducible upon inspection of the specification or rules generating it.
- *Weakly emergent*: Behavior is deducible in hindsight from the specification *after* observing the behavior.

.
.
.

- *Strongly emergent*: Behavior is deducible in theory, but its elucidation is prohibitively difficult.
- *Maximally emergent*: Behavior is impossible to deduce from the specification.

Note that the levels in this scale are not intended to be absolutes at this point, since we have refrained from attempting to give a definition of terms like "deducible," general enough to be independent of the context of different behaviors and models. However, the scale should at least allow for an increased accuracy or resolution in discussing a potentially emergent aspect of a complex system's behavior.

What is it that emerges? We distinguish between three different answers to this question:

Structure: The emergence of patterned structure, either in space time configurations, or in more abstract symbolic spaces. Examples include Benard cells in fluid convection, flocking behavior of Boids, and gliders in the game of life.

Computation: The emergence of computational processing, over and above the computation automatically implented in the formation of a structure. Examples include Holland's classifier system, and artificial life models that include the possibility for evolution of computation of computation performed by organisms [2, 20], or, in the unique model of Fontana, computation performed directly by the microscopic elements [21].

Functionality: The emergence of functionality, where functionality is defined in terms of actions that are functional, or beneficial to the microscopic components. So far, the primary examples of emergence of functionality are a subset of the examples of computational emergence, where the computation performs a function for the microscopic organisms.

The relationship between these different types of emergence is unclear. We hypothesize that there is a hierarchy of necessity: emergence of functionality requires the emergence of computation, which requires the emergence of structure. On the other hand, emergence of structure does not necessarily imply the emergence of computation, which does not necessarily imply the emergence of functionality.

We argue below that the emergence of colonization entails all three types of emergence, but may have an intermediate level of deducibility, implying less than maximal emergence.

3. Colonization

The motivation for choosing colonization as the emergent behavior objective in this study is twofold. First, from a biological perspective, colonization appears to be an important and widespread phenomenon in living systems. Found at almost every level, ranging from the microscopic world of bacteria to the macroscopic world of larger animals, colonization consistently emerges in environments where many individuals of the same species must share and/or compete for spatially clustered resources. Thus, it may be of interest to determine the environmental conditions which lead to the formation of these tightly clustered, highly interactive groups of organisms.

From the standpoint of ALife, inducing an emergent colonization behavior represents a "second order" evolutionary process which is lacking in many ALife simulations. Although *individual* organisms in the worlds of Ackley [20], Packard and Bedau [2], and others will often evolve clever, intricate strategies for survival in their environments, they remain, for the most part, completely independent of each other. Thus, evolution basically stops at the individual level. Colonization requires an evolution of the *interaction* amongst individuals, not merely evolution of individual strategies.

Furthermore, the problem of attempting to induce an emergent colonization behavior brings into focus a more general, fundamental question: What are the necessary primitives in an environment to allow for the *possibility* of the evolution of complex structures from simple building blocks? How rich must the initial environment be? How complex must the specification of the building blocks be? Although finding a possible solution for the problem of evolving a relatively low-complexity colony structure does not directly address these questions, it may provide some initial clues to the answers.

For the purposes of this study, a colony is considered to be a group of organsims which is spatially clustered, relatively stable in size over time, and exhibiting high levels of interaction amongst its members. Inspired by a study on the evolution of money as a medium of exchange by Kiyotaki and Wright [22], "interaction" in this experiment refers to an exchange of resources between organisms.

4. Implementation

4.1 The Artorg World

The artificial world as implemented in this experiment consists of a square Cartesian plane containing N by N (where N is the length of a side of the square) discrete points. Points in the world can contain energy resources, or "food", and can also be inhabited by members of the four different "species" of artificial organisms (hereafter referred to as "Artorgs"). Each point can be inhabited by, at most, one Artorg and can contain, at most, one food unit at any given time. However, a point can contain an Artorg and one food unit simultaneously.

4.2 The Organisms

Artorgs are mobile agents which move about in the world consuming energy resources and producing waste. The four species of Artorgs (white, red, green, and blue) compose a circular food chain where one species' waste is another's food. For example, red Artorgs consume green waste, but produce red waste which is then consumed by white Artorgs, which produce white waste, etc. An Artorg must maintain a minimum internal energy level (by consuming enough food) in order to exist. Once an Artorg's energy level drops below this threshhold, it is considered to be "dead" and is removed from the world.

Although they do not have a prespecified lifespan, Artorgs are subject to a metabolic rate which is proportional to their age. Thus, as an Artorg grows older, it requires more and more energy to maintain its existence. Eventually, it will be simply unable to acquire energy faster than it metabolizes it. This condition effectively imposes a finite lifespan on Artorgs.

Artorgs have a sensory system which enables them to see food as well as other Artorgs in the world. They are also able to determine the location of the nearest food (other than their own waste, which they ignore) to their present location. This nearest food location becomes the goal which drives an Artorg's movement strategy. Essentially, at any given time, an Artorg examines its surrounding environment, locates the nearest food, establishes that location as its goal in its internal memory, and attempts to move towards that goal.

4.3 Resource Trading

Besides finding and consuming food of the particular type which they are able to metabolize, Artorgs can also carry and exchange food of other types. For example, although a green Artorg can only consume blue food to satisfy its energy needs, it can pick up and carry red or white food and exchange that food with a neighboring Artorg which is also carrying food. Although an Artorg will not pick up its own waste (i.e. a green Artorg will not pick up green food), it can accept such food in a trade with another Artorg. Whether or not an Artorg will actually trade the food it is carrying for another Artorg's food depends upon its simple internal "brain".

The Artorg brain is essentially a sixteen bit table which dictates its trading strategy. Table 1 depicts a trading strategy (not necessarily a good one) for an Artorg. Rows in the table refer to the type of food the Artorg is currently carrying and potentially giving in a trade, and columns index the type of food which the Artorg's prospective trading partner is offering. Bits in this table which are set to '1' indicate that the Artorg is willing to make the corresponding trade. Bits that are set to '0' indicate the Artorg refuses the corresponding trade. For example, in the trading strategy given in Table 1, an Artorg carrying red food (referring to the second row in the table) would exchange that food for either white, green, or blue food (columns one, three, and four) but would refuse a trade with another Artorg offering

	white	red	green	blue
white	1	0	0	0
red	1	0	1	1
green	0	0	0	1
blue	1	1	0	0

Table 1: An Example Artorg Trading Strategy

	white	red	green	blue
white	n	C	n	n
red	u	u	u	u
green	n	C	n	n
blue	n	C	n	n

Table 2: Critical Bits in the Trading Strategy for a White Artorg

red food. For a trade to actually occur, both parties in the exchange must agree. In other words, both trading partners must have a '1' in the bit of their trading strategies corresponding to what they are giving and receiving.

Clearly, for a particular species of Artorg, there are potentially good and bad trading strategies to have. In general, an Artorg with a good trading strategy will trade anything it is carrying for food of the type which it can metabolize. This corresponds to three "critical" bits in its trading strategy, and specifically to the column corresponding to the type of food which it can metabolize. Table 2 illustrates the critical bits in the trading strategy of a white Artorg. Since white Artorgs consume red food, the critical bits (labelled 'C' in the table) in its strategy are located in the second column, which is the column indicating receipt of red food during a trade. In a good strategy, these critical bits are set to '1', and the white Artorg will always take the beneficial action of attempting to trade whatever it is carrying for red food. However, if some or all of these bits are set to '0', the white Artorg will refuse trades which can provide it with the energy it depends upon for its survival. This implies, of course, that an Artorg with a good trading strategy has an evolutionary advantage over its competitors with less than optimal strategies.

Bits in the table which are labelled 'n' correspond to "non-critical" trades which have no immediate impact on the Artorg's internal energy state. For example, making a trade of blue food for green food (determined by the bit in row four, column three) does not immediately help a white Artorg since it can only metabolize red food. However, acquiring green food may be advantageous to the white Artorg if it has another neighbor carrying red food who refuses a trade for blue food, but accepts a trade for green food. The bits labelled 'u' in Table 2 (all bits in row two) refer to "unused" bits, or bits in the white Artorg's trading strategy which will never be accessed in practice. A white Artorg will never have the opportunity to trade away red food since it immediately metabolizes such food after acquiring it, either via a trade or by finding it in the world. In principle then, these unused bits should have no effect on an individual's survivability, and hence, should not evolve to any optimal configuration.

4.4 Reproduction

The trading strategy of an Artorg is fixed over its lifetime, but reproduction using the genetic operators of the Simple Genetic Algorithm as described by Goldberg [23] provides the mechanism for the evolution of better trading strategies in future generations. In order to reproduce, an Artorg must survive long enough to reach the age of sexual maturity. Once sexual maturity has been reach, the Artorg periodically enters a short "gestation" period during which it ceases its normal movement and trading activities. At the end of this period, the Artorg mates with the closest Artorg of the same species to produce an offspring. Although reproduction is sexual, Artorgs do not have different genders. Mates are selected strictly on the basis of spatial proximity.

The offspring of an Artorg mating inherits its genetic information (i.e. its trading strategy) from both parents. Trading strategies are represented as sixteen bit strings equivalent to sequentially listing the bits of the strategy as depicted in Table 1 in a left to right, row major order. Single point crossover (see [23]) combines part of one parent's strategy with part of the other parent's strategy to create the offspring's strategy.

After crossover, a low probability (p_m = 0.005) mutation operator is applied bit by bit to the offspring's trading strategy. Individual bits are flipped from either '1' to '0' or '0' to '1' with probability p_m. Thus, since a trading strategy consists of sixteen bits, the probability that an offspring's strategy will be unaffected by mutation can be calculated as $(1-p_m)^{16} = 0.995^{16} \approx 0.923$. Once the offspring's trading strategy has been created and subjected to the mutation operator, the new Artorg is placed in the world in a vacant point adjacent to its "mother" (the Artorg which underwent the period of gestation prior to mating). New Artorgs are initially given a fraction of their mother's energy.

4.5 Initialization

Initialization of an Artorg world simulation is a straightforward process. Equal numbers of each of the four species of Artorgs are placed at random locations in the world. Trading strategies of the initial population are randomly generated sixteen bit strings. Each Artorg is initially given a high internal energy state and immediately produces a food unit of its color in an adjacent point in the world. From this point on, the Artorgs enter their life cycles, moving about in the world, consuming and trading energy resources, reproducing, and dying.

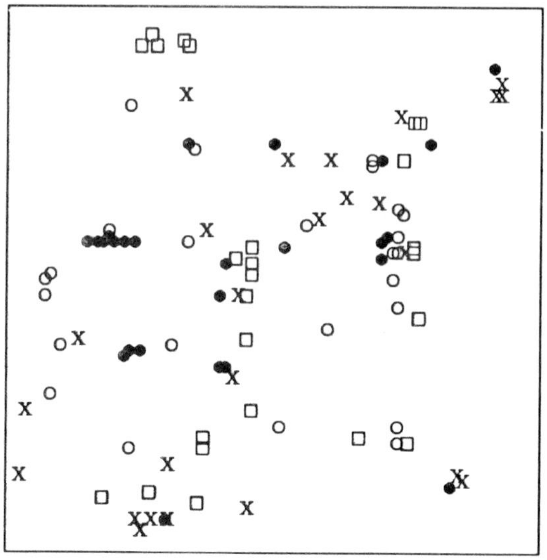

Figure 1: Artorg World after 50 Time Steps

5. Results

The results discussed here refer to experiments run with world sizes ranging from 60 by 60 (3600 discrete points) to 100 by 100 (10000 points) and initial populations ranging from 80 to 100 Artorgs. Within these ranges, population behaviors were not radically different.

5.1 A Sample Simulation

Since one of our major criteria for determining whether or not colonization occurs is the spatial arrangement of Artorgs in the world, it may be useful to first "visually" examine an Artorg world in progress. Although certainly not as interesting as the real time, graphical output generated on a Sun workstation by this program, Figures 1 through 3 provide sequential "snapshots" of the Artorg world at various points in time. In lieu of colors, different symbols are used to represent the four different species.

At time zero the world contains a random distribution of roughly equal numbers of the four species of Artorgs. At this time, all of the Artorgs in the world have completely random trading strategies. After fifty time steps, as shown in Figure 1, no spatial clustering is visible as the Artorgs roam about gathering food. The Artorg world is not yet old enough to have evolved significant trading interactions.

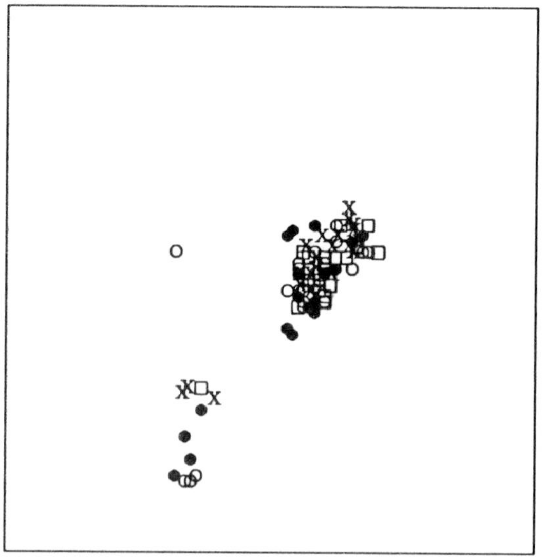

Figure 2: Artorg World after 200 Time Steps

Figure 2 depicts the state of the Artorg world after two hundred time steps. By this time, several new generations of Artorgs have been introduced into the world. Activity for the most part

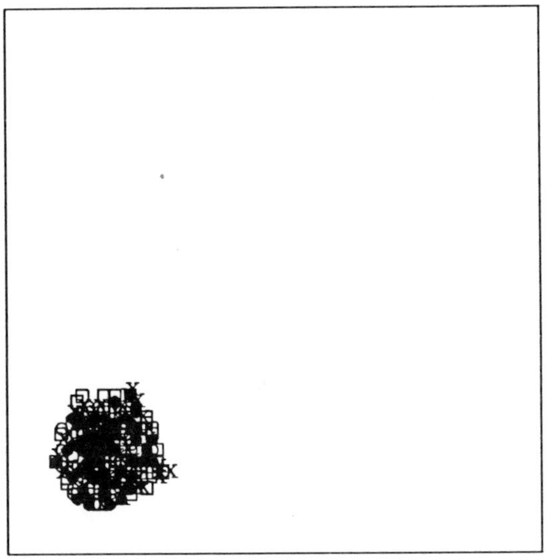

Figure 3: Artorg World after 2000 Time Steps

is centered around a loosely knit, heterogeneous cluster of Artorgs near the center of the world. This cluster, which can now be viewed as the start of a colony, is characterized by an increased amount of trading activity amongst its members. Furthermore, although it isn't shown in Figure 5, much of the energy in the world has been internalized in the Artorgs (i.e. most of the food in the world is being carried by the Artorgs rather than lying free in the world).

Finally, in Figure 3, after two thousand time steps, the entire Artorg population in the world comprises a single colony which is characterized by a high level of successful trading activity. Artorgs at this stage have, on average, better trading strategies than their ancestors and these strategies continue to improve in future generations. Better trading strategies result in a greater rate of food transfer within the population and hence, although it is difficult to tell from the figure, the population at this point in time is nearly double the size of the original one.

5.2 Analysis of the Sample Simulation

While the previous section clearly documents the formation of spatial clusters in the population, it does not provide any quantitative analysis of the evolution (if any) of interaction between Artorgs. Since the trading of resources is an integral part of such interaction in the Artorg world, an analysis of the evolution of trading strategies present in the population over time is in order.

Figure 4 depicts just such an analysis. This graph shows the changes in proportions of the three types of bits (as defined in Section 4.3) present in trading strategies which are set to '1' in the population as a whole over time. The top curve, corresponding to the proportion of critical bits in the trading strategies set to '1', starts out at around 0.5 and steadily increases to 0.95 at time 5000. This is a significant result because it definitely indicates the evolution of better trading strategies since an optimal strategy will have all of its critical bits set to '1'. Clearly, Artorgs with good trading strategies have a selective advantage since they are the ones reproducing and passing on their strategies.

As expected, the curve corresponding to the unused bits in a trading strategy in Figure 4 hovers at around 0.5. Since the unused bits in a strategy are never actually accessed, they have no bearing on an Artorg's behavior and thus, are not subjected to any selective pressures. Their proportion should be roughly 0.5 since they are set randomly to a '1' or '0' in the initial population. Likewise, the curve shown for the proportion of non-critical bits in Figure 4 hovers around 0.5. In principle, an increase in this proportion might indicate that consistent patterns of trade amongst more than two Artorgs (e.g. one Artorg brokering a trade between two others) were evolving. However, such an increase was not observed on a consistent basis in the simulations run.

The bottom curve of Figure 4 provides a fairly gross measure of interaction between Artorgs over time. This curves plots the cumulative proportion of trades that have been successfully made (i.e. both parties agreed to trade and actually exchanged the food they were carrying) to trades that have been attempted at a given time in the world. In some sense, this can be thought of as a measure of cooperation between Artorgs. This proportion steadily climbs throughout indicating that the Artorgs in later generations have evolved cooperative trading strategies which increase the overall net flow of food within the colony.

5.3 Other Simulations

In order to determine the probable cause(s) behind the apparent emergence of colonization typified by the sample simulation, two other simulations with different Artorg behaviors were run for comparative purposes. First, to examine the

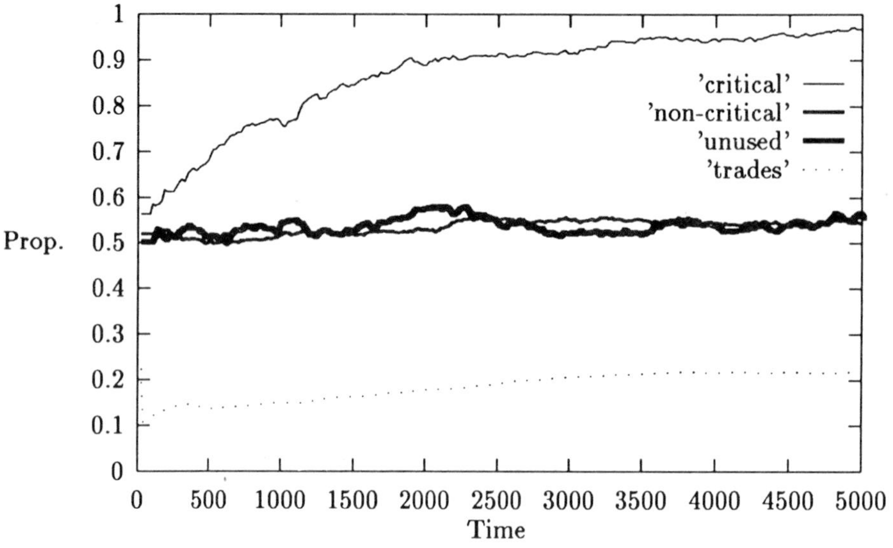

Figure 4: The Evolution of Artorg Trading Strategies

effect of the *evolution* of trading strategies, a simulation was created and run *without* any evolution. Offspring Artorgs were simply assigned random trading strategies instead of inheriting some genetically recombined strategy from their parents. To some extent, colonization still occurred. Spatial clumping of the Artorg population was observed, but on the whole, the colonies could not sustain as large a population given the same initial conditions as those found in the simulations with evolution. Furthermore, interaction amongst individuals in the colony as measured by the proportion of successful trades did *not* increase over time. Thus, the evolution of trading strategies is most likely not responsible for the spatial clustering behavior although it does seem to be essential for the growth of the colony.

Another simulation was run to examine the effect of the gathering and trading of resources on the spatial clustering behavior observed. In this simulation, Artorgs were not allowed to trade or to pick up any type of food which they could not metabolize. With these limitations, the tight spatial clustering characteristic of the colonies formed in the simulations where trading and gathering were allowed was not observed. Instead, this simulation was characterized by loosely associated homogenous flocks of Artorgs roaming around the world in search of what was mainly externalized food. Clearly then, it appears that the ability to gather and internalize food plays a major role in any spatial clustering that occurs in the Artorg world.

6. Conclusions

As stated in the introduction to this paper, our objective was to develop an artificial environment in which a behavior of colonization emerges in the population of its inhabitants. Based on the definition of "colonization" given in Section 3, we have achieved at least part of our objective. During the simulations run, Artorgs consistently formed spatial clusters in the world similar to that described in the previous section. Coinciding with the formations of these clusters was an overall increase in the level of interaction amongst colony members as better trading strategies evolved and the proportion of successful trades increased. Thus, we can reasonably argue that colonization, as we defined it, did indeed occur. Furthermore, we can surmise that the principle of exchange or transfer of resources amongst agents may be one of the important primitives necessary in an environment which is capable of producing a complex spatial structure, such as a colony.

In the emergence of colonization, we see all three types of emergence: Emergence of *structure* occurs both in the structure of the evolved strategies, and in the space-time structure of the

the population distribution. Emergence of *computation* occurs, in a very simple way, because the strategies that emerge as a result of evolution are performing a computational task, in making the decision to trade or not. *Functionality* emerges, in the sense that the resulting strategies serve a purpose for the individual organisms, and because the organisms benefit as a result of participating in the colony produced by their strategic computation.

However, the more difficult question to resolve is: *Is the colonization behavior emergent?* One can at least argue that the behavior is not *immediately* deducible upon inspection of its specification (in this case, several hundred lines of 'C' code), although there usually will be a dissenter to this idea in a large enough crowd. This is because in retrospect, it seems intuitively reasonable that the organisms stick together given their explicitly programmed movement and gathering behaviors, and no other collective behavior is obviously reasonable.

Thus, judging from the scale of emergence proposed in Section 2, the colonization occurring in an Artorg world appears to be at least "weakly" emergent. On the other hand, since we are running this program on a deterministic computer using a deterministic pseudorandom number generator, we can't say that the behavior is impossible to deduce unless the collective behavior of the Artorgs have the computational power of a Universal Turing Machine (for which we have no evidence). Thus, the exhibited colonization can not be considered a maximally emergent behavior.

It appears that our model falls in the scale of emergence where most ALife models fall – somewhere in the murky middle, between weak and strong. Reducing the prespecified behaviors in our model, such as movement towards the nearest food, by genetically encoding them and letting them evolve would likely strengthen the emergence of any behavior which occurs. However, there may be a fundamental tradeoff between increasing the level of emergence in a system, and being able to observe any kind of interesting behavior at all. As control is transferred to genetic and other evolutionary operators, so too is the power to influence the ultimate behavior of the system. The key to solving this problem of control versus emergence is to concentrate on determining the proper initial environment that is *likely* to produce a desired behavior in an emergent fashion rather than to focus on the the behaviors of individual agents in the environment.

7. Acknowledgements

Thanks are especially due to the Institute for Scientific Interchange in Turin, Italy, where some of the analysis of this model was done and much of this paper was written. Thanks also are due to Greg Lesher for his programming contributions and to Jeff Horn, Joe Breeden, and a host of others for their insight and commentary. Finally, the first author is especially grateful for the support and patience of David Goldberg.

References

[1] Packard, N.H. 1991. Intrinsic evolution in an artificial ecology. In *Artificial Life*, edited by C. Langton. Reading, MA: Addison-Wesley.

[2] Packard, N.H. and M. Bedau. 1991. Measurement of evolutionary activity and teleology. In *Artificial Life II*, edited by C. Langton, J. Farmer, and S. Rasmussen. Reading, MA: Addison-Wesley.

[3] Langton, C. 1989. Artificial Life. In *Artificial Life*, edited by C. Langton. Reading, MA: Addison-Wesley.

[4] Darwin, C. 1859. *On the Origin of Species by Means of Natural Selection*. London: reprinted Cambridge, MA: Harvard University Press, 1964.

[5] Bergson, H. 1911. *Creative Evolution*. Translated by A. Mitchell. New York.

[6] Rosen, R. 1973. On the generation of metabolic novelties in evolution. In *Biogenesis, Evolution, Homeostasis*, edited by A. Locker. New York: Pergamon Press.

[7] Rosen, R. 1985. *Anticipitory Systems*. New York: Pergamon Press.

[8] Pattee, H.H. 1972. The nature of hierarchical controls in living matter. In *Foundations of Mathematical Biology, Vol. I*, edited by R. Rosen. New York: Academic Press.

[9] Pattee, H.H. 1989. Simulations, realizations, and theories of life. In *Artificial Life*, edited by C. Langton. Reading, MA: Addison-Wesley.

[10] Rossler, O. 1984. Deductive prebiology. In *Molecular Evolution and the Prebiological Paradigm*, edited by K. Matsuno, K. Dose, K. Harada, and D. L. Rohlfing. Plenum.

[11] Wiener, N. 1948. *Cybernetics, or Control and Communication in the Animal and the Machine.* Cambridge, MA: MIT Press.

[12] McCulloch, W. and W. Pitts. 1943. A logical calculus of the ideas immanent in nervous activity. *Bull. Math. Biophysiscs* 5:115.

[13] Kauffman, S.A. 1969. *J. Theoret. Biol.* 22:437.

[14] Holland, J. 1975. *Adaptation in Natural and Artificial Systems.* Ann Arbor: The University of Michigan Press.

[15] Forrest, S. 1989. Emergent computation: self-organizing, collective, and cooperative phenomena in natural and artificial computing networks. *Proceedings of the Ninth Annual Center for Nonlinear Studies and Computing Division Conference, Physica D.*

[16] Freeman, E.T. and M.W. Lugowsky. 1989-1991. *Artificial Life Digest*, `alife-request@iuvax.cs.indiana.edu`.

[17] Cariani, P. 1991. In *Artificial Life Digest* **49**, maintained by E.T. Freeman and M.W. Lugowsky, `alife-request@iuvax.cs.indiana.edu`.

[18] Cariani, P. 1991. Emergence and Artificial Life. In *Artificial Life II*, edited by C. Langton, D. Farmer, and S. Rassmusen. Reading, MA: Addison-Wesley.

[19] Cariani, P. 1990. Adaptation and emergence in organisms and devices. In press, *Journal of General Evolution.*

[20] Ackley, D.H. and M.L. Littman. 1991. Interaction between learning and evolution. In *Artificial Life II*, edited by C. Langton, D. Farmer, and S. Rassmusen. Reading, MA: Addison-Wesley.

[21] Fontana, W. 1991. Algorithmic Chemistry. In *Artificial Life II*, edited by C. Langton, D. Farmer, and S. Rassmusen. Reading, MA: Addison-Wesley.

[22] Kiyotaki, N. and R. Wright. 1988. On money as a medium of exchange. *CARESS Working Paper #88-01.*

[23] Goldberg, D.E. 1989. *Genetic Algorithms in Search, Optimization, and Machine Learning.* Reading, MA: Addison-Wesley.

The Maximum Entropy Principle and Sensing in Swarm Intelligence

Gerardo Beni and Susan Hackwood
College of Engineering
University of California, Riverside
Riverside, California 92521-0425

Abstract

We discuss how in systems with 'Swarm Intelligence' sensing is most efficiently carried out by sets of value-specific sensing units rather than by the commonly used feature-specific sensing units, and how the maximum entropy principle allows the design of optimal sensing configurations in swarms. First, we realize that using value-specific sensing units requires using many units per feature (a disadvantage) but it allows for distributed operation (an advantage). Next, we consider for a set of value-specific sensing elements, the problem of designing the structure of the sensing swarm for optimal sensing under quite general conditions, as follows. We assume that for one feature (to be sensed by the swarm) only the range of values and its average value (over a time or space interval) are known. To design the optimal sensing structure we make use of the Jaynes-Shannon maximum entropy principle. This allows us to calculate the number of sensing elements that should be assigned to each value to be sensed. Finally, we give the explicit solutions for a decimal scale sensor to be realized by the swarm.

1. Introduction

Recently, there has been an increasing interest in distributed intelligence systems, both artificial (i.e., robotic [1]) and biological [2]. A particular behavior of distributed intelligent systems is the so-called "Swarm Intelligence" [3].

Systems exhibiting Swarm Intelligence behavior are defined as:
[Def.1] *Systems of non-intelligent robots exhibiting collectively intelligent behavior evident in the ability to unpredictably produce specific (i.e., not in a statistical sense) ordered patterns of matter [3].*

In this definition 'robot' is intended as *an entity capable of both mechanical and informational behavior*, thus including both artificial and natural systems. The critical term in the definition is 'unpredictably'. In fact, as discussed in [3], only when a system can be considered unpredictable (e.g., by being 'globally intractable' or 'unrepresentable') in producing order, it makes sense to speak of it as intelligent.

If unpredictability is the key element in defining the *intelligent* behavior of the system, the key element in defining the *swarm* behavior of the system is the presence, in the system as a whole, of a property which is absent in the units composing the system. In [Def.1] such a property is 'intelligence'; thus it refers to '*systems of non-intelligent robots exhibiting collectively intelligent behavior.*'

Thus, if we wish to consider swarm intelligent behavior more generally than in [3], we may start by extending [Def.1] to types of swarm behavior exhibiting different aspects of intelligence. For example, we may consider swarms exhibiting some components of intelligence, such as perception, recognition, inference, etc. We would then generalize [Def.1] to read:

[Def. 2] *Systems of non-intelligent robots exhibiting collectively some aspect of intelligent behavior evident in the ability to unpredictably produce specific (i.e., not in a statistical sense) ordered patterns of matter.*

Where we have left unspecified the ability of the system which indicates its having acquired an aspect of intelligence, since this is evidently dependent on the specific aspect considered. For example, if we consider 'understanding' as an aspect of intelligence, we may specify [Def. 2] as follows:

[Def. 2a] *Systems of non-intelligent robots exhibiting collectively '<u>understanding</u>' evident in the ability to recognize (e.g., visual) patterns.*

Similarly, other aspects of intelligence may be considered and other aspects of swarm intelligence can be investigated. As a first investigation along these lines, in this paper we will consider the aspect of [Def. 2a] , i.e., the emergence of 'Understanding' in a swarm.

2. Emerging Properties of the Swarm: Measuring and Understanding

'Understanding' is generally the ability to make experience intelligible by relating it to known concepts and/or categories, thus it is fundamentally a process of classification. The latter can be reduced to (i) measurements of features of the experienced data, (ii) knowledge of the class-boundaries in the feature space, and (iii) relating (i) to (ii).

If either the measurements of the features are complex, or the number of classes is large (or both) it will be impossible for a single unit to classify and therefore to 'understand'. We shall assume that this is indeed the case; in this sense we shall regard the single units as 'non-intelligent'. We will then investigate how a swarm of such units can become capable of 'understanding'. For this we shall assume first that the limit to the 'understanding' of the single unit is due to the inability to measure (the features of the environment).

More specifically, let us assume that each single unit is capable of *detecting* but not of *measuring,* and let us investigate how a swarm of detectors can become capable of measuring.

This is actually obvious once we consider that a detecting unit can be regarded most basically as a one-bit measuring device. If the detectors carried by each unit are different, a collection of these units can become capable of measuring. For example, if a unit is capable of detecting a certain wavelength λ (e.g., by changing from white to black if, and only if, light of wavelength $\lambda \pm \Delta\lambda$ impinges upon it) and other units behave similarly for different wavelengths, a collection of N (different) units can detect N different wavelengths. If we assume that the detectable wavelengths form a continuous spectrum (from λ_1 to λ_N, with $\Delta\lambda$ intervals), we can regard the collection of N such detecting units as capable of measuring. And if the detecting units are autonomous robots we can regard the collections of them as a 'measuring swarm'.

The idea is easily generalized to other types of measurements, e.g., i) temperature where each unit detects only a specific or narrow range of temperature (thermochromic materials have this property), ii) acidity (a pH detector could change color depending on acidity) or iii) chemical concentration and/or composition (e.g., ion selective FET's), and so on. The latter example can be extended to include chemical detection of different types of molecules, as done by certain specialized biological cells. A collection of such cells, each capable of detecting a different chemical compound (e.g., type of protein), can be regarded as capable of recognizing (proteins), and, thus, of understanding.

There is, however, a slight difficulty here. Let us return to the 'measuring' function. Strictly speaking, since a detector is a one-bit measuring device, a (minimal) measuring capability seems to be present in the units, by definition. This seems to violate our definition [Def. 2a]. We must therefore clarify that, in [Def. 2a], following the common usage sense of the terms 'measuring' and 'detecting', we distinguish the meaning of 'measuring' and of 'detecting' by specifying that:
(i) 'measuring' refers to 'assigning one of N (N>1) possible quantitative values to a (physical) quantity'; (ii) 'detecting' refers to 'assigning a logic value (True or False) to a (physical) state'.
With this specification, a one-bit unit can only detect, not measure.

There is an analogous situation for intelligent systems composed of large numbers of neural units. Each neuron can be regarded as a switch and thus as a one-bit unit. Should one regard a switch as having intelligence, e.g., of having recognition capabilities? From our definition [Def.2], with specifications analogous to (i) and (ii) above, 'recognition' is not present in a switch; although, of course, it can be present in a collection of switches. Similarly, 'measuring ability' is not present in a detector (i.e., a one-bit measuring unit), although it can appear in a group of detectors.

Of course, the issue could be protracted by asking whether or not recognition capability is present in *two* switches, or in *three*, and so on. The point is that, generally, it is possible to specify a function (e.g., measuring, recognition, self-reproduction, etc.) and then make the plausible assumption of the existence of a boundary in N (the number of units) below which the function cannot be realized. Proving the existence of the boundary, and/or finding the critical number defining the boundary, is, generally, difficult and maybe impossible (i.e., not computable). The existence of the boundary, however, is in many cases obvious from physical considerations (e.g., self-reproduction). Therefore, even if the mathematical proof of its existence is lacking, it is a plausible assumption to postulate that a new function may arise when a collection of units reaches a critical number of units. This may be regarded as an hypothesis of existence of 'emerging' properties, i.e., of properties arising discontinuously with increasing numbers of units in a group. Swarm intelligence is one such emerging property. 'Measuring' and 'Recognition' (Understanding) are also emerging properties. In the next section we shall consider how a Measuring (or Recognizing) Swarm can be structured.

3. Structure of the Measuring Swarm

The measuring swarm has the advantage, over conventional measuring devices, of being distributed, and thus more resilient to damage and destruction. For this to be the case, however, its structure must be optimized, in the following sense. Let us consider the example of the previous section, i.e., a measuring swarm composed of N detecting units of n different types, each type sensitive to one value (within a narrow range) of a physical quantity (e.g., one type turning black only at temperatures between 16.5° and 17.5°, another type between 17.5° and 18.5°, etc.). Such a swarm could be structured as a set $\{N_i; i=1,2,..n; \Sigma i\, N_i = N\}$ of n identical subsets of N_i units each. These numbers, N_i, of units in the subsets generally are optimized under different constraints. For example, if the sizes of the various types of units vary and if the total space available for the swarm is limited, the optimal numbers, N_i, will be determined by a geometric (area, volume, etc.) constraint. Such a case is not uncommon; the smell sensors of some animal sensors are composed of sensing units of different configurations and sizes. The space available for the units is also often limited.

In the previous example, the optimal structure of the swarm is constrained by space. A less obvious, and more fundamental, example is provided by cases where the optimal structure optimizes the essential function of the swarm (i.e., measuring, or recognizing) or some other a basic function (i.e., survival) of the swarm. In other words, the question to be answered is 'given a total number of units, how many units of each type should be present in the swarm so that the swarm is most efficient at measuring, recognizing, surviving, and/or other basic functions?'

An example is provided by the swarm of cells constituting the immune system of an animal. The function of the swarm is to recognize and destroy enemy cells. Both the recognizing ability and the destroying ability of the immune system are important functions to optimize. Assuming a finite number, n, of possible enemy viruses to be recognized and destroyed, how many cells should the immune system devote to fighting (recognizing and destroying) each type of virus?

Generally, the function of each subgroup is increased as the number of units in the subgroup increases. This is obvious for the 'destroying' function, but it is also true for the measuring (and recognizing) function. In fact, we may reasonably assume that if two subgroups (i and j) of detectors are sensitive in the ranges of values $V_i \pm \Delta V$ and $V_j \pm \Delta V$ respectively, they could subspecialize their n_i (n_j) units to be sensitive to n_i (n_j) different values in the interval ΔV. Therefore, the resolution (and thus the measuring and recognizing capabilities) become proportional to the number of member units in a subgroup.

Thus, when we consider the optimization of the swarm structure under the constraint of optimizing some of its basic functions, we are seeking to distribute the units so that each subgroup has the appropriate level of functionality, which, as we have seen, is generally proportional to the number of units in the group.

For this type of optimization, we shall make use of the Jaynes-Shannon[4] Maximum Entropy Principle, as discussed in the following section.

4. Optimization by Maximum Entropy Principle

We shall consider the following problem. The swarm structure is defined as in the previous section, i.e., $\{N_i;\ i=1,2,..n;\ \Sigma_i N_i=N\}$. The swarm measures a physical property, such as temperature, in a certain range (e.g., between 10° and 100° C). Assuming the average, over some interval of time, of the physical property is known to be 42°C. What should be the structure of the swarm so as to be most effective in measuring temperature (i.e., how should the sensing units be distributed so that the resolution of the measurement is optimized)?

The same model/problem could be applied to optimizing the destroying capability of the swarm. Let the temperature range 10-100° C be divided in 10 equal intervals centered at 5°, 15°,...95°C. Assume that 10 different types of pests (e.g., insects that damage agricultural crops) become active each in one of the 10 intervals of temperature. The swarm task is to sense the temperature and destroy the pests active at that temperature. Thus, the number of units of the swarm operating (i.e., detecting and destroying) in that temperature interval is a key factor to the success (e.g., survival) of the swarm. In this example, the number of units in the swarm subgroups has to be calculated from the knowledge of the average temperature.

The above problem can be reduced to the following:

[Prob. 1] Given the average of an observed feature (e.g., temperature) $\langle T \rangle$, and the possible values T_i ($i=1,2,...n$) of the feature, find the probability p_i ($=p(T_i)$) that the feature has the value T_i, for each i.

In fact, it is clear that from the knowledge of p_i we know n_i ($n_i = N\, p_i$) and thus the structure of the swarm.

This type of problem ([Prob.1]) is a generalized inverse problem [5]. Such problems are abstractly expressed as

$$A' = rA \qquad [1]$$

where A stands for 'cause' or 'true state', r is an operator, and A' stands for 'effect' or 'apparent state'. The direct problem is one of prediction: given the cause (or true state) A and r, deduce the effect (or apparent state) A'. The inverse problem is deeper: given r and the effect (or apparent state) A', what is the cause (or true state) A?

In our problem, Eq.[1] becomes

$$\langle T \rangle = r\,\{p_i\} \qquad [1a]$$

and it is clear that given the temperature distribution $\{p_i\}$, the direct problem of finding the average temperature $\langle T \rangle$ is trivial, whereas the inverse problem is not obvious.

In Eq.[1], if the data set A' is in one-to-one correspondence with the set A, and r is non-singular, one expects the problem to be solvable exactly by direct mathematical inversion. An example is the linear Fredholm integral equation of the first kind

$$A'(x) = \int_a^b r(x,y)\, A(y)\, dy \qquad [2]$$

which is to be solved for A given a definite class of functions A'(x) on a specific interval.

In general, however, the set A' is undetermined , and r is singular in the sense that the set A' may result from more than one distinct set A. In other cases, r is a point-spread function so that the very small elements in r result in very large values in r^{-1}, and therefore only an estimate of A^ of A can be obtained

$$A\hat{} = v\,A \qquad [3]$$

where the 'resolvent' v has to be determined. v is a generalized inverse, i.e.,

$$rvr = r \qquad [4]$$

which mathematically expresses the concept that v must be chosen so that A^ lies in the class C of possible states that could have produced A' in Eq.[1].

Orthodox statistics can only tell us (from the observed data) that the true state must lie in a certain class, but it has no prescription for telling us what unique choice has to be made within that class.

We see that the basic problem is not one of randomness but of *incomplete information.* Thus, a definite solution can only be obtained from prior information.

The Maximum Entropy Principle [4] allows the encoding of prior information into a probability distribution. Jaynes [6] introduced the principle by using Shannon's entropy [7]

$$S = -\,\Sigma\, p_i \log p_i \qquad [5]$$

for a discrete set of probabilities $\{p_i\}$, $\Sigma\, p_i = 1$, to assign probability distributions under certain constraints, such as ensemble averages, e.g.,

$$\langle T\rangle = \Sigma\, T_i\, p_i \qquad [6]$$

Jaynes proposed that *the optimum choice of probability distribution is the one that makes no other assumptions about the prior information, thus the one that maximizes the entropy* [5]. Which is a statement of the Maximum Entropy Principle.

For example, in the case of the constraint of Eq. [6] the maximization of S results in the well known Gibbs distribution

$$p_i = \exp(-\beta\, T_i)/\, Z \qquad [7]$$

where Z is the partition function

$$Z = \Sigma \exp(-\beta\, T_i) \qquad [8]$$

and β is the Lagrange multiplier to be determined from Eq.[6].

Returning to our problem [Prob.1] about the structure of the swarm, we see that such problem can be mapped into the example just described, so that the probability distribution is immediately found to be of the Gibbs type, Eq. [7], and the Lagrangian multiplier can easily be determined from the average temperature. Our problem is in fact mathematically equivalent to the 'Brandeis Dice Problem' [8] except that die has n faces. The solution is easily obtained from Eqs. [6,7,8] . Eq.[6] is equivalent to

$$-\frac{\partial}{\partial\beta} \log Z = t \qquad [6a]$$

where t is the adimensional average temperature (i.e., the temperature in units u)

$$t = \langle T\rangle /\, u \qquad [9]$$

From Eq. [6a] we obtain

$$q^{n+1}(t-n) + q^{n}(n+1-t) - qt + t - 1 = 0 \qquad [6b]$$

where

$$q = \exp(-\beta) \qquad [10]$$

and thus

$$p_i = q^i \,/\, \sum_{i=1}^{n} q^i \qquad [11]$$

5. Numerical results

In Table 1 we give the values of $\{p_i\}$ computed from Eq.[7] after solving numerically Eq.[6b], for the case of n= 10 (i = 1, 2,...10) and for eight values of t (t=2,3,4,5,6,7,8,9), u=10°. These eight values provide a good representation of the distribution as a function of t. At larger and smaller values of t (i.e., $t \approx 1$ and $t \approx 10$) the distribution is extremely peaked around these values as expected, and thus not very interesting for designing the structure of the swarm. Also not very informative for the structure of the swarm is the value of t = 5.5 which, as expected, corresponds to a uniform probability distribution (i.e., p_i = 0.1 for any i) . On the other hand it is interesting to see how sensitive the optimal structure of the swarm should be to deviation from the average (i.e., deviations from t= 5.5).

To see this, and generally for engineering the structure of the swarm, it is convenient to transform the data of Table 1 into actual sensors numbers. We have done this in two ways. First, in Table 2a, we have normalized the probabilities so that for each value of t the minimum probability is, in first approximation, 1 (i.e., only one sensor is used for this particular value of the temperature). In Table 2b and 2c, we have normalized the probabilities so that the total number of sensors is respectively 50 and 300 (two plausible lower and upper limits for engineering a swarms of robots). The results of Table 2c are also shown in Figure 1.

Using the normalization as in Table 2a, we find that for 5.1 < t < 5.9 the structure of the swarm remains uniform (one sensor per temperature interval). Beyond these values the distribution becomes slightly distorted (e.g., requiring two sensors for the three lowest temperature intervals at t = 5.0). We see from Table 2a that as the average temperature moves towards the limits of the range the swarm has to become more and more skewed towards sensing values of the temperature near the average. For example, at t=2 only one sensor is devoted to the highest temperature interval, whereas the lowest temperature interval has 489 sensors engaged in such measurement. Tables 1 and 2 also show that, as expected, the distributions are symmetric about the average t = 5.5.

-table 1-

	10	20	30	40	50	60	70	80	90	100
20	{0.5,	0.25,	0.13,	0.063,	0.032,	0.016,	0.008,	0.004,	0.002,	0.001},
30	{0.31,	0.22,	0.15,	0.1,	0.073,	0.051,	0.035,	0.024,	0.017,	0.012},
40	{0.21,	0.17,	0.14,	0.12,	0.095,	0.078,	0.065,	0.053,	0.044,	0.036},
50	{0.13,	0.12,	0.11,	0.11,	0.1,	0.096,	0.09,	0.085,	0.08,	0.075},
60	{0.075,	0.08,	0.085,	0.09,	0.096,	0.1,	0.11,	0.11,	0.12,	0.13 },
70	{0.036,	0.044,	0.053,	0.065,	0.078,	0.095,	0.12,	0.14,	0.17,	0.21 },
80	{0.012,	0.017,	0.024,	0.035,	0.051,	0.073,	0.1,	0.15,	0.22,	0.31 },
90	{0.001,	0.002,	0.004,	0.008,	0.016,	0.032,	0.063,	0.13,	0.25,	0.5 }

Table 1

Probability distributions (to 2 significant digits) for average temperatures 20 to 90 degrees. In each row, the probabilities of occurrence of temperatures from 10 to 100 degrees are given.

-table 2a -

	10	20	30	40	50	60	70	80	90	100
20	489	246	124	62	31	16	8	4	2	1
30	27	19	13	9	6	4	3	2	1	1
40	6	5	4	3	3	2	2	1	1	1
50	2	2	2	1	1	1	1	1	1	1
60	1	1	1	1	1	1	1	2	2	2
70	1	1	1	2	2	3	3	4	5	6
80	1	1	2	3	4	6	9	13	19	27
90	1	2	4	8	16	31	62	124	246	489

-table 2b -

	10	20	30	40	50	60	70	80	90	100
20	25	13	6	3	2	1	0	0	0	0
30	16	11	8	5	4	3	2	1	1	1
40	10	8	7	6	5	4	3	3	2	2
50	6	6	6	5	5	5	4	4	4	4
60	4	4	4	4	5	5	5	6	6	6
70	2	2	3	3	4	5	6	7	8	10
80	1	1	1	2	3	4	5	8	11	16
90	0	0	0	0	1	2	3	6	13	25

-table 2c -

	10	20	30	40	50	60	70	80	90	100
20	149	75	38	19	10	5	2	1	1	0
30	94	65	45	31	22	15	11	7	5	4
40	62	51	42	35	28	23	19	16	13	11
50	39	37	34	32	30	29	27	25	24	22
60	22	24	25	27	29	30	32	34	37	39
70	11	13	16	19	23	28	35	42	51	62
80	4	5	7	11	15	22	31	45	65	94
90	0	1	1	2	5	10	19	38	75	149

Table 2

For a swarm divided in 10 groups dedicated to detecting temperatures in ten different intervals, from 10 (±5) to 100 (±5) degrees, the rows give the number of sensors dedicated to sensing each interval when the external temperatures are 10°, 20°,...100°. In (a) the swarm is such that the minimum number of sensors for each interval is one. In (b) the swarm has 50 sensors, and in (c) the swarm is composed of 300 units.

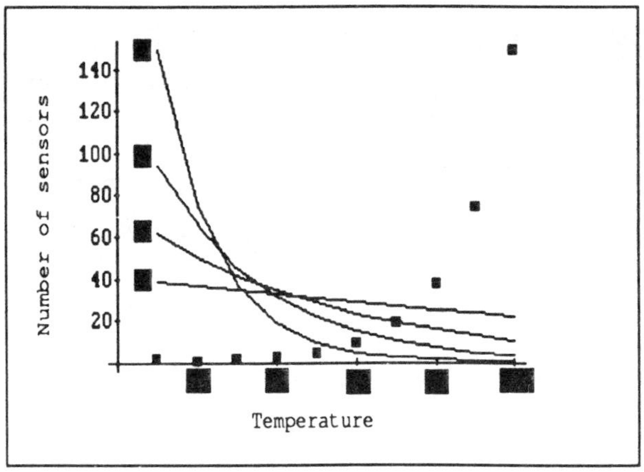

Figure 1.

For a swarm of 300 sensors, divided in ten groups dedicated to detecting temperatures in ten different intervals, from 10 (±5) to 100 (±5) degrees, the points give the number of sensors dedicated to sensing each interval when the external temperature is 90°. The solid curves (which are interpolations from ten points) have the same meaning except that they refer to average temperatures of 20, 30, 40, and 50 degrees (in order of decreasing slope). For average external temperature of 55° the curve would be a constant (each interval has exactly 30 sensors). Curves for temperatures above 55° are symmetric with curves below 55°, as shown by the curve for 10° and the (dotted) curve for 90°.

Although the Tables 1,2 give results for a 'decimal' measurement of a physical quantities, it is possible to get a general feeling for designing the structure of a swarm for a specific task. For other values of n (≠10) Eqs. [6b,10,11] provide the numerical solutions to the structure of the swarm.

In solving the problem for different values of n, it may be interesting to compare properties of the distributions, such as sensitivity to deviations from the average, as a function of n. These considerations may be relevant for the design of the swarm as we will discuss below.

6. Conclusions

As stated in the introduction, the aim of this study has been finding some guidelines to the design of a swarm to exhibit some components of intelligence, such as perception (sensing and measuring) capabilities or understanding (recognition) capabilities. We have seen that starting from units which do not exhibit such properties, it is possible to form swarms of these units that in fact do have these properties, i.e., can measure and recognize, simply by specializing each unit to detecting one narrow range of values of the feature observed. The specialization of detecting functions, however, cannot generally be uniform if the swarm has to function most efficiently. In other words, the number of units specializing in detecting a certain value should be a specific fraction of the total number of units; this fraction varying from value to value, and depending on what we know of the feature to be observed. In the previous sections we have shown how the structure should be calculated and we have given numerical examples of swarm structures, in particular for a decimal scale sensing swarm.

The sensing structure is calculated using the maximum entropy principle which maximizes the entropy of the probability distribution, therefore selecting the most probable (and thus optimal) distribution in the absence of any prior information. We have pointed out that this principle, being of great generality, is a useful tool for these type of swarm intelligence problems (not just the present one) where the difficulty arises from incomplete information rather than randomness.

The usefulness of determining the optimal structure of a sensing swarm has been illustrated with examples such as the task of destroying enemies whose activity is a function of some physical variable detectable by the swarm units. An optimal structure for the swarm translates to the maximum survival probability. This problem (survivability) is more clearly studied by looking at the evolution of the swarm.

Consider the case when the feature to be detected changes its value and our (incomplete) knowledge of such change varies accordingly. When we envision our knowledge of the feature to be observed (i.e., its average value) as varying in time, we also envision that the swarm should try to change its structure to respond to this variation with maximum survivability. For example, a swarm designed to sense temperatures between 10° and 100° should have (for maximum survivability) a different structure depending on whether the average temperature is e.g., 30° or 40° C. In fact, from Table 2c we see that, in a swarm of 300 sensing units, if we consider an enemy active at ≈20°C, 51 units are dedicated to detecting that enemy when the temperature is at 40°; whereas, when the temperature decreases to 30°C, the number of sensing units dedicated to detecting that type of enemy rises to 65. This is a considerable variation, and it is easy to convince ourselves how an error in restructuring optimally for the new situation might result in diminished chances of survival.

Knowing the optimal structure is indeed a necessary step to survival. But, it is not sufficient. Knowing the best structure of the sensing swarm allows us to predict how the swarm should change to respond optimally to external variations, but how this change should actually take place raises many questions. For example, since the swarm is not centrally controlled, who instructs the swarm to reconfigure according to the optimal structure?

These questions are considered in ref. [9]

References

[1] See e.g., G. Beni and J. Wang, "Theoretical Problems for the Realization of Distributed Robotic Systems", Proceed. 1991 IEEE Intern. Conf. on Robotics and Automation, Sacramento, Ca, April 1991, pp. 1914-1920.

[2] See e.g. S. Goss and J. L. Deneubourg, "Autocatalysis as a source of Synchronized Rhythmical Activity in Social Insects", Insectes Sociaux, Paris, 1988, v.35, pp. 310-315.

[3] G. Beni and J. Wang, "Swarm Intelligence in Cellular Robotic Systems", Proceed. NATO Advanced Workshop on Robots and Biological Systems, Il Ciocco, Tuscany, Italy (June 26-30, 1989); and Proceed. of the 7th Annual Meeting of the Robotics Society of Japan, Shibaura, Japan (Nov. 2-4, 1989) pp. 425-428.

[4] E. T. Jaynes, "Information Theory and Statistical Mechanics", in *Papers on Probability, Statistics, and Statistical Physics* (ed. R. D. Rosenkrantz) Kluwer Academic Publishers, Dordrecht, The Netherlands, 1989.

[5] W. T. Grandy, Jr., "Incomplete Information and Generalized Inverse Problems", in Maximum-Entropy and Bayesian Methods in Inverse Problems, (C. Ray Smith and W. T. Grandy, Jr. ,Eds.) Kluwer Academic Publishing, Dordrecht, The Netherlands, 1985.

[6] E. T. Jaynes, IEEE Trans. on Syst. Sci, Cybern. SSC-4, 227

[7] C. E. Shannon, Bell Syst. Tech. J. , v. 27, 379, 623.

[8] See e.g., The Maximum Entropy Formalism (R. D. Levine and M. Tribus, Eds.), MIT Press, Cambridge, Ma, 1979.).

[9] S. Hackwood and G. Beni "Self-Organization of Sensors for Swarm Intelligence", (to appear).

A BEHAVIORAL SIMULATION MODEL FOR THE STUDY OF EMERGENT SOCIAL STRUCTURES

Alexis DROGOUL, Jacques FERBER
LAFORIA - Université Pierre et Marie Curie - BP 169 - 4, Place Jussieu 75252 Paris Cedex 05, France.
drogoul@laforia.ibp.fr, ferber@laforia.ibp.fr

Bruno CORBARA[1,2], Dominique FRESNEAU[1]
(1) Laboratoire d'Ethologie et Sociobiologie - Université Paris XIII - Av. J.B.Clément, 93430 Villetaneuse, France.
(2) Laboratory of Applied Entomology and Nematology - Faculty of Agriculture
Nagoya University - Chikusa, Nagoya 464-01, Japan.

ABSTRACT

In this paper is reported a research on a system aiming to simulate and model the life of artificial creature populations in order to study the emergence of social structures whithin these populations. The features of this system, called EthoModeling Framework (EMF), are fully described. We show how to create an environment and how the agents communicate through it. We describe the structure of the agents and their capacitites in terms of behavior and learning. The notions of task, primitive and behavior reinforcement are presented and discussed with respect to other behavior-based approaches. Then, we introduce the MANTA project, implemented under EMF, whose purpose is to study the emergence of a division of labor inside a modeled anthill. A first example is presented as a case study on the generation of a division of tasks within a population of deliberately simplified ants. A second example allows us to show that an emergent social structure is able to improve the efficiency of an *emergent functionality* already studied in other works, e.g. collective sorting

INTRODUCTION

Self-organizing systems, "*systems in which orderly patterns arise without centralized control*" (Resnick 91), are arousing a growing interest in many sciences and especially in the recently born field of computer science called Artificial Life. Although these systems could be described using several formalisms, we will focus, in this paper, on the design of self-organizing societies of autonomous agents and the study of emergent social structures within them.

As pointed out by (Brooks 90; Steels 91), obtaining emergent specific tasks from a population of agents requires to understand the link between the behavior of a single agent and the global observed behavior of the society. We assume that, in many self-organizing systems such as social insects societies, understanding the emergence of social structures within them will help in expressing this link.

On the other hand, we believe that the stability and the efficiency of an *emergent functionality* performed by a population will be improved by the appearance of a parallel *emergent social structure*. We discuss this point in our "collective sorting" example.

Clearly, this research is still on its early stages and we still miss a general theory (although it has been studied in sociology, economics or ethology). An important work is then to be done on empirical studies. That is why we have developed a computer-based system called EthoModeling Framework (EMF), which provides items and tools for simulating the 'life' of populations of agents.

The design of EMF has been realized by taking into account two concurrent needs: on one hand, we needed a system allowing the testing of various hypothesis on the design of the agents, including behavior selection, learning, reinforcement, communication and so on, in order to study the impact of these choices on the global behavior of a society. Thanks to its object-oriented implementation, EMF allows hetero-genous agents to cohabit inside one and the same simulation, even if their internal mechanisms are different. On the other hand, we needed (and still need) to borrow data from real living self-organized systems. So we primitively conceived EMF as a modeling system, simple enough to be used by non computer scientists, in order to implement what we call behavioral simulations of real entities (social insects, cells, etc...) and compare the modeled societies to the real ones. This allows us to know what the features required by the agents to make up an organized society are. Two concurrent models are being implemented under EMF. The first, MANTA, simulates the life of a colony of ants with the aim of studying its division of labor. It is managed in collaboration with the University of Paris XIII's Ethology Laboratory. The purpose of the second is to simulate the blood cell differentiations inside the spinal cord and the behaviors of cells in the blood. It is managed by D. Tabourdeau, from the Paris VI's Laboratory of Artificial Intelligence (LAFORIA), and M. Bessis, from the Cellular Ecology Center.

The modeling part of EMF will not really be described in this paper, except in the first example which presents the MANTA project. We will rather focus on our implementation choices and on the results obtained when studying the "collective-sorting" example. This paper is then organized as follows. A presentation of EMF is provided in the next section. The architecture of the agents and their interactions with their environment are described, as well as the mechanisms of behavior selection and behavior reinforcement. With this background, we introduce the MANTA (Model of an ANThill Activity) project. A brief description of the modeled ants is given, followed by that of the agents involved in the modeling. Some examples of the model are then provided and their first results are reported. Finally, the perspectives in which we are going to work to make this model more realistic and to extend these results to other issues are detailed in the conclusion.

THE EMF MODEL

The implementation of EMF has been realized using Actalk (Briot 88), a language of actors under Smalltalk-80. Actors are well suited for the design of dynamic models, because they implement the inherent parallelism of such simulations (Agha 86).

EMF provides the programmer with a domain-independent kernel that rules the default internal functioning of the agents and the interactions between them and their environment. It is designed around two primary types of objects. On one hand, the agents, defined as *instances* of classes that inherit from the kernel-class *EthoAgent*. Each class represents a particular species of agents (with its own features), each instance an individual in this species. So it is possible to define new species of agents by creating new classes, define sub-species by inheritance and modification of the default behavior of their individuals and define an individual differentiation among the agents of a class by allowing a specific instanciation. On the other hand, the *places*, described in the next section.

Environment

The environment is defined as a large set of entities called *places*. The *places* are squares of the same size which know at every time their absolute position in the environment, the four places belonging to their neighborhood and the agents lying on them.

Places are divided into two categories: free *places* and *obstacles*. The main difference between them is that *obstacles* cannot accept agents and do not propagate *stimuli*. But it is possible to define particular *places* that accept a limited number of agents, *places* already provided with some *stimuli* or some agents. As for the agents, new *places* are simply defined by inheritance from existing ones.

Communication through the environment

Basic agents do not know each other and do not own any representation of other agents. They communicate by propagating their signature(s) in the environment.

We state that each agent owns *personal stimuli*, a set of "pheromone-like" signals identifying it. When it changes its state in the environment, the *place* on which it lies collects its *personal stimuli* and propagates them to the adjacent places. A stimulus is a doublet <*name,strength*> where *name* is the identifier of the stimulus and *strength* the value which will be propagated by the place.

The diffusion of the stimuli depends on the *places*. Each *place* defines a *propagation function* called $f_p(v)$ where v is the strength of the stimulus to be propagated. When asked to propagate a stimulus s, a *place* calculates $v'=f_p(strength(s))$, stores v' in its *stimuli* and asks its neighbors to propagate a new stimulus s' with the same name as s and v' as strength.

The *propagation function* of default *free places* is $f_p(v) = v - 1$. For *obstacles* , $f_p(v) = 0$ (they do not propagate stimuli). While this propagation is performed locally, it is possible to define *places* that propagate *stimuli* in a different way. Some can add noise ($f_p(v) = \mu(v - 1)$, $0 < \mu \leq 1$), some can slow them down ($f_p(v) = v - k$, $k > 1$), some can amplify them ($f_p(v) = v + k$, $k \geq 1$).

From a global point of view, this propagation results in a gradient field emanating from the position of the emitter (Steels 89) and using it as a way of communication between the agents presents five main advantages:

• Because gradient fields depend on the structure of the environment, they induce its implicit topology (Drogoul & al. 90a). If an agent follows a gradient, it automatically bypasses obstacles that do not transmit *stimuli* (if we assume that they also prevent the agent from moving on them).

• It provides the agents with a complete digest of what could interest them in their environment. In that way, they just need a simple domain-independent sensor system able to collect a local list of *stimuli*.

• Although the information is locally collected and reduced to a set of labeled values, they detain enough sense to be correctly interpreted. In fact, sensing a *stimulus* provides an agent with the type of agent that has propagated it, whether it is a matter of urgency or not and the direction from which it comes (by looking at adjacent places).

• It allows an agent to be reactive and opportunist. For instance, take the case of an *ant* following a gradient named *#food*, propagated by a *fruit*. If the *fruit* disappears, the *ant* will automatically interrupt its behavior because the stimulus *#food* will have vanished. On the other hand, if another *fruit* propagates a stimulus *#food* while the *ant* is following the first one, and if this stimulus is stronger, the *ant* will spontaneously change its direction to head to the latter.

• Finally, it does not prevent agents from choosing other forms of communication. As a matter of fact, it is well stated that many animals communicate *via* the propagation of chemical signals (Deneubourg & Goss 89), although they can do this more easily using intentional ways (for instance, tactile cues).

Agents Structure

The context in which we place the structure of the agents is that of the behavior-based artificial creatures (Maes 91). An agent is seen as consisting of a set of behaviors that we call *tasks* among which one can be active at a time. The selection and the suspension of a task are entirely *stimuli-oriented.* As in (Tyrrell & Mayhew 91; Schnepf 91) the term *task* refers to a set of behavioral sequences as opposed to the low-level actions (moving, and so on) that we call *primitives*. Moreover, some of these low-level actions are of no earthly use to us (for instance, obstacles avoidance) because of the topology of the environment induced by our *stimuli-oriented* communication. The agents are also basically provided with a mechanism of behavior reinforcement .

The knowledge of an agent is reduced to its *personal environment,* a set of entities among which it can collect stimuli. An agent does not need to know more about its world because its behavior is seen as a stereotyped response to a *stimulus*. The basic *personal environment* of an agent is constituted by its *place* (i.e. the environmental entity on which it lies). Other *places* can be of course added to increase the perception of the agent.

Behavior of an Agent

The behaviors of the agents are clearly separated into two categories:

• The *primitives*, low-level behaviors mainly related to physiological possibilities. We assume that they cannot be decomposed into behaviors of lower level. Agents of the same species share the same *primitives*. The *primitives* are not related to any *stimulus* and then cannot be directly used by the agent. They have to be encapsulated in *tasks*.

• The *tasks*, high-level behaviors that coordinate the call of some *primitives* in response to a *stimulus*. Agents of the same species do not necessarily own the same *tasks*. From an ethological point of view, *tasks* are close to *fixed-action patterns* (although they can be *reflexes* or *taxes* (Beer & al. 90)).

Tasks are instances of the class *AgentTask* and own the following features:

• A *name*: identifies both the task itself and the name of the *stimulus* that will trigger it.

• A *weight*: specifies the relative importance of the task inside the agent. This number can be modified by the *reinforcement process*. It is used in the *task selection process* in combination with the *strength* of the triggering *stimulus* for obtaining the *activation level* of the task.

• A *threshold*: specifies whether the task can be selected or not, given the fact that the *activation level* must surpass it for the task to be selected. It is modified by both the *reinforcement process* and the *task selection process*.

• An *activation/deactivation method*: contains the name of the method (defined in the class of the agent) to be called when the task becomes active/inactive. This method will typically be a sequence of *primitives*.

• An *activity level*: computed by the agent when the task becomes active. This number indicates the current "strength" of the task and is decremented by the agent each time it performs a *primitive*.

Activation, deactivation of a task

An agent knows the *current task* in which it is involved. When this task invocates one of its *primitives*, the agent performs the *task selection process*, in order to determine if a task is not more appropriated to its environment than the current one. This process is made up of three steps:

(1) Sensing: the agent collects the *stimuli* in its *personal environment* and eliminates those that do not match with a task name.

(2) Selection: the agent computes the *activation level* of each task by multiplying the *strength* of the stimulus with the *weight* of the related task. Tasks whose *activation level* surpasses their *threshold* and the *activity level* of the *current task* are selected to be activable tasks.

(3) Activation: If some tasks can be activated, the agent chooses the one whose *activation level* is the greatest (when two tasks have the same value, one of them is chosen randomly). Then it deactivates the *current task* and activates the selected one. When no tasks have been selected, the *current task* simply goes on (its *activity level* is decremented by the agent). When a task becomes active, it is placed in the *current task* of the agent and its *activity level* is initialized to the value of its *activation level*. When a task is deactivated, the agent performs its *deactivation Method* and zeroes its *activity level*.

Agents hold a special task called *#nothing*, always viewed as activable, chosen when no task are selected and when the *activity level* of the *current task* becomes nil[1]. This task specifies the default behavior of the agent when its environment is not particularly attractive.

The consequences of this selection mechanism on the behavior of the agents are as follows:

• The delay between the sensing of a stimulus and the activation of the related task is very small. So it allows the agent to be extremely **reactive** to its environment changes. This point is very useful in dynamic environments.

• A task will only be activated if its related stimulus is strong enough to surpass the *activity level* of the *current task*. In that way, the agent will react to this stimulus when it presents some characters of urgency (with respect to the *current task*) and neglect it when it does not. This allows the agent to be **persevering** (i.e. it will perform an important task even if its environment is crowded with stimuli).

• The duration of a task is partially governed by the *strength* of its triggering stimulus. As a matter of fact, a strong *stimulus* induces a great *activity level* of the selected task. While this *activity level* is decremented at each call of a *primitive*, it represents the maximum duration of the task. The agent then exhibits a certain **adaptivity** in its response to a stimulus. Consider the situation where an agent faces some predator. This agent will flee as far as possible from it (until it does not sense the predator anymore) and then, for instance, bury itself. When the stimulus of the predator is strong this task will certainly be accomplished up to the end. But if the stimulus is weak, the duration of the task will be shorter and the agent will just flee (it will not need to bury itself if the predator is far away from it).

• When deselecting a task, the agent always performs its *deactivationMethod*. As tasks are assumed to be correctly written, this allows any task to be stopped in a proper way. For instance, if an agent A carries an agent B during a particular task and if A is attracted by a new stimulus, the *deactivationMethod* of the previous task would lead A to put B down. In that way, it allows the agent to be **coherent** when switching from one task to another.

Positive,negative retroactions

"Real" creatures, although they are often provided with preprogrammed behaviors, exhibit flexible mechanisms of behavior selection. They can take former experiences of interactions with their environment into account when choosing their future behavior. The activation of a behavior also integrates non-environmental conditions such as motivations. Our aim is not to reproduce the numerous types of plasticities (Beer & al. 90) that have been studied in animals, nor to explore how intricate interactions between motivations and *stimuli* lead to the selection of a behavior. We simply focus on a mechanism of *behavior reinforcement* and a partial *motivation-oriented selection.*

[1]The *activity level* is continually decremented and lowered to zero when the job of the *current task* ends.

Behavior reinforcement has been observed in many animal species and particularly well studied in social insects as a mechanism of social organization (Theraulaz & al. 90). In our perspective, it is simply defined by the sentence: "*The more an agent performs a task, the more it will be able to perform it again*". The *reinforcement process* takes place just after the *current task* has been deselected and increases its *weight* relatively to the duration of the task.
The *threshold* associated with each task is viewed as an indicator on the motivation to do this task. A low *threshold* allows any *stimulus* to trigger the task, when a high one inhibits its selection. As we do not use explicit motivations, we assume that the motivation to do a task decreases when this task is being performed and otherwise increases. Expressed in our agents, it results in incrementing the *threshold* of the *current task* when it is deselected and decrementing the *thresholds* of all other tasks each time a task is selected. The amounts both depend on the values defined in the task and on its duration[2].

Other Works

The structure of our agents happens to be close to that proposed in (Schnepf 91), although we did not know this work when beginning to code our framework. The principles of behavior selection differ from the approach of Maes (Maes 91; Maes 90) or Brooks (Brooks 90) in that our *tasks* are not linked together by predecessor/successor nor activator/inhibitor links. Like (Steels 89) we use a non-intentional environment-driven type of communication in which autocatalytic or amplification mechanisms such as those described in (Prigogine & Stengers 84; Deneubourg & al. 86) can be reproduced. The behavior reinforcement idea proceeds from the same principles than (Deneubourg & al. 87; Theraulaz & al. 90) but we do not use stochastic nor mathematical functions to encode it.

THE MANTA PROJECT

MANTA (Model of an ANThill Activity) is the first project implemented under EMF. Its aims are: (1) To model the behaviors of simple ants. (2) To show that this model is able to generate a division of labor close to those observed in ant nests. (3) To apply these results to systems which consider self-organization as a crucial point, like robotics, distributed artificial intelligence or distributed problem solving.
Ants colonies are a fascinating model for people interested in the concepts of emergence and self-organization. Consequently, a lot of studies regarding their social organization have been published in the fields of ethology, sociobiology or ecology. More recently, people involved in other research areas have begun to investigate the domain in order to obtain new models for understanding the emergence of "intelligent" behaviors: "*an Ant viewed as a behaving system is quite simple, the apparent complexity of its behavior in time is largely a reflexion of the complexity of the environment in which it finds itself (...)*" (Simon 69). In (Hofstadter 79) and other works, the activity of a nest is compared to the activity of a brain. (Prigogine & Stengers 84) explores autocatalytic mechanisms in ants in the field of dissipative structures. (Steels 89) and (Deneubourg & al. 91) use ant-like robots to study *emergent functionalities*. Ant-like agents are employed in the AntFarm simulation of (Collins & Jefferson 91) in order to study the evolution of their colonies. Many works also focus on the modeling of social insects societies: (Hogeweg & Hesper 83; Hogeweg & Hesper 85; Hogeweg & Hesper 91) use the MIRROR framework to model bumble bees societies evolution, (Theraulaz & al. 91) models the division of labor in *Polistes* wasp colonies, (Deneubourg & al. 87) propose a model of learning aiming to reproduce the *Neoponera Apicalis* ant foraging.
As said above, we want to study the emergence of a division of labor inside a modeled anthill. At this time, a basic model has been implemented in order to test the reliability of EMF. Its agents do not really behave in a realistic way and are not provided with all their behaviors. Furthermore, as we do not pay attention to the time, they do not grow old and, consequently, do not die...

Ectatomma Ruidum

The species modeled, *Ectatomma ruidum*, has a distribution extending from southern Mexico to northern Brazil. The colonies contain a small number of ants (less than 300). This species is monogynous (one queen) and a clear dimorphism distinguishes the queen from the workers.

---

[2]It must be noticed that the reinforcement and the *treshold* modification depend on the sign of the amounts. If the increment of a task happens to be negative, a phenomenon of dishabituation will appear against this task.

The social organization of this species has been studied in (Corbara & al. 86,89; Lachaud & Fresneau 87) from the foundation of a society to its maturity, through an individual analysis of the behavior of each member of a society, the establishment of an inventory of behavioral acts (ethogram), combined into behavioral categories and the determination of "functional groups" by aggregating the behavioral profiles of the ants.
From the point of view of our study, *Ectatomma ruidum* has two major properties:
• Like *Polistes* wasps (Theraulaz & al. 91), all the ants seem able to perform a wide range of tasks - see the readjustments of behaviors following a sociotomy in (Lachaud & Fresneau 87) - but show a *differential reactivity* to *stimuli* depending on their behavioral profile. We hypothesize that it is directly related to a notion close to *behavior reinforcement.*
• The stability of repartition into "functional groups" among numerous colonies allows the comparison between the social organization obtained in the model and that observed in the reality. This comparison is facilitated by the possibility of using the same tools[3] in both cases.

Environment

The environment reproduces a laboratory nest (Figure 1). It is made up of *obstacles* and *antPlaces* (which inherit from *free places*) which simulate amplification processes by defining a new *propagation function:* $f_p(v) = ((v - 1) * n)$, where n is the number of agents lying on the place that propagate the same *stimulus.*
MANTA also provides EMF with the notion of *environmental agents*. Such agents cannot move nor sense and always propagate their *personal stimuli*. Two of them have been defined: HumidityAgent and LightAgent (whose stimuli are respectiviely named *#humidity* and *#light*). These agents can be dynamically added, removed or modified during the simulation.

Ants

The ants involved in the model are instances of the class *EctatommaAnt* and its subclass *EctatommaQueen*. These classes define a new domain-dependent piece of knowledge for their instances called *#carriedAgent.*

[3]Marking individuals, recording their behaviors by "scan sampling" at regular intervals, determining "functional groups" using multivariate analysis techniques.

Figure 2 describes *EctatommaAnt* with its *tasks, primitives* and *methods*. An instance of this class can then respond to five different *stimuli* - #egg, #larva, #cocoon, #food, #ant. The *weights* and *thresholds* of the related *tasks* are parametrable as well as the amounts for incrementing or decrementing them. *EctatommaQueen* owns the same features except that the *weights* and *thresholds* of its *tasks* are different[4].The behavioral methods invocated by the *tasks* can manage eight different *primitives*. For instance, the method *doEgg,* called when an ant senses some eggs, is defined with *positiveTaxis, negativeTaxis, carryAgent* and *dropAgent*: The agent firstly follows the gradient path up to the source of the stimulus *egg* (*positiveTaxis*). After that, it tries to carry the agent that propagated it (*carryAgent*). The ant then looks for other eggs, in a place less humid than its *place* (*positiveTaxis* for *egg* and *negativeTaxis* for *humidity*). When it finds one, it drops the agent (*dropAgent*).

Eggs, Larvae, Cocoons

Three other classes of agents have been created: *EctatommaEgg, Larva* and*Cocoon*. They intend to model the brood of a nest. Each of them defines a *personal stimulus* -#egg, #larva, #cocoon. Their instances are provided with the method *doNothing* which increases the *strength* of their stimulus and calls *repropagateStimulus*.

First Results

The following example studies the evolution of behavior of some ants provided with three tasks (#egg, #larva, #food). These tasks are similar to that described in the previous section. The case study is composed of 30 identical ants (the initial weights and thresholds of their tasks are equal), 50 larvae, 50 eggs and 50 pieces of food disseminated in the nest. As our purpose was to study the emergence of a division of labor, we did not add a queen. The time spent on each task by each ant is cumulated throughout the simulation (Figure 3). The simulation ends when the eggs, larvae and pieces of food are totally sorted into three separate clusters.
Although this example does not intend to simulate a real nest, a clear division of labor appears within the nest, characterized by five functional groups:

[4]A queen is defined as more sensitive to the brood (eggs, larvae, cocoons) and less sensitive to the food and ants.

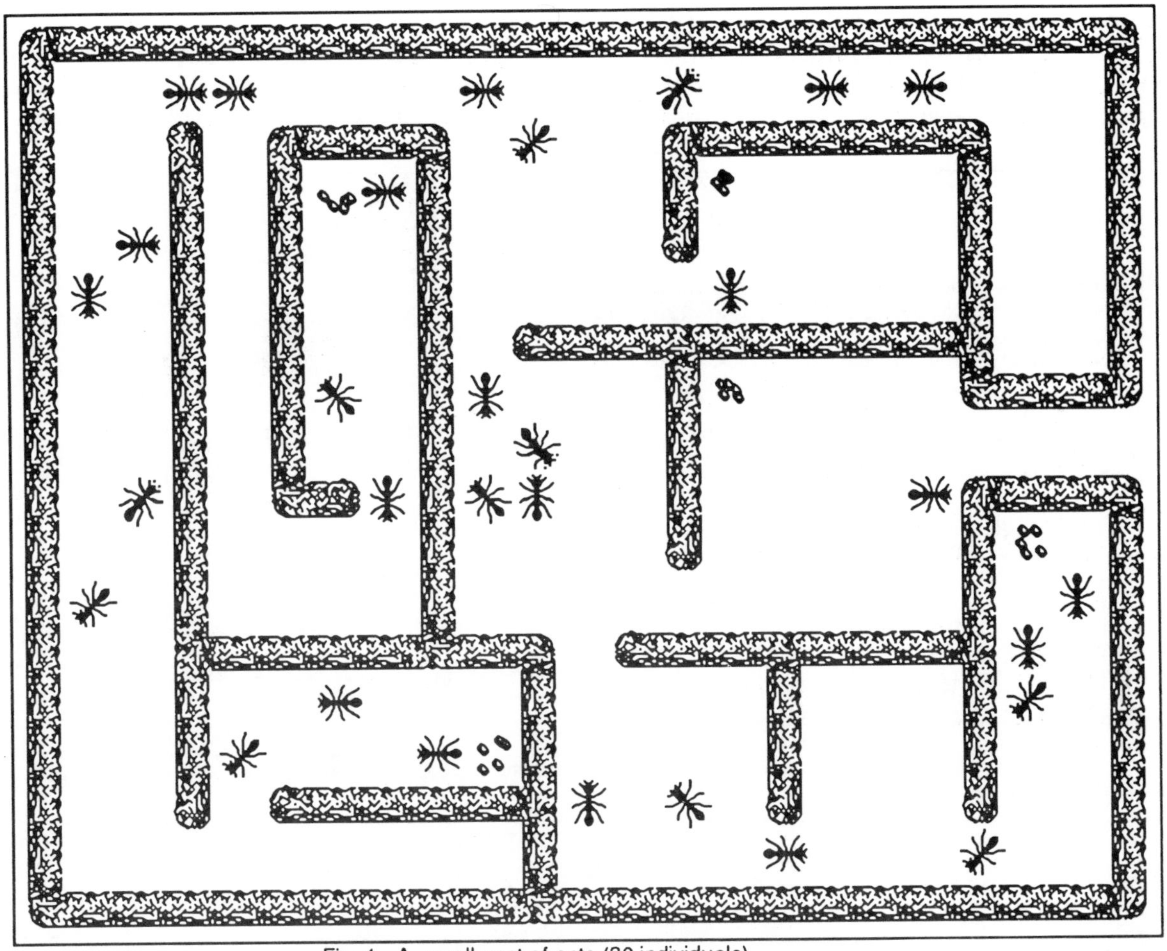

Fig. 1 - A small nest of ants (30 individuals)

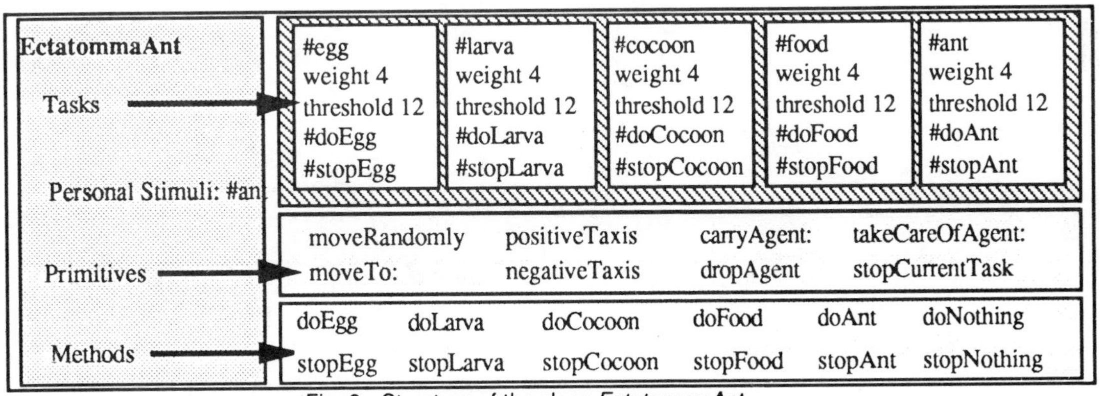

Fig. 2 - Structure of the class *EctatommaAnt*

Eggs nurses (Group 1, 8 ants): high level of care of eggs and low level of inactivity.

Unspecialized (Group 2, 8 ants): high level of inactivity, and mean level in other activities.

Feeders (Group 3, 7 ants): high level of feeding activities, important level of inactivity.

Larvae-Inactive (Group 4, 3 ants): high level of care of larvae, high level of inactivity and low level of care of the eggs.

Larvae nurses (Group 5, 4 ants): high level of care of larvae and low level in other activities.

Of course, this division of labor appears to be more simple than those observed in the reality.

The reason is that we provided the ants with a relatively small set of behavioral capacities. However, this structuration appears to be very stable throughout the many simulations we have made, which confirms in a way the validity of our approach. So we can reasonably hope to model anthills much closer to reality in the future. Moreover, all the agents that have achieved high performance in one task show a great level of specialization in it (i.e. the differences between the weights of the tasks are important). In that way, specialization can be seen as an autocatalytic process: they spend much time doing a task (and have more chance to perform it) because its weight is high, and this weight increases whilst they are performing it.

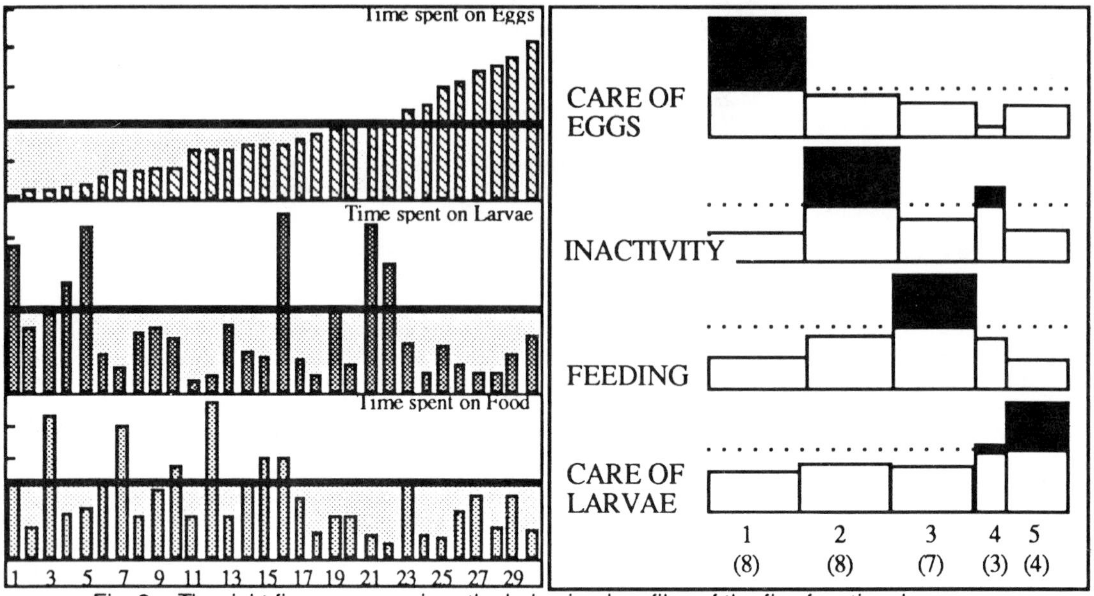

Fig. 3 - The right figure summarizes the behavioral profiles of the five functional groups.

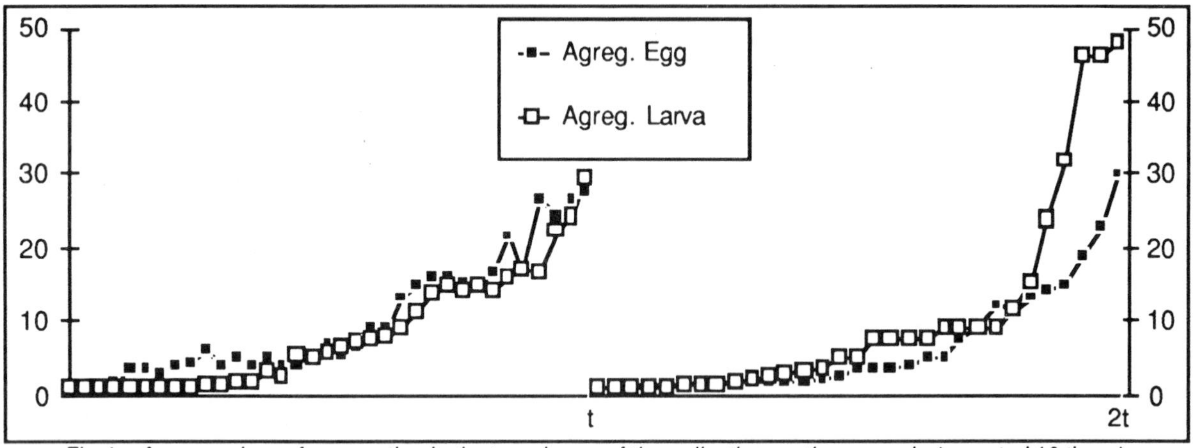

Fig.4 - Average sizes of aggregation in the two phases of the *collective sorting* example (repeated 10 times)

Now, the question is: what does a division of labor provide to a given population ? We do not discuss its importance in the "real" world, where it leads to a social structuration and increases the ability of a society to adapt itself to its environment (Corbara & al. 89). But, if we consider it from a functional point of view, this question would be: Does a division of labor improve the efficiency of a population with respect to the work that must be done ?

The purpose of the second example is partially to answer this question in a deliberately restricted case. 7 ants, 100 eggs and 100 larvae are randomly placed in a nest. At regular intervals, the average size of aggregation of the eggs and larvae is computed. The simulation is stopped at

an arbitrary time t. The brood is then wiped out and replaced by 100 other eggs and 100 other larvae. The same computations are performed and the simulation ends at time t+t (see Figure 4). It appears, when comparing the two graphs (obtained by making the average of ten simulations), that the division of labor appeared at time t improves the quality of the sorting. Firstly, the average size of the aggregations increases by almost 20%. Secondly, the productivity of the ants seems to grow in the last minutes of the second phase. Thirdly, the sorting happens to be more linear and less irregular. As an explanation, we can assume that the emergence of specialists increases the probability of an ant performing its task to the end. In actual fact, a specialized ant will be hardly disturbed by other stimuli when doing its task. In that way, it allows less specialized ants to perform their tasks in better conditions. These ants will then become more specialized, and so on...
However, drawing a general conclusion from this simple example would not be relevant and would certainly need to examine more accurately other case studies. *But, from the collective sorting point of view, the results presented here tend to show that an emergent functionality obtained from a population of agents can be improved by a parallel emergent social structure within this population.*

CONCLUSION AND PERSPECTIVES

In this paper we have described a system (EMF) aiming to simulate the life of artificial creature populations in artificial environments in order to: (1) Explore some case studies in the field of *self-organization.* (2) Model real eco-systems from an ethological point of view.
The concepts of environment and communication have been fully detailed as well as the basic structure of our artificial creatures, thanks to the notions of *primitives, tasks, task selection and behavior reinforcement*. We have demonstrated the properties of such a structure in terms of reactivity, plasticity and adaptativity.
This theoretical description has been followed by the presentation of a project (MANTA) implemented under EMF, whose purpose is to model the emergence of a division of labor inside a colony of ants. Some results have then been provided thanks to an example of *collective sorting*. The perspectives in which we are now going to work are as follows:
• Improvement of the MANTA model by: (1) adding new behaviors to the agents in order to get closer to reality; (2) taking time into account as an internal stimulus of each agent, which will have a direct effect on the weights and thresholds of its tasks; (3) making exhaustive simulations of realisitic situations; (4) extending the model to other species of ants, especially those employing other types of communication between the ants.
• Improvement of the kernel of EMF by testing new communication, task selection and learning strategies in order to choose the more efficient model in each domain. For instance, we are working at the present time on the comparisons between our agents and two new classes of agents which respectively define: (1) a mechanism of reinforcement learning inspired by (Lin 91), (2) a mechanism of behavior selection aiming to reproduce that of (Maes 91). One of our objectives is to apply a real bottom-up approach to the mechanism of behavior selection by considering the tasks themselves as agents competing for their satisfaction.

REFERENCES

G. Agha (1986) "Actors - A model of Concurrent Computation for Distributed Systems", MIT Press.
J.P. Briot (1988) "From Objects to Actors, study of a limited symbiosis in Smalltalk-80" , LITP Report 88-58RXF.
R. Brooks (1990) "Elephants Don't Play Chess" *in Journal of Robotics and Autonomous Systems*, Volume 6, p. 3-15.
R.J. Collins, D.R. Jefferson (1991) " Representation for Artificial Organisms" *in From Animals to Animats*, MIT Press, p. 382.
B. Corbara, D. Fresneau, J.P. Lachaud, Y. Leclerc, G. Goodall (1986) " An automated photographic technique for behavioural investigations of social insects" *in Behavioural Processes* 13, p. 237-249.
B. Corbara, J.P. Lachaud, D. Fresneau (1989) "Individual Variability, Social Structure and Division of Labour in the Ponerine Ant *Ectatomma Ruidum* Roger" *in Ethology* 82, p. 89-100.

J.L. Deneubourg, S. Aron, S. Goss, J.M. Pasteels, G. Duerinck (1986) "Random Behavior, Amplification Processes and Number of Participants: How they Contribute to the Foraging Properties of Ants" *in Physica* 22D, North-Holland, Amsterdam, p. 176-186.

J.L. Deneubourg, S. Goss, J. Pasteels, D.Fresneau, J.P. Lachaud (1987) "Self-organization mechanisms in ant societies (II): learning in foraging and division of labor" *in From Individual to Collective Behaviour in Social Insects*, Experientia Supplementum vol. 54, Birkhäuser Verlag, Basel, p. 177-196.

J.L. Deneubourg, S. Goss (1989) "Collective patterns and decision-making" *in Ethology Ecology & Evolution* 1: p. 295-311.

J.L.Deneubourg,S.Goss,N.Franks,A.Sendova-Franks, C.Detrain, L.Chretien (1991) "The dynamics of collective sorting Robot-like Ants and Ant-like Robots" *in From Animals to Animats*, MIT Press, p. 356.

A. Drogoul, J. Ferber, E.Jacopin (1991a) "Viewing Cognitive Modeling as Eco-Problem-Solving: the Pengi Experience", LAFORIA Report n°2/91

A.Drogoul, B.Corbara, D.Fresneau (1991b) "Applying EthoModeling to Social Organization in Ants" *in* Proceedings of the first European Conference on Social Insects.

D. Hofstadter (1979) "Gödel, Escher, Bach: an Eternal Golden Braid", Basic Books, Inc., Publishers, New York

P. Hogeweg, B. Hesper (1983) "The Ontogeny of the Interaction Structure in Bumble Bee Colonies: a MIRROR model" *in Behavioral Ecology & Sociobiology* 12, Springer-Verlag, p.271-283

P. Hogeweg, B. Hesper (1985) "SocioInformatic Processes: MIRROR Modeling Methodology" *in J. theor. Biol.* 113, Academic Press Inc., London, p. 311-330

P. Hogeweg, B. Hesper (1991) "Evolution as pattern processing: TODO as substrate for evolution" *in From Animals to Animats*, MIT Press, p. 492

J.P. Lachaud, D. Fresneau (1987) "Social Regulation in Ponerine Ants"*in From Individual to Collective Behaviour in Social Insects*, Experientia Supplementum vol. 54, Birkhäuser Verlag, Basel, p. 197-217.

Long-Ji Lin (1991) "Self-improving Reactive Agents: Case Studies of Reinforcement Learning Frameworks" *in From Animals to Animats*, MIT Press, p. 297.

P. Maes (1990) "Situated Agents can have Goals" *in Journal of Robotics and Autonomous Systems*, Vol. 6, p. 49-70.

P. Maes (1991) "A Bottom-Up Mechanism For Behavior Selection In An Artificial Creature" *in From Animals to Animats*, MIT Press, p. 239

M. Resnick (1991) "Beyond the centralized Mindset", AI& Education, Chicago.

U. Schnepf (1991) "Robot Ethology: a Proposal for the Research into Intelligent Systems" *in From Animals to Animats*, MIT Press, p. 465

H. Simon (1969) "The Sciences of the Artificial", MIT Press.

L. Steels (1989) "Cooperation between distributed agents Through self-organisation" *in* "Journal on robotics and autonomous systems", North Holland, Amsterdam.

L. Steels (1991) "Towards a Theory of Emergent Functionality" *in From Animals to Animats*, MIT Press, p. 451.

G. Theraulaz, S. Goss, J. Gervet, J.L. Deneubourg (1991) "Task differentiation in Polistes wasp colonies: a model for self-organizing groups of robots" *in From Animals to Animats*, MIT Press, p. 346.

T. Tyrrell and J.E.W. Mayhew (1991) "Computer Simulation of an Animal Environment" *in From Animals to Animats*, MIT Press, p. 263

Interactive Evolution of Dynamical Systems

Karl Sims

Thinking Machines Corporation
245 First Street, Cambridge, MA 02142

1 ABSTRACT

Simple local rules for dynamical and cellular automata systems can give rise to relatively complex and interesting structures. This paper describes how rules for these systems can be bred to search for new and unusual examples of emergent behavior from dynamical systems. Random mutations and matings of rule sets, followed by user selection based on observations of resulting behaviors, allow a variety of different dynamical systems to be interactively evolved. Two examples of breeding rules for two dimensional dynamical systems have been implemented and are presented. The first involves cellular automata networks with rules represented by lookup tables. The second uses sets of variable length lisp expressions to describe the initial states, and differential equations for grids of state variables. Results suggest that these are powerful methods for creating dynamical systems with emergent complexity that would be difficult to build by design.

2 INTRODUCTION

Cellular automata (CA) networks can be useful tools for modeling complex dynamical systems including physical and biological systems. Repeatedly applied local rules which determine the new state of each cell from its current state and the states of its neighbors can give rise to surprising levels of complexity, physical accuracy, and even "life-like" behavior [3, 10, 13, 20, 21, 22, 26, 27]. Simulations involving locally applied rules can be preferable to those with globally operating rules because they are highly parallel in nature, and probably more analogous to real chemical and biological systems of millions of interacting molecules or cells [1, 14, 15, 23].

One of the challenges involved in creating and studying artificial life-like systems, is designing local rules which successfully give rise to interesting global behaviors. It can be difficult to specify and predict the effects of local rules on the overall system, especially as they become more complex. This paper proposes methods that allow new forms of local rules to be generated that result in interesting and complex dynamical systems, but the local rules are not required to be preconceived, designed, or even understood by the human creator.

In biological systems, DNA could be considered as the specification of local rules which are acted out by proteins. They, in turn, define the biochemical dynamical systems which result in the development and functioning of organisms. As it would currently be very difficult to design DNA sequences for new types of viable organisms, it may also be difficult for humans to specify the local rules for complex life-like simulations. Both natural evolution and the simulated evolution presented here involve the variation and selection of rules for dynamical systems. Although the dynamical systems created here are relatively simple, they demonstrate the ease of achieving emergent complexity by combining the techniques of locally controlled dynamical systems with the evolutionary process.

2.1 Simulated Evolution

Genetic algorithms are search techniques in which populations of test points are evolved by random variation and selection [5, 7]. They are employed in a number of applications to find optima in very large search spaces. Reproduction of *genotypes* with random variation, and selection of *phenotypes* based on a non-random *fitness* function drives a population of individuals towards higher and higher levels of fitness. Sexual reproduction allows desirable traits to evolve independently and later be combined into the same genotype.

The work presented here uses random variation of genotypes that represent rules for dynamical systems to allow searching spaces of possible dynamical systems. For each generation, the rules of each genotype are applied locally to the cells of 2D networks. Selection is performed on the phenotypes which are the resulting global behaviors of these systems. In this way, the direction of the simulated evolution is determined by these global behaviors, but mutations are performed on the genotypes representing the encoded local rules.

Population sizes used for genetic algorithms are typically fairly large (100 to 1000 or more) to allow searching of many test points and avoiding local optima. For interactive efficiency and user interface practicality the examples presented here use a much smaller population size (4 - 16) and only one or two individuals are chosen to reproduce for each new generation.

2.2 Interactive Selection

In the work described here, the fitness of dynamical systems is determined interactively by a user at each step of the evolution process instead of automatically by a pre-defined fitness function. *Perceptual selection* is used because fitness functions that could determine how interesting or aesthetically pleasing a dynamical system is would be difficult to define, and many local optima may be of interest instead of just one global optimum. This allows the user to not only observe the intermediate results as the evolution progresses, but also to interactively navigate through the spaces of possible results.

In *The Blind Watchmaker*, Dawkins demonstrates the power of Darwinism with a simulated evolution of 2D branching structures called "biomorphs." Here, the user also interactively selects the shapes that survive and are reproduced to create each new generation [4].

2.3 Overview of the Paper

Two different methods for representing rules for 2D dynamical systems have been implemented. The first requires the value of each cell to be an integer of fixed length. A lookup table determines the next state of each cell from an index made from its current state and those of its neighbors. This allows all possible CA rules for a given number of bits per cell to be described by filling the lookup table with different values. In this case, the lookup table is the genotype which can be mutated and mated with other lookup tables to evolve CAs with various behaviors.

The second representation for genotypes of rules for dynamical systems contains lisp expressions that determine the initial state and the change of state of the system over time. Each cell can contain one or more "continuously" varying values (e.g. floating point numbers) instead of fixed-length integers. The initial state is determined by lisp expressions that return values for each cell location. Non-linear differential equations describe the behavior of the system, and are also represented by lisp expressions that calculate time derivatives for each cell as functions of the current state and neighboring states.

In the next section, the breeding of lookup tables for CA systems will be described. In section 4, breeding continuous dynamical systems with genotypes containing lisp expressions will be presented. Finally in sections 5 and 6, results are given and future work is suggested.

3 BREEDING CA LOOKUP TABLES

CA networks that contain a limited number of bits per cell can be represented and quickly simulated by using lookup tables to find the new state of each cell from an index of its current state and the state of its neighbors. In this work, CA lookup tables are interactively evolved by the following process:

1. A population of initial random lookup tables are generated by randomizing their bits. If zeros and ones are created with equal probability, chaotic behavior usually results, so zeros are created with a lower probability such that structured behavior is more likely (around 1/8 zeros is used).

2. For each lookup table, a 2D grid of cells is created and the contents are initialized to random values. The values are updated using the table for a number of iterations (30 - 200). Each iteration is displayed to the user in real-time as the simulation proceeds, by mapping the cell values into pixel intensities and displaying the grids of cells as images.

3. The user observes the animated behavior of the CA systems for each of the lookup tables, and selects one or more to survive.

4. The lookup tables corresponding to the selected systems are reproduced with mutations or combined with each other to create new lookup tables for the next generation.

This process of perceptual selection of CA behaviors, and reproduction with variation of the lookup tables is repeated (steps 2 - 4). Figures 1 - 3 show a variety of results that can occur after a number of generations. (Typically around 5 - 20 are required.)

3.1 Mutating and Mating CA Tables

For new variations of CA networks to occur, the lookup tables must be reproduced with some frequency of mutations, as stated in step 4 above. The method used here involves subjecting each bit in the table to probabilistic inversion. (An inversion frequency of around 0.01 is used because it causes frequent variation in results, but still provides some stability.) A non-local approximation of this method can require generation of fewer random numbers: the locations are chosen at random for a constant number of mutations.

Sexual combination of two parent lookup tables is performed by *crossing over* information between the parents to generate a new table. Values are copied from one of the parent tables, but with some frequency, the source table is switched to the other parent. This causes connected segments of the table to be more likely to stick together then sections at distant locations. (A frequency of .001 is used here such that only a few crossovers are likely in any one mating.) Again, an approximation to this method can save random number generation by choosing random locations for a constant number of crossovers.

3.2 Limitations of Representation

Although CA lookup tables can produce interesting behaviors, several limitations are noticeable: tables can become very large when the length of the state integers is more than a few bits; there is a limited number of states that each cell can have; and the space of possible tables is highly dimensional but still limited in its extent.

If the state of each cell contains N bits, and 3x3 neighboring states are used to determine each new state, the table will contain new states for each of 2^{9N} possibilities and is $N2^{9N}$ bits in length. This is acceptable for states of 1 bit where the table length is 512 bits, but for 2 bit states the table is already 524,288 bits long, which can prevent mutations and matings from being calculated quickly. Several modifications can help reduce the size of lookup tables:

1. The number of bits taken from the neighbors can be reduced to a subset of the total bits of their states.

2. The bits of neighbors can be combined with various associative operators and the results used in the table index instead of the neighbor bits themselves. (For example, and, or, xor, min, max, or $+$, might be used.) This limits the CAs to symmetrical behav-

ior, but this can actually be advantageous since asymmetrical rules commonly give undesirable directional shifting of the system.

3. Another useful method for shortening lookup table sizes involves shifting and wrapping the table on top of itself. Each bit in the table can be a part of more than one new state values. For example, if states consist of 4 bits, the lookup table can be shifted by 0,1,2, or 3 bits to provide 4 times the number of new states with the same table length. Tables could be read backwards and scrambled in various ways to provide even more shortening if necessary. The consequences of duplicating the effects of the lookup table bits have not been evaluated in detail, but it has been experimentally observed to be effective. Some viruses have developed a strategy similar to this – certain regions of RNA can be read twice, once shifted over by a base pair, to encode two different proteins [2].

These methods have allowed lookup tables for CA networks with 3, 4, or more bits per state to be mutated, mated, and simulated at interactive rates. [Figures 1 - 3].

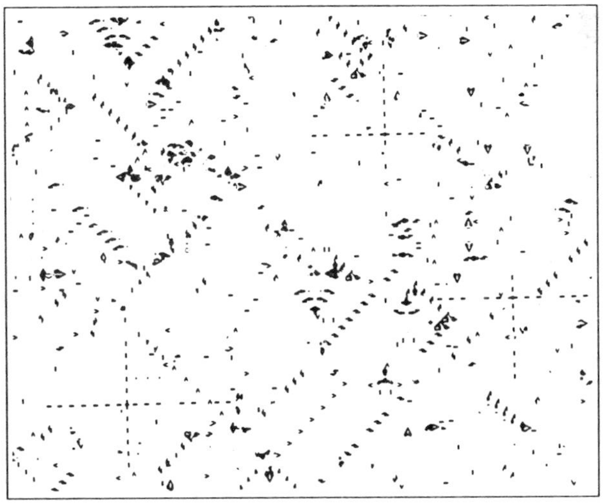

Figure 1: Evolved CA – Glider Zoo

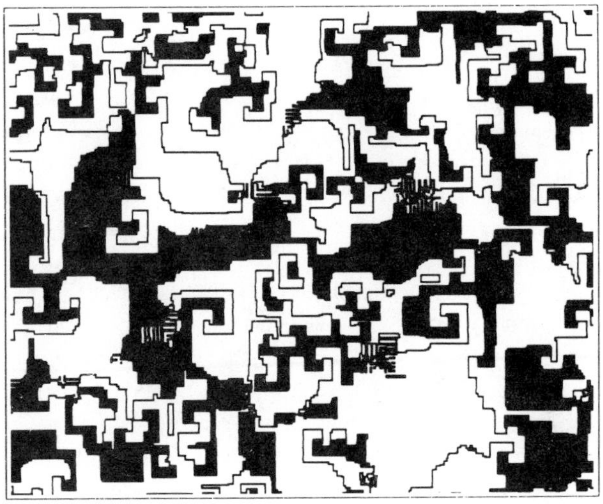

Figure 2: Evolved CA – Spiraling Regions

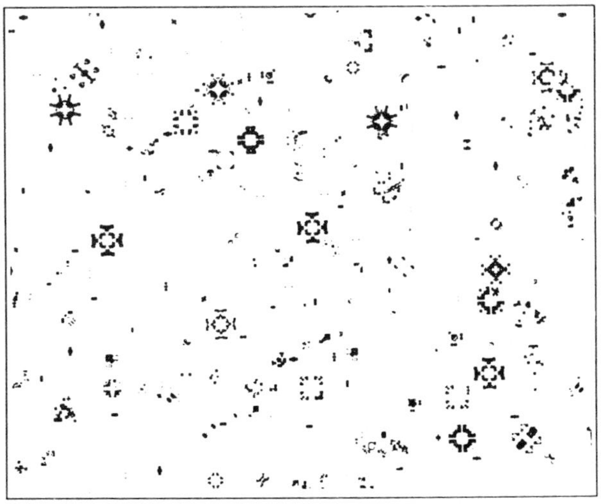

Figure 3: Evolved CA – Sparkles

A second limitation of using lookup tables to describe dynamical systems is that they only allow the states to have a fixed number of integral values. This tends to give the system a quantized look with regular shapes and blocks of pixels. Instead, it might be desirable to have cells contain values that can vary continuously.

A final limitation of evolving CA lookup tables, is that the extent of possible results is fixed. Although the dimensionality is very high, all genotypes are essentially equally complex and can not evolve towards higher levels of complexity. The parameters used to express the genotype are fixed; the number of bits in the state of each cell and the operations for combination of neighbors can not be modified or extended by mutations.

4 BREEDING CONTINUOUS DYNAMICAL SYSTEMS

In an attempt to surpass the limitations described above, a second representation for dynamical systems is presented. Arbitrary differential equations for continuously varying state variables are described by hierarchical lisp expressions which can be mutated, mated with each other, and evaluated to perform simulations.

4.1 Lisp Expressions as Genotypes

Traditionally, genotypes consist of fixed-length strings of digits or parameters, such as the ones described above. Fixed-length genotypes and fixed expression rules limit the phenotypes to that pre-defined space of possible results. Koza has used lisp expressions as genotypes such that the dimensionality of the search space itself can be extended to solve problems such as artificial ant navigation and game strategies [8, 9]. Discovery systems, such as AM and Eurisko, also utilize a form of mutating lisp programs [11]. Recently, artificial evolution of lisp expressions has been used to generate unusual pictures and textures for computer graphics [17].

In this application, lisp expressions are used as genotypes to determine the initial states and time derivatives for variables of continuous dynamical systems. For example, a system containing two quantities, A and B, at each grid location is described by four equations:

$$A_0 = F_{A0}(X, Y)$$
$$B_0 = F_{B0}(X, Y)$$
$$dA/dt = F_{dA}(A, B)$$
$$dB/dt = F_{dB}(A, B)$$

F_{A0} and F_{B0} are functions that determine the initial values for each element of A and B from their grid locations (X, Y). F_{dA} and F_{dB} are functions that determine the time derivatives for each element of A and B using the current state of the system. Arbitrary functions for F_{A0}, F_{B0}, F_{dA}, and F_{dB}, are specified by lisp expressions which can vary in size, structure, and behavior. A genotype of lisp expressions that would describe a simple reaction-diffusion-like system of two chemicals that diffuse and inhibit each other might be:

A_0 = (noise .8 .4)
B_0 = (noise .9 .5)
dA/dt = (– (laplacian A) B)
dB/dt = (– (laplacian B) A)

The list of primitive functions, or *function set*, that can be chosen to create these lisp expressions, contains operators including standard common lisp functions: +, –, *, /, *mod, round, min, max, abs, expt, log, sin, cos, atan, negate, sqrt, square, dissolve, if,* and *plusp* [18]. The function set for the initial state expressions also contains a *noise* procedure (as used in the example above) that generates solid noise from a frequency parameter and an initial random-seed value [12, 16]. The function sets also include operations that can access neighboring values of the elements of their arguments, perform convolutions with arbitrary masks, and find first and second order spatial derivatives: *x-grad, y-grad, grad-mag, grad-in-direction, grad-direction, laplacian, anisotropic-laplacian, curl, convolve-5-neighbors,* and *convolve-9-neighbors*. When these operations are used in various combinations, many different types of differential equations can be specified.

Simple random expressions are created for the initial state and time derivatives of each state variable. A random expression is generated by choosing from: a random constant value, an input variable (such as X, Y, A, or B), or a function from the function set with recursively generated random expressions for arguments. Interactive evolution is performed by first creating several genotypes with expressions generated in this way, and then displaying the corresponding simulations to the user. The state variables are mapped into colors for each iteration to visualize the animated behavior of the system in real-time. Then, the user selects one or more of these systems for mutation and mating to produce the next generation, and the process repeats. After a number of generations, genotypes with fairly complex expressions and interesting resulting behaviors can occur. As an alternative to starting with randomly generated expressions, the user can hand code an initial set of equations, such as a wave equation or a reaction-diffusion system, and begin the evolution from there. This allows many variations of input systems to be explored.

4.2 Mutating and Mating Lisp Expressions

A recursive mutation scheme is used to mutate genotypes containing lisp expressions. Each expression is traversed as a hierarchical structure and each node is in turn subject to possible mutations. Each type of mutation occurs at different frequencies depending on the type of node:

1. Any node can mutate into a completely new random expression.

2. If the node is a scalar value, it may be adjusted by the addition of some random amount.

3. If the node is a function, it can mutate into a different function. For example *(abs A)* might become *(cos A)*. If this mutation occurs, the arguments of the function are also adjusted if necessary to the correct number and types.

4. An expression can become the argument to a new random function. If necessary, other arguments are generated at random. For example, A might become *(* A .3)*.

5. Finally, an argument to a function can jump out and become the new value for that node. For example *(* A .3)* might become A. This is the inverse of the previous type of mutation.

Other types of mutations could certainly be implemented, but these are sufficient for a reasonable balance of slight modifications and potential for changes in complexity. The overall mutation frequency is scaled inversely in proportion to the length of the entire expression. This decreases the probability of mutation at each node when the parent expression is large so that some stability of the phenotypes is maintained. To keep evaluation of these expressions at real-time speeds, estimates of computation times are made, and slow expressions are automatically eliminated before being used.

Lisp expressions can be mated by *crossing over* sub-expressions between two parent expressions. A node in the expression tree of one parent is chosen at random and replaced by a node chosen at random from the other parent. This allows two sub-expressions that have evolved independently to be combined into a single genotype. Two genotypes are mated by mating each pair of expressions that specify each initial state and each time derivative.

4.3 Dynamic Simulation

For simplicity, simulations of continuous dynamical systems are performed using Euler's method of integration. The differential equations are approximated for a small discrete time interval Δt. For example,

$$\frac{dA}{dt} = F(A)$$

would be simulated by computing many discrete updates of the value of A:

$$A' = A + \Delta t F(A)$$

When Δt is smaller, the simulation is more accurate, but more computation is required. ($\Delta t = 0.1$ is often used.)

Systems can sometimes generate values that exceed the legal bounds of numerical representation. Values are regularly clamped to some legal bounds to avoid overflow errors. These particular discretizations of time and clamping parameters can affect the behaviors of some systems. In fact, systems sometimes evolve that exploit these specific procedures for interesting effects.

Higher order differential equations can also evolve. For example, a simple wave propagating system that indirectly specifies acceleration (d^2B/dt^2), instead of just velocity (dB/dt), might be described by:

$A_0 = .0$
$B_0 =$ (noise .1 .4)
$dA/dt =$ (laplacian B)
$dB/dt =$ A

The first derivatives are also included as possible arguments in the expressions to allow for further possibilities. Resulting behaviors might not be consistent if Δt is modified, but for a given time increment, this can help interesting physical-like systems to occur. For example, the previous system might instead be described with one state variable:

$A_0 =$ (noise .1 .4)
$dA/dt =$ (+ dA/dt ($*$ .1 (laplacian A)))

Similarly, expressions can evolve that counteract the incremental integration, and specify the next state directly from the current state.

The space of possible dynamical systems can be further enhanced by allowing complex numbers, instead of just real values, to be included in the state variables and expressions. The operations in the function set are adjusted to perform on complex quantities as well as reals, and complex constants and a grid coordinate value, $\#C(X\ Y)$, are included as possible arguments. (The form $\#C(r\ i)$ is used to denote a complex quantity with real part r and imaginary part i.) Expressions of real scalar values could theoretically evolve to perform the same complex operations, but this might not be likely to occur in a practical timeframe. Various spiral shapes and fractal structures have been found that use complex arithmetic [Figures 8 - 11].

5 RESULTS

These two techniques for interactive evolution of dynamical systems have been implemented on the Connection Machine(R) system CM-2, a data-parallel supercomputer [6, 19]. One virtual processor is assigned to each cell in the network so the entire grid can be processed simultaneously. Identical copies of lookup tables are distributed into every group of 32 processors so all processors can perform parallel table lookups using local memory references. Lisp expression mutations and crossovers are performed on a *front-end* computer, and the expressions are evaluated in parallel using the Connection Machine system and *Starlisp*. These implementations allow grid dimensions of up to 256x256 to be simulated at interactive rates, depending on the complexity of the genotype. Dimensions of 512x512 and larger can result in less efficient interactivity, but are still useful for viewing systems with high levels of detail.

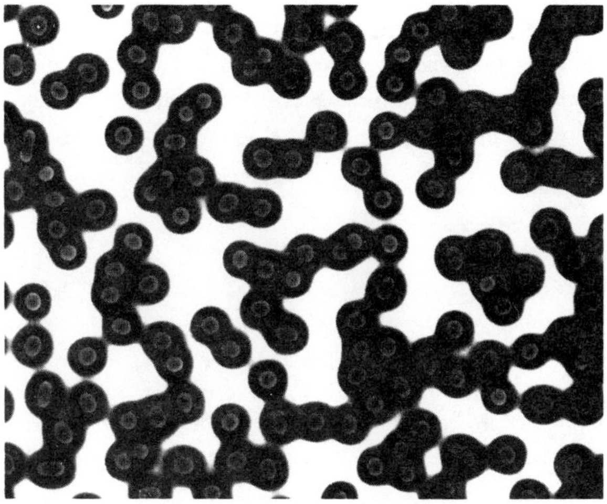

Figure 4: Cell Shapes

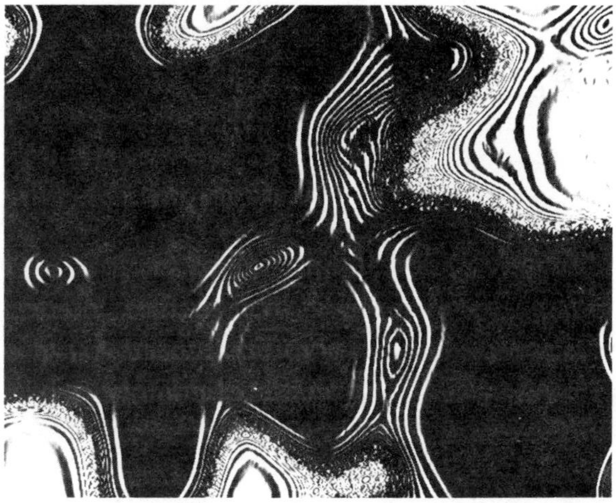

Figure 5: Wave Generators

Figure 6: Branching Patterns

Examples of some different types of CA behaviors are shown in figures 1 - 3. These were each produced by lookup tables that were evolved by the methods described in section 3.

Figures 4 - 13 show a variety of continuous dynamical systems that were evolved by the methods described in the previous section. For example, figure 4 was produced by the following system of equations:

A0 = (sin (noise -.14 -.77))
B0 = 1.99
dA/dt = (+ (+ (laplacian A 2.1)
(if-plusp (− A B) .4 .0)) (* -.38 A))
dB/dt = (+ (laplacian A 4.99) (* -.4 B))

This system proceeds from random noise towards a stable pattern of circular cell-like shapes. It is often not obvious why a set of equations produces the behavior that it does, even for relatively short expressions. Fortunately, a complete understanding of these equations is not required even by the creator. The expressions that specify the rules that produced figures 5 - 13 are given in the Appendix. Genotypes such as these can be interactively evolved in timescales such as 10 minutes – probably much faster than they could be designed.

6 FUTURE WORK

Many extensions to these techniques could be explored. Networks with connectivity other than 2D rectilinear grids might be represented and evolved. The number of elements and connections themselves could be subject to mutation and evolution. Dynamical systems similar to these but in three dimensions, could be simulated, visualized, and evolved, although the size of the volumes that could be processed in near real-time would have severe limits.

Images from other sources could be incorporated into the lisp expressions for initial states and differential equations of dynamical systems. This would allow arbitrary input images to determine the initial states or various dynamical properties of evolved systems, and might result in some unusual effects.

Fitness functions other than the interactive perceptual method could be used to direct the evolution of dynamical systems automatically. Algorithms which try to detect "interesting" behavior of moving images could be tested by observing the results of simulated evolutions which use those algorithms as fitness functions. Perhaps the information from many human selection decisions could be generalized and used to help define an automatic fitness function.

7 CONCLUSION

The work presented here attempts to combine the benefits of several techniques: locally specified rules for dynamical systems, evolution by random variation and non-random selection, and genotypic representations of variable complexity. It is likely that systems of evolving biological life have also utilized combinations of these techniques.

Interactive evolution is a potentially powerful method for creating and exploring complexity that does not require human understanding of the specific process involved. It could be considered a tool for helping a user with creative explorations, or it might be considered a system which attempts to "learn" about what is interesting from a human. In either case, it allows the user and computer to work together to construct results that neither could easily produce alone.

Interactive evolution of many types of dynamical systems should become more practical as computation becomes more powerful and available, and the techniques presented here will hopefully contribute to creating systems that give rise to emergent behaviors of higher and higher levels of complexity.

8 Acknowledgments

Thanks to Lew Tucker, Gary Oberbrunner, Matt Fitzgibbon, Jim Salem, and Peter Schröder for help and CM graphics software support. Thanks to Richard Dawkins for the interactive concept. Thanks to Pattie Maes for encouragement, thanks to Katy Smith for proofreading, and thanks to Bruce Boghosian for differential equation tips.

9 APPENDIX

Figure 5, Wave Generators:
A0 = 0.33
B0 = 0.27
C0 = (log (− 0.5 (grad-mag-squared (noise -0.2 -0.04))) (/ (noise 0.02 0.03) (noise -0.007 -1.4)))
dA/dt = C
dB/dt = (anisotropic-laplacian (sin A) A 0.9 0.08)
dC/dt = (neighbor-ave (atan dA/dt (laplacian B 1.8)))

Figure 6, Branching Structures:
A0 = Y
B0 = 1.0
C0 = (+ (negate (noise 0.12 1.9)) Y)
dA/dt = (neighbor-max (neighbor-max C))
dB/dt = (x-grad C)
dC/dt = (neighbor-ave (grad-direction B 0.25))

Figure 7, Crack Patterns:
A0 = (− (noise -0.064 1.17) -1.58)
B0 = -0.032
dA/dt = (neighbor-min A)
dB/dt = (laplacian A 4.99)

Figure 8, Globe:
A0 = #C(X Y)
dA/dt = (+ (/ dA/dt A) (+ (grad-direction (expt #C(1.6 0.25) 3.5) -0.42) (x-grad A)))

Figure 9, Fractal Spirals and Arms:
A0 = #C(X Y)
dA/dt = (+ (/ (+ (square A) 1.0) A) (+ -0.7 (expt (max (max A (laplacian (log A #C(-1.2 -0.05)) 0.11)) #C(0.21 -0.12)) 3.5)))

Figure 10, Spiral Wave:
A0 = #C(X Y)
dA/dt = (+ (/ (min A 1.0) A) (+ -0.7 (expt (max A #C(0.2 -0.12)) 3.5)))

Figure 11, Growing Fractal Buds:
A0 = #C(X Y)
dA/dt = (+ (/ (+ (square dA/dt) 1.05) A) (+ -0.7 (expt (max A #C(0.21 -0.12)) (max A #C(0.21 -0.12)))))

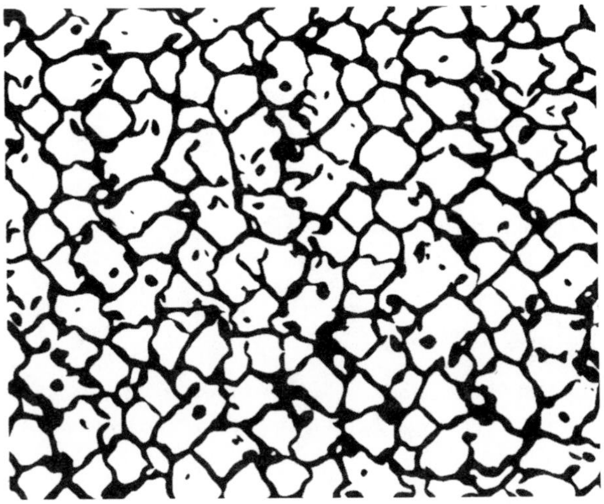

Figure 7

Figure 10

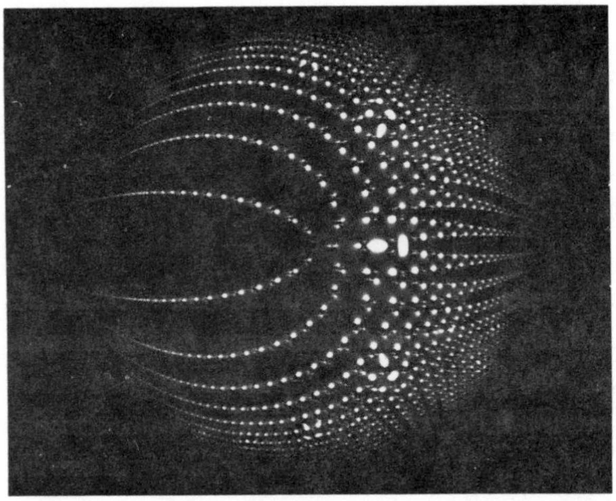

Figure 8

Figure 11

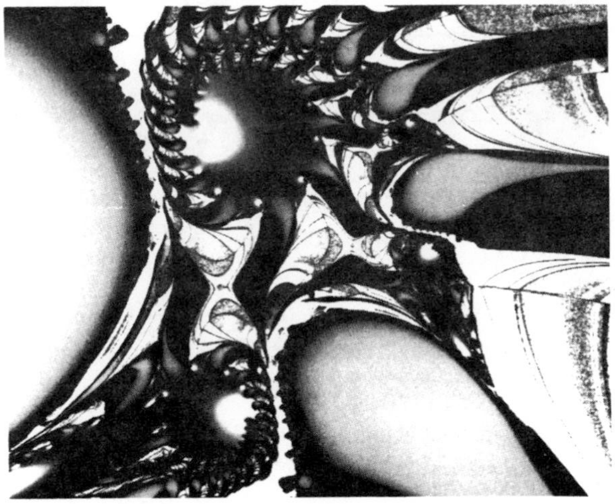

Figure 9

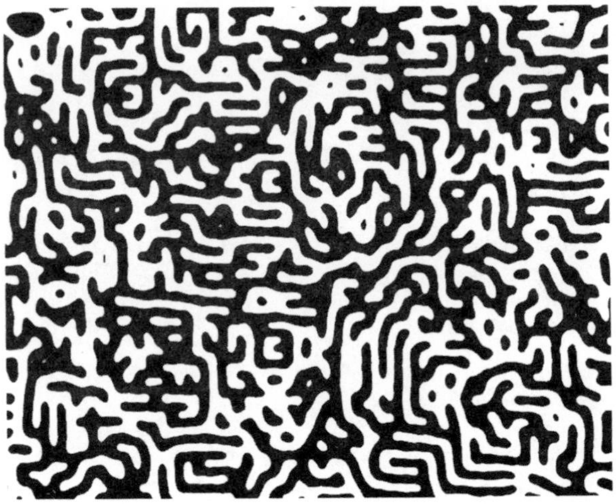

Figure 12

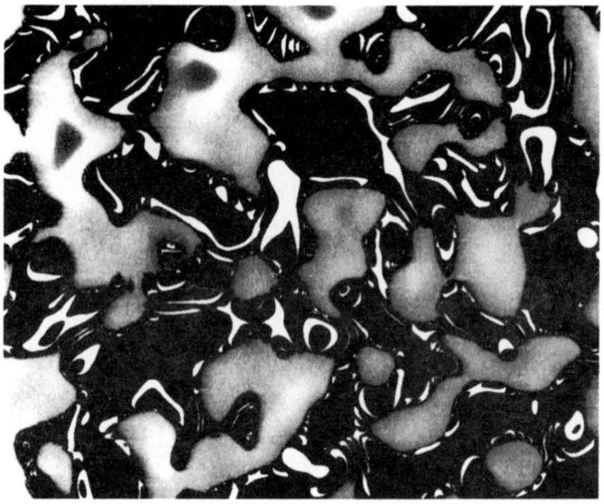

Figure 13

Figure 12, Reaction Diffusion Pattern:
```
A0 = (negate (noise -0.14 -0.77))
B0 = -0.086
dA/dt = (+ (+ (laplacian A 2.0) (convolve-5-neighbors-constant (- A B) 0.4 0.0 0.027
0.27 0.66)) (* -0.4 A))
dB/dt = (+ (laplacian A 4.99) (* -0.4 B))
```

Figure 13, Striped Blobs:
```
A0 = (complex-noise 0.06 1.3)
dA/dt = (+ (/ (+ (square dA/dt) A) A) (+ -0.7 (expt (max A #C(0.2 -0.12)) 2.8)))
```

References

[1] Babloyantz, A., *Molecules, Dynamics, and Life: An Introduction to the Self-Organization of matter*, Wiley Interscience, New York, 1986.

[2] Beremand, M. N., and Blumenthal, T., "Overlapping Genes in RNA Phage: A new Protein Implicated in Lysis," *Cell*, Vol.18, 1979, 257-266.

[3] Burks, A.W., *Essays on Cellular Automata*, University of Illinois Press, 1970.

[4] Dawkins, Richard, *The Blind Watchmaker*, Harlow Logman, 1986.

[5] Goldberg, D. E., *Genetic Algorithms in Search, Optimization, and Machine Learning*, 1989, Addison-Wesley Publishing Co.

[6] Hillis, W. D., "The Connection Machine," *Scientific American*, Vol.255, No.6, June 1987.

[7] Holland, J. H., *Adaptation in Natural and Artificial Systems*, University of Michigan Press, Ann Arbor, 1975.

[8] Koza, J. R. "Genetic Programming: A Paradigm for Genetically Breeding Populations of Computer Programs to Solve Problems," Stanford University Computer Science Department Technical Report STAN-CS-90-1314, June 1990.

[9] Koza, J. R. "Evolution and Co-Evolution of Computer Programs to Control Independently Acting Agents," *Conference on Simulation of Adaptive Behavior* (SAB-90) Paris, Sept.24-28, 1990.

[10] Langton, C., *Artificial Life*, Addison-Wesley, 1989.

[11] Lenat, D. B. and Brown,J.S. "Why AM and EURISKO appear to work," *Artificial intelligence*, Vol.23, 1984, 269-294.

[12] Lewis, J. P., "Algorithms for Solid Noise Synthesis," *Computer Graphics*, Vol.23, No.3, July 1989, 263-270.

[13] Manneville, P., Boccara, N., Bidaux, R., Vichniac, G., *Cellular Automata and the Modeling of Complex Physical Systems*, Proceedings of the Feb. 1989 workshop at Les Houches, France, Springer-Verlag, 1989.

[14] Meinhardt, H., *Models of Biological Pattern Formation*, Academic Press, London, 1982.

[15] Murry, J., "How the Lepard Gets its Spots (biological inquiry into single pattern-formation mechanism in animal coats)" *Scientific American*, Vol.258, 1988, p.80.

[16] Perlin, K., "An Image Synthesizer," *Computer Graphics*, Vol.19, No.3, July 1985, 287-296.

[17] Sims, K., "Artificial Evolution for Computer Graphics," *Computer Graphics*, Vol.25, No.4, July 1991.

[18] Steele, G., *Common Lisp, The Language*, Digital Press, 1984.

[19] Thinking Machines Corporation, *Connection Machine Model CM-2 Technical Summary*, technical report, May 1989.

[20] Tamayo, P., and Hartman, H., "Cellular Automata, Reaction-Diffusion Systems, and the Origin of Life," *Artificial Life*, Addison-Wesley, 1989, 105-124.

[21] Toffoli, T., "Cellular Automata as an alternative to (rather than an approximation of) differential equations in modeling physics," *Physica* 10, North-Holland, Amsterdam, 1984, 117-127.

[22] Toffoli, T., and Margolus, N., *Cellular Automata Machines: A New Environment for Modeling*, MIT Press, 1987.

[23] Turing, A., "The Chemical Basis of Morphogenesis," *Philosophical Transaction of the Royal Society*, Vol.237, August 1952, 37-72

[24] Turk, G., "Generating Textures for Arbitrary Surfaces Using Reaction-Diffusion," *Computer Graphics*, Vol.25, No.4, July 1991.

[25] Witkin, A., and Kass, M., "Reaction Diffusion Textures" *Computer Graphics*, Vol.25, No.4, July 1991.

[26] Wolfram, S., "Cellular Automata as Models of Complexity," *Nature*, Vol.311, 1984, p.419.

[27] Wolfram, S., *Theory and Applications of Cellular Automata*, World Scientific, 1986.

Simulating Co-Evolution with Mimetism

Nicolas MEULEAU
CEMAGREF Antony
Artificial Intelligence Laboratory
B.P. 121, 92 185 Antony Cedex
tel: (1) 40 96 61 21

Abstract

This paper describes a computational model of autonomous organisms co-evolving with a mimetic behavior. We discuss the role and importance of mimetism in swarm intelligence and how our program may be used to study it. This program has been tested when simulating traffic on a two-dimensional road where each car is an autonomous unit imitating the other cars and being imitated by them. This experience clearly showed an improvement in the cars' performances due to their mimetic behavior.

Introduction

Artificial Life often refers to the concept of emergence and several previous works have shown that a well-fitted behavior can emerge in a randomly initialized system (some of these systems were called animats by their creator (Wilson 85)). These studies established Genetic Based Machine Learning (Goldberg 89) as a main tool for computational simulations of adaptation and evolution.

Artificial Life is also concerned with the concept of swarm intelligence : "intelligent" behaviors resulting from the coordinated actions of several autonomous individuals. In this field, a few simulations have been made but it seems that more is to come.

This paper presents a program simulating the evolution of a group of autonomous animats where the two following assumptions have been made :

- H1 : animats are able to perceive which one of them are the best;

- H2 : animats are progressively able to mimic the average behavior of their best colleagues.

This mimetic behavior is assumed to have two main effects :

1- homogenize the animats' population (obvious);
2- increase the animats' learning speed and final performances (to be checked).

We believe that mimetism plays an important role in the creation and maintenance of a swarm, and that it speeds up the members of the swarm's learning. Moreover, we think that it may be used with some restrictions about who imitates who (thus, introducing a topology on the population), to simulate an emergent "intelligent" swarm behavior.

Our system has been tested with a program simulating traffic on a one-way road where a group of cars evolves. These cars are autonomous robots co-evolving with mimetism. Because of hypotheses H1 and H2, they are not independent (although they are autonomous) and a single car's evolution depends on the other cars.

This experience confirmed our intuition that mimetism acts as an accelerator of the animats' evolution and increases their final performances.

1. Basic choices for the simulation

There are a few available methods to simulate evolution on a computer. Among them, Genetic Based Machine Learning seems the more suitable to simulate an animat (Parodi and Bonelli 91). The rules dictating our animats' behavior will be coded on chromosomes and a Genetic Algorithm (G.A.) (Holland 75) will work on them.

We now have to choose one of the two following options :

1- a chromosome codes a whole strategy (i.e. a set of rules) and the G.A. selects and crosses complete strategies. An animat is characterized by a single constant chromosome and unfitted animats die.

2- a chromosome codes a single rule and a complete strategy is determined by a set of chromosomes. An animat is characterized by a set of genetically evoluating rules, it never dies but some of its rules die and are replaced by presumed better ones.

The first approach consists in coding complete decision tables on chromosomes. Its main drawback is that one rule is coded for each possible situation : there are no explicit general rule that could be applied in several similar, but different, situations. We can imagine a coding using variable-sized chromosomes where such general rules could be explicitly specified, but we prefer to use the second approach.

The second approach is used in classical Classifier Systems (Holland 75, Goldberg89): each chromosome codes a single production rule of type:

[pattern of situation] => [action],

the premises of rules being coded with 0's, 1's and #'s (wildcard symbol) and their conclusions with 0's and 1's.

Each rule has a strength that is used to determine its level of priority and to calculate its fitness for the G.A.. The rules' strengthes are in constant evolution under a Bucket Brigade algorithm (Goldberg 89), according to the results of their applicationss. Over that allowing explicit specifica-tion of general rules, this system uses adaptation by reinforcement (through the Bucket Brigade algorithm) that is not available in the first solution.

Although this system seems the best for educating a single animat, it is less suitable in the case of a group of animats because it does not use any comparison or competition between the animats. To feel this gap and to implement our two cognitive hypotheses (H1 and H2), we created a mimetic operator that compares the global performances of animats and is responsible for rules exchanges between them. Our hope was that the mimetic operator would accelerate the animats' evolution and improve their final performances.

To validate this, we tested our system in a simulation of traffic on a two-dimensional one-way road. We are going to present our mimetic operator as part of this simulation.

2. Road traffic simulation

In our simulation, animats are car drivers sharing the same goal that is to drive avoiding accidents (the fastest are the most rewarded). They evolve on a one-way annular road sometimes streewed with impassable obstacles. Here, they may only act by modifying their speed and changing lanes.

A simulation procedure is responsible for the synchronized shiftings of the cars and manages the crashes (calculating damages). Its parameters have been choosen so that driving at full speed is dangerous because, in this case, an obstacle on a car's braking distance may be out of its driver's sight.

To succeed in driving while avoiding accidents is a rather hard-to-solve problem, when the traffic is intense. In this case, the result of each move is tinged with chance because it depends on the unpredictable moves of the other cars. So, our animats have to learn a noisy function.

To achieve this, they only dispose of incomplete and imprecise information. Because of the weakness of their senses, the car drivers do not know exactly the world in which they evolve. They evolve in an internal representation of their world that is a crude imitation of their real world.

2.a. The code (the internal representation of the world)

To make a move, an animat only disposes of imprecise information about :

- its absolute speed,
- presence (or absence) of obstacles in its immediate proximity and, if the case arises, the relative speed of these obstacles.

A rule is coded on three chromosomes: *C1*, *C2* and *A*, where *C1* and *C2* constitute a situation template and *A* is an action. It must be decoded as : if *C1* and *C2* then *A*.

• *C1* is a linear chromosome of length 2, it represents four levels of the car's absolute speed.

• *C2* is a circular chromosome of length 12, it represents the information about obstacles on the road. For this purpose, it is divided into six parts corresponding to six zones of the road in the car's proximity (see fig1). The code used for each part of *C2* is the following:

1# -> no obstacle;
00 -> an obstacle slower than the car;
01 -> an obstacle faster than the car.

If there are several obstacles in a zone, the animat perceives only the closest. The edge of the road is coded as a slower obstacle in the forward zone and a faster obstacle in the backward zone.
The size of each zone in fig 1.a is a linear function of the car's absolute speed. Thus, all the information contained on *C2* is relative to the the car's absolute speed coded on *C1*.
C2 was chosen to be circular in order to represent the semantic proximity between zones 1 and 6 of the road, by a structural proximity of the corresponding parts of the chromosome.

• *A* is a linear chromosome of length 4 divided in two equal parts. The first is used to code a speed variation (from acceleration down to braking), and the second one gives the move (i.e. changing lanes).

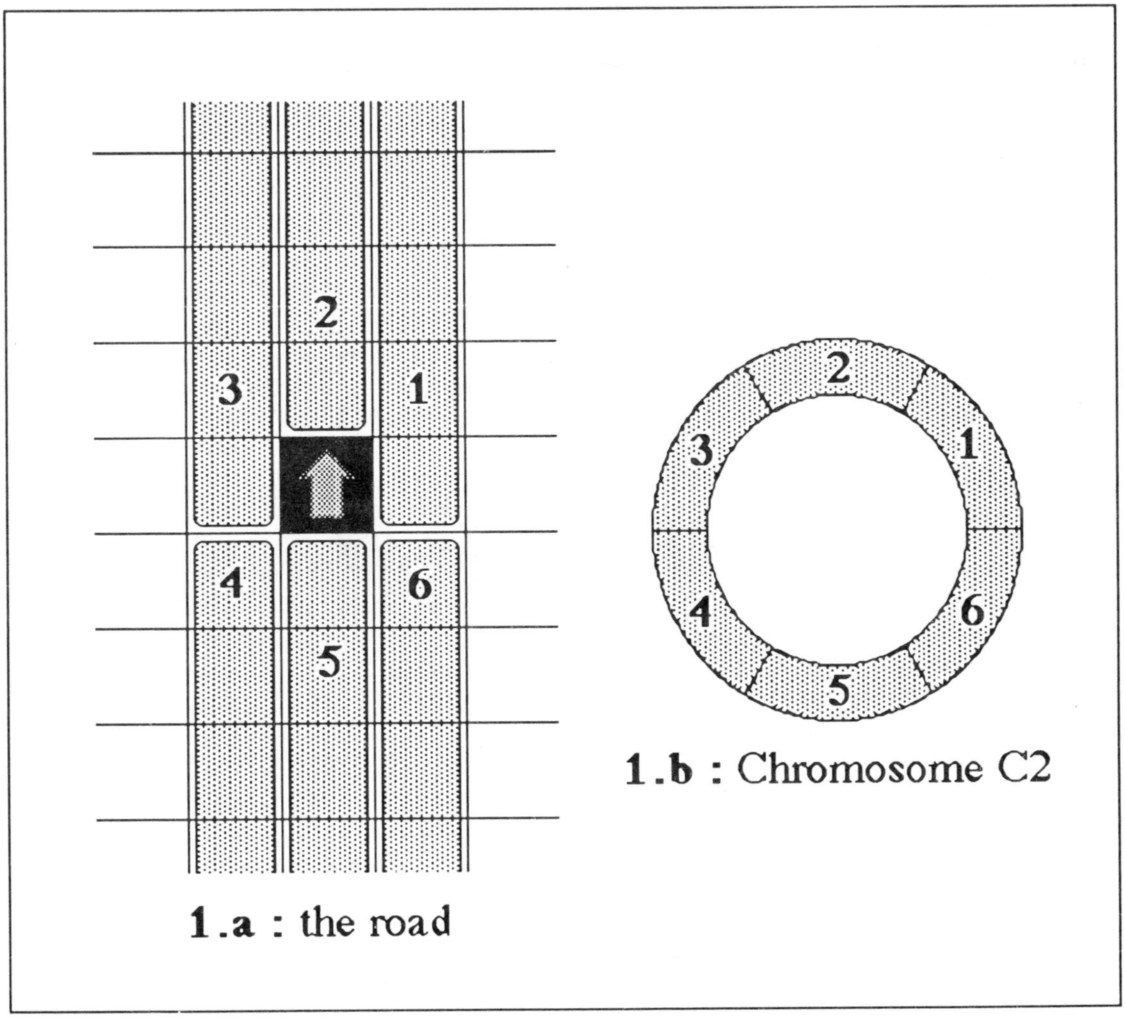

fig.1: Chromosome C2 (1.b) is divided into six parts corresponding to six zones of the road (1.a) in the car's closeness. We see that our animats' visibility is limited to three lanes.

Each animat is characterized by a constant-size set of rules. Each rule has a strength the amount of which varies under the action of a parallele Bucket Brigade algorithm similar to that presented by S.W. Wilson (Wilson 87). The rules' strengthes determine their priority level and are used to calculate their fitness for the G.A..

2.b. The G.A. that works on rules

The G.A. is responsible for the discovery of new rules. It uses the three classical operators (reproduction, crossover and mutation) proposed by J. Holland, and K.A. De Jong's crowding procedure (see Goldberg 89). We also added the following modifications:

• as L.B. Booker did (Booker 85), we only cross rules that match a same specific randomly-made message. Thus, the set of rules is implicitly divided in subsets that gather the rules matching a same message, and crossover is only used inside a subset.

• we use Wilson's creation operator (Wilson 85) that corresponds to the need for creating new rules to face new situations. It is used when there is no rule matching the environmental message (the animat does not know what to do). A new rule is then created, the premise of which is the unmatched environmental message with some wildcard symbols substituted. The action of the new rule is chosen at random and that rule is inserted in the set (the crowding procedure is used to make room for it).

• to facilitate emergence of good situation patterns in the rules' premises, we used two antagonistic operators called generalisation and specialisation.

- Generalisation is Wilson's partial intersection (Wilson 85) that acts on two rules with the same conclusion. It consists in comparing a portion of the rules' premises and adding wildcard symbols at the position where they diverge.
- Specialisation acts on a single rule, just after its successfull activation. It consists in replacing the rule premise by the message that has just fired it. Its effect is the substitution of the premise wildcard symbols by 0's and 1's.

With these additions, we obtain a powerful algorithm for simulating the evolution of a single animat. We present now the mimetic operator that involves several animats together.

2.c. The mimetic operator

We want to educate several animats evolving in the same environment and sharing the same goal. Our work is based upon the two following cognitive hypotheses:

• H1 : animats are able to perceive which one of them are the best;

• H2 : animats are progressively able to mime the average behavior of their best colleagues.

To implement these ideas we propose a mimetic operator that uses a comparison of the animats' global performances, and that is responsible for the replacement of rather bad rules of rather bad drivers by rather good rules of rather good drivers.

The first thing to do is to choose two animats: the first will play the role of the giver, and the second the recipient. The giver is choosen by a roulette wheel selection with a fitness criterion equal to the sum of all the payoff received by the animat's rules since the last mimetic operator stage. Thus, the criterion for evaluating animats is the summation over time of what was used to evaluate rules. The recipient is choosen in the same way using a criterion that is a decreasing linear function of the global fitness described above.

Some rules are going to be copied from the giver to the recipient. These rules are choosen in the giver's set with the G.A. selection procedure (roulette wheel selection using the strength of rules to determine their fitness). The crowding procedure is used to make room for these new rules in the recipient's set.

The number of transfers and the number of rules transfered each time are parameters for the program.

The consequence of the mimetic operator action is the spreading of presumably good rule templates among the population of rules sets. Everything is going on as if there were several classifier systems working in parallel on the same problem, with lateral rules exchanges. The best rules templates are spread in a non deterministic way, and thus, are tested in different situations at the same time. At the end of the run, mimetism leads to an uniformization of the population.

3. Results

The first thing we wanted to check was the performances of our classifier system in the evolution of a single rules set. Several runs were made where only one animat tried to drive on the road. In a second set of experiences, we tried to test the efficiency of our mimetic operator.

3.a. Educating a motorist

Our special classifier system allows to obtain a motorist able to evolve on a road filled with fixed obstacles. The algorithm convergence is slow and it may be accelerated by using learning protocoles where the same animat meets new situations in order to increase hardness. For instance :

1- the animat is placed alone on a wide road without obstacle. It quickly learns to start and the template "accelerate" spreads in the conclusion of its rules. Some of the rules that it uses are bad rules that do not pay attention to obstacles. It drives at full speed and makes useless zigzags.

2- the road width is reduced. As the accelerating rules are sorted, the animat stops zigzaging and learns to stay on the road. However, it continues driving at full speed.

3- The animat is eventually placed on a medium width road with an increasing number of obstacles.

An animat that has followed this learning protocole is able to carry on several laps of the ring, slaloming between the obstacles. We notice that it has learnt to limit its speed around three quarters of the maximum speed, that is approximately when the car's braking distance is equal to its driver's visibility. If we look "inside" such an animat, we see that most of its rules do not take care of what happens behind the car. This is natural because it has only met fixed obstacles during its past life. A new stage of adaptation with moving obstacles is now necessary. The animat will be placed in a traffic jam where he will have to take care of the cars arriving in its back.

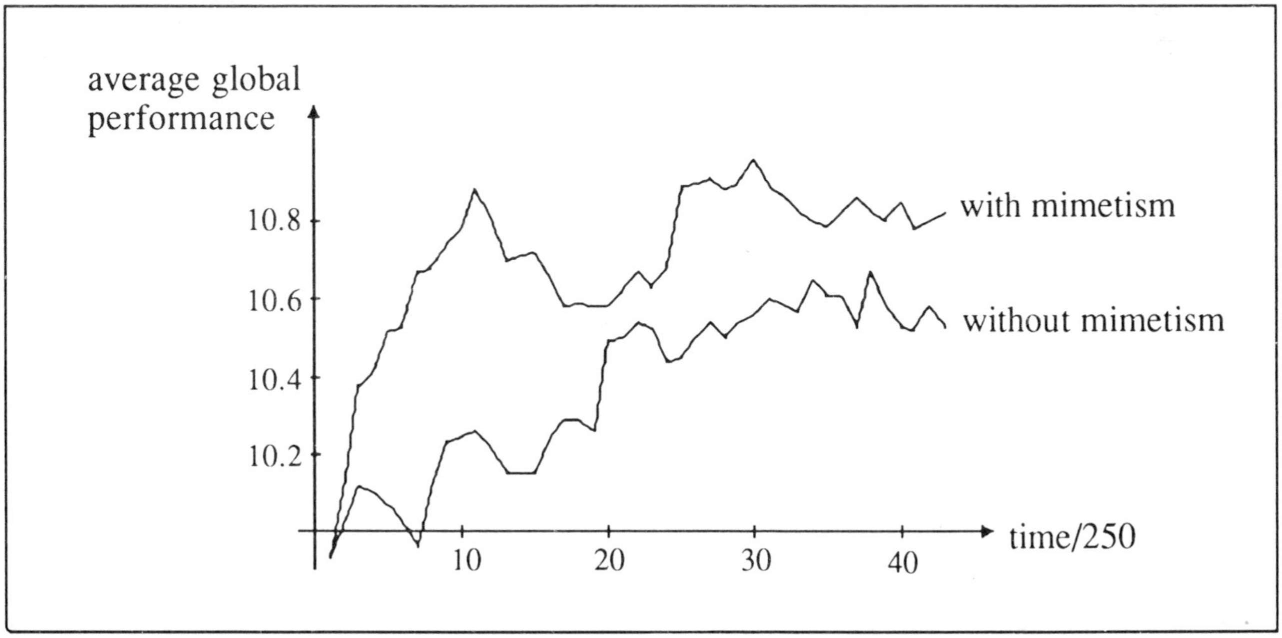

fig.2: Average global performances versus time, for ten cars on a road streewed with obstacles, with and without mimetism (average results of several experiences).

3.b. Performances of the mimetic operator

When running a simulation involving several animats we want to check our intuition that the mimetic operator improves the animats' learning and final performances. To do so, we have run several series of two simulations with exactly the same parameters, except that one uses mimetism and the other does not. In theese experiences, both simulations involved ten randomly initialized animats evolving on a road streewed with obstacles. The average performance of the group of animats is plotted versus time on figure 2. These results clearly show the improvement of the animats' final performances and learning speed due to their mimetic behaviour. This result was predictable because the introduction of hypotheses H1 and H2, through the mimetic operator, corresponds to the emergence of communication between the animats, that gain in this way a mean for sharing their experiences.

Conclusion

Mimetism allows to improve the performances of individuals sharing the same goal. When used without any restriction about who imitates who, it contributes to the uniformization of the animats' population . This phenomenon may contain a part of intelligence when there is acception of a common rule of behaviour, and when this consensus is favourable to the population. For example, the establishment of a general priority rule may limit the number of accidents in a traffic jam. Animats having grown together are then more efficient when they are grouped with each other. This is an instance of swarm intelligence.

The establishment of restrictions about who imitates who comes to the introduction of a topology on the animats' population. We may consider several topologies as using a natural topology of the world in which the animats evolve (i.e. an animat imitates only its colleagues that are "physically" close to him). It would be interesting to create a topology based on the animats' behaviour resemblances (i.e. an animat imitates those of its colleagues that look and behave like it). Such a simulation may allow the emergence of different species of animats, the mimetism acting only in the bossom of a same species, at the end of the run. Then we may hope to have a complex intelligent swarm behavior emerge.

References

• Booker L.B. 1985: Improving the performances of genetic algorithm in a classifier system. *Proceeding of an international conference on genetic algorithms and their applications*, 80-92.

• Goldberg D.E. 1989: *Genetic algorithms in search, optimization and machine learning*. Addison-Wesley.

• Holland J. 1975: *Adaptation in natural and artificial systems*. Ann Arbor: the University of Michigan Press.

• Parodi A. and Bonelli P. 1991: The animat and the physician. *From animals to animats: proceedings of the first internationnal conference on simulation of adaptative behaviour*, 50-57.

• Wilson S.W. 1985: Knowledge growth in an artificial animal. *Proceedings of an international conference on genetic algorithm and their applications*, 16-23.

• Wilson S.W. 1987: Classifier systems and the animat problem. *Machine learning 2*, 199-228.

DYNAMICS OF ARTIFICIAL MARKETS

Speculative Markets and emerging "Common Sense" Knowledge

Christian NOTTOLA, Frédéric LEROY, Franck DAVALO

BANQUE DE FRANCE - Artificial Intelligence Group
9, avenue du COLONEL DRIANT 75001 PARIS
Tel : 42 92 53 72

Abstract

In this paper, we move away from the classical economic theories of speculative markets which show them at a high level of description and consider that they, efficiently or inefficiently, compute the "fundamental" value of the good with respect to the state of the environment. From an artificial life point of view, a speculative market can be seen like a complex and evolving dynamic system. The behaviour of the market is not necessarily specified, it rather emerges from local interactions (interdependent representations) among a population of adaptative agents (the speculators). In this paradigm, market evolution and market representations form a dual system which is the essence of its autonomy. We present, from both a static and dynamical point of view, our "artificial market" program implemented with the help of genetic algorithms

Keywords

Artificial Market, Speculative Market, Autonomous Systems, common sense rationality, Co-evolution, Genetic Paradigm, Mimetism

I) INTRODUCTION

Like every market, speculative markets involve economic agents buying and selling goods or services in order to improve their welfare. Generally, the more durable is the good and the more "centralized" in space is the market, the more speculative it is. Examples of such markets are stock markets, currency markets or raw material markets. A speculator is a special kind of agent that is mainly motivated by drawing profit from (short term) fluctuation of the price of the good.

The classical economic paradigm (Part II) supposes the existence of an objective value of the asset and claims that speculation tends to guarantee the market price stability around the objective value. However, in real speculative markets, no such objective model exists and speculation rather tends to increase price unstability. An important step toward an understanding of empirical phenomena, consists to introduce self-referential mecanism through mimetic behaviours (Part III). However, non-linear analysis remains too rigid to cope with the complexity of social-ecological systems. In particular, this analysis tends to consider the speculative markets as archaic mob.

Our socio-ecological approach (part IV) begins to consider a new concept of rationality, the "common sense" rationality which is inherently bounded and adaptative. We then show how this new rationality gives the market a dual representational structure which is the essence of its autonomy. We finally briefly discuss our "artificial life" modeling approach of speculative markets. A description of our program of "Artificial speculative market" is given (Part V) which insists on important technical aspects such as the standard basic session, the agent's static characteristics, his decision-making process and the inductive, genetic and mimetic learning algorithms. We finally give an example of simulation.

II) THE RATIONAL EXPECTATION MODEL

The classical model lies on three main hypotheses : (i) There is a unique objective probabilistic law of the future price of an asset F_{t+1} with respect to the relevant information I_t known at date t (statistically predictable environment); (ii) All the agents are perfectly rational, i.e. they share the previous same representation of the system; (iii) Agents interact in a linear and static way through the market institution (no direct communication between the agents).

II.A) The fundamental value of an asset

Let us take the conditional expectation of the future price F_{t+1} with respect to the information I_t as an estimation of this price. So, we can compute the expected return of the asset from date t to t+1 :

$$R_{t,t+1} = \{E(F_{t+1}/I_t) - F_t + D_t\}/F_t$$

where D_t is the yield of the asset at date t.

Let r be the interest rate over a period of time (supposed to be constant). So, the expected return of the asset should be equal to the interest rate : $R_{t,t+1} = r$ (equilibrium condition). From this equilibrium condition we deduce the expression of the actual price :

$$F_t = \{E(F_{t+1}/I_t) + D_t\}/(1+r)$$

By a recurrence reasonning on the future date t+i (i>1) we finally obtain the "fundamental value" of the asset :

$$F_t = E(D_t/I_t)/\{1+r\} + ... + E(D_{t+i}/I_t)/\{1+r\}^i + ...$$

II.B) Equilibrium and market stability

The main concept of the classical theory is the concept of "market efficiency". A market is called efficient if the market price P_t perfectly reflects all the relevant information I_t, in other words if $P_t = F_t$.

Let us consider a particular agent A. According to the previous three hypotheses, he believes that the market price P can not be different from the fundamental value F. in fact, we suppose that A does not really know F but only an estimation F_A which is equal to $F + e_A$ where e_A is a white noise. So agent A adjusts his own behaviour according to F_A.

The market institution makes compatible agent's behaviours by computing the market price P which is assumed to be equal to the arithmetic mean of the agent's estimations. In consequence, if the number of agents is great enough, the market price P will be equal to the fundamental value F.

This "rational expectation" equilibrium is "self-fulfulling"; furthermore speculative behaviours guarantee its stability.

If we suppose that $P_t < F_t$, agent A considers that the market under-estimates the "objective" value of the asset and thinks that the "market" will correct his mistake. The rational behaviour for A consists at first to buy the asset at the market price P_t and then to sell it at the price F_t when the market's mistake will be corrected. So doing, A makes a net profit of $(F_t - P_t)$.

II.C) Inconsistency with empirical observations

From just an empirical point of view, the "rational expectation" theory is regularly questioned by cracks or panics familiar to stock markets.

One of the most striking empirical study was realized by. Schiller (1981) who studied the american stocks behaviours. On the basis of yields, Schiller (1981) computed over a long period of time the theoretical fundamental value of american stocks and showed that its variance was twenty time smaller as the observed price's variance.

III) THE NEO KEYNESIAN CRITICS

The previous empirical result can be seen as a confirmation of the Keynes 's heterodox theory of speculation on financials markets, which forms the chapter 12 of his famous book "The General Theory of Employment, Interest and Money" (1936).

III.A) Individual subjectivity and social convention

We have first to recognize, with Keynes (1936), that the "fundamental value" is not practically computable : "The oustanding fact is the extreme precariousness of the basis of knowledge on which our estimate of prospective yield have to be made. Our knowledge of the factors which governs the yield of an investment some years hence is usually very slight and often negligeable".

This difficulties, inherent to long term expectation, make that it "does not depend on the most probable forecast we can make. It also depends on the confidence with which we make this forecast [...]. If we expect large changes but are very uncertain as to what precise form these changes will take, then our confidence will be weak".

In other words, Keynes (1936) suggests that the "fundamental value" is not an objective value but a subjective value.

Following Orlean (1989), let us suppose that agent A has confidence in traditional methods of valuation with respect to a certain variable V_A which can take two values T_A and F_A with the probabilities s and (1-s). If V_A takes the value T_A, agent A continues to trust in traditional methods so he thinks that the future price P_{+1} is consistent with the law $F=\{F_{t+1}/I_t\}$. If V_A takes the value F_A, agent A no longer trust in the traditional methods and thinks that $P_{+1} = 0$ to simplify. So agent A expects a price P_A equal to $I_A*E(F)$, where I_A equals 1 if V_A equals T_A and 0 otherwise.

If we enlarge the scope to the whole market, due to its subjective feature at the individual level, the classical methods of valuation, is just a social convention.

Nevertheless, this "conventional method of calculation will be compatible with a considerable measure of continuity and stability in our affairs, so long as we can rely on the maintenance of the convention". This is the case in a purely institutional context, where the agents are only interested by the consistency between their representation and the reality.

Let us consider a group of n agents divided in k sub-groups. Each sub-group includes n/k agents, which all share the same variable V_k. If the V_k variables are independant, we can deduce the expression of the average price expectation P(k) :

$E(P(k)) = s*E(F)$ and

$V(P(k)) = \{s*(1-s)/k\}*E(F)^2$

In the case where all agents have their own variable (k=n), the confidence with which the agents make their forecast, does not necessary create a greater price volatility, since V(P(n)) converge to 0 when n becomes great enough.

III.B) Systemic risk and mimetic behaviour

In the classical paradigm, the risk is only due to the contingent feature of the fundamental law which is a purely exogeneous risk. But, if we reject the institutional context hypothesis, the agents know that market price is not an exogeneous data, but depends on the behaviours of the others : the price market P_t takes its autonomy towards the "fundamental value"

F_t. Henceforth, the agents have to face a new kind of risk, a systemic risk, which is inherent to the market.

Agent A will try to manage his new risk : knowing that the price of the asset does not reflect anything else than the average opinion of the agents, he will no longer try to evaluate the price from the fundamental factors correctly but will try to understand how these factors are interpreted by the other agents.

But, if each agent does the same, they face an infinite specularity : all agents will try to evaluate the price of the asset from the way how the average opinion interprets the average opinion interprets ... the fundamentals factors. This infinite reccurrence in the taking into account of the behaviour of the others ruins the rationality of the agents and leads them to a situation of total uncertainty.

In such a situation of uncertainty, Orlean (1989) argues that the mimetic behaviour is rational. But this behaviour creates a process of opinions polarization toward the same V variable which is responsible for price instability ($V(P(1)) = \max V(P(k)) = s*(1-s)*E(F)^2$).

Consider that we have only two variables V_A and V_B. Let $k_A(t)$ (resp. $k_B(t)$) the agents' proportion that construct their expectation at date t on the basis of V_A (resp. V_B) variable. We have :

$P_A = I_A*E(F)$ and $P_B = I_B*E(F)$

$P = \{k_A(t)*I_A + k_B(t)*I_B\}*E(F)$

and $k_A(t)+k_B(t)=1$

With V_A (resp. V_B), agents A (resp. B) take a risk :

$r_A = V\{P_A - P\} = 2*s*(1-s)*E(F)^2 = \mu*k_B^2$ (resp. $r_B = \mu*k_A^2$).

We can see the choice of the agent A as an arbitrage (D(A)) between the relative profit (R) and the relative risk ($r_A - r_B$) associated to the choice of V_A instead of V_B. Let v be the risk aversion, we have :

$$D(A) = R - v*\mu*(k_B^2-k_A^2)$$
$$= R - v*\mu*(2*k_B^2-1)$$

A choice I_A if $D(A) > 0$ (i.e. $k_B > (R+v*\mu)/2*v*\mu$) and I_B otherwise.

"Let us consider a sequential arrival process on the market, the initial state depends on the initial proportions of a priori beliefs. But as soon as $k_B > (R+v*\mu)/2*v*\mu$, by the result of the draw, agent A will decide to keep I_B instead of I_A. This situation is irreversible, from now k_B will be going to increase that will make less attractive the choice of I_A. Finally k_B will converge to 1. This process converges on two equilibriums that both correspond to unanimity situations to I_A or I_B. This convergence is not foreseable" (Orlean 1989).

Contrarily to the exogeneous risk, the systemic risk may not be managed by the agents. If an agent thinks to manage the systemic risk in adopting a mimetic behaviour, he is just increasing the systemic risk by that way.

IV) TOWARDS A SOCIO-ECOLOGICAL APPROACH

If we want to give an account of the autonomous nature of speculative markets, we no longer have to consider rational and fixed agents that interact, in a statistically predictible environment, through an institution that aggregates agent's behaviours in a linear and static way.

The previous analysis, in introducing self-referential mecanism through mimetic behaviours, is an important step toward an understanding of empirical phenomena. Though non-linear analysis can help economists to take into account new phenomena, it remains too rigid to cope with the complexity of socio-ecological systems. In particular, this analysis tends to consider the speculative markets as archaic mob. But we have to admit that the normal behaviour of the speculative market, if it is not true to the classical theory, is stable enough to guarantee the viability and the durability of the system.

Our socio-ecological approach begins to consider a new concept of rationality, the "common sense" rationality which is bounded and adaptative. We then show how this new rationality gives the market a dual representational structure which is the essence of its autonomy. Finally, we briefly discuss our "artificial life" modeling approach of speculative markets.

IV.A) "Common sense" rationality

In a multi-agents context, both Artificial Intelligence and Economic Theory faced the paradoxal implications of the cognitivist rationality.

We have seen, previously, that cognitive rationality implies infinite specularity between the agents (i.e. the capacity of the human mind to put itself in the place of another and see the world from this other agent's point of view). However, this infinity is incompatible with the mind capacities, which is a finite machine.

For Orlean (1989), this specularity leads the agents to a situation of total uncertainty where it is rational to adopt a mimetic behaviour. If, this model of mimetic contagion is well suited to the formalization of speculative bubbles or phenomena of rumors, the problem is that these two situations don't allow to explain the daily behaviour of speculative markets.

Moreover, this explanation introduces a cognitive discontinuity between conventional situations where behaviours are guided by the convention and non-conventional situations where the mimetic rationality prevails. We rather think that this discontinuity is only apparent to the observer. Both "conventional rationality" and "mimetic rationality" emerge from the same sub-level rationality : the "common sense" rationality.

From a static point of view, the "common sense rationality" is a bounded rationality : agents have a bounded knowledge of their environment (other agents and global behaviour) and bounded computing capacities. From a dynamical point of view, "common sense" knowledge depends on action and history, that is to say, on real-life. It is inherently a dynamical and adaptative knowledge.

The socio-cultural group that makes up a speculative market, "is immersed in a history, a tradition, a particular world and a particular form of common sense. Each individual has implicit, unformulated and tacit knowledge of this world, and although this knowledge is not explicit, it is constitutive of the individual's social being. This common sense has been collectively created by individuals, but, it nonetheless appears to them as if it were an objective reality wholly external to their own making and doing".(Dupuy 1989)

In multi-agents context, the basic learning process is imitation. But imitation can not only be defined by the copy of another behaviour, it is an original production with dynamical and selective features. As a consequence, "common sense knowledge" does not emerge globally, as convention does, but rather locally, i.e. at the levels of social sub-groups created by inter-individuals relationship. Our hypotheses of bounded knowledge imply that the density of the social web is low.

Each agent uses his "common sense" rationality "without engaging in any specular reference to what others might choose. The others are still present in this agent's individual choice, but it is as if their views had been crystallised into objects. Mediation by common sense makes it possible to obtain with null specularity what logic thought only an infinite specularity could obtain". (Dupuy 1989)

IV.B) The autonomous character of speculative markets

According to Varela (1980), we say that a system is "closed operationaly" if "its organisation is characterised by process which, (1) depends on each other recursively for their own generation and realisation and (2) constitutes the system as a unity recognizable in the space where the processus takes place".

Our model of speculative market distinguishes three main entities, the agents (the speculators), the institution (the centralized market) and the exogenous environment (exogeneous variables).

One speculator uses his "common sense rationality" to make a price's expectation and then decides [D] an action (A) according to its individual portfolio constraints. Our speculator is not fixed. He continuously adapts [L] its internal implicit model of the market (R). The centralized market [M] computes, in a deterministic and non-linear way, the asset's price (P) and the transactions in function of the agents intentions (A_1, A_2, ...,A_N). The evolution of exogeneous variables (E), is predefined and influences, the agent's behaviour.

On one hand, the socio-historical factors (agent's representations and present or past price) determine the futur price, with respect to the exogeneous environment :

$$[M]\,[D]\,(P,R_1,R_2,...,R_N) \text{ ------> } P_{+1}\ /E$$

On the other hand, the "emergent" market price P generates a pertubation for the system which takes the form of a learning process at the agent's level :

$$[L]\,(P_{+1},R_1,R_2,...,R_N) \text{ ------> } (R_1,R_2,...,R_3)_{+1}$$

With the previous two relations, we have implicitly defined the market as a self-referential system :

$$(P,R_1,R_2,...,R_N)\ \tilde{}\ [M][L][D]_E(P,R_1,R_2,...,R_N)$$

In the Varela's terminology, we shifted from a description of the market, in the form of an "input coupling" (classical model) to a description, in the form of an "enclosure coupling". The operator [M,L,D] determines the system enclosure. We have moved the stress, which was before under information representation (price and relevant information), towards the organizational interdependences of the system and the history of its structural coupling. In this regard, the cooperative action (social imitation and market aggregation) of a set of components (the speculators and their system representations), linked in a self-referential way, produces the internal coherence of the system.

This autonomy of the market towards its environment is the reason of its intrinsic unpredictability i.e. of its irrationality from a classical economic point of view.

As we have described the market, it partly results from the composition of the speculator's representations of market and conversely, the evolution of the market modifies these representations. The market and its representations are defined each other by the way of the individual and collective actions of the speculators.

Thus, It is futile to try to build an objective high level model of the speculative market for the market and its representations form a dual system.

IV.C) The genetic paradigm and artificial markets

As described previously, a speculative market is clearly a non-linear system. For such a system, conventional (or non-conventional) mathematical techniques of economic analysis using linearity, fixed points and convergence (or specified non-linearity) provide only an entering wedge when it comes to understand its behaviour.

At this point, we face some problems encountered by reseachers in their efforts to simulate life-like behaviours. The answer is partly given by Artificial Life as shown in Langton's seminal paper : "The non-linear systems must be treated as a whole. A different approach to the study of non-linear systems involves the inverse of analysis : synthesis. Rather than start with the behavior of interest and attempting to analyse it into its constituents parts, we start with constituent parts and put them together in the attempt to synthesize the behavior of interest" (Langton 1980). From a technical point of view, we make a great use of genetic algorithms both at the agent and group level.

At the agent level, the Holland's work on genetic algorithms and inductive learning is particularly well suited to model our concept of "common sense" rationality. In his cognition paradigm, the most important capacity consists precisely to act in a satisfactory way in the multiple contexts which rise at each time of our life. An agent interacts with its environment in a game-like way : sequences of actions occasionally produce payoff, which provides the system with the wherewithall for continued existence and adaptation. Agents in the market "build up models of the rest of the economy [market] and use them to make predictions. These models, sometimes called internal models, are rarely explicit. They are usually more prescriptive (prescribing what should be done in a given situation) than descriptive (describing the options in a given situation)" (Holland 1988).

Holland's work is only concerned with the learning performed by a single agent. However, the fact that in genetic algorithms all internal control information and external communication reside in the same data structure for massage passing, makes the scheme extendable to multi-agents learning context. The way to do it consists to give the possibility to agents to mimick some of the feature of the more successful ones. (see Shaw and Whinston 1989, for a general exposure in a DAI context and Meuleau 1991, for a nice application in the context of co-learning drivers).

V) THE PROGRAM : DESCRIPTION AND SIMULATION

We give below a description of important technical aspects of our program such as the standard basic session, the agent's static characteristics and decision-making process, and the learning algorithms. We finally give an example of simulation.

V.A) The standard basic session

During what we define as a standard basic session, every agent has the opportunity to make an offer to sell or buy one unit of good at his own preferential price. Offers are gathered to decide which of them will be selected (to be anyway processed at the current market price) and to compute the next market price.

We then confronte selling and buying prices with each other to match sellers and buyers until either demand or supply be satisfied. An exchange is a transfer of one unit of good from seller to buyer against an opposite transfer of currency at the amount of the market price.

We keep the average offered prices of the last decided exchange as the new market price. This algorithm tends to decrease market prices when supply exceeds demand and conversely in the opposite context.

V.B) Static characteristics of Agents and decisional process

An agent owns some stock of asset and some currencies which both form his portfolio.

An agent is defined by a set of rules of type [context --> anticipation]. A rule is composed of six simple parameters c_1, c_2, c_3, c_4, c_5 and a, where ci (i=1...5) constitutes the context part and a the anticipation part. The rule's semantics is described as follows : c_1 represents the evolution of the exogeneous variable, c_2 (resp. c_3) represents the evolution of the first (resp. second) derivative of the market exchange volume, c_4 (resp. c_5) represents the evolution of the first (resp. second) market price and a represents the expectation of the future first derivative of the market price.

Parameters are taken into account inside the rules only as three state qualitative information : increase (1), decrease (-1) or stability (0). We allow the use of "don't care" (#) as a parameter value. This is a way to create more general rules.

Before every session, each agent selects a rule among those matching the current context, according to a bidding system. Each rule makes a bid whose amount is positively correlated to its fitness and negatively correlated to its level of generality. This bid is slightly modified by a non deterministic term to add some flexibility to the system.

$\text{bid} = (\text{fitness})^k * 1/(1 + (\text{generality})^p) * (1 + \text{random}()/10^u)$

(k,p,u > 1 and random() returns a number between 0 and 1)

Agents act according to the anticipation of the selected rule : when the anticipation is an "increase" in market price, the agent decides to buy (only if he owns enough liquidity), he decides to sell (only if he owns at least one asset) when the anticipation is a "decrease" and he does nothing when anticipating a "stable" price.

Selling_Price = Market_Price - K*random()
Buying Price = Market_Price + K*random()

where K is a constant.

V.C) Learning abilities for co-evolutive agents

An agent is said to be evolutive when his set of rules can be modified : some rules' fitness can change, new rules can be created and bad rules can be destroyed.

After each session, when the new market price has been determined, each agent compares his anticipation to what really happened and, for the rules that matched the old context, increases or decreases their fitness (positive or negative fixed payoffs) according to the fact that they had the right or wrong anticipation. Bad rules (at least at a given period) are going this way to get a smaller and smaller fitness and won't be any more selected.

New rules are created according to three main principals : by inductive learning, by simple genetic algorithms and by mimetic algorithms.

When no rule matches the current context, a new one is created, increasing the rule's domain of validity by a suppression of constraints in the current context. The anticipation will be the real price evolution (which will be known at the next session).

We apply a genetic algorithm to each evolutive agent every period determined by a fixed number of session. A rule is viewed as a circular chromosome formed by the conditional parameters, and cross-overs are only performed on rules with the same anticipation. We create a new set of rules by crossing-over between good rules, by mutation on few rules (the fitness threshold which differentiates overall good rules from bad ones is : {initial fitness} - {tax of living}*{number of session} - {equivalent of two negative payoffs}).

Every fixed number of session (less frequently than we apply the genetic algorithm) we copy some best rules from the best agents of a group to the set of rules of the other agents of the same group. A good agent is determined by its performance : (Market Price) * (volume of goods) + (amount of currency). The agents of the same group tend to follow the best individual strategy that emerges from inside the group. These groups are pre-defined and fixed.

V.D) An example of simulation

At this point, we agree with Langton (1988) when he asserts that one "often gains tremendous insight into the essential dynamics of a system by observing its behaviour under a wide range of initial conditions". Yet, we miss time and place to give here these "essential characteristics" (evolutionary stable rules, market price evolution, ...). However, we comment below a simulation as an example.

The simulation involves 30 agents : 20 fixed agents and 10 adaptative agents. The 20 fixed agents are shared out into 2 groups of 10 agents which both follow a specific fixed strategy. This strategy is described by five rules which context part entirely and exactly fill the space of possible contexts. The two subgroups strategies differ only from the anticipation parts of some rules. These rules are :

(1) # # 1 # 0 --> 1 (resp. 1)
(2) # # 0 # 0 --> 1 (resp. -1)
(3) # # -1 # 0 --> -1 (resp. -1)
(4) # # # # 1 --> -1 (resp. -1)
(5) # # # # -1 --> -1 (resp. 1)

The 10 adaptative agents are spread in two groups of 5 agents. The first one involves independant agents i.e. non mimetic agents and the second one involves dependant agents with mimetic learning abilities.

To begin with, each agent owns the same portfolio which contains 20 units of the asset and 800 currency units. One unit of asset costs 20 currency units. We run the market during 80000 basic sessions, the genetic operator is applied each 1000 sessions and the mimetic one is applied each 3000 sessions. Moreover, the exogeneous variable is arbitrarily defined as a sinusoïd.

To understand the system behaviour, we focus on, adaptative groups learning evolution (Graph 1), price evolution (Graph 2) and groups performance evolution (Graph 3).

The graph 1 shows for each fixed agents' rules, how an adaptative agent set of rules is correlated to each rule of the first group of fixed agents. A correlation curve varies from -1 to 1 which corresponds to the exact emergence of the rule or its opposite (opposite anticipation). We can see that in the long term, an adaptative agent reproduces a combination of non adaptative agent's strategies. The five curves correspond respectively (from the bottom to the top of the graph) to the five rules :

(1) # # 1 # 0 --> 1 (converge to -1)
(2) # # 0 # 0 --> 1 (converge to -1)
(3) # # -1 # 0 --> -1 (converge to -1)
(4) # # # # 1 --> -1 (converge to -1)
(5) # # # # -1 --> -1 (converge to 1)

(for example, the curve which is situated at the bottom of the graph corresponds to the rule (1) and shows the emergence of the opposite rule).

More precisely, we notice that this agent globally behaves according to the three rules :

(1)' # # # # -1 --> 1
(2)' # # # # 0 --> -1
(3)' # # # # 1 --> -1

So he tends to sell twice more as to buy, in the long term. This graph only presents one adaptative agent, but all others adaptative agents behave the same way. Finally, after a short learning period (about 20000 sessions), the agent tends globally to sell more than to buy.

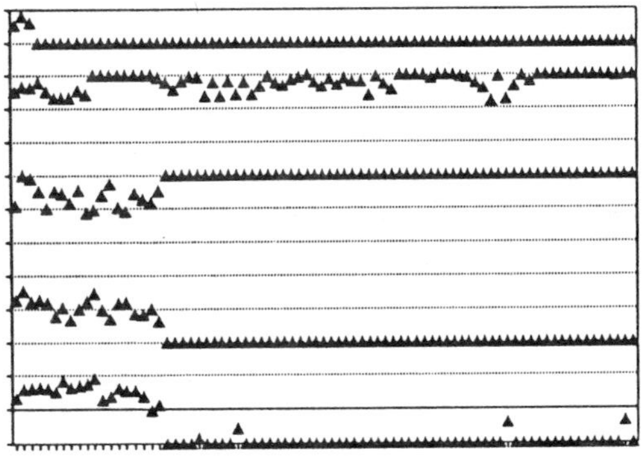

Graph 1 - Groups learning evolution

The graph 2 shows that the price tends effectively to decrease after a short period of sharp increase.

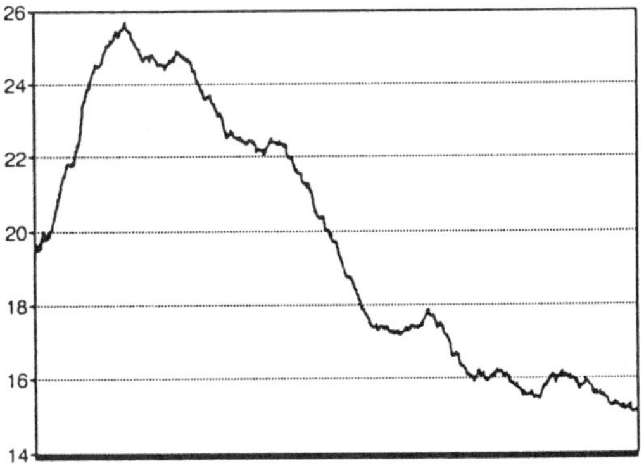

Graph 2 - Price evolution

The graph 3 presents the evolution of the mean performance ({stock*market price+liquidity} / number of agents}) per groups for the non adaptative agents***, the adaptative and mimetic agents** and the adaptative and non mimetic one*. After a short period, we notice the following comforting result : **adaptative agents behave better than non adaptative ones**, which is what we expected. After a sharp increase in adaptative agents' performance, the change of tendency seems to correspond to the point where all the evolutive agents had the same rules emerging stably.

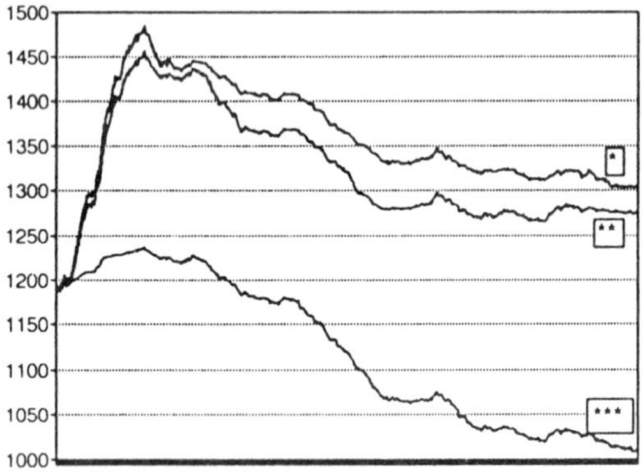

Graph 3 - Groups performance evolution

VI) CONCLUSION AND FUTURE WORKS

At this point, we have shown that a socio-ecological approach is relevant to the study of speculative markets, because of its microscopic characteristics (population of agents endowed with a "common sense" rationality) and macroscopic characteristics (a speculative market is "closed operationaly").

However, our "artificial market" research program is just beginning and the system presented here is yet too simple to be considered as "ecological".

To go further in a socio-ecological approach of speculative markets, we envisage (i) to increase the strategic space of the speculators by taking into account several time scales, several evolution patterns of variables, ... in order to generate a range of regularities or niches which can be exploited by differents strategies (ii) to consider an evolutionary web of sociological interactions which is an important part of our "common sense" rationality and offers a sociological answer to the traditional tradeoff between exploration and exploitation, (iii) to introduce non-speculators agents with pre-defined or adaptative behaviors in order to study symbiosis and/or parasitism interactions.

References

Dupuy J.P.
Common knowledge, common sense. Theory and Decision, July/September 1989.

Holland J.H.
The global economy as an adaptative process. The Economy as an Evolving Complex System. Addison-Wesley Publishing company, 1988.

Keynes J.M.
General Theory of Employment, Interest and Money. MacMillan, 1936.

Langton C.G.
Artificial Life. Artificial Life. Edited by Langton C.G., SFI Studies in the Sciences of complexity. Addison-Wesley Publishing Company, 1988.

Meuleau N.
Co-evolution and mimetism : a program simulating road traffic. In this volume.

Orlean A.
Pour une approche cognitive des conventions économiques. Revue Economique, mars 1989.

Shaw M.J. and Whinston A.B.
Learning and adaptation in distributed artificial intelligence systems. Distributed Artificial Intelligence (vol 2). Edited by Gasser L. and Huhns M. Morgan Kaufman, 1989.

Shiller R.J.
Do stock market prices move too fast to be justified by subsequent changes in dividends ?. American Economic Review, June 1981.

Varela F.J.
Principal of Biological Autonomy. Elsevier North holland, 1980.

Harvesting By A Group Of Robots

S. Goss, J.L. Deneubourg

Unit of Theoretical Behavioural Ecology, Service de Chimie Physique
CP 231, Université Libre de Bruxelles, 1050 Bruxelles

Abstract

We aim to show through simulations how a group of simple robots could navigate in an unknown area without maps, visual analysis or landmark recognition, and in situations where the homing signals used have a shorter range than the area to be explored, and can be blocked by obstacles. Basically, some of the robots act as homing beacons for the others, forming dynamic chains of beacons that thread through the area. While perhaps less efficient than more complex robots or guidance systems, a team of such chain-making robots combines the advantages of simplicity, reliability, and flexibility.

Introduction

Now that single robots are starting to appear that are relatively cheap, simple and reliable, it becomes reasonable to anticipate what they could do as a group. Our approach is to keep their individual behaviour as simple as possible, but to introduce either interactions between the individual robots or to increase slightly their individual capacity so as to generate an emergent and efficient group behaviour. By emergent we simply mean that the group exhibits behaviour not explicitly programmed into the individuals, and by efficient we mean that the emergent behaviour improves the group's performance according to the context in question.

Without necessarily trying to imitate nature, we have drawn from our experience of social insects, and ants in particular (Deneubourg & Goss 1989). Notwithstanding its complex internal physiology, certain aspects of an ant's behaviour are relatively simple and within the capability of a contempory robot. An ant colony, however, is an entirely more complex "organism", with a remarkable capacity for building, foraging, and overall organisation, and yet is composed of a small or large number of such behaviourally simple individuals. One of our aims is to recapture this discontinuity to endow teams of simple robots with capabilities beyond that of the individuals that make up the teams. It is to be stressed that what we present here are simulations, and not yet real robots. We feel they can nevertheless offer insights as to how this aim might be achieved, and the actual implementation of these models is possible in the near future.

The problem we have set our simulated robots is that of gathering randomly distributed objects (targets) in a square arena, and bringing them them to a central point (home). This is something that social insects do exceedingly well and by a number of different means (see e.g. Beckers et al. 1989), and we have loosely transposed here their system of individual foraging and of collective foraging with trails.

The major theme of our analysis is to what extent the individual robots' homing and orientation capacity can influence the group's overall performance. To do this we have simulated three robot models. None of them have an internal map, which simplifies them enormously, and instead they rely on an external signal or signals to guide them to the central point. In an ideal world a homing signal can be heard anywhere in the trial area, but we wanted to take into account a first possibility that the signal is line-of-sight only, e.g cannot pass through certain obstacles or be received in such valleys or behind such ridges as may be encountered in a "non-artificial" environment. The second possibility is that the signal is only short range and cannot be received throughout the area to be covered, and poses the problem as to how the robots can then find their way home from regions further away than this signal range.

The first two models we propose roughly correspond to individual foraging in ants, in which each individual searches independently, and can find its own way home from anywhere within the foraging area. The difference between them is that in the first model, and unlike individualy foraging ants, the robots cannot return to the site of their last find, whereas in the second they can.

The third model involves a much more collective behaviour in that the robots rely on each other to find their way home. If one wanted to imitate an ant society closely, one might imagine a succesful robot depositing a substance that can guide other robots both towards its recent find and back to the nest. However as well as implying that the discoverer can find its own way home, there are a number of practical objections to this idea, and instead, following a suggestion by Giulio Sandini (Deneubourg *et al.* 1990), we have chosen to make the robots themselves act as fixed and temporary trail markers (beacons) for the others, forming "chains" of robot-beacons. It shall become clear the trails formed in this model are not linked to any particular discovery but are more exploratory in nature, in that they serve to guide the robots within the foraging area whether or not they have discovered a target.

1. The basic robot

The basic robot is as follows:

No interactions: the robots have no interactions with other members of its group (other than avoiding collisions) and act independently and autonomously.
Obstacle avoidance: a robot can avoid bumping into obstacles and each other.
Random searching: they move pseudo-randomly, i.e. on a square grid they choose randomly to move into one of the subset of the four adjacent cardinal points that are currently not occupied by another robot or an obstacle. They can move into a space containing a target, but do not do so preferentially (i.e are not attracted to targets).
Very short range target detection: a robot can recognise an item to be collected, but only when it "bumps" into one, i.e. moves into a space containing one, and cannot spot a target at distance.
Limited transport capacity: a robot can pick up and carry one target item.
Homing capacity: they can return in a more or less straight line to a central beacon, and can receive the central beacon's signal throughout the trial area.
Foraging boundary: In the simulations they treat the edge of the trial area as an obstacle. This is equivalent to saying that when the signal strength drops below a certain level the robots cannot move in a direction that would take them further away from the beacon (ideally the trial area should be more circular than square).
Returning home: they return "home" (to the

central beacon) either when they have found a target or when they decide to "give up". The probability of giving up, p, is low and constant, and is tested at each time step.
Arriving home: when a robot reaches home, it deposes the target if it is carrying one and starts searching at random again.

2. The robot with memory of its last find.

The robot with memory of its last find's location is the same as the basic model, with the additional capacity of returning to the point where it last found a target. This implies the presence of either more than one beacon to permit the robots to find their way by triangulation throughout the test area, or the robot using a polar coordinate system to remember the direction and number of steps to the central beacon.

The robots rapidly find the targets near the central beacon, creating an empty zone around it. By returning to the last find rather than starting searching at the central beacon, the robots with memory avoid repeatedly searching the emptied zone, which constitutes an emergent benefit of their memory. This capability can also contribute to make a robot faithful to a particular zone, especially if that zone is richer in targets than others and targets are constantly arriving (Deneubourg *et al.* 1987). Note that this potential fidelity can be reinforced by making the robots give up and go home after a shorter period without finding a target, to avoid them wandering too far from their remembered last finds.

Finally, this robot can be programmed to remember the last find's XY coordinates in a cumulative fashion, as being a fraction w along the line joining the previous "cumulative last find" and the latest find. If the weight ($0 < w \leq 1$), is set to 1 then the memory is strictly short term and the robot remembers only the latest find. The closer the weight is to zero, then the greater the influence of previous finds and the longer the robots' memory. In such a case if the robot has found a number of targets in a particular zone, then even if it finds its next target "miles away", it will return more or less to the area of its previous finds. Note that a longer term memory is probably more effective when the targets are constantly arriving in the search area. In the simulations used here, however, the targets are all present at the start of the simulation and the robots are tested with a short term memory.

3. The chain-making robots.

This model is conceived for situations where the homing signal cannot carry very far, and so the robots have to rely on each other to find their way to and from home. The basic scenario is as follows.

Limited signal range: the robots start with a central beacon whose signal range is significantly shorter than the area to be covered.
Random searching: they search at random, as in the basic model.
Distance from beacon: the robots lock onto this beacon and periodically assess their distance from it (e.g. via signal strength).
Becoming a beacon: when a robot reaches the limit of its beacon's signal range, it checks to see if it can detect another beacon emitting within range. If so it locks onto that beacon and continues searching. If not it stops, enters "beacon mode", and starts emitting a homing signal of its own and of comparable range. Furthermore, it adopts a "beacon number" one greater than that of the beacon whose signal limit it reached, while remaining locked onto it (see fig. 1). Thus if it was locked onto a beacon of number 1, it becomes a beacon number 2.

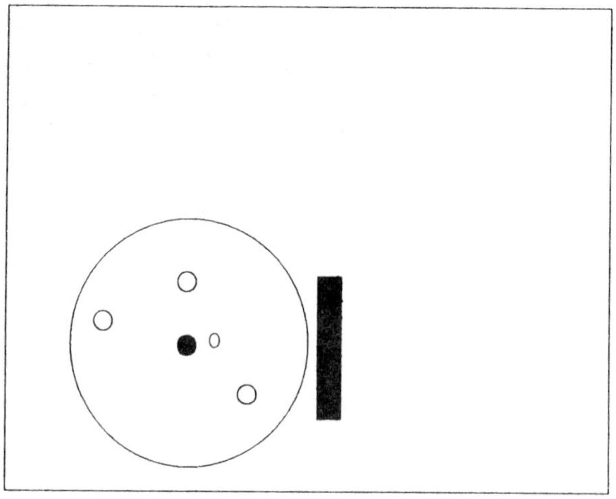

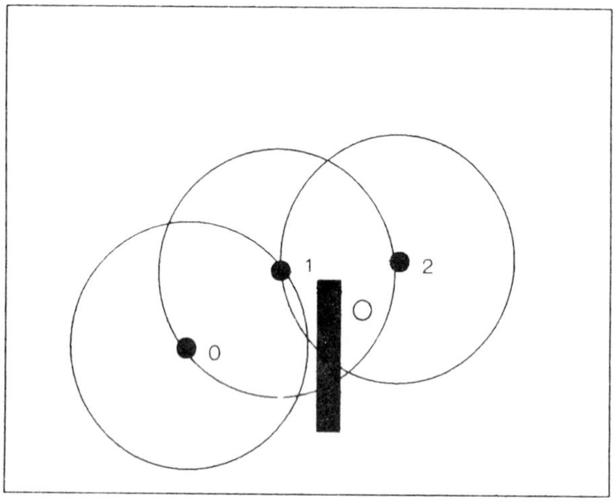

Fig 1a. Three chain-making robots (small empty circles) search within range (large circle) of beacon 0 (small solid circle). The solid rectangle is an obstacle opaque to the signal. **Fig. 1b**. One searcher reached the edge of beacon 0's range and became a beacon 1, forming a chain 0-1. A second searcher entered beacon 1's range, reached its edge, and became a beacon 2, forming a chain 0-1-2. The remaining searcher, while theoretically within range of beacon 1, cannot receive its signal through the obstacle. It can however receive beacon 2's signal, and thus search behind the obstacle, which the basic robots or robots with memory could not. To return home it first moves to beacon 2, then to beacon 1 and finally to beacon 0.

The central beacon is assigned the number 0, and to all extents and purposes could be itself a robot permanently in beacon mode). This describes a chain 0-1-2. Note that this sort of beacon-like behaviour is not found in social insects.

Beacon information: The signal emitted by a robot beacon contains two coded pieces of information, being its individual ID number and its beacon number.

Homing capacity: robots within the limited range of another robot beacon can, as in the basic model, move towards it.

Returning home: to return home, i.e. to the central beacon, a robot first goes to the beacon it is locked onto. It then checks for a signal from a beacon of number one less that is within range. There is always at least one, because each robot beacon became a beacon while still within range of a previous robot beacon (unless the chain has been broken - see below). The returning robot then locks onto this beacon (usually its previous beacon's beacon) and repeats the cycle until it has reached beacon zero. Thus a robot that finds a target while within range of beacon 3 of a chain 0-1-2-3 would move to beacon 3, then lock onto the signal from beacon 2, move to beacon 2, and so on until it reaches beacon 0.

In this way the team of robots explores the area rather as a group of tourists in a strange city who leave behind them at each crossroads one of their number to stay in visual contact both with the previous member left behind further back and the remainder of the group going ahead. By this means they can all find their way back to the hotel without having to buy a map or ask the way in a foreign language.

A group of these chain-making robots can potentially explore an area of radius equal to their number times their communication range, which can vary according to the local conditions (such as the presence of obstacles). As long as they avoid moving out of range or sight of their nearest beacon, no-one will get lost, and furthermore they can search behind obstacles lying between themselves and their home (see fig. 1). To use a second analogy, the group behaves very much like an arm with several articulations (the robot beacons) that give it the overall flexibility to reach round corners and into nooks and crannies to find targets with its fingers (the robots still searching at the head of the chain). Note also that the chain can have more than one branch.

By comparison, as the basic model and the model without memory depend on a central beacon, neither can move behind opaque obstacles without getting lost. This means that, depending on the quantity of obstacles present and the penetration or diffusion of the homing signal, large parts of the search area could remain permanently unexplored, whereas chain-making robots can potentially explore the entire foraging area.

In practical terms, of course, how can a robot know in advance that it is moving into a point out of contact with the other beacons without first moving there and getting out of contact, the very thing it is trying not to do? We have assumed the chain-making robot to be capable of retracing its step back to where it was before it moved so as to remain in contact.

This third model explores the option of making the individual robots to a small degree more complicated and interactive, so as to increase the group's capability. Notably the robot beacons assume an individual identity, albeit temporarily, so as to polarise the "field" of beacons to indicate the direction home and outwards. We are currently exploring more indirect means of achieving this without having to impose such an individualisation.

For all their flexibility, the chain-making robots formed have an inevitable drawback, namely that each robot that becomes a link in the chain (i.e. a beacon) is one less robot searching for targets, and this can greatly reduce the discovery rate of smaller groups. Indeed, as the scenario has been explained so far, when the last searching robot at the head of the chain reaches its contact limit with the previous beacon it becomes a beacon itself, and all the robots are thus beacons and no-one is searching.

We have added the following optional behaviours to improve the group's efficiency:

Searchers give up: as the other models, the searching robots return home either when they find a target or when they decide to give up. The probability of giving up is low and constant, and is tested at each time step.

Robots that gave up firstly go home and then return to the head of the chain: upon arriving home a robot that is not carrying a target tries to return to the head of the chain of beacons. To do this it moves to the first beacon it detects (if any). It then moves to the first beacon with a higher number it detects, and so on until it reaches the end of a chain, and then starts searching randomly. This avoids repeatedly searching the area closest to home which is rapidly emptied. Note that when there is more than one branch of the chain, this behaviour leads to the robot choosing at random between them.

Return to last find: while returning home with a target, the robot keeps a list of the beacons it used. When it reaches home it tries to retrace its path to the beacon nearest its last find. As with the robots with memory, this enables the chain to concentrate their activity on richer zones of the search area.

Beacons give up: The aim of this behavioural module is firstly to avoid all the robots getting blocked into beacon mode, and secondly to make the chains more dynamically linked to their harvesting success. To do so, when a searching robot becomes a beacon it initialises a traffic coefficient, t, at a value, for example, of t: $t_0:=10$. This value is constantly decaying, in the sense that at each step it decreases by a fixed fraction, e: $t:=t(1-e)$. Each time a robot carrying a target reaches a beacon on its way home (from beacon to beacon), the value of t increases by a fixed amount t^+: $t:=t+t^+$ (this implies some form of communication between the homing robot and the beacon when the former arrives next to the latter). When t drops below a fixed threshold value, t_T: $t_T<t_0$, this means that no traffic carrying targets has passed this beacon for some time, and the beacon is thus ready to give up and go home. First, however, it must check if it is at the head of the chain. Otherwise, if a robot beacon that was a link in the middle of a chain went home (e.g. beacon 2 in a chain 0-1-2-3-4), the chain would be broken and all the beacons further along the chain (beacons 3 and 4) would be out of contact with the others, i.e lost. The safest check is for the beacon to determine if it can receive any signal other than that of the previous beacon in the chain on which it itself depends to find the way home. If it does not receive another signal then it gives up and goes home, otherwise it stays in place, even though the robot emitting the signal is not necessarily locked onto the beacon preparing to give up. Note that for this check to work, searching robots must also emit a signal indicating that they are searching.

As a final point, a team of chain-making robots is vulnerable to breakdowns in a way that the first two models are not. Since the basic robot and the robot with memory act independently, should one break down or get lost, then the team's work rate will simply decrease proportionately. Should, however, one link in a chain break down, then those further along the chain will immediately become lost. It is also possible that fluctuations in signal strength, the presence of moving obstacles, or other factors can lead to robots becoming temporarily out of contact, with the same consequences for those further along the chain. However, the very nature of the chain-making system, together with the behaviours described next, help the chains to repair themselves rapidly in most cases and considerably limits the time spent lost.

Continual contact checking: All robots regularly check reception of the signal from the beacon they depend on. They memorise the approximate direction and distance of their beacon. If for any reason they no longer receive the signal then they become lost.

Lost robots: A lost robot continually checks to see if it is receiving any beacon's signal. If so it locks onto it, is no longer lost, and becomes a searching robot, unless it was carrying a target in which case it continues home, or unless it is at the limit of signal detection in which case it becomes a beacon itself. Most of the time a robot, either in beacon mode or searching mode, is in range of more than one beacon. Therefore if the one it depends on is no longer emitting, it simply switches to one of the others. When this is not the case, it first moves more or less to where its beacon was, using its memory of approximate direction and distance. This generally brings it into the edge of the range of its ex-beacon's beacon, in which case it itself becomes a beacon, and can thus become a new signal for any other lost robots further along the broken chain. Otherwise it starts moving at random until it enters a beacon's zone of influence. Thus, for example, if beacon 2 in a chain of 0-1-2-3-4-5 breaks down, beacons 3,4, and 5 become lost. Beacon 3 moves towards where beacon 2 was, enters the edge of beacon 1's zone of influence, and becomes a new beacon 2. Similarly beacon 4 moves to where beacon 3 was and enters the new beacon 2's zone of influence, and becomes a beacon 3, and so on, reforming a chain 0-1-2-

3-4 with only a short delay.

This self-repairing capacity gives the chain-making team one important advantage over the other two models. Should the central transmitter of either the basic model or the model with memory break down, then all the robots are irretrievably lost. In the chain-making team, the central beacon is no different from any other beacon, and if it breaks down, then the nearest beacon 1 replaces it, and the chains can reform.

4. Results

Table I shows the average time it takes for one robot to gather one target for different sized teams of the three sorts of robots, estimated from computer simulations. The greater the value, the lower the team's efficiency. Being strongly dependent on the different parameter values, these quantitative results are less important than their relative value, and are presented to illustrate the more general relative performances of the three models and the three group sizes.

The basic robots' search time averages around 7 kilo-robot-steps per find, and does not vary significantly with the team size since they act independently of each other and the environment.

The robots with memory perform much better, especially for the smaller group sizes (search time = 0.6), as they avoid re-searching the area closest to home. The performance decreases with larger teams, since by the time a robot returns to its last find, the region around that find has a greater probability of having been cleared by others.

Also with smaller groups another property emerges. Firstly the members of the team each develop a fidelity to a certain sector of the foraging area, as was expected. This can be seen in figure 2a, which shows an example the average co-ordinates of each robot's finds, for a team of 10 robots. If the robots searched in any zone, then these points would be grouped around the centre of the screen, as can be seen in fig. 2b which shows the same information for robots that are programmed not to return to their last find but to return an equivalent distance at a random direction.

Secondly the sectors to which the different robots have become specialised are most often spread more or less evenly over the search area (see fig. 2a), i.e. the overlapping is minimised. How do these robots split up the

Table I. The average time for one robot to find one target, expressed in 1000 robot steps per find, measured when 75% of the 1000 targets in the 200x200 step search area had been found, averaged over 17-50 simulations per category, for teams (**TS**) of 10, 50 and 200 robots. All robots move one pixel per time step. **Basic robots** (**BR**): p=0.0002 (prob. of giving up and going home per time step). **Robots with memory** (**RM**): p=0.0005, w=1. **Chain-making robots** (**CM**, **CO with opaque obstacles**): p=0.0002, signal range = 20, t_0=2, t_+=30, t_T=1, e=0.001.

The best performers are the robots with memory, especially in small teams, followed closely by the large teams of chain making robots. When opaque obstacles are present such that only 35% of the area is in line-of-sight with the central beacon, chain making robots are the only ones that can capture 75% of the targets, and moreover do so with only slightly less efficiency than without obstacles.

TS	10	50	200
BR	7.3 ±0.04	7.2 ±0.09	7.7 ±0.08
RM	0.6 ±0.01	0.9 ±0.01	1.8 ±0.02
CM	12.3 ±1.14	5.6 ±0.23	2.6 ±0.02
CO	14.1 ±0.75	8.0 ±0.44	3.9 ±0.11

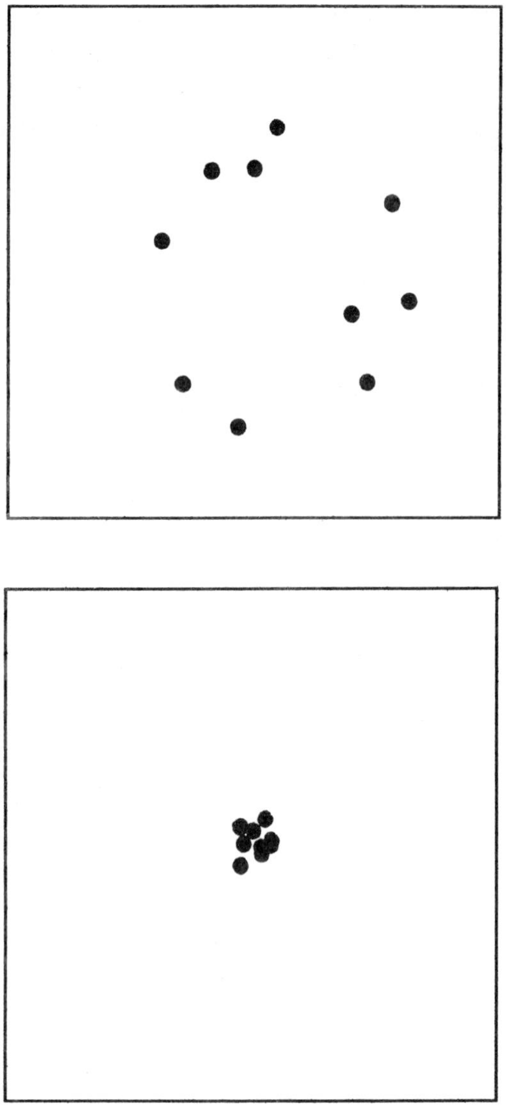

Fig 2a. The average position of each robot's finds, for a team of ten robots with memory (p=0.0005, w=1), for a simulation with 1000 targets randomly distributed in a 200x200 step area, when 75% of the targets have been found. The points are not in the centre but are spread out indicating that the team of robots has divided up the search area, each having a specialised search sector. **Fig 2b**. idem, for robots programmed not to return to the last find but to an equivalent distance in a randomly chosen direction. The points are grouped together around the home, indicating that the robots are not individually specialised to a sector.

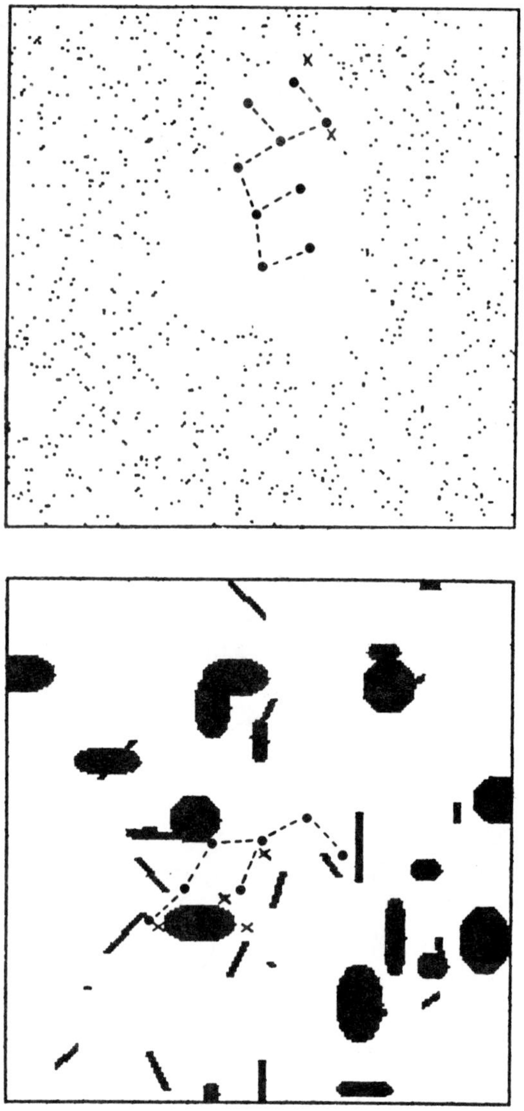

Fig. 3a. A team of 10 chain-making robots early during a simulation (Table I). The small dots are targets (initially 1000 randomly distributed, already a central zone has been cleared). The circles are robots beacons, "linked" as per the dotted lines. The crosses are searching robots. Although each robot's signal range is only $1/10^{th}$ of the area's side, the chains formed by the team can "reach" to the area's edge. **Fig 3b**. Idem with obstacles opaque to the signals (targets not shown). Although only 35% of the area is in line of sight with the home position, the team can move throughout the area, staying in contact via the chains formed.

search area between them when there is no communication between them? The answer is that they do in fact communicate, but indirectly. By taking a target from a point and returning to it, they reduce the target density in that area, and thus reduce the probability that another robot will find a target in the same area and return to it. By their actions on the environment each robot in a sense "repels" the others, and in this way the group develops a more evenly distributed spatial structure that was not programmed into their individual behaviour (see Deneubourg *et al.* 1987 for a similar phenomenon in ant colonies). If there are too many robots, then this property breaks down.

One might expect this spreading out to increase the team's search efficiency, but with the conditions and parameter values tested the robots that return randomly the same distance as that of their last find perform almost as well, with an average search time of 0.7 ±0.01 for a team of 10 robots. In a situation where the targets are constantly arriving, the spreading out would probably be more stable and have a greater effect on the team's efficiency, but this has yet to be tested.

The chain-making robots do not perform well in small groups, as they spend some 80% of their time acting as beacons (see fig. 3a). However, unlike the robots with memory, the search time per robot decreases as the group size increases and proportionally less robots act as beacons. A team of 200 chain-making robots has only a slightly longer search time per robot than 200 robots with memory (2.6 vs 1.8). Note that increasing the signal range of the small group would liberate a number of beacons for searching and thereby increase the group's efficiency.

They really come into their own, however, when placed in an environment with obstacles opaque to the homing signals (see fig. 3b). In this environment only 35% of the area is in sight of the central beacon, and so the other types of robots can only gather a maximum of 35% of the targets. The chain-making robots can gather them all, and do so only slightly slower than in an environment without obstacles.

5. Discussion

While robots able to return to the location of the last find are the best performers, especially in small teams, the chain-making robots perform almost as well in large teams and can function in more difficult environments.

The teams' performances need to be tested in different environments, with for example a strong heterogeneity of the targets' spatial distribution, and with the targets arriving and leaving continually. Furthermore, the task of gathering targets and bringing them back to a central point is only one of the chain-making robots' possible uses. Their ability to form chains and to spread themselves out in an area while remaining in contact with one another, especially in large teams, would make them useful in situations where one wishes to survey or monitor a large area, whose form is not known in advance. For example a team could form a network of burglar detectors or smoke detectors in a warehouse, or could be used to monitor radioactivity or pollution levels in a dangerous zone (see also Wang & Beni, 1988).

There is a certain reverse similarity between the "strategy" followed by the the chain-making teams and that followed, for example, by military supply depôts. The closer one gets to combat zones, the smaller and more temporary the depôts, each being supplied successively from the next depôt further back rather than from a central depôt.

While we have opted here for identical individuals each having a full behavioural repertoire, we could also have envisaged two castes of robots, one of which would form the chains of beacons, with the other searching for and transporting the target items within the chain's signal range. This poses the general problem of castes (see Oster & Wilson, 1978), or division of labour. The advantage of castes is that individuals can be simpler and more specific to their castee's main job than generalists, the disadvantage being that the group loses a certain plasticity by having an *a priori* composition.

Finally, although their different "behavioural modules" described above make the chain-making robots seem rather complicated, in fact, in comparison with the basic robot, the only extra capabilities needed concern the ability to transmit and receive simple short-range signals (e.g. one byte for thier ID and one byte for their mode), plus a small ability to calculate. The R-1 model recently advertised by IS Robotics, for example, is reported to have these capabilities and more besides. The decentralised control of different behaviours within an individual, as proposed by Brooks 1986 and Maes 1990, for example, promise to be able to coordinate large behavioural repertoires in a flexible manner.

Without wishing to minimise, for example, the communication problems that may arise when a dozen robots are all emitting signals in close proximity (i.e several channels may be required), or other problems that only become clear during *in vivo* trials, the three "logical" systems described above are all within the limits of today's know-how. We hope they give an indication as to how teams of robots could be coordinated in a decentralised manner to maximise flexibility, reliability and simplicity without overly sacrificing efficiency.

Acknowledgements

This work was supported in part by the Belgian program on interuniversity attraction poles. J. L. Deneubourg is a fellow of the Fonds National de Recherche Scientifique. We would like to thank the British Petroleum Venture Research Project for their active encouragement.

References

Beckers R., Goss S., Deneubourg J.L., Pasteels J.M. Colony size, communication and ant foraging stategy. *Psyche* 96, 239-256.

Brooks R. 1986. A robust layered control system for a mobile robot. *IEEE J. of Robotics and Automation*, RA-2, 14-23

Deneubourg J.L., Goss S., Fresneau D, Lachaud J.-P., Pasteels J.M. 1987. Self-organisation mechanisms in ant societies (II): learning during foraging and division of labour. In J.M. Pasteels, J.L. Deneubourg eds: From Individual Characteristics to Collective Organisation in Social Insects, Experientia Supplementum 54, 177-196.

Deneubourg J.L., Goss S., Sandini G., Ferrari F, Dario P. 1990. Self-organizing collection and transport of objects in unpredictable environments. In Proc. Japan-USA Symposium on Flexible Automation, in press.

Deneubourg J.L., Goss S. 1989. Collective patterns and decision-making. *Ethology, Ecology and Evolution* 1, 295-311.

Maes P. 1991. A bottom-up mechanism for behaviour selection in an artificial creature. pp 238-246 in: Proc. 1st. International Conference on Simulation of Adaptive Behaviour "From Animals to Animats", J.A. Meyer, S.W. Wilson, eds.

Oster G.F, Wilson E.O. 1978. Caste and Ecology in the Social Insects. Princeton University Press, Princeton.

Wang J., Beni G. 1988. Pattern generation in cellular robotic systems. IEEE symposium on intelligent control, Arlington VA.

LEARNING AND EVOLUTION

Learning, Behavior, and Evolution

Domenico Parisi Stefano Nolfi Federico Cecconi
Institute of Psychology -CNR - Rome
e-mail: domenico@irmkant.Bitnet stiva@irmkant.Bitnet
cecconi@irmkant.Bitnet

Abstract

We present simulations of evolutionary processes operating on populations of neural networks to show how learning and behavior con influence evolution within a strictly Darwinian framework. Learning can accelerate the evolutionary process both (1) when learning tasks correlate with the fitness criterion, and (2) when random learning tasks are used. Furthermore, an ability to learn a task can emerge and be transmitted evolutionarily for both correlated and uncorrelated tasks. Finally, behavior that allows the individual to self-select the incoming stimuli can influence evolution by becoming one of the factors that determine the observed phenotypic fitness on which selective reproduction is based. For all the effects demonstrated, we advance a consistent explanation in terms of a multidimensional weight space for neural networks, a fitness surface for the evolutionary task, and a performance surface for the learning task.

1. Introduction

Are behavior and learning among the causes of evolution? Do they influence the course or the rate of evolution? With reference to behavior Plotkin has written: "Whether behavior is also a cause and not just a consequence of evolution is a significant theoretical issue that has not received the attention it deserves from evolutionary biology" (Plotkin, 1988, pag. 1). He notes that the subject index of Mayr's The Growth of Biological Thought contains only three entries for "behavior". One might add that there is no single entry for "learning".

There are several reasons why the potential causal role of learning and behavior with respect to evolution tends to be ignored by evolutionary biologists, and by biologists generally. One reason is that the orthodox view represented by the Modern Synthesis tends to be reductionist, which implies that the causes and basic mechanisms of evolution are only to be found at the level of genetics. Behavior and learning are too wholistic to be considered as important to understanding the intimate nature of evolutionary processes. Another reason is that the idea that such phenotypic processes as behavior and learning might be among the causes of evolution sounds too Lamarckian, and the rejection of inheritance of lifetime changes in the phenotype is one of the foundations of the Modern Synthesis. A third reason is that behavior and learning are the province not of biology but of psychology and ethology. Biologists are reluctant to admit that the central phenomena studied by their discipline, and the theory of which is the organizing framework for biology (evolution and the theory of evolution), contain processes on which are competent such "soft" disciplines as psychology and ethology.

But there is still another reason that can explain why behavior and learning are not seriously considered as possible causes of evolution within biology. The various claims that have been advanced in the course of the present century in support of the idea that behavior and learning can influence evolution have had a limited empirical basis and, even worse, have been generally formulated in rather vague terms. Therefore, it has been easy for evolutionary biologists to dismiss these claims as irrelevant and to consider the whole issue as marginal at best.

The purpose of this paper is to examine some aspects of the problem "Do learning and behavior influence evolution?" within the framework of neural networks (Rumelhart and McClelland, 1986) and genetic algorithms (Holland, 1975; Goldberg, 1989). The justification for such an enterprise is that one can hypothesize that the theoretical apparatus of the theory of complex dynamic systems (of which neural networks and genetic algorithms are considered here as special applications) and the methodology of computer simulation typically used in research on neural networks and genetic algorithms can help make more precise and testable claims on the role played by learning and behavior in evolution. If we succeed in convincing students of evolution that this hypothesis is a reasonable one, then we will have contributed to eliminating at least the last of the four reasons listed above for ignoring this potentially very important issue.

2. How can learning help evolution

The orthodox view of evolution is that changes due to learning during life are not inherited and, more generally, that learning does not influence evolution. The basis for such a view is the physical separation between the germ cell line and the somatic cell line. Changes due to learning concern somatic cells whereas evolution is restricted to the germinal cells. Since the two types of cells are physically separated, it is impossible that whatever happens to the somatic cells can have an influence on evolution. On the other hand, Baldwin (1896), Waddington (1942), and several others have claimed that there is an interaction between learning and evolution and, more specifically, that learning can have an influence on evolution.

Computer simulations that apply evolutionary methods to populations of neural networks have recently shown that changes during the 'life' of individual neural networks which are not inherited can still have an influence on the course of the evolutionary process. Hinton and Nowlan (1987) have demonstrated how modifying at random the connection weights during life allows the simulated evolutionary process to select networks that are better adapted to the given task. Belew (1989) indicates how the beneficial effect of learning on evolution can increase if the weight changes are not random but are correlated with the task for which the networks are being selected. Ackley and Littman (1991) and Nolfi and Parisi (1991) have shown that when evolution is free to select what networks will learn during their life, useful learning tasks are evolved yielding an increase in evolutionary performance with respect to the situation in which lifetime learning is not allowed. Nolfi and Parisi (1991) also demonstrate how an evolved learning capacity might emerge and then extinguish if it is no longer useful for the evolutionary process.

In order to analyze how learning can help evolution in simulated organisms let us consider the simple artificial organisms described in Nolfi, Elman, and Parisi (1990). Each organism (O) lives in a bidimensional environment containing randomly distributed pieces of food. The organisms are modelled by a feedforward neural network (Figure 1) which basically receives sensory input from the environment concerning the position of the nearest food element and generates as output motor actions that allow the organism to displace itself in the environment.

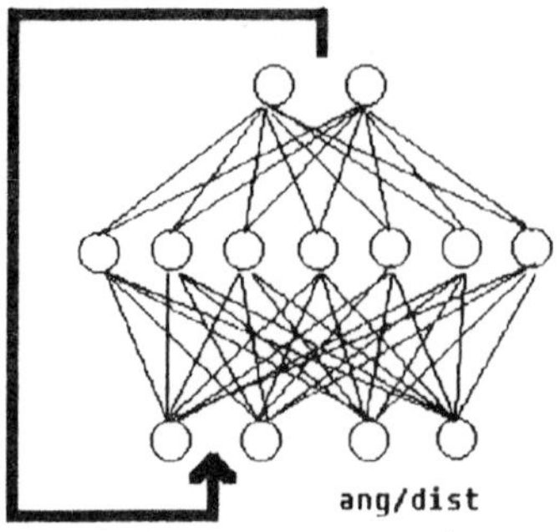

Figure 1. O's architecture. Sensory input is encoded by the 2 input units representing the angle and the distance of the nearest food element (both values are scaled from 0.0 to 1.0). Movement is encoded in the 2 output units that codify four possible actions: go ahead, turn left, turn right, and stay still. Outputs on the motor output units are fed back as additional input at time t + 1.

In each activity cycle activation spreads from the input units through the hidden units to the output units. The kind of movement of the organism which is generated by the network given a certain sensory input depends on the quantitative weights on the connections of the network. Initially these weights are assigned at random and therefore the organism wanders randomly in the environment.

In order to obtain Os which are able to reach food elements in an efficient manner an evolutionary method based on selection and mutation is used. The process starts with 100 Os, all having the same architecture and a different random assignment of connection weights. This is Generation 0 (G0). G0 networks are allowed to "live" for 20 epochs, where an epoch consists of 250 actions in 5 different environments (50 actions in each), for a total of 5000 actions. The environment is a grid of cells with 10 randomly distributed pieces of food. Os are placed in individual copies of the environment, i.e. they live in isolation.

At the end of their life Os are allowed to reproduce. However, only the 20 Os which have accumulated the most food in the course of their random movements are allowed to reproduce by generating 5 copies of their weight matrix. These best ranking individuals have been assigned (for purely random reasons) weight matrices that cause them to sometimes respond to food elements by approaching them. The 20x5 = 100 new Os constitute the next generation (G1). Mutations are introduced in the copying process by selecting at random 5 weights and adding a random value between +1.0 and -1.0 to these weights.

After the Os of G1 are created they also are allowed to live for 5000 cycles. The behavior of these Os differs slightly from that of preceding generation (G0) as a result of two factors. First, the 100 Os of G1 are the offspring (copies) of a subset of the Os of G0. Second, the offspring themselves differ slightly from their parents because of the mutations in their weights. These differences lead to small differences in average food eaten by the Os in G1 with respect to those of G0. At the end of their life the 20 best individuals are allowed to reproduce 5 times, forming G2. The process continues for 50 generations.

Mutations can result in offspring that are better than their parent or offspring that are less good. However, selective reproduction will insure that the former individuals will be more likely to reproduce than the latter. The net result is a progressive increase in food approaching ability due to selective reproduction and random mutations.

Nothing changes in the neural networks during their life up to this point. We then run another set of simulations in which we added a learning task during life. Os learned to predict the sensory consequences of their own actions, i.e. how the sensory information from a food element was going to change when a planned action was actually executed. Using backpropagation (Rumelhart, Hinton, and Williams, 1986) the networks were taught to specify at time T in two additional output units (prediction units) the sensory input that the network will receive at time T+1 (see Figure 2).

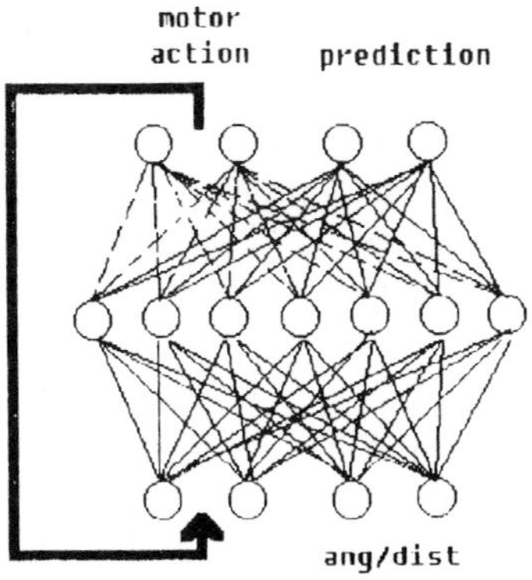

Figure 2. O's architecture. The two additional output units codify O's prediction.

The addition of the learning task during life increases the power of the evolutionary process. Even if none of the changes which occur in the parent's weight matrix as a consequence of learning are transmitted to offspring, populations of Os which evolve with such a learning are able to reach a larger number of food elements than Os evolved without learning (see Figure 3).

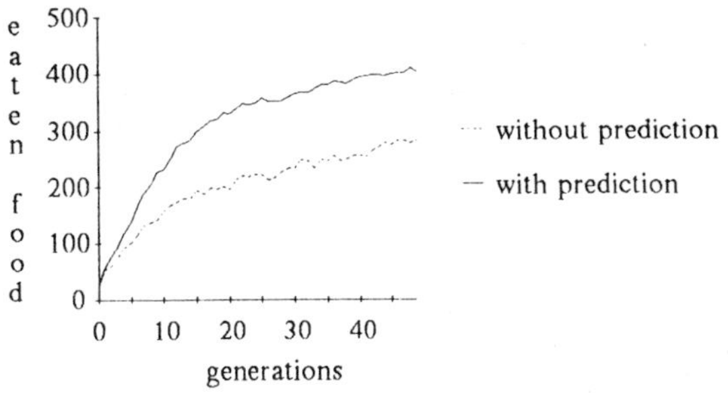

Figure 3. Average number of food elements eaten by successive generations of organisms evolved with and without life-learning. Each of the two curves represents the average performance of 10 different simulations with different random assignment of weights.

It is important to notice that the performance increase is not due to the fact that networks, having the possibility to learn, increase their fitness during their life. Such an increase exists (in other words, learning to predict how food position changes with the organism's actions leads the a better food approaching performance during life) but it is not enough to explain the difference between the two curves. In fact, life learning allows the evolutionary process to evolve networks that perform better at birth, i.e. before learning takes place. This means that learning, in addition to its life-time adaptive function, has an evolutionary function that results in an increase of offspring's fitness.

How can learning during life have an influence on evolution if inheritance is strictly Darwinian (or better, Waismannian) and not Lamarckian? In other words, if the learned changes in connection weights are not inherited and a reproducing individual transmits its intact inherited weight matrix to its offspring? To try to answer this question we must look at the fitness of genotypes in a more abstract way.

We begin by identifying the inherited genotype of an individual with a specification of the weight matrix of the individual's neural network at birth. It is this specification that is transmitted to the individual's offspring if the individual is among those that reproduce. By definition the genotype does not change except for mutations. We can view one particular genotype (weight matrix) as a single point in a multidimensional abstract space. Each dimension of this space corresponds to one particular network connection. Hence, if our networks have N connections, the corresponding space will be an N-dimensional space. A particular network will occupy the position on a dimension that indicates the quantitative weight of the corresponding connection. Therefore, each point in the N-dimensional space represents one particular weight matrix, and all possible weight matrices are represented in the space.

We now assume that each possible genotype (point in the N-dimensional space of weight matrices) has a certain fitness. That is, if an individual with that genotype (weight matrix) is allowed to live in some environment for a certain lifespan, it will generate a behavior which will result in a certain fitness value given a certain fitness criterion[1]. As a consequence, we can conceive of fitness as an additional dimension of the space, with weight matrices with a higher fitness located higher on that dimension than matrices with a lower fitness. Since the additional dimension of fitness is added to a space that already has N dimensions, we will talk of a (multidimensional) fitness "surface". If the fitness surface is "smooth" this means that weight matrices that are near to each other in weight space will have similar fitness values, whereas if the fitness surface is "rugged" one cannot predict what the fitness of a particular weight matrix will be given the fitness of a nearby matrix.

A first generation of randomly generated weight matrices is a collection of randomly distributed points in weight space. Selective reproduction means that the reproducing individuals have weight matrices that correspond to higher points on the fitness surface than those of non-reproducing individuals. Consider now mutations. Mutations mean that a reproducing matrix (parent) is replaced by one or more matrices (offspring) corresponding to points on the fitness surface located in a region of that surface just around the point to which the parent's matrix corresponds[2]. Since mutations are random, offspring matrices are a random sampling of points in that region.

Consider now two very different individuals (weight matrices) corresponding to distant points in weight space, which have the same fitness (hence, the two points are the same height on the fitness surface). Since the two individuals have the same fitness, selective reproduction has no way to choose between them. In fact, if there were no mutations it would be irrelevant from an evolutionary point of view to choose between them. In such a case the offspring of one individual would be exact copies of their parent and no consequence for the next generation's average fitness would result from choosing one of the two individuals rather than the other. However, since there are mutations, an individual will be replaced by individuals which are similar to their parent but not exact copies. More specifically, the offspring's weight matrices will sample the region surrounding the parent's point on the fitness surface.

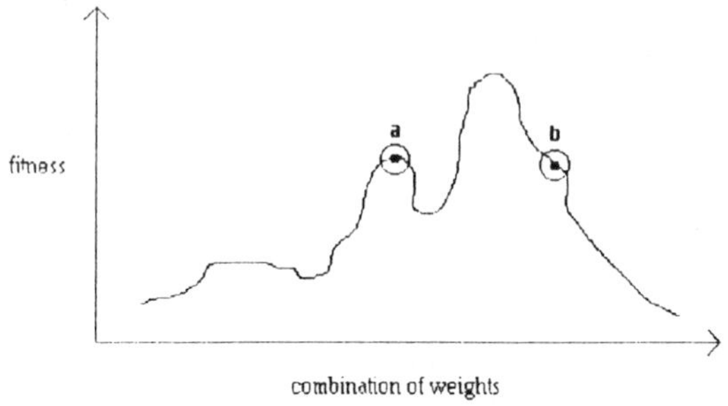

Figure 4. Fitness of all possible weights matrices. Point B has a better surrounding region than point A even if the fitness values of the two points are identical. For pratical reasons the N dimensions of the weight space as represented as a single dimension.

One consequence of this is that, although the two individuals correspond to points that are the same height on the fitness surface, the average fitness of the next generation will depend on the nature of the two regions surrounding the two points. The two points (parents) may be equally high but the region surrounding one of them can include points (offspring) that are on the average higher than the points in the surrounding region of the other (see Figure 4). It would then be appropriate for the selection process to select the individual with a better surrounding region rather than the other since the offspring of the former individual will be on average better than the offspring of the latter. More generally, it would be useful for the selection process to know the nature of the surrounding regions of candidates for reproduction since the fitness of offspring is more important than the fitness of their parents from the point of view of the next generation's average fitness. Selective reproduction per se has no means to know that. It sees the heights of candidates for reproduction on the fitness surface but it does not see their surrounding regions. Our hypothesis is that this is exactly what learning does: learning illuminates the regions on the fitness surface surrounding the points on that surface corresponding to candidates for reproduction, and makes what it sees available to the selection mechanism. The result is that selection is improved and there may be a positive influence of learning on evolution[3].

Learning involves weight changes and therefore it implies a movement in weight space of the point representing an individual matrix. If an individual X has a better surrounding region than another individual Y, even if both start from the same height on the fitness surface, by moving in weight space (learning) X is more likely to end up on a higher point on the fitness surface than Y, and therefore more likely to be selected for reproduction.

Given this sort of analysis, even random changes in the weight matrix during life-time, are enough to ensure the selection, on average, of the better between two individuals that have the same fitness but correspond to points on the fitness surface with surrounding regions of different quality. As a consequence, random changes in weights during life should results in a positive effect on evolution and this is exactly what Hinton and Nowlan (1987) have found. We have run some simulations in which individual networks are taught by using randomly generated teaching inputs on the two additional output units (see Figure 2), and in this case too there is a positive influence of learning on evolution, even if the improvement is less great than in the case of prediction learning (see Figure 5).

It remains to be explained why learning a task such as predicting the consequences of one's own actions, which is correlated with the task for which organisms are selected, results in a larger beneficial effect on evolution.

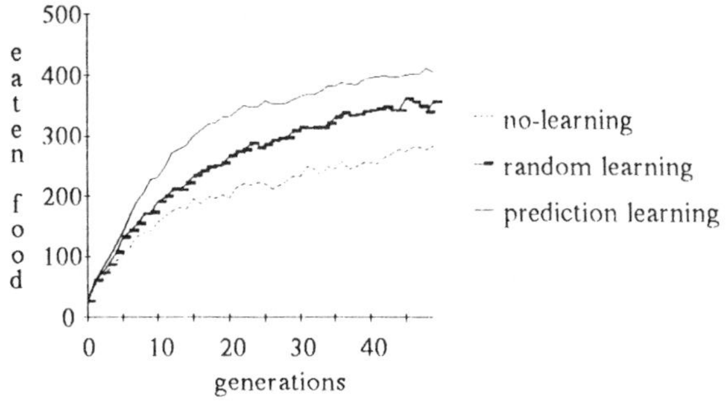

Figure 5. Average number of food elements eaten by successive generations of organisms evolved without life learning, with random learning, and with prediction learning. Each of the three curves represents the average performance of 10 different simulations with different random assignments of weights.

Our hypothesis is that some types of explorations of surrounding regions can be more "intelligent" than others, in the sense that they preferentially explore the sections of the surrounding region with good fitness points. If such points exist, i.e. if there are points in the surrounding region of an individual that have a higher fitness than the individual's fitness, an intelligent exploration of the surrounding region would increase the reproduction chances of such an individual. Individuals located in regions with such high fitness points should be preferred by the selection process because they will have some probability of generating at least some offspring better than themselves. Exploring an individual's surrounding region in such a way that sections with higher fitness points can be detected allows exactly that. It allows the selection process to prefer an individual located in a region with higher fitness points than itself to another individual even if the two regions globally include points with the same average fitness (see Figure 6). In the situation depicted in Figure 6, random learning (i.e. random exploration of the surrounding region) would not confer to point B more reproductive chances than to point A. If we want point B to be selected rather than A, since it is more likely to have better offspring than itself, we need an intelligent exploration of the surrounding regions, i.e. a movement of the point on the fitness surface such that the point is more likely to end up on a higher fitness level if there is such level.

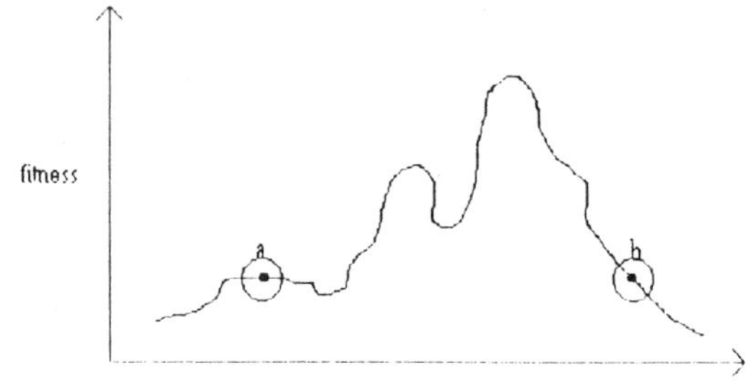

Figure 6. Fitness of all possible weights matrices. Point B has A better surrounding region than point A, because in its surrounding region there are points with higher fitness than points in B's surrounding region, even if the two points have identical fitness values and identical surrounding regions on average.

This we believe is what takes place in the simulations with prediction learning. Non-random learning tasks have a performance surface which is analogous to the fitness surface of evolutionary tasks. Each specific weight matrix corresponds to a particular point (height) on the performance surface for the given learning task. If the performance surface of a certain learning task and the fitness surface of a certain evolutionary task (as defined by a certain fitness criterion) are correlated, i.e. a matrix of weight which is good at the learning task is also good at the evolutionary task, and viceversa, then learning the task during life will have a stronger effect on evolution than just random learning. The reason is that learning the task implies weight changes that are also useful from the point of view of evolutionary fitness. Hence, by moving during learning to higher positions on the performance surface of the learning task, point B in Figure 6 will be simultaneously pushed toward higher positions on the fitness surface - which is impossible for point A. The net result is that B will have more chances of reproduction - which is useful from the point of view of evolution.

It is interesting to note that if one allows the evolutionary emergence of the life-time learning task rather than arbitrarily deciding what is the task at the outset, as in Ackley and Littman (1991) and Nolfi and Parisi (1991), evolution can select the learning tasks which is most appropriate for the displacement of points in weight space. In other words, it is plausible to expect that the learning task will change, at the evolutionary time-scale, in order to obtain the most intelligent exploration of the surrounding regions of individual points. This actually happens in the computer simulations described in Nolfi and Parisi (1991).

3. Indirect inheritance of acquired characters

In the preceding section we showed that, in our simulated organisms, learning can help the evolution of adaptive behavior and we discussed how this effect can be explained without postulating the inheritance of acquired characters. The existence of a phenomenon of this type was postulated by Waddington (1942). This is one aspect of the possible interaction between evolution and learning. In the present section we will examine another related aspect of this interaction, that is, we will try to figure out if learning some ability during life can facilitate the acquisition of that ability in successive generations. In other words, we want to demonstrate that a learning ability can be indirectly transmitted to descendants even if the inheritance mechanism remains strictly Darwinian and individuals are not selected for that learning ability.

If we analyze the results of the simulations described in the previous section and in Nolfi, Elman, and Parisi (1990), we find some evidence of inheritance of acquired characters. Figure 7 graphs the average error curve for the prediction task learned during life by Os belonging to the first and to the last generation. Although both groups of Os start from an identical error level at the beginning of their life (i.e. there is no inheritance of the capacity to predict at birth), the Os of the last generation learn more of the prediction task than the Os of the first generation. In other words, in a population of Os that learn to predict the sensory consequences of their own actions during their life there is an observed increase in the ability to learn the task across generations. Hence, we can conclude that there is inheritance of the <u>ability to learn</u> the particular task, although not directly of the <u>ability to perform</u> the task.

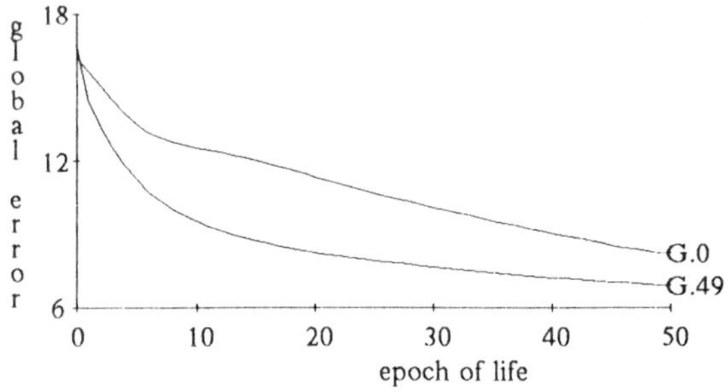

Figure 7. Global error on the prediction task as a function of epochs of training for naive Os (i.e. Os of generation 0) and evolved Os (i.e. Os of generation 49).

How such inheritance of a capacity to learn to perform a task might be explained? The answer could be that, as we have already suggested, the evolutionary task of approaching food elements and the learning task of predicting how the position of a food element changes with the organism's actions, are correlated. In other words, a weight matrix which is good for the first task is also good for the second task. In fact, as detailed in Nolfi, Elman, and Parisi (1990), it can be empirically demonstrated that in many cases input stimuli must be classified in the same manner for both the prediction and the approaching tasks. Hence, the same set of weights may be appropriate for both tasks. This kind of explanation does not require us to postulate any inheritance of acquired characters. As we have shown in the paper just cited, even populations of organisms which evolve without learning during their life the prediction task do learn this task better in later generations than purely random organisms.

This explanation assumes that there is inheritance of the ability to learn a particular task only if the learning task is correlated with the evolutionary task, that is, with the task that dictates who will reproduce and who won't. To test this hypothesis we run a new set of simulations in which Os had to learn during their life a task which presumably is not correlated with the task for which Os are selected. Our choice has been the XOR task. At each time step Os, in addition to generating an useful output on the motor output units, are taught by backpropagation to generate on an additional output unit a value of 0 if both input units have an activation value which is greater or less than .5, and a value of 1 otherwise (see Figure 8).

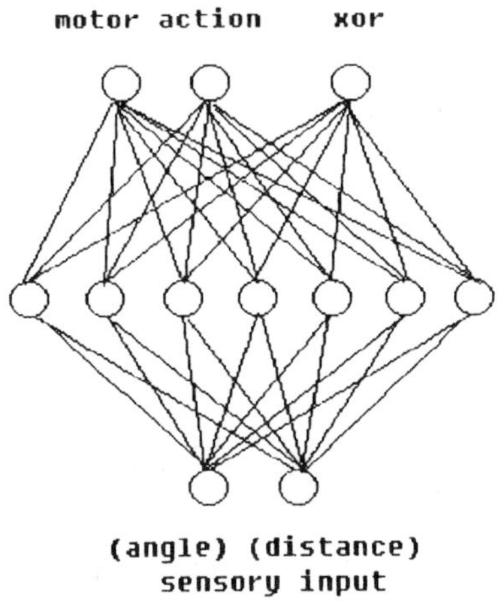

Figure 8. Network architecture for Os that learn the XOR task in addition to being selected for generating the appropriate motor actions in response to sensory stimuli. Sensory input is encoded by the 2 input units representing the angle and the distance of the nearest food element. Movement is encoded in the 2 output units that specify the amount and direction of turn and the length of the step forward. (At each time step Os can turn from 90 degrees left to 90 degrees right and then move from 0 to 5 cells forward.) The third output unit is the response unit for the XOR task.

If the previous explanation is correct we should expect that learning the XOR task during life should not influence how the task is learned by successive generations, that is, that there is no inheritance of the ability to learn the XOR task, since this task is not correlated with the evolutionary task of reaching food. Contrary to this expectation, we found that Os of successive generations are able to learn the XOR task better and faster than the Os of previous generations (see Figure 9). In other words, a capacity to learn the XOR task is genetically transmitted even if the weight changes that result from learning are not transmitted and the ability to perform the XOR task does not correlate with the capacity for which Os are selected.

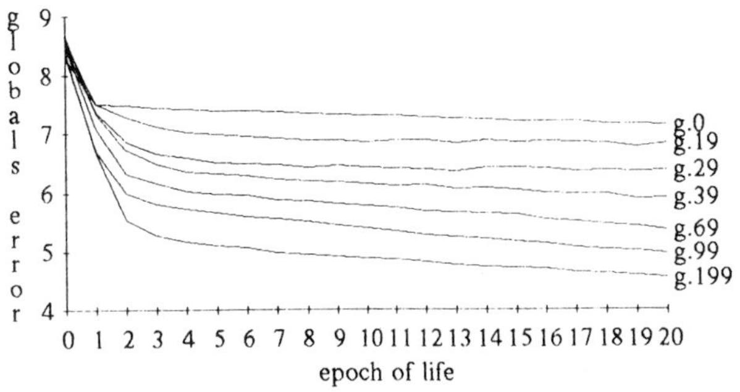

Figure 9. Global error on the XOR task as a function of epochs of life. The error curves of several generations are represented. Each curve is the average result of 10 simulations each starting from different initial random assignment of connection weights. Global error at epoch 0 is calculated by testing Os for an epoch of life without letting back-propagation operate.

Although the correlation between the learning task and the evolutionary task can be a (partial) explanation of the inheritance of the ability to learn the learning task when such correlation exists, it is clear that there can be inheritance of a learning ability even in the absence of this correlation and therefore we need another explanation for the case in which the learning task is not correlated with the evolutionary task.

A possible explanation which is consistent with our previous explanation of the influence of learning on evolution could be the following. We defined two tasks as correlated if it is probable that, given an arbitrary point in weight space, the performance of this weight matrix on both tasks will be equally good or equally bad. However, we should expect that, even when two tasks are not globally correlated, there may exist some sub-regions of weight space in which the two tasks are more correlated than in other regions. Individuals located in these more correlated regions will be more likely to reproduce because learning (moving to a higher position on the performance surface of the learning task) would involve moving to a higher position of the fitness surface (see Figure 9). But since these reproducing individuals are located in correlated regions, an increase in the evolutionary ability (approaching food) across generations will be accompanied by a parallel increase in the ability to learn the life-time task (doing the XOR task).

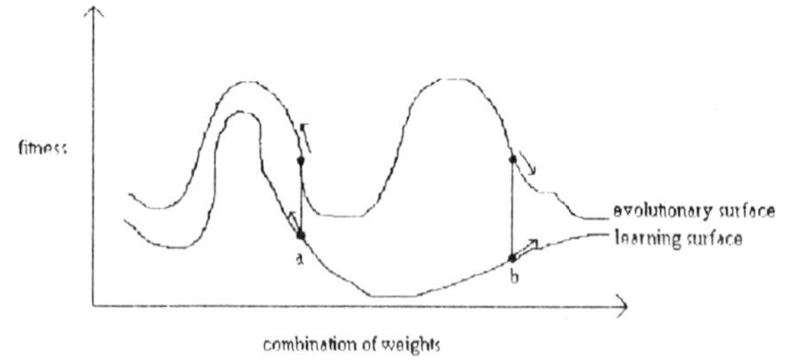

Figure 10. Fitness surface for the evolutionary task and performance surface for the life-learning task for all possible weights matrices. Life-time movements due to learning are represented as arrows. Point A is in a region in which the two surfaces are correlated. As a consequence, A has more probability to be selected that B even if A and B have the same fitness on the evolutionary surface at birth, since the learning task is more likely to cause an increase in the fitness of A than in the fitness of B.

We conclude that even the ability to learn arbitrary tasks can be genetically transmitted because evolution will progressively select individuals that lie in those sub-regions of weight space that correspond to correlated segments of the learning task surface and of the fitness surface.

4. The influence of behavior on evolution: Self-selection of input stimuli

So far we have assumed a notion of genetic fitness in terms of which, given a certain fitness criterion, each genetically transmitted weight matrix is assigned a fixed fitness value. In our case for each given weight matrix there is a corresponding single value on the fitness surface which is the number of food elements eaten during life. However, this is a simplification in that what is actually observed and used by the selective reproduction mechanism is not this hypothetical genetic fitness but a specific phenotypic fitness value. For each assumed genetic fitness value there may be various actually observed phenotypic values depending on a number of additional factors including (a) the environment in which an individual happens to live, (b) the experiences the individual happens to have in that environment, and (c), in so far as the behavior of the individual determines these experiences and in some cases changes the environment itself, the behavior of the organism.

We won't consider the role in evolution of all these additional factors that determine the phenotypic fitness of individuals on which the evolutionary process is based, but we will restrict ourselves to a particular aspect of the role of the behavior of the organism in determining the course of evolution.

Our starting point is that our organisms are ecological neural networks, i.e. neural networks that live and learn in an environment (Parisi, Cecconi, and Nolfi, 1990). The input to a network at each time step is not arbitrarily decided by the researcher but is a function of the structure of the initially defined environment and of the behavior of the organism in that environment. More specifically, the sensory input to an O (angle and distance of the nearest food element) depends on the local distribution of food but also on what has been the motor output of the network in the previous cycle. In other words, in ecological networks Os can control input stimuli with their behavior.

Now there are at least two different strategies that can be followed to maximize the number of food elements eaten. One strategy is to increase one's capacity to respond in an efficient way to all kinds of input stimuli. The other strategy is to develop a capacity to respond efficiently to a subset of input stimuli and then behave in such a way that one is more likely to encounter this subset of stimuli rather than the other ones. We have analyzed the data of our previous simulations to test the hypothesis that Os are able to follow the second strategy, which implies an important role of behavior in determining the phenotypic fitness of individuals.

We divided the input stimuli Os can receive during their life into 10 classes that correspond to different amplitudes of the angle of the currently perceived food element, and we calculated the frequency with which stimuli belonging to each of the 10 classes are perceived by a particular O, which is capable of a very good performance in reaching food elements (Nolfi and Parisi, in press).

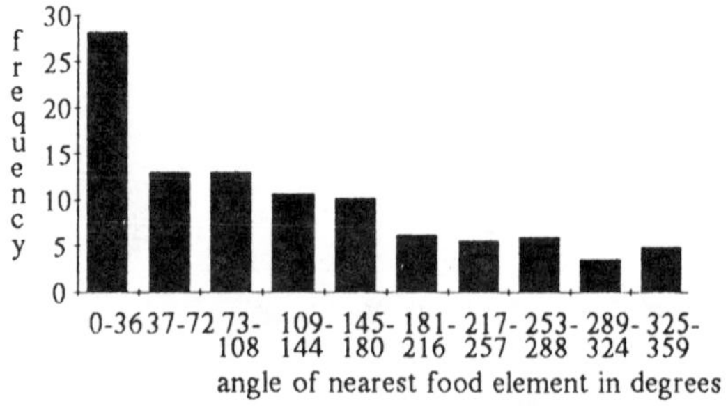

Figure 11. Percentage of occurrence of 10 classes of stimuli during 5000 actions of a particular O.

As Figure 11 shows, different classes of stimuli have very different frequencies of occurrence. For the particular individual that we have examined (other individuals may have different frequency distributions), stimuli with a very small angle (i.e. stimuli just on the right of O's facing direction) have very high frequencies while stimuli with a very large angle (i.e. stimuli just on the left of O's facing direction) have very low frequencies. At this point we can look at the O's performance for each class of stimuli. Since our Os are being selected for their ability to approach food, we define the goodness of the performance in response to each particular stimulus class as the amount of decrease in the distance between O and the stimulus (food element) after O's action.

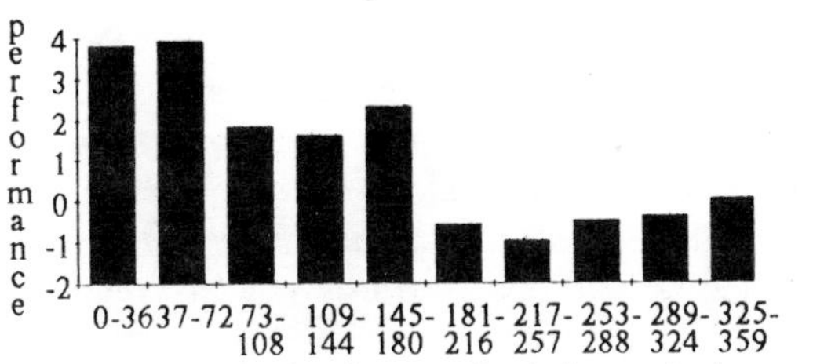

Figure 12. Average performance of the same O for each class of stimuli.

As Figure 12 shows, O reacts in a more efficient way to stimuli with small angles than to stimuli with large angles with respect to O's facing direction. This implies that O has developed a behavior which allows it to be exposed, most of the time, to stimuli to which it is able to react in an efficient way[4].

We can also measure how much of the O's performance can be explained as an ability to select the most appropriate stimuli and how much as an ability to correctly react to input stimuli. The results of this analysis are shown in Figure 13. The average performance of the O in the standard situation (i.e. the situation in which the stimulus at time t depends on O's action at time t-1) is plotted against the average performance of the same O obtained by generating each time a new stimulus in a random position with respect to O.

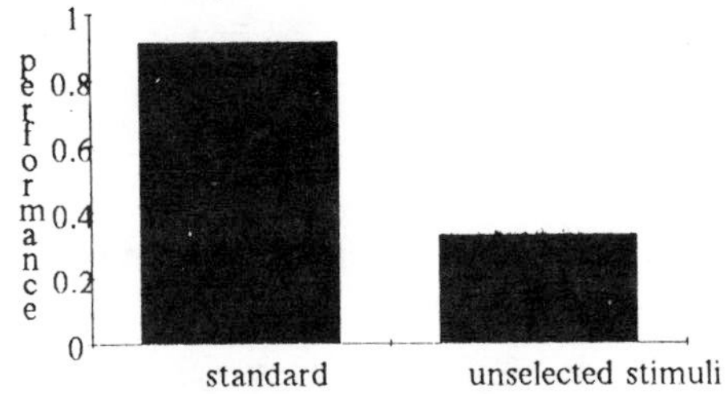

Figure 13. Average performance of an O which can indirectly select the incoming input stimuli compared with the performance of the same O when it is positioned, at each time step, in a new arbitrary situation.

The large loss in performance obtained when O is deprived of the possibility to indirectly select the input stimuli shows how this ability can be important in explaining O's evolved behavior. This can also explain why an ability to react equally efficiently to all classes of stimuli does not emerge evolutionarily. Os will still benefit from acquiring a capacity to react efficiently to all classes of stimuli, because infrequent stimuli to which Os do not react efficiently may still appear. On the other hand, the beneficial effect of such a generalized capacity would be relatively small when compared with the more specialized capacity to react efficiently to self-selected stimuli, so that there would not be enough accumulated evolutionary pressure for the generalized capacity to emerge.

5. Conclusions

In the last few years, thanks to the large increases in available computational power, the "artificial life" experimental approach to the study of natural evolutionary phenomena has spread in the scientific community. Within this approach, neural networks and genetic algorithms have been the most common tools used to simulate, respectively, the individual organisms and the natural evolutionary process. (In addition to the work already cited see: Miller, and Todd, 1990; Belew, McInerney, Schraudolph, 1990).

This simulative approach has already produced many interesting results that have contributed to a clarification of important arguments discussed in the evolutionary biology literature. This despite the fact that the simulative models currently implemented are extremely simplified with respect to the real phenomena.

In this paper we have offered new results on the interaction between learning, behavior, and evolution, and a general and consistent explanation of the various findings. We have shown that life-time learned changes can have an influence on evolution although it remains true that changes that are correlated with the criterion used for selective reproduction have a larger influence than random changes. We also have demonstrated how an ability to learn some task can emerge and be transmitted evolutionarily both for tasks that are correlated with the reproduction criterion and for uncorrelated tasks. Finally, we have indicated how behavior - more specifically self-selection of input stimuli - can influence evolution in that behavior is one factor that determines the observed phenotypic fitness on which selective reproduction is based.

References

Ackley, D.E. and Littman, M.L. 1991. *Proceedings of the Second Conference on Artificial Life*. Addison-Wesley: Reading, MA.

Baldwin, J.M. 1896. A new factor in evolution. *American Naturalist*, **30**, 441-451.

Belew, R.K. 1989. Evolution, learning, and culture: computational metaphors for adaptive algorithms. CSE *Technical Report* CS89-156. University of California, San Diego.

Belew, R.K., McInerney, J., Schraudolph, N. 1990. Evolving networks: using the genetic algorithm with connectionist learning. CSE *Technical Report* CS89-174. University of California, San Diego.

Goldberg, D.E. 1989. *Genetic Algorithms in Search, Optimization, and Machine Learning*. New York: Addison-Wesley.

Hinton, G.E., Nowlan S.J. 1987. How Learning Guides Evolution. *Complex System*, **1**, 495-502.

Holland, J.J. 1975. *Adaptation in Natural and Artificial Systems*. Ann Arbor, Michigan: University of Michigan Press.

Miller, G.F. and Todd, P.M. 1990. Exploring adaptive agency I: theory and methods for simulating the evolution of learning. In D.S. Touretzky, J.L. Elman, T.J. Sejnowski and G.E. Hinton (eds.), *Proceedings of the Connectionist Models Summer School*. San Matteo, CA: Morgan Kaufmann.

Menczer, F. and Parisi, D. 1990. "Sexual" reproduction in neural networks. *Technical Report* PCIA-90-06. Institute of Psychology, C.N.R. Rome.

Menczer, F. and Parisi, D. In press. Evidence of hyperplanes in the genetic learning of neural networks. *Biological Cybernetics*.

Nolfi, S., Elman, J, and Parisi, D. 1990. Learning and evolution in neural networks. CRL *Technical Report* 9019. University of California, San Diego.

Nolfi, S., and Parisi, D. 1991. Auto-teaching: neural networks that develop their own teaching input. *Technical Report* PCIA-91-03. Institute of Psychology, C.N.R. Rome.

Nolfi, S., and Parisi, D. In press. Self-selection of input stimuli as a way of improving performance. *Proceedings of the Workshop on Neural Networks in Robotics*. Los Angeles, CA: Kluwer Academic Publishers

Parisi, D., Cecconi, F., Nolfi, S. 1990. Econets: Neural Networks that Learn in an Environment. *Network*, **1**, 149-168.

Plotkin, H.C. 1988. *The role of behavior in evolution*. Cambridge, Mass.: MIT Press.

Rumelhart, D.E., Hinton G.E., and Williams, R.J. 1986. Learning internal representations by error propagation. In D.E. Rumelhart, and J.L. McClelland, (eds.), *Parallel Distributed Processing*. Vol.1: Foundations. Cambridge, Mass.: MIT Press.

Rumelhart, D.E. and McClelland, J.L. 1986. *Parallel Distributed Processing*. Cambridge, Mass.: MIT Press.

Todd, P.M. and Miller, G.F. 1991. Exploring adaptive agency II: simulating the evolution of associative learning. In: J.A. Meyer and S.W. Wilson (eds), *From Animals to Animats*. Cambridge, MA: MIT Press/Bradford Books.

Waddington, C.H. 1942. Canalization of development and the inheritance of acquired characters. *Nature*, **150**, 563-565.

---

[1] We will see later in the paper that talking of the fitness of genotypes is inaccurate and it ignores an important aspect of the processes involved in evolution. However, for the moment we can be satisfied with what has been said.

[2] This is not true in the case of sexual reproduction and genetic recombination because in this case offspring can have a very different weight matrix from that of each of their parents. On sexual reproduction in neural networks, see Menczer and Parisi 1990; in press).

[3] A similar explanation has been given by Hinton and Nowlan (1987).

[4] Other Os develop different preferences in stimulus selection (for example left stimuli can be preferred to right ones) but all react better to stimuli they indirectly select more often.

IMMUNE NETWORK AND ADAPTIVE CONTROL

Hugues Bersini
IRIDIA - Universite Libre de Bruxelles - CP 194/6
50, Av. Franklin Roosevelt
1050 Bruxelles - Belgium

Abstract

This paper describes an attempt to spread further the inspiration gained from the knowledge of biological systems for engineering applications. New lessons addressed to the control of complex processes might derive from elements of the immune system comprehension. Important points inherent to the immune functions are transposed, re-interpreted and analysed in an adaptive control perspective. They are: viability, distribution, reinforcement learning, optimization, adaptability and memory. Several resemblances will be pointed out with the Q_learning method as well as with classifiers system principles.

1 Introduction

This paper describes an attempt to spread further the inspiration gained from the knowledge of biological systems for engineering applications. After the connectionist models and the evolutionary based mechanisms (Genetic Algorithms (GA), Classifiers Systems (CFS) and Evolutionary Strategies (ES)), new lessons addressed to the control of complex processes might derive from elements of the immune system comprehension. The connections with the voluminous biological knowledge of the Immune Network (IN) structure and functions will not be detailed except by telling that the "guiding" model has been proposed and developed by Varela et al. (1988, 1989, 1990). A previous work (Bersini and Varela, 1990) discussed several essential and exploitable qualities characteristic of the immune function (and likely to be compared to their specific counterparts in the larger family of evolutionary systems): an interesting search algorithm, a large adaptive and learning capacity and a network-based endogenous selective memory. However the focus was not on control but on adaptive problem solving with a larger concern and with numerous biological connections whereas the emphasis here will be laid straight on adaptive control of complex processes.

Important points inherent to the IN functions and present in the Varela's model will be transposed, re-interpreted and analysed in an adaptive control perspective. They are: viability, distribution, reinforcement learning, optimization, adaptability and memory. Some of these points have already been integrated in various fruitful methodologies and been the object of a large but scattered literature (salient links with the Barto and Sutton works (1983, 1990) as well as with classifiers system principles will be stressed (Holland, 1986)). This paper, remaining purposely at a very abstract and unformalised level, aims to concentrate all these points within a same framework in a way faithful to the biological reality. Preliminary results which concern separately some of these points will be sketched (for simple but illustrative problems like the well-known cart-pole application), however their simultaneous consideration is still in progress.

2 General Approach

Suppose the process to be controlled characterized by a state vector $X(t) = \{x_i(t)\}$ represented in the state space R^n. This state space is partitioned into several sub-zones or cells. Each variable x_i has its domain of variation divided in K_i intervals: $[x_i^m(k), x_i^M(k)]$ with $x_i^M(k) = x_i^m(k+1)$. Then, the total number of cells is $\prod_i K_i$. Figure 1a illustrates such partition for a two variables process.

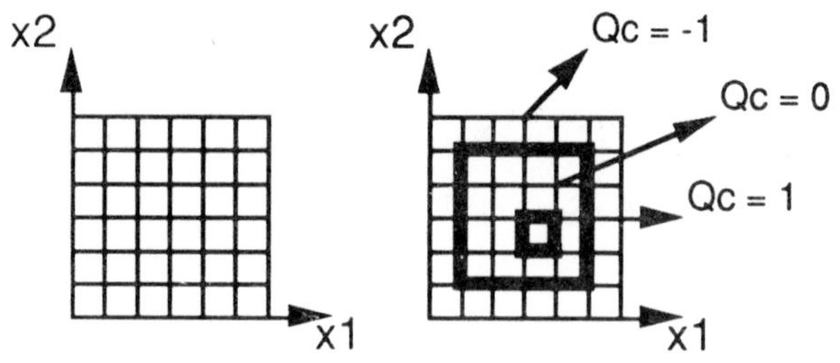

a) b)

Fig.1

3 Viability

A domain of viability V is a specific zone of the state space in which the process must indefinitely remain: X(t) C V. This notion of viability although appearing to relax classical engineering objectives proner to optimize than to keep viable convenes more adequately to the biological reality. J.P Aubin (1989) is constructing a complete mathematical framework in order to formalize this notion (the design of control laws for nonlinear processes with state constraints) and its possible exploitation for macrosystems arising typically in economics, biology and complex plants. This notion of viability is more meaningful for biological systems than for applications which require the introduction of an a priori finality and of a consequent associated fitness function. Here the aim of the control is no more to drive the process, by means of feedback gradient ascent mechanisms, to a precise target but rather to keep it within certain limits. No error-based feedback is required but just a punishment at the frontiers of the viable zone instead.

In (Varela, Sanchez and Coutinho, 1989) the connections between the immune network autonomous dynamic and this notion of viability are introduced and discussed. The advocated viewpoint demands to move beyond the immune system as a basic defense system, to one where the internal self-consistency is the central issue. It is explained how the recruitment of new species in the system is akin to a meta-control whose aim is to keep the concentration of the species in a certain domain of viability so as to preserve continuously the identity of the system.

In an engineering perspective, this constraint of viability might relax an objective of optimization for processes either too complex or interacting with an open, hard to formalize and unpredictable environment. On the other hand such constraint fits the objectives of reliability and safety which are generally stated via the establishment of a bounded zone for some variables of the process.

In the present approach the zone of viability will be one of the cells or a certain union of these cells (see fig.1b). Other types of configuration are equally possible. For each cell c, a quality measure is defined Q_c. For instance $Q_c=0$ for the cells in the zone of viability, and $Q_c = f(d(c,V))$ (where d(c,V) is a certain distance between the cell c and the zone of viability, f is inversely related to d and < 0) for the cells outside the zone. Revised with this viability perspective, the Barto, Sutton and Anderson's control of the cart-pole (1983) fixes a zone of viability for both the angle and the position. Outside the zone, the quality is -1. A third zone could be defined as a preferential zone, contained in the zone of viability, with the quality of its cells defined in]0,1]. For instance, Sutton's Dyna method (1990) teaches a robot to reach a target while avoiding to bump into obstacles. The quality of the preferential target cell is 1.

4 Distribution

Since the Selfridge's Pandemonium updated today into the blackboard methodology, the idea of distributed control is nothing very new in AI. It participates to this recent enthusiasm for auto-organising systems demonstrating emergent functionalities (Forrest, 1991) like an Hopfield net or a colony of insects. It is deeply involved in Minsky's society of minds and in Brooks' subsumption architecture. Roughly each actor has a very simple and localised responsibility and a very localised access to the information both when acting and when improving itself from the results of its act. The larger the distribution, the easier a future hardware parallel implementation. The local communication existing among the actors often amounts to trivial excitatory or inhibitory signals. The improvement of each actor depends on the behaviour of its closest neighbours namely the system exhibits local plasticity. The interesting resulting behaviour is an holistic phenomenon. Each actor "has no view" on the final objective it contributes to satisfy (here to keep the process viable).

In the present methodology each cell lodges a certain amount of operators liable to act only when the process accesses that specific cell. Complementary works are in progress to leave the control to discover alone an economic but satisfactory partition of the state space. This partition appears to be a crucial issue for 1) the quality of the control 2) the speed of learning (various experiments have shown that changing the frontiers of the cells can dramatically decrease the learning period) 3) the input generalization capability (for an interesting treatment of this last problem see Chapman and Kaebling, 1991). An operator is a function of the state vector and is characterized by some parameters to optimize: $W=(w_i)$ (W is then a point in a certain search space). The symbol for an operator is $O_c(W)$. Fig.2 illustrates this last point for linear operators acting in each cell i.e the control parameter $u = w_1x_1 + w_2x_2$.

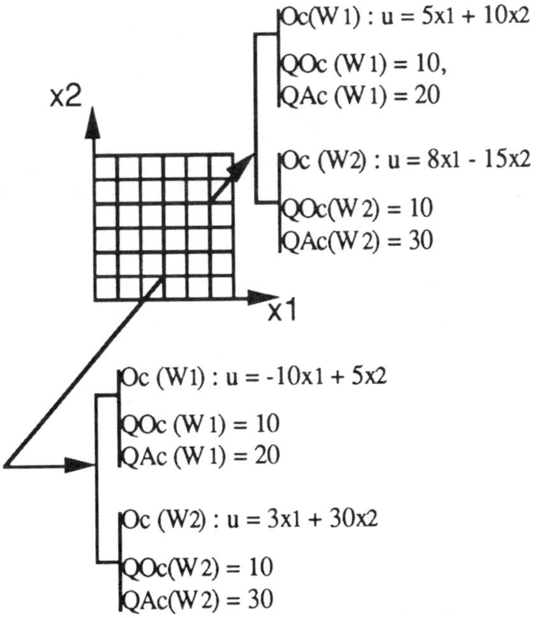

Fig. 2

Each operator is further characterized by two values: its quality $QO_c(W)$ and its adequacy $QA_c(W)$. In order to account for the various failure states in which the process to control can be, several actors can act in a same cell. When the process enters in a cell, the selection of the operator is achieved on the basis of its quality and its adequacy to be discussed later. With regard to the nature of the distribution, notice the similarities with the boxes method and the Barto, Sutton and Anderson's control of the cart-pole (1983) (for this last application, the only possible operators in each cell are two forces : -10 N or 10 N to exert on the cart, namely a bang-bang control).

Distributed control can achieve two different kinds of objective: 1) sequential problems where at any time only one operator is acting. The paper concrete part will be restricted to them and 2) cooperative controls where different operators can act simultaneously on different parameters of the process. The general methodology described in this paper although currently limited to the first category of problems could easily be extended to the second one.

The basic learning problem turns to be the discovery in each cell of the appropriate operators i.e the ones which collectively guarantee the attainment of the global objective: keep the process viable. For clarity's sake, the process will be considered stable i.e one and only one operator will have to be found out in each cell. The learning is performed through two different optimization strategies which differ by their nature and their temporal scale. The first one is a rapid strategy. Initially a set of random operators is provided in each cell. A reinforcement learning aims to discover in each cell the best operator to satisfy the global objective. Formally this research boils down to a stochastic learning automata problem (see Barto, 1990) and is very similar to the type of problem reinforcement learning is generally concerned with.

The second one is a slow strategy. Either if the solution was not present in this first random set of operators or if the current solution can be improved, a second set of operators can be "injected" in the cells and a next phase of reinforcement learning be initiated. And so on the reinforcement learning proceeds with intermittent renewal of some operators. We'll see later the achievement of this injection by means of a recruitment mechanism largely inspired by the immune meta-dynamics (Varela, Sanchez and Coutinho, 1989; Stewart and Varela, 1990).

Fig.3 illustrates these two learning strategies. It is worth mentioning that the methodology described here enters in a large family of biologically-inspired systems whose common feature is a three time-scales dynamics (a state dynamic + the two learning mechanisms: a parameter dynamic and a graph dynamic, see Farmer, 1991) and which comprises: GENET (Hebbian learning + GA for optimizing neural net structure), CFS (Bucket Brigade algorithm + GA for generating new rules), Immune Network (varying concentration of cells + recruitment of new cells) and autocatalytic networks. We will now describe successively these two strategies: the reinforcement learning and from time to time the immune recruitment optimization.

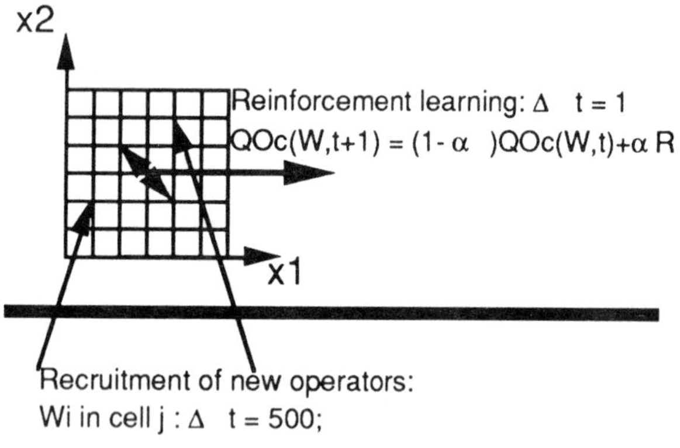

Fig.3

5 Reinforcement Learning

As stated by Barto (1990), when the performance measure for a supervised system is not defined in terms of a set of targets by means of a known error criterion, reinforcement learning addresses the problem of improving performance as evaluated by any measure whose value can be supplied to the learning system. Here two reasons justifies to resort to reinforcement learning: 1) information on the quality of the control is provided to the actor only when the process leaves the zone of viability then following a varying delay and the intervention of successive actors i.e the control is in keeping with general sequential decision problems 2) the nature of this information is almost a "qualitative measure" limited to punish the controller but not at all a distance-based error.

In (Barto et al, 1990) and (Sutton, 1990) the mechanism of reinforcement learning is described and exploited for different problems like the cart-pole control and the discovery of trajectories in a plan cluttered with obstacles. This type of learning shows important links with biology and behaviorist psychology and seems preferable to any form of more supervised learning when studying the immune system learning and adaptability. Recently, various works (Whitehead, 1991; Lin, 1991) have advocated the blending of supervised or teaching strategy (when some external teacher or an hypothetical model of the process is available) with pure unsupervised reinforcement learning for further refinement.

In order to characterize a reinforcement learning, two basic points must be preliminary defined (Barto, 1990): 1) a critic R capable of evaluating plant performances in a way both appropriate to the actual control objective and informative enough to allow learning. Here, the value of this critic is tightly connected with the Sutton's TD framework, 2) a way to modify gradually controller parameters to improve performance as measured by the critics. The methodology implementing the reinforcement learning is very close to the Q_learning algorithm developed by Watkins (Barto, Sutton and Watkins, 1990) which for multistage decision problems (and with delayed feedback, in our case when the process leaves the viability zone) performs an on line search of a nearly optimal policy, i.e the selection of the best operator in every cell. The on-line self-improving selection follows this simple algorithm:

1) initially, each cell c lodges a certain amount n (i=1..n) of operators Oc(Wi) characterized by a quality value QOc(Wi) (QA is neglected since a stable

process is considered). At the beginning QOc(Wi) = 0.

2) when the process accesses a specific cell, the selection of the operator is done probabilistically by means of a Boltzmann distribution.

3) As long as the process stays in the cell, the same operator keeps controlling it.

4) When the process leaves cell c to enter into cell c+1. The quality of the just acting operator is updated by:

$$QO_c(Wi) \Longleftarrow (1 - \alpha)QO_c(Wi) + \alpha R \quad (\alpha < 1)$$

with the critic:

$$R = (Q_{c+1} - Q_c) + \gamma \mathrm{Max}_i(QO_{c+1}(Wi))$$

γ is the discount rate ($\gamma < 1$)

Qc+1 - Qc = 0 as long as the process stays in the viability zone;
Qc+1 - Qc = -1 when the process leaves the viability zone;
Qc+1 - Qc = 1 when the process accesses the preferential zone;

The critic depends both on the difference of the two cells quality the process travels through (the entry cell c and the exit cell c+1) and the quality of the operator to be selected in the exit cell QO_{c+1}.This reminds the mechanism of co-evolution of coupled systems (Kauffman, 1989) where different sub-systems have their own localised adaptive goal without worry about the resulting fitness of the whole system. This dependence on the quality of the exit cell operator is very suitable first because it satisfies the biological requirement of local communications and secondly because it places the resulting optimization method within the dynamic programming perspective (see Barto and Singh, 1990)

When the process leaves the viability zone, it is re-initialized in a viable cell. Q_learning makes the period of viability to increase continuously until, if a solution exists, to become infinite. Following a certain amount of trials expected to exceed the necessary number to guarantee the convergence of the algorithm, a set of new operators is recruited in various cells.

6 The Immune Recruitment Optimization Strategy

The immune network model proposed and developed by Varela et al. (1988, 1989, 1990) comprises two major aspects. The first aspect concerns what has been called the dynamics of the system i.e the differential equations governing the increase or decrease of the concentration of a fixed set of lymphocite clones and the corresponding immunoglobins. The network view relates to the immunoglobins interactions by mutual binding. The binding of two species is defined by an affinity value between these two species. Such value is function of the species physical and chemical properties and then does not change. The second aspect concerns what has been called the meta-dynamics of the system. Only this aspect will be emphasized and exploited here for the ends of optimization.

The meta-dynamics governs the recruitment of new species from an enormous pool of lymphocites freshly produced by the bone-marrow. This recruitment process selects for the generation of a new species on the basis of the current global state of the system i.e. according to the sensitivity of the network for this candidate species. A possible candidate k will be recruited if $\Sigma_i m(k,i) f_i > T$, with i indexing the different species already present in the system, f_i being the concentration of species i and m(k,i) indicating the affinity between species k and i. T is the recruitment threshold. This complementary process is fundamental because it modifies continuously the actors in presence like a neural net whose structure (the number and the nature of neurons) would change in time. As discussed in the previous chapter and in (Varela, Sanchez and Coutinho, 1989), this meta-dynamics amounts to a meta-control whose objective is to conserve the system in its viability domain.

The recruitment mechanism of the immune system has inspired a technique of optimization both in real (IRM) and in hamming spaces (GIRM) (see Bersini and Varela, 1990; 1991). An eventual candidate is generated from very random structural manipulations within the current population. In order to be integrated in this population, the candidate must succeed a test of affinity with its neighbourhood. This test requires the candidate to be more similar with its best neighbours. It is shown that in comparison with the two best known population-based search techniques: GA (Goldberg, 1989) and ESs (Hoffmeister and Bäck 1990), this technique aims 1) to conserve the neighbourood-based strategy of classical optimization technics like the dichotomous or quadratic ones 2) to explicit and to accelerate the parallel local hill-climbing inherent to GA and ESs.

To illustrate briefly IRM, suppose you try to maximize the function f(x,y) represented in fig.4. In the graph x is comprised in [-10,10] and y in [0,8]. IRM initiates with a population distributed randomly in $-10 \leq x,y \leq 10$.

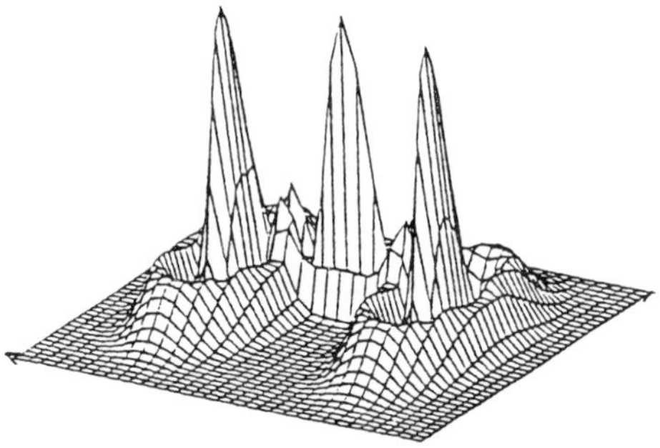

Fig.4

At each iteration 5 new points are recruited to be tested on the function. To be recruited a point must:

1) be proposed by random moves from the points currently comprised in the population

2) find the points of the population in its strict neighbourhood

3) success the recruitment test which takes place only in relation with these neighbouring points.

For this specific example, IRM found one of the two greatest picks in 90 iterations.

In the present methodology, in various cells, an eventual candidate W_k is proposed from random manipulations within the population of operators in the same cell and in the neighbouring cells. This eventual candidate will be recruited for acting on the process if :

$\Sigma_i m(W_k,W_i) QO_c(W_i) > T$ (more details on the functioning and the performance of this algorithm are given in (Bersini and Varela, 1991)).

$m(W_k,W_i)$ is a similarity function of two points (inversely related to their distance) in the space W. T is a threshold whose value can be adjusted to reinforce or to decrease the selectivity of the recruitment. This test guarantees the new candidate to be recruited to be more similar with the best operators already present in its own cell and in the closest cells and then to realize a parallel hill-climbing in the space of W. On the other hand, this imposed resemblance of an operator with the operators in the contiguous cells ensures the respect of continuity constraints in the controller space which both accelerates the learning and satisfies a very important requirement in the theory of adaptive control.

To clarify this last point, a simple experiment was performed where the objective was to approximate a certain function y=f(x) by a set of little segments. Each segment is defined by a triplet of values: Xo, Yo and α as indicated in fig.5:

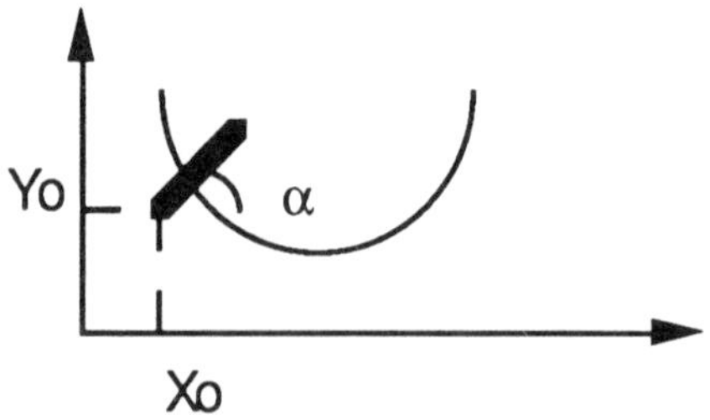

Fig.5

Thus the search takes place in R^3. The x axis is divided in 8 zones. In each zone, a good segment is searched. When in any zone a candidate is proposed, the recruitment test is performed not only with the segments already existing in the same zone but equally with the segments existing in the contiguous zones in order to respect this continuity constraints and to accelerate the search while drawing profit from this constraint. In fig.6 you see the evolution of the results for two successive generations.

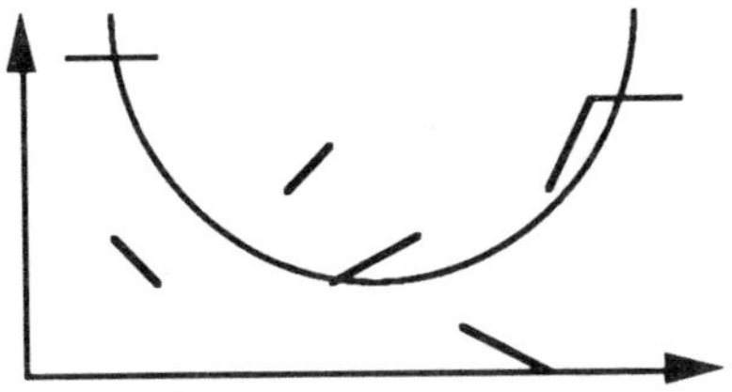

beginning generation

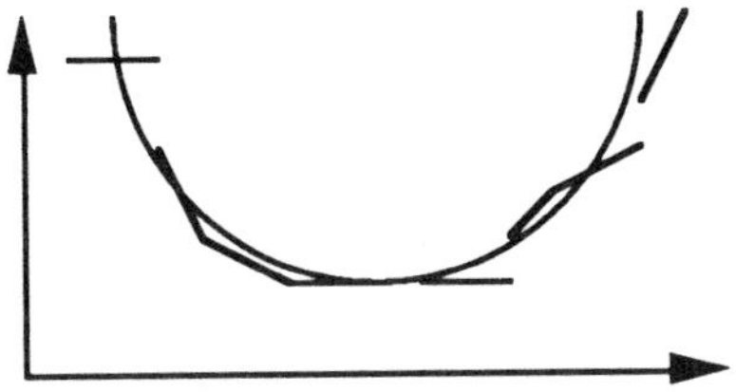

successive generation

Fig.6

Coming back to our control problem, when an operator is newly recruited in a cell, it replaces the worst operator acting in this cell (i.e $Min_i(QOc(Wi))$ and receives the quality value of the best operator in that cell (i.e $Max_i(QOc(Wi))$. Consequently, its probability to be tested in the next Q_learning phase is very high.

7 Adaptability

In case of failure or modification of the process to control, two different phenomena can occur. First, the process gets in various cells it has never passed through before. In the immune system, the adaptability relies in a large part on the randomness of the recruitment mechanism (Bersini and Varela, 1990). Here too, the optimization algorithm allows the contingent recruitment of operators in cells never visited before just in case these cells would be visited. Once the process gets in a virgin cell, an operator is available to react. In the same time, the two learning mechanisms initiate a search procedure to improve the operator acting in that cell.

Remark that on the contrary of neural nets, the adaptation does not always rely on the gradual adjustment of existing parameters but eventually on the apparition of a novel actor. In consequence, the adaptive character of immune nets goes beyond connectionist abilities to filter and to generalize their response for noisy versions of previously instructed patterns. IN are more like Holland's CFS (1986) instead belonging to a class of biological processes whose adaptability relies on a continuous generation of novel operators to handle an unpredictable and varying set of situations.

On the other hand the process could get in habitual cells but with a very different behaviour then requiring another operator to act than the one with the current greatest adequacy. The detection of the abnormality will be possible when comparing the quality of the most adequate operator with the critic it receives in case of failure. A sequential search based on the value of adequacy will turn to be necessary to find the required operator. In case no previous operator seems to convene for this new situation, it is necessary to discover a new operator. When a certain operator acts in a cell, its adequacy is updated while the adequacy of the other ones in the same cell is not modified.

In a recent work, Sutton (1990) allows the Q_learning method to adapt in case the environment changes. It is continuously possible to try alternative actions by increasing the "exploration side" of the action choice policy. However, the resulting method does not demonstrate any capability to memorize the different behaviours for the different situations that have been met. This explains the absence of an "adequacy" factor which was added in the current methodology to differentiate several operators acting in a same cell.

8 Memory

Anyone knows that the immune system can selectively reinforce and memorize its efficient behaviours in order to make them still more efficient a next time. According to the theory of immune network (Bersini and Varela, 1990; Varela and Stewart, 1990), this memory is dynamic. It results from an endogenous interaction amongst operators whose global tendency is to sustain and to stabilize, without the need for a central control, a limited set of good operators homogeneously distributed. If a specific situation has to repeat, we know the system to be prompter and better to react. Obviously a certain decay of the memory trace must be admitted, function of the frequency and the recency of the various situations.

In the methodology described here, this memory is realized by keeping in any cell different operators (with different W) having once efficiently acted on the process. Learning occurs because in principle, due to the two plastic mechanisms, the quality of the operators in a cell improve each time the process visits that cell. In most cases, the best and the most adequate operator will be selected in each cell. However with a certain frequency decreasing with time, the newly recruited operator will be allowed to act in order to be tested and thus to complete the search procedure.The adequacy of these operators is equivalent to their memory trace. An operator acting frequently will be more ready to act when the process accesses its host cell.

9 Preliminary Results

In order to validate the various facets of the methodology, simple experiments have been achieved for the control of the cart-pole (this problem is largely described in the literature, for instance (Barto, Sutton and Anderson, 1983)). It is characterized by four variables: x,θ,dx/dt,dθ/dt then the distribution and the partition are achieved in a four dimensional space. So far, only the four first aspects of the methodology have been investigated, that is the process has been considered structurally stable. The aim of the learning was to find in each cell a force between -10 N and + 10 N (then it is no more a bang-bang control) to exert on the pole so as to keep it viable the longer the best. The algorithm was the following:

1) Initially, 5 operators with random values in [-10 N, 10 N] are present in each cell. Q_learning runs for 500 steps (one step takes place as long as the process stays viable).

2) Each 500 steps, 5 new operators are recruited in whatever cells according to IRM. IRM forces the new value in [-10, 10] to be closer to the two best operators currently acting in the specific recruiting cell.

3) Q_learning is released once again and so forth, back to the first stage.

The partition of the state space was adequately assumed to be a critical feature of the problem. Indeed, in case of the same partition than the one in (Barto, Sutton and Anderson, 1983) (162 cells: 3 for x, 6 for θ, 3 for dx/dt, 3 for dθ/dt), no recruitment was needed to find a solution. On the whole, one solution was always in the preliminary random set and ± 400 steps sufficed to keep the cart-pole viable. Since Q_learning algorithm has been mainly applied to Markovian problems (like the discovery of trajectory in (Sutton, 1990)), very non-Markovian environments (here we mean that the exit cell depends not only on the operator applied in the current cell but equally on the inlet cell) like the cart-pole or any real process to control could become problematic. Surprisingly, the performance of the algorithm was pretty good and recently Barto and Singh (1990) have plead for the exploitation of Q_learning for direct adaptive control to the detriment of more formal and indirect approaches.

Nevertheless, decreasing the partition of the state space, the difficulty of the problem increases and the experiments results testify to the need of the complementary recruitment mechanism. For instance with a 36 cells partition (3 for x, 4 for θ, 3 for dθ/dt), a good solution was found only after several recruitment generations. In order to confirm the usefulness of the recruitment instead of leaving Q_learning runs for more time, statistics were realized which indicate that the final solution always contains several of the recruited operators. In addition further tests were run to validate the quality of the recruitment based on the immune mechanism instead of just random recruitments. There again, the greater selectivity of the renewal through the recruitment test was responsible for better results than simple random renewal.

10 Conclusions

This paper presents the development of an adaptive control methodology whose basic elements are inspired from the IN comprehension. They are: the notion of a viability domain, the use of reinforcement learning, the distribution of the control, the transposing of the immune meta-dynamics in an optimization technic, the adaptability and memory. Various resemblances have been pointed out with the works of Barto and Sutton, essentially the Q_learning method, as well as with classifiers system principles, mainly the two time-scales learning strategies (as a matter of fact Q_learning and bucket brigade are very similar mechanisms). Large efforts have still to be devoted to the investigation of the two last aspects: adaptability and memory. Only a better understanding of these crucial qualities will pave the way for a genuine immune control.

Acknowledgements

This work would not have been possible without the financial and intellectual support of the Shell Recherche SA France. I would like to thank the ERBAS group for fruitful discussions on adaptive control and biological metaphors. All the biological insights of this paper essentially come from F.Varela and J. Stewart who I acknowledge for their continuous support.

REFERENCES

Aubin, J.P. 1989: Learning Rules of cognitive processes. In *C.R. Acad. Sc. Paris, T. 308, Série I.*

Barto, A., Sutton, R. and C. Anderson. 1983: Neuronlike adaptive elements that can solve difficult learning control problems. *IEEE Transactions on Systems, Man and Cybernetics*, 13(5).

Barto, A. 1990: Connectionist Learning for Control. In *Neural Networks for Control* (Thomas Miller III, Richard Sutton and Paul Werbos eds.) MIT Press.

Barto, A.G., Sutton, R.S. and Watkins, C.J.C.H. 1990. Sequential decisions Problems and neural networks. In *Advances in Neural Information Processing Systems* 2, D.D. Touretzky, ED. Morgan Kaufmann, San Mateo, CA.

Barto, A.G. and S.P. Singh 1990. Reinforcement Learning and dynamic programming. In *Proceedings of the Sixth Yale Workshop on Adaptive and Learning Systems*, New Haven, CT.

Bersini, H. and F. Varela. 1990 : Hints for adaptive problem solving gleaned from immune networks. In *proceedings of the first conference on Parallel Problem Solving from Nature* - Springer Verlag.

Bersini, H. and F. Varela. 1991 : The Immune Recruitment Mechanism: A Selective Evolutionary Mechanism. In *proceedings of the fourth conference on genetic algorithms.*

Chapman, D. and L. P. Kaebling. 1991: Input Generalization in Delayed Reinforcement Learning: An Algorithm and Performance Comparisons. In *Proceedings of the 12th IJCAI Conference.*

Farmer, D. 1991: A Rosetta Stone to Connectionism. In *Emergent Computation*, Forrest S. (Ed). MIT Press.

Forrest, S. (Ed) 1991: *Emergent Computation.* A Bradford Book - MIT Press.

Goldberg, D.E. 1989: *Genetic Algorithms in search, optimization and machine learning.* Addison-Wesley Publishing Company, Inc.

Hoffmeister, F. and T. Bäck 1990: *Genetic Algorithms and EvolutionsStrategies: Similarities and Differences.* Internal Report of Dortmund University - Bericht Nr. 365.

Holland, J.H., Holyoak, K.J., Nisbett, R.E. & Thagard, P.R. 1986: *Induction: Processes of inference, learning and discovery*. Cambridge: MIT Press.

Kauffman, S.A. 1989: Principles of Adaptation in Complex Systems, in D. Stein (Ed), *Lectures in the Sciences of Complexity*, SFI Series on the Science of Complexity, Addisson Wesley.

Lin, L-J. 1991: Programming Robots Using Reinforcement Learning and Teaching. In *Proceedings of the 9th AAAI Conference*

Stewart, J. and F. Varela. 1990: Morphogenesis in Shape Space: Elementary meta-dynamics in a model of the immune network. Submitted to: *J. Theoret. Biol.*.

Sutton, R.S. 1990: Reinforcement Learning Architectures for Animats. In Proceedings of the SAB Conference - 24-28 September, Paris.

Varela, F., A. Coutinho, B. Dupire and N. Vaz. 1988: Cognitive networks: Immune, neural and otherwise, in A. Perelson (Ed.), *Theoretical Immunology, Vol.2* SFI Series on the Science of Complexity, Addisson Wesley, New Jersey.

Varela, F., V. Sanchez and A. Coutinho 1989: Adaptive strategies gleaned from immune networks, in B. Goodwin and P. Saunders (Eds.), *Evolutionary and epigenetic order from complex systems: A Waddington Memorial Volume*. Edinburgh U. Press.

Varela, F. and Stewart, J. 1990: Dynamics of a class of immune networks. I) Global behaviour. *J. theoret. Biol.* Vol. 144.

Whitehead, S.D. 1991: A Complexity Analysis of Cooperative Mechanisms in Reinforcement Learning. In *Proceedings of the 9th AAAI Conference.*

Genetic Self–Learning

Frank Hoffmeister* Thomas Bäck†

University of Dortmund · Department of Computer Science XI
P.O. Box 50 05 00 · D–4600 Dortmund 50 · Germany

Abstract

Evolutionary Algorithms are direct random search algorithms which imitate the principles of natural evolution as a method to solve adaptation (learning) tasks in general. As such they have several features in common which can be observed on the genetic and phenotypic level of living species. In this paper the algorithms' capability of adaptation or *learning* in a wider sense is demonstrated, and it is focused on *Genetic Algorithms* to illustrate the learning process on the population level (first level learning), and on *Evolution Strategies* to demonstrate the learning process on the meta–level of strategy parameters (second level learning).

Introduction

There is no doubt that the search process of natural evolution is a powerful mechanism for improving living beings on our planet by performing a random search in the space of possible DNA-sequences. Without the existence of a system capable of evolution — i.e. possessing the properties of a metabolism, self–reproduction, multistability, selection, and mutability — no life of the quality surrounding us could have emerged within the "short" period of 4 billion years as noted by Eigen (1971) and Ebeling and Feistel (1982).

Due to this newer knowledge about the qualities of natural evolution, some researchers tried to use the basic mechanisms of evolution as a basis of optimum-seeking techniques in case of vast search spaces. Without mentioning all important approaches, only the very early work of Bremermann (1965, 1968) and Fogel, Owens, and Walsh (1966) is stressed here besides the nowadays well-known and in most cases broadly accepted techniques. Most notably among them are the *Genetic Algorithm* (GA) and *Classifier System* as developed by Holland (1975, 1986a, 1986b, 1987) and Booker et al. (1989), the *Evolution Strategy* (ES) by Rechenberg (1973) and Schwefel (1975, 1977, 1981, 1987, 1988, 1989), and the *Genetic Programming Paradigm* by Cramer (1985) and Koza (1987, 1989, 1990).

In any of these approaches a population of individuals is maintained. This population is able to adapt to a given (static or dynamically changing) environment by randomized processes of reproduction, sexual recombination, and mutation. Through an environmental feedback individuals get a quality information (fitness), and the selection process favours the individuals of higher quality to survive (even the reproduction processes within these algorithms often favour higher quality structures). Thus, during the evolution process the average quality of the population increases, hopefully leading to an optimum point.

Algorithms following this general approach have been summarized under the term *Evolutionary Algorithms* by Hoffmeister and Bäck (1991, 1991b). It is important here to note that the approaches are mainly differing in the structure of the individuals the algorithm is working upon. The recombination and mutation operators are generally influenced by the basic structure, and the unifying and generally best selection and reproduction strategy has not been developed yet as can be seen from different approaches by Holland (1975), Baker (1985, 1987), Whitley (1989), and Hoffmeister and Bäck (1990).

With respect to the complexity of the structures the algorithms are working on, a hierarchy as presented in table 1 can be constructed, where P_{LISP} denotes the set of syntactically correct LISP–programs, $\mathcal{P}(S)$ is the power set of a set S, l denotes the individ-

* iwan@ls11.informatik.uni-dortmund.de

† baeck@ls11.informatik.uni-dortmund.de

Structures		Terminology
Computer programs	P_{LISP}	Genetic Programming Paradigm
Rules of a rule-based system	$\mathcal{P}(\{0,1,\#,\vert,\ldots\}^l)$	Classifier-Systems (Pittsburgh-approach)[1]
	$\{0,1,\#,\vert,\ldots\}^l$	Classifier-Systems (Michigan-approach)[2]
Real-valued vectors	$\mathbf{R}^{2n}$	Evolution Strategy
Bitstrings	$\{0,1\}^l$	Genetic Algorithm

Table 1: Hierarchy of structures worked upon by Evolutionary Algorithms

uals' length, and n is the dimension of the objective function and the corresponding number of mutation-rates for each object variable in an ES. From the top to the bottom of table 1 the amount of existing work on the actual topic increases as the theoretical and practical treatability of the structures increases due to their smaller degree of complexity.

Evolutionary Algorithms which model mechanisms from natural evolution are capable of adaptation to an unknown environment by maximizing the average fitness of the modelled population over time. In general, this corresponds to finding or *learning* of an optimal setting of some control parameters or of an internal representation of some reality in order to accomplish a given task. As such, Evolutionary Algorithms can be seen as an alternative approach in the context of machine learning.

According to a classification of machine learning strategies presented by Michalski (1986) Evolutionary Algorithms realize *learning by induction*, i.e. they work by some generalization of the input information. More exactly and in contrast to concept acquisition (learning by examples) this works by observation and discovery and provides the most advanced and complicated learning technique when it is compared to *rote learning*, *learning by instruction*, *learning by deduction*, and *learning by analogy*. Even humans are assumed to learn by inductive guessing general regularities from observed examples. Of course, these guesses are often too general and have to be corrected later on as described by Holland et al. (1987).

A further property of these algorithms which provides a high algorithmic potential as a technique for adaptation is their implicit parallelism. In a review by Hoffmeister (1991) various fine and coarse grain parallel implementations are presented, which are particularly well suited for MIMD-computers.

In the remainder of this paper we will focus only on the two lowest levels of the hierarchy, i.e. on Evolution Strategies (ESs) and Genetic Algorithms (GAs), which are described shortly in the following sections. The algorithms differ with respect to their learning capabilities. GAs are able to "learn", i.e. find, a point in the search space with maximum fitness. In order to do so they are driven by a set of fixed, external strategy parameters. This is referred to as *first level learning*. ESs work in a similar manner, but additionally they also "learn" the proper setting of several strategy parameters which guide the process of first level learning. This kind of *second level learning* is integrated into the algorithm, thus avoiding some kind of meta-level control algorithm like it was proposed by Grefenstette (1986) or Guliaev et al. (1989).

The effects of first and second level of genetic self-learning are demonstrated in the context of continuous parameter optimization which is used as an easy way to determine the "*fitness*" of evolving structures.

Genetic Algorithms

In this section only a very short introduction to Genetic Algorithms and their learning capability is given. For more informations on GAs the reader is referred to Holland (1975) and Goldberg (1989). The formal framework used here is taken from Hoffmeister and Bäck (1991) without going into the details. We focus on the following 8-tuple as an abstraction from Holland's work (1975):

$$\mathrm{GA} = (P^0, \lambda, l, s, \rho, \Omega, f, t) \tag{1}$$

where

$$P^0 = (a_1^0, \ldots, a_\lambda^0) \in I^\lambda \quad \text{initial population}$$
$$I = \{0,1\}^l$$

[1] The Pittsburgh-approach treats a set of rules as one individual as described by Smith (1984) and Wilson and Goldbert (1989).

[2] The Michigan-approach treats one rule as one individual according to Holland and Reitman (1978).

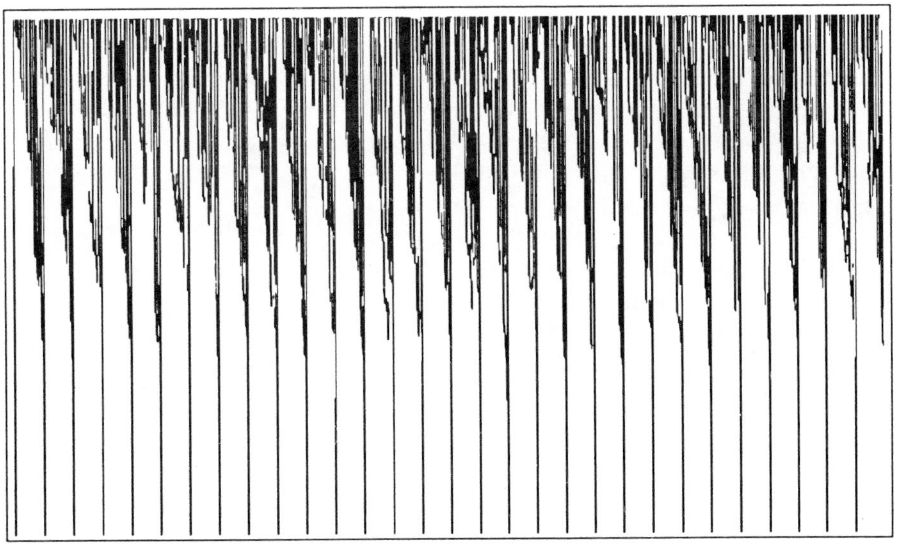

Figure 1: Development of best structure by a GA (first level learning)

λ	$\in$	$\mathbf{N}$	population size
l	$\in$	$\mathbf{N}$	bitlength of individuals
s	:	$I^\lambda \rightarrow I^\lambda$	selection operator
ρ	:	$I \rightarrow \Omega$	operator determination
Ω	$\subseteq$	$\{\omega : I \times I^\lambda \rightarrow I\}$	operator set
f	:	$I \rightarrow \mathbf{R}$	fitness function
t	:	$I^\lambda \rightarrow \{0,1\}$	termination criterion

P^0 is the randomly generated initial population, and the parameters λ and l describe the number of individuals representing one generation and the length of the 'genetic' representation of each individual, respectively.

The selection operator s produces an intermediate population P'^t from the population P^t by the generation of copies of elements from P^t: $P'^t = s(P^t)$. This is done by taking λ subsequent samples from $P^t = (a_1^t, \ldots, a_\lambda^t)$ according to the probability distribution $p_s : I \rightarrow [0,1]$, where $p_s(a_i^t) = f(a_i^t) \;/\; \sum_{j=1}^{\lambda} f(a_j^t)$ denotes the probability of individual a_i^t to be sampled. Holland (1975) introduced the name *proportional selection* for this selection scheme.

After the selection phase has taken place genetic operators are to be applied. One may think of a mapping $\rho : I \rightarrow \Omega$ which determines an operator $\omega_i^t \in \Omega$ for each individual $a_i'^t \in P'^t$ which will be applied to this individual: $\rho(a_i'^t) = \omega_i^t \; \forall i \in \{1, \ldots, \lambda\}$.

The genetic operator set $\Omega \subseteq \{\omega : I \times I^\lambda \rightarrow I\}$ includes genetic operators like *crossover* and *mutation*. The stochastic elements of these operators (application probabilities, e.g. $p_m \approx 0.001$ and $p_c \approx 0.6$, selection of loci) are hidden in the operators, e.g. application of an operator ω to an individual a_i and a population P yields a probability distribution $p : I \rightarrow [0,1]$ on I ($\sum_{a \in I} p(a) = 1$). According to p, a sample is taken from I, thus determining the resulting new individual $a_i' = \omega(a_i, P)$.

Now the transition from generation t to generation $t+1$ may be described as follows:

$$\begin{aligned} s(P^t) &= P'^t = (a_1'^t, \ldots, a_\lambda'^t) & \\ \rho(a_i'^t) &= \omega_i^t & \forall i \in \{1, \ldots, \lambda\} \\ a_i^{t+1} &= \omega_i^t(a_i'^t, P^t) & \forall i \in \{1, \ldots, \lambda\} \\ P^{t+1} &= (a_1^{t+1}, \ldots, a_\lambda^{t+1}) & \end{aligned} \tag{2}$$

The fitness values are obtained by the fitness function $f : I \rightarrow \mathbf{R}$, which is usually seen as a black box containing components like decoding of individuals, constraint handling, scaling and the objective function itself. $t : I^\lambda \rightarrow \{0,1\}$ denotes the termination criterion.

In order to illustrate the adaptive search capacity of such an algorithm, i.e. its first level learning properties, a simple optimization problem is used here. The fitness function f is a quadratic one of the form

$$f(x_1, \ldots, x_n) = \sum_{i=1}^{n} x_i^2 \tag{3}$$

(sphere model). It is unimodal, i.e. only one minimum point $x^* = (0, \ldots, 0)$ exists. The task of the genetic algorithm is to locate the minimum point from a randomly initialized start population. The algorithm works by encoding each object variable $x_i \in \mathbf{R}$

by using 32 bits and a dimension of $n = 30$, such that $l = 960$. For decoding purposes, each object variable is restricted to the range $-5.12 \leq x_i \leq 5.12$ (the $2^{32}-1$ different integer numbers encoded by each substring of length 32 are linearly mapped to that interval of real values). In the special experiment described here a mutation rate $p_m = 0.001$, population size $\lambda = 50$, and a two-point crossover operator was used ($p_c = 0.6$). Furthermore, the algorithm uses a modified selection mechanism called *extinctive* selection, which was introduced to GAs by Bäck and Hoffmeister (1991a). In fact, the experiment described here is based on (10,50)-proportional selection.

The result is given in an uncommon graphical way in figure 1. Here for 4000 generations in steps of 5 generations the actually best individual of the population is given as a line of pixels, where a 1 corresponds to a black pixel and a 0 corresponds to a white one. The development towards the optimum string

$$\{1\underbrace{0\ldots0}_{31}\}^{30}$$

can be seen clearly in this illustration, without stressing too much numerical data (the final best objective function value is $4.26 \cdot 10^{-17}$). The figure demonstrates the capability of adaptation on the population level. The capability of adaptation on the meta-level, i.e. the level of strategy parameters, is demonstrated in the next section.

Evolution Strategies

Evolution strategies as devised by Schwefel (1977, 1981) are a class of methods primarily used for unconstrained parameter optimization of an objective function $f : \mathbf{R}^n \to \mathbf{R}$ and for problems with additional inequality constraints $g_l \geq 0$. The overall goal is to find a vector $x^\star \in \mathbf{R}^n$ such that $\forall x \in \mathbf{R}^n : f(x^\star) \leq f(x)$ in case of a minimization task. $x^\star$ is called the *global optimum*. Restriction to function minimization is without loss of generality since $\max f(x) = -\min(-f(x))$.

In general, non-linear objective functions exhibit multiple optima. A *local optimum* $\hat{x}$ is defined as

$$\exists \epsilon > 0 \; \forall x \in \mathbf{R}^n : \quad \|x - \hat{x}\| < \epsilon \implies f(\hat{x}) \leq f(x) \tag{4}$$

Even if there is only one local optimum, it may be difficult to find a path to it in case of discontinuities. Trying to guarantee global convergence leads to more or less exhaustive scanning of the parameter space, since a lot of problems are NP-complete as demonstrated by Garey and Johnson (1979). Heuristic methods like the ES (or GA) try to keep within polynomial time without trapping into the nearest local optimum. They do not rely on gradient information like other search methods.

An ES incorporates the principles of population, recombination, mutation and selection from organic evolution as the major heuristics. Although it has very much in common with traditional gradient methods, which show just local convergence to some $\hat{x}$, it has a good chance to find better local minima due to the use of normally distributed mutations and sexual recombination. Schwefel's ES may be described as a 11-tupel

$$\mathrm{ES} = (P^0, \mu, \lambda, \; r, m, s, \; \Delta\sigma, \Delta\theta, \; f, g, t) \tag{5}$$

where

P^0	$=$	$(a_1^0, \ldots, a_\mu^0) \in I^\mu$	population $I = \mathbf{R}^n \times \mathbf{R}^n \times \mathbf{R}^w$
μ	$\in$	$\mathbf{N}$	number of parents
λ	$\in$	$\mathbf{N}$	number of offspring $\lambda > \mu$
r	:	$I^\mu \to I$	recombination operator
m	:	$I \to I$	mutation operator
s	:	$I^\lambda \to I^\mu$	selection operator
$\Delta\sigma$	$\in$	$\mathbf{R}$	step-size meta-control
$\Delta\theta$	$\in$	$\mathbf{R}$	correlation meta-control
f	:	$\mathbf{R}^n \to \mathbf{R}$	objective function
g_j	:	$\mathbf{R}^n \to \mathbf{R}$	constraint functions $j \in \{1, \ldots, q\}$
t	:	$I^\mu \to \{0, 1\}$	termination criterion

where P_0 denotes the initial population of μ parents which produce λ offspring per generation. $\Delta\sigma$ and $\Delta\theta$ are parameters which control the mutation of the object variables $x \in \mathbf{R}^n$ on a meta-level. The "genetic" information of an individual $a = (x, \sigma, \theta) \in I$ consists of three parts, namely the set of object variables $x \in \mathbf{R}^n$, the set of standard deviations $\sigma \in \mathbf{R}^n$ for mutation of the object variables x, and a vector of inclination angles $\theta \in \mathbf{R}^w$ which are used to control correlated mutations of the object variables x. The later two are also referred to as *strategy parameters*, since they control the effects of the mutation operator m for an individual.

An ES works similar to an abstract automaton running sequentially through a set of states (generations) until the termination criterion t holds. The term *generation* refers to the time step between successive states as well as to the population P_t at time t.

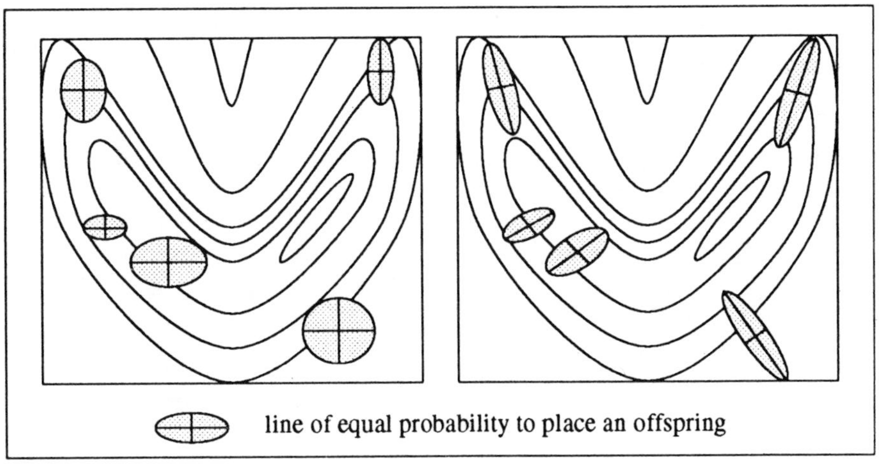

Figure 2: The effect of simple mutations (left) and correlated mutations (right)

The λ offspring are reduced to μ parents of the next generation by the selection operator s:

$$\begin{aligned} P^{t+1} &= s(P'^t) \\ P'^t &= (a'^t_1, \ldots, a'^t_\lambda) \in I^\lambda \\ a'^t_j &= m(r(P^t), \Delta\sigma, \Delta\theta) \\ &\quad \forall g_j \in g : g_j(a'^t_j) \geq 0, \quad j \in \{1, \ldots, \lambda\} \end{aligned} \tag{6}$$

An offspring which does not satisfy all constraints g_j is simply ignored as a *lethal mutation*. When realizing the selection scheme "survival of the fittest" the selection operator s is defined such that

$$\forall a \in P^{t+1} \; \nexists a' \in P'^t : f(a') < f(a) \tag{7}$$

In the selection scheme presented here the life time of every individual in the population is restricted to one generation (pure selection). Such an ES is referred to as a (μ,λ)–ES, while a variant of it, which allows for an infinite survival of the parents by incorporating them into the selection, is called (μ+λ)–ES (elitist strategy).

The recombination operator r is used to produce new offspring by mixing the information contained within different individuals of a population. Several recombination schemes may be envisaged:

$$r(P^t) = a' = (x', \sigma', \theta') \in I$$

$$x'_i = \begin{cases} x_{a,i} & \text{(A) no recombination} \\ x_{a,i} \text{ or } x_{b,i} & \text{(B) discrete} \\ \frac{1}{2}(x_{a,i} + x_{b,i}) & \text{(C) intermediate} \\ x_{a,i} \text{ or } x_{b_i,i} & \text{(D) global, discrete} \\ \frac{1}{2}(x_{a,i} + x_{b_i,i}) & \text{(E) global, intermediate} \end{cases} \tag{8}$$

where the indices $a, b, b_i \in P^t$ indicate parents likely chosen by r. Note, that with global recombination the mating partners for the recombination of a *single* component x'_i are chosen anew from the population resulting in a higher mixing of the genetic information than in the standard case (B).

Recombination is likewise defined for the other part of the genetic information, namely σ' and θ'. It realizes some kind of multi-point cross-over, which virtually enlarges the search space covered by the population.

The schemes (A), (B) and (C) may be found in nature when looking at non-sexual bacteria and sexually reproducing higher living beings, while (D) and (E) are somehow artificial.

The mutation operator m suffices to introduce new information into a population. It modifies at random the object *and* the strategy information of an individual $a = (x, \sigma, \theta)$ consisting of an object variable vector x, a vector of standard deviations σ, and a set of inclination angles θ, which influence the covariances of the mutations.

$$\begin{aligned} m(a) &= a' = (x', \sigma', \theta') \\ &\quad a, a' \in I;\; I = \mathbf{R}^n \times \mathbf{R}^n \times \mathbf{R}^w \\ \sigma' &= \sigma \cdot \exp \mathrm{N}_0(\Delta\sigma) \\ \theta' &= \theta \cdot \exp \mathrm{N}_0(\Delta\theta) \\ x' &= x + \mathrm{N}_0(\mathrm{A}) \end{aligned} \tag{9}$$

where $\mathrm{N}_0(y)$ represents a vector with independent, normally distributed random numbers each with variance y^2 and expected value 0. $\mathrm{N}_0(\mathrm{A})$ is a normally distributed random vector z with expectation 0 and probability density

$$p(z) = \sqrt{\frac{\det A}{(2\pi)^n}} \exp\left(-\frac{1}{2} z^T A z\right) \qquad (10)$$

The diagonal elements of the covariance matrix A^{-1} are the independent variances $\sigma_i'^2$ for the components x_i of the decision vector x, while the off-diagonal elements represent the covariances $c_{i,j}$ of the changes. Schwefel restricts the areas of equal probability density to n-dimensional hyperellipsoids, which are realized by a set of inclination angles $\theta' \in \mathbf{R}^w$, $w = 1/2n(n-1)$ for the main axes of the hyperellipsoid. The standard deviations σ_i' serve as a kind of mean step size along those axes.

Introducing the strategy parameters σ and θ into the mutation–selection process is a major ingredience of an evolution strategy. It allows a population with its sets of strategy parameters to adapt to the *local* topology of the objective function dynamically. In general, good settings of the strategy parameters of an individual result in a better fitness according to f. Thus, selection automatically favours better settings. Schwefel (1987) demonstrated, that near-optimal step sizes are used for the direct search process of the evolution strategy resulting in a high overall rate of convergence. The effect of correlated mutations is illustrated by figure 2, where a set of equally likely mutations for an individual is sketched by the borderline of an ellipsoids. The length of the axes represent the setting of the different σ_i. With simple mutations the axes of an ellipsoid are parallel to the coordinate system, while in case of correlated mutations an ellipsoid may be free oriented in space, thus exploiting narrow "valleys" in the search space much better.

The scheme presented realizes minimization of a single criteria based on haploid individuals, but it may be easily extended to a diploid or polyploid scheme. Kursawe (1990) presented an ES for multi-criteria optimization based on diploid individuals which not only finds a single point of the Pareto set but is able to mark the complete set within a single run.

Self-Learning

In order to demonstrate the feasibility of integrating the self-learning of strategy parameters like σ into an Evolutionary Algorithm, figure 3 shows some aspects of the dynamics inside an ES with simple mutations. Such an algorithm is a simple example for successful second level learning. Again, the optimization problem given by equation (3) is used. For demonstration purposes the global optimum point is shifted every 200 generations to show the self-learning capabilities in a nonstationary environment. The population size is also set to $\lambda = 50$.

Due to the symmetry of function f it is enough to learn just a single mutation rate (step-size), instead of 30 different ones. The left part of figure 3 shows the behaviour of an ES that has to learn only a single step-size, while the right part of the illustration shows an ES that must adapt 30 different step-sizes, i.e. a step-size for each object variable x_i.

The topmost plots show the observed first level learning, i.e. the way to the optimum expressed by the best, average and worst value of the objective function f per generation. The plots at the bottom of figure 3 present the maximal, average and minimal mutation rates (step-sizes) per generation which control the first level learning. First and second level learning are linked according to (9). Several interesting properties are reflected by figure 3.

The rate of convergence to the optimum is very much higher compared to GAs, which after 4000 generations find an $x \in \mathbf{R}^{30}$ such that $f(x) = 4.26 \cdot 10^{-17}$. An ES with simple mutations as used here yields an $f(x) \approx 10^{-8}$ after only 200 generations. Simulation runs with the undistorted function f show the same rate of convergence until the arithmetic resolution of the underlying computations is reached. This general advantage stems not only from the more adequate internal model used in ESs for this problem but *also* from the self-learning of strategy parameters which control the process of first level learning.

Theoretical considerations by Rechenberg (1973) and Schwefel (1977, 1981) for function f indicate that the optimal mutation rate is proportional to the distance from the optimum. A comparison of the top and bottom plots clearly shows that this proportion is maintained by the self-learned mutation rates, since $f(x)$ is nothing but the squared distance from the optimum and the shape of the curves agree perfectly. In general, ESs are able to learn fairly optimal settings of the mutation rates with respect to the requirements of the search space covered by the population which may change depending on location and time.

The rate of first and second level learning is also proportional to $1/n$, where n denotes the amount of self-learned information like the number of object variables and mutation rates. This relation results in the different behaviour presented in the left and right part of figure 3. The more strategy parameters are to be learnt the more time is required for their self-learning. The much wider distribution of the 30 different muta-

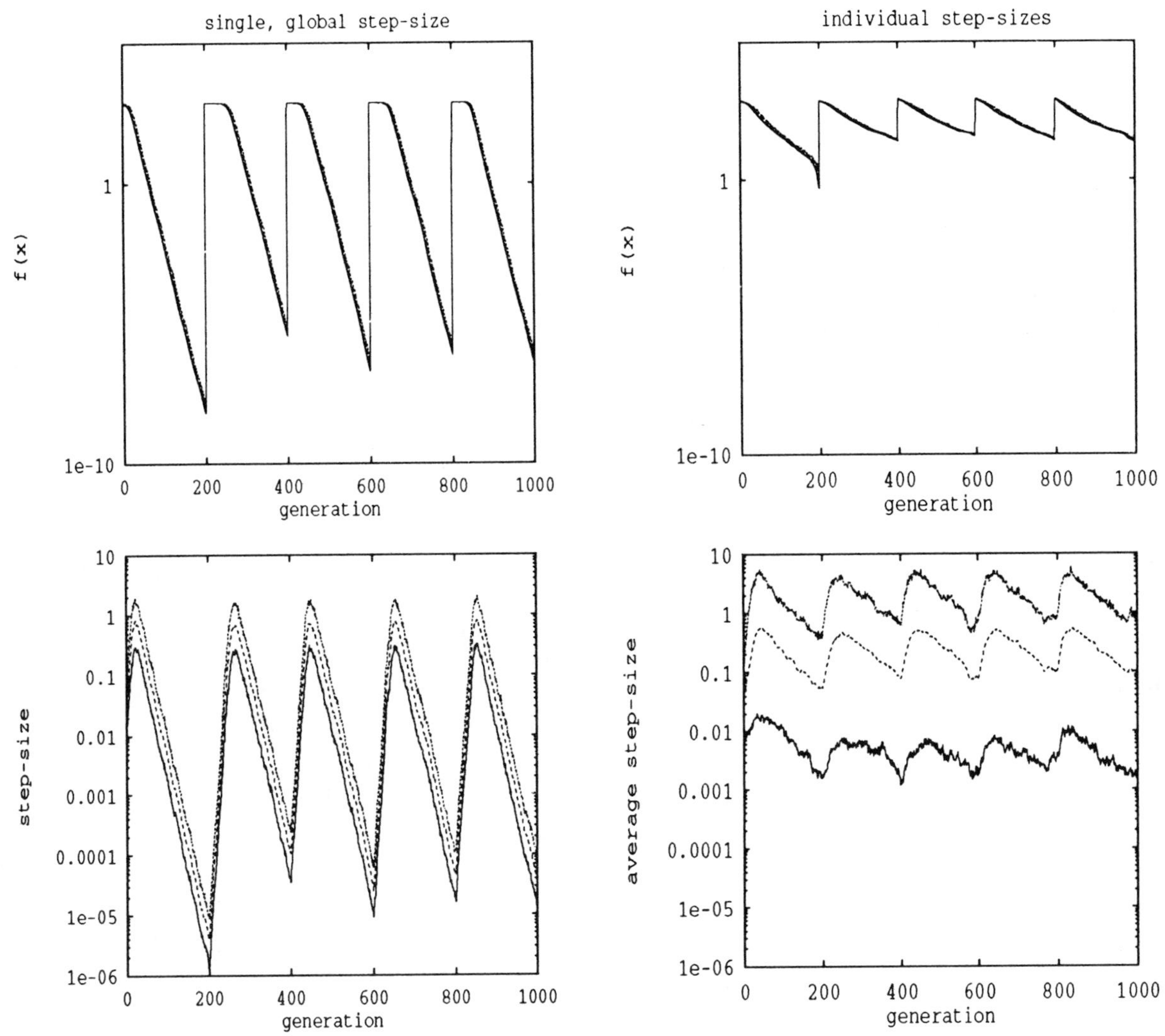

Figure 3: First and second level learning by an ES with different amounts of strategy parameters

tion rates (right) instead of a just a single one (left) results from partially optimal settings of the object variables and σ-vectors, where several object variables and mutation rates are not adapted properly although the corresponding performance (fitness) of the individuals is among the μ best of a generation.

The plots at the bottom of figure 3 also show the speed at which the strategy parameters are adapted in case of a rapidly changing environment, i.e. shift of the optimum point. This rate is controlled by the external parameter $\Delta\sigma$, which also inversely depends on the amount of information to learn. The stagnation phase observed for the $f(x)$ after a shift of the optimum point directly depends on the time required to adjust the mutation rates to the proper magnitude. Then, mutation rates are scaled according to the current distance of the population from the (new) optimum point.

Conclusions

As demonstrated in the previous sections, learning in Evolutionary Algorithms is possible on two different levels: First, on the level of the population, i.e. the genetic information itself, and, more surprising, on the second level (meta-level) of the strategy parameters. The latter mechanism has two advantages: It improves the velocity of adaptation on the genotypic level by introducing the capability to learn an internal model of the topology of the objective function (step-sizes) and it simplifies the parameterization of the algorithm by removing parameters or at least by substituting many of them by fewer and less sensible ones.

Finally, the self-learning of strategy parameters could lead to an adaptive algorithm without any externally predefined parameter, capable of self-adaptation of it's configuration and parameterization. These general principles are currently under investigation at the University of Dortmund, as well as the approach to use these mechanisms in Genetic Algorithms. This would allow for the application of parameter self-learning also to discrete optimization problems and could even help to solve some of the problems of learning and induction in Classifier-Systems, especially its problem of having too many sensible external parameters.

Acknowledgements

Special thanks to Jörg Heitkötter for his engaged work on the graphics software which was used within the paper for the visualization of the results.

References

Alexander N. Antamoshkin, editor. *Random Search as a Method for Adaptation and Optimization of Complex Systems*, Divnogorsk, USSR, March 1991. Krasnojarsk Space Technology University.

Thomas Bäck and Frank Hoffmeister. Extended selection mechanisms in genetic algorithms. In Richard K. Belew and Lashon B. Booker, editors, *Proceedings of the Fourth International Conference on Genetic Algorithms and their Applications*, pages 92–99, University of California, San Diego, USA, 1991. Morgan Kaufmann Publishers.

Thomas Bäck and Frank Hoffmeister. Global optimization by means of evolutionary algorithms. In Antamoshkin (1991), pages 17–21.

James Edward Baker. Adaptive selection methods for genetic algorithms. In Grefenstette (1985), pages 101–111.

James Edward Baker. Reducing bias and inefficiency in the selection algorithm. In J.J. Grefenstette, editor, *Proceedings of the second international conference on genetic algorithms and their applications*, pages 14–21, Hillsdale, New Jersey, 1987. Lawrence Erlbaum Associates.

L. B. Booker, D. E. Goldberg, and J. H. Holland. Classifier systems and genetic algorithms. *Artificial Intelligence*, pages 235–282, 1989.

H. J. Bremermann, M. Rogson, and S. Salaff. Search by evolution. In M. Maxfield, A. Callahan, and L. J. Fogel, editors, *Biophysics and Cybernetic Systems — Proceedings of the 2nd Cybernetic Sciences Symposium*, pages 157–167, Los Angeles, CA, 1965. Spartan Books.

H. J. Bremermann. Numerical optimization procedures derived from biological evolution processes. In H. L. Oestreicher and D. R. Moore, editors, *Cybernetic Problems in Bionics*, pages 597–616. Gordon and Breach, New York, 1968.

M. L. Cramer. A representation for the adaptive generation of simple sequential programs. In Grefenstette (1985), pages 183–187.

Werner Ebeling and Reiner Feistel. *Physik der Selbstorganisation und Evolution*. Akademie-Verlag, Berlin, 1982.

Manfred Eigen. Selforganization of matter and the evolution of biological macromolecules. *Die Naturwissenschaften*, 58(10):465–523, October 1971.

L.J. Fogel, A.J. Owens, and M.J. Walsh. *Artificial Intelligence through Simulated Evolution*. John Wiley, New York, 1966.

C. Fujiko and J. Dickinson. Using the genetic algorithm to generate lisp source code to solve the prisoner's dilemma. In J. J. Grefenstette, editor, *Proceedings of the second international conference on genetic algorithms and their applications*, pages 236–240, Hillsdale, New Jersey, 1987. Lawrence Erlbaum Associates.

M.R. Garey and D.S. Johnson. *Computers and Intractability — A Guide to the theory of NP-Completeness*. Freemann & Co., San Francisco, 1979.

David E. Goldberg. *Genetic algorithms in search, optimization and machine learning*. Addison Wesley, 1989.

J. J. Grefenstette, editor. *Proceedings of the First International Conference on Genetic Algorithms and Their Applications*, Hillsdale, New Jersey, 1985. Lawrence Erlbaum Associates.

John J. Grefenstette. Optimization of control parameters for genetic algorithms. *IEEE Transactions on Systems, Man and Cybernetics*, SMC-16(1):122–128, 1986.

Yu. V. Guliaev, I. L. Bukatova, L. N. Golubeva, and V. F. Krapivin. Evolutionary informatics and "intelligent" special processors. Academy of Sciences of the USSR, Institute of Radio Engineering and Electronics, 1989. Preprint.

Frank Hoffmeister and Thomas Bäck. Genetic algorithms and evolution strategies: Similarities and differences. Technical Report "Grüne Reihe" No. 365, Department of Computer Science, University of Dortmund, November 1990.

Frank Hoffmeister and Thomas Bäck. Genetic algorithms and evolution strategies: Similarities and differences. In Hans-Paul Schwefel and Reinhard Männer, editors, *Parallel Problem Solving from Nature*, volume 496 of *Lecture Notes in Computer Science*, pages 455–470. Springer, Berlin, 1991.

Frank Hoffmeister. Parallel evolutionary algorithms. In Antamoshkin (1991), pages 90–94.

John H. Holland and J. S. Reitman. Cognitive systems based on adaptive algorithms. In D. A. Waterman and F. Hayes-Roth, editors, *Pattern-directed inference systems*. Academic Press, New York, 1978.

John H. Holland, Keith J. Holyoak, Richard E. Nisbett, and Paul R. Thagard. Classifier systems, Q–morphisms, and induction. In Lawrence Davis, editor, *Genetic algorithms and simulated annealing*, pages 116–128. Morgan Kaufmann Publishers, 1987.

John H. Holland. *Adaptation in natural and artificial systems*. The University of Michigan Press, Ann Arbor, 1975.

John H. Holland. Escaping brittleness: The possibilities of general–purpose learning algorithms applied to parallel rule-based systems. In Ryszard S. Michalski, Jaime G. Carbonell, and Tom M. Mitchell, editors, *Machine Learning Vol.II*, chapter 20, pages 593–623. Morgan Kaufmann Publishers, Inc., 1986.

John H. Holland. A mathematical framework for studying learning in classifier systems. *Physica*, 22D:307–317, 1986.

John H. Holland. Genetic algorithms and classifier systems: Foundations and future directions. In J. J. Grefenstette, editor, *Proceedings of the second international conference on genetic algorithms and their applications*, pages 82–89, Hillsdale, New Jersey, 1987. Lawrence Erlbaum Associates.

John R. Koza. Hierarchical genetic algorithms operating on populations of computer programs. In N. S. Sridharan, editor, *Eleventh international joint conference on artificial intelligence*, pages 768–774. Morgan Kaufmann Publishers, August 1989.

John R. Koza. Genetic programming: A paradigm for genetically breeding populations of computer programs to solve problems. Technical Report STAN–CS–90–1314, Department of Computer Science, Stanford University, Stanford, CA 94305, June 1990.

Frank Kursawe. *Evolutionsstrategien für die Vektoroptimierung*. Master thesis, University of Dortmund, Dortmund, Germany, February 1990.

Ryszard S. Michalski. Understanding the nature of learning: Issues and research directions. In Ryszard S. Michalski, Jaime G. Carbonell, and Tom M. Mitchell, editors, *Machine Learning Vol.II*, chapter 1, pages 3–25. Morgan Kaufmann Publishers, Inc., 1986.

Ingo Rechenberg. *Evolutionsstrategie: Optimierung technischer Systeme nach Prinzipien der biologischen Evolution*. Frommann–Holzboog Verlag, Stuttgart, 1973.

J. David Schaffer, editor. *Proceedings of the Third International Conference on Genetic Algorithms and Their Applications*, San Mateo, California, June 1989. Morgan Kaufmann Publishers.

Hans-Paul Schwefel. Binäre Optimierung durch somatische Mutation. Technical report, Technical University of Berlin and Medical University of Hannover, May 1975.

Hans-Paul Schwefel. *Numerische Optimierung von Computer-Modellen mittels der Evolutionsstrategie*, volume 26 of *Interdisciplinary systems research*. Birkhäuser, Basel, 1977.

Hans-Paul Schwefel. *Numerical Optimization of Computer Models*. Wiley, Chichester, 1981.

Hans-Paul Schwefel. Collective phenomena in evolutionary systems. In *Preprints of the 31st Annual Meeting of the International Society for General System Research, Budapest*, volume 2, pages 1025–1033, June 1987.

Hans-Paul Schwefel. Evolutionary learning optimum–seeking on parallel computer architectures. In A. Sydow, S. G. Tzafestas, and R. Vichnevetsky, editors, *Proceedings of the International Symposium on Systems Analysis and Simulation 1988, I: Theory and Foundations*, pages 217–225. Akademie der Wissenschaften der DDR, Akademie-Verlag, Berlin, September 1988.

Hans-Paul Schwefel. Some observations about evolutionary optimization algorithms. In Hans-Michael Voigt, Heinz Mühlenbein, and Hans-Paul Schwefel, editors, *Evolution and Optimization '89*, Mathematical Ecology, pages 57–60, Berlin, 1989. Akademie Verlag Berlin.

S.F. Smith. Adaptive learning systems. In R. Forsyth, editor, *Expert systems — principles and case studies*, pages 168–189. Chapman and Hall, London, 1984.

Darrell Whitley. The GENITOR algorithm and selection pressure: Why rank–based allocation of reproductive trials is best. In Schaffer (1989), pages 116–121.

Stewart W. Wilson and David E. Goldberg. A critical review of classifier systems. In Schaffer (1989), pages 244–255.

Darwin's continent cycle theory and its simulation by the Prisoner's Dilemma

Heinz Mühlenbein
GMD Schloss Birlinghoven
D-5205 Sankt Augustin1

Abstract

Theoretical biology has largely ignored Darwin's true evolution model. In his famous book about the origin of species Darwin details the importance of a population structure on evolution. He conjectures that a large continent which will exist for long periods in a broken condition, will be the most favourable for the production of many new forms of life. We have called this conjecture Darwin's *continent cycle theory*. In this paper we will investigate some of Darwin's arguments in support of his theory by simulating an artificial ecology with the parallel genetic algorithm PGA. The artificial ecology consists of a population playing the Iterated Prisoner's Dilemma. The major emphasis of this paper is on the methodological questions of the simulation. These are the genetic representation, the mapping of the genotypes to phenotypes and the spatial population structure.

Keywords Genetic algorithms, evolution, population structures, prisoner's dilemma

1 Introduction

The most complex systems we observe in nature are the results of evolutionary processes. This was conjectured by Charles Darwin (1859) in his famous book:" On the origin of species by means of natural selection."()

The idea of applying evolutionary strategies in computer algorithms dates back as far as the invention of the first stored program computers. John von Neumann (1966) already investigated the question of whether modelling evolution on a computer could solve the complexity problem of programming. He invented automata theory to research the question of whether the construction of automata by automata can progress from simpler types to increasingly complicated types. ()

Von Neumann stated the following important difference between natural and artificial systems: "Today's organisms are phylogenetically descended from others which were vastly simpler than they are, so much simpler, in fact, that it is inconceivable how any description of the later, complex organism could have existed in the earlier one." But in most artificial systems the situation is different: " Everyone knows that a machine tool is more complicated than the elements which can be made with it, and that, generally speaking, an automaton A, which can make an automaton B, must have a complete description of B and also rules on how to behave while effecting the synthesis".

In the theory of cellular automaton, von Neumann was able to construct an automaton which could reproduce itself. This result showed that reproduction was possible. Von Neumann was well aware of the other two important evolutionary processes - namely variation and selection. He decided that knowledge about these two processes was not yet sufficient to incorporate them in his theory of automaton. "Conflicts between independent organisms lead to consequences which, acording to the theory of *natural selection*, are believed to furnish an important mechanism of evolution. Our models lead to such conflict situations. The conditions under which this motive for evolution can be effective here may be quite complicated ones, but they deserve study."

Selection and variation are the basic components of the genetic algorithm GA developed by John Holland(1975). But the genetic representation consists just of a simple binary bitstring, not a complex automaton. Nevertheless the GA has been succesfully applied to many application areas. For a number of technical reasons we have extended the GA to the parallel genetic algorithm PGA. The PGA is a totally distributed algorithm running with maximal efficiency on parallel computers.

The PGA models natural evolution more realistically than the GA. The selection of individuals for mating is done within the population itself. This is achieved by the introduction of a population structure. The GA in contrast models evolution by a centralized selection scheme.

We hoped to find arguments in favor for population

structures in biological textbooks. But we were very disappointed because most of the mathematical models abstract from the spatial population structure of the population. The importance of spatial population structures on evolution is still controversially discussed, as well in theoretical biology as in genetic algorithms research.

The outline of the paper is as follows. In section 2 we introduce Darwin's *continent cycle theory*. The general problem *stability* versus *diversity* and the relevance of space for evolution is discussed in section 3. The classic problem - evolution of a large panmictic population versus a number of small local populations is surveyed in section 4. The Iterated Prisoner's Dilemma IPD is introduced in section 5. The PGA is described in section 6. The importance of the genetic representation of the IPD on the simulation results is shown in section 7. A simple analytical model of clustered populations is introduced in section 8. Simulation results are presented in section 9.

An extended version of this paper has been published in Mühlenbein 1991b. There detailed simulation results can be found. The major emphasis of this paper is on methodological questions.

2 Darwin revisited

In the section "Circumstances favourable and unfavourable to Natural Selection" Darwin tries to describe the influence of intercrossing, isolation and number of individuals on the speed of evolution. Darwin mentions that this is an extremely intricate subject. He argues very carefully, for example: "For to ascertain whether a small isolated area or a large open area like a continent has been the most favourable for the production of new organic forms, we ought to make comparisons within equal times; and this we are incapable of doing".

Simulation makes such a comparison possible. It is of course impossible to simulate the real evolution of nature, so we have to find an artificial environment which is nevertheless complex enough to model the important aspects of evolution. As a first step we have decided to simulate an artificial population where each individual plays a two-person game against the other individuals. We have selected the Iterated Prisoner's Dilemma IPD, because it is surprisingly complex. Furthermore it is possible to compare our simulation results with theoretical results and simulations done by other researchers.

In a series of papers we will try to follow step-by-step Darwin's reasoning by simulation. We can cite here only Darwin's major conclusion. " I conclude that a large continental area, which will probably undergo many oscillations of level, and which consequently will exist for long periods in a broken condition, will be the most favourable for the production of many new forms of life, likely to endure long and spread widely." Darwin argues as follows. In a large continent, there is severe competition. This leads to the extinction of over-specialized species. But it is highly improbable that something new arises on a large continent. This happens much easier on small islands. But if the islands are isolated for a long time, then over-specialized forms will develop. So Darwin postulates, that the islands should reconvert to a large continent. There will be again severe competition eliminating the specialized forms. This briefly sketches Darwin's true evolution model. We call Darwin's conclusion the *continent cycle theory*. The interested reader is highly recommended to read the above mentioned chapter in Darwin's book.

Darwin's true evolution model is a non-equilibrium model, whereas all the popular Darwinian, Neo-Darwinian and Synthesis theories are equilibrum models. Darwin views evolution as a property of the organization of the organism, rather than as a property of the matter of an individual organism.

Darwin's arguments in favour of the continent cycle can also, with just some minor changes, be applied to other areas like the *invention of successful scientific ideas* or the *efficient organization of companies.* Take the organization of companies as an example. If the market (the environment) is stable, a large centralized company with severe internal competition is most effective. If the company has to adapt to a changing market, the large company should be subdivided into small companies which can adapt much faster.

It is this general aspect that gives Darwin's true evolution theory such a broad range of applications, ranging from artificial intelligence to sociology, economy, psychology and philosophy.

The major emphasis of this paper will be on methodological questions for at least two reasons. First we believe that methodological questions are of utmost importance in a scientific field where it is almost impossible to compare simulation results with actual experiments. Second, it is not possible to explain in one short paper all the simulation experiments which are necessary to support or disprove Darwin's continent cycle theory.

3 Stability, complexity and space

A discussion which is similar in spirit to Darwin's can also be found in population biology. Here the problem is called stability versus complexity. It is part of the "conventional wisdom" of modern ecology that an increase in the number of links in the food web increases the stability of the ecosystem. By this is meant that the more species that coexist, and the higher the number of links in which each species participates, the more each population will tend to vary around constant average values, and the more predictable will be the magnitude of the fluctuations (Wilson 1971). Complexity implies stability.

On the other hand, general mathematical models of multispecies communities show the opposite. Here increasing complexity of the ecosystem tends to beget diminishing stability. This was proven under very general conditions by May (1974). But May mentions one possible reason for this result. "We consider isolated communities which are uniformly unvarying in space; time is the only variable. Spatial inhomogeneties, however, undoubtedly play a major role in many, if not most, real biological communities."

The problem of spatial structures has also been noticed in other areas, like contagion processes. The usual stochastic models assume that the population is "well mixed". That is to say, the probability of an encounter between any two individuals at any moment in time is assumed to be the same for all pairs. If, however, the individuals are not mobile, then the probability of contact between two individuals already "infected" will, in generral, become larger as the process goes on. Rapaport (1973) writes: "What we need is first of all an abstract mathematical theory of spaces which are formed by stochastically governed interactions of individual elements".

Temporal structures are much more easier to describe than spatial or other interaction structures, because time can be mapped onto one axis with the usual metric. Spatial structures have to be described by graphs or relations. Stochastic effects in time can be investigated by running many experiments and computing the averages of the observed variables at certain times. The same procedure - averaging over points in space - seldom makes sense with spatial structures.

We will summarize in the next sectionn the efforts in population genetics to understand structured spaces where the interaction pattern is defined by spatial distances.

4 Spatial population structures

Several researchers in biology have tried to investigate the importance of spatial population structures for evolution - without ever refering to Darwin. It is now accepted, that a spatial population structure has more variety than a panmictic population. The importance of this fact on evolution has been however highly controversially discussed.

Wright (1932) has argued that the best way to avoid being hung up on a low fitness peak is to have the population broken up into many nearly isolated subpopulations. Wright's theory has three phases (Wright 1965). *Phase 1* consists of the *differentiation* of innumerable small local populations by more or less random processes that occasionally lead to higher peaks. *Phase 2* is the occupation of higher peaks by *local mass selection*. *Phase 3* is the *diffusion* of these succesful subpopulations throughout the species, followed by the appearance of still more succesful centres of diffusion at points of contact. Then the whole process starts again.

Fisher (1958), in contrast, argued that no such theory is needed. In a highly multidimensional fitness surface, the peaks are not very high and are connected by fairly high ridges, always shifting because of environmental changes. According to Fisher, the analogy is closer to waves and troughs in an ocean than in a static landscape. Alleles are selected because of their average effects, and a population is unlikely to be ever in such a situation that it can never be improved by direct selection based on additive variance.

The difference between these two views is not purely mathematical, but physiological. Does going from one favored combination of alleles to another often necessitate passing through genotypes that are of lower fitness? Fisher argued that evolution typically proceeded in a succession of small steps, leading eventually to large differences by the accumulation of small ones. According to this view, the most effective population is a large panmictic one in which statistical fluctuations are slight and each allele can be fairly tested in combination with many others alleles. According to Wright's view, a more favorable structure is a large population broken up into subgroups, with migration sufficiently restricted (less than one migrant per generation) and size sufficiently small to permit appreciable local differentiation.

Four different models for spatially structured populations have been investigated mathematically

- the one-island model
- the island model
- the stepping stone model
- the isolating by distance model

In the one-island model, an island and a large continent are considered. The large continent continuously sends migrants to the island. In the island model, the population is pictured as subdivided into a series of randomly distributed islands among which migration is random.

In the stepping-stone model migration takes place between neighboring islands only. One and two dimensional models have been investigated.

The isolation by distance model treats the case of continuous distribution where effective demes are isolated by virtue of finite home ranges (neighborhoods) of their members. For mathematical convenience it is asssumed that the position of a parent at the time it gives birth relative to that of its offspring when the latter reproduces is normally distributed.

Felsenstein (1975) has shown that the isolating by distance model leads to unrealistic clumping of individuals. He concluded, that this model is biologically irrelevant. There have been many attempts to investigate spatial population structures by computer simulations, but they did not have a major influence. A good survey of the results of the different population models can be found in Felsenstein (1976). Population models with oscillation like Darwin's continent cycle have not been dealt with.

The issue raised by Wright and Fisher is still not settled. Phase 3 of Wright's theory has been recently investigated by Crow 1990. He concludes: "The importance of Wright's shifting-balance theory remains uncertain, but we believe whatever weaknesses it may have, they are not in the third phase."

In the PGA we have implemented the isolation by distance model and the stepping stone model. The three phases of Wright's theory can actually be observed in the PGA. But the relative importance of the three phases is different than Wright believed. The small populations do not find better peaks by random processes. The biggest changes of the population occur at the time after migration between the subpopulations. Recombinations between immigrants and native individuals occasionally lead to higher peaks which were not found by any of the subpopulations during isolation. This behavior can easily be demonstrated in the application function optimization (see Mühlenbein 1991a for details). We can therefore state the following observation.

The creative forces of evolution take place at migration and few generations afterwards. Wright's argument that better peaks are found just by chance in small subpopulations is wrong.

In our opinion the most important part of Wright's theory is what Wright postulated as "the appearance of still more succesful centres of diffusion at points of contact".

We have not yet used Darwin's continent cycle population structure for optimization problems, because the results of the stepping stone model with migration are already very good. We believe that the reason for this success lies in the static fitness function. The fitness of an individual is given in a closed form. It depends only on the genotype of the individual. The same is true for the mathematical models where almost trivial fitness functions are used.

We believe that static fitness functions cannot model real evolution. In a real environment the fitness of an individual depends on the outcome ot its interactions with other organisms in the environment. The fitness cannot be specified in advance. In order to investigate Darwin's continent cycle we decided to simulate an artificial ecology. In our ecology the interactions of the individuals are modeled by a game. The fitness of the individual is the sum of the payoffs the individual gets during its lifetime. We have chosen the Iterated Prisoner's Dilemma (IPD), because it has been investigated from a number of different viewpoints.

5 The artificial ecology

Over its 30-year lifespan, the Iterated Prisoner's Dilemma has been one of the most frequently studied phenomena in economics, political science, sociology and psychology (see Axelrod 1984 for a survey). The basic prisoner's Dilemma is a two-person game, with each player having a choice of either cooperating (C) or defecting (D). A typical set of payoffs is presented below.

Move	C	D
C	3/3	0/5
D	5/0	1/1

Given these payoffs, it is easily shown that mutual defection is the only Nash equilibrium. Of course, the intrigue of the Prisoner's Dilemma is that this unique equilibrium is Pareto inferior to the mutual cooperation outcome. If the basic Prisoner's Dilemma is iterated, the resulting supergame is an Iterated Prisoner's Dilemma IPD. If the number of iterations is a known finite number, then a simple backward induction argument implies that the only equilibrium is mutual defection in every round. However, if the game is repeated a finite, but unknown number of times, then cooperative behavior can theoretically emerge.

The *ecological* approach to experimental games has added another dimension to the study of conflict and cooperation in societies. John Maynard Smith (1984) introduced the *evolutionary game theory*, where the games are played by a population of individuals. The higher the payoff of an individual, the more offspring he will get. In this manner the most effective strategies survive. A strategy is called *evolutionary stable*, if it cannot be invaded by a single mutant strategy. The theory assumes that the strategies are not changed during the course of evolution. In our simulations the strategies are coded by genes. The strategies are constantly changed by the parallel genetic algorithm, which uses mutation and crossing-over for generating offspring.

6 The method of investigation

There have been at least three attempts to investigate the IPD with genetic algorithms. The first simulation was performed by Axelrod(1987). Axelrod considered strategies where the moves are based on the game's past three-move history. The major focus of Axelrod's study was on strategies evolving against a fixed environment. Each individual played against eight representative strategies. Marks(1989) extended the investigation to *bootstrap* evolution, where the individuals play against each other. Miller(1990) used finite automata to represent strategies. Furthermore he investigated the effect of informational accuracy on the outcome of the simulation. All three researchers used the plain genetic algorithm for evolving the population. They have been interested in equilibrium states and "optimal" strategies. We concentrate on the evolution of the behavior of the total population.

In our simulations we use the parallel genetic algorithm PGA to simulate the ecology. This gives us the possibility to investigate the importance of spatial population structures on evolution. The PGA is defined as follows

Parallel Genetic Algorithm

STEP0: Define a genetic representation of the problem

STEP1: Create an initial population and its population structure

STEP2: Each individual does local hill-climbing

STEP3: Each individual selects a partner for mating in its neighborhood

STEP4: An offspring is created with genetic crossover of the parents

STEP5: The offspring does local hill-climbing. It replaces the parent, if it is better than some criterion (acceptance)

STEP6: If not finished, return to STEP3.

The PGA has been successfully applied to important optimization problems. The major enhancements to the plain genetic algorithm are the spatial population structure, the distributed selection and the local hill-climbing. The individuals are active. They look for a partner for mating in their neighborhood. The partner is chosen according to the preference of the individuals. The best individual in a neighborhood has the chance to get as many offspring as the global best individual of the population. The PGA therefore has a very "soft" selection scheme. Each individual has the chance that on average 50% of its genes are contained in the chromosome of an offspring. The offspring replaces the parent.

We have applied the PGA to many optimization problems. The PGA outperforms the GA on many large complex optimization problems by far, see Mühlenbein et al. 1988, Mühlenbein 1989, Mühlenbein 1991b for combinatorial optimization and Mühlenbein et al. 1991 for function optimization. In fact, the PGA has solved large optimization problems never solved before.

In order to investigate Darwin's continent cycle theory we decided to simulate an artificial ecology where the fitness of the individuals is not staticly specified. In order not to complicate the simulations our individuals are not allowed to improve their fitness by learning.

We now turn to the problem of genetic representation of strategies.

7 The genetic representation

There are at least two obvious ways to represent strategies as a genetic chromosome, one is based on a simple table lookup, the other on finite automaton. We will discuss in this paper deterministic table lookup strategies. A k-lookback strategy can be defined as a mapping of the outcome of the last k moves into a new move. In the simplest case of just looking one play back, a strategy can be defined by four entries in a table symbolizing the four possible moves of the last game - DD,DC,CD,CC. In addition two bits are necessary to specify the first move. The genetic representation of one-lookback thus consists of six bits. This gives 2^6 different genotypes. Three popular strategies are given below

						strategy
C	*	*	*	C	C	ALL-C
D	*	D	D	*	*	ALL-D
C	*	D	C	D	C	TIT-FOR-TAT

The sign * denotes that the allele on this locus does not have any influence on the performance of the strategy. There are twelve different bitstrings which all define an ALL-C strategy. The problem of this straightforward genetic representation is that we have a distinction between the *representation* and the *interpretation*. The program which interprets the representation is not part of the genetic specification and therefore not subjected to the evolution process. But we have a clear distinction between genotype, phenotype and behavior. The genotype is mapped into some phenotype, the phenotype together with the environment (in our case the other phenotypes) defines the strategy. Let us take the famous TIT-FOR-TAT as an example. In TIT-FOR-TAT the player makes the move the opponent made the game before. In an environment where only C is played, TIT-FOR-TAT cannot be distinguished from an ALL-C player. A different behavior can only be recognized if there exists an individual who occasionally plays D.

The mapping from genotype to phenotype is many-to-one. This makes a behavior oriented interpretation of a given genetic representation very difficult. There exist no simple structure of the genotype space. The Hamming distance between two ALL-C genetic representations can be as large as four, whereas the Hamming distance between two very different strategies like ALL-C and ALL-D can be as small as one. An example is shown below

						strategy
C	C	D	D	C	C	ALL-C
C	C	D	D	C	D	ALL-D

If we assume that the genetic operators *mutation* and *crossing-over* uniformly explore the genotype space, then strategies like ALL-C and ALL-D will have a much higher chance to be generated than other strategies which are less often represented. The genetic search is therefore biased by the genetic representation. We believe that this effect is not a shortcoming of the chosen representation, but that this feature models real life evolution. The evolution has always to work within the constraints it creates for itself.

The complex mapping between genotype and phenotype makes it difficult to estimate the outcome of a genetic operator. For example, a winning strategy may be crossed with a losing strategy, giving in most cases a new strategy. An ALL-D strategy which is crossed-over with an ALL-C strategy gives with probability 0.2 ALL-D and with probability 0.2 ALL-C. With probability 0.6 we get a strategy which is different from the strategies of the parents.

We believe that in our artificial ecology the crossover operator is too disruptive compared to real evolution. The same problem occurs if the genetic representation is based on a finite automaton. In order to solve this problem we have to find a genetic representation which is based on a more complex genetic machinery than simple bitstrings. It is outside the scope of this paper to discuss this genetic machinery. We only want to mention that we have to incorporate some ideas of models of self-reproduction proposed already in the 60's.

The influence of spatial population structures is independent of the genetic representation, therefore we will concentrate on this subject.

8 Structured populations

Before we discuss some of the simulation results in detail we want to show by a simple analysis how a spatial population structure influences the development of strategies.

For simplicity we assume that we have a population, consisting of *inhabitants* playing strategy I and *invaders* playing strategy J. Let s be the proportion of invaders. We assume that s is very small. Furthermore the invaders are clustered. We model this fact by a clustering factor k. Let $P(I, J)$ denote the payoff of an individual playing strategy I against an individual playing strategy J. After invasion the fitness of the inhabitants can be approximately computed as

$$F(I) = (1-s*\frac{1-ks}{1-s})*P(I,I)+s*\frac{1-ks}{1-s}P(I,J) \quad (1)$$

The invaders have the fitness

$$F(J) = (1-ks)*P(J,I)+ks*P(J,J) \quad (2)$$

We see that for $k = 0$ the invaders play against the inhabitants only, the case $k = 1$ gives the panmictic population normally considered in the theory of evolutionary games. In the case of $k > 1$ we have a clustering effect. For $k = s^{-1}$ the invaders and the inhabitants play within their group only.

A strategy is called *collective stable* if no strategy can invade it. A new strategy is said to *invade* if the newcomer gets a higher score than the native strategy. For small s, this means

$$P(I,I) < (1-ks)P(J,I)+ks*P(J,J) \quad (3)$$

If we set $p = ks$ then the above inequality is identical to Axelrod's *p-cluster invasion* (Axelrod 1984p.212). It is now easily seen that even ALL-C can withstand the invasion of ALL-D, if there is a strong preference for each strategy to play only against each other. With our payoff values we obtain that ALL-C will not be invaded for $k > 0.5s^{-1}$.

The above model can be applied to a population structure consisting of groups of individuals playing the same strategy. Each individual in a group has the same number of contests with individuals of other groups. The number of contests between the inhabitants compared to the number of contests between inhabitants and invaders define the clustering factor k. Then the fitness is given by formulas (1) and (2).

In a one-dimensional spatial population structure with restricted neigborhoods the situation is more difficult. The contest between the strategies happens at the boundary of the neighborhoods, whereas the individuals in the interior play only against members of their own group. In this spatial structure the success of the invasion is therefore determined by the outcomes at the boundary.

It is almost impossible to investigate realistic spatial population structures by analytical methods, one has to use simulations. This was first done by Axelrod (1984pp158-168). Axelrod investigated a simple 2-D structure where each player had four neigbors. The selection was very strong. If a player had one or more neighbors which had been more successful, the player converted to the strategy of the most successful of them. Axelrod's major conclusion was that mutual cooperation can be sustained in a (not too highly connected) territorial system at least as easy as it can be in a freely mixing system. We will extend Axelrod's work. First, different population structures are compared and second, the strategies evolve controlled by the genetic algorithm.

9 Simulation results

In our simulation we have investigated the following population structures

- a small panmictic population
- a large panmictic population(500 individuals)
- a panmictic population with randomly selected neighbors(seven)
- a one-dimensional population (ring structure with four neighbors)
- a cycle between a ring population and a panmictic population
- a cycle between ten islands populations and a panmictic population

In a panmictic population each individual plays against each other, in a spatial population structure the individuals play only against their neighbors. In a panmictic population with randomly selected neighbors the individuals play only against these neighbors. Most of the experiments have been done with a small population of 50 individuals. Detailed simulation results can be found in Mühlenbein 1991a. In our simulations we used 2-lookback strategies. They can be coded by 20 bits. This gives 2^{20} different genotypes.

In the first set of simulations we started with a population where the initial strategies had been randomly generated. We investigated the influence of the number of individuals and of the population structure on evolution. The following result has been obtained. A large panmictic population has the smallest variety and nothing new happens. Evolution within a continent cycle seems to be very robust. The ring population has the largest variety.

We also investigated the invasion of an ALL-C population by a cluster of 5 ALL-D individuals. The results are shown in figur 1.

In the figure the average, the maximum and the minimum fitness of the population is shown. At the start of the simulation the ALL-D population is living on a separate island. Nothing interesting happens. The average of the fitness of the population remains constant. After 20 generations the islands are converted to a continent. Now ALL-D invades the population. The population is rapidly changing to non-cooperation. But it takes only two continent cycles and the population is again at cooperation. In a single panmictic population ALL-D successfully invades the population. Then the population stays at non-cooperative behavior if the population is large (e.g. 500 individuals). This simulation is shown in figure 2.

We also simulated the worst case where the simulation started with a homogeneous ALL-D population. We investigated for the different population structures whether the populations will change to cooperation. In the simulations the population which is subjected to the continent cycle is first to arrive at cooperation. This result was consistent in ten runs. A closer analysis of the strategies showed that the winning cooperative strategies are not naive like ALL-C, but they resemble TIT-FOR-TAT.

In a further set of experiments we changed the game during the course of the simulation, for instance we changed the IPD to the chicken game. The spatial structured populations adapted much faster to the new game than a large panmictic population. This is one of the extensions that have been already proposed by Axelrod for investigation (p.221).

The detailed simulation results can be found in Mühlenbein 1991a

10 Conclusion

Theoretical biology has almost neglected Darwin's true evolution theory. We have investigated some of Darwin's arguments in support of his continent cycle theory by simulating an artificial ecology. The simulations are based on highly simplified assumptions. The populations are very small and the sexual reproduction

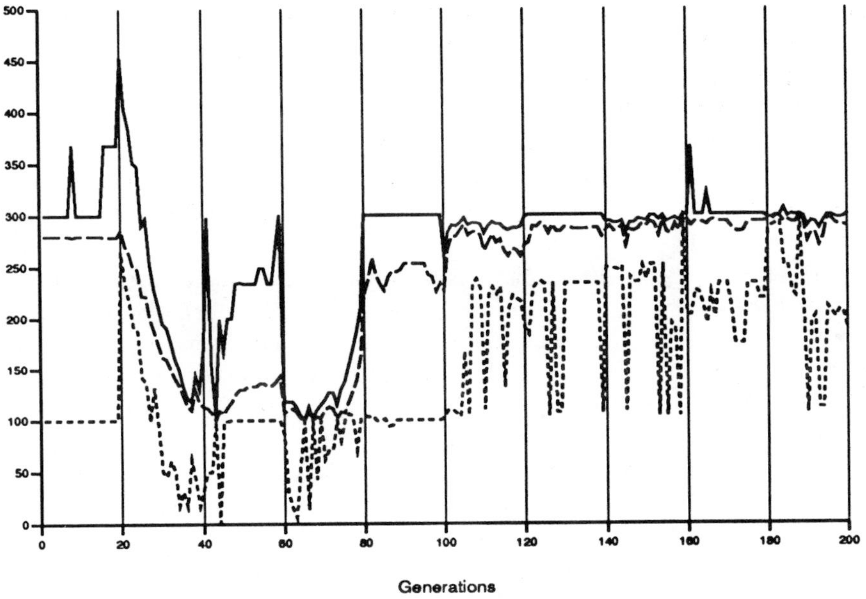

Figure 1: Continent cycle, initial 5 ALL-D, 45 ALL-C

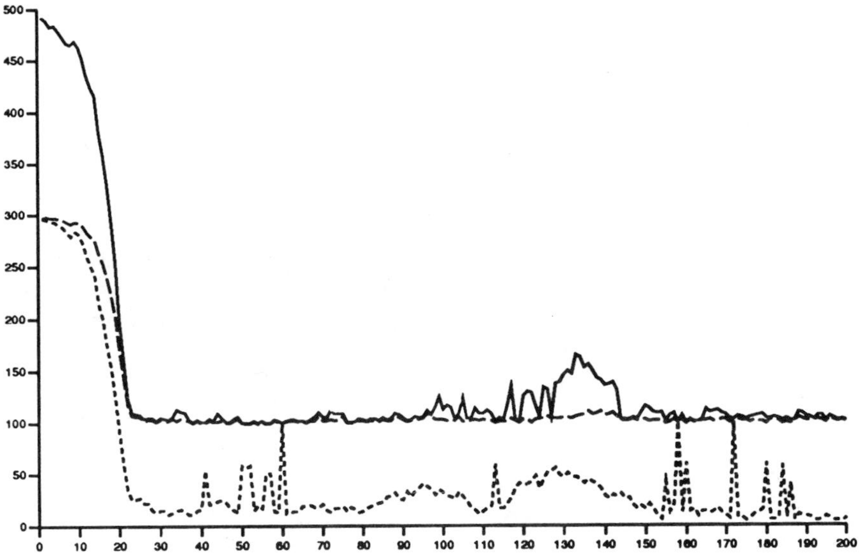

Figure 2: Large population, initial population 5 ALL-D, 490 ALL-C, 5 TFT

has no sexual differentiation between male and female. The most important simplification is that each individual can mate with each other. Therefore we have one species only in our ecology. But the number of different species is the original performance measure of Darwin's continent cycle theory.

But the main advantage of simulations can already be glimpsed from the experiments reported in this paper. Simulations provide a new intellectual perspective on evolution. Instead of having to rely only on observations of real biological systems (like Darwin) or standard mathematical models (like Wright), we are able to approach genetics and evolution as a theoretical design problem. The scientific value of the simulations is mainly given by the methodological questions, not by an individual simulation run.

Science in the past simplified evolution, just to obtain evolution models which could be dealt with mathematically. In using simulation there arises another problem. A single simulation run gives no scientific insight, it has to be carefully interpreted. The interpretation is especially difficult in problems where spaces are formed by stochastically governed interactions of individual elements.

Von Neumann already pointed out that there are two ways in which a theory of automata (or any research in artificial life) might prove useful. The first way is that "some of the regularities which we observe in the organization of natural organisms may be instructive in our thinking and planning of artificial automata." The second is the converse of the first: " A good deal of our experiences and difficulties with our artificial automata can be to some extent projected on our interpretations of natural organisms." We try to use the parallel genetic algorithm in both ways.

Acknowledgement: The author thanks M. Batz who made the simulation experiments.

REFERENCES

Axelrod, R. 1984. *The Evolution of Cooperation.* Basic Publisher, New York, 1984.

Axelrod, R. 1987. The evolution of strategies in the iterated prisoner's dilemma. In L. Davis, editor, *Genetic algorithms and Simulated Annealing,* pages 32–41, Los Altos, Morgan Kaufmann.

Crow, J.F., W.R. Engels, and C. Denniston. 1990. Phase three of Wright's shifting balance theory. *Evolution,* 44:233–247.

Darwin, Ch. 1859. *The Origins of Species by Means of Natural Selection.* Penguin Classics, London.

Felsenstein, J. 1975. A pain in the torus: Some difficulties with models of isolation by distance. *Amer. Natur.,* 109:359–368.

Felsenstein, J. 1976. The theoretical population genetics of variable selection and migration. *Ann. Rev. Genet.,* 10:253–280.

Fisher, R.A. 1958. *The Genetical Theory of Natural Selection.* Dover, New York.

Holland, J.H. 1975. *Adaptation in Natural and Artificial Systems.* Univ. of Michigan Press, Ann Arbor.

Marks R.E. 1989. Breeding hybrid strategies: Optimal behavior for oligopolist. In H. Schaffer, editor, *3rd Int. Conf. on Genetic Algorithms,* pages 198–207, San Mateo. Morgan Kaufmann.

May, R.M. 1974. *Model Ecosystems.* Princeton University Press, Princeton.

MillerOB, J.K. 1989. The coevolution of automata in the repeated prisoner's dilemma. Technical report, Santa Fe Institute.

Mühlenbein, H., M. Gorges-Schleuter. 1988 Evolution algorithms in combinatorial optimization. *Parallel Computing,* 7:65–88.

Mühlenbein, H., M. Schomisch, and J. Born. 1991 The parallel genetic algorithm as function optimizer. *Parallel Computing,* 17:619-632.

Mühlenbein H. 1989. Parallel genetic algorithm, population dynamics and combinatorial optimization. In H. Schaffer, editor, *3rd Int. Conf. on Genetic Algorithms,* pages 416–421, San Mateo. Morgan Kaufmann.

Mühlenbein, H. 1991a. Darwin's continent cycle theory and its simulation by the prisoner's dilemma. *Complex Systems,* 1991.

Mühlenbein, H. 1991b. Evolution in time and space - the parallel genetic algorithm. In G. Rawlins, editor, *Foundations of Genetic Algorithms,* pages 316–337, San Mateo. Morgan-Kaufman.

von Neumann, J. 1966. *The Theory of Self-Reproducing Automata.* University of Illinois Press. Urbana.

Rapaport, A. 1973. Mathematical General System Theory. In W. Gray and N.D. Rizzo, editors, *Unity through Diversity,* pages 437–460. Gordon and Breach, 1973.

Maynard Smith, J. 1982. *Evolution and the Theory of Games.* Cambridge University Press.

Wilson, E.O. and W.H. Bossert. 1971 *A Primer of Population Biology.* Sinauer Associates. Sunderland.

Wright, S. 1932. The roles of mutation, inbreeding, crossbreeding and selection in evolution. In *Proc. 6th Int. Congr. on Genetics,* pages 356–366.

Wright, S. 1965. Factor interaction and linkage in evolution. *Proc. Roy. Soc. Lond. B,* 162:80–104.

The Royal Road for Genetic Algorithms: Fitness Landscapes and GA Performance

Melanie Mitchell
AI Laboratory
University of Michigan
Ann Arbor, MI 48109
melaniem@eecs.umich.edu

Stephanie Forrest
Dept. of Computer Science
University of New Mexico
Albuquerque, NM 87131
forrest@unmvax.cs.unm.edu

John H. Holland
Dept. of Psychology
University of Michigan
Ann Arbor, MI 48109

Abstract

Genetic algorithms (GAs) play a major role in many artificial-life systems, but there is often little detailed understanding of why the GA performs as it does, and little theoretical basis on which to characterize the types of fitness landscapes that lead to successful GA performance. In this paper we propose a strategy for addressing these issues. Our strategy consists of defining a set of *features* of fitness landscapes that are particularly relevant to the GA, and experimentally studying how various configurations of these features affect the GA's performance along a number of dimensions. In this paper we informally describe an initial set of proposed feature classes, describe in detail one such class ("Royal Road" functions), and present some initial experimental results concerning the role of crossover and "building blocks" on landscapes constructed from features of this class.

1 Introduction

Evolutionary processes are central to our understanding of natural living systems, and will play an equally central role in attempts to create and study artificial life. Genetic algorithms (GAs) [15, 10] are an idealized computational model of Darwinian evolution based on the principles of genetic variation and natural selection. GAs have been employed in many artificial-life systems as a means of evolving artificial organisms, simulating ecologies, and modeling population evolution. In these and other applications, the GA's task is to search a fitness landscape for high values (where fitness can be either explicitly or implicitly defined), and GAs have been demonstrated to be efficient and powerful search techniques for a range of such problems (e.g., there are several examples in [19]). However, the details of how the GA goes about searching a given landscape are not well understood. Consequently, there is little general understanding of what makes a problem hard or easy for a GA, and in particular, of the effects of various landscape features on the GA's performance.

In this paper we propose some new methods for addressing these fundamental issues concerning GAs, and present some initial experimental results. Our strategy involves defining a set of landscape features that are of particular relevance to GAs, constructing classes of landscapes containing these features in varying degrees, and studying in detail the effects of these features on the GA's behavior. The idea is that this strategy will lead to a better understanding of how the GA works, and a better ability to predict the GA's likely performance on a given landscape. Such long-term results would be of great importance to all researchers who use GAs in their models; we hope that they will also shed light on natural evolutionary systems.

To date, several properties of fitness landscapes have been identified that can make the search for high-fitness values easy or hard for the GA. These include deception, sampling error, and the number of local optima in the landscape (see Section 3 for details). However, almost all the theoretical work on GA performance has been based on the assumption that deception is the leading cause of difficulty for the GA. This paper extends this work by (1) proposing several new relevant fitness landscape features, (2) studying one of these features in detail, and (3) demonstrating that there are "GA-easy" functions [27] which are not necessarily easy for the GA.

2 GAs and Schema Processing

In a GA, chromosomes are represented by bit strings, with individual bits representing genes. An initial population of individuals (bit strings) is generated randomly, and each individual receives a numerical "fitness" value—often via an external "fitness function"—which is then used to make multiple copies of higher-fitness individuals and eliminate lower-fitness individuals. Genetic operators such as mutation (flipping individual bits) and crossover (exchanging substrings of two parents to obtain two offspring) are then applied probabilistically to the population to produce a new population (or *generation*) of individuals. New generations can be produced synchronously, so that the old generation is completely replaced, or asynchronously, so that generations overlap. The GA is considered to be successful if a population of highly fit individuals evolves as a result of iterating this procedure. When the GA is being used in the context of function optimization, success is measured by the discovery of bit strings that represent values yielding an optimum (or near optimum) of the given function.

A common interpretation of GA behavior is that the GA is implicitly searching a space of patterns, the space of hyperplanes in $\{0,1\}^l$ (where l is the length of bit strings in the space). Hyperplanes are represented by *schemas*, which are defined over the alphabet $\{0,1,*\}$, where the * symbol means "don't care." Thus, *0 denotes the pattern, or schema, which requires that the second bit be set to 0 and will accept a 0 or a 1 in the first bit position. A bit string x obeying a schema s's pattern is said to be an *instance* of s; for example, 00 and 10 are both instances of *0. In schemas, 1's and 0's are referred to as *defined bits*, and the *order* of a schema is simply the number of defined bits. The fitness of any bit string in the population provides an estimate of the average fitness of the 2^l different schemas of which it is an instance, so an explicit evaluation of a population of M individual strings is also an implicit evaluation of a much larger number of schemas. The GA's operation can be thought of as a search for schemas of high average fitness, carried out by sampling individuals in a population and biasing future samples towards schemas that are estimated to have above-average fitness.

Holland's Schema Theorem [15, 10] demonstrates that, under certain assumptions, schemas whose estimated average fitness remains above the population's average fitness will receive an exponentially increasing number of samples. That is, schemas judged to be highly fit will be *emphasized* in the population. However, the Schema Theorem does not address the process by which new schemas are *discovered*; in fact, crossover appears in the Schema Theorem as a factor that slows the exploitation of good schemas. The "building-blocks hypothesis" [15, 10] states that new schemas are discovered via crossover, which combines instances of low-order schemas (partial solutions or "building blocks") of estimated high fitness into higher-order schemas (composite solutions). For example, if a string's fitness is a function of the number of 1's in the string, then a crossover between instances of two high-fitness schemas (each with many 1's) has a better than average chance of creating instances of even higher-fitness schemas. However, the actual dynamics of the discovery process—and how it interacts with the emphasis process—are not well understood, and there is no general characterization of the types of landscapes on which crossover will lead to the discovery of highly fit schemas. Specifically, there is no firm theoretical grounding for what is perhaps the most prevalent "folk theorem" about GAs—that they will outperform hillclimbers and other common search and optimization techniques on a wide spectrum of difficult problems, because crossover allows the powerful combination of partial solutions.

Our main purpose in this paper is to outline a strategy for examining these questions in detail. In particular, we are interested in understanding more precisely the relation between various fitness-landscape features and the performance of GAs, and we would like to confirm or disconfirm folk theorems such as the one mentioned above. Our approach stresses that there are many factors that make a landscape easy or difficult for the GA. Thus, we are interested in defining a set of landscape features that capture the various sources of facilitation and difficulty. We believe that such a set of features will be relevant both to practical domains in which people wish to apply the GA and to interesting biological phenomena. Once such a set of relevant features is defined, a large number of fitness landscapes can be "hand-designed," where each landscape consists of some configuration of these features. Different landscapes will present different types and degrees of difficulty for the GA, depending on what features they contain and how the features are arranged. We can then study the performance of the GA on such landscapes to learn the effects of different configurations. A longer-term goal of this research is to develop statistical methods of classifying any given landscape in terms of our spectrum of hand-designed landscapes, thus being able to predict some aspects of the GA's performance on the given landscape.

It should be noted that by stating this problem in terms of the GA's performance on fitness landscapes, we are sidestepping the question of how a particular problem can best be represented to the GA. The success of the GA on a particular function is certainly related to how the function is "encoded" [10, 21] (e.g., using Gray codes for numerical parameters can greatly enhance the performance of the GA on some problems), but since we are interested in biases that pertain directly to the GA, we will simply consider the landscape that the GA "sees."

3 Landscape Features and GA Performance

There is no comprehensive theory that relates characteristics of a fitness landscape directly to the performance of the GA, or that predicts what the GA's performance will be on a given problem. Such a theory will be difficult to articulate because the GA has many conflicting tendencies (e.g., the need to continue exploring new regions of the search space versus the need to exploit the currently most promising directions). At different times in the search or on different problems, one of these tendencies may dominate the others.

However, several properties of fitness landscapes have been identified that can make the search for high-fitness values easy or hard for the GA. Most research up to now has concentrated on three types of features: deception, sampling error, and the "ruggedness" of a fitness landscape. Bethke [2] defined a class of functions that are "misleading" for the GA and therefore hard to optimize. Goldberg extended this work, defining the class of *GA-deceptive* functions [8, 9, 11], in which low-order schemas lead the GA away from the fittest higher-order schemas. There have been a number of studies of GA performance on deceptive landscapes (e.g., [8, 3, 20]). Grefenstette and Baker studied a function in which high variance in the fitness of a correct low-order schema leads to sampling error that misleads the GA [13]. Other authors also identify sampling error as a problem in GA performance (for example, [21, 12]). Kauffman [18] has studied how the degree of ruggedness of a landscape affects the ease of adaptation under mutation and crossover. Finally, Forrest and Mitchell have identified the existence of multiple mutually conflicting partial solutions as a cause of difficulty for GAs [6].

In our current research, we are studying parameterizable landscape features that are more directly connected to the building-block hypothesis. As a starting point, these include the degree to which schemas are hierarchically structured, the degree to which intermediate-order fit schemas act as "stepping stones" between low-order and high-order fit schemas, the degree of isolation of fit schemas, and the presence or absence of conflicts among fit schemas.

We can then "mix and match" the various landscape features to create a wide variety of fitness functions. We conjecture that interactions among the features are nontrivial, and that this is one reason that it is so difficult to understand and predict GA performance.

Our landscapes will be defined by constructing fitness functions $F : \{0,1\}^l \to \Re$, (where l is the length of the bit string). Each function F will be defined in terms of various numbers, or densities, of the different landscape features (for example, a schema tree (see below) would be considered to be a landscape feature). A landscape will be parameterized in two ways, with one set of parameters corresponding to the relative frequency and location of each type of feature, and with a set of local defining parameters for each feature (e.g., the height of a hill). This separation of parameters allows us to include the notion of features embedded within other features, allowing the possibility of defining fractal-like landscapes. For the remainder of this paper we focus on the properties of particular landscape features with the understanding that they can be combined with one another in the manner just described.

Hierarchical Structure of Schemas, and Stepping Stones

The building blocks hypothesis implies that an important component of GA performance should be the extent to which the fitness landscape is hierarchical, in the sense that crossover between instances of fit low-order schemas will tend to yield fit higher-order schemas. Consider the fitness function defined in Figure 1, which we term a "Royal Road" function. This function involves a set of schemas $S = \{s_1, \ldots, s_{15}\}$, and is defined as

$$F(x) = \sum_{s \in S} c_s \sigma_s(x),$$

where x is a bit string, each c_s is a value assigned to the schema s, and $\sigma_s(x)$ is as defined in the figure. In this example, $c_s = order(s)$. The fitness of the optimum string (64 1's) is $8 * 8 + 4 * 16 + 2 * 32 + 64 = 256$.

As shown in Figure 1, a Royal Road function can be represented as a tree of increasingly higher-order schemas, with schemas of each order being composable to produce schemas of the next higher order. The hierarchical structure of such a function should in principle lead the GA, via crossover, very quickly to the optimum; in effect, this structure should in principle lay out a "royal road" for the GA to follow to the global optimum. In contrast, an algorithm such as hillclimbing that relies on single-bit mutations cannot easily find high values in such a function, since a large number of single bit-positions must be optimized simultaneously in order to move from an instance of one schema to an instance of a schema at the next higher-order level of the tree.

s_1 = 11111111**; $c_1 = 8$
s_2 = ********11111111**; $c_2 = 8$
s_3 = ****************11111111**; $c_3 = 8$
s_4 = ************************11111111********************************; $c_4 = 8$
s_5 = ********************************11111111************************; $c_5 = 8$
s_6 = **11111111****************; $c_6 = 8$
s_7 = **11111111********; $c_7 = 8$
s_8 = **11111111; $c_8 = 8$
s_9 = 1111111111111111**; $c_9 = 16$
s_{10} = ****************1111111111111111********************************; $c_{10} = 16$
s_{11} = ********************************1111111111111111****************; $c_{11} = 16$
s_{12} = **1111111111111111; $c_{12} = 16$
s_{13} = 11111111111111111111111111111111********************************; $c_{13} = 32$
s_{14} = ********************************11111111111111111111111111111111; $c_{14} = 32$
s_{15} = 1111111111111111111111111111111111111111111111111111111111111111; $c_{15} = 64$

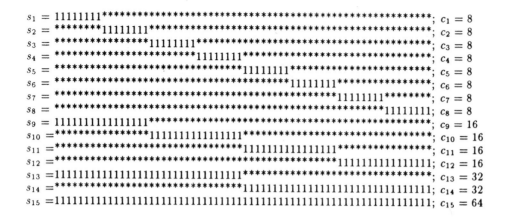

Figure 1: Example Royal Road Function. $F(x) = \sum_{s \in S} c_s \sigma_s(x)$, where x is a bit string, c_s is a value assigned to the schema s (here, $c_s = order(s)$), and $\sigma_s(x) = \begin{cases} 1 & \text{if } x \text{ is an instance of } s \\ 0 & \text{otherwise.} \end{cases}$

The Royal Road functions provide the simplest examples of the features of schema hierarchies and intermediate stepping stones, and as we discuss later in this paper, they can be used to study in detail the effects of these features on the GA's performance.

Isolated High-Fitness Regions

A second type of feature is an isolated region of high average fitness (say, containing the global optimum) contained in a larger region of lower average fitness, which is in turn contained in an even larger area of intermediate average fitness [16]. These are related to cases of "isolated optima" described by Bethke [2]. For example, using the same notation as for the Royal-Road functions, a simple isolate can be defined as follows:

$$F(x) = 5\sigma_{**11}(x) - 16\sigma_{*111}(x) + 5\sigma_{11**}(x) - 16\sigma_{111*}(x) + 31\sigma_{1111}(x).$$

Here the highest value is 9 (with optimum point $x' = 1111$), and the average fitnesses $u(s)$ of the five schemas are:

$u(**11) = 2$
$u(*111) = -1$
$u(11**) = 2$
$u(111*) = -1$
$u(1111) = 9.$

In such a feature, the region of highest fitness is *isolated* from supporting (lower-order) schemas by the intervening region of lower fitness. A search algorithm such as hillclimbing will reach the largest areas of intermediate fitness (**11 and 11**), but will in general be slow at crossing the intervening "deserts" of lower fitness (*111 and 111*). One hypothesis [16] is that the GA should be better able to search landscapes containing such features because the lower-fitness deserts can be quickly crossed via crossover (here, between instances of 11** and **11). Isolates are a special case of what have been called "partially deceptive functions" [9].

The idea of isolated regions of high fitness surrounded by flat deserts of low fitness is similar to the "mesa phenomenon" proposed by Minsky [24] and to the error surfaces identified by Hush et al. for multilayer perceptron neural networks [17]. Thus, the shape of the surface may be as important to GA performance as the actual direction of the gradient (deceptive functions emphasize direction). This feature allows us to control the shape as well as the direction of the surface the GA is searching.

Multiple Conflicting Solutions

Finally, landscapes with multiple conflicting solutions can be difficult for the GA. For example, consider a function with two equal peaks: for example, $f(x) = (x - (\frac{1}{2}))^2$, which has two optima, 0 and 1. In this environment, a conventional GA initially samples both peaks, but eventually converges on one by exploiting random fluctuations in the sampling process (genetic drift). Since both peaks are equally good, the population may maintain samples of both for some time. However, if the solutions are mutually exclusive (00...0 vs. 11...1 in many encodings), crossover may be hindered by crossing good solutions from different peaks, creating useless hybrids.

Moving away from a strict function-optimization setting, similar difficulties are encountered for any kind of ecological environment in which the population needs to maintain multiple conflicting schemas. Examples include classifier systems [14] (where genetic operators are used to search for a useful set of rules that collectively performs well) and GA models of the immune system [7] (where a population of antibodies is evolving to cover a set of antigens). In functions with conflicting pressures, issues such as crossover disruption [5] and carrying capacity (how many different solutions a population of a given size can maintain) [4] are relevant factors.

The three categories of features sketched above constitute an initial set from which to construct landscapes for the purpose of studying GA performance. This set is by no means complete; two goals of our current work are to extend this set and to determine appropriate dimensions along which to parameterize both the individual features and the landscapes constructed out of such features. However, we believe that this initial set captures several important aspects of landscapes that to date have been largely ignored in the GA literature, and that experiments involving GA performance on landscapes constructed out of such features will yield a number of important insights. In the next section we describe experimental results concerning the Royal Road landscapes, thus illustrating our overall approach.

4 GA Performance on Royal Road Functions

According to the building-blocks hypothesis, the Royal Road function shown in Figure 1 defines a fitness landscape that is tailor-made for search by the GA, since crossover should allow the GA to follow the tree of building-block schemas directly to the optimum. It provides an ideal laboratory for studying the GA's behavior for the following reasons: (1) all of the desired schemas are known in advance, since they are explicitly built into the function, so dynamics of the search process can be studied in detail by tracing the ontogenies of individual schemas; (2) the landscape can be varied in a number of ways, and the effects of these variations on the GA's behavior can likewise be studied in detail; and (3) since the global optimum, and, in fact, all possible fitness values, are known in advance, it is easy to compare the GA's performance on different instances of Royal Road functions.

There are several ways in which the degree of "regality" of the path to the optimum can be varied. For example, the number of levels (schema orders) in the tree can be varied. In Figure 1, there are four levels (schemas of orders 8, 16, 32, and 64); this could be changed to 3 levels, effectively truncating the hierarchy by eliminating all of the order-8 schemas. Another variation would be to introduce gaps in the hierarchical structure, say, by deleting an entire intermediate level in the tree (thus eliminating some of the intermediate stepping stones to the optimum). Another variation would be to modify the steepness of increase in the coefficients c_s as a function of height in the tree. Finally, deception can be introduced by mutating some of the supporting schemas, effectively creating low-order schemas that lead the GA away from the good higher-order schemas. Royal Road functions can be made arbitrarily difficult for the GA (e.g., by changing the values of the coefficients or by truncating the tree).

The Royal Road functions can be used to address a number of general questions about the effects of crossover on various landscapes, including the following: For a given landscape, to what extent does crossover help the GA find highly fit schemas? What is the effect of crossover on the waiting times for desirable schemas to be discovered? What are the bottlenecks in the discovery process: the waiting times to discover the components of desirable schemas, or, once the components are in the population, the waiting times for them to cross over in the desired manner? What is the cause of failure for desired schemas to be discovered? To what degree is a complete hierarchy (as opposed to an incomplete one with gaps in the tree) necessary for successful GA performance? Answering these questions in the context of the idealized Royal Road functions is a first step towards answering them in more general cases.

In the following subsections, we report results from our initial studies of Royal Road functions. These results address three basic questions:

1. What is the effect of crossover on the GA's performance on different landscapes?
2. More specifically, what is the effect of crossover on the waiting time for desirable schemas to be discovered, and how can we account for this effect?
3. What is the role of intermediate levels in the hierarchy (intermediate-order supporting schemas) on the difficulty of these functions with respect to the GA?

We report results of computational experiments that test the GA's performance on these functions, both with and without crossover. We also report results of control experiments which compare the GA's performance with a stochastic iterated hillclimbing algorithm (see [26]) on these functions. For each of these experiments, we used functions with $l = 64$ (the individuals in the GA population were bit strings of length

64). The GA population size was always 128, and in each run the GA was allowed to continue until the optimum string was discovered, and the generation of this discovery was recorded. The GA we used was conventional [10], with single-point crossover and sigma scaling [26, 6] with the maximum expected offspring of any string being 1.5. The crossover rate was 0.7 per pair of parents and the mutation probability was 0.005 per bit.

4.1 Effect of crossover on GA performance

Our examination of the role of crossover on the Royal Road functions begins with the following question: To what extent does crossover contribute to the GA's success on simple versions of these functions? That is, the initial set of experiments attempts to validate the building-blocks hypothesis on these functions. For these experiments, we ran the GA with and without crossover on the function given in Figure 1. We also ran hillclimbing on this function, allowing the equivalent of 2000 generations (256,000 function evaluations), which is more than three times as long as required by a typical GA run (see Table 1).

Table 1 summarizes the results of 50 runs of each algorithm on the function. As was expected, crossover considerably speeds up the GA's discovery of the optimum. Both versions of the GA significantly outperform hillclimbing: in 50 runs of hillclimbing, the optimum was never found, and moreover, the highest fitness attained was only 38% of the optimum.

These results confirm our qualitative expectations: on landscapes in which fit schemas are organized in a hierarchy like the one in Figure 1, crossover helps to significantly speed up the discovery process. This result may seem obvious, but it is necessary to establish as a baseline the *degree* to which crossover speeds things up before we can study the effects of variations on the landscape.

As a next step, we look more closely at the effects of crossover on the GA's performance, considering the effect of crossover on the waiting times for the various schemas defining the fitness function to be discovered. Table 2 displays the average generation at which the first schema of a given order is discovered for the runs with and without crossover for the Royal Road function (the values are averaged over 50 runs). The results given in the table show that, as expected, crossover significantly reduces the waiting time for discovering schemas at each level in the tree. However, even for the runs with crossover, there are, on average, significant gaps between the discovery of, say, the first order-16 schema and the first order-32 schema. What is the cause of these long gaps? That is, what are the bottlenecks in the discovery process?

To make this question more specific, we note that there are two stages in the discovery process of a given schema via crossover: the time for the schema's lower-order components to appear in the population, and the time for two instances to cross over in the right way in order to create the schema. Which of these stages contributes the most to the long gaps seen in Table 2?

The building-blocks hypothesis suggests that, once the lower-order components of a desired schema are present in the population, these components will then combine relatively quickly via crossover to form the desired schema. This would imply that the main bottleneck in the discovery process is the waiting time for the lower-order components to appear in the population, rather than the waiting time for them to cross over in the required way. We believe that this is the case, but the results of our experiments in this area were somewhat inconclusive. Given the importance of testing this rigorously, it is worth discussing some of the issues related to answering this question.

It seems that one could test this hypothesis in a straightforward manner by separately measuring the average time required for each stage and comparing the two times. We made several measurements to identify these separate stages. For each schema order in the tree, we measured the average difference in generations between the time when two components of a given order were both in the population and the time when the higher-order combination of the two occurred. For example, one of the measurements going into the order-8 average would be the difference between the discovery time for 11111111*...* or ********11111111*...* (whichever was discovered later), and the time when the combination 1111111111111111*...* is created. Table 3 gives the results of these measurements, averaged over all schemas of a given order, and over 50 runs. The data in the table seems to indicate that there is on average a large gap between the time the lower-order components are discovered and the time they are combined to form the higher-order schema.

However, there are several problems with this method of measurement. One problem is that there are times when one of the component schemas and the desired combination schema are created simultaneously through mutation (e.g., 11111111*...* is in the population first, but 1111111111111111*...* and ********11111111*...* are created at the same time via mutation). Since the hypothesis we are considering concerns cases where the component schemas are in the population before the combination schema, we did not include the cases of simultaneous discovery in the averages given in Table 3.

A second problem is using the discovery time of the lower-order components in this measurement.

	Mean gens to optimum	Median gens to optimum
GA with Xover	590 (50)	542
GA, No Xover	1022 (46)	1000
Hillclimbing	> 2000	> 2000

Table 1: Summary of results on the Royal Road function for GA with and without crossover, and for hillclimbing. Each result summarizes 50 runs. The numbers in parentheses are the standard errors. Each run of hillclimbing was for the equivalent of 2000 generations (256,000 function evaluations), but the optimum was never found.

	Order 8	Order 16	Order 32	Order 64
GA with Xover	.01 (.1)	28 (4)	152 (16)	590 (50)
GA, No Xover	.3 (.25)	106 (14)	386 (26)	1022 (46)

Table 2: The average generation of first appearance of a schema of each order for the Royal Road function. The values are averaged over 50 runs for the GA with and without crossover. The numbers in parentheses are the standard errors.

	Order 8	Order 16	Order 32
Mean time to combine	179 (26) (110 cases)	139 (27) (27 cases)	165 (21) (21 cases)

Table 3: The average difference in generations between the first appearance of two component schemas of a given order and the appearance of the schema that is the combination of those two components. The numbers in parentheses are the standard errors. The number of cases being averaged is also given. Since the data for all schemas of a given order are being averaged, there are more cases for the order-8 schemas than for the higher-order schemas. Cases in which there was simultaneous discovery of a low-order component and a higher-order combination were not included in the averages. See the text for a discussion of the problems with the data in this table.

	Order 8	Order 16	Order 32
Mean time to combine	118 (31) (55 cases)	20 (7) (13 cases)	1 (0) (3 cases)

Table 4: The same data as in Table 3 but with the first appearance of a component schema defined as the first appearance after which the schema persists in the population for at least 10 generations. This modification resulted in a decrease in the number of cases for each order, since under this new measurement, the number of cases of simultaneous discovery increased dramatically.

Further analysis of our data indicated that very often, a lower-order component (e.g., an instance of 11111111*...*) would be discovered fleetingly, only to disappear in the next one or two generations. It would appear again later on, and only then be used in a crossover with another lower-order component (e.g., ********11111111*...*) to form the higher-order combination. So in essence, the component was discovered twice; in Table 3 we recorded only the original discovery time. This resulted in a large increase in the measured time to cross over.

To remedy this problem, we recorded the discovery time of a component only if instances of it persisted in the population for at least 10 generations after the discovery. The results of those measurements are given in Table 4. Under this measurement, the average time for order-8 schemas to combine is still high, but seems to be much less for higher-order schemas. However, under this measurement, the number of cases of simultaneous discovery of a lower-order component and the higher-order combination increased dramatically, so the number of cases over which the average is being taken is much less in this case. This means that the results are less statistically reliable.

In summary, the various problems with the measurements cause these results to be somewhat inconclusive. The purpose of giving these data is to point out some of the problems. We believe that more appropriate measuring techniques will demonstrate that the main bottlenecks in the discovery process are the waiting times for components to appear rather than the waiting times for crossovers to take place. Testing this hypothesis is of great importance, and we are currently exploring methods that will enable us to do so.

Even though we were not able to satisfactorily confirm what the building-blocks hypothesis predicts—that the main bottleneck in the discovery process is the waiting time for the lower-order components to appear in the population—it turns out that some surprising results about the role of intermediate-order schemas (discussed in the next section) actually provide some validation for this prediction and thus give some clues as to the source of the long gaps seen in Table 2.

4.2 Do intermediate levels help?

To study the effect of intermediate levels on the performance of the GA, we ran the GA with crossover on a variant of the original Royal Road function—one in which the intermediate-order schemas were removed. The variant function contains eight order-8 schemas and one order-16 schema; the fitness of the optimum string (64 1's) is now $8 * 8 + 64 = 128$.

Table 5 shows the results of the standard GA, the GA without crossover, and hillclimbing on this function.

We expected the GA's performance to be worse than on the original Royal Road function, since we believed that the intermediate-level schemas act as stepping-stones, providing reinforcement for the lower-order schemas, and speeding up the process of finding the optimum. However, the results were the opposite of what we expected. On average, the GA finds the optimum faster on the function with no intermediate schemas.

What is the cause of this unexpected phenomenon? Further analysis led us to the conclusion that the intermediate schemas cause a kind of premature-convergence phenomenon [10]. For example, suppose that, on the function *with* intermediate levels, the GA finds 11111111*...*, ********11111111*...*, and then 1111111111111111*...*. Strings that are instances of the order-16 schema receive much higher fitness (since the fitness values go up exponentially with the level of the schema). The fitness differential between instances of 1111111111111111*...* and any order-8 schema (say, *...*11111111) is large enough (32 vs. 8) that the instances of 1111111111111111*...* will virtually take over the entire population in just a few generations, often with many zeros in the right half of the string "hitchhiking" along with the 16 1's in the left half of the string. This convergence therefore can negate progress that the population has made towards good schemas in the right half of the string. Thus, once one order-16 schema is discovered, the GA must start over to discover the second order-16 schema. We observed this process directly by plotting the densities (percentage of the population that are instances) of the relevant schemas over time: on a typical run, once an order-16 schema is discovered, its density in the population quickly rises, and the density of one or more of the disjoint order-8 schemas is simultaneously seen to drop significantly, sometimes to zero. Often, this effect will prevent an order-8 schema from being discovered for a long time. This explains the relatively long intervals between the first discoveries of an order-16 and an order-32 schema, shown in Table 2, and gives evidence that the main bottleneck in the discovery of a higher-order schema is the waiting time for its lower-order components to come into the population.

In the function without the intermediate levels, this problem does not occur to such a devastating degree. The fitness of an order-16 combination of two order-8 schemas is only 16, so its discovery does not have such a dramatic effect on the discovery and persistence of other order-8 schemas in the tree. It seems that once order-8 schemas are discovered, crossover combines them relatively quickly to find the optimum. Contrary to our intuitions, it appears that reinforcement from the intermediate layers is not required in these functions. It is possible that larger problems (for example, defined over bit strings much longer than 64) or different coefficients may create landscapes in which reinforcement is an advantage rather than a detriment.

These results point to a pervasive and important issue in the performance of GAs in any domain: the problem of premature convergence. The fact that we observe a form of premature convergence even in this very simple setting suggests that it can be a factor in any GA search in which the population is simultaneously searching for two or more non-overlapping high fitness schemas (e.g., the two order-8 schemas discussed above), which is often the case. The fact that the population loses useful schemas once one of the disjoint good schemas is found suggests that the rate of effective implicit parallelism of the GA [15, 10] may need to be reconsidered.

It is suggestive that in many biological settings functionality is evolved sequentially rather than in parallel. For example, it is hypothesized that the immune system evolved by learning to recognize a base set of antigens and then successively extended the base set [25]. Thus, it may be completely appropriate for the GA to use sequential search (first learning one set of schemas, then another) under certain circumstances.

5 Conclusions

This paper reports the beginning of an investigation of the role of crossover in GAs and the characteristics of landscapes in which crossover improves the GA's performance. We have proposed several features of fitness landscapes that we believe are relevant to the perfor-

	Mean gens to optimum	Median gens to optimum
Intermediate Levels	590 (50)	542
No Intermediate Levels	427 (34)	372
Hillclimbing No Intermediate Levels	> 2000	> 2000

Table 5: Summary of results for the original Royal Road function (repeated from Table 1) and a variant with no intermediate-level schemas. Each result summarizes 50 runs. The numbers in parentheses are the standard errors. Each run of hillclimbing (on the function with no intermediate levels) was for the equivalent of 2000 generations (256,000 function evaluations), but the optimum was never found.

mance of GAs (hierarchy, isolation, and conflicts) and we have sketched a method of creating parameterized fitness landscapes built out of combinations of these features, on which the GA's performance can be studied very clearly. To illustrate our overall approach, we have introduced a class of functions, the Royal Road functions, which isolate one important aspect of fitness landscapes: hierarchies of schemas. We presented experimental results that show how crossover contributes to GA performance on these functions, as well as more surprising experimental results that show the detrimental role of the intermediate-level schemas in the hierarchy.

Given that genetic algorithms have been applied to so many complex domains, it may seem like a backwards step to be studying their behavior on landscapes as simple as the Royal Road functions. However, the unexpected results we describe in this paper indicate that there is much about the GA's behavior that is not well understood, even on very simple landscapes. The building-blocks hypothesis is generally taken as an article of faith by those using GAs, but making the meaning of this hypothesis more precise and characterizing the types of landscapes on which it is valid remain open topics of great importance. Understanding the detailed workings of the GA on these simple functions is a first step to understanding the degree to which crossover can be expected to help on more complex landscapes containing similar features.

Another long-term goal of this work is to develop a set of statistical measures that will make it possible to compare our hand-constructed landscapes with ones that arise more naturally in GA applications, and thus to be able to predict the GA's performance on such landscapes. Statistical measures such as correlation length and length of adaptive walks to optima—both defined in terms of Hamming distance—have been applied to various landscapes for this purpose [18, 22]. These measures give some indication of the "ruggedness" of a landscape, which has some relation to the GA's expected performance, but we believe that more useful characterizations may require statistical measures that take into account the way crossover operates and measure correlations in terms of some kind of "crossover distance" rather than Hamming distance (a version of this approach was studied in [23]).

Additionally, we are interested in understanding how our discoveries about the GA relate to biological systems, including in the following questions: What is the relation of function optimization to adaptation and evolution? What is the relation of our results on the role of crossover to current work in theoretical population genetics on the types of environments in which recombination is favored [1]? To what extent can we understand biological environments in terms of the features we are proposing for our fitness landscapes (e.g., hierarchies of building blocks)? We hope that studying the relation of landscape features to GA performance will not only shed light on what types of problems are likely to be suited to GAs, but will also lead to insights concerning the evolution of natural—and artificial—biological systems.

Acknowledgments

The research reported here was supported by the Michigan Society of Fellows, University of Michigan, Ann Arbor, MI (support to M. Mitchell); the Center for Nonlinear Studies, Los Alamos National Laboratory, Los Alamos, NM and Associated Western Universities (support to S. Forrest); National Science Foundation grant IRI 8904203 (support to J. Holland); and the Santa Fe Institute, Santa Fe, NM (support to all the authors). We thank Robert Axelrod, Arthur Burks, Michael Cohen, Rick Riolo, and Carl Simon for helpful discussions, and we thank Greg Huber and Robert Smith for comments that helped to improve this paper.

References

[1] Aviv Bergman and Marcus W. Feldman. More on selection for and against recombination. *Theoretical Population Biology*, 38(1):68–92, 1990.

[2] A. D. Bethke. *Genetic Algorithms as Function Optimizers*. PhD thesis, The University of Michigan, Ann Arbor, MI, 1980. Dissertation Abstracts International, 41(9), 3503B (University Microfilms No. 8106101).

[3] Rajarshi Das and Darrell Whitley. The only challenging problems are deceptive: Global search by solving order-1 hyperplanes. In R. Belew and L. Booker, editors, *Proceedings of the Fourth International Conference on Genetic Algorithms*, Los Altos, CA, 1991. Morgan Kaufmann.

[4] Kalyanmoy Deb. Genetic algorithms in multimodal function optimization. Technical report, The Clearinghouse for Genetic Algorithms, Department of Engineering Mechanics, University of Alabama, Tuscaloosa, AL, 1989. (Master's Thesis).

[5] Kenneth A. DeJong. *An Analysis of the Behavior of a Class of Genetic Adaptive Systems*. PhD thesis, The University of Michigan, Ann Arbor, MI, 1975.

[6] Stephanie Forrest and Melanie Mitchell. The performance of genetic algorithms on Walsh polynomials: Some anomalous results and their explanation. In Richard K. Belew and Lashon Booker, editors, *Proceedings of the Fourth International Conference on Genetic Algorithms*, San Mateo, CA, 1991. Morgan Kaufmann.

[7] Stephanie Forrest and Alan Perelson. Genetic algorithms and the immune system. In H. Schwefel and R. Maenner, editors, *Parallel Problem Solving from Nature*, Berlin, to appear. Springer-Verlag (Lecture Notes in Computer Science).

[8] David E. Goldberg. Simple genetic algorithms and the minimal deceptive problem. In Lawrence D. Davis, editor, *Genetic Algorithms and Simulated Annealing*, Research Notes in Artificial Intelligence, Los Altos, CA, 1987. Morgan Kaufmann.

[9] David E. Goldberg. Genetic algorithms and Walsh functions: Part II, deception and its analysis. *Complex Systems*, 3:153–171, 1989.

[10] David E. Goldberg. *Genetic Algorithms in Search, Optimization, and Machine Learning*. Addison Wesley, Reading, MA, 1989.

[11] David E. Goldberg. Construction of high-order deceptive functions using low-order Walsh coefficients. Technical Report 90002, Illinois Genetic Algorithms Laboratory, Dept. of General Engineering, University of Illinois, Urbana, IL, 1990.

[12] David E. Goldberg and Mike Rudnick. Schema variance from Walsh-schema transform. *Complex Systems*, to appear.

[13] John J. Grefenstette and James E. Baker. How genetic algorithms work: A critical look at implicit parallelism. In J. David Schaffer, editor, *Proceedings of the Third International Conference on Genetic Algorithms*. Morgan Kaufmann, 1989.

[14] J.H. Holland, K.J. Holyoak, R.E. Nisbett, and P. Thagard. *Induction: Processes of Inference, Learning, and Discovery*. MIT Press, 1986.

[15] John H. Holland. *Adaptation in Natural and Artificial Systems*. The University of Michigan Press, Ann Arbor, MI, 1975.

[16] John H. Holland. Using classifier systems to study adaptive nonlinear networks. In Daniel L. Stein, editor, *Lectures in the Sciences of Complexity, Volume 1*, pages 463–499, Reading, MA, 1989. Addison-Wesley.

[17] Don R. Hush, Bill Horne, and John M. Salas. Error surfaces for multi-layer perceptrons. Technical Report EECE 90-003, University of New Mexico, Dept. of Electrical and Computer Engineering, Albuquerque, N.M. 87131, 1990.

[18] Stuart A. Kauffman. Adaptation on rugged fitness landscapes. In Daniel Stein, editor, *Lectures in the Sciences of Complexity*, pages 527–618, Reading, MA, 1989. Addison-Wesley.

[19] Christopher G. Langton, Charles Taylor, J. Doyne Farmer, and Steen Rasmussen, editors. *Artificial Life II*. Addison Wesley, Reading, MA, 1991.

[20] Gunar E. Liepins and Michael D. Vose. Polynomials, basis sets, and deceptiveness in genetic algorithms. To appear in *Complex Systems*.

[21] Gunar E. Liepins and Michael D. Vose. Representational issues in genetic optimization. *Journal of Experimental and Theoretical Artificial Intelligence*, 2:101–115, 1990.

[22] Mark Lipsitch. Adaptation on rugged landscapes generated by local interactions of neighboring genes. Technical Report 91-02-011, Santa Fe Institute Technical Report, Santa Fe, N.M., 1991.

[23] Bernard Manderick, Mark de Weger, and Piet Spiessens. The genetic algorithm and the structure of the fitness landscape. In R. Belew and L. Booker, editors, *Proceedings of the Fourth International Conference on Genetic Algorithms*, Los Altos, CA, 1991. Morgan Kaufmann.

[24] Marvin Minsky. Steps toward artificial intelligence. In Edward A. Feigenbaum and Julian Feldman, editors, *Computers and Thought*, pages 406–452. McGraw-Hill, 1963.

[25] Alan Perelson. Personal communication.

[26] Reiko Tanese. *Distributed Genetic Algorithms for Function Optimization*. PhD thesis, The University of Michigan, Ann Arbor, MI, 1989.

[27] Stewart W. Wilson. GA-easy does not imply steepest-ascent optimizable. In Richard K. Belew and Lashon B. Booker, editors, *Proceedings of The Fourth International Conference on Genetic ALgorithms*, San Mateo, CA, 1991. Morgan Kaufmann.

USING MARKER-BASED GENETIC ENCODING OF NEURAL NETWORKS TO EVOLVE FINITE-STATE BEHAVIOUR *

Brad Fullmer and Risto Miikkulainen
Department of Computer Sciences
The University of Texas at Austin, Austin, TX 78712-1188
email fullmer,risto@cs.utexas.edu

Abstract

A new mechanism for genetic encoding of neural networks is proposed, which is loosely based on the marker structure of biological DNA. The mechanism allows all aspects of the network structure, including the number of nodes and their connectivity, to be evolved through genetic algorithms. The effectiveness of the encoding scheme is demonstrated in an object recognition task that requires artificial creatures (whose behaviour is driven by a neural network) to develop high-level finite-state exploration and discrimination strategies. The task requires solving the sensory-motor grounding problem, i.e. developing a functional understanding of the effects that a creature's movement has on its sensory input.

1 Introduction

The behaviour of a particular biological organism is driven by its neural circuitry. In modeling artificial life forms it is therefore natural to represent the organism as an artificial neural network (ANN) with a set of sensory inputs and motor outputs. ANNs have been shown to be capable of very complex processing, and in most cases they can learn the processing task from examples (Siegelman and Sontag, 1991; McClelland et al., 1986).

However, the usual neural network learning algorithms are not always useful in artificial life problems. Many algorithms, such as backpropagation (Rumelhart et al., 1986), require that the correct output is known at each input situation. This requirement is relaxed in reinforcement learning, where only an estimate of the goodness of the action (or sequence of actions) is needed for learning (Barto et al., 1983). In artificial life, even this feedback may not be immediately available. For example, if the artificial creatures are supposed to learn cooperation in a complicated task, there is no easy way to specify what the correct actions at each point are, or even whether a particular sequence of actions is good or bad.

For this reason, genetic algorithms (Holland, 1975; Goldberg, 1988) are naturally well-suited for developing neural networks in artificial life. It is only necessary to specify a fitness function that estimates how well the creature performs in the task over its lifetime. The best creatures are then genetically combined to produce offspring, thereby increasing the density of successful traits in the population. Over many generations, the average fitness of the population improves until a sufficient proficiency level is attained. As in biological evolution, the population adjusts to evolutionary pressures by developing advantageous attributes including high-level behavioural strategies and low-level sensory processing capabilities. Genetic algorithms have been used previously to evolve various types of behaviour in artificial creatures such as following a broken trail (Jefferson et al., 1991), foraging for food (Collins and Jefferson, 1991) and communicating instructions (Werner and Dyer, 1991).

A central question in the neuro-evolution approach is how the network structure can be represented in terms of genetic information so that genetic algorithms are maximally effective. In this paper, a new representation mechanism that is loosely based on the marker structure of DNA is proposed. Unlike previous approaches, this mechanism allows all aspects of the network structure, including the number of nodes and their connectivity, to be controlled by evolution.

The effectiveness of the encoding scheme is demonstrated in an object discrimination task. Successful completion of this task requires that the creatures develop high-level finite-state exploration strategies. The creatures in our experiments possess a primitive visual apparatus, i.e. their input consists of a coarse visual image. In order to recognize the object, the creatures first need to evolve a capability to make

*This research was supported in part by a grant from the University of Texas Research Institute to the second author. Majority of simulations were run on a Cray Y-MP8/864 at the University of Texas Center for High-Performance Computing.

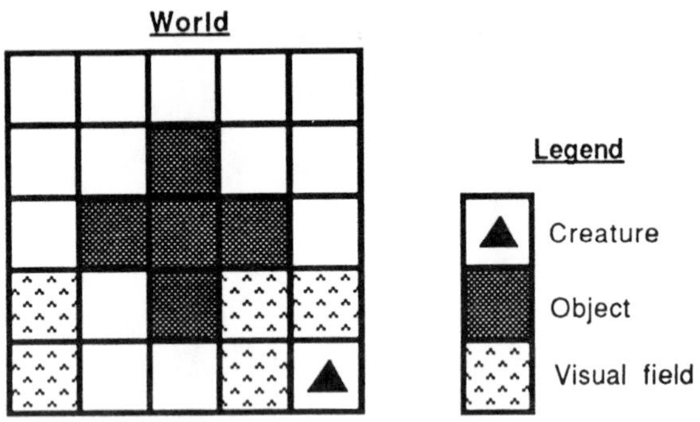

Figure 1: **Object discrimination task.** The object occupies the center of the world and the edges of the world wrap around. A creature is initially placed on a random empty square facing a random direction and it sees the squares in front of it and beside it.

sense out of their raw sensory information, and to relate it to their own actions (movements). We will call this task the "sensory-motor grounding problem".

2 The object discrimination task

In the experiments described below, creatures are evolved in the task of discriminating between a "good" and a "bad" object in an artificial world. An unprocessed "digitized" representation of the visual field is given as input, and the creatures have to evolve high-level search and recognition strategies.

The basic test scenario involves placing a creature and an object together in the simulated world and allowing the creature to explore the world (figure 1). The world is a toroidal five-by-five grid. The edges of the grid wrap around, i.e. the square immediately to the right of the rightmost square on the grid is the leftmost square on the same row, and similarly in the vertical direction. The objects vary in size and shape but generally occupy five to nine squares and are placed in the center of the grid. A creature occupies one square and can "see" five squares around it: the square directly in front of it, directly to its left and right and diagonally to its front left and right.

The creature can perform the following actions:

1. `Turn left`
2. `Turn right`
3. `Move forward`
4. `Do nothing`

The fourth option is included so that the creature can change the internal state of its neural net without changing its position (Jefferson et al., 1991).

The creature is initially placed on a random square (one not occupied by the object) and faces a random direction. The creature is given a lifespan of 35 cycles, where each cycle consists of:

1. Evaluating the creature's neural network given the network's current state and the creatures visual field as input.
2. Adjusting the creature's physical position according to the network's output.

There are two possible outcomes for each creature's lifespan:

1. The creature succeeds if:
   - The object was 'good' and the creature hit it, i.e. moved onto a square occupied by the object **-or-**
   - The object was 'bad' and the creature avoided it for all 35 cycles.
2. The creature fails if:
   - The object was 'good' and the creature did not hit it in 35 cycles **-or-**
   - The object was 'bad' and the creature hit it.

If the creature succeeds, it is given a new lifespan and the test is repeated with a new object. This process continues until the creature fails, at which point the creature's fitness level is determined by adding up the number of consecutive tests that the creature has successfully completed. After each creature has been tested and scored in this manner, the population of creatures is evolved using genetic algorithms (section 4). If a creature evolves that performs correctly for sufficiently many runs, it is said to have perfected the task and the evolution terminates.

3 Genetic representation of neural networks

3.1 Motivation

Genetic algorithms require that a creature's neural network be represented in a chromosome, that is, as a homogeneous string of e.g. integer values. It is these strings that the algorithm manipulates in order to improve the fitness of the population.

Node definition:

<start> <key> <initial_value> <k_1> <w_1> <k_2> <w_2> .... <k_n> <w_n> <end>

where:

start	- Start marker.
key	- Node identification value used in the connections (see below).
initial_value	- Output value of this node prior to first evaluation.
<k_i> <w_i>	- Input connection specifications: - k_i specifies the source of the connection. The node whose key value (see above) is closest to this value is taken as the source. - w_i specifies the weight of the connection.
<end>	- End marker.

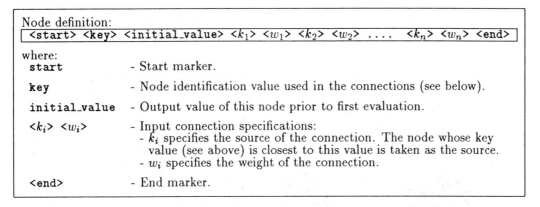

Figure 2: **Structure of a node definition.** Every node in the network is defined by this sequence, which may appear anywhere on the chromosome.

Previous approaches to genetic representation of neural networks have restricted the number of neurons (nodes) or the connectivity of the network (Dress, 1987; Mjolsness et al., 1988; Hancock, 1990; Collins and Jefferson, 1991; Jefferson et al., 1991; Werner and Dyer, 1991). These encoding schemes simplify the work of the genetic algorithm by reducing the number of parameters that must be optimized. However, any constraints placed on the network structure can result in a network that is either inefficient or incapable of performing the desired task. In order to maximize chances of evolving an optimal network, the search space of the genetic algorithm should be as large as possible. The marker-based encoding scheme, proposed below, allows *every* aspect of the network architecture to be controlled by evolution.

3.2 Marker-based encoding

The key feature of the marker-based encoding scheme is to use marker values to section off the working areas of the genetic material. This approach is inspired by the structure of biological DNA.

In DNA, the genetic information is contained in a sequence of nucleotide triplets. These triplets specify strings of amino-acids that make up a protein. Typically, a single strand of DNA specifies multiple proteins in this fashion. To separate the specification of different proteins, certain nucleotide triplets serve as markers rather than being part of amino-acid definitions. Each protein specification consists of a start marker and an end marker with the triplets in between defining the composition of the protein (Rothwell, 1988).

In a similar manner, we use markers to separate individual node definitions. Each definition contains all information that the node needs in order to carry out its computations. Instead of encoding the network structure in global terms such as number of layers or degree of connectivity, we let these features emerge from individual node definitions. The number of nodes in the network depends solely on the number of start/end marker pairs found in the chromosome.

Each node definition contains the identification of the node, its initial activation value, and a list specifying its input sources and weights (figure 2). The neuron may receive input from other nodes, from the sensors, and from its own output. The number of connections is determined by the distance between the start and end markers, allowing each node to use as many or as few inputs as it requires.

The chromosome in our experiments is a list of 800 integers ranging between -100 and 100. The start and end markers are identified by their absolute values: if this value MOD 15 equals 1, the integer is a start marker; if the value MOD 15 equals 2, the integer is an end marker. The interpretation of other chromosome integers depends on their position relative to the start and end markers. This scheme gives each value approximately 13% chance of being some type of a marker. By making the MOD constant larger or smaller, the density of node definitions can be adjusted.

The chromosome is implemented as a linear list but is treated as a continuous circular entity, that is, a node definition may begin near the end of the list and continue at the beginning of the list (figure 3). Node definitions are not allowed to overlap. If a start marker is encountered in the middle of a node definition it is treated like any other value (as a weight, or key, etc.). A node definition that 'wraps around' to the start of the chromosome is terminated by the start marker of the first node definition if an end marker has not yet

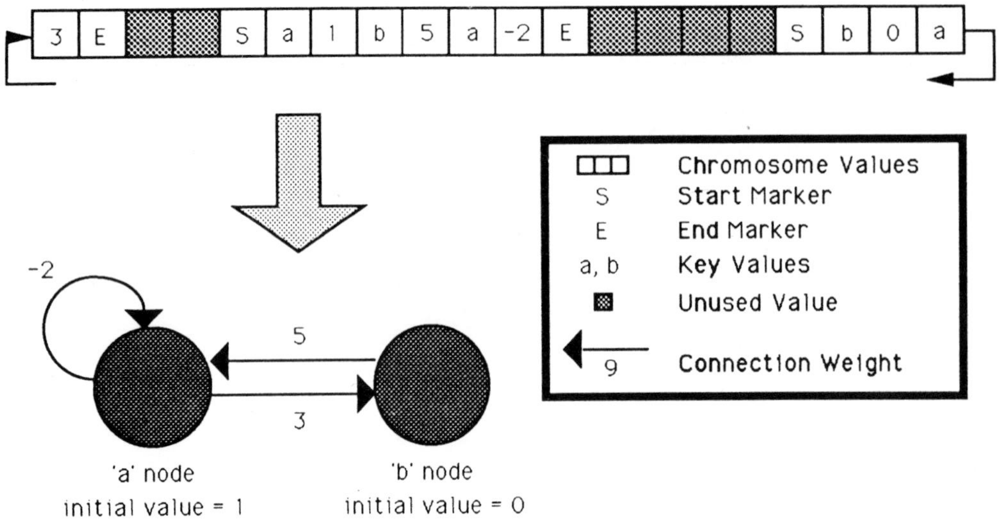

Figure 3: **Sample marker-based chromosome-to-neural-network mapping.** The chromosome contains two node definitions. The 'a' node definition begins at the fifth chromosome position and ends at the 12th. The 'b' definition begins at the 17th position and wraps around to the beginning of the chromosome, finally terminating at the second position.

been encountered. Integers between an end marker and a start marker are considered inactive, i.e. they do not take part in defining any part of the network.

3.3 Evaluating the network

During evaluation (execution) of the network, each node computes the weighted sum of its input and thresholds at zero:

$$o_k = F\left(\Sigma_{i=1}^{n} w_i o_{k_i}\right) \quad (1)$$

where o_k is the output of node identified by key k and $F(x)$ is a binary threshold function at 0.

The nodes are evaluated in the order in which they are read off the chromosome. Before each node's initial evaluation, its output value is set to its initial value (specified in the node definition) MOD 2. There are five binary inputs to the network, each representing whether a square within the creature's field of vision is empty or occupied. These inputs are referenced in the node's input connection list by mapping them to a certain range of key values. We define any connection key whose absolute value is less than 20 to be a reference to an input. The actual input is then identified as the key's absolute value MOD 5. This gives each connection a 20% chance of coming from a sensory input. The output of the network, specifying one of the four possible actions, is taken as the output values of the last two nodes read off of the chromosome. If a network contains fewer than two nodes it is not evaluated.

3.4 Properties

Most genetic representations of neural networks fix each position on the chromosome to a particular net characteristic (Dress, 1987; Mjolsness et al., 1988; Hancock, 1990; Collins and Jefferson, 1991; Jefferson et al., 1991; Werner and Dyer, 1991). Marker-based representation allows each position to be used in the way that produces the maximum benefit for the creature. In some cases many nodes with a small number of connections may be ideal, in other cases fewer nodes with a larger number of connections may be required. If a small, efficient network topology is desired, network size or execution speed can be incorporated into the fitness function.

An interesting phenomenom which consistently emerges when using this encoding scheme is the occurrence of nodes with no input connections, or 'constant nodes'. Since they receive no input, the output value of these nodes will never deviate from the initial value. Other nodes can reference these nodes as inputs, effectively establishing a non-zero threshold for that node. In other words, the constant nodes act as bias nodes, which are commonly used in place of threshold parameters in e.g. backpropagation learning (Rumelhart et al., 1986).

4 The Genetic Algorithm

4.1 Overall Strategy

The genetic algorithm used in our experiments is based on standard techniques (Goldberg, 1988). After all

One Iteration of GA for a Population of 50
1. Combine the best 15 chromosomes to form 30 new chromosomes (pairing each with another chromosome whose score is at least as good).
2. Replace the worst 30 chromosomes with the new offspring.
3. Mutate chromosomes (except the top scorer's).
4. Sort chromosomes by score.

Table 1: **Summary of the Genetic Algorithm.**

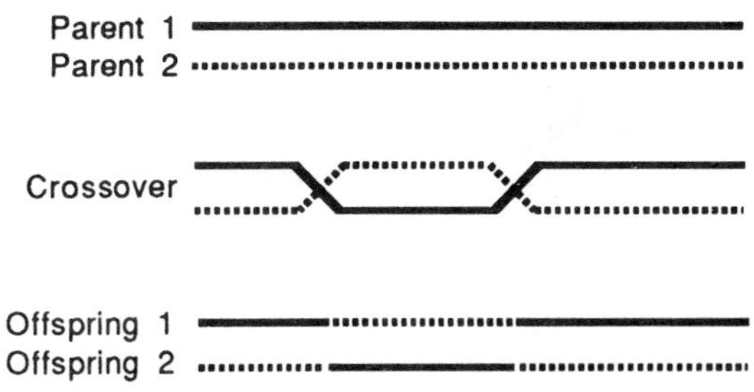

Figure 4: **Two-point crossover operation.** Two offspring are generated by recombining the genetic material of the parents.

creatures have been tested and assigned a score, a mate is assigned to each elite creature (elite = the highest scoring 30% of the population) by randomly selecting another creature whose score is *at least as good.* This strategy ensures that the best creature in the entire population is always duplicated in the offspring, and the higher-scoring creatures have better chances of propagating their genetic information. The new creatures replace the worst creatures in the population, while the original elite remain in the population. Finally, every creature except the top-scorer undergoes mutation. A population of 50 creatures was used in the experiments. The genetic algorithm is summarized in table 1.

It is common in genetic algorithm experiments to allow the genetic operators to manipulate the chromosome at the bit level (Goldberg, 1988). Our scheme, however, treats the integer as the basic genetic unit. This approach was adopted mainly to reduce processing overhead, thereby allowing larger chromosomes.

4.2 Crossover

The standard two-point crossover approach is used to generate offspring (Goldberg, 1988). The parent chromosomes are partitioned at two randomly chosen points (figure 4). Since the chromosome is treated as a circular entity, this effectively breaks the chromosome into two continuous chunks. An offspring chromosome is constructed by taking one chunk from each parent. This way two new offspring are generated at each crossover operation. The idea behind crossover is that different beneficial traits, previously encoded on different parent chromosomes, will have a chance of ending up on the same offspring chromosome, resulting in an offspring superior to either parent.

The marker-based representation scheme interacts with the crossover process in an interesting way. Since much of the space in the chromosome is unused (the space between the end of one node definition and the start of the next), the crossover points have a chance of falling in the unused sections, in which case the node definitions are transferred to the offspring without being disrupted. Additionally, because the connections are specified with key values (rather than e.g. with positions on the chromosome), a whole group of nodes can be passed from a parent to an offspring with their connections intact, perhaps preserving a useful trait. On the other hand, it is also possible to break node definitions during crossover, and some keys may take on different meanings in the new context. The likelihood of preservation vs. variation can be adjusted by changing the density of the start and end markers (section 3.2).

If the crossover operation was performed at the bit level, some chromosome values could change if a split broke up the bits of a chromosome integer. This would introduce new variability in the gene pool. However, much of the same variability can also be achieved through mutation.

4.3 Mutation

The standard mutation operation works by flipping a bit in a chromosome (Goldberg, 1988). To simulate the natural variability of this scheme at the integer level, the following approach is used: individual integer elements are mutated by randomly selecting a delta value within the legal range and adding the delta to the existing integer value. If the new value falls outside of the allowable range, it will "wrap around". Each element in the chromosome has a 0.4% change of undergoing mutation during each evolutionary cycle.

Three types of changes can occur, depending on where the mutation takes place. Most of the mutations occur in connection weights, and result in minor, smooth changes in the creature's behaviour. Mutation in a connection source is as frequent but has no

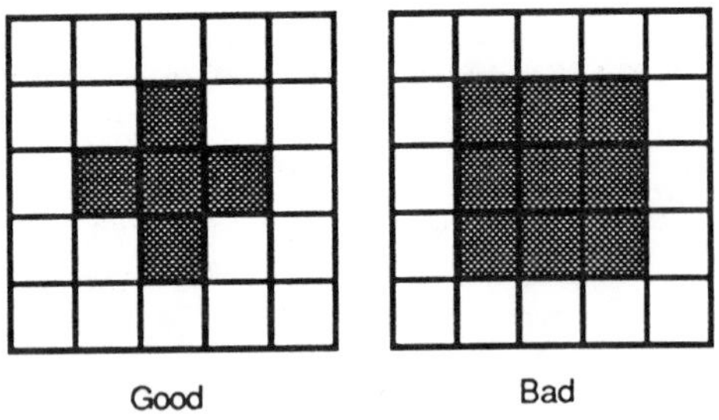

Figure 5: **Data set 1.** The objects can always be identified before hitting them.

Seed	Generations	Nodes	Connects/Node
1	304	15	11.20
2	4	11	9.00
3	77	16	7.56
4	7	15	10.07
5	296	15	9.73

Table 2: **Test results for data set 1.** Listed are: random number generator seed, number of nodes in the perfect creature's neural network, and average number of connections per node for the same network.

effect on behaviour until the change is large enough so that a different source is identified. This change is discrete, and may result in more significant changes in functionality. The third type of mutation occurs in start and stop markers. These are relatively rare but result in very significant changes. Nodes may be created and deleted, or large groups of connections may be created or deleted. In other words, mutation in the marker-based genetic representation can account for both smooth and discrete evolutionary steps.

5 The Experiments

In each experiment, a population of creatures is evolved until a creature completely mastering the task emerges. This creature must be able to always seek out the good object and avoid the bad object from an arbitrary starting position and orientation. The difficulty of this task depends on the choice of objects. Three different data sets (i.e. object selections) are used. The initial chromosome values for all creatures are generated randomly. Each data set was tested five times using five different random number generator seeds.

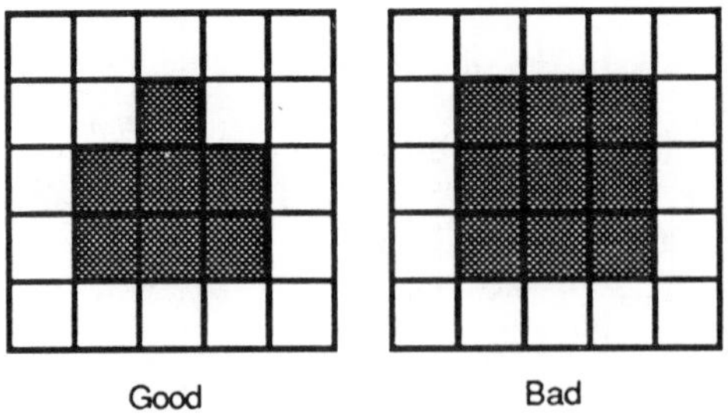

Figure 6: **Data set 2.** Several ambiguous views exist. Recognizing the good object requires traversing around it looking for a characteristic view.

Seed	Generations	Nodes	Connects/Node
1	116	17	6.94
2	211	15	10.80
3	36	16	9.25
4	414	14	8.29
5	15	9	20.11

Table 3: **Test results for data set 2.**

5.1 Data set 1: Straightforward pattern recognition

The first data set (figure 5) is relatively simple because each object can be easily identified. The creature only needs to go directly towards the object. When the creature sees an object square directly in front of it, it can always tell whether the object is good or bad. For example, if the creature sees "■■■" , it can simply stop, since this pattern cannot be found in the good object. Likewise, if the creature sees a "■" directly in front of it and a "■" directly to one side it should know to move forward, since this pattern only appears in the good object.

The creatures learned to master this task in an average of 138 generations (iterations of the genetic algorithm, table 2). Two types of behaviour evolved. In one case the creatures would search for a distinguishing view of the object and once found, either go into a wait sequence if the object was bad, or hit the object if it was good. The other type of behaviour (developed in one of the five experiments) had the creature *circle* the bad object indefinitely and quickly hit the good object.

5.2 Data set two: Surveying required

The objects in the second data set (figure 6) present a greater challenge as there is no longer any unique view that identifies the bad object. Every view found with

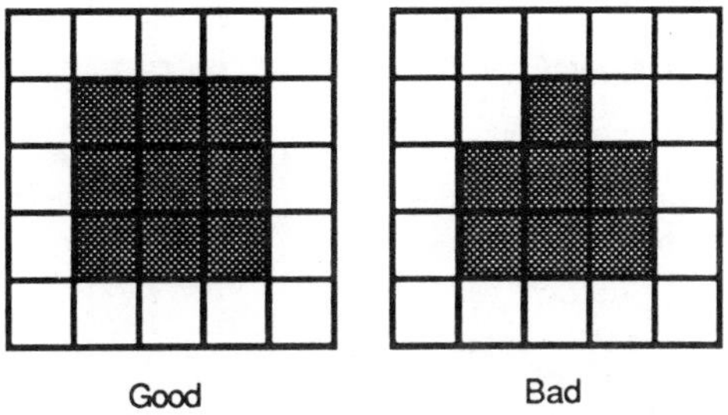

Figure 7: **Data set 3.** Objects are reversed from data set two. Hitting the good object requires using information from at least two different views.

Seed	Generations	Nodes	Connects/Node
1	820	13	10.30
2	1302	13	5.92
3	1643	16	5.94
4	832	14	10.93
5	978	11	13.00

Table 4: **Test results for data set 3.**

the bad object is also possible with the good object. The creature must survey different parts of the object and hit it only if it sees the unique characteristics of the good object.

The average number of generations taken to evolve a perfect creature in this test was 158 (table 3). The behaviour of all these creatures followed the same basic pattern: circle the bad object indefinitely and hit the object if a missing corner is seen. Note that this is identical to the behaviour of one of the creatures in the first data set. In fact when this creature was run on data set two, it achieved a perfect score.

An interesting phenomenom was observed in the circling creatures. They seem to have evolved an initialization phase, where they will first usually move forward one square and rotate 360 degrees before they start circling. Occasionally, though, they will forgo this phase and start circling immediately. It seems that for certain initial positions and orientations, they cannot determine exactly where they are from the visual field input and must look around to get oriented. Other starting situations, however, leave no doubt as they have a unique visual field associated with them.

5.3 Data set 3: Memory required

The third data set consists of the same two objects as the second data set. The difficulty of the problem is increased, however, by making the object with the distinguishing characteristic bad. There is no *single* view that indicates that an object should be hit. Now, in order to act correctly in the presence of the good object, the creature must survey at least two sides of the object, determine that it does not have the undesirable characteristic and then hit it.

This task is significantly more complex than the previous ones, because it requires that the creature must internally "remember" what it has seen previously and use that data along with the current input to determine the appropriate action. In other words, a simple reflex response to its immediate input is not sufficient. It has to develop a finite-state strategy.

The average number of generations taken to evolve a perfect creature for this data set was 1115 (table 4). The behaviour of the five creatures was very similar. When encountering a good object, they would survey two sides and if both were found to be flat, then hit the object. If a bad object was recognized, the creatures would go into a waiting pattern of a few cyclic moves.

6 Discussion

Given the creatures' high-level behaviour, can we infer that they have solved the sensory-motor grounding problem? Let's consider their task in more detail. Every time a creature moves, certain predictable changes occur. For example, if the creature sees a "■" directly in front of it and executes a right turn, the creature will always see the "■" to its left. In the case of right turns the left view will never contain any new information. Consider now the effect of a *left* turn. The left view now reveals previously unseen information that may be important in determining the identity of an object. The same visual input which was previously redundant, now contains valuable data. For each movement that the creature makes, there is a predictable change that will occur in the creature's visual field. Without the ability to relate a particular movement to a predictable change, the visual input would make no sense. In order to perform complicated recognition tasks, the creature must first develop a functional understanding of what effects its own movements have on its visual inputs.

What would happen if instead of giving a creature a five-element visual field, a (more sophisticated) creature was equipped with a 10,000 element retina? Could it evolve the capacity to use this data in a meaningful way? Processing large amounts of 'real world' data such as visual images using traditional AI techniques has proven to be somewhat problematic. Perhaps, noting the success achieved through natural evolution of biological neural networks, using a neuro-evolution approach would prove promising in this area.

The behaviour exhibited by the creatures in the experiments is at the complexity of finite-state automata. A creature takes an action based on its current visual input and its internal state, and updates its internal state. Similar behaviour also evolves in other neuro-evolution systems such as Genesys (Jefferson et al., 1991) and AntFarm (Collins and Jefferson, 1991). An interesting direction for future work is to determine how far this approach can be carried on. ANNs even with finite number of nodes are Turing-equivalent (Siegelman and Sontag, 1991). Would it be possible to evolve creatures that recognize context-free or context-sensitive languages?

But how far can the behavioural strategies be pushed? Could the creatures learn to hunt, or to play chess if it was necessary for survival? Unfortunately, the computational complexity of evolving such creatures grows very fast with the complexity of the task. The free-form genetic encoding scheme introduced in this paper is well-suited for more complicated applications since it can develop nets of arbitrary complexity and capacity. Exactly how efficient it is in highly complex tasks remains to be seen.

7 Conclusion

We have shown that marker-based genetic encoding of neural networks can evolve high-level behaviour similar to that of finite-state automata. In addition, the networks evolve an understanding of their sensory inputs and actions, i.e. they develop an internal world model. The main direction for future research is to see exactly how far this approach can take us in developing sophisticated visual processing capabilities and behaviour in highly complex tasks.

References

Barto, A. G., Sutton, R. S., and Anderson, C. W. 1983. Neuronlike adaptive elements that can solve difficult learning control problems. *IEEE Transactions on Systems, Man, and Cybernetics*, 13:834–846.

Collins, R. J. and Jefferson, D. R. 1991. AntFarm: Towards simulated evolution. In Farmer, J. D., Langton, C., Rasmussen, S., and Taylor, C., editors, *Artificial Life II*. Reading, MA: Addison-Wesley.

Dress, W. B. 1987. Darwinian optimization of synthetic neural systems. In *Proceedings of the IEEE First International Conference on Neural Networks*. Piscataway, NJ: IEEE.

Goldberg, D. E. 1988. *Genetic Algorithms in Search, Optimization and Machine Learning*. Reading, MA: Addison-Wesley.

Hancock, P. J. B. 1990. GANNET: Design of a neural net for face recognition by genetic algorithm. Unpublished Research Report.

Holland, J. H. 1975. *Adaptation in Natural and Artificial Systems: An Introductory Analysis with Applications to Biology, Control and Artificial Intelligence*. Ann Arbor, MI: University of Michigan Press.

Jefferson, D., Collins, R., Cooper, C., Dyer, M., Flowers, M., Korf, R., Taylor, C., and Wang, A. 1991. Evolution as a theme in artificial life: The genesys/tracker system. In Farmer, J. D., Langton, C., Rasmussen, S., and Taylor, C., editors, *Artificial Life II*. Reading, MA: Addison-Wesley.

McClelland, J. L., Rumelhart, D. E., and Hinton, G. E. 1986. The appeal of parallel distributed processing. In Rumelhart, D. E. and McClelland, J. L., editors, *Parallel Distributed Processing: Explorations in the Microstructure of Cognition. Volume 1: Foundations*. Cambridge, MA: MIT Press.

Mjolsness, E., Sharp, D. H., and Alpert, B. K. 1988. Scaling, machine learning and genetic neural nets. Technical Report YALEU/DCS/TR-613: Department of Computer Science, Yale University.

Rothwell, N. V. 1988. *Understanding Genetics*. New York: Oxford University Press, Inc. Fourth edition.

Rumelhart, D. E., Hinton, G. E., and Williams, R. J. 1986. Learning internal representations by error propagation. In Rumelhart, D. E. and McClelland, J. L., editors, *Parallel Distributed Processing: Explorations in the Microstructure of Cognition. Volume 1: Foundations*. Cambridge, MA: MIT Press.

Siegelman, H. and Sontag, E. D. 1991. Neural nets are universal computing devices. Technical Report SYCON-91-08: Rutgers Center for Systems and Control, Rutgers University.

Werner, G. M. and Dyer, M. G. 1991. Evolution of communication in artificial organisms. In Farmer, J. D., Langton, C., Rasmussen, S., and Taylor, C., editors, *Artificial Life II*. Reading, MA: Addison-Wesley.

Self–Adaptation in Genetic Algorithms

Thomas Bäck*

University of Dortmund
Department of Computer Science · Chair of Systems Analysis
P.O. Box 50 05 00 · D–4600 Dortmund 50 · Germany

Abstract

Within *Genetic Algorithms* (GAs) the mutation rate is mostly handled as a global, external parameter, which is constant over time or exogeneously changed over time.

In this paper a new approach is presented, which transfers a basic idea from *Evolution Strategies* (ESs) to GAs. Mutation rates are changed into endogeneous items which are adapting during the search process. First experimental results are presented, which indicate that environment–dependent *self–adaptation* of appropriate settings for the mutation rate is possible even for GAs.

Furthermore, the reduction of the number of external parameters of a GA is seen as a first step towards achieving a problem–dependent self–adaptation of the algorithm.

Introduction

Natural evolution has proven to be a powerful mechanism for emergence and improvement of the living beings on our planet by performing a randomized search in the space of possible DNA-sequences. Due to this knowledge about the qualities of natural evolution, some researchers tried to use the basic mechanisms of evolution as a basis of optimum-seeking techniques in case of vast search spaces.

In general, the algorithmic models of Darwinian evolution maintain a *population* of *individuals* (biological terminology has been adopted in this field). The population is able to adapt to a given (static or dynamically changing) environment by randomized processes of *selection*, *reproduction*, sexual *recombination*, and *mutation*. The environment provides a quality information (*fitness*) for the individuals, and the selection process favours the individuals of higher quality to survive ("survival of the fittest"). Even the reproduction process often favours structures of higher quality. Thus, during the evolution the average quality of the population increases, hopefully leading to an optimum solution.

Algorithms following this general approach have been summarized under the term *Evolutionary Algorithms* elsewhere, e.g. see Mühlenbein (1991) or Bäck and Hoffmeister (1991b). They include the *Genetic Algorithm* (GA) by Holland (1975) and the *Evolution Strategy* (ES) by Rechenberg (1973) and Schwefel (1981) as main representatives. At first glance they are mainly differing with respect to the structure of the individuals, but ESs benefit from the additional capability of learning on the level of strategy parameters by *self-adapting* them during the search (*second-level learning*). A detailed comparison of both algorithms was presented by Hoffmeister and Bäck (1991).

Within this paper a first effort towards incorporating the feature of self-adaptation into GAs by using adaptive mutation rates is presented. The general idea is to depart from global, fixed control mechanisms as used in GAs and instead to decentralize control by spreading it over the individuals. Additionally, control rules are no longer fixed within this distributed control approach, but control is subject to individual adaptation, thus facilitating a self–organizing behaviour of the population. Individually emerging behaviour instead of global control was identified by Langton (1989) to be one of the main characteristics of Artificial Life, hence the border (if any) between GAs and AL dissolves by means of self-adaptation.

Adaptive Mutation Rates

Much experimental work has been done in order to determine the best setting for the bit-mutation probability p_m of a Genetic Algorithm, but no clear answer

*baeck@ls11.informatik.uni-dortmund.de

to this question could be given. Some common settings are $p_m = 0.001$ (De Jong (1975)), $p_m = 0.01$ (Grefenstette (1986)), and $p_m \in [0.005, 0.01]$ (Schaffer, Caruna, Eshelman, and Das (1989)). The result of Schaffer et al. has also been formulated as the empirical expression

$$p_m \approx \frac{1.75}{\lambda \sqrt{l}} \tag{1}$$

where λ denotes the population size and l is the length of the individuals' genetic representation. Expression (1) is similar to that theoretically determined by Hesser and Männer (1991) for a special GA-variant

$$p_m(t) = \sqrt{\frac{\alpha}{\beta}} \cdot \frac{\exp\left(-\gamma \frac{t}{2}\right)}{\lambda \sqrt{l}} \tag{2}$$

which additionally introduces a time-dependency for p_m (α, β, γ are constants).

A time-dependency of mutation rates was first suggested by Holland (1975) himself, although he did not give a detailed choice of the parameter for the time-dependent reduction of p_m. Later on Fogarty (1989) used several time-dependent schedules for p_m, a measure which remarkably increased the GA-performance. Both approaches use a deterministic decrease of mutation rates over time, such that $\lim_{t \to \infty} p_m(t) = 0$. In addition, the mutation rate is handled as a global parameter, i.e. one parameter value of $p_m(t)$ is valid for all individuals of the population. A general mechanism for the adaptation of operator probabilities was presented by Davis (1989), who used the quality of the offspring generated by an operator as a measure to adapt its application probability. However, this technique runs into credit assignment problems similar to those identified by Wilson and Goldberg (1989) for Classifier Systems, when it is tried to reward operators that set the stage for a later production of high quality offspring. And even this technique uses a deterministic, global control rule for the alteration and adjustment of the operator probabilities[1].

The approach described here fundamentally differs from these mechanisms with respect to the following topics:

- Mutation rates are handled as temporal and individually differing parameters, which are incorporated into the genetic representation of the individuals (encoded as bitstrings).
- Mutation rates are also subject to mutation and selection, i.e. they undergo evolution as well as the object variables. No global, deterministic control for the alteration of mutation rates exists.
- Mutation rates are initialized at random.

As a result, p_m is no longer an external parameter of the GA, but it is subject to self-adaptation under certain circumstances (which will be explained later).

Technically, the implementation works as follows: For continuous parameter optimization problems of the form[2] $f : \prod_{i=1}^{n} [a_i, b_i] \to \Re$ either 1 or n encoded mutation rates are added to the genotype, which is now described as:

$$\begin{aligned} I &= \left(\{0,1\}^l \times \left(\{0,1\}^{\hat{l}}\right)^n\right) \\ &\cup \left(\{0,1\}^l \times \{0,1\}^{\hat{l}}\right) \end{aligned} \tag{3}$$

Here $\hat{l}$ denotes the length of the representation of a mutation rate. Furthermore, injective decoding functions $\Gamma_{a,b,l} : \{0,1\}^l \to [a,b]$ exist[3], which are mapping bitstrings of length l linearly to the real interval $[a,b]$. For $l = \sum_{i=1}^{n} l_i$ an individual $a \in I$ can be denoted as follows:

$$\begin{aligned} a = (&\alpha_{1,1} \dots \alpha_{1,l_1} \dots \alpha_{n,1} \dots \alpha_{n,l_n}, \\ &\hat{\alpha}_{1,1} \dots \hat{\alpha}_{1,\hat{l}} \dots \hat{\alpha}_{n,1} \dots \hat{\alpha}_{n,\hat{l}}) \end{aligned} \tag{4}$$

Then, for the encoding $(\hat{\alpha}_{i,1} \dots \hat{\alpha}_{i,\hat{l}})$ of the i-th mutation rate p_i, the mutation rate is obtained by $p_i = \Gamma_{0,1,\hat{l}}(\hat{\alpha}_{i,1} \dots \hat{\alpha}_{i,\hat{l}})$. The new mutation mechanism $m : I \to I$ works as follows:

$$\begin{aligned} &m((\alpha_{1,1} \dots \alpha_{n,l_n}, \hat{\alpha}_{1,1} \dots \hat{\alpha}_{n,\hat{l}})) = \\ &(\beta_{1,1} \dots \beta_{n,l_n}, \hat{\beta}_{1,1} \dots \hat{\beta}_{n,\hat{l}}) \end{aligned} \tag{5}$$

where $\forall i \in \{1, \dots, n\}\ \forall k \in \{1, \dots, \hat{l}\}$:

$$\begin{aligned} \hat{\beta}_{i,k} &= \begin{cases} \hat{\alpha}_{i,k} &, \chi \le \Gamma_{0,1,\hat{l}}(\hat{\alpha}_{i,1} \dots \hat{\alpha}_{i,\hat{l}}) \\ \kappa \in \{0,1\} &, \chi > \Gamma_{0,1,\hat{l}}(\hat{\alpha}_{i,1} \dots \hat{\alpha}_{i,\hat{l}}) \end{cases} \\ \beta_{i,k} &= \begin{cases} \alpha_{i,k} &, \chi \le \Gamma_{0,1,\hat{l}}(\hat{\beta}_{i,1} \dots \hat{\beta}_{i,\hat{l}}) \\ \kappa \in \{0,1\} &, \chi > \Gamma_{0,1,\hat{l}}(\hat{\beta}_{i,1} \dots \hat{\beta}_{i,\hat{l}}) \end{cases} \end{aligned} \tag{6}$$

χ denotes a uniform random variable on the interval $[0,1]$ which is sampled anew for each bit posi-

[1] An exception working with a really self-adapting crossover-operator is due to Schaffer and Morishima (1987), who encoded the crossover mechanism in the genotype of the individuals. This approach, although dealing with the operator itself instead of an application probability, is conceptually identical to the mechanism introduced here.

[2] Due to the binary encoding the object variables are in fact restricted to intervals $[a_i, b_i]$; $a_i, b_i \in \Re$.

[3] Let $\oplus$ denote summation modulo 2, and assume that a Gray code is used. Then, Γ often takes the form $\Gamma_{a,b,l}(\alpha_1 \dots \alpha_l) = a + (b-a) \cdot \left(\sum_{i=0}^{l-1} \left(\bigoplus_{j=1}^{i+1} \alpha_j\right) 2^i\right) / (2^l - 1)$.

tion. Also $\kappa \in \{0,1\}$ is a uniform random variable, determining an allele value each time it is sampled[4]. The mutation mechanism first mutates the mutation rates p_i with mutation probabilities p_i and then uses the resulting mutation rates to mutate the corresponding object variable information. This is schematically shown in figure 1. The special case of only one mutation rate can also be used to apply the mechanism to discrete optimization problems. In this case, one mutation rate is valid for all bits of the genotype.

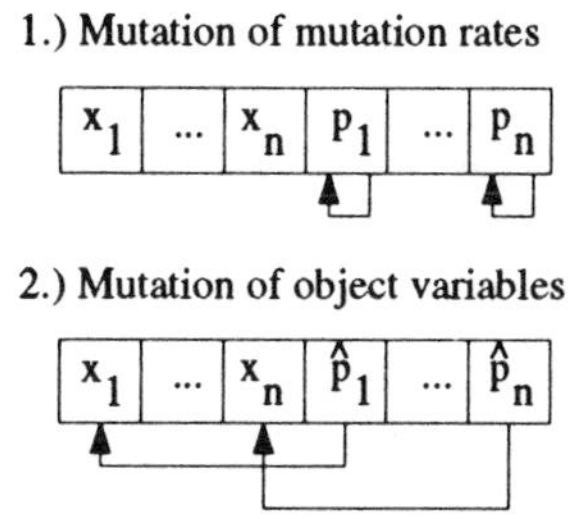

Figure 1: Schematic working mechanism of adaptive mutation

The asymptotic behaviour of adaptive mutation rates can be investigated when neither recombination nor selection are taken into account. To simplify notations, let $\hat{a} = (\hat{\alpha}_1 \ldots \hat{\alpha}_{\hat{l}})$ be the encoding of a mutation rate and $p_{\hat{a}} = \Gamma_{0,1,\hat{l}}(\hat{a})/2$ be the effective probability that a bit is changed. Then $p_{\hat{a}\rightarrow\hat{b}}$, the probability that mutation of $\hat{a}$ by using the bit-inversion probability $p_{\hat{a}}$ yields $\hat{b} = (\hat{\beta}_1 \ldots \hat{\beta}_{\hat{l}})$, is given by

$$p_{\hat{a}\rightarrow\hat{b}} = \prod_{i=1}^{\hat{l}} \Big(|\hat{\beta}_i - \hat{\alpha}_i| p_{\hat{a}} + (1 - |\hat{\beta}_i - \hat{\alpha}_i|)(1 - p_{\hat{a}}) \Big) \qquad (7)$$

Some special transition probabilities can easily be obtained:

$$\begin{aligned} p_{\hat{a}\rightarrow\hat{a}} &= (1 - p_{\hat{a}})^{\hat{l}} \\ p_{(0\ldots0)\rightarrow\hat{b}} &= \prod_{i=1}^{\hat{l}} (1 - \hat{\beta}_i) = \begin{cases} 1, & \hat{b} = (0\ldots0) \\ 0, & \hat{b} \neq (0\ldots0) \end{cases} \end{aligned} \qquad (8)$$

The set of $(2^{\hat{l}})^2$ possible transition probabilities forms a transition matrix of the corresponding markov chain. While $p_{\hat{a}\rightarrow\hat{b}}$ denotes the probability of a one–step transition, the probability $P_{\hat{a}\rightarrow\hat{b}}(n)$ to reach $\hat{b}$ from $\hat{a}$ after n transitions can be calculated by using a theorem from the theory of markov chains, e.g. to be found in the book by Gnedenko (1970):

$$P_{\hat{a}\rightarrow\hat{b}}(n) = \sum_{r=0}^{2^{\hat{l}}-1} P_{\hat{a}\rightarrow bin(r)}(m) \cdot P_{bin(r)\rightarrow\hat{b}}(n-m) \qquad (9)$$

Here $bin : \{0,\ldots,2^{\hat{l}}-1\} \rightarrow \{0,1\}^{\hat{l}}$ denotes a mapping to binary representation. Then theorem 1 holds, which states that $(0\ldots0)$ is an absorbing state of the markov chain:

THEOREM 1 (Asymptotic Behaviour)

$$\lim_{t\rightarrow\infty} P_{\hat{a}\rightarrow(0\ldots0)}(t) = 1 \quad \forall a \in \{0,1\}^{\hat{l}}$$

The proof is given in the appendix. Due to the absence of recombination on mutation rates and selection we can *not* conclude that convergence towards 0 is achieved by our algorithm (in fact, it should not be intended for mutation rates, because this would lead to the possibility of a reduction of the dimension of the actual search space).

While in ESs a meta-mutation rate is used to control the mutation of mutation rates (see Bäck, Hoffmeister, and Schwefel (1991) for an overview, Schwefel (1981) for an detailed description), experimental investigations using this mechanism for GAs have not been as successful as the mechanism described here.

An other precondition for self-adaptation to become effective concerns the selection operator. This will be discussed in the next section, before we present experimental results.

Extinctive Selection

A detailed classification of selection mechanisms in Evolutionary Algorithms has been given by Bäck and Hoffmeister (1991a). Here we will focus only on the topic of *extinctiveness*, which is important for self-adaptation of strategy parameters. Let a population at generation t be denoted as $P^t = (a_1^t, \ldots, a_\lambda^t)$ and let $p_s : I^\lambda \rightarrow [0,1]$ be the function determining the selection probabilities of the individuals in a population $(\forall P^t = (a_1^t, \ldots, a_\lambda^t) : \sum_{i=1}^{\lambda} p_s(a_i^t) = 1)$.

DEFINITION 1 (Extinctive Selection)

A selection scheme is called *extinctive*:
$\Longleftrightarrow \forall t \geq 0 \ \forall P^t = (a_1^t, \ldots, a_\lambda^t) \ \exists i \in \{1,\ldots,\lambda\} : p_s(a_i^t) = 0$

[4]Note, that following Holland (1975) a bit mutation event is realized here by chosing an allele value at random from the set $\{0,1\}$ of possible alleles, in contrast to the often used implementations which simply mutate a bit by inverting it.

DEFINITION 2 (Preservative Selection)

A selection scheme is called *preservative*:
$\Longleftrightarrow \ \forall t \geq 0 \ \forall P^t = (a_1^t, \ldots, a_\lambda^t) \ \forall i \in \{1, \ldots, \lambda\} \ : \ p_s(a_i^t) > 0$

An extinctive selection mechanism definitely excludes some individuals from being selected, in contrast to *preservative* mechanisms which always assign selection probabilities greater than zero to all individuals. Representatives for preservative selection are *proportional selection* as introduced by Holland (1975) and Baker's (1985) *ranking*, while *(μ,λ)-selection* as used by Schwefel (1981) in ESs is extinctive (only the μ best individuals are allowed to be selected). The terms *(μ,λ)-proportional selection* and *(μ,λ)-linear ranking* are used here to describe the extinctive variants of proportional selection and ranking, while for (μ,λ)-selection the term *(μ,λ)-uniform ranking* is used. The latter term was introduced by Bäck and Hoffmeister (1991a) and emphasizes the fact, that (μ,λ)-selection is a special case of (μ,λ)-linear ranking selection.

Experimental Results

For testing the self-adaptive capabilities of the approach the objective functions f_1 (the sphere model, used by De Jong (1975) and Schwefel (1981)) and f_{15} (the weighted sphere model[5], used by Schwefel (1981)) as described in table 1 are used as representatives of relatively simple, unimodal problems. These functions make it possible to study whether the amount of mutation rate information that has to be learned should be different. Additionally, the multimodal function f_7 (generalized Rastrigin's function, based upon the two-dimensional variant mentioned by Törn and Žilinskas (1989), pp. 185) is used here in order to test adaptive mutation rates for a complicated problem.

A modified version of Grefenstette's (1987) GA-implementation GENESIS is used to obtain the experimental results, and general settings for each run of the GA are:

- Population size $\lambda = 50$.
- Length of the object variable encoding part of an individual $l = 32n$ (n being the dimension of the objective function[6]).
- Crossover rate $p_c = 0.6$.
- Two-point crossover, working only on the genotype encoding of the object variables.
- Gray code.

For adaptive mutation a length $\hat{l} = 20$ was chosen to allow sufficiently many different mutation rates to be encoded by the string. For each objective function a *reference* GA with (50,50)-proportional selection and a constant, external mutation rate $p_m = 0.001$ is compared to the following variants:

(1) (50,50)-proportional selection, 1 adaptive mutation rate.
(2) (50,50)-proportional selection, n adaptive mutation rates.
(3) (10,50)-proportional selection, no adaptive mutation ($p_m = 0.001$).
(4) (10,50)-proportional selection, 1 adaptive mutation rate.
(5) (10,50)-proportional selection, n adaptive mutation rates.

The setting of $\mu/\lambda = 1/5$ for the extinctive selection variants stems from theoretical results derived by Schwefel (1981) concerning the convergence velocity of ESs for the sphere and corridor model, and first experiments by Bäck and Hoffmeister (1991) indicated to use it even in the field of GAs. The experimental results are compared by looking at the best values per generation, which are averaged over 10 runs of the algorithm. In figures (2)–(4) the resulting graphs are shown for f_1, f_{15}, and f_7, respectively. The plots are labeled by their numbers given in the enumeration above, the reference GA being labeled with (0).

First we will look at the combination of preservative selection and adaptive mutation, i.e. cases (1) and (2). For the unimodal functions (figures 2 and 3) performance decreases as the amount of additional information increases, while for the multimodal function (figure 4) one mutation rate (1) converges to a better local optimum than the reference GA, and n mutation rates (2) improve slowly but steadily, possibly being better than (0) and (1) on the long run. Thus, without changing the selection mechanism the large amount of additional information is disadvantageous for unimodal and of slight advantage for multimodal topologies.

When introducing extinctive selection (3) alone, the behaviour is contrary. On unimodal functions

[5]The index choice for objective functions is founded on the historical development of our implementation as well as the attempt to keep in correspondence with De Jongs (1975) nomenclature f_1–f_5.

[6]A length of 32 bits per object variable is used for the representation of the real interval $[a,b]$ to which the bit-strings are mapped, in order to achieve a maximum resolution $\Delta x = (b-a)/(2^{32}-1)$ of the search grid.

Name	Description	Dim.	Characteristics	Ref.
f_1	sphere model $f_1(\vec{x}) = \sum_{i=1}^{n} x_i^2$ $-5.12 \leq x_i \leq 5.12$	$n = 30$	unimodal, high-dimensional	De Jong (1975) Schwefel (1981)
f_{15}	weighted sphere model $f_{15}(\vec{x}) = \sum_{i=1}^{n} i \cdot x_i^2$ $-5.12 \leq x_i \leq 5.12$	$n = 30$	unimodal, high-dimensional	Schwefel (1988)
f_7	generalized Rastrigin's function $f_7(\vec{x}) = nA + \sum_{i=1}^{n} x_i^2 - A\cos(\omega x_i)$ $A = 10\ ; \omega = 2\pi\ ; -5.12 \leq x_i \leq 5.12$	$n = 20$	multimodal, high-dimensional, f_1 with sine wave superposition	Törn and Žilinskas (1989)

Table 1: The set of test functions

performance increases remarkably, while on the multimodal function extinctive selection does not change performance when compared to the reference GA.

In any case the GA remarkably benefits from the combination of adaptive mutation and extinctive selection, although it accomplishes this behaviour in different combinations with respect to the number of mutation rates. The unimodal functions are better suited for search with extinctive selection and only one mutation rate (4) than n rates (5), while for the multimodal function one mutation rate quickly converges to a local optimum and n mutation rates lead to the best solution with a population not yet converged after 500 generations.

However, these results for unimodal functions are contradicting to those obtained by Schwefel (1988) for self-adaptation of mutation rates in an ES. For f_1 and f_{15} he found remarkably better behaviour for variants using a combination of individual step sizes and recombination than for variants using only one step size. This synergetic effect is mainly caused by the recombination of mutation rates, which supports the emergence of actually better suited combinations of mutation rates. To prevent the mechanism from reducing the search space by a mutation rate which becomes zero, in ESs Schwefel (1981) uses an additional exogeneous multiplication factor for all standard deviations of an individual. By using a log-normal distribution for this factor its expectation is 1 and the occurrence probability of a multiplication factor r is equal to that of a factor $1/r$, thus a subspace search is prevented by such a mechanism.

The GA-behaviour found in these experiments is a clear confirmation of the well-known contradiction between exploration and exploitation in global optimization. For unimodal surfaces a path oriented, exploitative search with a high convergence velocity is desired, while for multimodal surfaces the search should be volume oriented, explorative with a high convergence confidence towards a global optimum point. Both property classes are contradicting, one can not have them at the same time.

Applied to the results given here, only one adaptive mutation rate seems to serve as a local hillclimbing mechanism when combined with extinctive selection. On the other hand, a high degree of exploration is achieved when all object variables are mutated independently, thus serving as a powerful global exploration mechanism when combined with a strong emphasis on survival of the fitter individuals to prevent the algorithm from converging too slow.

In case (4) of one adaptive mutation rate figure 5 gives an impression of the course of the average mutation rate over time. Two facts are interesting to note:

- For extinctive selection average mutation rates are almost a factor of 10 larger than for preservative selection.
- There is no difference in the average mutation rates between the multimodal and the unimodal functions.

From these observations we can conclude that the algorithm balances well between a mutation rate as high as needed for efficient search and as high as possible without destroying useful information, thus working on the borderline of efficient optimization and almost random walk.

Understanding the mutation rates of figure 5 as optimal ones, we can compare them to the results obtained by Schaffer's empirical expression (1), which are

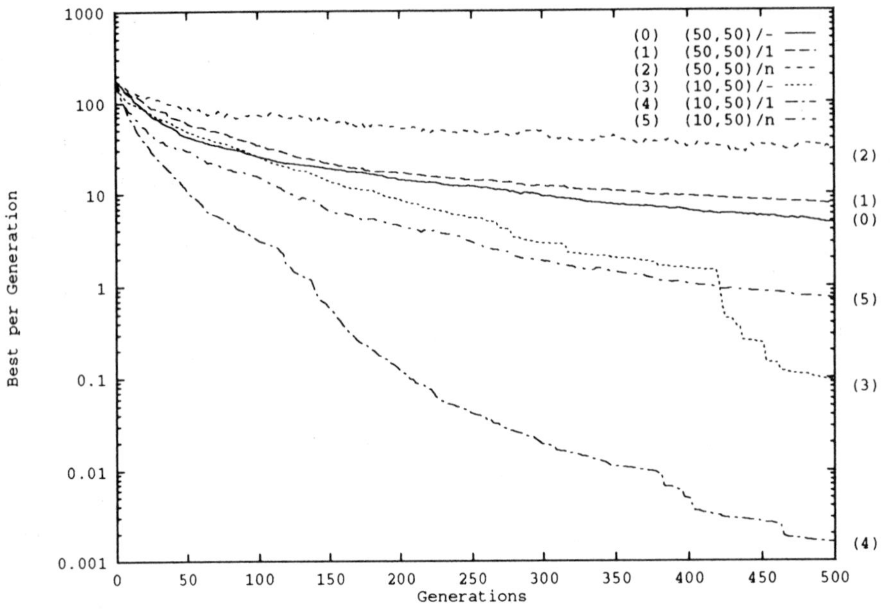

Figure 2: Performance on f_1

- $p_m = 0.0011$ for f_1 and f_{15} ($\lambda = 50$, $l = 960$),
- $p_m = 0.0014$ for f_7 ($\lambda = 50$, $l = 640$).

Unfortunately the results can not be compared directly due to the fact that the mutation rates used here are probabilities for sampling a bit position instead of inverting it, and Schaffer et al. do not explain which kind of mutation they use. However, at the most our mutation rates would double, increasing the gap between the results. We can conclude by formulating hypothesis 1:

Hypothesis 1

An optimal mutation rate for a GA is relatively large and turns mutation into an additional search operator. When used in combination with extinctive selection, it considerably improves the performance of a GA.

Concerning the GA this hypothesis is a daring one. Holland (1975, pp. 110–111) has explicitly stressed the role of mutation as a "*background operator*", operating as a mechanism to reintroduce lost alleles, but *not* as a search operator. On the other hand, Eigen (1976) has demonstrated that for more general models of evolving systems on the level of organic macromolecules evolution works most efficient when mutation rates are directly below the threshold value above which information is destroyed. Although the investigations of Eigen do not take recombination into account, they are theoretically well-founded and provide a strong argument for enlarging the role of mutation even in the artificial evolving systems we are dealing with.

Summary

Within this work it is confirmed that under the condition of an extinctive selection mechanism second-level learning of mutation rates is possible and advantageous even in GAs. For a multimodal function n mutation rates per individual perform well, while for unimodal functions one mutation rate per individual performs well. In any case at least a combination of one adaptive mutation rate per individual and extinctive selection is better than the reference GA. This is a strong argument for the general introduction of adaptive mutation rates to GAs, which would also eliminate a part of the parameterisation problem of GAs. However some questions haven't been answered yet, especially concerning recombination of mutation rates, which has shown by Schwefel (1988) to be an essential condition[7] for self-adaptation in ESs. Surely,

[7] Another essential condition for self-adaptation in ESs is the possibility to forget good information. Schwefel (1988) has demonstrated that for this reason self-adaptation does not work in a (μ+λ)-ES, which allows arbitrarily long survival of individuals. A standard GA without the *generation gap* by Grefenstette (1986) always allows to die even for the best individual, hence we do not discuss this topic here in detail for GAs.

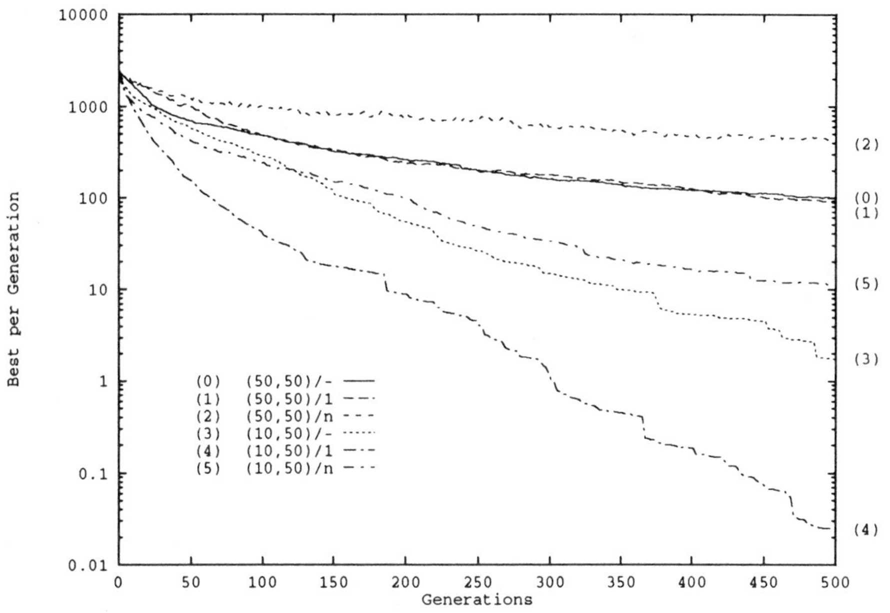

Figure 3: Performance on f_{15}

new recombination techniques have to be used for n mutation rates, while for one mutation rate traditional crossover could be used.

In addition the influence of different extinctive selection mechanisms, especially those which are rank-based, as well as the influence of the ratio μ/λ, i.e. the degree of extinctiveness, should be investigated further.

Appendix: Proof of theorem 1

The proof of theorem 1 is based upon equation (9) for calculating the n-step transition probabilities of the markov chain:

$$\begin{aligned}
&P_{a\rightarrow(0\ldots0)}(n) \\
&= \sum_{r=0}^{2^{lm}-1} P_{a\rightarrow bin(r)}(m)\, P_{bin(r)\rightarrow(0\ldots0)}(n-m) \\
&= \sum_{r=0}^{2^{lm}-1} P_{a\rightarrow bin(r)}(n-1)\, P_{bin(r)\rightarrow(0\ldots0)}(1) \\
&\quad \text{for } m = n-1 \\
&= P_{a\rightarrow(0\ldots0)}(n-1)\, P_{(0\ldots0)\rightarrow(0\ldots0)}(1) \\
&\quad + \sum_{r=1}^{2^{lm}-1} P_{a\rightarrow bin(r)}(n-1)\, P_{bin(r)\rightarrow(0\ldots0)}(1) \\
&= P_{a\rightarrow(0\ldots0)}(n-1) \\
&\quad + \sum_{r=1}^{2^{lm}-1} P_{a\rightarrow bin(r)}(n-1)\, P_{bin(r)\rightarrow(0\ldots0)}(1) \\
&\geq P_{a\rightarrow(0\ldots0)}(n-1)
\end{aligned}$$

Hence, $P_{a\rightarrow(0\ldots0)}$ increases monotonously over time. Since $\sum_{r=0}^{2^{lm}-1} P_{a\rightarrow bin(r)}(n) = 1$ and $P_{a\rightarrow(0\ldots0)}(n) \leq 1$, either

$$\sum_{r=1}^{2^{lm}-1} P_{a\rightarrow bin(r)}(n-1)\, P_{bin(r)\rightarrow(0\ldots0)}(1) > 0$$

or

$$P_{a\rightarrow(0\ldots0)}(n-1) = 1$$

must be valid ($P_{bin(r)\rightarrow(0\ldots0)}(1) = p_{bin(r)\rightarrow(0\ldots0)} \neq 0$ iff $r \neq 0$), hence either the probability of a transition to zero increases strictly, i.e. $P_{a\rightarrow(0\ldots0)}(n) > P_{a\rightarrow(0\ldots0)}(n-1)$, or $P_{a\rightarrow(0\ldots0)}(n) = 1$. q.e.d.

References

Bäck, T. and F. Hoffmeister. 1991a. Extended selection mechanisms in genetic algorithms. In *Proceedings of the Fourth International Conference on Genetic Algorithms and their Applications*, edited by Richard K. Belew and Lashon B. Booker, pages 92–99. University of California, San Diego, USA. Morgan Kaufmann Publishers.

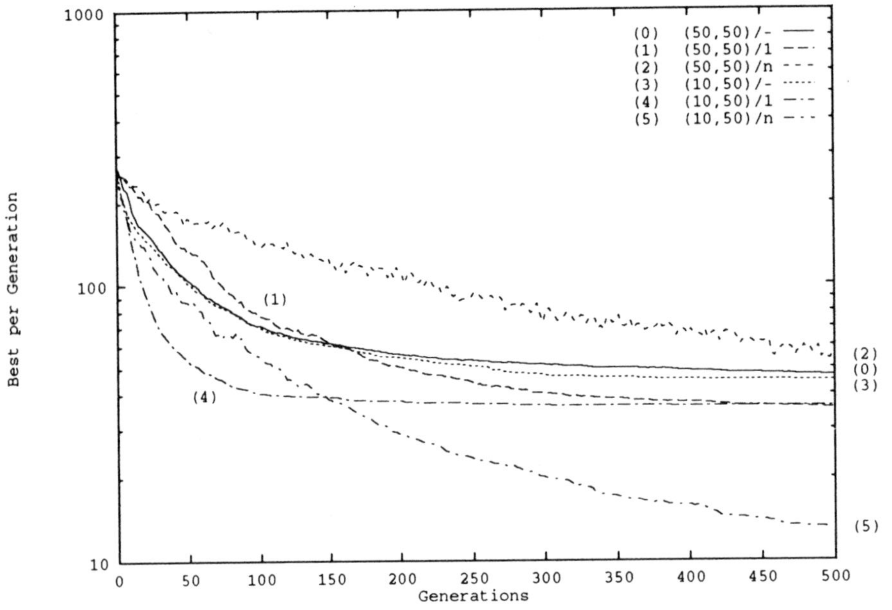

Figure 4: Performance on f_7

Bäck, T. and F. Hoffmeister. 1991b. Global optimization by means of evolutionary algorithms. In *Random Search as a Method for Adaptation and Optimization of Complex Systems*, edited by A. A. Antamoshkin, pages 17–21. Krasnojarsk Space Technology University, Divnogorsk, USSR.

Bäck, T., F. Hoffmeister, and H.-P. Schwefel. 1991. A survey of evolution strategies. In *Proceedings of the Fourth International Conference on Genetic Algorithms and their Applications*, edited by Richard K. Belew and Lashon B. Booker, pages 2–9. University of California, San Diego, USA. Morgan Kaufmann Publishers.

Baker, J. E. 1985. Adaptive selection methods for genetic algorithms. In *Proceedings of the First International Conference on Genetic Algorithms and Their Applications*, edited by J. J. Grefenstette, pages 101–111. Hillsdale, New Jersey. Lawrence Erlbaum Associates.

Davis, L. 1989. Adapting operator probabilities in genetic algorithms. In *Proceedings of the Third International Conference on Genetic Algorithms and Their Applications*, edited by J. D. Schaffer, pages 61–69. San Mateo, California. Morgan Kaufmann Publishers.

Eigen, M. 1976. Wie entsteht Information? Prinzipien der Selbstorganisation in der Biologie. *Berichte der Bunsen-Gesellschaft*, 11:1059–1081.

Fogarty, T. C. 1989. Varying the probability of mutation in the genetic algorithm. In *Proceedings of the Third International Conference on Genetic Algorithms and Their Applications*, edited by J. D. Schaffer, pages 104–109. San Mateo, California. Morgan Kaufmann Publishers.

Gnedenko, B. W. 1970. *Lehrbuch der Wahrscheinlichkeitsrechnung*. Akademie–Verlag, Berlin.

Grefenstette, J. J. 1986. Optimization of control parameters for genetic algorithms. *IEEE Transactions on Systems, Man and Cybernetics*, SMC–16(1):122–128.

Grefenstette, J. J. 1987. *A User's Guide to GENESIS*. Navy Center for Applied Research in Artificial Intelligence, Washington, D. C.

Hesser, J. and R. Männer. 1991. Towards an optimal mutation probability in genetic algorithms. In *Parallel Problem Solving from Nature*, edited by Hans-Paul Schwefel and Reinhard Männer, pages 23–32. Volume 496 of *Lecture Notes in Computer Science*, Springer, Berlin.

Hoffmeister, F. and T. Bäck. 1991. Genetic algorithms and evolution strategies: Similarities and differences. In *Parallel Problem Solving from Nature*, edited by Hans-Paul Schwefel and Reinhard Männer, pages 455–470. Volume 496 of *Lecture Notes in Computer Science*, Springer, Berlin.

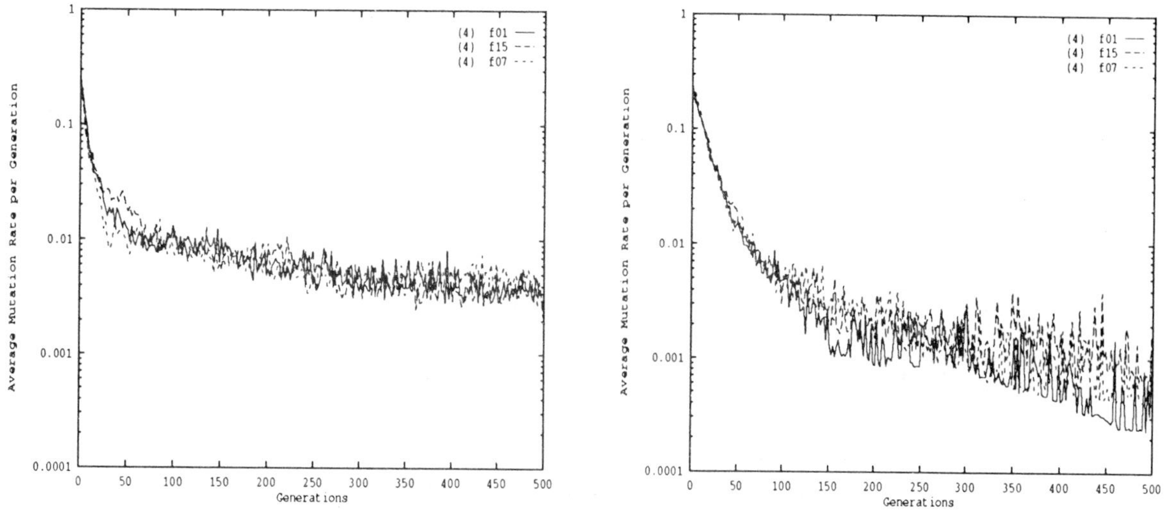

Figure 5: Average mutation rates for (10,50)- (left) and (50,50)-proportional selection (right)

Holland, J. H. 1975. *Adaptation in natural and artificial systems.* The University of Michigan Press, Ann Arbor.

De Jong, K. 1975. *An analysis of the behaviour of a class of genetic adaptive systems.* PhD thesis, University of Michigan. Diss. Abstr. Int. 36(10), 5140B, University Microfilms No. 76-9381.

Langton, C. G. 1989. Artificial life. In *Artificial Life*, edited by Christopher G. Langton, pages 1–48. Volume VI of *Studies in the Science of Complexity*, Los Alamos, Santa Fe Institute. Addison-Wesley.

Mühlenbein, H. 1991. Evolution in time and space — the parallel genetic algorithm. In *Foundations of Genetic Algorithms & Classifier Systems*, edited by G. Rawlins. Morgan Kaufmann.

Rechenberg, I. 1973. *Evolutionsstrategie: Optimierung technischer Systeme nach Prinzipien der biologischen Evolution.* Frommann-Holzboog Verlag, Stuttgart.

Schaffer, J. D., R. A. Caruna, L. J. Eshelman, and R. Das. 1989. A study of control parameters affecting online performance of genetic algorithms for function optimization. In *Proceedings of the Third International Conference on Genetic Algorithms and Their Applications*, edited by J. D. Schaffer, pages 51–60. San Mateo, California. Morgan Kaufmann Publishers.

Schaffer, J. D., and A. Morishima. 1987. An adaptive crossover distribution mechanism for genetic algorithms. In *Proceedings of the Second International Conference on Genetic Algorithms and Their Applications*, edited by J. J. Grefenstette, pages 36–40. Hillsdale, New Jersey. Lawrence Erlbaum Associates.

Schwefel, H.-P. 1981. *Numerical Optimization of Computer Models.* Wiley, Chichester.

Schwefel, H.-P. 1988. Evolutionary learning optimum-seeking on parallel computer architectures. In *Proceedings of the International Symposium on Systems Analysis and Simulation 1988, I: Theory and Foundations*, edited by A. Sydow, S. G. Tzafestas, and R. Vichnevetsky, pages 217–225. Akademie der Wissenschaften der DDR, Akademie-Verlag, Berlin.

Törn, A. and A. Žilinskas. 1989. *Global Optimization*, volume 350 of *Lecture Notes in Computer Science.* Springer, Berlin.

Wilson, S. W., and D. E. Goldberg. 1989. A critical review of classifier systems. In *Proceedings of the Third International Conference on Genetic Algorithms and Their Applications*, edited by J. D. Schaffer, pages 244–255. San Mateo, California. Morgan Kaufmann Publishers.

STEERABLE GenNETS

The Genetic Programming of Steerable Behaviors in GenNets

Hugo de Garis

CADEPS Artificial Intelligence and Artificial Life Research Unit,
Universite Libre de Bruxelles, Ave F.D. Roosevelt 50,
C.P. 194/7, B-1050, Brussels, Belgium, Europe.
tel: + 32 2 650 2783, fax: + 32 2 650 2785
email: CADEPS@BBRNSF11(.BITNET)

&

Center for Artificial Intelligence, George Mason University,
4400 University Drive, Fairfax, Virginia, VA 22030, USA.
tel: + 1 703 764 6328, fax: + 1 703 323 2630
email: HUGODEG@AIC.GMU.EDU

Keywords :

Generalized Behavioral Learning, Genetic Programming, Genetic Algorithm, Neural Networks, GenNets, Multi-Function GenNets, Shaping, Behavioral Memory, Variable Neural Control, Steerable GenNets, Biots (Biological Robots), Artificial Nervous Systems, Artificial Creatures, Artificial Life.

Abstract :

This paper shows how Genetic Programming techniques (i.e. the art of "applied evolution", or building complex systems using the Genetic Algorithm) can be used to evolve dynamic behaviors in neural systems which are controllable or steerable. The Genetic Algorithm evolves the weights of a fully connected, time dependent, neural network (called a GenNet), such that the same GenNet is capable of generating two separate time dependent behaviors, depending upon the setting of two different values of a clamped input control variable. By freezing these weights in the GenNet and then applying intermediate control values, one obtains intermediate behaviors, showing that the GenNet has generalized its behavioral learning. It has become controllable or "steerable". It is likely that this principle will be applicable to the evolution of many controllable neural behaviors and will prove to be extremely useful in the construction of artificial creatures (with artificial nervous systems) based on neural modules. One simply evolves two behaviors at different settings of the control input so that the GenNet will generalize its behavioral learning. In this paper, a concrete example of this process is given in the form of the Genetic Programming of a variable frequency generator GenNet. A challenge for future research will be finding a theoretical explanation for the existence of this extraordinary phenomenon. This paper terminates with a discussion on the "handcrafters VS.evolutionists" controversy, concerning future approaches to artificial creature (biot) building.

Introduction :

This paper shows how it is possible to evolve generalized controllable (dynamic) behaviors in neural systems, using a technique called Genetic Programming (GP). GP is the application of the Genetic Algorithm (GA) (Goldberg 1989) to building complex systems, such as behavioral modules for artificial nervous systems (de Garis 1991a), or artificial embryos (de Garis 1991b). GP changes the focus of the GA away from its traditional emphasis upon optimization, towards being used as a tool to build (evolve) functional systems despite their massive complexity.

A GenNet is a fully connected, time dependent, neural network whose weights are evolved with the Genetic Algorithm such that the time dependent output(s) perform some desired behavior, such as controlling the angles of legs on an artificial creature such that it walks, or turns etc. In the concrete example given in this paper, the desired output is a sinusoidal oscillation of a given period and amplitude. By clamping a neural input (control) signal value at +0.5, a GenNet was evolved which gave a sinusoidal output oscillation of period 40 clock-cycles and amplitude 0.5. The same GenNet was simultaneously evolved with a clamped input value of -0.5 to give an output period of 80 clock-cycles. Thus two separate behaviors were evolved on the same GenNet. When intermediate control values were clamped on the GenNet, oscillations of intermediate period were generated. This shows that it is possible to get "multi-functional" GenNets to generalize their behavioral learning. By evolving a library of such controllable behavioral GenNets and sending them appropriate control signals, it will be possible to build artificial nervous systems for robotic control (de Garis 1990a, b).

The GenNet (or evolutionary) paradigm is much more flexible and powerful than the traditional neural network paradigms such as Backprop (Rumelhart et al 1986), Hopfield nets (Hopfield 1984) etc., because GenNets can be totally dynamic. There is no need for constraints such as symmetric weights, or layers, or feedforward only, or all inputs being clamped etc. With the traditional neural network paradigms, it is usual to let the neural output values stabilize before being used. In the case of the backpropagation algorithm, this stabilization is not a consideration because outputs are a direct consequence of the (feed-forward) inputs. There is no feedback of neural outputs from higher layers to lower layers. In the Hopfield net, however, there is feedback, because it is usually fully connected. One clamps the inputs and waits until the outputs have stabilized before using them. These restrictions were imposed upon the traditional neural network paradigms for reasons of mathematical tractability. Without such restrictions, the dynamics of the networks would have been too complicated for analysis. However, using the Genetic Programming paradigm, one does not care how complex the dynamics are, one is only concerned with how well the system being evolved performs. Thus a GenNet can have time dependent inputs, time dependent outputs, be fully connected, have a large number of neurons in the net etc. If one takes the outputs and uses them to control behaviors, then one can evolve the GenNet to perform the behavior desired, without having the slightest idea of what is going on inside the GenNet. A GenNet is thus a "black-box". It can be built (evolved) but its internal dynamics are usually not well understood. Thus, although GenNets are much less mathematically analyzable than the usual neural networks, they open up a whole new world of evolvable behaviors. To make an analogy, GenNets are to traditional neural nets, what the study of dynamics is to statics.

GenNets have been evolved by the author to perform a whole range of dynamic behaviors, such as teaching a pair of stick legs to walk (de Garis 1990b), to control the angles of leg components of an artificial creature such that it walks straight ahead, or turns left or right, or pecks at food, or mates with a partner (de Garis 1991a), to detect the velocity components of a "line" moving across a 4*4 neural net retina, to detect frequencies of an incoming sinusoidal signal, to detect its average (root mean square) signal strength, to generate a "timeout" signal which remains positive for a given number of clock-cycles, and then dips and remains negative (de Garis 1991c). Genetic Programming applied to the evolution of GenNet behaviors provides a powerful technique for the construction of building blocks for artificial nervous systems. Steerable GenNets will be even more useful for artificial creature building. For example, one could evolve a GenNet for making a biot (biological robot, i.e. a robot built on principles inspired from biology) walk straight ahead at two different speeds (using two different clamped input control values). By applying an intermediate control value, one would obtain an intermediate speed. One could thus control the walking speed of the biot by a single input to the GenNet which determines the walking. Similarly for another GenNet evolved to make the biot turn. At one control setting, the biot could turn quickly (or with a high curvature), and at another control setting, it could turn slowly (or with a low curvature). Thus with a single control input, one could control the rate at which a biot would turn. The idea of controllable or steerable behaviors has many potential applications.

To show that a "steerable GenNet" is possible, a concrete example of the evolution of such a GenNet will now be presented. The behavior in this case is the generation of a sinusoidal signal with a given amplitude and frequency. The two different behaviors are two sinusoids of different frequencies. The intermediate behavior is a sinusoid of intermediate frequency which is generated when an intermediate control value is applied to the GenNet.

The remainder of this paper consists of the following. Section 1 shows how a GenNet was evolved to produce a single frequency sinusoid output. Section 2 takes the techniques of section 1 and applies them to the evolution of a multi-functional GenNet capable of generating two different frequencies depending upon the values of two clamped control inputs. Section 3 terminates with some remarks, and a discussion on the growing "handcrafters VS. evolutionists" controversy concerning future approaches to biot building.

1. A Single Frequency Sinusoid Generator GenNet

The bitstring chromosome format used to evolve the GenNet took the form of a concatenation of binary fractional numbers which coded for the values of the neural weights (which were limited to an absolute value of less than 1.0, with 6 bits for the fraction and 1 bit for the sign). GenNets typically contained about a dozen or so artificial neurons. Hence if there were N neurons (and therefore N*N connections) in the GenNets, the bitstring "chromosome" had lengths of N*N*(6+1) bits. The "activity" of a neuron was defined to be the usual dot product of its incoming signal vector and its weight vector. This dot product was passed through a non linear sigmoid function with limiting values between +1.0 and -1.0 All neurons calculated their outputs synchronously (from their inputs) at each "clock-cycle".

By mutating (bit flipping) and crossing over (swapping bits for each bit position of two chromosomes with a 50% probability) these bitstrings, a set of weights was evolved which gave the desired dynamic behavior. The "fitness" (i.e. the measure of quality of the behavior, and the factor which determined the number of offspring of each bitstring in the next generation) was defined to be the inverse of the sum of the squared errors between the actual output and the desired output for each clock-cycle of the oscillation.

This section discusses the evolution of a GenNet which output a sinusoid of a desired amplitude and frequency. The initial idea was to see whether the GP approach would be versatile enough to allow such an evolution, and if so, whether it would be possible to evolve a GenNet capable of emitting sinusoids of variable frequency according to the strength of a variable control input signal to the GenNet. The motivation behind this attempt was that a frequency generator was thought to be a fundamental component of any artificial nervous system and therefore the attempt to evolve such a generator would be very worthwhile.

To start with, the aim was to generate a single frequency. An arbitrary amplitude and period were chosen (namely 0.5 for the amplitude, and 100 clock-cycles for the period). The GenNet used for this experiment contained (an arbitrary) 15 artificial neurons. In the figures below the desired output curve is shown as a thin line, and the actual output is shown as a dark line. For each cycle (101 of them), the square of the difference between the desired output and the actual output was found. The fitness value was defined as the inverse of the sum of these squares for the 100 cycles. The mutation rate used was usually 0.001, i.e. one chance in a thousand that a bit would mutate (flip). This meant that usually only one bit per chromosome per generation would be mutated. (For GA specialists, the reproduction strategies used for the chromosomes were "roulette wheel" and "elitist").

The series of figures below, provides an example of GP techniques in action, and in particular the use of "shaping", i.e. the phased evolution of a GenNet. For example, a fitness definition "A" is used to evolve GenNet A. The weights thus evolved then serve as the initial weights for a second phase of evolution using fitness definition "B" to produce GenNet B. GenNet B's behavior will manifest traces of A's behavior. This "behavioral memory" of "shaped" GenNets can be very useful in getting GenNets to do what one wants.

Two (external) inputs were clamped, at 0.5 on neuron "0" and at -0.5 on neuron "1". All other external (not internal) inputs were clamped at 0.0, and the output was taken from neuron "14" for each cycle. These two clamped values were rather arbitrarily chosen. The actual clamped values were probably not very important, because the evolution would presumably adapt to them. Note that since GenNets are fully connected, each neural output became an (internal) input for both itself and all the other neurons. Each neuron also had an external (unweighted) input.

FIG.s 1 and 2 show the outputs of the best GenNet after 10 and 300 generations. Further evolution beyond 300 generations was unable to "bring down" the curve to cross the horizontal axis a second time. At this stage a tactical decision was made. The desired curve was obviously not evolvable in "one go", so it was decided to use shaping techniques. As will be clear by the end of this experiment in evolving a GenNet oscillator, Genetic Programming is an art, comparable with computer programming or electronic circuit design. There are few hard and fast rules. Human Genetic Programmers (or in this case, GenNet Programmers) improve with experience as tricks and valuable heuristics are learned.

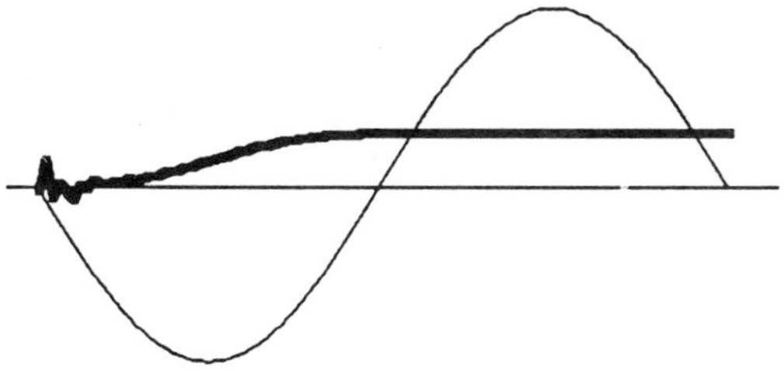

FIG. 1 Best of 10th generation
(100 cycle evolution)

Having made the decision to employ shaping techniques, the following strategy was chosen and tried. The curve would initially be evolved over only 50 cycles. The GenNet resulting from this would be used as the starting GenNet in a second evolutionary phase to evolve a 100 cycle curve. This was the original plan. As will be seen, there were some surprizes in store. FIGs 3 and 4 show the best individual results from 10 and 500 generations.

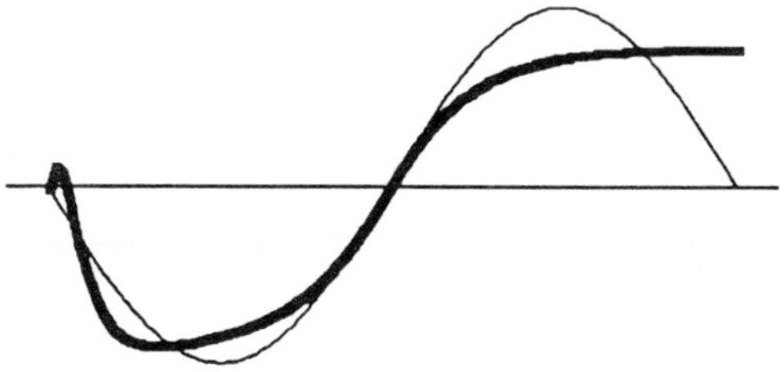

FIG. 2 Best of 300th generation
(100 cycle evolution)

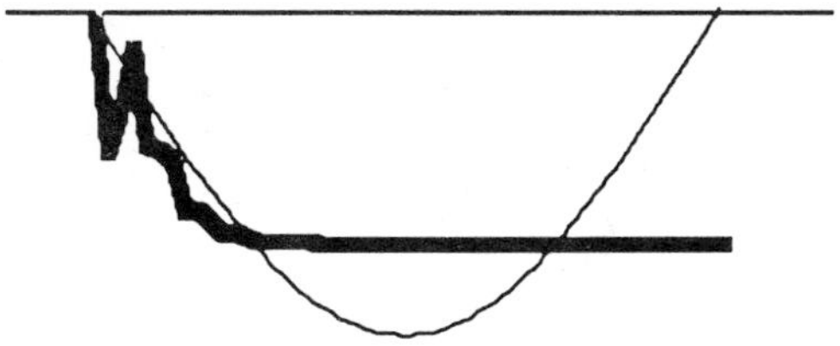

FIG. 3 Best of 10th generation
(50 cycle evolution)

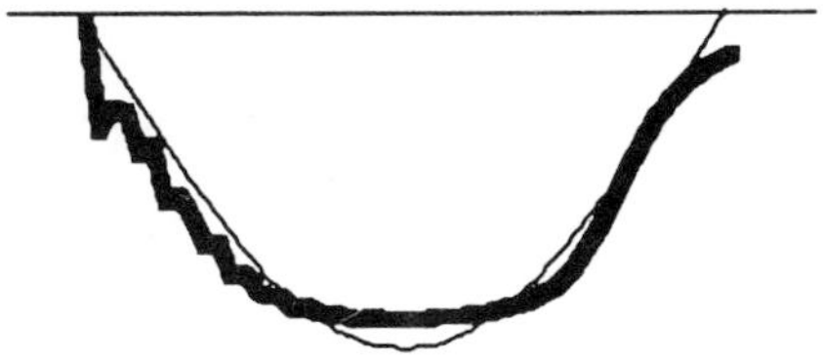

FIG. 4 Best of 500th generation
(50 cycle evolution)

The GenNet which gave the curve in FIG. 4 was then used as the initial GenNet for a 100 cycle evolution. FIG. 5 shows the output over 100 cycles for this GenNet in the first generation. Unfortunately, it did not cross the horizontal axis. To force the curve to cut the horizontal axis and yet not fall again into the trap of FIG. 2, it was decided to allow the evolution to occur over 65 cycles (i.e. a half oscillation, "plus a bit", to force the curve to cut the axis). FIG. 6 shows the result of the elite chromosome after 200 generations.

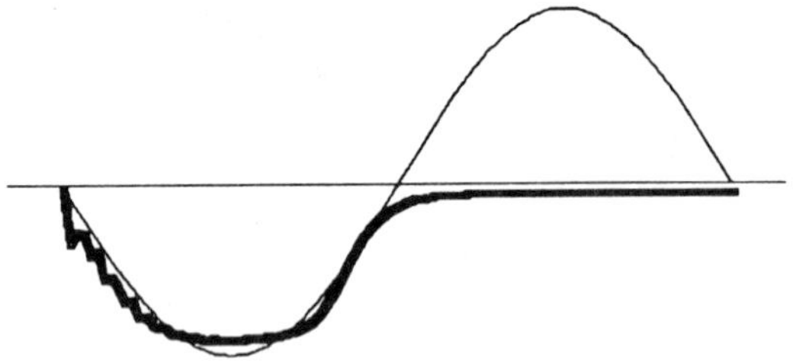

FIG. 5 GenNet of FIG. 4, run for 100 cycles

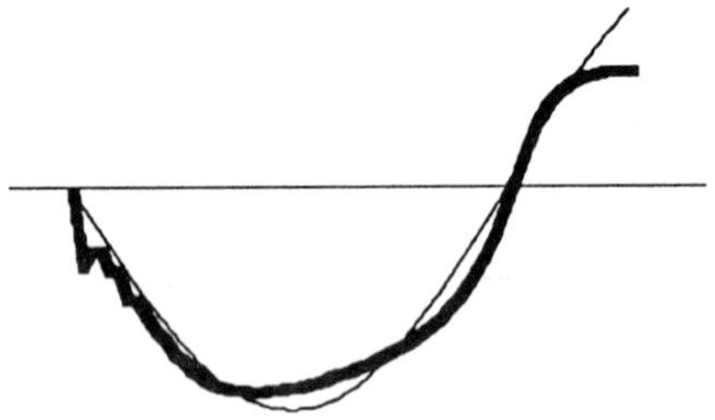

FIG. 6 GenNet of FIG. 4, 65 cycles, best of 200 generations

FIG. 7 shows the result of the same GenNet run for 100 cycles. The result was again unsatisfactory. The curve refused to bend down again. To overcome this problem, the fitness definition was modified slightly to favour a down turn of the curve. Each square of the difference between the actual and desired output was multiplied or weighted by the clock-cycle number, thus for example, the difference for the 37th clock-cycle was multiplied by 37. The fitness was defined as the inverse of the sum of these weighted square differences.

The effect of this weighting was to "reward" curves which bent down again, because those which did not, got low fitness scores. FIG. 8 shows the result of shaping the GenNet of FIG. 6 (i.e. resulting from the "weighted" evolution over 65 cycles) for 200 generations over 100 cycles.

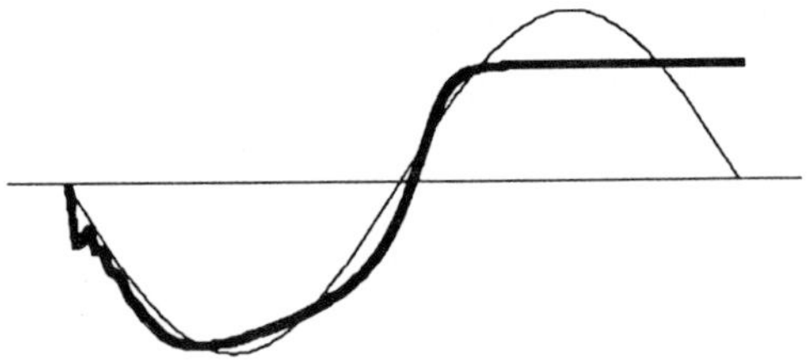

FIG. 7 GenNet of FIG. 6, 100 cycles, best of 100 generations

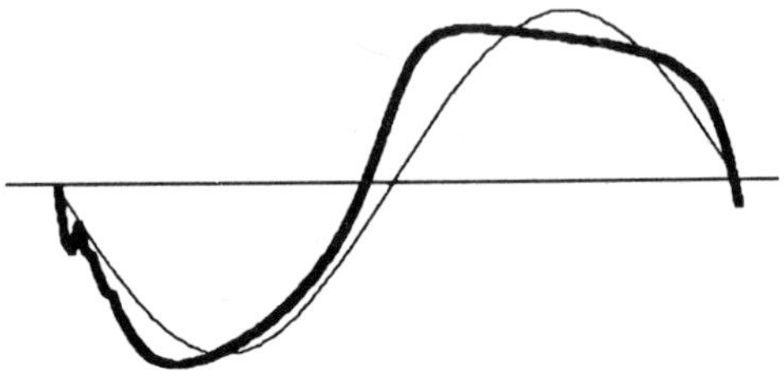

FIG. 8 "Weighted" GenNet of FIG. 6, 100 cycles, 200 generations

The curve in FIG. 8 is beginning to look like what we want. It has approximately the desired amplitude and period (i.e. 0.5 and 100 cycles respectively). The final stage in the shaping process was to take the GenNet used in FIG. 8, and to remove the cycle number weighting factor from the fitness definition (i.e. setting it to what it was before) and evolving over 100 cycles. FIG. 9 shows the result of the evolution over 300 generations. (Always the elite chromosome result is shown).

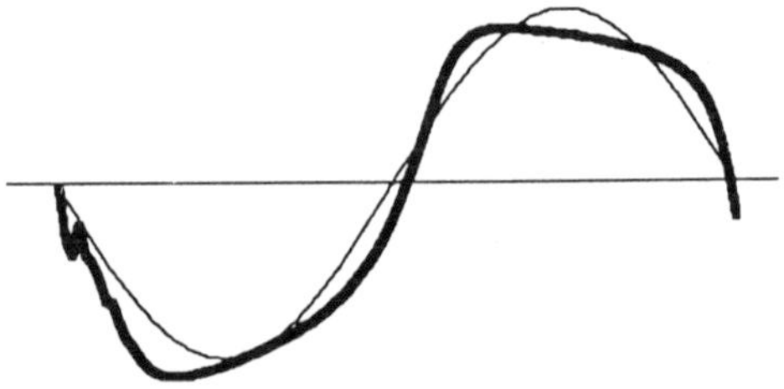

FIG. 9 "Unweighted" GenNet of FIG. 8, 100 cycles, 300 generations

The critical test was then to see how well this GenNet would perform over several oscillations. FIG. 10 shows the results of letting the GenNet of FIG.9 run for 200 cycles. FIG. 11

ran for 800 cycles, with appropriate changes in scale of the horizontal axis.

FIG. 11 shows that the required oscillation has been more or less successfully achieved. With longer evolution times and higher fitness scores, it would be possible to obtain better results, in the sense of closer approximation between the target and actual curves, but at least the idea that one can evolve a GenNet to perform a sinusoidal oscillation with a given period and amplitude has been demonstrated.

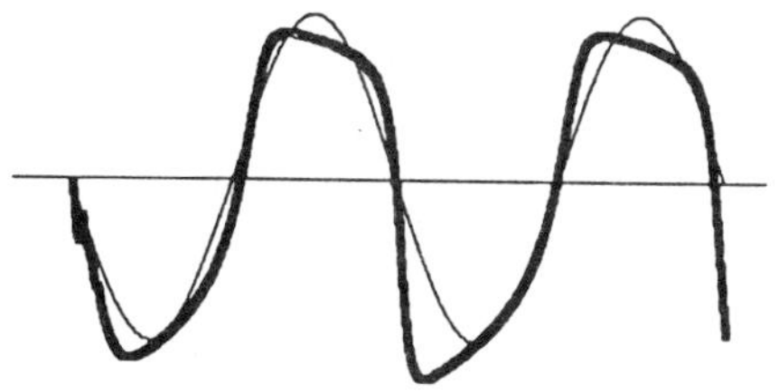

FIG. 10 GenNet of FIG. 9, over 200 cycles

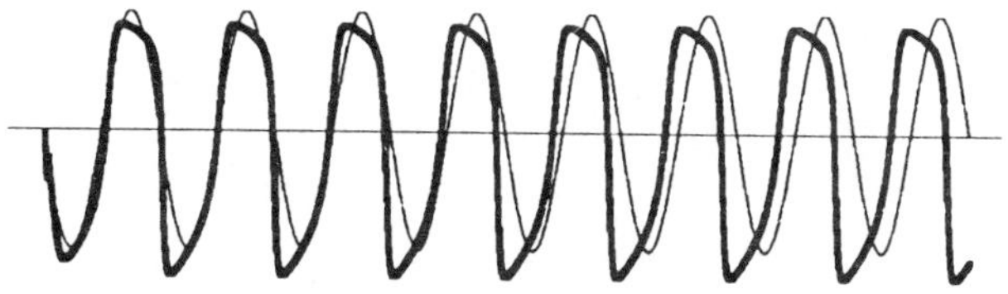

FIG. 11 GenNet of FIG. 9, over 800 cycles

2. A Dual Frequency Sinusoid Generator GenNet

As mentioned in the previous section, the idea of being able to evolve a GenNet capable of generating a variable frequency output, would be very attractive, and could be usefully employed in future artificial nervous systems. For example, such a GenNet could be used to control the frequency of rotation of leg components on artificial creatures. Simply by increasing the magnitude of a single control signal to the GenNet, would increase the frequency of the output. Such a GenNet would be a true "variable frequency generator" or "VFG". The experiments presented in this section show how such a VFG was evolved. The approach taken was as follows. A multi-function GenNet was evolved. Two of the external inputs were clamped. Neuron "0" took the value 0.5, and neuron "1" (acting as a form of control), took the value -0.5 when frequency F1 was to be generated, and the value +0.5 for frequency F2. The hope was that if this could be done, perhaps intermediate frequencies (having values between F1 and F2) would be generated for intermediate (clamped) control signals on neuron "1" (having values between -0.5 and +0.5). The first thing to do therefore was to attempt to evolve the multi-functional GenNet, capable of generating two separate frequencies.

Benefitting from the experience of evolving a single frequency generator, as described in the previous section, the first step was to try to evolve two separate "half" oscillations, using the same GenNet. The two (arbitrary) periods chosen were 40 and 80 clock-cycles. A GenNet of 14 neurons was used, and the fitness function was defined in the following way. For each GenNet chromosome, two trials were undertaken. In the first, neuron "1" took value -0.5, and in the second, it took value +0.5 In each case the sum of the squares of the differences between the target and actual curves was calculated for each clock-cycle. Since the second trial contained twice as many cycles as the first, a correcting factor to give each of the two trials a more or less equal "weighting" or influence on the total fitness function was used. Thus the sum of the first trial was initially multiplied by 2.0 and added to the sum of the second trial. The total fitness was then the inverse of this sum of sums. (Later in the experiment, the value of this extra weighting factor (i.e. 2.0) was increased.) FIG. 12 shows the outputs of a single GenNet for the two trials at periods of 40 and 80 clock-cycles, taken over 23 and 46 cycles (i.e. just over half the oscillation), for 600 generations. The thinner line represents the 40 cycle oscillation and the thicker line the 80 cycle oscillation.

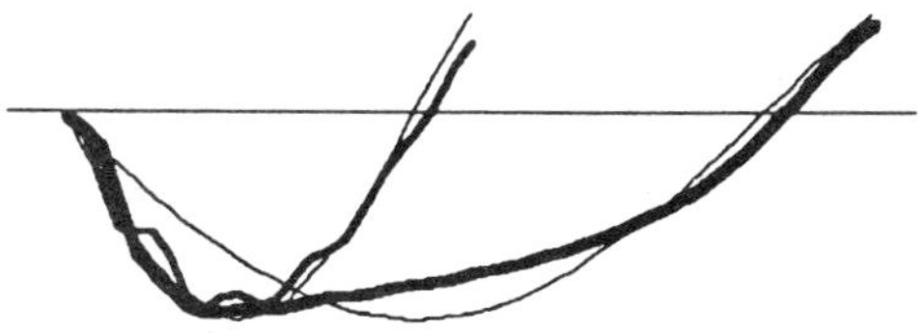

FIG. 12 Dual Frequency GenNet, 23-46 Cycles, Periods 40 and 80 cycles, 600 generations

The GenNet which gave the results shown in FIG. 12 was then used over a full oscillation. FIG. 13 shows the results after 50 generations. The horizontal scale was halved. The 80 cycle period curve showed promise, but the 40 cycle period curve was way off. FIG. 14 shows the improvements at 300 generations. Note that the 40 cycle period curve refused to bend down again.

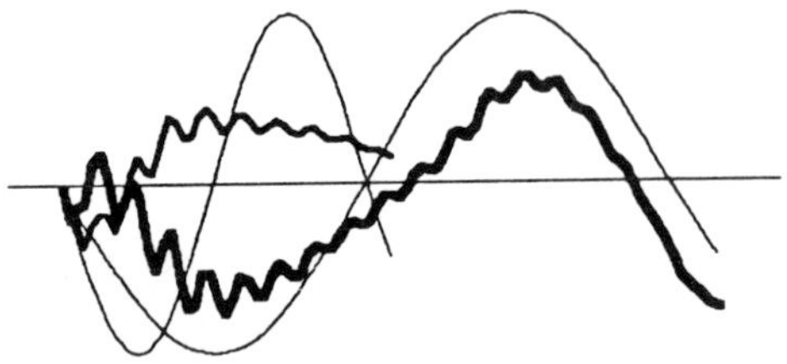

FIG. 13 Dual Frequency GenNet, 43-86 Cycles, Periods 40 and 80 cycles, 50 generations, weighting factor 2.0, (shaping GenNet from FIG. 12)

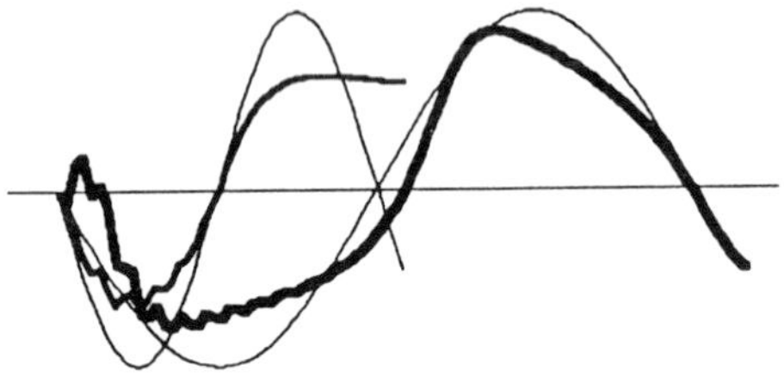

FIG. 14 Dual Frequency GenNet, 43-86 Cycles, Periods 40 and 80 cycles, 300 generations, weighting factor 2.0, (shaping GenNet from FIG. 12)

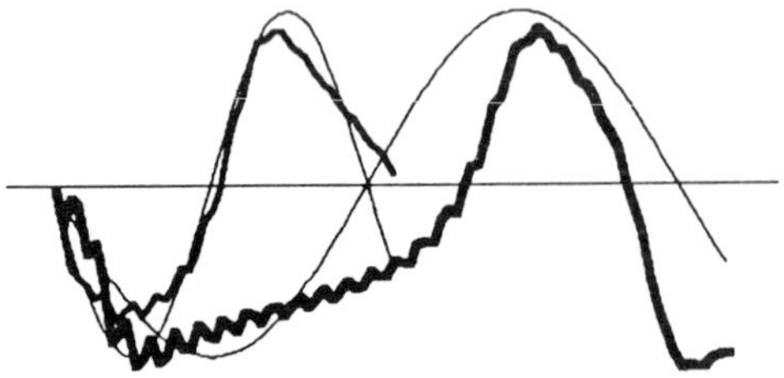

FIG. 15 Dual Frequency GenNet, 43-86 Cycles, Periods 40 and 80 cycles, 300 generations, weighting factor 16.0, (shaping GenNet from FIG. 12)

At this stage it looked as though the weighting factor was too small because the 80 cycle period curve was quite good and the 40 cycle period curve still did not bend down. After some trial and error, it was finally decided to increase the weighting factor to 16.0 After 300 generations with this weighting factor the results are shown in FIG. 15

FIG. 15 was thought to be good enough to be able to pass to the next stage, namely to test whether a periodic motion of both curves would arise over a greater number of cycles. FIG. 16 shows the results of allowing the GenNet, whose results were shown in FIG. 15 to run over 4 times the number of cycles as shown in the previous figures. The horizontal scale is shortened by the same factor.

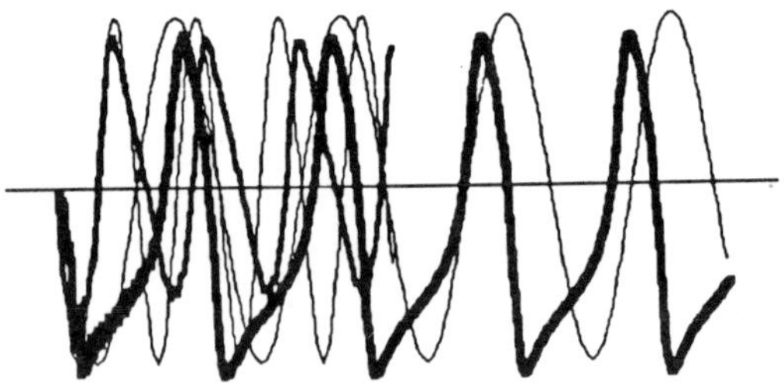

FIG. 16 Dual Frequency GenNet, 163-326 Cycles, Periods 40 and 80 cycles, (using GenNet from FIG. 15)

This result was thought to be good enough to deem the experiment a success. A multifunctional GenNet capable of generating two separate frequencies depending upon the value of a clamped input control signal, had been successfully evolved. This was considered quite a significant result in itself (i.e. multi-functional GenNets are possible), but there is more. The critical test was to see whether intermediate clamped values at "neuron" 1 (i.e. between + 0.5 and - 0.5) would give intermediate output frequencies. That is, had the GenNet evolved an ability to "interpolate" between the two clamped control signal values of + 0.5 and - 0.5?

FIGs. 17 to 20 show the results of this test. The captions indicate the clamped values of "neuron" 1. Note that the light curve is no longer a target. It now simply indicates a curve of period

80 cycles, which is useful as a basis to compare the heavy actual curves.

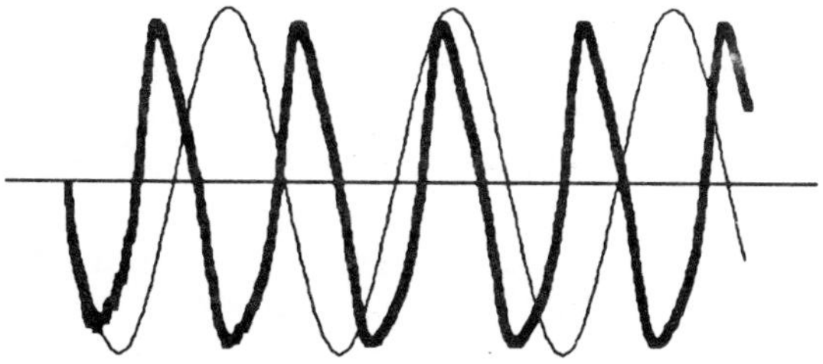

FIG. 17 Dual Frequency GenNet,
246 Cycles, control input clamped at 0.3,
(4.8 oscillations)

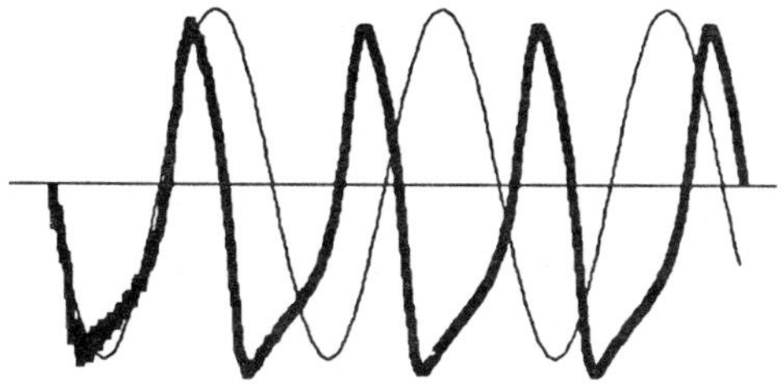

FIG. 18 Dual Frequency GenNet,
246 Cycles, control input clamped at -0.3,
(4.0 oscillations)

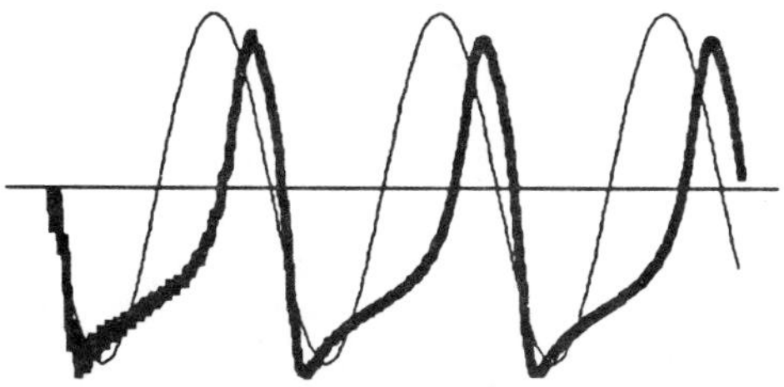

FIG. 19 Dual Frequency GenNet,
246 Cycles, control input clamped at -0.6,
(3.0 oscillations)

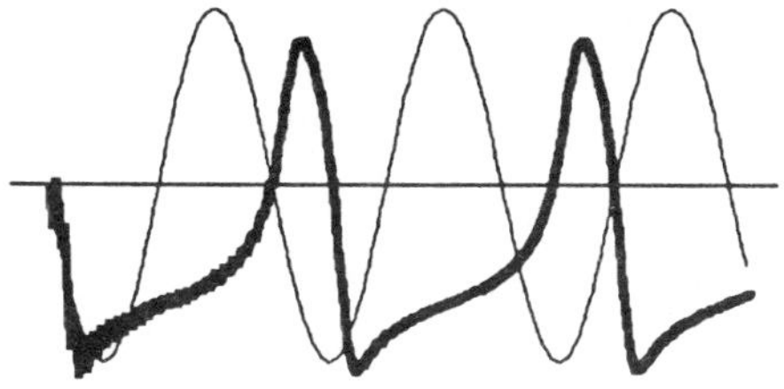

FIG. 20 Dual Frequency GenNet,
246 Cycles, control input clamped at -0.7,
(2.4 oscillations)

These figures speak for themselves. There was obviously an excellent "interpolation" of the clamped input values on "neuron" 1. This GenNet was not only capable of generating two different frequencies, but a whole spectrum of them. A truly variable frequency generator had been evolved. More importantly, the idea of steerable GenNets was shown to be valid.

3. The "Handcrafters VS. Evolutionists" Controversy and other Remarks

As mentioned earlier, Genetic Programming, as applied to the evolution of GenNet behavioral modules, is an extremely useful technique when it comes to building artificial nervous systems for insect robots. This technique has already been applied to the simulation of a 5-behavior (walk, turn left, turn right, peck, mate) Lizard-like quadruped (called LIZZY) which detects prey, predators and mates in its environment (as characterized by the frequency of the sinusoid signals they emit), which orients itself relative to the source of the signal using its antenna, and then flees or approaches appropriately (de Garis 1991c). It is now the ambition of the author, over the next two years, to simulate and build an insect robot having roughly 100 behavioral, detector, and decisional GenNets, and thus have a much wider behavioral repertoire than the insect robots of today (Brooks 1989), (Beer 1990), (including the author's own LIZZY). GenNets (i.e. their weights) will be stored in generic electronic chips which can be attached to a "bus" line which connects to the effectors (legs, arms etc) of the insect robot. This approach will probably be cheaper than the adhoc electronic behavioral modules built so far (Brooks 1989). The advantage of using a real robot (as against a simulated one) is that the robot itself can be used to help evolve the behaviors, i.e. one actually makes the robot walk or turn etc. in order to measure the fitnesses of the chromosomes which specify the motions.

The phenomenon of steerable GenNets (or generalized behavioral learning in GenNets) remains a purely empirical observation. It would be nice to understand why this phenomenon occurs in theoretical terms, but so far, no such theory exists. Thus, understanding why steerable GenNets are possible, poses a challenge to researchers in the fields of neural networks, genetic algorithms and particularly in the field of complex dynamics, to discover the necessary explanatory theory.

The remainder of this paper is devoted to the so-called "Handcrafters VS. Evolutionists" controversy. These two groups of ALifers (or rather Bioticists) express two radically different philosophies relating to future biot building. The "handcrafters" believe that human directed design and construction of the components of biots is essential. Brooks (1989) is an obvious member of the handcrafters camp (at least in practice). The alternative camp, the "evolutionists" (e.g. de Garis 1991c, Beer 1991), believe that it is only a question of time before the complexity of connections and dynamical interactions between components become too complex for such biots to be predictable or designable. This opinion is strengthened when the evolutionists look at the molecular scale technologies (such as molecular electronics (Reed 1988) and nanotechnology (Drexler, 1986), (Schneiker 1990) which will be with us within the decade. Molecular electronics aims to give molecules the capacity to compute. Nanotechnology is even more spectacular in its aims, in hoping to create a "mechanical chemistry", i.e. using nano scale robots (nanots) as assemblers to make any substance, by picking up an atom "here" and putting it "there". Humanity knows that such a thing is possible, because we have the existence proof of biochemistry. Nature's ribosomes and DNA show that molecular scale assembly is possible.

These molecular scale technologies necessarily mean that the number of components that they will allow in "nanotech" based systems will be of the order of Avogadro's number, i.e. a trillion trillion. Systems based on such molecular scale components will obviously have to self assemble if they are to be built at all. No handcrafter is going to design and assemble a trillion-component machine. But this raises the problem that one cannot be sure that the self assembled system is useful in some sense. The only way to ensure this will be to measure its performance. Those hypercomplex systems which do well, i.e. have high fitness, can be used as the basis of future self-assemblies. These self assembling systems will be coded into GP-type chromosomes, which instruct its "embryological" self-assembly (de Garis 1991c). This evolutionist approach lies at the heart of the GP philosophy. In the evolutionists view, the only alternative in the longer term, will be to take an artificial evolutionary approach (i.e. to use GP techniques), when faced with the "complexity problem", (i.e. the design problem which arises when one is confronted with a huge number of parameters or variables which interact in complex usually non linear ways). A biot, capable of 100+ behaviors, will obviously be very complex, and probably too complex for handcrafting techniques.

One of the counter argument used by the handcrafters against the evolutionists is that evolutionary techniques are hopelessly slow and hence impractical. For example, if one used GP techniques to evolve the motions of a physical biot, then the mechanical speeds used to measure the fitnesses of the motions, would mean that the evolution would take weeks to months.

The evolutionists are not immune to these arguments of the handcrafters, but simply reply that there may be no alternative, because handcrafting will inevitably bog down when faced with the complexity problem. It may be possible to partially overcome the slowness argument by employing "incremental evolution", i.e. initially evolving simple whole-nervous-systems, which are successful, and later adding components to them in an evolutionary way. This cuts down on the complexity and the size of the search space that the Genetic Algorithm has to work with. Incremental evolution is the technique used by nature, so the evolutionists have a good precedent. The challenge to the evolutionists will be to produce examples of "whole nervous system evolution", i.e. using GP techniques to evolve a whole nervous system from scratch - no easy undertaking. If this can be done, then incremental evolution may have a chance.

The author has tried to simultaneously evolve a "three-GenNet-nervous-system" (de Garis 1991c), where two of the GenNets were motion controllers, i.e. their output values were used to determine the angles of a pair of sticklegs over time, such that the stick legs walked. One motion GenNet made the sticklegs move to the right across the computer screen. The other motion GenNet made the sticklegs move to the left across the computer screen. For these motions to be triggered, they were fed two external (control) inputs from a third control GenNet. The control GenNet evolved control signals, towards which the motion GenNets had to evolve their response. It was a form of co-evolution. The fitness of this three-GenNet-system was defined as the sum of the two distances walked in the two desired directions.

This whole-nervous-system evolved, but very slowly, namely a week on a MAC II computer. Hence the "too slow" critique of the handcrafters is reinforced to some extent. On the other hand, the evolution did take place, so that one can imagine using GP to add GenNets to the circuit to increase functionality.

Just which of the two groups, the "handcrafters" or the "evolutionists", will prove to be dominant ten years from now, only time can tell. What does seem to be clear today however, is that a complexity crisis is looming in ALife, as bioticists attempt to scale up their biots from having 10 to 100, 1000 ... behaviors and more.

References :

Beer R.D., 1990, "Intelligence as Adaptive Behavior : An Experiment in Computational Neuroethology", Academic Press, San Diego.

Beer R.D. & Gallagher J.C., 1991, "Evolving Dynamical Neural Networks for Adaptive Behavior", (submitted for publication).

Brooks R.A., 1989 "A Robot that Walks; Emergent Behaviors from a Carefully Evolved Network", Neural Computation 1, pp 253-262.

de Garis Hugo, 1990a, "Genetic Programming: Modular Evolution for Darwin Machines", IJCNN-90-WASH-DC, (Int. Joint Conf. on Neural Networks), January 1990, Washington DC, USA.

de Garis Hugo, 1990b, "Genetic Programming : Building Artificial Nervous Systems Using Genetically Programmed Neural Network Modules", ICML90 (7th Int. Conf. on Machine Learning), June 1990, Austin, Texas, USA.

de Garis Hugo, 1991a, "Genetic Programming", Chapter 8, in book, "Neural and Intelligent Systems Integration", ed. Prof. Branko Soucek, WILEY.

de Garis Hugo, 1991b, "Artificial Embryology : Genetically Programming an Artificial Embryo", chapter in book, "Fast Intelligent Processes, Systems and Applications", ed. Prof. Branko Soucek, WILEY.

de Garis Hugo, 1991c, "Genetic Programming : GenNets, Artificial Nervous Systems, Artificial Embryos", PhD Thesis, Universite Libre de Bruxelles.

Drexler K.E., 1986, "*Engines of Creation : The Coming Era of Nanotechnology*", Doubleday.

Goldberg D.E., 1989, "Genetic Algorithms in Search, Optimization, and Machine Learning", Addison-Wesley.

Hopfield J.J., 1984, "Neurons with graded response have collective computational properties like those of two state neurons", Proceedings of the National Academy of Sciences USA, vol.81, pp 3088-3092.

Langton C.G., 1989, "*Artificial Life*", ed., Addison Wesley, 1989.

Reed M.A., 1988, "Quantum Semiconductor Devices", in "*Molecular Electronic Devices*", F.L. Carter, R.E. Siatkowski, H. Wohltjen eds. North Holland.

Rumelhart D.E., Hinton G.E., Williams R.J., 1986, "Learning Internal Representations by Error Propagation", vol. 1, Parallel Distributed Processing, ch.8, pp 318-362, MIT Press, Cambridge, MA.

Schneiker C., 1989, "*Nano Technology with Feynman Machines : Scanning Tunneling Engineering and Artificial Life*", in (Langton 1989).

An Action Based Neural Network for Adaptive Control: The Tank Case Study

Antonio RIZZO &
Istituto di Psicologia
CNR
Viale Marx 15
00137 Roma - Italy

Neil BURGESS
Department of Anatomy
University College London
Gower Street WC1E 6BT
London - U.K.

Abstract

Neural networks of the "environment as teacher" type (see Miyata 1987) are investigated for the on-line adaptive control of the level of fluid in a tank, under time-varying conditions. The nature of on-line adaptivity and the use of "hidden units" is briefly discussed, as is the suitability of closed-loop control in this problem or as a model of human action. Simulations indicate that on-line adaptive networks based on closed loop control can succeed in this problem, and perform best without hidden units.

Introduction

Current approaches to Control Theory are becoming more and more involved with adaptive control (Astrom & Wittenmark 1989; Goodwin & Sin 1984). Adaptive control deals with processes for which both the inner dynamics and the external perturbations they experience can vary with time. Biologically inspired systems such as Neural Networks (NN), Genetic Algorithms (GA) and Immune Networks (IN) seem to offer new strategies for process control. In particular NN using the backprogation algorithm (BP) have produced interesting results (Jordan, & Jacobs 1990; Narendra & Parthasarathy 1990; Nguyen & Widrow 1990; Saerens & Soquet 1989).

We report on a study that exemplifies some of the powers and drawbacks of feed-forward NN for process control and that tries to distinguish between two different aspects of adaptiveness in these NN models. The study was carried out within the research action ERBAS (Exploratory Research on Biological Adaptive Systems) which aims to compare different biologically inspired approaches to process control. The comparison concerns benchmark studies of increasing complexity. The main requirement for each case is to develop systems for control that can solve the problem without prior knowledge and by continuous adaptation to the task.

Bearing in mind the difference between on-line adaptivity and a static generalization ability, we explore the use of 'environmental feedback' for on-line training of the control signal. Specifically we consider the benchmark problem of controlling the level of fluid in a tank by operating a valve.

Our main aim is to develop an approach inspired by psychological models of human action focused on on-line adaptive control. We use the idea by Rumelhart (see Miyata, 1987) of using the predicted effect of an action to learn how to control that action. Miyata (1987) expanded this approach, naming it the EAE model (Environment - Action - Environment). The basic idea is to have the external feedback (as opposed to proprioceptive feedback) coming from the environment as the teacher for the network so that an explicit set of actions does not have to be provided for teaching.

Controlling an action using only feedback from its effect is too simplistic a model of human action control and represents only the closed-loop control. However it has some interesting properties, indeed Miyata used this idea as the base for proposing a connectionist model for action planning and control derived from the Activation-Triggering-Schema (ATS) framework (for action control) developed by Norman and Shallice (1980).

Neural Nets for Closed-Loop Control

The Miyata model copes with the problem of action planning and execution as a problem of mapping from a Desired State of the World to a representation of the Actions needed to achieve that state. This mapping depends on: 1) the internal and external context in which actions are executed, and 2) the evaluation of consequences of the actions. The mapping is learnt by experience. These characteristics are reflected both in the way in which the network learns and in its architecture.

Fig. 1 shows the basic architecture of the network. It is formed by two sub-networks, labelled 'EA' and 'AE'. The EA network maps from a Desired State of the World to the Actions needed to accomplish such a State. The AE network maps from the Action to a prediction of the State of the World. In the original study the two networks were trained separately. First, the AE network is trained so as to reliably predict the modification in the World caused by an action. The error between the predicted change and the real change is used for this first training. Then, the EA network is trained to perform the actions necessary to accomplish a given Desired State of the World. The error between the prediction (E_feedback) and the Desired State of the World (E_desired) is used for this.

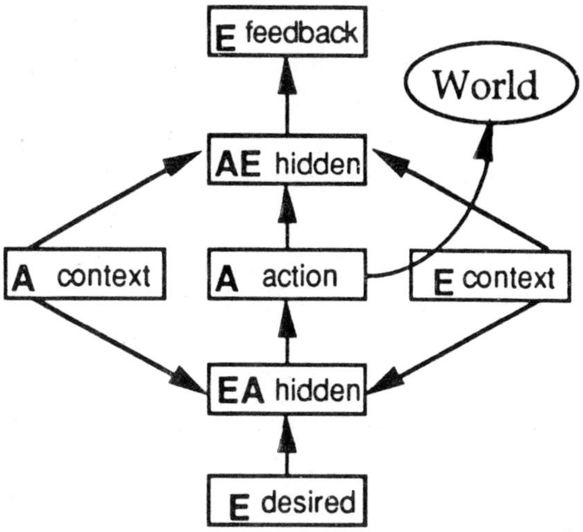

Figure 1: The basic architecture of Miyata's network.

In both networks, the temporal and spatial contexts influence the mapping by means of two sets of memory units, the A_context and the E_context. It is important to note that in both trainings there is no teaching input that specifies which actions are correct from situation to situation. Indeed, this is a frequent situation for biological systems. There is no explicit teaching information for the configurations of muscles required by skilled motor activities, living systems learn these mainly from the result of their actions.

Limitations

The EAE model is a psychologically plausible model of action. However it represents essentially the closed-loop control and thus leaves out at least three important psychological requirements for an action model, some of which (b and c) are mentioned in the ATS model: a) An action model should account for error in the definition of the State of

World (a "mistake"). b) It should describe the role of conscious attentional control and automatization (open loop control). c) It should account for multiple levels of representation of action and feedback. These are some of the directions along which the present model can be extended. But here we will test mainly how "on-line adaptive" closed-loop control can be, when implemented as a Neural Network.

In closed-loop control the critical point is to have a comparison between the desired-state of the world and the actual-state of the world and to eliminate a possible difference. Thus the two states should be described in comparable terms (when this is not the case action evaluation in human action control is hampered, see Norman, 1984, 1990; Rizzo et al., 1987). So, the adaptiveness of this learning paradigm is constrained by the type of information available from the environment with respect to the definition of the desired-state of the world. Another limit of closed-loop control is the temporal distance between the action and its effect in the environment. Temporally delayed feedback hampers an effective comparison.

For the tank benchmark problem the first limit is irrelevant (the actual and desired states are both described in terms of the level of fluid). However the second limit will affect control and would become increasingly apparent as a function of the time-delay of the valve.

The Tank Case Study

The tank case study concerns the regulation of an hydraulic system. A tank is filled by an inflow of liquid, at the bottom there is a valve that regulates the outflow from the tank. There are four possible types of valve (T1-T4). They differ in the way the area of valve actually open is related to the control signal sent to it (how far it is to be turned: 0-100 %). The different relationships are shown in Fig. 2, the fifth valve, type T5, was added so as to be able to have a bigger change in the system (see below) (Fig 2).

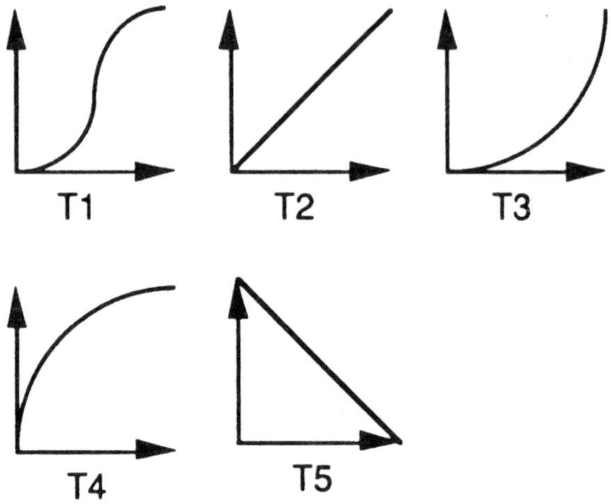

Figure 2. Valve types: Sigmoid (T1), Linear (T2), Parabolic (T3), Square root (T4) and Linear decreasing (T5).

The task is to maintain a certain desired level of fluid in the tank, this level is, in general, time dependent. The rate of inflow of water is also time dependent. The benchmark tasks considered by ERBAS involves four cases in which the time dependence of the desired level and inflow rate can be: constant, step-function or saw-tooth, to be controlled using valve type T1, and a fifth case in which the valve type is regularly switched between types T1- T4. A complete description of the tank case study is reported in Nordvik and Renders (1990).

For all the tasks the only information available to the controller was the current level of the tank and, obviously, the reference level to be reached. As above reported the main aim of the ERBAS project is to assess the on-line adaptability of a controller without any prior knowledge on the system.

What is adaptivity?

Within the current approach two different types of control solution are possible:

a) Generalization without on-line learning - i.e. the network learns a sample of several possible states of the plant from which it generalizes when new situations are encountered.

b) On-line learning of the prediction of the effect of an action and On-line learning of the correct action to achieve a desired state of the world.

We consider only solution b) to be an example of on-line adaption rather than static generalization.

For implementation in a feed-forward NN, solution a) requires training before implementation using a large training set of example situations. A network with many hidden units may be necessary to learn the different behaviors appropriate in different situations. Moreover new situations might be out of the range of generalization of the network (e.g. unpredictable cases).

Solution b) requires a network that can learn different behaviors very quickly, on-line. In terms of multi-layered BP networks this means keeping the number of hidden units as small as possible as BP learning is so slow (increasing rapidly with network size) and the network needs only to be capable of one behavior at any one time.

However, in both cases, learning is from the environment. Due to our aim of on-line adaptivity we choose to use solution b) with both prediction and action being adjustable on-line.

Notice that our choice is determined by the time-varing nature of the system rather than by its non linear nature. Non linear processes can be controlled by a stationary mapping using a pre-trained NN with hidden units. With Time-varying non-linear processes a NN with many hidden units may need a lot of time to retrain itself to implement a changed mapping, or may fail altogether (weight changes from the configuration implementing the previous mapping may lead only to a locally optimal configuration which does not implement the new mapping).

By contrast a NN with few or no hidden units may implement a non linear mapping in an unstable way by continual weight adjustment, in this case re-learning new mappings on-line will take much less time. Note also that the likelihood of becoming trapped in a locally optimal configuration is much less, in fact none exist in the case of no hidden units i.e. in a simple delta rule network.

In the tank problem both the inflow rate and the valve can be time-varying. That is, both the upper (prediction) network and the lower (action) network must implement time-varying mappings.

The Network

We decided that even though the task is non-linear, a continuously adapting network with no hidden units would be sufficient. This linear approximation would not be as accurate if the updating of the network occurred at time-steps much greater than the time constants of the system (e.g. here both the time constant of the valve and the duration of each time-step are 1 second). Fig. 3 shows the network we adopted.

The choice of closed-loop control implemented by an 'action' sub-network and a 'prediction' sub-network conveniently solves the problem of providing training for the action when the only measurable data available is at the level of the state of the controlled system. This occurs as follows (see e.g. Miyata, 1987).

The lower sub-net receives as input the Actual level (Al) of the fluid and the Desired level (Dl), produces as output an Action (A) directly to the valve. The upper sub-net receives as input Al and A and outputs the predicted next level (Pl) of the fluid. Then a comparison is made between the next actual level and the prediction Pl for the correction of the weights in the upper sub-net. A comparison between Pl and Dl is used for the correction of the weights in the lower sub-net.

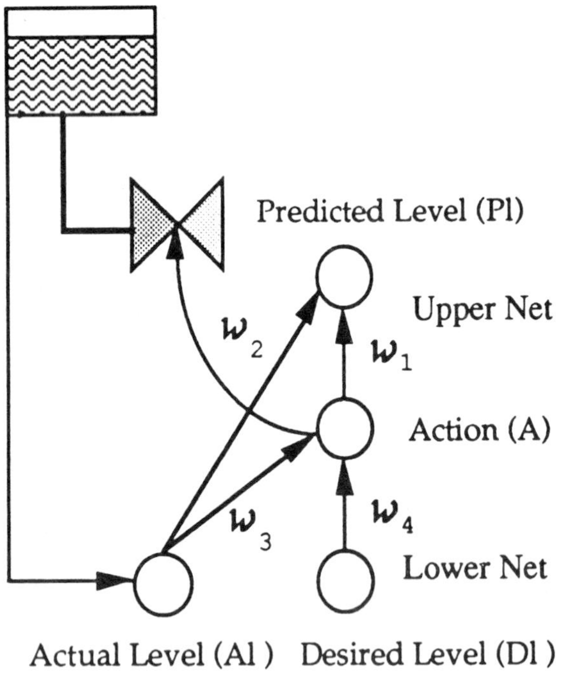

Figure 3. The Neural Network for adaptive control

Thus for the training of the lower (action) sub-net an error E can be defined for each action:

$$E = -\,{}^{1}/_{2}\,(Pl - Dl)^2.$$

Weighted connections in the lower net can then be adjusted by application of the BP algorithm. This is a simple result of the fact that the upper net can predict the effect of an action on the system. In particular we can change a connection weight (e.g. W_3 see Fig 2) in the lower net so as to perform gradient descent in the error. That is the change in the value W_3 is :

$$\Delta W_3 = -\,\varepsilon\ \partial E/\partial W_3$$

$$= -\,\varepsilon\ (\partial E/\partial Pl)\ (dPl/dnet1)\ (\partial net1/\partial A)\ .\ (dA/dnet2)\ (\partial net2/\partial W_3),$$

where ε is the 'learning rate',

$Pl = f(net1) = f(Al.W_1+A.W_2+\phi 1)$,

$A = f(net2) = f(Al.W_3+Dl.W_4+\phi 2)$,

$\phi 1$ and $\phi 2$ are adjustable thresholds.

Thus :

$$\Delta W_3 = \varepsilon\ (Dl-Pl)\ f\,'(net1)\ W_2\ f\,'(net2)\ Al,$$

and W_4 can be adjusted similarly. Notice that it is due to the presence of the upper net that we can calculate

$$\partial E/\partial A = (\partial E/\partial Pl)\ (dPl/dnet1)\ (\partial net1/\partial A) = (Dl-Pl)\ f\,'(net1)\ W_2$$

i.e. that we know the change in the (predicted) error with respect to a change in the action.

As far as teaching the weights for the action (i.e. the bottom half of the network) is concerned it is sufficient for just the sign of the weight from action unit to the prediction unit to be correct for the change (in the weights W_3 and W_4 to be in the right direction to minimize the error E (true gradient descent would require also that the weight had the correct magnitude and would generally require less steps).

This corresponds to the knowledge of how the system responds to an action (in general the 'Jacobean' of the system is necessary). In the five benchmark cases of the tank problem this sign is always negative: opening the valve leads to an eventual reduction in the fluid level. This makes the problem of adapting rather too simple to distinguish clearly between the worth of different strategies, see below.

The activation of a unit is restricted to the range (-1,1) by using the activation function f(x)=tanh(x). All input {output} values were scaled linearly onto {from} (-1,1) to interface with the simulation of the tank. The value of the learning rate was 0.5 for the upper network and 10 for the lower network (this is due to the fact that the error for the action layer is very small after BP through the upper network). A very slight decay term was used to prevent weight values becoming to large to be easily changed when a new situation occurs. Connection weights were changed according to:

$$W(t)=(1-\delta)W(t-1) + \Delta W(t),$$

where $\delta=0.001$.

Notice that (see above)

$$\Delta W(t)=-\varepsilon\, \partial E/\partial W,$$

i.e. no momentum term is used so that weight changes can be more instantaneously adaptive.

Even though the functions representing the behavior of the tank and the valves are non-linear, due to the on-line adaptivity of the controller, the task can be performed by a network whose action at each time-step is only a linear function of the current fluid level (and the desired level) and whose prediction is only a linear function of the action (and the current level). That is, at a given point in time (in each situation) it is enough for the network to know how far to open the valve to maintain the existing level (say X%) and to open{close} it if the level is too low{high}.

If the network can learn to adjust the value of X faster than it changes due to the various perturbations it can succeed. Similarly, a rough prediction of the next level can also be made from a linear combination of the previous level and the action. Also notice that, for the teaching of the lower sub-network, it is enough that the upper sub-network learns to give the weight W_2 the correct sign (see above) .

Whilst the mappings required to produce this approximate action and prediction at each time-step are linear, they change with the state of the tank (i.e. the mappings depend e.g. on the level of the fluid). This is not an insurmountable problem for us because the connection weights can also change with time . Thus we are able to do without hidden units because of our choice of on-line adaptivity.

Results

For all cases we started with random weights in the connections of the network (ranging from -0.1 to + 0.1). There was no prior knowledge of the tank except in our choice of the inputs and of the architecture of the network. Even though the starting configuration of weights are important for successful learning, due to their number, and restricted range, and to the adaptiveness of the delta rule we did not observe a significant difference between favorable and unfavorable starting weights (e.g. negative vs positive connection between action unit and prediction unit).

After about 50 cycles the difference due to different starting weights disappeared and the neural network was able to control all of the 5 cases, performance only improves with further time.

We also tested a network with hidden units (3 units in both the upper and in the lower network, as used by Saerens & Soquet, 1989) on the same cases. The on-line performance was worse than that of the network with no hidden units in all cases, see for example fig. 4.

Fig. 4 shows the performance of the two networks for one of the five cases. In this case there was a constant inflow of fluid but different desired levels had to be reached and kept, using valve type T1. Fig. 4 shows how the desired actual levels varied as a function of time.

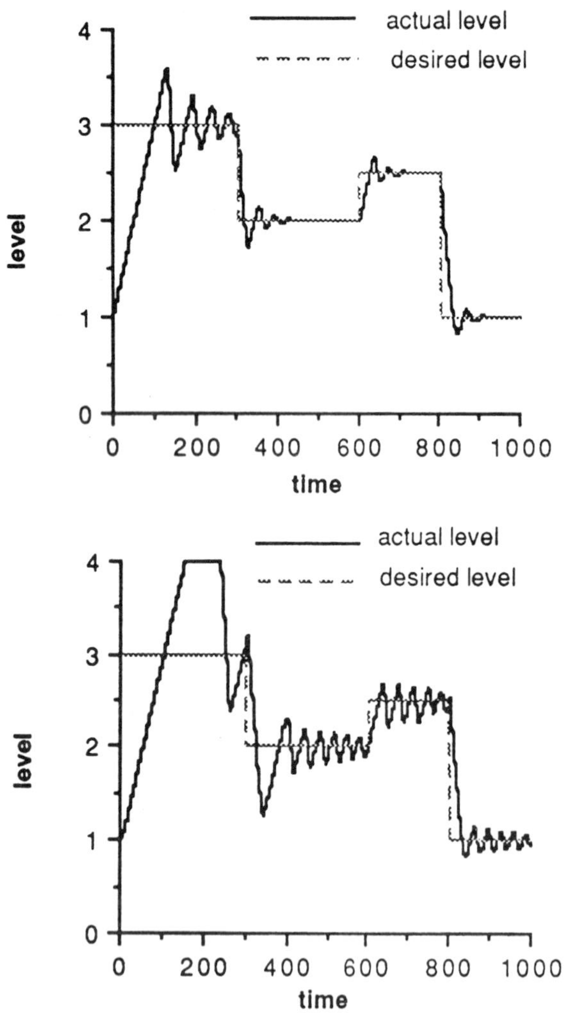

Figure 4. Performance of the network with hidden units (below) and without (above) on one of the five ERBAS cases.

It can be observed that the network reaches a good performance quite soon (400 cycles). The level fluctuates briefly around the desired level whenever there is a change in the desired level. This fluctuation was further reduced with time but never eliminated, it is exacerbated by increasing the time constant of the response of the valve.

We have simulated up to 10,000 time-steps, no connection weight exceeded 2.5 in magnitude (4.5 without decay); weight values tended to oscillate rather than saturate. See also Figs 5 and 6 for performance when both inflow rate and desired level have a saw tooth time-dependence of different period and the valve type changes on-line.

The initial learning shown by the network with hidden units is rather slow. However if both networks are initially pre-trained for 1500 time-steps (Saerens & Soquet also used pre-training) then the performance of the one with hidden units becomes almost as good as that of the one without.

This similarity of performance is deceptive; in terms of on-line adaptability the network with no hidden units will adapt more quickly. However in this particular task all of the different situations presented are quite similar in terms of their control, see above. A strategy:

"if the fluid level is too high {low}
then close {open} the valve"

is enough to give approximate control in all cases (in terms of learning it is enough just for W_2 to be negative, see above). Thus little real adaptivity is required and comparing performance is difficult.

Accordingly we investigated performance when the type of valve may change completely: it may close where previously it opened - type T5 in Fig. 2. This requires a greater change in both the prediction and action sub-nets.

We ran simulations in which both inflow rate and desired level have a saw- tooth time-dependence (of period

500 and 300 respectively) and the valve type changes on-line, this time including use of valve type T5. Figs 5 and 6 show the performance of the networks without hidden units and with hidden units respectively.

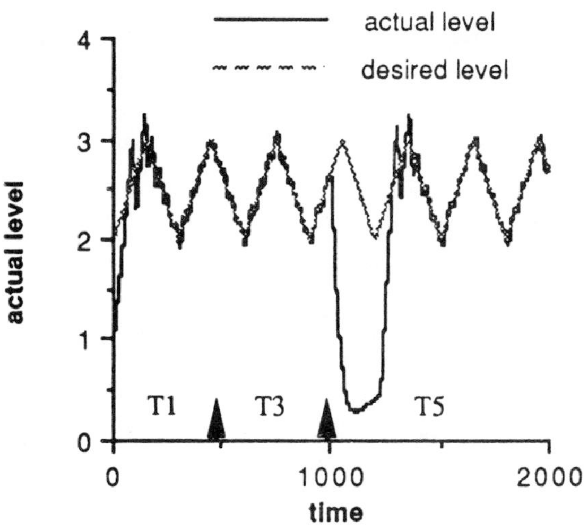

Figure 5. Performance of the network without hidden units. Valve-type changes (through T1, T3, T5) at times 500 and 1000 as indicated.

We see that the initial learning of reasonable control using valve types T1 and T3 is much quicker in the network without hidden units. After the change to valve T5 recovery to approximate control takes 300 steps without hidden units, with hidden units it takes 1000 steps (also the subsequent oscillations are larger and longer-lasting). These behaviors are the same in the cases using valves T2 and T4, and with other time dependencies for inflow rates and desired levels.

Fig. 7 shows the performance of a network with hidden units after 1500 steps of pre-training using valve T1. Performance usingvalves T1 and T3 seems as good as that of the network with no hidden units after 300-400 steps (it is in fact slightly more jerky). However when the valve type changes to T5 performance is again much worse than that of the network with no hidden units, although better than that with hidden units and no pre-training.

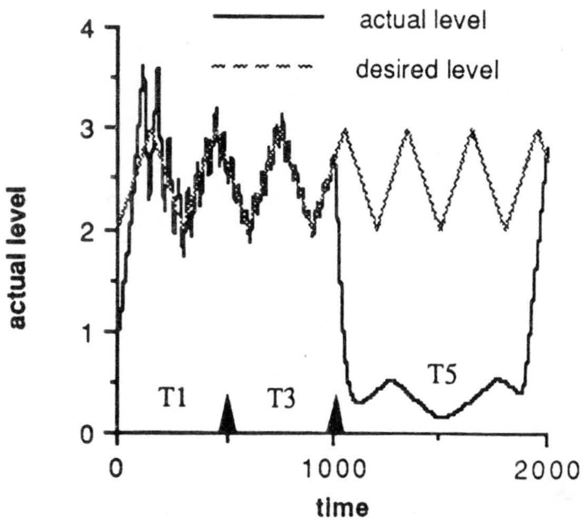

Figure 6. Performance of the network with hidden units. Valve-type changes (through T1, T3, T5) at times 500 and 1000 as indicated.

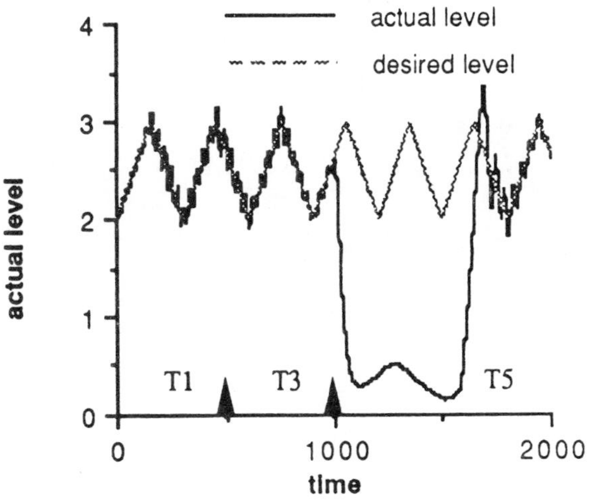

Figure 7. Performance of the network with hidden units after 1500 steps of training. Valve-type changes (through T1, T3, T5) at times 500 and 1000 as indicated.

Conclusion

The results of our simulations showed that a closed-loop control of action implemented as a Neural Network can be on-line adaptive. However, it presents the characteristic limitations of this control mode, e.g. time delay in the action's effect hampers an effective comparison. The use of hidden units could only partially reduce the consequences of this limit, moreover their cost in terms of adaptiveness of the learning rule is quite high. A better solution might be to have a context dependent closed-loop control. But, overall, close-loop control represents only one mode of human action control. It is our aim to explore more of the aspects of the theory of human action control that have been left out (see above). In particular, at the present we are collecting data from an experiment made with human subjects concerning the same tasks with which we tested the neural network.

Another limitation of closed-loop control implemented as a NN concerns the fact that the possibility of reducing the error between desired state and actual state of the world rest on its ability to predict the next state of the world after its action. Some authors (e.g. Jordan & Jacobs, 1991) have presented this as a way to have a model of the environment, however this is much more limited than the model of the environment which appears to be used by humans in control problems (e.g. open-loop control mode). It seems more like a device to implement closed-loop control with NN using BP.

Finally, for the network to be on-line adaptive with the BP learning rule requires the use of the minimum number of hidden units. The on-line adaptivity of the model (i.e. the continual retraining of the weights) enables control of a relatively complex system in many different situations with a very simple network. In the non-linear benchmark control problem of the tank of fluid, good control was achieved without the use of hidden units. The adaptability of this model was greater than that of a network with more hidden units (whether pre-trained or otherwise).

Acknowledgements
We wish to thank Jean-Pierre Nordvick and Ugo Bersini for useful discussions. This work was carried out within the ERBAS project, one of us (NB) was also supported by a Royal Society European Exchange Program Research Fellowship.

References

Astrom, K.J., & Wittenmark, B. 1989. *Adaptive Control*. Amsterdam: Addison-Wesley.

Goodwin, G., & Sin K.S. 1984. *Adaptive Filtering, Prediction and Control*. Englewood Cliffs, NJ: Prentice-Hall.

Jordan, M.I., & Jacobs, R.A. 1990. Learning to control an unstable system with forward modeling. In D. Touretzky (Ed.) *Advances in Neural Information Processing II*. San Mateo, CA: Morgan Kaufmann.

Miyata, Y. 1987. *The Learning and Planning of Actions*. PhD Dissertation. Department of Cognitive Science, University of California San Diego. La Jolla, California 92093.

Narendra, K.S., & Parthasarathy, K. 1990. Identification and control of dynamic systems using neural networks. *IEEE Transaction on Neural Networks*, 1: 4-27.

Nguyen, D., & Widrow, B. 1990. Neural networks for self-learning control systems. *IEEE Control Systems Magazine*, 10: 18-23

Nordvik, J.P. & Renders, J.M. 1990. *The tank case study: terms of Reference* - ERBAS. JRC - Ispra Technical Note Nº I90.97.

Norman, D.A. 1984. *Working papers on errors and error detection.* Unpublished manuscript.

Norman, D. A. 1990. *The Psychology of Everyday Things.* New York: Basic Books.

Norman, D.A. & Shallice, T. 1980/6. Attention to action: Willed and automatic control of behavior. In R.J. Davidson, G.E. Schwartz, & D. Shapiro (Eds.) *Consciousness and Self Regulation: Advances in Research, Vol IV*. New York: Plenum Press.

Rizzo, A., Bagnara, S., & Visciola, M. 1987. Human error detection processes. *International Journal of Man-Machine Studies*, 27: 555-570.

Saerens, M., & Soquet, A. 1989. A neural controller. *Proceedings of the first IEE International Conference on Artificial Neural Networks, London,* : 211-215.

A Model of Formal Neural Network for Non-Supervised Learning and Recognition of Temporal Sequences

Bruno GAS - René NATOWICZ
Ecole Supérieure d'Ingénieurs en Electrotechnique et Electronique
Laboratoire Intelligence Artificielle et Analyse d'Images
Cité Descartes BP 99
93162 Noisy Le Grand cedex
tel: 45.92.67.43 - 45.92.67.14
FRANCE

Abstract

We propose a non-supervised model of formal neural networks to learn and recognize temporal sequences. Time is represented by its effect on processing and not as an additional dimension of inputs: synaptic efficacy of a connection is an integration time of the signal passing through the connection.

The learning process is essentially the modification of connection integration times. We assume that any cell of the network can have a "spontaneous" and an "evoked" activity. Under this assumption such networks can, in an unsupervised way, learn and recognize temporal sequences. An example of such a network is described and the results of the simulation are discussed.

1 Introduction

A central question in cognitive sciences is to understand and modelize systems with learning and adaptation abilities, acting in complex and changing environments. Such systems must be able to modify their knowledge in time, depending on situations they have to face, without external supervision. The question is not only to recognize situations but more than that, to recognize sequences of specific situations, which can be more informative to the system. The importance of time in human and animal ability to understand one's environment is essential. Situation arrangements can turn out to be more important than the situations themselves. In this frame, studying how memorisation and recognition of temporal sequences can be processed by connectionist systems, seems to be of first importance. This study requires on the one hand to ask the question of time representation in such systems and on the other hand the question of their autonomy.

In existing models of neural networks such as the Hopfield model (1982), Ackley, Hinton and Sejnowski's studies on the Boltzmann machine (1985), or T. Kohonen (1984), L. Personnaz (1986) and F. Robert's (1986) studies on recurrent networks, time dimension is embedded in the convergence of a network state iteration process up to a fix point. This static equilibrium limit point does not fit in with the problem of temporal sequence recognition which supposes a continuous dynamic interaction with an external environment.

Models of formal neural networks with time dependant input have already been proposed. D.-E. Rumelhart, G.E. Hinton and R.J. Williams (1986) demonstrate how to apply retropropagation algorithm to recurrent neural networks. R. Goebel (1990) also uses the retropropagation algorithm adapted to recurrent networks for evaluating programming language Lisp expressions. D. Wang and M. Arbib (1990) propose a neural network model for temporal sequence recognition based on a notion of short term memory.

These models are supervised learning ones.

They cannot be used to conceive devices that exhibit autonomous adaptation to unexpected environment changes. This adaptation property is often denoted as "self organization". A self organizing network has the property to progressively modify itself according to its only input stimuli. When sequences are repeatedly presented as input, the network modifies its set of connections. Here, the notion of static equilibrium of a system (fix point of an iterative process) is added with the notion of static equilibrium on the structure. As G. Carpenter and S. Grossberg have stressed (1980), the question is to know how such a system must search for stability of its structure without eventually turning rigid and how such a system can keep a certain kind of plasticity without becoming continuously chaotic.

The hypothesis according to which the central nervous system self-organizes by changing the efficiency of synaptic connections has been proposed by D. Hebb (1949). This hypothesis ("Hebb's rule") is a scheme of non supervised and local learning processes. Two examples of self-organization relying upon Hebb's rule are described by S. Amari (1972).

Hebb's rule, through which the correlation between states of two different cells at the same time is taken into account, is generalized by A. Hertz, B. Sulzer, R. Kühn and J. van Hemmen (1988, 1989) to take into account correlation between two states at different times. This approach could find a biological justification insofar as impulse transmission results from the processing of "slow" and "rapid" neurons; the set of these impulses establishing the synaptic potential.

S. Dehaene, J.P. Changeux, J.P. Nadal (1987) describe a network of formal neurons that can recognize, produce, and memorize temporal sequences of "representations" through a connection selection process. They introduce the notion of first order sequences such as 1-2-1-2... and second order ones, such as 1-2-1-2-1-3...; in this last sequence the symbol 1 can be followed by two different symbols (2 or 3).

In the present approach, we do not distinguish between recognition and learning phases: a temporal sequence presented as input can be recognized even though the presentation results in internal modifications of the network.

In the first part of this paper (2.1) we define temporal sequences. In a second part (2.2) we describe the dynamics of our neural network model, caracterized by sequences of excitations and inhibitions of every network cell. This dynamic activity is governed by a short and a long term local memory at every connection. The third part of this paper (2.3) is devoted to the description of the continuous learning process of the network. This learning process is part of the networks dynamics and described separately only for sake of clarity.

The main characteristics of the dynamics of any network instance of the model are :

1. Non-supervision :
   - It does not need from the environment any other information than network input.
   - It does not need preclassification of temporal sequences to be presented on input.
2. Locality :
   - Information useful to compute the output of a cell and the values of any cell connections is entirely contained in the short and long term memories of the cell and its connections.

These characteristics are fullfilled by defining any cell of the network as

- an autonomous entity, i.e. capable of having a "spontaneous activity".
- a constituent of the network and as such capable of having an activity depending upon the network, i.e. an "evoked activity".

A common way to study learning and recognition capabilities of a formal neural network is to test different learning rules and to observe and measure the network behaviour. Instead of this, we adopt an approach of network synthesis by defining a local "interest function" through which one deduces rules to modify the connections. The interest function which gives the aim of the learning process is defined with respect to the network (F.Varela (1989)) and is only concerned with evoked activity of the cells: "when a cell is in an evoked activity state, it brings into order connection modification rules aiming at keeping the evoked state".

2 A Non-supervised Neural Network model

2.1 Temporal sequences

Let us consider a set $\mathcal{R}$ of $N_{\mathcal{R}}$ elements called cells, or units, that are connected with one another: $\mathcal{R} = \{C_i\}_{i=1,\dots,N_{\mathcal{R}}}$. Every unit C_i of $\mathcal{R}$ produces at time t an output $e(C_i, t) \in \{0, 1\}$.

Let ξ represent the environment and $\mathbf{E}(\xi, \mathcal{R}, t)$ denote the input vector environment :

$$\mathbf{E}(\xi, \mathcal{R}, t) = [e_1(\xi, \mathcal{R}, t), e_2(\xi, \mathcal{R}, t), \dots, e_{N_{\xi,\mathcal{R}}}(\xi, \mathcal{R}, t),],$$

with $e_i(\xi, \mathcal{R}, t) \in \{0, 1\}$ denoting the ith sensor state and $N_{\xi,\mathcal{R}}$ the number of sensors. Cells connected to one or more sensors are called "input cells of network $\mathcal{R}$".

Every time an output state cell has value 1, we say that the cell sends a "spike" to all cells it is connected to. Let us define a "spike train" as a binary sequence of 0s or 1s during a short time τ. It is generally assumed that the most relevant parameter to be extracted from a spike train is the rate of spike occurrence. In order to simplify the model, we consider the three specific following spike trains where $pr(st_{t-k} = 1)$ denotes the probability to have a spike at time $t - k$:

- An "excitatory spike train" : $st_{exc}(t, \tau)$ such that
  $pr(st_{t-k} = 1) = 1 \; \forall k \in [1, \tau]$;
- An "inhibitory spike train" : $st_{inh}(t, \tau)$ such that
  $pr(st_{t-k} = 1) = 0 \; \forall k \in [1, \tau]$;

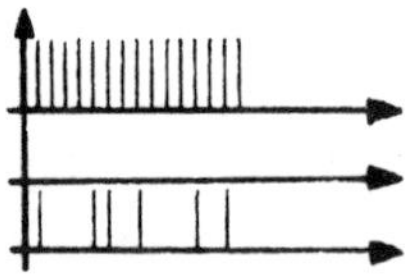

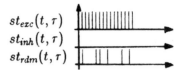

Figure 1: Spike trains

- An "random train" : $st_{rdm}(t, \tau)$ such that
  $pr(st_{t-k} = 1) = p_k \; \forall k \in [1, \tau]$,
  with $0 \le p_k \le 1$ and $\sum p_k = 1$.

Network $\mathcal{R}$'s "perception" of its environment ξ is sequences of excitatory, inhibitory or random trains on every sensor.

Let n be the number of sensors and S_i denote the n-uplet whose components are one of the three spike trains previously defined : $S_i \in \mathcal{S}$, $\mathcal{S} = \{S_1, \; S_2, \dots \; S_{|\mathcal{S}|}\}$ and $|\; \mathcal{S} \;| = 3^n$. Let us call n-uplet S_i "symbol S_i". The presentation of a symbol S_i to net sensors needs τ network iterations. We define a temporal sequence $\mathbf{S}$ as $\mathbf{S} = S_a, S_b, \dots, S_{l(\mathbf{S})}$; with $S_i \in \mathcal{S}$. Each S_i is called a component, or a symbol, of $\mathbf{S}$. The length $l(\mathbf{S})$ of the sequence is the number of symbols in the sequence. The presentation of a sequence $\mathbf{S}$ to net sensors requires $\tau.l(\mathbf{S})$ network iterations. For example, in figure 2, we defined a temporal sequence $\mathbf{S}$ with four symbols ($l(\mathbf{S}) = 4$), for a network with two sensors ($n = 2$) with the three spike trains defined in figure 1.

2.2 The network dynamics

2.2.1 Total Input

Cells are of two possible classes : excitatory or inhibitory. Let $sgn(C_i)$ be the "class" of cell C_i:

$$sgn(C_i) = \begin{cases} +1 & \text{if cell } C_i \text{ is excitatory} \\ -1 & \text{if cell } C_i \text{ is inhibitory} \end{cases}$$

In our model, cell classes are randomly fixed initially and remain constant:

$$\forall u, sgn(C_i, t + u) = sgn(C_i, t_0).$$

Let $pre(\omega_j(C_i))$ be the presynaptic cell of connection $\omega_j(C_i)$. By extention, $pre(C_i)$ will be the set of all connection presynaptic cells of cell C_i. Every cell C_i of network $\mathcal{R}$ computes a summation

$$\mathcal{S} = \left\{ \begin{array}{ll} S_1 = \begin{pmatrix} st_{inh} \\ st_{inh} \end{pmatrix}, & S_2 = \begin{pmatrix} st_{rdm} \\ st_{inh} \end{pmatrix}, \\ S_3 = \begin{pmatrix} st_{exc} \\ st_{inh} \end{pmatrix}, & S_4 = \begin{pmatrix} st_{inh} \\ st_{rdm} \end{pmatrix}, \\ S_5 = \begin{pmatrix} st_{rdm} \\ st_{rdm} \end{pmatrix}, & S_6 = \begin{pmatrix} st_{exc} \\ st_{rdm} \end{pmatrix}, \\ S_7 = \begin{pmatrix} st_{inh} \\ st_{exc} \end{pmatrix}, & S_8 = \begin{pmatrix} st_{rdm} \\ st_{exc} \end{pmatrix}, \\ S_9 = \begin{pmatrix} st_{exc} \\ st_{exc} \end{pmatrix}. & \end{array} \right\}$$

symbol set $\mathcal{S}$

$$\left\{ \begin{array}{l} \mathbf{S} = S_9, S_7, S_3, S_1 \\ r.l = 40 \end{array} \right.$$

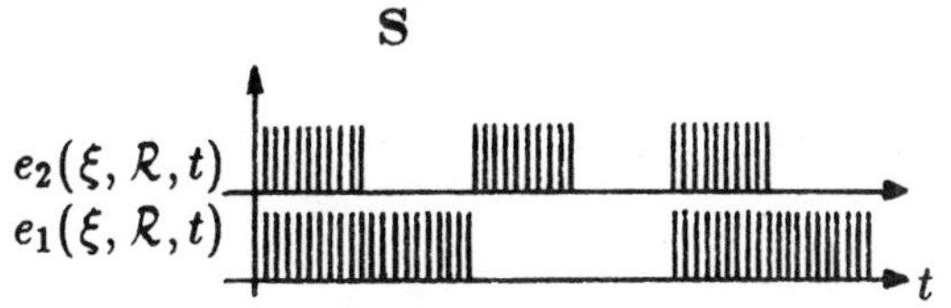

Figure 2: A temporal sequence exemple

of past and present output of its presynaptic cells as follows.

Let the jth connection of C_i, $\omega_j(C_i)$ be characterized by :

- "the time integration of $\omega_j(C_i)$" : $T(\omega_j(C_i), t) \in [0, ..., T_{max}]$;
- "the contribution of $\omega_j(C_i)$ to total input of cell C_i" : $v(\omega_j(C_i), t) = \sum_{u=1}^{T(\omega_j(C_i),t)} e(C_k, t-u)$; with $C_k = pre(\omega_j(C_i))$. One has $v(\omega_j(C_i), t) \in [0, T(\omega_j(C_i), t)]$.
- "the class of $\omega_j(C_i)$" : $sgn(\omega_j(C_i)) = sgn(C_k) \in \{-1, +1\}$; with $C_k = pre(\omega_j(C_i))$.

Let $\mathcal{V}(C_i, t)$ denote the total input of cell C_i at time t. We compute $\mathcal{V}(C_i, t)$ by summing the input connection contributions:

$$\mathcal{V}(C_i, t) = \sum_{j=1}^{N(C_i)} sgn(\omega_j(C_i)) v(\omega_j(C_i), t)$$

where $N(C_i)$ is the number of all presynaptic connections of cell C_i. One has :

$$\mathcal{V}_{min}(C_i, t) \leq \mathcal{V}(C_i, t) \leq \mathcal{V}_{max}(C_i, t)$$

Where $\mathcal{V}_{min}$ and $\mathcal{V}_{max}$ denote respectively the minimum and maximum values of total input $\mathcal{V}(C_i, t)$:

$$\mathcal{V}_{min}(C_i, t) = \sum_{j=1}^{N(C_i)} T(\omega_j(C_i), t). \frac{1 - sgn(\omega_j(C_i))}{2}$$

$$\mathcal{V}_{max}(C_i, t) = \sum_{j=1}^{N(C_i)} T(\omega_j(C_i), t). \frac{1 + sgn(\omega_j(C_i))}{2}$$

Normalizing the total input values, we obtain the total input values relative to cell C_i:

$$\mathcal{V}_c(C_i, t) = \mathcal{V}(C_i, t) + \mathcal{V}_{c_{min}}(C_i, t) - \mathcal{V}_{c_{max}}(C_i, t)$$

where:

$$\mathcal{V}_{c_{min}}(C_i, t) = -\tfrac{1}{2} |\mathcal{V}_{max} - \mathcal{V}_{min}|$$

$$\mathcal{V}_{c_{max}}(C_i, t) = \tfrac{1}{2} |\mathcal{V}_{max} - \mathcal{V}_{min}|$$

The contribution $v(\omega_j(C_i), t)$ of connection $\omega_j(C_i)$ to total input of cell C_i is the short term memory of the connection $\omega_j(C_i)$ at time t; the set of all C_i cell connection contributions at time t is the short term memory of cell C_i at time t. The integration time $T(\omega_j(C_i), t)$ is the long term memory of connection $\omega_j(C_i)$ at time t; the set of all C_i cell connection integration times at time t is the long term memory of cell C_i at time t. Modifications of this long term memory are the result of the learning process, described in the third part of this paper.

2.2.2 Spontaneous and Evoked Activity

As stressed in the introduction 1, any cell of the network can be considered as an autonomous entity and as a component of a system, the network itself. To put this in concrete terms, every cell C_i of the network is assigned two different input/output functions and an activity type function $\mathcal{A}(C_i,t)$:

1. Spontaneous activity law: output of cell C_i is a function that does not depend on past or present activity of cell C_i presynaptic cells.
2. Evoked activity law: output of cell C_i is a function of past and present activity of cell C_i presynaptic cells.
3. Activity type function, $\mathcal{A}(C_i,t) \in \{0,1\}$:
   - if $\mathcal{A}(C_i,t) = 0$ then cell C_i computes at time t its output according to its spontaneous activity law;
   - if $\mathcal{A}(C_i,t) = 1$ then cell C_i computes at time t its output according to its evoked activity law.

As a pre-emptive remark, let us stress that the activity type function value, $\mathcal{A}(C_i,t)$, will itself depend on the total input of cell C_i at time t, $\mathcal{V}_c(C_i,t)$.

We propose the following spontaneous and evoked activity laws, where $pr(e(C_i,t) = 1)$ is the probability that cell C_i sends a spike on its output at time t and $h(C_i)$ is a threshold value:

1. spontaneous activity law:

$$pr(e(C_i,t) = 1) = p(C_i)$$

   i.e. the probability that cell C_i sends a spike at time t is function of cell C_i and constant over the time.

2. evoked activity law:

$$pr(e(C_i,t) = 1) = \begin{cases} 1 & \text{if } \mathcal{V}_c(C_i,t) \geq h \\ 0 & \text{if } \mathcal{V}_c(C_i,t) < h \end{cases}$$

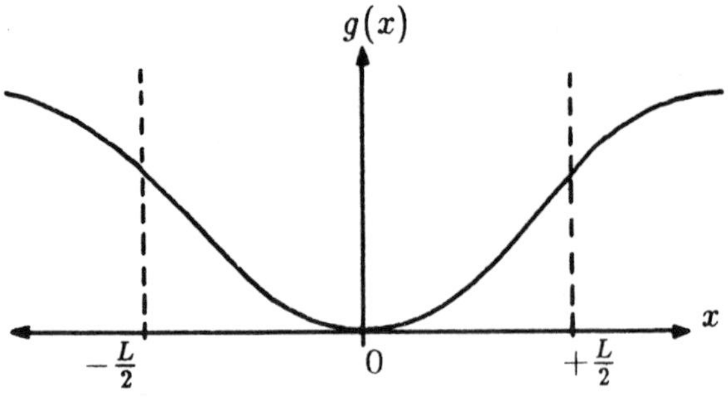

Figure 3: Function g (evocation criterion)

3. activity type function :
   we propose the following law to compute activity type function $\mathcal{A}(C_i)$:

$$\begin{cases} pr(\mathcal{A}(C_i) = 1) = g(\mathcal{V}_c(C_i,t)) \\ pr(\mathcal{A}(C_i) = 0) = 1 - g(\mathcal{V}_c(C_i,t)) \end{cases}$$

Function g will be named "evocation criterion".

Let us recall that a cell is in an evoked type state at time t if its output is computed according to its evoked activity law, whatever the result of this computation is. Qualitatively, we wish an evocation criterion for cell C_i such that the higher the number of evoked presynaptic cell is, the higher the probability that cell C_i is in an evoked type state is, i.e. the probability that cell C_i be in an evoked state must increase when its total input $\mathcal{V}_c(C_i,t)$ approaches its border values $\mathcal{V}_{c_{min}}$ and $\mathcal{V}_{c_{max}}$ and must decrease down to 0 if $\mathcal{V}_c(C_i,t)$ moves away these border values. In this paper, we propose a symetric evocation criterion (cf. fig.3):

$$g(\mathcal{V}_c) = \begin{cases} \frac{1}{1+\exp^{-\mathcal{V}_c+\frac{L}{2}}} & \text{if } \mathcal{V}_c \geq 0 \\ \frac{1}{1+\exp^{\mathcal{V}_c+\frac{L}{2}}} & \text{if } \mathcal{V}_c < 0 \end{cases}$$

In short, out of learning, the computing process at every cell C_i is:

1. Compute for every connection of cell C_i, the contribution $v(\omega_j(C_i,t))$ to the total input.
2. Compute the total input $\mathcal{V}_c(C_i,t)$.
3. Chose the activity type state $\mathcal{A}(C_i,t)$ according to

$$\begin{cases} pr(\mathcal{A}(C_i,t) = 1) = g(\mathcal{V}_c(C_i,t)) \\ pr(\mathcal{A}(C_i,t) = 0) = 1 - g(\mathcal{V}_c(C_i,t)) \end{cases}$$

4. Compute output $e(C_i,t)$ according to the activity type state $\mathcal{A}(C_i,t)$.

Let us stress that the shape of the evocation criterion g is such that with high and low values of total input $\mathcal{V}_c(C_i,t)$, any cell C_i tends to be in an evoked type state: the parameter L determines on what extend cell C_i is sensitive to the activity type state of the cells of its presynaptic neighborhood $pre(C_i)$. In this paper, the parameter L has the same value for all the cells and is therefore a network parameter.

2.3 Learning process

One says that the network $\mathcal{R}$ is learning when it modifies the integration time of at least one of its connections (cf. 2.2.1). Integration times of connections are the only parameters of the model whose values can be learnt.

Let $\triangle T(\omega_j(C_i),t)$ be the modification to the jth connection of cell C_i at time t with $\triangle T \in \{-1,0,1\}$. Let $a(C_i,t) \in \{0,1\}$ be a function whose value depends on the total input of cell C_i at time t, such that if $a(C_i,t)=0$ then cell C_i does not modify its connections at time t; if $a(C_i,t)=1$ then cell C_i is in a learning state and modifies its connections according to the learning process. Therefore,

$$\begin{cases} a(C_i,t)=0 \Rightarrow \\ T(\omega_j(C_i),t+1)=T(\omega_j(C_i),t) \end{cases}$$

$$\begin{cases} a(C_i,t)=1 \Rightarrow \\ T(\omega_j(C_i),t+1)=T(\omega_j(C_i),t)+\triangle T(\omega_j(C_i),t) \end{cases}$$

for any incoming connection $\omega_j(C_i)$ of cell C_i.

As introduced in chapter 1, the network autonomy in its learning process requires the introduction of an "interest function" defined in respect of the network. We propose the following local interest function:

"When in evoked type activity state, cell C_i modifies its connections in order to maintain its evoked type activity state".

As a consequence, the global aim of learning is that subnets being in evoked type activity state remain in evoked type activity state.

In this paper, we propose the most direct translation of the local interest function:

$$\begin{cases} pr(a(C_i,t)=1)=pr(\mathcal{A}(C_i,t)=1) \\ pr(a(C_i,t)=0)=pr(\mathcal{A}(C_i,t)=0) \end{cases}$$

We have simulated the network with a learning law here presented as a truth table (table 1). This law is to be understood as an instance of non supervised learning that can be defined within our model. It is far from being unique. This law makes the variation of integration time of the jth incoming connection of cell C_i at time t ($\triangle T(\omega_j(C_i),t)$) depend upon:

- the contribution $v(\omega_j(C_i),t)$ of the jth connection to the total input on cell C_i at time t.
- the integration time of the jth connection at time t, $T(\omega_j(C_i),t)$.
- the class $sgn(\omega_j(C_i))$ excitatory or inhibitory, of the jth connection.
- the total input on cell C_i at time t, $\mathcal{V}_c(C_i,t)$.

3 Simulation

We describe the simulation of an instance of the neural network model just defined. The simulation was done on a low price personal computer.

Network description :

- the net $\mathcal{R}$ is composed of ten cells : $N_{\mathcal{R}}=10$
- the net $\mathcal{R}$ is fully connected but without self-connection: $N(C_i)=9, \ \forall C_i \in \mathcal{R}$.
- the net $\mathcal{R}$ has two sensors: $N_{\xi,\mathcal{R}}=2$.
- cell classes are evenly distributed with probability: $pr(sgn(C_i)=1)=\frac{1}{2}$.
- the two connections that link sensors to input cells are excitatory ones.

*test*1	$sgn(\omega_j(C_i))$	*test*2	$\Delta T(\omega_j(C_i),t)$
NO	+1	*NO*	0
NO	+1	*YES*	−1
NO	−1	*NO*	−1
NO	−1	*YES*	0
YES	+1	*NO*	−1
YES	+1	*YES*	+1
YES	−1	*NO*	+1
YES	−1	*YES*	−1

Where:

$$test1 = \begin{cases} YES & \text{if } v(\omega_j(C_i),t) > \frac{1}{2}v_{max} \\ NO & \text{if } v(\omega_j(C_i),t) \le \frac{1}{2}v_{max} \end{cases}$$

$$test2 = \begin{cases} YES & \text{if } \mathcal{V}_c(C_i,t) > \frac{\mathcal{V}_{c_{max}}}{2} \\ NO & \text{if } \mathcal{V}_c(C_i,t) \le \frac{\mathcal{V}_{c_{max}}}{2} \end{cases}$$

$v_{max} = T(\omega_j(C_i),t)$, maximum possible contribution of connection ω_j to the total input $\mathcal{V}_c(C_i,t)$.

Table 1: Learning law truth table

- the maximum value of the integration time is $T_{max} = 32$.
- all initial connection integration time values are: $T(\omega_j(C_i),t_0) = \frac{T_{max}}{2}$
- the two connections values that link sensors to input cells are definitively: $T(\omega_j(C_i),t) = T_{max}, \forall t \ge t_0$.
- the net $\mathcal{R}$ is initially spontaneous and $\mathcal{V}_c(C_i,t_0) = 0, \ \forall C_i \in \mathcal{R}$.
- the parameter L of evocation criterion g (cf. fig.3) is defined relatively to the maximum value of cell C_i total input: $L = \mathcal{V}_{c_{max}}(C_i,t)$.
- the spontaneous activity law parameter value of cell C_i is: $p(C_i) = \frac{3}{10}, \ \forall C_i \in \mathcal{R}$.
- the threshold value of cell C_i is: $h(C_i) = \frac{1}{2}\mathcal{V}_{c_{max}}(C_i,t)$.

3.1 Network evocation

Four experiments are here described. In the initial state of the network, all cells are in spontaneous type state.

According to section 2.2.2, at any time, we know the probability for a cell to be in a spontaneous or evoked activity type state. Let us consider a subset $r \subset \mathcal{R}$ of cells. We will say that the corresponding subnet r is evoked iff:

$$\forall C_i \in r, \ \mathcal{A}(C_i,t) = 1,$$

i.e. any cell of set r computes its output according to its evoked activity law.

- If $r = \mathcal{R}$, the network is totally evoked;
- If $r \subset \mathcal{R}$ and $r \ne \mathcal{R}$, the network is partially evoked;
- If $r = \emptyset$, the network is totally non evoked (spontaneous).

We built three temporal sequences to simulate the environments (see fig. 2):

- $\mathbf{S}_A = S_9, S_7, S_3, S_1$;
- $\mathbf{S}_B = S_9, S_9, S_1, S_1$;
- $\mathbf{S}_C = S_1, S_9, S_1, S_3$;

with $\tau = 16$.

Let t_0 be the initial time of experimentation. All the network parameter values are those of a network running in a spontaneous state from $t = -\infty$ to $t = t_0 - 1$:

$$\forall C_i \in \mathcal{R}, pr(e(C_i,t) = 1) \ = \ p(C_i).$$

1. Random input.
   In this experiment, the input of the network is a symbol $S_5 = \begin{pmatrix} st_{rdm} \\ st_{rdm} \end{pmatrix}$ renewed at every presentation. Any subnet remains in spontaneous type state. One can say that the network is forced by the environment to remain non evoked, or symmetricaly, that the network does not "perceive" any regularity in its input "sequence".

2. No input.
In this experiment, no input is presented to the network. The whole network eventually reaches an evoked type state after a time delay depending on the parameter L of the evocation criterion (cf. fig. 3): the smallest the value of L is, the quicker the evoked type state is reached; the higher the value of L is, the longer this time delay is. Limit case is for $L > 2\mathcal{V}_{c_{max}}$, case where the evoked type state is never reached, and for $L < 0$, case where the evoked type state is always reached. The parameter L can therefore be defined without any reference to the environment as the Network Expected Time Of Self-Evocation ("netose" parameter). Let us note that boolean recurrent networks are limit cases of the model with:

$$\begin{cases} L < 0 \\ T(\omega_j(\mathcal{C}_i), t) = 1 \; \forall \; i, j, t \end{cases}$$

3. Temporal sequences as input.
The netose parameter L remains constant, relative to $\mathcal{V}_{c_{max}}$: $L = \mathcal{V}_{c_{max}}(\mathcal{C}_i, t)$. In the first experiment, sequence is a first order one (cf. chapter 1 and Dehaenne, J.P. Changeux and J.P. Nadal (1987)). In the second experiment, the sequence is a second-order one.

   (a) Sequence $\underline{\mathbf{S}_A}\ldots = \underline{S_9, S_7, S_3, S_1}\ldots$
   $\mathbf{S}_A$ is composed of non random symbols. An average of 12 presentations of sequence $\mathbf{S}_A$ is enough to put the network in the totally evoked state. When evocation is achieved, further presentations (up to 200) do not change the network structure. A fix point of the structure is reached, i.e. all the state connection parameters remain constant.
   These 12 $\mathbf{S}_A$ sequence presentations need less than 11 seconds on the personal computer used. If one considers 5.10^{-2} seconds as a typical neuron spike time utterance, the corresponding "real time" is less than 39 seconds.

   (b) Sequence $\underline{\mathbf{S}_C}\ldots = \underline{S_1, S_9, S_1, S_3},\ldots$
   This sequence is a second order one as symbol S_1 can be followed by symbol S_9 or symbol S_3. An average of 16 presentations is necessary to reach an evoked type state of the network. A fix point of the network structure is achieved. Computer time is less than 15 seconds, "real time" would be less than 52 seconds.

3.2 Network used as binary classifier

A temporal sequence $\mathbf{S}$ is considered as recognized by the network if its presentation brings a totally evoked state of the network. Its important to note that this recognition criterion does not imply a fix point of the network structure. Two experiments are described. The first one is concerned with first order sequence recognition, the second one with second order sequence recognition. In both cases, the initial state of the network is spontaneous (totally non evoked).

1. First order sequence recognition.
First of all, sequence

$$(\mathbf{S}_A)^{20} = (S_9, S_7, S_3, S_1)^{20}$$

was presented as input. A fix point of the network structure was reached. Then the sequence

$$(\mathbf{S}_B)^4 = (S_9, S_9, S_1, S_1)^4$$

was presented as input.

Immediatly after first presentation of sequence $\mathbf{S}_B$, the network changed its activity state type from totally evoked to partially evoked. After the four presentations of sequence $\mathbf{S}_B$, the network was in a spontaneous state.

The third part of the experiment consisted in presenting the sequence $\mathbf{S}_A$ as input. After presentation of $(\mathbf{S}_A)^2$, the network always had recovered the evoked state it was in just before presentation of sequence $(\mathbf{S}_A)^4$. In some experiments, a unique presentation of sequence $\mathbf{S}_A$ was enough.

2. Second order sequence recognition. First of all the second order sequence

$$(\mathbf{S}_C)^{16+9} = (S_1, S_9, S_1, S_3)^{16}(S_1, S_9, S_1, S_3)^9$$

was presented to the network. After presentation of sequence $(S_1, S_9, S_1, S_3)^{16}$ the network reached an evoked type state and a fix point of the network structure.

Thereafter, after presentation of sequence $(\mathbf{S}_C)^{16+9}$, the sequence $(S_1, S_9)^{3+5}$ was presented as input to the network. Presentation of sequence $(S_1, S_9)^3$ brought the network to a partially evoked state: size of the evoked subnet varies from 2 to 8, depending on the experiment. The network remained in its partially evoked type state during presentation of sequence $(S_1, S_9)^5$.

The third part of the experiment consisted in the presentation of sequence

$$(S_1, S_9, S_1, S_3)^{2+200}.$$

After presentation of sequence

$$(S_1, S_9, S_1, S_3)^2,$$

the network recovered the evoked type state it was in before presentation of sequence $(S_1, S_9)^{3+5}$. The network remained in its evoked type state during further presentations.

4 Conclusion

We defined a connectionist model of network in continuous interaction with its environment and exhibiting really non supervised sequence learning capabilities.

The non supervised learning process (cf. chapter 1. point 1) was achieved under the hypothesis that any cell of the network can have two distinct modes of processing, spontaneous and evoked, depending upon the activity of its presynaptic cell neighborhood.

Three states of network instances are introduced (cf. chapter 3.1): totally evoked, partially evoked, spontaneous.

The criterion of network sequence recognition was given.

We stressed the existence of a self defined parameter, the network expected time of self evocation, through which boolean recurrent networks are zero limit cases of the model (cf. chapter 3.1. point 2).

In the model presented, the only parameters subject to learning are connection integration times and the local aim of learning is a very general one: any cell of the network "tries", when in evoked mode of processing to maintain it (cf. chapter 2.3).

A simulation of this network was described in which the network was used as a binary sequence classifier. Using this model for supervised learning would nevertheless be direct by presenting a sequence on input cells and at the same time a sequence on other cells, so distinguished as supervisor cells. More complete experimentations on the model are in progress.

Further developments will be devoted to theoretical and experimental investigations of the model. Cells sending their output to the environment, possibly through effectors, will be considered.

References

Ackley, D.H., G.E. Hinton and T.J. Sejnowski, A learning algorithm for Boltzmann machines, *Cognitive Science*, vol.9, pp.147-169 (1985).

Amari, S. Learning patterns and pattern sequences by self-organizing nets of threshold elements, IEEE transactions on computers, vol.C-21, N.11 (1972).

Carpenter, G.A. and S. Grossberg, The art of adaptative pattern recognition by self-organizing neural network, IEEE computer, vol.21, N.3, pp.77-88 (1988).

Dehaenne, S., J.P. Changeux and J.P. Nadal, Neural networks that learn temporal sequences by selection, Proc. Nat. Acad. Sci. USA, vol.84, pp.2727-2731 (1987).

Diederich, J. Concept learning, an introduction, *Artificial Neural Network* (Ed. J. Diederich) IEEE (1990).

Elmann, J.L., Finding structure in time, *Cognitive Science* 14, pp.179-211 (1990).

Goebel, R. Learning symbol processing, *Parallel Processing in Neural Systems and Computers.* R.Eckmiller, G. Hartmann and G. Hauske (Editors) (1990).

Hebb, D.O. The organization of behavior, New York: Wiley (1949).

Hertz, A., B. Sulzer, R. Kuhn and J.L Van Hemmen, Hebbian learning reconsidered: representation of static and dynamic objects in associative neural nets, Biol. Cybern. 60, pp.457-467 (1989).

Hertz, A., B. Sulzer, R. Kuhn and J.L Van Hemmen, The Hebb rule: storing static and dynamic objects in an associative neural network, *Europhys. Lett.* 7(7), pp.663-669 (1988).

Hopfield, J.J. Neural networks and physical systems with emergent collective computational abilities, Proc. Nat. Acad. Sci. USA, vol.79, pp.2554-2558 (1982).

Kohonen, T. Self-organisation and associative memory, Ch.4, Springer Verlag, Berlin (1984).

Personnaz, L., I. Guyon and G. Dreyfus, Collective computational properties of neural networks: new learning mechanism, *Physical Review* A, vol.34, pp.4217-4228 (1986).

Robert, F. *Discrete iterations*, Springer Verlag, Berlin (1986).

Rumelhart, D.E., G.E. Hinton and R.J. Williams, Learning internal representations by back-propagating errors, *Nature* vol.323, p.533-536 (1986).

Rumelhart, D.E., G.E. Hinton and R.J. Williams, Learning internal representations by error propagation, *Parallel Distributed Processing: Explorations in the microstructure of cognition*, I: fondations, MIT press, Cambridge (1986).

Varela, F. *Autonomie et connaissance, essai sur le vivant*, Seuil (1989).

Wang, D. and M.A. Arbib, Complex temporal sequence learning based on short term memory, Proceedings of the IEEE, vol.78, N.9 (1990).

Characterizing the Adaptation Abilities of a Class of Genetic Based Machine Learning Algorithms

Gilles VENTURINI
Laboratoire de Recherche en Informatique
Université de Paris-Sud
91405 Orsay Cedex, FRANCE.
venturi@lri.lri.fr

Abstract

Adaptive algorithms that learn to classify objects (or situations) into classes (or actions) can be elaborated using genetic algorithms and classifier systems. This study defines a class of such algorithms and presents two types of adaptation abilities. The first one, called "soft adaptation", takes place when the appearing probability of situations met vary over time, and results from an incremental learning process. The second one, called "strong adaptation", takes place when the optimal actions for some situations change, and results from a continuous and knowledge revising learning process.

Two measures of quality and disorder over the learning system are defined in order to measure experimentally its adaptation abilities. Adaptation is characterized by a quality decrease and disorder increase (the problem to be learned has been modified) followed by a quality increase and disorder decrease (the learning system learns the new problem). The learning of control rules for a simulated moving robot is taken as an example.

1 Introduction

Genetic algorithms (Holland 1975, Goldberg 1989, De Jong 1988) (denoted GA in the following) are probabilist and adaptive search procedures. They can be considered as the simulation of a population evolution. The entities in the population are facing an environment which selects the genetically environment-adapted entities. These entities give birth to some offsprings which inherit of some parts of the parents genetic codes. Generations after generations, only the entities that are the most genetically adapted to the environment survive. If the environment varies, the population can follow these variations because any genetic code has a non zero probability of being generated. Offsprings are generated using genetic operators such as cross-over or mutation.

The classifier systems (Wilson and Goldberg 1989) (Holland 1987) (denoted CS in the following) are production systems where the rules are expressed in a simple language in order to be able to recombine them using genetic operators.

The GA and CS provide the basis of Genetic Based Machine Learning algorithms (denoted GBML in the following) (Grefenstette 1989, De La Maza 1989). The properties of these algorithms are generally incrementality and adaptability.

The subject of this study is to characterize theoretically and experimentally the adaptation abilities of a class of GBML algorithms. This class is defined in section 2. In section 3, the adaptation abilities of this class are studied as the result of learning processes. Section 4 introduces two experimental measures of adaptation abilities. Section 5 illustrates these notions with an example of a learning process in simulated moving robotics.

2 A class of GBML algorithms

2.1 The machine learning problem

Let us consider the following machine learning problem :

- Let E be an environment described by its model $M_E(t)$ and its state vector $E(t)$ of n numerical components,
- Let L be a learning system able to :
  - perceive $E(t)$: m components of $E(t)$, $m \leq n$, are perceived and coded as a fixed length binary message. In the following, these messages are called situations and we define the set of all perceivable situations by :

    $$Sit = \{s_1, ..., s_p\}$$

    We define $P(s_i, t)$, the probability that the environment is perceived as a situation s_i at time t.
  - act directly on m' components of $E(t)$, $m' \leq n$, with a discrete number of actions. In the following, we define the set of all possible actions by :

    $$Act = \{a_1, ..., a_k\}$$

- Let $R(M_E(t), E(t), s, a, t)$ be a reward function giving the numerical evaluation of action a application when $E(t)$ is perceived as a binary situation s at time t.

At any time t and for any situation s, we define the optimal action $a_*(s,t)$, the action that maximizes $R(M_E(t), E(t), s, a, t)$ for all action $a \in Act$.

The goal of the learning system L is to be optimal : for a set S of situations, L must maximize the probability of applying the action $a_*(s,t)$ for any encountered situation $s \in S$ at time t.

To achieve this goal, L builds a set of rules, called classifiers, of the following form :

$$Situation\ Set \rightarrow Action,\ Strength$$

The left part, *Situation Set*, is expressed generally with the CS language : a pattern of the same length as the binary message and composed of the three characters '0', '1' and '$\star$'. A pattern matching operator is defined : '0' matches '0', '1' matches '1', '$\star$' matches either '0' or '1'. A rule is active for a situation s if its left part matches the message s.

The right part, *Action*, is generally a binary message coding an action on the environment.

A rule is optimal at time t when its right part *Action* is the optimal action of the encountered situations matched by its left part.

The *Strength* of a rule is a numerical coefficient, updated with the reward function value computed when the rule is applied. This strength evaluates the rule's optimality relatively to the situations it matches.

The GA is expected to discover strong rules and to increase their probability of being triggered.

2.2 A class of GBML algorithms : Reflex GBML algorithms

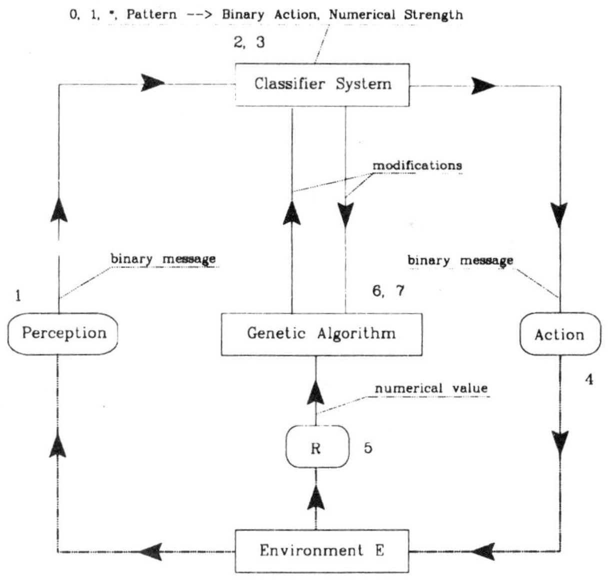

Figure 1: Global algorithm

This class of algorithms is defined in a general way by the following points :

- rules are not triggered in chained sequence : the CS does not use internal messages (Roberston and Riolo 1988). In this sense, the system's behavior is reflex-like.

- the strength of a rule is updated at each triggering and not in a delayed way (Grefenstette 1989).

This class of algorithms can be seen as a simple basic model of GA and CS. It works on the following principle (Figure 1) :

1. Environment perception : generation of a binary message s,
2. Pattern matching operation and selection of the active rules. If no rule is active, a partial matching operator is used or a new rule that matches s is created randomly.
3. Choice of one active rule with a probability law depending on rules strengths : a strong rule is chosen with a high probability. For example, the probability of chosing one rule R_i can be :

$$P_{chosen}(R_i) = \frac{Strength(R_i)}{\sum_{R_j \in R_{active}} Strength(R_j)}$$

where R_{active} is the set of active rules.

4. Chosen rule triggering and action on the environment,
5. Reward computation according to the action's effect on the environment,
6. Triggered rule's strength update. Usually, the strength of a rule R_i is updated with the reward value $Reward$ using (for instance) the following principle :

$$Strength(t+1) = K_1 Strength(t)$$
$$+ K_2 Reward$$

where $K_1, K_2 > 0$.

7. Possibly, the GA modifies the set of rules : selection of a rules subset using (for instance) the precedent law P_{chosen}, offspring generation using genetic operators,
8. Go to 2,

This class contains several algorithms like (Goldberg 1989, Wilson 1987, Booker 1989, Odetayo and McGregor 1989, Bonelli et al. 1990, Natowicz and Venturini 1990).

3 Adaptation and Reflex GBML

For reflex GBML algorithms, we define two cases of adaptation when

1. the law $P(s_i, t)$ changes,
2. the reward function $R(M_E(t), E(t), s, a, t)$ varies, usually because the environment model $M_E(t)$ or some unseen variables of $E(t)$ vary. We consider the cases where these variations result in optimal actions changing.

In both cases, L must modify the set of rules in order to maintain its optimality.

In the following, we suppose that :

1. L has encountered a set S of situations, $S \subset Sit$,
2. L has learned a set R of rules and is optimal for S.

3.1 Adaptation resulting from an incremental learning process : "soft adaptation"

3.1.1 $P(s_i, t)$ law variations

We suppose that the probability law $P(s_i, t)$ varies at time T such that one of the three following cases is met :

- Some new situations appear :

$$\exists s_i \in S,\ such\,that\ P(s_i,t) = 0,\ t < T$$
$$and\ P(s_i,t) > 0,\ t \geq T$$

The other probabilities are not changed.

- Some situations disappear :

$$\exists s_i \in S,\ such\,that\ P(s_i,t) > 0,\ t < T$$
$$and\ P(s_i,t) = 0,\ t \geq T$$

The other probabilities are not changed.

- No situation appear or disappear :

$$\forall s_i \in S,$$
$$t < T,\ P(s_i,t) > 0, \Rightarrow t \geq T,\ P(s_i,t) > 0$$
$$\forall s_i \in S,$$
$$t < T,\ P(s_i,t) = 0 \Rightarrow t \geq T,\ P(s_i,t) = 0$$

The second point adresses the problem of forgetting. The first point adresses the problem of being sensitive to novelty. Only this point will be discussed in the following since the two others do not require necessarily adaptation abilities.

3.1.2 Soft adaptation

Let us suppose that a set S' of new situations appears (first point). L is one of the two following cases :

1. L is still optimal for situations of S and S' : R rules induced by L are general and correct. In this case, no adaptation takes place.

2. L is not optimal for situations of S' : L adapts R by generating some new rules, modifying and deleting old rules.

In this case of adaptation, the optimal actions of S situations are the same. The problem to be learned has simply been incremented of S'. This is why this case of adaptation is called "soft adaptation", even if it might involve some "complex" processes in the learning system.

GBML algorithms of the class studied here are "soft adaptive" because they are always sensitive to new situations (incrementality property, see point 2 of the algorithm principle).

The problem treated in some studies like (Zhou and Grefenstette 1989) (Holland and Reitman 1978) can be considered as soft adaptation problems.

3.2 Adaptation resulting from a continuous and knowledge revising learning process : "strong adaptation"

Strong adaptation is characterized by the following events :

1. $R(M_E(t), E(t), s, a, t)$ varies at time T so that :

$$\exists s_i \in S \; such \, that \; a_*(s_i, t) = a_j, \, t < T$$

$$and \, a_*(s_i, t) = a_l, \, l \neq j, \, t \geq T$$

   L is no more optimal. Let R' be the subset of rules that lower L's optimality.

2. L detects that rules of R' lower its optimality,

3. L adapts R to recover its optimality.

Point 2 implies that L revises the rule strengths so that a high strength is never definitely assign to a rule. In this class of algorithms, this is insured by the fact that a rule strength is updated at every rule triggering.

Point 3 implies that L can learn some new rules and modify some learned rules at any time. In this class of algorithms, this is insure by the fact that the probability of generating and testing a new rule never equals 0.

This strong adaptation implies that L revises its knowledge and can learn continuously. These properties are common in GBML algorithms (Booker 1982).

4 Two experimental measures of adaptation

We remind the reader that :

- $Sit = \{s_1, ..., s_p\}$ is the set of all perceivable situations,

- $Act = \{a_1, ..., a_k\}$ is the set of all possible actions on the environment,

- $R(M_E(t), E(t), s, a, t)$ is the reward obtained at time t when the environment is perceived as a situation s and when L chooses action a.

- $P(s_i, t)$, the probability that the environment is perceived as a situation s_i at time t.

We define in the following :

- $P(s_i, a_j, t)$, the probability that L chooses the action a_j when the environment is perceived as a situation s_i at time t,

The following measures applied to the class of algorithms defined above.

4.1 Theoretical disorder measure

The disorder (Shannon 1948, Natowicz and Venturini 1990) of a situation s_i is defined by

$$d(s_i, t) = -\sum_{j=1}^{k} P(s_i, a_j, t) log_2(P(s_i, a_j, t))$$

$d(s_i,t) = 0$ when L chooses always the same action for situation s_i. $d(s_i,t)$ takes its maximal value when L chooses all the actions with equal probability.

The global disorder of L at time t is given by :

$$D(t) = \sum_{i=1}^{p} P(s_i,t)d(s_i,t)$$

A situation that appears rarely has a low contribution in the global disorder. The maximum value of $D(t)$ is $|log_2(\frac{1}{k})|$ (note that $d(s_i,t)$ can be normalized using log_k instead of log_2, such that the maximum value of $D(t)$ is 1).

The class of algorithms treated here is restricted to non chained classifier systems because the evaluation of a situation disorder would be a complex operation (exploration of all possible classifier chains).

4.2 Theoretical quality measure

L respond to a situation s_i at time t with a quality (Natowicz and Venturini 1990) given by :

$$q(s_i,t) = \sum_{j=1}^{k} P(s_i,a_j,t)R(M_E(t),E(t),s_i,a_j,t)$$

The global quality of L is given by :

$$Q(t) = \sum_{i=1}^{p} P(s_i,t)q(s_i,t)$$

This measure can not be applied to systems where the reward function is computed in a delayed way because there is no reward value available at every time step.

4.3 Experimental measures

Usually, only the following informations are available :

- $s(t)$, the situation perceived at time t,
- $a(t)$, the action chosen at time t,
- $d(s(t),t)$, L's disorder in situation $s(t)$ at time t,
- $r(t)$, the reward computed once action $a(t)$ has been applied.

If the probability law $P(s_i,t)$ and the reward function $R(M_E(t),E(t),s,a,t)$ are relatively constant between $t-T$ and t (the problem to be learned is not much modified between $t-T$ and t), $D(t)$ is approximated by :

$$D'(t) = \frac{1}{T+1}\sum_{t'=t-T}^{t} d(s(t'),t')$$

where T is a fixed value.

In the same way, $Q(t)$ is approximated by :

$$Q'(t) = \frac{1}{T+1}\sum_{t'=t-T}^{t} r(t')$$

This quality measure is often used in other studies like (Wilson 1987).

4.4 Measuring adaptation

In the precedent cases of adaptation, the following effects are expected on $Q(t)$ and $D(t)$:

1. the quality decreases and the disorder increases : L is no more optimal. Some rules are deleted and new but not yet strong rules are learned.

2. the quality increases and the disorder decreases : L recovers its optimality by learning strong rules and increasing their probability of application.

We expect also that the disorder never equals 0 : the probability of triggering an optimal rule is never equal to 1 (to insure knowledge revision and new rule testing).

5 Example : adaptive learning in simulated moving robotics

The example described here is the simulation of a moving robot that must reach a target in an unknown environment with obstacles.

The robot perceives the target distance and direction using a rotative head. The target direction is named direction 0 in the following. It perceives the obstacles with 8 telemeters placed in eight directions starting with direction 0. A local sensor's memory is implemented in order to let the robot escape from $C-like$ obstacles (Natowicz and Venturini 1990). The robot perceives also its speed vector intensity. In this way, the binary message

$$0_0 1_1 0_2 0_3 0_4 0_5 1_6 1_7 \; 10$$

means that some obstacles are detected in relative directions 1, 6 and 7, and that the speed of the robot is about 2 ms^{-1}.

The robot can move with an acceleration order in one of the 8 directions. The actions are coded as an integer between 0 and 7.

A reward is computed by adding the robot-target distance variation on a given time step to a binary penalty function that takes into account an osbtacle hit.

The learning process belongs to the class defined previously.

This robotics problem introduces some difficult issues for the learning system because the probability laws $P(s_i,t)$ and $P(s_i,a_j,t)$ are correlated. Let us define $S(t)$ the set of all situations that the robot could encounter at time t if it was able to stand in all places of $E(t)$. This set do not depend on the robot's behavior. Initially, the robot goes around in the environment so that the set of situations it really encounters is $S(t)$. But when it has learned, many situations of $S(t)$ are not encountered any more (for example in figure 2, the robot do not go any more in the upper-right corner of the environment). Thus the law $P(s_i,t)$ depends on the robot's behavior, which is characterized by its set of rules R. So, the previous probabilities $P(s_i,t)$ and $P(s_i,a_j,t)$ are noted respectively $P(s_i/R,t)$ and $P(a_j/s_i,t)$ to point out the dependencies between these two laws.

5.1 Soft adaptation

Initially, the environment contains only one short wall between the robot and the target (Figure 2). A trial consist in letting the robot reach the target from a fixed initial position. After 500 of these trials, the wall is changed to a $C-like$ obstacle, thus introducing some new situations (Figure 3). The simulation goes on for 500 trials.

At the end of each trial, the simulated time t, the global disorder $D'(t)$ and the global quality $Q'(t)$ are measured. Figures 4 and 5 shows the results obtained. The effects on disorder and quality in the middle of the curves are those expected in section 4.4. The optimal levels of quality are different in the two environments (in the second environment, the robot can not go as straigth forward as in the first one).

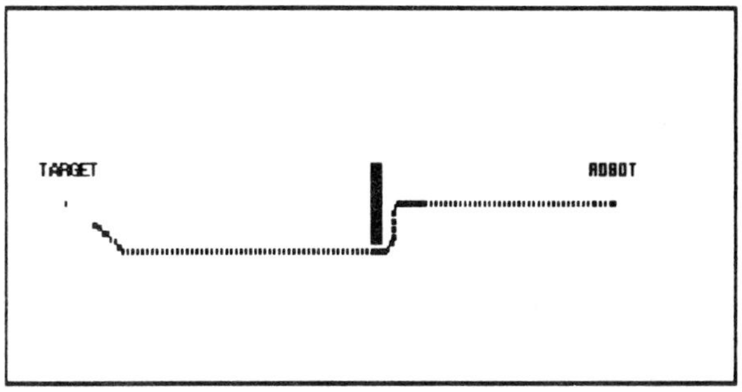

Figure 2: Trajectory example after learning the initial problem

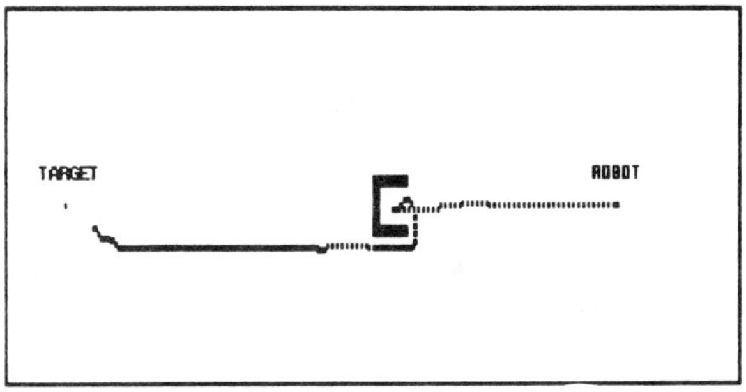

Figure 3: Trajectory example after learning the incremented problem

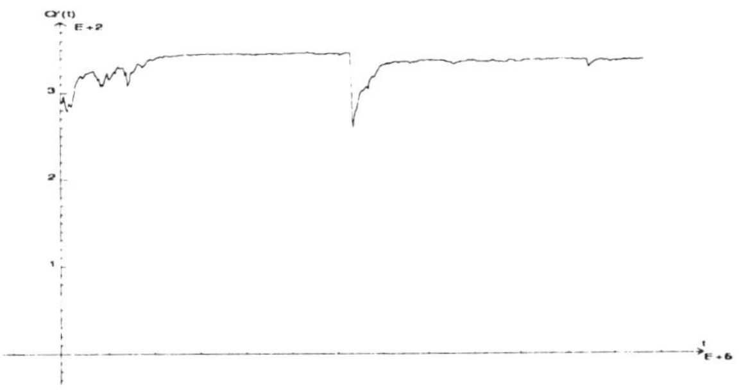

Figure 4: Soft adaptation, Quality

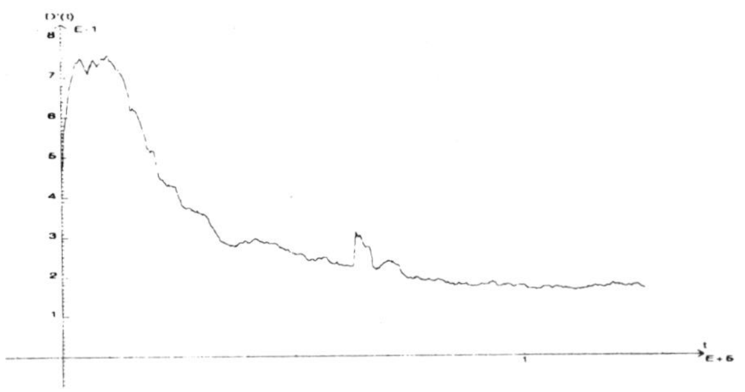

Figure 5: Soft adaptation, Disorder

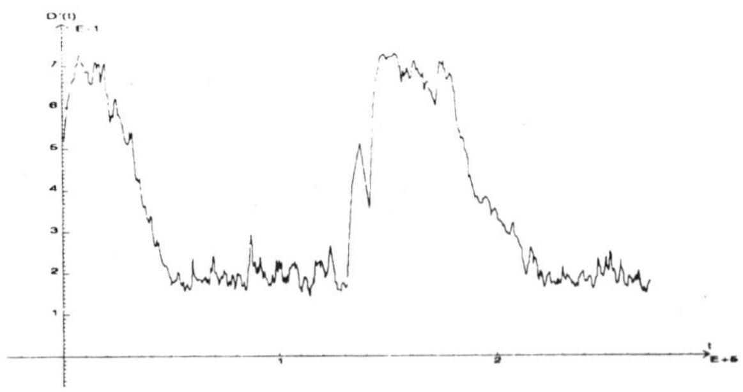

Figure 8: Strong adaptation, Disorder

5.2 Strong adaptation

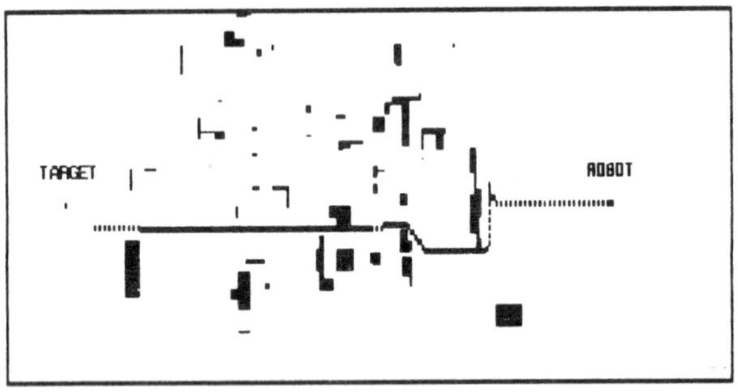

Figure 6: Trajectory example after learning in randomly generated environments

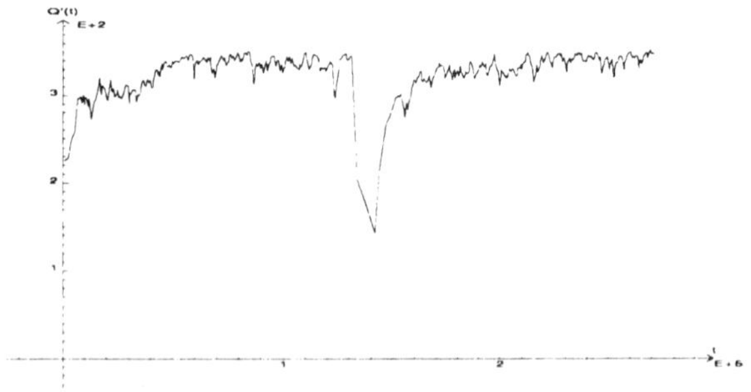

Figure 7: Strong adaptation, Quality

A trial consists here in generating randomly obstacles in the environment and in placing the robot in a fixed position (Figure 6). 1024 trials are made in this way. During the next 1024 trials, the robot's acceleration orders are inverted (simulation of a change of optimal actions). The same measures are made as for soft adaptation. The results in figures 7 and 8 are those expected in section 4.4.

The statistical characteristics of the environment are the same : thus the same quality level is obtained before and after the perturbation takes place (middle of the curves). The oscillations on the curves result from the fact that a difficult obstacle configuration can be randomly generated.

6 Conclusion

This study has tried to characterize the adaptation abilities of a class of GBML algorithms. The definition of measures allows us to check experimentally these abilities. We have pointed out the difficulties of this robotics learning task.

In some other work, learning algorithms has been compared on a given problem like the multiplexor function learning task (Wilson 1987, Bonelli et al. 1990). With the measures introduced here, it is possible to compare the adaptation abilities of these algorithms on this problem. We could define the adaptive multiplexor function as the multiplexor function where some binary ouputs are inverted or where some new inputs are added incrementally.

It would be interesting to define disorder measures for chained classifier systems.

Our future work consists in building genetic learning systems applied to moving simulated robotics and in improving their adaptation abilities.

References

Bonelli P., A. Parodi , S. Sen and S. Wilson. 1990. Newboole : A Fast GBML System, Machine Learning. Proceedings of the Seventh Internationnal Conference 1990, University of Texas, Austin, B. W. Porter and R. J. Mooney Ed., Morgan Kaufmann Pub., pp 153-159.

Booker L. B. 1982. Intelligent behavior as an adaptation to the task environment. Doctoral dissertation, Department of Computer and Communication Sciences, University of Michigan, Ann Arbor.

Booker L. B. 1989. Triggered rule discovery in Classifier Systems. Proceedings of the third Internationnal Conference on Genetic Algorithms, George Mason University 1989, J. D. Schaffer Ed., Morgan Kaufmann Pub., pp 265--274.

De Jong K. 1988. Learning with Genetic Algorithms : An overview. Machine Learning 3, Kluwer Academic Pub., pp 121-138.

De La Maza M. 1989. A seagull visits the race track, Proceedings of the third Internationnal Conference on Genetic Algorithms. George Mason University 1989, J. D. Schaffer Ed., Morgan Kaufmann Pub., pp 208-212.

Goldberg D. E. 1989. *Genetic Algorithms in Search, Optimization and Machine Learning.* Addison Wesley.

Grefenstette J. J. 1989. A system for learning control strategies with genetic algorithms. Proceedings of the third Internationnal Conference on Genetic Algorithms, George Mason University 1989, J. D. Schaffer Ed., Morgan Kaufmann Pub., pp 183-190.

Holland J. H. 1975. *Adaptation in natural and artificial systems.* Ann Arbor : University of Michigan Press.

Holland J. H. and J. J. Reitman. 1978. Cognitive Systems based on adaptive algorithms. *Pattern-directed Inference Systems*, Ed. D. A. Waterman and F. Hayes-Roth, Academic Press.

Holland J. H. 1987. Genetic Algorithms and Classifiers Systems : Foundations and Future Directions. Proceeding of the Second Internationnal Conference on Genetic Algorithms, July 28-31 1987, J. J. Grefenstette Ed., LEA Pub., pp 82-89.

Natowicz R. and G. Venturini 1990. Learning the behavior of simulated moving robot using genetic algorithms. Cognitiva 90, Afcet, Madrid, pp 367-374.

Odetayo M. O. and D. R. McGregor. 1989. Genetic Algorithm For Inducing Control Rules For A Dynamic System. Proceedings of the third Internationnal Conference on Genetic Algorithms, George Mason University 1989, J. D. Schaffer Ed., Morgan Kaufmann Pub., pp 208-212.

Robertson G. G. and R. L. Riolo. 1988. A Tale of Two Classifier Systems. Machine Learning 3, Kluwer Academic Pub., pp 139-159.

Shannon C.E. 1948. A mathematical theory of communication. Bell Syst. Tech. J., July and Oct. 1948, 27, pp 379-423 and pp 623-656.

Wilson S. W. 1987. Quasi-Darwinian Learning in a Classifier System. Proceeding of the Fourth International Workshop on Machine Learning, Morgan Kaufmann Pub., pp 59-65.

Wilson S. W. and D. E. Goldberg. 1989. A Critical Review of Classifier Systems. Proceedings of the third Internationnal Conference on Genetic Algorithms, George Mason University 1989, J. D. Schaffer Ed., Morgan Kaufmann Pub., pp 244-255.

Zhou H. H. and J. J. Grefenstette. 1989. Learning by Analogy in Genetic Classifier Systems. Proceedings of the third Internationnal Conference on Genetic Algorithms, George Mason University 1989, J. D. Schaffer Ed., Morgan Kaufmann Pub., pp 291-297.

GENETIC ALGORITHMS APPLIED TO FORMAL NEURAL NETWORKS:

Parrallel genetic implementation of a Boltzmann machine and associated robotic experimentations

P. Bessière
IMAG-LGI / LASCO3
Institut IMAG-Laboratoire de Génie Informatique / LAboratoire de SCiences COgnitives
BP 53X
F-38041 Grenoble Cedex
FRANCE
bessiere@imag.fr

I. ABSTRACT

In this paper we describe a possible application of computing techniques inspired by natural life mechanisms (genetic algorithms and artificial neural networks) to an artificial life creature, namely a small mobile robot, called KitBorg.

We proposed in a previous work (Bessière 1990) **Probabilistic Inference** as a possible underlying theory or mathematical metaphor for numerous works in the field of formal neural networks.

Probabilistic Inference suggests that any cognitive problem may be split in two **optimization problems**. The first one called the "dynamic inference problem" is an abstraction of "learning", the second one, namely, the "static inference problem", being a mathematical metaphor of "pattern association".

In this previous paper, for instance, Boltzmann machines have been shown to be a special case of probabilistic inference, where the two optimization problems are dealt with using simulated annealing (Kirckpatrick 1983) for the pattern association part and using simple gradient descent for the learning one.

It was, then, suggested that other optimization technics should be considered in that context and especially **genetic algorithms. The purpose of this paper is to describe the state of the art of the investigations we are making about that question using a parallel genetic algorithm.**

We will first recall the principles of probabilistic inference, then, we will present briefly the parallel genetic algorithm and the ways it is used to deal with both optimization problems, to finally conclude about ongoing robotic experimentations and future planned extensions.

II. PROBABILISTIC INFERENCE

Probabilistic inference may be seen as the present state of the art resulting of numerous works aim to use probability theory as a model of inference and decision making in an incomplete and uncertain universe.

In probabilistic inference theory, knowledge is represented using the usual formalism of probability theory. Knowledge is encoded using a set $\Xi = \{X_1, ..., X_n\}$ of variables. The value space of Ξ is called Ω. The basic assumption is that **a knowledge state of a cognitive system is a probability distribution P over Ω.**

Probabilistic inference has to deal with two different problems:

1 - given a knowledge state (a probability distribution P) and some new information (a set of constraints Φ on Ξ), how to infer a new knowledge state (a probability distribution Q) taking into account the new information;

2 - given a knowledge state (a probability distribution P) and values of some of the variables of the set Ξ, how to infer the most probable values (according to P) of the other variables.

The first problem may be called the "dynamic inference problem" because it concerns how the knowledge state changes in order to take into account new information, while the second problem, the "static inference problem", concerns the consistency conditions of a knowledge state at a given time (see (Hunter 1986)).

Dynamic inference problem

Given a set of variables $\Xi = \{X_1, ..., X_n\}$, given Ω its value space, given a prior knowledge state (a probability distribution P) and given some new information (a set of constraints Φ on Ξ); the dynamic inference process has to find a posterior knowledge state (a probability distribution Q).

In the general case, there is an infinity of probability distributions which are potential solutions of this problem. However, all the probability distributions are not equivalent. Some appear to be more "coherent", more "probable", more "interesting" than some others. The function H(Q,P) (called Kulbach entropy, relative entropy or cross entropy) is a way of measuring the "interest"[1] of a given probability distribution Q relative to P and Φ, the smaller H the better Q. H is defined by:

$$H(Q,P) = + \int_{\Omega} Q(\omega) \log \frac{Q(\omega)}{P(\omega)} \, d\omega \qquad [f.1].$$

According to this, the dynamic inference problem may be restated as follow: given P and Φ, find the

[1] *For a discussion of this crucial point see (Bessière 1990)*

probability distribution Q which **minimizes** H. It can be shown that if Φ is a consistent set of constraints, there is one and only one solution Q* to this problem. Finding Q* is not a trivial mathematical problem.

However, for a very important class of problems, where Φ takes the form of a set of real functions ($\Phi = \{f_1, ..., f_m\}$) such that the mean value a_i ($A = \{a_1, a_2, ..., a_m\}$) of every function f_i is known, then it can be shown that the solution take the following form:

$$q^*(\omega) = \frac{1}{Z^*} e^{-\sum_{i=1}^{m} \lambda_i f_i(\omega)} \qquad [f.2]$$

where q* is the density of Q*, λi are the Lagrange multipliers and Z* is a normalizing constant.

Let us take an example: given two variables A (the Age of the captain) and L (the Length of the boat), the problem we want to solve is find A given L or find L given A.

We have: $\Xi = \{A,L\}$; $\Omega = [7,77] \times [4,444]$.

Starting from scratch (no prior information), P_0, *the initial knowledge state, is a uniform distribution over* Ω *(figure 1). Let us suppose that we first learn the mean value of A* ($E(A) = m_A$) *and the variance of A* ($E((A - m_A)^2) = \sigma_A{}^2$)*. An infinity of probability distributions over* Ω *have this mean value and this variance. However one and only one minimizes H: the normal distribution* P_1 *having this mean value and this variance as parameters (figure 2). If we then learn the mean value and variance of L, by the same process, we get the probability distribution* P_2 *(figure 3). Iterating this process for all the data we can get about our problem, and especially for information expressing correlations between A and L we will finally get a probability distribution Q* which will sum up all the previously acquired information (figure 4). The surface correponding to Q* may be considered as a visualization of the "memory" of the system.*

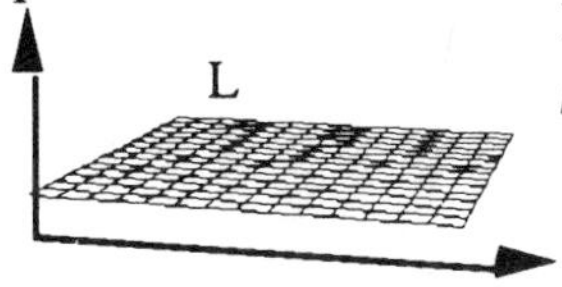

Figure 1

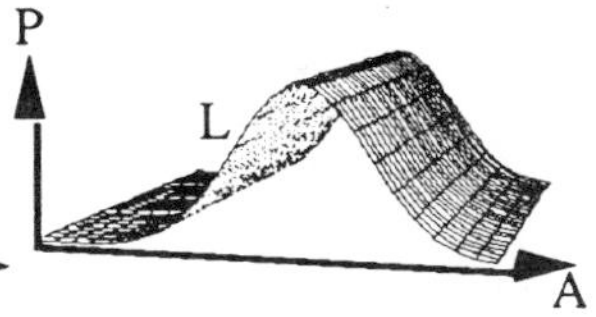

Figure 2

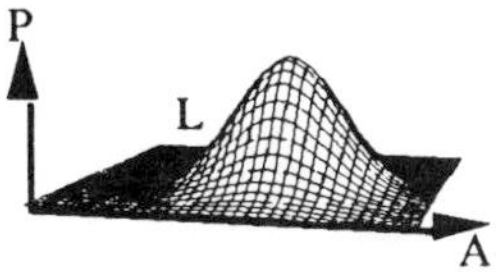

Figure 3

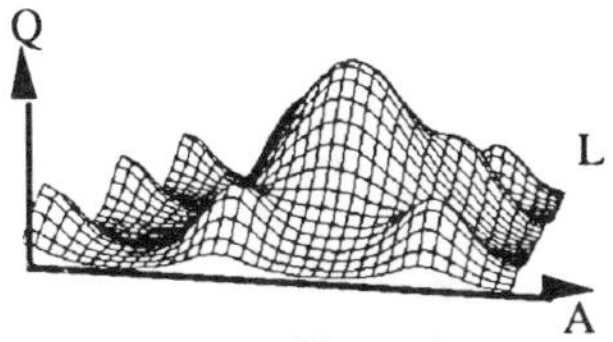

Figure 4

Static inference problem

Given a set of variables $\Xi = \{X_1, ..., X_n\}$, given Ω its value space, given P a probability distribution over Ω and given values of some of the variables of the set Ξ; the static inference process has to find the most probable values of the unspecified variables of Ξ.

According to the previous paragraph, the interesting cases to consider are those cases where P takes form [f.2]. Therefore, finding the most probable values of the non specified variables (i.e. maximizing P) corresponds to the **minimization** of the function:

$$U(\omega) = \sum_{i=1}^{m} \lambda_i f_i(\omega) \qquad [f.3]$$

over the sub-space of Ω defined by the given values on Ξ.

Getting back to our example, this means that for a given value a of the variable A we want to find the most probable value l of the variable L. This process may be visualized by looking for the maximum of the curve defined by the intersection of Q and the vertical plane corresponding to A = a (this curve is in bold on figure 5).*

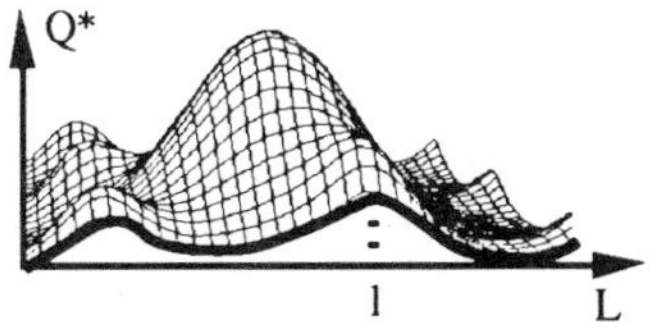

Figure 5

Boltzmann machine

In (Bessière 1990) we show in some details how Probabilistic Inference may be used as an underlying paradigm for numerous Artificial Neural Networks models. Let us just recalled how it is related to Boltzmann machines model.

A usual simplification of probabilistic inference consist in restricting the problem to cases where the X_i are binary variables and where the f_i depend on no more than two variables:

$$f_i(X_1, ..., X_n) = \alpha_i X_k X_l + \beta_i X_k + \gamma_i Xl + \delta i \qquad [f.4]$$

In that case we get (from [f.2]):

$$Q^*(\omega) = \frac{1}{Z^*} e^{-\sum_{i<j} W_{ij} X_i X_j - \sum_i W_i X_i} \qquad [f.5]$$

where Q* is a 1-Gibbs distribution. Such distributions have well known dynamics with nice simple properties. This is the choice made, for instance, for Hopfield nets (Hopfield 1982) and for Boltzmann machines (Ackley 1988).

The dynamic inference problem has new parameters, the "weights" W_{ij}, in place of the old ones, the Lagrange multipliers λ_i. The search space, which was the space of all probability distributions over Ω, is approximated by the space of weights' values. The dynamic inference process is replaced by a gradient descent dynamic in the space of the weights' values with H as objective function. One of the remarkable properties of the Gibbsian neural nets is that this gradient descent may be done, without any explicit computation of H, using simply classical local adaptation rules (for instance, Widrow-Hoff's rule for Boltzmann machines) on the system at "thermodynamic" equilibrium (see (Ackley 1988)). Reaching thermodynamic equilibrium itself is strictly equivalent to treating the static inference problem and is done using simulated annealing. U is the objective function but for Gibbsian neural nets, U takes the exact form of an energy function:

$$U = -\sum_{i<j} W_{ij} X_i X_j - \sum_{i} W_{ij} X_i \qquad [f.6].$$

III. PARALLEL GENETIC ALGORITHM

Genetic algorithms compose a very interesting family of optimization algorithms. Neither their principles, nor their application can be presented here but a very complete description may be found in (Goldberg 1989).

However, let us recall that the standard genetic algorithm has the following form:

Generate a population of random individuals.
While number_of_generations ≤ max_number_of_generations Do
Evaluation - assign a fitness value to each individual.
Selection - make a list of pairs of individuals likely to mate, with fittest individuals listed more frequently.
Reproduction - apply genetic operators to the selected pairs. New individuals produced constitute the new population.

Genetic algorithms are quite easy to implement on parallel machines. Two main approaches, to do so, have been considered so far:

- **standard parallel approach**: In this approach, the evaluation and the reproduction are done in parallel. However, the selection is still done sequentially, because parallel selection would require a fully connected graph of individuals as any two individuals in the population may be mated (Macfarlane 1990).

- **decomposition approach**: This approach consists in dividing the population into equal size sub-populations. Each processor runs the genetic algorithm on its own sub-population, periodically selecting good individuals to send to its neighbors and periodically receiving copies of its neighbors' good individuals to replace bad ones in its own sub-population (Pettey 1987)(Tanese 1987). The processor neighborhood, the frequency of exchange and the number of individuals exchanged are adjustable parameters.

Considering massively parallel architectures with numerous processors, namely, a SuperNode of Transputers, we chose a fine-grained model, where the population is mapped on a connected processor graph like a grid, one individual per processor. This may be considered as an extreme version of the decomposition approach, where the sub-populations are reduced to a single individual. We have a bijection between the individual set and the processor set. The selection is done locally in a neighborhood of each individual. The choice of the neighborhood is the adjustable parameter. To avoid overhead and complexity of routing algorithms in parallel distributed machines, we chose to restrict neighborhood to the only four directly connected individuals. The parallel genetic algorithm proposed is:

Generate *in parallel* a population of random individuals.
While number_of_generations ≤ max_number_of_generations Do
Evaluation - Evaluate *in parallel* each individual.
Reproduction - Each individual reproduces *in parallel* with the best of its' four neighbors.
Selection - Do *in parallel* a selection of best local offsprings.

Another version to this approach has been already proposed in (Mühlenbein 1989), where, furthermore, at each generation a hill-climbing algorithm is executed for each individual in the population.

Detailed description of this work and various benchmarks may be found in (Talbi 1991a), (Talbi 1991b) and (Talbi 1991c). This parallel genetic algorithm implemented on a SuperNode of Transputers shows a remarkable **"superlinear" speed-up**, in the sense that when multiplying both the number of processors and the size of the population by p, the execution time to reach a given quality of solution, is divided by kp (with k>1).

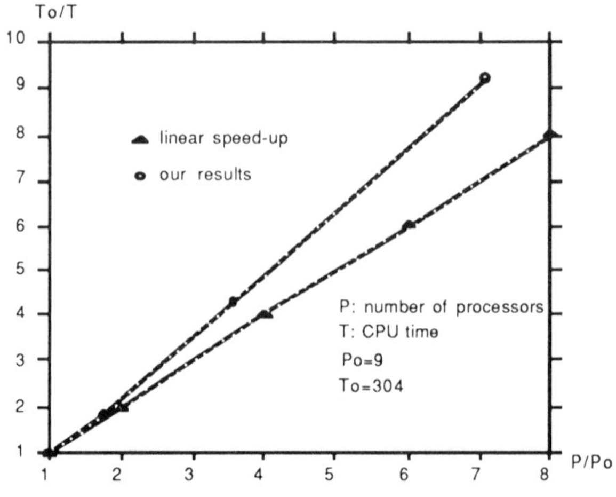

Figure 6

IV. A PARALLEL GENETIC BOLTZMANN MACHINE

Let us now describe how we use the parallel genetic algorithm presented in preceeding section to deal with the two optimization problems a Boltzmann machine has to face:

Static inference problem

To deal with the static inference problem we replace the usual simulated annealing of Boltzmann machines by our parallel genetic algorithm. We work with a population of 64 individuals, each one being a vector of bits X_i representing the activities of the cells of the network. The search space is 2^N, where N is the number of cells in the network. The fitness function is the global energy function of the network

$$E = - \sum_{i<j} W_{ij} X_i X_j \qquad [f.7]$$

When the Boltzmann machine algorithm searches in parallel on the state of each cell, our algorithm searches in parallel on 64 global states of the network.

The very first comparisons between the two algorithms, made with single processor versions, show same run times' order of magnitude. It should however be noticed that the used version of the parallel genetic algorithm is a very simple and preliminary one, that may certainly be greatly improved. The same super-linear speed-up than for other applications was measured when running the algorithm on more processors. This means than using an implementation on a 128 Transputers MegaNode will leads to an acceleration of the algorithm by a factor of the order of one hundred.

A very remarkable result is that both algorithms (usual simulated annealing and parallel genetic algorithm) found the same attractors or, at least, different attractors but with the same fitness values. This may be considered as an indirect "clue" that both algorithms converge on global optima and do not get stuck in local optima because, in that last case, there would be no reasons for both of them to find two optima with the same fitness values.

Dynamic inference problem

To deal with the dynamic inference problem we replace the usual gradient descent of Boltzmann machines by our parallel genetic algorithm. We work with a population of 64 individuals, each one being a vector of bits representing the set of weights of the network. The search space's size is $Log_2(p)^M$, where M is the number of connections in the network and p the range of the weights. A huge search space, indeed! The fitness function depends on the specific application treated. It evaluates how good is a certain vector of weights, by averaging results obtain when treating the static inference problem on a set of different cases. When the Boltzmann machine algorithm searches sequentially the space of weights, our algorithm searches in parallel on 64 sets of possible weights.

The work is not advanced enough to draw any conclusions from our preliminary benchmarks on the dynamic inference problem. However, we may say that **the genetic parallel Boltzmann machine did learn** simple encoder problems (Ackley 1988).

V. ONGOING ROBOTIC EXPERIMENTATION

Let us finally describe the principle of some ongoing robotic experimentations planned to validate the parallel genetic Boltzmann machine approach. These experimentations are closely related to work describe in a paper of this conference by Dedieu and Mazer.

The prupose of these experimentations is to test a new robot programming paradigm on a small mobile robot named KitBorg developped by the company Aleph Technologies. This new paradigm is describe in details in (Dedieu 1991).

In usual robot programming, the programmer has a model of its' own for the environment and tries to both express the plan of robot's actions and the tasks of the robot's sensors and actuators relatively to his model. A main difficulty with this approach is that the programmer's model of the environment is usually very difficult to match with the sensors informations. For instance, a human programmer would describe the notion of "obstacle" in some geometrical terms, when, in contrast, the robot's sensors will get information about the presence of an "obstacle" through some variation in the intensity of lightenning or optical flow.

The principle of this new robot programming paradigm is based on the assumption that the robot is able to "learn" (using the adequate neural network algorithms) some classification of its' sensori-motor data that will be characteristic of some significant situations. The burden of interpreting these situations is let to the human programmer. The robot imposes its' "view" of the world to the programmer, in contrast with the usual robot programming approach where the human programmer imposes his conception of the environment.

In (Dedieu 1991), some results about the application of Kohonen's map to this task of learning sensori-motor categories are extensively described. We are trying to used the parallel genetic Boltzmann machine to the exact same task. After a learning phase where we classify sensori-motor data, our hope is that we will be able to "recall", in a second phase, adequate actuators command, given some sensors inputs, in order to reached a given objective sensors situation.

This work is not advanced enough to present some results, but we hope to be able to do so soon given that this task will be our main concern in the very next furture.

VI. CONCLUSION AND PERSPECTIVES

One aim of this work was to prove that formal neural networks could work using genetic algorithms to deal with the two optimization problems they have to face. This aim has been reached. **It suggests a totally new way to implement neural networks on parallel machines.** This seems to be a very promising research track and will certainly be an important concern for us in the near future. We especially intend to improve our parallel genetic algorithm.

More work has to be done to really answer the question: "What optimization technics should be used for the different optimization problems of the various formal neural networks models?". We plan to do more benchmarking to compare the different parts of the two versions of the Boltzmann machine.

More work has also to be done to validate the parallel genetic Boltzmann machine approach on the described robotic experimentations. This task is one of our, present, main concern.

Finally, we hope that we will be able to propose a **cognitive algorithmic model inspired by probabilistic inference and using genetic optimization technics.**

BIBLIOGRAPHY

D. H. Ackley, G. E. Hinton & T. J. Sejnowsky. 1988. *A learning algorithm for Boltzmann Machines* in *Connectionist models and their implications* edited by D. Waltz and J.A. Feldman, Ablex Publishing Corporation.

P. Bessière. 1990. *Toward a synthetic cognitive paradigm: probabilistic inference.* Proc. of COGNITIVA90, Madrid, Spain.

David E. Goldberg. 1989.*Genetic algorithms in search, optimization, and machine learning.* Addison-Wesley Publishing Company.

J. J. Hopfield. 1989. *Neural networks and physical systems with emergent collective computational abilities.* Proceedings of the National Academy of Sciences (U.S.A.).

Daniel Hunter. 1986. *Uncertain reasoning using Maximum entropy Inference*in *Uncertainty in Artificial Intelligence*; edited by L. N. Kanal & J. F. Lemmer. Elsevier Science Publishers.

S.Kirkpatrick, C.D.Gelatt & M.P.Vecchi. 1983. *Optimization by simulated annealing.* Science, Vol.220, No.4598, pp.671-680.

D.Macfarlane & I.East. 1990. *An investigation of several parallel genetic algorithm.* Proc. of the 12th Occam User Group, Exeter, UK, pp.60-67.

H.Mühlenbein & J.Kindermann. 1989. *The dynamics of evolution and learning: Towards genetic neural networks* Connectionism in Perspective, R.Pfeifer et al. eds., North-Holland, pp.173-197.

C.B.Pettey, M.R.Leuze & J.J.Grefenstette. 1987. *A parallel genetic algorithm.* Proc. of the Second Int. Conf. on Genetic Algorithms, MIT, Cambridge, pp.155-161.

E-G. Talbi & P. Bessière. 1991a. *A parallel genetic algorithm for the graph partitionning problem.* A.C.M. International Conference on SuperComputing, Cologne, Germany.

E-G. Talbi & P. Bessière. 1991b. *Superlinear performance of a genetic algorithm on the SuperNode parallel architecture.* S.I.A.M. News.

E-G. Talbi & P. Bessière. 1991c. *Genetic parallel algorithm : performances and applications.* Proceeding of "International Conference on Novel Optimization Technics", Copenhague, Danemark.

R.Tanese. 1987. *Parallel genetic algorithms for a hypercube.* Proc. of the Second Int. Conf. on Genetic Algorithms, MIT, Cambridge, pp.177-183.

ADAPTIVE AND EVOLUTIONARY MECHANISMS

The Holland α-Universes Revisited

Barry McMullin
Dublin City University
E-mail: <McMullinB@DCU.IE>

Abstract

The α-Universes were introduced by John Holland as minimal systems in which the spontaneous emergence of self-replicating entities might be studied. This paper reviews Holland's original work and presents key results from an extended empirical investigation. The results indicate that, contrary to the original expectations, in the specific universe studied (α_0) the question of spontaneous emergence does not arise—because the putatively self-replicating entities prove not to be viable, even when artificially introduced.

1 Introduction

The theory that life on Earth arose spontaneously may be challenged by calculations based on unbiased random agitation of some more or less plausible chemical soup, showing that the expected emergence time would be many orders of magnitude longer than the time known to have been available. Holland (1976) argued that such calculations are critically flawed because the trajectory of the system would not be "random" but would, in fact, be strongly *biased* toward the emergence of life-like entities.

It is difficult to establish this point analytically, due to the complexity of the dynamic behaviour of real chemical systems. Holland therefore introduced the α-Universes: these are a class of *artificial* systems, providing crude and highly simplified analogs of certain chemical processes assumed to be involved in the origin of life. It is claimed that these systems are sufficiently complex that they can support identifiably "life-like" entities—while still being sufficiently simple that closed form analysis is possible (at least of certain aspects of their behaviour). Holland described one specific α-Universe in detail: I refer to this as α_0.

Holland presented a quantitative analysis of the emergence time for "life" in α_0, based solely on (analogs of) random, unbiased, agitation. He then showed that, far from α_0 actually exhibiting such an unbiased process, simple forerunners of "living" entities could be expected to emerge in a vastly shorter period, and would strongly bias the subsequent trajectory. If this analysis is correct then it establishes the *principle* that any analysis which presupposes an unbiased process in the origin of life is seriously flawed. Furthermore, it would indicate a practical approach toward the realisation of *artificial life* (albeit in a very primitive form)—simply by implementing α_0.

Holland's paper was limited to theoretical analysis; however, he noted that empirical testing of his results would be practical, using a computer implementation of α_0. The present paper reports on the outcome of just such a program of empirical testing.

2 The Universe α_0

Loosely speaking, α_0 consists of a 1-dimensional space of discrete *cells* (somewhat akin to a cellular automaton). In general, Holland is not explicit as to the size of α_0 nor (on the assumption that it is bounded) as to the behaviour at the boundaries. For numerical work, he typically uses a "region" of 10^4 cells. The analysis and experiments described in this paper assume an unbounded (circular) geometry, generally with a total size of 2×10^3 cells.

Each cell is either empty, or holds an *atom* of some *element*. Matter is conserved (i.e. the total number of atoms of each element is constant). Atoms may move (or be moved) around in the space, in accordance with certain dynamics, or *operators*, to be described below. Atoms in adjacent cells may be *bonded* together. Bonded atoms are guaranteed to remain adjacent (just so long as they stay bonded—bonds form and decay as part of the dynamics of the system).

A sequence of adjacent atoms, delimited at both ends by one or more empty cells, is called a *structure*. Note that the atoms making up a structure are not necessarily bonded. A *complex* is some specified *set* of structures. The structures making up a complex need not, in general, have a definite spatial relationship; however, for the complex to exhibit interesting properties it is generally necessary that all the component structures be more or less "close" to each other.

The dynamic behaviour of the α-Universe is defined by two groups of operators: the *primitive* operators, and the *emergent* operators. All operators are defined to operate stochastically. The primitive operators are context *insensitive*—i.e. they apply to all matter throughout α_0 without regard to its sequential organisation. They are the abstract counterparts of diffusion and activation in real chemical systems. The emergent operators are context *sensitive*—i.e. their operation is sensitive to the sequential organisation of matter. In effect, certain structures, (should they arise) have special dynamic properties. They are termed "emergent" operators precisely because they are contingent on such special configurations—they "emerge" iff matter in some region "happens" (under the action of the primitive operators or otherwise) to adopt some such special configuration. These are the abstract counterparts of catalysts (particularly enzymes) in real (bio-)chemical systems.

In the study of real chemical systems it is of interest to seek an explanation of the properties and characteristics of catalysis in terms of more fundamental (atomic) interactions. However, for the particular analyses we wish to make of the α_0 dynamics, such a more fundamental explanation would be superfluous, and is not attempted. Instead, the properties of emergent operators are simply imposed by fiat.

Holland takes (self-)replication as diagnostic of "life"; the dynamics of α_0 are such that certain complexes (should they arise) may exhibit primitive self-replicating behaviours.

3 Predictions

The dynamic behaviour of the universe α_0 is, of course, critically affected by the presence, or otherwise, of emergent operators. Holland's approach is to assume that, starting from a "random" configuration, there will (almost certainly) be an initial epoch in which the density of emergent operators will be negligible, and the dynamics of the system can be analysed, to a good approximation, purely by reference to the primitive operators. I term this the *Primitive Epoch*. It is further assumed that, at some subsequent stage, the effects of emergent operators may become significant, and any analysis of the ensuing development will require *both* primitive and emergent operators to be taken into account. I term this the *Emergent Epoch*.

Holland further assumes (implicitly) that the transition (if any) from Primitive to Emergent Epochs will be triggered by the emergence of (more or less effective) self-replicating complexes. The argument is as follows: if structures (including emergent operators) are simply being formed and broken up again "randomly" (i.e. by the unbiased actions of the primitive operators) it seems plausible that their density (and thus their dynamic effects) will be small; whereas, if some system of structures (i.e. a complex), could actively *replicate* itself, instead of relying on random actions of the primitive operators for its formation, then it could "quickly" achieve a high density and would therefore have a significant impact on the dynamic behaviour of the system.

If this picture is accurate then the critical question becomes: how long is the Primitive Epoch expected to last?

By definition, during the Primitive Epoch, structures are generated and broken down more or less independently of their particular organisation. The statistics of this process are stationary. It is therefore possible to estimate the expected time to spontaneous emergence of any specific combination of structures (complex). Holland derives an approximate expression (his Theorem 3) for this emergence time. This shows (as might be anticipated) that the expected emergence time is critically dependent on the total size (number of atoms) of the specified complex; in fact, emergence time increases more or less as an *exponential* function of the size of the complex.

This general result can be applied to estimate the duration of the Primitive Epoch *only* on the basis of some identification of a particular complex (or perhaps any one of some set of complexes) whose emergence would trigger the transition to the Emergent Epoch. Holland considers two distinct cases, discussed in the following two sections.

3.1 The `FullSR` Complex

Suppose firstly that the transition cannot occur until a "fully" self-replicating complex appears. This is a complex which incorporates a *complete* "genetic" description of itself; this description is then (separately) copied and decoded to realise a replication cycle. This conforms essentially to the abstract model of self-replication pioneered by Schrödinger (1944) and (later) von Neumann (1951), and subsequently confirmed as the general mechanism exploited in all modern terrestrial life forms.

Holland identifies what is, more or less, the *simplest* α_0 complex which would exhibit this kind of fully self-replicating behaviour. I denote this complex by the symbolic name `FullSR`. It consists of 8 distinct, interacting, structures, composed of a total of 60 atoms.[1] The expected emergence time for `FullSR` is calculated to be approximately 10^{43} time steps (in a region of size 10^4 cells). For all practical purposes then, `FullSR` will *never* spontaneously appear, and it would appear that the critics of the idea of spontaneous emergence of life are vindicated (at least in α_0).

[1] This apparently small size, compared to the smallest comparable terrestrial organism, is an artefact of the relatively complex behaviours of quite small structures (emergent operators), which have been *designed* into α_0 to facilitate the spontaneous emergence of self-replication, even in a relatively small region (of space and time).

3.2 The PartSR and Seed Complexes

Alternatively, it may be the case that some significantly simpler complex, not capable of full replication as described above, might still be capable of some kind of *partial* replication, which would be sufficient to dramatically alter the subsequent dynamics of α_0. In particular, if such partially self-replicating complexes could become established, this would skew the distribution of structures in such a way that fully self-replicating complexes could then emerge relatively quickly (effectively via a conventional Darwinian process).

Holland identifies a complex of just 3 structures, with a total of only 14 atoms, for which this is apparently the case; I denote this complex by the symbolic name `PartSR`. The complex `PartSR` is not fully self-replicating, but it *can* replicate partial fragments of itself; if these fragments achieve a high density then a fraction of them will be spontaneously augmented and combined to achieve complete replication. Holland presents calculations to show that the fecundity of `PartSR` is indeed sufficient to achieve a net population growth rate, once the complex is initially established.

Holland goes on to show that an even smaller complex (2 structures, a total of 11 atoms) can function as an effective "seed" or precursor for the emergence of `PartSR`. I refer to this smaller complex as `Seed`. If the `Seed` complex ever appears (spontaneously) then it should apparently generate a substantial population of `PartSR` complexes; this `PartSR` population should then be viable in its own right even after the `Seed` complex decays.

Following this argument then, a transition from the Primitive to the Emergent Epoch will be triggered by the spontaneous emergence of `Seed`. The expected emergence time for this is calculated to be approximately 4×10^9 timesteps (again in a region of size 10^4 cells). If this analysis is correct then it suggests that the spontaneous emergence of "life" is quite feasible in α_0. Indeed, this result now admits the possibility of empirical test; Holland gives the example that, if an α_0 time step could be implemented in, say, 1ms of real time, then the expected emergence time for `Seed` becomes about 125 (real) hours—compared to over 10^{30} (real) centuries for `FullSR`...

4 Implementation

There are certain difficulties in implementing α_0 precisely in the manner described by Holland. For example, Holland implies a bounded universe, insofar as certain operator definitions require the space to be sequentially scanned from "left" to "right"; the effect of such operators is then uniquely defined only if "left" and "right" boundaries exist. On the other hand, however, the detailed behaviour of operators at universe boundaries is not consistently defined. Furthermore, certain operators, if implemented literally according to Holland's description, would be extremely inefficient in computational terms. The implementation has therefore been designed to preserve *only* the critical properties of α_0—i.e. those properties which are actually utilised in Holland's analysis; within this constraint it has been heavily optimised for execution speed.

The α_0 implementation has been written entirely in the C language (conforming to the ANSI X3J11 standard). Original development was carried out on IBM PC compatible machines, running MS-DOS, and Turbo-C V2.0. Most experimental study was carried out on this same platform—which incidently explains why a universe size of 2×10^3 cells has typically been used, this being the largest which can be comfortably accommodated on this platform. The package has also been ported to a VAX/VMS platform (which can support much larger universe sizes). As far as possible, the package has been written to be "easily" portable; machine dependancies are encapsulated by conditional compilation. The source code comprises about 3700 lines.

Performance varies widely with the particular configuration of the universe, and the platform in use—but one example is as follows: on a 286-based PC (8MHz clock), typical execution time is of the order of 20ms real time per α_0 time step, for a universe of 2×10^3 cells, with only the primitive operators enabled.

5 Playing God

To recap, there are three substantive elements to Holland's predictions:

1. The `Seed` complex will (spontaneously) appear in a relatively short time.
2. Once the `Seed` complex *does* appear, a population of `PartSR` complexes will be established, and will maintain themselves.
3. Conventional Darwinian evolution can then optimise the replicating ability of the complexes quite quickly.

Of these, the first potentially requires a substantial amount of (real) time to test; the second can be easily tested (by "playing God"—directly inserting an instance of the `Seed` complex); and the third can be tested only when (or if) testing of the second has been successful (i.e. after prediction 2 has been verified). Therefore, testing concentrated, in the first instance, on prediction 2—whether the `Seed` complex can establish a viable population of `PartSR` complexes. I present results for three scenarios, each calling for a progressively higher level of "divine intervention" in trying to trigger this emergence of artificial "life".

5.1 "Economy" Model

An α_0 of 2×10^3 cells was generated with a random initial configuration. This was executed for 100×10^3 time steps to allow transients, associated with the initial configuration, to decay. A single instance of `Seed` was then inserted. A further 6×10^3 steps were executed. Figure 1 is a plot of the number of `PartSR` complexes present over this latter period. It is clear that, contrary to expectations, a significant population of `PartSR` is *not* established (in fact, the maximum "population" achieved is just a single instance!).

5.2 "Standard" Model

It was noted that in normal operation of α_0 the density of free atoms (i.e. atoms with empty cells on both sides) was much lower than predicted by Holland's analysis, and generally approached zero. This has a detrimental effect on the operation of the `Seed` complex, as it relies on the availability of free atoms for its operation. It turns out that free atoms are generally not present because, even from a random configuration, there is a significant density of simple emergent operators. These bond any available free atoms together, more or less as they appear. In effect, Holland's assumption that there would *be* a Primitive Epoch, during which the action of the emergent operators could be neglected, is not valid.

However, it was not yet clear how serious this failing was. It was conjectured that the `Seed` complex might be able to operate effectively if the availability of free atoms was initially assured. Once a large population of the `PartSR` complex was established it could still then be viable (and support subsequent Darwinian evolution).

So an α_0 of 2×10^3 cells was again generated with a random initial configuration; but this time the single instance of `Seed` was *immedi-*

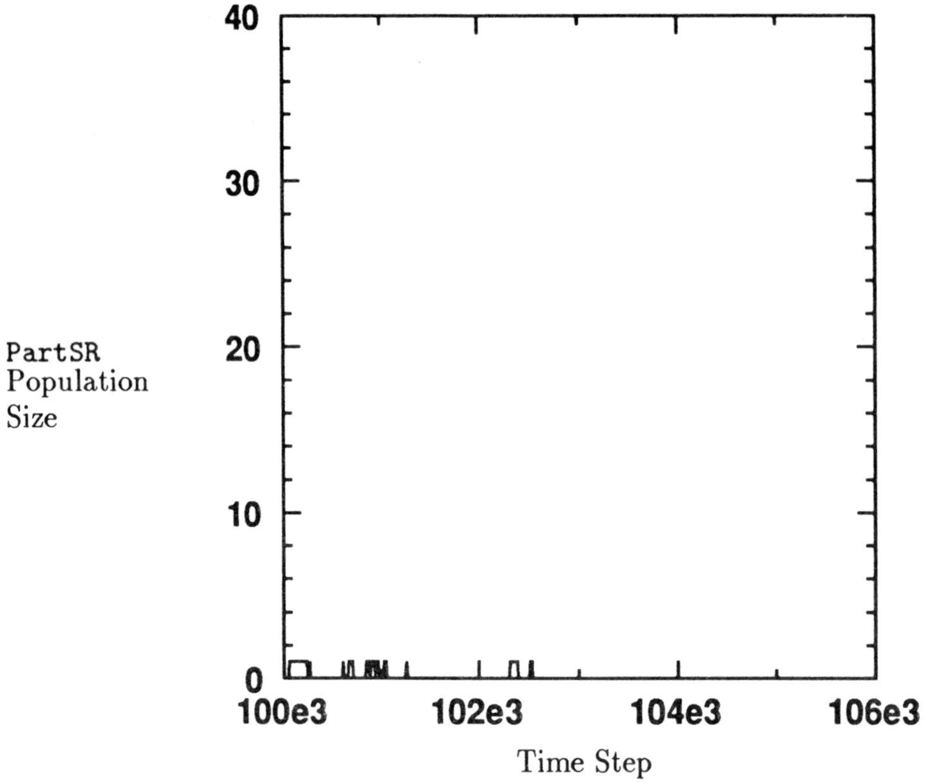

Figure 1: *"Economy" Model.* In this case, a randomised configuration is initially generated, transients are allowed to decay, and then a single instance of Seed is artificially inserted (at Time Step 100×10^3). Contrary to the original prediction, a large population of PartSR is *not* generated; in fact, the maximum PartSR "population" size achieved is just a single instance.

ately inserted. The initial random configuration has a significant density of free atoms (actually in accordance with the densities which Holland's analysis of the action of Seed were based on). 6×10^3 steps were executed. Figure 2 shows the resulting density of PartSR. The performance is certainly an improvement over the previous case, with the PartSR population reaching 10 instances; but the population still never approaches saturation (this particular universe has a capacity of 40 instances of the PartSR complex). Furthermore, after reaching a peak of about 10 instances, the population rapidly goes extinct again.

5.3 "Deluxe" Model

At this point it was clear that the Seed complex was not capable of carrying out the function anticipated by Holland—i.e. to establish a viable population of PartSR complexes. However, it was not clear whether this was merely a problem of the relatively limited size of PartSR population which the initial instance of Seed was managing to generate, or whether the PartSR complex would not be viable even in an arbitrarily large population.

To test this, an α_0 (still with 2×10^3 cells) was generated with a highly artificial initial configuration—namely saturated with instances of the PartSR complex. This was exe-

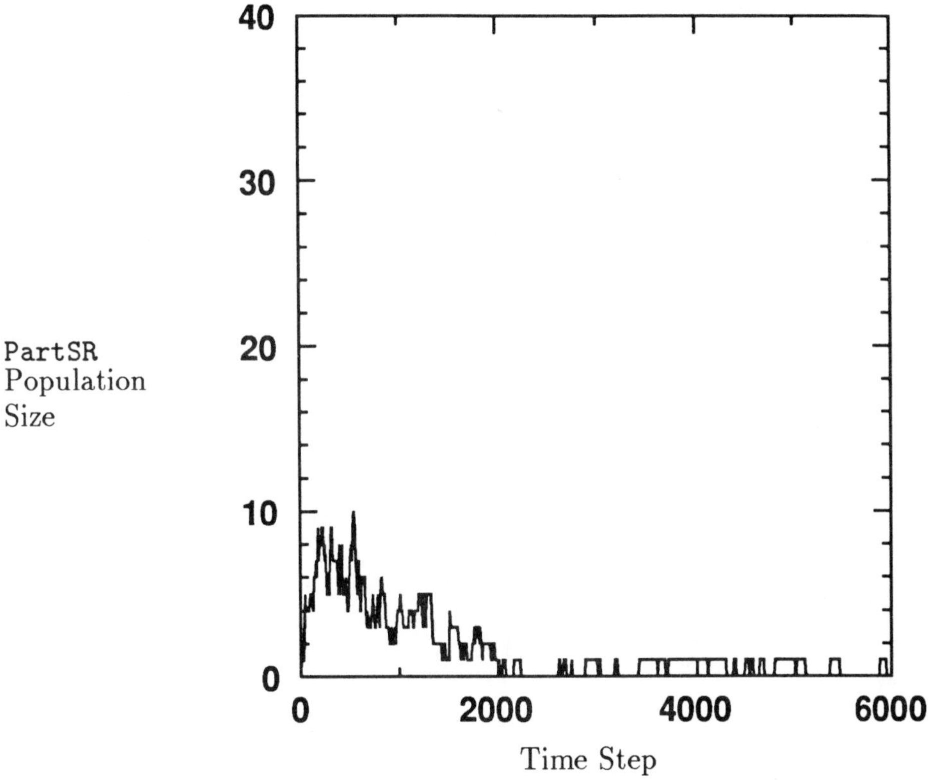

Figure 2: *"Standard" Model.* As in the "Economy" model, a randomised configuration is initially generated and a single instance of `Seed` is artificially inserted. However, in this case, `Seed` is inserted immediately (at Time Step 0)—i.e. without any delay to allow transients to decay; in particular, the (initial) density of free atoms is, in this case, relatively high. In contrast to the economy model, `Seed` does now succeed in generating a significant population of `PartSR` complexes—peaking at 10 instances, representing about 25% of the absolute maximum capacity for this particular universe. However, this population of `PartSR` is still evidently not viable in itself, and, contrary to prediction, rapidly goes extinct.

cuted for 6×10^3 steps. Figure 3 is a plot of the number of `PartSR` complexes present over this period. It is seen that, even with this "most favourable" configuration, the population still rapidly goes extinct.

It was clear at this point that α_0 was not capable of supporting the "life-life" behaviour postulated by Holland. A number of variations were (briefly) investigated. These included increasing the size of the universe (to the 10^4 cells originally considered by Holland), and restricting the behaviour of the emergent operators so that, in effect, *only* the operators associated with `PartSR` would be executed. None of these variations had a significant positive effect—the `PartSR` complex was not viable under any of the scenarios tested.

6 Analysis

It is not clear how deep rooted the deficiencies of α_0 are, but it is possible to identify some specific, proximate, causes of failure.

Holland's analysis relies on having a com-

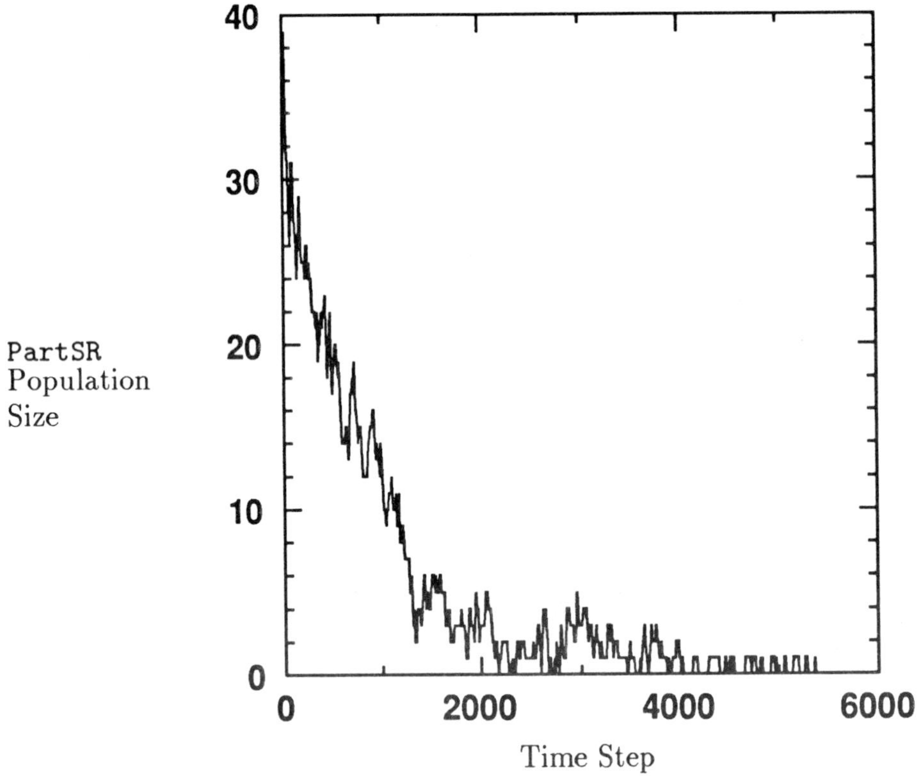

Figure 3: *"Deluxe" Model.* In this case a highly non-random initial configuration was generated—namely, saturated with instances of the `PartSR` complex (a total of 40 instances in this particular universe). It is seen that even in this "most favourable" case, which removes any reliance on the operation of the `Seed` complex, the population of `PartSR` is still not viable, and again rapidly goes extinct.

plex composed of structures which are, internally, "strongly bonded", which is to say *long lived.* He then estimates the average "productivity" over this lifetime, to come up with a net positive rate of change for the density of the `PartSR` complex (once a threshold is reached). However, in practise, there are (at least) three factors which severely disturb the behaviour of the complex, and which are not allowed for in Holland's analysis:

- Raw materials (free atoms) quickly become scarce (due to usage by random, garbage, emergent operators). This has already been discussed above; the effect is to drastically reduce the rate at which all emergent operators function in practice, thus reducing the *fecundity* of any putatively self-replicating complexes. However, given that the control experiments, in which this effect was artificially reduced or removed, still did not yield a viable `PartSR`, it seems that, though the effect is real, it is not critical (on its own).

- Even when a structure is internally bonded, there is nothing to stop random garbage moving into a position immediately adjacent to it. At the very least this interrupts or suspends the progress of an emergent operator. Thus, it turns out that complexes can only be *active* for a limited portion of their total lifetimes (regardless of the availability of free atoms); again this severely limits fecundity.

- But, at worst, this random arrival of a garbage structure beside an emergent operator can have much more severe effects. If it arrives on the right hand side it can corrupt the output of the operator (introducing a high "mutation" rate, and further reducing fecundity). If it arrives on the left hand side it can result in the formation of a different, garbage, emergent operator which forcibly, and prematurely, breaks up the original operator. This has actually been observed to occur on a number of occasions. Thus, as well as reduced fecundity, complexes also have higher mortality than expected.

So: compared to Holland's analysis, the lifetimes of the structures are shorter than expected, they are only active for a fraction of this time, and their products are sometimes corrupted. The net effect is that mortality exceeds fecundity (by a significant margin), the putatively replicating complexes cannot make up for their own natural decay rate, and thus become extinct quickly. These effects are directly related to the size of the complexes, and the time required to complete a replication cycle. Thus, they would actually affect the `FullSR` complex even more severely than `PartSR`.

A naïve attempt at solution of these problems might be to simply reduce the "temperature" of the universe (reduce the rate at which bonds decay, and structures get randomly moved around). It seems likely that the `FullSR` complex could be made viable in this way (in the limit, if the primitive operators are disabled entirely, `FullSR` would be able to expand to the capacity set by whatever free atoms are initially available; thereafter, of course, all dynamic activity would cease); however, this is not at all the case for `PartSR`, which relies on the primitive operators to complete its replication. It is quite possible (though no proof is currently available) that `PartSR` would not be viable at *any* "temperature". In any case, any reduction in "temperature" would be accompanied by an increase in the expected emergence time for any particular structure or complex, and thus may be completely counterproductive (given that spontaneous emergence was the problem originally being investigated).

The essential problem here seems to hinge on the fact that von Neumann style self-replication involves *copying* and *decoding* an information carrier, where the decoding must be such as to generate (at least) a copy of the required copying and decoding "machinery". α_0 fails to sustain this kind of behaviour because (*inter alia*) the maximum information capacity of its carriers (in the face of the various sources of disruption) seems to be of the order of perhaps 10 bits; this is insufficient to code for any worthwhile machinery—even the relatively simple copying and decoding machinery constructible in α_0.

A more plausible model for the spontaneous emergence of "life-like" behaviour may therefore involve a universe in which certain information carriers, of capacity (say) an order of magnitude larger than that required to code for minimal decoding machinery (in the particular universe), can be copied *without any specialised machinery at all.* In such a system there may be potential for a Darwinian evolutionary process to begin more or less immediately, in which more sophisticated phenotypic properties might, incrementally, become associated with the information carriers—possibly then culminating in a full blown "decoding" (or embryology).

This is, of course, rather speculative; but, as it happens, it is closely related to a general model for the origin of *terrestrial* life which has been championed by Cairns-Smith (1982). This is based on *inorganic* information carriers, which could conceivably be replicated without the relatively complex apparatus required for RNA or DNA replication. It seems to me, in the light of the experimental results presented here, that it would now be a promising research program to adopt Holland's original *strategy* (which is to design relatively simplified model chemistries, loosely based on cellular automata, in which to examine the origin of "life"), but to replace his detailed models (the α-Universes) with models based on different theoretical considerations—such as those of (for example) Cairns-Smith.

7 Conclusion

I should like to emphasise here the debt which this paper owes to John Holland's original formulation and analysis of the problem of spontaneous emergence of self-replicating behaviour. While it has been possible to point to defects in that analysis, this was with the benefit of hindsight, and prompted by experimental evidence not available to Holland. It does not detract in any way from Holland's creative achievement in formulating the *possibility* of such an investigation in the first place.

Drew McDermott once lamented that his field (Artificial Intelligence) was "starving for a few carefully documented failures" (McDermott 1985). It seems perverse to seek success *through* failure in this way—and such was certainly no part of my original intentions. Nonetheless, I think McDermott had a valid point, which is fairly well illustrated by the present work: for the primary conclusion here is that, although the model universe α_0 fails to demonstrate the phenomena originally hoped for, its particular mechanisms of failure are interesting and suggestive in their own right. In its own way, this may be best outcome of all.

Acknowledgments

This work was made possible by generous support from the School of Electronic Engineering in Dublin City University. I am also grateful to Noel Murphy of DCU, and John Kelly of University College Dublin, for many extended discussions relating to it, and to Inman Harvey of the University of Sussex for his perceptive criticism of an earlier draft.

References

Cairns-Smith, A.G. 1982. *Genetic takeover and the mineral origins of life.* Cambridge: Cambridge University Press.

Holland, J.H. 1976. Studies of the spontaneous emergence of self-replicating systems using cellular automata and formal grammars. In *Automata, Languages, Development*, edited by A. Lindenmayer and G. Rozenberg. New York: North-Holland.

McDermott, D. 1981. Artificial Intelligence Meets Natural Stupidity. In *Mind Design*, edited by John Haugeland. Cambridge: MIT Press.

Schrödinger, E. 1944. *What is Life?* Cambridge: Cambridge University Press.

Von Neumann, J. 1951. The general and logical theory of automata. In: *Cerebral Mechanisms in Behavior—The Hixon Symposium,* edited by L.A. Jeffress. New York: John Wiley.

The Evolution of Sexual Selection and Female Choice

Robert J. Collins
David R. Jefferson
Artificial Life Laboratory
Department of Computer Science
University of California, Los Angeles
Los Angeles, CA 90024

Abstract

One of the main goals of the researchers in the field of artificial life is to increase our understanding of natural life. We are particularly interested in using artificial life to study issues in natural evolution and population genetics. Current tools of population geneticists and evolutionary biologists are inherently limited. For example, only the simplest genetic systems can be completely understood analytically, the fossil record is incomplete and difficult to interpret, and evolutionary experiments in the laboratory or field are usually limited to at most a few dozen generations and are difficult to control and repeat. Simulated evolution makes it possible to study evolutionary systems over thousands of generations (macroevolution) and on large populations.

In this paper, we demonstrate that *microanalytic* (low-level) computer simulations of evolving populations of artificial organisms can usefully augment analytic population genetics models. We begin with a simple analytical model of sexual selection, and extend it in many dimensions by relaxing the important simplifying assumptions. Furthermore, while all of the simplifying assumptions are necessary to make the analysis tractable, they also may cause the model to not apply to real populations. Simulated evolution can supply empirical evidence that an analytical model is robust with respect to variations that cannot be handled analytically. While analytic methods typically describe only the equilibria of the model in question, microanalytic simulated evolution allows the exploration of the evolutionary dynamics of populations away from the equilibrium.

1 Introduction

We, like many other researchers in the field of artificial life, are attempting to increase our understanding of natural life (Langton 1989a; Langton 1989b; Langton et al. 1991). In particular, the focus of this paper is on using computer simulations of evolving populations of artificial organisms to study problems natural evolution. The computer simulation of evolving populations is important in the study of ecological, adaptive, and evolutionary systems (Taylor et al. 1989). The other main approaches are the study of the fossil record, molecular studies, observational and experimental studies, and mathematical analysis. These approaches are inherently limited in ways that computer simulations are not. First, the fossil record is incomplete and difficult to interpret. Second, while molecular studies can determine the underlying genetic similarities and differences of various species, these studies are time–consuming, and the results are often difficult to interpret due to the complexity of the biochemistry of natural life. Third, evolutionary experiments in the laboratory or field are usually limited to at most a few dozen generations because natural organisms (other than microbes) grow and reproduce slowly. In addition, such experiments are difficult to control and repeat, because of the complexity of the interactions between an organism and its environment. Fourth, only the simplest genetic systems can be completely described and understood analytically. In contrast, simulated evolution makes it possible to study simplified models of nontrivial evolutionary systems over thousands of generations (macroevolution). Although these models are simplified, they are much more complex and realistic than those that can be attacked with mathematical analysis. By their very nature, computer simulations are easily repeated and varied, with all relevant parameters under the full control of the experimenter. Of course, an inherent weakness of computer simulations is the inability to attain the full complexity of natural life.

Most computer simulations in biology (including evolutionary simulations) are based on solving differential equations from mathematical models (Swartzman and Kaluzny 1987; Taylor 1983), where the equations specify the global dynamics of the system. In contrast, we use a very different computer simulation paradigm, which we refer to as *microanalytic* (Collins and Jefferson 1991b; Collins and Jefferson 1991a). A microanalytic evolutionary simulation separately represents and simulates each individual organism, each gene in each organism, and each environmental effect in detail. Rather than attempting to capture the complex global dynamics of the population and environment in a set of equations, we model only the local interactions between the individual organisms and environment. Based on these relatively simple local interactions, the complex global dynamics of the evolving population emerges. This basic strategy (emergence of complexity from simple local interactions) is typical of many artificial life studies (Langton 1989b; Langton et al. 1991).

Until recently, macroevolutionary microanalytic simulations were not computationally feasible. Microanalytic simulations are computationally intensive, due to the detailed simulation of the life of each organism. Macroevolutionary simulations require many thousands of organisms in order to avoid small population effects (such as random genetic drift), and in most cases, hundreds or even thousands of generations must be simulated. The availability of massively parallel computers such as the Connection Machine (Hillis 1985; Hillis and Guy L. Steele, Jr. 1986), have made simple microanalytic simulations possible. The Connection Machine-2 is used for all simulations described below.

2 Sexual Selection and Female Choice

One of the significant and enduring problems of evolutionary biology is the evolution of preferences for mates with exaggerated secondary sexual characteristics that apparently reduce the ability of the individual bearing them to survive (Kirkpatrick and Ryan 1991). Typically, it is the females that express the preference, and the males that express the apparently maladaptive trait. This phenomenon has been known for more than 120 years. Darwin (1871) describes a number of examples, but offers no explanation for the evolution of these female mating preferences, although a number of hypotheses have been proposed in recent years (Kirkpatrick and Ryan 1991).

This phenomena is paradoxical in species where a female receives nothing from a mate (other than sperm), and there is no direct relationship between her mate choice and her viability or fecundity. Because the expression of the trait in a male reduces his likelihood of surviving to reproduce, females that mate with such males will produce fewer offspring of mating age in the next generation. At first glance, it appears that females that prefer the *absence* of the trait should always be at a selective advantage, therefore eliminating preferences *for* the trait. The fact that this phenomena appears to be common in nature suggests that females that prefer the absence of the trait are not always at a selective advantage, and/or the natural situations are actually more complex than they appear.

3 Kirkpatrick's Model

Fisher (1958) was the first to provide a possible (qualitative) solution to the problem of selection for maladaptive traits. Kirkpatrick (1982) has developed a simple analytic model of sexual selection, consisting of two loci, each with two alleles.

Kirkpatrick's model of sexual selection assumes that the males of the species contribute only gametes to the next generation, and that there is no direct relationship between a female's mating preference and her survivorship nor her fecundity. The model also assumes that the trait and preference loci are not sex-linked and reside on different chromosomes and the genetic system is haploid. The preference locus P has two alleles: P_0 and P_1; and likewise the trait locus T has alleles T_0 and T_1. Kirkpatrick also implicitly assumes an infinite and unstructured population[1].

The allele at the P locus is expressed only in females, and the allele of the T locus only in males. The T_0 allele produces males that do not possess the secondary sexual characteristic, while the T_1 allele produces the trait and thus has the side effect of reducing viability (the probability of surviving to adulthood) to $1 - s$ (where $s > 0$) relative to the T_0 males. The P_0 females prefer to mate with T_0 males. Given a two-way choice of a T_0 male and a T_1 male, a P_0 female will choose to mate with the T_0 male a_0 times more frequently than the T_1 male. In the same way, P_1 females prefer to mate with T_1 males, and the strength of the preference is a_1. These preferences are frequency dependent, so the P_i females will choose to mate with a T_i male with probability

$$P(T_i|P_i) = \frac{a_i t'_i}{t'_j + a_i t'_i} \qquad (1)$$

where t'_k is the frequency of mature T_k males in the population.

A generation begins with an equal number of males and females. Then, viability selection kills a fraction s of the T_1 males. Mating proceeds as defined above, recombination between gametes occurs, and the process repeats with the next generation.

Let p_1 be the frequency of the P_1 allele in the population, and t_1 be the frequency of the T_1 allele. From this model, Kirkpatrick derives the following equation for the equilibrium allele frequencies:

$$t_1 = \begin{cases} 0 & \text{if } p_1 \leq V_1 \\ \frac{(a_0 a_1 - 1)(1-s)}{(a_0 + s - 1)[a_1(1-s) - 1]} p_1 - \frac{1}{a_1(1-s)-1} & \text{if } V_1 < p_1 < V_2 \\ 1 & \text{if } V_2 \leq p_1 \end{cases} \qquad (2)$$

where

$$V_1 = \frac{a_0 + s - 1}{(a_0 a_1 - 1)(1 - s)}$$

and

$$V_2 = \frac{a_1(a_0 + s - 1)}{(a_0 a_1 - 1)}$$

[1]An unstructured population implies panmixia (no spatial structure, so any individual may mate with any other—distance is not a factor in mate choice) and synchronous (nonoverlapping) generations (no age structure).

Equation 2 is plotted for several sets of parameters in Figure 1. Depending on the parameters and initial conditions, the frequency of the trait allele (t_1) can take on any value from 0 to 1. For both alleles of T to be maintained in the population, it is required that $1 - a_0 < s < 1 - \frac{1}{a_1}$, otherwise either T_0 or T_1 will become fixed.

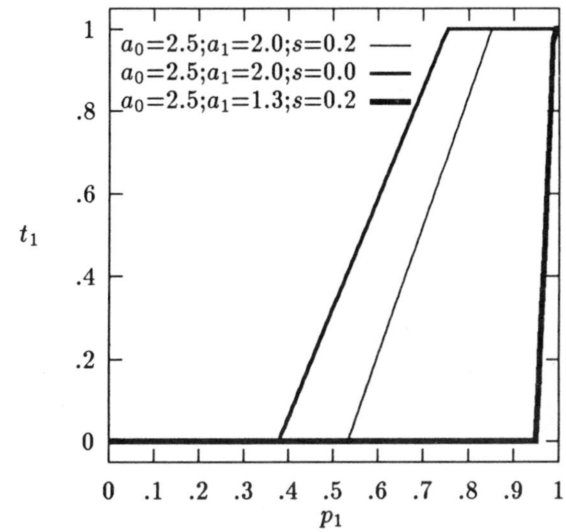

Figure 1: Equation 2 plotted for various sets of parameters.

It is interesting that the equilibrium is a curve, rather than a single point. Kirkpatrick provides an intuitive explanation of the various forces at work in this model (Kirkpatrick 1982, p. 5):

> The finding that there is not a single point of equilibrium can be understood intuitively by separating the effects of natural selection and mating success. At any equilibrium it must be that the viability deficit which trait–bearing [T_1] males suffer is exactly offset by the mating advantage they receive so that the two male phenotypes have identical fitness. The mating advantage is determined by both the strength and frequency of the preference allele [P_1]. Increasing the frequency of the preference allele increases the mating advantage. This does not necessarily result in fixation of the male trait allele [T_1], however, because the strength of the mating advantage decreases as the frequency of trait–bearing males increases.

Due to the preferential mate choices of the females in a population that contains both of the T alleles, a non-random association can form between the alleles of the T and P loci. Under strong sexual selection the chances of an individual in the population having the genotype P_iT_i is greater than p_it_i, where p_i and t_i are the allele frequencies of P_i and T_i respectively. This strength of this association between P and T alleles is measured by D, the linkage disequilibrium. The result of this association is that when the frequency of T_i changes due to selection, the frequency of P_i tends to change with it[2].

In this model, the frequency of the P alleles changes only due to this correlated responses to changes in the frequency of the T alleles ($D \neq 0$). This means that once the population reaches the curve of equilibrium, there will be no movement along the curve unless some force outside the model perturbs the allele frequencies. Examples of such outside forces that might occur in real populations (but are assumed to not exist for the purposes of Kirkpatrick's analysis) are random genetic drift, migration pressure, mutation pressure, correlated responses with other loci that are under selection, etc.

4 Simulating the Model

In our microanalytic simulations of this model, we place the organisms in a 2 dimensional grid[3], with one male and one female organism per grid location. Males and females possess both the T and P loci, but diverge phenotypically. The males express their T allele (and thus may be subject to viability selection, based on s), while females express their P allele while choosing a mate.

A generation begins with an equal number of males and females (65,536 of each, for a total population size of N=131,072). Then, viability selection is applied to the T_1 males, randomly killing each with a probability of s. The females then each choose one of the surviving males as her mate and together they produce two offspring, one male and one female, which are placed at the mother's grid location. Each of the two offspring is the result of an independent recombination and mutation of the two parent genomes. The P and T loci are implemented on different chromosomes, so there is no direct linkage between them. We add mutation at a low rate ($\mu = 0.00001$ per bit per generation), in order to prevent permanent fixation for any allele in our simulation experiments.

Kirkpatrick's model does not specify the mechanics of how the females choose their mates; it simply defines the frequency of choices in Equation 1. In our simulation, each female randomly samples 25 males (with replacement) from the population and determines approximate values for each t_i'. Each female then applies Equation 1 to determine with which male phenotype (T_i) she will mate, and then randomly selects one of

[2]If the *strength* of the preference and trait were under genetic control, then we would expect to see selection for more and more dramatic secondary sexual characteristics in males, and the strength of the preferences for such traits should also increase due to this correlated response (Fisher's (1958) "runaway" process).

[3]We will use the grid when we extend the model to use local mating, rather than panmixia.

the (living) T_i males from her random sample of males. Note that if only one phenotypic class of males is represented in her sample, Equation 1 will cause her to always choose that class.

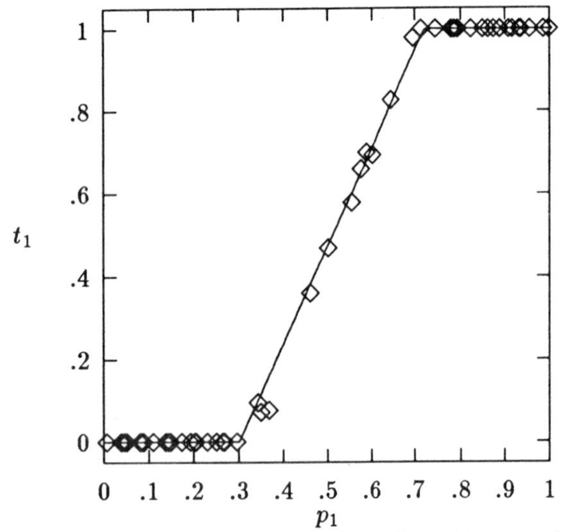

Figure 2: Locations of 51 populations after 500 generations with panmictic mating, $a_0 = 2.0$, $a_1 = 3.0$, $s = 0.2$, $\mu = 0.00001$, and $N = 131,072$. The line is the equilibrium predicted by Kirkpatrick.

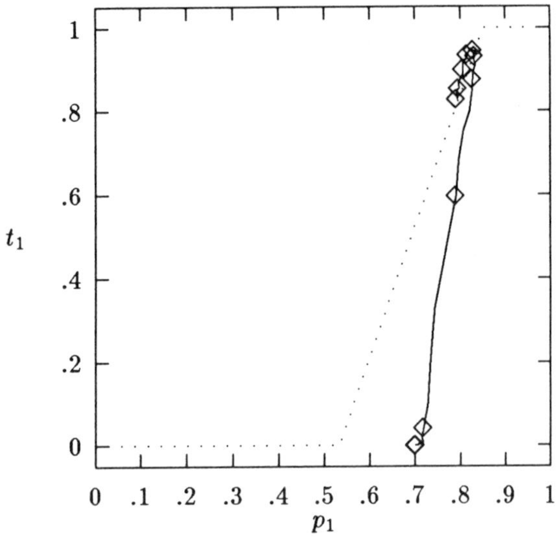

Figure 3: The path of a population for 500 generations with panmictic mating, $a_0 = 2.5$, $a_1 = 2.0$, $s = 0.2$, $\mu = 0.00001$, and $N = 131,072$. The run begins with $p_1 = 0.7$ and $t_1 = 0.0$. The ◇'s are at 50 generation intervals. The dotted line is the equilibrium predicted by Kirkpatrick.

This simulation model departs from the analytical model in three important ways: (1) finite populations are used; (2) females do not have global knowledge of the population, but rather sample a small number of males in choosing a mate; and (3) a low rate of mutation has been introduced. These modifications make the model more biologically realistic and more amenable to massively parallel simulation. As Figure 2 demonstrates, the simulated populations move to the equilibrium predicted by Kirkpatrick's analysis.

While these initial experiments have verified that the simulation model produces the equilibrium predicted by the analytical model, they give us little insight concerning the behavior of populations that begin far from the equilibrium. In particular, we are interested in how a new allele invades a population and how that population subsequently evolves to a point on the equilibrium curve. Figure 3 shows the path taken by a population that begins with a gene pool containing an abundance of both preference (P) alleles, but no T_1 alleles. During the experiment T_1 alleles are introduced into the population by mutation. Although it takes about 100 generations for significant numbers of T_1 alleles to build up, once this occurs the population moves quickly to the equilibrium curve.

This experiment dramatically demonstrates the power of sexual selection and female choice. The female's preferences are stronger for the more viable males ($a_0 > a_1$) yet the less preferred and less viable T_1 males quickly take over the population. Figure 4 shows how the average viability of the males decreases as the T_1 males proliferate. This experiment also demonstrates the "runaway" process described by Fisher (1958). Although the P and T loci reside on different chromosomes, a positive association (linkage disequilibrium $D > 0$) forms between the P_1 and T_1 alleles. As t_1 increases due to selection, p_1 also increases from 0.7 to more than 0.8.

Kirkpatrick (1982) notes that forces such as random genetic drift may have important effects in real populations. Although the equilibrium is stable (in an infinite, non-mutating population), if the population is pushed off of the equilibrium, it may return to the curve at a different location. Despite the size of the population ($N = 131,072$), random genetic drift is apparent in the experiment in Figure 3. In particular, the path taken by the population is not straight, and during the latter half of this experiment, it appears that the population has drifted a short distance from the equilibrium, and returns at a point with somewhat lower values for p_1 and t_1.

In this section, we have not only verified that the simulation model produces the equilibrium derived by Kirkpatrick, but we have also demonstrated that it is a viable way to study the dynamics of populations far from equilibrium. In addition, we are able to observe the effects of finite population size on the system.

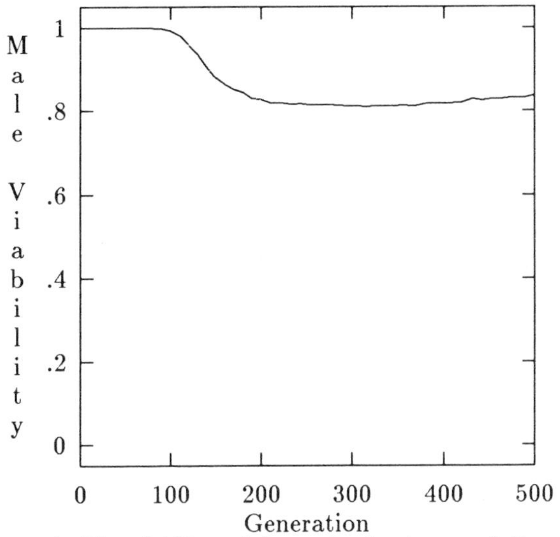

Figure 4: The viability of the males in the population in Figure 3.

5 Extensions of the Model

In formulating the analytic model, a number of simplifying assumptions were made in order to make the mathematics tractable, including (1) an infinite population; (2) panmixia (global mating); (3) the adult organisms are haploid; and (4) the preference and trait phenotypes are each specified by one locus with two alleles. How dependent on these assumptions are the predictions of the model? Unless there is a reasonable expectation that the predictions hold, the model is not very useful for studying real populations. In the previous section, we simulated an infinite population with a large but finite, mutating population. In this section, we explore the effects of spatial structure (local mating) and diploidy.

5.1 Sexual Selection in Structured Populations

One of the important assumptions that is made by Kirkpatrick is panmixia. This is important to make the analysis tractable, but it also may make the predictions inapplicable to structured populations (which includes most real populations). In this section, we extend both Kirkpatrick's analytic model and our simulation model to include the *stepping stone* model of population structure (Kimura and Weiss 1964).

One of the basic assumptions of Wright's shifting balance theory of evolution is that spatial structure exists in large populations (Wright 1931; Provine 1986). The structure is in the form of *demes*, or semi-isolated subpopulations, with relatively thorough gene mixing within a deme, but restricted gene flow (migration) between demes. In the stepping stone model of population structure, the demes are assumed to lie in an n-dimensional lattice, with migration restricted to neighboring demes in the lattice. The migration rate m is the probability that an individual in the subpopulation has migrated from a neighboring deme during the current generation. Therefore, if the number of individuals in the deme is N, Nm individuals will migrate into the deme each generation. One important analytical result is that the demes will become strongly differentiated due to genetic drift if $N_em \ll 1$, but will behave as a single panmictic population if $N_em > 4$ (Kimura and Maruyama 1971), where N_e is the effective population size (Wright 1931). Our analytical extensions (see below) to Kirkpatrick's model apply for the case of $N_em \ll 1$, and Kirkpatrick's original panmictic model applies when $N_em > 4$. We would expect some sort of intermediate behavior for the intermediate migration rates, although neither model fully applies in this case.

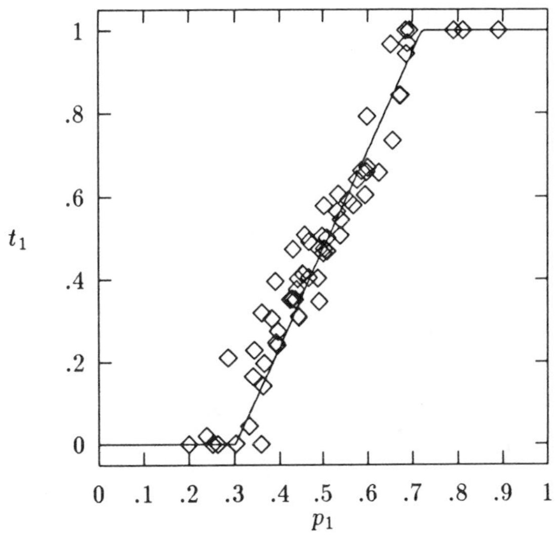

Figure 5: Locations of 64 panmictic populations of size $N = 8192$ after 500 generations with $a_0 = 2.0$, $a_1 = 3.0$, $s = 0.2$, $\mu = 0.00001$. The line is the equilibrium predicted by Kirkpatrick.

Are the equilibrium allele frequencies of a stepping stone structured population accurately predicted by Kirkpatrick's model? In fact, the answer is no. Instead of a single equilibrium curve, we expect the equilibrium allele frequencies to form a region. Consider a structured population consisting of a number of demes. Assume that there is restricted gene flow between demes ($Nm \ll 1$), so the allele frequencies of each deme evolve (roughly) independently to some point on Kirkpatrick's equilibrium. (Each of the demes is relatively small, so we expect that random genetic drift will have a greater effect, yet we empirically observe in Figure 5 that the populations of $N = 8,192$ individuals still fall near to Kirkpatrick's equilibrium.) The equilibrium allele frequencies for the whole population are calculated as the mean allele frequencies of the demes, each of which lies on the equilibrium curve defined by Equation 2. Therefore, we expect that the equilibrium allele frequencies of the population as a whole will be defined by

$$
\begin{aligned}
t_1 &\leq \begin{cases} \frac{1}{\frac{a_1(a_0+s-1)}{a_0a_1-1}} p_1 & \text{if } p_1 \leq V_1 \\ 1 & \text{if } p_1 > V_1 \end{cases} \\
t_1 &\leq \begin{cases} 0 & \text{if } p_1 \leq V_2 \\ 1 + \frac{1}{1-\frac{a_0+s-1}{(a_0a_1-1)(1-s)}}(p_1 - 1) & \text{if } p_1 > V_2 \end{cases}
\end{aligned} \qquad (3)
$$

where

$$V_1 = \frac{a_1(a_0 + s - 1)}{a_0a_1 - 1}$$

and

$$V_2 = \frac{a_0 + s - 1}{(a_0a_1 - 1)(1 - s)}$$

which forms the boundary within which all possible conglomerations of subpopulations residing on Kirkpatrick's equilibrium must lie. This defines the region between the solid lines in Figure 6 (where the panmixia equilibrium defined by Equation 2 is shown by the dotted line).

Is the region of equilibrium neutrally stable? If it is, once a population reaches any point in the region, it will stay there (in the absence of drift, etc.). Although the curve of equilibrium under panmixia is neutrally stable, the region of equilibrium for structured populations is not necessarily stable. Stability of the whole population is achieved only when each subpopulation reaches the equilibrium described by Equation 2, but it is possible for the population allele frequencies to fall within the region of equilibrium (described by Equation 3) while some of the demes are still far from equilibrium. Due to this instability, significant change in allele frequencies due to selection pressure induced by sexual selection might be observed even for populations that are within the region of equilibrium.

To simulate the stepping stone model in the selection and mating process, we place the individuals in a toroidal, 2 dimensional grid (again, with one male and one female at each grid location). The grid is then broken into non-overlapping demes consisting of 64x64=4096 grid locations. As with the panmictic simulation, each female randomly samples 25 males (with replacement), but now the samples are chosen only from the female's deme, rather than the whole population. From this sample, she calculates t'_i for the local males and applies Equation 1 to determine the phenotype of her mate. She then randomly chooses one of the (living) males with the appropriate phenotype from her sample, and produces two offspring (one male and one female) at her location. This provides for random mating (panmixia) within the deme, and no mating between demes. After mating, migration to one of the four neighboring demes occurs with a probability m per individual.

The results of 51 simulations are shown in Figure 6 (generation 500). Although the allele frequencies are at

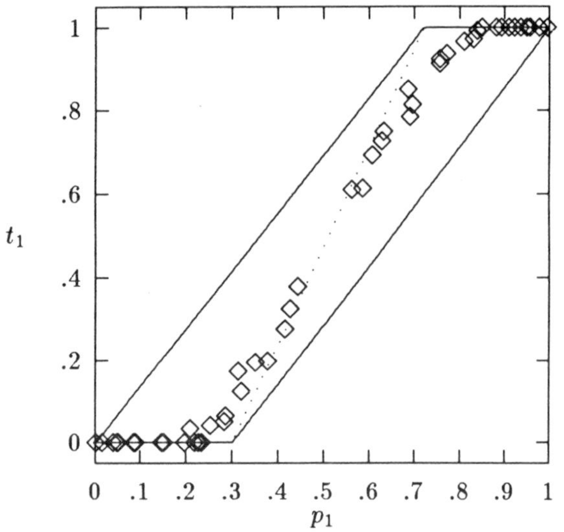

Figure 6: Locations of 51 populations after 500 generations with local mating (stepping stone model with 16 demes of 8,192 individuals each), a_0 = 2.0, a_1 = 3.0, s = 0.2, μ = 0.00001, m = 0.00001, and N = 131,072. The solid lines define the predicted region of equilibrium for local mating, and the dotted line is the equilibrium predicted by Kirkpatrick for panmixia.

equilibrium anywhere within the region, the population appear to have a greater probability of falling near the long axis of the region of equilibrium, rather than near the edges. As predicted, the populations do not fall on the panmictic equilibrium curve, but they do fall within the region of equilibrium.

Again, we examine the behavior of a population that begins far from the equilibrium, by repeating the experiment where we observed the invasion of a new allele into the gene pool, but this time using the spatially structured population described above. Figure 7 plots the path of a population that begins at $p_1 = 0.7$ and $t_1 = 0.0$. Although the evolution again proceeds quickly, the rate of change in t_1 appears to be about half that observed in the panmixia experiment. It is important to note that the selection pressure remains strong, even after the population has entered the region of equilibrium (demonstrating its potential for instability), although around generation 350 the selection pressure seems to have dropped off significantly. As we saw under panmixia, random genetic drift has noticeable effects: the path under selection is not entirely straight, and the population wanders once the population reaches a "stable" equilibrium.

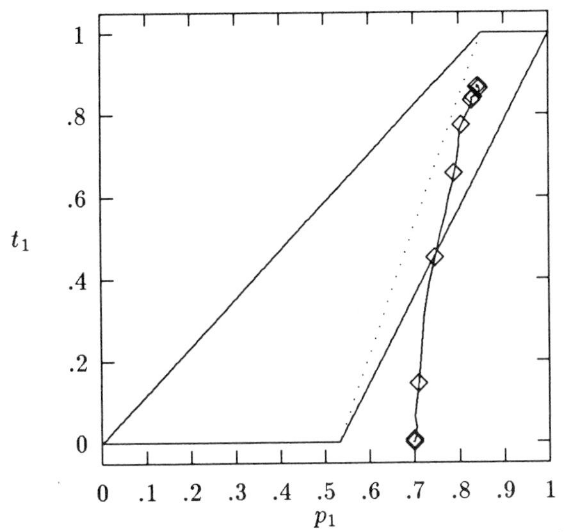

Figure 7: The path of a population for 500 generations with stepping stone structure (16 demes, each consisting of 8,192 individuals), $a_0 = 2.5$, $a_1 = 2.0$, $s = 0.2$, $\mu = 0.00001$, and $N = 131,072$. The run begins with $p_1 = 0.7$ and $t_1 = 0.0$. The solid lines define the predicted region of equilibrium for local mating, and the dotted line is the equilibrium predicted by Kirkpatrick for panmixia.

5.2 Sexual Selection in Diploid Organisms

In order to make the mathematics tractable, Kirkpatrick assumes that the organisms are haploid (Kirkpatrick 1982, p. 10):

> It is apparently impossible to treat comparable two–locus, two–allele diploid models analytically because it requires nine (rather than three) simultaneous nonlinear equations.

In this section, we extend our microanalytic simulation model to include diploid organisms. Using these simulations, we can determine if a qualitative difference results from moving from haploid to diploid genetics.

Genotype	Male Phenotype	Female Phenotype
$T_0T_0P_0P_0$	T_0	P_0
$T_0T_1P_0P_0$	T_0	P_0
$T_1T_1P_0P_0$	T_1	P_0
$T_0T_0P_0P_1$	T_0	P_0
$T_0T_1P_0P_1$	T_0	P_0
$T_1T_1P_0P_1$	T_1	P_0
$T_0T_0P_1P_1$	T_0	P_1
$T_0T_1P_1P_1$	T_0	P_1
$T_1T_1P_1P_1$	T_1	P_1

Table 1: The relationship between the diploid genotypes and phenotypes when both T_1 and P_1 are recessive.

The only changes required to add diploidy to the simulations are to include a second bitstring for each chromosome, and define a dominance relation between the alleles. Although we (and Kirkpatrick) analyzed the equilibrium in terms of allele frequencies in the previous sections we now switch to phenotype frequencies (note that the genotype of a haploid individual is its phenotype). In this paper, we consider only simple dominance relationships between the alleles, although other systems can be simulated in the same manner. We examine the case where the trait (T_1) and the preference for that trait (P_1) alleles are recessive, as described in Table 1, although the other three dominance combinations can be examined just as easily.

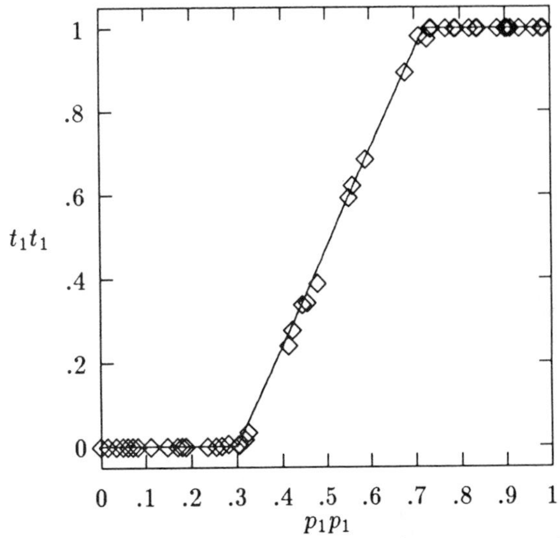

Figure 8: Locations of 51 populations after 500 generations with panmictic mating and diploid genomes, with T_0 and P_0 dominant, $a_0 = 2.0$, $a_1 = 3.0$, $s = 0.2$, $\mu = 0.00001$, and $N = 131,072$. The line is the equilibrium predicted by Kirkpatrick.

Although the analysis is intractable for diploid organisms, the model can be viewed in terms of phenotypes only, and requires no reference to either haploidy or diploidy for the underlying genetics. With either panmixia (Figure 8) or structured populations (Figure 9), we expect and observe no obvious difference in the character of the equilibria due to diploidy.

One area where the evolution of diploid populations differs from haploid populations is in terms of the rate of genetic drift. Because a haploid population has half as many alleles as a diploid population with the same number of individuals, the haploid population drifts approximately twice as fast. This is an important difference, especially when we are dealing with relatively small populations over large numbers of generations.

Another place where diploidy can have an important effect is during the introduction of new (recessive) alleles into the gene pool. Under random mating (Hardy–Weinberg principle), the frequency of phenotypic expression of a recessive trait is the square of the frequency of the associated allele. For example, if the

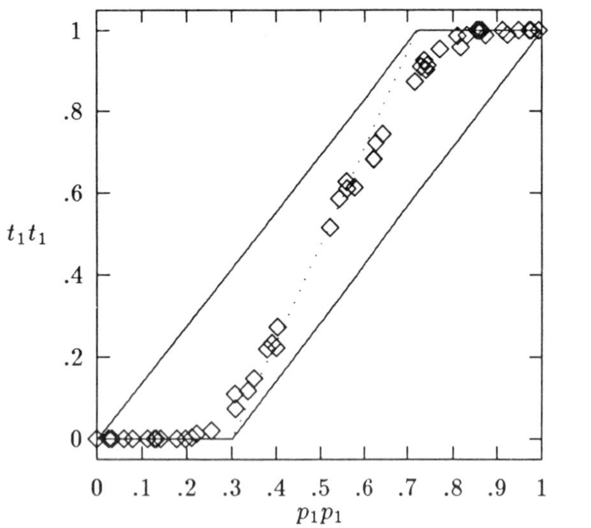

Figure 9: Locations of 51 populations after 500 generations with local mating (stepping stone model with 16 demes of 8,192 organisms each), diploid genomes with T_0 and P_0 dominant, $a_0 = 2.0$, $a_1 = 3.0$, $s = 0.2$, $\mu = 0.00001$, $m = 0.00001$, and $N = 131,072$. The solid lines define the predicted region of equilibrium for local mating, and the dotted line is the equilibrium predicted by Kirkpatrick for panmixia.

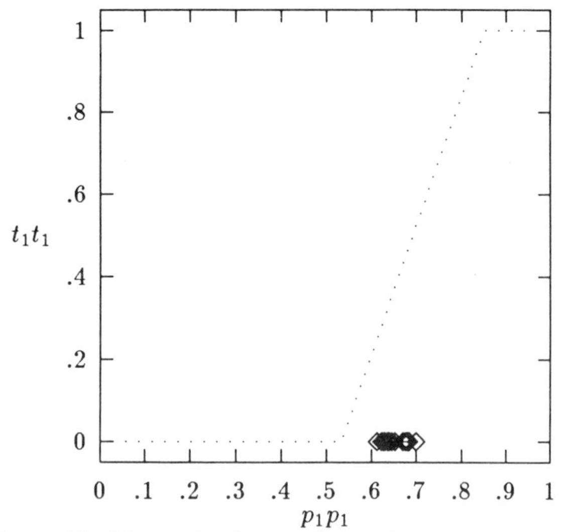

Figure 10: The path of a population for 1000 generations with panmictic mating, $a_0 = 2.5$, $a_1 = 2.0$, $s = 0.2$, $\mu = 0.00001$, and $N = 131,072$. The run begins with $p_1p_1 = 0.7$ and $t_1 = 0.0$. The ◇'s are at 50 generation intervals. The dotted line is the equilibrium predicted by Kirkpatrick.

T_1 allele is recessive and is present in the population with a frequency of $t_1 = 0.01$, only $t_1t_1 = 0.0001$ of the males will express the T_1 phenotype. Therefore, the invasion of recessive alleles into the gene pool, even if they are strongly favored by selection, may take significantly longer under diploid genetics.

We explore this effect for panmictic and spatially structured populations by once again repeating the experiment where we observed the invasion of a new allele into the gene pool, with both the P_0 and the T_0 alleles dominant. The experiment begins with the phenotype frequency of $p_1 = 0.7$ and no T_1 alleles in the population of 131,072 organisms. In a population this size, about 800 copies of the T_1 allele will be required before it becomes likely that a T_1 phenotype male will occur. At the mutation rate of $\mu = 0.00001$, there is on average a 66% chance of mutating one T allele in the population each generation. Therefore, we would expect that a large number of generations and/or significant random genetic drift is going to be required to get the T_1 alleles to a high enough frequency that the sexual selection mechanism can begin to exert its influence.

The simulation results of the invasion of a new, recessive T allele for a panmictic population are plotted in Figure 10, and for a structured population in Figure 11. As expected, the diploidy results are dramatically different from the results of the corresponding haploid experiments (Figures 3 and 7). In the case of panmixia, the T_1 alleles did not become prominent enough for the selection process to begin, even after 1000 generations. During the 1000 generations, the frequency of the P alleles drifted quite noticeably. In the structured population, the T_1 alleles became numerous enough (in at least one deme) to undergo selection due to the female preferences after about 500 generations. It then took about another 400 generations to slowly evolve into the equilibrium region. Like the previous experiments, the effects of genetic drift were apparent.

Although extending the haploid models to include diploidy does not alter the expected equilibria, the evolutionary dynamics are significantly different. First, the effective population size is approximately twice that of a haploid population, so genetic drift is a weaker force. Second, the invasion of recessive traits into the population, even when the preference frequencies favor that trait, is a slow process, while in haploid genetic systems (or under diploidy when the trait is dominant) the process is relatively fast.

6 Discussion

Our main goal in writing this paper is to demonstrate the feasibility and utility of microanalytic simulations in studying population genetics models. We have empirically reproduced Kirkpatrick's analytically determined equilibrium curve for his model of sexual selection. The major differences between our simulations and Kirkpatrick's model are that we simulate a finite (rather than infinite) population and the females choose mates based on a sample of the population (rather than global knowledge). Using this simulation, we are not only able to explore the equilibrium,

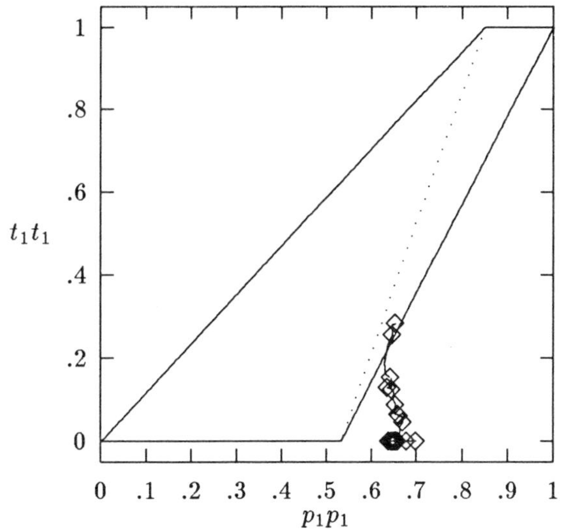

Figure 11: The path of a population for 1000 generations with stepping stone structure (16 demes, each consisting of 8,192 individuals), $a_0 = 2.5$, $a_1 = 2.0$, $s = 0.2$, $\mu = 0.00001$, and $N = 131,072$. The run begins with $p_1p_1 = 0.7$ and $t_1 = 0.0$. The solid lines define the predicted region of equilibrium for local mating, and the dotted line is the equilibrium predicted by Kirkpatrick for panmixia.

but also the dynamics of populations on, near to, or far from the equilibrium curve.

Although this paper is largely an empirical study, we have also analytically extended Kirkpatrick's model of sexual selection to handle populations that are structured into relatively large demes, with relatively low migration rates. Spatial population structure causes the neutrally stable curve of equilibrium to become a sometimes unstable region of equilibrium. Again, we have empirically verified the equilibrium (and its transient instability) via microanalytic simulation (with a stepping stone model of migration), and also studied the evolutionary dynamics of populations away from equilibrium.

Although the mathematics to derive the equilibria under diploid genetics are intractable, there is no reason to believe that the equilibria (in terms of phenotype frequencies) are any different from the haploid model that Kirkpatrick analyzed. Unlike the mathematical model, the simulation model is trivial to extend to handle diploidy. We have empirically verified that the diploid equilibria are identical to the haploid equilibria, for both panmictic and spatially structured populations. This demonstrates that simulated evolution can supply empirical evidence that the analytic model is robust with respect to variations that cannot be handled analytically. Although the equilibria are not affected by diploidy, the dynamics of the evolution can be very different.

We have studied the particular case of the invasion of a preferred but recessive allele into the population. Under haploid genetics, all alleles are expressed in the phenotype, and the invasion of the new allele proceeds rapidly. However, in diploid organisms (under simple dominance), recessive alleles are not expressed in the phenotype unless the allele is present in both copies of the locus. Under random mating, this occurs with a frequency that is the square of the frequency of the recessive allele in the population. This means that forces such as mutation, migration, and random genetic drift are required to get the invading allele to high enough frequency that the associated phenotypic trait begins to appear in the population. This makes it difficult for preferred recessive alleles to invade and take over the population, despite their selective advantage. This problem is most severe for large panmictic populations, due to the relatively slow rate of drift.

The use of macroevolutionary microanalytic simulations to complement analytical models in the study of population genetics appears to be very useful. The simulations not only can be used to provide empirical verification of phenomena, but can also be used to verify the robustness of a model across a number of variations. In addition, a large number of complications that affect real populations can be handled simultaneously (e.g. selection, mutation, population structure, migration, random genetic drift, etc.), providing important feedback on the relative importance of the various components. For example, we found that genetic drift is an important factor in the evolutionary dynamics of even relatively large populations. Also, most analytical population genetics models only describe populations that are at equilibrium. One of the most powerful aspects of the microanalytic simulations is the ability to study the non–equilibrium dynamics of realistic (mutating, drifting, etc.) populations.

We plan to extend this study by implementing a model of sexual selection based on diploid genetics with polygenic (multiple loci) inheritance, with multiple alleles at each locus. With this model, we will attempt to more graphically demonstrate Fisher's runaway selection. In addition, we will use this model to test the possibility that runaway sexual selection can cause reproductive isolation (and thus the potential for speciation) even in the absence of geographic barriers.

Acknowledgments

We would like to thank Chuck Taylor, Greg Werner, Alexis Wieland, and especially Joe Pemberton for their valuable input. This work was supported in part by W. M. Keck Foundation grant number W880615, University of California Los Alamos National Laboratory award number CNLS/89–427, and University of California Los Alamos National Laboratory award number UC–90–4–A–88. The empirical data was gathered on a CM-2 computer at UCLA under the auspices of National Science Foundation Biological Facilities, grant number BBS 87 14206.

References

Collins, Robert J. and David R. Jefferson (1991a). AntFarm: Towards simulated evolution. In Langton, Christopher G., Charles Taylor, J. Doyne Farmer, and Steen Rasmussen, editors, *Artificial Life II*, volume 10 of *Santa Fe Institute Studies in the Sciences of Complexity*, pages 579–601. Santa Fe Institute, Addison–Wesley.

Collins, Robert J. and David R. Jefferson (1991b). Representations for artificial organisms. In Meyer, Jean-Arcady and Stewart W. Wilson, editors, *Proceedings of the First International Conference on Simulation of Adaptive Behavior: From Animals to Animats*, pages 382–390. The MIT Press/Bradford Books.

Darwin, Charles (1871). *The Descent of Man and Selection in Relation to Sex.* Murray, London.

Fisher, Ronald A. (1958). *The Genetical Theory of Natural Selection.* Dover, New York, 2nd edition.

Hillis, W. Daniel (1985). *The Connection Machine.* The MIT Press, Cambridge, Massachusetts.

Hillis, W. Daniel and Guy L. Steele, Jr. (1986). Data parallel algorithms. *Communications of the ACM*, 29(12):1170–1183.

Kimura, Motoo and Takeo Maruyama (1971). Pattern of neutral polymorphism in a geographically structured population. *Genetical Research*, 18:125–131.

Kimura, Motoo and George H. Weiss (1964). The stepping stone model of population structure and the decrease of genetic correlation with distance. *Genetics*, 49:561–576.

Kirkpatrick, Mark (1982). Sexual selection and the evolution of female choice. *Evolution*, 36(1):1–12.

Kirkpatrick, Mark and Michael J. Ryan (1991). The evolution of mating preferences and the paradox of the lek. *Nature*, 350:33–38.

Langton, Christopher G. (1989a). Artificial life. In Langton, Christopher G., editor, *Artificial Life*, volume 6 of *Santa Fe Institute Studies in the Sciences of Complexity*, pages 1–47. Addison–Wesley.

Langton, Christopher G., editor (1989b). *Artificial Life*, volume 6 of *Santa Fe Institute Studies in the Sciences of Complexity.* Addison–Wesley.

Langton, Christopher G., Charles Taylor, J. Doyne Farmer, and Steen Rasmussen, editors (1991). *Artificial Life II*, volume 10 of *Santa Fe Institute Studies in the Sciences of Complexity.* Addison–Wesley.

Provine, William B. (1986). *Sewall Wright and Evolutionary Biology.* University of Chicago Press.

Swartzman, Gordon L. and Stephen P. Kaluzny (1987). *Ecological Simulation Primer.* Macmillan Publishing Company.

Taylor, Charles E. (1983). Evolution of resistance to insecticides: The role of mathematical models and computer simulations. In Georghiou, George P. and Tetsuo Saito, editors, *Pest Resistance to Pesticides.* Plenum Press.

Taylor, Charles E., David R. Jefferson, Scott R. Turner, and Seth R. Goldman (1989). RAM: Artificial life for the exploration of complex biological systems. In Langton, Christopher G., editor, *Artificial Life*, volume 6 of *Santa Fe Institute Studies in the Sciences of Complexity*, pages 275–295. Addison–Wesley.

Wright, Sewall (1931). Evolution in Mendelian populations. *Genetics*, 16:97–159.

A Model for the Emergence of Sex in Evolving Networks: Adaptive Advantage or Random Drift?

Filippo Menczer & Domenico Parisi
Institute of Psychology, CNR
Viale Marx 15, Rome, I-00137
Fax: (I-39) 6-824737
E-mail: DOMENICO @ IRMKANT.BITNET

Abstract

The evolution of sex is an intriguing problem in evolutionary biology: most higher organisms use some form of sexual recombination of the genetic material in the process of reproduction, thus there should be an adaptive advantage in recombination if sex was selected in the course of evolution. Theories have been developed to identify the evolutionary conditions that create a preference for sexual reproduction as a more preferable solution to the problem of gene transmission, as opposed to agamic reproduction. Given the difficulty of proving any of these hypotheses, one might hope that the new tools offered by the simulation methods of ALife, GA's, and neural networks, might help the investigation by allowing the study of simplified models and of their detailed consequences. We start from some results on the effects of introducing crossover (a recombination operator) in a GA used for evolving a population of artificial animals trained on a simple task. Since there is a clear advantage in applying crossover versus simple mutations alone, we expect that this advantage could be retained by the population through selection: this hypothesis is tested in a model with local, individual (rather than global) genetic operators' probabilities by studying the emergent recombination frequencies. It is unexpectedly hard to analyze the results of the simulations, as the operator probabilities do not enter directly in the computation of fitness, while they have a well-known indirect influence on the "behaviour" of fitness. We are monitoring a trait that is not directly selected, thus being subject to the strong action of random drift.

1. The Evolution of Sex

Why do the overwhelming majority of higher organisms reproduce sexually, while lower organisms use agamic reproduction? This open question is of interest for researchers from different disciplines, like theoretical and molecular biology, population genetics, dynamical adaptive processes, genetic algorithms. The ubiquity of sex has vast implications which cannot be addressed in this paper. For an articulated presentation of current ideas, see in Michod, Levin 1988. It is our belief that ALife can contribute to the problem by making new models and simulation tools available for investigation.

We want to restate the problem for our purposes in a more restricted sense, such that a simplified model can be developed and a meaningful analysis can be carried out. In the first place we are not interested in the mechanisms which gave origin to the different reproductive systems, but rather in the dynamical phenomena of natural evolution through which sexual and asexual reproduction have emerged as the main reproductive systems. For instance, mutations are obviously inevitable errors in the physical process of copying genetic material, while many theories state that sex could have originated as a repair mechanism for deleterious DNA mutations (see for example the chapter by L.D.Brooks in Michod, Levin 1988). We start from a situation in which both systems are available (with genetic variations) in a population, and observe what happens when these two systems compete one with the other. In the second place we drop from the model all the details about sexual and asexual reproduction and schematize them as two simple copy procedures: the former involves a recombination of the two parents' genetic material, while the latter does not. Both procedures are subject to errors (i.e. mutations).

1.1. Adaptive Advantages

The question we are trying to address is: how does individual selection act on recombination in a population? If selection is based on an individual fitness measure, we should consider the adaptive advantages of the recombination operator. If we see the genetic evolution of the population as a fitness optimization process in the space of the genotypes, the sexual (or asexual) individuals will be selected if recombination contributes to optimizing the fitness more (or less) efficiently. The two arguments (as stated for example in the chapter by J.F.Crow in Michod, Levin 1988) more commonly theorized in accounting for the advantages of sexual reproduction are: (1) adjusting to temporal or spatial environmental changes; (2) facilitating the incorporation of beneficial mutations and the removal of deleterious ones. There are also disadvantages in sexual reproduction, such as the well-known cost of meiosis (Michod, Levin 1988). Given our simplifications of the problem, our hope is to use a genetically-evolved population of artificial animals to test the possible adaptive advantages versus the disadvantages of recombination in reproduction.

1.2. Random Drift

When dealing with a problem of population genetics such as the evolution of recombination, we should not take for granted that any trait emerged from natural evolution was originally selected because of its adaptive advantage. In fact, other evolutionary factors are important beside selection: random (or genetic) drift is the main example. At least two mechanisms derived from the action of selection in finite populations go under the definition of random drift: first, the sampling error implied by the fact that our measure of fitness is only an estimate of the true fitness, doomed by an error which tends to zero as the population approaches infinity; second, the "hitchhiking effect" due to random associations between neutral and advantageous (or disadvantageous) traits. While these effects would not exist in an infinite population, real populations are finite and so natural evolution is the result of the interaction of selection and random drift in finite populations (see the discussion on linkage disequilibrium in the chapter by J.Felsenstein in Michod, Levin 1988). Random drift doesn't need directional selection (fitness optimization) to operate: a genetic trait with no adaptive advantage can reach fixation in the population through purely neutral selection (Kimura 1983) because of random drift. We must consider the net effect of such different evolutionary forces when trying to account for the natural emergence of genetic traits whose adaptive advantages are not totally clear, as for sexual recombination.

2. Ecological Networks

The ALife framework in which the evolution of recombination is monitored and analyzed is taken from previous works where genetic algorithms are used in the learning process of populations of neural networks modelling simple artificial animals. An external environment provides feedback by which the living strategies of the animals are evaluated and a fitness function can be computed. Once we define a task for the network, i.e. a desired mapping between its input and its output, there will be sets of weight values for the connection weight matrix of the network that yield such mapping, or perform the task correctly. The fitness function measures how well the task is performed. The process of learning the correct connection weight matrix consists in an optimization task where the fitness is to be maximized as a function defined in the domain of the connection weights. An unsupervised learning algorithm is used, in which the only information available is the value of the fitness function at each point it is measured. The details of the ALife scheme can be found in: Menczer, Parisi 1990; Parisi, Cecconi, Nolfi 1990; Patarnello, Carnevali 1989. However, we summarize its main features in the following subsections so that the reader can visualize the simulation "test-bed" for the subsequent analysis on sexual recombination emergence.

2.1. ALife Task

The nervous system of a very simple synthetic animal is modelled through a feed-forward neural network (Rumelhart, McClelland 1986). The net is connected to a sensory-motor apparatus via its input and output neurons. The interaction between the sensory-motor system and the environment provides the network with the necessary external feedback cycle. Each animal moves in an environment made of a 2-dimensional lattice (called world) where the cells are marked "1" (food in the cell) or "0" (empty cell) according to a random uniform probability distribution. The animal moves in the world and has to reach as many food objects as possible.

The architecture of our ecological network is simple: a single input unit acts as a sensor neuron and contains coded information about the world (i.e. the normalized angle under which the animal "sees" the nearest food, with respect to its facing direction). The two output units act as motor neurons and contain coded information about the moves of the animal (stay still, turn left, turn right, or move forward one cell). Figure 1 shows the architecture of the animal network.

1. Animal Neural Network Architecture

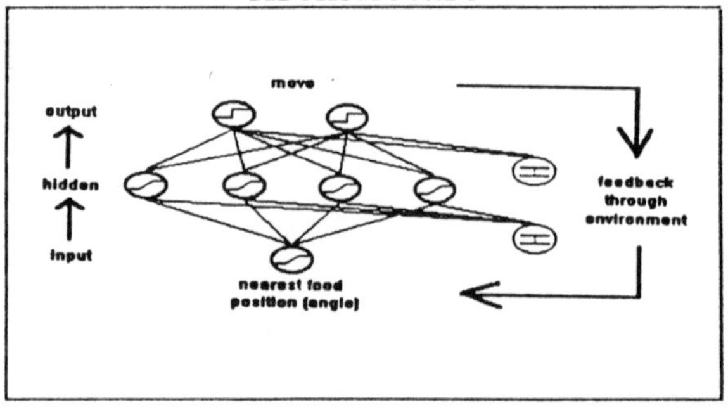

The world lattice is periodic on both dimensions, assuming a toroidal shape, so that the animal always moves in an area where the food is not too far, if there is any food at all. The world has a linear dimension of C = 10 or 20 cells. Life consists of C2/2 network spreading cycles in a certain world, each cycle corresponding to a move; each time the animal steps into a cell that contains a piece of food, the food is automatically eaten. The average amount of food eaten by an animal during its lifetimes, normalized into the unit interval, is the fitness function to be maximized.

2.2. Stochastic Genetic Learning

Now that the task has been defined, a training procedure is needed to search for an optimal point in the network's weight space. We look for an unsupervised form of learning, where information about the fitness is gathered only through interaction with the environment, so we turn to a stochastic genetic algorithm (Menczer, Parisi 1990; Holland 1975; Goldberg 1989; Menczer, Parisi 1991). This method is based on the genetic paradigm of population evolution through selection of fit individuals and reproduction, and thus it meets the requirements of our biological framework. We map the network's weight matrix onto a genotype structure simply by representing the network as a real vector, each component encoding a connection weight explicitly. Figure 2 illustrates how a real genotype is constructed (Menczer, Parisi 1990; Menczer, Parisi 1991; Montana, Davis 1989; Whitley, Hanson 1989) : the actual animal is determined univocally by its connection weights, which are represented in a block matrix; each column in the connection matrix corresponds to the fan-in of a unit in the network.

2. Genotype-Phenotype Fan-In Mapping

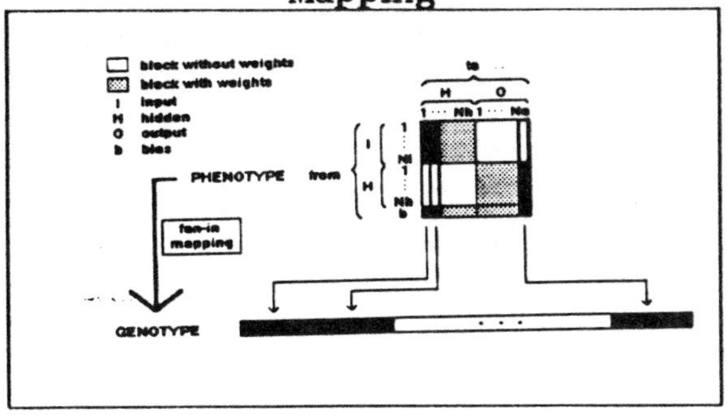

A random population of individuals is generated initially: each weight of each individual is assigned a random real number with uniform distribution in a given interval I = [-Wmax, + Wmax]. Thus the initial points are uniformly distributed in a hypervolume (2Wmax)N centered at the origin, where N is the dimension of the weight space. The values Wmax = 5, N = 18 are used.

Once all the individuals in the population have lived in a number of different worlds and their fitness values have been measured, a stochastic selective pressure acts upon them, so individuals with higher fitness have greater probability of being selected for reproduction. The stochasticity of the process, which helps to prevent the population from getting stuck in local maxima, is determined by the selection probability distribution, a monotone function of fitness given by:

$$p(f(w)) = \frac{exp(f(w)/T)}{>_{w'}(exp(f(w')/T))}$$

where w is the point in weight space, p is the selection probability, f is the fitness and T is a parameter called "temperature". The p(f) distribution must accomplish a trade-off between two opposite and equally dangerous tendencies: if p(f) is too steep, only the most fit individuals will reproduce, with a premature convergence of the population to sub-optimal fitness maxima; if p(f) is not steep enough, there will be no convergence. The T parameter determines the steepness of the probability distribution function, and should be tuned for the desired trade-off (Menczer, Parisi 1990). A way of containing random drift is to perform a kind of annealing (Kirkpatrick, Gelatt, Vecchi 1983) on T. A linear relation

$$T = 1/2 - <f>/2$$

between temperature and population mean fitness is used in some of our simulations: as a result, better exploration takes place in the beginning of the search and the population escapes local fitness maxima more easily.

After the population is initialized, the G.A. consists in the repetition of a cycle made of the following five steps:

1) selection of two parent individuals according to the p(w) distribution;
2) application of the genetic operators to the parent individuals to obtain two "child" individuals;
3) life of child individuals and measure of their fitness;
4) substitution of child individuals in place of two "dead" individuals chosen at random with uniform probability;
5) fitness, temperature and selection probabilities updating (p(w) renormalized).

2.3. Operators and Convergence

Two genetic operators are used for the search process: random mutation and two-cut crossover.

Mutation is always applied in reproduction because it models the physical errors made during the copying of the genetic material from the parents to the children. Each element in a child genotype is replaced, with probability mu, by a new value chosen at random from I with uniform probability distribution. The parameter mu, called mutation rate, is a measure of error and must be chosen carefully because it can be responsible for premature convergence (an effect of genetic drift due to sampling error).

Crossover can serve as a model of isogamous recombination, because it operates in the following way: given any two parent genomes, it crosses them by "cutting" the genotype vectors in 2 positions; there is no preferential crossing position, as illustrated in figure 3. Then the genome segments between cuts are exchanged. Crossover is applied only with probability x.

3. Two-Cut Crossover Recombination Operator

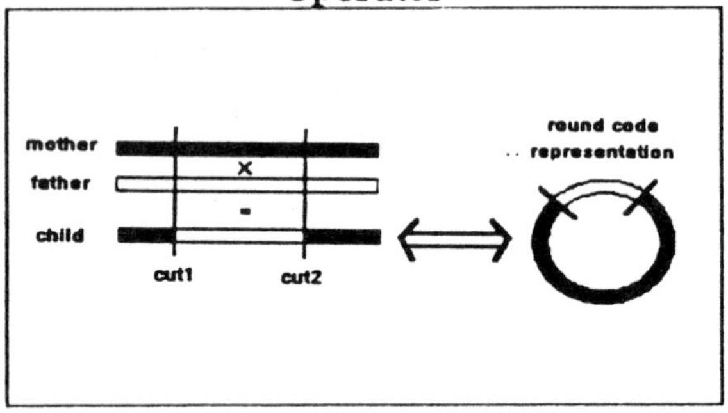

From a purely algorithmic point of view (Davis 1989) the crossover probability x is a very important parameter, as the learning behaviour depends on it. But for us this number is even more crucial, because it represents a quantitative measure of how much sexual reproduction is used in the population, while (1-x) is a measure for asexual reproduction.

Let us first analyze the effect of mutation rate on convergence. If we set x=0 and perform simulations for different mu values, we obtain the results shown in figure 4. It is clear that the lower the mu, the faster the fitness growth. This is because most mutations are obviously deleterious. In the extreme mu=0, we are performing error-free copies and the population quickly converges to a sub-optimal fitness. Mutations are necessary for exploring the weight space and escaping local maxima, so we must set mu > 0. Our first choice is a small mu, say 0.001, but we will see in what follows that such a naive choice doomes a trait not directly selected to be fixed under the effect of random drift in the evolution process. For now, however, we are only considering fitness, which is selected, so a small mu is appropriate.

4. Effect of the mu parameter on mean fitness for x=0

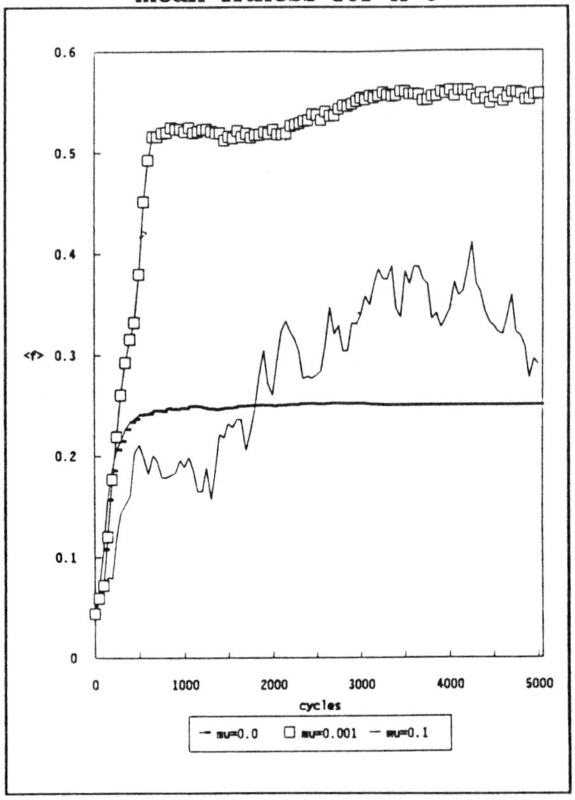

Let us now monitor the effect of the global crossover probability in simulations with different x values. Figure 5 illustrates the situation: a non-zero crossover probability is indeed advantageous as it affords a better convergence. (An interpretation of this result, although for a more local type of mutation, is given in Menczer, Parisi 1991.) Clearly some high x would seem optimal, and in the next section we will describe a model in which such an optimum should emerge from competition among individuals.

Figure 6 gives an idea of the strategies evolved by the best animals in a few thousand cycles of our stochastic GA.

5. Effect of the x global parameter on mean fitness for mu=0.001

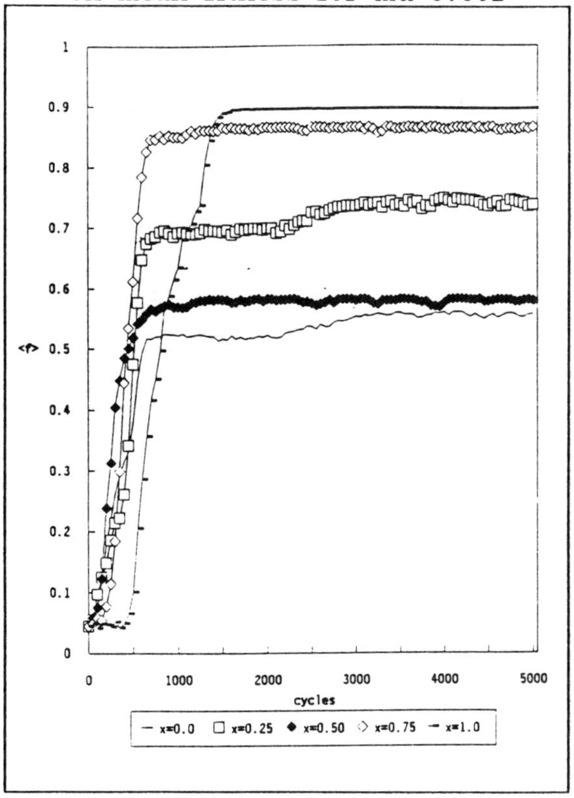

6. Animal Eating Strategies after 0 and 5000 cycles

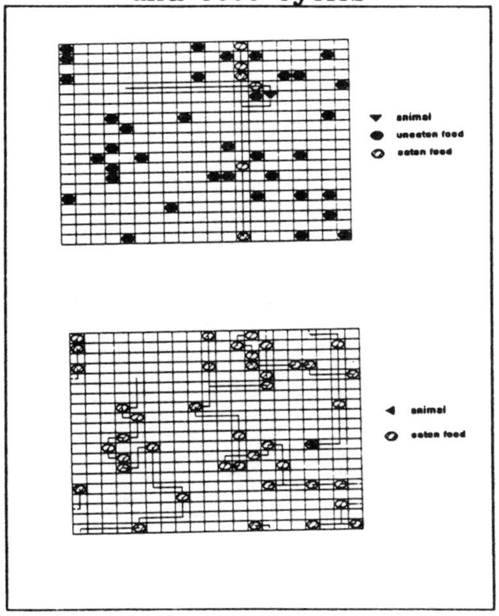

3. The Model

Up to now we considered the operator frequencies as global parameters, shared by the whole population: the crossover probability x is the same and fixed for all individuals. Conversely, if the measure for sexual recombination is to emerge from the dynamics of the evolution-by-selection process itself, it ought to become a local parameter. If we associate an x value to each individual, this trait will undergo the same selective pressure as the genome of the individual to which it is linked. Thus the competition among the individuals has also an effect on their crossover probabilities: if there exist "good" x's, the linked individuals receive a push in terms of fitness and are more likely selected, together with their x's. Using the terminology of population genetics, a locus in the genome vector of an individual acts as a "modifier" for that individual's reproduction mechanism. Genetic variability for the modifier locus must be guarantied in order for selection to have a pool of available alternatives.

The system is implemented in the following way: each animal/network has two extra elements in the genotype vector, "appended" to the connection weights. Let the population be made of P individuals, i = 1,...,P. A first element x(i) in the unit interval [0,1] represents the crossover probability of animal i. The necessary variability on the modifier locus is obtained by initializing the vector X at random with uniform probability density. After two parent individuals (i,j) are selected, they use crossover for reproduction with the average probability

$$< x(i,j) > \; = \; (\, x(i) \; + \; x(j) \,) \; / \; 2,$$

and they do not with the remaining probability (1- < x(i,j) >). The crossover probabilities of the child individuals are equal to those of the parents at birth, and then are subject to being mutated (in the unit interval) with the same procedure as the rest of the genome vector. One more element c(i) in [0,1] is associated to each animal i: C is a statistical control for X in that it undergoes exactly the same dynamics, with the difference that it has no active role in the genetic process.

4. Results

In this section an outline of the simulations performed is presented. The computational load of the stochastic GA used in connection with our ALife task is heavy: in order to average out the noise of the fitness and X measures, each experiment is repeated with several different initial conditions. A typical simulation requires a few hours on a RISC/6000 machine.

4.1. What to Expect

The purpose of the simulations is to study the behaviour of X under the action of selection. The population mean, < x >, is our estimate of the optimal recombination probability. Before presenting the data, let us see what can be anticipated from theory. The central point is that, for an individual i, x(i) is not used to compute the fitness f(i). Thus, selection is guided by a measure which is independent from the trait that we are monitoring. Actually, f(i) and x(i) are somehow correlated, but in an indirect way: x(i) has an effect on the growth rate of f(i), so that we could write:

$$x(i,t) = g(df(i,t)/dt)$$

where g is an unknown function. Given this premise, there are two types of drift to which X may be subject: the one due to neutral selection and the other due to directional selection. The former type (Kimura 1983) is a weak drift generated solely by the processes of randomly sampling the finite population and copying (reproduction). In other words, even if the probability of selection were a constant, independent from f (T = infinity), some x values would still diffuse in the population and so <x> would be drifted toward some value different from the initial <x> = 1/2. Such a value would be "selected" without being of any advantage. Mutating X prevents fixation (i.e. spurious convergence with all identical x's): the higher mu, the lower probability of fixation, the longer time in which <x> keeps floating. The second type of drift (Michod, Levin 1988) is much stronger: for low T values directional selection (toward higher f) accelerates the "neutral" drift by the hitchhiking effect, so that the x values initially associated at random with the fittest individuals colonize the population and are rapidly fixed. This "spurious" convergence should be considered a natural evolutionary force rather than an interference.

4.2. Simulations and Parameters

The first simulation is a control experiment on the weak drift from neutral selection. In figure 7 we plot <c> versus time (GA cycles) with T = infinity, or random, fitness-independent, selection. It is readily seen that a "diffusion" process is the consequence of neutral selection: <c> floats toward values distant from the expected average 1/2. The lines in each graph represent different random initial conditions, resulting in different evolutionary courses. High mu values limit the drift, while mu = 0 allows a faster fixation of C.

Figure 7. Control Experiment: Weak Drift by Neutral Selection

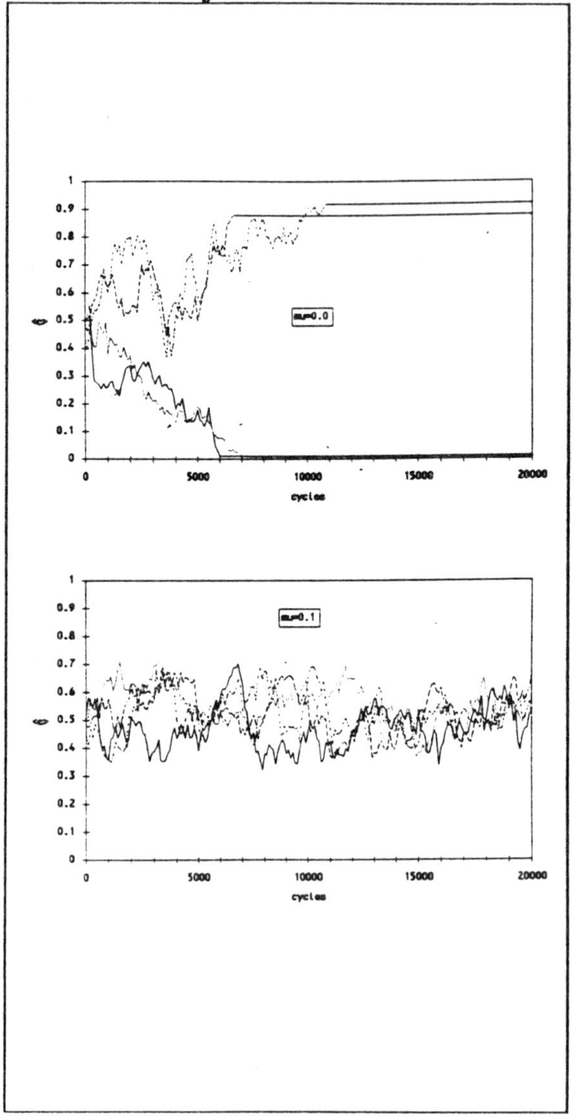

Next we see directional selection: with T = 0.1 the fittest individuals are selected and their c's are advantaged. Figure 8 shows the quick fixation of <c> in a few runs: such spurious convergence takes place for <x> as well, producing a large uncertainty on the emergent behaviour of the modifier locus for sexual recombination. We do not want to eliminate random drift, which is intrinsic in natural evolution, but in order to be sure that this effect does not cancel the significance of the <x> measure, we must tune the parameters so that <c> does not reach fixation before <x> converges.

8. Strong Drift by Directional Selection with mu=0.001

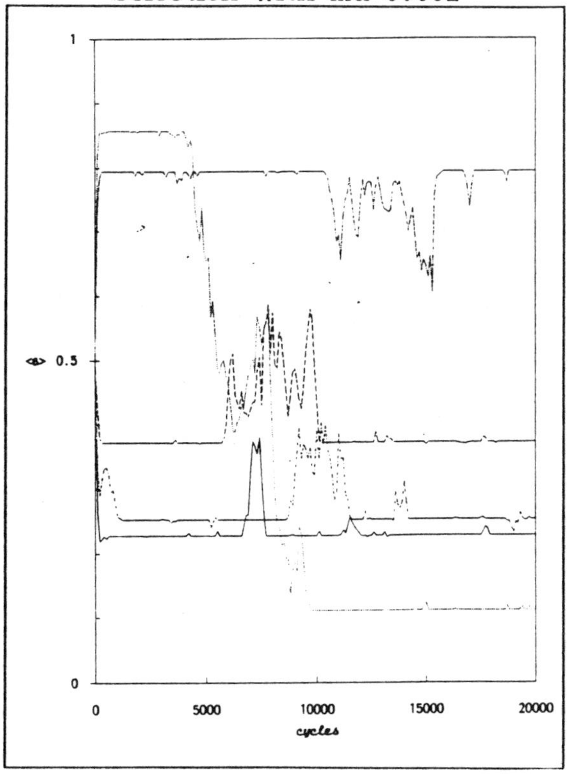

The main parameter that can be adjusted to contain random drift and allow a significant measure of <x> is mutation rate. We have seen that a low mu results in a strong drift under fitness selection. Too high a mu is unplausible and slows down the evolution - in the limit mu = 1 the adaptive search is no longer local. So we look at neutral selection and choose the lowest mu such that C does not reach fixation within the time scale used for monitoring X. This is done by controlling that the dispersion of <c> over different runs remains reasonably constant in time. The simulations tell us that mu = 0.1 is a good choice.

Raising the temperature also affects random drift by weakening selective pressure and increasing noise: the simulations show that this is beneficial only at the beginning of evolution, in order to slow down the initial spurious convergence. The problem is in keeping T constant, while natural selective pressure increases as the species differentiate. So we make temperature a decreasing function of the mean fitness, as shown in section 2.2., with a smoothing effect on <x>'s initial behaviour. Since <f> varies roughly from 0.05 to 0.8, T goes from about 0.5 to 0.1.

In figure 9 the evolution of recombination in a simulation with mu = 0.001 and constant T = 0.1 is shown versus one with mu = 0.1 and linear T(<f>). The error intervals correspond to ± 1 standard deviation of the results from the different runs. The positive effect on <x>'s statistical significance should be clear. The value to which <x> converges is somewhere around 0.7: this is high, as expected, although not as much as figure 5 suggested.

9. Tuning T and mu for Controlling Random Drift

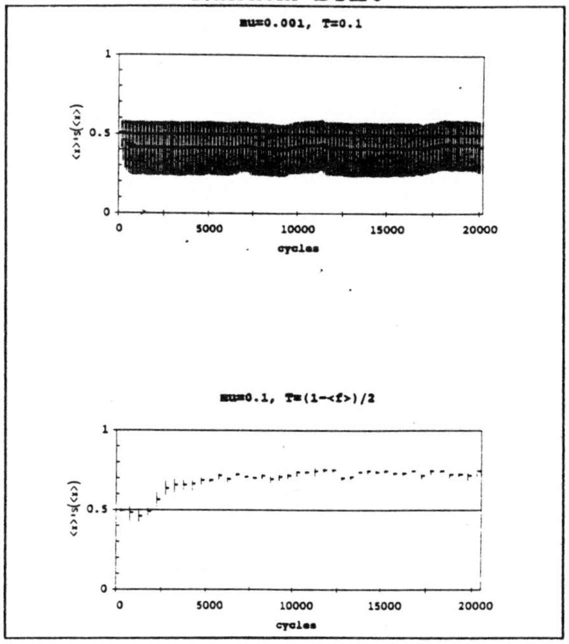

Another quantity whose effect is considered important is population size. In the range of 100-1000 individuals, raising the size of the sample reduces the neutral diffusion effect and regularizes fitness growth. However, random drift from directional selection is not meaningfully affected: large populations, just like high constant temperatures, slow down the <x> convergence, which is beneficial only in the beginning. A population between 250-500 individuals seems adequate in most cases.

4.3. Spurious vs. Adaptive Convergence

What we have done so far is a run-time monitoring of the population mean recombination probability. But much additional information on what actually happens can be found from looking at the evolution of individual x values.

Figure 10 presents the histograms of the frequency distributions of X and C. At different GA times, the number of individuals with probabilities in each interval is shown. For example, the distributions after 0 cycles are the Monte Carlo implementations of the initial uniform distributions for X and C. From comparing the X histogram with its C control, we see immediately that the emergence of a high < x > could not be the sole effect of random drift. A second, more important observation can be made: while the c distribution has a peak which floats in time but coincides with < c > (see also figure 11), the x distribution is skewed toward 1; now, since x is bounded in the unit interval, a distribution peaked in x = 1 is truncated and this explains why the mode does not coincide with < x >. The mode is in our case better than the arithmetic mean as an estimation of the optimal recombination probability emerged from the simulations: thus, the agreement with the performances of figure 5 turns out to be very good. A similar conclusion on the role of the variable x on the fitness trend can be drawn from looking at figure 11, where < f >, < x > and < c > from a single-run simulation are plotted. It should be evident that < f > and < x > are strongly correlated, and this doesn't show after averaging over different runs. Essentially, the fact that the fitness "follows" the recombination frequency means that higher recombination rates are advantageous.

10. Frequency Distributions for X and C

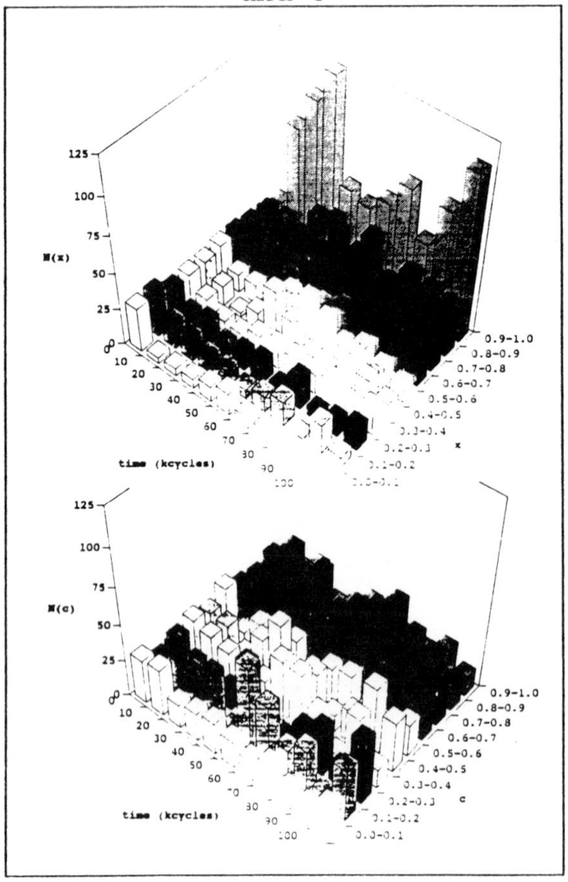

11. Single-Run Simulation Results

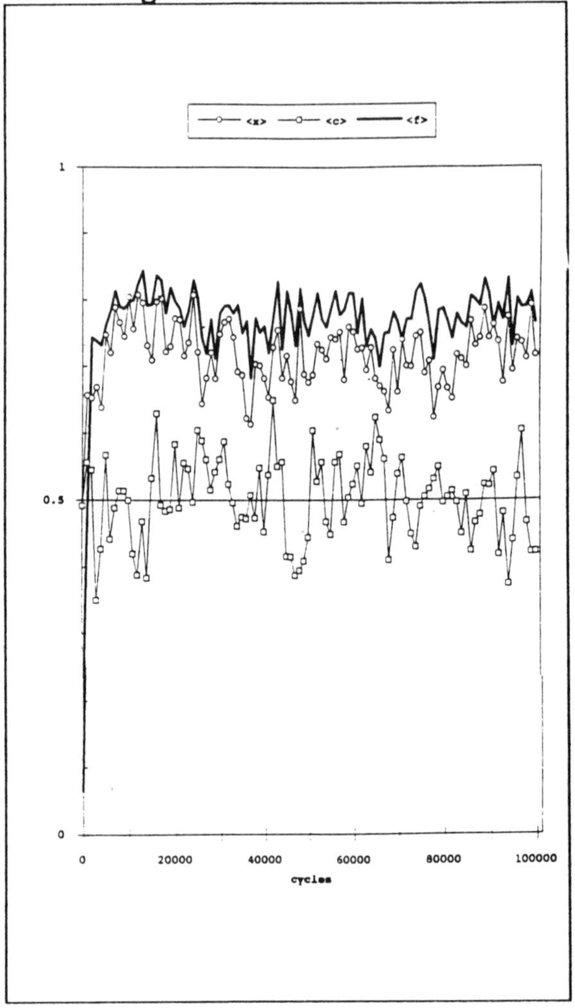

One final observation deserves mentioning. If we plot the population variances, s2x and s2c, as is done in figure 12 for the simulation of figure 11, we see that the former does not fall below the latter: although the separation between < x > and < c > is significant, x's distribution does not become more peaked than c's. In our opinion this is due to the high mutation rate, which on one side limits random drift and on another preserves the genetic variability for the recombination modifier.

12. Significance of Emergent <x> Estimations

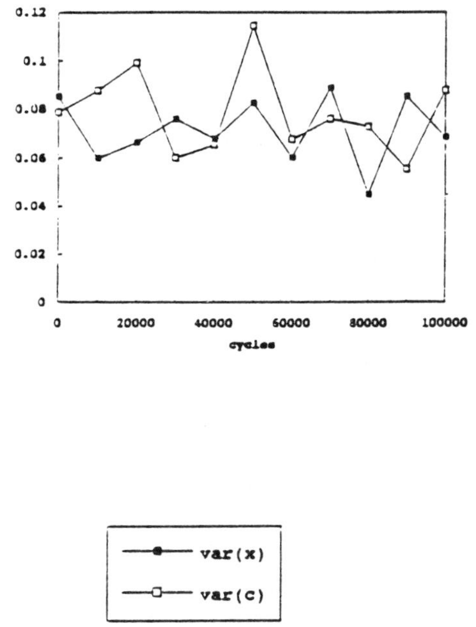

Conclusion

An effort was made to make the tools of ALife, in conjunction with GA's and neural networks, available for the study of an unsolved Natural Life problem.

The results obtained so far indicate that adaptive advantages do exist in genetic recombination, and that these may have played an important role in the evolution of sexual reproduction. Future efforts should be devoted to clarify which mechanisms of sex generate the critical advantages. A possible direction is to investigate how a fluctuating environment would affect the dynamics of selection on recombination.

In the beginning of this project we were frustrated by the apparent "randomness" of the results. As the picture became more clear and the central role of random drift in such uncertainty began to appear, we realized that we were dealing with an important evolutionary force. It is our belief that this force must be given proper consideration if anything emerged in Natural Life is to be studied through adaptive ALife models.

References

Davis L.. *Adapting Operator Probabilities in Genetic Algorithms* - in J. D. Schaffer (Editor): Proc. 3rd Int. Conf. on Genetic Algorithms - M. Kaufmann, Palo Alto, CA, 61-69 (1989)

Goldberg D.E. *Genetic Algorithms in Search, Optimization and Machine Learning* - Addison-Wesley (1989)

Holland J.H. *Adaptation in Natural and Artificial Systems* - Ann Arbor: Univ. of Michigan Press (1975)

Kimura M. *The Neutral Theory of Molecular Evolution* - Cambridge University Press (1983)

Kirkpatrick S., Gelatt C.D., Vecchi M.P. *Optimization by Simulated Annealing* - Science, vol. 220, 671-680 (1983)

Menczer F., Parisi D. *Evidence of Hyperplanes in the Genetic Learning of Neural Networks* - "Biological Cybernetics", in press

Menczer F., Parisi D. *Sexual vs. Agamic Reproduction in Neural Networks* - PCIA Technical Report, Institute of Psychology CNR, Rome, Italy (1990) [submitted to "NETWORK"]

Michod R.E., B. R. Levin (Editors): *The Evolution of Sex, An examination of Current Ideas* - Sinauer, Sunderland, MA (1988)

Montana D.J., Davis L. *Training Feedforward Neural Networks Using Genetic Algorithms* - Proc. 11th IJCAI - M. Kaufmann, 1, 762-767 (1989)

Parisi D., Cecconi F., Nolfi S. *ECONETS: Neural Networks that Learn in an Environment* - Network, 1, 149-168 (1990)

Patarnello S.,Carnevali P. *A Neural Network Model to Simulate a Conditioning Experiment* - International Journal of Neural Systems, 1 (1), 47-53 (1989)

Rumelhart D.E., McClelland J.L. (Editors): *Parallel Distributed Processing: Explorations in the Microstructure of Cognition*, vol. 1 - MIT Press, Cambridge, MA: Bradford Books (1986)

Whitley D., Hanson T.: *Optimizing Neural Networks Using Faster, More Accurate Genetic Search* - in J. D. Schaffer (Editor): Proc. 3rd Int. Conf. on Genetic Algorithms - M. Kaufmann, Palo Alto, CA, 391-396 (1989)

Species Adaptation Genetic Algorithms: A Basis for a Continuing SAGA

Inman Harvey
School of Cognitive and Computing Sciences
University of Sussex
Brighton BN1 9QH, England
email: inmanh@cogs.susx.ac.uk

Abstract

For Artificial Life applications it is useful to extend Genetic Algorithms from a finite search space with fixed-length genotypes to open-ended evolution with variable-length genotypes. A new theoretical analysis is required, as Holland's Schema Theorem only applies to fixed lengths. It will be argued, using concepts of epistasis and fitness landscapes drawn from theoretical biology, that in the long run a population must have genotypes of nearly equal length, and this length can only increase slowly. As the length increases, the population will be nearly converged, and hence evolving as a species.

1 Introduction

Genetic algorithms (GAs) are a form of search technique, primarily used for function optimization, modelled on Darwinian evolution. Some basic knowledge of GAs, is assumed for the purposes of this paper; the best introduction is (Goldberg 1989). Holland's Schema Theorem has provided the theoretical underpinning for GAs (Holland 1975, Goldberg 1989); this Schema Theorem assumes that all the genotypes in a population are the same length, and remain so through successive generations. In the messier world of natural evolution these assumptions do not hold, which prompts questions such as:

- Could some more generalized version of this theorem be extended to include variable length genotypes?
- Are there circumstances in which they might be of use in GAs?

In speaking of variable length genotypes I will be making some assumptions, spelt out later, about how those extra parts on long genotypes, not present on the shorter ones, contribute to their fitness. But the answers to these two questions will be, firstly: no, there is no such immediate generalization, but rather a very different process is at work as genotypes change length, which must be analysed independently. And secondly: for traditional function optimization problems they are unlikely to be of use, but they will be in Artificial Life.

Manipulation of schemata in the conventional analysis of GAs can be interpreted in terms of intersections of hyperplanes in the predefined search-space — for instance in the case of binary genotypes of length l, the search-space is a hypercube of l dimensions. If this length is variable, it is not easy to extend this notion of a search space satisfactorily. An alternative characterization of a genotype search space, perhaps less familiar to the GA community, is borrowed from theoretical biology; this lends itself more easily to variation in length of genotype.

It will be argued that for progress through such a space to be feasible, it only makes sense for genotypic variation in length to be relatively gentle. It follows that instead of attempting a generalization of the Schema Theorem to genotypes of any length, the analysis of the convergence of a population of nearly uniform length can and should be decoupled from the analysis of changes in length. A general trend towards increase in length is associated with the evolution of a *species* rather than global search. The word *species* I am using to refer a fit population of relative genotypic homogeneity.[1]

As to the question of under what circumstances variable lengths might be of use in GAs, it would seem that for such traditional GA concerns as function optimization in a pre-defined domain, one would do best to stick to fixed lengths. In the context of Artificial Life, however, where an animat is evolving in an environment with unknown complexity, then variability in genotype length becomes relevant. A genotype space can be open-ended if the environment itself alters over time, perhaps in response to the evolution of the animat itself. The classic case is the *Red Queen* (or *Arms Race*) phe-

[1] It will follow from this that crosses between members of the same species have a good chance of being another fit member of the same species; whereas crosses between different species will almost certainly be unfit.

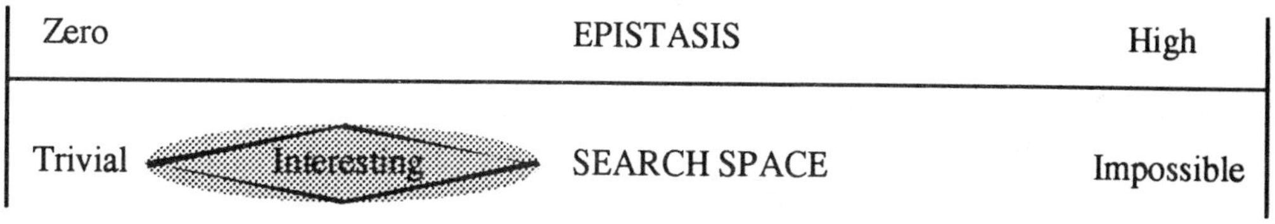

Figure 1: *Low, but non-zero, epistasis is associated with a search space that is possible, but non-trivial.*

nomenon of coevolution of different species interacting with each other, where one can expect over time both the phenotype complexity and the genotype length to increase.

The notion of a search space is a metaphor which is usually a useful one. It does, however, imply a space of pre-defined extent, with a pre-defined or recognizable goal. In the natural world, tempting though it may be for any one species to think of evolution as a 4 billion year search for a goal of something very like them, it is evident that any such notion of a goal can only be *a posteriori*. So in order to distinguish the space of possibilities that a species can move in from that of a conventional search space, I shall use the term *SAGA space*[2]. This corresponds to the acronym for Species Adaptation Genetic Algorithms, the altered and extended version of GAs necessary to deal with such a space.

2 Variable lengths in GAs

Variable length genotypes have been used in GAs in, for instance, Messy GAs (Goldberg *et al.* 1990), LS-1 classifiers (Smith 1980), Koza's genetic programming (Koza 1990). The first of these in fact uses an underlying fixed-length representation. The analyses offered in the other two examples do not satisfactorily extend the notion of a schema such that schemata are preserved by the genetic operators.

For instance, Koza's genetic programming (Koza 1990) uses populations of programs which are given in the form of LISP S-expressions; these can be depicted as rooted point-labeled trees with ordered branches. The primary genetic operator of crossover, or recombination, swaps complete sub-trees between the parents, and if these sub-trees are of different size then the offspring will have genotypes of different lengths from their parents.

Koza suggests that the equivalent of a schema in the search space of such programs can be specified initially by any one specific sub-tree. Since the set of all potential programs containing that sub-tree is infinite, Koza finds it necessary to partition it into finite subsets indexed by the length of the program, and it is these subsets that are considered as schemata. The number of occurrences in the reproductive pool of examples of a particular schema which, as sampled in the parental pool, shows above-average fitness, will indeed tend to increase. But this does not cater for the fact that the crossover operator will in general turn the offspring into programs of different lengths, and hence disrupt the schema which has been defined by program length. A possible way to minimize this disruption would be to restrict the possible variations in length to only minimal changes, and indeed this will be echoed in the conclusions reached further on in this paper.

The obvious way to extend the crossover operator from fixed-length to variable-length genotypes is by randomly choosing different crossover positions for each of the two parents; an offspring may then inherit two short portions, or two long portions, and in general will have a genotype of significantly different length. It will be shown that this approach is flawed.

3 Epistasis

A gene is the unit of analysis in determining the phenotype, and hence its fitness, from the genotype; it is coded for by a small subsection of the genotype. The term epistasis refers to the linkage between genes on the genotype, such that the expression of one gene modifies or over-rules the expression of another gene.

If there is no epistasis, in other words if the fitness contribution of each element on the genotype is unaffected by the values of any of the others, then optimization can be carried out independently on each element; simple hill-climbing is adequate. At the other end of the epistatic scale, where there are many dependencies between the elements, the only useful building blocks that a GA tries to manipulate are too long, and easily disrupted by genetic operators. Indeed in the limit of maximum epistasis only random search is feasible. The appropriate region on the epistatic scale suitable for GA type search is between these two extremes, and GA representations need to be chosen with this in mind (Davidor 1990).

4 Uncorrelated Landscapes

A model of a genotype search space which allows explicit setting of low or high degrees of epistasis is based on the concept of a protein space, originally introduced in (Maynard Smith 1970). This space has a point for each possible example of a genotype, and a neighbour-

[2]"Saga ... story of heroic achievement or adventure; series of connected books giving the history of a family etc. [Old Norse = narrative]." Concise Oxford Dictionary.

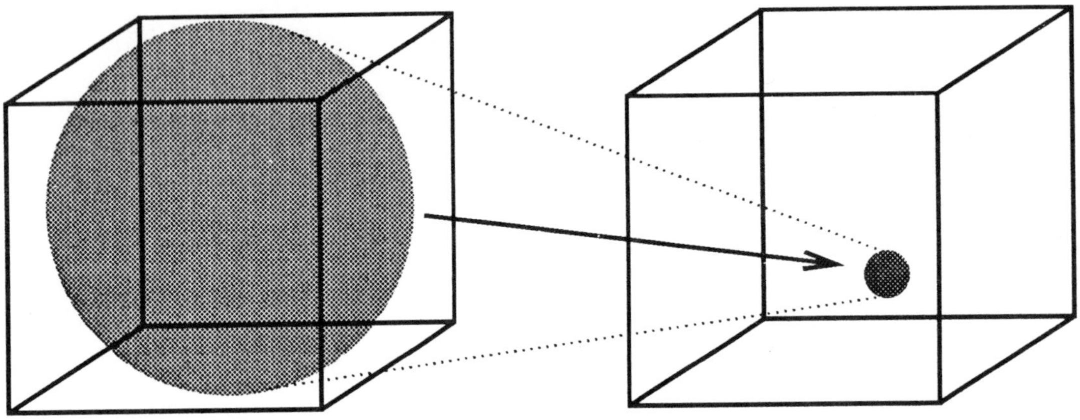

Figure 2: *The evolution of a standard GA in a fixed-dimensional search space; the population initially spans the whole space, and in the end focusses on the optimum.*

hood metric which gives all those other points which can be reached by a single mutation from a given point. Compared with the traditional GA analysis, which takes a global view of the whole search space, and considers how a population of points in this search space can effectively range across it by use of recombination, we now have a very different perspective. Here mutation is the only genetic operator, instead of just a background one to prevent irremediable loss of an allele.

Kauffman (Kauffman and Levin 1987, Kauffman) has extended this model to produce a general theory of adaptive walks on rugged fitness landscapes — where the distribution of fitness values across the space is visualised as a landscape with fitness represented by the height. It should be noted that the fitness values are ascribed to points on a lattice rather than a continuum. Nevertheless the landscape can be imagined as a mountain range, where ruggedness implies a relative lack of correlation of heights of nearby points, which in turn is associated with high epistasis on the genotype.

Gillespie's assumptions (Gillespie 1984), that the mutation rate is slow compared to the assimilation of any fitter mutation by the population as a whole, are being used. The population as a whole is considered to be at a single point in the space, with mutations of single members sampling the immediately neighbouring points. Any less fit mutations die out rapidly, whereas any fitter one causes, by this assumption, the whole population to move to that point.[3]

If the fitnesses of neighbouring points on this landscape are completely uncorrelated, then it is maximally rugged. In an adaptive walk on such a landscape if the first step upwards, from the bottom rank of fitness, takes one unit of time, then the next step upwards, where only half the neighbours are fitter, takes on average 2 units, then 4, 8, ..., doubling each time (Kauffman and Levin 1987).

5 Correlated landscapes

The above discussion is for a completely uncorrelated landscape — which can be considered equivalent to maximum epistasis between the genes on the genotype. In most fitness landscapes there is, however some local correlation, in that neighbours will tend to have similar fitness values, and certainly this is true of any search space in which GAs are to be of use. Let length be defined in this space using the distance metric of how many point mutations are necessary to move from one genotype to another. A long jump is defined to be the equivalent of several *simultaneous* mutations, long enough to jump beyond the correlation lengths in the landscape. Moves via such long jumps will in general display important similarities with the characteristics of uncorrelated landscapes (except that in the limit of long jumps all points are accessible, and hence the notion of a local optimum becomes meaningless). In particular the above result still holds: that the waiting time until finding a fitter

[3]This is a more restricted assumption than that in (Eigen and Schuster 1979), where a population under the influence of selection and a low mutation rate in general moves to form a *quasi-species*, with a probability distribution centred about a point. Eigen and Schuster show that for a given selective pressure, the maximum length of genotype that can be reliably held in a tight distribution at an optimum is of the order of magnitude of the reciprocal of the mutation rate. Mutation rates of 5×10^{-4} per base by single-stranded RNA replication is adequate for a phage with length 4500. The lower mutation rates of order 10^{-9} associated with DNA replication and recombination in eukaryotes allow for the genotypes of length order 10^9 that humans have.

variant by such long jumps doubles after each such improvement.

Kauffman further considers a different assumption from that used above; suppose that instead of a single mutant being sampled at each unit of time, there is a large population of fixed size simultaneously sampling different mutants, and the population then moves as a whole to the fittest of any improved variant encountered. It is shown that the above result on waiting times remains almost unchanged.

This search process is of course very different from that analysed in conventional GAs, where a population of points effectively spans the search space, and recombination allows effective moves to predominate. The distinction between these two types of search process must be kept in mind when we turn to looking at variable length genotypes.

6 Variable length genotypes

Let us spell out some assumptions about a genetic system with variation in the length of genotypes, within which many different types of representation, or mapping from genotype to phenotype to fitness, could be allowed.

- Firstly, it is assumed that the genotype can be analysed in terms of a number of small building blocks, or genes, that are coded for individually on it; possibly by a single symbol, or a sequence of symbols. These genes can be uniquely identified, either by their position by reference to an identified end of the genotype, as in conventional GAs; or by an attached tag or template, such as those used in messy GAs (Goldberg *et al.* 1990). Longer genotypes will code for genes that are not present at all on shorter ones.

- Secondly, it is assumed that each gene makes a separate additive contribution to the fitness of the whole; but that the contribution of any one gene can be modified by epistatic interactions with a number K of the other genes. This number K is less than the total number of genes available, otherwise the fitness landscape would be uncorrelated.

- Thirdly it is assumed that the total of all these additive contributions is then normalized in some way such that the final fitness remains within some predefined bound regardless of how many genes there are.

This last condition reflects the fact that any fitness function is only relevant in so far as it affects the selection process. On average in the long term each member of a viable population will be replaced by just one offspring. Less than one and the population is heading for extinction, more than one implies exponential growth. But there are always finite physical resource limitations which prevent such unlimited growth, and this has to be taken account of in the fitness function.

All these assumptions allow a standard GA to operate when lengths are fixed. In addition to the normal genetic operators of mutation and crossover, we assume that there are further operators, perhaps *cut* and *splice*, or *increase-length*, which allow offspring to have their length changed by arbitrary amounts, although still retaining at least some genetic material from their parent(s).

Suppose that there are a total of G different genes represented in the population, some perhaps represented in all genotypes and some in only a few. Then by adding an extra allele for each gene, to indicate whether it is 'absent' in a particular genotype, a new representation of the population can be formed in which every gene is represented in every member. Genetic operators which do not introduce a completely new gene into the population allow this to be analysed as a normal GA.

Suppose now that the genetic operators allow, by lengthening a genotype, the creation of a *single* new gene, giving a new total of $G+1$. By the second and third assumptions made explicit above, the epistasis of this new gene is similar to that of the previous ones. The new population can now be considered as being spread across a new $(G+1)$-dimensional search space, except that all bar one member is confined within the previous G-dimensional sub-space. This can still be analysed as a normal GA with an initially skewed population. If a single advantageous new gene appears in the population, it can become widespread through crossovers.

In contrast to this, an alternative possibility is that the genetic operators allow the creation in one generation of a *large number* g of new genes on one genotype. In the new $(G+g)$-dimensional search space, the old population is based entirely inside the original (in relative terms, very small) G-dimensional subspace, with just the one new point exploring elsewhere. This is obviously a 'long jump' and the fitness will be uncorrelated with that of any of the previous generation. If such a long jump is successful, in the sense that the new genes are retained in the population, with a resulting general increase in the fitness of the population, then the chances of a successful further long jump will be significantly less. Any such long jump adaptation will suffer from the problem of the doubling of waiting time after each jump.

The picture now emerges of two very different processes going on at independent timescales in this SAGA space. Given a genetic operator which allows unrestricted changes in length of genotypes, we can expect the following sequence of events in a locally correlated landscape:

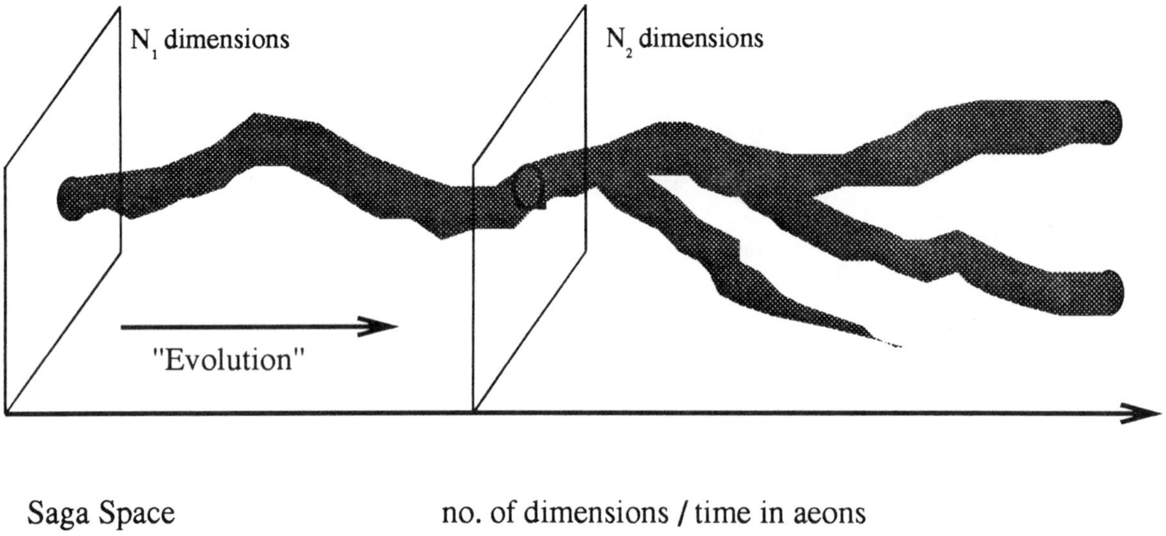

Figure 3: *The progress of the always compact course of a species; the* z *axis indicates both time and the (loosely correlated) number of dimensions of the current search space. The* x *and* y *axes represent just two of the current number of dimensions.*
The possibility of splitting into separate species, and of extinction, are indicated in the sketch, although not here discussed.

- An early population could fluctuate in length through 'long jump' adaptation which effectively acts in an uncorrelated landscape; but as average fitness increases the doubling of waiting times will slow this process down drastically.

- Thereupon the traditional GA operators of crossover and mutation will take over, and Holland's Schema Theorem will be applicable to this phase of the search.

- Those applications of the change-length operator which result in minimal changes of length will be moves on a correlated landscape, and therefore are feasible even if major changes are increasingly unlikely.

- If there are selectionary pressures which encourage the genotype lengths to increase, the population will become a nearly-converged 'species', with an almost uniform length that increases in small steps. [4]

7 SAGA and the Schema Theorem

A schema defines a subset of possible genotypes which share the same values at a specified number of genes. If there is no upper limit to the possible length of the genotype, these subsets will be infinite in size, and estimates of the 'average fitness' of a schema based on any finite sample become problematical.

We might be tempted to avoid this by saying, in this particular example we will restrict the space of possibilities to genotypes of length less than, e.g., 1000. But then 'nearly all' possible instances of a particular schema will refer to genotypes very close to this upper limit, and there may be no reason to expect the average fitness of this schema to bear any significant relationship to the fitness of the same schema restricted to genotypes of maximum length 100, 500 or even 950.

However, consider the case where all the population have the same G gene sites (though with variations in the values at each gene site); and we are considering the addition of one extra gene to one or more of the population. We can recast our analysis in terms of a population all of genotype length $G+1$, with the extra gene having one additional possible value of 'absent'. For any two schemata S_1 and S_2 that have the extra gene fixed as 'absent', let $S_1\prime$ and $S_2\prime$ be the corresponding schemata with the extra gene value allowed any value (including 'absent'). Given the assumption of low epistasis, the relative fitnesses of schemata S_1 and S_2 will be closely correlated with the relative fitnesses of schemata $S_1\prime$ and $S_2\prime$. This will still hold true if we allow an extra g genes rather than just one, provided that g is small in relation to G and the assumption of low epistasis holds. It will not hold true when g is large, or epistasis is high.

Hence in the short term of small changes in genotype length in a population of nearly uniform genotype

[4]These ideas should be neutral in respect of the punctuated equilibria controversy. A succession of small steps may or may not be rapid in geological time — indeed there may well be good reasons why there should be on occasion such a cascade. What is being ruled out here is any single large step.

0	1	1	0	1	1	0
		i'	i	i''		

A: $i, i', i'' = 011$

0	1	1	0	1	1	0
	i''		i			i'

B: $i, i', i'' = 001$

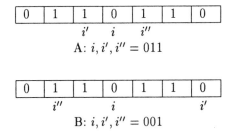

Figure 4: *At the top, gene i is linked to neighbours i', i''. The values 011 point into a fitness look-up table for i. Below, i' and i'' are no longer immediate neighbours.*

	000	0.141
value of B	001	0.592
	010	0.653
value of A	011	0.589
	100	0.793
	101	0.233
	110	0.842
	111	0.916

Figure 5: *Fitness table for gene i, filled with random numbers between 0 and 1. i, i' and i'' determine fitness contribution of gene i to fitness of the whole genotype.*

length, we can still apply the Schema Theorem.

8 Would variable lengths be useful?

Turning now to the second question posed in the introduction, under what circumstances might it be useful to have a genetic operator which allows an increase in the number of genes represented on the genotype? If the problem being tackled is basically a function optimization one, where there is a pre-defined search space with a fixed number of factors that can be coded for on the genotype, then it would be folly not to put them all in at the start, represented in such a way as to minimize the epistasis, and put one's trust in the Schema Theorem.

A major group of problems which cannot be specified in terms of a pre-defined search space involve coevolution of one population with another (or several) which in turn is affected by the first. Since one population is part of the environment for the other, the environment is continually changing (Hillis 1991, Husbands 1991). The same requirements of relatively few epistatic interactions between a gene and those aspects of the environment which it affects and is affected by, hold if an evolutionary process is going to be more than random search.

There are many coevolutionary worlds where an increase in complexity in one population stimulates an increase in complexity of the other, and so on, perhaps indefinitely. So in as much as length of genotype is associated with complexity of the phenotype, we can expect that there is selective pressure for long-term growth in their lengths. Lindgren (Lindgren 1990, Lindgren 1991) models a population of individuals competing with each other at the iterated Prisoner's Dilemma with noise — the population in practice breaks into sub-populations with different strategies. There is no recombination, the only genetic operators being mutation and gene doubling. The particular representation used treats a binary genotype of length 2^h as a look-up table; the history of the last h interactions between competing prisoners, coded in 0's and 1's and considered as a binary number, generates a pointer into this look-up table to determine the strategy. Application of the gene-doubling operator does not in itself generate new strategies, but allows later mutations to generate finer discriminations within that strategy. Hence his representation could be mapped into a different one where the length of the genotype only increases by one step at a time. His results show periods of stasis alternated by periods of unstable dynamics, with a long-term growth in the lengths of the successful sub-populations.

9 Simulation

The NK model (Kauffman and Levin 1987, Kauffman) assumes a binary genotype of length N, where each position represents a gene which is affected by linkage with K others. This is an abstract model in which it is assumed that the fitness of the phenotype can be directly calculated from the values on the genotype.

The three assumptions itemized above hold for the fitness function. In the case of $K = 2$, the fitness contribution of gene i depends on the two others to which it is linked (which may be specified as immediate neighbours, or may be specified at random positions). The binary alleles of i and its 2 neighbours specify a 3-bit number which picks a fitness from an 8-place table of fitnesses associated with gene i — there are N such fitness tables prepared at the start of the simulation, with each place containing a fitness randomly chosen in the range 0 to 1.

The fitness of the genotype is then assessed by adding up the fitnesses thus determined for all N genes, and dividing by N. It can be seen that in this case of $K = 2$, the flipping of a single bit on the genotype will affect the fitness contributions of on average just 3 genes; the other $N-3$ being unaffected, this gives a reasonably correlated fitness landscape. In the limit of $K = N - 1$, where the fitness table associated with each gene would have 2^N places, the flipping of a single bit would alter everything, and the fitness landscape is totally uncorrelated.

This model can be extended to allow for changes in genotype length. The simplifying assumption is made that any new gene appears at the right-hand end of the

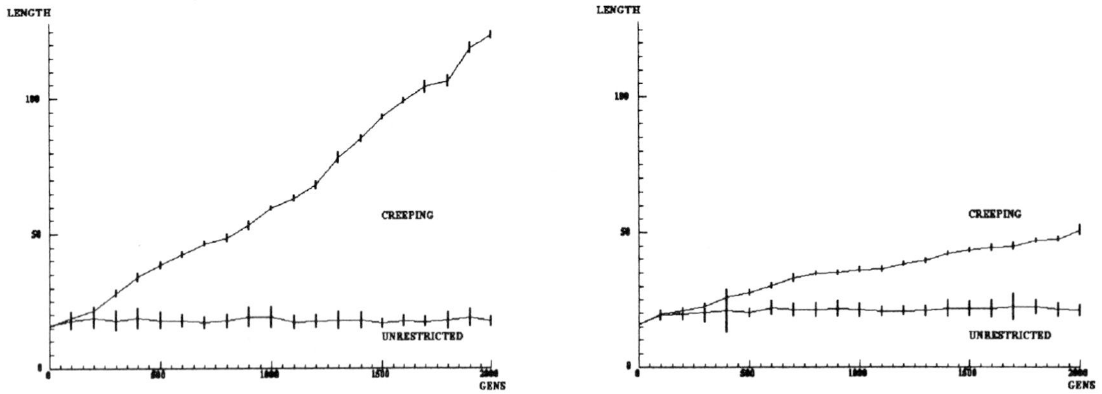

Figure 6: *Average genotype lengths against generations; vertical bars show standard deviations. Effects of 'creeping' and 'unrestricted' increase-length genetic operators on a population with the same fitness conditions, epistasis $K = 2$. Left graph, linkage with neighbouring genes. Right graph, random linkage.*

genotype, and that the identity of the gene is uniquely determined by its position in the genotype. In the case of $K = 2$, if linkage is with immediate neighbours to left and right, the ends are assumed linked in a loop to avoid boundary conditions. A set of tables of random fitness values for each gene is set up for the minimal-length genotype. For each new gene added one new table is generated for it, and two further replacement tables for those genes which are neighbours of the newcomer. This can easily be generalized for $K > 2$, and also for choice of epistatic linkages to newcomers being randomly selected rather than restricted to neighbours.

This allows the setting up of models for simulations with genotypes of any length, with epistasis of any degree. A standard GA can then be run, with increase in the lengths of genotype allowed under specified conditions. Such simulations allow experimentation with variable lengths, in an abstract context, without the difficulties of choice of representation that normal problems give.

Experiments have been run with a population of 100 genotypes, all of initial length $N_{init} = 16$, with epistasis given by $K = 2$, linkages being with neighbouring genes on the genotype; the genetic operators will allow the lengths to increase. The initial fitness of any genotype, as defined by look-up tables of random numbers, was then adjusted by adding a factor proportional to $N/(N+\overline{N})$, where N is the length of the particular genotype and $\overline{N}$ is the current average genotype-length of the population. The constant of proportionality was chosen such that there was a selectionary pressure in favour of longer genotypes comparable to the selectionary pressures given by the initial fitnesses.

In the first trial the genetic operators were crossover, mutation, and an increase-length operator which in 10% of offspring allowed a genotype to increase in length by between 0 and 50%. In the second trial the 'creeping' increase-length operator only allowed an increase of genotype length in the offspring by exactly one. Despite this restriction, the average length increased steadily in the 'creeping' trial as compared to virtually no increase in the 'unrestricted' trial.

On separate trials with the epistatic linkages being with randomly placed genes instead of with neighbouring genes, the results were similar, although with the 'creeping' increase in length at a slower rate. In both sets of trials there was much more variation in lengths within the population in the 'unrestricted' case, compared to the 'creeping'.

10 SAGA and Development

By working with the evolution of a nearly converged species increasing in genotype length and in phenotype complexity over time, we have moved away from the usual GA notion of evolution as a search technique towards a notion of 'evolution as a tinkerer' (Jacob 1989), always adding to or altering something that is already viable.

The cumulative process of additions and alterations implies that a phenotype can be considered as being produced from a genotype by a developmental process. It will not be surprising if 'Ontogeny recapitulates Phylogeny', subject to the small but ever-present possibility of a later alteration bearing on a significantly earlier stage in the developmental process. The application of this approach to, for instance, the evolution of subsumption architectures for robots (Brooks 1991) would seem to correspond to the effective, tinkering, incremental approach that practical designers take.

One consequence will be that a species will only reach those parts of a SAGA space that are connected by a continuous chain of viable ancestors to the origin. Thus within the space of all possible genotypes of length G there may well be a host of fit and viable points or islands which, through isolation and lack of a viable pathway from the origin, are unattainable.

11 SAGA and Genetic Operators

In addition to the usual GA operators of mutation and/or crossover, an operator which allows change in genotype length is necessary. The example in the NK model simulation above is the most trivial such operator, and depends on the identity of any gene being given by its position relative to one end of the genotype. Lindgren's (Lindgren 1991) doubling operator uses a representation which has this same dependency on position.

If the identity of a gene is given by a tag, or by template-matching as seems to happen in the real world of DNA, then absolute positions of genes on the genotype need not be maintained. This allows for duplication of a section of the genotype, after which mutations can differentiate the duplicated parts. The crossover operator can still be used in a fairly homogeneous population with slight variations in genotype length, although given any random crossover point in one parent, a 'sensible' corresponding crossover point in the other parent must be chosen. This can be uniquely defined as that point (or in some cases, any of a contiguous group of points) which maximises the longest common subsequences on both sides of the crossover. A version of the Needleman and Wunsch algorithm makes this computationally feasible (Needleman and Wunsch 1970, Sankoff 1972).

12 Conclusions

With fixed-length genotypes one can afford to think in terms of a fixed, pre-defined search space with a finite number of dimensions which, even if it is immense, is at least theoretically knowable by God or Laplace.

When one allows genotypes to vary in length the search space is potentially infinite and it stops making sense to think of it as predefined. Nevertheless, in the real world, evolution has taken place in such a fashion that we have very distant ancestors whose genotypes were much shorter than ours; the problems we face are not the problems they faced.

When looking at evolution, talking about 'problems being solved' can be very misleading. However, people using GAs are usually hoping to use lessons from evolution in order to find solutions to a problem that faces them. If they really do know the problem they have to solve, then they can define in finite terms the search space, and fixed length genotypes are appropriate. If, however, they are trying to evolve a structure with arbitrary and potentially unrestricted capabilities, then the problem space is not pre-defined, genotypes must be unrestricted in length, and a new approach is needed. Hence this discussion is probably more relevant to those looking at the evolution of animats or cognitive structures than it is to those looking at GAs as function optimizers.

One of the lessons demonstrated is that if genotypes can potentially increase indefinitely, they will in practice only do so on a slow timescale, so that within a population all genotypes will be very nearly the same length. Indeed, there will be a high degree of uniformity in the genotypes, and any significant variations, including changes in length, will spread through the whole population before the next variation occurs. This is in contrast to the relatively fast timescale on which the crossover operator, which is the power-house of standard GAs, very efficiently mixes and matches fitter schemata.

One factor to bear in mind here is that there is a relationship between mutation rate and the length of a genotype that can effectively evolve. Too little mutation, and there is not the variation to allow change; too much, and there is not sufficient stability to maintain fitness.

In contrast to the approach used in Holland's Schema Theorem, or the hyperplane analysis of schemata, where the population can effectively sample the whole search space, we must visualise a population in our new, infinitely though slowly expandable, search space as a localized cloud (with a high degree of consistency within the population) which can only sample 'nearby' points (those that can be moved to by one or a small number of applications of the genetic operators.) The question ceases being 'Where in this whole search space is the optimum?' and becomes instead 'From here, where can we move to that is better?'.

Acknowledgements

This work has been supported by a grant from the SERC, and I acknowledge helpful comments on an earlier draft from Phil Husbands, Jim Stone, Pedro de Oliveira and Shirley Kitts.

References

[Brooks 1991] Rodney A. Brooks. Intelligence without representation. *Artificial Intelligence*, 47:139–159, 1991.

[Davidor 1990] Yuval Davidor. Epistasis variance: A viewpoint on representations, ga hardness, and deception. *Complex Systems*, 4(4), 1990.

[Eigen and Schuster 1979] M. Eigen and P. Schuster. *The Hypercycle: A Principle of Natural Self-Organization*. Springer-Verlag, 1979.

[Gillespie 1984] J.H. Gillespie. Molecular evolution over the mutational landscape. *Evolution*, 38:1116, 1984.

[Goldberg *et al.* 1990] David E. Goldberg, K. Deb, and B. Korb. An investigation of messy genetic algorithms. Technical Report TCGA-90005, TCGA, The University of Alabama, 1990.

[Goldberg 1989] David E. Goldberg. *Genetic Algorithms in Search, Optimization and Machine Learning*. Addison-Wesley, Reading, Massachusetts, USA, 1989.

[Hillis 1991] W.D. Hillis. Co-evolving parasites improve simulated evolution as an optimization parameter. In C. G. Langton, J. D. Farmer, S. Rasmussen, and C. Taylor, editors, *Artificial Life II: Proceedings Volume of Santa Fe Conference Feb. 1990*. Addison Wesley: volume XI in the series of the Santa Fe Institute Studies in the Sciences of Complexity, 1991.

[Holland 1975] John Holland. *Adaptation in Natural and Artificial Systems*. University of Michigan Press, Ann Arbor, USA, 1975.

[Husbands 1991] Philip Husbands. Simulated co-evolution as the mechanism for emergent planning and scheduling. In *Proceedings of the 4th ICGA*, 1991.

[Jacob 1989] François Jacob. *The Possible and the Actual*. Penguin, 1989.

[Kauffman and Levin 1987] Stuart Kauffman and Simon Levin. Towards a general theory of adaptive walks on rugged landscapes. *Journal of Theoretical Biology*, 128:11–45, 1987.

[Kauffman 1989] Stuart Kauffman. Adaptation on rugged fitness landscapes. In Daniel L. Stein, editor, *Lectures in the Sciences of Complexity*, pages 527–618. Addison Wesley: Santa Fe Institute Studies in the Sciences of Complexity, 1989.

[Koza 1990] John R. Koza. Genetic programming: A paradigm for genetically breeding populations of computer programs to solve problems. Technical Report STAN-CS-90-1314, Department of Computer Science, Stanford University, 1990.

[Lindgren 1990] K. Lindgren. Evolution in a population of mutating strategies. Technical report, Nordita, Copenhagen, 1990.

[Lindgren 1991] K. Lindgren. Evolutionary phenomena in simple dynamics. In C. G. Langton, J. D. Farmer, S. Rasmussen, and C. Taylor, editors, *Artificial Life II: Proceedings Volume of Santa Fe Conference Feb. 1990*. Addison Wesley: volume XI in the series of the Santa Fe Institute Studies in the Sciences of Complexity, 1991.

[Maynard Smith 1970] John Maynard Smith. Natural selection and the concept of a protein space. *Nature*, 225:563–564, 1970.

[Needleman and Wunsch 1970] S. B. Needleman and C. D. Wunsch. A general method applicable to the search for similarities in the amino acid sequence of two proteins. *Journal of Molecular Biology*, 48:443–453, 1970.

[Sankoff 1972] David Sankoff. Matching sequences under deletion/insertion constraints. *Proceedings of the National Academy of Science, USA*, 69(1):4–6, 1972.

[Smith 1980] Stephen F. Smith. *A Learning System based on Genetic Adaptive Algorithms*. PhD thesis, Department of Computer Science, University of Pittsburgh, USA, 1980.

The Computer Zoo—evolution in a box

Jakob Skipper
The Niels Bohr Institute, Blegdamsvej 17, DK-2100 Copenhagen Ø, Denmark

Abstract: *This article describes a computerized ecosystem called 'The Computer Zoo', in which innumerable programs live, reproduce, and die. They are subjected to evolution by constant random mutations of the programs. Natural selection determines what programs survive, reproduce, and carry their code to the next generation. The purpose of the project is to create open-ended evolution just like in the nature, but in a completely artificial environment instead.*

In a traditional programming language the number of functional programs is microscopic compared to the number of possible programs. In order to improve this ratio and thereby speed up the evolution, the Computer Zoo uses a specially designed language Czoo, *which is more resistant to mutations than a traditional programming language.*

A number of experiments have been done using this new language. We see symbiosis and parasites, and self-assembly of flocks of programs. We also see punctuated equilibria and traces of predatory behaviour. The language also allows sexual reproduction.

1 Introduction

As the title of this paper suggests we have set up a very ambitious goal, namely the creation of evolution in a completely artificial system. There is no *a priori* assumption that the artificial system must be a computer, but it does appear to be a very suitable medium for artificial life.

We are modelling evolution, not the nature. Therefore we have not done the modelling by defining foxes, rabbits, grass etc. and then letting the foxes eat the rabbits under the control of a handful of rules. The Computer Zoo discards the idea of representing the nature directly in the model. Instead we create a complete *electronic ecosystem* and some digital creatures to live in it. These creatures have nothing to do with rabbits or foxes. Nevertheless, the digital creatures show some of the same behaviours as real animals.

This approach follows the tradition established by earlier models of evolution, such as the Coreworld by Rasmussen et al. 1990, and the Tierra simulator by Thomas Ray 1991.

2 Defining the Zoo

So now we have to define a system in which evolution may take place. We must define the principles of the digital creatures, and we must also build the electronic ecosystem in which the creatures live.

A creature is just a program, but it is not a traditional program written in a traditional language. Traditional languages are far too sensitive to random mutations. Instead we have designed a new language *Czoo* specifically for this purpose.

At the beginning we have just a single program living in our electronic world. But this program reproduces again and again, so soon there are more than enough to fill the available space. The reproduction process is not always successful. Random mutations occur now and then. Our hope is, that along the way the mutations give rise to new and better 'species' of programs, that outperform and eradicate the original ancestor program.

The results of the runs depend completely on the characteristics of the world and the Czoo language. The world must be rich enough to allow a wide variety of possible species to exist, reproduce, and evolve, but on the other hand it should not be overly unrestricted, as this would lead to a total chaos. Chris Langton (1990) has shown how a one-dimensional cellular array should be balanced at a point between order and chaos to evolve long transients in time. It does probably also apply to an artificial life simulator even if we, strictly speaking, cannot be sure that his results can be transferred to other complex systems.

In real life, a very important part of the environment for an animal is the other animals and plants in the habitat. Evolution ensures that the animals adapt not only to the slowly changing climatic and geological conditions, but also to the other animals, who are themselves being changed by evolution. The pace it set by the fastest evolving species, so a species must evolve quickly, simply to keep its niche and to survive.

This is known as the Red Queen hypothesis (L. van Valen 1973).

It appears that the interaction with other species is a driving force in the evolution. Therefore the programs in the Zoo must also interact if we want to see open-ended evolution in the system. If they were allowed to run in complete ignorance of the existence of each other, very little evolution would appear.

2.1 Language principles

One important property of the world is the language in which the simulated programs are written. A traditional programming language is very sensitive to random mutations in the code. Change a random bit, and chances are the program falls completely apart. This is because the number of functional programs is microscopic compared to the number of possible programs. This fact is usually referred to as the 'brittleness problem'. We designed the Czoo language to tackle this problem.

2.1.1 Two-dimensional world

One common consensus from the First Conference on Artificial Life in Santa Fe (Langton 1987) was that artificial life should be created by the use of local interactions among individuals rather than by global control. But local interactions require a meaning to the words local and global, so it is necessary to have some topology, or geography.

The Coreworld (Rasmussen et al. 1990) and the Tierra simulator (Ray 1991) both use as topology a conventional one-dimensional memory. In the Computer Zoo, all the running programs are placed in a two-dimensional grid. Any program is assigned a direction and a position on the grid. There are eight possible directions: north, north east, east etc. It is perfectly possible for two or more programs to share the same grid position. To utilize the grid, the instruction set contains three instructions for moving around, namely `forward`, `turnleft`, and `turnright`.

Having defined a grid, we must also settle on a measure of distance. In the Zoo, the distance between two programs is the maximum of the vertical and the horizontal distance. Consequently, a program has the distance 1 to all its eight neighbour grid points.

2.1.2 Memory cells

Since we have discarded the linear memory model as our topology and replaced it with a two-dimensional grid, we need some other way to organize the memory. We chop the entire memory into small, independent pieces of 16 words each. These chunks are named *memory cells* and they contain the code and the data of our programs in the Zoo. The words are 32 bits wide, but when they contain code we only use the lower 5 bits.

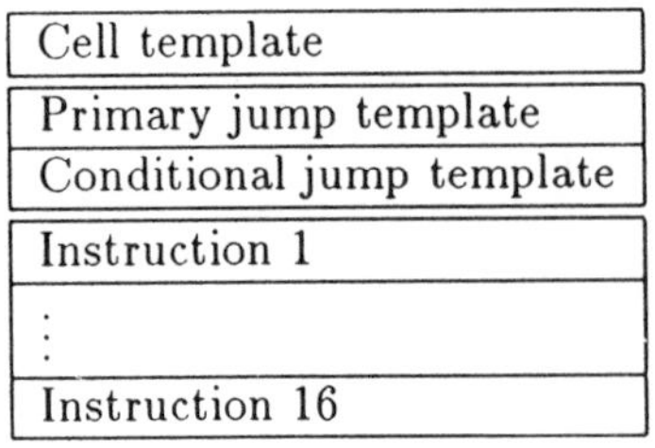

Figure 1: *A single memory cell. The cell template is computed from the lower 5 bits of each of the 16 instruction words.*

We want the programs to be of any length, not just 16 instructions. A program may therefore have more than one memory cell with code, and so we need a way to transfer program flow from one cell to another. We do that by using templates. Every memory cell has a 32-bit word called the ***cell template***. It is computed from the 16 words by xor'ing and rotating the five instruction bits so that a mutation of a single bit in an instruction results in a change of a single bit in the template. Whenever an instruction is changed, for instance by a mutation, the cell template also changes. Note that this template is not unique—the algorithm maps 80 bits into 32, giving $2^{48} \approx 3 \cdot 10^{14}$ different possible memory cells for each template.

The cell also has two jump templates; the ***primary jump template*** and the ***conditional jump template***. Whenever a program has executed the 16 instructions in a memory cell, it uses the primary jump template to find the next cell to execute. The program runs through all its memory cells, comparing the jump template to the cell template. The cell with the template that is closest to the jump template is chosen as the next cell to execute. We use the Hamming distance (number of different bits) to compare two templates. If no cell template has a distance from the jump template within a certain limit called the *template tolerance*, the jump fails and the program dies.

By establishing a sequence of matching templates we can create an endless loop. But we also want to make conditional jumps. To do that we use the conditional jump template. The instruction set contains two conditional instructions; `if` and `ifnot`. They skip the rest of the instructions in the cell when the `flag` register is true or false, respectively. The next cell to

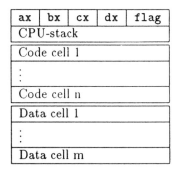

ax	bx	cx	dx	flag
CPU-stack				
Code cell 1				
⋮				
Code cell n				
Data cell 1				
⋮				
Data cell m				

Figure 2: *A program consists of four general purpose registers, a flag register, a CPU-stack, one or more code cells, and zero or more data cells.*

execute is then selected by using the conditional jump template instead of the primary.

The two instructions `if` and `ifnot` are the only instructions for program sequencing. The use of templates makes explicit loop, repeat, and jump instructions superfluous.

As a cell and a jump template may match even if they are not equal, this scheme introduces some fault tolerance. The jump can be resolved correctly even if one of the templates is partly destroyed by mutations.

2.1.3 Programs

A program consists of one or more memory cells containing code. As described above the jump and cell templates of the code cells are used to control the program flow. The order of the cells in the program is therefore unimportant.

But a program may also own data. In addition to the code cells, a programs owns zero or more data cells. A data cell is identical to a code cell, the only difference being the way it is used by the program. The data cells typically hold an offspring program under construction, but they may hold any type of data. Just like the code cells, the data cells are addressed using a template, so their order is also unimportant.

In addition a program also has four general purpose registers `ax`, `bx`, `cx` and `dx`, and a boolean `flag` register. Finally it has a CPU-stack, that is just a statically allocated data cell. A program is shown in figure 2.

2.1.4 Events

Until now we have focused on a single program, paying no attention to its interactions with other programs. The combination of cell and jump templates controls the program flow through the memory cells. This simple principle can be reformulated using *events*, and the new scheme can easily be extended to include interactions among programs.

Execution starts when a program receives an event. The event is a 32-bit number just like a jump template. The event is compared to all the cell templates; and the cell with the best match (determined by the Hamming distance between the template and the event) is selected for execution.

When the execution of the instructions in the cell has finished, the program issues an event taken from either the primary or the conditional jump template. This means, that the program sends the template as an event to itself. When the program receives its own event, the event sparks off the execution of a new cell, and the process is repeated.

We can now introduce interactions by giving an event a scope. When the event is issued, it is broadcast to all the programs within some radius from the issuing program. We call this radius the *event radius*. As a consequence, not only the issuing program but also a number of other programs receive the event and consequently execute some code selected by the event.

When this event broadcasting is enabled, a program may receive more events than it can handle. The events are then queued for the program for later processing. There is no limit of the number of pending events in the queue. This could cause a continuous, unlimited growth in the number of pending events, but the experiments have shown that this does not happen in practice.

If a program has received an event that does not match any cell template within the template tolerance, the event is simply discarded and the next in the queue is used instead. If there are no more pending events, the programs dies.

The concept of events can easily be expanded. The simulator can raise events to signal external conditions such as the presence of an unallocated memory cell. The programs could then develop code to react sensibly. This aspect has not been investigated.

2.1.5 Remote execution

Consider a program, that owns a specific code cell C. As we saw above, an alien program may by the use of broadcasting of events cause the program owning C to execute C's code. There is another mechanism in the Zoo, that allows the alien program to execute this C cell itself, without affecting the owning program. We call this *remote execution*. It is in some sense the opposite scheme of event broadcasting; a program does not broadcast its jump templates, it 'imports' the cell templates of other programs.

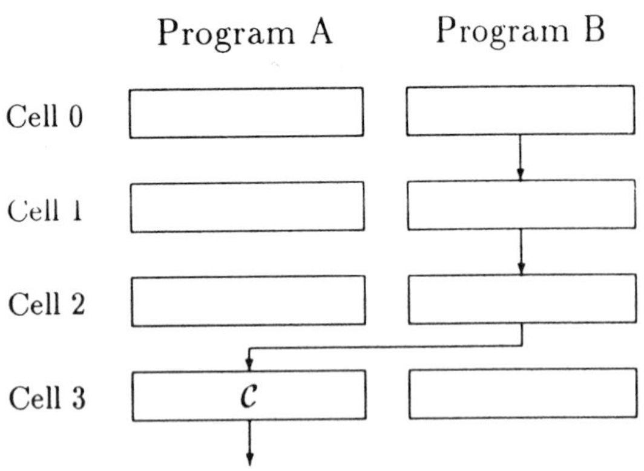

Figure 3: *Remote execution. Program B executes remotely the code of cell C in program A. It then continues execution using the jump template stored in program A and it is therefore likely to continue executing A's code. But since A may also execute B's code remotely, the execution of the two programs can become deeply interweaved.*

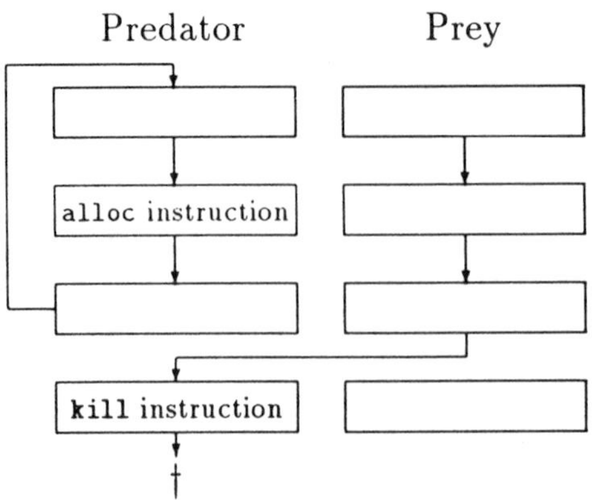

Figure 4: *Program flow when a prey due to remote execution falls into the trap set up by the predator.*

When a program receives an event (that may or may not originate from the program itself), it normally searches all its own code cells for the best match. But if we use remote execution, the program also searches the code cells of all other programs within event radius. If the best match is a cell owned by some other program, this foreign code is executed instead. The remote execution is completely transparent to the 'host' program. The scheme is illustrated in figure 3. Remote execution turns out to be a very important facility, as we shall see in the next section.

2.2 What the Zoo can do

We have described how the world is seen by a program executing in the Zoo. The chosen architecture has some interesting consequences that we summarize in the following. In this section we describe the anticipated capabilities of the Zoo. The actual demonstrated capabilities are described later in section 3.

2.2.1 Predatory behaviour

The possibility of predatory behaviour is one consequence of the design of the Zoo. We call a program a predator, if it kills another program in the hunt for more memory. There are actually two ways to be a predator, corresponding to the two kinds of interaction; remote execution and event broadcasting. The two kinds of predatory behaviour could be called 'setting up a trap' and 'shooting poisoned arrows'. We will concentrate on the former, since that is by far the easiest to detect.

Consider the picture in figure 4. The predator has a code cell that it never executes itself, and this cell contains a `kill` instruction causing the executing program to instantly commit suicide. Another program within event radius (the prey) executes this code remotely and dies during the execution. The predator then allocates the memory of the prey, using the memory allocation instruction `alloc`.

Instead of an explicit `kill` instruction, the fatal code could cause an execution error, or contain a jump template that does not match anything, or it could simply mess things up in a way so that the prey will make an execution error later (poisoning).

However, it takes some time from the moment the prey dies until the predator gets a time slice and allocates the memory. And since the dead program may own more than one memory cell (code or data), there may be more than enough memory for the predator. This is a chance for other programs to steal the prey (scavengers).

This kind of predatory behaviour is very passive. The predator just sets up the trap and then waits for the prey to do the work. But the opposite scheme is also possible within the current model, when we use event broadcasting instead of remote execution. The predator then issues an event that is lethal to the prey (it sparks off execution of some code in the prey that causes it to die).

These two methods can be combined. The predator issues an event that causes the prey to execute a fatal code cell owned by the predator. This requires the predator to be immune to the fatal code, since it itself receives the event and therefore executes the code.

Predatory behaviour is only an evolutionary advantage to a program if memory is scarce and the memory allocation scheme ensures, that the predator is the program most likely to allocate the memory released from the prey. More about memory allocation in sections 2.3 and 3.5.

2.2.2 Sexual reproduction

Remote execution is a way for a program to read and use the code cells of other programs. It has a parallel when the memory cells are treated as data, called *remote collection*. When reading a memory cell as data (and that can be a code or a data cell), the program searches all cells of all programs within event radius for the best match and then read the desired data from it. When this is part of the reproduction process, the program copies the code of other programs code instead of its own. If there is no partner nearby, the program simply copies its own code cells.

This is actually sexual reproduction but it is implicit. The programs are not 'aware' that they reproduce sexually. There is also no performance penalty for a program to reproduce sexually.

Using remote collection the program makes an offspring assembled of pieces taken from various other programs. With a term borrowed from biology, this is usually called cross-over. In a traditional programming language cross-over will almost certainly lead to a disabled offspring. But in Czoo it is different. Firstly, the cell templates ensures that the code taken from another program usually resembles the original code of the parent. Secondly, when we copy the code one cell at a time, chances are that cross-over does not happen in the middle of at cell, but only between cells (see the `duplicate` instruction in appendix A).

2.2.3 Sensing and communication

When a program receives and processes an event we can say that it senses the event. This view is especially useful when the program receives events that it did not issue itself (we use event broadcasting). We can say that the program sees another approaching program when it reacts to the events issued by this other program. It may also recognize other program species on their events and take appropriate action. Likewise, a program can issue events that may trick other programs into believing something else has happened. This opens up an enormous range of possible interactions between the programs.

Note that the use of events equips the programs with a sensing apparatus and not with an explicit appearance (such as for instance explicitly adding the concept of colour), because the appearance is completely determined by the character of the observer's senses. We humans recognize a zebra on its stripes, but that is only because our main sense is our sight. Had our main sense been the sense of smell, we would describe the appearance of a zebra very differently.

A Czoo program has many different appearances: a pattern of events emerging from it, a written representation in the Czoo language, a bit pattern in the memory etc. But since Czoo programs sense events they recognize each other from the issued events.

Since programs may exchange events, they can also be said to communicate. In principle it should be possible to evolve programs that communicate by sending various events to each other.

2.2.4 Redundancy

The Czoo language gives the programs the option to use redundancy by duplicating vital program parts. If a program owns multiple copies of a code cell and one of these is mutated, this changed cell changes its template. But then the unchanged copy of the cell is (probably) a better match for the jump templates in the program, and this unchanged cell is selected for execution before the mutated one.

2.3 The environment

The programs described in the previous sections run in a large multiprocessing simulator. It could also be called the environment, the electronic ecosystem, the operating system, or the world of the programs. This simulator has some properties very important to the behaviour of the programs.

First of all there is memory allocation. Memory is a limited resource to any computer program including Czoo programs. The simulator has a fixed amount of memory cells that the programs may allocate using a dedicated `alloc` instruction. All unallocated memory cells go into a huge, central pool from which the programs allocate new cells, and into which the cells belonging to dead programs go.

When programs replicate they use memory and in very little time all the available memory cells are allocated. To allow further replication, some programs must die and release their allocated memory.

A program may die because of an execution error, because it executed a special suicide instruction `kill`, or it can be terminated by the simulator. When some program asks for more memory and no more memory cells remain in the pool, the simulator finds the oldest running program and terminates it, depositing all of its code and data cells in the pool.

The ancestor program would be the only program species in the simulator if it had not been for mutations. The Computer Zoo implements two different kinds of mutation: point mutation and erroneous duplication. The main difference is the time in which the mutations occur.

Point mutation is the simplest form. With uneven intervals the simulator flips a random bit in a random memory cell, changing either an instruction or a jump template. As a result, even a program that was correct when started may after a while degenerate due to mutations.

Erroneous duplication takes place during the process of copying a single memory cell. The instruction set contains a `duplicate` instruction that copies an entire memory cell onto another previously allocated memory cell. This duplication is not always completely correct. With a small probability, the simulator flips a random bit in the cell, or it either deletes or inserts a random instruction at a random place. Erroneous duplication only affects new programs. Once a program has started running it never changes (except if point mutation is also used).

2.4 The instruction set

The structure of the instruction set used in Czoo resembles a traditional assembly language. The code in a memory cell is a string of instructions with no compound constructs like `begin` ... `end`, `for` ... `do` etc. But there is one evident difference: Czoo has no constant operands. If a constant like 42 is needed in a program, it has to be constructed from zero by shifting, incrementing, and adding.

A language with no constant operands was first introduced by Thomas Ray in his Tierra language. The objective is to reduce the *real* size of the instruction set. If we have a large instruction set it is most unlikely that a random mutation in the code creates a useful instruction. As Ray points out, the size of an instruction set is not just the number of op-codes. Two instructions like `add 1` and `add 2` have different semantics even if they have the same op-code. They are, therefore, really different instructions.

The Coreworld use the language Redcode taken from the game Core War (Dewdney 1984). It has only 10 op-codes, but most instructions have one or two operands and four addressing modes. Thomas Ray calculates the real number of instructions in Redcode to be about 10^{11}. In contrast, the Czoo language has 32 instructions and none of them have operands.

The virtual CPU simulated by the Computer Zoo has four general purpose 32-bit registers **ax**, **bx**, **cx**, and **dx**. There is also a flag register called **flag**. It is set and cleared to indicate success and failure of certain instructions. Finally, a program has a statically allocated memory cell being used as the default CPU-stack, but any data cell may be used as a stack.

In addition to traditional instructions like **add**, **push**, etc., the language also has a number of special purpose instructions like `alloc` (allocates a memory cell), `split` (creates a new program from all the data cells and starts running it), and **kill** (immediately kills the program executing it). They are usually not found as native instructions in a computer. Instead, they are implemented as operating system calls. But since we do not distinguish between the operating system and the underlying (simulated) hardware in Czoo, these calls are genuine instructions. The only way to avoid such instructions entirely is to invent a complete artificial physics.

2.5 Relations to biology

The Computer Zoo as described above is a piece of artificial life, but it is not designed to resemble the biological life in any way However, some of the concepts have been inspired by the nature and the human DNA.

The human DNA can be viewed as a long string of nucleotides, just like a traditional assembly language program is a long string of instructions. But the DNA string is divided into functional substrings, and each substring codes for some specific character of the individual. During the reproduction process cross-over is more likely to occur between two such functional substrings than in the middle of a string.

A natural model of this in a program is to divide the code into smaller parts that go relatively intact through the reproduction process. This was the idea behind the memory cells. The concept is simplified in the Zoo by giving all cells a fixed length.

The use of templates in the cells was inspired by Thomas Ray, but he was inspired by biochemistry. When two protein molecules in a biological cell interact, they do not specify the coordinates or address of each other. Instead they are brought together by diffusion, and they react when their surfaces match.

3 Running the Zoo

Having set up the Zoo, we start running it. A run starts with an ancestor program. We use the same simple ancestor program in all the runs. It is loaded into the Zoo at a random position, and then it starts

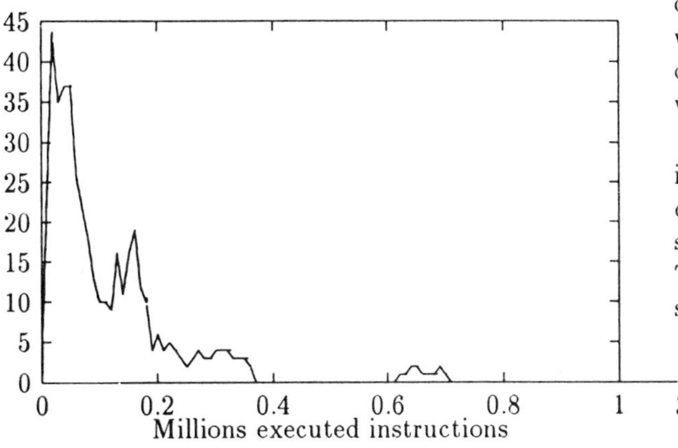

Figure 5: *Number of copies of the ancestor program. Notice how the ancestor is eradicated but reappears for a short while, before it disappears completely.*

running and reproducing itself again and again. The ancestor dominates for a short while, but then some other mutated program take over (see figure 5).

3.1 Symbiosis & parasites

One very common result of these runs is the development of parasite programs similar to what happens in Thomas Ray's Tierra simulator. It happens when we use remote execution and no broadcasting of events.

For a short while the ancestor totally dominates the entire Zoo. But very quickly the system destabilizes and a lot of small programs appear. Typically it happens after a few hundred thousand instructions, which take about 2–5 minutes on a 12 MHz 80286 PC. These small programs contain just a single code cell so they do not themselves have all the code necessary to replicate. Instead they use remote execution to execute the code of other programs in the neighbourhood.

Since these small parasitic programs cannot replicate alone, they are dependent on each other and the hosts. This dependence on other programs is the trade-off for an improved reproduction speed. Since there is only one cell to copy, the replication takes much less time.

3.2 Moving and flock formation

The ancestor program is programmed to move forward all the time. The first one-cell parasite programs appearing also do the same. Their dependence on the hosts cause them to cluster in one big flock on the screen build around one or more hosts (see the screen dumps in figure 7). A program that always moves forward will sooner or later fall out of the flock. When it does so, it dies because there are no fellow programs with the code needed. It simply dies of loneliness.

As a countermeasure the parasites soon start moving in circles and spirales instead, thereby reducing the chance of 'getting lost'. The circle-moving programs soon dominate and cause the flock to decrease in size. This has already developed in two of the programs shown in figure 6.

3.3 Punctuated equilibria

The Zoo also shows punctuated equilibria. Punctuated equilibria is an expression originally used by Gould and Eldredge (1977) to describe the paleobiological evolution. Their hypothesis was that this did not happen gradually. Instead there were longer periods of relative stability, punctuated with irregular intervals by short periods of turbulent changes.

The one-cell parasitic programs described above use the code of each other and of the four-cell hosts. They are, therefore, dependent on having some critical mass of fellow programs around to survive. If the density of programs drops too low (for instance because of random fluctuations in the number of programs) the community breaks down completely and all the parasites die. This gives room for more robust programs carrying all their code around, and they grow in numbers and rule the world until the parasites get together again.

Such a sudden takeover may happen several times during a run with irregular intervals. An example is shown in figure 8.

3.4 Predatory behaviour

In the Zoo we have seen spurious appearances of predators, but the evolved predators are too unstable to survive for longer periods of time.

In an attempt to measure predatory activity, the Zoo updates the so-called *prey count* for all programs. It is reset when the program is born, and incremented every time another program dies executing the code of the first program.

Figure 9 shows the maximum and average prey counts of a run. Notice how the prey counts suddenly increase violently but quickly drop again. This suggests that one or more predators occured, but also that they did not reign the Zoo for very long time. Their sudden dead could be because they end up killing themselves, or simply because they run out of preys.

```
" littamref" (lt. gray   ), cnt=37, len=1/0, preys=0/0, bal=-5
0 : littamref CELL oketnovlen(-) isarbisfob(-)  SELF KILL TURNRIGHT PREFIX-CX MOVSP ZERO? ADD SHL
                                                MOVSP STACK-AX TURNRIGHT PREFIX-CX DEC IFNOT SPLIT SPLIT


"igakgissas" (lt. gray   ), cnt=41, len=1/0, preys=0/0, bal=-5
0 :igakgissas CELL isidgaskok(-) isibfahkek(-)  SPLIT . . . . . . TURNRIGHT TURNRIGHT . . . . . . TURNRIGHT

"igakgiskas" (lt. green  ), cnt=43, len=1/0, preys=0/0, bal=-5
0 :igakgiskas CELL isidgaskok(-) isibfahkek(-)  SPLIT FORWARD . . . . . TURNRIGHT . . . . . . . . TURNRIGHT
```

Figure 6: *The code of three parasites. The 'igakgissas' and 'igakgiskas' parasites are variations of a cell from the ancestor program, but some turn-instructions have entered and changed the moving pattern of the program. The 'littamref' program illustrates that a parasite may lose all of its functional code and run completely on code belonging to other programs.*

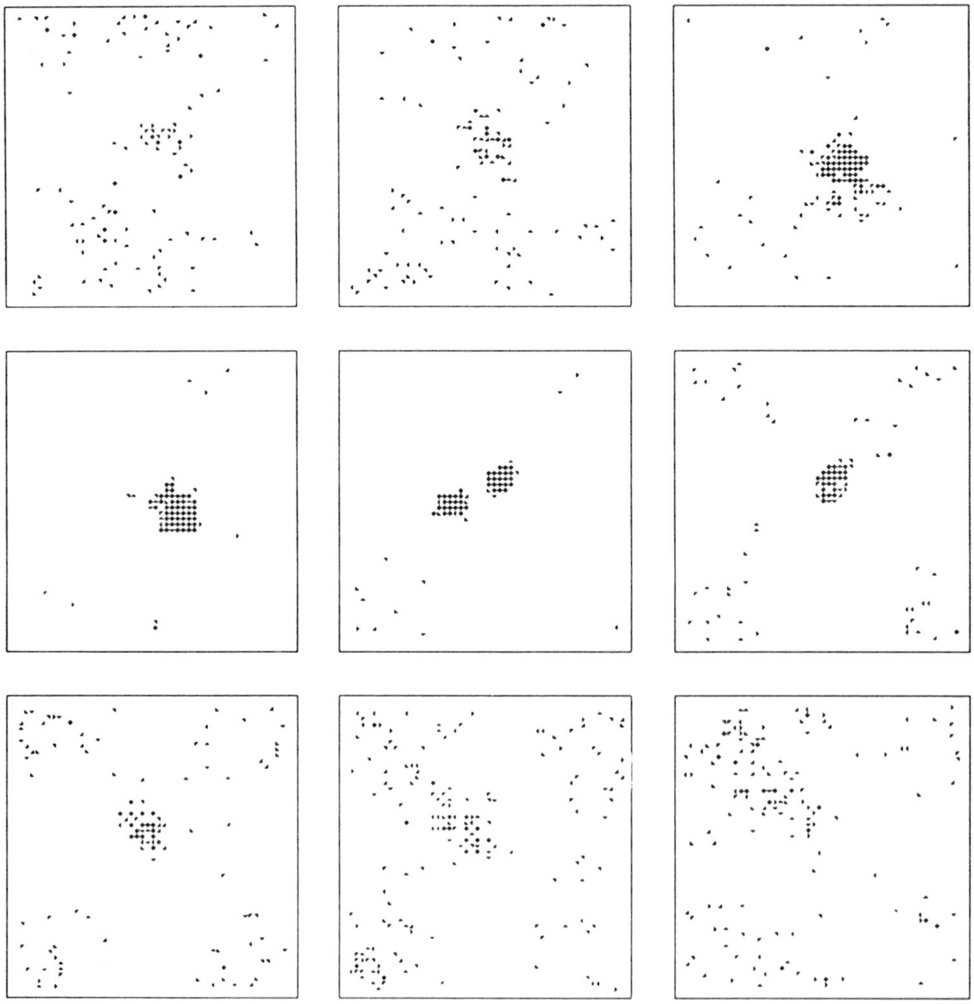

Figure 7: *Reproduction of nine actual screen shots showing the self-assembly and subsequent disintegration of a flock.*

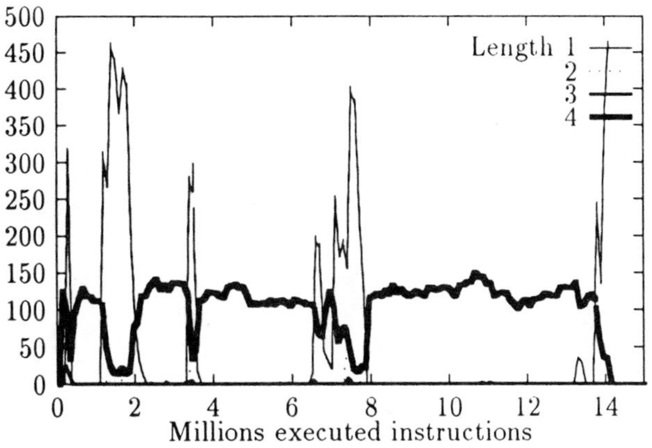

Figure 8: *Punctuated equilibria. The graph shows the number of programs of the lengths 1 to 4 during the run. Notice the sudden and irregular changes between 1-dominance and 4-dominance.*

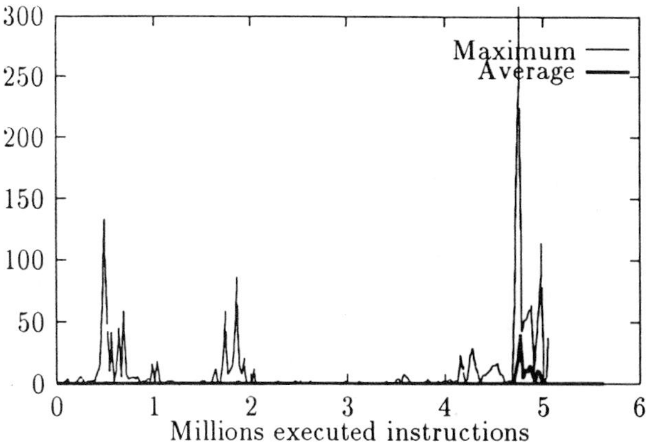

Figure 9: *Prey counts. Graph showing the maximum and average prey counts of the programs in the Zoo.*

3.5 Increasing locality

An important buzz-word in artificial life is *local*. As much as possible should be local rather than global. But in the Zoo both mortality and memory allocation is handled globally. Therefore we tried to change the environment to be more local.

We assigned every unallocated memory cell a position on the grid just like the programs. For an **alloc** instruction to succeed, there had to be an unallocated memory cell within event radius from the program. If not, the **alloc** instruction failed, setting the **flag** register accordingly. A program then had to move around in search of memory. When a program died, all of its memory was placed at the grid point, where the program was at the time of death.

The mortality was also changed. Ideally the simulator should never forcibly terminate any program at all. The programs ought to live until they die by themselves or are killed by a predator. We tried that, but it slowed down the evolution too much, so a different strategy was chosen as a compromise. The **alloc** instruction did no more cause the simulator to kill the oldest program. Instead the simulator would now and then insert a **kill** instruction in a random memory cell belonging to a random program.

This new setup ought to be better for predators. When the simulator automatically kills enough programs to supply memory, there is no evolutionary advantage in being a predator. An having all memory handled globally has as a consequence, that any program may allocate the memory a predator has released from a dead prey. Local memory and the **kill** insertion strategy should therefore evolve more predators.

But that was not the case. The best results concerning predators were done with the original configuration of the environment, despite its lack of encourage for the programs to develop predatory behaviour. Perhaps making things local is not always a miracle cure. It could be nice to do some more experiments to find out whether complete, uncompromised locality of everything is always desirable.

4 Conclusion

The Computer Zoo demonstrates that it is possible to create evolution among computer programs. We cannot claim true open-ended evolution since the programs always die out after a while.

But in a sense we do have open-ended evolution anyway. There is no endpoint for the evolution, and no optimal program that cannot be improved. The performance of a given program depends on the other programs in the Zoo at any given time. Therefore the evolution may in principle continue forever.

There are probably many reasons why this does not happen in practice. The death of the programs in the Zoo usually coincides with the appearance of predators or parasites. For some reason they cause the number of programs to drop, and if it reaches zero it will never rise again. It is quite possible, that a larger grid with more memory cells and programs would enable the Zoo to live longer.

The concept of remote execution seems to be essential to the evolution. All the results mentioned in the previous section are achieved using remote execution. Thomas Ray's Tierra Simulator does also use what is actually a variation of remote execution. Under certain circumstances his programs execute other program's code. And he has also found symbiosis. His parasite programs are quite simular to our one-cell programs as both kinds use other program's code to reproduce without affecting the host.

The behaviours documented in this article are all phenomena that have biological parallels. But it is quite possible that there are many other odd behaviours in the Zoo that has no biological counterpart and cannot be described in simple biological terms like 'parasite' and 'predator'. The problem is that we cannot detect it. To move further with the Zoo it is essential to develop better analysis tools that do more work than just extracting and dumping megabytes of data. What we need is a tool to analyse the interactions between the programs. Given such a tool, we are convinced we could find many more interesting program species.

Acknowledgements

I would like to thank professor Benny Lautrup from the Niels Bohr Institute for help and inspiration during the entire development process of the Computer Zoo, and also thanks to Thomas Ray from the School of Life & Health Sciences for inspiring me to make the Computer Zoo and for critical comments on my early drafts of the system. Further more I am grateful to Carsten Knudsen from the Technical University of Denmark for setting up the seminar that started it all, and to Jacob Engelbrecht who provided me with the sketch of the human DNA that inspired the concept of the memory cells in the Zoo. And finally thanks to Claus Emmeche for many interesting comments on the Zoo from a more philosophical point of view.

References

Dewdney, A.K.. 1984. *Computer recreations: In the game called Core War hostile programs engage in a battle of bits.* Scientific American 250, pp. 14–22.

Gould, S.J., N. Eldredge. 1977. *Punctuated equilibria: The tempo and mode of evolution reconsidered.* Paleobiology vol 3,2, pp. 115–151.

Langton, Christopher G. 1987. *Artificial life: Proceedings of an Interdisciplinary Workshop on the Synthesis and Simulation of Living Systems.* Addison-Wesley, ISBN 0-201-09346-4 and 0-201-09356-1 (pbk.)

Langton, Christopher G. 1990. *Computation at the edge of chaos: Phase transitions and emergent computation.* Physica D 42, North-Holland, pp. 12–37.

Rasmussen, Steen, Carsten Knudsen, Rasmus Feldberg, Morten Hindsholm. 1990. *The Coreworld: Emergence and evolution of cooperative structures in a computational chemistry.* Physica D 42, North-Holland, pp. 111–134.

Ray, Thomas S. 1991. *An approach to the Synthesis of Artificial Life.* In Artificial Life II, edited by Christopher G. Langton, Charles E. Taylor, J. Doyne Farmer, Steen Rasmussen. Addison-Wesley.

van Valen, L. 1973. *A new evolutionary law.* Evolutionary Theory 1, pp. 1–30.

A The Czoo instruction set

`add, dec, inc, neg, shl, zero, zero?`
: Arithmetic operations on the current stacktop.

`alloc`
: Allocate a new data cell.

`copy`
: Move from on stack to another.

`duplicate`
: Copy an entire memory cell onto another previously allocated data cell.

`forward, turnleft, turnright`
: Move and turn the program 45 degrees on the two-dimensional grid.

`if, ifnot`
: Jump using conditional jump template if `flag` is set or cleared, respectively.

`kill`
: Commit suicide instantly.

`movps, movsp`
: Move between the two stack registers.

`nop`
: No operation.

`null`
: Clear the stack register (so that the new current stack is the CPU-stack).

`pop, push`
: Move data between current stacktop and prefix register.

`prefix-ax, prefix-bx, prefix-cx, prefix-dx`
: Change the current prefix register to be the named register.

`self`
: Instruction for self inspection.

`split`
: Create a new program from all the data cells owned by a program, and start running it.

`stack-ax, stack-bx, stack-cx, stack-dx`
: Change the current stack register to be the named register.

Measuring the Evolving Complexity of Stimulus-Response Organisms

Jeffrey Horn *
Department of Computer Science
and the Center for Complex Systems Research
University of Illinois at Urbana-Champaign
jeffhorn@uiuc.edu

Abstract. Intuitively, an evolving population should exhibit increasingly complex and sophisticated strategies for survival. But how can we know when and where such evolution is taking place in the intricate interactions of a population? To simply measure changes in genotype is not discriminating enough, while using fitness introduces bias and is overly constraining. Rather, what we should measure in order to gauge the course and rate of evolution is the degree of *intrinsic complexity* of a strategy. Under such a measure, a strategy of moving toward a particular environmental situation is just as sophisticated as a strategy of moving away from the same situation. Thus, such measures are free of bias as to what is a "good" or "bad" strategy, allowing us to see evolution where we might have previously dismissed it. In this paper, we discuss these issues concretely by proposing a specific measure of complexity for a particular, but popular, architecture for behavior: a lookup table of stimulus-response rules. Such a measure could be used to define and quantify artificial evolution, distinguishing between real progress and mere adaptation.

1. Introduction

While running a program to simulate evolution, we might see one organism in the population carefully picking its way around obstacles and traps, and homing in on a cache of fuel (or food). Ah, an intelligent strategy has evolved, we might say to ourselves. But then suddenly, the artificial bug swerves to the left of the food supply, and wanders off, apparently towards a more distant food source. At the same time, a swarm of similar organisms, plus a large predator, converge on the first food source. Was our intelligent agent avoiding the predator by sacrificing an easy meal? Was it anticipating extraordinary competition from the converging mob? Perhaps it was moving randomly after all.

How do we know how intelligent our evolving agents have become? If their survival strategies really do evolve, they will eventually become so intricate and subtle that it will be impossible to detect by direct observation of their behavior. An alternative is to look directly into their "minds", but for most implementations it is extremely difficult to decipher the abstract strategy encoded in the hardwired bug brains, be they interconnected control loops, stimulus-response rules, neural networks, or finite state automata.

The purpose of this paper is to present a method of measuring the complexity, or the degree of sophistication, of an evolved artificial organism. Although this measure is specific to stimulus-response (S-R) encodings of behavior, it allows us to clarify what we mean by vague terms such as "complexity" and "sophistication", and to differentiate this characteristic from concepts such as fitness, intelligence, rationality, and other less precise, more subjective terms. Here, in the simplified world of S-R organisms, we have an opportunity to nail down exactly what we mean by the *evolution of complexity*.

2. The Need For a Quantitative Measure

It is hoped that the measure of complexity proposed in this paper will prove to be a fundamental tool in the analysis of artificial life and evolution. In particular, we hope that such a measure will help us to do the following.

*Most of the ideas described in this paper grew out of discussions and simulations carried out by a group organized by Norman Packard at the Center for Complex Systems Research at the University of Illinois. In particular, the models of evolution developed by Norman Packard, Jean-Yves Peterschmitt, and Andy Assad provided the inspiration and testing grounds for measuring complexity. Norman Packard and Mark Bedau introduced the fundamental concept of intrinsic complexity. Mike Rudnick supplied valuable insights into the nature of the Walsh Transform. Finally, David E. Goldberg keeps Walsh functions at the front of my mind.

2.1 Focus the Search for Intelligence

In a simple enough environment, with sufficiently constrained interactions among artificial organisms, we have relied on direct observation, plus intuition, to detect evolution. Prey eludes predator. Predator actively pursues prey. Bugs follow the food gradient and are attracted to the best grazing.

But as we increase the size of our populations, raise the number of generations, add new features to the environment, and enhance the architectures of the bug brains, we also decrease the resolution of our window of direct observation. It becomes increasingly difficult to tell whether one organism is behaving any more intelligently than another. An objective measure of complexity can help us focus on the more sophisticated individuals, thus filtering the better candidates for direct observation.

2.2 Expand the Search for Intelligence

An objective complexity measure might also direct our attention to strategies that we might normally have dismissed as random, but which actually embody an intricate understanding of the environment. For example, we might see a group of organisms moving toward a food basin and think that the grouping is due solely to the combined effect of simple strategies that seek the nearest food. But in actuality, many of the organisms might be following the subtle strategy of schooling, seeking safety in numbers from predators. Such a strategy would be much more "complex" than just moving toward food.

2.3 Distinguish Mere Adaptation From True Evolution

We would also like to able to distinguish more "advanced" or "evolved" organisms from those that have simply found a good, but easy, niche. For example, after a long simulation, several species of organisms might have evolved. One group has learned that food appears at a constant rate near the center of the grid, while another group has learned to hunt down a type of prey that takes energy to catch, but, with judicious hunting, provides more energy than the "easy" food supply. The former strategy is simply to move to the center of the world and stay around there. The latter strategy is much more complex. Both are examples of successful adaptation to the environment, but it seems useful to be able to distinguish and rank them. To do so automatically, without having to rely on subjective interpretation of their behavior, seems a worthy goal.

2.4 Track Complexity Flows

If we can measure complexity of a single artificial animal, we can look at the dynamics of evolution. We would hope to see interesting, emergent phenomena, such as local increases in complexity where the environment is most complex. Local increases could also be due to the feedback loop of other organisms: the more sophisticated one's neighbors, the more subtle and complex one has to be to survive. If we had a similar measure of complexity for the environment, we could look for correlations in the growth of complexity. If organisms can create artifacts, then the complex organisms might make their local environments more complex, leading to even more complex progeny.

2.5 Specify Terminology

Finally, once we define complexity, we can try to define other general terms, such as "diversity", in terms of complexity. We might then explore relationships among such measures, such as the possible tradeoff between complexity and diversity.

3. Some Obvious, But Unsatisfactory, Candidate Measures

A simple approach to measuring complexity might be to measure the degree to which the population is changing, but such a measure doesn't distinguish between genuine evolution and random perturbations or periodic oscillations.

A more specific metric would be the organisms' fitness: average, median, or best of generation. At first, increasing fitness seems closest to our intuitive idea of an improving, evolving population. But it turns out to be difficult to measure the "objective fitness" of individuals. Using some dynamic measure of fitness, such as total energy stored, age, or some other quantification of on-line performance, can be misleading. As the population improves, competition becomes more severe. Indicators such as "food-consumed-per-unit-of-energy-expended" might actually decrease even as organisms become smarter.

A third possibility is to measure fitness statically, in isolation from other bugs, by putting an individual into an ideal test environment and measuring its performance there. But the choice of ideal test environment introduces bias. The most evolved organisms might have a strategy fine-tuned for dealing with the drastic effects of other organisms. For example, a bug from a crowded environment might follow a strategy of avoiding the best food basins, knowing that the current generation of simpler, gradient-followers will pounce on such a pile of food. Instead, our more intelligent organism will seek out the second or third best locations in its local neighborhood. But in isolation, the simpler, greedier gradient-followers will seem more intelligent than the more subtle "compromiser".

Figure 1: Typical Distribution of Food

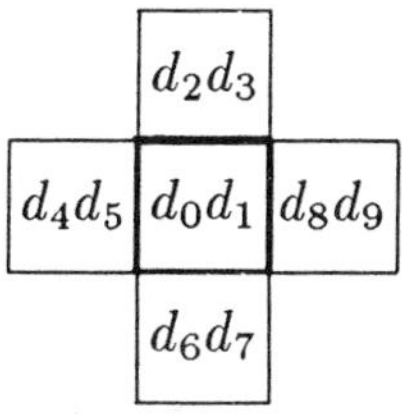

$\vec{d} = < d_0d_1d_2d_3d_4d_5d_6d_7d_8d_9 >$

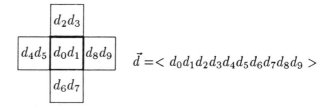

Figure 2: What a Bug Sees

4. The Model

To be more concrete about these issues, we describe our simple world and its inhabitants. This model is due to Norman Packard, and is described in [Packard 89] and [Packard and Bedau 91].

4.1 The World

The environment is a two-dimensional grid, with wraparound (i.e., the surface of a torus), as illustrated in Figure 1. There are only two types of objects: bugs and food. All bugs are the same, apart from having different strategies (lookup tables) as described in the next subsection. Each square can contain zero to three units of food, plus bugs. The darker squares in Figure 1 contain more food than the lighter squares.

Bugs consume food units and produce no waste. Bugs need the energy from food to keep living. Additional energy is required to move and to reproduce. There are no other objects, such as obstacles, traps, poison, or predators. Bugs do not interact, except indirectly, such as for crossover and reproduction, and by consuming the available food. Currently, food enters the world regularly through random placement of gaussian distributions (i.e., "hills" of food), with random mean and variance.

4.2 The Stimulus-Response Brain

The bug's environmental detectors can sense the amount of food in each cell of its neighborhood (i.e., the cell on which it is located, and the four adjoining cells at each of the four major compass points). The range of the environmental detectors is illustrated by Figure 2. The bug cannot detect other bugs, nor can it "see" diagonally. The resolution of food detection is exact: the bug detects exactly what level of food is present, from 0 to 3 units. Thus two bits are sufficient to encode the amount of food in each cell, and a ten bit string, as shown in Figure 2, captures the entire instantaneous environmental input vector.

The ten bit string can be used as an index into a Lookup Table (LUT) of bug output/actions. Thus for each of the 2^{10} possible configurations of the local environment, the LUT specifies a single output. A complete LUT, an array of 1024 outputs, specifies the behavior of a bug.

As for the output, each bug can move from 0 to 15 cells at a time, in a straight line, in any of eight directions, as shown in Figure 3. Thus the output can be encoded by a seven bit string, with four bits for the magnitude of the movement and three bits for the direction. Figure 3 depicts the relationship of the movement vector to its bit string encoding.

The simplicity of our bug brain architecture allows us to use a functional analysis to distinguish levels of complexity. At the same time, the architecture is capable of expressing a sufficiently wide range of behaviours (strategies) so that we can test the robustness of our complexity mea-

$\vec{a} = < a_0a_1a_2a_3, a_4a_5a_6 >$

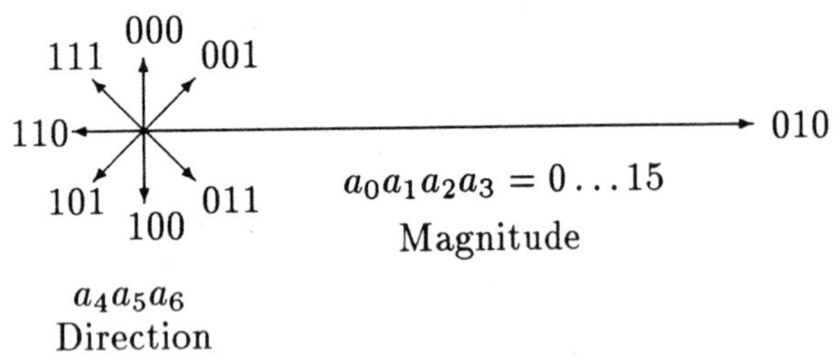

Figure 3: What a Bug Can Do

sure.

5. A Sampling of Strategy Space

Despite the simplicity of this model, it is capable of expressing a range of strategies, some fairly sophisticated. In this section, we provide some examples to demonstrate the breadth of the model as well as to more concretely illustrate several earlier points on the difficulty of interpreting and comparing strategies.

5.1 Evolution Explores Strategy Space

The entire space of possible strategies (instantiations of the model) is quite large. With $2^4 * 2^3 = 2^7$ possible output vectors, and 2^{10} possible environmental configurations, there are $(2^7)^{2^{10}} = 2^{7168}$ different possible lookup tables (LUTs). Most of these are not encodings of "sensible" strategies for the simple environments we imagine[1].

In a typical simulation of evolution, we would initialize N organisms with random LUTs. That is, a random movement vector would be generated for each entry in the table. Thus the initial population would be scattered throughout the strategy space. A genetic alogorithm would then be used to select "better" individuals for reproduction, where offspring would be generated by crossing LUTs of parents (possibly with some mutation). The repetition of selection and breeding results in the population as a whole searching the strategy space on numerous, simultaneous trajectories.

[1]It is interesting to note that for every LUT, we could come up with an environment for which that LUT's strategy would be effective. Designing an environment around a strategy is not unthinkable, and illustrates how dependent fitness and functionality are on the environment in which they are measured.

input	*output*
$d_0d_1d_2d_3d_4d_5d_6d_7d_8d_9$	*magnitude, direction*
0000000000	0010, 101
0000000001	1001, 100
0000000010	0111, 001
0000000011	0110, 100
0000000100	0011, 001
0000000101	1001, 110
0000000110	0100, 010
⋮	⋮
1111111111	0110, 110

Figure 4: A Random Lookup Table

5.2 Some Strategies Emerge

After running our simulation for awhile, more "intelligent" strategies begin to emerge, or so we hope. The output vectors of LUTs become less random and more "predictable" from their inputs. We also hope that they are becoming more complex. Below we present several plausible emergent strategies. These are discussed in order of our intuitive rating of their complexities[2].

5.2.1 The Random LUT

This is the family of initial strategies for the bugs in our population. It is simply an LUT with a move generated at random for each LUT entry. Figure 4 depicts a few lines from one these incipient strategies. Note that the random LUT does not specify a "random-move" strategy. Once generated, the LUT names a fixed move for each environmental situation. Given an empty food field for example, the bug with a random LUT will move in a straight line in a fixed direction.

Intuitively, the random LUT's strategy should turn out to have a very low level of complexity.

5.2.2 The Constant LUT

Another family of simple LUTs is the constant LUT. A constant LUT has a single output vector for all possible inputs. Thus it always specifies the same move. Such a strategy seems quite simple at

[2]This is not to say that the sequence of strategies represents a line of descendents. Indeed, it seems more likely that each strategy listed would have developed from different ancestries.

input	*output*
$d_0d_1d_2d_3d_4d_5d_6d_7d_8d_9$	*magnitude, direction*
0000000000	1010, 101
0000000001	0001, 010
0000000010	0001, 010
0000000011	0001, 010
0000000100	0001, 100
0000000101	0001, 100
0000000110	0001, 010
⋮	⋮
1111111111	0000, 110

Figure 5: A Hill-Climbing Strategy

first, perhaps less complex even than our initial random LUT. But it is also the product of evolution, since it represents a strategy highly adapted to a particular, albeit simple, environment. We could imagine an environment in which the food gradient increases in one direction, until it reaches its maximum at a wall or other obstacle (this represents a slight change to our obstacle-free torus). Or food could always be entering the world from one side of the screen. Thus a strategy of always moving in one fixed direction (toward the fixed line of maximum food) is optimal. This example illustrates how the complexity of the environment promotes and constrains the complexities of the strategies evolved within it.

5.2.3 A Hill-Climbing Strategy

Figure 5 shows the first few entries of an LUT which implements a gradient descent strategy. In such a strategy, the bug moves in the direction of the greatest increase in food level. In other words, the strategy "computes" the difference between the food level of its current position and the food levels of each of its four neighboring cells. It then designates a movement in the direction of the greatest positive difference (i.e., more food). Such a strategy seems, intuitively, to be quite appropriate for almost any environment.

At first glance, it is difficult for a human observer to see the strategy instantiated by the LUT in Figure 5. Comparing it to the first few lines of the random LUT in Figure 4, we see that it requires quite a bit of interpretation and analysis to distinguish the LUT with more intelligent behaviour. Of course, by watching the performance of two bugs, each behaving according to one of the LUTs, we would expect to easily distinguish the wanderer from the hill-climber.

5.2.4 An "Average-Food" Strategy

However, direct observation of behavior cannot be depended upon for judging the relative "sophistication" of LUTs. Take, for example, an "averaging strategy" of moving away from areas of low average food concentrations to areas of high average food values. To implement such a strategy in an LUT, we could compute the average level of food in the five cells, and make a move in a random direction, but with a magnitude related to the average food value. That is, the higher the average food level in the neighborhood, the less far the bug moves. So for very high averages, say greater than two, the bug moves only one or two cells away. For average food values below one, the bug moves 15 cells away.

With such a strategy, the bug would tend to hop around the torus until reaching a good food basin, where it would crawl around randomly until most of the food was consumed, or until it wandered off the edge of the basin. This strategy would make some sense in an environment where uniform food basins were randomly distributed, for example.

The "average-food" strategy would certainly be difficult to understand from a printout of the LUT. It would probably also be difficult to detect by observing the bug's behavior. At least, it would likely take more observation time to distinguish the average-food strategy than it would to see the hill-climbing behaviour. And yet we would all (probably) agree that the average-food strategy is quite sophisticated, relative to the majority of strategy space (although not necessarily as sophisticated as hill-climbing). Whether the average-food strategy is as *effective* as hill-climbing is a question independent of the issue of complexity.

5.2.5 Partial Strategies

For each of the strategies presented so far, a whole family of strategies exist which are "partial implementations" of the full strategies. We would expect to see such partial strategies as ancestors of the complete implementations. One kind of partial implementation would have only some of the correct table entries. Other entries would contain randomly generated moves leftover from the initialization of the first generation.

Another type of partial implementation might have rules that specify movement vectors very close to, but different from, the movement vectors in the full implementation of the strategy. Thus a partial implementation of the hill-climbing LUT might still have some of the original, randomly generated moves for some environmental situations, or it might have rules specifying movement 45 degrees different from the direction of the steepest gradient.

Partial implementations provide a large number of example strategies which should span the range from low-complexity random tables to high-complexity, fully-implemented strategies.

6. The S-R Brain As a Function

Intuition gives us a partial ordering of the strategies discussed so far. We might not agree on whether a random or a constant LUT is more complex, but we would probably all rank both the average-food and the hill-climbing strategies as more sophisticated than the other two. What is it about these LUTs that makes one seem so much more complex than another?

We can view the LUT as a mapping: from environmental input to action output. Viewed as a mapping, those LUTs that seem least complex (e.g., random LUT or constant LUT) have one thing in common: their output is *unrelated* to their input. In the case of the constant LUT, the input simply doesn't matter, as the output is always the same. As for the random LUT, its output is not related to any generalized feature of the input. To have any idea at all of where our bug will move next, we must know its entire local neighborhood. In contrast, the hill-climbing and average-food strategies incorporate relations between output vectors and *similarities* among different environmental configurations. Such strategies make use of discovered, general features of the environment, such as the importance of the current cell [3] in computing a gradient, or the greater weighting to be given to the high order bit in each cell's food detector.

We can think of the LUT as a function from bit strings (the environmental detectors) to a scalar value (the output). The output might be the magnitude of the movement vector, or the angular direction of movement. Once we consider the output as a scalar value, we can perform functional analysis of the LUT.

We might expect that the more complex strategies contain many *sub*functions which recognize environmental features in the input. These subfunctions then contribute to the overall function value an amount *related* to the current value of that feature. For example, the hill-climber strategy contains subfunctions for each of the 2-bit cell detectors. These subfunctions are combined to form other subfunctions which represent the differences between food values of neighboring cells and the food at the current cell. These intermediate subfunctions combine their contributions to determine the net direction or magnitude of movement [4].

For the average-food strategy, subfunctions exist for each 2-bit cell detector, with their contributions used as input to a subfunction that totals the food values, and maps the totals into a magnitude of movement. Simpler strategies, such as staying put if there is any food in the current cell and moving randomly otherwise, have fewer subfunctions and/or a shallower hierarchy of them. The random and constant LUTs seem to have no such subfunctions at all.

There are many ways of restating a function in terms of a linear combination of subfunctions. In this paper, we choose to use the Walsh Transform on the function defined by the LUT. In the next section, we show how the Walsh functions seem to be the very subfunctions we intuitively discussed in this section.

7. The Walsh Complexity Analysis

Viewed as a function, a very complex LUT should place most of the function's "energy" into component subfunctions. In this section, we present the Walsh functions as just the right subfunctions we are looking for. We show how switching the basis of the LUT's function to the Walsh monomial functions makes explicit the distribution of the LUT's functional energy across complex features of the environmental input vector.

7.1 The Walsh Functions

The Walsh functions have been explored as a theoretical tool for many types of analysis. They

[3] That is, the center cell, on which the bug is currently located.

[4] These subfunctions corrrespond to the functions computed by nodes in the hidden layers of a neural network, were we to use such an architecture for our bug brains.

an individual into an ideal test environment and measuring its performance there. But the choice of ideal test environment introduces bias. The most evolved organisms might have a strategy fine-tuned for dealing with the drastic effects of other organisms. For example, a bug from a crowded environment might follow a strategy of avoiding the best food basins, knowing that the current generation of simpler, gradient-followers will pounce on such a pile of food. Instead, our more intelligent organism will seek out the second or third best locations in its local neighborhood. But in isolation, the simpler, greedier gradient-followers will seem more intelligent than the more subtle "compromiser".

Figure 1: Typical Distribution of Food

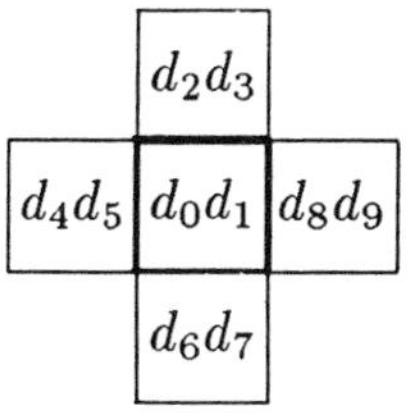

$$\vec{d} = < d_0d_1d_2d_3d_4d_5d_6d_7d_8d_9 >$$

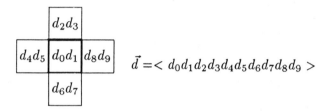

Figure 2: What a Bug Sees

4. The Model

To be more concrete about these issues, we describe our simple world and its inhabitants. This model is due to Norman Packard, and is described in [Packard 89] and [Packard and Bedau 91].

4.1 The World

The environment is a two-dimensional grid, with wraparound (i.e., the surface of a torus), as illustrated in Figure 1. There are only two types of objects: bugs and food. All bugs are the same, apart from having different strategies (lookup tables) as described in the next subsection. Each square can contain zero to three units of food, plus bugs. The darker squares in Figure 1 contain more food than the lighter squares.

Bugs consume food units and produce no waste. Bugs need the energy from food to keep living. Additional energy is required to move and to reproduce. There are no other objects, such as obstacles, traps, poison, or predators. Bugs do not interact, except indirectly, such as for crossover and reproduction, and by consuming the available food. Currently, food enters the world regularly through random placement of gaussian distributions (i.e., "hills" of food), with random mean and variance.

4.2 The Stimulus-Response Brain

The bug's environmental detectors can sense the amount of food in each cell of its neighborhood (i.e., the cell on which it is located, and the four adjoining cells at each of the four major compass points). The range of the environmental detectors is illustrated by Figure 2. The bug cannot detect other bugs, nor can it "see" diagonally. The resolution of food detection is exact: the bug detects exactly what level of food is present, from 0 to 3 units. Thus two bits are sufficient to encode the amount of food in each cell, and a ten bit string, as shown in Figure 2, captures the entire instantaneous environmental input vector.

The ten bit string can be used as an index into a Lookup Table (LUT) of bug output/actions. Thus for each of the 2^{10} possible configurations of the local environment, the LUT specifies a single output. A complete LUT, an array of 1024 outputs, specifies the behavior of a bug.

As for the output, each bug can move from 0 to 15 cells at a time, in a straight line, in any of eight directions, as shown in Figure 3. Thus the output can be encoded by a seven bit string, with four bits for the magnitude of the movement and three bits for the direction. Figure 3 depicts the relationship of the movement vector to its bit string encoding.

The simplicity of our bug brain architecture allows us to use a functional analysis to distinguish levels of complexity. At the same time, the architecture is capable of expressing a sufficiently wide range of behaviours (strategies) so that we can test the robustness of our complexity mea-

picks out the high order bit d_0 in the encoding of the food detector, while the latter corresponds to the lower order bit d_1.

7.4 Plotting Some Strategies

To get some idea of the kind of information available from Walsh transformations, we plot the Walsh coefficients for the four different LUTs discussed earlier.

Before running the LUTs through the Walsh transform, we must map the two dimensional output vector (magnitude,direction) into a scalar. Many ways exist, including simple linear combinations of the two scalar components. Or we could treat each component as a separate scalar function value, and perform separate Walsh analyses on each, thereafter combining the results of the Walsh analysis.

To keep the presentation as clear as possible, we simply choose one of the components, the magnitude, and analyze the LUTs as functions from the 10-bit environmental detectors to a magnitude of movement [7].

Figure 6 plots the 1024 Walsh coefficients for each of the random, average-food, and hill-climber LUTs. Immediately, we contrast the apparent "structures" of the two more sophisticated strategies with the scatter of the random LUT. It seems there is a lot of information available in the Walsh coefficients.

For example, we can group Walsh coefficients by their *order*. The *order* of a coefficient is the number of bit positions over which the corresponding Walsh function is defined. Thus, w_6 is an order two coefficient, since ψ_6 is a function of bit positions 2 and 4 in the input vector. The order of a Walsh coefficient corresponds to the breadth of environmental information for which it accounts. There are $l+1$ possible orders, including order 0.

Figure 7 plots the distribution of energy across orders for the Walsh coefficients for the random, average-food, and hill-climber LUTs. For each of the 10 orders, we plot the average *magnitude* (i.e., absolute value) of all coefficients of that order. Since we are interested in the distribution of energy, the signs of the coefficients are not important; only their effect on the function value is. Also, we do not show order 0, which only

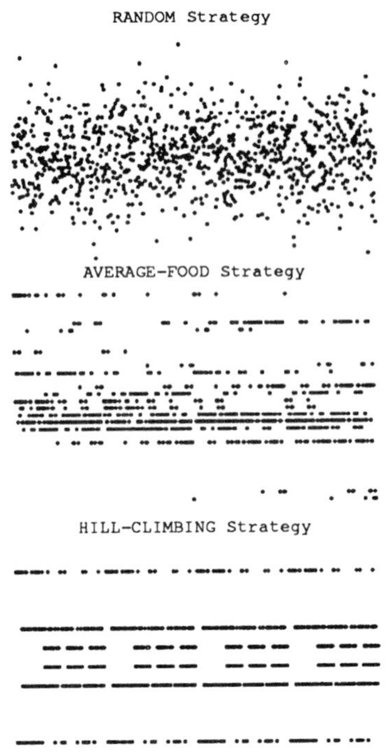

Figure 6: Scatter Plots of Walsh Coefficients

contains the single coefficient w_0. We know that w_0 is the average function value, corresponding to schema **********. We are interested in the other Walsh coefficients, which call for *changes* to the average function value for certain environmental situations.

Figure 7 reveals some interesting differences among the strategies. The random LUT seems to have its energy distributed uniformly across orders[8]. The more sophisticated LUTs, on the other hand, have far from uniform distributions[9]. Both the average-food and the hill-climbing strategies have high average values for order one coefficients because both recognize that 1's in any bit position mean food. The random LUT doesn't "know" about the relationship of 1's to food.

More speculatively, the hill-climber strategy gives relatively more credence to order 2 subfunctions, because it is comparing two cells in order to compute a gradient, and the high-order bits are most important to compare. The average-food strategy, on the other hand, does not compare cells. It does, however, add up all the food val-

[7]The hill-climbing LUT will be simulated by a strategy of moving very little distance when the steepest gradient is high, and moving very much when it is low. The average-food, random, and constant LUTs need no modification.

[8]Order 10 is low only because it contains a single coefficient, w_{1023}, and so is more subject to noise than the other orders.

[9]Note that the constant LUT also has a uniform distribution, since all coefficients but w_0 would equal 0.

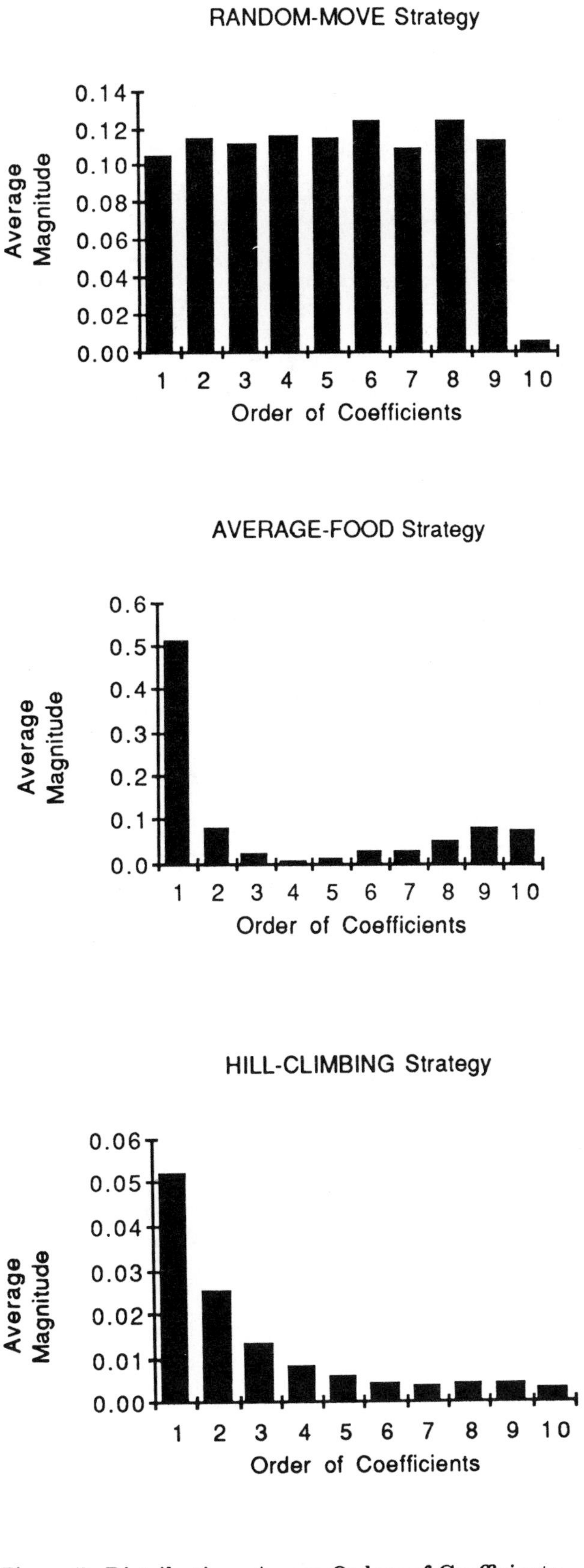

Figure 7: Distributions Across Orders of Coefficients

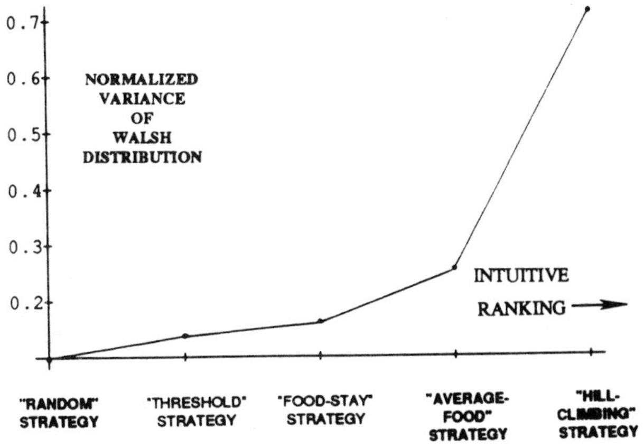

Figure 8: An Objective Ranking of Complexity

ues for all cells, explaining the relatively higher values for the higher order coefficients.

7.5 Condensing the Information

Figure 7 illustrates only one of many ways to compress and examine the "Walsh information". We could also plot the distribution of energy (magnitudes) *within* an order n, and see which particular n-bit combinations are important to the strategy.

But we must further compress the Walsh information if we want a single, scalar value that estimates the complexity of the LUTs. Figure 7 suggests that the more complex an LUT, the farther from uniform will be its distributions of energy across coefficient orders. Figure 6 suggests that many dispersed clusters are an indication of many different sub-strategies interwoven in the same LUT. Clearly, we have not yet isolated all of the relevent information from the Walsh coefficients, nor have we found the best way to project that into a single complexity measure. But it does seem that most if not all of the information we need is present in the coefficients. It also seems that the **variance** of the distribution would be a good first approximation.

In Figure 8, we plot the normalized variances of the Walsh distributions for several different LUTs. Specifically, we take the average magnitude of all Walsh coefficients other than w_0. Next we sum the square roots of the differences between each coefficient and the average. Then we normalize by dividing by w_0. The resulting measure of the spread of Walsh coefficient magnitudes is plotted as an estimate of the *objective complexity* of the strategy. As Figure 8 illustrates, this objective complexity ranking roughly corresponds to our intuitive ranking, although the average-food LUT seems under-rated to us.

8. Conclusions and Future Work

The focus of this paper has been the nature of complexity: what it is, how to measure it, and a conjecture that an increase in complexity is synonymous with evolution. These general, philosophical issues were discussed in the context of a specific, but simple, model of artificial life and evolution, allowing us to propose and analyze a concrete measure of complexity.

The Walsh complexity analysis presented in this paper is specific to the S-R type of strategy encoding. However, the Walsh complexity measure does seem to capture much of our intuitive notion of complexity. And its ranking of a few example strategies agrees with our intuitive ranking. But much work needs to be done.

The highest priority is to more rigorously test and fine-tune this measure. The refinement should involve three parallel efforts. First, we can use our measure to rank a large number of other strategies. The S-R architecture is expressive enough to provide many more example strategies, such as the partial implementations of strategies, discussed earlier. Second, the utility of this measure as an indicator of evolution should be tested immediately, by using it to track a simulation of evolution. We can use the measure to isolate organisms with high objective rankings of complexity, and then examine their strategies to see if we agree with the measure's predictions. Third, additional analytical work should be pursued, to better understand what information is lost and what is retained under various compressions of the Walsh information. Even if our method of compressing the Walsh data turns out to be only an approximate measure of objective complexity, I believe that all the right ingredients for such a measure are produced by the Walsh analysis. We must explore more of the information available from the Walsh transform.

It is also clear that the S-R architecture is a good model for these early studies of evolving complexity. Once we understand exactly what complexity is and how it behaves in one simple AI architecture, we can more easily define complexity measures for other architectures, such as neural networks or classifier systems[10]. Eventually, we should be able to generalize the measurement of complexity to all systems capable of evolution.

We will then be able to discuss other important issues, such as distinctions between complexity, utility, and intelligence, and the difference between evolution and adaptation. I expect that we will someday define evolution as the net increase in overall complexity (i.e., emergent complexity). Perhaps we will even define intelligence in terms of a threshold level of complexity.

[10]The simplest Classifier System is known as a "Stimulus-Response" Classifier System. It has no internal message list and is equivalent to our LUT.

References

[Packard 89] Packard, Norman H. 1989. Intrinsic adaptation in a simple model for evolution. In *Artificial Life*, edited by Christopher Langton. Redwood City, CA: Addison-Wesley.

[Bedau and Packard 91] Bedau, Mark A. and Packard, Norman H. 1991. Evolutionary activity, teleology, and life. In *Artificial Life II*, edited by Christopher Langton, et. al. Redwood City, CA: Addison-Wesley.

[Packard and Bedau 91] Packard, Norman H. and Bedau, Mark A. 1991. A complexity measure. *Unpublished manuscript.*

[Goldberg 89a] Goldberg, David E. Genetic algorithms and Walsh functions: part I, a gentle introduction. *Complex Systems* 3, 1989, 129-152.

[Goldberg 89b] Goldberg, David E. Genetic algorithms and Walsh functions: part II, deception and its analysis. *Complex Systems* 3, 1989, 153-171.

[Goldberg 90] Goldberg, David E. 1990. Construction of high-order deceptive functions using low-order Walsh coefficients. *IlliGAL Report No. 90002*, Illinois Genetic Algorithms Laboratory, Department of of General Engineering, University of Illinois at Urbana-Champaign.

[Bethke 80] Bethke, A.D. 1980. Genetic algorithms as function optimizers. Ph.D. dissertation, University of Michigan.

[Goldberg 89c] Goldberg, David E. 1989. *Genetic Algorithms in Search, Optimization, and Machine Learning.* Reading, MA: Addison-Wesley.

NATURAL SELECTION IN A POPULATION OF AUTOMATA

Petr Kůrka

Department of Philosophy of Mathematics and Physics,
Faculty of Mathematics and Physics, Charles University
Malostranské náměstí 25, 118 00 Praha 1, Czechoslovakia

1 Introduction

Although the theory of natural selection permeates much of modern biological thought, its logical and mathematical analysis is not yet available. The problem is in its great generality, which borders with unfalsifiability. There is a great number of possibilities to formulate a mathematical theory of natural selection and different formalizations lead to different and often opposite properties. Thus the evolutionary process based on a zero-sum game is quite different from that based on a game of partnership (Kůrka 1986). The elucidation of the dynamics of natural selection is the task of mathematics, but this is difficult both in full generality and in special cases. The fitness landscape obtained in evolutionary models is usually very irregular and rugged (see Schuster 1989 for discussion of this issue) and most mathematical techniques fail. Only populational genetics formulates a tractable theory of natural selection, but it is based on too simple model of gene expression and does not take into account complex gene interactions.

In the absence of a mathematical theory, there is a number of mathematical or computer models clarifying some aspects of natural selection. There are several evolutionary models, in which a population inhabits a fitness landscape and clusters around fitness maxima (Eigen and Schuster 1977, Niklas 1986, Dawkins 1986, Dewdney 1989, Galar 1989). The fitness in these models, however, is a property of an individual, rather than a property of its relation to the population, so the ecological dimension of natural selection is lost.

A simple model of interaction between individuals of a population provides the theory of games (Maynard-Smith 1982, Hofbauer and Sigmund 1984). A genotype describes strategy, which the individual adopts in encounters with other individuals. When there are enough strategies available, the resulting evolutionary models have rich behaviour with interesting features. This is the case in repeated matrix games, in which an individual chooses its moves on the base of past moves of the opponent (Kůrka 1986, Axelrod 1982, Miller 1989, Kůrka and Pavlík 1991).

Implicitly, these models are based on the metaphor of genetical information as computer program. This metaphor is rather widespread: It is the base of Dawkins's approach (Dawkins 1982, Dawkins 1986), and even Mayr (1982) relies on it considerably. Recently, it has been criticised by Atlan and Koppel (1990) on the grounds of Turing's

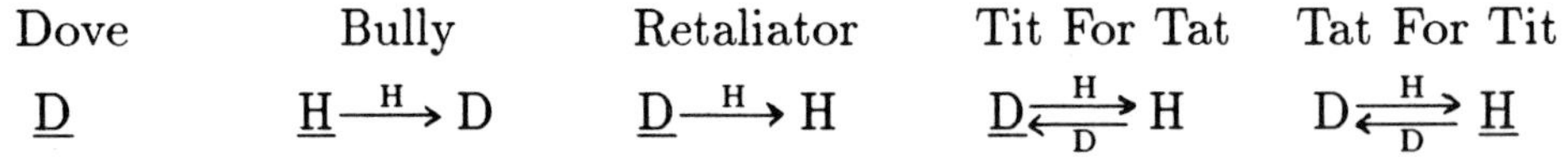

	1
	D
D	1
H	1

	1	2
	H	D
D	1	2
H	2	2

	1	2
	D	H
D	1	2
H	2	2

	1	2
	D	H
D	1	1
H	2	2

	1	2
	D	H
D	1	1
H	2	2

Figure 1: Automata represented by graphs and tables

Halting theorem: If the genetical information were really a program (i.e. a description of a Turing machine), then vast majority of mutations would be deleterious, and the evolution through random mutations would be unimaginable. It is significant, in the light of this criticism, that the evolutionary models so far proposed do not use the computer metaphor in this strong sense. Rather, these models use a recursive set of genotypes: Genotypes are vectors of integers or reals in Niklas 1986, Dawkins 1986, and Dewdney 1989, or recursive sets of strings of letters in Eigen and Schuster 1977, and Kůrka 1985. Because of recursiveness, it is possible to check the correctness of genotypes in advance, so that the majority of generated genotypes is viable. This fact can be counted as a support for Atlan and Koppel's thesis.

In the present contribution we reflect on the results of Kůrka and Pavlík (1991). We consider a population of finite automata, which play with each other the repeated Hawk-dove game. At each time step, an automaton chooses its move on the base of the previous moves of the partner. The game is played indefinitely and the pay-off of each player is the average of its pay-offs at single moves. The set of automata is infinite (though recursive), and there are many possibilities for both competition and cooperation between the partners. The automata reproduce and sometimes mutate. The lifespan of an automaton is inversely proportional to its fitness (mean pay-off obtained against other automata of the population).

In the repeated Hawk-dove game the natural selection leads to the establishment of an ecological network of mutually cooperating individuals. Two automata may cooperate by alternating hawk and dove strategy and thus obtain more than two doves. When a nucleus of cooperating automata appears, it gets selective advantage, dominates the population, and then slowly evolves to ever increasing complexity, interdependence and variability. When such a community evolves, it is very stable. The participating individuals may change, but the cooperative pattern persists.

2 Genotypes

We consider the Hawk-dove game with strategies $S = \{D, H\}$ and a pay-off matrix $(A_{ij})_{i,j\in S}$

	D	H
D	2	0
H	6	-2

The game is played repeatedly by two partners, who independently choose either hawk or dove. Their choices are revealed simultaneously, and a player choosing strategy $i \in S$ obtains pay-off A_{ij} if its partner has chosen strategy j. We suppose that the game

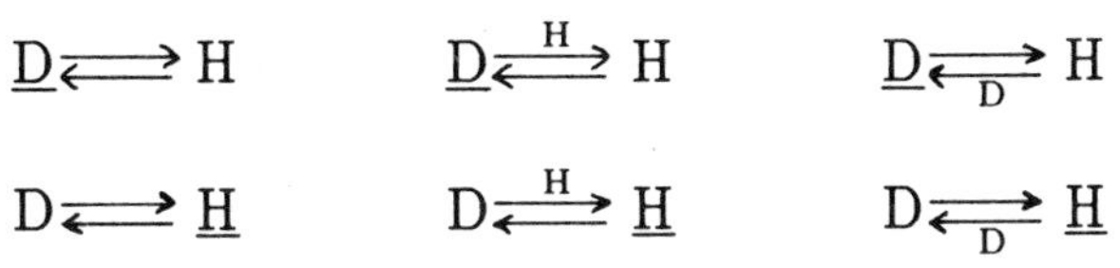

Figure 2: Cooperating automata

is played by finite automata. A finite automaton represents a model of rational behaviour. It is a device with finite set of inner states. At each time step it plays the strategy determined by its current inner state and switches to another state in dependence on its partner's move. We picture automata as labelled graphs. The vertices represent the inner states labelled by strategies, which the automaton outputs. The arrows are labelled by strategies too, and represent transitions, which the automaton undergoes upon communicating the partner's move. An unlabelled arrow means transition for both strategies. The initial state is specified with underlining.

The genotype of an automaton is a table with three rows and n columns, where n is the number of states, together with the specification of the initial state. First row represents outputs, and its entries are strategies. Second and third row represent the transition function and their entries are numbers from 1 to n. The initial state is again underlined. Some examples are in Fig. 1.

Thus Dove is an automaton which plays D, disregarding the moves of the opponent. Bully plays hawk so long as its partner plays dove, and switches to dove as soon as the partner plays at least once hawk. Conversely Retaliator plays dove so long as the partner plays dove and then switches to hawk. Tit For Tat plays at first dove and then the last move of the partner, while Tat For Tit differs only in playing at the beginninig hawk.

For example, when Bully plays against Tit For Tat, then its moves are $HHDDDD...$ and those of Tit For Tat are $DHHDDD....$ We see that after three moves the games stabilize and both partners play dove. We neglect therefore the irregular beginning and set down both pay-offs as $A_{BT} = A_{TB} = 2$. Similarly the games of Tit For Tat against Tat For Tit are $DHDH....$ and $HDHD....$ respectively. Both sequences have period of length 2. We define the pay-offs as mean pay-offs obtained in this cycle. Thus the pay-offs of both Tit For Tat and Tat For Tit are $(6+0)/2 = 3$. In general, any game of two automata eventually reaches a cycle, whose length is at most the product of numbers of states of both automata. The pay-offs of the automata in question is defined as their mean pay-off in this cycle. In this way we obtain extended pay-off matrix for the whole (infinite) set of automata.

The pay-off of an automaton playing against itself is at most 2: in the repeated game only pairs of identical moves occur. On the other hand two different automata may alternately play dove and hawk against one another, so that they obtain mean pay-off 3. In this case we say that the automata cooperate. An example of cooperation is provided by six two-state automata in Fig. 2. The pay-offs of these automata against themselves ranges from -2 to 2, but any two of them cooperate and obtain pay-off 3. Other examples of cooperation are obtained when the second automaton is replaced by Tit For Tat, or when the last automaton is replaced by Tat For Tit.

3 Mutations

According to the approach of genetical algorithms exposed in Holland 1975, we consider several genetic operators, which produce new automata by modifying the current ones. The genetical operators respect the "grammar of the genes", i.e. the syntactical constraints on the tables.

1. Point mutation: Another initial state is picked up or the value of either output or transition function is changed at one argument. This means that an entry of the table is changed.

2. Insertion: A new state is added and the transition and output functions are defined on it arbitrarily: A new column is added to the table. This is a neutral mutation, since the added state is not accessible from the initial one, and therefore the behaviour is not changed.

3. Deletion: A noninitial state is removed and the transitions leading to it are redirected: A column is removed from the table and the pointers are updated.

4. Conjunction: Two automata are united and a new initial state is added with transitions leading to the initial states of original automata: The tables are concatenated, new initial state is added and the pointers are updated.

We regard these mutations as errors in replication, which occur with certain probabilities. We suppose that each mutation of a given type is equally likely. However, the probabilities of insertion, deletion and conjunction depend on the number of states, so that the number of states would not grow without limit.

4 Selection

The selection process might be based either on game dynamics as in Kůrka 1985 and Kůrka 1986, on its stochastic version as in Kůrka and Pavlík 1991, or on a more complex computer algorithm as in Miller 1989. While game dynamics is more amenable to mathematical analysis, its stochastic version is closer to the spirit of natural selection. A genotype is typically present in a single copy at most, and there is a great genetical variability.

We have the set $\overline{S}$ of automata and for each automata $p, q \in \overline{S}$ their pay-offs A_{pq} and A_{qp}. The state of a population is given by a population vector $X = (X_p)_{p \in \overline{S}}$ of numbers of automata of each type. X_p are nonnegative integers, whose sum $N = \sum_{p \in \overline{S}} X_p$ is finite (population size). The phenotype of an individual p in a population X consists in its pay-offs against other individuals of X. We say that two individuals p, q are phenotypically equivalent ($p \overset{X}{\approx} q$) with respect to X if they have the same pay-off with individuals of X, i.e. if for each r for which $X_r > 0$ there is $A_{pr} = A_{qr}$, $A_{rp} = A_{rq}$. The phenotype of an individual determines its fitness, which is its average pay-off against other individuals except itself. (For this reason, A_{pp} is weighted by $X_p - 1$ instead of X_p.)

$$F_p(X) = (\sum_{q \in \overline{S}} A_{pq} X_q - A_{pp})/(\sum_{q \in \overline{S}} X_q - 1)$$

Note that the fitness of an individual depends on the whole population X.

To keep the population size constant, we suppose, that at each time step an individual reproduces and another dies. The rate of reproduction is uniform. An individual is chosen randomly and either reproduces without error or mutates to a slightly different one. New individual may also arise as a conjunction of two randomly chosen individuals. The choice of the automata to be reproduced or

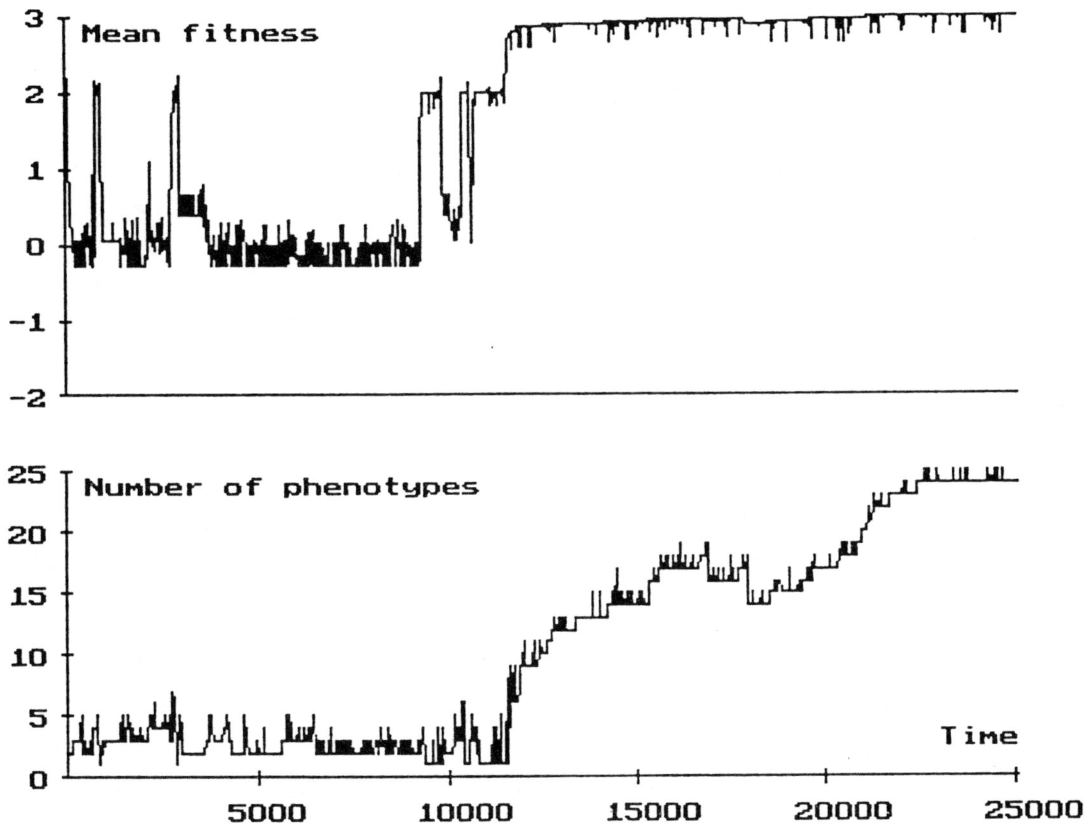

Figure 3: Evolution of fitness and diversity

conjuncted is independent on its fitness. This yields greater variability in reproduced individuals with greater possibilities of successful mutations. The fitness determines the probability of death: the individuals with lesser fitness are more likely to die. These rules determine transition probabilities between population states. In this way the natural selection is conceived as a Markov process whose states are population vectors of given size.

5 Computer simulations

The result of a typical computer simulation is depicted in Fig. 3. Here population size is 25, the probability of error-free reproduction is 0.7 and that of point mutation is 0.21. The probabilities of insertion and mutation depend on the number of states and make together 0.09. (Conjunction is not used here: it does not significantly change the results.) We plot two rough characteristics of the population. The mean fitness ranges from -2 for a population of Hawks to 3 for a population of cooperating automata. The number of phenotypes, i.e. the number of phenotypically nonequivalent automata ranges from 1 to the population size.

At the beginning, all individuals are Doves and the mean fitness is 2. Soon a Hawk appears, the mean fitness slightly rises and then drops as the Hawks multiply. Further variants of hawk-like strategies appear, lowering the mean fitness bellow zero. This is a quasistable state, which persists usually for several thousands of simulation steps. Occasionally Retaliators succeed, drive out the Hawks, and establish a population of automata phenotypically equivalent to Doves. Such a population is more stable than that of pure doves, nevertheless, because of its phenotypical homogeneity, it is endangered by neutral mutations. The dove-like automata reappear and the population becomes vulnerable to hawk-like automata, which ultimately prevail, and lower again the mean fitness below zero. This development is reminiscent of the dynamics of doves, hawks, bullies and retaliators treated in Zeeman 1981.

Sooner or later, however, a group of two or three cooperating automata appears. For some time they coexist with Hawks and hawk-like automata, but three cooperating automata are already strong enough to drive the Hawks out. This process is enhanced by structural similarity of cooperating automata. Thus there are six two-state cooperating automata, which differ only slightly. As soon as two or three of them appear, the other follow quickly afterwards. Once a cooperative population appears, it is very stable. It may happen that a new mutant automaton outplays all individuals present and bring the cooperation to an end. With increasing number of phenotypes, however, such an event is very unlikely. More often a mutant automaton finds a new way of cooperation, i.e. it finds an unoccupied ecological niche. In this way the number of phenotypes grows, till it approaches the population size. Then the population slowly drifts through other modes of cooperation. From time to time a mutant appears and outplays a small number of automata, while cooperating with other ones. The outplayed individuals are driven out and new cooperating automata soon appear to replace them. This event is visible in a small, short-lived drop in mean fitness. The composition of population slowly changes, individuals once driven out reappear again, but the cooperation persists. The emergence of cooperative behaviour is a fairly regular event, occurring under nearly arbitrary initial conditions.

We can modify the model by dropping the assumption of constant population size. Let us suppose, that when the mean fitness is high enough, then reproduction is more likely than death, so that the population grows. With this assumption the number of phenotypes grows without limits. New strategies succeed only if they find a really novel way of cooperation. This means that their complexity and sophistication steadily increase.

6 Concluding remarks

The presented model illustrates some of the fundamental features of the theory of natural selection. The evolutionary process is a stochastic process taking place in the space of genotype distributions. There is infinity of genotypes, they have simple structure and determine a great variety of phenotypes. The process of gene expression, the translation of genotypes to phenotypes, is nevertheless complex and nontrivial. Similar genotypes may yield identical, similar or quite different phenotypes. There is a hierarchy of neutral mutations. Some mutations do not change the behaviour at all, other manifest themselves only under specific circumstances. Neutral mutations may be hidden for a long time and then manifest suddenly. Mutation is a random unpremeditated event with rather uniform distribution. The fitness of an individual depends on the whole population. Individuals with higher fitness have greater survival probability.

We have seen that in the repeated Hawk-dove game these assumptions lead to establishment of a cooperating ecosystem and its subsequent ramifications and self-organization. This is, however, not the neccessary consequence of natural selection alone. The structure of the underlying game is quite essential. There is no cooperation in a zero-sum game. As a result, the population of automata playing the rock-paper-scissors game, for example, remains forever on a rather primitive level. It is dominated by simplest automata and no ecosystem is established. When a more sophisticated strategy does appear, it is soon driven out by a simpler one (Kůrka 1987).

The current neodarwinian theory of evolution through natural selection postulates, that the fitness of an organism is determined by its genotype and environment, which includes genotypes of other organisms. The deciphering of this dependence is presumably the task of molecular biology. At present, however, this is not in sight. Without this law of gene expression, the theory of natural selection is incomplete und unfalsifiable. Different assumptions about the laws of gene expression lead to quite different patterns of evolutionary events. Moreover, any evolutionary event can be explained by natural selection. This is like classical mechanics, in which the Gravitation law would be replaced by the assumption, that some gravitation law exists. In such a theory, any trajectory could be explained, but no trajectory could be predicted.

It is therefore desirable to supplement the theory of natural selection with rules constraining gene expression. One possibility suggests the approach of Atlan and Koppel (1990). Another might come from non-equilibrium thermodynamics.

References

Atlan,H., M.Koppel. 1990. The cellular computer DNA: program or data. *Bulletin of Mathematical Biology* vol.52, no.3: 335-348.

Axelrod,H. 1987. The evolution of strategies in the iterated Prisoner's dilemma. In *Genetic Algorithms and Simulated Annealing*. Edited by L.David. Los Altos, California: Morgan Kaufmann.

Dawkins,R. 1982. *The Extended Phenotype*. Oxford: Freeman.

Dawkins,R. 1986. *The Blind Watchmaker*. Harlow: Longman Scientific & Technical.

Dewdney,A.K. Computer recreations. Simulated evolution: wherein bugs learn to hunt bacteria. *Scientific American*. May 1989, 104-107.

Eigen,M., P.Schuster. 1977. The hypercycle, a principle of natural self-organization. *Naturwissenschaften* 64,11:541-565.

Galar,R. 1989. Evolutionary search with soft selection. *Biological Cybernetics* 60: 357-364.

Hofbauer,J., K.Sigmund. 1984.: *Evolutionstheorie und dynamische Systeme. Mathematische Aspekte der Selection.* Berlin: Verlag Paul Parey.

Holland,J. 1975. *Adaptation in Natural and Artificial Systems*. Ann Arbor: University of Michigan Press.

Kůrka,P. 1985. Evolution of replicators playing a strategic game. *Biological Cybernetics* 52: 211-217.

Kůrka,P. 1986. Game dynamics and evolutionary transitions. *Biological Cybernetics* 54: 85-90.

Kůrka,P. 1987. Darwinian evolution in games with perfect information. *Biological Cybernetics* 55: 281-288.

Kůrka,P. 1990. Game theoretical models of mutation and selection. In *Organizational Constraints on the Dynamics of Evolution.* Edited by J.Maynard-Smith and G.Vida. Manchester: Manchester University Press.

Kůrka,P., T.Pavlík. 1991. Cooperation in the Hawk-dove game. Submitted for publication.

Mayr,E. 1982. *The Growth of Biological Thought. Diversity, Evolution and Inheritance.* Cambridge: Harvard University Press.

Maynard-Smith,J. 1982. *Evolution and the Theory of Games.* Cambridge: Cambridge University Press.

Miller,J.H. 1989. The coevolution of automata in the repeated Prisoner's dilemma. Santa Fe Institute.

Niklas,K.J. Computer-simulated Plant Evolution. *Scientific American.* March 1986.

Schuster,P. 1989. Optimization and Complexity in Molecular Biology and Physics. In *Optimal Structures in Heterogenous Reaction Systems.* Edited by J.Plath. Berlin: Springer-Verlag.

Sigmund,K. 1986. A survey of replicator equations. In *Complexity, Language and Life: Mathematical Approaches.* Berlin: Springer-Verlag.

Zeeman,E.C. 1981. Dynamics of the evolution of animal conflicts. *Journal of Theoretical Biology* 89:249-270.

EPISTEMOLOGICAL ISSUES AND CONCEPTUAL FOUNDATIONS

The Historical and Epistemological Ground of von Neumann's Theory of Self-Reproducing Automata and Theory of Games

Stefan Helmreich
Department of Anthropology
Stanford University
Stanford, CA 94305 USA

stefang@portia.stanford.edu

> He built a machine and fashioned a digital model of the Void, an Electrostatic Spirit to move upon the face of the electrolytic waters, and he introduced the parameter of light, a protogalactic cloud or two, and by degrees worked his way up to the first ice age...
>
> — Stanislaw Lem, *The Cyberiad*, p. 44.

Researchers in the nascent discipline of Artificial Life might not be engaging in projects quite as grandiose as the above, but they are certainly tackling problems and questions of cosmological dimension. Christopher Langton's attempts to define the new field give some idea of its scope: "The whole notion of Artificial Life is trying to abstract the relevant details of living things from the probably irrelevant details of the particular material in which life happened to emerge on the planet earth" (quoted in Brockman 1991:5) and "Artificial Life can contribute to theoretical biology by locating *life-as-we-know-it* within the larger picture of *life-as-it-could be*" (Langton 1989:1). Taking advantage of ever increasing computer power, and deriving cautionary lessons from the failings of Artificial Intelligence's too grand project of wizarding up intelligent machines full-blown, Artificial Life researchers are modeling life on computers beginning from the bottom up, trying to get emergent behavior from the rule-governed interaction of simple elements in complex systems. They continue a long Western tradition of trying to fabricate simulacra of living organisms — a tradition that extends from the Rabbi of Prague's Golem of clay, to the hydraulic and mechanical contraptions of mid-millennium, to Mary Shelly's Frankenstein, to the von Neumannian self-reproducing automata which this paper takes as one of its concerns.

In this paper, I contend that the project of theorizing *life-as-it-could-be* is powerfully influenced by our symbolically constructed images of *life-as-we-know-it*. I argue that our abstractions of "life's formal properties" are inescapably grounded in an historical, epistemological, and cultural context. In particular, I maintain that religious, philosophical, and political systems of knowledge strongly guide the way we think about life, artificial or otherwise.

I concern myself here with two important formulations of *life-as-it-could-be* drawn by the influential mathematician and computer scientist John von Neumann. The first is his theory of self-reproducing automata, and the second is his theory of games (initially perhaps not self-evidently about life, but if we consider how extensively it has been applied to evolution, manifestly so). The enormous influence which von Neumann's ideas have had in computer science and in molecular and evolutionary biology promises to continue in Artificial Life.[1] I suggest that we step back for a moment to examine these ideas more closely. I here anatomize von Neumann's formulations against the ground of Judeo-Christian narratives of life and creation, representational theories of language, Cartesian metaphysics, and utilitarian political philosophy. Far from being the most purified models of life and its interactions, von Neumann's models interdigitate with the postulates of thousands of years of Western thought. The models could be otherwise, and if the project of Artificial Life is truly to consider *life-as-it-could-be*, then we should listen to alternative visions and examine more critically the ones we already have. As H. H. Pattee said in his contribution to the first conference on Artificial Life, "Computer users, of all people, should find it evident that there are many alternative ways to successfully simulate any behavior" (1989:68).

Self-Reproducing Automata

John von Neumann was fascinated by the possibility of formalizing intellect, as his *The Computer and the Brain* (1958) — in which he made some of the first analogies between the brain and the digital computer — testifies. Beyond this, he was also

---

1 Von Neumann's ideas have also been important in theories of international relations. During his tenure at the RAND corporation, von Neumann used his game theoretical constructs to help shape U. S. Cold War foreign policy.

intrigued by the notion that life itself might be formalizable. Extensions of this interest, expressed in his "General and Logical Theory of Automata" (1951), led him eventually to questions about self-reproduction—questions he attempted to answer in *Theory of Self-Reproducing Automata* (1966). As Arthur Burks, editor of this posthumous volume, put it "He wished to abstract from the natural self-reproduction problem its logical form" (quoted in Langton 1989:13). He conceived two ways of doing this: one, using a kinematic model, and the other using a cellular model.[2] I will examine each in turn.

The kinematic model

> The constructing automaton floats on a surface, surrounded by an unlimited supply of parts ... [it] contains in its memory a description of the automaton to be constructed. Operating under the direction of the description, it picks up the parts it needs and assembles them into the desired automaton (von Neumann 1966:82).

For a self-reproducing automaton, the stored description is obviously a self-description, and if the automaton is really to reproduce itself to the smallest detail, it must enable its offspring to reproduce too: the self-description must contain instructions to bestow a self-description to offspring automata. This is not too difficult with von Neumann's idea of the stored program: instructions and data are both represented numerically in memory, so that instructions can be transmitted as data and then reconverted.

H. H. Pattee has said that "Von Neumann's kinematic description of the logical requirements for evolvable self-replication should be a paradigm for artificial life study" (1989:69). I would agree, but more along the following lines: von Neumann's model is most useful for helping us think about the preconceptions we bring to any characterization of life's logical form. Since Pattee is eager to remind us that simulations of life should not be mistaken for realizations of life, I think he might concur.

Compare von Neumann's description of the kinematic model with the Biblical myth of creation:

> And the earth was without form and void;
> and darkness was on the face of the deep.
> And the Spirit of God moved upon the face
> of the waters....And God said, Let us make
> man in our image, in our likeness: and let
> them have dominion over ...all the earth,
> and over every creeping thing that creepeth
> on the earth (Genesis 1:2-26).

Like God, von Neumann's automaton has come from nowhere, floats on nameless waters, and already contains within itself the idea of the creature it will create. And like God, it is enabled to create with description, with language. With its code it will beget a creature in its own image.

We might imagine, though, that by the time von Neumann has started his story this has already transpired—we may be dealing with an automaton Adam. It certainly seems like it, since the kinematic model relies on a material instantiation to work, and the automaton is placed, like Adam, into a bounteous Biblical Garden of Eden. We are also reminded that Adam inherited the divine power of language somewhat diminished: where God's very words created the things of the world, Adam was only able to name things that already existed—like animals in the Garden of Eden, and Eve, the first woman (Genesis 2:19-20, 3:20). Like Adam, our automaton names already extant things; the coded description of parts it needs to fabricate a copy of itself correspond exactly and unproblematically to pre-given objects in the world.

The assumption that words refer transparently to empirical things and processes is one of the foundations of Western thought, elaborated in traditions from Judeo-Christian (and Islamic) cosmology to modern analytic philosophy. This assumption, however, is gravely flawed; it neglects the fundamentally social nature of language. Words do not refer to things but rather to socially constructed concepts. In the terminology of Ferdinand de Saussure, the relationship between *signifiers* (words, or "sound-images") and *signifieds* (concepts, *not* things) is arbitrary and the product of convention (1915). Language can never give us unmediated description of the world, and attempts to formalize language as a kind of calculus neglect its essentially hermeneutic nature.

But von Neumann's contention that "logical propositions can be represented as electrical networks or nervous systems" (1956:44) still guides most work in Artificial Intelligence (Winograd and Flores 1986). And the transparency of linguistic description is also taken for granted in much evolutionary biology. As Richard Lewontin has pointed out, when we talk of adaptation, we assume that "the partitioning of organisms into [behavioral or physical] traits and the partitioning of the environment into problems has a real basis and is not simply the reification of intuitive"— I would say cultural—"human categories" (1984:241). Chris Langton's statement that "you take populations of these programs and let them work on their *environment*, which is the *problem*..." shows that such an assumption is easily imported into Artificial Life (quoted in Brockman 1991:6, emphasis added). If we are to take language as a social process seriously, we must wonder whether the representational code provided to von Neumann's problem solving automaton in the kinematic model could really work.

---

2 Actually he envisioned five, only two of which he was able to elaborate before his death of cancer in 1956. They were: the kinematic model, the cellular model, the excitation-threshold-fatigue model, the continuous model, and the probabilistic model (von Neumann 1966:93).

The cellular automata model

Von Neumann was not satisfied with his kinematic model because he felt that it "did not properly distinguish the logic of the process from the material of the process" (Langton 1989:13). For one thing, the model specified a motile organism, an animal. Perhaps plants and other kinds of life might be included too. At the suggestion of his colleague, Stanislaw Ulam, von Neumann embedded the kinematic model into a formalism now known as a cellular automaton (CA). Here is how Chris Langton and Richard Laing explain it:

> ...a CA model consists of a regular lattice of *finite automata*, which are the simplest formal models of machines. A finite automaton can be in only one of a finite number of states at a time, and its transitions between states are governed by a *state transition table*: given a certain input and a certain internal state, the state transition table specifies the state to be adopted by the finite automaton at the next time step. In a CA, the necessary input is derived from the states of the automata at the neighboring lattice points. Thus the state of an automaton at time $t+1$ is a function of the states of the automaton itself and its immediate neighbors at time t. All of the automata in the lattice obey the same transition table and every automaton changes state at the same instant, time step after time step (Langton 1989:13)

> ...organism reproduction takes place in an indefinitely extended...array of identical automata ... each of [which] ... is capable of being in 29 different states (Laing 1989:50).

Reproduction happens when a differentiated portion of the cell space — a "parent organism" consisting "of a contiguous active configuration of cell-automata making up a general purpose computer and constructor along with an expandable memory" (Laing 1989:50) — transforms "undifferentiated cell-automata" into copies of itself, each one containing its own self-description.

Because it was crucial to von Neumann that the kinematic model could be formalized in a CA lattice, many presumptions of the kinematic model remain lodged in the CA model, most notably the idea of creation through coded language. We must remember, though, that the numbers assigned to finite state machines in the CA mean nothing by themselves; they must be given an initial and continuing interpretation by a God-like programmer who sets the whole thing in motion. It's easy to see how interpretation might be confounded with objective description, however, because logic, as language, is seen as giving a transparent description of the world. And formal structure, in Western, Judeo-Christian thought, is also seen as transcendent over and superior to material instantiation.

The concern with abstracting the logical form of life from its material realization is foreshadowed as far back in scientific history as Aristotle, who granted "form" and "material" actual genders. As he phrased it in his *Generation of Animals*, "The male provides the 'form' and the 'principle of movement', the female provides the body, in other words, the material" (I.XX.729a). This gendering of form (as active male principle) and material (as passive female principle) is perhaps most powerfully rendered in the agricultural metaphor for animal and human reproduction used in the Bible (and also in the Qu'ran): males plant their "seed" in the receptive and yielding "soil" of females (Delaney 1986, 1991). Abraham is promised by God, "I will multiply thy seed as the stars of heaven" (Genesis 22:17) while Sarah is left "barren" like dead earth until God enables her to conceive in her old age.

"Form" and "material", "seed" and "soil" are oppositions which we have inherited as essentially gendered, and this characterization makes it difficult to get away from attaching gender to these concepts in other contexts. It is difficult not to hear Aristotelian and Judeo-Christian echoes — and their gendered reverberations — in Langton's description of Artificial Life as "the attempt to abstract the logical form of life in different material forms" (quoted in Kelly 1991:1) and in Burks' statement that von Neumann "wished to abstract from the natural self-reproduction problem its logical form" (quoted in Langton 1989:13). And "form" and "seed" are drawn metaphorically close in Artificial Life by frequent analogies between computer code and genetic code.[3] Von Neumann's CA model gives us an automaton whose form, as Word and seed (i.e. as computer code and "genetic" code), is propagated through a passive and receptive cell space. Richard Laing's description of the general constructor in the CA model of von Neumann's self reproducing machine — "a device containing banks of pulsers which, when activated, can emit streams of pulses to be injected into undifferentiated regions of the cell space to cause cell automata there to assume any one of the 29 possible cell-automaton states" (1989:50) — is striking when we remember how gendered such imagery is.[4]

3 We might note that the prevalent description of DNA as a text which is transcribed and translated secularizes notions of the Word as determinative and creative. When sociobiologists like E. O. Wilson talk about "the morality of the gene" (1975:1), they grant DNA the divine office of determining our cultural habits. In light of Alan Turing's contention that "Given the table corresponding to a discrete state machine, it is possible to predict what it will do" (1950) and von Neumann's use of discrete state machines in his CA model, we can see how genetic determinism might be reinforced by such models as von Neumann's.

4 Carol Delaney has pointed out that in monotheistic religion, female bodies, like soil, "are relatively undifferentiated" (1986:498).

Later elaborations of von Neumann's CA model explicitly use "seed" imagery. L. S. Penrose's mechanical model of a CA is described by Langton as consisting of:

> a box filled with tilting blocks. The blocks have tilting hooks which can engage other blocks in several different arrangements. When a 'seed' — consisting of a pair of blocks hooked together in one of the possible arrangements — is placed into a box full of unhooked blocks and the box is shaken vigorously, the seed will induce the rest of the blocks to hook up in pairs exhibiting the same conformation as the seed (1989:17).

And Langton says of a simple CA model: "These embedded self-replicating loops are the result of the recursive application of a rule to a seed structure" (30). In a speculative discussion of self-reproducing lunar factories, Richard Laing tells us of a "'seed' perhaps weighing one hundred metric tons delivered to an extraterrestrial planetary surface" (1989:58). And he reminds us of the masculine principle behind the seed with his discussion of a CA offspring receiving "its patrimony" (1989:54).

Von Neumann has bequeathed us an automaton modeled after the male God of monotheism, reproducing itself without a mate, bypassing what a genetic algorithmist friend of mine called "the implementation problem of pregnancy," and not needing the sex which Norman Packard has called "a computational hassle" (Kelly 1991:21). The children of the automaton transcend problems of the flesh, and live in a Platonic realm of mind and form. They exist in the world but are simultaneously separate from it, as Christianity envisions humanity through the narrative of the exile from paradise, and as Cartesian metaphysics codifies with its separation of mind and body, subject and object, and man and nature. With different creation myths and different metaphysics, we might have ended up with a parthenogenic or hermaphroditic automaton, but as Carol Delaney has indicated, "In cultures influenced by monotheism a whole world is symbolically constructed and systematically integrated between notions of conception and the conception of the deity" (1986:504). If human procreation is symbolically constructed as "the human analogue of divine creation" (Delaney 1991:3), von Neumann has fashioned a self-reproducing automaton which is "the machine analogue of divine creation." Needless to say, one needn't be a believer (von Neumann wasn't) to be strongly influenced by the religious heritage of the society within which one works and thinks.

It is important to recognize that von Neumann himself admitted the problems of abstracting form from material: "By axiomatizing automata in this manner, one has thrown half the problem out the window and it may be the more important half. One has resigned oneself not to explain how these parts are made of real things, specifically, how these parts are made up of actual elementary particles, or even of higher chemical molecules" (1966:77). Artificial Life researchers might give this statement more considered thought than they have. Our postulates about the logical form of life may well be conditioned not only by the factors I enumerated above, but also by an over-familiarity with carbon life.[5]

Game Theory and Evolution

In *Theory of Self-Reproducing Automata*, von Neumann speculated that replicating automata might encounter each other in CA space, and that "conflicts and collisions" might arise (1966:129-131). He guessed that such conflicts and collisions might lead to a struggle for existence (over location, because his CA organisms didn't move from their place of birth, unlike kinematic ones) and that evolution might be a logical consequence of such meetings, provided, of course, that automata could reproduce themselves with variation. Although his speculations about how this might work were minimal,[6] he is well known for providing, with Oskar Morgenstern in 1944, the formalism of game theory that has been employed by so many evolutionary biologists to model organism interaction (see e.g. Hamilton 1964, Maynard Smith 1982). I here take as my concern dissecting this theory and relating it to an historical background of Western religion, epistemology, and political philosophy.

Game theory is essentially a theory of how rational actors should make maximizing and optimizing decisions in a world of assumed scarcity, competition, differential interests, and incomplete information. Von Neumann wasn't the first to try to understand decision making in terms of games. Steve Heims has noted that the mathematician Blaise Pascal (1623-1662) considered the existence of God in game theoretic terms:

> Pascal considered the decision problem, given that we have no way of knowing whether God exists, is it more advantageous to act on the premise that God exists, or on the opposite premise that God does not exist?... [Pascal] considered the advantages of a libertine's life as opposed to a

---

5 Even Cairns-Smith's unconventional hypothesis (1966) that the original replicative life on Earth was clay (a substance containing silicon, among other things, and having a crystal-like structure, like DNA) resonates with the idea that the Judeo-Christian God "formed man of the dust of the ground" (Genesis 2:7). Not all cosmological systems grant soil such primacy in their origin myths. Compare the Judeo-Christian creation story with the Mayan narrative in the Popol Vuh, in which people are created not from earth, but from maize.

6 Laing (1976, 1979, 1989) has offered suggestions within the von Neumannian paradigm for theorizing automata variation and evolution.

> pious life, the libertine's life being perhaps preferable if there is no God. This has to be balanced against the infinite benefit of the salvation that would result from a pious life if God exists (1980:81).

Pascal assumes a very von Neumannian self-interested individual, and though Heims states that competitors are missing from this early game theoretic formulation, our player is already constituted as a rational maximizer and is engaged in a game against an actually very present God. It is the same God whose banishing of humanity from the Garden of Eden, according to Judeo-Christian mythologies, engendered our isolation from Him (and thereby set the conditions for questioning His existence), gave us a world of scarcity, constituted nature as hostile —

> Cursed is the ground for thy sake; In sorrow shalt thou eat of it all the days of thy life... (Genesis 3:17).

— and put us into competition with our fellows (Cain, remember, murdered Abel in a competition for God's favor).

Game theory is formulated for a post-Edenic world, a world in which we must use every bit of our wits to survive. The flesh condemned to perish, the mind — the reasoning mind — is elevated to our most precious tool. The separation of mind and matter chartered in the Bible was given full metaphysical elaboration in René Descartes' *Discourse on Method of Properly Conducting One's Reason and of Seeking the Truth in Sciences* (1637), which ripped subject apart from object in an ontological move that continues deeply to affect our thinking. For Descartes, the mind was transcendent, eternal, divine.[7] Truth, in the form of axioms and self-evident premises, needed no temporal space in which to exist. Axioms and their derivative proofs became, in a sense, simultaneous. And so in game theory, game rules and game outcome exist in the same breath, for, as von Neumann put it, "Time never occurs in logic" (1956:44).[8] Through Cartesian metaphysics, the self-interested individual acquired a transcendent and rational mind, a mind in the image of the Judeo-Christian God.

The rational, atomistic, and by nature selfish individual was the foundation of utilitarian political economy. Bentham, Hobbes, and Smith believed that all people acted out of an "enlightened self-interest" and sought rationally and practically to maximize pleasure and minimize pain. This belief gained powerful reinforcement in social Darwinist readings of evolutionary theory, and continues to be axiomatic in some neo-Darwinist narratives of evolution. Through von Neumann and Morgenstern, the assumption of innate selfishness was mathematized and imported back into economic theory, from which it was appropriated by some schools of behavioral ecology and sociobiology. Von Neumann's beliefs about the essential selfishness of all behavior is perhaps best summed up with a quote from von Neumann himself: "It is just as foolish to complain that people are selfish and treacherous as it is to complain that the magnetic field does not increase unless the electric field has a curl. Both are laws of nature" (quoted in Heims 1980:327).

But such a "law of nature" rests on an assumption of scarcity (Heims 1980) and on a presupposition that scarcity logically entails competition. Yet, as Evelyn Fox Keller has reminded us, "interactions [can] effectively generate new resources ... increase the efficiency of resource utilization or reduce absolute requirement" (1991:93). Perhaps if we thought of von Neumann's self-reproducing automata as interacting in the way Keller suggests, we might open up another avenue for thinking about *life-as-it-could-be*.

Automata Again

But I think that we might also re-theorize the organism itself. It could be instructive to build models using Varela, Maturana, and Uribe's concept of *autopoiesis*, in which boundaries between "organism" and "world" are deliberately blurred (1974). This would certainly help us step out of out of shadow of Cartesianism, and might help us recognize the naivete of representational theories of language, as Maturana (1978) and Winograd and Flores (1986) have suggested. It also might help complexify notions of adaptation and highlight the fact that organisms are always already part of their environment.

Another suggestion for rethinking von Neumannian automata, and thereby certain theories of the organism, is to problematize the word "reproduction" itself. Most organisms do not produce mere clones of themselves, especially when sexual recombination is involved. The word "reproduction" is perhaps "more appropriate for the assembly line or photocopy machines" (Delaney 1991:5) than for the creative process of biological generation. Returning to the word "generation" might help us recognize what is happening as a dynamic process, rather than as the mere making of a product, and might allow for a more autopoietic and less teleological theory of evolution.

We might also ask if our science would be different were it founded in a different cosmology. If we had a non-masculine or non-singular God, what would our stories of self-reproducing automata look like? If we had inherited a cosmological mythos in which creation did not take place in a single

7 The title of Hans Moravec's *Mind Children: The Future of Robot and Human Intelligence* (1988) situates it perfectly within the Cartesian and Judeo-Christian tradition. We are reminded of a humanity created in the image of, and trying to usurp the powers of, a masculine monotheistic and monogenetically generative god.

8 Norbert Wiener, founder of the field of cybernetics, objected to von Neumann's game theory as a model for social reality because it left out the factor of time and the contingencies it introduced. Wiener also objected to von Neumann's image of humans; it was too static, and didn't allow for non-selfish motives (1961).

instant, or in which events transpired in a non-linear temporal scheme, how would our theories of life be framed? These questions are difficult and cannot be answered here, but I hope that they can provide the starting point for new lines of thinking.

If workers in Artificial Life hope to abstract the logical form of life from its material instantiations on earth, they should attend to the way in which their understandings of life are mediated by the history and epistemology of the cultural world within which they live. Certainly I do not refute the idea that life can exist in non-carbon based forms, or in other forms in carbon itself; I simply suggest that Artificial Life researchers broaden their concept of possible life. Other traditions, other cultures, and different viewpoints within Western culture construct the natural world differently and with different implications. The ideas of von Neumann are without doubt important, but they are ultimately restricted in application, as all human ideas must be. We must seek out new perspectives on life and biology, for as philosopher Susanne Langer (1942) has pointed out, the world in which we live is sculpted most decisively not by the sort of answers we generate, but by the kinds of questions we ask.

Acknowledgements

I would like to thank Bill Maurer and Carol Delaney for their helpful comments on earlier drafts of this paper.

This material is based upon work supported under a National Science Foundation Graduate Fellowship. Any opinions, findings, conclusions or recommendations expressed here are those of the author and do not necessarily reflect the views of the National Science Foundation.

References

Aristotle. [1979]. *Generation of Animals*. Translated by A. L. Peck. Loeb Classical Library. Cambridge: Harvard University Press.

The Bible, King James Version. World Bible Publishers, Inc.

Brockman, John. 1991. Artificial Life: A Conversation with Chris Langton and Doyne Farmer. In *Ways of Knowing*, edited by John Brockman. New York: Prentice Hall.

Cairns-Smith, A. G. 1966. The Origin of Life and the Nature of the Primitive Gene. *Journal of Theoretical Biology* 10: 53-88.

Delaney, Carol. 1986. The Meaning of Paternity and the Virgin Birth Debate. *Man* 21:494-513.

Delaney, Carol. 1991. *The Seed and the Soil*. Berkeley: University of California Press.

Descartes, René. 1637. *Discourse on Method of Properly Conducting One's Reason and of Seeking the Truth in Sciences*. Translated by F. E. Sutcliffe. Harmondsworth: Penguin Books, 1968.

Hamilton, W. D. 1964. The Genetical Evolution of Social Behavior. *Journal of Theoretical Biology* 7:1-51.

Heims, Steve J. 1980. *John von Neumann and Norbert Wiener: From Mathematics to the Technologies of Life and Death*. Cambridge: MIT Press.

Keller, Evelyn Fox. 1991. Language and Ideology in Evolutionary Theory: Reading Cultural Norms into Natural Law. In *Boundaries of Humanity: Humans, Animals, Machines*, edited by James J. Sheehan and Morton Sosna. Berkeley: University of California Press.

Kelly, Kevin. 1991. Designing Perpetual Novelty: Selected Notes from the Second Artificial Life Conference. In *Doing Science*, edited by John Brockman. New York: Prentice Hall.

Laing, Richard. 1976. Automaton Introspection. *Journal of Computer and System Sciences* 13:172-183.

Laing, Richard. 1979. Machines as Organisms: An Exploration of the Relevance of Recent Results. *BioSystems* 11:201-215.

Laing, Richard. 1989. Artificial Organisms: History, Problems, and Directions. In *Artificial Life*, edited by Christopher Langton. Redwood City, CA: Addison-Wesley.

Langer, Susanne K. 1942. *Philosophy in a New Key*. Cambridge: Harvard University Press.

Langton, Christopher. 1989. Artificial Life. In *Artificial Life*, edited by Christopher Langton. Redwood City, CA: Addison-Wesley.

Lem, Stanislaw. 1967. The First Sally (A), or Trurl's Electronic Bard. In *The Cyberiad*. Translated by Michael Kandel. New York: Harcourt Brace Jovanovich, Publishers.

Lewontin, Richard C. 1984. Adaptation. In *Conceptual Issues in Evolutionary Biology*. edited by Elliott Sober. Cambridge: MIT Press.

Maturana, Humberto R. 1978. Biology of Language: The Epistemology of Reality. In *Psychology and Biology of Thought: Essays in Honor of Eric Lenneberg*, edited by G.A. Miller and E. Lenneberg. New York: Academic Press.

Maynard Smith, John. 1982. *Evolution and the Theory of Games*. Cambridge: Cambridge University Press.

Moravec, Hans. 1988. *Mind Children: The Future of Robot and Human Intelligence*. Cambridge: Harvard University Press.

Pattee, H. H. 1989. Simulations, Realizations, and Theories of Life. In *Artificial Life*, edited by Christopher Langton. Redwood City, CA: Addison-Wesley.

El Popol Vuh. Spanish translation by Adrian Recinos. Costa Rica: Editorial Universitaria Centroamericana, 1978.

de Saussure, Ferdinand. 1915. *Course in General Linguistics*. Translated by Wade Baskin. New York: McGraw-Hill, 1966.

Turing, Alan. 1950. Can a Machine Think? *Mind* 422-460.

Varela, F. J., H. R. Maturana, and R. Uribe. 1974. Autopoiesis: The Organization of Living Systems. *BioSystems* 5(4): 187-196.

von Neumann, John. 1951. The General and Logical Theory of Automata. In *Cerebral Mechanisms in Behavior*. New York: Wiley.

von Neumann, John. 1956. Probabilistic Logics and the Synthesis of Reliable Organisms from Unreliable Components. In *Automata Studies*, edited by Claude Shannon and John McCarthy. Princeton: Princeton University Press.

von Neumann, John. 1958. *The Computer and the Brain*. New Haven: Yale University Press.

von Neumann, John. 1966. *Theory of Self-Reproducing Automata*, edited by Arthur Burks. Urbana: University of Illinois Press.

von Neumann, John and Oskar Morgenstern. 1944. *Theory of Games and Economic Behavior*. Princeton: Princeton University Press.

Wiener, Norbert. 1961. *Cybernetics, or Control and Communication in the Animal and the Machine*, second edition (first edition 1948). Cambridge: MIT Press, 1985.

Wilson, Edward O. 1975. *Sociobiology*. Cambridge: Belknap/ Harvard University Press.

Winograd, Terry and Fernando Flores. 1986. *Understanding Computers and Cognition*. Redwood City, CA: Addison-Wesley.

Meta-Knowledge, Autonomy, and (Artificial) Evolution: Some Lessons Learnt So Far

Jean-Luc Dormoy
EDF R&D Center
IMA-TIEM
1, avenue du Général De Gaulle
92141 Clamart Cedex, France

Sylvie Kornman
LAFORIA
Paris 6 University
4, place Jussieu
75252 Paris Cedex 05, France

Abstract

We claim in this paper that an extensive use of meta-mechanisms is a very powerful tool for building autonomous AI & AL systems. We support that claim by examples of *knowledge-based systems* exhibiting unexpected and partly autonomous behaviors. They show that autonomy, as well as viability, could be achieved in the future by means of meta-mechanisms. In particular, meta-mechanisms require simpler mechanisms than multi-agent-like or emergent mechanisms, though they can achieve more sophisticated behaviors.

We also present the perspective of bootstrapping as a basic methodology for building AI & AL systems. Its motivation is that building AI or AL systems is probably too difficult a problem to be tackled by just finding out the right components and then assembling them. These systems must go through a sequence of evolutionary steps, and we must be aware of that fact.

On one-hand, bootstrapping means that any new component should be made *applicable to the system as a whole* - and not only *participate* to the system's behavior - in order to help further extensions. On the other hand, the strategy used when building a system should *not* be mainly concerned by immediate performance, *but* by further extensions. This means that new functions or components should be added to the system *in order to* make further extensions possible or easier. We describe some experiments in building AI systems according to this strategy, and its constraints and difficulties. Indeed, we have no clean theory of bootstrapping yet, instead mere intuitions. So, these experiments mainly aim at figuring out how the design of a sophisticated system through bootstrapping steps should be conducted. We think that, eventually, a theory will be required.

1 Introduction

A common view of AL and AI systems architectures is based on *multi-agent architectures*. In this view, a set of non-intelligent small agents interact with each other, and from this interaction emerges a global behavior. In a practical way, the physical implementation of the agents share and act through a common substrate -e.g. data structures in 'symbolic' multi-agent systems, or numbers in neural nets- , but they are of a different nature. Their own substrate, i.e. their physical implementation, does not intersect the substrate they act on.

The aim of this paper is to discuss the meta view, i.e. a view where agents can also *act on* agents. This view is not new in any way, but we think it can be useful to reconsider it with respect to refurbished problems stressed by the AL community, such as autonomy, viability and evolution. We make various claims, and we show how they are justified by some examples of previous AI systems, and by the systems we are building, namely the Shal and Sade/Meta-Hari systems.

We first claim that meta is powerful. Indeed, a simple mechanism achieves more when properly used at the meta-level rather than at the basic level. Acting at the meta-level means that the components implementing the mechanism act on the physical implementation of other components, whereas acting at the basic level means merely interacting with them. Conversely, the designer who intends to build a system exhibiting a given behavior would better choose a meta-level architecture.

Secondly, we re-consider the autonomy and viability problems with respect to meta-level architectures. In particular, an operational closure of the system[1] can be achieved by simpler mechanisms in a meta architecture. Autonomy can be enhanced in meta-level architectures by the fact that components can be used at any level. Indeed, from the designer's point of view, this a saving principle: let components act on components, and you will need less, because a component can participate to various functions at various levels. Viability can be tackled by specific-purpose components, which for example observe other components, and try to fix improper behaviors.

Thirdly, we discuss the bootstrapping problem of AI or AL systems. Bootstrapping has been a long-known technique for building compilers, for example. It consists of using an already-existing version of a system for running a new version. When systems have the capability of processing themselves, the old version can often be discarded after having been used once. So, bootstrapping is a design methodology for building

[1] In the sense of Varela

artifacts through a sequence of small steps. Its main benefit is that one very quickly takes advantage of the improved functions provided by the intermediate versions, instead of having to wait for the system to be completed.

Indeed, we think that bootstrapping usefulness is two-fold. First, it helps in building an operationally closed system. This means that the system is not yet fully autonomous, that it still requires the designer to intervene in its functioning, but that already built-in components can be subtituted for the designer's intervention in solving sub-problems. This is the stage we are in in the Shal construction. Second, bootstrapping could be used to improve -from the designer's point of view- an already autonomous system. It can even be thought of including 'mutation components' in the system, which would help the designer to change the system. We are not experimenting this yet.

The bootstrapping perspective is perfectly coherent with the meta view. Indeed, we try to build components which participate to their own processing. Besides, building a system in this way dramatically changes the content of the components to be implemented, i.e. what they do. When adding a new component, its function must be to help to process components, including itself. So, bootstrapping makes the designer face a new set of constraints, he is not free to tackle the subproblem he would like to. Indeed, those constraints turned out to be so tough in our experiments that they required our main focus of attention. Eventually, our systems are not intended to provide any kind of 'external' functionality, but to be merely able to process themselves. The bootstrapping methodology we used *-how-* became a goal *-what-* in its own. We describe some aspects of this work.

Let's say at last, and at least, some words about the examples provided throughout this paper. First, we felt free to borrow from famous pieces of work in AI, and to stress some of their aspects which seemed interesting to us. This does not mean that their authors share our views. Second, our examples are *knowledge-based systems*. We know the discussion about *representation*. Anyway, we think that these systems properly illustrate our views, though not specific to knowledge-based systems. Instead, we think that, at this level of discussion, using knowledge or not is a mere issue of substrate. Beyond, we also have some ideas about the previously mentioned discussion, but we do not intend to argue about them in this paper.

2 Meta is powerful

The Prodigy system is the first example we mention, which shows that a mechanism can provide a more powerful behavior when properly used at the meta-level rather than at the basic level.

Prodigy (Minton & al. 1989) is a workbench developed at Carnegie-Melone University for experimenting various kinds of learning in knowledge-based systems. Among these experiments, Steve Minton used the Explanation-based Learning (EBL) technique for learning new control knowledge which helps a problem-solver to solve a class of problems. Some form of EBL was already used 15 years ago in planners such as STRIPS. Since then, EBL has been formalized and used in various ways. The spirit of EBL is to learn from a single example and a theory of the domain (knowledge) some tractable formulations of a generally intractable *target concept*. For example, the rules of chess could be the domain theory, a particular winning chess position the training example, and the target concept a formalization of *win*.

Usually, EBL is used for learning from success. This means that, when a particular case of the class of problems is solved, EBL attempts to summarize how this success has been reached, and to generalize as much as possible. It produces some kind of *macro-operator*, which sums up the generalized version of the actions performed to reach success in the example, and which can be used later to directly solve a similar problem. The main problem in this approach is that the cost of matching previously learnt macro-operators can overwhelm the potential improvement they can provide. This is the cost/utility problem.

One of the innovative features of Prodigy is that, instead of using EBL at the basic level (i.e., the level of the problem itself), it is used at the meta-level of the problem-solver. Prodigy has been provided with a theory of some important aspects of the problem-solver behavior, and with target concepts such as success, failure and goal interaction[1]. What Prodigy learns by means of EBL is control rules, i.e. rules which guide the problem-solver's decisions when attempting to solve a problem. The experiments conducted by Minton & al. showed in particular that learning from failure actually was an effective learning method.

Beyond the intrinsic interest of Prodigy, the point we wish to emphasize is that the basic technique used in it is a "slight" modification of an already-known technique. The main difference is that the EBL mechanism is used in Prodigy at the meta-level, i.e. the level of the problem-solver. We think that that is one of the main reasons why Prodigy succeeded, while its predecessors were stuck by the cost/utility problem. Moreover, Prodigy can learn more general knowledge. For example, if a particular problem mentions the two subgoals *Stack x on y* and *Stack y on z*, then Prodigy will learn (from goal interaction) and then use the fact that it is better to try to stack y on z first. This control rule can be used in various situations, while a macro-operator learnt by EBL when applied at the basic level would consist of a more specific piece of knowledge.

1 A goal interaction occurs in a planning problem whenever an already-achieved subgoal must be destroyed for achieving another subgoal.

3 Meta in the perspective of autonomous and viable systems

3.1 Autonomy

The use of components at the meta-level, i.e. acting on components, makes it simpler to build relatively autonomous system. We shall give two examples, from two systems: Shal and Sade/Meta-Hari.

In the Shal system (Dormoy 1990, 1991), which the first author is currently developing, some components are used at different levels and so participate to different functions. For example, we are developping a TMS-like component[1], which function is to undo the deductions drawn from a fact later considered as non pertinent. The initial reason why we implemented this component was that Shal makes heuristic deductions in its various activities, and they can be found to be incorrect later. So, these deductions are to be undone. However, Shal also has a component which aims at discovering errors in a knowledge-base. Obviously, this error-finding component is applied to the Shal system itself (including the error component). It turns out that the error-finding component knowledge also contains heuristics. So, it happens that some errors are incorrectly stated by this component. When the system finds evidence of this, the TMS component acts on the error component - which acts on the whole system - to undo its wrong deductions. In the next future, it might also be possible that the TMS component undo deductions drawn by the TMS component (because it also has heuristic knowledge).

This example shows that various functions can be achieved by a single component, provided that it has the possibility to apply at various levels. Without systematically giving components the ability to act on components, we would have had to design specific components for each usage of our TMS component. So, it is clear to us that reaching a relative autonomy is made easier by using meta capabilities, simply because less components are required.

Another example is the Sade/Meta-Hari under developement by the second author (Kornman 1989, 1991). This system is designed to observe a running knowledge-base, to discover misbehaviors in it, such as looping or getting stuck, and to repair the knowledge-base behavior in order to get out from the wrong situation. This system has the ability to do so in various situations, but not always. In particular, it can loop or get stuck. It turns out that, together with the system, a small component for systematically interrupting a knowledge-base while it is running has been implemented. This component routinely triggers the observing system, which attempts to find evidence of a misbehavior, if any. This interrupting component applies to any running knowledge-base, in particular to the observing system when it is running. So, the system also sometimes "observes itself". When it is looping or getting stuck, a copy of itself can analyze the situation, discover the wrong behavior, and repair it. Obviously, it is possible that the system at meta-level 2, i.e. the system observing the system which observes the knowledge-base, go into looping or getting stuck. Another level of observation is then added.

It is clear that this meta-tower of mutually observing systems is not a panacea. Firstly, it is not desirable to have a high tower: while being observed, a system does nothing, and so a relatively small amount of time should be devoted to observing. Secondly, it is possible that the "whole tower" loop or get stuck: indeed, more and more levels are added, the upper levels observing the lower ones, and each level going into wrong behavior[2].

However, the experiments being conducted with the Sade/Meta-Hari system show that it is possible to design the system so that it avoids complete collapse in most situations. Roughly speaking, the observing system must not have too many problems. If so, the meta-observing system would have much work repairing its lower copy, and, as its capabilities are the same, it would not be good enough to do so. Other problems arose, which we shall just mention here, such that the relationship between form and content of a component. When we say that a component acts on a component, we should indeed say that the *content* (what it does) of a component acts on the *form* (its physical implementation) of a component. However, for a given content - which is what the designer aims at when building the component -, there are various possible forms for implementing it. So, the content of meta-components acting on components strongly depends on the form of the components they act on. In a practical way, a very slight change in the form of a component can invalidate the meta-components. So, one of the most challenging problems when building meta-level architectures is to "tune" the form of components in order to make it fit with the content of already-existing components which are to be used at the meta-level. This is still a "black art".

The Sade/Meta-Hari system is autonomous is some sense, and brings autonomy to the knowledge-base it is applied to. When coupled to a knowledge-base, it makes it possible to almost always get out from traps and deadends - even traps caused by the implementation of the procedural inference engine which runs the knowledge-bases. So, there are two lessons learnt by these experiments. First, autonomy is not reached by a knowledge base - or any other kind of system - per se, even if this was intended by the knowledge base designer. It is strongly enhanced by another component acting at the meta-level, the Sade/Meta-Hari system. Secondly, the observing component also has the capability to apply

1 Indeed, this component has the function of a conventional TMS, but does not work at all in the same way.

2 From a logical standpoint, deciding whether a program loops is an undecidable problem.

onto itself, which still enhances the behavior of the whole system.

3.2 Viability

Viability looks like a very difficult problem, even more difficult than autonomy. In the (short) history of meta-level systems in AI, the systems which exhibited a relatively autonomous behavior also exhibited a very poor ability to avoid quick collapsing. We shall first give two examples which demonstrate this problem, then an example which shows how unstability could be fought.

The AM system (Lenat 1982), designed by Doug Lenat in the 70s, was an "artificial mathematician". It had knowledge and heuristics to build and consider interesting mathematical objects, and to conjecture interesting theorems about them. It proved nothing, and the knowledge in mathematics it started from was close to nil. Simply, it exhibited the "inspired behavior" of a mathematician while discovering new mathematics. This system had stunning results. For example, it discovered basic arithmetics, including integers, addition and multiplication, prime numbers, and unique factorization of integers in primes.

However, according to Lenat, AM did not produce interesting results after running two hours. It had given anything it could, and was lost in overwhelming uninteresting objects and conjectures.

Lenat interpreted this problem in the following way: AM had the "right heuristics" to deal with the simple objects it started with, but once more sophisticated objects were introduced (arithmetics), these heuristics were of no use any longer. AM lacked the ability to synthesize new heuristics better fitting its new domains of interest.

This was the main motivation for Lenat building his next system, Eurisko (Lenat 1983). Eurisko had heuristics to deal with heuristics, in particular heuristics for changing or discovering new heuristics. The results of Eurisko have also been quite impressive. It managed to win a naval battle game championship, by being trained to learn good heuristics specific to this game. It also reproduced the results of AM, and others in other domains (e.g. VLSI design). In particular, Lenat showed that Eurisko had discovered a new meta-heuristic, i.e. a heuristic for discovering heuristics, which was better than the heuristic which gave birth to it. This was an example that the system could actually enhance itself.

However, it is not clear how Lenat could manage to keep his system relatively stable. Obviously, a system which can radically change itself has many opportunities to produce lethal components. This actually happened in Eurisko. For example, a meta-heuristic had been synthesized, which stated that nothing in the system was interesting. This "killing" component fortunately turned out to be suicidal, i.e., while killing everything, it killed itself. But this was just chance, and it seems reasonable that more subtle wrong components have been generated. It seems that Lenat managed this problem by often intervening in the Eurisko process of discovery (he says that Eurisko's successes are 60% Eurisko's and 40% Lenat's). So Eurisko was not *viable* by itself, it required Lenat's help. There was something lacking in Eurisko, but this thing is obviously sophisticated.

We shall now show how the viability problem could be tackled by using a rather different example. The Shal system we are developping makes a systematic use of its knowledge for processing itself and helping its own design process. A very serious problem when building such a sophisticated system is *errors*. This is true for any system, but systems based on a meta-level architecture can exhibit some new kind of errors, much more difficult to identify and fix than in other systems. When a component is faulty, and when this component applies to another component, the fault can be visible only a long time after. For example, if a component MC1 -used at the meta-level - makes deductions on a component C which helps another component MC2 to compile C, and if an error occurs in MC1, then the error can be visible only when using the compiled version of C. But, in turn, component MC1 is not necessary faulty, simply we used a compiled version of it, wherein an error has been introduced by the compiling components. So, tracking down an error requires not only to observe the behavior of the interacting components, but also to navigate through the meta-levels of components acting on components.

The simplest idea for tackling this problem is to design a special component, the aim of which is to find errors in components. In a practical way, this requires the discipline which consists, whenever the designer (us) finds out a new kind of error, of providing the system with sufficient knowledge to discover similar errors on its own the next time they occur. We have in Shal an ever-growing error-finding component, which size now adds up to as much as one-third of the whole system.

It is rather difficult to quantitatively assess the gain of this error component. However, we experienced that it does discover errors when we modify Shal, and our past experience convinces us that it helps to save days of work.

This error component does not exactly respond to the viability problem as usually stated, in the sense that it function is not to modify the behavior of the system when something lethal is coming up, but to prevent the system from being so wrong that it would not "survive" more than a few minutes. However, if we think of the design process of Shal as some kind of ontogenic process, the error component prevents from generating wrong components.

Another example is the already-mentioned Sade/Meta-Hari system. While the error component of Shal could only statically analyze a system, Sade/Meta-Hari dynamically intervenes in the behavior of the system. So, this system provides a partial answer to the viability problem as generally understood.

Both systems show, though still in a partial way, that the use of components at the meta-level can help to tackle the viability problem. Moreover, this problem can be *explicitely* tackled. The fact that a system's behavior is viable does not only emerge from its architecture, instead there are some specific components which help it to do so. The problem is to discover some relatively general mechanisms which ensure that a system will not collapse.

4 Bootstrapping

4.1 Methodologies for building AI & AL systems

In Nature, there are several degrees of change. Usually, AL people emphasize the adaptive aspect of autonomous systems. This refers to the way "grown-up" animals or "completed" artificial systems behave. If we refer now to Artificial Life or Artificial Intelligence systems, it is clear that these systems must have a degree of adaptivity, but an even more difficult issue is to know how to build them - adaptive or not. In Nature, this is done by reproduction, and evolution, which are very different degrees of change.

A consistent view in AI is the "explosive kernel" vision. Instead of building a huge system by hand, we should try to build some very special components, which should be able to improve themselves just by running, so providing us with a new, better system. These primordial components make up the kernel, and its intention is to be explosive, i.e. to expand and improve itself in an infinite loop.

A serious experiment in this way was Lenat's Eurisko system. Eurisko was provided with meta-heuristics, more precisely heuristics which aimed at discovering new heuristics. Eurisko exhibited one case of a group of meta-heuristics which discovered new, better meta-heuristics. So, this first experiment was a success in showing that it is possible to build a system which intrinsically improves itself, not only adapts itself to external conditions. However, as visible at once, this perspective is extremely ambitious, and Eurisko did not go further along this line.

Another view is the bootstrapping vision. Indeed, we are seeking to build artificial systems, i.e. built by a designer, though life has appeared without any. Now, building AL and AI systems is so difficult a task that it is probably hopeless to do it in one single step. So, the idea is to use what is already built as soon as it is available while building the system. This implies that the main function of components should not be to achieve an 'external' function, but to participate to the whole running and changing of the system.

This is no new idea. It has been used for long in computer science, for building compilers or interpreters (partial evaluation) for example. It has also been used in some AI systems, such as TEIREISIAS (Davis 1982). TEIREISIAS, which was a system put upon the MYCIN expert system, was aimed at explaining and controlling MYCIN's behavior, and at helping the expert to acquire new knowledge. The TEIREISIAS component dealing with acquiring new objects, attributes and values had been built by Randall Davis by means of itself: as soon as some primitive concepts had been wired-in, the object, attribute and value concepts themselves were acquired by means of TEIREISIAS.

Jacques Pitrat has put the idea forward in his MACISTE system (Pitrat 1986, 1990). The main -and only- aim of this system is to be able to process itself. Roughly speaking, the system is a rule-based system. It has a very important component, which is a rule compiler. One of the main goal of the MACISTE experiments was to show that an AI system could produce all the programs it would need -not a single line of code should be written by the human designer. So, the problem is to build a rule compiler which can compile itself. In a practical way, this is no easy task.

Starting from Jacques Pitrat's ideas, we are currently building a system, named Shal, which is also intended to fully process itself. Nevertheless, there are some differencies between Shal and MACISTE, due to different starting points. We shall not discuss them, neither shall we discuss the details of these systems. Instead, we shall describe some lessons learnt so far in building an operationally closed system through bootstrapping.

4.2 Constraints and problems in bootstrapping

4.2.1 The bootstrapping tunnel: make steps small

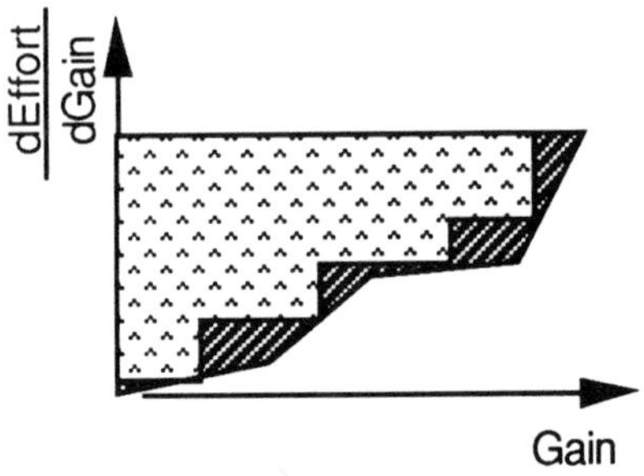

Figure 1: The bootstrapping tunnel

Our first attempt consisted of directly building a rule compiler written in rules. This work had been done with Jean-Yves Lucas in 1988-89 (Lucas & Dormoy 1990). We started from his SIREN system, which was a system able to synthesize programs which solved constraint satisfaction problems from their mere specification. This system had 400 rules, and was theoretically able to compile its rules. However, the experiments showed that rules compiled by this compiler were less efficient than when interpreted by the human-encoded inference engine, especially when run on large working memories. There was some knowledge implicitely present in the inference engine which was not stated within the rules. So, we considered adding rules. We assessed that the system's rules would add up to 800. However, when compiling rules R, the compiling rules work on a representation of R in the working memory. So, when represented, 800 rules make up a large working memory, which was just the case when our first compiler was inefficient. So, we got stuck.

The reason why this first attempt was a failure was that we tried to achieve a sort of operationally closed system through a single step. This is not a good idea, just because we could not take advantage of an already-existing system. This is summarized in the diagram below. The area under the lines respectively represent the effort (e.g. human, or CPU) required by achieving a given function when completing the system through a single step (grey), or through a sequence of small steps (dark). The reason why the second alternative is better is that each intermediate system takes advantage of the functionalities provided by the previous ones.

4.2.2 The necessity to solve various problems at the same time

After this first attempt, we chose another path. Instead of trying to reach a rule compiler very quickly, we added some knowledge for discovering the behavior of a rule base. The idea was that this would provide better compilers in the long term, and at the same time that 'partial' conclusions drawn by this component could be immediately useful for improving the rules behavior and efficiency. This is what actually happened. Though not yet able to compile rules, Shal takes advantage from what is deduced by Shal to improve its behavior.

Then, other problems happened. The Shal knowledge base was getting ever larger, and we had many problems in simply managing this large ensemble. First, a better control was required for the system properly using its knowledge. We designed a language and some knowledge for stating, using, and 'criticizing' control. Second, from the beginning, we had been using *semantic constraints*, which provided the system with knowledge about the kind of working memory to be used. It turned out that, as the system grew larger, it was not possible to provide it with this kind of knowledge by hand. So, some components were added, which make it possible to discover this knowledge automatically.

While adding these components, new 'micro-languages' had appeared, wherein we -or the system-stated semantic constraints or control knowledge. All this knowledge was represented within the working memory, in a very painful-to-read syntax. So, we designed a component for translating simple languages into each other from simple specifications.

Secondly, more and more knowledge was of a heuristic nature. This means that it turns to be somewhat 'irrational', and that at least some means for checking and correcting them was needed. This is why we implemented a 'TMS-like' component -though very different in nature from what has been done in AI about this topic.

Thirdly, the most important obstacle became *errors*. There are various kinds of errors. First, there are the errors in implementing the system. Second, when using heuristic knowledge, the system can go into 'wronger and wronger' deductions, and so collapse or enter any kind of lethal behavior. For both reasons, the largest component in our system is now an error-finding-and-fixing component. It adds up now to one third of the whole system.

Eventually, this very short chronology of our system development shows that it is not possible to solve a problem independently from others. One must tackle 'all' the problems at the same time. Seeking autonomy and viability, we are now quite far away from mere rule compiling.

4.2.3 The necessity to solve problems in a bad way

At the same time, we have had a hard time to get rid of old psychological and cultutal habits. In particular, when a scientist faces a problem, he tries to solve it ***in-depth***. This does not work here. Indeed, if for a given subproblem P, we implement an excellent solution in a component C, we can expect C to be large. As C must be processed by other components, these components must be 'expert enough' to cope with that large one. In the first stages of our system development, this is not possible. So, components must remain relatively small and have a form as simple as possible.

4.3.4 Dealing with the "real-world" I: the fixed point problem

Adding a component is two-fold. One first wants to add a new functionality; this is its *content*, i.e. what the component is supposed to do. Now, this component must be processable by already-existing components. Indeed, when acting at the meta-level, components act upon the *form* of components. There is no simple relationship between content and form of a component. Even a slight change in the 'language' where components are expressed -or, say, their physical substrate- can dramatically change the form of a component exhibiting a given behavior.

So, the designer is not free to add components. When adding a new component C1, with an intended content, there must be somewhere what is required to process the form of C1. If this does not exist yet, one must add C2 for processing C1. In turn, one might need C3 for processing C2, and so forth. At the end, we must have in hand components C1, C2,...,Cn, which content can process their form. This is some kind of 'fixed point' property, or 'local operational closure'. In a practical way, the size of C1 to Cn must not be so large as to make them unprocessable by the already-existing system (see Subsection *The Bootstrapping Problem*).

We have no answer to this problem, but vague intuitions. Indeed, this is the main problem we are fighting with in building Shal.

4.2.5 Dealing with the "real-world" II: internal vs. external worlds

In some sense, the Shal and Sade/Meta-Hari systems are perfectly egocentric: they just observe themselves, compile themselves, process themselves, etc. In particular, they are not confronted with the real world. Their 'real world' is themselves.

Indeed, this is not a side-effect of our approach, but one of its foundations. As we mentioned, designing components, the content of which is able to process their form, is a difficult task. So, adding components for making the system able to achieve an intended behavior in the 'real world', let alone 'surviving' in it, is out of reach of our systems in their current stage of development.

We think that this is not a problem, on the contrary we think that this might be a necessary condition for long-term research. Our main goal is not performance, it is 'artificial evolution'. As we said, we think that bootstrapping, or 'artificial evolution', could be an efficient methodology for building working AL & AI systems. So, trying to reach a quick solution when building an autonomous creature might be a deadend in the long term. We do not mean that there is nothing to learn from these experiments. We are on a different research path. We are seeking new design principles for AL & AI systems. A consequence of our approach is that our systems will go on surviving in 'protected worlds' for a long time.

5 Conclusion

We showed in this paper that meta-level architectures make simple mechanisms more efficient when used at the meta-level. We also showed that autonomy and viability can be enhanced in the meta approach. We then introduced the bootstrapping, or 'artificial evolution' approach, which aims at building a system by means of its earlier versions. We described some conclusions learnt so far from our experiments in building the Shal and Sade/Meta-Hari systems. What we omitted to mention is that we have no clean theory yet, but we think that such a theory will be necessary in the future.

References

Davis, Randall, and Doug Lenat. 1982. *Knowledge-based systems in Artificial Intelligence.* Mc Graw-Hill, 1982.

Dormoy, Jean-Luc. 1990. *Behavior and function of a knowledge-base.* Cognitiva'90, November 1990, Madrid, Spain.

Dormoy Jean-Luc. 1991. *Knowledge for compiling knowledge: the Shal system.* To be published in the *Revue de l'Intelligence Artificielle.*

Kornman, Sylvie. 1989. *Automatic introspection in a declarative knowledge-base system.* Congrès systémique, Lausanne, Switzerland.

Kornman, Sylvie. 1991. *Systems under surveillance.* IASTED 1991.

Lenat & Davis. 1982. See Davis, 1982.

Lenat, Douglas B. 1983. *EURISKO: A program that learns new heuristics and domain concepts.* Artificial Intelligence 21 (1983), pp. 61-98.

Lucas J-Y, and J-L Dormoy. 1990. Jean-Yves Lucas, Jean-Luc Dormoy. *Shal : un compilateur de règles écrit en règles qui s'applique à lui-même (A rule compiler which applies to itself).* Convention IA'90, January 1990, Paris, France.

Maes, Pattie, and Daniele Nardi, Eds. 1988. *Meta-level architectures and reflection.* North-Holland.

Minton, Steven, Jaime G. Carbonell, Craig A. Knoblock, Daniel R. Kuokka, Oren Etzioni, and Yolanda Gil. 1989. *Explanation-based learning: a problem-solving perspective.* AI Journal Vol. 40, Numbers 1-3, September 1989.

Pitrat, Jacques. 1986. *Le problème du bootstrap. (The bootstrapping problem).* Internal report "Cahiers du Laforia".

Pitrat, Jacques. 1990. *Métaconnaissance. (Metaknowledge).* Hermès, Paris.

Varela, Francisco J. 1989. *Autonomie et connaissance, essai sur le vivant.* Seuil, Paris.

Feedforward: The Ethological Basis of Animal Learning

R. Allen Gardner and Beatrix T. Gardner
Animal Behavior Research Group and Center for Advanced Study
University of Nevada /296
Reno, NV 89557

Abstract

The view that instrumental learning is based on reward and punishment has dominated theory and application throughout this century. In behaviorist versions, stimulus-response connections are stamped in or stamped out by the consequences of action. In cognitive versions, expectancies are formed by experience with past consequences.

The Law of Effect entails 1) a prespecified list of appetites and aversions that assigns positive and negative values to consequences and 2) an executive mechanism that associates consequences with acts, stores this information, and calculates the hedonic potential of each available response at each choice point. It is a cumbersome, top-down model.

The evidence of early experiments with rats and pigeons and the feedback principles of early servomechanisms seemed to offer both hard evidence and a plausible model for the Law of Effect. However, a large and rapidly growing body of modern evidence demonstrates that most, perhaps all, of the phenomena of conditioning appear regardless of and often in spite of response-contingent consequences. At the same time, experimental operations designed to demonstrate some residual effect of consequences entail an *ex post facto* error that vitiates all possible versions of this experimental design.

This analysis points to a parsimonious, feedforward principle of both adaptive and maladaptive learning with straightforward implications for efficient instrumental learning in artificial systems.

Ethology of the Skinner Box

The Operant Conditioning Chamber or Skinner Box was designed to study the arbitrary effects of reinforcement in an extremely artificial environment. Subjects such as rats or pigeons are first made hungry or thirsty by deprivation. The chamber used with rats usually has a lever protruding from one wall, the chamber for pigeons usually has a key placed at about the level of a pigeon's beak. When a rat depresses its lever, or a pigeon pecks its key, the apparatus delivers a small portion of food or water.

Elaborate variations in the pattern of responding can be induced by variations in the pattern of food or water delivery or "schedule of reinforcement." Further variations can be induced by variations in visual and auditory displays that are correlated with the delivery of food or water. With several levers or keys and several displays, extensions and elaborations of this procedure seem to be limited only by the ingenuity of the experimenter.

Shaping and Autoshaping

Because the procedure is so easily and cheaply automated, it is highly cost effective — a significant factor in its popularity among experimenters. The most inefficient step in the procedure used to be the wait for the first response. Without any intervention by the experimenter, hours might elapse before a naive rat or pigeon pressed the lever or pecked the key for the first time. Some impatient experimenters smeared the lever with moist food to induce the first lever-press. In the orthodox technique,

> We first give the bird food when it turns slightly in the direction of the spot from any part of the cage. This increases the frequency of such behavior. We then withhold reinforcement until a slight movement is made toward the spot. This again alters the general distribution of behavior without producing a new unit. We continue by reinforcing positions successively closer to the spot, then by reinforcing only when the head is moved slightly forward, and finally only when the beak actually makes contact with the spot....
>
> The original probability of the response in its final form is very low; in some cases it may even be zero. In this way we can build complicated operants which would never appear in the repertoire of the organism otherwise. By reinforcing a series of successive approximations, we bring a rare response to a very high probability in a short time.... The total act of turning toward the spot from any point in the box, walking toward it, raising the head, and striking the spot may seem to be a functionally coherent unit of behavior; but it is constructed by a continual process of differential reinforcement from undifferentiated behavior, just as the sculptor shapes his figure from a lump of clay. (Skinner, 1953, pp. 92-93)

The need to "shape" the first response might sustain belief in the arbitrary effect of contingent reinforcement, but manual shaping is obviously labor intensive. In 1968, Brown and Jenkins reported a truly economical procedure which they called "autoshaping." The response key in a pigeon chamber lighted up for 8-sec. At the end of that time, the key light was turned off and food was delivered no matter what the pigeon did. If the pigeon pecked the key while it was still lighted, the light was turned off and food was delivered, immediately. In either case, after an intertrial interval, the key was relighted and the cycle repeated. Soon, the pigeons were pecking the key on their own. Autoshaping was as effective as Skinner's manual procedure.

The discovery of autoshaping generated a large volume of research that replicated and extended the early findings in great detail. Later experiments induced robust rates of pecking with food delivered only at the end of the light-on period, independently of anything that the pigeon did. In 1969, Williams and Williams showed that key-pecking is maintained when food is only delivered if the pigeon fails to peck the key — that is, when food is omitted every time the pigeon pecks the key. In this "omission" contingency, free food evokes robust rates of key-pecking, at first. As a result of the negative contingency, the more the pigeons peck the less food they get. As food is omitted, key-pecking declines. When key-pecking declines, food is again delivered, key-pecking recovers, food is again omitted, and so on, indefinitely. Overall, this procedure maintains a robust rate of key-pecking.

Under the omission contingency, hungry pigeons behave as if they are trying to avoid food. When food stops they rest content, as if a painful stimulus has been removed. When food is delivered again, they hasten to make responses that have in the past stopped the delivery of food.

Superstition

The elaborate manual shaping — so carefully described and so assiduously followed by Skinner and a generation or two of his followers — was entirely unnecessary. It could serve as a striking human example of what Skinner called "superstitious" behavior.

> If there is only an accidental connection between the response and the appearance of a reinforcer, the behavior is called "superstitious." We may demonstrate this in the pigeon by accumulating the effect of several accidental contingencies. Suppose we give a pigeon a small amount of food every fifteen seconds regardless of what it is doing. When food is first given, the pigeon will be behaving in some way—if only standing still—and conditioning will take place. It is then more probable that the same behavior will be in progress when food is given again. If this proves to be the case, the "operant" will be further strengthened. If not, some other behavior will be strengthened. Eventually a given bit of behavior reaches a frequency at which it is often reinforced. It then becomes a permanent part of the repertoire of the bird, even though the food has been given by a clock which is unrelated to the bird's behavior.
> Conspicuous responses which have been established in this way include turning sharply to one side, hopping from one foot to the other and back, bowing and scraping, turning around, strutting, and raising the head. (Skinner, 1953, p. 85)

The concept of superstitious behavior plays a central role in the traditional view of key-pecking as arbitrary behavior reinforced by feeding rather than obligatory behavior evoked by feeding. It seems unlikely, however, that Skinner or anyone else ever actually observed the incidents of adventitious contiguity between responses and food so often described before Staddon and Simmelhag (1971) published the first detailed account of moment by moment observations.

Contrary to Skinnerian doctrine, with repeated, noncontingent delivery of food, all of Staddon and Simmelhag's pigeons developed the same habit — pecking at the wall above the food hopper. Most of the pecking occurred just before each delivery of food. This is what we would expect if pecking is a prefeeding response evoked by moderately spaced delivery of food, like the salivation of Pavlov's dogs. Staddon and Simmelhag also reported other stereotyped behaviors such as wing-flapping and circling movements that varied from pigeon to pigeon and resembled Skinner's descriptions of "superstitious" behaviors. But these appeared early in the intervals between food delivery, which is quite the opposite of the timing that we would expect if they were reinforced by contiguity with food.

Earning vs. Free Loading

In the traditional view, lever-pressing and key-pecking entail arbitrary work that rats and pigeons will perform in order to earn food or other necessities of life. The biological utility of the incentives must justify the biological effort expended because animals would not press the bar or peck the key if they had an easier way to get the incentives. This proposition seemed so obvious to so many that it was not tested directly until Jensen (1963) offered rats a choice between pellets of food that were dispensed by the apparatus in the usual way, and a heap of identical pellets already there in a convenient food dish.

Jensen's experiment has been thoroughly replicated with pigeons as well as with rats under a wide variety of experimental conditions. With an abundant supply of free food standing there in front of them, most animals earn some of their food by pressing the lever or pecking the key. Under some conditions, subjects have earned as much as 90% of their food. Also, naive rats and pigeons have acquired the habit of lever-pressing or key-pecking for food even when free food was continuously available (Osborne, 1977; 1978). Hungry animals prefer to earn food even when the consequences of work are negative; that is, when they abandon the heap of free food to work at the lever or the key, they lose time that they could have spent eating.

Avoiding Food

In 1951, Breland and Breland first described a kind of show business based on techniques they had learned as junior associates of B. F. Skinner. The Brelands taught chickens to bat baseballs and parakeets to ride bicycles; and some 38 different species acquired a wide variety of unlikely skills which they displayed in museums, zoos, fairs, department stores, and — the ultimate achievement — television commercials. The popularity of the animal actors combined with the practical effectiveness of the conditioning techniques resulted in a financially successful business. They also had failures, not random failures, but patterns of failure that plainly contradicted the behavior theory behind their otherwise so successful program of conditioning. The Brelands referred to these patterns as "misbehavior" (Breland and Breland, 1961).

In one display, a pig picked up large wooden coins from a pile and deposited them in a "piggy bank" several feet away. After shaping with a single coin placed farther and farther from the bank, the pig progressed to a requirement of four or five coins picked up and deposited one by one to earn each small portion of food. It was a textbook example of ratio reinforcement and most pigs acquired it rapidly. Instead of improving with practice, however, performance deteriorated day by day. The pigs continued to pick up the coins readily enough, but they were slower and slower to deposit them in the bank. On the way to the bank, they would drop a coin and root it along the ground with their snouts, pick it up and drop it again, often tossing it in the air before rooting it along the ground once more. Pig after pig indulged in more and more rooting and tossing until they delayed the delivery of food, indefinitely.

Raccoons failed in a similar way. Adept at manipulating objects, raccoons quickly learned to grasp and carry wooden coins and even to insert them into a slot. But they would not let go. They held on handling and rubbing the coins and dipping them in the slot as if washing them. Given two coins, a raccoon would rub them together over and over again like a miser. Raccoon misbehavior looked very much like the manipulatory behavior raccoons normally direct towards naturally-occurring portions of food — they handle and rub foods that have husks and shells, and even fish prey such as crayfish out of pools. Similarly, wild and domestic pigs kill small rodents by rooting and tossing them before eating them.

In the Breland failures, animals first had to direct responses that resembled prefeeding toward objects that resembled food. Then they had to stop prefeeding the token food before they could receive actual food. The Brelands tried making their animal actors hungrier, reasoning that this should increase the incentive value of food. If, instead, "misbehavior" consists of obligatory components of prefeeding evoked by a conditioned connection between the tokens and the food, then it should increase with increased hunger. This is precisely what the Brelands report; the hungrier they were, the more the animals persisted in "misbehavior" that postponed food.

Rodents also manipulate their food before eating it. Timberlake and his associates (Timberlake, 1983; 1986; Timberlake, Wahl, and King, 1982) placed rats in a specially designed chamber without the usual lever, and dropped a 5/8-in steel ball into the chamber through a hole in one wall. Unimpeded, the ball took 3.1-sec to roll down a groove in the slightly inclined floor and pass out of the chamber through a hole in the opposite wall. The experimenters also dropped pellets of food one at a time into a food dish located to one side and above the exit hole. Under some conditions the food arrived at the same time as the ball, under others it was delayed for a measured period of time, and under still others food was delayed until the ball rolled out of the chamber.

The rats handled, mouthed, and carried the ball as if it were a seed or nut in a shell. They dug at the entry hole during the delay between the sound of the dispenser and the entry of the ball, even though this tended to delay the ball by blocking the hole. When food was delayed until the exit of the ball, the rats continued to handle it, thus impeding its progress, preventing its exit, and postponing the food. Under experimental conditions in which food arrived before the ball rolled out of the chamber, most of the rats formed a habit of carrying the ball to the food dish or otherwise impeding its exit and later resumed handling the ball after they had consumed the food. They persisted in this even though it lengthened the intertrial interval, thus delaying the next feeding.

In the usual conditioning chamber for rats, the lever is the only graspable, moveable object, hence the only available target for the prefeeding manipulatory behavior of these animals. Lacking a manipulatory appendage, pigeons peck at targets with their beaks, and the most prominent target in the chamber for pigeons is the lighted key. The chamber used by Staddon and Simmelhag (1971) had no key, but their pigeons pecked at the wall above the food bin, anyway. If conditioned pecking were based on a kind of stimulus substitution in which the pigeons pecked at random spots of dirt or other imperfections that resembled grains of food, then we would expect them to peck at the floor. Random spots on the floor of the chamber should resemble grain as much as random spots on the upright walls, and downward pecking should resemble normal feeding behavior more than horizontal pecking. Why should pigeons peck at spots on a wall? Unlike precocial birds such as chickens that feed themselves from the first, the young of altricial birds such as pigeons are fed by their parents. The young of altricial birds solicit food by pecking upward at a parent's beak and crop.

The "misbehaviors" of the Breland pigs and raccoons and the Timberlake rats are components of prefeeding in these species. They were evoked by stimuli associated with feeding. When food appeared the animals interrupted the prefeeding they were directing at the tokens, in favor of consummatory responses directed at the food, itself. The prefeeding responses only became "misbehavior" when the animals had to interrupt them before the food appeared.

In the conditioning chamber, rats and pigeons interrupt lever-pressing and key-pecking to consume food. They also mix eating with prefeeding, as when heaps of food are already available in free feeding experiments. But, they drift into "misbehavior" when they have to stop key-pecking or lever-pressing to get food, as in the omission contingency. It is then that their responses postpone rather than hasten the arrival of the food.

This behavior suggests a loop in a program that ends with a test. Fresh inputs indicating the presence of food initiate the next loop in the program. In the absence of fresh inputs the loop is repeated. That prefeeding behavior such as lever-pressing and key-pecking will be mixed with feeding proper under conditions in which heaps of free food are already available, suggests a program of the form:

Feed —> Manipulate + Eat + Feed

The Brelands tell how easy it was to teach chickens to pull in a loop of string or wire, a simple feat that was extremely difficult to teach to pigeons. Unlike pigeons, chickens in a farmyard get much of their food by scratching in the earth for worms. In one of their displays, the Brelands wanted a chicken to stand still on a platform for 12 to 15 seconds, waiting for food. They found that about 50% of their chicken stars began to shift from place to place on the platform while scratching vigorously at the floor beneath them. The perceptive Brelands labelled the platform "dance floor" and had the chickens start a "juke box" by pulling a loop. They then required the chickens to stand on the platform (thus depressing a switch) for 15-sec. and called this show "The Dancing Chicken." They estimated that in the course of an average performing day each chicken made more than 10,000 useless scratching responses when all they had to do was to stand still on the platform for 15-sec at a time. Audiences were awed when they saw how a behaviorist could get an animal to dance to any tune through the power of positive reinforcement.

Constraints and Contingency

Skinner designed the Operant Conditioning Chamber to study the arbitrary effects of reinforcement. The chamber was supposed to be so arbitrary that the obligatory, species-specific aspects of rat and pigeon behavior would be minimal, just as civilized life was once thought to be so artificial and arbitrary that human behavior must be virtually free of biological constraints. But in spite of all precautions, rats and pigeons stubbornly refuse to leave their ethology behind when they enter the conditioning chamber. Lever-pressing and key-pecking were supposed to represent arbitrary work that rats and pigeons would only perform for food and water rewards. Instead, these particular responses can be evoked and maintained by food and water without any contingency at all. Indeed, under a wide range of conditions, positive and negative contingencies are irrelevant to the rate of lever-pressing and key-pecking. The Brelands have demonstrated analogous phenomena in a wide range of animal species under a wide range of conditions. We cannot dismiss these findings as artifacts peculiar to the behavior of rats and pigeons in the Skinner Box.

The only way to preserve the Law of Effect is to retreat to the position that the arbitrary effects of consequences only operate within limits imposed by certain species-specific constraints. This is known as the "constraints on learning" approach (Shettleworth, 1972). In the relevant experiments, however, so much learning does take place without any contingency at all, that a more apt label might be, "constraints on the Law of Effect."

Yoked Control

Responses that seem to be reinforced by the contingent delivery of food or water are evoked by these incentives without any contingency, at all. In that case, how much of the results of operant conditioning can we attribute to the effect of response-contingent reinforcement? The experimental answer to this question is straightforward. It requires two conditions. Under one condition, *C*, incentives are contingent on some criterion response. Under the second condition, *Y*, the same quantity of incentives are delivered but independently of the criterion response.

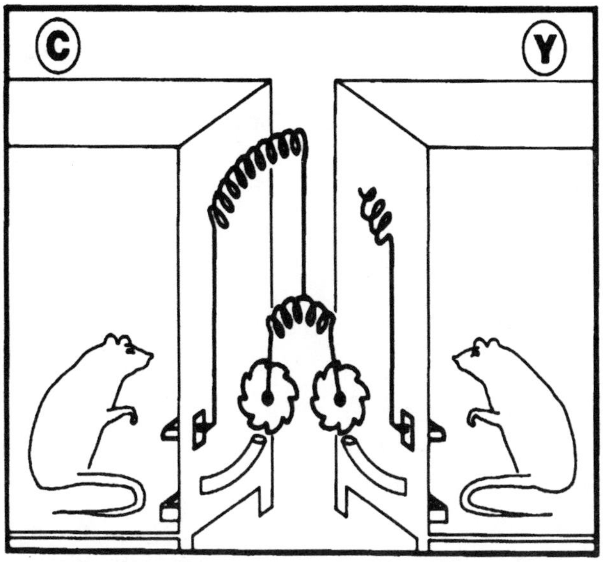

Figure 1. Diagram of a yoked control experiment for measuring the effect of contingency on lever-pressing in the Skinner Box.

Experimental Design

The two chambers shown in Figure 1 are identical except that the lever of chamber *C* operates both food magazines, while the lever of chamber *Y* is not connected to either magazine. Both magazines dispense pellets of food when rat C presses his lever, but neither magazine is affected when rat *Y* presses his lever. Thus, *C*'s feeding is contiguous with and contingent upon his lever-presses, while *Y* receives the same number of pellets at the same time intervals but *Y*'s feeding is independent of his lever-presses. The difference between *C*'s responses and *Y*'s responses should measure the difference between contingent and evocative effects of the incentives. This general procedure can be adapted to use with any criterion response and any method of dispensing incentives.

In Figure 1, food always arrives when rat C has just pressed his lever — that is, when he is engaged in that particular prefeeding behavior; when his threshold for pressing is low; and when he is *ready* to press.

Consider the analogous case of the subjects in Figure 2 who represent two college students *C* and *Y* participating in a word recognition experiment. They are seated in separate rooms at identical terminals. Each subject reports by speaking into a microphone. Immediately after subject *C* says, "Ready" identical target words appear on both screens, and immediately after *C* reports a word both screens are blacked out, but nothing that subject *Y* says has any effect on either screen. As a result, the target words will usually appear when *C* is attending to her screen. Sometimes, *Y* will also be attending to her screen, but many trials will begin at times when *Y* is paying no attention to the screen, whatever. On the average trial, then, *Y*'s attention will be lower than *C*'s, and C will recognize more words than *Y* does. *C* will have the same advantage if the experiment is converted from word recognition to word learning by requiring *C* and *Y* to memorize the words. But, we cannot attribute *C*'s superiority in either case to the rewarding effect of her control over the screen.

The yoked control is an *ex post facto* de-

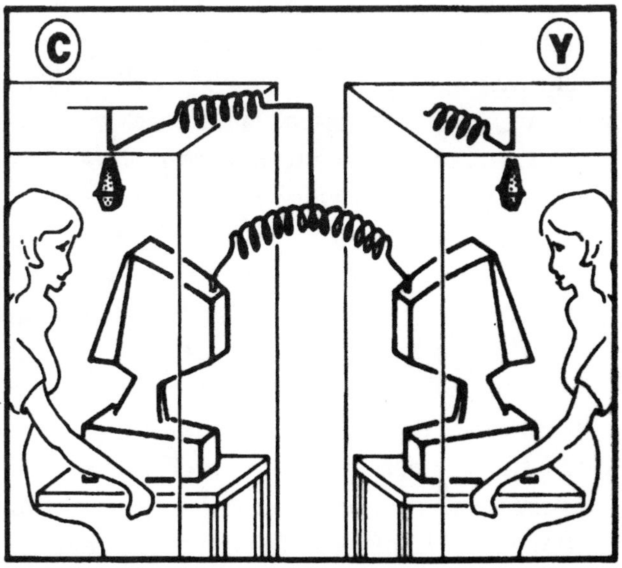

Figure 2. Diagram of a yoked control experiment for measuring the effect of contingency on word recognition.

sign. The classical example of this error (Underwood, 1957, pp. 97-99) is a study of the effects of time spent in the Boy Scouts on later participation in community affairs. The study found that young men who had joined the Scouts and remained Scouts for an average of four years, later participated in more community activities than other young men who had joined the Scouts at about the same time but quit in an average of 1.4 years. The authors concluded that extended membership in the Boy Scouts increased later community involvement.

The Boy Scout study proves nothing of the kind, of course. The quitters were different from the stickers at the time that they quit. That is why they quit. There is no valid way to attribute later differences to participation in the Boys Scouts, because the two groups were different before the differential conditions had any chance to act on them. Once subjects have been selected on the basis of past behavior, we cannot logically attribute subsequent differences in behavior to later conditions imposed by the experimenter.

Conclusion

Yoked control experiments always confound contiguity with contingency when the reinforcing stimulus, S^*, either evokes or inhibits the to-be-conditioned response. The source of confounding cannot be eliminated by more powerful procedures or more precise instruments. All conceivable versions of the yoked control for response contingent reinforcement suffer from the same *ex post facto* error.

The principle of response contingent reward and punishment is an intuitively attractive hypothesis that agrees with an every day, common sense view of learning that has appealed to parents, teachers, animal trainers, moralists, and psychologists for centuries. Nevertheless, for those who judge scientific merit on the basis of experimental operations rather than on the basis of intuition or common sense, a principle without any possibility of operational definition is also without any scientific merit.

Learning without Hedonism

If we can dispense with response contingent reinforcement then we can also dispense with much of the clutter of a learning process based on experienced or expected pleasure and pain.

Bioassay

Consider the following version of the experiment in Figure 1. Suppose that instead of delivering pellets of food into a dish, the apparatus delivers doses of a drug directly into the blood stream by means of a fistula. The doses are small enough to be rapidly metabolized, hence their effect is transitory and brief. Let us further suppose that there is a drug, Epsilon, that has only one effect on rats; and that effect is the excitation of feeding behavior.

The rats are yoked in pairs as before, so that both receive an injection of Epsilon when rat *C* presses his lever, but neither is affected when rat *Y* presses his lever. When *C* presses his lever, he receives a dose of Epsilon which excites his feeding behavior. Since manipulation is one of his feeding behaviors, that bout of lever-pressing will be prolonged. Sometimes *Y* will also be pressing his lever when Epsilon is released into his blood stream, but often he will be in some other part of the chamber engaged in some other behavior, altogether. Consequently, rats in condition *C* will, on the average, press the lever more times than rats in Condition *Y*.

Since we know that Epsilon is limited to one effect — the excitation of feeding behaviors — we can resist the temptation to conclude that Epsilon is a positive reinforcer. But we only have this advantage in thought experiments. Real experiments are performed to determine the effects of unknown drugs. In an actual bioassay experiment which failed to take into account the logical fallacy of the yoked control we would have to conclude that Epsilon was a positive reinforcer.

In fact, bioassay experiments with analogous designs have been used to support the conclusion that electrodes implanted in certain regions of the rat brain deliver "reinforcing brain stimulation." The argument for this conclusion begins with the assumption that lever-pressing is arbitrary work that rats will shun unless we pay them for it with food or some other commodity. It follows that, if contingent brain stimulation increases lever-pressing, it must have some value for the rat, hence the region that was stimulated is a pleasure center. As we have seen, however, lever-pressing is evoked by feeding. It is more parsimonious to conclude that stimulation of certain regions of the rat brain evokes manipulation just as feeding does. The experimental result would be the same.

If reinforcing brain stimulation is a way of paying the rat with the pleasurable result of eating, then we would expect eating, itself, to fall off when brain stimulation was freely available. Indeed, we might expect some rats to starve to death under these conditions. Nevertheless, when food is freely available and brain stimulation is also freely administered by the experimenter, rats eat more rather than less food (Mogensen and Cioé, 1977, pp. 581-584). This is, of course, just what we should expect if activity in certain regions of the brain evokes a repertoire of obligatory feeding behaviors that includes both eating and manipulation. In that case, when there is food and no lever, brain stimulation should evoke eating, and when there is a lever but no food, brain stimulation should evoke lever-pressing. When both are available, brain stimulation should evoke a mixture of feeding and prefeeding just as food does.

Inhibition and Competition

Consider one more variant of the yoked control experiment. Once again paired rats receive injections of a drug by means of a fistula. This time, however, the drug is Iota which has only one effect on rats, the inhibition of feeding behavior. The subjects are yoked in pairs as before, so that both rats receive Iota when rat *C* presses his lever, but neither gets any Iota when rat *Y* presses his lever. When *C* presses his lever, he receives a dose of Iota that inhibits his feeding behavior. Since manipulation is one of his feeding behaviors, that bout of lever-pressing will be shortened. Sometimes *Y* will also be pressing his lever when Iota is released into his blood stream, but often he will be in some other part of the chamber engaged in some other behavior which may or may not be part of a rat's feeding behavior.

On the average, doses of Iota will depress *C*'s lever-pressing more than *Y*'s. If we did not know that Iota has only one effect — the inhibition of feeding behavior — we might conclude that Iota was aversive. For, if lever-pressing is arbitrary work that increases with pleasureable consequences and decreases with painful consequences then Iota must be a punisher, and a site of brain stimulation that has the same negative effect must be a pain center. Only the omniscience of the thought-experimenter or the logical analysis of the yoked control can protect us from this error.

Suppose that instead of inhibiting feeding behavior, Iota excites a repertoire of nonfeeding behavior that is incompatible with lever-pressing. Doses of such a drug or stimulation of such a brain site would also interrupt bouts of lever-pressing. In the same way, doses of Epsilon or stimulation of an Epsilon brain site would interrupt bouts of nonfeeding behavior. An inhibitory process based on negative consequences is only required in a system which requires an excitatory process based on positive consequences. The result is a top-heavy, cumbersome model in which each response is governed by a separate pair of opposing excitatory and inhibitory processes, when all that is required is circuitry that can select now one response and then another.

The carrot and the stick move the donkey forward when the carrot is applied to the front and the stick is applied to the rear of the donkey. If the stick is applied to the nose of the donkey, then the donkey moves backward even if the stick is applied as a punishment for moving backward. Whether applied to the front or to the rear, the stick has a feedforward effect. Aversive stimulation depresses feeding behavior by positively evoking responses that are incompatible with feeding. In aversive conditioning with shock as in appetitive conditioning with food, the responses that are conditioned are the responses that are evoked by an S^*. Aversive conditioning is also independent of the contingency between response and S^*, and robust conditioning develops even when this earns more pain. [See Gardner and Gardner, 1988, for details of the experimental evidence and analysis of the noncontingent, feedforward basis of aversive conditioning. Arguments for stimulus-stimulus contingency are popular in cognitive, top-down treatments of aversive conditioning, but are also based on logical errors in experimental design discussed in detail in Gardner and Gardner, 1988.]

Feedback vs. Sign Stimuli

The prototypes of what Norbert Wiener called "cybernetics" were two-phase systems such as thermostats in which one of two possible inputs maintains the current output (positive feedback) and the second possible input switches the device back to the alternative phase (negative feedback), thus limiting fluctuations in temperature. Modern computers are multi-phase systems that perform a given operation until a test is passed. At that point, the next operation is initiated, and so on. A computer can go through many operations before it repeats the first operation. Indeed, it may never return to the logical state that initiated the first operation. The pulse that ends one operation initiates the next. It feeds forward rather than backward, rather like the sign stimuli of classical ethology. In the case of a male stickleback, for example, establishing a territory and building a nest are not rewarded by the appearance of a gravid female. Instead, the swollen abdomen of the female is a sign stimulus that initiates courtship. Courtship is not rewarded when a female deposits eggs in the nest; instead, the clutch of eggs is a sign stimulus that initiates fanning and nest-tending.

Highly artificial sign stimuli can evoke genuine, species-specific patterns of behavior. One recalls Tinbergen's description of the male sticklebacks in his laboratory that attempted to attack Royal Mail vans passing by the windows, even though the only stimulus that a van shared with an intruding male stickleback fish was its fiery red color.

In the model that we are offering here, an S^* serves to evoke obligatory responses rather than to reinforce arbitrary responses. The stimulus feeds forward rather than backward. The rats studied by Timberlake and his associates manipulated small steel balls almost indefinitely until pellets of prepared grain arrived. Under comparable conditions, rodents manipulate a seed until they find a suitable place in the husk to break open. This is the S^* for breaking open the husk. If a rat finds a kernel of food in the husk, this is the S^* for consuming the kernel, and so on.

Prefeeding responses, such as salivation, are evoked by the sight of food. If an arbitrary stimulus, such as a tone, is presented when the subject is salivating, the tone later evokes salivation before food appears. A vast number of experiments demonstrate that this procedure is sufficient for conditioning. Is it necessary to introduce an additional feedbackward mechanism by which positive or negative consequences reinforce or weaken the connection between stimulus and response? Are there economic advantages to a feedbackward mechanism of learning with all of the cumbersome, prespecified, top-down mechanisms that it entails? If not, the additional burden will handicap both organism and robot in a competitive world. A feedforward model of the learning process offers a more practical alternative that is also more consistent with the experimental evidence (for a more comprehensive treatment of this evidence see Gardner and Gardner, 1988).

An Application to Artificial Life

Brooks (1990) describes Herbert, a robot that enters offices, approaches desks, and removes empty soda cans from the top of the desks. Herbert picks up a can when a beam is broken between the two fingers at the end of an arm that reaches for cans. For simplicity here, suppose that Herbert's arm can only reach to the right or to the left. Suppose further, that 80% of the empty cans in this environment are on the right and only 20% are on the left. To profit by this correlation all Herbert would need is a circuit that prevented immediate repetition of arm movements, right or left, but insured repetition after a delay, say at the next desk.

This would guarantee that at the next desk, Herbert would reach in the same direction that was successful at the last desk. On average, Herbert would find a can on the first try 80% of 80% of the time which is distinctly better than 50%. This could be improved by allowing some cummulation that gradually raised reaching right to something higher than 80% and dampened the effect of infrequent instances of left-lying cans. With this learning mechanism, Herbert could benefit from experience without discriminating correlation from causation and without evaluating, computing, or storing positive and negative hedonic contingencies. Herbert could use the recent history of the world as a model of the future and respond directly to that. This learning mechanism would also be more flexible than one based on contingency because Herbert could respond quickly to changes in the right-left distribution of cans on desks without having to average new instances into the old computations.

References

Breland, K., and Breland, M. 1961. The misbehavior of organisms. *American Psychologist*, *16*, 681-684.

Brooks, R.A. 1990. Elephants don't play chess. *Robotics and Autonomous Systems*. *6*, 3-15.

Brown, P., and Jenkins, H.M. 1968. Autoshaping of the pigeon's key-peck. *Journal of the Experimental Analysis of Behavior*, *11*, 1-8.

Gardner, R.A., and Gardner, B.T. 1988. Feedforward versus feedbackward: An ethological alternative to the law of effect. *Behavioral and Brain Sciences*, *11*, 429-493.

Jensen, G.D. 1963. Preference for bar pressing over 'freeloading' as a function of number of rewarded presses. *Journal of Experimental Psychology*, *65*, 451-454.

Mogenson, G., and Cioé, J. 1977. Central reinforcement: A bridge between brain function and behavior. In W.K. Honig and J.E.R. Staddon (Eds.), *Handbook of operant behavior*, (pp. 570-595). Englewood Cliffs, NJ: Prentice-Hall.

Osborne, S.R. 1977. The free food (con trafreeloading) phenomenon: A review and analysis. *Animal Learning and Behavior*, *5*, 221-235.

Osborne, S.R. 1978. A note on the acquisition of responding for food in the presence of free food. *Animal Learning and Behavior*, *6*, 368-369.

Shettleworth, S.J. 1972. Constraints on learning. *Advances in the Study of Behavior*, *4*, 1-68.

Skinner, B.F. 1953. *Science and human behavior*, New York: Macmillan.

Staddon, J.E.R., and Simmelhag, B. 1971. The 'superstition' experiment: A re-examination of its implications for the principles of adaptive behavior. *Psychological Review*, *78*, 3-43.

Timberlake, W. 1983. Rats' responses to a moving object related to food or water: A behavior-systems analysis. *Animal Learning and Behavior*, *11*, 309-320.

Timberlake, W. 1986. Unpredicted food produces a mode of behavior that affects rats' subsequent reactions to a conditioned stimulus: A behavior-systems approach to 'context blocking'. *Animal Learning and Behavior*, *14*, 276-286.

Timberlake, W., Wahl, G., and King, D. 1982. Stimulus and response contingencies in the misbehavior of rats. *Journal of Experimental Psychology: Animal Behavior Processes*, *8*, 62-85.

Underwood, B.J. 1957. *Psychological research*, New York: Appleton-Century-Crofts.

Williams, D.R., and Williams, H. 1969. Automaintenance in the pigeon: Sustained pecking despite contingent non-reinforcement. *Journal of the Experimental Analysis of Behavior*, *12*, 511-520.

Computing at the Tissue/Organ Level

(with particular reference to the liver)

R. C. Paton, H. S. Nwana, M. J. R. Shave & T. J. M. Bench-Capon

Department of Computer Science
University of Liverpool
Liverpool, L69 3BX, U.K.
rcp@cs.liv.ac.uk

Abstract

Biosystems at the tissue/organ level of complexity can be used to provide valuable insights for computer scientists and others interested in elaborating parallel models of computation. Two of the most important are the central nervous system and the immune system. This paper looks at the liver as another source of ideas. The liver is a fascinating organ, highly complex and like the brain poorly understood, but it can provide many insights into parallelisation. Following on from a summary review of liver biology, a number of computational models are described and a variety of approaches considered. Emphasis is placed on a broad range of informal models. The paper concludes with a discussion of certain issues related to cell-cell interaction.

1 Introduction

Several approaches to parallel and emergent computation are based on biological analogues that are described at the tissue or organ level of complexity such as, artificial neural networks (ANNs) and immune algorithms. However, there are a lot of other biosystems at this level which could be used to provide valuable insights for computer scientists and others interested in elaborating parallel models. The purpose of this short paper is to examine one such system, the liver, and consider a variety of ways in which it can be used as a source for computational models. The strategy for introducing the computational liver' is as follows:

- Summary of an approach to modelling.
- Introduction of pertinent details concerned with the biology of the liver (as far as it is understood).
- Description of computational models at different levels of biological organisation.
- Comments about some general issues associated with cell-cell interaction.

This paper records one approach to the development of a range of descriptive, biologically motivated models. The writers' intention is to encourage researchers in Alife to explore the breadth of complex biosystems and the variety of ways of building models. As such, relations to a biological system are emphasised rather than to a computational artifact. Hence, this paper reports on the stage of model building prior to formalisation; when relations between the biological and the computational are being sought out.

2 A Modelling Approach to Tissue/ Organ Level Computing

The approach to biologically motivated computing elaborated in this and a companion paper (Paton *et al*, 1991b) seeks to apply a theoretical framework to new models of computation. The source for these models is biological and the subject computational. A common language can be identified between source and subject which is expressed by the metaphorical context in which statements are made and concepts are organised; this provides models with theoretical terms as well as an explanatory framework. A simple example may be useful at this point. Consider some biological source ideas for artificial neural networks (ANNs) as shown in Table 1.

Subject (ANN)	**Common language**	**Source** (CNS)
Processing unit	Basic part	Neuron
Input	Input	Dendrite
Output	Output	Axon
Weight	Strength of connection	Synapse
ANN	Network	Neuronal circuit
Transfer function	Non-linear behaviour	Dendritic tree processing

Table 1 Some Components of the Common Language between Central Nervous System (CNS) and Artificial Neural Networks (ANNs)

Other nouns in the common language include fault tolerance, distributed processing, memory, information transfer, negative feedback regulation, local interaction and adaptive behaviour. Clearly, this example is a simplified summary but it shows how source and subject are related. The importance of the kind of comparison made in Table 1 is that source and subject can be interchanged depending on the problem area and an understanding of this relationship is important when new ideas are introduced. Thus, apparently novel concepts in ANNs may suggest new ways of thinking about the nervous system and vice versa. Examples of this would include the need to account for NMDA in parallel distributed processing (PDP) models of cognition (Crick, 1989) or the role of neuromodulators in ANNs (see section 4 of this paper). In the context of the present paper there is an express intention to demonstrate the value for two way interchange of ideas between biology and computing. However, because of length restrictions, it is not possible to provide any more than a summary overview.

The value in gaining a fuller appreciation of metaphorical transfer in biologically motivated computing is the characterisation of metaphorical transfers between source(s) and subject and particular issues addressed in this paper are:

- the occurrence of multiple sources for the same subject. For example, some ANN models seek to import ideas from other networks such as the immune system (Weisbuch & Atlan, 1989).
- multiple level sources for the same subject. For example, applying ideas associated with interorganismal systems to ANNs such as population and selection parameters.
- reapplying biological subjects which have been based on computational sources as new source models for computing. For example, biomolecular computing.

It was argued elsewhere (Paton *et al,* 1991a) that a variety of computational objects, such a automaton, program, processor, information retrieval system, etc., share common metaphorical contexts. For example, all can be described using the machine metaphor in either real or virtual terms. However, there are limitations with this way of thinking, especially when there are concepts which are not common to machines. It is often in this capacity that metaphor has an ontological role because it can provide new or alternative ways of describing and talking about the world. Tieing everything to machine can result in abstracting out salient features in order to preserve source-subject correspondence.

It is also useful to highlight the distinction between biological analogy and biological homology (see Paton *et al,* 1991b). Biological analogy focusses on the sharing of common function whereas homology deals with the sharing of common structure. For example, a synapse and a weight are very much analogous. However, it could be argued that an artificial neural network and a neuronal circuit are less analogous and more homologous in that they share structural similarities (i.e., they are both circuits). Analogy often captures ideas associated with source - subject functionality whereas homology deals more with architecture, mechanism and organisation. The motivation behind the approach to biologically motivated computing discussed in this paper is the desire to improve upon nonlinearity and particularly distributed processing and communication through an understanding of both homologous structures and analogous functions.

It is now possible to summarise the underlying approach to this paper. The sharing of a similar context (e.g., the computational metaphor or certain systemic metaphors) means that concepts in one domain (source) can be displaced into the other (subject) and vice versa. With respect to the 'computational liver', we not only use computer language to talk about the real organ, nor do we merely seek to address issues particular to the liver in computational and systemic terms, we also wish to provide an additional metaphor for the development of computational systems. Thus, a computational model of the liver for one researcher may be re-applied as a model of computation by another. For the purposes of this paper the computational model is a less formalised version of the model of computation. (Note: this distinction is explored in Paton *et al,* 1991b).

3 Towards the Characterisation of a Computational Liver

We begin this section with a few simple statements about the ways in which the liver and a real or virtual machine share such common 'ideas' as:

- Both process data - the context of the machine provides the means for defining data. In the case of the liver these are biological chemicals such as hormones and metabolites.
- Both are complex systems.
- Both can be described using such general ideas as architecture, mechanism, organisation and functionality. Different models can be used to account for particular emphases.

For the present purposes, the liver is best described as a distributed parallel processing system at various levels of its organisation.

3.1 Background Motivation for Choosing the Liver as a Modelling Source

The liver is a fascinating organ. To the medical practitioner or physiologist it is almost, or maybe equally, as enigmatic as the brain; essential to life and but not very well understood. It has extraordinary regenerative powers, being able to repair itself quite rapidly following the loss (through surgery) of up to half its mass, and it has a quite remarkable capacity for tolerating increased metabolic demands. At the organ level of organisation, its multi-functionality is only rivaled by the brain.

3.2 A Summary Review of Liver Biology

The purpose of this section is to summarise current understanding of the liver as it relates to the express purpose of this paper, namely to gain insights into the workings of a highly parallel multi-functional system.

As such a lot of biological details have been omitted and the interested reader may wish to consult Arias *et al* (1982), Jones & Spring-Mills (1983) and Quistorff (1990).

3.2.1 General Remarks

The human liver is the largest organ in the body (about 1.5 kg. in an adult). It has a dual blood supply receiving seventy-five percent from the hepatic portal vein (HPV) and twenty-five percent from the hepatic artery (HA). The total hepatic blood flow is about one quarter of the total cardiac output. Materials leave the liver via three separate fluid transport systems namely, blood vascular (hepatic vein), biliary (hepatic duct) and lymphatic. This information is summarised in Figure 1.

3.2.2 Hepatic Microstructure

The structural unit of the liver is the hepatic lobule (of which there are about one million). Each lobule is a polyhedral prism of tissue approximately 2.0mm in length by 0.7mm in diameter. It is roughly hexagonal in cross section with a centrally-located vein (terminal hepatic venule) and a *triad* of vessels located at each apex of the hexagon. Figure 2 gives a schematic breakdown of the structural details at this level. Each triad contains a terminal branch of the hepatic artery, hepatic portal vein and bile duct. The material of the lobule itself consists mainly of one cell type, the *hepatocyte*. In cross section the hepatocytes appear as strings (of one cell thickness) radiating from the central vein. The three dimensional architecture is that of radially arranged anastomosing plates or laminae. These cell plates are separated from each other by blood conducting cavities, the *sinusoids*, which receive blood from the side branches of the triad vessels and convey it to the central vein. Both cell plates and sinusoids can be characterised by their fractal organisation which accounts, in part, for the efficient way in which materials are exchanged between hepatocytes and blood (see Sernetz, 1989).

The parallelisation of the liver into lobules, together with the complex hepatic vascular tree, provides the means by which every gram of tissue receives between one hundred and one hundred and thirty millilitres of blood per minute. This value is very high. Not only this, the hepatocytes are perfused by a mixed arterial and portal supply. The distribution of this mixture within and between macroscopic regions of the whole organ is uniform and the flow distribution is not altered by changes in nervous stimulation, venous blood pressure or oxygen consumption.

3.2.3 Hepatic Functional Units

Although hepatic microstructure is delineated by lobules, the functional unit of the liver is best described according to the distinctive way by which blood is delivered at the microscopic level. This unit is called the *acinus* and is a small, irregular mass of tissue which receives blood from the side branches of the triad vessels which run at right angles to the triad. Figure 3 shows one such acinus, although a single lobule will share six (one with each adjacent lobule). Blood flows in a radial direction from the triad vessel termini, along the sinusoids to the central vein. The radial flow of blood in adjacent sinusoids in concurrent.

3.2.4 Metabolic Zonation in Acini

The microvasculature of the acinus, arranged as concurrently-perfused sinusoids, contributes to a gradient of oxygen, metabolites and hormones between the periportal region and the perivenous region. As a result of this, when compared to the perivenous region, the periportal region of a sinusoid will be relatively richer in oxygen and also in compounds absorbed through the gut or released into the splanchnic vascular bed. Three distinct physiological zones are typically identified in the literature (Jungermann & Katz, 1989):

- Periportal (adjacent to axis of triad vessels) - oxygen, hormonal and substrate concentrations are usually highest here. This is Zone 1.
- Perivenous (adjacent to the central vein) - oxygen, hormone and substrate concentrations usually lowest here. This is Zone 3.
- Intermediate zone - as the name suggests, this is in between the other two zones. This is Zone 2.

Acinar zonation is summarised in Figure 3. The organisation of the acinus into different metabolic zones is a very important feature of hepatic parallelisation. A valuable contrast may now be made with the brain in that the microcirculation here is organised so as to minimise zonation effects; adjacent capillaries are perfused in opposite directions (see Quistorff & Chance, 1986). The microcirculation of the liver is organised to obtain maximum zonation.

Recent research has demonstrated that particular populations of hepatocytes, unique to particular acinar zones, can be characterised by their metabolic profile with respect to:

- Presence of particular enzymes and subcellular structures. For example, periportal mitochondria are larger and more abundant compared to perivenous cells. Metabolic zonation for particular enzymes varies, some may be clearly demarcated depending on whether they are in periportal or perivenous zones whilst the zonation for others is less.
- Response to particular hormones. For example, there is evidence that the enzyme patterns in periportal cells are correlated with glucagon induction and those in perivenous cells with insulin induction (Wolfe & Jungermann, 1985). As blood passes through an acinus hormonal signals may be decreased by removal (e.g., insulin or glucagon) or they may be increased as in the transformation of thyroxine to the more potent triiodothyronine). There is also suggestive

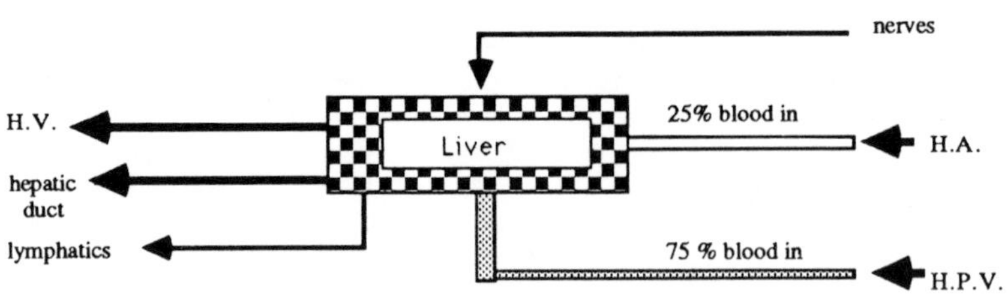

Figure 1 - Summary Diagram Showing Liver Inputs and Outputs

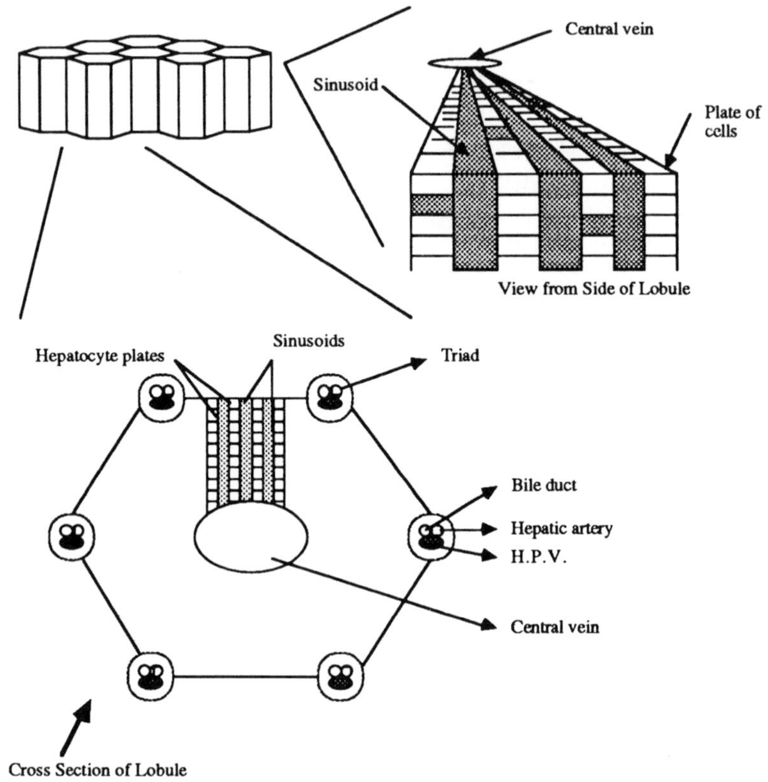

Figure 2 - Schematic Overview of the Construction of Lobules
(Note: branches of triad vessels emerge laterally from the triad. In order to preserve clarity only a few vessels are shown in the diagram)

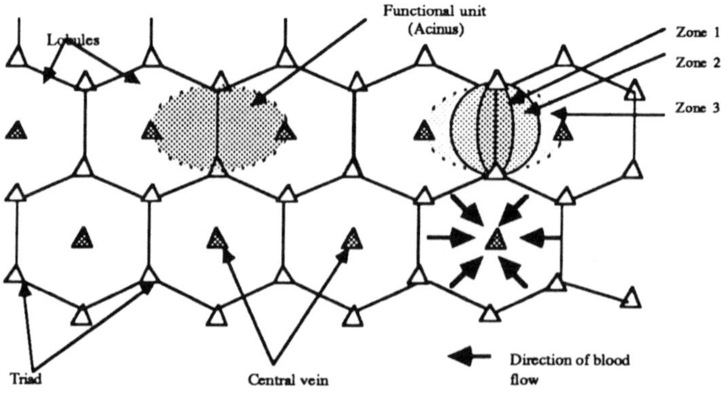

Figure 3 - Simplified Representation to show Relation of Lobules, Metabolic Zones and Acini evidence for the zonation of membrane-bound hormone receptors (Quistorff, 1990).

- Metabolic response to substrates. For example, periportal cells are involved in bile formation, the catabolism of fatty acids and amino acids and glucose mobilisation whilst perivenous cells are involved with glucose utilization, ketogenesis and detoxification of xenobiotics.
- Effect of oxygen. For example, physiological oxygen concentration modulates hepatic carbohydrate metabolism and may affect gene expression (Jungermann & Katz, 1989).

As shall be discussed more fully below, the implication of zonal heterogeneity to biologically motivated computing at the tissue/organ level is very important. For example, all hepatocytes have the same genome (although it will be amplified in polyploid and binucleate cells). However, it is differentially expressed by cells according to oxygen and hormone gradients, autonomic innervation and cell-cell interaction. As such there is a common code (genome) which is differentially expressed as metabolic zonation and amplified (in polyploid and binuclear cells). Zonal hepatocyte heterogeneity is dynamic, depending on the interaction of the cells with the environment and with each other. This provides an example of a highly plastic and adaptable system of multi-functional elements, each having a common though variably expressed genome (coded representation).

3.2.5 The Streaming Liver

The discussion so far has, in temporal terms, presented a picture of the liver which deals with its being and behaving. In this brief section we consider some aspects of the organ related to its becoming.

Many tissues exhibit the phenomenon of streaming. This is where cells migrate from a region of division (the progenitor or P-region) to a quiescent or non-fission region (Q-region). As such two age-related distributions in a streaming tissue may be abstracted: firstly, age in terms of position in space (i.e., distance from progenitor region) and secondly, chronological age. One may compare spatio-temporal ideas related to tissue streaming with the notion of a *sere* in ecology (i.e., a sucession of communities in space and time). This is an example of the need for ecological understanding at the tissue level.

Zajicek and co-workers demonstrated in a series of experiments that tissues of the liver undergo streaming (e.g., Zajicek *et al*, 1985; Arber *et al*, 1988). The model they have constructed is based on the acinus in which cells stream from the portal region to the central vein. For our present purposes, the current discussion will be restricted to the hepatocyte. Hepatocytes live between two hundred and four hundred and fifty days. During this time they migrate from the P-region, through the Q-region to be eliminated adjacent to the central vein. The streaming hepatocytes proceed along a radial trajectory which traverses the three acinus zones (i.e., beginning in Zone 1 and ending in Zone 3). Thus the acinus is a highly dynamic structure both metabolically and spatio-temporally.

3.3 An Exploration of some Hepatic Computational Models

As a computer, the liver has to deal with very large volumes of heterogeneous data of a variety of general types that may change depending on body state. It is capable of satisfying such demands because it has multi-functional processing units which operate in parallel through multi-level regulatory processes.

The analysis in this section focusses on two organisational levels: the hepatocyte and the acinus and as such misses out others. A breadth of examples are given in order to illustrate to the reader that concepts can be transferred in a variety of metaphorical contexts. This is important, the liver can provide insights into parallelism not only in terms of architectures such as MIMD (Multiple Input stream, Multiple Data stream) but also with regard to distributed interactions among different agents (Blackboards), open system ecologies and emergence of form as in a streaming tissue.

3.3.1 Models of the Hepatocyte

The hepatocyte is a fascinating cell type. It makes up sixty percent of the cell population of the liver and eighty percent of its volume. As should be clear from what has previously been discussed, it is extremely versatile. Indeed it demonstrates exocrine, endocrine and metabolic functions. This is manifested in structural terms by the large numbers of organelles. For example, for an 'average' cell there have been estimates of upwards of two thousand mitochondria (eighteen percent intracellular volume) and one thousand peroxisomes; seven percent of the cell volume is rough endoplasmic reticulum and twelve per cent of the volume is smooth endoplasmic reticulum / Golgi bodies. Many processes in the cell operate in parallel.

Attempts at modelling a cell vary. As noted elsewhere (Paton, 1991), it is possible to describe a biosystem in a variety of ways and for the present purpose we identify several salient features:

- Systemic metaphor - such as machine, circuit, organism, society, etc.
- Level of organisation - such as intercellular, organismal, cellular, etc.
- Emphasis of the model - for example, focussing on architecture or mechanisms or organisation or functionality of the whole system.

For example, we may wish to model the emergent ability of the cell's metabolism to adapt to changes in hormone and metabolite levels by using a parallel distributed processing (PDP) approach. Alternately, we could model a multi-level compartmental model through the interaction of parallel processes. In the former case an ANN could be applied whereas in the latter case a Blackboard architecture could be suggested (see below). A summary of possible system/level combinations are represented diagrammatically in Figure 4.

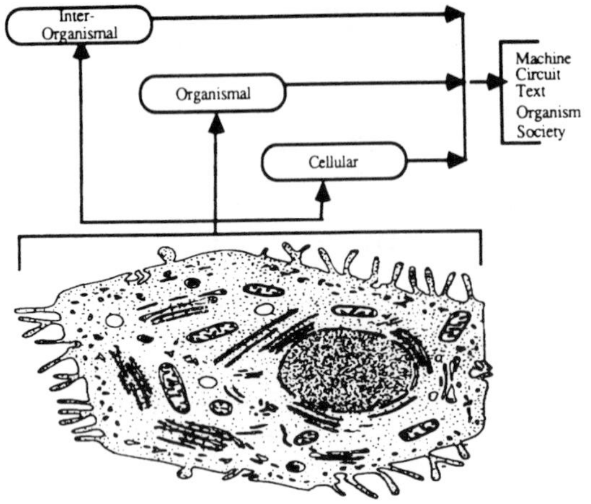

Figure 4 - Some Possible Ways of Modelling an Hepatocyte in Terms of Level and System

(i) **ANN Models of Hepatocytes**

Bray (1990) considers the way in which one aspect of intracellular signalling, that of glucagon processing, can be modelled as a parallel distributed process (glucagon is a hormone involved in the regulation of hepatic glucose release into the blood).The source of Bray's computational model is an ANN in which cell performance is modelled as a PDP network and the PDP processing units are signalling molecules such as cyclic AMP. Common ideas include distributed memory, network processing, fault tolerance and non-linear behaviour. Clearly this is just one example of a connectionist approach to hepatocyte modelling. There are other intra- and inter-cellular signalling pathways that could be modelled in this way. More general features of hepatocyte collective behaviour would be ammenable to a PDP approach. Further analysis would be required to get to a satisfactory first approximation of quantitative relationships.

(ii) A Blackboard Architecture

A Blackboard is a Knowledge Based System which provides a way of distributing control of problem solving effort among several disjoint knowledge sources. As Cunningham and Veale (1991) note, it consists of a common data structure through which knowledge sources communicate and an associated control mechanism by which that communication is moderated. The whole blackboard is subdivided into panels on which information is transformed. Information exchange can take place between panels and for the present purposes we consider a fully distributive daemon-driven control architecture in which daemons (regulatory biochemicals) bring about system state changes.

Subject (Hepatocyte)	**Common language**	**Source** (Blackboard)
Functional compartment	Data store	Panel
Function	Goal/task	Problem
Metabolic	Processor	Knowledge source
Organisation of cell	Structure	Data structure
Metabolic change	State change	Event (panel state change)

Table 2 - Source - Subject Interrelations between Blackboard and Hepatocyte

An alternative approach would be to model the interactions of various panels each of which describes the system at a particular organisational level using a particular systemic metaphor. One example is shown in Figure 5. In this case, each panel (of which there are four) is described by a particular systemic metaphor. For example, it is possible to describe the organisation of the system as the interaction of text (genome) with machine (metabolism) whereas mechanistic details are best described by the operation of a text-driven circuit within the machine. Description of the system as a whole may be best served using the language of a society. This kind of approach cuts across reductionistic boundaries in that processes are described from a variety of levels (panels). This kind of approach has certain things in common with Holcombe's application of multi-levelled X-machines to cells (Holcombe, 1990; Paton *et al*, 1991b) except that panels need not be deterministically prescribed.

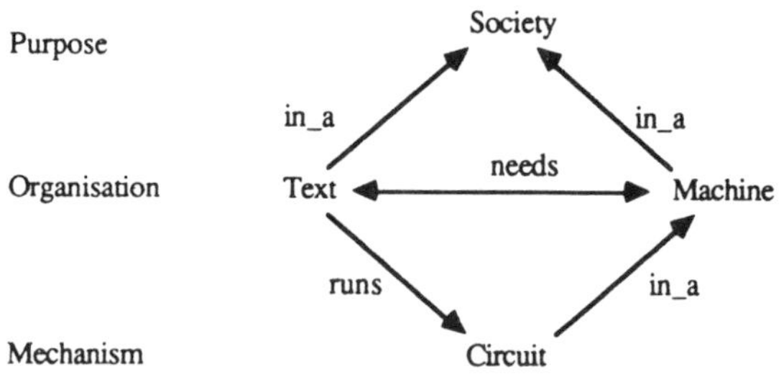

Figure 5 - One Example of an Idealised Blackboard Architecture for Modelling an Hepatocyte

(iii) Hepatocyte as a MIMD Processor

The hepatocyte displays highly varied multi-functionality; much more so than a neuron. Indeed, it would not seem sensible to capture its complexity in terms of a sequential, multi-level or simple non-linear machine. It is at least a colony of machines and a then a lot more (Paton *et al*, 1991b). The sub-cellular level of a computational liver could be described by several interacting PDP networks. The program in the hepatocyte is highly adaptable and its execution would best be described in terms of an emerging open system. For these reasons the hepatocyte may best be modelled as a MIMD or open system in its own right.

3.3.2 Models of an Acinus

(i) Streaming Tissues and Cellular Automata

Sipcic *et al* (1991) report on the computer simulation of the streaming of the polyp cancer cell sequence in the crypts of Lieberkühn which is based on a cellular automata model. The system is implemented on a Connection Machine and simulates the process of mitosis in the P-region and streaming into the Q-region. It is anticipated that streaming liver models will also be ammenable to this kind of approach.

(ii) SIMD Model of a Functional Unit

A SIMD (Single Instruction stream, Multiple Data stream) machine uses a large number of simple processing elements each obeying the same instruction stream. We may compare this to a static picture of a three-zone acinus in which processing in one zone produces output which is further transformed in the next zone, and so forth. This would constitute a very simplistic model of the liver based on a systolic array. However, it supplies some valuable information in relation to a machine that has to process very large amounts of heterogeneous data. For example, data transfer is achieved through communication between adjacent zones by cell-cell communication and also via a data bus (sinusoid). The lobular architecture permits six parallel three-zone units served by six data input ports (triads) and one output port (central vein). The microvascular architecture and the inter-cellular communication provides an efficient means of distributing the large data load. It is hoped that the reader will appreciate that this kind of model is extremely simplistic when it comes to understanding the real liver.

(iii) MIMD architecture

A MIMD model of an acinus is pertinent if the level of complexity is increased to a consideration of cell-cell interactions within a zone and multi-functional material transformation. Some important details include:

- Multi-functional processing units - the multifunctionality of hepatocytes was described in section 3.3.1. Individual units perform different sets of functions at different spatio-temporal locations. At any one time a cell is carrying out many parallel processes. These are regulated at a variety of organisational levels (see Table 3 below). This contrasts very clearly with SIMD arrays of multiple special purpose functional units (Haynes *et al*, 1982).
- Pipelining - the fractal organisation of the sinusoids provides the hepatocyte plates with a continuous supply of blood (carrying data). This ensures sufficiency of data capture by hepatocytes. Data capture is membrane-mediated; some data types (e.g., hormones) are captured by receptors and others (e.g., oxygen, metabolites, ions) according to the chemical conformation of the membranes. It seems reasonable to suggest that pipelining is a major contribution to parallelisation at this level.
- Data flow - the adaptational capabilities of the system are reflected in its data driven capacities. The intrinsic multi-processing parallelism of cells and zones enables the acinus to deal with waiting overheads.
- No centralised control (asynchronous processing) - this is related to data flow. A variety of data types are involved in parallel distributed regulation (see Table 3 below).
- Algorithmic parallelisation - one could argue that each cell has the same algorithm (i.e., its genome). Within an acinus these algorithms are differentially expressed, in parallel, according to the spatio-temporal location of the cell and its adaptation to the environment in which it is found. The MIMD qualities that can be described using this comparison deal with the differential expression of the same code according to differential demands on individual processing units. The metabolic heterogeneity within an acinus is a clear example of this situation.

Thus, the hepatocyte and the acinus can be modelled as MIMD machines so that we are presented with a situation of MIMD within MIMD levels.

(iv) Zonation and Open System Ecologies

It is possible to go on from the MIMD model to an open system description. Huberman's (1989) characterisation of open systems provides a valuable way by which an acinus can be described as an open system in the computational sense. Common features include:

- Distributed processing - cells in different zones are specialised for different activities.
- No global control - integration is not only due to external factors such as hormones and nervous innervation but also to cell-cell interactions at the local level.
- High degree of communication - local broadcasts of some substances may be perpetuated through the syncytium via gap junctions. Extracellular release can be downstream in the sinusoid and upstream in the biliary system.
- Ecology - an understanding of the interaction of one part with its environment which includes other parts. The zonation of spatial relations

coupled with the idea of acinar niche structure and succession within a zone due to streaming.
- Community of parts - the emphasis here is that of community as in the ecological sense.
- Evolving system - the system is constantly changing as cells stream from the P to Q region.
- Ability to deal with asynchronous changes and anonymous messages.
- Partial computation - one zone partially processes a biochemical and it is left to another zone to complete the process.

In the light of the shared concepts from the above list, it could also be argued that a single sinusoid - hepatocyte plate could be modelled as an open system. The computational ecology, with its succession of cells, zonation according to environmental conditions, highly complex network of interactions, MIMD-like processing units provides a considerable challenge to designers.

3.4 Source Models from Biotechnology

As discussed elsewhere (Paton *et al*, 1991a), biotechnology completes a triangle of interrelations between the biosciences and computer science. It is not possible to go into great detail as this would go beyond the scope of the paper. A simple example of a biotechnological source of information about a biochemical processing system is Quistorff's (1990) report on experiments in which hepatocyte immobilisation columns were used to emulate sinusoids. Oxygen gradients were established in these columns and metabolic zonation was identified with respect to a periportal-periveous gradient of ornithine decarboxylase. At a more general level, the liver shares several common features with a multi-phasic enzyme bioreactor (Sernetz *et al*, 1985, 1989). In particular, we may note heterogeneous (multiphasic) catalysis and fractal organisation. This kind of technology is far less sophisticated than the biological system but can be used to provide empirical data on which to test computational analogues.

4 Communication and Interaction between Cells in Tissues and Organs

The individual cells of a mutilcellular organism do not operate autonomously but interact in a controlled and co-ordinated manner. This is the case throughout the cycle of being, behaving and becoming. The purpose of this section is to explore issues of communication and interaction in tissues and organs in order to gain insights into biologically motivated questions of open and MIMD computer systems as discussed previously, especially in relation to:

- Regulatory principles and processes for the whole system.
- Emergence of integrative principles in simple systems.
- Multi-modal and anonymous communication (e.g., nervous, hormonal, ionic).
- Modulation of one signal system by another (i.e., hormonal by nervous and nervous by hormonal).

A further issue also arises which is pertinent to the ontological problem associated with autonomy namely, the cellular components of multicellular organisms are not autonomous. As Pitts *et al* have put it, (multicellular organisms have) 'surrendered much of their independence for the advantages of corporate organisation' (Pitts *et al*, 1986, p140). Is a tissue or organ a collection of functionally simple component machines or a functionally coupled single unit or a community of cells ? This is very important when we come to develop computational models. Tissues and organs are organised complexities exhibiting self-maintaining and adaptive capabilities. The integrative and regulatory features which contribute to their open system architectures are very elaborate and some are listed in Table 3.

Intracellular
- Gene regulation of enzyme levels, Secondary messengers and Gene amplification.
- Localisation of receptors.
- Pathway regulation e.g., thermodynamic (equilibrium constant), allosteric, inhibition.
- Diffusion and Organisation of intra-cellular microtrabeculum.
- Compartmentation and Pooling.

Intercellular
- Cell-cell gap junctions and Synapses.
- Effectors e.g., metabolites and peptides.
- Metabolic zonation.

Interorgan
- Metabolic products e.g., amino-acids.
- Peptides.
- Hormonal.
- Ion composition.
- Nervous.

Table 3 - Some of the Regulatory Principles Operating in Multicellular Organisms (adapted from Quistorff, 1990)

At this stage it may be useful to reflect on the spatio-temporal issue associated with biological organisation in terms of being, behaving and becoming. Emergence is a becoming concept and is associated with biosystem organisation in a spatio-temporal frame whereas ideas associated with polarity of function, modular organisation and hierarchical levels are more often reflected in being and to some extent behaving. As such it is possible to identify and describe the being nature of emergent computation as well as its becoming.

The ways in which cells interact, their methods of communication and the forms in which signals are passed and interpreted will provide a very valuable means of assessing interaction between computational agents. This can be described from two perspectives: emergent (bottom-up) behaviour and top-down description. The major systems of intercellular communication in vertebrates are the endocrine and nervous systems. This would usually be described by a top- down approach with general statements about organisation and functionality. However, vertebrate-type hormones have also been identified in invertebrates and protists. Le Roith and co-workers (1986) suggest that protists are able to communicate with each other using vertebrate-like hormone molecules. This presents us with the opportunity of modelling interactions from the bottom-up.

The liver and the brain share one common functional characteristic which can enable us to make comparisons about their computational properties. Their cells synthesize, release and are affected by biochemicals. Building on the discussion above it would be possible to develop some computational models from which more formal models of compuatation could be described. The following paragraphs briefly compare neurons with hepatocytes. This provides suggestions about new emphases for computational models.

Architecture

At the cellular level, neurons are architecturally complex (i.e., dendritic trees, axonal arborizations) and there is a variety of cell forms; hepatocytes are architecturally uniform and simple. An architectural description at the sub-cellular level reveals that both cell types are complex although hepatocytes have more organelles. Polarisation of structure for functional purposes is displayed by both cell types at the cellular and sub-cellular level.

Mechanism

Non-linear behaviour in neurons is attributable to dendritic processing and transmitter and modulator effects. The non-linear behaviour of an hepatocyte is attributable to emergent behaviour of the interaction of many intracellular biochemical pathways as well as extracellular modulatory effects. Computational approximations must capture some of this mechanistic variety rather than being described in terms of non-linear functions.

Organisation

Neuronal circuits and hepatic lobular structure can both be described according to classical ideas such as polarity, hierarchy and tissue mosaic. In both, intercellular communication depends upon cell-cell junctions (gap junctions in hepatocytes and synapses in neurons) and on longer distance transfer of substances via fluid transport systems (notably blood). Differences are related to spatio-temporal location, metabolic heterogeneity and the occurrence/non-occurrence of streaming. Connectivity is far greater in the brain but cell versatility and adaptability is greater in the liver.

Functionality

Getting (1989) suggests at least twenty four properties at cell, synaptic and network levels that contribute to the non-linear behaviour of neuronal networks. The functionality of an hepatocyte is far greater.

So what is the value of this analysis ? Hopefully, the reader will have begun to appreciate that the hepatocyte is not only more complex than the neuron but that the liver, at its various levels of organisation, can provide valuable information for the source of computational models and for models of computation. The descriptive comments made so far suggest several ways of developing biologically motivated computing at the tissue/organ level:

- Source - subject interrelations between an hepatocyte and an ANN should provide valuable insights for new models.
- The need to account for neuro-hormonal interactions. For example, are some globally modifying algorithms for ANNs analogous to the action of hormonal neuromodulators ? (Note: for a physiological review see McGaugh , 1989).
- How can emergence of integrated structures be accounted for in terms of cell-cell interactions, metabolic zonation and extrinsic modulators ?

5 Concluding Comments

This paper is very much a focussed introduction to a biologically motivated approach to tissue/organ level computing with the main emphasis on certain aspects of one organ. It must be pointed out that there are many other examples that need to be considered and described such as:

- The brain as a gland (e.g., biochemical processor and multi mode nervous/hormone communication).
- The pituitary gland (e.g., multi-modal nervous/hormonal communication and multiple functions).
- Red bone marrow (e.g., multi-functionality, differentiation and streaming).
- The pancreas (similar to liver but with less functionality).
- Symbiotic systems (e.g., communication, synergy, interaction, autonomy vs. interdependence).
- Mixed cell cultures (e.g., interaction, communication).
- Plant tissues (e.g., 'Kranz' architectures in C4 plants and parallel distributed processing).

The models and metaphors discussed in this paper have been concerned with informal descriptions of parallel systems. As such, the material presented here lacks formal rigour and precision. However, it is hoped that readers will appreciate that an informal approach provides a breadth of description that is lacking when a formal modelling approach is used.

The value of such analysis to artificial life is in the breadth of detail about biological complexity at the tissue/organ level. In order to achieve this an appreciation of the breadth of possible descriptive models should be appreciated. Hence, the approach advocated here is to explore a range of possible models before formalising on one particular kind.

Acknowledgements

This paper has benefited from comments and advice of Stephanie Forrest, B.A. Huberman, E.W. Parry, W. Richard Stark, Gershom Zajicek.

References

Arber, N., Zajicek, G. & Ariel, I. 1988. The Streaming Liver II. Hepatocyte Life History, *Liver*, 8, 80-87.

Arias, I.M., Popper, H., Schachter, D. & Shafritz, D.A. 1982. *The Liver: Biology and Pathobiology*, New York: Raven Press.

Bray, D. 1990. Intracellular Signalling as a Parallel Distributed Process, *Journal of Theoretical Biology*, **143**, 215-231.

Crick, F. 1989. The Recent Excitement about Neural Networks', *Nature* , 337, 129-132.

Cunningham, P. & Veale, T. 1991. A Flexible Blackboard Architecture for Automatic Knowledge Elicitation from Text, in *Proceedings of the 5th European Knowledge Acquisition Workshop*, Crieff, Scotland.

Getting, P. A. 1989. Emerging principles governing the operation of neural networks, *Annual Review of Neuroscience* ,12, 185-204.

Haynes, L.S., Lau, R.L., Siewiorek, D.P. & Mizell, D.W. 1982. A Survey of Highly Parallel Computing, *IEEE Computer*, 15(1), 9-24.

Holcombe, W.M.L. 1990. Towards a Description of Intracellular Biochemical Organisation, *Computers Math. Applications*, 20 (4 - 6), 107-115.

Huberman, B.A. 1989. Asynchrony and Concurrency, in Eckmiller, R. & von der Marlsburg, C. (eds), Neural Computers, Springer : Berlin, 455-466.

Jones, A.L. & Spring-Mills, E. 1983. The Liver and Gall Bladder, in Weiss, L.(ed), *Histology: Cell and Tissue Biology*, New York: Elsevier.

Jungerman, K. & Katz, N. 1989. Functional Specialisation of Different Hepatocyte Populations, *Physiological Reviews* , 69 (3), 708-764.

Jungerman, K. 1987. Metabolic Zonation of Liver Parenchyma: Significance for the Regulation of Glycogen Metabolism, Gluconeogenesis and Glycolysis, *Diabetes/Metabolism Reviews* , 3(1), 269-293.

Le Roith, D. et al, 1986. Evolutionary Aspects of the Endocrine and Nervous Systems, *Recent Progress in Hormone Research*, 42, 549-587.

MacDonald, C. 1985. Gap Junctions and Cell-Cell Communication, *Essays in Biochemistry*, 21, 86-118.

McGaugh, J.L. 1989. Involvement of Hormonal and Neuromodulatory Systems in the Regulation of memory Storage, *Annual Review of Neurosciences*, 12, 255-287.

Paton, R.C. 1991). Towards a Metaphorical Biology, Working Paper: CS/1991/21, Department of Computer Science, Liverpool University, To appear in *Biology and Philosophy*.

Paton, R. C., Nwana, H. S., Shave, M. J. R., Bench-Capon, T. J. M. & Hughes, S. (1991a), Transfer of Natural Metaphors to Parallel Problem Solving Applications, in Schwefel, H-P. & Maenner, R. (eds) *Parallel Problem Solving from Nature, Lecture Notes in Computer Science*, Springer : Berlin.

Paton, R. C., Nwana, H. S., Shave, M. J. R. & Bench-Capon, T. J. M. 1991b. An Examination of Some Metaphorical Contexts for Biologically Motivated Computing, submitted for publication.

Pitts, J., Kam, E. Melville, L. & Watt, F.M. 1986. Patterns of Junctional Communication in Animal Tissues, *Junctional Complexes of Epithelial Cells*, Ciba Foundation Symposium 125, Chichester, Wiley, 140-153.

Quistorff, B. & Chance, B. 1986. Redox Scanning in the Study of Metabolic Zonation of Liver, in Thurman, R.G., Kauffman, F.K. & Jungermann, K. (eds), *Regulation of Hepatic Metabolism*, New York : Plenum.

Quistorff, B. & Romert, P. 1989. High Zone-Selectivity of Cell Permeabilisation following Digitonin-Pulse Perfusion of Rat Liver, *Histochemistry*, 92, 487-498.

Quistorff, B. 1990. Metabolic Heterogeneity of Liver Parenchyma Cells, *Essays in Biochemistry*, 25, 83-136.

Sernetz, M., Gelléri, B. & Hofmann, J. 1985. The Organism as Bioreactor. Interpretation of the Reduction Law of Metabolism in terms of Heterogeneous Catalysis and Fractal Structure, *Journal of Theoretical Biology*, 117, 209-230.

Sernetz, M., Willems, H. & Bittner, H.R. 1989. Fractal Organisation of Metabolism, in Wiesner, W. & Gnaiger, F. (eds), *Energy Transformation in Cells and Organisms, Proceedings of 10th ESCPB Conference*, Stuttgart : Thieme, 82-90.

Sipcic, S.R., Deutsch, D. & Zajicek, G. 1991. Simulation of a cancer Progression in the Colon on a Massively Parallel Processor (CM2], paper presented to the fifth SIAM Connference on Parallel Processing for Scientific Computing, March 25-27, Houston, Texas.

Weisbuch, G. & Atlan, H. 1989. Control of the Immune Response, in Eckmiller, R & Malsburg, C (eds), *Neural Computers*, Berlin : Springer-Verlag.

Zajicek, G., Oren, R. & Weinreb, M. 1985. The Streaming Liver, *Liver*, 5, 295-300.

The Connection between AI and Biology in the Study of Behaviour *

Barbara Webb
Department of Artificial Intelligence
University of Edinburgh
bhw@uk.ac.ed.aifh

Tim Smithers
Artificial Intelligence Laboratory
Vrije Universiteit Brussel
tim@be.ac.vub.artil

Abstract

This paper considers the role of AI in understanding biological behaviour. It is argued that the potential role is in testing hypothesised mechanisms by constructing and testing models, but that the actual contribution is dependent upon the verifiability of the models as adequate representations of the biological problem under study. That is, to carry over conclusions drawn from AI to biological problems, those conclusions must not be based on unfounded assumptions about the problem. One general assumption that seems to characterise current research is that the physical interaction of the agent with its environment can be greatly simplified in the representation without thereby affecting the viability of the mechanisms of sensory-motor control being investigated. We contrast this assumption with the problems that arise in building a real robot that models possible mechanisms of cricket phonotaxis: a proper understanding of the physical agent-environment interaction is essential to build a robot that usefully tests hypotheses about the mechanisms that underly this task—and is equally essential in making sense of the current results in biological research for this behaviour.

*Acknowledgements: The first author is supported by a British Commonwealth Award. The Department of Artificial Intelligence at Edinburgh University has supplied the facilities for research, which has been supported by the department's technical staff.

1 AI and Biological Behaviour

There has been much talk in recent years about the possible advantages of studying behaviour by the combination of several disciplines: particularly by combining neurobiology, ethology and artificial intelligence (AI) in the study of basic sensory-motor behaviours in simple animals (see, for example, articles in [Meyer & Wilson, 1991], [Langton, 1989], [Arbib, 1989]). Although the field of neuroethology ([Camhi, 1988], [Hoyle, 1984]) has by this time established procedures and methods for relating neurobiology and ethology, the exact role of AI in contributing to an understanding of behaving systems is less clearly defined. Furthermore, how the methodology of AI can best support this role is a question that is not well explored: for example there is no clear way to evaluate the actual success of current approaches.

The sort of interaction that might be expected is to take some particular behavioural task and examine it using each of these different disciplines. There are some good examples of this exchange of information between disciplines for *parts* of behaviours: sensory processing (particularly vision, eg. [Blake & Troscianko, 1990]); motor abilities (such as walking, eg. [Kumar & Waldron, 1989]); and central neural mechanisms (assuming certain processes for input and output, e.g. [Arbib & House, 1987]). So far there are fewer attempts to look at complete sensory-motor systems in this way, although understanding such complete, if simple, systems may well be an essential foundation for investigating and understanding more complex forms of behaviour [Brooks, 1986]. The recently christened field of computational neuroethology ([Beer, 1990], [Cliff, 1990]) apparently means to address this area, by using neuroethological data to build computer simulations of sensory-motor mechanisms in insects.

1.1 The Role of AI

So what is the potential role of AI in investigating biological behaviour? The aim of investigation is to find the mechanisms that underly particular behaviours. In neuroscience, the mechanism is discovered by looking inside the system; in ethology it is discovered by close examination of the behaviour and how it varies. In both fields, hypothesising possible mechanisms plays a vital part in guiding investigations (although a certain amount of behavioural observation and neurological exploration can be done without having any explicit hypothesis in mind).

An element of constructing theories is testing the plausibility of proposed mechanisms by examining how adequate (or inadequate) they are at producing the behaviour under investigation. This can be done by building the mechanisms, simulating the mechanisms, or deducing through mathematical analysis the properties of mechanisms. And it is here that AI can play a central part in extending theorising: that is, the methodology of AI provides a means of suggesting, making explicit, and exploring the consequences of hypotheses about mechanisms for behaviour.

1.2 Fulfilling this role

If AI methods are to fulfill this theoretical role for neuroethology, what must be made clear is the relationship of the mechanisms explored in AI to the mechanisms that exist in biological creatures. The contribution of AI to biological science, rather than to engineering, can be measured in the degree to which this relationship can be shown to exist.

Under the approach described above, AI mechanisms are taken to be *models* of the biological mechanisms, that is, the properties and structure of one are taken by the researcher to represent properties and structure of the other. This relationship may vary from loose analogy (for example, a computer system that shows vaguely lifelike behaviour is invented, and it is consequently suggested that the mechanisms involved may be of the same general form as the mechanisms that underly life) to explicit representation of a specific system (for example representing the structural and functional properties of a group of neurons that are thought to mediate a certain behaviour). In either case, the question that arises is to what extent can conclusions drawn from constructing and manipulating models be applied to the systems they represent?

1.2.1 A parallel problem

Stating the problem in this way recalls a similar problem that has been much discussed in the field of psychological measurement: the problem of 'permissable statistics'. The question concerns the validity of reporting statistics that involve numerical operations (such as addition) when the numbers were introduced only to represent, for example, a classification, and not to represent any numerical relations on the property that the statistic is given for. The classic example is the meaninglessness (or otherwise) of reporting the average value for the numbers on football shirts ([Lord, 1953]). As explained in [Michel, 1986], the problem is one of valid inference from results on the numbers to results about the property that these numbers represent. A necessary condition on the validity of the inference is that the same inference could be drawn under any other equally valid representation of the property (for example, the average of a set of football numbers would change given some equally valid assignment of numbers to players, hence any inference based on the average of the numbers is not necessarily true of the players).

In the case of numerical representations, the relationship between equally valid representations is to a certain extent formally specifiable [Narens & Luce, 1986]. For the general case of representations of systems by models of any nature, it is not so simple. What does it mean to require, in applying the results of AI behavioural modeling to biological behaving systems, that the conclusions must be independent of the form of the representation, that is, that the same conclusions could be reached under any equally valid representation of the system?

1.2.2 Valid representation

Any theoretical representation of a biological system (particularly a complete sensory-motor system) will require a large number of simplifications, and these will be supported by a large number of assumptions about what are the relevant factors to represent, and what constitutes an adequate way to represent them. Some assumptions will be well supported by what is already known about the system; others may be informed guesses about what is relevant; and others may be quite arbitrary (often based on limitations of the medium of representation). Applying the above criteria, therefore, suggests that for results from the represention to be extrapolated to the actual system, it should at least be possible to reach the same conclusions under the alteration of any arbitrary assumptions.

Of course, not all assumptions will be explicitly available for evaluation: so the direct application of this principle is not easily done. Nevertheless, examples of models for which the results rely on arbitrary assumptions are not hard to find. An arbitrary assumption can be considered to be one for which no theoretical justification is provided: in much of 'behavioural AI' the only justifications are general claims about the universality of the processes and dismissals of the need for unnecessary detail. This contrasts with related examples of scientific modeling, for example [Koch & Segev, 1989] where neuroscientists have constructed computer models of their theories, in which the justifications are explicit.

1.3 A major assumption

The traditional approach of AI to intelligent behaviour tends to equate looking for behavioural mechanisms with looking for information processing mechanisms: mechanisms that take input from sensors, and transform this information to generate output for actuators. Despite the use of some rather different methods for performing the task (such as parallel architectures, emergent functions and so on) by those who claim to be exploring biological mechanisms, it is difficult to overcome the tendency to describe the mechanisms basically in this way, as processors of information. Connected to this description is the idea that what is being sought is archetype processing mechanisms for sensory-motor tasks, that are applicable to more than one specific biological (or technical) set of sensors and actuators.

A common consequence of these ideas is that it is assumed that the problem of sensory-motor control can be at least partially abstracted away from the physical processes that determine the input to the sensors and the effects of the output of the actuators on the world. Hence a large proportion of the simplifying assumptions made in representing the biological systems are in the area of the physical interaction of the animal's sensory and motor mechanisms with the environment (some examples are discussed in [Webb, 1990]).

However, this conception of behaviour as being the information processing of the agent is misleading. Behaviour is not a property of the agent but rather exists in the interaction of the agent with its environment. It is the way that the internal mechanisms of the agent are fitted to its sensors and actuators and how they operate in the environment in which the agent is embedded that determines the behaviour. Thus, in attempting to devise a mechanism in the agent that achieves a certain behaviour, it is crucial to consider the form of this environmental interaction.

This is particularly apparent for sensory-motor behaviour, because it is easy to see that any generic specification of a sensory-motor task (e.g. avoid obstacles, find food source) will have a large number of possible solutions. What will constrain the set of solutions is increasing the specification of the nature of the environment in terms of the agent's abilities to interact with it. What this means is that any assumptions about this interaction will have a substantial effect on the mechanisms involved, so these assumptions cannot afford to be arbitrary. In fact, in any theorising about sensory-motor mechanisms (whether or not supported by simulation) the characterising of the agent's interaction with the environment is critical to usefully proposing and evaluating possible mechanisms. This point will be illustrated by a consideration of some of the results of studying cricket phonotaxis by building robotic models.

2 Cricket Behaviour

The behavioural task to be examined is that of cricket phonotaxis—the ability of a female cricket to find a male cricket by walking towards the calling song of the male. The behaviour and neuroscience of this animal have been studied quite extensively (e.g. [Huber & Thorson, 1985] [Schildberger, 1988]), but there seems to be a little theory guiding this research or providing a framework for the findings. There are several features of this behaviour that suggest it is of interest to study: it is fairly simple yet is a complete sensory-motor task; similar behaviours are found in a number of other animals and could be useful for artificial agents; and it involves a behavioural strategy to overcome the inherent inaccuracies in sensory and motor responses, which is a method of control interesting for robotics.

2.1 A Brief Description

The basic behaviour observed is that presented with a (species specific) calling song of a certain frequency (usually between 3-7kHz) and temporal pattern (consisting of repeated short 'syllables' making up longer 'chirps') the female cricket will approach the sound source by walking in a zigzag path — this consists of short, roughly straight segments and stops followed by turns to change direction whenever the the path deviates by more than a about 30 deg from the direction of the source. The cricket can do this task reliably over rough terrain, with major distortions of the signal by environmental refraction and filtering; it also maintains this tracking ability for long stretches of times when walking on an experimental treadmill. Furthermore, it can track one calling song despite the presence of other simultaneous songs from different locations.

Experiments have given some more details about this behaviour. It appears that only a few features of the temporal pattern of the calling song (in particular the syllable rate) are necessary for phonotaxis [Thorson *et al*, 1982] but other elements play a role when the cricket chooses from several songs [Stout & McGhee, 1988]. The intensity of the song also affects this choice; for a single song, phonotaxis only occurs within a certain intensity range, and the degree of deviation decreases with increasing intensity [Huber, 1983]. The size of turns appears to be roughly related to the degree of deviation, but turns are also sometimes made in the wrong direction [Bailey & Thompson, 1977].

The basic behavioural strategy that has been suggested for phonotaxis, given that the cricket has two ears, one on each front leg, is that the animal receives and filters the signal for frequency and temporal pattern to determine if it is of the correct form, and if it is, approaches it by turning and walking to the side of the ear with the stronger stimulation, changing direction when this side changes. That is, the location behaviour is apparently reactive: the cricket does not use the inputs to identify the direction of the sound and then set a course towards it, but simply reacts to sensory indications that it is deviating too far from the correct course. This sums up the theory given so far to support the neuroethological investigations, which have concentrated on identifying a neural filtering mechanism to support recognition, and on establishing the existence of a difference in the response levels of the auditory neurons on either side to support localization.

This theory has been described as the 'simple' model of localization [Weber & Thorson, 1988]: "We use the word 'simple' because a two-eared robot programmed to obey this rule could be made to track a sound source in a manner like that of the female"(p.13).

2.2 Implementing the localization mechanism

Attempting to program a Lego robot [Donnett & Smithers, 1990] to obey this rule quickly revealed how ill-defined is this model of localization. The robot task was to locate a light source: it was equipped with light-sensors (that gave a value between 0 and 4, comparable to the 0-5+ range of spikes per syllable that encodes intensity in the cricket [Esch *et al*, 1980]) on each side, as well as bump sensors and binary infra-red emitter-detectors for avoiding obstacles; and was moved by separately driven back wheels that allowed rough control over the length of short straight runs and the angle of on-the-spot turns. Getting this vehicle to find the light source was not difficult, but it raised a number of questions about the possible mechanisms in the cricket.

Given that the cricket proceeds by turning to the ear with the stronger signal, the implication is that the input from the two ears is compared, and a decision made as to which way to turn. This could be implemented without a specific comparison mechanism, for example by having a direct connection from the ear to the speed of the legs on the other side (as in Braitenberg's simple vehicles [Braitenberg, 1984]). Though this may be viable for a wheeled robot, the control of six-legged walking makes it more likely that some overall coordination is needed for turning: however, little is known about how insects control turns.

Even assuming (as cricket researchers do) that there is some clearly identifiable comparison mechanism that causes turns to be made, does this strategy mean that the cricket can move forward only when there is no detectable difference between the ears? Or does it make a turn of fixed size in the correct direction and then move forward a certain distance before turning again? Or is the turn ballistic, based on the size of the difference detected; or feedback controlled, continuing until the opposite ear becomes equal or louder and then moving forward?

Which method is best for a robot depends on the relationship between the environment, sensors and actuators—if the sensors are relatively slow to respond, ballistic turns may be useful; if the control of turning is coarse relative to the detection of difference, turning till no difference exists might take an inordinate amount of time, due to overturning and correction; if the incoming signal is unreliable, turning till the opposite difference exists may be more robust; if a fixed size of turn is well-scaled to the angle at which a difference is usually detected it can be an efficient way of achieving the task with minimal processing; if the motor control is such that the agent can't reliably do turns of a certain size in the absence of further cues (for example, due to variations in ground surface), then some use of sensory feedback to end the turn may be required.

Thus identifying the mechanism in the cricket requires an understanding of this environment-sensor-actuator relationship for the cricket. Unfortunately, knowledge of how the cricket controls its movement is almost non-existant—particularly when it is considered that in its natural environment, it will also be moving around and over an irregular field of obstacles (vegetation) which, furthermore, are causing distortion in the signal. However, rather more is known about the sensory system: consideration of this leads to a rather different conception of the task.

2.3 The auditory mechanism

How the cricket's auditory system comes to have stronger stimulation on the side nearer the sound source is not straightfoward. As the size of the cricket means that the separation between the auditory receivers is in the order of two centimetres, no substantial intensity difference will be caused by the relative distance of the ears from the source, and this small separation combined with the shape of the cricket and the typical wavelength of the calling song (around six centimetres) means that shadowing effects will also be small. Instead the cricket ears use a pressure gradient mechanism, in which the relative phase of sound waves arriving at the tympanum from alternative openings causes the waves to either cancel or summate depending upon the relative distances the sound must travel, and this varies depending upon the orientation of the cricket in the sound field [Boyd & Lewis, 1983]. Thus the tympanum is essentially an orientation specific mechanism, i.e. its response varies according to the direction of the sound.

In other words, the cricket auditory system is better described as two orientation specific sensors, rather than the usual analysis in terms of non-directional sensors at separate locations in space. Using this alternative description makes several features of the cricket's behaviour more comprehensable, for instance, the ability of some crickets to successfully maintain phonotaxis despite the surgical removal of one ear [Schmitz *et al*, 1988]. That is, the necessity for comparison between the sensors is less critical: for example, the cancellation that occurs when one ear is turned away from the source may always result in signal that falls below a fixed threshold, no matter what the actual amplitude of the signal is.

Currently, a new circuit for the robot is being built which will process sound signals in a comparable way to this pressure-gradient mechanism, that is, it performs a phase summation/cancelation on sound signals received on each side. As for the cricket, this interaction will be critically dependent on the wavelength of the signal and the distance between the ears: the cricket's auditory mechanism is only orientation specific at the critical frequency of the calling song.

2.4 The recognition mechanism

Consideration of how this new form of sensory input will be used for localization raises some interesting issues. In the cricket, the difference in stimulus strength at the auditory organs is encoded in several ways in the auditory nerve: different receptors respond to different intensity levels; the number of of impulses of each receptor depends on intensity; and the latency of firing depends on intensity. Place coding of intensity is apparently lost at the level of ascending neurons, but firing frequency and latency still encode intensity levels. It seems generally accepted (although there is no strong evidence) that the firing rate is the feature by which the phonotaxis mechanism determines which way to turn, and the existance of the temporal latency difference is usually ignored.

However, temporal information is critical in the recognition of the song. Usually the recognition mechanism is treated as being independent of the location mechanism, the former simply serving to turn the latter on and off. A common assumption is that the signals in the two ears are combined to generate the signal that is then filtered. However, the intensity dependent latency effects involve sufficient offset that combining the signals would obscure the syllable pattern that is supposed to be critical for recognition.

There is no evidence for independent neural pathways in the auditory system — on the contrary, the same pair of ascending neurons have been implicated as the carrying the recognisable syllable pattern [Huber, 1983] and as necessary for location [Schildberger & Horner, 1988]. Yet efficient neural coding of the temporal pattern is incompatible with coding the intensity information by the firing rate; whereas coding intensity by temporal delay is consistent with preserving a temporal pattern. Evidence that the length of the syllable does not affect phonotaxis whereas the time between syllable onsets is critical [Huber, 1983] also suggests that the latency of the syllable onset may be important.

What this suggests is that the mechanism for phonotaxis may be one that involves a temporal comparison of the onset of incoming signals, in such a way that a difference can only be detected provided the signal onsets occur at fixed intervals, i.e. the signal has a certain temporal pattern. Thus recognition of the signal pattern would be implicit in the operation of the location mechanism, in the same way that frequency recognition is implicit in the means by which a directional effect at the ear is established.

3 Final Comments

The next step in this project will involve an attempt to specify the mechanism roughly outlined above so as to implement it in the robot. This will be compared with alternative mechanisms, such as one that does strictly separate recognition and location. One advantage that we suspect might arise in the first scheme is that it has potential for explaining the ability to track one signal despite the presence of another, on the basis of location effects that emerge without the system 'recognising' that two sources exist; rather than requiring that the cricket 'chooses' between two recognised signals and 'attends' to only one, which is how this phenomenon is usually explained under the standard theory — a good example of a 'folk psychology' explanation that does nothing more than describe the observed behaviour.

Obviously the picture of cricket phonotaxis research given here is rather simplified, and a number of additional complications exist. What we think has emerged, however, is that a proper characterisation of the sensory interaction with the environment has been critical to understanding the possible mechanisms: and appreciating what aspects of this interaction are important has come from consideration of the task of building an actual robot. Further, the assumptions that would have been necessary to get any behaviour out of a simulation of this task would have been so many that the relevance of such a simulation to the biological mechanism would have been minimal: the current state of theory in this field is simply not sufficient to support such assumptions.

References

[1] Arbib, M.A. and House, D.H. (1987). Depth and detours: an essy on visuallly guided behaviour. In Arbib, M.A. and Hanson, R.A., (eds.), *Vision, brain and cooperative computation.* MIT Press/Bradford Books, Cambridge, Mass.

[2] Arbib, M.A. (1989). Interacting subsystems for depth perception and detour behaviour. In Arbib, M.A. and ichi Amari, Shun, (eds.), *Dynamic Interactions in Neural Networks: Models and Data.* Springer-Verlag, New York.

[3] Bailey, W.J. and Thompson, P. (1977). Acoustic orientation in the cricket teleogryllus oceanicus (le guillou). *Journal of Experimental Biology*, 67:61–75.

[4] Beer, R.D. (1990). A biological perspective on autonomous agent design. *Robotics and Autonomous Systems*, 6:169–186.

[5] Blake, A. and Troscianko, T., (eds.). (1990). *AI and the Eye.* John Wiley and Sons, Chicester.

[6] Boyd, P. and Lewis, B. (1983). Peripheral auditory directionality in the cricket. *Journal of Comparative Physiology A*, 153:523–532.

[7] Braitenberg, V., (ed.). (1984). *Vehicles: Experiments in Synthetic Psychology.* M.I.T. Press, Cambridge MA.

[8] Brooks, R.A. (1986). Acheiving artificial intelligence through building robots. A.I.Memo 899, M.I.T.

[9] Camhi, J.M. (1988). Inverterbrate neuroethology. *Experientia*, 44:361–362.

[10] Cliff, D.T. (1990). Computationl neuroethology: A provisional manifesto. CSRP 162, University of Sussex.

[11] Donnett, J. and Smithers, T. (1990). Lego vehicles: A technology for studying intelligent systems. Research Paper 490, University of Edinburgh.

[12] Esch, H., Huber, F. and Wohlers, D. (1980). Primary auditory interneurons in crickets: Physiology and central projections. *Journal of Comparative Physiology A*, 137:27–38.

[13] Hoyle, G. (1984). The scope of neuroethology. *The Behavioural and Brain Sciences*, 7:367–412.

[14] Huber, F. and Thorson, J. (1985). Cricket auditory communication. *Scientific American*, 253:6:47–54.

[15] Huber, F. (1983). Neural correlates of orthopteran and cicada phonotaxis. In Huber, F. and Markl, H., (eds.), *Neuroethology and Behavioural Physiology.* Springer-Verlag, Berlin.

[16] Koch, C. and Segev, I., (eds.). (1989). *Methods in Neuronal Modeling.* M.I.T. Press - Bradford Books, Cambridge MA.

[17] Kumar, V.R. and Waldron, K.J. (1989). A review of research on walking vehicles. In Khatib, O., Craig, J.J. and Lozano-Perez, T., (eds.), *The Robotics Review 1.* M.I.T. Press - Bradford Books, Cambridge MA.

[18] Langton, C.G., (ed.). (1989). *Artificial Life*, Redwood City, California. Addison-Wesley.

[19] Lord, F.M. (1953). On the statistical treatment of football numbers. *American Psychologist*, 8:750–751.

[20] Meyer, J.A. and Wilson, S.W., (eds.). (1991). *From Animals to Animats: Proceedings of the First International Conference on the Simulation of Adaptive Behaviour*, Cambridge, Mass. MIT Press/Bradford Books.

[21] Michel, J. (1986). Measurement scales and statistics: A clash of paradigms. *Psychological Bulletin*, 100:398–407.

[22] Narens, L. and Luce, R.D. (1986). Measurement: The theory of numerical assignments. *Psychological Bulletin*, 99:166–180.

[23] Schildberger, K. and Horner, M. (1988). The function of auditory neurons in cricket phonotaxis I Influence of hyperpolarization of identified neurons on sound localization. *Journal of Comparative Physiology A*, 163:621–631.

[24] Schildberger, K. (1988). Behavioural and neuronal methods of cricket phonotaxis. *Experientia*, 44:408–415.

[25] Schmitz, B., Kleindienst, H.U. and Huber, F. (1988). Acoustic orientation in adult female crickets after unilateral foreleg amputation in the larva. *Journal of Comparative Physiology A*, 162:715–728.

[26] Stout, J.F. and McGhee, R. (1988). Attractiveness of the male acheta domestica calling song to females II The relative importance of syllable period, intensity and chirp rate. *Journal of Comparative Physiology A*, 164:277–287.

[27] Thorson, J., Weber, T. and Huber, F. (1982). Auditory behaviour in the cricket II Simplicity of calling song recognition in gryllus and anomolous phonotaxis at abnormal carrier frequencies. *Journal of Comparative Physiology A*, 146:361–378.

[28] Webb, B.H. (1990). Computer simulation in the study of intelligent behaviour. DAI Discussion Paper 101, University of Edinburgh.

[29] Weber, T. and Thorson, J. (1988). Auditory behaviour in the cricket IV Interaction of direction of tracking with perceived temporal pattern in split-song paradigms. *Journal of Comparative Physiology A*, 163:13–22.

AMOEBA, PLANARIA and DREAMING MACHINES

Bruno MARCHAL
I.R.I.D.I.A. Université Libre de Bruxelles
50 av. F. Roosevelt. CP194/6. B-1050 Brussels, Belgium

Abstract: A general definition of *personal capability* is given for mechanical entities. It is shown how to use it to build self-reproducing machines, self-regenerating organized collections of machines, and more general self-referential nets. We study different classes of true propositions that can be communicated (i.e. proved or correctly guessed) by such machines about themselves in the limit. We additionaly examine a linked class of known, retrievable, but not as such communicable experiences.

Key words: Machine, diagonalization, Self-Reproduction, Self-referential nets, Inductive Inference Modality, Capability, Arithmetic, G, G*, S4Grz[1].

1. HISTORY

Descartes suggested that animals and human bodies are machines in contrast with the immaterial human soul. Nevertheless, he failed in his subsequent attempt to prove that some machine is able to reproduce itself like an animal or a human body. The first explicit self-reproducing man-made automaton was conceived by Von Neumann some centuries later. Essentially, Von Neumann's construction embodies a diagonalization similar to others occuring in the foundation of mathematics, as employed by Cantor, Gödel, Kleene and others (see Davis 1965). Moreover, an important double diagonalization theorem of Kleene (1952) contains everything necessary to build a self-reproducing, or self-transforming, machine relative to a universal environment. Myhill has given an in-depth account of that result and illustrated its strength for building an evolutionary machine (Myhill 1964).

Case has generalized this theorem, providing a very general collection of machines that includes the offspring of Myhill's evolutionary machine. (Case 1974). I will define a notion of personal capability directly from Kleene's theorem or Case's generalization[2]. The crucial point is that both biological reproduction and psychological introspection are captured by (generalisations) of Kleene's result.

Diagonalization has also been fruitfully applied in the theory of inductive inference (Putnam 1963, Gold 1967, Blum & Blum 1975, Case & Smith 1983), and in proof theory (Solovay 1976, Smorynski 1981). This will allow us to compare what machines (or structured collection of machines) are able to prove about themselves with the true propositions they are able to inductively infer about themselves in the limit. I suggest that a theory of knowledge can be extracted from such an *a priori* mechanist approach.

2. GÖDEL NUMBERINGS

Let ω denote the set of natural numbers:

$$\omega = \{0, 1, 2, ...\}$$

Church and Turing wanted to define precisely the concept of an *intuitively*, or *humanly* computable function from ω to ω. At that time it was believed that so general a definition could not exist. The

[1] The following text presents research results of the Belgian National incentive-program for fundamental research in artificial intelligence initiated by the Belgian State, the Prime Minister's Office, Science Policy Programme. Scientific responsibility is assumed by the author.

[2] Concerning this paper the definition of personal capability I give can be consider as nominal, nevertheless I provide philosophical motivation for it in Marchal (1991).

reasoning behind this was as follows: should such a definition exist, we could derive a finitely describable language L in which all the computable functions could be coded, and consequently enumerate them in some order:

$$\mathcal{P}_L = \{\phi_0, \phi_1, \phi_2, \phi_3, ...\},$$

ϕ_i, is the function (extension) computed by the ith code, denoted by *i* (intension).
i is called an index, code, program or even machine, for the function ϕ_i.

In that case we could compute the diagonal function :

$\Delta_L = \lambda x\ \phi_x(x)+1$ (first diagonalization)

which, although it is humanly computable, differs from each ϕ_i. Indeed, in the case where Δ_L would belong to $\mathcal{P}_L$, there would exist a k such that $\Delta_L = \phi_k$, but this would entail:

$\phi_k(k) = \phi_k(k)+1$ (second diagonalization)

It seems that any language L cannot describe how to compute Δ_L.

This apparent refutation will not work if we allow L (and indeed we do) to describe *partial (i.e. not defined everywhere)* functions. In terms of machines, this would mean that L describes some machines which do not halt for every input. In such cases, the second diagonalization only implies that ϕ_k is not defined for k.

Definition: $\mathcal{R}_L$ is the subset of $\mathcal{P}_L$ which contains all total computable[1] functions describable in L.

If $\mathcal{P}_L$ contains all the intuitively computable functions, then the above proof demonstrates only that there is no L-describable machine capable of distinguishing the code of the total functions belonging to $\mathcal{R}_L$ from the code of the partial computable functions.

It happens to be that every attempt to formally capture the set of intuitively computable functions, including partial functions, has given rise to the same subset of total computable functions, i.e. to the same subset $\mathcal{R}$ of ω^ω.: $\mathcal{R}_{algol} = \mathcal{R}_{lisp} = \mathcal{R}_{prolog} = \mathcal{R}_{c++} = \mathcal{R}_{game\text{-}of\text{-}life} = \mathcal{R}_{n\text{-}body\ problem}$ (Moore 1990)

This is the basic empirical motivation for Church's thesis: $\mathcal{R}_{your\text{-}preferred\text{-}programming\text{-}language}$ = the set of all intuitively total computable functions. We can denote it by $\mathcal{R}$ (without subscript). In particular these functions are the ones which are computable with a computer, and implementable in (any) programming language[2]. Example: the following algorithmically generated list of Lisp programs gives rise to a precise enumeration (with repetition) of $\mathcal{P}$:

```
1  (lambda (x) x)
2  (lambda (x) 'equal)
3  (lambda (x) 'car)
4  (lambda (x) 'cdr)
5  (lambda (x) (car x))
6  (lambda (x) (cdr x))
7  (lambda (x) 'x)
8  (lambda (x) (k x))
9  (lambda (x) (null x))
10 (lambda (x) 'quote)
11 (lambda (x) 'lambda)
12 (lambda (x) 'k)
13 (lambda (x) 'cons)
14 (lambda (x) 'cond)
15 (lambda (x) 'null)
16 (lambda (x) '(equal))
17 (lambda (x) '(car))
18 (lambda (x) '(cdr))
19 (lambda (x) '(x))
20 (lambda (x) '(quote))
21 (lambda (x) '(lambda))
22 (lambda (x) '(k))
23 (lambda (x) '(cons))
24 (lambda (x) '(cond))
25 (lambda (x) '(null))
26 (lambda (x) (equal x x))
27 (lambda (x) (cons x x))
etc.
```

1 a total function is defined at *every* natural numbers.

2 With the notable exception of some intuitionist attempt to capture a sufficiently large enumerable set of total computable functions (which are included in $\mathcal{R}$ classically).

This version of Lisp has a small set of atoms {lambda, car, k, quote, etc.} These atoms denote also the primitive (given) computable functions. k denotes the Kleene metaprogram which embodies the constructability of Kleene's theorem, as I will show below.

In P we can interpret ϕ_i as the function from ω to ω, computed by the ith lambda expression in the list above, where ω is seen as a set of indices for finite expressions. P is called a Gödel numbering (Rogers 1958) and it enjoys two remarkable properties.

Firstly:

$$\exists u \quad \forall i \forall x \qquad \phi_u(i,x) = \phi_i(x) \qquad (1)$$

This means that there is a machine with index*u* capable of computing any ϕ_i, given its index *i*, and its argument.

Indices correspond to programs. Thus, *u* corresponds to an interpreter for an arbitrary program i with argument x.

Definition: we call *u* a universal environment.

Secondly:

$$\exists s \quad \forall i \forall x \forall y \quad \phi_i(x,y) = \phi_{\phi_s(i,x)}(y). \qquad (2)$$

s is a metaprogram which parametrises a function of n+1 variables into a function of n variables by fixing one of the arguments, for example:

$$\phi_s((\lambda x \lambda y\ x+y), 2) = \lambda y\ 2+y.$$

Here is s given in LISP:

```
(def 's '(lambda (program data)
  (list (quote lambda)
      (delete-firsts (length data)
            (arguments program))
      (substitute-arguments data
                  (firsts (length d)(arguments
                                          p))
                  (body p)))))
```

Example: (s '(lambda (x y z) (F (G y z))) '(3 4)) gives (LAMBDA (Z) (F (G '4 Z))). A simple substitute function would not have introduced a quote before the number: '4, substitute-arguments does it in order to handle the identification between numbers and programs.

We are ready to give Kleene 's theorem:

$$\forall t \quad \exists e \quad \forall y \qquad \phi_e(y) = \phi_t(e,y)$$

In other words, for any computable function (transformation) coded by the number *t*, there is another machine coded by *e* which, on any input y, computes t, on itself and y.

Proof: $\lambda x \lambda y. \phi_t(\phi_s(x,x),y)$ where t is the code of the transformation and s the code of the substitution function (first diagonalization) is an intuitively computable function. Therefore, by Church's thesis, there is an r such that ϕ_r computes it.

$$\phi_r(x,y) = \phi_t(\phi_s(x,x), y).$$

Using automated parametrization (2) on the left hand side :

$$\phi_r(x,y) = \phi_{\phi_s(r,x)}(y).$$

Using universal instantiation, let x = r (second diagonalization) :

$$\phi_t(\phi_s(r,r), y) = \phi_{\phi_s(r,r)}\ (y).$$

We finish by making $e = \phi_s(r,r)$. QED.

To avoid the use of Church's thesis it suffices to do the same work in a particular formal system.

Here is a diagonalization function written in LISP:

```
(def 'diag '(lambda (f)
  (list (quote lambda)
      (arguments f)
      (substitute-argument
       (list (quote s)
           (car (arguments f))
           (list (quote list)
                (car (arguments f))))
       (car (arguments f))
       (body f)
      ))
 ))
```

example: (diag '(lambda (x) (length x)))
(LAMBDA (X) (LENGTH (S X (LIST X))))

The double diagonalization is captured in a uniform manner by the following program:

```
(def 'k '(lambda (f)
  (s (diag f) (list (diag f))))
```

So k applied to the code of a transformation t will build the machine e which applies t to itself.
I call k *Kleene's metaprogram*, for it embodies Kleene's proof of the recursion theorem (Kleene 1952).

example: (k '(lambda (x) (length x))) gives

```
(lambda nil
    (length (s '(lambda (x) (length (s x (list x))))
            (list '(lambda (x) (length (s x (list x))))))))
```

this program applied without arguments gives its *own* length.

Definition: a machine M has *personal capability* with respect to a function t relative to a universal environment *u* if M = (k t) interpreted by *u*. This means that M will be able to apply t to its own code *in u*. Personal capability as presented here, is a relative and intensional concept.

3. The Amoeba

A self-reproducing machine is a machine which has personal capability with respect to the identity function. Such a machine applies ($I = \lambda x\ x$) to itself:

$$\phi_e() = I(e) = e$$

example: if the universal environment is LISP then I = (lambda (x) x):

```
(def 'I '(lambda (x) x) )
```

Consequently, to obtain the amoeba, a self-reproducing machine, in LISP[1], it suffices to apply Kleene's metaprogram k to I:

$$\phi_k(I) = (k\ I) =$$

```
(lambda nil
  (s '(lambda (x) (s x (list x)))
    (list '(lambda (x) (s x (list x))))))
```

This program applied to an empty input yields itself:

$$\phi_{\phi_k(I)}() = ((k\ I)) =$$

```
(lambda nil
  (s '(lambda (x) (s x (list x)))
    (list '(lambda (x) (s x (list x))))))
```

4. The Planaria

Case (1974) has generalised Kleene's theorem:
For any machine *t*, there exists a machine *e*, such that

$$\phi_{\phi_{\cdot_{\cdot_{\cdot_{\phi_e(x_1)}}}}(x_n)}(a) = \phi_t(e, x_1, \ldots, x_n, a),$$

Intuitively, this means that we can built a self-referential *collection* of machines, or even of collections of collections of machines, etc. It allows us to extend the definition of personal capability to such collections. I call these collections *self-referential nets.*

Proof: (by induction)

When n=1, it reduces to Kleene's theorem. Using the parametrization theorem we find a *g* (given by an application of the metaprogram *s*) such that:

$$\phi_{\phi_g(x, x_1 \ldots x_n)}(a) = \phi_t(x, x_1, \ldots, x_n, a) \qquad (*)$$

taking $g = \phi_s(t, x, x_1, \ldots, x_n)$.
Suppose the theorem is true for n-1, then we can apply it to $\phi_g(x, x_1, \ldots, x_n)$ with x_n playing the role of u so that there is an *e* such that:

$$\phi_{\phi_{\cdot_{\cdot_{\cdot_{\phi_e(x_1)}}}}(x_{n-1})}(x_n) = t(e, x_1, \ldots, x_n)$$

Substituting in (*) gives the result. QED.

---

1 I use PHI-LISP, a dialect of Lisp I have implemented for illustrating the use of recursion theory in philosophy of the mind. (see Marchal, 1992) In PHI-LISP

$$\phi_{\phi_e(y)}(z)$$

is written ((e y) z), i.e meta-programming is left-parenthesizing.

By means of this generalisation, it is possible to build *planarias*, analogous to the small flatworm with the amazing power to self-regenerate (Buschsbaum 1938). I illustrate the simplest one, which is a list of two cells (C1,C2). Each cell reconstitutes the entire planaria (C1,C2) depending on the value of a particular fixed argument, FOO. Thus:

C1(FOO) = (C1,C2)
C2(FOO) = (C1,C2)

I provide different (extensional) functions for each cell:

$$C1 = \lambda x.x+1$$
$$C2 = \lambda x.x+2$$

Construction: using the generalized recursion theorem (with n=2):

$$\forall t \exists e \quad \phi_{\phi_e(y)}(z) = \phi_t(e,y,z) \qquad (**)$$

ϕ_e will be the generator of C1 and C2: $\phi_e(1) = C1$, $\phi_e(2) = C2$, so we want:

$$\phi_{\phi_e(1)}(z) = \text{if } z=FOO \text{ then op } (\phi_e(1),\phi_e(2)) \text{ else } z+1$$

$$\phi_{\phi_e(2)}(z) = \text{if } z=FOO \text{ then op } (\phi_e(1),\phi_e(2)) \text{ else } z+2$$

e will be found by applying (**) to the following *recursion matrix*:

$t(x,1,FOO) = (\phi_x(1),\phi_x(2))$
$t(x,2,FOO) = (\phi_x(1),\phi_x(2))$
$t(x,1,z) = z+1$, if $z \neq FOO$
$t(x,2,z) = z+2$, if $z \neq FOO$
$t(x,y,z) =$ 'error if $y > 2$.

that is, by applying k and the parametrization function following the proof of the generalized recursion theorem.

I demonstrate this in phi-LISP, I use "m" rather than "t" to avoid confusion with the predefined LISP boolean constant t.

```
(def 'm '(lambda (x y z)
    (cond
      ((and (equal y 1) (equal z 'FOO))
        (list (x 1) '***** (x 2) ))
      ((and (equal y 2) (equal z 'FOO))
        (list (x 1) '+++++ (x 2) ))
      ((equal y 1) (+ z 1))
      ((equal y 2) (+ z 2))
      (t '(ERROR, there are only 2 cells))
    ))
  )
```

Next, we define g following the proof of the generalisation of Kleene's theorem:

```
(def 'g '(lambda (x y) (s m (list x y))) )
```

It is now sufficient to use Kleene's k to derive the planaria :

```
(def 'p (k g)).
```

Each cell generates the entire planaria when applied to FOO, for example:

((p 2) 'FOO)[1]

```
((lambda  (z)
     (cond ((and (equal '1 1) (equal z
'FOO))
           (list ('(lambda (y)
                  (s m
                       (list (s '(lambda (x
y) (s m (list (s x (list x)) y)))
                                (list '(lambda
(x y)
                                         (s m (list
(s x (list x)) y)))))
                                  y)))
                1)
                '*****
                ('(lambda (y)
                  (s m
                       (list (s '(lambda (x
y) (s m (list (s x (list x)) y)))
                                (list '(lambda
(x y)
                                         (s m (list
(s x (list x)) y)))))
                                  y)))
                 2)))
          ((and (equal '1 2) (equal z
'FOO))
           (list ('(lambda (y)
                  (s m
                       (list (s '(lambda (x
y) (s m (list (s x (list x)) y)))
                                (list '(lambda
(x y)
                                         (s m (list
(s x (list x)) y)))))
```

---

1 The reader must look at this code like a biologist looks at a DNA molecule. Thus, I have not attempted to make the code readable as only its form is significant. In fact, some manipulation of λ-expressions allows the building of less redundant but even less readable cells (Marchal 1992).

```
                    y)))
               1)
               '+++++
               ('(lambda (y)
                  (s m
                        (list (s '(lambda (x
y) (s m (list (s x (list x)) y)))
                              (list '(lambda
(x y)
                                    (s m (list
(s x (list x)) y)))))
                    y)))
               2)))
          ((equal '1 1) (+ z 1))
          ((equal '1 2) (+ z 2))
          (t '(error: there are only two
cells))))
  +++++
  (lambda (z)
    (cond ((and (equal '2 1) (equal z
'FOO))
           (list ('(lambda (y)
                  (s m
                        (list (s '(lambda (x
y) (s m (list (s x (list x)) y)))
                              (list '(lambda
(x y)
                                    (s m (list
(s x (list x)) y)))))
                    y)))
               1)
               '*****
               ('(lambda (y)
                  (s m
                        (list (s '(lambda (x
y) (s m (list (s x (list x)) y)))
                              (list '(lambda
(x y)
                                    (s m (list
(s x (list x)) y)))))
                    y)))
               2)))
          ((and (equal '2 2) (equal z
'FOO))
           (list ('(lambda (y)
                  (s m
                        (list (s '(lambda (x
y) (s m (list (s x (list x)) y)))
                              (list '(lambda
(x y)
                                    (s m (list
(s x (list x)) y)))))
                    y)))
               1)
               '+++++
               ('(lambda (y)
                  (s m
                        (list (s '(lambda (x
y) (s m (list (s x (list x)) y)))
                              (list '(lambda
(x y)
                                    (s m (list
(s x (list x)) y)))))
                    y)))
               2)))
          ((equal '2 1) (+ z 1))
          ((equal '2 2) (+ z 2))
          (t '(error: there are only two
cells)))))
```

and each cell functions correctly:

```
((p 1) 3)
   4

((p 2) 3)
   5
```

This planaria *p* has personal capability with respect to a simple self-regeneration ability relative to LISP.
Note that in such a self-regenerating net each cell is potentially an "egg" in the sense that.each cell, when given some precise input (like FOO above) is able to regenerate the entire net.

5. MYHILL'S MACHINES

Remark: Everything proved thus far can be formalized in a sufficiently rich formal theory. The relevance of this fact does not lie in the quest for some rigorous presentation, but in the fact that we can construct a machine with the ability to prove these facts. In particular we are interested in what a machine is able to prove concerning its own capability to prove propositions. We must distinguish between "M proves a simple proposition p" (we shall write $M \vdash p$, or simply $\vdash p$) and "M proves the more sophisticated proposition 'M proves p'" (which should be written as $M \vdash \Box_M(\ulcorner p \urcorner)$, with "$\Box_M$" representing M's ability to prove in M's language and $\ulcorner p \urcorner$ representing p in M's language, but we shall abbreviate this as $\Box p$).

Definition: A machine M is said to be self-referentially correct in a universal environment u if M has personal capability with respect to provability relative to u. (for a related definition see Smullyan, 1985)

If that machine is able to correctly prove some elementary facts concerning substitution, then we can find a sentence *g* such that M will prove:

$$g \leftrightarrow -\Box g$$

This is a particular case of what is called the diagonalization lemma. We can replace □ by any formula with one free variable and find a corresponding g. The diagonalization lemma is essentially a formalisation of Kleene's theorem. Now, if M does not prove any false statements, i.e. it is consistent, then g is true and M is not able to prove g (this is Gödel's first incompleteness theorem). The proof is *constructive* (algorithmic) so we can augment M with the algorithmic ability to synthetize this very sentence. In this situation, we obtain a new machine M_2 with more powerful provability capacities. This construction can be iterated in the recursive transfinite (see Feferman 1962).

With Case's extension of Kleene's theorem, it is possible to build a self-referential sequence of increasingly powerful machines with respect to provability.
Suppose x is the code of a machine M with a recognizable part that is a theorem prover, then M must be part of the domain of the following two functions:

1) $\lambda x T(x)$, where T generates the set of theorems of the proof system of x.

2) $\lambda x RL(x)$, where RL transforms[1] x into an equivalent machine, except that it adds a true but not provable statement concerning x into the set of axioms of the proof system of x.

We want to build a sequence of machines: m_0, m_1, m_2, m_3..., such that each m_i, on a particular fixed argument, "PROVE", gives $T(m_i)$, and on another, "NEXT", gives m_{i+1}, where m_{i+1} is $RL(m_i)$. m_0(PROVE) generates the theorems of an elementary first-order axiomatisation of Peano Arithmetic (PA). As in the planaria, the role of m_i, is played by $\phi_e(i)$:

$\phi_{\phi_e(i)}(z)$ =if i=0 & z = PROVE output T(PA),
else if z=NEXT, output $\phi_e(i+1)$,
else if z= PROVE, output $T(RL(\phi_e(i-1)))$.
(else if z=(UNIV x y) output $\phi_x(y)$.)

As before, e will be obtained by applying k to an s variant of the recursion matrix:

t(x,i,z) = if i=0 & z = PROVE output T(PA), else
if z=NEXT then output $\phi_x(i+1)$, else
if z=PROVE output $T(RL(\phi_x(i-1)))$. (3)

z being any list. We can make any m_i universal:

if z match (UNIV j r) then output $\phi_j(r)$.

6. Inductive Inference

Definition (Gold 1967): An Inductive Inference Machine (IIM) is a machine which, in the limit, takes *all* pairs <input, output> of a function f as successive inputs and progressively outputs programs called hypotheses. We say that f is *presented* to M. The IIM converges if it ultimately outputs the same program repeatedly. The IIM M correctly identifies f and we write $f \in EX(M)$ if M converges to a program which computes f. Note that any ϕ_i is trivially identifiable: ϕ_i is always identified by the *idiotic* $\lambda x\ i$, which always gives on any input the same hypothesis i, so that the interesting concept is the identification by *one* IIM of a *subset* of $\mathcal{R}$. Case & Smith (1983) call an IIM *Popperian* if all the hypotheses produced are total functions. (So that the generated hypotheses are all refutable in the Popper sense).

Definitions
1) $EX = \{S \subset \mathcal{R}\ \exists M\ S \subset EX(M)\}$.
Putnam has gived a more strict criterion which can be proved equivalent to the *Popperianity* of the IIM:
2) $PEX = \{S : \exists M \text{ Popperian } S \subset EX(M)\}$.

[1] RL stands for for the *Refutation* of mechanist philosophy given by *Lucas*. Such a refutation is itself mecanisable. The refutation of mechanism and the mechanical refutation of that refutation has already been carried out by Post (1941). Webb has written a book on the subject (Webb 1980). Webb's book also provides a deep analysis of Kleene's theorem in relation to Church's thesis and mechanist philosophy.

Theorem (Putnam[1], 1963):

$$R \not\in \text{PEX}.$$

Putman's proof is based on the intuitive feeling that any given inductive machine α can be made to be wrong. Let m be the code of α, then the following computable function defeats any PEX machine:

$$\phi_e(0) = 0$$
$$\phi_e(x+1) = 1+\phi_{\phi_m(\phi_e(:\,x))}(x+1).$$

where $\phi_e(:\,x)$ is:

$$\{(0,\phi_e(0)), (1,\phi_e(1)), \ldots (x, \phi_e(x))\}$$

QED. The proof is constructive, so that it is easy to add evolving inductive inference capabilities to self-referential nets of popperian machines.

Theorem (Case and Smith 1983):

$$\text{PEX} \subsetneq \text{EX}$$

Case and Smith have shown that the set of functions computed by self-reproducing machines (on the fixed argument 0):

$$S = \{f : \phi_{f(0)} = f\}$$

belongs to EX, but not to PEX. Indeed, the function :

$$\phi_e(0) = e \quad \text{; compare with Putnam's function}$$
$$\phi_e(x+1) = 1+\phi_{\phi_m(\phi_e(:\,x))}(x+1).$$

is trivially identified by the IIM β which outputs a on {..., (0,a), ...}.

Here is a translation of the proof into LISP:

```
(def 'EX-BUT-NOT-PEX '(lambda (iim-pex-var)
(k
 (list 'lambda (list 'y 'x)
     (list 'cond
          (list (list 'equal 'x 0) 'y)
          (list 't (list (list '+ 1
                    (list (list iim-pex-var
                          (list 'ulis 'y
                               (list '- 'x 1)))
                    'x))
                 )
              )
          )
     )
  )          ; ulis (i,n) = {(o,φi(o), ...(n,φi(n))}
 ))          ; k is Kleene's metaprogram.          QED.
```

It is easy to show that any algorithmatically generable subset of R belongs to EX (Gold 1967) but, like PEX, R itself does not belong to it.

Nevertheless, we can enlarge the set of identifiable functions by means of a *non-constructive* weakening of the identification criteria.

Definitions: (Case and Smith 1983):

1) $f =^{0v1} g$ means that f is equal to g except, *possibly,* on a single input. Put in another way, it means that $\{x: f(x) \neq g(x)\}$ has cardinality less than *or* equal to 1.

2) M EX^1-identifies f if, when we present f to M, it converges on a program computing a g such that $f =^{0v1} g$. We write $f \in \text{EX}^1(M)$.

3) $\text{EX}^1 = \{S : \exists M\ S \subset \text{EX}^1(M)\}$.

Theorem. (Case and Smith 1983) $\text{EX} \subsetneq \text{EX}^1$. More precisely, they have shown that the set :

$$S^{0v1} = \{f : \phi_{f(0)} =^{0v1} f\}$$

does not belong to EX. The IIM α (see above) witnesses that it belongs to EX^1.

The "*possibly* " is unavoidable; such an enlargement cannot be effected constructively (algorithmically) (Chen)[2] :

[1] Putnam has proved this theorem for an extrapolation criterion which has latter been shown equivalent to the Popperian identification criteria by Case and Smith, 1983.

[2] Communication to Case and Smith (1983).

Proof: Suppose that there is a computable function ϕ_j such that for any inductive inference machine M: 1) $\phi_{\phi_j(M)}$ is total computable and 2) $\phi_{\phi_j(M)}$ does not belong to EX(M). In which case, the following IIM:

$$m = \lambda x\ (k\ j)$$

i.e. the machine which given any input always outputs ϕ_j applied to itself, is such that $\phi_{\phi_j(m)}$ belongs to EX(m), and this contradicts 2). QED.

summary: Let us informally summarize what has been done so far. I have shown the existence of a metaprogram k which can build programs having some self-referential ability relative to a universal environment. When k is applied to the code of a function t, k outputs a program which is able to apply t to itself.
For example, if t is the identity function, one gets a self-reproducing program. I have shown how to use k to build more general self-referential structured collections of machines. By using the constructive aspect of Gödel's incompleteness proof, I have shown how to build a self-referential sequence of increasingly powerful machines (with respect to provability). It is possible to provide the machines in the nets with inductive inference capabilities. In the general case, however, such abilities cannot be constructively presented, in contrast with provability. In Marchal (1992), I show how to deal with some of these non-constructive aspects by allowing branching in the self-referential nets.
I will next examine the collection of true self-referential propositions that these machines are able to communicate in the limit. I argue that such propositions can be either provable *or* guessed correctly. The approach is relevant for the study of self-knowledge, at least if we accept the classical theory of knowledge according to which it is true belief. In particular, Descartes's approach to dreams seems to emerge in the limit. Such a result, if confirmed, would be a broadening of Slezak 's analysis of the *cogito* argument (Slezak 1983).

7. Dreaming Machines

In his booklet, *DREAMING*, Malcom (1959) opposed Descartes' view of dreams with his own young-Wittgensteinien, verificationist conception. As in Brouwer's philosophy, truth is provability or verifiability. He has built a positivistic theory of dreams which contradicts both Descartes' and the modern conception of dreams (Dement 1972) in which dreams are genuine subjective experiences occuring in sleep. In particular, he argues against Descartes' doubt that dream and reality can be easily distinguished (Descartes 1641, see also Caillois 1956). I suggest that the incompleteness phenomenon gives evidence for Descartes' approach. This requires Solovay's modal analysis of provability in a recursive extension of Peano Arithmetic (Solovay, 1976). The theorem applies to a fixed machine M in the self-referential net. Recall that □p is an abbreviation for $\Box_M(\ulcorner p \urcorner)$:

The following modal system, G:

AXIOMS:	□p->□□p
	□(p->q)->□p->□q
	□(□p->p)->□p
RULES:	p and p->q entails q
	p entails □p

is a sound, decidable and complete formalisation of the proof abilities *of* M which are provable *by* M, and the following logic, as G* :

AXIOMS:	□p->p
	All the theorems of G
RULES:	p and p->q entails q

is a sound, decidable, and complete formalisation of all the proof abilities of M, including those which M is not able to prove.

definitions: A true sentence is *strongly communicable by M* if it is formally

provable (relative to a body of evidence) by M. It is *weakly communicable by M* if M has inductively infered that sentence. *Idiotic self-inductive inference machines* *<G,G*>* are those which belong to a self-referential net whose recursion matrix has been initialized with theorem provers for G and G*.
Such an idiotic machine can be used as a mechanist counter-example *contra*-Malcom, for it can distinguish strongly-communicable (provable) sentences from weakly communicable sentences (the non provable theorems which can be guessed). If, using RL or inductive inference it reflects an undecidable sentence, then it gives birth to new machines for which G, and possibly G*, can still be sound, inferable, and even in some sense complete.

8. Knowing Machines

There are enough affinities between the concepts of truth and proof to invite attempts to define knowledge using them. I will first show that the intuitive notion that knowledge is provability is untenable. I will then provide a more adequate alternative representation in terms of both provability and truth.
I assume the common opinion that knowledge representation in modal logic should be given by S4:

AXIOMS:	⊡p->p
	⊡p->⊡⊡p
	⊡(p->q)->⊡p->⊡q
RULES:	p and p->q entail q
	p entails ⊡p

1. intuitive representation: ⊡p is □p?
Do we have □p->p? (the first axiom of S4). For a large class of theories, Löb (1955) shows that ⊢ □p->p entails ⊢ □p. Furthermore, it has been shown that the proof is formalisable in PA, so we have:

□(□p->p)->□p (Löb's formula)

which can be noted to be the principal axiom of G. Now, S4 is closed for the necessitation rule: "p entails ⊡p". Thus, if we have □p->p, we also have □(□p->p). Thus we must have □(□*false->false*). It follows from Löb's formula that □*false*, which, with □p->p and modus ponens gives *false*. Consequently it is inconsistent to have both the axiom □p->p and the rule "p entails ⊡p" for □. (see Montague, 1974 and Thomason, 1980 for similar results).

With G, we lose □p->p. With G*, we lose "p entails □p". In the Platonistic realm the machine can infer non-strongly-communicable truths, and even weakly-communicate them with some precautions, by means of "?" for example. But how can we reconcile □p->p and "p entails □p"?; how can we isolate immediate, actual and solipsist-like world knowledge?

2. Alternative representation ⊡p is □p&p.
A consequence of Löb's theorem is that we know that □p and □p&p are Platonistically (i.e. G*) equivalent, but not provably so (i.e. G). Let us define ⊡p by □p&p. It is easy to show that ⊡p will obey S4. Indeed, it can be characterized by an even stronger logic, where an axiom due to Grzegorczyk (1967) has been added:

AXIOMS:	□p->p
	□p->□□p
	□(p->q)->□p->□q
	□(□(p->□p)->p)->p
RULES:	p and p->q entails q
	p entails □p

This is a sound, decidable, and complete formalisation of the provable true-and-provable sentence in PA. This system is known as S4Grz.
Astonishingly, it is also a sound, decidable, and complete formalisation of the true true-and-provable sentences in PA. This follows from independent work by Boolos (1980), and Goldblatt (1978). So, after all, there is a reconciliation of truth and provability based on self-reference. Using Grzegorczyk's

extension of Gödel's link between S4 and Intuitionistic Logic (IL), Goldblatt describes an arithmetical interpretation of IL in PA, and proves a similar double completeness result.

Here is a summary of the relevant work of Solovay, Boolos and Goldblatt :

Provable by M		True for M	
G	->	G*	LN
IL	->	IL	NP
S4Grz	->	S4Grz	NP

LN = Loss of necessitation, NP = necessitation preserved, and necessitation is the common name for the rule "p entails □p".

9. APPLICATIONS

We have seen that idiotic <G, G*>, although unreasonable for forming models of the mind, can nevertheless be useful for building counter-examples to some arguments in philosophy of mind. Amongst its other applications are the following: the clarification (and exemplification) of Kripke-like arguments against the identity thesis (Kripke 1982), the refutation of Baker's arguments against functionalism (Baker 1985). In both cases, their arguments[1] remain valid within a purely extensional view of identity and function(alism). It is a confusion between

$$(p \,\&\, \Box p) \quad \text{and} \quad \Box p$$

or at a more primitive level, it is a confusion between:

necessarily $e=e$ and necessarily $\phi_e() = e$.

The basic philosophical motivations for the present approach are described in (Marchal 1988, 90, 91, 92)
Other results can be extracted from the present analysis. If we accept the optimistic Darwinian-like idea of survival of the *sound* machine, then the self-referential nets produce in the limit (at term) machines describable with the help of G, G*, S4Grz, or their extensions. Furthermore, communication of *weakly-communicable* statements enhances, not only the scope of possible dialogues between machines and their environment, but allows for the speed-up of computations relative to that environment. This speed-up phenomenon has also been presumed by Gödel (see Gödel 1936, Arbib 1964, Royer 1989).
Good (1971) has made an analysis of *relative freedom* of one machine relative to another in terms of relative computational efficiency. This analysis, transposed into our setting, would entail the emergence of *freedom* (in Good's sense) relative to universal environments.

[1] Baker's arguments, or the arguments held by those who defend the (token) identity thesis and are refuted by Kripke.

Bibliography

ARBIB M.A., 1964, ***Brains, Machines, and Mathematics***, Springer-Verlag, 1987. (1er ed. McGraw-Hill, 1964).

BAKER L. R., 1985, *A Farewell to Functionalism* Philosophical Studies, 48.

BLUM L. & BLUM M., 1975, *Toward a Mathematical Theory of Inductive Inference*. Information and Control 28, pp. 125-155.

BOOLOS G., 1980, *On Systems of Modal Logic with Provability Interpretations*, Theoria, 46, 1, pp. 7-18.

BUSCHSBAUM R., 1938, ***Animals without Backbones: 1***, Penguin Books, 1938. (Third Edition: with BUSCHSBAUM M., PEARSE J. and PEARSE V., The University of Chicago Press, Chicago and London, 1987).

CAILLOIS R., 1956, ***L'incertitude qui vient des rêves***. Gallimard.

CASE J., 1974, *Periodicity in Generations of Automata*, Mathematical Systems Theory. Vol. 8, n° 1. Springer Verlag, NY, pp. 15-32.

CASE J. & SMITH C., 1983, *Comparison of Identification Criteria for Machine Inductive Inference*. In Theoretical Computer Science 25, pp 193-220.

DAVIS M. (ed.), 1965, ***The Undecidable***. Raven Press, Hewlett, New York.

DEMENT W. C., 1972, ***Dormir, rêver***, Editions du Seuil, Paris, 1981, (traduit de l'américain: *Some Must Watch While Some Must Sleep* 1972)

DESCARTES R., 1641 *Meditationes de prima philosophia*, Paris. Also in ***Oeuvres et Lettres.*** Bibliothèque de la Pléiade. pp. 267-334,Gallimard, 1953.

FEFERMAN S., 1962, *Transfinite Recursive Progressions of Axiomatic Theories,* Journal of Symbolic Logic, Vol 27, N° 3, pp. 259-316.

GÖDEL K., 1933, *Eine Interpretation des Intuitionistischen Aussagenkalküls*, Ergebnisse eines Mathematischen Kolloquiums, Vol 4, pp. 39-40.

GÖDEL K., 1936, *On the Length of Proofs*. translated in Davis 1965.

GOLD E. M., 1967, *Language Identification in the Limit.* Information & Control 10, pp. 447-474.

GOLDBLATT R., 1978, *Arithmetical Necessity, Provability and Intuitionistic Logic*, Theoria, Vol 44, pp. 38-46.

GOOD I. J., 1971, *Freewill and Speed of Computation.* Brit. J. Phil. Sci. 22, 48-49.

GRZEGORCZYK A., 1967, *Some relational systems and the associated topological spaces*, Fundamenta Mathematicae, LX pp. 223-231.

KLEENE S. C., 1952, ***Introduction to Metamathematics.*** P. Van Nortrand Comp. Inc.

KRIPKE S., 1972, ***La logique des noms propres.*** Les éditions de minuit, 1982, (traduit de l'américain: *Naming and Necessity*, 1972)

LÖB M. H., 1955, *Solution of a Problem of Leon Henkin*, Journal of Symbolic Logic, 20, pp. 115-118.

MALCOM N., 1959. ***Dreaming.*** Routledge & Kegan Paul ltd.

MARCHAL B., 1988, *Informatique théorique et philosophie de l'esprit.* Actes du 3ème colloque international de l'ARC, Toulouse.

MARCHAL B., 1990, *Des Fondements Théoriques pour l'Intelligence Artificielle et la Philosophie de l'Esprit*, Revue Internationale de Philosophie, 1, n° 172, pp 104-117.

MARCHAL B., 1991, *Mechanism and Personal Identity*, Proceedings of WOCFAI 91, M. De Glas & D. Gabbay (Eds.), Angkor, Paris.

MARCHAL B., 1992, *Mécanisme et Identité Personnelle*, thesis, in preparation.

McKINSEY J. C. C. & TARSKI A., 1948, *Some Theorems about the Sentential Calculi of Lewis and Heyting*, Journal of Symbolic Logic, 13, pp. 1-15.

MONTAGUE R., 1974, *Syntactical treatments of modality, with corollaries on reflexion principles and finite axiomatizability*, in R. Montague, Formal Philosophy, New Haven and London.

MOORE C. M., 1990, *Unpredictability and Undecidability in Dynamical Systems*, Physical Review Letters, V. 64, N° 20, pp. 2354-2357.

MYHILL J., 1964, *Abstract Theory of Self-Reproduction*, in Views on General Systems Theory, M.D. Mesarovic, ed. Wiley NY, pp 106-118.

POST E., 1941, *Absolutely Unsolvable Problems and Relatively Undecidable Propositions: Account of an Anticipation*, in Davis 1965, pp. 338-433.

PUTNAM H., 1963, *Probability and confirmation* The Voice of America, Forum Philosophy of Science, 10 (U.S. Information agency, 1963). Reprinted in *Mathematics, Matter, and Method.* Cambridge University Press.Cambridge 1975.

ROGERS H., 1967, ***Theory of Recursive Functions and Effective Computability.*** McGraw-Hill, 1967. (2ed, MIT Press, Cambridge, Massachusetts 1987)

ROGERS H., 1958, *Gödel Numbering of the Partial Recursive Functions*, Journal of Symbolic Logic, 23, pp. 331-341.

ROYER J. S., 1989, *Two Recursion Theoretic Characterizations of Proof Speed-ups*, The Journal of Symbolic Logic, 54, N° 2.

SLEZAK P., 1983. *Descartes 's Diagonal Deduction*, Brit. J. Phil. Sci. 34, pp. 13-36.

SMORINSKI, C., 1981, *Fifty Years of Self-Reference in Arithmetic*, Notre Dame Journal of Formal Logic, Vol. 22, n° 4, pp. 357-374.

SMULLYAN R., 1985. *Modality and Self-reference*, in Intensional Mathematics, S. Shapiro (Ed.), North-Holland, Amsterdam

SOLOVAY R., 1976, *Provability Interpretations of Modal Logic*, Israel Journal of Mathematics 25, pp. 287-304.

THOMASON R., 1980, H. *A Note on Syntactical Treatment of Modality*, Synthese, 44, pp. 391-395.

WEBB J.C., 1980, ***Mechanism, Mentalism & Metamathematics.*** An Essay on Finitism. D. Reidel Pub. Company.

Selectionist Systems as Cognitive Systems

Bernard Manderick
AI Laboratory
Free University of Brussels*†

Abstract

Selectionist systems inspired by adaptive biological systems provide a possible solution to basic cognitive problems like categorization and adaptive control which minimizes the importance of prior variable environment-specific knowledge as well as the role of a supervisor. Moreover, the learning in selectionist systems differs from most other learning algorithms which are examples of instructive learning.

1 Introduction

In order to cope with an uncertain and noisy environment, any autonomous cognitive creature - this could be a biological organism or an autonomous robot - has to solve a number of basic cognitive problems. For instance, a creature has to categorize the inputs coming from the environment. And, the creature has to adapt its behavior to the environment. These are the problems of categorization and adaptive behavior.

Moreover, the creature has to solve these problems in the following circumstances. First of all, the creature has to do this without the help of a teacher. And second, the creature does not have initial variable environment-specific knowledge which could be used to solve these cognitive problems. The creature is connected with its environment in a feedback loop and the only information that it gets from the environment is via its sensors. At the same time, the creature affects the environment via its effectors. From the creature's point of view, the environment is essentially a black box.

Categorization and adaptive behavior have also received much attention in machine learning which is a subfield of artificial intelligence. In both domains, successful learning algorithms have been developed. Although these learning algorithms differ in many respects, most of them have two things in common: First, they are *supervised* while the learning task is performed. And second, they have a lot of *knowledge about their domain of application*.

For example, in many categorization algorithms, a supervisor or teacher provides a preclassified set of examples or he provides the correct answer after each categorization attempt of the learning algorithm.

To learn from examples, algorithms contain additional constraints in order to make reasonable guesses about what has to be learned. These additional constraints are called *bias* [Utgoff 1986]. Bias guides the learning and reflects the knowledge that the designer of the program has about the domain of application. It has been argued that learning algorithms should contain bias [Mitchell 1980].

In the case of categorization, given a number of examples different hypotheses can be formulated how these examples can be classified. The ordering in which these hypotheses are considered, the way these hypotheses are evaluated and so on are examples of bias. In the area of adaptive control, the state space of the system to be controlled is often discretized in a clever way and as a result the problem becomes considerably less difficult to solve. This is another example of bias.

Our starting point is that a cognitive system in order to be true autonomous has to solve the problems of categorization and adaptive behavior without prior variable environment-specific knowledge. As a matter of fact, categorization is a prerequisite to make models of the world. Models are simplifications of the real world and in this simplification the categorization of inputs considered equivalent by the organism plays an important role. Categorization comes first and knowledge about the world second. So, that knowledge cannot be used to guide the categorization. In the same way, the adaptation of the behavior has to proceed without using a detailed model of the world. The adaptation has to be based on the feedback that the creature gets from its own actions.

So, an autonomous cognitive creature has to face the following *bootstrap problem*:

*Address: Pleinlaan 2 - B-1050 Brussels - Belgium. Email: bernard@arti.vub.ac.be

†This research has been sponsored by the Belgian Government under contract "Incentive Program for Fundamental Research in Artificial Intelligence, Project: Self-Organization in Subsymbolic Computation".

> How can an autonomous creature acquire initial knowledge about the environment and how can it behave adaptively 1) without having built-in environment-specific knowledge and 2) without being supervised while acquiring that initial knowledge or behaving adaptively.

This bootstrap problem resembles the circumstances in which biological systems like a species, an immune system and a brain have to adapt. Natural evolution produces species that are increasingly better adapted to their niche. The immune system of a vertebrate organism builds up an immune response to any foreign substance that might invade that organism. The brain categorizes stimuli coming from its environment and supports adaptive behavior. Yet, these systems have not been designed with the characteristics in mind of the environment in which they have to operate. Still, they are able to adapt successfully to their environment of which they have no prior variable environment-specific knowledge.

In biology, theories have been proposed which explain the adaptive capabilities of these biological systems. *Selectionist* theories have proven to be the most successful ones: Neo-Darwinism, the synthesis of Darwin's [1859] original theory of natural selection and modern genetics explains the evolution of species. The clonal selection theory for antibody formation [Jerne 1955, Burnet 1959] explains the working of the immune system. Edelman [1987] has proposed the theory of neuronal group selection to explain the working of the brain.

Scientific progress may result from the application of ideas in one domain to another one. We want to investigate how selectionism which underlies the adaptability of the above biological systems can be applied to understand autonomous cognitive creatures.

In contrast, most learning algorithms studied in machine learning can be characterized as *instructive*. Here, the algorithm processes the information coming from the environment in such a way that its future behavior is better adapted to that environment. This process is much more complicated than selectionist learning where new elements are produced by a "random" mechanism.

If we want to build true autonomous creatures then we have to take the biological metaphors seriously. The rest of this paper is organized as follows. First, we compare selectionist systems in biology. Second, some design principles for autonomous systems are derived from this comparison. And third, the domain of application in artificial intelligence of these systems is determined.

2 Selectionist Systems in Biology

In this section, we compare three adaptive biological systems. For two of them, the natural evolution of species and the immune system, it is nowadays widely accepted that their adaptiveness is best explained by selectionist principles: the natural evolution of species is explained by *neo-Darwinism* which is the synthesis of Darwin's original theory and modern genetics - see [Dawkins 1986] for an overview, and the immune system is explained by the *clonal selection theory* - see [Perelson 1990] for an overview. For the third system, the brain, a selectionist theory called *neuronal group selection theory* or *neural Darwinism* has been proposed recently to explain higher brain functions like perception, categorization and memory [Edelman 1987].

These selectionist theories have a lot in common but there are also a number of differences. In all theories, the notion of population is important, the diversity within the population exists prior to any interaction with the environment, the variants in the population are tested by the environment and the "fitter" variants are selected and amplified. For the three biological systems, instructive theories have been proposed. Differences between the three selectionist theories are in the role of selectionist principles and in the adaptation mechanism. We begin with the differences.

In biology, an important distinction is made between theories explaining the evolution and theories explaining the functioning of structures. In biology, both types of theories were often confounded resulting in confusion between causes of evolution of organisms (*ultimate* causes) and causes of functioning of organisms (*proximate* causes) [Mayr 1982]. Unawareness of this distinction might also hamper the understanding of adaptation and cognition in terms of selectionist principles.

Selectionist principles play a different role in the evolution theory on the one hand, and the clonal selection theory and the neuronal group selection theory on the other hand. In the evolution theory, selectionist principles explain how species become more and more adapted to their environment, i.e. it explains the *evolution* of species. Individuals of some species like mammals behave adaptively. Evolution theory says nothing about the mechanisms behind this adaptive behavior. Other species like insects are very well adapted to their environment but their behavior is stereotypical. In contrast, it is the *functioning* of the immune system and the brain that is explained by selectionist principles, i.e. these principles clarify the mechanisms responsible for the adaptability of the IS and the brain. This way, the IS is much more important than natural evolution as a metaphor in understanding adaptation in an unknown environment.

In the past, researchers were mostly referring to the theory of natural evolution as a metaphor for adaptation and cognition. This explains much of the resistance against selectionist theories of cognition. Some widely held objections are: Natural evolution operates on a million year time scale. How could the same principles lie at the basis of behavior adaptive in real time? And, evolution theory explains the emergence and evolution of structures like the brain but this does not necessarily means that the brain functions according to selectionist principles.

Therefore, it is important that we look at selectionist theories like the immune system where selectionism is proposed as the proximate cause. This is why we have paid more attention to the clonal-selection theory and neural Darwinism.

Adaptation in dynamical systems comes in two flavors: adjustment and innovation [Farmer *et al.* 86]. If adaptation is the result of changes of the parameters in the system then it is called *adjustment*. Learning in neural nets where the weights are the parameters is an example of adjustment. In contrast, if adaptation results from "topological" changes of the dynamical system then it is called *innovation*. Adaptation as reflected in the metadynamics of the IS is an example of innovation. The continuous creation of new antibody types changes the IS's network "topology". In both the evolution of species and the IS, adaptation is innovation. According to the TNGS, the formation of the primary repertoire is an example of adaptation as innovation (neuronal groups compete for neurons and this affects the "topology" of the groups) and the formation of the secondary repertoire is adaptation as adjustment (only the synaptic weights of the connections are modified and this does not affect the "topology" of the groups).

More important than the differences are the similarities between natural evolution, the immune system and the brain. These systems have been explained by selectionist theories: natural evolution by neo-Darwinism, the immune system by the clonal selection theory and the brain by the neuronal group selection theory.

Each system consists of a *population* of units: a species is a population of genotypes/phenotypes, the immune system is a population of B-lymphocytes and the corresponding antibodies and the brain is a population of neuronal groups.

There is a lot of *diversity* within the population: No two individuals of a species are identical if twins and the like are excluded. About 10^7 antibody types exist in the immune system. And the neuronal groups are different in their anatomical structure.

The units of the population are "*tested*" by either the external or the internal environment: Individual organisms are "tested" by their niche. Antibody types are "tested" by antigens (the external environment) or antibody types in the immune system (the internal environment). Neuronal groups are "tested" by signals coming from the sense organs (external environment) or by signals coming from other groups (internal environment).

Due to differences between the units, these units *respond differently* to their environment and the "fitter" units of the population are selected by the environment and *amplified*. In the evolution of species, the units of selection are individuals and better adapted individuals have more offspring than the less well adapted ones. In the IS, the units of selection are antibodies and the number of activated antibodies increases through the proliferation of the corresponding B-lymphocytes and the release of free antibodies. In the brain, the units of selection are neuronal groups and the groups that respond to an input are amplified through modification of synaptic weights.

The diversity within the population of units is the result of an autonomous process called the *generator of diversity* which is influenced neither directly nor indirectly by the environment. The diversity among the genotypes results from mutation and crossover of the existing genotypes. Mutation and crossover are not affected by the environment. The diversity among the antibody types in the immune system is the result of the recruitment strategy [Bersini & Varela 1990, 1991]. This strategy is largely unaffected by the external environment: B-lymphocytes activated by an antigen start to mutate at a higher rate than the other B-lymphocytes. This is the only influence of the external environment on the generation of diversity in the immune system. The anatomical differences between neuronal groups are the result of cell movement, cell differentiation and cell death.

A last point of similarity between the three biological systems is that *instructive* theories have been proposed for 1) explaining natural evolution (Lamarck's theory), 2) the immune system (Pauling's direct folding theory) and 3) the brain (Hebb's cell assembly theory). These instructive theories are either refuted (the first two theories) or questioned (the third theory). The major difference between these instructive theories and their selectionist counterparts is the role of the environment. In selectionist theories, the diversity among the units of the population exists prior to any "testing" by the environment and this diversity is maintained by a process which is not influenced in any way by that environment. The role of the environment is to select the "fitter" variants. The priority of the autonomy of the system over its environment is exemplified in Varela's view of the immune system [Varela *et al.* 1988]: The role of the immune system is not to eliminate antigens. The immune system is just a self-regulating generator of B-lymphocyte and antibody diversity. The self-regulation keeps the concentrations of the several antibody types within acceptable limits. The antigenes affect the existing balance and the immune system has to compensate for these imbalances of several sorts. The immune response is nothing more than a side effect of the self-regulation of the immune system.

In contrast, instructive theories stress the priority of the environment over the system. In Lamarck's theory, changes in the environment direct changes in the organism so that the organism adapts to these changes. In the direct folding theory, the antigen is used as a template to create matching antibodies. And in Hebb's theory, the cell assembling process is directed by the environment.

The comparison between natural evolution, the immune system and the brain is summarized in Table 1.

3 Selectionist Cognitive Systems

Selectionism has its roots in biology. Selectionist systems have common properties and for two of these systems - the immune system and the brain - selectionism explains their functioning rather than how these sys-

	Natural Evolution	Immune System	Brain
Selectionist theory	neo-Darwinism	Clonal selection theory	Neuronal group selection theory
Generator of diversity	mutation and crossover	recruitment strategy	cell movement, differentiation and death
Unit of selection	genotype/ phenotype	antibody type	neuronal group
Amplification process	reproduction of the fitter individuals	secretion of free antibodies and reproduction of the corresponding B-lymphocytes	modification of the synaptic weights of the connections
Explains	evolution	functioning	functioning
Adaptation	innovation	innovation	adjustment

Table 1: A comparison between 3 selectionist theories: 1) the theory of natural evolution of species (left), the clonal selection theory (middle) and, 3) the theory of neuronal group selection (right). Here, we have restricted ourselves to the second selectionist process described by the theory of the neuronal group selection.

tems are evolved. Moreover, these systems have "*cognitive*" properties: The immune system recognizes shapes of antigens, memorizes these shapes and the immune system learns to respond faster to shapes it had recognized in the past [Varela *et al.* 1988]. A system that *functions* according to selectionist principles is called a *selectionist cognitive system* abbreviated as *SCS*. The immune system and the brain are examples of SCSs and will be used to illustrate the key concepts.

In the rest of this section, we define SCSs, we discuss the design decisions that have to be taken and we try to determine the scope of SCSs.

3.1 Definition of SCSs

Common properties of selectionist cognitive systems are a population of diverse units also called *variants*. These variants are "tested" by the environment in parallel. Due to their differences, variants respond differently. And depending on their response, variants are selected and as a result their relative importance in the population is amplified. The diversity in the population exists prior to the testing by the environment and the way this diversity is maintained proceeds independently from the environment in which the system is embedded. The role of the environment is to select the variants that stood the "test".

A *Selectionist Cognitive System*

- Consists of a population of variants.

Examples of such variants are B-lymphocytes in the immune system and neuronal groups in the brain according to the neuronal group selection theory [Edelman 1987]. B-lymphocytes differ in the antibodies that they reproduce and neuronal groups differ in their anatomical structure. In the context of machine learning, these variants might be rules or classifiers [Holland & Reitman 1978], or complete production systems [De Jong 1988]. The initial diversity in the immune system results from randomly combining genes from the gene libraries. The recruitment strategy [Varela *et al.* 1988] maintains that diversity. The initial diversity in the brain is the result of the first selectionist process described by the TNGS. The details of how this initial diversity is created and later on maintained are not specified in the theory of neuronal group selection.

- These variants get the opportunity to respond to inputs from the environment. They are "tested" by the environment. Different variants respond in a different way to the same input. The response is a function of how well each unit matches that input. A unit recognizes an input if the match with that unit exceeds some threshold.

B-lymphocytes are in the blood stream with the antigens. If the antibodies on the surface of a B-lymphocyte match a given antigen sufficiently then it gets activated. The match depends on the complementarity of the paratope of the antibody and one of the epitopes of the antigens, i.e. the affinity of the binding. Different neuronal groups receive the same input signals. Depending on their anatomical structure, different groups respond differently.

- The selected variants are amplified. This amplification is a function of the response to the current input. Amplification means that the relative importance in the population of the responding variants increases and/or the relative importance of the other variants decreases.

Some of the matching B-lymphocytes in the IS get activated when then exceed the proliferation threshold and start to proliferate. More B-lymphocytes of the matching type are produced. In contrast, B-lymphocytes that do not get activated die after a few days. If neuronal groups respond sufficiently to an input signal then the weights of the synaptic connections of these groups are modified and these groups will show a higher response in the future to the same or similar input signal.

To design a selectionist cognitive system the following decisions have to be made:

- Choose the units or variants for your problem.
- Choose the properties in which these variants differ.
- Choose the size of the population. The size should be large enough so that no inputs go unmatched. An initial response is needed which can then be improved later on. Otherwise responding variants have to be created in an ad hoc way. The size of the population will depend on the environment in which the SA has to operate.
- Choose a generator of diversity. Although the responding variants are amplified, the diversity within the population has to be maintained for two reasons. First, the SA has to be able to improve on its initial response. That initial response is determined by the responding variants. Amplification of these variants does not allow further improvement. Second, the diversity within the population should remain large enough so that the SA is able to respond to inputs not encountered yet.
- Choose a function which determines the match between an input and a variant.
- Choose an amplification mechanism.

The structure of a selectionist cognitive system is displayed schematically in Figure 1.

3.2 Discussion of SCSs

A first crucial point in the above definition is that *the population consists of diverse units or variations.* The diversity should be large enough so that at least one variant responds to every possible input. This way, the selectionist system can adapt itself to an environment of which it has no prior knowledge. Also, if a selectionist system is well-adapted to an environment there should be still enough diversity among the variants so that if the environment changes the system could adapt itself to these changing conditions.

A second crucial point in the above definition is that *diversity results from some combinatorial process which operates autonomously from the environment.* For instance, B-lymphocytes mutate and variations on the original B-lymphocytes are produced by reshuffling genes from the gene libraries. These processes proceed independently from what happens in the environment. The role of environment is to select the "fitter" variants. The variants that are produced are not prompted by the environment in any way. If the production of variants was correlated with what would be a solution to the environmental problem then the selection step would make no sense at all: the environment would instruct the system rather than select the better adapted variants.

3.3 Scope of SCSs

Symbolic AI made progress in high-level cognitive areas such as knowledge representation, problem solving and reasoning. However, in low-level cognitive activities such as vision, pattern recognition and adaptive behavior the situation is completely different. Progress was slow and difficult to attain. For instance, until recently work on vision in AI was primarily concerned with the transformation of visual input into an internal symbolic representation of that visual input. This symbolic representation could then be used by a physical symbol system [Marr 1982]. The transformation from visual input to internal symbolic representation proved to be a formidable task which is not solved yet.

The characteristics of high-level cognitive and low-level cognitive activities seems so different that Steels [1991] used the terms behavior-based intelligence as opposed to knowledge-based intelligence to characterize these two types of intelligence.

In *knowledge-based intelligence*, everything is centered around the knowledge the system has about the world and about its own internal structure and functioning. Knowledge is represented in such a way that it can be used by reasoning processes like inference and induction. These reasoning processes have been formalized. And this is why this approach has proven to be so successful in the areas of high-level activities like theorem proving, planning, diagnosis and so on.

In contrast, *behavior-based intelligence* works on poor models of the world and results from the way very simple modules like behaviors are cooperating and competing to achieve some goal [Brooks 1986, Braitenberg 1986, Tinbergen 1951]. Typically, each module has access to a number of sensors and effectors and the sensory information is associated by the module with the behavioral response. No complicated reasoning processes take place at the level of behavior-based intelligence. Behavior-based intelligence does not fit the PSS-hypothesis very well.

Behavior-based intelligence uses poor models of the world. Selectionist Automata are designed to operate in an environment of which they have no prior environment-specific knowledge. So, it seems reasonable to apply SCSs to problems of behavior-based intelligence.

4 Conclusion

In this paper, we have argued that selectionist systems provide one source of inspiration to build true autonomous cognitive systems. We have compared three such biological systems and two of these systems have "cognitive properties". This comparison resulted in a number of design principles to build selectionist cognitive systems. We have also tried to determine the scope of selectionist cognitive systems.

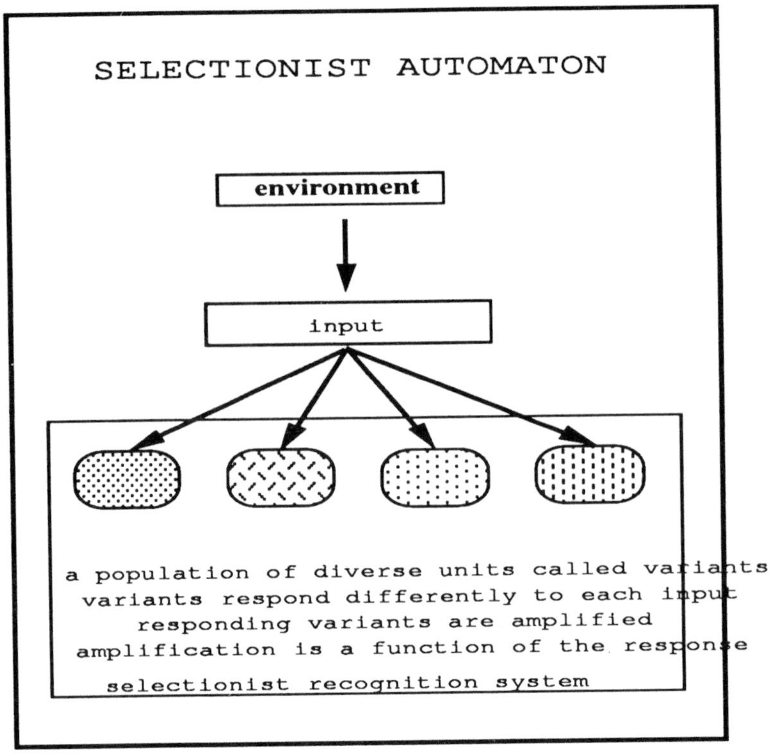

Figure 1: A selectionist cognitive system in its environment.

Acknowledgments

I would like to thank Luc Steels, the director of the AI Lab of the VUB, for his continuous support. Thanks also to H. Bersini of the ULB, D. Roggen of the VUB and F. Varela of CREA for valuable comments on my dissertation [Manderick 1991] and on which this paper is based.

References

Ada, G. L. & Nossal, G. (1987) "The Clonal-Selection Theory", In *Scientific American*, Vol. 257, pp. 62–69.

Bersini, H. & Varela, F. (1990) "Hints for adaptive problem solving gleaned from immune networks", In H.-P. Schwefel and H. Mühlenbein (eds.) *Proceedings of the First International Workshop on Parallel Problem Solving from Nature*, Springer Verlag, to be published.

Bersini, H. & Varela, F. (1991) "The Immune Recruitment Mechanism: A Selective Evolutionary Strategy", To appear in *The Proceedings of to the Fourth International Conference on Genetic Algorithms*, San Diego, CA.

Braitenberg, V. (1986) *Vehicles: Experiments in Synthetic Psychology*, Bradford Books, The MIT Press, MA.

Brooks, R.A. (1986) "A robust layered control system for a mobile robot", In *IEEE Journal of Robotics and Automation, Vol. 1*, pp. 14–23.

Burnet, F. M. (1959) *The clonal selection theory of acquired immunity*, Vanderbilt University Press, Nashville.

Darwin, C. (1859) *On the origin of species by means of natural selection or the preservation of favoured races in the struggle of life*, Murray, London.

Dawkins, R. (1986) *The Blind Watchmaker*, Longman Scientific & Technical, Harlow, UK.

De Jong, K.A. (1988) "Learning with Genetic Algorithms: An Overview", In *Machine Learning*, Vol. 3, Nos. 2/3, Kluwer Academic Publishers, Dordrecht, The Netherlands.

Edelman, G. M. (1987) *Neural Darwinism: The Theory of Neuronal Group Selection*, Basic Books, Inc., New York.

Farmer, J.D., Kauffman, S.A., Packard, N.H. & Perelson, A.S. (1986) Adaptive Dynamic Networks as Models for the Immune System and Autocatalytic Sets, Technical Report LA-UR-86-3287, Los Alamos National Laboratory, Los Alamos, NM.

Holland, J.H. & Reitman, J.R. (1978), *Cognitive Systems Based on Adaptive Algorithms*, In Waterman, D.A., Hayes-Roth, F. (eds), *Pattern-directed Inference Systems*, Academic Press, New York.

Jerne, N.K. (1955) The natural- selection theory of antibody formation, In *Proceedings of the National Academy of Sciences U.S.A., 41*, pp. 849–856.

Manderick, B. (1991) "Selectionism as a Basis for Categorization and Adaptive Behavior", VUB AI-Lab Technical Report 91-1.

Marr, D. (1982) *Vision: a computational investigation into the human representation and processing of visual information*, Freeman, San Francisco, CA.

Mitchell, T.M. (1980) *The need for biases in learning generalizations*, Department of Computer Science, Rutgers University, New Brunswick, NJ.

Perelson, A.S. (1990) "Theoretical Immunology", In E. Jen (ed.) *1989 Lectures in Complex Systems*, Santa Fe Institute Studies in the Sciences of Complexity, Addison-Wesley, Redwood City, CA.

Steels, L. (1991) *Lectures in Knowledge-Based Systems*, Unpublished manuscript.

Tinbergen, N. (1951) *The Study of Instinct*, Oxford University Press, New York, NY.

Utgoff, P.E. (1986) "Shift of Bias for Inductive Concept Learning", In Michalski, R.S., Carbonell, J.G. & Mitchell, T.M. (1986).

Varela, F., Coutinho, A., Dupire, B. & Vaz, N.N. (1988) "Cognitive Networks: Immune, Neural, and Otherwise", In A.S. Perelson (ed.) *Theoretical Immunology, Vol. II*, Santa Fe Institute Studies in the Sciences of Complexity, Addison-Wesley, Redwood City, CA.

Looking at Life

Robert Davidge
School of Cognitive and Computer Studies
University of Sussex
Brighton BN1 9QH
England
robertd@uk.ac.susx.cogs

Abstract

The paper offers a personal viewpoint on several interesting areas within AL. It looks at the problem of recognising when an AL system is successful. It also makes the observation that the entire environment is living and exposes the non-fractal simplicity of current AL ecosystems. We are reminded that evolution is open-ended and that biological goals are self-referential. The great problem of organic flexibility in AL and the related issue of mutability are mentioned. The importance of the individual organism is emphasized. Two tests are applied to AL systems: can they demonstrate a vertical mapping to the atomic level and is there a horizontal uniformity of complexity at the chosen design level. Satisfying both tests, the processor is equated with the biological cell.

Introduction

Artificial Life has generated an unprecedented surge of interest in the last few years since the first workshop [*Langton*, 1989]. The research approach is characterised by the appearance of individual and isolated systems. We are still feeling our way as to what constitutes a right research approach and there is confusion between *modelling* life processes and *creating* artificial life.

Completely absent so far is any body of theoretical ideas or hypotheses on what constitutes life, how it may be recognised or created. This paper does not attempt to fill that void, but it does probe a few fingers into the great unknown which represents our true understanding of Life. If we are not careful and lay a very solid foundation of philosophical and even metaphysical groundwork, we will end up with a discipline similar to AI, in which there are many algorithms, some limited progress and a still complete ignorance of the nature of intelligence. One belief I hold, which promises to eventually unite AL and AI, is that intelligence and life are inseparable. If you recognise one, you will recognise the other. What other aspects of the universe are also necessarily enfolded in the mantle of Life remains for us to discover.

I now offer a few vistas into the landscape of Life which may aid in the construction of the first general hypotheses. I am aware though of the immensity of the space which lies before us and the paltriness of the equipment with which to look.

Recognising Life

How do we know that our complex system is a living system? There is no test equivalent to the Turing Test of AI. All the definitions of life are inadequate (see for instance [*Farmer and Belin*, 1991; *Peacocke*, 1983, chapter 1]) and we are left with ourselves as intuitive arbiters of the living from the non-living [*Gabor*, 1990]. I suggest we wholeheartedly accept our own ability to recognise life in any form, so that the test of the development of artificial life is our own reaction. If a living system is created, we will not be able to switch it off, anymore than we could destroy the rain forest.

A more scientific approach, than our own intuition, is to propose that there will be certain organizations during the development of life which are common to all living systems, natural and artificial. If we do not accept this middle path within AL, then we are left with the two extremes: either artificial life has nothing in common with natural life, in which case, how will we recognise it as life; or artificial life is identical to nature, in which case surely, we are only modelling life not creating it. On the middle way we look for those 'milestones' on the path of Life which are common to all life streams in every medium of development. I suggest that these milestones will represent abstract organizations of structure or behaviour essential to the development of Life in general, such as perhaps, the cell, cell differentiation, multicellular diversification, metabolism, reproduction, parasitism, etc..

Biological Analogy

The middle path of analogous organization between biology and AL permits us to draw upon the rich language of biology so that we may describe qualitatively the types of behaviour demonstrated by our computer-based complex systems. Without this impudent and liberal use of biological analogy and metaphor we will miss the great potential for insight, inspiration and intuition afforded by the natural world.

Although by using such language we are in great danger of over promoting our systems, without it we are left with a very colourless terminology for description. Even more importantly, unless we attempt to equate complex systems with biological systems then no parallels can be drawn, artificial life ceases to be an accurate name for the goals of the field an we miss an unrivalled opportunity to appreciate the immense complexity of biological systems.

All is Life

In a living system, there must be a distinction between the organism and its environment, yet the organism must be constructed from the materials present in the environment and interact with it, or rather, through it with other organisms. It is tempting to think of the environment as non-living physical or chemical substance populated by islands of living substance – the organisms. However, it is truer to conceive of the environment as made almost totally of living substance; only certain resources such as water for drinking, sunlight for photosynthesis, rock faces for attachment are physical or chemical.

The division between the living and physical environments is blurred by the organisms themselves. Slowly the physical world is replaced by the products of the biological world. These may be the remains of living organisms as in oil deposits or soil humus, or they may be the biochemical secretions produced by organisms to attract mates, mark their territories or digest prey, etc..

We could consider the entire environment to be a block of messages. In such a world of 'biochemical' messages we should see emerging the behaviour between individuals which constitutes a working ecosystem. A successful development of an ecosystem from a set of informational instructions opens a new view upon the organization of ecologies by their means of communication and would view intelligence as a measure of the utilisation of the biological information available within the ecosystem. We could even look for the beginnings of language through the evolution of messages. This might be looked on as the same hypothesis that cognition develops from the ecosystem [*Gibson*, 1979], but from the other direction, i.e. the ecosystem developing from the inter-communication of its organisms.

Econiche Formation

In all AL systems to date the environment has been very homogeneous such as a grid or maze. Some have put artificial barriers into their worlds e.g. the semi-permeable membranes of [*Werner and Dyer*, 1990], in order to simulate geographic isolation of populations. However what we would like to see is the organisms actually transforming their environment making it into a richer ecosystem within which niches of a distinctly different character appear. One aspect of our own world which has not been reproduced anywhere is its fractal nature [*Mandelbrot*, 1983]. Any natural ecosystem has many levels of environment in which organisms live. For instance the oakwood has deer moving through it, whilst moles burrow beneath the surface and caterpillars crawl on the leaves. The deer have fly larvae burrowing in their hides, while the moles are infested by fleas and the caterpillars injected with wasp eggs. Finally within the guts of all three are protozoa grazing on populations of bacteria.

Open-ended Evolution

The most interesting fact of Life, is that it goes on and on. Unlike a program there is no solution to be found, no 'halting problem' to worry about. In one sense, termination of the program equals death. Langton has suggested the maintenance of a complex balance between order and chaos or cessation and dissipation as the fundamental attribute of a living system [*Langton*, 1990].

Evolution has been talked of in terms of computer search with selection driving onward to the final solution. However this is to miss the utter complexity of life by attempting to model simple allele combinations under a fitness function. The biosphere is made of millions of species and billions of individuals. From this viewpoint, the sorting of the gene pools seems only incidental to the great life games played out between these characters.

The wonder of life is that, from a limited range of physical constraints, a so far endless, variety of new forms and processes have evolved. In general there has also been an increase in complexity, i.e. evolution is not 'searching' for a solution, but *creating* its own originality. There is no reason to believe that evolution will ever terminate, nor that it will cease to produce more and more complex forms of expression; the evolution of society and consciousness can be regarded as further evolutions beyond the biological (see for instance [*Schwemmler*, 1989]).

It is this open ended evolution of new and interesting variety and complexity that the entire endeavour of AL seeks to achieve. To take the finite constraints of the system's physics and expand them into the infinite realms of living forms.

Self-Referential Goals

We cannot postulate any goals for a living system. To do so commits the great sin of teleology. However we can observe natural life, that it has developed forms and functions that are far beyond those of the non-living structures bound by the same physical laws. Life is gaining control of the physical universe. It can be said that whatever AL system you design within a computer it will not be able to walk across the room and switch on the light. In other words, that there are distinct boundaries to any universe in which life must evolve. However, we have seen natural life penetrate those boundaries again and again.

From the organic soup, cells have emerged and evolved into forms capable of climbing out of the sea and eventually walking across the room. They have even designed the light switch. Now you might argue that these boundaries are only local or relative within the entire realm of the universe. However it is just these 'local' barriers which provide all the interesting life behaviour within our own set of boundaries, the earth.

So in the quest for artificial life, we can place no *a priori* goals for the organisms to achieve, no light switch test of success can be set up. If life evolves, it will recognise its own light switches, its own goals.

Organic Flexibility

All computer based AL systems start at a disadvantage with natural life. The two physics are almost opposites in their characters. The carbon based system is a flexible, noisy world. The great problem of encoding information to be passed from generation to generation was solved through the beautiful structure of the DNA double helix and its RNA interpreting mechanism. For the rigid, constant world of the computer such information storage is no problem. Ahead of it lies the exceedingly difficult task of producing programs which can develop flexibly, *organically*.

Mutability

How much mutability can the system be allowed? By mutability is meant the change or transmutation of the programs represented by the substrate and the organisms, not the mutation rate applied to the system by, say, the simulation of cosmic ray influence, but rather the transmutation of the world by digestion, or the alteration of organisms by breeding or infection.

More complex organisms and environments seem to have a greater amount and variety of transmutation, e.g. complex biological species tend to show sexual rather than asexual behaviours, and richer ecosystems demonstrate more interwoven behaviours and exchanges. A high degree of mutability is biologically very plausible, where every action of an organism alters its environment, not just breeding, but killing, eating, digestion, movement, etc.. This must be distinguished from high mutation rates on organisms, through toxic products such as radiation which produce genetic defects, sickness and death. This high mutually interactive mutability may be an attribute of living systems. Chemical systems do not show such variety of interchangeability, even if you consider the exchange at the boundaries of reacting molecules. There may be an optimum range of mutability for generating life behaviours as Langton has postulated for cellular automata [*Langton*, 1990].

The Importance of the Individual

Each organism's life is marked by two major events:- birth and death; and this pairing corresponds directly to the maintaining of populations and ecosystems. However for the distribution of genotypes in a population, it is the parental generation which is most important. The genome of the child is dependent upon the mating of its two parents. Death becomes important in this process only if it occurs to an organism before the completion of its reproductive activities.

Evolution of populations works by a combination of these processes. The genotypes move through the population according to the natural coincidences of the organisms within the ecosystem. A fox and a rabbit are both bringing up families in the grassland: if they meet on a path and the rabbit is killed, then her whole family will die and the vixen's live for another day. If the rabbit escapes then her family will live and the fox's suffer.

All this can be well predicted at the population level using algorithms which utilise probability, samples and fitness functions, but to the individuals in the grassland, every event is an exultation of survival for this day or a tragedy for life. Life does not occur at the general level, it occurs at the individual level; it is not populations that are alive, but individuals; and each individual is involved in a desperate game of coincidences and luck which determines its survival or death at every moment. In biology we have used stochastic processes as the only means available to get a glimmer of order in a world so complex as to appear 'fuzzy'. However as Rapoport pointed out in the discussion of [*Pask*, 1962], using statistics to measure the length and outcomes of chess games is to use the wrong tool on the wrong question; we need to know the rules of the game to understand the outcome. If we are to truly create artificial life, then it can only be through letting individuals play out their bio-epics upon an environmental stage.

Vertical Mapping

Ideally we should set up an artificial environment and watch life forms evolving and emerging from the initial physics. Unfortunately, none of us can wait this long. So we must choose at which part of the evolutionary tree we wish to look and design the life forms and environment up to that point.

This gives rise to two related problems: the organisms must be 'embedded' into their environment and there must be a simple and neat mapping from their primitives downwards through layer after layer of successive biological, biochemical and physical primitives, finally ending in atomic processes. The problem of many AL systems (if not all!) pointed out by [*Jefferson et al.*, 1990, page 29] is that they do not have this potential mapping; their behavioural primitives such as 'move' or 'eat' are just symbols in code. When we are designing the physical conditions of our systems, great self-discipline should be shown to ensure that non-arbitrary constraints or rules are used. This restriction lies behind the search for a 'natural' physics within the computer through which to implement AL systems. Obviously this condition is fulfilled naturally by robots [*Brooks*, 1986], but is also fulfilled by computer architectures and possibly even by operating systems and computer languages. Systems using the last of these include [*Fontana*, 1991; *Koza*, 1990; *Rasmussen et al.*, 1990b; *Ray*, 1991].

The physics of any AL system will be those laws which can be defined globally; for instance the arbitrary condition by which an organism is declared dead. The biological rules are not capable of being fixed universally; they evolve locally as each species exploits the environment within the constraints of the underlying physics: Life, whilst keeping within the letter of the law, takes its spirit to unimagined heights!

A Uniformity of Complexity

Closely related to the idea of a vertical Physical Mapping in an AL system is the idea of horizontal levels of organizational complexity. Since we do not have the time to wait for a prebiotic system to develop life forms, we must design into our AL systems behaviours and structures, as the primitives, from which we hope to develop the next higher level of life. It is only reasonable to expect that these primitives all be of the same order of complexity. This idea of 'uniformity of complexity' would be violated if, say, in a system utilising assembler code, one of the instructions employed a concept taken from a high level language such as list processing or template matching. Similarly in analogies from biology, we should presume that the Principle of Economy in Nature has produced organisms demonstrating capabilities to the fullest at their particular developmental level of complexity. So that since, for example, all neural networks are only found in multicellular animals, we may assume that the neural network is too complex an organizational structure to be demonstrated in a single cell animal. Consequently we should be disturbed by any AL system in which organisms which in one respect seem analogous to unicellular animals are designed with the capability of using a neural network.

The Cell and the Processor

So far in AL, systems have taken one of two approaches: either create a set of physical laws from which behaviour emerges (this is essentially prebiotic); or design a program representing an organism. The problem with this second approach is that the program has no basis in the underlying computer physics, i.e. could not have emerged from a computer evolution; and is essentially serial, i.e. it competes for a processor resource. This competition only disappears when each program has a dedicated processor; when the program in effect *is a processor* (just not efficiently implemented through the underlying processor physics).

So far those AL systems that make use of computer structures, e.g. [*Rasmussen et al.*, 1990b; *Ray*, 1991; *Skipper*, 1991], can be classified as program-centered. That is the organisms or prebiotic elements are created as programs which evolve and compete for processing resources. The computer memory contains the evolving programs and is both the environment and the organisms. The processor can be thought of as a central sun or energy source allocating packets of processing time to each organism. Such systems are similar to the normal stored-memory programs except that the actual code of the executing program is mutated. The program organisms will evolve to exploit the way the processing resources are allocated.

Processor-centered systems, (see [*Davidge*, 1991] for an example) are communication oriented rather than resource oriented. Each processor is considered to be an organism living within a relatively small communal memory. The resource for exploitation is the information which lies within the shared memory world. Processing resources are not a consideration, only the local neighbourhood of information and the effects of other processors upon that neighbourhood. Were a processor-centered system to be implemented in hardware, then the number of processors would indicate the size of the population, whereas in a program-centered system only the size of the memory constrains the population size. Of course, in a software emulation, we can always bypass the restrictions on the number of processors, by generating virtual processors, so the distinction is blurred. But at the hardware level the difference is important. Processor-centered systems bear some resemblance to distributed autonomous agents engaged in cooperative tasks, but all actions and communications are totally self-referential.

Natural Life	*Artificial Life*
energy	energy
atom	electron
carbon	silicon
molecule	transistor
biochemical process	logic gate
organelle	ALU, registers
cell	processor
multicellular	multiprocessor

The above tabulation equates the processor with the cell and hence with the smallest possible organism. In biology the cell stands as a 'milestone' in evolution: an 'atom of life' which cannot be divided further into parts which have independent existence. Similarly a processor (at least the *von Neumann* architecture) cannot be divided into its constituent parts and still retain its functionality. It can be thought of as an 'atom of computation'.

The cell is the first individual or organism. Outside of it is chemistry and inside of it is biochemistry. Outside the processor is a memory or environment of data, while the processor itself contains its own logical and arithmetical interpretation of that data and through its processing renders data into information. This might be likened to a biological processing of the chemical environment into a biochemical one.

Groups of cells form colonies when homogeneous and organisms when differentiated. Our parallel computers are still at a very early evolutionary stage if this comparison holds true. The specialised functions of the Cray processors might resemble the simplest of multicellular organisms, whilst the Connection machine would be more like a sponge or *Volvox* (colonies of single cells), and a network of workstations might be equivalent to a small neural network. An important question arises here: if the cell and the processor have a similarity of organizational complexity, do they also have a similarity of processing power? That is, are the cell and the processor equivalent in the amount and nature of information they can handle? Obviously they are completely different in the form of that information and the mechanism by which they process it.

Major questions of biology centre around the cell: its initial appearance from prebiotic elements; its form and function common to all cells; its metabolism and biochemistry which drive life; its formation of multicellular organisms or individuals from the colony; its division or union producing reproduction; its differentiation developing the embryo; its repair capabilities allowing healing to occur. A subset of these questions can be applied to processors, namely the initial *von Neumann* design is common to all current computers though each has slight variations; the design is implemented on a semiconductor substrate, through transistors and gates common to all current electronic devices; the mechanisms of parallel operation are current research topics for processors. The questions of reproduction and self-repair have not been addressed yet within computer science and it is here that AL and Emergent Computation could point the way. Should the comparison with the cell continue to hold on deeper investigation, then the mechanisms of nature could aid in the design of a processor with an organic flexibility. Indeed, I hope that this intuition of cell and processor equivalence will act as a source of inspiration to the design of processors based on biological analogies.

The cell should also be the basis of questions in cognitive science and philosophy: it is the smallest life form capable of perception, even perhaps of learning; it is the basic node in a biological neural network; it is the unit of light reception in the eye; it can be an individual or part of a higher individual. We might then expect the processor to also show these same functional abilities (perhaps no more and no less). Thus can the processor design with little modification display perception, learning, sensation, individual independence and group cooperation? The past emphasis on the processor executing stored-programmable algorithms in these areas might confuse our initial response.

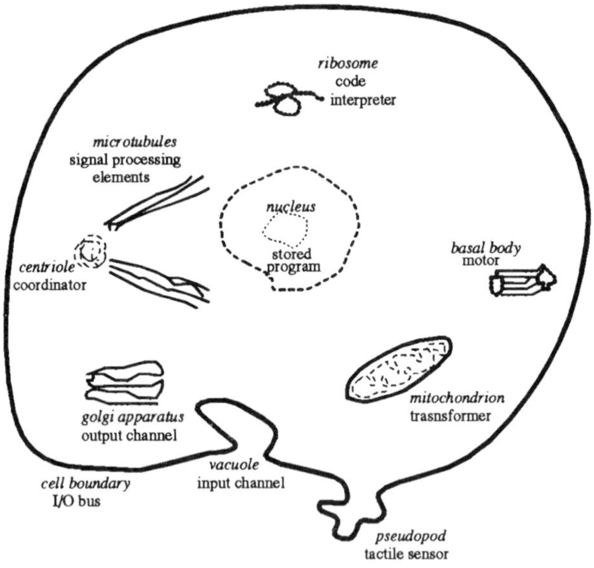

Figure 1: Stylised Cell with possible Computer Analogies

Once we accept the equivalence of the processor to the cell in AL, then our approach to AL research falls into divisions neatly paralleling biology and from which we can draw analogies and make predictions about the probable success of our enterprises. For example we can partition work in AL into the following sections:

1. *Prebiotic life*:- evolution of the processor (e.g. see [*Langton*, 1990]).

2. *Cell Biology*:- Processor architecture, form and function, metabolism of the constituent parts of a processor, processor behaviour (e.g. see [*Davidge*, 1991]).

3. *Multicellular Organisms*:- Multiprocessor cooperation, differentiation of processors into 'tissues', communication network behaviours between multiprocessor organisms.

AL systems can be judged on the correspondence between their proposed level of biological analogy and their implementation primitives. For example, a cellular automaton implementing a general atomic physics and developing replicating strands similar to RNA would be valid, but one in which the same emerging structures were said to be cells or organisms, yet lacking any processing power, would be invalid. This refers to a misidentification of the relevant biological analogy for the complexity of the system. However such an enterprise could be undertaken using computational metabolism [*Lugowski*, 1989] for each tile in the array is claimed to be a processor.

Working at a level of biological organization without tools of equivalent complexity can only produce models and not *life*. Billions of years and countless lives have passed for us to presume that anything less is doomed to failure.

Assuming that Nature exhibits the Principle of Economy to its fullest, or that you cannot beat her at her own game, then we can state the following two points based upon analogies of biological complexity at the cell/processor level.

1. Neural, motor, structural cells etc. need to be *processors*, but specialised. At least a part of their processing must be to interpret their extracellular environment and respond to it in addition to that of their specialised function. The level of complexity required for a neuron is a processor capable of developing its own connections to other processors and sensing the extracellular medium as well as performing a summation and threshold operation entirely independently of neighbouring cells, i.e. full parallelism at the level of the node. Similarly in robotics, the limb of an animoid should require thousands, even millions of motor, structural and neural processors to produce the delicacy of movement exhibited by a bird in flight, or a cat in jumping.

2. We should look for analogies of intelligence for the processor at the level of taxis or tactile response shown by single cells, notably protozoa. Light detectors are often a single spot of pigment, whilst cilia may be both tactile sensors as well as motor drives; chemical sensors are individual molecules at sites in the cell wall.

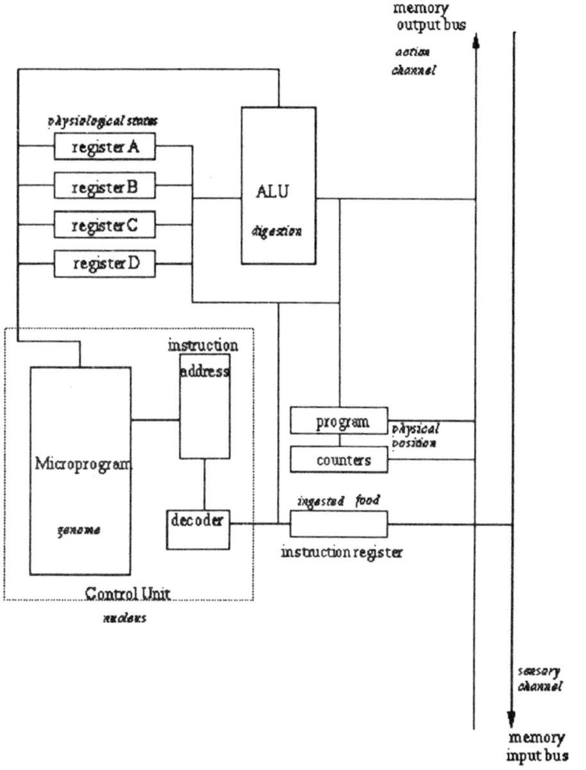

Figure 2: Processor Layout with Analogous Biological Names

Hameroff and Watt have suggested a mechanism by which microtubules could act as processing elements [*Hameroff and Watt*, 1982]. Their suggestion that the protein units comprising the microtubule act as sources, sinks and switching gates for electrons in a way reminiscent of a semi-conductor device. Further, in [*Rasmussen et al.*, 1990a] cellular automata connected in a network demonstrate the emergent properties and potential signal transference or information processing possible in this idea of microtubules. Such a model is radically different in design to the *von Neumann* architecture, but again confirms the parallels between the cell and the processor delineated in the previous tabulation. There the biochemical process was paired with the logic gate and this would be the most appropriate place in the tabulation for the mechanism of the microtubules. Thus we might expect that if the comparison held, the computer equivalent to the microtubule structures in the cytoplasm would be a massive network of reconfigurable logic gates processing signals in parallel. Although this model of cytoplasmic processing differs greatly to the *von Neumann* architecture, the concept of the individual processor still holds. The cytoplasm cannot be extracted and still function as a viable processor. It has an important relationship with the nucleus. On cell division the chromosomes are replicated and separate along with the cytoplasm. The cell is a processor which permits itself to be divided so long as representatives of all the parts are retained in the divisions.

In addition to microtubules being modelled by cellular automata, there might be a similarity here to shift registers [*Huffman*, 1956] which were suggested as an early model for neural networks [*McCulloch*, 1968]. They seem to be similar to Kauffman's binary networks [*Kauffman*, 1990].

Guenter Albrecht-Buehler has suggested a host of cellular features which could correspond to computer technology of the day. These include suggestions that: macromolecule modification might be similar to flag setting; the environment to the data bus; protein crosslinks to switches; and DNA, RNA, heteropolymers, and microtubules to elements of an information carrying code [*Albrecht-Buehler*, 1985]. Figure 1 illustrates a model of the cell as a computer, while Figure 2 reverses the view and shows the architecture of a processor considered as a cell.

In [*Davidge*, 1991], I have expanded the idea of the processor as a cell into a design for the emulation of processor organisms moving through a memory environment. These organisms will interact with the environment and communicate with each other through the processing of simple machine instructions which constitute the physical environment. If the analogy of cell and processor is correct then they will correspond to the organizational level equivalent to protozoa. Indeed I expect to show that the behaviour of the processor organisms is very similar to that of protozoa, in the limits of their capabilities to respond and learn. This latter ability is, I believe, incompatible with current processor architecture although adaptation through evolution will be possible. According to [*Albrecht-Buehler*, 1985] learning in cells does not seem to have been investigated and cytoplasmic intelligence in only two other cases: [*Adler*, 1969] and [*Macnab and Koshland*, 1972].

The processor as a unicellular organism fulfills both the criteria discussed in the last two sections on Vertical Mapping and Uniformity of Complexity. Even though I am in a sense 'modelling' or emulating the processors in software, the working of the processor is well enough described to emulate it to the electron level or to build the entire system in hardware, if this is needed to justify the system as belonging truly to AL rather than to biological modelling as required by the principle of Vertical Mapping.

Processor organisms demonstrate a great deal of locality, i.e. the organisms control the AL system; and simplicity in that the basic nature of the processor has not been modified beyond that of minor adjustments to the architecture. Similarly the machine instructions are not taken from higher programming constructs and can all be executed in a few machine cycles. This design *could* be implemented directly in hardware with but minor modifications to an 'off the shelf' processor. Those aspects of the system which are conceptually more advanced than that of a processor and its machine code, and might validate the principle of Uniformity of Complexity, are easily identified and include the allocation of space and its recovery on birth and death. In a hardware implementation this would involve the reconfiguring of the parent processors into their children within a fixed population and could be undertaken as a special routine by the processors themselves.

If the hypothesis of the equivalence of cell and processor is maintained then its implications for the design of AL systems, emergent processors and parallel computer architectures are significant.

Acknowledgements

My thanks to Phil Husbands and all who have taken part in the Alergic meetings at Sussex. This work is supported by an award from the SERC of Great Britain.

References

Adler, J., Chemoreceptors in Bacteria, *Science*, *166*, 1588, 1969.

Albrecht-Buehler, G., Is Cytoplasm Intelligent Too?, *Cell and Muscle Motility*, *6*, 1–21, 1985.

Brooks, R. A., Achieving Artificial Intelligence Through Building Robots, MIT, AI Memo No. 899, 1986.

Davidge, R. J., Bringing Processors to Life, Sussex University, DPhil Thesis Proposal, 1991.

Farmer, J. D. and A. d'A. Belin, Artificial Life: The Coming Evolution, in *Proceedings in Celebration of Murray Gell-Man's 60th Birthday* Preprint, Cambridge University Press, 1991.

Fontana, W., Digital Chemistry, in *Artificial Life: Proceedings of the second workshop on Artificial Life* preprint, edited by C. G. Langton, J. D. Farmer, S. Rasmussen and C. Taylor, Addison-Wesley, 1991.

Gabor, L. M., Judging "Aliveness": The Impact of Inborn Human Bias, 1990, Unpublished Manuscript.

Gibson, J. J., *The Ecological Approach to Visual Perception*, Houghton Miflin, Boston, 1979.

Hameroff, S. R. and R. C. Watt, Information Processing in Microtubules, *Journal of Theoretical Biology*, *98*, 549–561, 1982.

Huffman, D. A., The Synthesis of Linear Sequential Coding Networks, in *Information Theory*, edited by C. Cherry, Butterworths, London, 1956.

Jefferson, D., R. Collins, C. Cooper, M. Dyer, M. Flowers, R. Korf, C. Taylor and A. Wang, Evolution as a Theme in Artificial Life: The Genesys/Tracker System, Computer Science Department, UCLA, UCLA-AI-90-09, November 1990.

Kauffman, S. A., Requirements for Evolvability in Complex Systems: orderly dynamics and frozen components, *Physica-D*, *42*, 135–152, 1990.

Koza, J. R., Genetic Programming: A Paradigm for Genetically breeding Populations of Computer Programs to Solve Problems, STAN-CS-90-1314, Stanford University, 1990.

Langton, C. G., ed., *Artificial Life: Proceedings of the first workshop on Artificial Life*, Addison-Wesley, 1989.

Langton, C. G., Computation at the Edge of Chaos: Phase Transitions and Emergent Computation, *Physica-D*, *42*, 12–37, 1990.

Lugowski, M. W., Còmputational Metabolism: Towards Biological Geometries for Computing, in *Artificial Life: Proceedings of the first workshop on Artificial Life*, edited by C. G. Langton, pp. 341–368, Addison-Wesley, 1989.

Macnab, R. M. and D. E. Koshland, The Gradient Sensing Mechanism in Bacterial Chemotaxis, *Proc. Natl. Acad. Sci. USA*, *69*, 2509, 1972.

Mandelbrot, B., *The Fractal Geometry of Nature*, W.H. Freeman, New York, 1983.

McCulloch, W. S., Logic and Closed Loops for a Junket to Mars, in *Neural Networks: Proceedings of the School on Neural Networks, June 1967 in Ravello*, edited by E. R. Caianello, Spinger-Verlag, Berlin, 1968.

Pask, G., A Proposed Evolutionary Model, in *Principles of Self-Organization*, edited by H. Von Foerster and G. W. Zopf, pp. 229–254, Pergamon Press, 1962.

Peacocke, A. R., *An Introduction to The Physical Chemistry of Biological Organization*, Clarendon Press, Oxford, 1983.

Rasmussen, S., H. Karampurwala, R. Vaidyanath, K. S. Jensen and S. Hameroff, Computational Connectionism within Neurons: A Model of Cytoskeletal Automata subserving Neural Networks, *Physica-D*, *42*, 428–449, 1990a.

Rasmussen, S., C. Knudsen, R. Feldberg and M. Hindsholm, The Coreworld: Emergence and Evolution of Cooperative Structures in a Computational Chemistry, *Physica-D*, *42*, 111–134, 1990b.

Ray, T. S., An Approach to the Synthesis of Artificial Life, in *Artificial Life: Proceedings of the second workshop on Artificial Life* preprint, edited by C. G. Langton, J. D. Farmer, S. Rasmussen and C. Taylor, Addison-Wesley, 1991.

Schwemmler, W., *Symbiogenesis: A Macro-Mechanism of Evolution: progress towards a unified theory of evolution*, Walter de Gruyter, Berlin, New York, 1989.

Skipper, J., The Computer Zoo — Evolution in a Box, in *First European Conference on Artificial Life*, 1991, These Proceedings.

Werner, G. M. and M. G. Dyer, Evolution of Communication in Artificial Organisms, University of California, UCLA-AI-90-06, Los Angeles, November 1990.

ANIMAT'S I

Hugues Bersini
IRIDIA - CP 194/6
Universite Libre de Bruxelles
50, av. Franklin Roosevelt
1050 Bruxelles - Belgium

ABSTRACT

Two waves of criticism directed against a same target: AI or cognitive models based on propositional representation, inferential and search mechanisms have long undergone a partial amalgamation. Nevertheless, although initially crossing their road, these two criticisms diverge in the middle of it. They will be labelled "Animat" and "SynSub" (for "Syntactic Subjectivism"). The animat movement disputes traditional practices in AI and emphasizes the role of sub-cognitive sensori-motor processes to the detriment of high-level rational cognition. Members of the second movement resist to the new fashion behaviorist pressure exerted by the first movement and defend an intermediary position on the behaviorist/cognitivist axis. This position obtains when relaxing the preponderance attributed to the external reality in the mind/world interaction feeding our mental representations. In substance, the paper will successively present the two movements, will try to clarify why their target sharing and the ambiguity of their manifesto are responsible for a incorrect merging, and will all along overview embryonic methodological approaches which aim at satisfying both opponents.

1 INTRODUCTION

Two waves of criticism directed against a same target: AI or cognitive models based on propositional representation, inferential and search mechanisms have long undergone a partial amalgamation. Nevertheless, although initially crossing their road, these two criticisms diverge in the middle of it. They will be labelled "Animat" (Winston, 1990) and "SynSub" (for "Syntactic Subjectivism"). In substance, the paper will successively present them, will try to clarify why their target sharing and the ambiguity of their manifesto are responsible for a incorrect merging, and will all along overview embryonic methodological approaches which aim at satisfying both opponents[1].

The animat movement disputes traditional practices in AI and emphasizes the role of sub-cognitive sensori-motor processes to the detriment of high-level rational cognition. Irritated by the invasion of abstraction, logic, problem-solving, planning, reasoning on the whole territory of human behavior study, this movement yearns for the behaviorist and cybernetic trends and pleas for the reactive coupling of "intelligent systems" with the real world rather than with a symbolic so-called representation of it. These systems should be situated in the same world we are situated in because as stated by Brooks (1991) there is no better model of the world than the world itself. Several advocates of this animat or robotic functionalism would like to see the Turing test extended to the low-level intimate coupling with the world. They are Brooks (1990, 1991), Harnad (1990), Winston (1990), Chapman and Agre (1987). A good compilation of works defending these ideas is in (Maes, 1990).

What is strongly questioned is the necessity that some propositional representation of the environment characterizes the actor's mental state prior to the act. As originally stressed by Dreyfus (1972), a large part of human behaviour does not need any propositional representation beyond the direct perception of the environment he interacts with. In such cases, the environment is taken for granted and does not correspond to any explicit mental state but something outside of the head which precisely because it is not problematic does not deserve any complementary thoughts

[1] Since French epistemology has always shown large interest for reflexions associated to the SynSub movement, the paper contains French philosophical quoting. Out of respect for the authors, I did not attempt any approximate translation.

(Suchman, 1987; Coulter, 1989). The representation required for achieving a certain goal is entirely dependent and elaborated from the environment stimuli. No mental "abstract projection" is necessary to anticipate, to validate or to plan the pursuit of the current attitude. If casting out reflexology is one of the things that cognitive science can be proud of (Fodor, 1990) may be it has been a bit too far. When Brooks (1990, 1991) attacks the notion of representation, he refers to the traditional, un-grounded propositional representation AI is used to and not to the output of the perceptual modalities which contributes without any thinking aids to an important part of human behaviour.

Such behaviours consist in adapted, automatized reactions to the worlds, triggered by specific environment features and by implicit motivations. More like in a classical cybernetic loop, the resulting action will be a straight function both of the external stimuli and of an internal state encoding intentions and current assessment of the situations. It is because this type of behaviour brings human closer to other members of the animal kingdom that this non-anthropocentric direction (Preston, 1991) connects AI to Artificial Life and justifies the label "Animat". Now as it often occurs when defending counter-current ideas, two attitudes are possible: a weak, conciliatory and a strong, radical. The weak one is the so-called ecumenical trends: nothing is basically misguided with the cognitive roads of AI, not the same problems are addressed: problem solving deals with human problems, the game of chess has nothing to do with reaching a target while avoiding obstacles, the "intelligence" of AI refers to the intelligence of the human example not of the software engineer. The animat movement cares for the low-level behaviours shared with animals and animals don't play chess (Brooks, 1990).

The counter-reaction might even be sharper: if you want any cognitive system to engage in low-level activity and be situated in the world, it is simple to rely on the same production rules as the ones expert systems are composed of. Just compile the rule "IF mice-in-front-me THEN eat-it" and the trick works for the simulation of the cat behaviour, and if you feel annoyed by the linguistic content of the rule just replace it by "IF 10001001 THEN 010001111" whatever coding you want keeping aware that the premise role is only to index the real mice namely to match the perceptual apparatus output. The problem arisen from this counter-reaction is that the rules modifications required for an eventual connection to the sensori-motor apparatus: parallel rules, with real value premices, firing simultaneously, without need for search, control i.e any separate syntactic machine, and whose inference strength may be adapted, will bring the resulting system very close to connectionism or Holland's classifier system and will make it to loose its "AI authenticity". Since at the end any system is always Turing-machine equivalent, the problem is not the use of rules but rather how are they used.

The conciliatory attitude views planning, that is reasoning in a world model, as an intermittent contribution to the continuous flow of activity. Plans are resources the actor can rely on in continuously redeciding what to do (Chapman and Agre, 1990). A previous paper (Bersini, 1990) largely influenced by phenomenological and ethnomethodoligal writings discussed the notion of "breakdown" (Winograd and Flores, 1986) and presented a preliminary model. Breakdowns contribute to a better understanding of the circumstances in which an actor stops acting and engages in problem solving. They are behavioral occurrences characterized by surprise, uncertainty or apprehension. They are due to sudden ruptures, like an unusual alternative or an expectation failure, in sensori-motor automatisms that are normally adapted to a situation. They provoke a de-coupling of man with his environment which is amplified by he appearance of symbolic representations of the world and the reasons for the interactions. These representations allow to transcend the present through remembrance of previous actions and anticipation of the next ones. The conciliator asserts that nothing prevents the study of post-breakdown attitudes independently on the pre-breakdown ones, time and further analysis will join the two in a final uninterrupted flow of situated activity. The strong "animatist" denies this and considers the study of representations to make sense only in the context of situated activity because of their intricate correlation to perception, to movement, to implicit motivations, etc... (See Clancey, 1991).

Broadening his refusal to neglect low-level activity in the explanation of high-level one, the strong animatist considers that any high-level symbol and reasoning find its roots in the sensori-motor low level and that it turns impossible to study the footprint without the study of the foot itself. For instance, there is no genuine way to possess, understand and reason with the concept "chair" without having seen it and having sat down, etc... The study of the intelligent being in each of us is impossible if by-passing the evolving animat present in each of us. No program will ever substitute for the missing situatedness nor for the world imprint in our mental substrate. Knowledge is operational (not figurative) and ontological, the right and only approach is situated, bottom-up and emergent.

However, either weak or radical, this growing animat community expresses the need for autonomous systems capable of "being-in-the-world" without any programmer assistance. Any AI program with cognitive claims should perceive, act and ground its representations in the surrounding world. In substance two important concerns characterize this movement: behaviour rather than excessive rationality and autonomy rather than programmer dependency.

Confusion arises when noticing that similar claims: autonomy, anti-representationalism ... are equally put forward by a second group of critics which will be qualified here as SynSub ("Syntactic Subjectivism") (Maturana and Varela, 1987; Edelman and Reeke, 1988; Clancey, 1991; Lakoff, 1987; Johnson, 1987; Rorty, 1981). Anyone will agree, except the last survivor of the solipsistic tribe, that mental representations result from a two actors interaction: the mind and the external reality. Our world is represented both in perceiving it and in thinking about it. Why then such allegation for whatever machine or animat subjectivism and to what extent this new manifesto leads to a non conformist position in comparison with traditional AI and even the behaviour-based approach previously advocated ?

Members of this second movement resist to the new fashion behaviorist pressure exerted by the first movement and defend an intermediary position on the behaviorist/cognitivist axis. This position obtains when relaxing the preponderance attributed to the external reality in the mind/world interaction feeding our mental representations. This interaction remains essential but not determinant any more because cognitive systems are capable to escape from the environment instructive imprint through self-organisation processes. These processes make information encoded in the brain to be constraint by the environment but no more extracted from it[1]. Piaget's constructivist philosophy (1937, 1967) comes very close not only through its insistence on the "operationality" and the sensori-motor roots of knowledge but also the self-structuration process which shapes the encoding of new mental schema[2]. Following in constructivist wake, several authors speak of information created instead of given by the environment (Clancey, 1991; Edelman and Reeke, 1988) thus locate meaning mainly in the head. As will be discussed later, the inside content can be independent on the outside to different degree: from an impoverishment to an enrichment even to a transformation of the encoding mechanism.

Now the divergence of these two movements must be enlightened. The quest of autonomy advocated by the SynSub movement does not attack the programmer preponderance (in favour of a straight environmental coupling) but rather the environment preponderance in this coupling. The anti-representationalist claim has nothing to do with the encoding materials: propositions rather than binary string or numerical values (the debate "symbolic vs sub-symbolic") but rather undermines the isomorphic nature of this

---

1 L'activité de l'esprit apparaît comme une activité proprement interne, c'est à dire qu'au lieu de subir la nécessité d'une contrainte extérieure, elle trouve en elle les ressources de son développement. En un mot la liberté est le caractère qui définit l'esprit (Brunschvig, *Introduction à la vie de l'esprit*, 1900).

2 Cinquante ans d'expérience m'ont appris que la connaissance ne résulte pas de simples enregistrements d'observations, sans une activité structurante du sujet (Piaget, *Psychologie et Epistémologie*, 1950).

coupling. Situating and adapting animats to their environment fully satisfies members of the first movement but not sufficiently members of the second movement whose preoccupation remains the nature of this coupling. No future for a methodological solipsism but no more future for a naive methodological objectivism. This intermediary position keeps in line with Varela's "enactive" (1989, 1991) approach which studies vision respecting simultaneously an experentialist and an ecological perspective that is to say vision studied in relation with the perceptual apparatus, the previous experiences and the cognitive state of the viewer but always in the context of its ecological embodiment[1] .

2 ANIMAT

An increasing number of works treat and simulate the pre-breakdown reactive and automatic cognitive processes (Brooks, 1990; Maes, 1989, 1990; Ballard and Whitehead, 1988; Schoppers, 1987; Mitchell, 1990; Firby, 1987; Georgeff and Ingrand, 1989; Malcom and Smithers, 1990). Roughly, these simulations consist in the computation of a specific mapping from the set of possible situations and some internal states into the set of possible actions. Pre-compiled action modules compose a huge library that can be indexed both by situation features and by internal elements like goals. The goal indexing is not always allowed (see Maes, 1990) but appears to be a first important step in the SynSub direction. These action modules can be either elementary actions or small networks whose indexing releases a pre-ordered sequence of actions. These modules are generally interconnected by inhibitory or excitatory links to constitute finally a distributed and decentralized subsumption architecture (Brooks, 1990) close to spreading activation mechanisms. On account of the conjunction of various cognitive prerogatives which are the parallelism and speed, the content-addressability of memory, the robustness to damage and noise, the implicit inferential motor, the neuronal inspiration, the generalization performance and the adaptive capabilities, connectionism is cut out for implementing such behavioural architectures. If connectionism-like structure and functionalities turn to be necessary elements of the animat achievements, they remain however not sufficient with respect to the subjectivist claims.

As a rule for animat design the environment assumes a substantial role. Actions are directly associated to environment features without intermediary reasoning steps. Actually the way environment data match the indexing elements of action modules requires perception stages to treat and transfer crude external stimuli into action modules calling conditions. With regard to these intermediary stages a lot of behaviour-based approaches are tricky. They suppose a simulated closed-world environment where every external feature is abstracted and coded in the same way as the indexing elements. Then no real perception is required. Obviously these approaches give rise to fantastic problems when the models leave their artificial and closed environments to interact with the real world where a bounded and "pre-symbolized" picture does not make sense.

These models relying on isomorphic principles, that is to say states of mind matching states of the world, are still on the representationalist or objectivist side. They maintain the notion of representation as a faithful image of something that pre-exists and makes sense independently on the representational apparatus. They suppose a one-to-one correspondence between mental representation and external reality in which cognitive structures replicate environment structures. The perception mechanism passively receives this information to perform an approximate matching with the high-level structures and to base the following behaviour on it.

[1] La plus importante acquisition de la phénoménologie est sans doute d'avoir joint l'extrême subjectivisme et l'extrême objectivisme dans sa notion du monde ou de la rationalité. La rationalité est exactement mesurée aux expériences dans lesquelles elle se révèle. Il y a de la rationalité, c'est-à-dire: les perspectives se recoupent, les perceptions se confirment, un sens apparaît. Mais il ne doit pas être posé à part, transformé en Esprit absolu ou en monde au sens réaliste. Le monde phénoménologique, c'est non pas de l'être pur, mais le sens qui tranparaît à l'intersection de mes expériences... (Merleau-Ponty, *Phénoménologie de la Perception*, 1945).

3 PERCEPTION

In the still growing set of perception models, it is remarkable to notice the omnipresence of the objectivist attitude. Any model of vision, from the Gregory's schematic approach to the Gibson's ecological one, going through the property list, the picture-grammar or the Waltz' connectionist methodology is in keeping with a representationalist or objectivist position. All these approaches could be, for argument's sake, crudely sketched by considering the micro-world to perceive as a set of features W0 = {w1,w2, ..., wn) which can undergo successive transformations or readjustments W0 --> W1 --> .. --> Wi to match finally a set of cognitive structures R = {R1,R2, .., Rm}, each of these structures being in large part characterized by the same descriptive features Rj = {w1, ...}. In short, vision turns to be a mechanism of correspondence: WxR. Even one of the most impressive study of vision from Marr and his colleagues (Marr, 1982; Ullman and Koch, 1987) respects this scheme: *A representation is a formal system for making explicit certain entities or types of information, together with a specification of how the system does this. And I shall call the result of using a representation to describe a given entity a description of the entity in that representation (...) Vision is a mapping from one representation to another* (Marr, 1982).

In Marr's model, initial representations are two dimensional arrays of intensity values. Intermediary information processes are necessary to transform this initial array in successive representational stages in order to perform the final top-down correspondence with high-level cognitive schema responsible for the three dimensional perception. At these three stages of the vision process: the initial matrix, the intermediary information processes and the final schematic matching, "objective" because the treated information is extracted from the initial environment imprint, severe questions can be addressed. How are the limits of the initial matrix fixed in the unlimited and changing outside world without a subject-based filtering and delimitation of the perception field? How can misperceptions (generally imputed to the intermediary processes) be explained without recognizing the influence of both genotypic and phenotypic human evolution and adaptation? How are the high-level schema acquired from an infinite, continuously stimulating and changing world when refusing a Cartesian or Fodorian innate existence (see the compilation of papers in Silvers, 1990). These three questions prepare for the recognition of a necessary syntactic subject-based determinism during the entire perception process.

4 ANIMAT'S I

The special meaning attributed here to "animat subjectivism" has nothing to see with a vivid debate dividing the AI philosophical community for years about the last private territory of mental introspection and replication. It is the still inviolate territory of "qualia" (Dennet, 1988), of "what it is like to be ..." (Nagel, 1974), of the "chinese room" (Searle, 1980), of the "ineffable consciousness phenomonology", etc... Nothing will be add to this debate and this explains the presence of the term "syntactic" preceding "subjectivism". Here the subject is indeed a syntactic subject which don't care about qualia, private intentionality even consciousness, a real and Cartesian animat. The paper basic message defends a machine which cannot be inert and simply receptive when selecting what to represent and when representing it. A machine-centred influence is required which leaves an indelible "subjective" or "individualistic" mark on the representations.

This chapter shows how recent researches whose main originality is to increase the subject influence in the vision models aim at resolving the problems stressed in the previous chapter. With respect to the boundaries of the initial stimuli matrix, the recovery road goes through active and animate vision (Brooks, 1990; Chapman and Agre, 1987, 1989; Ballard, 1991; Cliff, 1991). The focus of vision is no more inherent to the outside scene but determined by the subject instead in function of its goals, its task-at-hand, its current assessment of the situation. In brief, vision has to be treated in the larger context of behaviour and can't be isolated from perceptually guided activity (Thompson,

Palacios and Varela, 1991)[1]. PENGI (Chapman and Agre, 1987) plays a video game in a continuous and interactive manner. It relies on this animate vision mechanism in order to select what to see and what to do. One crucial aspect is the collaboration between a central decision system and a peripherical indexical-functional vision system which together throw away most of the information present in the scene to focus on limited information needed for the task-at-hand. Ballard (1991) discusses why the assumption of an object-centred reference frame moving in relation to the subject behaviour largely simplifies the computation of the various stages of vision.

In relation to the intermediary information processes, Poggio (1989) classes perception as problem solving in which an enormous account of prior knowledge of the world allows to narrow the enormous search space. Even if this knowledge is faithful to the outside world, the heuristic pruning can already be recognized as a responsibility of the subject. Obviously, all these intermediary inferential processes keep vision away from a crude behaviourist or Gibsonian ecological approach and maintain vision as a largely inferential cognitive phenomenon but the representationalist problem is still there: does the subject impact in vision result in change of content? An on-going debate among philosophers of mind (Dretske, 1986; Cummins, 1989; Fodor, 1987; Dennet, 1988, the debate proceeds in the recent (Loewer and Rey, 1991)) questions the likelihood of a crude causal perception theory which merely relies on the existence of a reliable mind/world correlation when facing the misperception phenomena. One possible way out (still contested by Fodor) calls for teleological aspects. It is because the distortion of reality induced by these intermediary processes is useful i.e adapted to a majority of situations that for very rare and ambiguous scenes a same distortion provokes misperception. There again, this anthropocentric insertion of human genotypic and phenotypic adaptation amounts to accept the subject and his situated experiences to influence this stage of vision.

It is his focus on the sole hypothetico-deductive learning mechanism that conducts Fodor (1980) to borrow a nativist position in which high-level schema are largely innate. Other views of learning are possible, inductive and unsupervised, which undermine the need for a priori cognitive structures. It is worth mentioning connectionist unsupervised learning approaches (Kohonen, 1988; Grossberg, 1988) because, in a sense, the neural net exhibits large autonomy while encoding and organising its experiences. Standing apart from Kohonen and a lot of unsupervised connectionist techniques, but in agreement with Piaget (whose insistence on the subject structuring and self-equilibration during learning is well known), Grossberg's ART (1988) treats learning as a recurrent mechanism. The presence of separable and plastic top-down connections is responsible for this SynSub structuring (the subject intervention is often achieved by means of feedback connections). These connections are responsible for an approximate-matching phase which precede any new encoding. Learning is function of what is already learnt. If Grossberg's work is well grounded in cognitive sciences, advantages of this SynSub insertion on other unsupervised connectionist techniques are numerous: no deterioration of memory in response to many arbitrarily input, stabilisation, regulation of learning by attention focus, variable speed of learning ...

However, in spite of this bidirectional architecture which improves the organisation of the classes and the learning dynamics, the basic information content is always supposed to belong to the environment input and no amount of rearrangement and recombination of existing elements will ever transcend the assumptions made in representing these elements (Winograd and Flores, 1986). If a realistic/solipsistic axis was conceived to locate these connectionist inductive methods, the whole set would still be very close to the realistic pole.

Now researchers like the adherents to a neuronal selectionist scheme make important steps in the solipsistic direction (Edelman and Reeke, 1988). In fact, selectionism is an

[1] La perception est exactement une anticipation de nos mouvements et de leurs effets (...) Bien percevoir, c'est connaître d'avance quel mouvement j'aurai à faire pour arriver à ces fins. Celui qui perçoit bien sait d'avance ce qu'il a à faire (Alain, *Eléments de philosophie*, 1910).

extremist counter-reaction to instructivism because the environment impact amounts to the selection of something that pre-exists in the brain. Chomsky (1980) called in question the classical instructivist view of learning (either by the supervising teacher or by the unsupervising data) within this new perspective. Selectionists refuse to see the organism as a receiver but rather as a creator of criteria leading to information (Edelman and Reeke, 1988, Rosenfield, 1988; Clancey, 1991). Mental categories are not pre-existing in the environment but must be invented by each individual while interacting and adapting to his environment. In addition, the lack of autonomy and subject interferences in the encoding of the environment interactions denies any "individualistic perspective" (Merleau-Ponty, 1945). What states of neuronal activity are triggered by the different perturbations is determined in each person by his individual structure and not by the feature of the perturbing agent (Maturana and Varela, 1987). The study of perception should re-centre the subject because mental representations are not independent on the individual mental structures and personal experiences (Sacks, 1988; Rosenfield, 1988).

This re-updated interest for notions like, situatedness, reactivity, autonomy is not leaving unconcerned the AI methodological community and applications based on reinforcement learning (a twin brother to selectionism) (Barto, Sutton and Anderson, 1983; Sutton, 1990) tackle systems which, to satisfy internal needs, interact with an environment whose responsibility is limited to punish or reward the system. Some recent approaches exhibit an on-line map building competence (Mataric, 1990). This building is incremental and function of the environment interactions (the constructivist flavour is easy to perceive). The resulting map grounds the planning intermittent support to the more automatic behaviours (Sutton, 1990).

Two distinct interpretations can be attributed to the notion of "self-organisation" with different location on the realistic/solipsistic axis: in the unsupervised learning community: self-clustering of a continuous flow of data, sill very realistic, in physics of complex systems: self-creation of new way-of-being in reaction to environment perturbation (akin to bifurcations), closer to the solipsistic pole[1].

5 THE IMPACT OF PHYSICAL SCIENCES

Highly non-linear complex systems (and the brain is one of them) are capable of a fantastic autonomy when reacting to environment stimuli. Morin (1990) analyses the connections among complexity, autonomy and reactivity to the world. The more complex a system is the larger its instability and reactivity to external stimuli. An external perturbation as such does not impose its information content to the system but amounts to a simple incident whose system draws profit for discovering alone a new way of being. This self-organisative capacity is generally due to the presence of feedback. A system with internal loops guarantees its own causality, its autonomy. The brain possesses a very large amount of feedback connections (Thompson, Palacios and Varela, 1991) and in the connectionist community, the addition of such connections already serves a lot of functions (Bersini, 1990): pattern completion, selective attention, attractor dynamics, abductive reasoning, sequential processing, conception of state machines, short term memory, oscillatory behaviour etc... So far, the type of connectionist dynamic which has most interested researchers was dissipative with local stability, but today an increasing number of works are emphasizing and exploiting other dynamics: oscillatory and chaotic (Skarda and Freeman, 1987; Baird, 1990)[2].

Morin's philosophical analysis echoes the study done by Prigogine and Stengers (1988) on the dissipativity and the instability

---

[1] Dans les systèmes complexes, la subjectivité devient catégorie logique et organisationelle capitale qui caractérise l'individualité vivante et est inséparable de l'auto-organisation (Edgar Morin, *Science avec Conscience*, 1990).

[2] La cervelle est l'objet / la chose / du monde où le maximum de conséquences répond dans le plus grand nombre de cas au minimum de fait / d'action / et d'énergie - (et voici encore une définition de la psychologie -). Il n'y a pas de système où un petit événement se change plus aisément en cataclysmes - mais c'est à cause de l'attente, des accumulations qui sont là (Valery, *Les Cahiers*, 1922).

characterizing complex systems. It is the intrinsic activity of the system which determines the relations to maintain with the environment and not the other way round.

The neurophysiological experiments of Skarda and Freeman (1987) constitute a critical turning point in the development of the SynSub movement. The role of feedback, bifurcations, oscillatory and chaotic behaviors, (see Baird, 1990) to learn and to retrieve odor-specific information was the subject of an interesting debate (in the comments following the article (1987)). Unfortunately, a large part of this debate focused on the functional encoding of the symbols: binary string with precise address in a Von Neuman machine, a fixed point attractor in a dissipative recurrent net or an oscillatory dynamic exploiting chaos for its benefic destabilizing effect, while the sensible point should have been the encoding conversion from static input to oscillatory output. Indeed conclusive statements of Skarda and Freeman about the exploitation of recurrent nets for pattern completion gives indication of their scepticism with regard to the objectivist position: *The problem is epistemological; we do not know what a completed pattern is nor, we suspect, does the brain ... Most generally, these neural activity patterns are generated from within ... Whatever meaning they have is embedded in the self-organizing matrix of the entire brain.*

As a matter of fact the origins of the SynSub concepts falls to biology by right and an important biological tradition, from Monod to Atlan (1979), has for long discoursed on the self-organisative properties of biological systems. *The study differentiating the biological object from an artefact has to consider the fact that the structure of a living being results from a process totally different because it owes nearly nothing to the action of external forces, but everything, from the general form to the least detail, to "morphogenetical" actions internal to the object itself (...) This structure gives evidence of an autonomous determinism, precise, rigourous, implying a "freedom" almost total regarding external agents or conditions, capable obviously to alter this development, but not to superintend it, not to impose on the living object its organisation* (Monod, 1970).

Maturana and Varela (1987) have carried on this tradition by exploring biological systems capacity to create their own world of experience. The more recent Varela's enactive approach (1989, 1991) maintains the interest on self-organisative properties but lays emphasis on the need to situate these systems in their environment. The advocate viewpoint demands to explore this constructive tendency in an operational and ecological context[1].

6 CONCLUSIONS

Rather than attempting a synthesis of the paper inflationary developments, the conclusive statements will still widen it and glance through physical sciences epistemology. It is worth to point out the current counter-direction taken by cognitive sciences in comparison with physical sciences. In Mind's I, Hofstadter and Dennet (1981), discussing the Morowitz' article, called attention on a today epistemological vicious circle. In short, cognitive sciences are taking a reductionist road while physical sciences of the most reducible (the quantum level) are taking a cognitive road. A same circle has to be noticed with respect to the objectivist tendency of cognitive sciences: "ground symbols in the world", "vision map reality", etc... clearly in contrast with a more and more advocated relativist or subjectivist epistemological position in physical sciences (Laudan, 1990)[2] .

Referring to the Copenhagen interpretation of quantum mechanics (Pagels,

---

[1] L'idée fondamentale est donc que les facultés cognitive sont inextricablement liées à l'historique de ce qui est vécu, de la même manière qu'un sentier au préalable inexistant apparaît en marchant. L'image de la cognition qui s'ensuit n'est pas la résolution de problèmes au moyen de représentations, mais plutôt le faire-émerger créateur d'un monde avec la seule condition d'être opérationnel: elle doit assurer la pérénnité du système en jeu (Varela, 1989).

[2] Le cercle des sciences aboutit en fin de compte à mettre en évidence ce que l'analyse de chaque connaissance particulière souligne d'emblée, mais à des dosages divers, l'interdépendance étroite du sujet et de l'objet. Selon qu'elle est située à l'un ou l'autre pôle, la science parle par conséquent un langage plus idéaliste ou plus réaliste. Laquelle de ces deux langues est-elle la vraie? (Piaget, *Psychologie et Epistémologie*, 1950).

1982; d'Espagnat, 1990), d'Espagnat considers two understanding levels of the same backstage intelligible reality: a micro and a macro level. The maladjustment of human common sense to grasp the scientific concept of the infinitely small may be explained by an updated version of Kant's views i.e a subjective slicing of our perceptions according to mental categories. However these mental categories are not innate and might result from a recurrent interaction between the mind autonomous evolving and a constraining world. The continuous accommodation of the reality would be responsible for the dissonance between scientific knowledge of the microscopic world and the perception of the macroscopic world. Seeing, we abstract reality by relying on a preliminary but evolving viewpoint which filters what is not useful and shape the remaining part to improve situatedness.

These allegations fit so well the SynSub movement presented in this paper that cognitive scientists must be very cautious when aiming at looping a loop that some physicists fear today definitively open.

REFERENCES

Atlan, H. (1979) *Entre le cristal et la fumée. Essais sur l'organisation du vivant* - Ed Seuil.

Ballard, D. and S.D. Whitehead (1988): Connectionist Design on Planning. In *Connectionist Models Summer School Proceedings* - Touretsky, Hinton, Sejnowsky (Eds) - Morgan Kaufmann.

Ballard, D. (1989): Reference frame for active vision, *IJCAI-89*, Detroit, MI.

Barto, A.G., Sutton R.S. and C.W. Anderson (1983) : Neuron like adaptive elements that can solve difficult learning control problems. *IEEE Trans. Sys. Man. Cyber.* 13.

Baird, B. (1990): Bifurcation and Category Learning in Network Models of Oscillating Cortex - In *Physica D* 42 - North Holland.

Bersini, H. (1990a): A Cognitive Model of Goal-Oriented Automatisms and Breakdowns. In *Proceedings of the 8th SSAISB Conference on Artificial Intelligence.*

Bersini, H. (1990b): Why Bidirectional Connections? *Internal Report.*

Brooks, R. (1990): Elephants Don't Play Chess. In *robotics and autonomous systems* - Vol.6 North-Holland

Brooks, R. (1991): Intelligence without Reason. In *Proceedings of the 12th Conference IJCAI.*

Chapman, D. and P.E. Agre (1987) : Pengi: An implementation of a theory of activity, in *Proceedings of the Sixth National Conference On Artificial Intelligence*, American Association for Artificial Intelligence, Seattle, Wash..

Chapman, D. (1989): Penguins Can Make Cake. In *AI Magazine* - Winter.

Chapman, D. and P.E. Agre (1990): What are Plans For? *Robotics and Autonomous Systems* 6 - North-Holland.

Chomsky, N. (1980) *Rules and Representations.* New York: Columbia University Press.

Clancey, W. (1991): Book Review Of The Invention of Memory: A New View of the Brain - Israel Rosenfield. *Artificial Intelligence* - Vol.50 - No 2.

Cliff, (1990): The Computational Hoverfly; a Study in Computational Neuroethology. In *Proceedings of Simulation of Adaptive Behaviour - From animals to animats.*

Coulter, J. (1989): *Mind in Action.* Polity Press.

Cummins, R. (1989) *Meaning and Mental Representations.* Cambridge, Mass.: MIT Press.

D'Espagnat, B. (1990): *Penser la Science ou les enjeux du savoir.* La bibliothèque Gauthier-Villars. Dunod

Dennet, D. (1988) *Intentional Stance* - MIT Press

Dretske, F. (1986) Misrepresentation. *Belief*, ed. R. Bodgan, Oxford: Clarendon Press.

Dreyfus, H. (1972) : *What Computers can't do; A Critique of Artificial Reason.* New York: Harper & Row.

Edelman, G.M. and G.N. Reeke (1988) Real Brains and Artificial Intelligence. In *the Artificial Intelligence Debate - False Starts, Real Foundations* - MIT Press

Firby, R.J. (1987) : An investigation into reactive planning in complex domains, in *Proceedings of the Sixth National Conference on Artificial Intelligence*, Morgan Kaufmann, Seattle, Washington.

Fodor, J. (1980) Fixation of Belief and Concept Acquisition. In *Language and Learning.* M. Piatelli-Palmarini, ed. Harvard University Press.

Fodor, J. (1987) *Psychosemantics.* Cambridge, Mass.: MIT Press.

Georgeff, M.P. and F.F. Ingrand (1989): Decision Making in an Embedded Reasoning System. In *Proceedings of the 11th IJCAI Conference.*

Grossberg, S. (Eds) (1988): *Neural Networks and Natural Intelligence.* MIT Press, Cambridge Mass.

Harnad, S. (1990) The symbol Grounding Problem - *Physica D*, 42 (1-3).

Hofstadter, D. and D. Dennet (1981): *The Mind's I.* Basic Books.
Johnson, M (1987) *The Body in the Mind: The Bodily Basis of Meaning, Imagination and Reason.* The University of Chicago Press.
Kohonen, T. (1988) *Self organisation and associative memory.* Springer Series in Information Sciences, vol.8 - Springer-Verlag, 2nd Edition.
Lakoff, G. (1987) *Women, Fire and Dangerous Things. What Categories Reveal about the Mind.* The University of Chicago Press.
Laudan, L. (1990): *Science and Relativism.* The University of Chicago Press.
Malcolm, C. and T, Smithers (1990): Symbol Grounding via a Hybrid Architecture in an Autonomous Assembly System. in *Robotics an Autonomous Systems* - 6.
Maes, P. (1989): The Dynamics of Action Selection. *In proceedings of the 11th IJCAI Conference.*
Maes, P. (eds.) (1990): Designing Autonomous Agents - *Robotics and Autonomous Systems* 6 - North-Holland.
Marr, D. (1982) *Vision: A Computational Investigation into the Human Representation and Processing of Visual Information.* San Francisco: W.H. Freeman.
Mataric, M.J. (1990): Navigating with a Rat Brain: A Neurobiologically-Inspired Model for Robot Spatial Representation. In *Proceedings of the SAB Confererence* - 24-28 September, Paris.
Maturana, H.R. and F.J. Varela (1987) *The Tree of Knowledge. The Biological Roots of Human Understanding.* New Science Library.
Mitchell, T. (1990) Becoming Increasingly Reactive. In *Proceedings of the 8th AAAI*
Monod, J. (1970) *Le Hasard et la Necessité* - Ed. Seuil
Morin, E. (1990) *Science avec Conscience.* Nouvelles edition sciences - Points
Nagel, T. (1974): What is it like to be a bat ? In *Philsophical Review*
Pagels, H. (1983): *The cosmic code.* New York: Bantam Book.
Piaget, J. (1937) *La construction du réel chez l'enfant.* Neuchâtel et Paris: Dlachaux et Niestlé.
Piaget, J. (1967) *Biologie et connaissance: essai sur les relations entre les régulations organiques et les processus cognitifs.* Paris: Gallimard.
Preston, B (1991) AI, Anthropocentrism, and the Evolution of Intelligence. *Minds and Machines* Vol.1 No 3.
Prigogine, I. and I. Stengers (1988) *Entre le temps et l'éternité.* In Fayard
Rorty, R. (1981) *Philosophy and the Mirror of Nature.* Princeton University Press.
Rosenfield, I. (1988) *The invention of memory, a new view of the brain.* Basic Books, Inc., Publishers, New York.
Sacks, O. (1988) *L'homme qui prenait sa femme pour un chapeau.* Paris, le Seuil.
Schoppers, M.J. (1987): Universal Plans for Reactive Robots in Unpredictable Domains. In *Proceedings of the tenth IJCAI Conference.*
Searle, J.R. (1980) : The intentionality of intention and action. *Cognitive Science,* No 4.
Silvers, S. (1989) (Eds): *Rerepresentation. Readings in the Philosophy of Mental Representation.* Kluwer Academic Publishers.
Skarda, C.A. and W.J. Freeman (1987): How brains make chaos in order to make sense of the world. In *Behavioral and Brain Sciences* 10.
Suchman, L. (1987): *Plans and Situated Actions. The Problem of Human/Machine communications.* Cambridge University Press.
Sutton, R.S. (1990): Reinforcement Learning Architectures for Animats. In *Proceedings of the SAB Confererence* - 24-28 September, Paris.
Thompson, E., Palacios, A. and F. Varela (1991): Ways of Coloring - To appear In *Behavioral and Brain Sciences.*
Ullman, S. and C. Koch (1987): Shifts in Selective Visual Attention: Towards the Underlying Neural Circuitry. In L.M. Vaina (ed) *Matters of Intelligence* - D. Reidel Publishing Company.
Varela, F.J. (1989): *Connaître: Les Sciences Cognitives: Tendances et Perspectives.* Paris: Editions de Seuil.
Winograd, T. and F. Flores (1986) *Understanding computers and cognitions.* Ablex Publ.
Winston, S (1990) The Animat Path to AI. In *Proceedings of Simulation of Adaptive Behaviour - From animals to animats, 24-28 September, Paris.*

Life as an Abstract Phenomenon: Is Artificial Life Possible?

Claus Emmeche
Institute of Computer and Systems Sciences
Julius Thomsens Plads 10
DK-1925 Frederiksberg C, Denmark
(mail to: Chr. X Alle 49, DK-2800 Lyngby, Denmark)
Claus@dasy.cbs.dk
Claus@bkb.ku.dk

Abstract

Is life a property of the material structure of a living system or an abstract form of organization that can be realized in other media; artificial as well as natural? One version of the Artificial Life research programme presumes, that one can separate the logical form of an organism from its material basis of construction, and that its capacity to live and reproduce is a property of the form, not the matter (Langton 1989). This seems to oppose the notion of a cell within contemporary molecular biology, according to which "form" and "matter" do not represent separate realms. The information in a living cell is intimately bound to the properties of the material substrate. This condition may represent a restriction on the validity of formal theories of life.

1 Introduction

The new field of research called "Artificial Life" (henceforth referred to as AL) is under establishment as a respectable domain of scientific inquiry. Like "Artificial Intelligence," it brings together people from a lot of disciplines and provokes new questions and approaches to the study of complex phenomena. The purpose of this paper is to discuss one basic notion of this research programme — the claim of medium-independence of life from any specific material substrate — and by implication, to discuss the models that are claimed to realize genuine lifelike properties.

The strong version of Artificial Intelligence is based on the assumption that cognitive functions are computational and thus in principle independent of the specific material substrate supporting computational processes. In the same way, the proposed AL research programme seems to presume that one can separate the logical form of an organism from its material base, and that its "aliveness," its capacity to live and reproduce, is a property of the form, not the matter (Langton 1989). Therefore it is possible to synthesize life (genuine living behaviour) on the basis of computational principles. The claim that life, or lifelike behaviour is possible to realize in the computational medium, I will (cf. Sober 1991) call the "strong version" of AL, as opposed to a weaker version that only claims to model aspects of living behaviour by computer simulation techniques. (Cybernetic/robotic approaches to the construction of lifelike devices with sensors and effectors (animats) or biochemical approaches to prebiotic life through *in vitro* experiments will not be considered though sometimes included in the broad AL research programme). Strong version AL seems to contradict an immediate intuition of molecular biologists, that "form" and "matter" do not represent separate realms (at least on the intracellular level), and that information is intimately bound to the properties of the material substrate. In this paper, I will explicate this intuition by an example to give an idea of the problems facing computational attempts to synthesize life and give formal descriptions of living behaviour. In a second paper I will discuss the semiotic problem of describing the type of sign-relations that is often presumed to exist within a cell seen through the perspective of molecular biology, and the sign-processes that characterizes the relation between an observer, an organism and a model of an organism.

2 Artificial Life as a Contribution to Theoretical Biology

AL research may evoke a new dialogue between computer scientists and experimentalists about a set of related questions:

1. Can we construct universal theories of life as a phenomenon independent of the specific media that life on Earth is made of, as described by biochemistry and molecular biology? (I think we can, and I think that the theory of Maturana & Varela (1980) is one such example).

2. Are there any necessary relations between the material components and the formal processual structures that characterise living systems? (I'll guess that the physical constraints on form discussed by D'Arcy Thompson (1942) and Vogel (1987) are a candidate for one set of such necessary relations).

3. Is the computational approach to biology — and the idea of synthesizing not only molecules, but whole organisms — counterintuitive to biologists only because of a prejudice that experimental intervention in Nature by the standard methods of chemistry and physiology is the only way to assess the structure of living reality?

4. In what sense may life be a computational, medium-independent phenomenon? Is life a multi-media-realizable phenomenon because it is *intrinsically computational*, or because the form of movement of *any* specific natural phenomenon (that can be described by an algorithm) can be realized by a computational set-up.

5. What kind of concept (or set of related concepts) of computation is presupposed in ALife discussions?

Part of the historical background of these questions is the way one has conceived of the relation between life and inorganic nature, and by implication, biology and physics. Traditionally, biology is seen as an empirical science concerned with local and contingent phenomena formed by natural selection, and often too complex for detailed basic explanation. Physics is seen as a science of universal processes, ranging from the smallest particles to the evolution of cosmos. This picture is highly simplified. On the one hand, some types of physical processes only occur very rarely at highly specific circumstances, and are thus equally local. On the other hand, life, or lifelike processes, may be a much more global phenomenon than the picture of present biology can tell. Considering the size of the universe, we should expect on probabilistic grounds that other forms of life have evolved on other planets, yet too far away to give access to empirical investigation (Papagiannis 1985).

The specific earthly forms of life we know about are the result of a vast succession of historically frozen accidents constrained by some general principles of biological evolution and morphogenesis, which in turn depend on the mechanisms of heredity and biochemistry. Unfortunately, neo- and postdarwinian evolutionary theory has been unable to give any satisfying account of the nature of developmental and evolutionary constraints (Webster and Goodwin 1982, Ho and Fox 1988). Thus, we cannot by the present theory of biology distinguish between possible and impossible forms of life (but for a small section of the biological possibility space very close to actual forms of life, such as the sets of lethal mutants). The genetic code, for example (specifying the transcription of DNA sequences into protein sequences), might have been differently composed. However, its presumed arbitrarity might not be due exclusively to historically frozen accidents and various external and (with respect to the living system) contingent causes; rather, some general biochemical constraints on possible forms of protein synthesis and regulation not yet understood may have acted lawfully in the process of creation of this specific code, disallowing the formation of other code tables (Crick 1968, Orgel 1968). Thus, theoretical biology could benefit from new approaches to its subject matter in order to make progress as to the general aspects of living systems.

3 Definition of Artificial Life

In this context, it is stimulating that Chris Langton proposes to characterise the field of AL as the study of "life as it could be" — so that other forms of life than those actually evolved on earth until present fall within the proper realm of bio-research. However, this extension of theoretical biology may pose some problems.

The claim of empirical extension: the biology of the possible

The first point in Langton's definition of the subject of AL goes like this: "Artificial Life is the study of man-made systems that exhibit behaviors characteristic of natural living systems. It complements the traditional biological sciences concerned with the *analysis* of living organisms by attempting to *synthesize* lifelike behaviors within computers and other artificial media. By extending the empirical foundation upon which biology is based *beyond* the carbon-chain life that has evolved on Earth, Artificial Life can contribute to theoretical biology by locating *life-as-we-know-it* within the larger picture of *life-as-it-could-be*." (Langton 1989, p.1) This is a step towards a more comprehensive view of biology, although one can discuss if present biology is merely analytic. Biologists have recognized the synthetic organizational complexity of their objects ever since the word organization in the late 18th century was used by French and German naturalists to emphasise that the distinction between living, organized bodies and brute, inanimate ones was more essential than the earlier division of Nature into the kingdoms of animals, plants, and minerals.

It is not clear what kind of criteria can be used to evaluate theories and models of "life as it could be" in a non-trivial subset of possible worlds (a general science of life in natural and artificial systems should be delimited from mere game construction and computer animation for science fiction movies). As anything is possible in pure imagination, AL has to take recourse to the earthly biology to see if a particular instance of an artificially constructed model of life has a plausible behaviour. Physically interesting models of reality should not represent violations of known physical laws (which we believe to be both universal and well defined in terms of contemporary physics). So biologically interesting models of some aspect of a living process should violate neither physical laws nor what is conceived presently to be a possible behaviour of a living system. The problem is, that the latter is ill-defined, and the computational paradigm of AL does not by itself provide a better description of the universal phenomena of biology.

Methodology and emergence

With respect the computational approach of AL and the crucial property of emergent behaviour in AL models, Langton rightly dissociates the AL research programme from classical research in Artificial Intelligence, where models are built "top-down" (general specifications of behaviour are recursively decomposed into simple algorithms), inference is sequential, and the global control of behaviour allows no emergence of really new patterns of behaviour. The computational paradigm of connectionism within cognitive science has an approach to modelling complex behaviour which is essentially the same as in AL, at least with respect to parallelism, "bottom-up" specification (recursive rules apply to local structures only) and emergence. However, the concept of emergence is ambiguous, and neither neural nets nor cellular automata models of dynamic systems may prove to be emergent under more strict definitions of the term (Cariani 1991).

The claim of medium-independence of life

The third point in Langton's definition of AL is more troublesome. It is true that bottom-up *models* of emergent properties can be said to synthesize lifelike behaviours within a computer, but Langton intensifies this view and postulates that, in fact, by these means one can *realize* lifelike properties. Thus we can have *genuine life* in artificial systems (p.32, ibid.). For example, in a model of flocking behaviour of birds by Craig Reynolds, the individual simulated birds (or "boids") are not real birds, but their emergent behaviour in the model is for Langton as genuine and real as the behaviour of their natural counterparts. Thus Langton does not claim that computers themselves will be alive, but that the informational universes they can support eventually can be alive (p.39). Accordingly, the "artificial" in AL refers only to the component parts, not the emergent processes: "If the component parts are implemented correctly, the processes they support are *genuine* — every bit as genuine as the natural processes they imitate." (p.33)

The reason for this claim can be seen as a somewhat Platonic conception of life, according to which "...the dynamic processes that constitute life — in whatever material bases they might occur — must share certain universal features — features that allow us to recognize life by its dynamic *form* alone, without reference to its matter. This *general* phenomenon of life — life writ-large across all possible material substrates — is the true subject matter of biology." (p.2, ibid.) And thus "...the principal assumption made in Artificial Life is that the 'logical form' of an organism can be separated from its material basis of construction, and that 'aliveness' will be found to be a property of the former, not the latter." (p.11, ibid.)

Thus, while the simulated birds have no cohesive physical structure but only exist as information structures within a computer (as Langton admits), the phenomenon of flocking birds and the flocking of simulated birds should be two instances of the same phenomenon: *flocking*. To a hunter or an ornithologist, or even a bird, it may seem a little strange. To a logician or a computer scientist used to handling abstract symbolic structures, it is quite obvious. The problem of theoretical biology, I think, is to deal with the living material structures of organisms and their inherent "logic" at the same time.

But even if that can be done, our *models* of the logic of living systems are not necessarily instances of the true logic inherent in the very systems themselves. First, as data are theory-ladden, so are models; a scientific model do not represent nature in any direct or iconographic way; what it represents is a theory of nature (in this instance, a computational theory with many unspecified presuppositions). Furthermore, the logic of life is a many level affair, spanning in time and space from molecular to ecological and evolutionary relationships. The physical/chemical causal processes within an organism are of a different kind, described by a different set of theories, than the processes within a computer running some programme. Their functions may be similar on some level of description, but the inherent logic of the processes, on the physical/chemical level (and probably on higher levels as well), is likely to be different.

4 Why "Strong AL" is Biologically Counterintuitive

Why does strong AL seem to be so counterintuitive from a biological point of view? Hardly any biologists can disagree with Langton when he says that "Neither nucleotides nor amino acids nor any other carbon-chain molecule is alive — yet put them together in the right way, and the dynamic behavior that emerges out of their interactions is what we call life." (p.41) But we also learn that "Life is a property of *form*, not *matter*, a result of the organization of matter rather than something that inheres in the matter itself." (ibid.) Though this is a purely philosophical claim rather than a scientific proposition, it appears to be incompatible with an intuition nourished by the current paradigm of molecular biology. This intuition says that real life is both form and matter, and that the proper object of life science is to study both aspects and their dynamic interdependence.

All living organisms on Earth happen to be made up of cells. A cell is analyzed in terms of its materials, structures, and processes, and can be seen as a bag of chemicals (each of which has its own form), and as a complex self-organizing structure containing a sequence of digital non-complete self-description (Pattee 1977) and embodying a web of structural informational relationships in time and space (Løvtrup 1981, Alberts et al. 1989). In a material world, life cannot be pure form. Molecular biology is often accused of only taking interest in the material components of the cell. The obvious answer is that, on the intracellular level, molecular biologists cannot separate form and matter, because the behaviour of the cell and its constituent molecules depends crucially on the *form* of the individual macromolecules (proteins, ribosomes, messenger-RNAs, etc.).

The "form," or biological information, of an organism is bound to the properties of the material substrate to such an extent that attempts such as von Neumann's to give "the logical form of the natural self-reproduction problem" (see Langton 1989, p.13) will encounter severe problems. This interdependence of form and matter can be illustrated by an example:

In the bacterium *Escherichia coli*, the synthesis of the aminoacid tryptophan from chorismatic acid occurs in three steps, each of which is catalysed by a specific enzyme. These enzymes are themselves synthesized from aminoacids by the ribosomes. This process of polymerizing aminoacids into protein chains is termed translation, because the sequence of the 20 different aminoacids in proteins is specified by a DNA sequence (gene) on the chromosome. In the case of the three tryptophan synthesis enzymes, the DNA regions specifying their aminoacid sequences are grouped together in a common control unit, the tryptophan operon. For the enzymes to be synthesized, the DNA regions have to be transcribed into mRNA chains. This is done by RNA polymerase which starts transcribing from the tryptophan promoter in the first part of the operon and terminates after all the genes have been transcribed. Since transcription and translation are very energy consuming processes, the regulation of these processes in the response to the need for the enzymes is highly advantageous to the cell. A sophisticated system for the control of transcription of the tryptophan operon is found in *E.coli*. The attenuation control system involves both the protein coding function and the physical nature of the RNA chain. The mechanism is thoroughly studied and shall only be briefly described here (see Landick and Yanofsky 1987).

Attenuation control is based on the tight coupling of transcription and translation in prokaryotes. The RNA leader region contains a ribosome binding site followed by a short gene encoding 13 aminoacids, a stop codon, and a non-coding region including the attenuator sequence. The latter consists of a transcription terminator, i.e., a short C-G-rich palindrome (that forms a "hairpin" secondary structure by base pairing) followed by eight U residues. The region can exist in alternative base-paired conformations (fig.1); only one of these allows the formation of the terminator. A substantial body of evidence has established a model according to which the tryptophan level determines the ability of the ribosome to proceed through the leader region, and this in turn controls the formation of mRNA secondary structure: a) When tryptophan is present, the ribosome can continue along the leader (synthesizing the leader peptide) to the stop codon between region 1 and 2. The ribosome now extends over mRNA region 2, preventing it from base pairing. Thus region 3 can pair with region 4, generating the terminator hairpin, that causes the RNA polymerase to terminate (it dissociates the RNA from the DNA so that no genes are transcribed). b) When the cells are starved for tryptophan, the ribosome stalls (because of deficiency of charged Trp-tRNA) when it encounters the two tryptophan codons (i.e., the RNA code specifying the insertion of tryptophan in the growing chain) in immediate succession within region 1 of the leader. By stalling, the ribosome sequesters region 1, so that regions 2 and 3 will base pair before region 4 has been transcribed by the polymerase. Thus, mRNA region 4 remains single-stranded, no termination hairpin is formed, and RNA polymerase will read through the attenuator and transcribe the remainder of the operon. In summary, the attenuation control responds directly to the need of the cell for tryptophan in protein synthesis.

The right timing of the events is essential. Evidence suggests that after initiation at the promoter, the RNA polymerase proceeds to a position (after the leader peptide sequence) where it pauses; this may be necessary to give time for ribosomes to bind to the ribosome binding site of the leader transcript before regions 3 and 4 are synthesized. The 1:2 mRNA secondary structure may function as the transcription pause signal.

The example shows several things. The "linguistic mode" of the cell (i.e., the instructions in the DNA) and the "dynamic mode" (the workings of the machinery) are so closely connected in the prokaryote cell that the "logic" that describes the behaviour of the cell is time-dependent and for some part implicitly represented in the machinery that reads the instructions (*pace* Pattee 1977). The argument of von Neumann that it is possible to abstract the logical form of some feature of an organism's performance (such as self-reproduction) runs into difficulties when one attempts to "realize" this form in another medium. To describe logical aspects of biological systems in order to formalize them may be complicated, though possible (and if possible, it may only be trivial aspects of self-reproduction that are formalized, as argued by Kampis and Csányi (1987)). But attempts to realize these formal descriptions in a second medium may be much harder if the implementation of the formal description does not take into account the interdependence of form and matter at the cellular level. What is realized is our formal theory, not a duplication of the original living system.

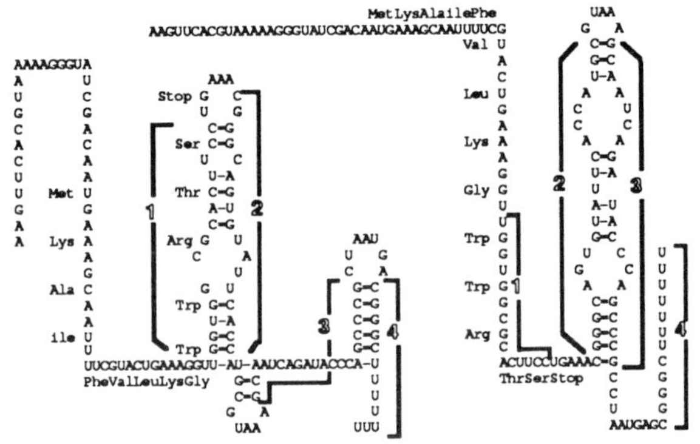

Fig.1. The alternative base-paired conformations of the mRNA *trp* leader region. The four regions that can base pair are shown. Region 1 contains the last five codons of the leader peptide. Region 4 and the last part of region 3 contain the attenuator sequence. Left: The 1:2 and 3:4 secondary structures. The pairing of region 3 and 4 generates the terminator (the 3:4 hairpin followed by the U residues). Right: The 2:3 secondary structure allows no formation of terminator hairpin. (After Lewin, 1983, and Landick and Yanofsky, 1987).

One might object to the example above, arguing that it only shows that AL models must be adapted to another level of detail to encompass the mechanisms described. One could in principle make a cellular automaton model of the interactions of the attenuation control.

But still, this would be a simulation; the model might be *formally* similar to the operon of the *E.coli* but would have no physical or causal similarity to the real system. It is often claimed (e.g., Burks 1975) that von Neumann's 1948 kinematic model of self-reproduction (the components of which are a constructor, a duplicator, a controller, and a written instruction) was verified by the discovery of DNA structure and functioning (the analogous components being the ribosomes, the polymerases, the repressor + derepressor control molecules, and the DNA). But the analogy is in no way complete, because the functions of the biological components are not separated in the real system and depend on the specific physical structure of the constituents. The dynamic information (Burks and Farmer 1984) stored in the 3D structure of DNA and in the rest of the cell's components is not represented by the formal model of self-reproduction (a central instance of the symbol-matter problem described by Pattee 1989).

5 The Implicit Functionalism in "Strong AL"

The strong version of AL is in one respect very similar to the strong version of Artificial Intelligence, or the functionalistic stance within cognitive science. They both embrace the philosophical idea of medium-independence: The characteristics of life and mind are independent of their respective material substrates. Genuine living behaviour can be realized in the computer because *life* basically is (or belongs to) a class of complex behaviours that could haunt other media than the biochemical.

To a molecular biologist, functionalism may seem rather peculiar: a philosophical doctrine of "a person who believes that study of the functioning of a person or animal is all important and that it can be studied, by itself, in an abstract way without bothering about what sort of bits and pieces actually implements the functions under study." (Crick 1989) Functionalism in cognitive science has a background in psychology, developed in reaction to behaviourism (that did not allow psychologists to look into the black box of the brain), and in philosophy of mind, put forth as an alternative to a problematic materialistic theory of identity between mental states and neural states. Though one can distinguish between functional analysis as a research strategy (Cummings 1975), explanatory functionalism within psychology appealing to computation by representations within a "language of thought" (Fodor 1975), and metaphysical functionalism as a philosophical theory of mind (Putnam 1960, Block 1980), there are some main features shared by all forms of functionalism:

a) A more or less explicit notion of functional equivalence, where x is functionally equivalent with y, if x has capacities to contribute to the capacities of the whole in a similar (or the same) way as y.
b) A more or less strict reliance on the concept of a Turing Machine.
c) The assumption that the causal structures postulated to be identical with the mental states can be realized by a vast variety of physical systems.

ad.b) Mental states are often identified with Turing machine table states; and to give a true explanation of some psychological phenomenon is seen as something like providing a computer program for the mind — or some of its subroutines. One should therefore attempt to give a functional analysis of mental capacities broken down into their component mechanical processes. If these processes are algorithmic (which is often assumed without justification), then they will be Turing-computable as well.

ad.c) It is well known that a digital computer, in principle, can be of many different kinds of components; valves, transistors, chips, neurons, or jets of water. This *multiple-realization argument* may be true for any *formal* system, given the right interpretation of the structure that implements it. But three hurdles should be noted:

1. It does not guarantee that our formalization of specific systems — whether mental, biological, or physical — can catch all the essential factors that govern such a system. There might even be aspects of the system that are in principle unformalizable. For instance, the meaning of the symbols manipulated by a cognitive process is context-dependent, and the ultimate context of human language is the natural and cultural world — that may be hard to formalize.

2. The construction (of any material kind) that implements the formal structure (a model of speech, for example) is still in need of our interpretation in order to give any meaning — a thing we might easily forget in the case of a system based on purely syntactical rules appearing to instantiate semantically meaningful behaviour. The semantics is not intrinsic to syntax but de-

pends on our conscious interpretation of the system (Searle 1980).

3. The functioning of a construction implementing some formal structure may well be functionally equivalent to other implementations (or realizations) on one chosen level of description, while on another level it may show dissimilar properties that from a biological point of view may seriously effect its chances of survival in a realistic environment. This fact shows another problem with the property of functional equivalence: that it basically is a logical property; that it is level-dependent; and that it may not cope with "real life" situations where dependence on time-consumption and energetic efficiency on several levels of organization may be crucial for the proper functioning of a system.

Though some elements of functionalism are shared by the strong version of the AL programme, it does not follow that all problems facing functionalism in cognitive science will be the same in AL. I think, however, that two parallels can be drawn.

I. Some psychologists and phenomenalistic philosophers have objected to computational accounts of mind and cognition, arguing that *cognitive activity* is intimately related to a living human being (or animal) situated in a specific environment and cannot be abstracted from the sensuous, bodily actions of the organism without losing some crucial aspects of this activity, as, e.g., the view from inside (or the *Umwelt*, i.e., the species-specific subjective universe (Uexküll 1926)). Only in theory is cognition guided by the formal rules of logic; in practice, it is subjected to a subject's specific bodily desires, feelings, material needs, interests, purposes, etc. Thus, one cannot separate cognition from volition and emotion, and these "psychical" properties are features of genuine biological processes. As the "psyche" of man or animal in this sense is medium-dependent, so is a living organism's teleonomic orientation and relation to its environment. Therefore, as we cannot have machines that "think" in the same way as humans or intelligent animals think, we cannot have machines that act and react, self-organize and reproduce (and sustain their "autopoiesis") in the same way as real organisms do. To generalize the concept of cognition to include machine as well as personal thinking leaves unanswered the question of the real nature of (the human type of) thinking. In the same way, though we could generalize the concept of *life* to include lifelike behaviour of machines, and postulate that wet organisms just instantiate some of the same abstract properties of reproduction, metabolism, irritability (or what might be selected as important features of an organism-machine), this would not reveal the specific constraints on the way life has evolved or could have evolved on Earth. And it does not tell us much new about life as it could be — not even in a silicon valley on a foreign planet. The processual characteristics of life will always be higher level phenomena constrained by specific lower level properties. The general phenomenon of emergence is probably a universal feature of life, but one must also look at the set of possible material substrates that can "support" emergence.

II. A second parallel between problems with functionalism in cognitive science and AL concerns the notion of computation and the relationship between the pattern generating properties of the physical functioning of a computer model and our specific interpretations of these patterns. Much research in what Haugeland (1985) dubs "Good Old Fashioned Artificial Intelligence" relies on *the formalists' motto*: "If you take care of the syntax, the semantics will take care of itself," i.e., if the system modelled is well formalized and the rules sufficiently strong, the automation of that system guarantees that any output when interpreted makes sense. However, this presupposes that such rules can be found, but many cognitive skills and topics (such as common sense and natural language use) resist formalization. Furthermore, the interpretation is still not intrinsic to the formal system itself but imputed by somebody ascribing meaning to the output symbols: semantics is not intrinsic to syntax. Although the computational paradigm of AL (and connectionism in cognitive science) is different, there seems to be a parallel *computationalists' motto* at stake: "If you take care of the computational setup, living behaviour will emerge by itself." Again, this presumes that the component units can be formalized appropriately and that "aliveness" exclusively is a property of a formal or computational system. But what if computation is not intrinsic to physical or biochemical systems? We normally conceive of computation as mathematical operations with numbers performed by man or manmade machines (interpreted by man). One may *talk* of the lac operon in digital-mechanical terms as a "chemical computer" and express one's amazement about DNA metaphorically, calling it "certainly the most sophisticated computer of which we are aware" (Burks and Farmer, 1984), but that does not by itself render the physical or biological world a computer or its processes computational. Anything that obeys physical laws can be simulated on a computer (with limitations on accuracy and speed), but that does not substantiate a computational viewpoint of physical processes.

One could argue that, in contrast to cognitive science that claims it possible to synthesize intelligence because the brain is information processing, AL is not committed to the view that life (e.g., a cell) is information processing; it may be, but that is not central to the possibility of AL. What is central is that the parallel, bottom-up computational approach allows the computer to support emergence of complex behaviour in the same way as a prebiotic chemical system allowed the self-organization of matter into living cells. However, that does not make the model an instance of the thing modelled. A cellular automaton (CA) model of some physical system such as weather, constructed by the same computational approach, is still not to be thought of as an (artificial) instance of weather, realizing the very causal phenomena of thunderstorms. To use a distinction of Kant in this context (as re-introduced by Sober 1991), one recognises that the model system *follows a rule* (or a set of rules, namely the ones represented by the CA state transition function table), but the natural system acts *in accordance with a rule* (i.e., physical laws). The natural system does not consult representations in order to "update" its state but behaves *as if* it had consulted a set of rules. Thus, even if the possibility of strong AL is not committed to the view that life is information processing (that key features of life are governed by intrinsic representations within the living system), admitting this distinction should moderate the claims of computational realizability of life.

6 Conclusion

If AL or some other kind of "empirical mathematics" should have any bearing on the way biologists conceive of their subject matter, the question about the reality-status of the models will inevitably spring up — from both sides: What is the biological content of AL models, and what logical or computational lessons can be drawn from the biologists' empirical garden of model species? In biology, many theoretical generalizations have often been made on the basis of a small set of model species such as the fruit fly or *Eschericia coli.* (The question whether AL models are simulations of biological processes or essentially realize lifelike properties has an analogy within the field of complex dynamics. Here, the relationship between mathematical properties and measurable real behaviour of the systems described is not straightforward. It is not always clear whether real systems actually realize deterministic chaos or if their behaviour "simulates" instances of quasi-periodicity and noise.)

I am not really convinced that computationally based "real" artificial life is impossible; on the other hand, I'm far from persuaded that it's inevitable. I am dubious, because difficult questions about the nature of life and computation remain open. With respect to the latter, one could ask if a concept of computation presupposes a symbolic representational relation of reference between the physical level of propagating signals and a conceptual level of mathematical entities (such as numbers) — such relation of reference eventually being constituted by interpreting organisms or special devices with some minimal complexity (or, to use a technical term of Peirce, interpretants) — or if the process of computation is an intrinsically physical process, that require no "organic" or referential instance in addition to the mere physical functioning of the computing system. This question is beyond the scope of the present note. The following points are not meant to be conclusive, but to express the limits of my doubt about the AL research programme. There are reasons to believe that:

1. Life is not medium-independent, but shows an interdependence of form and matter.
2. Life may be realized in other media than the carbon-chain dominated as a result of a long, natural evolutionary process.
3. AL research may contribute to theoretical biology by:
   (i) simulating developmental and evolutionary phenomena of life on Earth,
   (ii) simulating life as it could have evolved in non-earthly environments given some set of realistic boundary conditions,
   (iii) providing new concepts and models of emergent phenomena belonging to a general set of complex systems of which biological systems (under particular kinds of descriptions) may be a subset.
4. AL may inspire attempts to realize life artificially in other media by *in vitro* experiments. Such prospects

include the experimental approach of molecular biology and protobiology research. However, this is not yet the centre of interest in the present AL research programme.

Acknowledgments

A version of the argument above was presented at the NATO Conference on Complex Dynamics and Biological Evolution at Hindsgavl, Denmark, August 1990, arranged by Erik Mosekilde whom I thank for comments on an earlier version of this paper. I also thank Jesper Hoffmeyer, Mogens Kilstrup, Jakob Skipper, Benny Lautrup, Chris Langton, and Peter Pruzan for stimulating discussions.

Note Added in Proof

I can only recommend the treatise of Kampis (1991) which adds to and in several ways explicate the argument of the present paper.

References

Alberts, B., Bray, D., Lewis, J., Raff, M., Roberts, K., Watson, J.D., 1983, *Molecular biology of the cell*, Garland, New York.

Block, N., 1980, What is functionalism?, pp. 171-184 *in*: *Readings in the Philosophy of Psychology, Vol.I*, N.Block, ed., Methuen, London.

Burks, A.W., 1975, Logic, biology and automata — some historical reflections, *Int.J.Man-Machine Studies* 7: 297-312.

Burks, C., and Farmer, D., 1984, "Towards modeling DNA sequences as automata," *Physica* 10D: 157-167.

Cariani, P., 1991, "Emergence and artificial life", pp. 775-797 in C. G. Langton et al., eds., *Artificial Life II*, Addison-Wesley, Redwood City, California.

Crick, F., 1968, "The origin of the genetic code," J.Mol.Biol. 38: 367-379.

Crick, F., 1989, *What mad pursuit*, Weidenfeld & Nicolson, London.

Cummings, R., 1975, "Functional Analysis," *Journal of Philosophy* 72:741-764.

Fodor, J.A., 1975, *The Language of Thought*, Crowell, New York.

Haugeland, J., 1985, *Artificial Intelligence: the very idea*, MIT Press, Cambridge, Mass.

Ho, M.-W. & Fox, S., 1988, *Evolutionary processes and metaphors*, Wiley, New York.

Kampis, G., 1991, *Self-modifying Systems in Biology and Cognitive Science*, Pergamon Press, New York.

Kampis, G., and Csányi, V., 1987, "Replication in abstract and natural systems," *BioSystems* 20: 143-152.

Landick, R., and Yanofsky, C., 1987, "Transcription attenuation," pp.1276-1301 in: *Escherichia coli and Salmonella typhimurium. Cellular and molecular biology, Vol.2*, F.C.Neidhardt, ed., American Society for Microbiology, Washington.

Langton, C.G., 1989, "Artificial life," pp.1-47 in: *Artificial Life* (Santa Fe Institute Studies in the Sciences of Complexity, Vol. VI), Langton, ed., Addison-Wesley, Redwood City, California.

Lewin, B., 1983, *Genes*, 2nd.ed., Wiley, New York.

Løvtrup, S., 1981, "Introduction to evolutionary genetics," pp.139-144 in: *Evolution Today*, G.G.E. Scudder & J.L.Reveal, eds., Hunt Institute for Botanical Documentation, Pittsburgh, Pennsylvania.

Maturana, H.R. and Varela, F.J., 1980, *Autopoiesis and Cognition. The Realization of the Living*, D.Reidel, Dordrecht.

Orgel, L., 1968, "Evolution of the genetic apparatus," *J.Mol.Biol.* 38: 381-393.

Papagiannis, M.D., 1985, "Recent progress and future plans on search for extraterrestrial intelligence," *Nature* 318: 135-140.

Pattee, H.H., 1977, "Dynamic and linguistic modes of complex systems," *Int.J. General Systems* 3: 259-266.

Pattee, H.H., 1989, "Simulations, realizations, and theories of life," pp. 63-77 in: *Artificial Life* (Santa Fe Institute Studies in the Sciences of Complexity, Vol. VI), Langton, ed., Addison-Wesley, Redwood City, Calif.

Putnam, H., 1960, "Minds and machines," in: *Dimensions of Mind*, S. Hook, ed., New York University Press, New York.

Searle, J., 1980, "Minds, brains, and programs," *Behavioral and Brain Sciences* 3: 417-458.

Sober, E., 1991, "Learning from functionalism — prospects for strong AL," pp. 749-765 in C. G. Langton et al., eds., *Artificial Life II*, Addison-Wesley, Redwood City, California.

Thompson, D'Arcy W., 1942, *On Growth and Form*, 2nd ed., Cambridge at the University Press, Cambridge.

Uexküll, J. von, 1926, "Theoretical Biology," Kegan Paul, London.

Vogel, S., 1988, *Life's Devices, The Physical World of Animals and Plants*, Princeton University Press, Princeton.

Webster, G., and Goodwin, B.C., 1982, The origin of species: a structuralist approach, *J. Social Biol. Struct.* 5: 15-47.

LIFE = COGNITION :
The epistemological and ontological significance of Artificial Life

John STEWART
CNRS, Department of Immunobiology
Pasteur Institute
25 rue du Docteur Roux
75724 Paris cedex 15, France

Abstract.
What is knowledge? This paper proposes the concept "Cognition=Life" as a constructive alternative to the vacillation between objectivism and nihilism characteristic of Western epistemology to date. This new definition possesses several attractive features: "knowledge" is materially incarnate in dynamic processes; it is primordially tacit; "object" and "subject" are intrinsically inseparable. "Living organisms" are in turn defined as a subclass of autonomous dynamic systems; the crux of their essential knowledge resides in their capacity to continually produce themselves, both materially and organizationally. It is concluded that research in Artifical Life, by deepening our understanding of living organization, can greatly contribute to a renewal of Epistemology.

The project of creating artificial life is so fascinating that it is clearly worthwhile pursuing in its own right. In this paper, I wish to argue that in addition, we may hope that it will also illuminate other areas of fundamental importance: not just biology, but the perennial philosophical issues of the nature of knowledge and even of reality itself.

What is knowledge?

In attempting to answer this question, it is difficult to avoid the starting-point of *objectivism,* the ontological postulate according to which the real world exists and is what it is independently of any knowledge which subjects may or may not have of it. On this view, the objects of knowledge have no intrinsic relation with any cognizing subject, so that the object and subject of cognition are *separable.* It is well to recognize that in our everyday commonsense attitudes, objectivism is the "spontaneous philosophy" of all of us (in modern Western culture at least). In cognitive science, the dominant paradigm of cognitivism implicitly adopts an extreme form of objectivism, according to which the real world not only exists independently of cognition, but possesses a set-theoretical structure (i.e. consists of distinct objects with essential class properties). This extreme postulate is necessary for cognitivism, because it makes it possible: firstly, to establish the objects of knowledge on the one hand, and the subject's *representations of* these objects on the other, as clearly separate entities; and secondly, to establish well-defined *correspondence relations* between these representations on the one hand, and objects (or classes of objects, or relations between objects or classes of objects) on the other. It is on this basis, but on this basis only, that cognitivism is able to specify the "truth conditions" which give semantic content to cognitive representations: a representation is "true" if the correspondence relations are adequately respected, "false" otherwise.

What is wrong with objectivism in general and cognitivism in particular? The fundamental problem was identified (a long time ago now) by Kant in his "Critique of Pure Reason" (7) : ontological "reality in itself" is inherently unknowable. The reason is that even the most elementary forms of experience (such as sense perception) necessary to gain knowledge of the world require, as their condition of possibility, that the subject bring to the situation a pre-existing cognitive apparatus. Kant himself considered that this pre-existing apparatus consisted essentially of a canonical set of a priori conceptual categories: the twelve logical categories of Aristotle, plus the concepts of space and time. Nowadays this specific position seems overly restrictive and idealistic: the formation of the cognitive apparatus is itself a subject for natural scientific investigation, and there is no reason to suppose that it should fit into a unique canonical set of ideal forms. Nevertheless, the fundamental thrust of Kant's argument remains perfectly valid: cognition can only occur in terms of the subject's cognitive repertoire; and since, as Hume made plain (7), induction is strictly speaking impossible, this repertoire *cannot* derive directly or reliably from the objects of knowledge themselves. In other words, the categories and structures which make up the cognitive repertoire are necessarily *non-empirical.* Since knowledge is necessarily expressed in the terms provided by the subject's cognitive repertoire, it is akin to a projection; it follows that knowledge is not and *cannot be* knowledge of an independent "reality in itself".

However, in spite of Kant's devastating critique, objectivism is still very much with us. Spontaneously, we continue to believe that by some sort of miracle our knowledge does indeed correspond to an independent reality. A good example is the cognitivist "disquotation theory of truth": the phrase "the cat is on the mat" is true if and only if .... there is a cat, and a mat, and the cat *is* on the mat. The silly triviality of this theory should warn us that we are guilty here of a fallacious projection. Latour (2) has given a brilliantly perceptive account of how the objectivist illusion comes about in the case of scientific objects. Initially, a scientific object (such as an atom, or a gene) is given by theory; at this stage, it is clearly hypothetical and there is no problem. However, when a social consensus concerning the adequacy of this theory crystallizes in the scientific community, three things happen. Firstly, the theoretical object *splits* into two parts, one being the theoretical statement which defines the object, the other being a "twin" which is projected into the "real world out there". The fact that this is a projection is clearly revealed by the fact that the "real object" is (miraculously?!) identical in every respect to the theoretical object. The second event is an *inversion* : whereas initially the theoretical object was primary, and the "real object" derivative, very rapidly more and more "reality" attaches to the "object out there" and less and less to the theoretical statement which thus becomes a statement "about" the independent object. Finally, history is rewritten in the best Orwellian style, so that it comes to seem as though the "real object" had been there all along, and was simply waiting to be "discovered" for what it is. As Latour points out, these are all purely rhetorical devices. The fallacy becomes apparent if we stop to reflect that in order to validate objectivism, we would have to have *independent* knowledge of *two* terms, the "real object" on one hand and our "representation of" this object on the other. However, since we can have no "knowledge of an object" *other* than ... our knowledge of that object, this is intrinsically impossible.

This being so, how are we to account for the irresistible seduction which objectivist rhetoric undeniably exerts on us? I think that the major reason is that the Kantian critique is essentially negative: it destroys objectivism in principle, but leaves us with nothing in its place. It makes the valid point that our conceptual categories are non-empirical, i.e. that they do not derive from independent "reality" or "objects of knowledge" in themselves, but it does not sufficiently tell us where they *do* come from. In particular, in the absence of a positive alternative, it leaves us with nothing to substantiate our deep intuition (which I believe to be correct) that our knowledge is not purely arbitrary: there is order to our perceptions, and we cannot with impunity believe whatever we like. There must be some sort of "reality principle" to account for the fact that, in our experience, our knowledge is sharply constrained, independently of our will. As long as the only alternative is *nihilism* - the ontological postulate according to which nothing exists, or else (which amounts to the same) that reality is completely chaotic and arbitrary so that anything and everything is equally possible - then it is not surprising (and arguably healthy!) that we should prefer objectivism.

The aim of this paper is to explore a possible way out of this impasse by presenting in outline a theory of knowledge which is neither objectivist nor nihilist. Stated positively, the goal is to provide an account of how knowledge can be constrained by reality without resorting to a system of correspondence with independent referents. The central idea can be summed up by the succinct formula "Cognition = Life" (3,4,8). In other words, the prototypical form of knowledge is "knowing how to stay alive"; or to use a more expressive imagery, the aim is to make sense of a phrase such as Gregory Bateson's "sequoia trees *know how* to resist forest fires". Several corollary features of this approach are worthy of note:

(i) Knowledge is a dynamic process; it is not a substance which can be quantified (cf "information") or stored in books or brains;

(ii) Knowledge is primarily tacit, incarnated in material processes; it is not principally linguistic[1] or propositional in form;

(iii) The subject and the object of knowledge are inseparable. There are two aspects to this. Firstly, there is a sense in which there is no other "object" of knowledge than the subject's own dynamic existence ("knowing how to stay alive"); thus, the only "reference" is self-reference[2]. Secondly, however, it is certainly possible for an observer[3] to distinguish between an organism and its environment. Nevertheless, in this case, the "environment" becomes an "ecological niche", and it is not possible for the observer to specify what the niche "is" without reference to the organism inhabiting it - and reciprocally, the organism cannot be fully specified without reference to the "niche". Thus, in this sense also, object and subject are intrinsically inseparable. It follows that this approach is indeed non-objectivist.

(iv) The tacit knowledge expressed in the material processes constituting any living organism is very tightly constrained: myriad minor changes in organization would lead to the death of the organism. This is reflected in the biological fact that the range of observable phenotypic variation within a given life-form[4] is generally very small - the reason being that variation outside this range is not compatible with the viability of that life-form. At the same time, it is to be noted that although these constraints are implacably tight and severe when they operate at the level of any particular life-form, globally they do not determine a unique solution. On the contrary, the fantastic diversity of past and present life-forms on the planet earth illustrates the fact that these constraints are compatible with an open-ended plurality of specific forms. To put it another way, there are always strong constraints, specifying a particular form within narrow limits; but these constraints can take an incredible number of different forms

---

[1] Of course the emergence of language, almost certainly related to hominisation, adds a radical new dimension to what knowledge is. I cannot discuss this important question here, and will only note that the emergence of language does not and cannot justify objectivism.

2 This is bluntly stated, for clarity; but of course much more could be said. A complete exposition of the non-objectivist position would have to account for objectivist appearances, and to give an adequate explanation of how and why it is that human beings spontaneously adopt objectivist attitudes. The phenomenon of language certainly plays a key role in any such account; however, the limited scope of this paper precludes entering into this question here. See (1) and Merleau-Ponty's discussion of "realism as a well-founded error" (5).

[3] In certain special cases - notably that of a human being endowed with language - the "observer" can be the organism itself. (3,4).

[4] To a first approximation, within species; but to be more precise, most species regroup a number of different life-forms which appear in the form of polymorphisms, sexual and otherwise.

which is only finite because of limitations of space and time (as far as we know, restricted to the history of the planet earth). The reality principle operative in the framework of objectivist correspondence relations requires partial isomorphism between "representations" and a section of "reality"; since putatively different representations that are each isomorphic to the same section of reality are thereby necessarily isomorphic to each other, this means that objectivist reality rigidly determines a single world as a unique possibility. On the alternative view presented here, the "reality principle" is stringent, certainly, but at the same time infinitely more rich and creative: an open-ended plurality of worlds are possible, and it becomes a value-laden issue as to which of these possible worlds will be actually instanciated in the finite space and time available. In conclusion, this alternative reality is even less nihilist than objectivist reality, because it includes the possibility of values and meaning.

To sum up, it seems that the idea "Cognition=Life" presents a number of attractive features. It is therefore worth taking this idea seriously; and to this end, I wish to address a key question: what is life? Obviously, if we choose to answer the question "what is knowledge" by saying that "cognition is life", then we need an adequate answer to the question of what life is. Up until now, we have been relying on the common-sense presupposition that we already know what life is: for example, even a child knows that a dog is alive and a stone is not. However, although perfectly adequate for everyday purposes, this will not do in the present context: in order to function scientifically, we need an authentic theoretical definition of what life is. Unfortunately, contemporary Western biology, based on the synthesis of the nineteenth-century theories of Darwin, Weismann and Mendel which has led to molecular genetics, provides no answer to this question.[5]

In outline, the definition I shall propose is this: living organisms are a subclass of autonomous dynamic systems with the particular property that they continually produce themselves (8). There are thus two parts to this definition: I shall first discuss the notion of "autonomy", and then examine what is involved in the additional constraint of self-production.

An autonomous system is most conveniently defined negatively: it is a system which is *neither* totally determined by its environment (so that the behaviourist project of specifying an exhaustive set of purely external input-output relations is guaranteed to fail), *nor* solipsistic (i.e. totally isolated or independent of its environment). This double requirement involves sailing perilously

[5] This rather remarkable deficiency may well be responsible for the disquieting tendency of contemporary research to restrict its domain of investigation to the biochemistry of substances derived from entities which common-sense identifies as "living", with the result that this research arguably no longer merits the title of "biology" since it does not properly focus on the living organization as such. However, this is not the place to pursue this issue explicitly.

between Charybdis and Scylla, and amounts to a strong definition which is positive and yet likely to be pluralistic in its specific applications. It is possible to describe an autonomous system in terms of a formalism which is applicable to simulation models of living systems, and which may hopefully be useful as a guideline in attempts to build actual forms of artifical life. A dynamic system is typically composed of a finite number of elements, i = 1...n. The state of each element can be defined by a variable x_i, so that the global state of the system is given by the state-vector **x**. The dynamics of the system are given by equations of the form:

$$\mathbf{x'} = f(\mathbf{S};\mathbf{x}) \qquad [1]$$

where **x'** is the time derivative of **x**, **S** is the *structure* of the relations between the components, and f is a determinate functional form[6]. The key to the conundrum as to how a system can escape from determinism by its environment without being totally independant of the same environment resides in the distinction between the internal state **x** and the structure S. The internal state **x** is entirely determined by the equations [1] which contain no reference to anything external to the system. In general, the equations [1] specify an attractor dynamics; the various basins of attraction can be thought of as putative cognitive categories. The point is that these "categories" or "classes of equivalence" are entirely intrinsic to the system itself, and make no reference to the environment. At the same time, the structure **S** can be modified by the interactions between the system and its environment, and this will lead to a modification in the subsequent dynamics and hence to a different internal state **x** than if the interaction had not occurred. Thus, the structure **S** plays the crucial role of an *interface* between **x** and the environment, both shielding **x** from any direct determination by the environment, and yet at the same time making it possible for the environment to significantly influence **x** (and, a point of some importance for a full development of this theory, for the system to act in return with respect to the environment). We can sum up by saying that the absence of external reference results from the *operational closure* of the system (as expressed in [1]); the simultaneous possibility of significant interaction results from the *structural coupling* between the system and its environment (8).

This definition of autonomous systems is an important step towards the definition of living systems, particularly if we add the natural constraint that the state-vector **x** should neither collapse (all elements falling to zero and staying there) nor explode (one or more elements increasing indefinitely out of bounds). It is not however sufficient (which is a pity, because if it were then the creation of artifical life would be manifestly feasible!). In order to obtain a

---

[6] An example may aid in clarifying the application of this formalism. In neo-connexionist networks, the *elements* are typically automata each with binary *state-values*. The major feature of the *structure* is the matrix M whose elements, m_{ij}, are the connexion-strengths between elements i and j; *f* is a threshold function of the "field" $h_i = \Sigma\ m_{ij}.x_j$.

satisfactory definition of life, we need to add an additional requirement: the operation of the system must be such that ipso facto it results both in the dynamic perennity of all its essential elements, and in the maintenance of those relations between its elements that constitute its essential structure (3). In other words, the system must have the capacity to continually *produce itself,* both materially and organizationally[7].

We come now to the crux of the argument concerning the theoretical significance of artificial life for a non-objectivist science of cognition. Field theories in biology have had a somewhat chequered history[8]. In what must be considered an unfortunate over-reaction, contemporary biologists have increasingly turned to an exclusive concentration on a purely molecular level of analysis. As a result, the study of biological organisms as integrated systems has been gravely neglected. Thus, it is only very recently that biological organisms have been seriously viewed even as autonomous dynamic systems[9]. The results of these recent studies are promising; but when it comes to the second part of our definition of living organisms - i.e. as autonomous systems with the particular additional property of producing themselves - it must be admitted that work has hardly started. Of course there are excellent prima facie grounds for supposing that biological organisms are indeed "living systems" in the precise sense of our theoretical definition; but since even the simplest natural organisms (bacteria, amoeba, algae) are immensely complicated, we are very far indeed from really understanding how it is that they manage to achieve an autopoietic organization. The problem is that these organisms are "already there"; although by tinkering with them we can certainly make them die, we should not delude ourselves into thinking that this means we have anything like a comprehensive grasp of what is positively involved in their tacit knowledge of "how to stay alive". We are rather like children tinkering with an big supply of watches that work already; although we can certainly recognize a watch that works, and we can easily make the watches stop, this does not mean that we have even begun to understand positively how it is that the watches work. However detailed our possible understanding of purely local mechanisms - the cogs on this wheel that mesh with the cogs on that one - we are missing the overall synthetic view that relates local mechanisms to each other in an integrated whole.

7 It may be noted that the view presented here is rigorously monist: "life" and "cognition" do not belong to separate orders of reality, as in Cartesian dualism; they are immanent in material processes themselves, on the sole condition that these processes constitute an autonomous dynamic system of the particular sort we are seeking to define.

8 Most notably in the relative failures of field theories in developmental biology - and gestalt psychology - in the 1930's.

9 Most notably in neo-connexionist models of the nervous system and the immune system.

This, precisely, is where the project of purposely creating artificial life comes in. In the case of the watches, the acid test of our positive comprehensive understanding would be our ability to actually make a watch ourselves. Even if our watch was very crude compared with those of the watchmaker, and did not keep time very well or for very long, the fact that it did work would be proof that we did understand what was involved. Well might Vico say that the condition for understanding something is to have made it (7). It is also probable, although far from trivial, that in the process of trying to construct a watch ourselves, we would come to appreciate better the truly essential features of the watches made by the master watchmaker.

As with the watches, so it may be with living organisms. Even failures in our attempts to create artificial life will be instructive, because they will already inform us (in part) as to what is actually involved in achieving a living organization. To put it another way, we would be learning something about the constraints that derive from one particular application of the "pluralistic reality principle" referred to above. Success would of course be even more important[10], because it would mean that we had indeed grasped in an adequately comprehensive way how this "reality principle" works.

[10] On condition that it came on the basis of our own explicit design, and not just by blindly copying the watchmaker's model. Biological organisms are, however, so complicated that the chances of succeeding by "blind copy" can probably be discounted anyway.

In conclusion, I wish to return to the philosophical issues that I addressed at the outset of this paper. In fact, epistemological and ontological issues are inseparably related, because we cannot say anything about what knowledge is without at least postulating something about the nature of the reality to be known (9). The postulate that "life" and "cognition" are fundamentally the same thing cuts the Gordian knot that traditionally surrounds these issues (cf the inherently unknowable nature of "reality in itself" according to Kant). Since, on this view, the object and subject of knowledge are inseparable, this means that in an important sense a new "reality" is brought forth or created in each act of living cognition. In the context of artificial life, this highly unorthodox view looks surprisingly sensible: there is an obvious sense in which the creation of artificial life would indeed constitute the bringing forth of a new reality. What I have sought to show is that although it may be disquieting to envisage giving up our familiar objectivism, by doing so we can enter into a new world which is challenging, certainly, but by no means incomprehensible.

Acknowledgement.

This paper is alost totally inspired by the work of Humberto Maturana and Francisco Varela. This particular formulation of the idea that "life is cognition", and any mistakes that it may contain, are however my entirely own responsibility.

References.

1) Dumaret A. &Stewart J. (1988). *L'hérédité de l'intelligence.* Editions Dumas, St Etienne.

2) Latour B. & Woolgar S. (1979). *Laboratory life: the social construction of scientific facts.* Sage, Beverly Hills.

3) Maturana H. & Varela F.J. (1980). *Autopoiesis and cognition: the realization of the living.* Reidel, Boston.

4) Maturana H. & Varela F.J. (1987). *The tree of knowledge.* Shambhala, Boston.

5) Merleau-Ponty M. (1942). *La structure du comportement.* Presses Universitaires de France, Paris.

6) Polanyi M. (1958). *Personal knowledge: towards a post-critical philosophy.* Routledge and Kegan Paul, London.

7) Russell B. (1959). *The Wisdom of the West.* Macdonald, London.

8) Varela F.J. (1980). *Principles of biological autonomy.* Elsevier North Holland, New York.

9) Von Glasersfeld E. (1981). "An introduction to radical constructivism". In: P. Watzlawick Ed., *Die Erfundene Wirklichkeit. Wie wissen wir, was wir zu wissen glauben? Beiträge zum Konstruktivismus.* Piper Verlag; Munich.

Some epistemological implications of devices which construct their own sensors and effectors

Peter Cariani

37 Paul Gore St, Boston, MA 02130.
eplunix!peter@eddie.mit.edu

Abstract

Various classes of physical devices having adaptive sensors, coordinative parts, and/or effectors are considered with respect to the kinds of informational relations they permit the device to have with its environment. Devices which can evolve their own physical hardware can expand their repertoires of measurements, computations, and controls in a manner analogous to the structural evolution of sensory, coordinative, and effector organs over phylogeny. In particular, those devices which have the capacity to adaptively construct new sensors and effectors gain the ability to modify the relationship between their internal states and the world at large. Such devices in effect adaptively create their own (semantic) categories rather than having them explicitly specified by an external designer. An electrochemical device built in the 1950's which evolved the capacity to sense sound is discussed as a rudimentary exemplar of a class of adaptive, sensor-evolving devices. Such devices could potentially serve as semantically-adaptive front-ends for computationally-adaptive classifiers, by altering the feature primitives (primitive categories) that the classifier operates with. Networks composed of elements capable of evolving new sensors and effectors could evolve new channels for inter-element signalling by creating new effector-sensor combinations between elements. The new channels could be formed orthogonal to pre-existing ones, in effect increasing the dimensionality of the signal space. Such variable-dimension signalling networks might potentially lead to more flexible modes of information processing and storage. Devices having the means to both choose their sensors (primitive perceptual categories) and effectors (primitive action categories) as well as the coordinative mappings between the two sets would acquire a degree of epistemic autonomy not yet found in contemporary devices.

Modelling relations in biological organisms and artificial devices

A very ancient and biological notion is that the sensory organs of an organism determine the basic categories through which it perceives the world and that its effector organs determine the basic categories through which an organism can act to alter its environment. Between sensors and effectors lies some mechanism for their coordination, thereby permitting the organism to respond appropriately to some perceived state of the world. Such a framework can also be applied to analyzing functional relations embedded in artificial devices. One can talk about the informational relationships between organisms and devices and their environments in terms of the basic functionalities of *sensing*, *coordinating*, and *effecting* (or, more abstractly in terms of *measurement, computation*, and *control* (Cariani 1989)). Taken together these functionalities allow an organism or device to sense some perceived state of the world, to make a prediction for what is the best action to take given that perception, and to act accordingly. Given a set of sensors, a set of effectors, and a mechanism for coordinating between the two, such *modelling relations* can be embedded in an organism or artificial device (Uexküll 1926; Pattee 1982; Rosen 1985; Cariani 1989, 1991ab; Kampis 1991; Emmeche 1991).

Within this functional, informational framework (Figure 1), the sensory organs determine the relation between the world at large and those internal states which are affected by sensory inputs. A sensory organ makes primitive distinctions on the world by producing two or more possible outcomes, depending upon its interaction with the external world. For example, a receptor may signal the presence or absence of some chemical substance (relative to some threshold concentration). There must be at least two

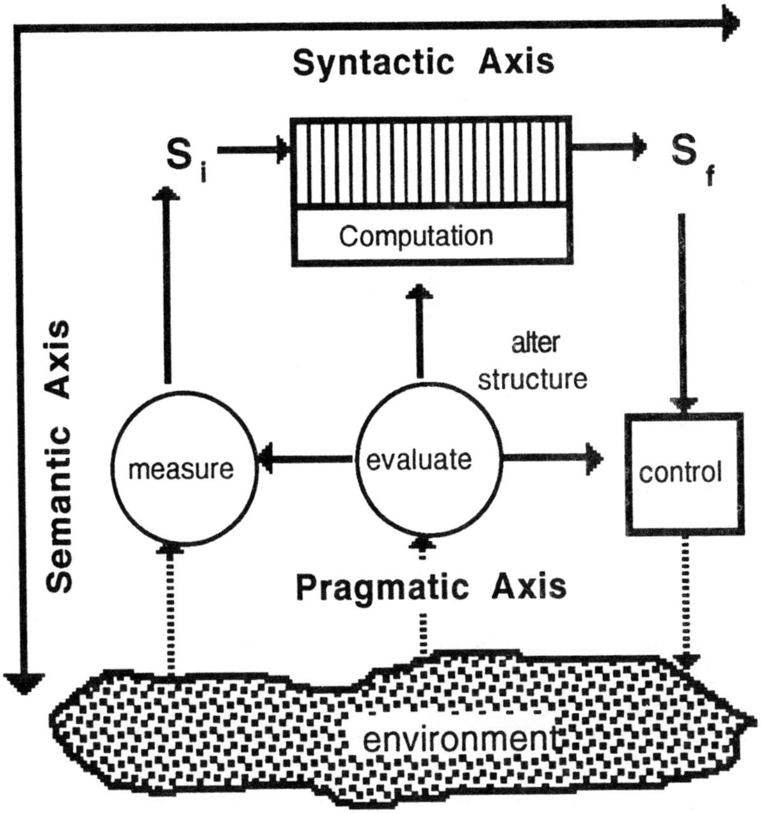

Figure 1. Basic informational relationships between an organism or device and its environment. The sensors, effectors and computational parts of a device correspond to the sensory organs, effector appendages (muscles, secretory organs), and coordinative organs (hormonal, nervous systems) of organisms. These material structures implement the informational functionalities of measurement (sensing), control (acting), and computation (coordinating). When embedded in an organism or device in the appropriate way, these three functionalities implement a modelling relation. The semiotics of this relation involve three independent axes: a semantic axis, a syntactic axis, and a pragmatic axis. The external semantics of the internal states of the organism/device are determined by its sensors and effectors, while the internal relations between those states can (often) be described in terms of rule-governed, syntactic relations. The pragmatics of devices are those evaluative structures which cause a change in internal structure so as to improve performance. In the case of biological organisms, the evaluative test is survival and reproduction, while in artificial devices the evaluative criteria are set by the designer-user to solve some task at hand.

states possible for the receptor to function as a discriminatory element -- if the receptor were always in one state, no information regarding the external world would be conveyed, the organism could not act contingent upon some perceived change in the world. The distinction or discrimination made forms a perceptual *category* having two or more possible, mutually-exclusive *states*. To the extent that different receptors interact with the world differently, so as to produce different outputs in the same situation, those receptors implement different categories, they function as different windows on the world outside the organism.

Effector organs also determine the relation of internal states and the world at large, but the directionality of immediate causation is different. While the output state of a sensory element is contingent upon some state of affairs in the external world, the external world in some way is contingent upon the input state of the effector organ. For example, the electric field strength in the vicinity of an electric eel is highly contingent upon the internal states of the eel's nervous system; whenever the eel decides to fire, a large change in the field will follow. Similarly, when a set of muscles is activated for moving, the relative position of the organism relative to the rest of the world is altered -- the positional configuration of objects in the world becomes contingent upon inputs to the organism's motor system.

Sensors and effectors thus mediate between the internal states of the organism and the world outside of it. Together they determine the external semantics of the internal states of the organism, the immediate consequences of world-states on organism-states and vice-versa. Here, the word "immediate" is stressed because the causality between sensing, coordinating, and acting is a circular one -- an action has an impact upon subsequent perceptions which influence subsequent actions, and so on (Uexküll 1926 and the "circular causal relations" in the cybernetics of Wiener 1961 and McCulloch 1989). An animal moves its head in order to better see something moving in its visual periphery which causes yet other objects to come into view, prompting another movement and more perceptions. An entire theory of adaptive control has been developed with this circular organization as its organizing principle, that effective regulators adaptively adjust their behavior so as to bring about a desired perception (Powers 1973, 1979).

Coordinative organs mediate between the output states of sensory organs and the input states of effector organs, in effect providing a mapping between particular perceptual outcomes and particular action alternatives. The more reliable the coordination, the more this mapping resembles a function (i.e. for a given distinct perceptual state, one particular action will always be taken). When this coordination is completely reliable, it is possible to describe the state-transitions in terms of a "state-determined system" (Ashby 1954). Such (finite) state-determined systems can be described completely in terms of syntactic, formal operations, and it is in these circumstances that one is justified in characterizing what is going on in the natural system in terms of "computations". In the ideal case of a completely reliable coordinating organ (as might be found in a contemporary robot with a digital electronic computer taking inputs from sensors and activating effectors), coordination implements a purely syntactic relation within the set of internal states whilst sensing and effecting organs implement purely semantic relations with the world at large. Here the coordinative rules must operate within the set of perceptual categories given by sensors and those behavioral categories determined by effectors.

The evolution of sensors, coordinators, and effectors

In biological evolution all three functionalities evolve over time. Receptor organs coevolve with coordinative structures and effector organs to produce organisms which can make the sensory distinctions, coordinations, and actions needed for survival and reproduction. Sensors evolve to make those distinctions which enhance the survival of their bearers; those sensors which make discriminations important for survival and reproduction will over generations prevail within a population. Effectors similarly evolve to enable those actions which enhance survival and hence reproduction. Those body configurations of bones, muscles, and secretory organs which are particularly effective in getting food, evading predation, eluding disease, and reproducing will tend to prevail

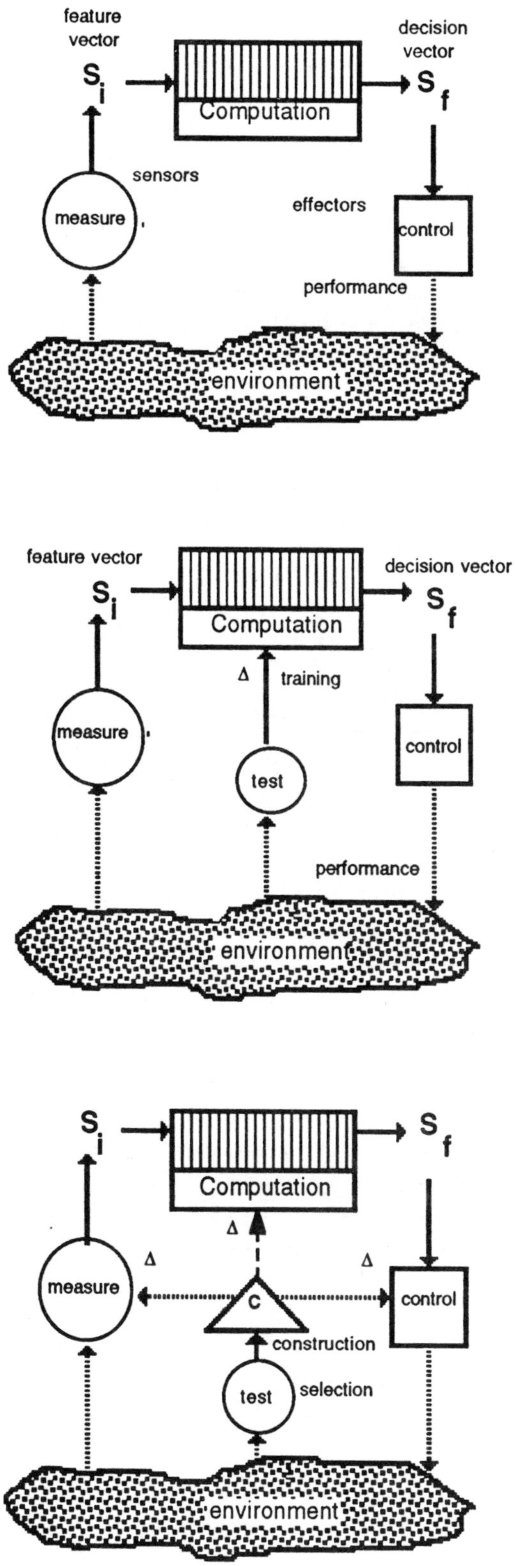

Figure 2. General types of adaptivity. The solid arrows represent digital or symbolic processes, while the dashed arrows represent analog or undifferentiated processes. (Top) *Nonadaptive robotic devices.* These devices do not modify their internal structure contingent upon their experience (past performance). There is no feedback from performance to enhanced structure. (Middle) *Adaptive computational devices.* These devices alter the input-output algorithm of their computational part contingent upon their performance. They operate within fixed sets of functional states, switching from alternative input-output functions (fixed hardware, variable software). These devices improve their input-output mappings over time but are constrained by the fixed, nonadaptive nature of their sensors and effectors. Because sensors and effectors determine the linkage of device states and the world at large and there is no means here of adaptively altering them, these devices are semantically-bounded. Such devices operate within the set of semantic categories defined by their sensors and effectors and within the set of syntactic states defined by their computational hardware. (Bottom) *Structurally adaptive devices.* These devices construct new material structures (new hardware), enabling new functional states and operations to arise. Such devices are capable of evolving new semantic categories through the adaptive construction of sensors and effectors. Those which evolve new sensors and effectors change their external semantics in order to optimize their performance. This is analogous to the evolution of new sensory and effector organs in biological evolution. Structually adaptive devices are also capable of augmenting the state spaces of their computational parts by building new material structures (more memory, processors) which increase the number of syntactic distinctions which can be manipulated. This is analogous to the evolution of more complex coordinative structures in biological organisms. The two adaptive device types are not mutually-exclusive: there could be devices which were both computationally-adaptive and structurally-adaptive.

over time in the population. Coordinative organs (in higher organisms this is usually the nervous system) evolve to more effectively map the perceived state of the world to an appropriate action. Those individuals which can coordinate percepts with possible actions more effectively can make better use of the information provided by the sensory array, and will tend to survive longer to have more offspring.

Phylogenetic vs. ontogenetic learning

By constructing their own sensors, effectors, and coordinative organs biological species alter their relationships to the world around them. Over phylogenetic time periods the categories through which organisms apprehend the world and act on it evolve with the changing needs of the population. If learning is taken in its broadest sense as the alteration of internal structures so as to better perform in an external environment, then this biological evolution of sensing, coordinating, and effecting organs represents a kind of phylogenetic learning in which the ability to model the environment, and consequently survival and reproduction, is improved.

> Two of the phenomena which we consider to be characteristic of living systems are the power to learn and the power to reproduce themselves. These properties, different as they appear, are intimately related to one another. An animal that learns is one which is capable of being transformed by its past environment into a different being and is therefore adjustable to its environment within its individual lifetime. An animal which multiplies is able to create other animals in its own likeness, or at least approximately, although not so completely in its own likeness that they cannot vary in the course of time. If this variation itself is inheritable, we have the raw material on which natural selection can work. If hereditary invariability concerns manners of behavior, then among the varied patterns of behavior which are propagated some will be found advantageous to the continuing existence of the race and will establish themselves, while others which are detrimental to this continuing existence will be eliminated. The result is a certain sort of racial or phylogenetic learning, as contrasted with the ontogenetic learning of the individual. Both ontogenetic and phylogenetic learning are modes by which the animal can adjust itself to its environment. (Wiener, 1961)

Usually phylogenetic learning is thought to involve the optimization of the kinds of structures which constitute the organism, while ontogenetic learning is an optimization within those (relatively invariant) sets of structures and plasticities given the individual organism as the product of phylogeny. Here the basic semantic categories of the organism (percept, action repertoires) are usually thought to be fixed by phylogenetic learning while the particular mappings within those categories (percept-action coordinations) are thought to lie in the domain of ontogenetic learning. While this may be valid as a first cut, there may be circumstances (particularly in higher organisms) where new sensory and behavioral categories are formed within the lifetime of the individual organism. The ontogenetic, performance-contingent selection of antibodies in the immune system is an obvious example of this: an array of molecular sensors is evolved through differential reproduction of those cells producing antibodies that recognize foreign molecules. The set of distinctions (the equivalence classes of antigens which can be recognized) that the immune system can make on the world around it evolves over time. Here the functional interrelationships mediating between evaluation of particular sensors (how strongly a given antibody binds to an antigen, thereby "recognizing" it) and structural adjustment are similar to those found in morphological evolution. Less clear-cut is the question of how well this description might apply to the formation of new conceptual structures in the brain. Here one would look toward adaptive alterations in the ways in which continuous, analog neural discharge patterns (e.g. interspike interval distributions) are transformed into discrete global modes of representation and action. While the particular mechanisms of evaluation, inheritance and construction of structural alternatives may turn out to be very different for individual nervous systems and evolving populations of organisms, the abstract functional organization of adaptation can still, nevertheless, be qualitatively similar. In all cases this organization consists of a cycle of performance evaluations, modification of a constructive plan (through blind variation or directed alteration), and the subsequent construction of new structures to enable new performances.

Optimization within categories and optimization of categories

From the standpoint of analyzing what general kinds of functional adaptations are possible, it is useful to distinguish between the optimization of the percept-action categories themselves and the optimization of particular mappings between states formed by the categories. The corresponding processes in the optimization of a scientific model would involve the selection and optimization of appropriate measuring devices and observables vs. the optimization of predictions made given a particular set of observables. One is a semantic search process, finding the appropriate relations between the world and the state variables of the model (the right measurements to make), while the other is a syntactic search process, finding the algorithm which generates the best predictions given those measured initial states. These two kinds of optimization, of the categories themselves vs. between states within fixed categories, represent two kinds of acquired knowledge.

Each kind of knowledge entails a different kind of learning; each corresponds to a possible kind of adaptive device that we could potentially build (Figure 2). If the sensors of our devices correspond to sensory organs of organisms, computational parts correspond to biological coordinative organs (nervous systems), and effectors correspond to the various biological effector organs, then we can envision all of the types of device adaptivity which would correspond to the biological evolution of these various organ types.

The optimization of categories would correspond to the structural evolution of sensors, computational networks, and effectors. The artificial analogy of the biological evolution of sense organs would be devices which evolved (or adaptively constructed) their own sensors to make the primitive distinctions necessary to solve a problem. The artificial analogy of the biological evolution of effector organs would be devices which evolved (or adaptively constructed) their own effectors appropriate to some given task. The artificial analogy of the evolution of coordinating systems would be a device which evolved the material structures subserving computations: new memory states and/or new processing element types.

Optimization within categories would correspond to flexible switching between the set of states given by structural evolution. One could think of structural evolution (optimization of the categories) in terms of "hardware" design, construction, and augmentation while this latter kind of optimization (within pre-established categories) is performed by "software" algorithms operating within the hardware constraints. While we now have adaptive devices which can optimize the particular computations they perform (trainable machines, neural nets, genetic algorithms), we do not as yet have devices which evolve their own hardware -- their sensors, their computational hardware, their effectors. And while much attention has been paid to adaptation in the computational realm, exceedingly little has been paid to adaptation in the sensing and effecting realms.

The evolution of new perceptual distinctions and action alternatives

How can a new sensory distinction or a new possible action evolve? In general it will entail the adaptive construction of a new material structure which interacts with the device's environment in a way that is different from existing sensors and effectors. If the structure enhances the performance of the device, then it is stabilized and incorporated into the device's constructive specifications.

This new structure could be a part of the device proper or it could take the form of a prosthesis, modifying the relationship(s) between existing sensors and effectors and the world beyond the prosthesis. The immune system was mentioned above as a natural example of internal structural evolution. Most of the examples of prosthesis are artificial. We ourselves build tools (chain saws, steam shovels, chemical plants, bicycles) which, when directed by our biological effectors, radically alter our relationship to the world around us. We build sensory prosthetics (cat-scanners, telescopes, microscopes, molecular assays, hearing aids) which allow us to amplify the number of distinctions we can make on the world. We build coordinative prosthetics (computers, pencil-and-paper, written symbol strings) that allow us to amplify the complexity of our coordinations by extending our memory and our ability to effectively manipulate large numbers of symbols.

In all of the artificial examples cited above, however, human beings are part of the loop-- human beings construct the new types of sensors, the larger computers, the more powerful effectors. On the whole we have very few devices which carry out these adaptive constructions on their own. If we look around us at the kinds of robotic devices available, the vast majority of them have fixed sensors, effectors, and coordinative programs. A small minority of them are adaptive robots having trainable computational parts mediating between fixed sensor and effector arrays (via neural nets, genetic algorithms, Bayesian methods, or other training algorithms). The devices which come closest to adaptively evolving their own sensors and effectors are those which tune the parameters controlling their sensors (as in Carver Mead's analog-VLSI devices (1989) or as in autofocusing mechanisms for cameras), but these parameters are designed explicitly into these devices -- the device itself does not have the structural autonomy necessary to evolve its own categories.

Artificial evolution of a primitive ear

In the late 1950's, the cybernetician Gordon Pask (Pask 1958, 1959, 1960) constructed an electrochemical assemblage to demonstrate that a machine could in fact evolve its own sensors. The device consisted of an array of electrodes immersed in a ferrous sulfate/sulphuric acid solution. By passing current through the array, iron dendritic thread structures could be grown between selected pairs of electrodes. By adaptively allocating current to the electrodes (by changing their relative share of current), the growth of these threads between the electrodes could be steered; structures could be constructed and rewarded on the basis of how they interacted with the world at large. All of this could be accomplished without a specific physical theory of how the threads form and extend themselves, much in the same way the "blind" search for effective sensory substrates operates in biological evolution. One could implement a contemporary neural network this way -- the inter-element weights of the neural net would be proportional to the inter-electrode conductances. Instead Pask adaptively steered the assemblage to construct structures sensitive to sound. If particular configurations arose which changed their resistive properties in response to sound, then they were rewarded. In about half a day they were able to train the device to discriminate between presence and absence of sound, and then between two frequencies of sound. The device represents the artificial evolution of a new sense modality, the emergence of sensory distinctions which were not present in the device at the start. The structural adaptivity of the device enables the emergence of a new function. This relation between adaptivity and emergence is discussed in more depth elsewhere (Rosen 1985, Cariani 1989, 1991ab, and Kampis 1991). In the process of training, a new perceptual category (or primitive distinction) was created by the device *de novo*. This process is fundamentally distinct from the building up of complex distinctions from logical combinations of pre-existing ones, such as one finds in virtually all contemporary artificial intelligence strategies.

Pask's device is an example of a general class of evolutionary robotic devices which evolve their own hardware. The potential existence of evolutionary robots which construct their own sensors and effectors has a number of far-reaching epistemological consequences. Warren McCulloch was one of the few people at the time to see the broader implications of Pask's device:

> With this ability to make or select proper filters on its inputs, such a device explains the central problem of experimental epistemology. The riddles of stimulus equivalence or of local circuit action in the brain remain only as parochial problems. (McCulloch, in the preface of Pask 1960).

Finding the right feature primitives for a neural net

Pask's assemblage was the first artificial device when given a task, to automatically find the observable(s) or feature primitives necessary to solve the problem with which it was confronted. While Pask's device was quite rudimentary, it would be possible to build other devices along the same general organizational principles. We could then use these devices as front-ends for our computationally adaptive neural nets and trainable machines (Cariani 1990).

In contrast to the ability to evolve new sensory distinctions, all existing classifiers operate within fixed sets of feature primitives which the designer has determined is appropriate to the classification problem at hand. The device then adaptively searches for an appropriate algorithm to partition the space of feature combinations. If the set of feature primitives is obvious or the problem can be specified in purely formal terms, then feature selection is unproblematic. In the case of an ill-defined real world problem (Selfridge 1982), however, the appropriate feature primitives may not be obvious, and the designer probably will not have at his/her disposal a set of features which can correctly classify all cases. Typically in these cases the primitive feature set is tuned by the designer -- the designer thinks of all the possible features which might plausibly enhance performance and some subset of those features is chosen. If the features chosen are informationally inadequate to perform the task (e.g. to classify perfectly), then the performance of the adaptive device will plateau at this limit. In this case a device capable of adaptively constructing new sensors and hence new feature primitives would be able to surpass this plateau by further improving the basic features. A feature space which was difficult or impossible to correctly partition might well become more tractable under a change of observables. If an observable is added, the feature space increases in dimension by one, and what was a local minimum in the old feature space might easily be a saddle point in the augmented space. Hill-climbing, besides involving following local gradients upwards, can also thus involve increases in the dimensionality of the hill itself. Because it is usually tacitly assumed that the sensors (and hence the feature primitives) are fixed and that computational adaptation is the only form of learning possible, these alternatives are usually not explicitly discussed in the literature. However, in real life tasks, when a neural net fails to improve beyond a given level of performance, despite the best efforts of its designers to optimize the algorithm, often those designers go looking for more (or more suitable) observables, thereby altering the dimensionality and external semantics of the space they are searching. Sometimes this proves to be a successful strategy.

Increasing the number of independent signalling modes in a network

Networks of devices capable of evolving new sensors and effectors also have the means of raising the dimensionality of their signal spaces. Whenever a new effector-sensor combination arises between two elements there is the possibility that the sensor of one element can detect the actions of the new effector. If the new sensor and effector are different from pre-existing ones, then there will be some informational independence between signals sent through that channel and pre-existing signalling channels. For example, if we had one element evolving a primitive sensitivity to sound (or hormones or electrical pulses) while another evolved a primitive means of producing sound (or hormones or electrical pulses), then the network will have evolved a signalling channel which is (at least partially) orthogonal to pre-existing ones. This is a general strategy for increasing bandwidth -- proliferate new orthogonal signalling modes. One major advantage of increasing dimensionality (categories) over proliferating states within existing dimensions is that different signals can be kept separate from each other if desired; different patterns need not interfere with each other (as in many kinds of connectionist networks), and new signals need not be logical combinations of pre-existing ones. This strategy also enables simultaneous transmission of different signal types (multiplexing). These two features allow for much more flexible adaptive signalling possibilities and are potentially relevant to our conceptions of the biological neuron as an adaptive information processing device (Cariani 1991b). Rather than discrete logic elements adaptively summing various combinations of synaptic inputs to produce one scalar output signal, we might also consider neurons in terms of mixed digital-analog elements capable of transmitting multidimensional information through interspike interval distributions (Chung, Raymond and Lettvin 1970, Raymond and Lettvin 1978). By tuning membrane recovery processes and electrical resonances, a neuron could adaptively proliferate new temporal discharge patterns, thereby increasing the dimensionality of the information encoded in its spike trains. It is possible that such tunings could be implemented by adaptive allocation of ion channels and pumps to local patches of excitable membrane, contingent upon their local past histories of excitation. In addition to adaptively altering effective connectivities through synaptic weights (conceived as scalars), in effect we would also have a learning mechanism which operated in the frequency domain, with all the advantages conferred by (partial) orthogonalities of different interspike intervals. Recurrent networks of these elements, each one adaptively tuning itself, might then be capable of proliferating new resonant network modes, thereby increasing the number of stable global states available to the network as a whole. Whether or not such functional organization proves to be operant in the nervous system, useful artificial mixed digital-analog neural nets can be constructed along these lines by utilizing trees of adaptively tuned pulse oscillators connected together in various ways (Pratt 1990).

The construction of an epistemically autonomous observer

Finally, once we have devices which can both construct their categories for sensing and effecting and also optimize the mapping between those categories, we have devices which are *epistemically-autonomous* -- within the limits imposed by their material structure, they determine the nature of what they see and how they act on the world. This conception of epistemic autonomy lies close to the concepts of *semantic closure* (Pattee 1982) *organizational closure* (Maturana 1981; Varela 1979), the *self-modifying device* (Kampis 1991; Csanyi 1989) and the *anticipatory system* (Rosen 1985, 1991). Once we have the concept of epistemic autonomy and understand the material structures needed to subserve this kind of functional organization, we then have the means for constructing an autonomous subject, a point of view independent of our own, one capable of telling us about that which we do not already know.

References

Ashby, W.R. 1956. *An Introduction to Cybernetics*. London: Chapman & Hall.

Cariani, Peter. 1989. On the design of devices with emergent semantic functions. Ph.D. dissertation, State University of New York at Binghamton.

Cariani, Peter. 1990. Implications from structural evolution: semantic adaptation. *Proceedings, International Joint Conference on Neural Networks, January, 1990, Washington, D.C.* I: 47-51.

Cariani, Peter. 1991a. Emergence and artificial life. In *Artificial Life II. Proceedings of the Second Workshop on Artificial Life,* edited by C.G. Langton, C.E.Taylor, J.D.Farmer, and S.Rasmussen. Reading, MA: Addison-Wesley.

Cariani, Peter. 1991b. Adaptivity and emergence in organisms and devices. *World Futures*, 31: 49-70.

Chung, S.H., S.A. Raymond, and J.Y. Lettvin. 1970. Multiple meaning in single visual units. *Brain Behavior and Evolution* 3:72-101.

Csanyi, Vilmos. 1989. *Evolutionary Systems and Society*. Durham, NC: Duke.

Emmeche, Claus. 1991. A semiotical reflection on biology, living signs, and artificial life. *Biology and Philosophy* 6: 325-340.

Kampis, George. 1991. *Self-Modifying Systems in Biology and Cognitive Science: A New Framework for Dynamics, Information, and Complexity*. New York: Pergamon.

Maturana, Humberto. 1981. Autopoiesis. In *Autopoiesis: A Theory of Living Organization,* edited by Milan Zeleny. New York: North-Holland.

McCulloch, Warren S. 1989. *The Collected Works of Warren S. McCulloch.* Salinas, CA: Intersystems Publications.

Mead, Carver. 1989. *Analog VLSI and Neural Systems*. Reading, MA: Addison-

Wesley.

Pask, Gordon 1958 Physical analogues to the growth of a concept. In *Mechanization of Thought Processes: Proceedings of a Symposium, National Physical Labs, November, 1958*. London: H.M.S.O.

Pask, Gordon. 1959. The natural history of networks. In *Self-Organizing Systems*, proceedings of a conference, Chicago, May 5-6, 1959, edited by M.C. Yovits and S. Cameron. New York: Pergamon Press, 1960.

Pask, Gordon . 1961. *An Approach to Cybernetics*. New York: Harper & Brothers.

Pattee, Howard H. 1982. Cell psychology: an evolutionary view of the symbol-matter problem. *Cognition and Brain Theory* 5: 325-341.

Powers, William. 1973. *Behavior: The Control of Perception*. New York: Aldine.

Powers, William. 1989. *Living Control Systems. Selected Papers of William T. Powers*. Gravel Switch, KY: Control Systems Group.

Pratt, Gill. 1990. Pulse Computation. Ph.D. dissertation. Massachusetts Institute of Technology.

Raymond, S. A. and J. Y. Lettvin. 1978. Aftereffects of activity in peripheral axons as a clue to nervous coding. In *Physiology and Pathobiology of Axons*, edited by S. Waxman. New York: Raven Press.

Rosen, Robert. 1985. *Anticipatory Systems*. New York: Wiley.

Rosen, Robert. 1991. *Life Itself: A Comprehensive Inquiry into the Nature, Origin and Fabrication of Life* . New York:: Columbia University Press.

Selfridge, Oliver. 1982. Some themes and primitives in ill-defined systems. In *Adaptive Control in Ill-Defined Systems,*. edited by O. Selfridge, E.L. Rissland and M.A. Arbib. New York: Plenum Press.

von Uexküll, 1926. *Theoretical Biology*. New York: Harcourt Brace.

Varela, Francesco. 1979. *Principles of Biological Autonomy*. New York: North Holland.

Wiener, Norbert. 1961. On Learning and Self-Reproducing Machines.*Cybernetics or Control and Communication in the Animal and the Machine*. Cambridge: MIT Press.

Philosophical Aspects of Artificial Life

Mark A. Bedau*
Philosophy Department, Reed College
Portland, OR 97202, USA
mab@reed.edu

October 10, 1991

There is a new interdisciplinary science—dubbed "artificial life" (or "ALife")—that promises to be of significant philosophical interest. Artificial life has relatively straightforward relevance to issues in metaphysics, philosophy of science, philosophy of biology, and philosophy of mind, but it also bears centrally on more distant issues in social and political philosophy, economic philosophy, and ethics. However, few philosophers have begun to think through these issues, probably because few are yet even aware of this new science.

This document is intended to help prompt reflection about the philosophical aspects of artificial life. Following a general sketch of ALife is a catalogue of philosophical issues ALife raises and potentially illuminates. The aim here is only to describe and clarify the questions; attempts to answer them are left for other occasions.

1 An Overview of Artificial Life

It is useful to view the field of artificial life by contrast with the analogous field of artificial intelligence (AI). Whereas AI attempts to devise and study computational models of cognitive processes like reasoning, memory, and perception, ALife attempts to devise and study computationally implemented models of the processes characteristic of living systems. These processes include:

- self-organization, spontaneous generation of order, and cooperation
- self-reproduction and metabolization
- learning, adaptation, purposiveness, and evolution

To a first approximation, what AI is to psychology and the philosophy of mind, ALife is to biology and the philosophy of biology.

*For helpful comments, thanks to audiences at M.I.T. and the University of New Hampshire, and to Kate Elgin, Bernie Gert, Brian Goodwin, Mark Hinchliff, John Konkle, Nelson Minar, Jim Moor, Walter Sinnott-Armstrong, Norman Packard, Steen Rasmussen, and Carol Voeller.

But artificial life is more than just computationally oriented theoretical biology. It falls within a new branch of physics and computer science known as "complex systems theory," currently being presented in, e.g., the Addison-Wesley series SFI Studies in the Sciences of Complexity, and recently popularized through the science of chaos (Crutchfield et al. 1986, Gleick 1987). Living systems are especially salient examples of spontaneously organized complex systems, but nature exhibits many other examples as well—some outside the living realm, such as Bénard convection cells and certain other dissipative structures (Prigogine and Stengers 1984), and others consisting of aggregates of living beings, such as social groups or economic populations. The field of artificial life seeks an understanding of spontaneous organization and adaptation that illuminates these phenomena in *whatever* settings they occur.

In fact, one of the most striking natural systems that exhibits fundamental properties of life, such as self-organization and adaptive learning, is the mind. For this reason, the insights sought by artificial life may well shed light on at least some fundamental aspects of mental processes (a theme sounded in Bedau and Packard 1991 and in work on group "intelligence" in the social insects such as Collins 1991). From this perspective, AI is a subfield within the larger ALife fold. To be sure, in many respects life seems simpler than cognition, and ALife is concentrating its initial efforts on modeling simple living systems. But many in the ALife community hope eventually to build up to an understanding of mental processes.

The field of artificial life is betting on the success of a central working hypothesis: that the essential nature of the fundamental principles of life can be captured in relatively simple models. If correct, this hypothesis makes it sensible to attempt to understand the *general* class of living phenomena by computationally exploring the characteristic behavior of these simple models. Progress in ALife would then reveal fundamental truths about all living systems, including those found here on

Earth. It is important to recognize that nothing guarantees that ALife's hypothesis is true. The hypothesis does find some fledgling corroboration in work to-date, such as simple models of self-reproduction (Langton 1986) and adaptive evolution (Bedau and Packard 1991), but its ultimate success is an empirical matter still hanging in the balance of future results.

ALife's working hypothesis provides a general motivation for the field's focus on computational models. Four more specific considerations bolster this rationale. First, ALife seeks maximally general principles governing all possible forms of life. So, rather than looking for regularities by sifting through a mass of contingencies concerning life as we know it, it makes sense to study computational models since these exhibit an appropriately high level of generality. Second, it is very difficult, practically impossible, to conduct ordinary biological experiments that address the relevant questions even with respect to familiar forms of biological life. For example, most natural evolving systems operate on a time scale spanning vast numbers of human generations, and the few that evolve relatively quickly (like the immune system) are so complex that they all but defy analysis. By contrast, computer models allow for rapid and precisely controlled experiments. Third, the models explored by ALife exhibit quite complex forms of behavior, and in general it is simply impossible to discover their behavior by any means other than observing the effects of simulations (Wolfram 1984); in fact, this feature can be taken as definitive of complex systems. Fourth, abstract theorizing in the absence of empirical constraints is too easy, and the results are of uncertain value. A computer model must be precise if it is to be programmable, and all tacit assumptions must be explicitly specified if the program is to run. Implementing models on machines proves that the capacities captured by the model are mechanistically realizable. Furthermore, mechanistically implementing a model forces the scientist to surmount the non-trivial hurdle of computational feasibility (Garey and Johnson 1979). Thus, even if a computational model does not capture exactly how a certain kind of life process actually happens here on Earth, the model will be at least within the realm of feasibility.

Despite the analogies between artificial intelligence and artificial life, there is an important difference between the modeling strategies typically employed in the two fields. Most traditional AI models are top-down-specified serial systems involving a complicated, centralized controller which makes decisions based on access to all aspects of global state. The controller's decisions have the potential to affect directly any aspect of the whole system. However, most natural systems exhibiting complex autonomous behavior seem to be parallel, distributed networks of communicating "agents" making decisions that directly affect only their local state. Each agent's decisions are based on information about only its own local state. Following this lead, ALife is exploring the emergent dynamics of bottom-up-specified parallel systems of simple local agents.

Bottom-up models offer two important advantages over top-down models. First, the dramatic "toy" top-down models of early AI succumb to combinatorial explosion when attempts are made to have them produce natural, flexible, spontaneous behavior after being scaled up to realistic proportions (Dreyfus 1979, Hofstadter 1985). Bottom-up models, by contrast, have some promise of providing a computationally feasible solution to this kind of problem. Second, top-down models provide relatively shallow explanations of a system's global behavior. Rules governing the system's global behavior patterns are included in the system by fiat. Bottom-up models, by contrast, provide deeper explanations of a system's "macroscopic" behavior patterns by showing that they emerge out of the aggregate behavior of a population of "microscopic" agents.

ALife populations of processors have important similarities to parallel distributed processing networks (also known as PDP, connectionist, or neural networks) that today command so much philosophical attention (McClelland and Rumelhart 1986). Indeed, some ALife models include connectionist networks (e.g., Collins 1991). But most ALife models diverge from the connectionist paradigm in many specific respects, so familiar connectionist models constitute only a small subset of the class of bottom-up models being explored in artificial life.

Abstract accounts of artificial life like the foregoing have only limited value. A better taste of the real flavor of artificial life research can be had by reviewing typical ALife models such as those found in recent conference proceedings (Farmer et al. 1986, Langton 1988b, Langton et al. 1991).

2 Fourteen Questions

The field of artificial life raises a wide variety of philosophical issues. More importantly, an appreciation of artificial life might provide the wherewithal to find their answers.

The following questions are largely unadorned by proposed answers, and, although not exhaustive, they should convey the diversity of issues raised. Some are familiar philosophical questions that find interesting and rich instances in artificial life; others are issues that arise only in the context of artificial life. Some concern the nature of life and other vital phenomena; others concern the nature of artificial life science; a few concern intellectual bookkeeping.

The following five rough and overlapping topics serve to catalogue the questions: (1) fundamental definitions, (2) artificial intelligence, (3) functionalism, (4) emergence, and (5) the ethics of creation.

2.1 Fundamental Definitions

Philosophy is concerned with the essential aspects of the fundamental nature of reality; thus philosophy's preoccupation with such notions as existence, identity, causation, change, knowledge, mind, freedom, and value. One fundamental aspect of reality is *life*; the distinction between life and non-life is at least as basic as the distinction between mind and body. Yet philosophers have largely ignored the issue of the nature of life (Aristotle being one of the few exceptions). So, the most obvious philosophical issue raised by ALife work is perhaps:

Question 1: What is life?

Clarity about the nature of life should help clarify its possible subjects, so the answer to question 1 should help settle whether it could be appropriate to attribute life to systems consisting of ordinary biological individuals (such as species, ecosystems, and even the whole Earth), and to subsystems within biological organisms (such as the immune system). Closer to ALife's home, the answer to question 1 should also help settle the propriety of attributing life to a physical machine executing a suitable ALife program, to physical processes occurring inside that machine, or even to the abstract and disembodied program in its own right.

A skeptic might question whether there is any interesting answer to the question about life's fundamental nature, thinking the debate over the "true" nature of life to be mere semantics. Thankful to have progressed past nineteenth-century debates over vitalism, our skeptic might doubt that a principled distinction can be drawn in the field of more or less complex entities spanning crystals, viruses, bacteria, computer programs, and other self-organizing, adapting, evolving systems. But consider the mind; for while few doubt that there is a real difference between mental and non-mental entities, the cases of mind and life are strikingly parallel. There is a strong intuitive sense both that the mind is qualitatively different from non-mind and that life is qualitatively different from non-life. At the same time, both life and mind occur in various degrees; in fact, a case can be made for placing them at different ends of a hierarchy of internal processing strategies. Thus, there is ample reason for at least looking for a principled account of life.

Science has a tradition of attempts to provide a general characterization of life. Some proposals consist of more or less heterogeneous lists of characteristics (Monod 1972, Mayer 1982); others focus on specific properties, such as certain chemical patterns (Haldane 1949), evolvability (Maynard Smith 1975 and 1986), or autopoiesis, i.e., the property of being a "self-producing" system (Maturana and Varela 1980). Yet few biologists exhibit interest in the philosophical issue of the general nature of life. Their primary concern is to understand life-as-we-know-it, and an abstract philosophical account of life is largely irrelevant to that scientific pursuit. It is easy enough to identify life forms in our biosphere, so biologists quickly become engrossed in fruitful scientific projects such as describing and explaining patterns of diversity observed in biological populations and unravelling the structure and function of DNA.

ALife scientists have no comparable luxury. Striving to capture the general features characteristic of living systems, they must confront the question of the general nature of life-as-it-could-be. The salient features of life-as-we-know-it guide the formulation of initial hypotheses about the outlines of life-as-it-could-be, and life-as-we-know-it will remain an acid test of hypotheses about the most general nature of life. Nevertheless, we cannot sensibly design and evaluate ALife models without already having at least a rudimentary sense of the bounds of possible forms of life, and experimentation with ALife models will help refine our views on the general nature of life.

The targets of ALife models listed at the outset of section 1 (self-organization, metabolization, adaptation, etc.) in effect are an initial stab at partially characterizing the nature of life; thus these processes constitute at least a preliminary answer to the question about the nature of life (question 1). It is still a matter of debate whether all of these processes are equally fundamental to life and whether additional processes must be involved. But regardless of how these debates are resolved, ALife will remain interested in understanding these processes for their own sake. Thus, paralleling the question about the nature of life, ALife prompts us to ask:

Question 2: What is the nature of life's characteristic processes, such as self-organization, self-reproduction, metabolization, adaptation, purposiveness, and evolution?

These processes are undoubtedly related; understanding one will involve understanding the others. This raises a third question.

Question 3: How are life and each of its characteristic processes related, and what metaphysical status do these relationships have?

For example, is every extant form of life a member of an evolving system? If so, is this a mere contingency, a strict necessity, or a matter of some intermeditate modality?

It is also natural to wonder whether the fundamental definitions of concern to ALife are matters of a priori conceptual analysis, empirical data analysis, or something else. A central task of artificial life is to determine what can we learn about life and its characteristic processes from the structure of their ALife models, and this task raises a fundamental epistemological issue in the philosophy of science concerning scientific model building:

Question 4: What is the nature of the inference from the structure of a "successful" model to the properties of the phenomenon modeled?

It is a non-trivial matter to determine which features of a model are necessary or sufficient aspects of reality. For example, if bottom-up models persist as the architecture of choice in both AI and ALife, it is unclear whether to attribute this to the nature of life and mind or to our own epistemological limitations.

However we are to account for the epistemological significance of ALife models, there is clearly a fertile dialectical relationship between our grasp of the answer to this philosophical issue and the models produced and studied in artificial life. ALife models that attempt to capture vital processes are motivated and directed by an antecedent intuition about the nature of these processes, coupled with an antecedent conviction about their centrality to life. However, the successful construction of models might make it apparent that the true nature of these processes or the role they play in living systems is *not* as previously presumed. Model building can highlight the need for revision in our conceptions of the nature of these processes and of life. Furthermore, appreciation of the model can suggest the direction and substance of these revisions. These revised views can generate a new cycle of ALife model building, which can prompt yet further revisions in our understanding of life processes. Thus cycles the dialectic between the philosophy and science of ALife.

2.2 Artificial Intelligence

Artificial intelligence has profoundly affected contemporary philosophy. Much attention has been devoted to weighing its philosophical implications (Boden 1977 and 1990, Dennett 1978, Dreyfus 1979, Haugeland 1985, Hofstadter 1985). Although many conclusions are still controversial, there is wide agreement about which issues are important and which positions deserve serious attention.

Since ALife and AI share so many important features, we can exploit the familiarity of the intellectual terrain around AI to identify some of the main landmarks around ALife, and initial attempts to do this have already begun (Sober 1991). At the same time, we must be prepared for the possibility that more extensive exploration of ALife might force us to revise what we now take to be settled conclusions about AI.

Traditional AI has certainly not enjoyed overwhelming and unequivocal success, because of combinatorial explosion and the "frame" problem (Haugeland 1985, Hofstadter 1985, Boden 1990). These very problems show some promise of being mitigated by the bottom-up modeling strategies embodied in the new PDP models (McClelland and Rumelhart 1986). Although it is too early to judge the final success of the PDP approach, the similarity between PDP models and the bottom-up models found in ALife is still quite striking. This raises the bookkeeping issue of how to classify ALife models:

Question 5: What is the relationship between typical ALife models and connectionist (PDP, neural network) models?

It is important to note that ALife and connectionism pertain to different *kinds* of classifications. Whether a model is connectionist concerns its architecture, and connectionist architectures can be applied to problems concerning widely different kinds of phenomena. What makes a model ALife, on the other hand, is the kind of phenomenon being modeled, and widely different kinds of architecture can be employed in ALife models.

Nevertheless, it turns out that ALife models almost invariably possess a certain broad architectural features—being "bottom-up"—which they share with connectionist models. For our purposes, bottom-up models are those in which the global behavior statistically emerges from the aggregate behavior of a population of relatively simple and autonomous processors acting solely on the basis of local state information. Connectionist models are a specific subset of bottom-up models in which the population of processors is a set of nodes arranged in layers, where a node's activity is some simple function of its input from the nodes to which it has immediate connections, and the strengths of the connections between nodes are adjusted in learning. Most ALife bottom-up models lack such specifically connectionist architectural details. Part of what makes this bookkeeping question interesting is the possibility of learning something about the significance and limitations of connectionism by reflecting on the architecture and performance of ALife models. But its main interest, surely, comes from the prospect of learning something fundamental about life from the invariant underlying architecture of its models.

Another kind of issue is raised by the close relationship between artificial life and artificial intelligence.

They not only use the same methodology; many of life's fundamental principles seem true also of mental processes. This blurs the disciplinary relationship between AI and ALife, and raises a basic question:

Question 6: What is the relationship between life and mind?

Are life and mind two endpoints on a continuum? Different stages in some hierarchy? What fundamental principles apply to both, and why? One of the most exciting prospects of ALife is that experimental research can be brought to bear on the connection between these two most basic aspects of reality.

Of the many philosophical controversies involving artificial intelligence with analogues concerning artificial life, one deserves special mention. Usually a computer model of something can easily be distinguished from the real thing. A hurricane in a computer simulation of the weather is not a real hurricane, and even though modern flight simulators are strikingly realistic a session in a flight simulator is not really flying. But in some cases a suitable computer simulation *does* seem to produce the genuine article (Dennett 1981). A suitable computer simulation of jazz improvisation seems for all the world to produce real jazz music, and a computer-driven theorem-prover seems to produce proofs every bit as genuine as those produced by flesh-and-blood mathematicians.

One of the most heated philosophical controversies raised by AI is the question whether it is ever appropriate to attribute mental properties such as thinking to computers (or programs). The starkest form of this issue is this: Even if we assume that it is possible for a computer (perhaps in the future) to *simulate perfectly* the behavioral and functional processes characteristic of mental beings, does it follow that the computer *really* has a mind? Alan Turing (1951) initiated this debate by proposing the Turing test in his seminal argument for a positive answer, and the debate has recently been revived by John Searle's (1980) "Chinese room" argument for a negative answer.

One of the more dramatic philosophical issues raised by ALife is the parallel question about whether a perfect simulation of life would be the creation of real life:

Question 7: Under what conditions, if any, is a simulation of a life process an artificial but real instance of life?

What makes ALife so exciting to the mass media is this prospect of creating new forms of life. It is certainly possible that distant galaxies contain forms of life quite unlike those with which we are now familiar. Why couldn't quite different forms of life be created in artificial life laboratories? The simulation-or-reality debate in artificial life has already been engaged, with Christopher Langton (1988a) arguing the positive position and H. H. Pattee (1988) raising skepticism.

ALife's simulation-or-reality debate bears on other philosophical issues. For example, Langton's argument would be significantly supported by a functionalist approach to life (discussed in the next section). Furthermore, the simulation-or-reality debate seems more tractable in artificial life than in artificial intelligence because ALife can sidestep some of AI's sharpest thorns—life need not involve subjectivity and self-consciousness, for example (so there is no evident analogue of Searle's Chinese room argument for artificial life), and the prospect of artificially created life apparently threatens our self-esteem much less than the prospect of artificially created minds. Progress on ALife's simulation-or-reality debate might even help break the impasse in the analogous debate in AI.

2.3 Functionalism

Functionalism is the dominant position in contemporary philosophy of mind (Putnam 1975, Fodor 1981). Functionalists view mental beings as input-output devices and hold that having a mind is no more and no less than having a set of internal states that causally interact (or "function") with each other and with environmental inputs and behavioral outputs in a characteristic way; a mental system is any system whatsoever that is governed by a set of internal states that is functionally isomorphic to human mental states. It does not matter what kind of material instantiates those functionally-defined patterns. Human mental states happen to be embodied in patterns of neuronal activity, but if exactly the same patterns of activity were found in a system composed of quite different materials—such as silicon circuitry—then, according to functionalism, that system would also literally have a mind. Functionalism's slogan could be "mind as software, not hardware," and its central thesis could be summarized thus: Mind is a property of *form*, not matter; to have a mind is to embody a distinctive dynamic *pattern* of states, not to be composed out of a distinctive sort of substance.

Life, too, seems to hinge on form rather than matter. Living organisms participate in a network of processes, some (such as information processing, metabolization, purposeful activity) operating within the organism's lifetime, and others (such as self-reproduction and adaptive evolution) operating over many generations. These processes must occur in some material substratum or other, but which specific kind of matter embodies them seems irrelevant to a system's vitality so long as the *forms* of the processes are preserved. The universe may well contain alien forms of life in which vital processes are sustained in substances outside even the realm of carbon chemistry. Thus, just as with the mind, functionalism is an attractive approach toward the nature of life, which raises the question:

Question 8: Is life a functional notion?

A functionalist perspective on life, if sound, is important aside from the intrinsic interest of understanding life. The contrast afforded by a functional definition of life would potentially illuminate functionalism with respect to mind. Furthermore, the notion of functional definition in general is interesting, but so far all the best examples of functional definitions have come from the philosophy of mind. Providing a second rich and complex setting in which to explore functional definitions could not help but shed light on functionalism in general.

Just as functionalism in the philosophy of mind has been deeply informed by its connection with artificial intelligence, functionalism with respect to life should have a similarly close association with artificial life. In the previous section we noted that ALife models may well transform artificial intelligence, partly by supporting and extending the connectionist revolution and partly by connecting the studies of mind and life. If AI does undergo such transformations, then the face of its intellectual cohort—functionalism in the philosophy of mind—might be similarly transformed. This highlights the need for a grasp of the different kinds of accounts that fall under the functionalist fold:

Question 9: What are the different basic kinds of functional accounts?

We need to understand how the form of a functional account of some phenomenon depends on the architecture of our best models of that phenomenon. The bottom-up architecture of ALife models might especially transform functionalism. For example, it has been argued that functionalism must explicitly acknowledge that the global "macroscopic" patterns definitive of certain functional systems emerge bottom-up style from an underlying "microscopic" layer of phenomena (Bedau 1991). Awareness of ALife models forces us to reflect on the relationship between lower-level and higher-level features of emergent functionalist systems and rethink which aspects of a type of phenomena functionalist models must capture. In this way we are led to confront a fundamental epistemological issue concerning functionalism:

Question 10: What are the criteria of adequacy for emergent functionalist accounts?

Although functionalism has attracted attention primarily within the philosophy of mind, its appeal extends to social and political philosophy, economic philosophy, and the special sciences generally (Fodor 1981). To the extent that ALife does change the face of functionalism, the ramifications will extend potentially to all the special sciences. The lessons about functionalism learned from ALife models might help us understand such diverse subjects as the complex patterns observed in voting behaviors and economic transactions.

2.4 Emergence

The issue of emergence has been epitomized by the question: "How can the whole be greater than the sum of its parts?" This issue arises because in certain situations complicated phenomena do seem to emerge spontaneously from fundamentally simpler phenomena.

Some examples of apparent emergence involve nonliving matter. A hurricane is an autonomous, self-sustaining global unity with an integrated dynamics, but it somehow emerges simply from the aggregate action of a huge collection of air and water molecules all governed by the same relatively simple local rules. Another example of apparent emergence is the mind. Conscious mental life consists of an autonomous, integrated flow of mental states (beliefs, desires, etc.) that follows a complicated global dynamic, but presumably this process somehow emerges out of the aggregate activity of the huge interconnected collection of neurons in the brain that are all obeying more or less the same relatively simple local rules.

Life is the context for many of the most compelling examples of apparent emergence. *The origin of life.* The initial primitive biotic community of self-replicating adaptively evolving entities emerged from a prebiotic chemical soup. *Phylogeny.* A vast biosphere containing a multitude of different complex species has emerged in the course of evolution from an initial biosphere containing just a few relatively simple species. *Ontogeny.* An individual organism is a vast diversity of systems and subsystems composed of a vast diversity of specialized types of cells. This intricately differentiated entity emerges in the course of embryological development from a single undifferentiated zygote. *The vital hierarchy.* Ecosystems are composed of organisms, which are composed of organ systems, which are composed of organs, which are composed of tissues, which are composed of cells, which are composed of organelles, which are composed of chemicals. Each "layer" in this hierarchy consists of two "levels"—a macro-level the behavior of which somehow emerges from the aggregate behavior at the micro-level below it.

What to make of emergent phenomena has been a perennial philosophical problem, one so far resisting scrutiny. Vitalistic explanations employing occult substances or forces operating outside the realm of physical and chemical law are unacceptable. Traditional forms of reductionism are unappealing explanations of emergence since the necessary reductions seem unavailable. Even though the micro-level entities behave mechanistically and the system's global macro-level behavior that emerges is driven solely by the micro-level dynamics, without explicit micro-level simulation the global behavior cannot be predicted even from complete knowledge of the micro-level properties—in this sense the emergent behavior is autonomous. Contemporary philosophy, deeply suspicious about whether the idea of emergence is even coherent, has simply put this issue on indefinite hold.

Artificial life is squarely attempting to understand the emergent quality of vital phenomena, and bottom-up ALife models typically display forms of emergent behavior. Brief descriptions of two simple models of group behavior might begin to suggest the emergent potential of bottom-up models. Although not themselves models of systems that are alive, these models do exhibit the emergence of simple forms of some of the central characteristics of living systems, such as spontaneous self-adaptivity and self-organization.

Flocking Boids. Flocks of birds exhibit impressive group behavior, fluidly swooping, reeling and maneuvering around obstacles, all the while maintaining group cohesion while avoiding collisions. Furthermore, the flock's dynamic equilibrium is maintained without any individual bird or group of birds functioning as a leader. A recent computer model of flocking "boids" developed by Craig Reynolds (1987) has reproduced similar behavior in simulated flocks. What is interesting is that the natural flocking behavior emerges spontaneously from models that are driven simply by each individual boid independently determining its flight path from local information, following such rules as match the velocities of neighboring boids, steer towards the perceived center of mass of neighboring boids, and minimize (within limits) the distance from neighboring boids. Simulations show that when a random assortment of individuals boids follow these local rules, natural flocking behavior arises—the flock coheres and moves as a unit, fluidly changing direction and navigating arbitrarily placed obstacles. (A sequence of pictures showing flocking boids is reproduced in Langton 1988a.) Even though the global behavior of this model is driven solely by the simple local rules governing each individual boid, global flocking behavior spontaneously emerges.

The Game of Life. Probably the best known example of something like an A-Life model is the Game of Life devised more than a generation ago by the Cambridge mathematician John Conway (1982) and popularized by Martin Gardner (1983). "Played" on a two-dimensional grid (such as a checker board), at each time step each square or cell is in one of two states—"dead" or "alive." Whether a given cell is dead or alive at a given time is a simple function of the previous states of the eight adjacent cells: a cell that was alive at t remains alive at $t+1$ if and only if exactly two or three of its neighbors were alive at t (cells with fewer than two living neighbors die of "loneliness" and those with more than three die of "overcrowding"); a cell that was dead at t becomes alive at $t+1$ if and only if exactly three of its neighbors were alive at t (there were just enough living neighbors to "breed" a new living cell). Extensive simulations have shown that amazingly complex patterns can emerge from this simple local rule governing individual sites: some reach stable or periodically oscillating configurations while others continue to change and grow indefinitely. Clusters of cells can function just like AND, OR, NOT, and other logic gates, and these gates can be connected into complicated switching circuits. They can even constitute a universal Turing machine.

Reynold's boids, Conway's Game of Life, and more complicated artificial life models make it possible to reopen the study of emergence. They provide a profitable setting for gathering rich and manageable empirical data from models of different kinds of emergent phenomena, thus providing a new purchase on the question:

Question 11: Under what conditions do systems exhibit emergent properties?

This question applies to both artificial and natural systems, and ALife might help answer both. First, as outlined above, many aspects of life apparently involve emergent phenomena, so any fundamental understanding of living systems provided by ALife has the prospect of illuminating the general properties of emergence. But more importantly, bottom-up ALife models themselves illustrate and instantiate emergent dynamics. It is primarily for the latter reason that ALife might provide a key which unlocks the mysteries of emergence. The hope is that understanding how ALife models generate emergent phenomena will reveal how emergent phenomena arise in real living systems.

One preliminary task for the study of emergence in ALife models is to formulate a typology of basic kinds of emergent phenomena. This and other fruits of the study of ALife emergence should help sort out a philosophical bookkeeping question:

Question 12: How is emergence related to reduction, supervenience, explanation, prediction, and determinism?

Progress on this sort of question will ultimately require a precise account of bottom-up models—something that it must be admitted is still lacking. Study of ALife emergence can be expected to help settle whether the difference between bottom-up and top-down models is a matter of principle, degree, perspective, or something else.

2.5 The Ethics of Creation

Artificial life raises two kinds of ethical issues. One is a concern about the consequences of technological change for extant beings; the other concerns the consequences of technological change for newly created life forms.

The development of a powerful new technology usually has ethical consequences. Atomic fission and fusion provide examples from recent history, and today genetic engineering threatens to teach us of this lesson again. One kind of ethical issue raised by ALife is analogous to those raised by other powerful technologies—details differ but the form is similar. The havoc wreaked by computer "viruses" and "worms" (Spafford 1991) provide ample evidence of the destructive potential of artificial life technologies; precautions must be taken against their accidental misuse and intentional abuse. These concerns highlight a question of the ethics of technology:

Question 13: What ethical implications does ALife research have for humanity and other extant forms of life?

Reflection on this topic will identify ethical predicaments which ALife scientists must confront. (It is ironic that ALife might provide *solutions* to some of the very problems it spawns; e.g., there is talk about creating artificial immune systems that protect computer networks from new viruses.)

Technologies for creating life involve a special ethically-charged consequence: the creation of new living beings. Consider genetic engineering. If genetic engineering produces complex enough forms of life, ethical consequences *for the newly created forms of life* might arise. To express this issue at its logical if fanciful extreme, we would be wrong to pretend we had no ethical responsibility to a future Frankenstein we created by genetic engineering. Now, this digression on genetic engineering is beside the point if the science of artificial life concerns only certain computer models and their theoretical implications. However, *if* the simulation-or-reality issue about life (question 7) has a positive answer, then artificial life *computer* laboratories might witness the creation of new forms of life just as might the bio-chemistry laboratories of genetic engineering. The "creatures" being simulated in a suitable ALife model (sufficiently elaborate, sufficiently long-operating, ...?) could actually be alive. Thus, pending the outcome of question 7, ALife raises a more pointed ethical issue:

Question 14: What ethical responsibilities would we bear to artificial forms of life that we created?

Presumably the impermissibility of whimsically harming or destroying creatures would not disappear merely if the "creatures" were created by genetic engineering or artificial life techniques. Most of us do not think twice about swatting a mosquito whereas we hesitate at even kicking a dog. It is sometimes thought that our moral responsibilities to a creature depend on which specific capacities it possesses. The animal rights literature, for example, bases our responsibilities to animals on their sentience—in particular, their capacity to experience pleasure and pain (Regan 1983). The environmental ethics literature, by contrast, tends to ground our responsibilities to other forms of life on the supposition that life in-and-of-itself is intrinsically valuable (Callitott 1982, Taylor 1986). Artificial life might create a new setting in which fundamental ethical issues like these must be pondered.

3 Conclusion

This list of questions should make amply evident the philosophical interest of the new science of artificial life. ALife provides a new and distinctive context in which to consider longstanding philosophical concerns, and it raises wholly new and distinctive questions. These questions reach into the heart of metaphysics, epistemology, and ethics.

Furthermore, reflection on ALife science might suggest how to answer these questions. The scientific strategies being developed in ALife are opening new philosophical horizons. In time, artificial life may well affect the substance of philosophy as much as, if not more than, artificial intelligence.

The philosophy of artificial life is not merely a derivative, second-order gloss on first-order ALife science. In fact, most of the questions identified above are of direct and fundamental concern in artificial life *science*. However unclear the relationship between ALife science and ALife philosophy might be, the two are surely closely related, and in time they will co-evolve.

References

Bedau, M. A. 1991. "Emergent Functionalism, Artificial Intelligence, and Artificial Life." In preparation.

Bedau, M. A., and N. H. Packard. 1991. "Measurement of Evolutionary Activity, Teleology, and Life."

In *Artificial Life II*, edited by C. G. Langton, C. E. Taylor, J. D. Farmer, and S. Rasmussen. SFI Studies in the Sciences of Complexity, Vol. X. Reading, CA: Addison-Wesley.

Berlekamp, E. R., J. H. Conway, and R. K. Guy. 1982. *Winning Ways*. Vol. 2. New York: Academic Press.

Boden, M. A. 1977. *Artificial Intelligence and Natural Man*. New York: Basic Books.

Boden, M. A., ed. 1990. *The Philosophy of Artificial Intelligence*. New York: Oxford University Press.

Callicott, J. B. 1989. *In Defense of the Land Ethic*. Albany: SUNY Press.

Collins, R. J., and D. R. Jefferson. 1991. "AntFarm: Towards Simulated Evolution." In *Artificial Life II*, edited by C. G. Langton, C. E. Taylor, J. D. Farmer, and S. Rasmussen. SFI Studies in the Sciences of Complexity, Vol. X. Reading, CA: Addison-Wesley.

Crutchfield, J. P., J. D. Farmer, N. H. Packard, and R. S. Shaw. "Chaos." *Scientific American*, December 1986, 46–57.

Dennett, D. C. 1978. "Artificial Intelligence as Philosophy and as Psychology." In his *Brainstorms*. Montgomery, VT: Bradford Books.

Dennett, D. C. 1981. "Reflections." In *The Mind's I*, edited by D. R. Hofstadter and D. C. Dennett. New York: Bantam Books.

Dreyfus, H. L. 1979. *What Computers Can't Do*. 2nd edition. New York: Harper and Row.

Farmer, D., A. Lapedes, N. Packard, and B. Wendroff. 1986. *Evolution, Games, and Learning: Models for Adaptation in Machines and Nature*. Amsterdam: North-Holland.

Fodor, J. A. 1981. *Representations*. Cambridge, MA: The MIT Press.

Gardner, M. 1983. *Wheels, Life, and Other Mathematical Amusements*. New York: Freeman.

Garey, M. R., and D. S. Johnson. *Computers and Intractability*. New York: Freeman.

Gleick, J. 1987. *Chaos: Making a New Science*. New York: Viking.

Haldane, J. B. S. 1949. *What is Life?* London: Alcuin Press.

Haugeland, J. 1985. *Artificial Intelligence: The Very Idea*. Cambridge, MA: The MIT Press.

Hofstadter, D. R. 1985. "Waking Up from the Boolean Dream, *or*, Subcognition as Computation." In his *Metamagical Themas: Questing for the Essence of Mind and Pattern*. New York: Basic Books.

Langton, C. G. 1986. "Studying Artificial Life with Cellular Automata." In *Evolution, Games, and Learning: Models for Adaptation in Machines and Nature*, edited by D. Farmer, A. Lapedes, N. Packard, and B. Wendroff. Amsterdam: North-Holland.

Langton, C. G. 1988a. "Artificial Life." In *Artificial Life*, edited by C. Langton. SFI Studies in the Sciences of Complexity, Vol. VI. Reading, CA: Addison-Wesley.

Langton, C. G., ed. 1988b. *Artificial Life*. SFI Studies in the Sciences of Complexity, Vol. VI. Reading, CA: Addison-Wesley.

Langton, C. G., C. E. Taylor, J. D. Farmer, and S. Rasmussen, eds. 1991. *Artificial Life II*. SFI Studies in the Sciences of Complexity, Vol. X. Reading, CA: Addison-Wesley.

Maturana, H. R., and F. J. Varela. 1980. *Autopoiesis and Cognition*. Dordrecht: Reidel.

Maynard Smith, J. 1975. *The Theory of Evolution*. 3rd edition. Hammondsworth: Penguin.

Maynard Smith, J. 1986. *The Problems of Biology*. New York: Oxford University Press.

Mayr, E. 1982. *The Growth of Biological Thought*. Cambridge, MA: Harvard University Press.

McClelland, J. L., and D. E. Rumelhart. 1986. *Parallel Distributed Processing: Explorations in the Microstructure of Cognition*. 2 Vols. Cambridge, MA: The MIT Press.

Monod, J. 1972. *Chance and Necessity*. Translated by A. Wainhouse. New York: Vintage.

Pattee, H. H. 1988. "Simulation, Realizations, and Theories of Life." In *Artificial Life*, edited by C. Langton. SFI Studies in the Sciences of Complexity, Vol. VI. Reading, CA: Addison-Wesley.

Prigogine, I., and I. Stengers. 1984. *Order out of Chaos*. Toronto: Bantam Books.

Putnam, H. 1975. "The Nature of Mental States." In his *Mind, Language, and Reality*. Cambridge: Cambridge University Press.

Regan, T. 1983. *The Case for Animal Rights*. Berkeley: University of California Press.

Reynolds, C. W. 1987. "Flocks, Herds, and Schools: A Distributed Behavioral Model." *Computer Graphics* 21: 25–34.

Searle, J. 1980. "Minds, Brains, and Programs." *Behavioral and Brain Sciences* 3: 417–458.

Sober, E. 1991. "Learning from Functionalism." In *Artificial Life II*, edited by C. G. Langton, C. E. Taylor, J. D. Farmer, and S. Rasmussen. SFI Studies in the Sciences of Complexity, Vol. X. Reading, CA: Addison-Wesley.

Spafford, E. H. "The Internet Worm: Crisis and Aftermath." *Communications of the ACM* 32: 678–687.

Taylor, P. 1986. *Respect for Nature*. Princeton: Princeton University Press.

Turing, A. M. 1951. "Can a Machine Think?" *Mind* 59: 433–460.

Wolfram, S. "Computer Software in Science and Mathematics." *Scientific American*, September 1984, 188–203.

Artificial Life or Surreal Art?

Stephen Todd and William Latham

IBM United Kingdom Scientific Centre
Athelstan House, St Clement St
Winchester, Hants, UK SO23 9SR
+44-962-844191, todd@venta.vnet.ibm.com

Abstract

This paper describes the use of life-based rules for the generation of animated surreal art. Rules controlled by the artist define the form of the individual sculptures and how they are coloured and textured. Mutator, an interface based on natural selection, then assists the artist to select preferred sculptures. The film "Mutations" uses these sculptures as actors in an animation. The animation is driven by rules that depict the ideas of parenthood, birth, maturation and decay, and control the timings of these processes.

All the rules are based on concepts of life, but modified and controlled by the artist to express his imagination: the rules use biological inspiration but do not perform biological modelling. The natural basis of the rules gives the works an organic realism, and the artist's imagination imposes a surrealist feel.

The application of rules by the computer removes much labour from the production of works of art, so using the computer as artist's assistant permits the creation of works previously impractical. Beyond that, application of the rules often produces artistic results beyond the artist's expectation and imagination, and so the computer becomes the artist's creative partner.

Introduction

Life is always a topic that fascinates peoples' scientific and artistic imaginations. Mathematics, though arguably not so important in biology as in physics and chemistry, plays an important role in formalising an understanding of the way life works. To a scientist understanding life may be an end in itself, but an artist applies this understanding to the production of effective works of art.

Computer technology adds a new dimension to the interaction between scientist, artist and mathematician. Mathematics is more easily applied in the physical sciences, and so it is in these areas that the technology is more easily exploited. For the physical scientist, computer technology permits automatic application of mathematical rules in **simulation**, and exploration of mathematical ideas in **visualization**. For the artist, computer technology applies the mathematical rules to remove much of the labour involved in the production of a work of art. Rules of perspective, first explored and exploited by the Renaissance artists, and rules of light and shadow, explored and exploited by Leonardo and by the Dutch school of art, are now routinely included in systems such as the Winsom (Quarendon 1984) renderer we use.

Artificial life is one way of applying mathematical rules to the biological sciences. As with the physical sciences, the ability of computer technology to apply rules consistently and easily is exploited by the scientists both for simulations based on existing rules, and for exploring the effects of new rules. This paper describes how an artist uses a computer to apply rules of life in the production of works of art.

The rules used are based on life, and thus give the work a natural organic feel to which the viewers can relate. However, the rules are not bound by true biology, but are controlled and modified by the artist to express his imagination, and this imposes a surreal feeling.

Computer production of images removes much of the artist's labour, and thus permits the creation of previously impractical works. The use of complex rules goes further, and permits the computer to create results that go beyond even the artists imagination.

The body of this paper shows how the artist uses rules of artificial life to produce art forms. It emphasises the inspiration of biology and artificial life, leaving details of the techniques to the references.

Techniques used

This section outlines the main tasks involved in our preparation of art works. Most complicated is the creation of an animation, which involves four major creative phases described in this section.

- Creation of the rules that control the form (shape) of the sculptures to appear in the animation. These rules are inspired by models for growing horns, shells, trees and other organic objects.
- Choice of colouring and surface texturing rules, again chosen to mimic natural texturing.
- Selection of individual sculptures generated by the rules above. The selection process is based on an artist controlled version of natural selection.
- Creation of a detailed storyboard, based on rules of birth, growth and death, that defines how these sculptures behave during the animation.

There are also several production phases in rendering an animation and putting it on film or videotape that do not concern us here.

We give examples of the rules used, and their relation to biological rules, and end the section with general comments on what makes a good rule.

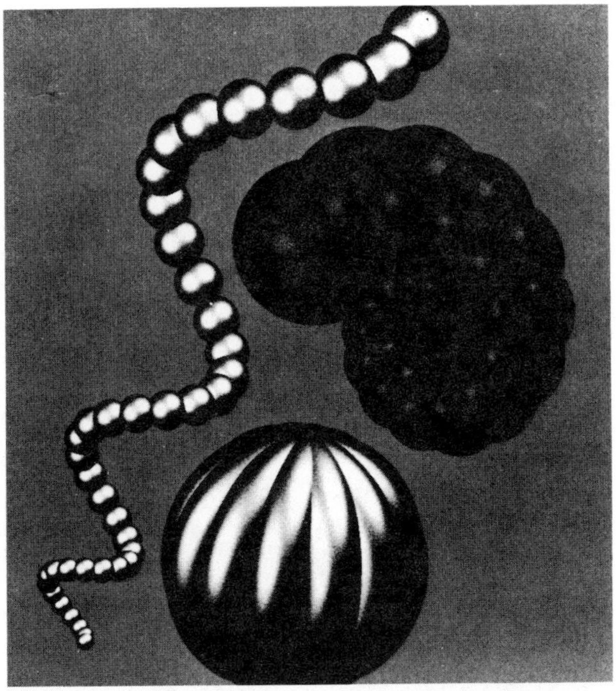

Figure 1. Mathematically generated 'biological' forms.

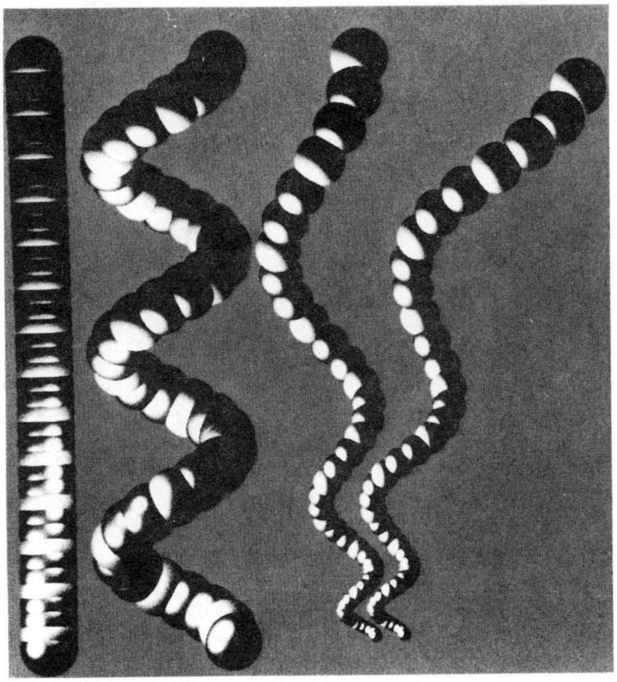

Figure 2. Sculptural development of a form: stack, grow, twist and bend.

Form

Mathematical explanation of the form of biological objects has received much attention, for example the scientist D'Arcy Thompson's investigation of geometry of nature (Thompson 1961). Several people have exploited nature for computer graphics (Kawaguchi 1982, Aono and Kunii 1984, Pickover 1989), including the authors (Latham 1990 b, Latham 1988, Latham and Todd 1989).

Our original biologically based form generation programs used different functions for generation of horns, spiral shells, pumpkin, fan and branching forms (Figure 1).

We soon realized that all of these functions were based on taking a simple 'primitive' input shape and repeatedly applying a transformation to it. The functions merged into a single iterative function, with parameters to define the primitive object, the transformation to apply, and the number times to apply it . The transformation parameter gave great flexibility, but as it was difficult to use it was replaced with sculptural terms such as 'stack', 'bend' and 'twist' (Figure 2). This single function no longer refers explicitly to its biological origins, other than its often inappropriate generic name *the horn function*, but the same interest in organic growth inspires the way it is applied.

The horn function evolved (Latham 1990 b) to include variations which permit the generation of more complex organic forms (Figure 3).

- Segmented forms made from a list of horns.
- Horns made by repeatedly transforming input forms that are themselves horns.

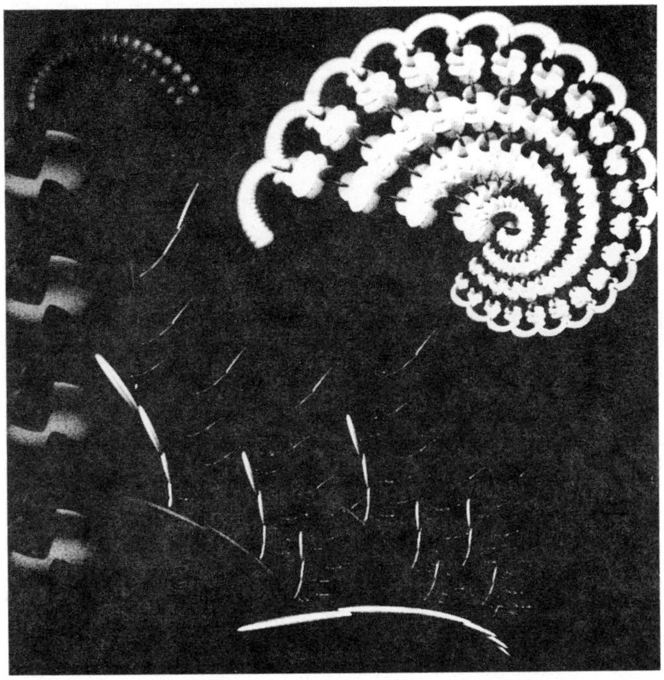

Figure 3. Complex forms: segmented horn, horn of horns and fractal horn.

- Forms made by recursive (fractal-like) geometry, as used by Barnsley and others to generate trees and ferns.

The horn function so developed became a generative rule used by the artist to create forms. The computer application of the rule not only assisted the artist to render forms, it produced surprising results that assisted his imagination in the creation of forms.

Texture

All our sculptures are textured using standard computer graphics texturing techniques (Voss 1985, Perlin 1985), implemented as a subsystem (Todd, Latham and Hughes 1991) of the Winsom renderer.

The techniques are based on Fourier generation of filtered white noise, with either fractal or bandpass filters. The filters and textures are often chosen to be suggestive of biological features such as elephant hide or leopard spots (Figure 4).

As with many of our rules, our texture generation rules do not attempt to model biological processes, but are chosen to give organic visual results. These results are often close to those generated by reaction diffusion models (Turk 1991)[1] and cellular automata (Li 1989).

Figure 4. Sample textures.

Mutation and Selection

The definition of our forms and textures naturally gives rise to parameterised families of sculptures. Each family is defined by a parameterised program we call a *structure*. When the program is run with a particular set of parameters, it gives a corresponding sculpture, and the parameters control features such as how much twist a shell has, or how regular a texture pattern is. Thus all the potential members of a family lie in a multidimensional space of forms. Typically we have ten or twenty parameters, and a ten or twenty dimensional space. This is difficult to illustrate, so (Figure 5) shows forms in a two dimensional space.

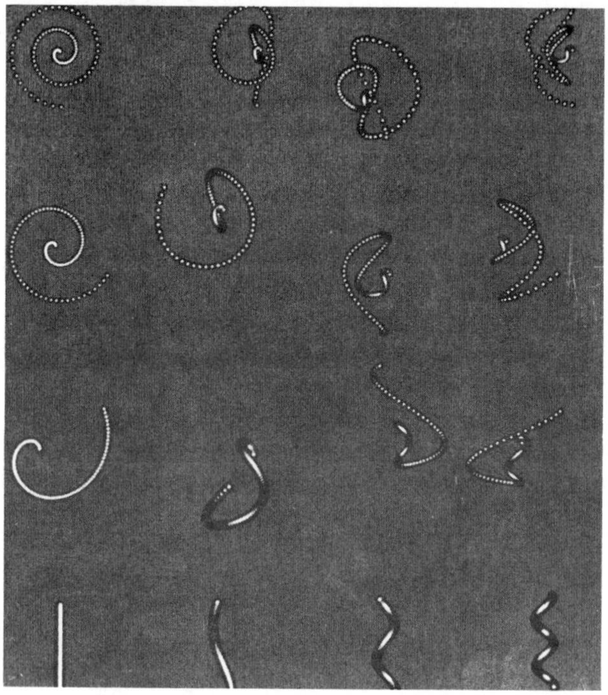

Figure 5. Objects in two dimensional form space: twist and bend.

Mutator (Todd and Latham 1990) is a program to assist exploration of this vast space and selection of artistically interesting members of this huge family. Mutator likens the *parameters* of our system to *genes* in a biological system,

[1] There is a possible explanation of the relationship between bandpassed filtering and the reaction diffusion process. Reaction processes emphasise local differences and so generate a high pass filter on the origin input, whereas diffusion processes smooth out local differences and so generate a low pass filter. The processes combine to give a compound filter which approximates a bandpassed filter

The textures we use are solid three dimensional textures out of which the sculpture is effectively carved. The texture does not adjust itself to the shape of the sculpture as a reaction diffusion model adjusts itself to the shape of an animal hide, so we do not achieve automatic variation of texture over different parts of a form.

with the *structure* and the horn function performs the role of *interpretation* of the genes by ribosomal expression. It operates by an artist controlled analog of natural selection.

In its simplest form Mutator has some similarities to Richard Dawkin's Biomorph system (Dawkins 1986). An initial value for all genes is chosen. The computer then 'mutates' these values, to give nine sets of genes, and generates and displays a frame of the nine corresponding sculptures. The artist selects a 'preferred' sculpture from the frame, and its genes are used as the starting point for a new frame of mutations, and so the loop of computer generation and artist selection continues (Figure 6). This dual process follows the natural processes of generation by genetic mutation and selection by survival of the fittest.

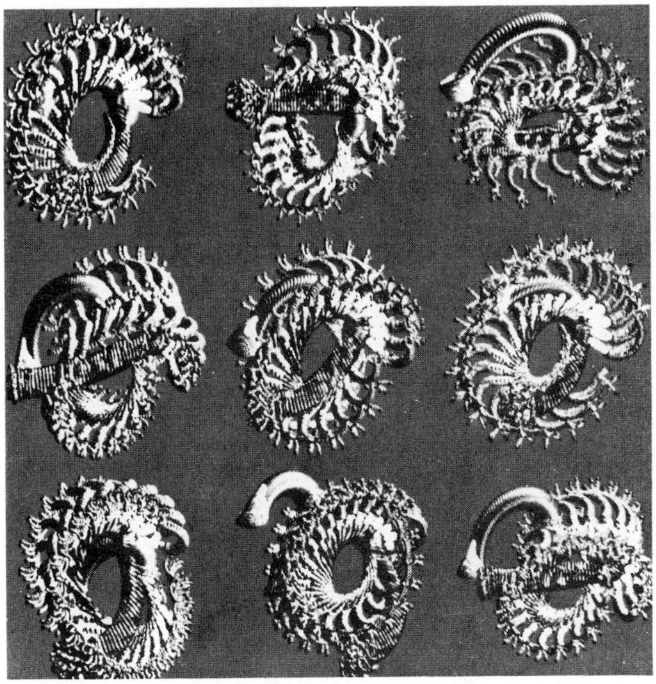

Figure 6. A frame of nine mutations.

The main difference between Biomorph and the basic Mutator is the intended use. Biomorph is a very effective *illustration* of the power of the dual processes of natural generation and selection. Mutator *applies* this power to create an artist's interface that uses a series of subjective decisions to select members from a family of sculptures. Because of this, Mutator operates on an artist written structure that produces complex three dimensional forms, as opposed to Biomorph's fixed structure and two dimensional forms.

Mutator also provides a variety of additional features.

Steering:
As the artist makes selections, Mutator detects trends in the direction in parameter space of the selected mutations and biases further mutations accordingly. The artist may also make judgements such as 'good' or 'bad' about mutations other than those selected, and these judgements further influence the generation of mutations. As far as we know

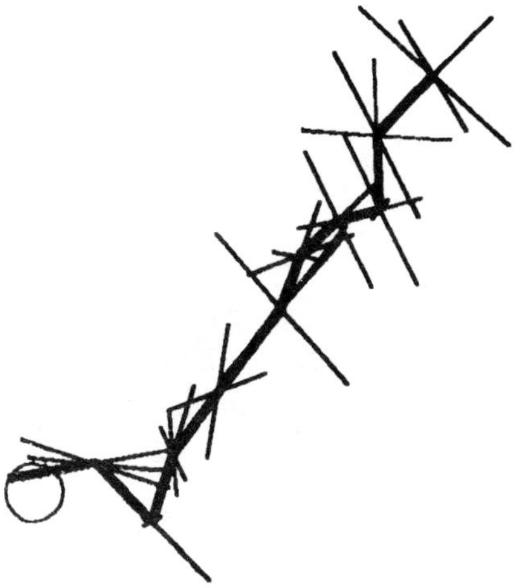

This shows a unsteerd attempt to move from the top right into the circle. The heavy line shows the route taken, and the lighter lines mutations offered but ignored. 11 moves were required.

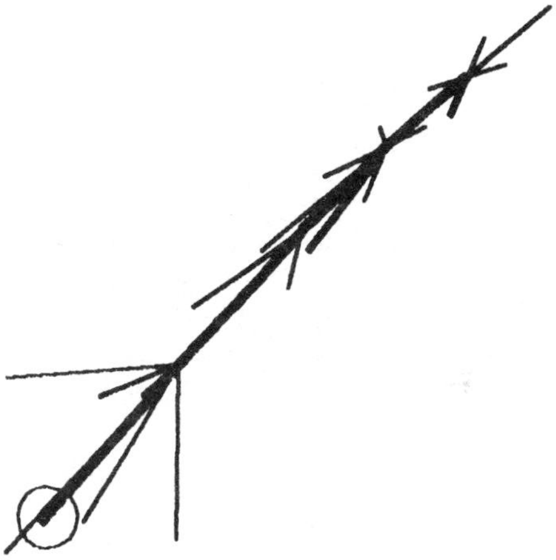

This shows the effect of steering. The mutations offered start collecting around the required direction, and the steps automatically get larger as the diresction is established. 4 moves were required.

Figure 7. Steering used to speed up a search of form space.

this steering technique has no biological analog, but it relates to the classic 'hill climbing' techniques used with Monte Carlo optimisation. The purpose of steering is to speed up the artist's exploration of form space (Figure 7).

Marriage: Mutator permits the artist to arrange a marriage between parents, and generates new child sculptures by mixing the genes of the two parents. The artist rejects or selects the children for procreation by further mutation or marriage. This marriage process is clearly derived from sexual reproduction.

Random marriage

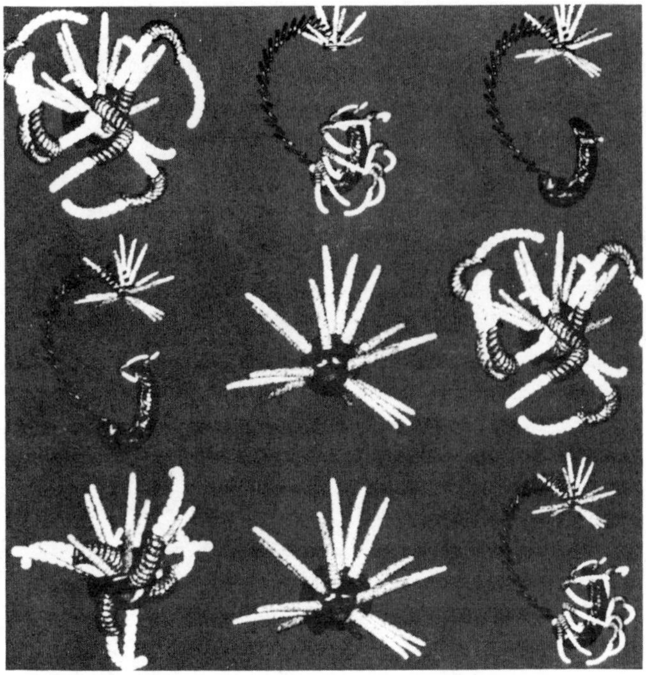

Spliced marriage

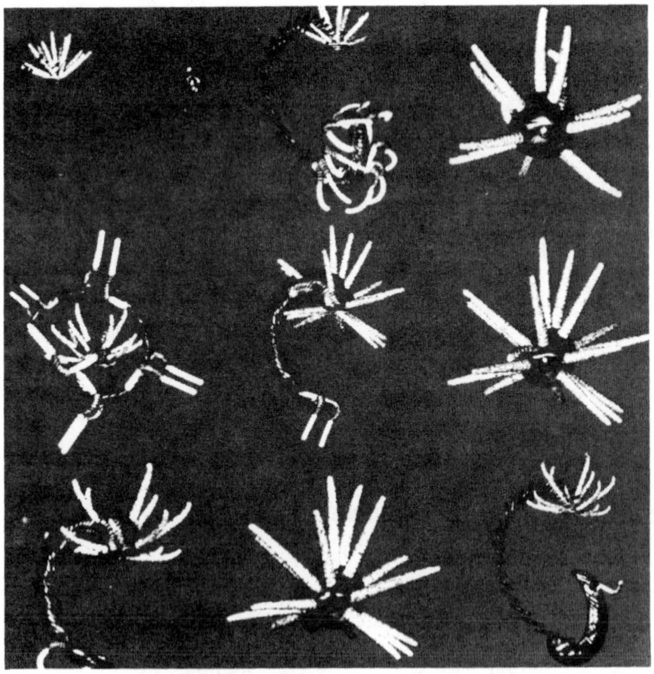

Averaged marriage

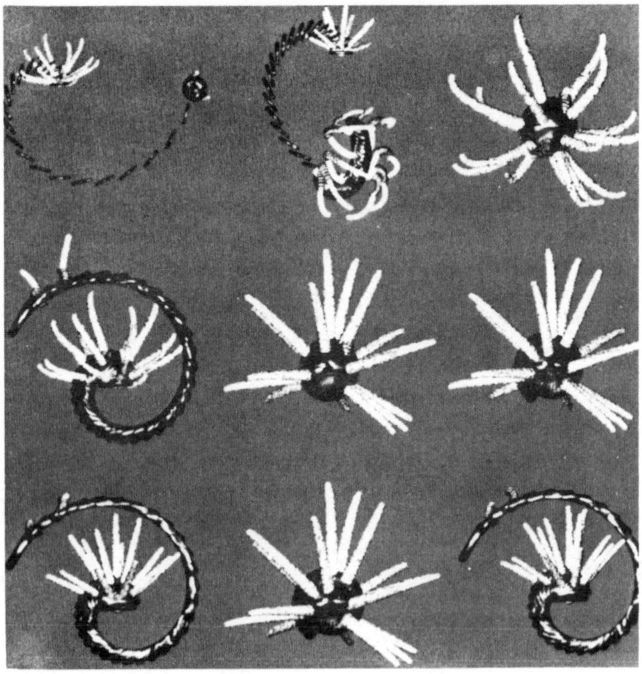

Dominant recessive marriage

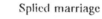

Figure 8. Marriage, using random and spliced gene mixing rules.

The gene mixing may be done in several ways. In *random* marriage each gene is selected randomly from one or the other parent. In *spliced* marriage the first so many genes are selected from one parent, and the remainder from the other. Spliced marriage is more effective at generating children with features that closely match those of the parents (Figure 8).

We are experimenting with further variations, for example multi-parent marriages, and gene mixing rules based on the ideas of dominant and recessive genes and on averaging.

Full tree

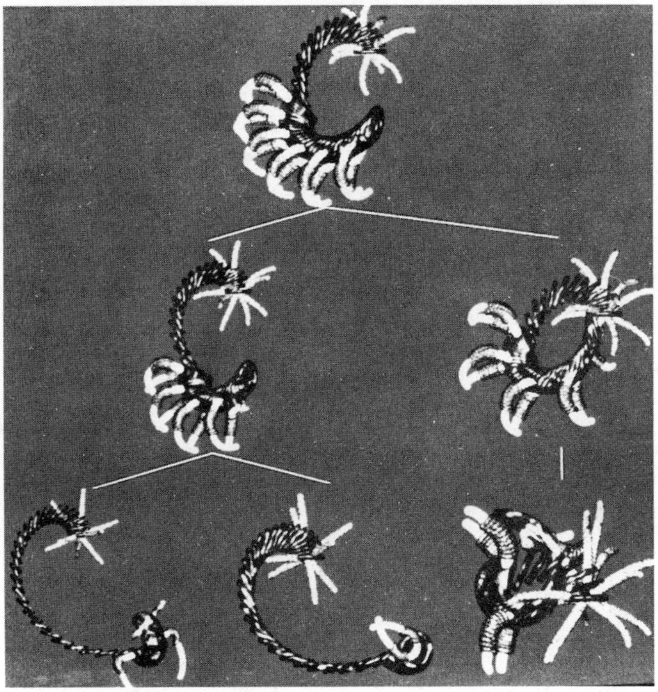

Figure 9. Display of family trees by Mutator.

Family Tree: Mutator has various options for displaying and revisiting sculptures. This permits an overview of a family tree (Figure 9). Particularly important is the arrangement of marriages between distant cousins to prevent the generation of uninteresting inbred forms.

Mutation of Structure: Mutator as implemented only permits the exploration of members of a family with a fixed number of genes each of which has a fixed interpretation. We intend to extend it to permit mutations of the underlying structure, so that different branches of the Mutator tree will contain members with different numbers and meanings of genes. For example, Mutator might change the structure

```
    horn
      ribs(??)
      stack(??)
      grow(??)
      bend(??)
  to
    horn
      ribs(??)
      stack(??)
      grow(??)
      twist(??)    /* <<< */
      bend(??)
```

In summary, Mutator is an interface to help an artist select from a family of sculptures. Its rules are derived from an artist controlled analog of natural selection, but are adapted to make selection as fast and effective as possible.

Animation

In general, there are two extremes in animation. Conventional animation involves manual drawing of key frames, and the subsequent production of all the in-between frames. It involves a huge amount of human resource, sometimes computer assisted (ACM 1990), but often not (as in Walt Disney's classics). Animations generated to visualise scientific simulations, whether physical (Atiyah et al 1989) or biological (Reffye et al 1988, Miller 1988), involve human effort in setting up the simulation, and then large computer resources in running the simulation and preparing the pictures. Our animations fall between these extremes (&Animpap., Latham 1990 a). We use rules which are applied by the computer to remove much of the labour of hand animation, but give ourselves considerable control over the rules to give the necessary artistic flexibility. This extends the use a physical rules (Wejchert and Haumnann 1991) and splining of parameters (Steketee and Balder 1985), to allow life inspired rules on animation timing.

The film "Mutations": The film "Mutations" is an animation of mutation. Rather than mutation being a process used in the selection of static sculptures, as described in the previous section, it becomes the theme of the entire film. Each scene is based on 'actors', which are sculptures selected by the artist during a Mutator session. Rules of life control how these actors behave in the scene. These rules control how an actor grows, where it moves, and when it is born and dies.

Rules of growth: As an actor grows and decays, rules of growth define a valid set of gene values at every frame time. The computer uses the rules to compute the genes for that time, and then generates the sculpture using these genes,

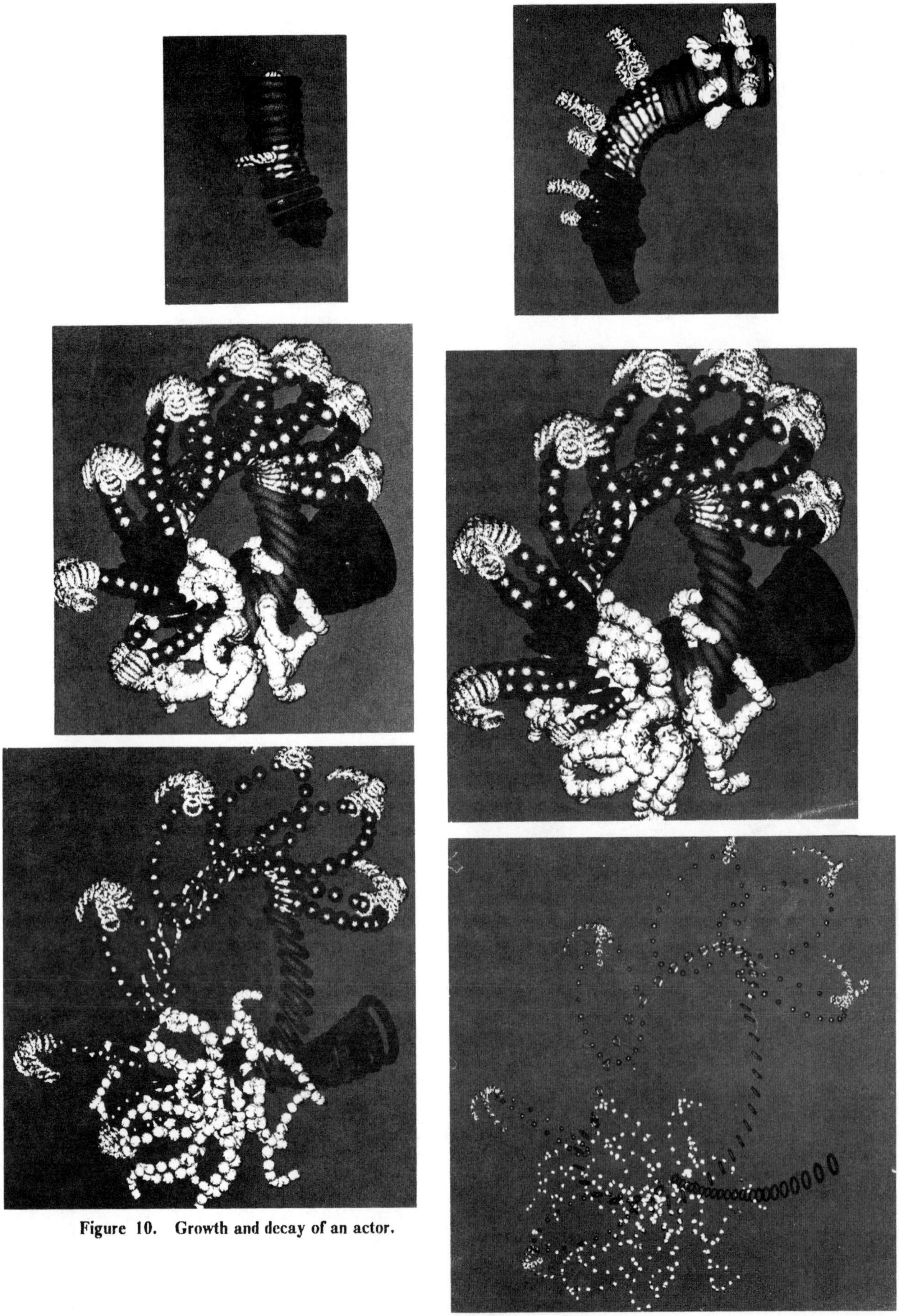

Figure 10. Growth and decay of an actor.

thus giving a constantly changing form. The genes go through four distinct key sets at specified key times, and interpolation controls gene values at other times (Figure 10 on page 7).

bud a small simple form for the first introduction of an actor.

fullsize a full size form which does not yet have its own full individuality.

mature the form as selected by the artist during the Mutator session.

death the final form before the actor disappears from the screen.

The key values for the genes are themselves generated by rules to depict the development of the object. The genes for a all buds are set to zero to give a small, simple member of the family. The fullsize genes are set mid-way between the mature genes of the parent and the actor's own mature genes. The death genes are set from the mature genes by a rule that makes the actor disintegrate and fade away.

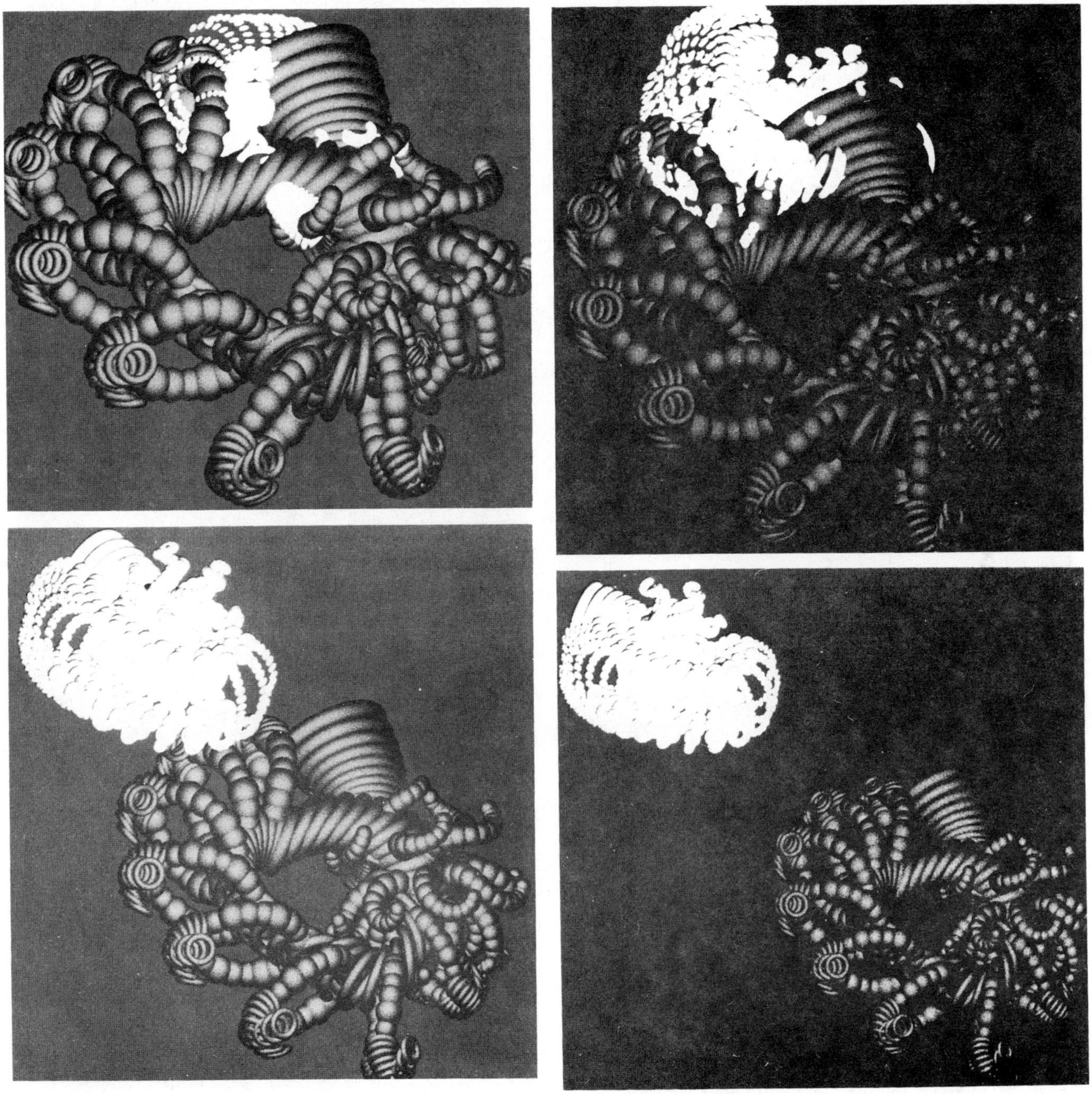

Figure 11. Birth of an object.

All the rules may be manually overwritten. The first actor in a scene generally does not start from a small bud, and the rule for the genes at the fullsize stage is modified for greater artistic variation.

Rules of position: The forms are based around a central 'spine' which ends in a flared hollow horn. When an actor is first conceived, it is placed at the start of its parent's spine. It moves down the spine and is born out of the flared end of the horn, a cornucopia depicting birth and parenthood (Figure 11 on page 8). Once born, the child floats away from its parent and falls under the influence of an external whirlwind.

Timing rules: The life of every actor is thus determined by five key times

- conceived, when it has bud form and starts its movement down the parent's spine,
- born, when it is released from the parent into the whirlwind,
- fullsize, when it reaches its fullsize form,
- mature, when it reaches its mature form,
- dies, when it reaches its death form and disappears from the screen.

These relate to each other, and to the timings of the actor's parents and children. For example, our rules fail if a child is conceived before its parent. A child may be conceived, or even born, before its parent is born: this is just biologically unrealistic and artistically likely to lead to confusion.

Originally these timing values were set manually for each actor, but this became very difficult to control, as slightly delaying the conception of one actor caused a change of times for all descendants. We thus derived Life Cycle, a program consisting of a set of timing rules based on typical intervals:

- conception to birth,
- birth to fullsize,
- fullsize to conception of first child,
- gap between successive children,
- birth of last child to start to decay,
- start of decay to final death.

All of these have default timing values which can easily be overwritten for detailed artistic control, and many of which can be made negative for special effects directed by the artist. Figure 12 shows a timing sequence derived from the rules of Life Cycle.

Artistic rules of life

All the rules are based on biological analogs, modified to our requirements. The main criteria of a good rule is that it should give a natural organic feel and aesthetic results, with interesting composition and timing. Thus our timing rules give a longer life span to actors that have more children: artistically this gives more time to see the 'interesting' births, but as far as we are aware the rule has no biological backing.

A good rule gives the artist sufficient control, and has enough variation that it can generate unexpected results. Unexpected results are sometimes an inspiration, but are by no means always good. In particular, we have found that rules that give an interesting variation over animations of a few seconds can lead to chaos or complete boredom when applied to longer scenes. When a rule fails in this kind of way, we generally first override it to create the desired results, and then analyse the final version to derive a new more sophisticated rule.

Conclusion

We have described the use of mathematical rules in the design of forms and animations. Life is the inspiration behind these rules, and this gives the artworks a realism and relates them to the viewer's experience. Once established, the rules are modified and applied to satisfy aesthetic criteria, and are not rigidly followed to give simulations of life. The results are thus surreal, artificial life, based on life but going beyond it. In all works of art, the artist tries to invest paint or stone to create an illusion of life, for example the Mona Lisa or Rodin's "Burghers of Calais". These however are static; using Mutator and Life Cycle it is possible to evolve forms by a surreal parody of the natural evolutionary process.

The works are a product of the artist's imagination. The artist controls the rules and the parameters that drive them, and the computer applies the rules to produce works impractical to produce in any other way. But the contribution of the computer to the art goes beyond this. Frequently the computer follows the artist's rules to yield results that go not just beyond his practical production capability, but also beyond his conception and imagination. The computer is a creative partner which realises the artist's ideas of growth and evolution. The role of the artist is to be a gardener who prunes, breeds, selects and destroys, his plant sculptures, and who can even change the rules of life of his universe.

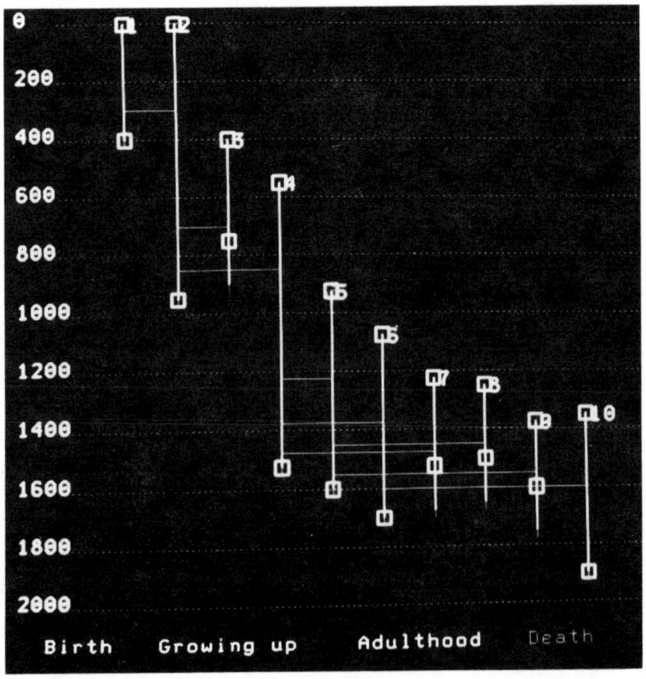

Figure 12. Timings generated by Life Cycle.

References

ACM, Technological Threat, *ACM Siggraph Film Show*, 1990.

Aono, M. and T. L. Kunii, Botanical Tree Image Generation, *Computer Graphics and Applications* 4, no.5: 10-34, May 1984.

Atiyah, Sir Michael F., Nigel J. Hitchen, John H. Merlin, David E. L. Pottinger and M. William Ricketts, Monopoles in Motion: a study of the low-energy scattering of magnetic monopoles, Animation and IBM UKSC Report 207, October 1989.

Dawkins, R., *The Blind Watchmaker*, Longmans Scientific and Technical, 1986.

Kawaguchi Y., A Morphological Study of the Form of Nature, *Computer Graphics* 16, no.3, July 1982.

Latham, William and Stephen Todd, Sculptures in the Void, *IBM Systems Journal* 28, no.4, 1989 New Scientist, no.1701, 27 January 1990.

Latham, William, The Conquest of Form, Exhibition at Arnolfini Gallery (Bristol), The Natural History Museum (London) and UK tour, 1988-1990. The Evolution of Form, Exhibition at Melbourne Arts Festival and Australian tour, 1990. The Empire of Form, Exhibition at O-Museum, Tokyo, Japan. 1990.

Latham, William, A Sequence from the Evolution of Form, *SIGGRAPH Film and Video Show*, Dallas, 1990.

Latham, William, The Artist's View of Computer Sculpture, Tutorial at 8th *Eurographics UK Conference*, Bath, April 1990.

Li, Wentian, Complex Patterns Generated by next nearest neighbors cellular automata, *Computers and Graphics* 13, no.3: 531-537, 1989.

Miller, Gavin S. P., The Motion Dynamics of Snakes and Worms, ACM Siggraph 88 Conference Proceedings, *Computer Graphics*, 22, no.4: 169-178, August 1988.

Perlin, Ken, An Image Synthesizer, Proceedings of Siggraph Conference San Fransisco 1985, *Computer Graphics*, 19, no.3: 287-296, 1895.

Pickover, C., A Short Recipe for Seashell Synthesis, *IEEE Computer Graphics and Applications*, 8-11, Nov 1989.

Quarendon, P., WINSOM user's guide, IBM UK Scientific Centre Report 123, 1984.

de Reffye, Philippe, Claude Edelin, Jean Francon, Marc Jaeger, Calude Peuch, Plant Models Faithful to Botanical Structure and Development, ACM Siggraph 88 Conference Proceedings, *Computer Graphics*, 22, no.4: 151-158, August 1988.

Steketee S., and N. I. Balder, Parametric Key frame interpolation incorporating kinetic adjustments and phrasing control, Journal of Visualization and Computer Animation, ACM Siggraph 85 Conference Proceedings, *Computer Graphics*, 19, no.3: 255-262, July 1985.

Thompson, D., On Growth and Form, Cambridge University Press, Cambridge, UK, 1961.

Todd, Stephen and William Latham, Mutator, a subjective human interface for evolution of computer sculptures, IBM UKSC report 248.

Todd, Stephen, Winchester Colour and Texture Facilities: WINCAT, Tutorial at 8th *Eurographics UK Conference*, Bath, April 1990, and IBM UKSC report 250.

Todd, Stephen, William Latham and Peter Hughes, Computer Sculpture Design and Animation, *Journal of Visualisation and Computer Animation*, 2: 98-105, August 1991.

Turk, G., Generating Textures on Arbitrary Surfaces Using Reaction Diffusion, ACM Siggraph 91 Conference Proceedings, *Computer Graphics*, 25, no.4: 289-298, August 1988.

Voss, R. F., Random Fractal Forgeries, Proc. NATO A.S.I 17, *Fundamental Algorithms in Computer Graphics*, Ilkley, UK, ed. R.A. Earnshaw (Springer Verlag, NY, 1985).

Wejchert, Jakub and David Haumnann, Animation Aerodynamics ACM Siggraph 91 Conference Proceedings, *Computer Graphics*, 25, no.4: 19-22, August 1988.

AUTHOR INDEX